HUMAN RACE
GET OFF YOUR *KNEES*
The Lion Sleeps No More

First published in April 2010

3 9082 13139 6031

 David Icke Books Ltd
185a High Street
Ryde
Isle of Wight
PO33 2PN
UK

Tel/fax: +44 (0) 1983 566002
email: info@davidickebooks.co.uk

Cover illustration by Neil Hague
and political art by David Dees

**British Library Cataloguing-in
Publication Data**
A catalogue record for this book is
available from the British Library

ISBN 978-0-9559973-1-0

Printed and bound in India by Thomson Press India Ltd

HUMAN RACE
GET OFF YOUR *KNEES*
The Lion Sleeps No More

David Icke

Original Illustrations in this book are by

Neil Hague

Neil is a British artist, illustrator and visionary, whose
work is dedicated to the 'truth vibrations'.
For over 15 years Neil's work has appeared on book covers
all over the world and he has had numerous exhibitions
of his highly individual and imaginative paintings across the UK.
Those that have seen Neil lecture have often described
his work as neo-shamanic, healing and from the heart.

He has also written three books including recently his first
Illustrated Graphic Novel
Kokoro - *The New Jersusalem & the Rise of the True Human Being*
For more information about his books, lectures, prints, workshops
and original paintings found in this book visit

www.neilhague.com

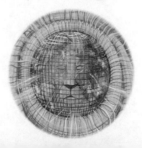

Dedication

To the extraordinary Linda, my rock in every storm.

To the wonderful Yeva, my great, great friend, who left us during the writing of this book.

To Kerry, Gareth and Jaymie for all their support no matter what.

To Carol Clarke and Linda Smith for their unwavering support.

To Credo Mutwa ... I am so proud to call you my friend.

To my mates, Neil Hague and Mike Lambert.

To the self-obsessed and destructive liars, fakes and frauds who have come into my life and done so much damage to my health, work and finances while claiming to 'support' me. I have done what I have done and I will do what I will do *despite* you, and you will have to live with that for the rest of your lives – and beyond.

Other books and DVDs by David Icke

Books

The David Icke Guide to the Global Conspiracy (and how to end it)

Infinite Love is the Only Truth, *Everything* Else is Illusion

Tales from the Time Loop

Alice in Wonderland and the World Trade Center Disaster

Children Of The Matrix

The Biggest Secret

I Am Me • I Am Free

… And The Truth Shall Set You Free – 21st century edition

Lifting The Veil

The Robots' Rebellion

Heal the World

Truth Vibrations

It Doesn't Have To Be Like This

DVDs

Beyond the Cutting Edge – Exposing the Dreamworld We Believe to be Real

Freedom or Fascism: the Time to Choose

Secrets of the Matrix

From Prison to Paradise

Turning Of The Tide

The Freedom Road

Revelations Of A Mother Goddess

Speaking Out

The Reptilian Agenda

Details of availability at the back of this book

*and through the website **www.davidicke.com***

Rise Like Lions

What is Freedom? – ye can tell
That which slavery is, too well –
For its very name has grown
To an echo of your own.

Tis to work and have such pay
As just keeps life from day to day
In your limbs, as in a cell
For the tyrant's use to dwell,

So that ye for them are made
Loom, and plough, and sword, and spade,
With or without your own will bent
To their defence and nourishment.

Tis to see your children weak
With their mothers pine and peak,
When the winter winds are bleak –
They are dying whilst I speak.

Tis to hunger for such diet
As the rich man in his riot
Casts to the fat dogs that lie
Surfeiting beneath his eye;

Tis to let the Ghost of Gold
Take from Toil a thousandfold
More that eer its substance could
In the tyrannies of old.

Paper coin – that forgery
Of the title-deeds, which ye
Hold to something of the worth
Of the inheritance of Earth.

Tis to be a slave in soul
And to hold no strong control
Over your own wills, but be
All that others make of ye.

And at length when ye complain
With a murmur weak and vain
Tis to see the tyrant's crew
Ride over your wives and you –
Blood is on the grass like dew.

Then it is to feel revenge
Fiercely thirsting to exchange
Blood for blood – and wrong for wrong –
Do not thus when ye are strong.

This is slavery – savage men
Or wild beasts within a den
Would endure not as ye do –
But such ills they never knew.

What art thou Freedom? O! could slaves
Answer from their living graves
This demand – tyrants would flee
Like a dreams dim imagery:

Let a great Assembly be
Of the fearless and the free
On some spot of English ground
Where the plains stretch wide around.

Let the blue sky overhead,
The green earth on which ye tread,
All that must eternal be
Witness the solemnity.

Ye who suffer woes untold,
Or to feel, or to behold
Your lost country bought and sold
With a price of blood and gold –

Let a vast assembly be,
And with great solemnity
Declare with measured words that ye.

Are, as God has made ye, *free*
And these words shall then become
Like Oppression's thundered doom
Ringing through each heart and brain,
Heard again – again – again.

Rise like Lions after slumber
In unvanquishable number –
Shake your chains to earth like dew
Which in sleep had fallen on you –
Ye are many – *they* are few.

Selected verses from *The Mask of Anarchy* by Percy Bysshe Shelley. It was written after the Peterloo massacre carried out by the British government in Manchester in 1819 against people who had gathered to demand the reform of parliamentary representation.

If...

If you can keep your head when all about you
Are losing theirs and blaming it on you,
If you can trust yourself when all men doubt you,
But make allowance for their doubting too;
If you can wait and not be tired by waiting,
Or being lied about, don't deal in lies,
Or being hated, don't give way to hating,
And yet don't look too good, nor talk too wise;

If you can dream – and not make dreams your master;
If you can think – and not make thoughts your aim;
If you can meet with Triumph and Disaster
And treat those two impostors just the same;
If you can bear to hear the truth you've spoken
Twisted by knaves to make a trap for fools,
Or watch the things you gave your life to, broken,
And stoop and build 'em up with worn-out tools;

If you can make one heap of all your winnings
And risk it on one turn of pitch-and-toss,
And lose, and start again at your beginnings
And never breathe a word about your loss;
If you can force your heart and nerve and sinew
To serve your turn long after they are gone,
And so hold on when there is nothing in you
Except the Will which says to them: 'Hold on!'

If you can talk with crowds and keep your virtue,
Or walk with Kings – nor lose the common touch,
If neither foes nor loving friends can hurt you,
If all men count with you, but none too much;
If you can fill the unforgiving minute
With sixty seconds' worth of distance run,
Yours is the Earth and everything that's in it,
And – which is more – you'll be a Man, my son!

Rudyard Kipling

Now I Think I Know…

Starry, starry night
Paint your palette blue and grey
Look out on a summer's day
With eyes that know
The darkness in my soul
Shadows on the hills
Sketch the trees and the daffodils
Catch the breeze and the winter chills
In colours on the snowy linen land.

Now I understand
What you tried to say to me
And how you suffered for your sanity
And how you tried to set them free
They would not listen
They did not know how
Perhaps they'll listen now.

Starry, starry night
Flaming flowers that brightly blaze
Swirling clouds in violet haze
Reflect in Vincent's eyes of China blue
Colours changing hue
Morning fields of amber grain
Weathered faces lined in pain
Are soothed beneath the artist's loving hand.

Now I understand
What you tried to say to me
And how you suffered for your sanity
And how you tried to set them free
They would not listen
They did not know how
Perhaps they'll listen now.

Don McLean

The Human Story

There is an Eastern tale that speaks about a very rich magician who had a great many sheep. But at the same time this magician was very mean. He did not want to hire shepherds, nor did he want to erect a fence about the pasture where the sheep were grazing. The sheep consequently often wandered into the forest, fell into ravines and so on and, above all, they ran away, for they knew that the magician wanted their flesh and their skins, and this they did not like.

At last, the magician found a remedy. He hypnotised his sheep and suggested to them, first of all, that they were immortal and that no harm was being done to them when they were skinned; that on the contrary, it would be very good for them and even pleasant; secondly, he suggested that the magician was a good master who loved his flock so much that he was ready to do anything in the world for them; and in the third place, he suggested that if anything at all was going to happen to them, it was not going to happen just then, at any rate not that day, and therefore they had no need to think about it. Further, the magician suggested to his sheep that they were not sheep at all; to some of them he suggested that they were lions, to some that they were eagles, to some that they were men, to others that they were magicians.

After this, all his cares and worries about the sheep came to an end. They never ran away again, but quietly waited the time when the magician would require their flesh and skins.

This tale is a very good illustration of man's position.

G I Gurdjieff, quoted by P D Ouspensky in his book, In Search of the Miraculous, *1949.*

Nothing Is Impossible – Unless We Think It Is

Imagine being able to walk through walls.
You wouldn't have to bother with opening doors; you could pass right through them. You wouldn't have to go around buildings; you could enter them through their walls and pillars and out through the back wall. You wouldn't have to detour around mountains; you could step right into them. When hungry, you could simply reach through the refrigerator door without opening it. You could never be accidentally locked outside your car; you could simply step through the car door.

Imagine being able to disappear or reappear at will.
Instead of driving to school or work, you would just vanish and rematerialize in your classroom or office. You wouldn't need an airplane to visit far-away places, you could just vanish and rematerialize where you wanted. You would never be stuck in city traffic during rush hours; you and your car would simply disappear and rematerialize at your destination.

Imagine having x-ray eyes.
You would be able to see accidents happening from a distance. After vanishing and rematerializing at the site of any accident, you could see exactly where the victims were, even if they were buried under debris.

Imagine being able to reach into an object without opening it.
You could extract the sections from an orange without peeling or cutting it. You would be hailed as a master surgeon, with the ability to repair the internal organs of patients without ever cutting the skin, thereby greatly reducing pain and the risk of infection. You would simply reach into the person's body, passing directly through the skin, and perform the delicate operation.

Imagine what a criminal could do with these powers. He could enter the most heavily guarded bank. He could see through the massive doors of the vault for the valuables and case and reach inside and pull them out. He could then stroll outside as the bullets from the guards passed right through him.

With these powers, no prison could hold a criminal. No secrets could be kept from us. No treasures could be hidden from us. No obstructions could stop us. We would truly be miracle workers, performing feats beyond the comprehension of mortals. We would also be omnipotent.

What being could possess such God-like power?
The answer: a being from a higher-dimensional world.

Physicist Dr Michio Kaku, author of Hyperspace: A Scientific Odyssey Through Parallel Universes, Time Warps, and the Tenth Dimension

Contents

Humanity is at a fork in the road, and we can no longer stand there staring at the map pondering which direction to take. It is hardly a choice, after all.

One road leads to a global fascist/communist dictatorship that would control every aspect of our lives, including our thoughts. The other will open the door to freedom and potential on a scale never experienced in the 'world' as we have known it.

Hard one, isn't it?

A choice between a prison and a paradise?

Wow! Decisions, decisions, decisions.

To put your head in the sand you have to be on your knees

If a tornado is coming, what is the most effective response? To bury your head in the sand and convince yourself it's not coming?

That would be fine for a while, but the tornado is still coming and your backside is in the air and right in its flight path. Ignorance appears to be bliss, and then …

Is it not more intelligent to acknowledge the tornado, get off your knees, turn around and face it? In doing so, you are taking control of the situation and giving yourself the power to take avoiding action.

This is the choice that humanity is faced with today.

Remember: ignorance may be bliss … but only for a while.

Knock, knock, knock.

'Darling, who can that be at this time of night?'

1

I Am Not David Icke

The only tyrant I accept in this world is the 'still small voice' within
Mahatma Gandhi

I have lived a strange life; well, *very* strange by most people's standards, but it doesn't feel strange to me at all now. It did once, to be sure. One minute I was a respected television anchorman, the next I was possibly the most widely-ridiculed figure in British history. What happened? I woke up. Ironically, while the world was dubbing me 'insane', I was in the process of *regaining* my sanity. I was becoming conscious, or at least more so.

In fact, the 'I' in the context of these words is not an 'I' at all. It is an *experience* called 'David Icke'. The real 'I', the eternal 'I', is the Consciousness I was 'becoming' – reconnecting with – while 'David Icke', my human 'personality', or 'experience', was being labelled the 'crazy man'. Humanity is so desperately confused about the difference between the real 'I' – the Consciousness that is their eternal self – and what we call the human body/mind/personality. One is who we *are* and the other is what we are *experiencing*. It is this confusion that leads to billions of people living out their false identities, believing that this is who they are. I am Ethel Brown … I am Charlie Smith … I was born here … work there… like to go to Spain for my holidays. Thus, they see themselves overwhelmingly in terms of limitation – I can't, little me, 'Joe Public', I have no power. This suits the networks of global manipulation and control because, to state the obvious, it is far easier to shepherd and suppress billions of 'Ethel Browns' and 'Charlie Smiths' than billions who know that their primary state is eternal Consciousness, *All That Is, Has Been and Ever Can Be*. We are not our bodies; we are Infinite Consciousness having an experience through our bodies (Fig 1 overleaf).

Let me make it clear where I am coming from in this book right at the start, because everything you will read relates to this, including my own 'story' (experience). We live in a virtual-reality universe, very well symbolised by the *Matrix* movie trilogy, although there is far more to it than that. We are not our bodies, nor even our minds. These are the vehicles that allow us to experience the virtual-reality universe, a fantastically advanced version of the Internet in many ways, as we shall see. If you want to access the Internet and 'experience' what it has to offer, you can't just log-on by yourself. You need a conduit, or interface, that lets you go 'online'. We call this interface a computer, and the virtual-reality universe operates in much the same way, though, of course, on an infinitely greater level of sophistication. We are talking spaceships to counting-beads by comparison, and

Illustration by Neil Hague (www.neilhague.com)

Figure 1: *The human body is only one level of our Infinite Consciousness. The body is not who we are, it is a vehicle to experience this virtual-reality universe.*

then some. The real 'I' – Consciousness – has no form in its eternal, infinite state. It is just *awareness*. The interface employed by Consciousness is the computer system that we call the human mind and body. The body is a most obvious computer when you look at the evidence, and its communication system is what we call 'mind'. Or, rather, what I refer to as *The* Mind. We talk about 'my' mind, 'his' mind, 'her' mind, 'their' minds and so on, but I would suggest there is *one* mind – *The* Mind. It is the interface between Consciousness and the virtual-reality universe, and everyone from a New Ager to a Wall Street banker is expressing different aspects of *The* Mind – unless they become conscious and realise that mind and body are not who they are. Then they can *open* the Mind to Consciousness and become aware of their real self (Figs 2 and 3). You might call this a state of 'real-self consciousness', as opposed to fake-self mind.

Who Am I?

Very few people have this realisation (though that is changing) because they are pressured and manipulated to see themselves as their minds and their bodies. They look in the mirror and say 'that's me', and they listen to the endless thought-chatter in their heads and say 'that's me'. But it isn't. That 'me' is not a 'me' at all. It is the vehicle for the *real* 'me' – Consciousness – to experience this reality. Humanity has been deceived on so many levels and in many ways to identify the 'me', the 'I', with mind and body. This fake identity entraps our focus of attention, our awareness, in the mind/body and disconnects it from the true 'I' – Consciousness. This is crucial to both our own experience and the world we collectively create, given that their perspectives are so vastly different. Consciousness knows that everything is One, while the Mind sees everything in terms of separation and division. Mind, as a *servant* to the experience of Consciousness, is fine – that's the role it is meant to play. It is when we think we *are* our minds and bodies that the trouble starts. We are then caught in an illusion that we think is real. It is Mind that gives us the experience of this realm of form, or of 'things', by decoding vibrational reality into illusions like 'time', 'space' and apparent 'physicality', much as a computer decodes information on a software disk into pictures, text and graphics onto a computer screen. Time, space and physicality do not exist except as an illusory construct, and we experience them through the decoding

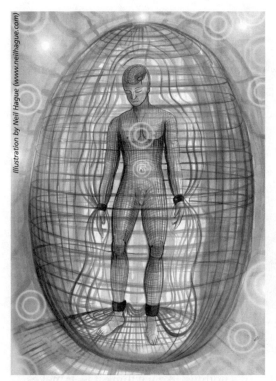

Figure 2: *Most of humanity has a self-identity that relates to their body/mind and this makes them a prisoner of the five senses as they close their mind to their higher levels of awareness. They are entrapped in what I call the 'eggshell' or the 'bubble'*

systems of mind and body, as I will be explaining in detail. It is so simple when you see how it all works, and extraordinary when you realise how 'physical' reality is so different to what we think it is. The 'physical' world you see as 'outside' of you only exists (in that form) in your brain. Ridiculous? Impossible? No, simply *true*.

We don't see with our eyes; we see with the decoding systems of the brain. The eyes turn vibrational information into electrical signals which the brain decodes to construct our 'physical' reality (Fig 4 overleaf). Everything is the same information in different forms, be it vibrational, electrical, chemical, whatever. The means of communication is different, but it's the same information in different forms. It is like a man in a

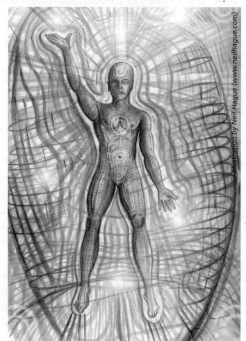

suit passing a piece of paper to a woman in a dress who gives it to a bloke in a t-shirt. The means of communication may look different, but it is the same information. The principle applies to the body-computer that communicates and decodes information vibrationally, electrically, electromagnetically and chemically. The book you are looking at now only exists in its apparent 'physical' form inside your brain, and the same with everything else that you 'see', including the Sun, Moon and stars that seem so far away. All the sight, sound, touch, smell, taste, colours, temperature, and the experience of distance, solidity, even movement, are all vibrational information – waveforms – decoded via the five senses and the brain into the illusion of

Figure 3: *When we open our minds we can connect with the greater 'I' and access expanded levels of understanding, insight and awareness. The 'world' then looks very different from the one perceived by those still in the 'bubble'*

Illustration by Neil Hague (www.neilhague.com)

Figure 4: *The 'physical' world as we perceive it does not exist except as vibrational and electrical information decoded by the body/brain into illusory physicality in our 'heads'. It is like a computer decoding information on a software disk to appear on the screen as colours, text, pictures and graphics*

physicality 'out there'. The fact is there is no 'out there' when it comes to the 'physical' world. It feels like you are physically holding the book, I'll grant you, and the same for me as I tap this keyboard; but your hands and mine are converting vibrational information from the book and from the keyboard into electrical signals which the brain decodes into the sense of 'physically' holding the book and tapping the keys. I will be going into this in much more detail as we go along. It is fundamental to understanding what is really happening in this 'world'. Much of the information I shall be revealing across many subjects will seem extraordinary and 'far out' to most people, but what the hell else can be more 'far out' than the fact that you are not even physically holding the book you are reading? The world is not just a little bit different to how we think it is; it's nothing like we think it is. It makes me smile when I hear comments like 'Icke's a madman' in response to views

which, when it comes to weirdness, are not in the same league as reality itself. 'Icke's crazy!' Oh really? Do you think that's air you're breathing now?

Mind perceives reality in terms of apartness, structure, language, hierarchy, laws, time, space and individuality. This is its job – to give Consciousness an experience of such things. The problem is that humanity has identified so totally with Mind and its sense of perception that people think that their experience is who they are. It is like being at the keyboard, mouse in hand, seeing everything as the computer sees it. Suddenly, all our creativity and uniqueness would be lost to the universal software behind all computers. So it is with humans when we identify with mind and body and forget our true and infinite nature. It is, however, more than just forgetting. We have been manipulated to forget, generation after generation, by the network of interbreeding bloodline families that I have been exposing all these years. The Shadow People, as I call them, know how we create reality and their goal is to keep us in Mind and out of Consciousness. In that state we become controllable en masse. They lock us into the mind-body computer level of perception and then program the computer's sense of reality by controlling the information and electrochemical influences that we receive. Once again, I will explain all as we proceed. People talk about the conscious mind and subconscious mind and they use phrases like 'regaining consciousness', and suchlike. I am using the term 'Consciousness' in a very different way, not least with a capital 'C' to emphasise that all Consciousness is one Consciousness expressing itself in infinite ways. When I talk about Consciousness, I mean that level of awareness that is

Figure 5: *'Mind'-people see almost everything from the perspective of the five senses and so become entrapped by the illusions of the 'physical' world. This makes them so easy to manipulate and control. Conscious people retain their connection to their higher levels of awareness and see everything from another point of observation. They are 'in' this world, but not 'of' it. Mind-people often call Conscious people 'crazy' or 'dangerous' because of their very different perspectives of reality*

eternal and infinite – our primary state. It is All Knowing, All Possibility, Infinite One-Consciousness in awareness of itself. Everything is an expression of that One Consciousness; it has to be because that's all there is. But not everything is in the same state of awareness and, compared with Consciousness in awareness of itself, Mind is a village idiot. It is said that self-awareness, being aware of one's own existence, is the definition of being conscious. I disagree. Self-awareness may mean you are aware of your own existence, but it doesn't mean you are Conscious in the sense that I am using the term here. Mind has self-awareness, not least through its false identity of being Ethel Brown or Charlie Smith and the 'life stories' that go with them; but if Mind becomes a closed circuit, a 'closed mind', as it is with most people, it will not be truly Conscious in the sense of eternal Consciousness, or Infinite Awareness. It will be operating with a fundamentally limited sense of awareness, possibility and self-identity (Fig 5). If you are new to this, it can be a lot to take in, but it really is very straightforward when you connect the dots, as I will.

'Great Minds' Think Alike (And the Not So Great)

Mind communicates via thought. It never stops thinking. Humans are addicted to thinking because they are addicted to Mind and believe that this is who they are. In turn, the thoughts become emotions, the body-mind reaction to thought, and so humans are addicted to emotion, too. You don't even have to experience something directly to trigger an emotional response; you just have to think about it. We live in a Mind-made world, full of Mind-made people, and so the Mind is God: 'He's got a great mind'; 'She has an incredible mind'; 'What a brilliant mind'. The Mind is everything in a Mind-made reality and that's why the intellect is a focus of worship in what we call the modern world. Being an 'intellectual' or an 'academic' is confirmation, according to our distorted understanding, that you are 'clever'. Well, it depends what you mean by clever. The dictionary definition is: 'mentally quick and original; bright'. Mentally quick, okay, but that's the role of Mind, to work things out through thought. Original? Not true. Originality comes from Consciousness, not Mind. Bright? Again, what is meant by 'bright'? If it means the ability to hold lots of facts in the memory and pour them forth at will, well that's just Mind again. What we call 'cleverness' comes from Mind, while wisdom comes from Consciousness and, as I have been saying for years, cleverness without wisdom is the most destructive force on earth. For example, it is very clever to build an atomic bomb, but it is not wise to do so. We have lots of clever people, but not many wise ones, and that's because the perception of humanity is dominated by Mind, the computer-like conduit and not the true self.

I have been speaking to different types of audiences for 20 years in more than 50 countries, and beyond question it is the intellectuals and academics that are the most unresponsive to anything 'outside the box'. That 'box' is Mind. They are so imprisoned by Mind that they cannot compute information and awareness inspired by Consciousness. It is an alien world to them, like something from the Twilight Zone. Yet they are the ones who are celebrated for their intelligence and it is they who run the institutions that control and direct society. The Mind-made system spews out Mind-made robots to administer the Mind-made system. Round and round it goes, decade after decade. While Mind communicates through thought, Consciousness speaks to us as 'knowing'. This is also called 'intuition'. It is not something you think; it is something you feel, something you just *know*. We all have this intuition to an extent. It is that feeling that you know something, but you don't know why you know. 'I just know I have to meet this person', 'go here', 'be there'. There are usually no words (Mind) to explain this knowing, this urge to do something, but it comes from somewhere deep within. Yes, from Consciousness. The dominance of Mind over our sense of reality closes the door to intuition, because if we follow that feeling then Mind is no longer the governor, no longer in control. Of course, it is going to fight to protect its pre-eminence. How many times have you had an intuitive knowing or a powerful urge to do something only for the chatter in your head to talk you out of it?

> You can't do that; what will your family think, and the neighbours and the people at work? It's irresponsible; you have commitments, duties, and what about your career? You will be letting people down, and yourself. You can't just up and go on a whim. It's not logical.

Ah, yes, logic – 'a system of reasoning'. But what is 'reason'? The dictionary definitions are classic: 'The capacity for logical, rational and analytic thought; intelligence; good judgment; sound sense; a normal mental state; sanity'. Mind, Mind, Mind. 'The capacity for logical, rational and analytic thought; intelligence' refers quite obviously to the intellect or Mind, but 'good judgement, sound sense'? By whose criteria, pray? The Mind-domination of our reality means that everything is defined from the perspective of Mind. 'Good judgement, sound sense' is simply the Mind's definition of what that is. What if Mind, as is the case, knows a fraction of what there is to know? Would you take a village idiot's definition of 'good judgement, sound sense' and live your life accordingly without question? This would be crazy, but the best part of seven billion people is doing just that every day. If you looked out of the window on a fine sunny morning you would think it sound judgement, good sense, to ask the family round for tea in the garden, or to pull out the deckchairs to work on the tan. If you had a greater awareness of events, say that a hurricane was coming, what appeared at first to be sound judgement, good sense, would suddenly be revealed as potential suicide. So it is with the vastly different scale of awareness between Mind and Consciousness. When you open Mind to Consciousness you realise how limited, and even stupid, Mind really is when operating as a closed circuit and 'consciously' aware of only five-sense reality. You also see that to accept Mind as the arbiter of 'good judgement, sound sense' is simply insane. Talking of which, I love that third definition of 'reason': 'a normal mental state; sanity'. The delusory perspective of Mind is the point from which everyone and everything is filtered and judged. If you are saying things that are beyond the capacity of Mind to understand, you must, by definition, be insane and not in a 'normal mental state'. This is why I have said so often that I welcome being called insane, because that is confirmation of my sanity. Thank you to all concerned.

Don't be so Dense

Everything is energy in different forms. Experiments by Japanese scientists have shown how the body 'glows' and emits light that rises and falls with the passage of the day. Five healthy male volunteers were placed bare-chested in front of cameras in complete darkness for twenty minutes every three hours. The researchers found the body-glow rose and fell over the day, with its lowest point at 10am and its peak at 4pm, dropping gradually after that. It is thought that these fluctuations in energy emissions are connected with the principle of the body clock. The body-mind is energy, as everything is, and it can be free-flowing (open mind), or dense and heavy (closed mind) depending on our state of being. Nothing induces this energy density more than fear and rigid belief. A phenomenon known as 'brain mapping' means that rigid beliefs are self-perpetuating as the brain filters reality to fit the belief. Those in the shadows seeking to control world events are after your mind – your belief. They pretty much don't care what rigid belief you have – religious, political, whatever – so long as you have one. Any of them will limit your ability to see the big picture, and they can also play belief against belief to divide and rule. Open minds that can expand to consciously connect with Infinite Awareness are the worst nightmare of the manipulators and they have structured society to do everything possible to suppress such an awakening, such an opening of Mind. Rigid belief can even be seen in the way the neuron cells connect in the brain. They form an electrical web that represents the rigidity of perception, and the neurons fire in accordance with the sequence that represents the belief. These networks are called 'brain maps' and they can be summed up by the phrase: 'Neurons that fire together, wire together'.

David Shainberg, an American psychiatrist from the William Alanson White Institute of Psychiatry in New York, says that thoughts are vortices of energy that can become fixed and rigid. These vortices are another level of the process that connect with the neuron networks and create the rigid, repeating sequence in how they fire. Shainberg suggests that these fixed, dense vortices reveal themselves as fixed opinions, a rigid sense of reality and unchanging views. It also goes the other way with fixed opinions and beliefs creating the dense vortices and fixed neuron networks. It is these networks and low-vibrational energy fields (different expressions of the same beliefs) that close the channels, hold us in five-sense reality and block the conscious connection to Infinite Awareness. They are the electrical and vibrational levels of the filtering process where information is constructed by the brain to fit belief. It means that some people see the glass half-full, and others see it half empty; some see the positive in everything, and others the negative. These 'brain maps' of neuron networks firing in a repeating sequence are like software programs playing out on a computer. They never change until you re-write the software codes or change the disk. Most people never do, and that is why they are so predictable and limited in perception and behaviour. When we break out of such rigid thought, the neuron web snaps and another is formed to match the new reality. With that, the filtering process changes and other fields of possibility are decoded that were not being accessed before. We experience this as a 'life-changing' event, or a sudden surge of new opportunity in our life that hadn't presented itself before. This 'opportunity' was always there in the mass of energy within All Possibility; it was just that the person's belief was causing their brain not to 'read' it and bring it into 'physical' experience. Rigid thought and low-vibrational states, especially fear, cause our energy fields to fall into slow-vibrational density and this creates a 'firewall' to Infinite Awareness. What do we call people who aren't very 'bright'? We call them 'dense'. After I had my initial awakening in 1990, I was saying things that were way outside the belief systems of most people, and their brain maps fired to decode me as crazy, even dangerous. What was happening, in fact, is that I was in the process of going 'out of my Mind' and into Consciousness.

Lying to Yourself

A major expression of these brain maps is a phenomenon known as 'cognitive dissonance'. It is an imbalance of the mind and emotions that maintains humanity in ongoing ignorance and servitude. To understand cognitive dissonance is to understand so much about the human condition. It may sound very highbrow and spawned from the often twilight world of intellectual jargon, but it is really very simple. It means to be in two 'minds', basically, with one contradicting the other. This mostly takes the form of a belief contradicted by experience, information or behaviour. Cognitive (knowledge, awareness) dissonance (discord) is the state of inner stress and unease caused by a person's belief not matching their experience, behaviour or the facts before them. In that one short sentence I have described most of humanity and why the world is as it is. This state of unease insists that we square that circle by resolving the contradiction and this is done mostly by lying to ourselves, or what I would call self-deception. Humans are in a constant state of cognitive dissonance and this is mercilessly exploited by those who wish to control us. 'Shut up, I don't want to hear it' is one expression of cognitive dissonance, or an effort to avoid it. How often we hear this said when a rigid belief system is faced with information that contradicts its reality. Those words betray what happens when beliefs and perceptions are challenged by evidence. To remove the dissonance, the stress of contradiction, people mostly either (a) dismiss the belief-challenging information as untrue, without further investigation, or (b) change their beliefs and assumptions in the light of new information or experience. If you do the latter, cognitive dissonance is a positive thing. You learn from new information and experience and expand your awareness. Unfortunately, however, most people take the other route and try to protect their belief system from all challenge (Fig 6). You see this

Figure 6: *Cognitive dissonance can be a form of schizophrenia in which two contradictory views or facts are both believed to be true – war is peace, freedom is slavery, ignorance is strength*

most powerfully with religious believers, academics, scientists, doctors and those with a rigid political or cultural worldview. If they have to choose between their belief system and greater understanding, the belief system wins every time. This means that they must discredit the messenger in their own mind – 'That Icke's a nutter' – to somehow explain away the information while leaving the belief system intact. The Sceptics Society is really the Cognitive Dissonance Society. It is not there to question information and beliefs that challenge its own, but only to discredit them out of fear of their own belief system being flawed. The more that we understand about the true nature of reality, the more ludicrous are the 'explanations' from the belief-system groupies of academia. There is a 'parapsychologist' at a UK university who has constantly dismissed the so-called paranormal and 'near-death experiences' in terms that make the head shake. She has said that near-death experiences – when enormous numbers of people have reported leaving the body and then returning – are the brain remembering its 'life' as it dies. Well, how can it be remembering floating above its body looking down on itself? It's crazy! But that's how cognitive dissonance works. The belief-system clouds the judgement as the neurons fire in their repeating sequence, and even the most obvious contradictions cannot be seen. George Orwell described what we now call cognitive dissonance as 'doublethink' – the ability to hold two contradictory beliefs and accept that both are true. His phrase: 'war is peace, freedom is slavery, ignorance is strength', captures the self-delusion of cognitive dissonance. It is a human pandemic and crucial to the ongoing success of the global control system that I have spent 20 years exposing. It is also a phenomenon of Mind, not Consciousness.

The Silent Voice

Most people are so enslaved by Mind that they rarely, if ever, feel the urgings of their intuitive knowing – what some call the Silent Voice. The Mind 'does' loud, you see, and the LOUDER THE BETTER. It loves to keep the noise going, upping the decibels as necessary, to make sure the endless, mostly irrelevant and nonsensical mind-chatter drowns out the Silent Voice of Consciousness. WHAT DID MY INTUITION SAY? PARDON? CAN'T HEAR YOU. I SAID, WHAT DID MY INTUITION SAY? OH, FORGET IT, IT'S GONE NOW. Everything has awareness of some kind, and Mind certainly does. It is aware that if it allows Consciousness to express itself within this reality, its days of domination are over. It doesn't want that and it has become so deluded, for reasons I will explain, that it works to close the channels to Consciousness, encouraged by the elite families of the global conspiracy and their secret society networks. They use the knowledge I am outlining here to entrap the population in prisons of Mind. I will detail later how they do this, but one key way is to destroy the silence and make people frightened of the silence. Quite obviously, it is in the silence that the Silent Voice speaks most clearly, communicating not in words so much, as in awareness and 'knowing'. Yet how many people sit in silence any longer? Everywhere the silence is being broken by the 'modern world', and in the deep inner sanctums of the conspiracy this is no accident.

Consciousness talks to us through the heart and that's why we tend to 'feel' intuition in the chest area. I don't mean the physical heart, but the 'spiritual' one that can be felt in the centre of the chest. It is a vortex, or 'chakra' (meaning 'wheel of light'), which connects the 'physical' level with our higher levels of awareness beyond the five senses (Fig 7 overleaf).

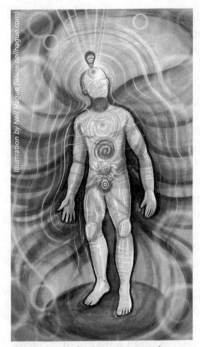

Figure 7: *The body is connected to multiple energy fields (levels of awareness) through the 'chakra' vortices. These are the seven main ones*

This is the origin of why the 'physical' heart is used to symbolise love. It comes from the lost understanding of what 'heart' really means in this context. When you feel great love or compassion notice again how you feel it in the centre of the chest – the location of the heart chakra or vortex through which we also feel our intuitive 'knowing'. When someone is trying to make a decision, we say: 'What does your heart tell you?' or 'Does it feel right?' The heart chakra is our major connection to Consciousness beyond this 'world' of illusory form, while our 'head', the conditioned Mind, is caught in the trap of 'thinking' in accordance with the rules and regulations of five-sense reality. Most people are imprisoned by their 'head', which is indoctrinated to believe the official version of what is right and wrong, moral and immoral, sane and insane – the 'norms' of society. This is an expression of the earth-bound awareness, the 'five-sense' Mind, which is manipulated daily to accept a version of reality and possibility that suits the agenda of those seeking to control. It is based on limitation, rules and regulations and the 'I can't', 'you can't', mentality. It sees why something cannot be done or should not be done, and rarely why it can or should. It is also frozen by fear, and this holds humanity in a mental and emotional prison cell. The 'heart', the intuition, however, is our connection with the Infinite Self beyond the five senses. It has its own electromagnetic field and its own sense of reality. The 'heart' feels rather than thinks and it has 'knowing' rather than second-hand 'knowledge' gleaned from the indoctrination machine. Some call it 'innate intelligence', intelligence beyond mere 'knowledge'. Most people have an inner 'war' going on between what they think and feel – what their head tells them to do and what they intuitively feel to do. Almost every time, the head is the winner. It is easier that way, or appears to be, in a Mind-society founded on the imposition of thought and belief. Once the 'norms' are decided and imposed by the system through 'education', 'science', the media, medicine and so on, any rebels or freethinkers are subjected to ridicule or condemnation (in my case, both) for the crime of being different, or challenging this ludicrously limited version of reality and possibility. This process is captured superbly by a Japanese saying: 'Don't be the nail that stands out above the rest because that's the first one to get hit'. Mind keeps its head down; Consciousness says, 'Hey, guys, I'm over here.'

Psychological Fascism

Anyone who seriously follows intuitive 'knowing' rather than the indoctrinated, fearful head/mind is going to face the ridicule and condemnation of the psychological fascists. These are not only people with jackboots and silly moustaches; they are parents, 'friends', colleagues, and, if you are in the public eye, 'journalists' and the public in general – anyone, in fact, who makes it difficult or unpleasant for you to be different.

This reaction is clearly widely-encoded in the human psyche through the power of genetic programming and domination of Mind. Look at how cruel even small children can be to anyone who is 'different' at school. Most of the human race is utterly indoctrinated by the externally implanted 'norms' which bombard the Mind from cradle to grave; they have no comprehension that their 'normal' thinking is their individual, and collective, prison. Such is their bewilderment, they not only contribute minute by minute to their own enslavement, but they also defend the Control System ferociously from anyone who questions or challenges the foundations and assumptions on which it stands. As Morpheus says in the first *Matrix* movie:

> The Matrix is a system, Neo. That system is our enemy. When you're inside, you look around, what do you see? Businessmen, teachers, lawyers, carpenters. The very minds of people we're trying to save, but until we do, these people are still a part of that system, and that makes them our enemy. You have to understand, most of these people are not ready to be unplugged. And many of them are so inured, so hopelessly dependent on the system that they will fight to protect it.

I don't go with the stuff about enemies – that's classic Mind – but it pretty much describes the human perception of the system that enslaves them. It is what I call the 'flat-earth mentality'. When the norm was that the Earth was flat, anyone who claimed it was round was subjected to ridicule and condemnation, even imprisonment and death. When the norm changed with the deluge of evidence that the Earth was a sphere, the roles immediately reversed and anyone who claimed it was flat then got the treatment. Norms rule, OK? Set the norms and you control human perception and behaviour. This is why exposing norms for the nonsense they are is so important. Those who live life through their intuition always attract the attention of the Thought Police, because the 'head' and the 'heart', Mind and Consciousness, view reality from completely different points of observation. Five-sense Mind disconnected from Consciousness is engaged in a constant and furious battle with intuition through fear of losing its perceived power over events and behaviour. If someone said their intuition told them that there were bandits around the corner and that they should turn back, the Mind of others would ask them for the 'proof'. They would be told not to be so silly and to stop spoiling the trip. In the same way, people have refused to get onto aircraft that were later to crash, because they had a 'feeling' – intuition from Consciousness. Even if these people had told the other passengers what they felt, most would have still got on the plane. Their heads would tell them the likelihood of crashing was miniscule and, anyway, they needed to get to their destination to attend a business meeting or to make a dinner date. Also, the great breakthroughs in understanding, including those in science, are invariably the result of intuition, of 'gut feeling', rather than of intellect alone. The intuition is the inspiration, and the intellect – or Mind – only confirms it.

Daring to be Different

When we follow our intuition, we often find ourselves behaving in ways that the conditioned, imprisoned minds of people around us find impossible to understand. They have to 'rationalise' your words and behaviour by saying you are 'mad' or 'dangerous'. In fact, you are merely different, viewing reality from another point of observation. It is like the scene with Robin Williams in the 1989 movie, *Dead Poets Society*, where he told his pupils in a 'norm'-dominated school:

I stand upon my desk to remind myself that we must constantly look at things in a different way. You see, the world looks very different from up here ... just when you think you know something, you have to look at it another way. Even though it may seem silly or 'wrong', you must try ...

... We all have a great need for acceptance, but you must trust that your beliefs are unique; your own, even though others may think them odd or unpopular. Even though the herd may go, "That's baaaaad".

With perfect timing, just before my own 'awakening', I had some experiences that led me to decide that if ever my mind and intuition, my head and heart, were in conflict again I would always go with my intuition. I have never wavered from that to this day. As I was soon to find, this commitment to relying on intuition can land you with serious challenges in a world that operates through head and Mind. In the midst of such experiences the head is screaming at the heart: 'I told you so! Look what happens when you don't listen to me!' This is where most people pull back and return to the head – experiment over. But when you stay with it and continue to follow your intuitive knowing in the face of all the consequences that may follow, a wonderful, liberating transformation begins to manifest. Mind is judging events only from the perspective of seeing to the next bend in the river, but your intuition (Consciousness) is viewing the entire river from source to sea. It knows that while things might seem bad at this point, the experience is leading somewhere really positive a little downstream. This has happened to me constantly, and never more so than in the opening years of the 1990s. Sometimes you get angry and frustrated because, to Mind, something has gone 'wrong'; but you later see that what went 'wrong' was actually perfect in the light of what came from it, or the gift of experience that it gave to you. For instance, using the river analogy, you might have been swept to the shore by the current or have sprung a leak in your canoe and had to stop. You might be furious, curse your 'luck' and say, 'Why me?' Then, along comes a local who tells you what good fortune you've had because just around the next bend was a massive waterfall that would surely have killed you. When you become more sensitive to your intuition you don't even need 'hints' like a leaky boat, you just 'know' that you should head for the shore and go no further.

The challenge is to read the signs and messages that intuition and life experience give to us and act upon them instead of letting Mind have its way. 'There is no reason to stop,' Mind would say. 'There is no evidence that there are waterfalls or rapids in this river and until I see the proof we are going ooooon ... aaaagggghhhhhhh ...' If you open to Consciousness you can bring Mind into line as an ally and not an enemy. It can be restored to its rightful place as a servant to the experience of Consciousness and no longer be the master. As a result of going with my intuition, no matter what, my five-sense Mind has been able to observe 'logically' that while following intuition can throw up enormous challenges, the experience always turns out to be what was necessary from the bigger perspective. It sees that what appears to be self-destruction actually

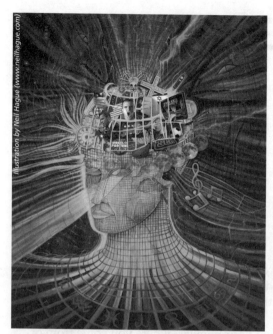

Illustration by Neil Hague (www.neilhague.com)

Figure 8: *Humanity is overwhelmingly disconnected from Consciousness by manipulated diversions and belief-systems designed to focus perception on the five senses. When we do this we block out infinity and perceive a fraction of what there is to 'see' and know*

leads to a positive outcome, and this happens *because* of the 'self-destructive' experience, not despite it. With this realisation, head moves into harmony with intuition and the war between what you think and feel, think and know, comes to an end. The two become One, and you follow your intuitive 'knowing' without the head symbolically banging its fist on the table.

Life is less about learning than about unlearning, or deprogramming. Consciousness in its highest state is already All-Knowing. Becoming Conscious is not something we need to strive for; it is our natural state. People spend so much time seeking that they never stop to find. We *are* Consciousness; there is no need to search for it. What we need to do is remove the illusory barriers and diversions (so well symbolised in Figure 8) that block our connection to who we really are and so keep us in Mind. The foundation on which all the diversions are constructed is the attachment to Mind, and the belief that this is who we are. Break that addiction, that illusion, and Consciousness floods in without you doing anything else. You can hold a ball on the bottom of a tank of water, but once you let go (free yourself from Mind) it flies to the surface in an instant. It has to. That is its natural state. It is not that we need to destroy Mind, not at all. It has an important part to play, indeed crucial, in being the interface, the computer system, that allows our Consciousness to experience this world of 'form' and 'things'. It is Mind that decodes this reality into what we think is a 'physical' landscape; it decodes what we call words and language; and it basically allows us to function within the illusion. There is nothing wrong with a 'brilliant mind' so long as it is *part* of our perception and not the governor of it.

Once we think we are the Mind, that's when our arse and the sticky stuff make contact and secure a firm connection. That's when we become Ethel and Charlie. I refuse to identify with such fake personas. I am not David Icke. I am Infinite Consciousness, and David Icke is my current experience within this 'physical' reality. The inner shift that takes place when you make that distinction will change your life forever.

2

No Brick in the Wall

Freedom is the right to tell people what they do not want to hear
George Orwell

My own 'life story' (experience) is an illustration of what I am talking about here. Like everyone else, I thought I was the mind-body called David Icke until a series of extraordinary experiences that continue to this day showed me that I was something far greater: Consciousness.

This is what you are, too. I don't care what your name is, where you come from or what you have done or not done. These details are just your experience. What you *are* is Consciousness, indeed the same Consciousness that I am. We are One, and the apparent divisions between us of race, age, culture, religion, job or income bracket are mere illusions, as we shall see, which enslave us in a false identity that allows the few to control the many. A prince or pauper, it matters not. The prince is the pauper and the pauper is the prince, for they are expressions of the same One Consciousness. This is the revelation, the realisation, that will set us free. Imagine an infinite ocean. The body of water is the same, but the perspective of reality when viewed from different parts of this ocean will be different and be given different names – Atlantic Ocean, Pacific Ocean, South China Sea … The only difference between us is the point from which we choose to observe reality from within Infinite Consciousness. We are the same ocean, the same One Consciousness, but we observe reality from different perspectives, different points of awareness. The loss of this understanding, over at least thousands of years (as we perceive 'time'), has meant that the language has not been developed to adequately describe the nature of the real 'I'. Whenever we talk of 'I', the Mind immediately relates this to the human body/personality and its name. I trust it will be

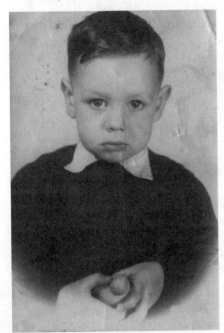

Figure 9: *You can see how delighted I was to be on Planet Earth*

clear in the text which 'I' is being referred to in the various contexts and I will use terms like real 'I' or true 'I' for Consciousness to make it clearer when necessary.

Figure 10: *My mother, Barbara – 'me mam'*

The David Icke 'I' was born in Leicester, England, at around 6.15pm on 29th April 1952. I grew up in what they call in Britain a 'working class' family (Fig 9). This is often another way of saying 'skint', and in our case it certainly was. My father, Beric, was the product of the toughest of lives, and the biggest influence on me in those early years. My mother, Barbara, was the opposite of my father (Fig 10). He was domineering and wanted to control, and she went quietly along doing whatever was necessary for her family. If you needed someone in a trench with you, she was among the first you should call. My father was extremely sharp intellectually, but his background of poverty and daily survival meant that he could never achieve his ambition to become a doctor. Only people with money had any chance of that, and my father had to leave school to provide an income for his family after his own father did a runner and left them. These times left scars with him that he carried for the rest of his life; and so did his experiences in the Great Depression of the 1930s, when he once walked from London to Blackpool, a distance of some 200 miles, looking for work during the (manufactured) 'slump' in which unemployment soared while those responsible for it added massively to their wealth. He joined the Army Medical Corps during the Second World War and won the British Empire Medal for pulling airmen from a blazing plane that crash-landed at the Chipping Warden airbase in Northamptonshire, England, in 1943. He also served in the Middle East and moved on through Italy as the fascists retreated. He was shocked to see wealthy Roman Catholic churches, in places like Naples, surrounded by unbelievable poverty while those in such dire need went on giving to their merciless religion. It made him vehemently anti-religion for the rest of his life; unfortunately, though, he also rejected any idea of life after 'death' because he equated that with the view of the religions he so despised. His many stories, including those of Naples, shaped my outlook on life from a very early age. Any expressions of unfairness, injustice and imposition have always pressed my buttons. I was a rebel from the start, questioning the established order. I now see that my childhood experiences were preparing me for what I was going to do much later. To the 'Mind Me' I was just a boy growing up, but to the greater 'Me', my life was a chain of experiences leading to what it knew was to come. It's like the analogy again of the canoe on the river with Mind seeing to the next bend and Consciousness seeing from source to sea. The question is, do we 'learn' (deprogram from Mind domination and become Conscious) as a result of our experiences on the 'river', or do we ignore them and let the Mind go on dictating our perception? They say there's no fool like an old fool and to an extent that is true. The 'old fools' are those who have been through the most years of experiences, but who have learned little (deprogrammed hardly at all).

My earliest memory is of sitting at a battered old table in a dark and dingy room. On the table was a bottle of sterilised milk – much used by the British 'working class' of the 1950s because it lasted longer than the other sort. This memory has come flooding back whenever I have smelled the distinctive whiff of sterilised milk. The scene was in a tiny terraced slum of a house in Lead Street, just off Wharf Street, in the run-down centre of Leicester, an industrial city in the English East Midlands. I lived in Lead Street for the first three years or so of my life, and the sterilised milk is all I can recall. My second memory is of running for the bus when we moved to a big new council estate on the outskirts of Leicester – the house where my younger brother, Paul, still lives more than 50 years on. It is directly across the road from Leicester General Hospital where I was born. Money was short, seriously short, throughout my childhood and I remember going with my mother around the back of the Gents clock factory on 'pay day Thursdays' so my father could sneak out and hand over his wages to buy that night's dinner. On a number of occasions when there was a knock at the door, my mother would tell me to hide under the window or behind a chair. There we would stay, still and quiet, until she gave the all-clear. I had no idea what this was all about until later when I realised the knock was the council rent-man coming to collect the money we didn't have. It's funny when people look so enviously at those who appear to have easier lives or who are born into rich families, when both are just Consciousness having an experience. If I needed to be born into a rich family to do what I do now then I would have been, but I wasn't. The upbringing I had was what best served my 'journey'. So chill out if you don't like your life, or didn't like your childhood, and ask why it is, or was, necessary. Why did it happen to you and not someone else? Why are you living the life that you are and not someone else? Acknowledge the answer and your life will change because the lesson is 'learned' (the Mind program deleted) and you can move on. There is no need to go on experiencing something once the reason for it has gone, and so you won't. If the same things keep happening to you then you haven't seen what they are telling you and, until you do, the cycle will continue.

Throughout my childhood I always felt 'different', although I didn't know why. I felt there was something I was here to do, but I didn't know what. I was a loner, and I spent hours, day after day, playing by myself with little push-along metal trains on the windowsill, lost in my own world. These 'Lone Star Locos', as they were called, were my best friends. My mother often recalled how I was so shy that I would cross the street to avoid speaking to people I knew. All these years and many public professions later, I still prefer my own space and privacy, and once a public event is over I just want to get away and disappear from view. This has always been an apparent contradiction with me. I have been in the public eye as a professional soccer player, a national television presenter, a politician, and now an author and challenger of conventional thought; yet all along I have been a person who dislikes the 'limelight' and prefers to be anonymous. I just love peace and quiet. One thing I knew right from childhood was that I would refuse to be one of the crowd. I was going to be different, and if I couldn't be different I didn't want to be here. I wasn't going to accept a future based on the fact that I was 'working class' and therefore destined for a factory or some low-paid job doing what someone else told me to do. I am not knocking those who do that – not at all. Without such people all those things we buy in the shops, including food, would not be there and I think the wages paid for these essential and hugely undervalued jobs is a disgrace. Keep the streets clean and they pay you a pittance; play the casino in Wall Street or the City of London, gambling with the very survival of millions of people, and they pay you a fortune. I am not demeaning those who work in factories and find themselves pawns in a dictatorial and unjust system. It is simply that I decided early in my life that this was not going to be for me. Then again, what I took to be 'I', the boy called 'David Icke', was actually being guided by a level of 'me' that I had no idea about at the time. My determination to be different came from the fact that this was my 'destiny', my 'journey', what I was here to do.

'Hey, can any of you lads play in goal?'

How I would escape from the fate that awaited most people from my background was not exactly clear. I just knew that I would. I failed the so-called 11-plus exam that decided if my latter years at school would be in an elite grammar school (for the 'brightest' and the 'best') or a secondary modern (for all the rest). I had no interest in school; it bored me rigid, and I only went because I had to and it allowed me to play for the football team. I rarely did better than average in exams. I couldn't care less what grades I achieved. I really didn't give a damn about logarithms or algebra or any of the other stuff they were telling me to absorb or expecting me to believe. Writing always interested me, as did history and geography, but little else. The only time I did well was one year at primary school when the teacher ridiculed and humiliated me in front of the class and said I was basically stupid. Immediately after this public put-down, the teacher set a spelling test – hardly my best subject even to this day (round of applause for Spell Check, I say). But at the end of the lesson, the poor guy had to somehow announce to the class that the child he had just ridiculed as stupid had scored highest in the test. I can still hear him choking. That year I came top of the class in the annual exams, and with a point proven to myself and to the miserable teacher, I went back to snoring through the rest of my time in the appalling school system. It is not there to educate, but to indoctrinate, and impose a false identity on its hapless victims. It is so splendidly captured in that superb song by Pink Floyd: 'Hey, teacher, leave those kids alone … All in all you're just another brick in the wall.' I was not going to be in the wall. I would have jumped off it first.

Football was my salvation, my escape from the net that trawled the schools of 'working class' kids and poured them into the system's sausage machine. A teacher at primary school spotted me playing in a kick-about soccer game in the playground. He asked me to go for a trial for the school team. If he hadn't have asked, I wouldn't have gone. The thought that David Icke would get into the team never occurred to me. I thought those things happened to others – not to me – but I was picked, and my self-confidence soared. I was about nine or ten and I knew then what my escape route would be. I was going to be a professional footballer. It seemed a ridiculous ambition given that the number of kids who make it to the professional game is a tiny fraction of those who want to be footballers; but I 'knew' from the start that it was going to happen. Even then, as I look back, there was this 'knowing' that was guiding me, something beyond the usual thought-chatter that we constantly hear. It is indeed like a silent voice. I would spend hours every day with a football. My father would say on many occasions that I was never going to earn a living kicking a ball about and I should think about what I was really going to do when I finished school. I didn't consider anything else – not once. I knew I was going to be a professional footballer and that was it. I was a goalkeeper, which suited my personality perfectly. Usually, it's not easy finding kids who want to be goalkeepers. They all want to be outfield players scoring the goals. Often it was the lad who was the worst player who got shoved in goal, but from the beginning I always wanted to be the goalkeeper. In many ways it is a loner's position, a part of the team, yes, but with a very different role and with different skills required from the other players. That instinctively appealed to me and so did the responsibility that came with being the last line of defence. If other players make mistakes they still have the keeper to get them out of trouble, but when a keeper makes an error it is invariably punished with a goal and recorded on the score sheet. I liked that sense of being on the edge with the difference between hero and villain so finely balanced.

I went on playing for school teams but, by the time I was 13, just two years before I was to leave for the dreaded adult world, there was still no sign that I would be heading for a professional football club. Then, right on cue, a 'lucky break' set me on my way. This has been such a feature of my life – my experience. Just when I have needed help to achieve something, bingo! There it was, often at a late hour when all seemed lost. I don't like using the word destiny because it sounds so grand, but if you take its definition of 'a predetermined course of events considered as something beyond human power or control', it does fit the bill pretty much. Destiny sounds grand because it is associated with fame or perceived great achievement, like being President of the United States for instance, but destiny can also apply to a guy who drives a bus, or to a hospital nurse. It is your journey of experience and you can miss your 'destiny' when you listen to Mind instead of following your intuition and urgings of Consciousness. People say 'no' far too often. If you say 'yes' to your intuition, and put Mind in its place when it cusses and complains, your 'destiny' will manifest, whatever that may be. Destiny so often gets lost, suffocated by enslavement to Mind.

In those days, in the 1960s, if you wanted to attract the attention of professional football clubs you had to be playing for your town or city schools representative side. The big clubs didn't bother looking below that level. They figured that if you were not good enough to represent your city you would be of no interest to them. I was 13, a crucial age for impressing the scouts looking for the best young talent, and I was nowhere near playing in the standard of games that they were watching. By now, I was attending Crown Hills Secondary Modern School in Leicester and spending most of my time staring out of the classroom window, daydreaming away the boredom of the curriculum, little of which ever registered. Then, one day, the sports teacher told me he was sending me for a trial for the Leicester schoolboys' under-14's team, but I would be going as an outfield player. There was a highly-rated goalkeeper at the trial who was certain to be selected, he said, and it wasn't worth me trying to compete with him. This was a lad who was already playing for the older under-15's Leicester team and it was obviously taken for granted that he would play for the younger side, too. 'Fate', however, as usual in my life, was about to intervene. One thing we need to understand if we are to see 'life' as it really is: there are no coincidences. There is only creating your own reality and your willingness, or otherwise, to follow your intuitive knowing and cease to be controlled by Mind.

I played outfield in the first trial game and was pretty hopeless. My heart was not in it. I only wanted to be the goalkeeper. I was asked to go and kick around with the other rejected boys while the second trial match was played. That was the end of that, I thought. Then I heard a shout from where the trial was continuing. 'Hey, can any of you lads play in goal?' bellowed the team manager. 'Yes!' I shouted and I ran towards him as quickly as I could before anyone else could lay claim. One of the two goalkeepers had been injured and could not continue, and when I took over I did so well that the manager asked me to come to the next trial a week later as a reserve goalkeeper to the one so highly rated. That next trial game was to change my life. I played as well as I have ever played in my entire

Figure 11: *A professional footballer, but it didn't last for long*

career. The teams were seriously mismatched and I was bombarded with shots from every angle. It was one of those days when if I had dived the wrong way, the ball would have found the end of my foot and been deflected away. It was almost as if I could not let in a goal even if I had tried. Something intervened that day, for sure, but only decades later did I begin to appreciate what that something was. I was picked for the team above the lad everyone thought was a certainty. The next year I played for the Leicester under-15's team, and the professional clubs began to knock on my door. I signed for Coventry City, then in England's top division, and I left school to earn my living doing exactly what I wanted to do. I was a professional footballer, just as I always knew – for reasons I didn't understand – that I would be (Fig 11).

As it turned out, my football career was soon to be in trouble when I developed what doctors told me was rheumatoid arthritis at just 15 and a half years old. It started in my left knee and soon progressed to both knees and both ankles. In the years after my football career ended, the pain and swelling went on to infiltrate my wrists, hands and all my fingers. For years I refused to bow to the doctors' verdict that I should stop playing. Staggeringly, as I look back, I continued to play successfully for Coventry for four years despite the arthritis, before I was told to either stop playing or face life in a wheelchair. I was 19 when they gave me that verdict, but still determined to play on. I joined another club – Hereford United – and enjoyed a year of great success before the end came literally overnight. The arthritis was extremely painful in that final year and the daily training sessions were agonising until my joints had warmed up. I would be limping at the start of each session, and every day I would have some excuse to hide the common cause. It would be a blister or a stiff calf muscle or something. I knew that if the club discovered the real cause they would be looking for a new goalkeeper. The buzz and adrenalin would get me through the games and I was playing well, so no questions were asked. We won promotion to a higher division. I was playing in a professional league football team at just 20 and some bigger clubs were beginning to show an interest. Then, one night, I looked down at my knees before I got into bed and saw that the swelling in my left knee had disappeared – for the first time since I was 15. I was elated and thought to myself: Hey, I'm beating it! The following morning as I began to stir from sleep, I realised that I could not breathe. I tried for what seemed an age to take in air and I thought I was going to die. I tried to nudge my wife, Linda, lying beside me, but I was unable to move a single muscle. Suddenly, I gasped a breath and, as my body came back to life, I realised that what seemed like every joint in my body was in sheer agony. I could not move on the bed, let alone walk, and, although the pain and lack of mobility were to ease with the days, I was never to play football again.

If I look at what happened from the perspective of Mind, of being a human being with one shot at 'life', it was a tragedy for a youngster to see his dream destroyed. How sad. Don't get me wrong, it bloody hurt I can tell you; but life often presents you with your greatest gifts brilliantly disguised as your worst nightmare. Football had given me what it was meant to give me, and the next step of the journey now beckoned. Once again, the little 'I', the Mind 'I', had no idea that this was so. To the little 'I', seeing only the next turn in the river, my life had fallen apart. To the big 'I', the true 'I', it was job done, move on. Football had given me many things, not least the focus and discipline necessary to progress, but also confidence in myself and the ability to live with the pressure of expectation from a very early age. This gave me emotional strength, as did, to a massive degree, the arthritis. To live with almost constant pain – and it was to get much worse with the years – activated an unshakable will to keep going, whatever. If you can live with that level of pain, when even putting your socks on is a daily agony, everything else is a cinch. The end of my football career also presented me with an enormous emotional disappointment to overcome … and a challenge: do I look for a new dream, or fall apart because the last one died?

Er, new dream, please.

'Hello, good evening and welcome'

I had just turned 21: an ex-professional footballer virtually crippled with arthritis, and, to my knowledge, with no other potential skill or profession with which to earn a living. Happy days. In such dire straits I did what anyone would do: I decided I was going to be a network television presenter. I was interviewed on a live TV programme about the ending of my soccer career, and I thoroughly enjoyed the atmosphere and the whole deal. This is for me, I thought, and I set my target of presenting the BBC's *Grandstand*, then the biggest and best sports show on British television. This was apparently even more ludicrous than my ambition to play soccer for a living. At least there were around a hundred goalkeepers in professional teams, but you could count the BBC sports presenters on one hand. Now this guy, who loves privacy and anonymity, wanted to be a national television anchorman. Bizarre on the face of it, but something just drove me on and, once again, I knew it was going to happen. My whole life experience has been like that. As soon as one door closes, there's a chink of light as another creaks open. It has been like walking through a maze, with some force – Consciousness – guiding me through. Until the turn of the 1990s, I thought I was just following my 'ambitions'.

I was told that the way into television news and sport would be by first working in newspapers and on the radio. There was an immediate problem, however. With no academic qualifications of any shape or form it was not going to be easy finding a newspaper to hire me. Having worked in the media, and having seen it from the outside, I can safely confirm that academic qualifications are absolutely no measure of intelligence; nor do they give you the ability to be a competent journalist. But examination passes confirm that you have successfully passed through the indoctrination machine and so that's what the system demands. Anyway, eventually I got a job, by 'coincidence' (there are no coincidences), back in my home city of Leicester. It was a weekly newspaper called the *Leicester Advertiser*, which was just about read by the people who wrote it. If its circulation had been human it would have been on a life-support machine. I got the job because no one

Figure 12: *I made it into television, but, as it turned out, it was just another step on a much greater journey*

else wanted it, but soon I was moving on with doors opening and closing to perfection to speed me through to radio and then television. I worked as a news reporter and presenter with BBC regional and national news before, in 1982, becoming a nationally-known anchorman with BBC Television Sport, the very job I had targeted all those years earlier when I was told my soccer career was over. I remember driving to the BBC in tears the day I first presented *Grandstand*, which I had set my sights on in those dark times at the age of 21. It was nothing to do with fronting a television show; it was about achieving what I had set out to do when my life and health were in tatters (Fig 12). My father used to say to me that you are never finished until you tell yourself you are finished, no matter what others may say. I would recall those words many times in the years to come. What he was saying, without knowing he was speaking a profound truth, is that we create our own reality. What we believe is reality will manifest as experienced reality. This is something the global manipulators exploit to great effect.

'Politics' (poly = many; ticks = blood-sucking creatures)

Soon after I had achieved my long-held ambition to work in television, the job lost its appeal. I found television to be a deeply insincere world full of insecure, often shallow, and sometimes vicious characters. They used to say that television people got so confused they stabbed each other in the chest (as opposed to the back, which was the usual route). There were, and are, many exceptions, but they are not usually in the positions of hire and fire. To make it that far you need to have no problem with trampling over others or with licking arse, mostly both. Within a few years I wanted out, and, from the little Mind 'I' perspective, it would seem that I was never satisfied with anything and always flitting from one thing to another. I thought about that myself sometimes and so, I'm sure, did Linda, my incredibly supportive wife for 29 years. Linda went along with my apparently insatiable desire to pursue new ambitions so soon after I had achieved the last one. She has been so important to my journey, and remains so to this day as the owner of the company that publishes my books. She is the greatest friend I have ever had or could ever want. We don't attract people into our lives by accident. They are either here to support us, or to offer us the chance to look at ourselves in a way we wouldn't normally do. Often the latter are called 'pains in the arse'. Yes, they can seem like that and I have been there (playing both roles), but they can be essential to deprogramming from Mind domination, making you face aspects of yourself that need deleting, and pointing you in a new direction. Look at the people in your life who give you a hard time. What is it saying about you? Okay, acknowledge that and either they will change in their attitude towards you or drift from your life.

I continued to work for the BBC, in body if not spirit, for another eight years, but my real focus was now elsewhere. From childhood I had loved 'nature' and what has now been termed the 'environment'. I would ride for hours on my bike through the Leicestershire countryside enjoying the beauty and the solitude. As the 1980s progressed, the protection of the environment became the centre of my life. I began an environmental pressure-group on the Isle of Wight, just off England's south coast, where I have lived for nearly 30 years; but I realised that no matter how good your arguments were about an environmental issue, or any other, the only thing that mattered was the number of hands in the air at the local council meetings when the vote was taken. If you didn't have the majority supporting your case, its strength or validity was irrelevant. I also began to understand that the councillors' decisions about which way to vote were often being agreed at the local Freemasons' temple before the 'debate' in the council chamber had even been heard. The next stage of my life was already beginning to stir. I decided that the environment needed a voice on the local council, and my career in politics, if you can call it such, had begun. What happened next is another example of the way an unseen force has been weaving my life experience. I rejected all the major political parties because I didn't trust any of them. Instead, in 1988, I wrote to the little-known UK Green Party, which made the protection of the environment the centre of its policies. They sent me some information that seemed to be sensible and I sent off my membership fee and began to organise public meetings to start a branch of the Greens on the Isle of Wight.

Things began to move very fast. Within a couple of weeks I received a letter from the Green Party's regional organiser asking us to send a representative of the new Isle of Wight branch to their next meeting. I went along, and at the end it was announced that their regional representative on the national party council was resigning and they needed nominations for his replacement. With no one wanting the job I said I would do it, and even so two people voted against me! I think they believed that being in television was 'ungreen'. Anyway, another two weeks later I turned up at my first national council meeting in a building near Regent's Park, in London, and found it awash with navel contemplators who could talk for England while never reaching a conclusion. I could completely understand why the Green Party had been such a nonentity in British politics. Just before lunch, the 'chairperson' said they were looking for party spokesmen and women, or 'Party Speakers' as the Greens called them, to represent the party in the media for the coming year, and nominations would be taken in the afternoon. During lunch, I was approached by a man who said he thought it would be good to have someone well-known in the media to represent the party and asked if I would be interested. I said, 'OK, I'll give it a try.' An hour or so later I was elected a National Speaker for the UK Green Party. I had been a member for a matter of weeks (Fig 13).

My appointment coincided with a surge of interest in the Environment, fuelled by a series of prime-time television programmes highlighting the plight of rainforests and the consequences of pollution. By the summer of 1989 this reached a peak of public concern, and suddenly the UK Green Party was big news. We won 15 per cent of the national vote in elections to the European Parliament. The party had rarely registered more than one per cent up to this point. From empty press conferences and empty halls, the party and its official speakers were thrust onto the national news and into the political limelight. The Green Party had arrived, but, as it transpired, not for long. A battle ensued between those in the party who wanted to be true to its original beliefs (the 'fundis', or

Figure 13: *A national spokesman for the British Green Party – the last step before the real work began*

fundamentalists) and those who liked the success and were pressing to drop policies they believed were preventing even more support (the 'realos', or realists). I was a 'fundi-realo' in that I wanted to stick with the values, but present them to the public in a much more effective way. I wrote a book called *It Doesn't Have to be Like This* with this end in mind. It set out Green Party policy in words that the public could understand without all the enviro-jargon I was hearing all the time. I still agree with some of the premise of that 'policy book', but as I awakened to the world as it really was, I saw that the core agenda behind the creation of the 'green movement' was to exploit, and invent, environmental concerns as an excuse to advance the global control system. The Big Lie about human-caused 'climate change' is the prime example. The infighting within the Greens sickened me, and more so when it became clear that while the Green Party claimed to be the 'new politics', it was just another version of the old politics with the same old methods, manipulations and reactions. The Green Party set out to challenge the system and ended up joining it. Many times it has been reported that I was 'sacked' by the Green Party for what was now to unfold in my life, but the truth is that I never renewed my membership because I could see that the Greens were clearly not going to change anything. Another reason why I distanced myself from the party in the months which followed was that some very strange things were happening to me and I knew that when I spoke about them publicly I was going to be in for some serious ridicule which, by association, would affect the Green Party.

I had reached the most pivotal point in my Mind 'I' life, and what I had experienced this far was going to be so important in what was to come. As I look back from today's perspective, I can see how perfect it has all been – the 'bad' bits and the 'good'. These are just labels that come from the perspective of Mind that sees everything as duality and polarity, while Consciousness sees the unity of everything. The 'bad' bits have been just as important, often more so, as the 'good'. They are all threads in the same tapestry called experience. There were things I had to know and understand for what was about to unfold, and I needed the emotional strength that was vital to surviving the next stage. None of this I knew about, but the big 'I' did and it played out to perfection. I had felt, and overcome, the emotional trauma of seeing my dreams of being a footballer shattered by arthritis. In pursuing a cure, I had been introduced to the ancient Chinese healing art of acupuncture and that had opened me to an understanding that there is far more to the human being than just a body. Playing in such pain had triggered a determination to overcome adversity and to keep going, no matter what the challenges and the odds. Journalism had shown me how the media works, and how much the 'news' is manipulated. I was able to see how the media was structured to confirm the official version of events, and not to question or investigate this official reality. I could see that most journalists were some of the most uniformed, conditioned and imprisoned people you could ever meet. How can they report the world as it is when they have not got a clue how it is? Journalism is such a blatant creation of Mind. The overwhelming majority of journalists are stuck solid in Mind, and report events from that perspective. Anyone who lives outside of that minute little box is immediately ridiculed or condemned, because the box doth not compute. A quote I saw said: 'Those who danced were thought to be quite insane by those who could not hear the music.' Journalism also allowed me, through the demands of newspaper space, to develop the ability to write concisely and communicate to an audience spanning the whole spectrum of knowledge on the subjects in question. My television career presented insights into that medium's manipulations, techniques and often unbelievable shallowness, both on the screen and off. The national public profile it gave me also ensured that I would be widely-reported when the time came for me to consciously awaken and see beyond the illusion. My time in the Green Party showed me politics from the inside, and how it is a game of power, not principle, no matter what the name on the door may be. I saw how many politicians who opposed and condemned each other in public 'debate' were very much closer in private.

My life experience this far had given me all that I needed for what was to come and, oh, my God, what was to come.

3

What's Goo-in' On, Our Dave?

If you want to tell people the truth, make them laugh, otherwise they'll kill you
Oscar Wilde

I began to be aware of strange happenings around me from the time I was writing my environmental book, *It Doesn't Have to be Like This*, in 1989. I was writing very quickly, often a chapter a day, and when I read it back each evening I would keep thinking to myself: Where did this come from? and: I don't remember writing that! It was like I was writing it all in a dream.

At this same time I began to feel a presence around me. When I was alone in a room it felt like somebody else was present, and this went on for months. Eventually, I was sitting on the side of the bed in a hotel room in London in early 1990 and the presence felt so strong that I actually said out loud, 'If you are there will you please contact me because you are driving me up the wall!' Soon afterwards, events began to accelerate. In March 1990, I was playing soccer with my son, Gareth, then aged eight – now a brilliant singer-songwriter – on the seafront near my home in Ryde, on the Isle of Wight. I said to him that we would go for lunch at the railway station cafe nearby, but it was full and, as we headed for an alternative, somebody recognised me from the television and began to ask me questions about football. When the conversation was over, I couldn't see Gareth, but I knew he would be in the newspaper shop at the station looking at books about steam trains – which we both had an interest in. I stood at the entrance to the shop and said to Gareth that we would go and find another cafe, but, as I turned to leave, my feet were stuck to the ground as if two magnets were anchoring them to the floor. It was a very weird feeling, almost as if, as I now understand, another reality had manifested around me. As I stood there, my feet fixed to the spot, I heard a very clear 'voice' in my head say: 'Go and look at the books on the far side.' Shit, what was that? What the hell is going on here? I knew this shop very well and the books in that 'far side' section were of no interest to me. They were invariably romantic fiction of the Barbara Cartland variety. I went over to see what would happen, not least because that was the only direction my feet would go, and I was immediately attracted to a book with a woman's face on the front. It was as if that was the only book I could see, a feeling I have had endless times since. I turned it over to read the blurb and saw the word 'psychic'. The author was a professional psychic and 'hands-on' healer and I thought immediately of the presence I had been feeling around me for all those months. Would this lady be able to tell me what was going on? I read the book in 24 hours and contacted her to make an appointment. I said nothing about the presence, only that I had arthritis and I wanted to see if her healing could help. I was not going to say anything about what had been happening to me unless she picked up on it herself.

Wavelength 'Worlds'

I only saw her four times and in the first two visits nothing happened of note, except that I talked with her about other dimensions or frequencies of existence and a much wider vision of life and possibility. I had always rejected religion and also the absurd idea peddled by 'science' that we are all 'accidents' of 'evolution' who cease to exist at 'death'. Unbelievable rubbish, but that is largely still the claim of establishment 'science', despite the wealth of evidence and research, including that of open-minded real scientists, which demolishes such claptrap. Up to this point, I had never really pondered on an alternative to this nonsense, but, as I talked with the psychic lady, I was immediately at one with what she was saying about the multidimensional nature of reality, and the ability of one dimension to communicate with others. It was as if she was telling me what I already knew, which is exactly what she was doing. We all know this information, but we have been conditioned to forget who we really are, and what we really know, by becoming so consumed by five-sense Mind. For those new to all this, some background is necessary. We don't live in a 'world' so much as a frequency range – the one that our five senses can perceive. This five-sense range of perception is tiny and known as 'visible light'. Creation is not structured like a chest of drawers, one level on top of another; it is made up of frequencies sharing the same 'space', in the same way that all the radio and television frequencies do. Broadcast frequencies are not just around your body at this moment, they are sharing the same 'space' as your body, and this is possible because they are operating on a different wavelength to your body and to each other. Only when the wavelengths, or frequencies, are really close do we get 'interference' and become aware of another station. Apart from that, all are oblivious to each other's existence. They operate in different frequencies, 'realities' or 'worlds'. When you tune your radio to a station, say Radio 1, that's what you get. You don't hear Radio 2, 3 or 4. Move the dial and change the frequency from Radio 1 to Radio 2 and now, obviously, you hear Radio 2. But Radio 1 does not cease to broadcast when you move the dial from its wavelength. It goes on broadcasting – existing – while your focus, your awareness, is tuned to something else.

This is precisely the principle on which this virtual-reality universe operates. The five senses through which we see, hear, smell, touch and taste can perceive an infinitesimal fraction of that which exists in the 'space' you think you are 'seeing' now. This is why animals, such as cats, jump around reacting to what appears to us to be 'empty space'. To the cats, the 'space' is not empty at all. They have a greater visual frequency range and they can see entities and activity that are beyond the frequency limits of the human five senses. When people say that everything is within you or, symbolically, the Kingdom of Heaven is within you, this is correct. All infinity is within us because all infinity shares all 'space', or our sense of it. The point is, however, that we can't see all infinity with our five senses, just as you cannot hear all the available radio stations by tuning in to one of them. We see only that tiny part of infinity that is vibrating to the frequency range of those senses – what we see, hear, smell, touch and taste. This is what I call the five-sense prison. Most people are so trapped in its manufactured and manipulated illusions that they believe that this is all that exists, and is all that they are. It is their only reality – the reality of Mind. This is further ingrained and conditioned by the 'education' system, the media and 'science', all of which are dominated by the belief that the 'world' of the five senses is basically all that there is. When energy is vibrating slowly it appears to us to be 'dense' and 'solid', say like steel, but look at it under a powerful microscope and, no matter how 'solid' something seems to be, it is still vibrating energy. As the speed of vibration increases, the energy becomes less and less dense until it is vibrating so quickly that it leaves the frequency range of the five senses and, to human perception, 'disappears'. It has not disappeared; it has simply left the range that human senses can access. This explains why people have seen ghosts or 'UFOs' which 'appeared' out of nowhere and then 'disappeared'. There are endless virtual realties that interpenetrate each other like radio or televisions stations and, when you know what you are doing, you can move between them. Scientists call them 'parallel universes'. The conditioned five-sense reality of Mind thinks that those who talk of seeing something appear and then disappear must be mad. 'It's not possible!' they cry. Oh, but it is. The 'nowhere' from which such manifestations come and go is simply another frequency, or wavelength, of existence that our five senses cannot access. Understanding all this is crucial to appreciating that the 'far out' world of the so-called 'paranormal' is perfectly and simply explainable. The longer this book goes on the simpler it will become.

Houston, We Have Contact

On my third visit to the psychic I was lying on a medical-type couch or 'bed' during the healing session when I felt something like a cobweb on my face. I had remembered reading in her book that this can happen when 'spirits' are trying to make contact. Funnily enough, I have never felt it since. I said nothing to her, but within 10 to 15 seconds she pushed her head back and said: 'Wow! This is powerful; I'll have to close my eyes for this one!' My backside was slipping down the bed and I was asking myself what on earth I'd gotten myself into. She said she was seeing a 'Chinese-looking' figure in her psyche who was saying: 'Socrates is with me'. Socrates (469–399 BC) was the Greek philosopher whose most famous pupil was Plato. At the age of 70, Socrates was charged by the authorities with heresy, and corruption of local youth, and he carried out his death sentence himself by drinking hemlock. Amongst a library of famous quotes, Socrates said: 'Wisdom is knowing how little we know'. Brilliant. The 'Chinese-looking' figure was only a projection from another reality into the perception of the psychic to give her a familiar image to focus on. The communicator was an expression of Consciousness from beyond the realm of the 'physical' body; it can take any form it chooses. This is what we all are in our higher forms – pure Consciousness and Awareness. Other-dimensional communicators project information, or thought, into a psychic's energy field / brain and he or she decodes that into human language. This is what was happening to me when I heard the 'voice' in the newspaper shop. It is the same principle as radio programmes being broadcast from the transmitter in waveform and decoded into words by the radio. An Italian psychic will 'hear' the thought projections in Italian, an English one in English, and so on. This is how the psychic reported some of what the 'Chinese-looking' figure communicated that day in March, 1990:

He is a healer who is here to heal the Earth and he will be world famous.

He will face enormous opposition, but we will always be there to protect him.

He is still a child, spiritually, but he will be given the spiritual riches.

Sometimes he will say things and wonder where they came from. They will be our words.

Knowledge will be put into his mind and at other times he will be led to knowledge.

He was chosen as a youngster for his courage. He has been tested and has passed all the tests.

He was led into football to learn discipline, but when that was learned it was time to move on. He also had to learn how to cope with disappointment, experience all the emotions, and how to get up and get on with it. The spiritual way is tough and no one makes it easy.

We know he wanted us to contact him, but the time wasn't right [this was a reference to what I said in the 'empty' hotel room, which the psychic didn't know about]. He was led here to be contacted, not to be cured. But one day he will be completely cured.

He will always have what he needs [this could have been 'wants'], but no more.

In my next session with the psychic, the figure appeared to her again and these words were given to me:

One man cannot change the world, but one man can communicate the message that will change the world.

Don't try to do it all alone. Go hand in hand with others, so you can pick each other up as you fall.

He will write five books in three years.

Politics is not for him. He is too spiritual. Politics is anti-spiritual and will make him very unhappy.

He will leave politics. He doesn't have to do anything. It will happen gradually over a year.

There will be a different kind of flying machine, very different from the aircraft of today.

Time will have no meaning. Where you want to be, you will be.

I was a BBC television presenter introducing sport, and a national spokesman for the Green Party. Yet here I was being told that I was a healer who was here to heal the Earth; and that one man cannot change the world, but one man can communicate the message that will change the world. Huh? Come again? On one level it seemed mad and ridiculous. Even so, something within me, my intuitive 'knowing', told me I had to go with this and see where it led. Funny, just before this happened I made an investment – with my head and against my intuition – and lost some money. It wasn't a lot, but, as I mentioned earlier, it was enough for me to say that if ever my head and my heart were at odds again I was going with my heart, my intuition, every time. This is what I decided to do when faced with the apparently crazy things I was being told via the psychic. As a result of the unstoppable urge I had to walk this path, my life went through upheavals that were almost too much for my emotions to bear. But all these years and so much pain later, what I was told would happen either has happened or is happening, except for the line about being 'completely cured'. I'm still waiting for that. The idea that I would write five books in three years on subjects I knew nothing about seemed especially absurd. Yet, as it turned out, I was to complete those books in three years to the very month, although I didn't realise that until I remembered those words and counted back.

When I told some of the Green Party leadership about these experiences, their reaction was just as closed-minded, ignorant and uninformed as you would find anywhere in the system the Greens were claiming to challenge. 'David is going crazy', was the rumour that began to circulate from those I had told. Yeah, right. Welcome to the new politics! Like all political parties, by the very fact they are in politics, the Green Party is a Mind construct and utterly dominated by the intellect while talking of spirituality. By that, I don't mean every member – just the structure, and those who let Mind dominate their perception, which is most of them. They think they are different from other political parties, yet they are just another expression of the same Mind. Jonathan Porritt, the best-known UK 'Green', is a blueprint Mind intellectual who was scathing about me and my experiences. Of course he was, and, of course, so many other 'Greens' were, and are. They are Mind people and their awareness is confined to the box that entraps their perception. When I see Green Party spokespeople on television, it is like watching politicians from any other party. They parrot policies that are straight from the agenda of the global manipulators, including centralisation of power (though they claim otherwise) and the Big Lie of human-caused 'global warming'. They have joined the club they claimed to be dedicated to replacing, and the sad thing is they think they've done the opposite. One notable exception was Justin Walker, who was quite a prominent member of the Green Party when all this happened. He is still a friend all these years later and campaigning in many of the areas related to what I am doing. He allowed his mind to open to new possibilities and he has taken a lot of flak from the 'different' Greens for having anything to do with me. Good on you, Justin. The reaction to my experiences by the Green Party hierarchy in the 'no-hierarchy' party was a very mild precursor of what was to follow.

It's All Organised

After those initial visits to the psychic, events began to move quickly. 'Coincidences' would lead me to other psychics in this early awakening period and they did not know what the others had told me. The themes were extremely consistent. There was a shadow across the world that had to be lifted, a story that had to be told, and I, for whatever reason, was going to tell it. Among these communications were:

> Arduous seeking is not necessary. The path is already mapped out. You only have to follow the clues … We are guiding you along a set path. You are learning according to our teaching of you. It was all organised before you incarnated.

> True love does not always give the receiver what it would like to receive, but it will always give that which is best for it. So welcome everything you receive whether you like it or not. Ponder on anything you do not like and see if you can see why it was necessary. Acceptance will then be very much easier.

> He is a solidifier of thought who helps the Word to surface in people he meets.

> You are being asked to change. You are being asked to change in a total way. It is not a matter of small changes, of a little thing here, a little thing there. You are really being asked to turn [yourself] inside out. There is a massive shadow which must be cleared and it is up to [people] such as [yourself] to focus … on that challenge.

> Those of you who are at the forefront of this, you are rather like a snowplough. You are the thin end of the wedge. You really have… how shall I put this? To a certain extent, I suppose, you have the shitty end of the job. You have got to do an awful lot, but nevertheless you are capable of doing an awful lot. That is why you have chosen to come; that is what you are here for, to really shovel some shit, and therefore make some space behind you to make it easier for the others.

Another constant theme was of great upheavals that were to come, and a transformation of human consciousness into a truly awakened state. This theme continues in my life and work to this day. There was no sign of any 'transformation of consciousness' back in 1990, but, away from the concrete Mind of the mainstream media, there is a massive and gathering awakening happening today all over the world. No, it's not the majority, nor even nearly so, but it's expanding faster with every week. People in vast numbers are looking at themselves and the world in a new way and encompassing information and ideas they would have dismissed with laughter and derision not so long ago. I was told through these psychic communications that we had been trapped in a 'freeze vibration' and that this low vibrational 'solidity' was being broken by an energetic transformation. I learned much later that many ancient traditions say that the 'physical world' was once far more fluid and less dense than we experience today; and the Aborigines in Australia say the Earth is destined to return to this higher vibrational state, which they call 'Dreamtime'. We are certainly in the midst of fantastic change that will set this 'world' free of its subservience, ignorance and density (in every sense). Much more about this later.

'What I am going to say has nothing to do with that…'

Within a few weeks of that first contact through the psychic healer, the BBC told me it was not renewing my contract and, in effect, I was fired. This was a shock given all the letters of commendation I had received from BBC staff, and the fact that I was still very young to be doing the job and should have had decades ahead of me. The main reason was clearly pressure from the BBC hierarchy to get rid of me because of my Green Party activities, and especially my refusal to pay the Poll Tax that was introduced during the dictatorial reign of Prime Minister, Margaret Thatcher. It demanded that rich and poor pay the same … a blatant injustice, and I was one of millions who withheld payment in protest at its unfairness. These millions eventually had to appear in court and there was enormous media interest when the first cases were heard. Here, fate stepped in again. The first cases could have been heard in a courtroom anywhere in the United Kingdom. But where were they heard? In Newport, a little market town on the Isle of Wight, and my case was among those on the list. I arrived at the court to a blur of television cameras and newspaper reporters and photographers as they came to record the first Poll Tax protestors being prosecuted. Except that they weren't, as it happened. I waited for hours as row after row of protestors were dealt with for their refusal, and often inability, to pay. They couldn't deal with us individually because there were too many.

Then, at last, I was called, and I stood before the magistrates with six or seven others to face the charges. One in the group, a man I had met at Poll Tax protest meetings, put his hand in the air for permission to speak. He pointed out the date by which the payments should have been made and the date on which the summonses were sent out to non-payers ordering them to appear in court. He then revealed that, according to the law, period between the two dates was too short and that the prosecutions happening that day were therefore illegal. The atmosphere in the court changed immediately and the magistrates adjourned for discussions. When they returned around half an hour later, they had to announce that the man was correct and all prosecutions that day were invalid and everyone was free to go. I pointed out to the magistrates that it was not that simple. People had been brought to court illegally and had lost a day's earnings and incurred transport costs as a result. What about the compensation? The authorities had no choice but to agree. Loss of earnings was repaid and I was to receive a cheque for £2.50 for my bus fare. These events were emblazoned across the front pages of all the newspapers and dominated the television news, and Margaret Thatcher's Poll Tax became a national joke. From this point, with its credibility demolished, it had no chance of survival and had to be replaced with a system more in tune with people's ability to pay. I had to pinch myself that night. Not only had the first cases been heard on the Isle of Wight, when they could have been anywhere in Britain, but the prosecutions were thrown out at the very point that I was standing in line waiting for my case to be dealt with! Coincidence, or what? I can see now that it wasn't, but then it was like: what are the chances of that?!

The morning after the court hearing, I arrived at the BBC to discuss my 'future' with the corporation's Head of Sport. Spread across his table were the morning papers, recording the Poll Tax fiasco in Newport, with my face on most of them. 'What I am going to say has nothing to do with that,' he said, pointing to the papers. Hmmm. I was told, basically, that I had no future at the BBC, and a few weeks later we parted company after eleven years with not even a 'thank you' or a 'best of luck'. The BBC is actually an arrogant and often vicious organisation that treats its staff like cattle, just like other television and media organisations. But, once again, there are many levels to the same experience. From the perception of the five-sense 'I', the BBC was callous and arrogant in the way it treated me. From the perception of the true 'I', however, I was being set free from the television treadmill so I could go wherever it was my life was taking me. I thank them for that because if I was still presenting TV programmes all these years later, as many of my then colleagues still are, I would be in search of a clifftop to leap from and the higher the better. Good luck to them, but, loss of income apart, I was so glad to be out of it.

Where Now?

My old life was over, just as it was meant to be. I may have been out of a job, with no alternative income, but I felt liberated. Working in the soulless media had become a living nightmare, and now I was free. I only survived the next few years financially because I lived well below my income from television and had enough money in the bank to see my family and I through – just. It was a time when trusting the flow of life was a major challenge, with everything I had worked years to build now falling around me. And it was about to get a whole lot worse. In many ways, symbolically, I *had* jumped from a clifftop and I was about to find out if I could fly. It didn't seem like it for a long time, but in the end I realised that I could – just as we all can. Linda and my children were, of course, even more confused than I was. At least I had directly experienced the strange happenings; they knew only what I had told them.

Here was their husband and father, a well-known face on national television for a decade, suddenly out of a job, talking about weird events and ideas, and soon to be publicly ridiculed on a scale rarely seen in all British media history. The fact that they stood by me and did not once waver in their support, no matter happened, was one of the key factors in my ability to survive what was about to be unleashed. They were there for me because they were meant to be there for me, as I am for them. It is the same for everyone, whether they are in 'good' or 'bad' relationships, much as it may not seem that way from the perception of Mind. People do not come into our lives by accident, especially our families. Once again, if you are having problems with your family, ask yourself why, and what it says about you. Maybe it's that you need to change, or it could be that you are being challenged to cut loose the illusory blood-ties of family and realise that the real connection between us is through Consciousness. From this perspective you can have more in common with, and feel a greater connection with, someone you met ten minutes ago than with the family you have lived with all your life. Even close family bonds are through Consciousness, not blood, which is just an illusion of Mind.

My only desire was to follow the rapidly-changing course of my life. Strange as it all was, there was a force within me that knew that this was the way I had to go. Through the latter months of 1990, I wrote my first book about these events, called *Truth Vibrations*. The title referred to the vibrational change that I was told was coming to awaken humanity from its coma-like state and lift the veil on the lies and deceit behind 'life' on Planet Earth. All that had been secret and hidden would be revealed, I was told. Two decades later, this is clearly happening all over the world. When the book went to the printers just before Christmas of 1990, the sequence began that led to a transformation of my sense of awareness that changed almost everything I had ever thought or believed. I suddenly had the tremendous urge to go to Peru. I had no idea where this came from at the time, but I do now – Consciousness, the Silent Voice that speaks through 'knowing' and intuition. I knew nothing about Peru and had never thought about the place until now. In this same period I kept seeing the word 'Peru' everywhere – in books, in newspapers, in travel agent windows … I met another psychic lady who said without any prompting from me: 'Have you ever thought about visiting Peru?' She said I would be going there and 'drinking of the holy waters'. This comment came back to me a few weeks later when I was drinking water from the Urubamba River, the 'holy river', which flows through the Sacred Valley of the Incas and passed Peru's ancient and formerly 'lost' city of Machu Picchu. Everything I did after those first communications through the psychic was decided by intuition. I didn't know why I was going to Peru, only that I had to for some reason. My head, my 'logic', told me that I should not be spending money I could not afford to make such an expensive trip, but by now my 'head' was no match for my 'heart'.

Purely on intuition, I flew to Lima, Peru, at the start of February 1991, for the experience that re-wrote my life. When I stepped off the plane at Lima airport and collected my luggage, I was like a little-boy-lost. What now? I had a feeling to head for Cusco in the Andes, the centre of the ancient Inca civilisation, and I saw on the departure board that a plane was leaving for there in around 35 minutes. The airport was a mass of people and I had yet to buy a ticket. No chance of getting that flight, I thought. Then, a Peruvian guy, speaking pretty good English, emerged through the crowd and asked me where I was going.

'Cusco,' I said.

'You have hotel?'

'No.'

'You have ticket?'

'No.'

'I get you ticket; I get you hotel.'

This he did in a ridiculously quick time, taking his commission on the way, of course. By now the flight was close to leaving and I went to the back of a long line of people waiting to check in. It was clearly impossible for me to make the departure time, but, as I prepared for a long wait, my fixer said, 'No, no, follow me.' He took me down to the front of the queue where his friend on the check-in desk immediately stopped what he was doing and began to check me onto the flight. Less than an hour after arriving in Lima, I was walking back across the tarmac to board the plane to Cusco. Such 'coincidences' and synchronicities were to be constantly repeated for the next three amazing weeks and have continued ever since. I arrived at my rundown hotel and sat on the bed wondering what to do next. Someone I had met a few days earlier had given me the telephone number of a friend in Cusco, and I made a call to see what would happen. She turned out to be the manager of a local travel agency and within an hour my basic travel plans and arrangements were sorted. She also called a Peruvian guide she knew who would show me around the country. The next day, I arrived at his home to meet him and to begin what was to be an incredible adventure. The door was open and I walked in to find him asleep on the floor. As he opened his eyes, his first words were not 'hello' or 'good morning', but, 'Did you have any dreams last night?' After recovering from the surprise of his opening remark, I said that yes, I had. The dream was very vivid and included one of my front teeth falling out.

'Is your father or grandfather still alive?' he asked.

'Well, yes, my father is. Why?'

'That dream is often symbolic of your father or grandfather dying.'

Making an international phone call in Peru outside of Lima is far from easy; it certainly was then anyway, but a week later when I finally managed to ring home, I found that my father had died back in England – at the same time as the dream. His funeral had taken place before I even knew he had died. I was to stay longer than planned in Peru and, for the next three weeks, as I travelled around much of the country, a daily sequence began to repeat itself. Each morning, I would tell the guide where I intuitively felt to go and he would invariably tell me it wasn't possible, yet every day we would somehow end up there. I went to some stunning locations, not just the famous tourist sites like the extraordinary Machu Picchu, but many other unforgettable places. Eventually we arrived in a town in southern Peru called Puno, not far from Lake Titicaca, which is said to be the highest navigable lake in the world. The guide had booked us into a hotel called the Sillustani, named after an ancient Inca site about an hour's drive away. For obvious reasons, there were pictures of the place around the hotel and I told the guide I wanted to go there. True to form, he said it was not possible at that time of year without spending a lot of money, but my intuition to go was so strong that I said I would do whatever was necessary. I had to hire a tourist minibus for myself (or so the guide told me) and off I went with him and the driver.

'It will be over when you feel the rain'

Figure 14: *The Inca ruins at Sillustani, Peru*

The Sillustani ruins are located on a hill skirted on three sides by a beautiful lagoon (Fig 14). The area was uninhabited and surrounded by distant mountains. It was quiet, with only a couple of children waiting with a llama, hoping to sell photographs to tourists; but there were none, apart from me. After I walked around the ruins for an hour or so under the piercing Peruvian sun, I went back to the tourist bus to return to Puno. I thought the trip was over and I felt deflated and disappointed. As lovely as this place was, what I had experienced did not begin to match the power of the intuition that had compelled me to go there. About three minutes down the road, I was pondering on my experience and looking out of the window, when a mound to the right attracted my attention. As I looked at the mound, a voice in my head began to repeat: 'Come to me … come to me … come to me.' *What?* Now a bloody mound was talking to me! I asked the driver to stop the bus. 'I'll only be a few minutes,' I said. At the top of the mound I encountered a circle of standing stones, which couldn't be seen from the road. They were about waist high and I stood in the centre of the circle looking back across to Sillustani and to the mountains way off in the distance. There was not a cloud in the sky and the sun was extremely hot, burning my face. Suddenly, I felt my feet being pulled again like magnets into the ground. It was the same as in the newspaper shop in Ryde, but this time it was far more powerful. My arms then stretched out above my head without any conscious decision from me. If you put your arms above your head, slightly outwards at about 45 degrees you'll see how they start to ache within a minute. My arms were like that for over an hour. I felt nothing until it was over, and then my shoulders were in agony. I felt a drill-like sensation in the top of my head and I could feel a flow of energy going the other way, too, up from the ground through my feet and out through the top of my head. It was like a two-way flow. I heard a voice in my mind that said: 'They will be talking about this moment a hundred years from now.' This was followed by: 'It will be over when you feel the rain.' What was that about rain? What rain? There was not a cloud to be seen, just a brilliant sun in a clear blue sky. What was happening to me?

I stood there, unable to move as the energy increased to the point where my body was shaking as if plugged into an electrical socket. Time became meaningless. There was no 'time' as we perceive it, no past, no future, only the moment I was experiencing. I kept moving in and out of conscious awareness, much like when you drive a car and wonder where the last few miles have gone. The car has been driven by your subconscious while the conscious was off in a daydream. In one of my returns to awareness I saw there was a light grey mist over the distant mountains and, as I watched, it became darker and darker. My god, it was raining over there, although far away. Soon the rain clouds emerged from the mountains with extraordinary speed. I can only describe it as like pulling a curtain across the sky as a straight line of cloud moved towards me, covering the Sun. I saw faces in the clouds as they billowed like dry ice in a stage show. By now, my body was shaking so fiercely from the energy passing through me that I could hardly stand. As the storm approached, I watched a wall of stair-rod rain getting closer and closer, moving in a straight line. The moment I felt the water on my face the surges of energy stopped as if a trip-switch had been flicked. I staggered forward, my legs like jelly, my shoulder and arm muscles now stiff and painful. It was only at this point that I noticed that the Peruvian guide was standing next to the circle, tired of waiting for me in the bus. If a facial expression ever said 'mad Englishman', his was it! Energy was pouring from my hands with tremendous power and I went down to the bus to grab a crystal in an effort to diffuse some of it. I only had the crystal because I had walked into a shop in Glastonbury, England, two or three weeks earlier and the owner had picked it up and given it to me for free. 'I think you should have this,' he said. When I replied that I could not afford to spend that money, he said, 'No, just take it.' My feet also continued to burn and vibrate for some 24 hours. The discomfort kept me awake for most of that night.

The next day, I arrived at an astonishing place called Sun Island in Lake Titicaca, which spans the Peruvian and Bolivian borders and is claimed to be the highest navigable lake in the world at some 13,000 feet. According to Inca legend, Sun Island and nearby Moon Island were the birthplace of the Sun and the Moon, and these bodies took human form as the first Inca, Manco Capac, and his sister-wife, Mama Ocllo. There was no electricity on the island and without the visual pollution of neon light the stars can be seen with incredible clarity. I stepped out of a little fishing boat and onto the shore, still trying to make sense of what had happened to me on that mound the previous day. There I met a blonde lady from Argentina who had been in La Paz, Bolivia, the day before when she had felt strongly that she had to go to Sun Island. She arrived only half an hour before I did. When I shook her hand to say hello she wouldn't let go and, although she couldn't speak English, she made gestures to my hand saying something like, 'What is this I can feel?' What was she talking about? What could she feel? What had happened to me on that mound? In the weeks that followed, my life and perceptions went through a transformation that took me to the limits of mental and emotional survival. It was like a dam had burst in my head and, if we are talking vibrationally, it had. My five-sense Mind was suddenly flooded with new perceptions, thoughts and ideas as my psyche opened to other levels of awareness. It was just too much to process all at once to make any sense of it. Looking back, I can liken the experience to pressing too many keys on a keyboard too quickly and when the computer can't process all the data, it freezes. This is how I felt.

'He thinks he's Jesus'

Unfortunately for my short-term self-respect, but perfect for my long-term awakening, my book *Truth Vibrations* was published early in 1991 in precisely the period when I could hardly tell you what planet I was on. The book, and my public behaviour and statements, led to unimaginable national ridicule. It was blasted across the front pages of the newspapers and on television and radio programmes galore. I could not walk down any street in Britain without being ridiculed. I lived my life at this time to the sound of laughter. Go to a bar? Forget it. There was uproar. I would stop at traffic lights and look across to see whole families laughing at me in the cars alongside, and television comedians only had to say my name to trigger riotous laughter – no joke necessary. My children were laughed at in the street and at school and they were followed by tabloid journalists trying to dig the dirt. One freelance 'journalist' on the Isle of Wight was especially appalling, gleefully taking money from the tabloids to do their sleazy work while claiming to be my friend. The hysteria reached its peak when I appeared on a live prime-time television chat show hosted by Britain's then best-known TV 'personality', Terry Wogan. He took the ridicule route and the audience was laughing within a minute or so of me sitting down. That pretty much continued for the whole of the interview. I became famous for wearing turquoise clothes because after the experience on the mound I began to want to wear only turquoise. I didn't know why I was doing that, I just felt compelled to. I later realised that turquoise is a very powerful and sacred colour to many native and esoteric beliefs. Native Americans are an example of this. Years later when I met my now great friend, Credo Mutwa, a 'Sanusi', or shaman, and the official historian of the Zulu nation in South Africa, he was decked from neck to toe in brilliant turquoise. At the time I knew nothing of the esoteric meaning of turquoise, only that I felt strongly to wear it (Fig 15). Funny, some of the media could not even get that right and many articles reported my obsession with 'purple'. Where they got that from, goodness knows.

The other foundation of the ridicule was that I had referred to myself using the term 'Son of God', implying that I was Jesus or something. Ironically, 'Jesus' is a 'man' I have no doubt never existed, as I have explained in detail in some of my books. I used the term 'Son of God' in the sense of being an aspect, as I understood it at the time, of the Infinite Consciousness that is everything. We are like droplets

Figure 15: *The 'turquoise period' ... but the ridicule set me free*

of water in an ocean of Infinite Consciousness, or Awareness. We are 'individual' at one level of perception, but still part of the infinite whole. More than that, we *are* the infinite whole, just as a droplet is the ocean and the ocean is the droplet. I was not trying to say I had come to save the world or anything, only that, like everyone and everything else in all existence, I was an aspect of the Infinite and not just a physical 'personality'. If you call the Infinite Consciousness 'God', I was trying to say, we are all the symbolic 'sons' and 'daughters' of 'God'. Obviously, my awareness of these matters has increased dramatically since then, but that was the basis of my comments about being a 'Son of God'. However, I was misrepresented in the media and, with my mind downloading so much information following the mound experience in Peru, I wasn't grounded or 'here' enough to articulate clearly what I was trying to say. I was walking around in a daze, really. This led to even greater misrepresentation and misunderstanding amongst those who ridiculed and laughed. All I can say to 'Jesus' is don't for goodness sake come back, mate, because they'll bloody crucify you – Christians as much as anyone. And if you do return, I would definitely do the coming-on-a-cloud deal to give yourself any chance at all. Some comedians were funny rather than vindictive, though, and I recall the British comic, Jasper Carrott, saying that I couldn't be the Son of God because you'd never find three wise men and virgin in Leicester. The Mayor of Leicester apparently took exception to that, poor man. Carrott's piss-take was done with good humour and wit, and my children were in hysterics. The rest of the media coverage and most of the public reaction was just gratuitous ridicule and bile. I remember my mother ringing me in the middle of this media storm to ask in her broad Leicester accent, 'What's goo-in' on, our Dave? What's goo-in' on?' I couldn't help her. I didn't know. I was just certain that I had to go with it, whatever 'it' was.

I clearly remember being aware during the Wogan television interview of two very different expressions of myself. I can now see that they were Mind, caught in the conditioned illusions of this five-sense 'world', and Consciousness observing these events from a very much higher perspective of knowing. While the audience was laughing at me on the Wogan show, my five-sense Mind, the illusory 'personality' called 'David Icke', was in emotional turmoil and agony, but there was another level of me that I also recall very clearly. It was saying: 'It's OK, everything is fine, this is leading somewhere, don't worry'. Many times I had a major problem believing those words, I must say, but so it has proved to be. I understand why people thought I had self-destructed and why, even now, with the fast-growing recognition my books are enjoying, the 'turquoise', 'Son of God' period is seen as an unfortunate disaster that has made my subsequent work far more difficult in terms of public credibility. People who say that miss the point. This period of unbelievable ridicule did not make my subsequent work more difficult – it made it *possible*.

Ridiculed to Freedom

Here again, we have the two perspectives of Mind and Consciousness. Mind can see a few paragraphs on a page, while Consciousness has read the book. In fact, it has written it. To do what I was to do a few years down the line I had to free myself from the prison that almost everyone lives in. It is a prison that disconnects Mind from Consciousness, and one that daily holds humanity in slavery to a system created and orchestrated by the few to this very end. It is the fear of what other people might think. Most human beings are not living the lives they want to lead or speaking their own undiluted truths. They are frightened of how others would react – parents, teachers, 'friends' and neighbours – if their views and lifestyles are at odds with the 'norms' on which this lunatic asylum is founded. They keep their heads down and their mouths shut. (Don't be the nail that stands out above the rest because that's the first one to get hit). In short, they are not living their truth or expressing their uniqueness and desires; they are conforming to what society and its parent, teacher, 'friend' and neighbour – Thought Police – dictate should be the limits of their lives and views. How could I write and talk about the challenging and often 'bizarre' concepts in my books and at public events if I still cared what anyone thought of me? Impossible! I would be editing information, even leaving out great swathes, because of my concern with what others would think. Thanks to that onslaught of ridicule in the early 1990s, the prison door opened. I was going to speak my unfiltered truth and if people didn't like it, well that was just too bad. They must believe something else then, it's all the same with me. When you are faced with the level of ridicule that I endured, year after year, you either 'go under' and have a breakdown, or you ditch any concern with what other people think, and have a break*through*. You escape the sheep pen called 'What will other people think?' The ridicule may have been a nightmare at the time to my insecure, bewildered Mind, but Consciousness knew why it had to happen. It was to set me free and deprogram my Mind so that it could open to Consciousness. This was essential for what I had to do. As that 'psychic' communication said in the earliest days of my awakening:

> True love does not always give the receiver what it would like to receive, but it will always give that which is best for it. So welcome everything you receive whether you like it or not. Ponder on anything you do not like and see if you can see why it was necessary. Acceptance will then be very much easier.

With hindsight …

It was many months before I began to understand what had happened to me, and many years before the bigger pieces were put together. On the mound in Peru, I had a monumental 'kundalini' experience. As I said earlier, the 'physical' body is connected to its other energy 'bodies' and Consciousness beyond the five senses, by those spinning vortices known as 'chakras'. Even this is only one perception of reality, as we shall see.

We have these chakra vortices all over the body, but there are seven main ones. Each chakra represents a different level of being. For instance, the one just above the navel, the solar plexus chakra, is the connection to our emotional level and this is why we feel emotions like fear and worry in the stomach area. We call it having 'butterflies in the tummy' or 'getting the shits', but really the sensation is coming from the solar plexus chakra and this is transferred to the 'physical'. The chakras interconnect with the body through the glands of the endocrine system, like the pineal, pituitary and thyroid, and the vibrational state of the chakra affects the body in countless ways. The balance point of the three lower ('physical') chakras and the three higher ('mental and spiritual') ones is the heart chakra. It is from here that we can balance the physical and non-physical levels of being and this is a connection to our highest levels of intuitive knowing – Consciousness. A kundalini experience is when tremendously powerful energy is released through the base chakra at the bottom of the spine. This process is described by Itzhak Bentov in his book, *Stalking the Wild Pendulum*:

> The kundalini, as described in yoga literature, is said to be an 'energy, coiled up like a serpent at the base of the spine'. When this energy is 'awakened', it enters the spine, rises up along it, and is seen or perceived as a luminous serpent by the person having the experience. Once it has risen into the head, the luminous rod hopefully pierces the top of the head; that is, the rod-like energy beam is seen as projecting through the skull pointing upward. When this happens, the person is said to be 'illuminated'. Eventually, such a person may become highly intuitive and develop some psychic powers, such as clairvoyance, clairaudience or healing abilities.

This is what happened to me on the mound in Peru, and subsequently. It was the cause of my 'dam burst'. The kundalini exploded up through my spine, activating all the chakras and my brain into a more profound level of awareness that I call Consciousness. This is happening to rapidly-growing numbers of people across the world at this time of collective awakening. It doesn't always happen in the way I experienced it, as a mind-blowing explosion, but it is happening to more and more people as the energetic transformation continues with what I call the Truth Vibrations. With that initial 'explosion' came the apparent chaos in the mind as I was transforming from one energy state to another. It was this activation that caused me to suddenly see myself and the world in a totally different way, and I was bombarded with information and concepts I could not process for months. Public ignorance of these matters led me to be labelled 'mad'. This is the usual defensive response to anyone who is significantly different, and I was now seriously different. We are back to the dancer appearing crazy to those who cannot hear the music. What they called 'madness' was really transformation. Itzhak Bentov points out that the psychological symptoms of the more extreme kundalini experience (which mine was) 'tend to mimic schizophrenia' and many people are sent to mental institutions because 'modern' medicine does not understand what is happening. He goes on:

> It is ironic that persons in whom the evolutionary processes of Nature have begun to operate more rapidly, and who can be considered as advanced mutants of the human race, are institutionalised as subnormal by their 'normal' peers. I dare to guess, on the

basis of discussions with my psychiatrist-friends, that this process is not as exotic and rare as one would like us to believe, and possibly 25 to 30 per cent of all institutionalised schizophrenics belong to this category – a tremendous waste of human potential.

Bentov rightly says that the diagnosis of 'schizophrenia' stems from the kundalini activation of other levels of awareness:

> The reason for this is that they have been catapulted suddenly into a situation in which they are functioning in more than one reality. They can see and hear things occurring in our neighbouring realities, that is the astral or other higher realities, because their 'frequency response' has been broadened … The onslaught of information may be overwhelming, and they begin to mix and confuse two or three realities.

It was years after my 'turquoise period' that I read those words, but they describe my own experience so well. I went through this process in public without understanding what the hell was happening to me. When eventually the nature and effects of the kundalini awakening were explained, it made complete sense of what I had experienced, although the emotional debris around me at the time was no less painful. For months after my mental and emotional 'dam' collapsed, my life was in chaos. On every level there was turmoil and I said and did many things which the David Icke that people knew would never have contemplated. It was all reported across the front pages of the national newspapers and by the end of this experience there was little left of my old life and identity. Every bridge to the 'past' was ablaze and there was no going back. Not that I wanted to. As messed up as my life seemed to be, something inside drove me on. I was not going to run. I knew that this was all meant to be, but why, and to what end? After about three months, the chaos in my mind began to subside and I became 'normal' once again. Well, on the surface I did. Inside I was transformed. What happened to me on the mound in Peru, and the 'downloads' that followed, began to integrate with 'David Icke'. I realised that I could see so much that I hadn't seen before. I was looking through the same eyes and hearing through the same ears, but what I saw and heard were dramatically different. I began to see beyond the movie, the conditioned version of reality that those in power sell us as the 'truth'. I could see the manipulation with an increasing clarity and, as my understanding expanded, I could see that the world was nothing like what we were led to believe it was. The 'world' we thought to be real was a manufactured illusion. But why, and by whom, or by what?

Bring it on …

By mid-1991, my feet were back on the ground, but all people and media remembered were the crazy days of my very public transition. Once you are labelled and placed in the pigeonhole, that's it. Once 'crazy', always 'crazy'; black and white, no shades of grey. The ridicule and laughter continued wherever I went and the 'normal' course of action would have been to stay out of sight. Instead, I embarked on a speaking tour of British universities, aware of what my reception would be like. Did I want to go? Of course not (Mind). Did I know it was necessary? Yes (Consciousness). The events sold out, sometimes weeks in advance, because these 'decision-makers of tomorrow' came to laugh and ridicule. One night, it was 15 minutes before I could begin speaking.

There was uproar, and beer cups were thrown at the stage. I waited for this to die down and then I said:

'You think I'm mentally ill, don't you?'

'YEEEEESSS,' came the collective reply.

'So what does that say about you then? You have paid to ridicule someone you have been conditioned to believe is mentally ill!'

You could have heard a pin drop. It had dawned on them that their behaviour was not a statement about me, but about themselves. It is a revelation we would all do well to remember: what we do and say is not a reflection of those we ridicule and condemn, but of ourselves. I was heard in respectful silence for the rest of that night, apart from a small group at the back near the bar who continued to heckle in the darkness. I asked for the lights to be switched on so everyone could see where the noise was coming from and I asked for a microphone to be taken to the group so they could say what they wanted to say in the full view of the audience. You would have thought the microphone was on fire such was the vehemence of their refusal to take it. These talks to university students showed me much about myself and the conditioned human responses that imprison the collective psyche. It confirmed that I had begun to purge my concern with what other people thought of me. I really didn't give a damn any more, no matter how I was received. What a liberation that was. I began to see what an illusion I had been living and how the entire human race, except for a few, was caught in a virtual-reality game that dictated the rules. In this period, I had to smile to myself whenever I was interviewed by a British TV host called Eamonn Holmes, a chap I knew from my days in television. He could not compute how anyone would give up a successful career in television to do what I had done. The fact that television was not the be all and end all of life, or that such a version of 'success' was illusory, seemed beyond his comprehension: 'But you could still be in television.' Yes, Eamonn, but I don't want to be, mate. 'But…' Another Mind-made man in a Mind-made profession. Virtually all of them are in the media, it goes with the job.

Right 'place', right 'time'

Those first psychic communications in 1990 have proved to be prophecy indeed, not least the one about 'knowledge will be put into his mind, and at other times he will be led to knowledge'. In the years that followed, I embarked upon a daily journey of often breathtaking coordination, or 'synchronicity', in which I would meet people, read books and documents, or have experiences that would continually increase my understanding of what was going on in the world, and the nature of life itself. Also, thoughts which have suddenly appeared in my head about people and events have later proved with hindsight or research to have been correct. I have been guided with synchronistic precision, and it all comes from the intuitive level. Without this, I could never have compiled so much information and made so many connections so quickly. There is a force that wants to open the Mind of humanity, that's for sure. It has certainly opened mine and I am passing on what I discover to those who wish to hear. I'll give you one example of the outrageous 'coincidences' that have become commonplace since the mound experience in Peru. By mid-1995, I had completed the manuscript for a book called … *And The Truth Shall Set You Free* in which I had mentioned quite extensively the background of former US President Jimmy Carter. As the book was about to go to press, I travelled to Ireland to see a wonderful show called *Riverdance* at the Point Theatre, in Dublin. This was before it became a world-wide phenomenon. The tickets were bought at the box office like everyone else's. I walked up the steps into the arena to find my seat. I had a friend who worked on the show as a masseuse and when I reached the top of the steps I was surprised to see her standing there. She was looking bewildered and bemused. She said she should have been backstage but had felt intuitively – that word again – to come and wait for me. While she waited, she had overheard a security guard say the 'security seats' were in row S – numbers 25, 26, 27 and 28. I could now understand why she was bemused because she knew that the tickets for another friend and I were for S 25 and S 26. I was in the 'security' seats? What was going on? She also said that she had never seen these security people before. They were not the ones that usually worked at the theatre. I decided to go to the seats to see what would happen. There were only minutes to go before the start of the show and the arena was packed, but when I reached row S it was empty from end to end. Spooky. I sat down with my friend, and the people in front of us began to turn around and look to the back of the theatre. When I turned to look, I could see a ring of 'heavies' coming down the stairs; they were surrounding somebody, and there were camera flashes going off like machine-gun fire among the audience. Clearly somebody famous was involved here. This entourage then stopped at the far end of my empty row, and the people inside the circle of security men began to walk towards me.

As they got closer I could see that it was President Jimmy Carter and his wife, who proceeded to sit down beside me in the other two security seats. Unbelievable! According to the newspapers I read the next day, Carter was in Ireland to meet with the then Irish President, Mary Robinson, and had taken the opportunity to see *Riverdance*. Here were he and his wife sitting next to me in 'security seats', when my tickets had been bought in the same way as every other member of the audience that night and no-one at the theatre would have known who they were for. I stood up and shook Carter's hand, and something urged me to look into his eyes. To my astonishment, and I can only describe this from my own experience, it was like looking into an empty shell. It seemed to me that there was no-one home and it was a very weird experience indeed. I resisted the urge to tell him I had a book coming out soon that he might like to read. I sat there contemplating the hilarious thought that here I was sitting in security seats next to an American President I was exposing in my books, while surrounded by CIA security men. Consciousness, as I have experienced many times, has a terrific sense of humour and irony. This is the kind of 'coincidence' that has happened constantly since I began to follow my heart in 1990 and investigate what was really happening in this world, who was really in control and to what end. When people ask how I have compiled so much information on these subjects, this is how: I don't have to look for it; it comes to me. As I was told in those early days:

Arduous seeking is not necessary. The path is already mapped out. You only have to follow the clues … We are guiding you along a set path … It was all organised before you incarnated.

This is not to say it is easy. It takes a tremendous amount of work and commitment and some days I have virtually been in a trance with all the information that needed to be processed, assimilated and fitted together. At the end of a long day it has been like, 'Where am I? What's my name?' It is the guiding force that makes it possible to lift a veil of secrecy that is desperate to remain hidden from public view and has managed to be so for thousands of years. For my part it has been vital to follow my intuition, my 'knowing', at all times. This is the means through which Consciousness 'speaks' to all of us if we are prepared to listen. If my intuition says I must go here, do something, or meet a person, this is what I do. No questions, no consultations with the 'logical' head – I just do it. There is always a good reason, either obvious at the time or when looking back, for why that action was necessary. I would stress here, however, that synchronicity can have a negative side, too, as I will explain later on. It is not necessarily all 'meant to be'.

Never give up

The big audiences that came to ridicule me in the immediate aftermath of the 'turquoise period' soon drifted away once it became clear that there was actually nothing to laugh at when the information was explained at length. For years after that, I would speak to a handful of people in small, cold halls and leave poorer than when I had arrived. Any income from the 'audience' rarely matched the expenses of the event. At the same time I heard people say that I was 'only doing it for the money'. My determination to continue was seriously challenged in this period, I can tell you. It all seemed so pointless, but that inner 'knowing' never left me and constantly assured me that all would be well. Even when I was earning little or no money throughout most of the 1990s I managed, through 'out of the blue' invitations, to visit more than 40 countries (it is now 50). This helped me to compile an increasingly massive library of information about the background, methods and personnel behind the covert manipulation of the world and its people. I began to see that a global conspiracy was no wacky 'theory', as portrayed by the media. This has led to a long series of books through the years since the publication of *Truth Vibrations*. They include: *Heal the World*; *Days of Decision*; *The Robots' Rebellion*; … *And The Truth Shall Set You Free*; *I am me, I am free*; *The Biggest Secret*; *Children of the Matrix*; *Alice in Wonderland and the World Trade Center Disaster, Why the Official Story of 9/11 is a Monumental Lie*; *Infinite Love is the Only Truth – Everything Else is Illusion*; and *The David Icke Guide to the Global Conspiracy (and how to end it)*.

Especially since the publication of *The Biggest Secret* in 1999, and even more so since the attacks of 9/11 and the invasion of Iraq, there has been a gathering of interest in what I am communicating. My website: **www.davidicke.com**, attracts millions of visits, and my talks all over the world enjoy large and rapidly-growing attendances. I could hardly fill a telephone booth at one time, but now I speak to thousands all over the world. It is all a long way from speaking at a venue near Chicago to just eight people, or cancelling events to avoid having to talk to myself. People are beginning to wake up on an ever-increasing scale and I have almost been a barometer of this with the interest in my own work. One of the first things I was told about in 1990, in fact the very theme of *Truth Vibrations*, was that a transformation – an awakening – of human consciousness was upon us. I can now see this manifesting more obviously every day. People are opening to a truth that we all know, but have been manipulated to forget: who we really are. I hope that my experience will encourage people to express their infinite uniqueness and to cease to conform to what the world of Mind tells them they should be. Anyone can do it. We don't have to be 'special', because we already are 'special', if only we'd realise it. A blade of grass, a breath of air, the flight of an eagle – everything is special. All it needs is a refusal be ridiculed, hounded, condemned and feared into conceding your connection to Consciousness to the domination of Mind.

Do what your heart intuitively tells you, for it is Consciousness speaking – the Silent Voice. Follow that and the adventure begins.

4

'You only have to follow the clues…'

Each generation imagines itself to be more intelligent than the one that went before it, and wiser than the one that comes after it
George Orwell

The confusion and bewilderment of my mega 'awakening' began to morph into the early stages of clarity, and I found myself on what was truly to become an incredible journey.

Synchronicity, or apparent 'coincidence', led me to people, books, documents and experiences that were handing me the pieces to a gigantic puzzle; and from the turn of 1992, a pattern was becoming clear. A major theme from the beginning was the region called Mesopotamia, the 'Land Between Two Rivers' – the Tigris and the Euphrates, which has been known variously as Sumer, Babylon, Chaldea and now Iraq (Fig 16 overleaf). I was constantly seeing references to Sumer and Babylon in books that I read, and hearing about them from psychics I met and people who came into my life, often very briefly. Ancient Egypt often appeared, also. But what did it all mean? Another theme involved 'elite' bloodlines, or families, who were controlling world events with the goal of imposing a centralised global dictatorship along the lines of George Orwell's 'Big Brother' classic, *1984*. Where did all this fit in? What was going on, and what was I supposed to do about it? I had so many questions. As the weeks became months, and then years, however, the mist began to clear and an astonishing story emerged. I have revealed in my other books what I have been so guided to uncover since the early 1990s, not least in my biggest work: *The David Icke Guide to the Global Conspiracy (and how to end it)*. I am going to include here only enough information from previous books to show how the pieces fit together, and I am going to concentrate the focus on taking the story forward to new levels of clarity. This is especially so with regard to 'reality'. What is 'reality'? Who are we? Where are we? How is our sense of reality manipulated and conditioned so that we see the 'world' as others want us to see it? How can we break out of Mind and into Consciousness, and transform this prison into the paradise it once was and will be again? To those new to my work, much of what I say will appear to be, at first hearing, fantastic and impossible. I understand that; but suspend your incredulity, stick with it, and the dots will connect with each turn of the page. The world is nothing like it appears to be, and there are some big surprises in store even for those who have walked the journey with me this far.

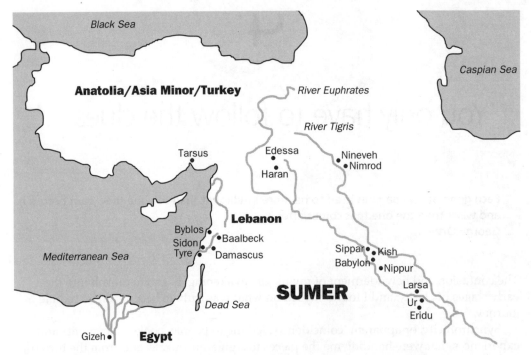

Figure 16: *The land of Mesopotamia, and especially Sumer and Babylon, entered my life very soon after my initial 'awakening'*

Okay, this is the story that the incredible synchronicity of my life since 1990 has led me to uncover, and I will tell it as much as possible in the order that it has been given to me. In this chapter, I will outline the basic facts and then add the layers of detail as we go along.

The 'Golden Age'

There are endless myths and legends across the world about lost lands that sank beneath the sea amid earthquakes, volcanoes and tidal waves. Different cultures have different names for these once highly-advanced civilisations, but the most common are Atlantis and Mu, also known as 'Lemuria'. Atlantis is said to have been located in the Atlantic Ocean, and Mu in the Pacific (Fig 17). Some researchers even suggest that these stories refer to a lost planet, the remnants of which are known today as the asteroid belt. I am open to anything if the evidence can be produced to support it, but what is without question is that the Earth has been subject in geologically-recent times to just the kind of cataclysmic events described in the stories and legends about the demise of Atlantis and Mu. These catastrophes are recorded in ancient myths and legends all over the world and in the geological and biological record. They are described in the Bible as the 'Great Flood', a story that was taken from much older accounts. The tale of Noah and the Great Flood is an almost verbatim repeat of stories told in Sumer (4000 BC to 2000 BC) and other ancient Mesopotamian civilisations, including Babylon (2000 BC to 300 BC). These accounts have been found on clay tablets recovered from what is now Iraq, and they originate from thousands of years earlier than the biblical version. They tell of a man called Gilgamesh, which the Bible re-names 'Noah', and the Mesopotamian *Epic of*

Gilgamesh sounds rather familiar: there was a great flood, and Gilgamesh built an ark to save animals and his family and sent out birds to see if the flood was receding. The ark eventually came to rest on a mountain. Another version is the Flood story which tells of how 'the gods' decided to destroy humanity, and a god called 'Enki' warned the priest-king Ziusudra of a coming flood. He told him to build a great ship and take aboard 'beasts and birds'. After the rains and flood, Ziusudra bowed in thanks before the sun

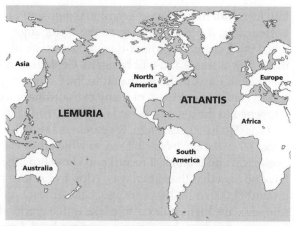

Figure 17: *The approximate locations of where Lemuria and Atlantis are believed to have been*

god, Utu. The ancient Indian 'Noah' was called Manu, and similar accounts, using different names, can be found in Babylon (where 'Noah' is 'Atrahasis') and in Chaldea, Egypt, Assyria, Greece, Arcadia, Rome, Scandinavia, Germany, Lithuania, Transylvania, Turkey, Persia, China, New Zealand, Siberia, Burma, Korea, Taiwan, Philippines, Sumatra, Islamic belief, Celtic lore, and among native peoples throughout North, South and Central America, Africa, Asia, Australia and the Pacific. These stories tell of extraordinary geological upheavals that include: heat so fierce that it boiled the sea; mountains breathing fire; the disappearance of the Sun and Moon and the darkness that followed; the raining down of blood, ice and rock; the Earth flipping over; the sky falling; the rising and sinking of land; the loss of great continents; the coming of the ice; and virtually all of them describe a fantastic flood, a wall of water which swept across the Earth. The ancients said that this brought an end to the 'Golden Age'. There are endless legends and accounts all over the world of a Golden Age destroyed by cataclysm, and the subsequent 'Fall of Man'. The ancient Greek poet, Hesiod, described the world before this 'fall':

> Man lived like Gods, without vices or passions, vexation or toil. In happy companionship with divine beings they passed their days in tranquillity and joy, living together in perfect equality, united by mutual confidence and love. The Earth was more beautiful than now and spontaneously yielded an abundant variety of fruits. Human beings and animals spoke the same language and conversed with each other [telepathy]. Men were considered mere boys at a hundred years old. They had none of the infirmities of age to trouble them and when they passed to regions of superior life, it was in a gentle slumber.

Hindu tradition tells of different 'epochs' or 'eras' it calls 'Yugas'. The Krita Yuga was their 'Golden Age', a time when there were no 'worldly desires', disease or fear. There was constant joy and happiness, it is said, and what people needed just spontaneously 'sprang from the earth everywhere and always whenever the mind desired it'. Then the paradise ended and the subsequent Yugas have seen what the Bible calls the 'Fall of Man' into fear, suffering, disease, emotional pain and an obsession with materialism – five sense reality. It is hard to imagine the 'Krita Yuga' world from the perspective of today when the focus is on competition and survival, life is short and infirmity a pandemic; but that's how it was – and will be again. Geological catastrophe, and the intervention of a malevolent force, brought an end to the Golden Age. Earth's geological and biological record confirms evidence of many extraordinary upheavals, including three that happened in the general periods of 14,000 to 15,000 years ago; 11,000 to 13,000 years ago; and 7,000 to 8,000 years ago. Researchers D S Allan and J B Delair produced an excellent book, *When the Earth Nearly Died*, in which they compare the ancient accounts with the geological and biological record and show how they tell the same story. Most people have no idea that the Himalayas, Alps and Andes only reached their present height around 11,000 to 13,000 years ago. Lake Titicaca on the Peruvian-Bolivian border is now said to be the highest navigable lake in the world at some 13,000 feet, but around 13,000 years ago much of that region was at sea level. I remember seeing David Attenborough, Britain's best-known natural history documentary-maker, pointing out fish and other sea fossils high up in a mountain range. How come? Those mountains were once at sea level, and recently so in geological terms.

The ancient Greek philosopher, Plato (who lived in the period 427-347BC), wrote about Atlantis and its demise, and he said in his work *Laws* that agriculture began at high elevations after a gigantic flood covered the lowlands. The botanist, Nikolai Vavilov, studied more than 50,000 wild plants collected from around the world and concluded that they originated from only eight different areas – all of them mountainous terrain. It is plainly obvious when you put all the tangible evidence and ancient accounts together that the Earth has experienced a series of fantastic geological cataclysms, not just once but many times. This could easily have confused the timescale of Earth's perceived 'evolution' because a tidal wave on the scale described by the ancients could have produced pressures on the Earth's surface of two tons per square inch, creating mountain ranges and fossilising everything within hours. Artificial stone today is created by pressures of this magnitude. There is widespread evidence that some fantastic event changed the Earth's surface in little more than an instant. Intact trees have been found fossilised, and that would be impossible unless it happened immediately because the tree would disintegrate before it could be fossilised in the time period that scientists talk about. There was also an instant freezing of some regions and this is why mammoths have been found embedded in ice, still standing up and in the process of eating. All this supports the accounts passed down from ancient peoples in every corner of the world. In the course of writing this book I came to understand how, and by what means, this geological devastation was triggered. I will explain all later and it is a shocker.

Atlantis would appear to have been located on the Mid-Atlantic Ridge, which is part of a fracture line that continues for 40,000 miles. The Mid-Atlantic Ridge is in the region where four vast tectonic plates – the Eurasian, African, North American and Caribbean – all meet and collide. It is extremely geologically unstable and one of the main locations for earthquakes and volcanoes. The region where Mu/Lemuria is said to have been located is surrounded by fault lines and geological activity in the so-called 'Ring of Fire' (Fig 18). Islands like the Azores are said to be remnants of Atlantis, and the Pacific islands are said to be part of the land mass known as Mu/Lemuria. The Azores and the Canary Islands (named after dogs – 'canine' – and not canaries) were subject to

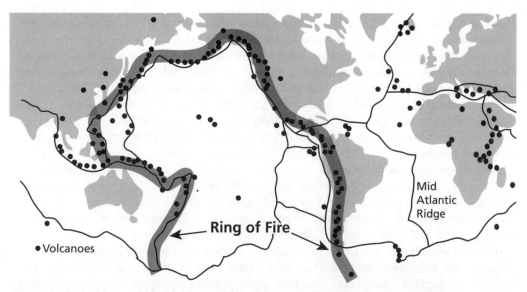

Figure 18: *The highly unstable Mid-Atlantic Ridge passes through the suggested location of Atlantis while Mu/Lemuria was in the same region as the Ring of Fire*

widespread volcanic activity in the time period that the ancient Greek philosopher, Plato, suggested for the end of Atlantis. In his works, *Timaeus* and *Critias*, Plato appears to date the end of Atlantis at about 11,000 years ago. The seabed around the Azores confirms geologically-recent upheavals. Tachylite lava, which disintegrates in sea water within 15,000 years, can still be found there. Other evidence confirms that the seabed in this region was above sea level within the period we are talking about. This includes studies of beach sand gathered from depths of 10,500 – 18,440 feet. An article in *National Geographic* by the oceanographer, Maurice Ewing, concluded: 'Either the land must have sunk two or three miles, or the sea must once have been two or three miles lower than now. Either conclusion is startling.' The volcanic activity that sank the land around the present-day Azores has been connected by geological and biological evidence to the same period that saw the break-up and sinking of the land mass known as Appalachia, which connected what we now call Europe, North America, Iceland and Greenland. Even the degree of submergence is closely related. What applies to the suggested location of Atlantis can also be found in the Pacific and the former land of Mu/Lemuria. Much has been written over the years about the so-called Bermuda Triangle – the region between Bermuda, southern Florida and Puerto Rico – and this is an area that has often been linked with Atlantis. The speculation has been fuelled by the discovery of submerged buildings, walls, roads and stone circles, even what appear to be pyramids, under the waters of the Bahama Banks near Bimini and within the 'triangle'. Walls or roads creating intersecting lines have also been discovered. In fact, all over the world evidence has been found of sunken cities and other structures.

Golden Age to Stone Age

What we (often mistakenly) call 'intelligent life' on this planet goes back much further than is believed by mainstream science. So much evidence has been found to confirm this, but the 'scientific' establishment simply ignores it to protect the official version of human history. The 'pre-Flood' world was a 'Golden Age' global society that was far more advanced technologically than what we are today. I know that sounds far-fetched because advances only happen with the passage of 'time', right? It goes without saying that where we are today must be the 'cutting edge' of human development. But, hold on, why must it? Look around the world at the former lands of civilisations still acknowledged to be highly advanced for their time. Look at Egypt today compared with the incredible civilisation that once occupied that land; it's the same with Sumer, now Iraq; the Inca Empire of present-day South America, and so many other places around the world. The point is that human 'civilisation' and knowledge can decline as well as advance. Imagine what would happen to today's global society if we were faced with the staggering upheavals that were unleashed to end the 'Golden Age'. Within seconds, we would be a comparatively primitive society. Remove electricity from today's world and think what that would mean for the way we live our lives. Remember what happened in the immediate aftermath of Hurricane Katrina in New Orleans, and with every other such disaster. Think about the scenes of devastation we see after earthquakes, like the one in Haiti, and imagine what would happen in all these examples if there was no rescue operation coming because the rest of the world was in the same state. It would be a dog-eat-dog, everyone-for-themselves, find-your-own-food, shelter and warmth, free-for-all. In the thousands of years that followed, the memory of the technological world we have today would fade, ever more rapidly, and only be preserved in stories and myths which would, more and more, be seen as crazy tales and figments of the imagination. Most people would deny such a world ever existed because it would be so at odds with their daily experience. We would have the same we-can't-do-it-so-it-can't-be-done mentality that once laughed at the very idea that we could fly into space. The official history in that post-cataclysmic society would only begin with the records left by humanity once it had re-advanced to a certain level. Only then would they write or symbolise accounts of what had gone before, and this would be based on stories passed down verbally through the earlier generations. Such a point could take thousands of years after the global geological destruction. *Could?* This is precisely what did happen after the events that devastated the Earth and ended the 'Golden Age'.

'Primitive' Genius

Evidence of advanced knowledge from the ancient and prehistoric world is staring at us, while mainstream 'science' tries to explain it away, or just ignores it in order to maintain the status quo. There are the 'mystery' structures built thousands of years ago all over the world that 'primitive' people could never have constructed. Some are beyond the capability of even modern technology. At Baalbek, northeast of Beirut in the Lebanon, three massive chunks of stone, each weighing 800 tons, were moved at least a third of a mile and positioned high up in a wall. This was done thousands of years ago. Nearby is another block, weighing 1000 tons – the weight of three jumbo jets (Fig 19). How was this possible? Official history does not wish to address such questions because of where it might lead. In Peru, there are ancient temples and other sites built with stones weighing 440 tons, and at the ancient city of Tiahuanaco there are blocks weighing 100 tons and connected by metal clamps. The site is dated at some 11,000 years ago. Also in Peru are the mysterious Nazca Lines formed when the ancients scored away the top surface of the land to reveal the white subsurface. By this method were created incredible depictions of animals, fish, insects and birds (Fig 20). The images are made with one continuous line, and some are so big they were only seen in their entirety after 1939 when aircraft began to fly over the region. Rock carvings dating back more than 10,000 years were found during an expedition to the Marcahuasi plateau, northeast of

Figure 19: *Baalbek in the Lebanon where the ancient builders used a stone weighing the equivalent of three jumbo jets. 'Primitive people' did this? Yeah, sure they did*

Lima, Peru, and these included sculptures representing people and animals, most of which are not native to the country. They included a polar bear, walrus, African lion, penguin and the stegosaurus dinosaur. Dinosaurs were unknown to science until the 1880s and the stegosaurus was not identified until 1901. The knowledge which allowed wonders like Nazca, Baalbek, the Great Pyramid at Giza and other amazing creations to be built with such precision and scale was available to the Atlanteans and Muans of the Golden Age, and to 'chosen people' after the Flood, too, as we shall see.

These amazing ancient structures, temples, stone circles and standing stones were not only lined up precisely with the Sun, Moon and certain star systems … they were aligned just as precisely in relationship to each other all over the planet. Often the building techniques and designs were the same in different parts of the world because, if you go back far enough, ancient societies were not isolated and disconnected. A precisely-machined and shaped cube of metal was found in the centre of a block of coal in Austria in 1885 and, based on the age of that coal seam, it must have been made some 300,000 years ago. A piece of gold thread was found embedded in eight feet of rock in Rutherford Mills, England, in 1844, and that rock was estimated to go back 60 million years. Electric batteries have been found in ancient Egyptian tombs, and prehistoric bones of animals have been discovered with bullets in them. An imprint of a modern shoe with a heel was found in mineral deposits 5.5 million years old. A human face carved on a seashell was discovered in red rock dated at between 2 and 2.5 million years ago. Hundreds of perfect metal spheres were unearthed by South African miners in mineral deposits some three billion years old. Humanoid footprints were discovered with dinosaur remains in the same layer from the Cretaceous period of

Figure 20: *The extraordinary Nazca Lines in Peru which can only be seen in their entirety from an aircraft*

Figure 21: *The advanced civilisations that emerged after the Earth recovered from the 'Great Flood' cataclysms. They included the post-Flood Inca period in South America, West Africa, Egypt, Sumer, the Indus Valley and China*

between 65 and 135 million years ago. You can find countless other examples of the world's high-tech history in excellent books like *Forbidden Archaeology* by Michael A Cremo and Richard L Thompson. Why don't all these discoveries re-write official 'history'? Why isn't this taught in schools? Mainstream 'science' is controlled by the elite bloodline families I have been exposing for 20 years, not least by control of funding, and it is there to sell a fake history, not to discover the true one. Why the families want to do this will become clear. The history of the Earth and humanity is nothing like the one taught in the schools and universities and accepted as 'fact'. The author and researcher, Colonel James Churchward, who specialised in the history and existence of Mu, wrote:

> Civilisations have been born and completed and then forgotten again and again. There is nothing new under the Sun. What is, has been. All that we learn and discover has existed before; our inventions and discoveries are but reinventions, re-discoveries.

There was a lot of rediscovering to be done after the devastation that the ancient legends describe. Humanity basically had to start again. Accounts by the Inca people, compiled by Fernando Montesinos, one of the earliest Spanish chroniclers in South America, say there were two distinct Inca empires – one before and one after catastrophic land upheavals. Survivors who had sheltered in a mountaintop sanctuary, possibly the famous 'lost city' of Machu Picchu, which fits the bill perfectly, returned to Cusco in the Andes to begin again, the accounts maintain. The pre-Flood peoples were more technologically advanced than those who followed, and the purity of the original knowledge was lost as the generations came and went. Eventually, the memories were largely retained as myths and legends symbolised in endless ways around the world.

All roads lead to Sumer

It was thousands of years before new civilisations appeared that were well ahead of their contemporaries, although these did not even nearly reach the heights of the pre-Flood age (Fig 21). They included those in Central America, the post-Flood Inca period in South America, West Africa, Egypt, Sumer, the Indus Valley and China. Mainstream historians describe Sumer, the Biblical land of 'Shinar', as the 'cradle of civilisation' – but it wasn't. It was one of the most advanced post-Flood civilisations that re-emerged after the 'Golden Age' was destroyed by geological catastrophe. Sumer, however, is extremely important to the human story and this is why the land of Mesopotamia was coming at me from all angles and many sources almost immediately after meeting the psychic in March, 1990. The Sumerian period is estimated to have spanned the millennia between 4000 BC and 2000 BC, although opinions vary about the detail, and it was followed in the same land by others like Chaldea, Assyria and Babylon. The Sumerians arrived from mountainous terrain to settle in the 'Fertile Crescent' of what is now Iraq, and some believe they were earlier located in Africa. The Sumerians were the first post-Flood – or postdiluvian – people to live in cities and build walls, roads and ocean-going ships. The Sumerians appeared, apparently out of nowhere, at an already highly advanced level of knowledge and sophistication. More than a hundred 'firsts' that we take for granted today can be traced to Sumer six thousand years ago. Sumerians were the first-known people to study the stars, to develop the written word, to enforce a legal code with a court system, and to introduce agriculture and animal husbandry. They recorded the existence of planets that were only officially 'discovered' in the last 200 years. History speaks widely about how the ancient Egyptians, Romans and Greeks were ahead of their time, but all these cultures were based on the knowledge they inherited from Sumer and, as I shall explain, the so-called 'gods' of Sumer.

The real origin of what are called Sumerians goes back much further than a few thousand years and into the Golden Age that lasted hundreds of thousands of years in our version of 'time'. Their history has been reconstructed mainly from clay tablets, and other evidence unearthed since the 19th century. I will refer to these clay tablets as the 'Sumerian Tablets' to keep it simple. The 2003 invasion of Iraq and the systematic looting of the museums led to the loss of thousands of these priceless artefacts, and the significance of that will be seen as we proceed. After the fall of the last dynasty around 1900 BC, Sumerian scribes wrote chronicles of their long and distant history from before they located in Mesopotamia and became known as Sumerians. Their accounts, edited into later Babylonian chronicles, claim that their kings go back more than 240,000 years. To understand what happened, we need to appreciate that the advanced post-Flood societies were continuations of the knowledge and people-streams of the advanced societies before the flood. It was just that the cataclysmic events and the long period of recovery meant that the purity of the knowledge was much diluted. There are other reasons for this, too, which I will come to later. Civilisations of great advancement suddenly appeared elsewhere at around the same time in Egypt and the Indus Valley in what is now the Indian continent (Fig 22 overleaf). I present evidence in other books that in the earlier stages these were, contrary to official history, part of a single empire ruled and influenced from Sumer.

Same knowledge, different route

Before the cataclysms, there was a global society based on a common religion and knowledge. This was replaced by largely isolated communities in the aftermath of the upheavals. The original knowledge was then expressed in different ways and changed and diluted with the millennia, but you can still see the common themes if you look at the connections between the countless myths, names and rituals in the various cultures. I saw this myself when the Zulu shaman, Credo Mutwa, 'threw the bones' for me a couple of times. He has a basket of animal bones carved into various symbols and he reads the 'future' for people from where the bones land in relation to each other after he casts them across the floor (Fig 23 overleaf). I realised that I was looking at another version of casting the rune stones in Europe, or reading the tarot cards. It is the same knowledge expressed in different ways. The foundation of this common understanding

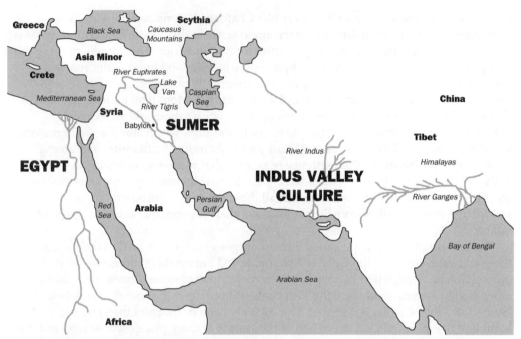

Figure 22: *Three advanced civilisations that 'suddenly' appeared after the Great Flood. Sumer/Babylon, Egypt and the Indus Valley were closely connected*

Figure 23: *The bones are thrown onto the floor and where they land in relationship to each other is 'read' by Credo Mutwa*

is that everything is vibrating energy, as I said earlier. All may seem to be 'solid', but at deeper levels it is all energy vibrating at different frequencies. The same applies to the human body, mind and emotions. There are no exceptions – in this reality, anyway. The Credo bones are also vibrating energy-fields and the symbol they are carved to represent dictates their frequency or resonance. Thought creates form, and if you symbolise something to have a certain meaning it will vibrate to that frequency. Before Credo threw the bones, he asked me to put my hands over them while they were still in the basket. This was to connect my energy field with those of the bones. The human energy-field holds the information of not only what is happening in the moment, but also the possibilities and probabilities that are likely to follow unless we change our thoughts and emotions – our vibrational state. There is no future as such … only the potential of this moment, and skilled people can read that potential through various techniques, including 'throwing the bones'. As I put my hands over the basket, the bones were connecting energetically with my energy field, and the frequencies represented by the bones locked into the same frequencies within my 'aura' or auric field. I call this vibrational magnetism and it can be likened to radio stations on the same wavelength – they connect. Where the bones are going to fall in relation to each other on the floor is determined while they are still in the basket by the energetic connections they make with the person's own energy field. Where the bones end up on the floor is a symbolic representation of the person's energy field. People like Credo are not really 'reading the bones' – they are reading you.

It is the same with rune stones and tarot cards. This is why you will choose one card from the pack and not another. One magnetically connects with your energy field, and another does not. Be careful, though. It takes a skilled reader to interpret the meaning, be they tarot cards, bones, whatever, and many who claim to be 'experts' are nothing of the kind. I have had books fall from shelves in front of me in bookshops that have given me important insights, and the same principle is involved here, too. Books are energy fields and their frequency is decided by the content, which is thought expressed as words. Deeper levels of me connected vibrationally with the books that fell from the shelves because my five-sense awareness needed to read them. To my eyes, the books fell on the floor miraculously; but in fact it was an energetic connection that made it happen, no miracles necessary. When I have seen a book and known immediately that I have had to read it, or when I hear something and know I have to act upon it, the same principle applies. There is a vibrational connection being made. There will be many reading this who will be saying: 'Hey, something like that happened to me.' It's far more common than people realise. How ironic that the carriers of the knowledge through the generations from the ancient world, shamans like Credo Mutwa, are dubbed 'primitive' or 'witch doctors' when their work is based on an understanding that is way ahead of mainstream science. I am not for a moment saying that such people know everything, and most of the spiritual leaders of native peoples are now way back from the cutting edge themselves, but they still retain the basic understanding that mainstream science ignores and is encouraged to ignore by those who write the cheques: the primary state of this reality is vibrating energy and not the 'physical' world that we think we see. Mainstream science is obsessed with only the 'physical' level of perception which, as I shall show, is an illusion constructed by the mind/brain. It was the original pre-Flood knowledge, myths and beliefs that went their different ways in the isolated post-Flood societies that explain, in part, how the same themes can be found in ancient and native communities around the world that had never officially 'met'. When the Christian powers of Europe began to conquer the globe they were bewildered to find their virgin-mother-and-child story almost wherever they went. This is why, or one major reason why, that happened.

The Bloodline

By the mid-1990s, another major layer of understanding began to emerge in the synchronicity of my life. This was to powerfully connect with the earlier information about the significance of the land called Mesopotamia and the consequences of the 'Great Flood'. I began to realise that certain bloodlines were seeded in the pre-Flood world, and also later as the Earth recovered. Today they control world society. Their aim is to control everything and everyone down to the finest detail in a global Orwellian 'Big Brother' state. Look around – it is happening so fast. When I first began to write about this agenda for world dictatorship, most people found it hilarious; but the laughter is diminishing rapidly now that what I have outlined since 1993 has become daily experience. The Mind-made mainstream media is still laughing at what I have said, even though it is reporting the fast-advancing Big Brother state in its newspapers. What can you say? 'Elite' bloodlines were seeded all over the world before the upheavals and reseeded later, especially in those advanced civilisations that began to emerge in places like South and Central America, Egypt, the Indus Valley, China and Sumer. They are all significant to the world as it is today, but those bloodlines that originate in Sumer-Mesopotamia, now Iraq, appear to be of especial importance to the direction that humanity has taken in the last six thousand years. The forces behind the invasion of Iraq in 2003 were these same ancient bloodlines, and while there are many reasons for that collective atrocity – oil, conquest, control of the Middle East and others – this land is of fundamental importance to the bloodlines for historical and other reasons. They also took the opportunity to raid Iraqi museums and steal priceless, irreplaceable artefacts from ancient Mesopotamian societies, including Sumerian clay tablets, to hoard for themselves and to prevent any true reading of their significance in ways that would demolish the fake official 'history' they have imposed upon the population. I will deal with the origin of these bloodlines later, and why they believe themselves to be 'special', but I want to keep the sequence in the order that it was given to me. I'll just refer to them as the 'elite' or 'the bloodlines' for now, but they have a particular genetic origin that makes them different to the main body of the human population.

The 'elite' bloodlines became the leaders of the ancient societies – the kings, queens and emperors, who claimed the right to rule because of what? Their bloodline. Have you ever wondered why royal and aristocratic families are so obsessed with interbreeding, or why the same often happens with the families that control government, banking, business and the media? It is to maintain a genetic code that is different from the rest of the population. The bloodline can be diluted very quickly if it is interbred with others. Still today we have the kings and queens qualifying to be heads of state because of their bloodline. Take the House of Windsor family in Britain (really the German House of Saxe-Coburg-Gotha). Queen Elizabeth II is only sitting in Buckingham Palace because of her family line and this makes monarchy the most racist institution on the planet. You can only become Head of State in Britain if you are white (in effect), come from one family bloodline and practice (at least officially) Protestant Christianity. This is happening in a country that is constantly passing new laws to stamp out alleged racial and religious discrimination. A head-shaker, I know, but true. One day, I visited the website of the UK Commission for Racial Equality (it now has a new name), which is supposed to prosecute cases of racial discrimination, including those involving work and job applications. They asked people to report examples of racial discrimination for them to investigate and I reported the Queen and the monarchy and asked the head of the Commission, Trevor Phillips, why he had accepted an honour, an Order of the British Empire, from such a blatantly racist institution. All I received was a vacuous letter from a Commission lawyer which demonstrably failed to address the question and, of course, they decided not to investigate. Throughout history to the present day there has been one law for the bloodline families and another for everyone else.

The Sumer Empire became the Babylonian Empire and the term 'empire' followed the elite bloodlines of Mesopotamia wherever they located. They began to travel great

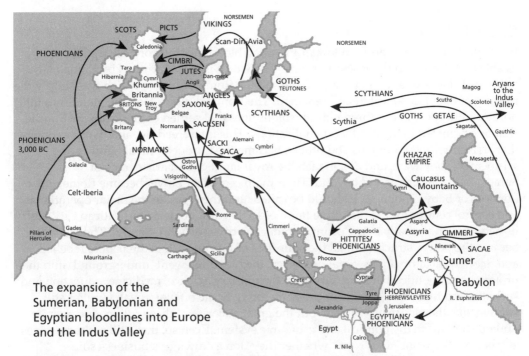

The expansion of the Sumerian, Babylonian and Egyptian bloodlines into Europe and the Indus Valley

Figure 24: *The bloodline and peoples of Sumer, Babylon and Egypt became known by many other names as they migrated from Mesopotamia and the Middle East over thousands of years*

distances by land and sea from around 3000 BC and one of their destinations was Europe, particularly Britain. This is why so many of the classic 'symbols of Britain' come from the Middle East and what was once known as Asia Minor, now Turkey. These include the flag of England with its red cross on a white background; the patron saint of England, 'St George'; and even the 'Scottish' and 'Irish' bagpipes. These sea-farers travelled and settled far and wide and went under the name of Sumerians, Egyptians, Phoenicians, Danaans and many others, but they were basically the same peoples. Their leaders certainly were, because they were spawned from the same bloodline families with the same origin. It was these peoples, and the advanced knowledge of their political and esoteric leadership, that, in league with the force behind them, which I will reveal later, built the great stone circles and structures in Britain, Europe and elsewhere. These included Stonehenge, Avebury, Carnac in Brittany, France, with its 3,000 standing stones, and the 'mysterious' round towers of Ireland. They aligned the stones with energetic force-lines, known as 'ley lines' or 'meridians', which surround and interpenetrate the Earth; and also with the Sun, Moon and planets. Sumerian artefacts confirm their highly-developed knowledge of the solar system. Before and after the Sumerian and Babylonian societies ended, their peoples settled in these other lands (Fig 24) and their travels included, it would seem, sailing to the American continent thousands of years before Christopher Columbus. He was an agent for the bloodlines and he knew basically where he was heading. The claim that he was 'looking for India' and stumbled over America is just a cover story to hide the common bloodline thread behind major historical and current events (see *The Biggest Secret*).

Global Babylon

It was the 'elite' Sumerian-Babylonian-Egyptian bloodlines (all connected) that established Rome and the Roman Empire. The world is still controlled by Roman law today, as I shall explain. They also established the Roman Church, which was simply the religion of Babylon relocated and renamed. The Roman Empire took the bloodlines into northern Europe and interbred with the bloodlines that settled earlier from the Middle East or originated in the pre-Flood civilisations. This interbreeding, and the newcomers that arrived with the Romans and others, became the European royal families and aristocracy. They were, and are, in fact, the royal families and aristocracy of Sumer/Babylon/Egypt and beyond. Their main centres of power became Rome and London, or Babylon-don, as it should be called, and they remain the major operational and control centres for the bloodline families to this day, not least the Vatican City with its networks in virtually every country under the cover of 'Christianity'. The bloodlines became the power structure in all the countries of Europe. When the people rebelled and rejected dictatorship by royal dynasties, the bloodline went 'underground' into the professions of politics, banking, business, the military, science, medicine, education and suchlike, and that's where most of them are today. Some official 'royal' families still survive, like the House of Windsor, but the great majority of these ruling elite operate undercover within the political and economic system. Even so, they still see themselves as 'special', 'superior' and 'royal' whether they don a crown or a business suit.

The bloodlines of Sumer, Babylon and Egypt 'went global' with the European colonial empires. Prime among them was the British Empire on which 'the sun never set', so vast was its domain of control and occupation. The Sumerian Empire, Babylonian Empire, Roman Empire and British Empire are all expressions of the same force which has had, all along, the ambition of global conquest and control. It is no coincidence that wherever the bloodlines located their 'headquarters', an empire would follow. They are obsessed with acquisition, control and domination, for reasons that will become clear. The British Empire and its smaller counterparts imposed by France, Germany, Spain, Belgium, Portugal and others, allowed the bloodlines to be exported across the world, together with the secret society network that manipulates them and their place-people, agents and gofers into the positions of power. This network of secret societies originates before the Flood in deeply malevolent secret societies established in Atlantis and Mu in the latter stages of the Golden Age. The wonders that were Atlantis and Mu descended into infamy, chaos and sheer evil before the cataclysms brought them to an end, and these secret societies and their black magicians were behind it all. The secret societies of Atlantis and Mu continued as the Mystery Schools of the post-Flood world, especially in Sumer, Babylon and Egypt. Not all Mystery Schools were of ill-intent, but the bloodline versions were and even the benevolent ones were gradually taken over. Manly P Hall, the Freemasonic historian, describes what happened in Egypt when the 'black magicians of Atlantis' seized control of the Mystery Schools. It was the same story everywhere:

> While the elaborate ceremonial magic of antiquity was not necessarily evil, there arose from its perversion several false schools of sorcery, or black magic, [in Egypt] … the black magicians of Atlantis continued to exercise their superhuman powers until they

had completely undermined and corrupted the morals of the primitive Mysteries ...
they usurped the position formerly occupied by the initiates, and seized the reigns of
spiritual government.

Thus black magic dictated the state religion and paralysed the intellectual and spiritual
activities of the individual by demanding his complete and unhesitating acquiescence in
the dogma formulated by the priest craft. The Pharaoh became a puppet in the hands
of the Scarlet Council – a committee of arch-sorcerers elevated to power by the
priesthood.

This is what happened in the latter period of the Golden Age, and from these 'arch-sorcerers' came the world religions and the global secret society network of today. Knowledge about the true nature of reality and how it can be manipulated is not good or bad. It just is. How it is used is what matters, and the bloodlines have sought to hijack this knowledge and use it to entrap the human population. When the bloodline-controlled European empires took over a country, they sought out the shamans and carriers of the ancient knowledge and verbal history and had them killed. Christianity was the vehicle to justify destroying the 'agents of Satan' and to wean the people from the influence of their own religious leaders and carriers of the knowledge and into service to 'Jesus'. In truth, they were using this as an excuse to take ancient knowledge out of circulation so they could replace it with a fraudulent version of life, reality and history. Meanwhile, the secret society networks of the bloodline families became ever more powerful as they hoarded the knowledge, and the people became increasingly ignorant as it was taken away. I hear many Christians going on and on about the 'occult', a word that just means 'hidden', as if all esoteric awareness is 'the work of the Devil'. It is just knowledge and can be used for good or ill. The very fact that they will not encompass these understandings themselves leaves them open to be controlled by those who use the knowledge malevolently. The bloodlines want to keep people ignorant of what they know, and here we have Christians and so many others keeping themselves in ignorance because of their religious beliefs that also originate with the bloodline families. Religion is their most effective form of mind and perception control. 'No, I can't read that or do this. What would the Pope say, or the Rabbi or the Imam?' Who gives a shit? Unfortunately, billions do.

The secret society network today operates globally with groupings like the Jesuits, Knights Templar, Knights of Malta, Opus Dei and Freemasonry, working as one unit at their highest levels. This 'unit' or force that connects all the major secret societies is known as the 'Illuminati', or 'Illuminated Ones'. It is a series of degrees into which the other secret societies feed their chosen few, and entry to at least the upper echelons of the Illuminati pyramid is by bloodline only (Fig 25 overleaf). The great majority of secret society initiates have no idea that the Illuminati degrees even exist. They think the top of their own secret society is as far as they can go. They don't know the true agenda, because the knowledge is so compartmentalised in a maze of different 'degrees', groups and symbols. If you misinterpret the symbols you have no chance of knowing what it all means, and the lower ranks are systematically misled to keep the real knowledge exclusive only to the bloodlines. They need to have outsiders in their secret societies, corporations and governments, because there are not nearly enough of them to do what

The Illuminati Pyramid

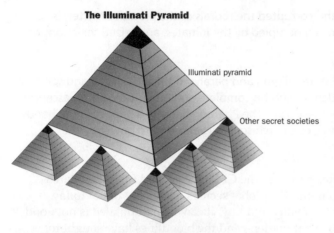

Illuminati pyramid

Other secret societies

Figure 25: *Carefully chosen initiates of the 'individual' secret societies progress through to the Illuminati pyramid which is not acknowledged to exist. The structure is strictly compartmentalised and entry to at least the upper levels of the Illuminati is by bloodline only*

is necessary to advance their agenda of global control. They also need them as ignorant cover, especially in secret societies, and so they have had to create a structure that stops those people knowing what *they* know. The Illuminati have always hidden the truth in a complex mass of degrees, levels, contradictions, mystique and lies. Carl Claudy, executive secretary of the Masonic Service Association in Washington DC, said: 'Cut through the outer shell and find a meaning; cut through that meaning and find another; under it, if you dig deep enough, you may find a third, a fourth – who shall say how many teachings?' Everything is compartmentalised to ensure that only a few understand what is happening. The Illuminati is a name the bloodlines have for their network, but they prefer not to use a name at all. It makes discovery far more difficult. Many people get confused between the Illuminati, the bloodline network of secret societies going back thousands of years and more, and the Bavarian Illuminati, officially formed in 1776. This had a highly significant influence over many world events, including the French Revolution, but the Bavarian Illuminati is a strand in the web, not the web itself.

The Hidden Dictatorship

The bloodline plan for global control advanced by giant leaps after the European powers began the process of giving 'independence' to their former colonies, especially the United States. This would seem to be an obvious contradiction, but it isn't. By apparently, emphasis *apparently*, giving 'independence' to the colonies, they were actually exchanging one form of control for an even more effective one. When you are living in a dictatorship, whether it be communism, fascism, apartheid or colonial rule, at least you have the advantage of knowing where you stand. You know you are controlled and pretty much who the controllers are. This form of dictatorship has a finite life, because eventually the desire for freedom will bring it down, even though it can take a long time to harness the required unity of response. The most powerful form of control is one you cannot see and are not aware exists. People are given the illusion of freedom by being allowed a vote every four or five years, but behind the scenes the same few are in control whichever party or shade of government is officially 'voted' into office. Democracy is supposed to be 'rule by the majority', which is a tyranny in itself, but it's not even that. It is a dictatorship by the few hiding behind the smokescreen of a free and open society. Boy George Bush and Barack Obama, for example, are controlled ultimately by the same people and it doesn't matter if the

Republicans or the Democrats are theoretically in the White House. Either way, the same Shadow People are dictating policies and events on behalf of the bloodline cabal and this also applies to the Labour and Conservative parties in the UK and their equivalent everywhere. They might have different names, but they are masks on the same face. As the saying goes, it doesn't matter who you vote for, the government still gets in – the secret government, the Hidden Hand that pulls the strings of those who appear to be in power and making the decisions. The idea is to kid the people they are free when they are fundamentally controlled. You don't rebel about not being free when you think you *are* free. If you sit in a cell and you can see the bars you know you are in a prison. If you are in a cell and you can't see the bars you think you are free to leave whenever you want. Until you try, that is, and most people never do. Governments talk endlessly about freedom and the 'Free World' because they are selling the prison without the bars. What they say is bollocks, of course, but we have to believe it or we might realise that, in truth, we live in one-party dictatorships controlled by a handful of bloodline families. Mind you, as the Orwellian global state moves on with an ever-gathering speed, the bars are becoming more obvious by the day to anyone with a brain to call their own.

It can now be seen why many of the 'wars of independence' were engineered by the very colonial powers that were apparently being challenged. They wanted to be challenged as they sought to instigate the prison without the bars. The Boston Tea Party, which was used to promote rebellion in the American colonies, is recorded by official history as simply a protest against the tax imposed by the British on tea and other commodities. Men dressed as Mohawk Indians boarded three ships of the bloodline-controlled East India Company and threw 342 chests of tea into Boston Harbor, but the whole stunt was planned and carried out by Freemasons who were connected to the 'Mother Lodge' in Great Queen Street, London (see *The Biggest Secret* for the detailed background). The British, or rather the Sumerian-Babylonian-Egyptian bloodlines controlling Britain, set out to lose the American War of 'Independence' and further increase their ongoing dictatorship by ruling covertly from the shadows. They left in their 'former' colony both the bloodline, under many different names, and the secret society network through which they manipulate themselves and their agents into the positions of power and influence. The British elite did this in every colony, as did other European governments under the direction of the same bloodline clique. African 'independence' to this day consists of the bloodlines manipulating, or imposing through war, black leaders who will dance to their tune. Robert Mugabe in Zimbabwe is a great example. His tyrannical rule was imposed on that now tragic people by the manipulations of British Foreign Secretary, Lord Carrington, and his cohort, the former US Secretary of State, Henry Kissinger, both major agents of the bloodline network. Africa has never been 'free' since 'independence', and neither have any of the 'former' colonies, including the United States. Overt control has been replaced by the even more sinister covert control; physical occupation has been replaced by financial occupation.

The bloodline families have constructed a global control system piece by piece, century after century, and today it is astonishing in its reach, depth and detail. They have enslaved humankind in a prison without bars, or, rather, without bars they can see – at least until very recently. Most still can't see them, no matter how blatant they may be. As long ago as 1923, the writer, Aldous Huxley, said: 'Liberty? Why it doesn't exist. There is no liberty in this world, just gilded cages.' He was so right. Those 'cages' are the closed and padlocked minds of the people, systematically disconnected from Consciousness, as I shall show. Humans live their lives in a prison of perception, and the goal of the bloodlines is to keep them there.

5

'Will You Walk Into My Parlour?' said the Spider to the Fly

Political language … is designed to make lies sound truthful and murder respectable, and to give an appearance of solidity to pure wind
George Orwell

The Illuminati bloodlines control world events through what is now a global network of secret societies and semi-secret groups that is structured like a transnational corporation. The 'corporate' headquarters dictates the policy and the subsidiary networks in each country impose it upon the people in their sphere of influence.

The operational headquarters are in Europe, especially Rome and London, although Paris, Berlin, Brussels and Amsterdam are very significant, too. By 'Europe', I don't mean the here-today-gone-tomorrow European governments, but the web of secret societies that has its operational centre in Europe. The subsidiary networks in each country are 'subcontracted' to control and direct their nation's politics, business, banking, media, military, medicine, 'science', 'education', etc., and ensure they conform to the blueprint dictated by the 'headquarters'. In this way, they are able to introduce the same policies across the world at pretty much the same time (Fig 26). These national subsidiary networks, headed by the bloodline families in each country, have their own subsidiaries, or 'branches', in the towns, cities and communities and this structure allows the centre of the web, the 'headquarters', to manipulate and influence all levels of

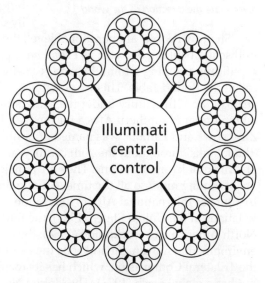

Figure 26: *The world is controlled by the centre of the Illuminati web in the same way that a corporate headquarters dictates global policy to all of its subsidiaries. In the case of the Illuminati, these 'subsidiaries' are secret society networks and bloodline families in every country, which themselves have networks that influence all levels from national government to local community*

Figure 27: *Neil's Hague's superb portrayal of the spider's web structure through which the few dictate the direction of the world*

global society. Most of the people involved don't know they are part of a grand conspiracy to enslave the world. They only have enough information to do what they are told to do, nothing more. It is the same technique that they use to build secret technology. Different people are employed to make the various parts, without knowing what the end product will be. Only the few who put the parts together know that. The technique is known as 'compartmentalisation' or 'the need to know'.

The Illuminati network is like a gigantic spider's web and the strands represent different secret societies, semi-secret organisations and others that operate openly in the public domain. The latter includes governments, transnational corporations and the banking system. The closer the 'strands' are to the 'spider' in the centre, the more secretive and exclusive they will be. The network expands out from the centre to organisations that directly interact with mainstream society; but all the strands, near and far, are controlled by the 'Spider' and its 'Shadow People'. The key 'Shadow People' at operational level, the enforcers of the 'Spider', are the House of Rothschild banking dynasty, as I shall be explaining in detail (Fig 27). One highly significant grouping within the web is a series of organisations based on a secret society called the Round Table. This was established by the Rothschilds in London in the latter years of the 19th century under the leadership of the Rothschild agent, Cecil Rhodes, who plundered southern Africa for them and for the Illuminati. Rhodesia, now Zimbabwe and Zambia, was named after him. The Round Table spawned a series of 'think tanks' throughout the 20th century, and continues to do so. Keep a very close eye on 'think tank' organisations. They are a major conduit for bloodline manipulation and are becoming more so all the time. Among these Round Table satellites are: the Royal Institute of International Affairs in London (established in 1920); the Council on Foreign Relations in the United States (1921); the Bilderberg Group which operates in Europe, North America and worldwide (1954); the Club of Rome which manipulates the environmental movement and sells the lie of human-caused global warming (1968); and the Trilateral Commission, which has its focus on Europe, the United States and Japan, but has a global reach (1973). The United Nations, founded in 1945, was the creation of this network, as was the European Economic Community, now the European Union, which was established in 1957 through the Treaty of Rome. Members and attendees of these Round Table groups occupy key positions in national governments, the European Union and NATO. They are also found throughout banking, business, the media, and so on. This allows a common perception and strategy to be developed and introduced through central coordination. In July 2009, the US Secretary of State, Hillary Clinton, made a speech at the Council on Foreign Relations to mark the opening of a new office in Washington DC. She said:

> I have been often to, I guess, the mothership in New York City, but it's good to have an outpost of the Council right here down the street from the State Department. We get a lot of advice from the Council, so this will mean I won't have as far to go to be told what we should be doing and how we should think about the future.

'Told' is the operative word. Zbigniew Brzezinski, the former US National Security Advisor to President Jimmy Carter and a mentor to Barack Obama, was a co-founder of the Round Table's Trilateral Commission with David Rockefeller. The Rockefeller family is a Sumerian bloodline and they are interbred with the Rothschilds, from whom they take their orders. The role of the Rockefellers is to run the United States 'subsidiary', and the family's bigger players, like David Rockefeller, operate worldwide. The names Rothschild and Rockefeller will be constant companions throughout the book with regard to engineered wars, economic crashes and the control and manipulation of government, banking, global corporations, medicine, pharmaceutical and biotech industries, the media, intelligence agencies, secret societies, and so much else. Banking is their main vehicle for manipulation and John F Hylan, Mayor of New York in the early years of the 20th century, said of this Rothschild banking cabal:

> The real menace of our republic is the invisible government which, like a giant octopus, sprawls its slimy length over our city, state and nation. At the head is a small group of banking houses, generally referred to as 'international bankers'.

For 'international bankers', read 'Rothschild'. The Rothschilds and the bloodline families own the banks and corporations through financial control and place-people directors who run the organisation according to instructions. This way the full extent of ownership by the same families can be hidden. How many know that the Rothschilds control at least most of the Vatican's wealth or that they are financial advisors to the Chinese government? According to the late researcher, Eustace Mullins, who spent decades investigating the Rothschilds, they took over the worldwide financial operations of the Catholic Church in 1823. Rothschild agents are everywhere; it's just that you don't see who their real masters are.

The Fabian Society

Another Illuminati organisation that merits especial mention is the Fabian Society. It is described as a 'British intellectual socialist movement, whose purpose is to advance the principles of social democracy via gradualist and reformist, rather than revolutionary, means'. Put another way, it was committed from its founding in 1884 to the drip, drip, drip of 'change' that would lead to the world we have today. It is said that the name 'Fabian' comes from 'Fabius', the Roman general, Quintus Fabius Maximus Verrucosus, who employed carefully-planned strategies to wear down the enemy over long periods of time and avoided battles that could prove decisive either way. This is the technique that I call the 'Totalitarian Tiptoe'. The Fabian Society emblem is a wolf in sheep's clothing, which sums up its whole modus operandi (Fig 28 overleaf). Fabians also use the

Figure 28: *The oh, so appropriate logo of the Fabian Society*

technique of what they call 'permeation', which we know today as manipulating the consensus. The early inspirations of the Fabian Society were Sidney and Beatrice Webb, and members included famous figures like George Bernard Shaw, H G Wells, Virginia Woolf, Bertrand Russell and Ramsey MacDonald, who would be Britain's first Labour Party Prime Minister in 1924. Other Fabian Society Prime Ministers include the deeply Illuminati, Harold Wilson (see *… And The Truth Shall Set You Free*). The Fabian, George Bernard Shaw, wrote: 'This new and complete revolution we contemplate can be defined in a very few words. It is outright … world-socialism scientifically planned and directed.' The Fabian Society is a secret society at its core and it was the force behind the creation in 1900 of the British Labour Party, which it still controls today. Former Prime Minister, Tony Blair, is a Fabian and a blatant front-man for its agenda. The Fabian Society was behind his appointment as leader of the Labour Party in 1995 after the very convenient death of his predecessor, John Smith. Blair then spent ten years as British Prime Minister during which he introduced the Fabian agenda with extraordinary breadth and speed. Some 200 Fabians have been members of the UK Parliament since Blair's election in 1997, including his successor as Prime Minister, Gordon Brown, and cabinet ministers, Robin Cook, Jack Straw, David Blunkett, Peter Hain, Patricia Hewitt, John Reid, Ruth Kelly, Alan Milburn and Clare Short. The controlling force in the Labour Party today, Peter Mandelson, is extremely close to the Fabian Society. Fabians are not confined to Labour or socialist parties. The organisation operates covertly across the political spectrum as it builds its 'permeation' – manipulating the 'consensus' behind the Fabian/Illuminati agenda. This is why you can't tell political parties apart any more.

Four Fabians, Beatrice and Sidney Webb, Graham Wallas and George Bernard Shaw, founded the Illuminati university college known as the London School of Economics and Political Science (LSE). Among those who have studied at the LSE are major Illuminati names like David Rockefeller and the billionaire financier, George Soros, both of whom will get many mentions in this book. Another is Richard Perle, one of the leading members of the infamous neoconservative cabal that controlled the Boy Bush administration and instigated the 'war on terror'. President Kennedy also studied there, albeit briefly, and people you would never expect turn up as students at the LSE. These include Saif al-Islam Gaddafi, the second son of Libyan dictator Colonel Muammar Gaddafi and his widely predicted successor. If you go to Appendix I, you will see the extraordinary number of famous and influential world leaders, politicians, government advisors and adminstrators, economists, journalists and so on who have been educated at the Fabian Society's London School of Economics or have been connected to the organisation. It is, like Oxford and Cambridge universities, a place where Illuminati assets can be recruited and developed, many of them with no clue how and why they are subsequently used. The Fabian Tony Blair is married to Cherie Blair, who was educated at the London School of Economics. They met while training as barristers in the nearby Knights Templar-controlled centre of law known as The Temple. They were both pupil

barristers at the chambers founded by
Blair's future Lord Chancellor, Derry
Irvine, who taught law at the London
School of Economics. Blair unveiled the
'Fabian Window' at the LSE in 2009. The
window was designed by George
Bernard Shaw in 1910 and portrays two
leading Fabians helping to build a 'new
world' (Fig 29). It was lost for 25 years,
but turned up in Phoenix, Arizona and
was put on display at the LSE. The image
shows the Fabians hammering the Earth
with an anvil below the wolf in sheep's
clothing, and the motto: 'Remould it
nearer to the heart's desire'. The Fabian
Society is the premier 'think tank' behind

Figure 29: *The Fabian Window – building a 'New World'*

the new Labour movement in Britain and it operates officially in other countries, too, like
Australia, Canada and New Zealand, and unofficially through other groupings in the
United States and elsewhere. It interfaces with the families of the banking elite, most
notably the House of Rothschild. Australian Prime Minister Bob Hawke was a Fabian
and one of many overseas leaders under its patronage and control. The Australian
Labour Party Senator, Chris Schacht, is reported to have told a government joint standing
committee on treaties inquiry in June, 2001 that he had been a member of the Fabian
Society for 20 years. He added: 'You probably were not aware that us Fabians have taken
over the CIA, KGB, MI5, ASIO (Australian Security Intelligence Organization), IMF, the
World Bank and many other organizations.'

The Fabian Society is a major strand in the web, that's for sure, and has known from
its creation about the long-term agenda for the global fascist/communist global
dictatorship (fascism and communist are interchangeable when you cut through the
crap about their 'differences'). The Fabian access to the long-term agenda for the world
becomes extremely relevant when you consider this: I have been saying for years that if
you put together George Orwell's book, *1984* (published in 1948), and Aldous Huxley's
Brave New World (1932) you have pretty much got the fix on the global society the
Illuminati are seeking to impose today. What a 'coincidence', then, that both Orwell and
Huxley were members of the Fabian Society. As I have long contended, their books were
not written from imagination, but from knowledge of what was coming. This is why
they have proved to be so extraordinarily accurate. George Orwell (real name Eric Blair)
was taught French by Aldous Huxley at the elite Eton College, where the royal children
go, and they became life-long friends (Figs 30 and 31 overleaf). Huxley introduced him
to the Fabian Society, but Orwell became disillusioned and his Fabian 'expose', *1984*, is
based on what he gleaned from his association with them. Some believe that Orwell's
Big Brother society was really set around the turn of the 21st century, but it was called
1984 as a code to link it to the Fabian Society. 1984 was the society's centenary year. It is
obvious when you look at this background where Huxley and Orwell got their
inspiration for their prophetic 'novels'. The Fabian Society acquired and sealed the
archives of Orwell when his second wife, Sonia, died. Representatives of the publishing

Figure 30: *Aldous Huxley*   **Figure 31:** *George Orwell*

Both were members of the Illuminati Fabian Society and both wrote 'novels' that proved to be extraordinarily accurate about the global Control System that is now fast emerging

company, Harper Collins, are reported to have said that the Fabians will control the copyright of *1984* to the year 2025. Even rights to Orwell's estate are under the control of the Fabian Society. They don't want the truth of what he was really writing about to be made public. I will explain later how it is possible for these groups to know the Illuminati agenda for the world at least many decades, even a hundred years and more, ahead of time.

The Global Dictatorship

You can symbolise the global control structure as a spider's web, or a system of pyramids within bigger pyramids. Virtually every organisation is structured as a pyramid and only the few at the top, in the 'capstone', know the real agenda and goals. There are more and more people the lower you go in these pyramid structures, but with each step down they know less and less about the true motives of the organisation they work for. It is compartmentalisation again. They are just 'doing their job' and know only enough to do that. The few at the top can manipulate the rest of the pyramid to advance their agenda while everyone else has no idea there even *is* an agenda, let alone that they are unknowingly playing a part in it. Only the 'capstone' knows how all the pieces fit together, and when you connect the dots between all the apparently 'innocent' individual contributions you find a deeply sinister pattern. These compartmentalised pyramids (governments, banks, corporations and other organisations and groupings) are

themselves part of a bigger structure. This can be likened to 'Russian dolls' with smaller pyramids encompassed by bigger and bigger pyramids (Fig 32). The structure means that the banks, plural, become one bank if you go high enough. It is the same with governments, political parties, transnational corporations, media organisations, etc.

The Pyramid of Manipulation

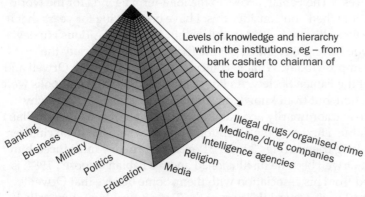

Levels of knowledge and hierarchy within the institutions, eg – from bank cashier to chairman of the board

Banking / Business / Military / Politics / Education / Media / Religion / Intelligence agencies / Medicine/drug companies / Illegal drugs/organised crime

All the major institutions and groups that affect our daily lives connect with the Illuminati, which decides the coordinated policy throughout the pyramid.

People in the lower compartments will have no idea what they are part of.

Figure 32: *The 'Russian Doll' structure of global control*

Sitting at the top of the biggest pyramid, which encompasses all the others, is the House of Rothschild, enforcing and orchestrating the agenda of the 'Spider'. The pyramid-within-pyramid structure means they can impose the same agenda on all the pyramids and this agenda is founded on the incessant centralisation of power in all facets of human life. Here we have the true origin, and the engine room, of what is called 'globalisation'. If you are the few and you want to control the many you must centralise decision-making. The more you do so, the more power you have to centralise even quicker. This is why the speed of globalisation gets faster and faster. An important point to make here: controlling the pyramids that control the other pyramids is where the real power lies. For example, if you control the pyramid that encompasses the banking and financial system, you control all the banks and financial houses within it. Different banks under different names may come and go as you engineer booms and busts to transform society, but they are just chips in the game. When you control the system you always win. If you control the European football championship it doesn't matter if Manchester United beat Real Madrid or the other way round. You control the game and so you can't lose. It is worth remembering this when a bank goes under. The people who work at the bank might lose out, but not the Rothschilds, Rockefellers and those who control global finance. In fact, the fewer banks there are the easier it is to control the system and this is why we have seen the emergence of mega banks, like the Rothschild-dominated Goldman Sachs.

You can see in Figure 33 the structure of the global dictatorship that the bloodlines want to impose. There are likely to be additions to this here and there, but the theme is clear. They want to install a world government that would dictate to every country via 'international law' and 'international regulation'. It is for this reason that you hear so much about the need for international law and the 'harmonisation' of regulations. It is

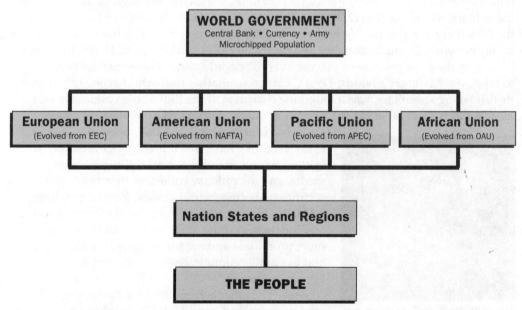

Figure 33: *The planned top-down structure of global control, headed by a world government, central bank, currency and army*

the agenda unfolding. The dictates of the world government would be imposed on any 'rebel' countries by a world army that is planned to emerge from the fusing of NATO and the UN peacekeeping operations. National armies would become mere units of the world army, which would work in unison with a planned world police force. We are seeing the steps towards this now and they will become much clearer as it progresses. A world central bank would oversee all global finance, and a world electronic currency would replace all other currencies. This has enormous implications for freedom, as it is meant to. If your credit card is refused by a computer system today you still have the option to pay cash, but what about when there is no cash and the computer says no to your card or microchip? You would have no means of purchase, and that's the idea – control. I have been warning for so long about the plan to microchip the entire global population, including all babies at birth, and now it is being openly suggested. This is not just about electronic tagging and constant surveillance, either, though that is obviously part of it. The main reason is even more sinister, as I will be explaining.

The Superstates

The next level of this global structure, below the world government, is planned to be a series of superstates like the European Union dictatorship that already controls the countries of Europe. Something like 75 per cent of the laws imposed on British people today originate with the unelected bureaucrats in Brussels, and it is illegal for the British Parliament, or any parliament within the Union, to introduce laws that are at odds with those decided by the ever-expanding European fascist/communist state. I have been writing since 1994 that the European Union is the creation, to a large part, of the Illuminati's secretive Bilderberg Group and you can read the background in detail in *… And The Truth Shall Set You Free*. The Bilderberg Group secretly coordinates a common policy between governments, banks, corporations, the media, intelligence agencies and the military, including NATO (Fig 34). It was established by the Rothschilds in 1954 at the Bilderberg Hotel in the Netherlands and is run on their behalf by the Rockefeller family network. David Rockefeller and Rothschild/Rockefeller agent, Henry Kissinger, have been the most prominent players over the decades, and others are now beginning to take over. Kissinger's buddy, Lord Carrington, another Rothschild agent and former British Foreign Secretary, was a long-time chairman of the Bilderberg Group. He was also Secretary General of NATO, a position utterly dominated by Bilderberg assets.

There is a central core group that meets regularly and every year they have the 'Bilderberg Conference' when leading figures in politics, banking, business, the media, and the military come together amid intense security to discuss 'world affairs'. Researchers have had increasing success in exposing the Bilderbergers and the names on the attendee list, but many of the more prominent and sensitive figures are slipped in and out of the 'conferences' in secret and do not appear on the list.

Figure 34: *The Bilderberg Group is a very significant strand-in-the-web*

Leaked documents from the 1955 Bilderberg conference at the Grand Hotel Sonnenbichl in Garmisch-Partenkirchen, Germany, confirmed the

Bilderberg plan for the European Union when they came to light in 2009. The documents talk of the 'pressing need to bring the German people, together with the other peoples of Europe, into a common market'; and 'to arrive in the shortest possible time at the highest degree of integration, beginning with a common European market'. Note the word beginning. The Bilderberg papers say that 'it might be better to proceed through the development of a common market by treaty rather than by the creation of new high authorities'. The Common Market, or European Economic Community, was indeed created two years later in 1957 by the Treaty of Rome, a major centre of Illuminati power and home to the relocated Church of Babylon, established in Rome by the bloodlines of Sumer, Babylon, and Egypt and renamed the Church of Rome. The 'treaty' technique has been used ever since, as we see with the Lisbon Treaty in 2009 that is designed to turn the now European Union into a fully-fledged dictatorship with its own president, foreign policy, army, police force and bureaucratic control system. The leaked Bilderberg documents from 1955 talk of the need for a single European currency, and the Bilderberg network has been manipulating for decades to bring this about. Even the current Bilderberg chairman, the aristocrat and bloodline, Viscount Etienne Davignon, said in a rare interview that Bilderberg introduced the policy agenda for a single currency, what became the euro, in the early 1990s.

In fact, the manipulation goes back 50 years and then some. One of the most significant conspirators behind the creation of the European Union is Otto von Habsburg, head of the bloodline Habsburg dynasty. He is still the head of the Pan European Movement founded in 1923. The Habsburgs are a thoroughbred Illuminati bloodline who ruled much of Europe for centuries. The Habsburg dynasty was awarded the title of Holy Roman Emperor and produced emperors of Austria; dukes of Austria; kings of Germany, Hungary, Spain, Portugal and Bohemia; grand dukes of Tuscany; and even an emperor of Mexico. Otto von Habsburg was born in 1912 with the title Archduke Franz Joseph Otto Robert Maria Anton Karl Max Heinrich Sixtus Xaver Felix Renatus Ludwig Gaetan Pius Ignatius of Austria. The bloodlines love their titles and they are obsessed with status, power and hierarchy. Habsburg was the eldest son of Karl of Austria, the last emperor of Austria and last king of Hungary. He lives in Bavaria, Germany and, like many operating at high levels of the conspiracy, he has lived well into his 90s. He has made it clear that he wants a Roman Catholic (Church of Babylon) Europe and a European head of state elected (appointed) for life. Another document that revealed the true nature and background to the European Union was written by the Nazis in 1944. The document, known as the Red House Report, or EW-Pa 128, is an account of a secret meeting at the Maison Rouge Hotel in Strasbourg on 10th August 1944, when Nazi officials and bloodline German industrialists planned for a Fourth Reich just as the Third was crumbling around them. The plan was to replace the physical occupation of Europe, which Hitler and company had sought through miltary conquest, with the economic occupation of centrally-controlled European community, summed up in the words of Nazi propaganda chief, Joseph Goebbels: 'In 50 years' time nobody will think of nation states.' His timescale was a little out, but his theme was not. The plan was described right at the start by Jean Monnet, the 'Founding Father' of the EU, and a Rothschild frontman. He wrote in a letter to a friend on 30th April 1952:

Europe's nations should be guided towards the superstate without their people understanding what is happening. This can be accomplished by successive steps, each disguised as having an economic purpose, but which will eventually and irreversibly lead to federation.

The EU is controlled by an unelected bureaucracy called the European Commission (which mirrors the Politburo in the Soviet Union) and it proposes all the laws. These are then discussed at secret meetings of more bureaucrats, known as the Committee of Permanent Representatives, and rubber-stamped by the Council of Ministers. National parliaments have no say whatsoever and the European Parliament is only there to give an image of elected representation. It's all a sham and members of the European Parliament, or 'MEPs', have an extremely limited time to even speak before their microphone is switched off. The Union claims, hilariously, to be 'democratic' when you have Hans-Gert Pöttering, the outgoing President of the Parliament, urging MEPs in 2009 to unite to freeze 'anti-Europeans' out of the decision-making process. A fifth of the irrelevant MEPs are in groups that support either less integration or complete withdrawal from the Union. That is their right, or it would be if the EU were not a dictatorship. Mr Pöttering said: 'I think it is very important that the pro-European MEPs cooperate well so the anti-Europeans cannot make their voices heard so strongly.' I think it is more important that you get a life, mate. Ten per cent of the fantastic EU budget (115 billion euros in 2008) is lost to fraud every year, and the pay and expenses for bureaucrats and MEPs is extraordinary. Take the case of Neil Kinnock, the former leader of the UK Labour Party, and his wife, Glenys, who was a member of the European Parliament. Kinnock is famous for being a wind-bag and never using one word when there are thousands to choose from. He started out as a 'firebrand Welsh socialist' who condemned what became the European Union until he discovered the money was good. He also condemned the British House of Lords and then joined it. His missus became an MEP while he became a bureaucrat at the Commission, and it was revealed in 2009 that together they earned £10 million from the EU and now qualify for substantial pensions for life. What a fraud Kinnock is, one of the most obvious club-joiners you could ever see, but he is typical of the gravy train/pig trough that is the European Union.

We Don't Care What You Think

The story of the European Union is a wonderful example of how easy it has been for the few to dictate to the many, and how the rules are changed to suit the situation. The EU bureaucracy first proposed a European 'Constitution' to install its long-planned dictatorship, but they made the mistake of actually giving the public a say about this in the Netherlands and France in 2005. Both populations rejected the Constitution in referendums because they could see what the implications were of the creation of a President of Europe, a European Foreign Minister and the vast erosion of national powers to veto and opt out of bureaucrat-dictated laws and regulations. What normally happens when referendums about the EU go the 'wrong way' is that they wait a while, pour resources, people and propaganda into the country, and then force another vote. This has happened a number of times. They could see with the French and Dutch, however, that the feeling against the Constitution was so strong that this was not going

to work. So, they simply changed the name of the document from the European Constitution to the Lisbon Treaty. Some 98 per cent of the content was the same, but they said that because it was now 'just' a treaty and not a constitution, it was not affected by the French and Dutch votes and the promise of the Tony Blair government in Britain to 'guarantee' a public vote on the Constitution no longer applied. A spanner was thrown in this cosy little 'works', albeit sadly temporarily, by the only nation given a referendum on the Treaty – Ireland. Even the EU bully boys couldn't stop this because it was in the Irish Constitution that there had to be a public vote on such a transfer of power. It was thought that a 'yes' vote would be a breeze, but the Irish voted 'no' in June 2008 and the Brussels toilet roll order did soar. Oh my God! Every EU government had to agree to the Treaty for it to become law and the truly useless Irish leader Brian Cowen could not do so in the light of the public decision. Cowen was given his orders by the EU leadership to have another vote and get the right answer this time. It was a perfect opportunity for the Irish to say 'no' again and deliver a blow for 'power to the people'. What did they do? They voted 'yes' for the Lisbon Treaty in the second referendum of October 2009. It was an absolutely mind-boggling decision and testament to how easy it is for the few to control the many when the many are not conscious. What can you say about people who are so publicly abused and insulted by having their first decision rejected by the EU tyranny and then vote again to agree to give control of their lives and their country to the very same EU tyranny? And a few people can't control the world?? The Irish 'yessers' were actually voting to dismantle their own country, hand complete control over anything that matters to Brussels bureaucrats and, irony of ironies, ensuring that they will never get the chance to vote again on increased EU powers because that right is deleted by the Lisbon Treaty. Many people think it is impossible for so few to control the lives of the global population. Unfortunately, because of Mind-dominated humanity, it isn't.

Network of 'Unions'

The same agenda is close to being introduced in North America and Mexico under the title of the North American Union (NAU). This is replacing NAFTA, the North American Free Trade Agreement (their version of the Common Market), and will unify the United States, Canada and Mexico under a single government, as in Europe, and replace the US and Canadian dollars and the Mexican peso with a single currency said to be called the 'amero'. The front organisation for this has been the Security and Prosperity Partnership signed into being in 2005 by US President George W Bush, Canadian Prime Minister Paul Martin and Mexican President Vicente Fox. Lou Dobbs, a long-time CNN presenter, is a rare mainstream journalist who has exposed this group and the real agenda behind it and there is no doubt that this was connected to him being fired in 2009. The open government foundation, Judicial Watch, obtained official documents under the Freedom of Information Act to prove that not only is the North American Union coming, it is already here behind the scenes. Many agencies refused the Judicial Watch information request, citing 'national security' (the plot's security), but eventually they received thousands of pages of documents. They detail how all areas of life in the United States, Canada and Mexico are being covertly merged, including law enforcement and the military. The documents stress that this establishment of the Union has to be done through 'evolution by stealth' – the classic Fabian Society technique so

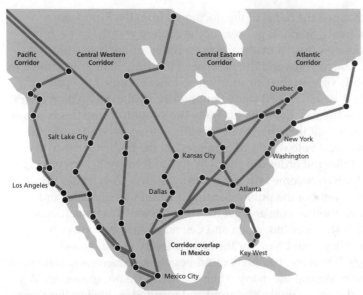

Pacific
Corridor
Central Western
Corridor
Central Eastern
Corridor
Atlantic
Corridor
Quebec
New York
Washington
Salt Lake City
Kansas City
Los Angeles
Dallas
Atlanta
Corridor overlap
in Mexico
Key West
Mexico City

Figure 35: *The planned North American Union 'Super Highway' network*

Illustration by David Dees (deesillustration.com)
NAFTA Super Highway
Driving A Stake Through America's Heart

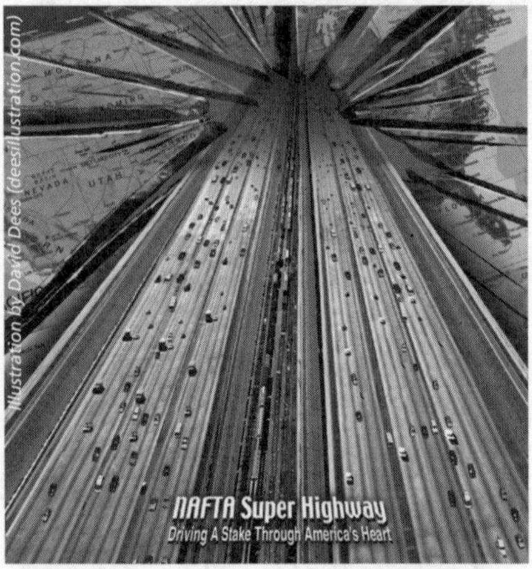

Figure 36: *The Super Highways will spell the end for America as a sovereign State.*

well described by Jean Monnet in his letter about the European Union in 1952. Documents also describe how fears of 'climate change' would be used to impose a carbon tax to fund the Union. This is what the bloodline frontman, Barack Obama, is now seeking to impose. The transport infrastructure for the North American Union can be seen in the emerging 'NAFTA' (in truth, North American Union) superhighway connecting the major seaports of Mexico with the United States and Canada (Figs 35 and 36). It is being constructed through government confiscation of fantastic areas of land, including homes and other buildings, which are then given to the overseas corporations building the infrastructure. These foreign corporations are being given the power to levy tolls on even those roads that are already built and paid for by American taxpayer money. We are seeing foreign companies buying up land, businesses and infrastructure in every country to dismantle sovereignty and self-determination on the way to the centralisation of global control. The long list of corporations that have relocated from North America to Mexico in more recent times were doing so in preparation for what they knew was going to happen. The plan is to extend the North American superstate eventually to the whole of the Americas. One other point about these massive new road networks in America: they are controlled by the Pentagon, not the civilian administrations that only deal with the paperwork. The original highway network in America was designed by the Pentagon. One reason for this is that the old and new highways are there to aid troop movements around North America. I know for a fact that new railway systems being built in Eastern Europe (with money illegally provided by the European Union) are for the use of World Army troops, and that people officially called 'railway executives' overseeing the construction actually work for NATO.

The European Union was manipulated into place via a free trade area, the European Economic Community, or Common Market, and the same is happening in North America with the NAFTA free trade zone, the North American Free Trade Agreement. The Asia-Pacific Union, to include Australia and New Zealand, is following the same modus operandi via the merger of APEC (Asia-Pacific Economic Cooperation) and ASEAN (the Association of South-East Asian Nations). The African Union took the same route when it was created out of the African Economic Community and the Organization of African Unity. The African Union is moving towards a central government for the whole of Africa, and an African army and financial system all subordinate to the global system. These superstates would answer to the world government, and the present structure of countries and nations would be broken up into much smaller regions to dilute any unified challenge to this edifice of power. We can see other elements of this global dictatorship already in place like the World Trade Organization (WTO), which can levy massive fines on countries that seek to protect their own economies from the merciless global system. The idea is to make sure that no country is allowed to be self-sufficient and all are dependent on the world system over which they have no say or control whatsoever. Dependency = control and that's why we see manufactured dependency everywhere, especially through engineered scarcity when we could have abundance. The equation is simple: abundance = choice = freedom; scarcity = dependency = control. They sell this grotesque human exploitation as 'free trade' when that's the last thing it is. Illuminati 'free trade' involves exploiting the poorest peoples on the planet to produce their products for pennies and then shipping them to the richer regions of the world to sell them for as much as they can get. Globalisation, and the dismantling of trade barriers, means that these criminal corporations can now move their products almost wherever they want without financial penalties. If anyone tries to protect their own people from this commercial tyranny and occupation, the WTO moves in to stop them. The only 'free' in 'free trade' is the freedom to exploit and abuse. As a result of this criminal activity, 25,000 people a day die of hunger in a world of plenty in which gluttony abounds. The next stage of integrating the economies and governments of the United States and the European Union is underway with the signing of a transatlantic economic integration agreement and the establishment of the Transatlantic Economic Council with the aim of creating a single market.

Long in the Planning

The bloodline plan for the world is not made up by the year, or even by the decade. It's all been playing out for centuries, but unless you can connect the dots you would never see it. I have come across many accounts over the years of how insiders or semi-insiders have described the global society that was planned. The books of George Orwell and Aldous Huxley are just the most famous examples, but far from the only ones. Nor is the agenda only about centralisation of global power, as I will explain at length as we go along. It seeks to impose a total transformation of global society to create a world prison state controlling the fine detail of people's lives, including their very thoughts. Couldn't be done? It already has been to a large extent. In 1969, Dr Richard Day was the national medical director of the Illuminati-front, Planned Parenthood, a creation of the eugenics-supporting Rockefeller family, and he was also Professor of Paediatrics at Mount Sinai Medical School in New York. On 20th March 1969, he addressed the Pittsburgh

Paediatric Society with an audience of about 80 doctors. Dr Day asked everyone to turn off tape recorders and stop taking notes so that he could tell them about a coming a new world system and how American industry was going to be sabotaged. One member of the audience, Dr Lawrence Dunegan, a Pittsburgh paediatrician, did take notes and detailed what he had heard in a series of taped interviews. Dr Dunegan, who died in 2004, said.

> The stated plan was that different parts of the world would be assigned different roles of industry and commerce in a unified global system. The continued pre-eminence of the United States and the relative independence and self-sufficiency of the United States would have to be changed ... in order to create a new structure, you first have to tear down the old, and American industry was one example of that.

> Each part of the world will have a specialty and thus become inter-dependent. The US will remain a centre for agriculture, high tech, communications, and education, but heavy industry would be 'transported out'.

This is what has been happening for decades in the European Union as the economies and industries in the various countries have been targeted to destroy diversity and self-sufficiency and replace it with 'specialisation'. This makes everyone dependent on everyone else and allows a single control-centre to dictate the world economy. Dr Dunegan reported how Richard Day said the plan was also to cull and control the population through medicine, food, new laboratory-made diseases and the suppression of a cure for cancer. 'We can cure almost every cancer right now,' he said in 1969. 'Information is on file in the Rockefeller Institute, if it's ever decided that it should be released.' Why do you think so many of those involved in the conspiracy live for so long? A CIA scientist I met in the late 1990s told me how he had been cured of cancer by a secret serum not available to the public. Letting people die of cancer, Day said, would slow down population growth. 'You may as well die of cancer as something else.' Like all the bloodline families, Day believed in eugenics and the 'survival of the fittest'. Unless it affected them, of course. He said in 1969 that abortion would no longer be illegal and it would be accepted as normal. The food supply would be monitored so that no-one could give it to a 'fugitive of the system'. Growing food privately would be banned by saying it wasn't safe. Young people would spend longer in school, but not learn anything, and the family would 'diminish in importance' – by manipulation. There would be restrictions on travel and private home-ownership would disappear. The conspirators would increase violence, pornography and obscenity in the media and movies and this would desensitise people to violence and porn and make them feel that life is short, precarious and brutish. Music would 'get worse' and would be used for programming perception. Society would be fiercely controlled and people would be electronically tagged. Long-established communities would be destroyed by unemployment and mass immigration. Weather modification would be used as a weapon of war and to create drought or famine. Day himself had been involved in weather modification during the war. 'People will have to get used to the idea of change, so used to change, that they'll be expecting change. Nothing will be permanent.' This is a summary of his predictions posted at **overlordsofchaos.com**:

Population control; permission to have babies; redirecting the purpose of sex – sex without reproduction and reproduction without sex; contraception universally available to all; sex education and carnalising of youth as a tool of world government; tax-funded abortion as population control; encouraging anything goes homosexuality; technology used for reproduction without sex; families to diminish in importance; euthanasia and the 'demise pill'; limiting access to affordable medical care makes eliminating elderly easier; medicine would be tightly controlled; elimination of private doctors; new difficult to diagnose and untreatable diseases; suppressing cancer cures as a means of population control; inducing heart attacks as a form of assassination; education as a tool for accelerating the onset of puberty and evolution; blending all religions ... the old religions will have to go; changing the bible through revisions of key words; restructuring education as a tool of indoctrination; more time in schools, but pupils 'wouldn't learn anything'; controlling who has access to information; schools as the hub of the community; some books would just disappear from the libraries; changing laws to promote moral and social chaos; the encouragement of drug abuse to create a jungle atmosphere in cities and towns; promote alcohol abuse; restrictions on travel; the need for more jails, and using hospitals as jails; no more psychological or physical security; crime used to manage society; curtailment of US industrial pre-eminence; shifting populations and economies – tearing out the social roots; sports as a tool of social engineering and change; sex and violence inculcated through entertainment; implanted ID cards – microchips; food control; weather control; knowing how people respond – making them do what you want; falsified scientific research; use of terrorism; surveillance, implants, and televisions that watch you; the arrival of the totalitarian global system.

Day also said that people who don't want to go along with the new world system would be 'disposed of humanely'. There would be no 'martyrs', he said. 'People will just disappear.' Are we going to sit around and meekly wait for this? Or are we going to stand up, speak out and stop taking this crap? Make no mistake, this is what is planned and it is unfolding around us now.

By 1994/95, when I wrote the first edition of ... *And The Truth Shall Set You Free*, I could clearly see what was in store for humanity if nothing intervened. A guiding force was handing me the puzzle-pieces and they made so much sense of the world. What appeared to be bureaucratic 'incompetence' could be seen in a new light. It was only 'incompetence' if the goal was to serve the best interests of the people. Once you realise the agenda is about the control and exploitation of the people, and the constant centralisation of power, the apparent incompetence becomes genius because of what it leads to. As the magnitude of what I was uncovering became ever more obvious, it was deeply frustrating to be laughed at and dismissed for saying what I knew to be true. It wasn't the laughter and dismissal of me personally that mattered – I was well used to that. It was the knowledge of what was planned for humanity and what was coming in just a few years unless people woke up to what was happening. I don't have that frustration any more because things are as they are and all you can do is your best. It is also now clear, and getting clearer by the day, that so many more people are at last seeing what they could not see before.

6

Spider Men

All the war-propaganda, all the screaming and lies and hatred, comes invariably from
people who are not fighting
George Orwell

In the early years of my journey after Peru, the recurring themes were Sumer and
Babylon and the bloodline families who came out of there – one name in particular:
Rothschild. You simply cannot understand the global conspiracy without knowing the
background to this vicious bunch of interbreeding global criminals and power-crazed
genocidal maniacs.

Over the top? Far too mild, if anything.

'Genocide' is defined as: 'The deliberate and systematic destruction of a racial, political
or cultural group'. This captures the ambitions of the House of Rothschild so perfectly,
and the 'racial group' in their sights is called 'humanity'. They operate at the centre of
the web and they act like conductors of the orchestra. The Rothschilds are not the origin
of the power that drives the conspiracy, because the rabbit hole is much deeper than
that. They are, however, the prime dispensers of that power within human society on
behalf of the 'Spider'. Almost everyone will have heard of the Rothschilds, yet almost
no-one knows what they actually do. They are bankers, aren't they? Yes they are, but
that's like saying that Hitler was a painter. It doesn't tell anything like the full story. The
Rothschilds have a horrific record of engineering wars, including the world wars,
instigating financial crashes and manipulating countries across every continent via the
networks they control. There is not a single man, woman or child whose life is not
affected, often disastrously, by the Rothschilds. Their power and influence was once
well known, and politicians cowered before them in the knowledge that without their
sanction they would either never experience high political office, or stay there for long if
they did. Their control and manipulation became so obvious that their plans were in
danger of exposure, and since the early years of the 20th century they have brilliantly
disguised the extent of their ownership and power structure by using nominee directors
and other front people, including the Rockefeller family and 'independent' industrialists
and tycoons like J P Morgan, Andrew Carnegie, Edward R Harriman and a stream of
others. When you see those names you are looking at another word for Rothschild. The
Rockefellers are a Rothschild bloodline and subordinates to the main family. J D

Rockefeller's Standard Oil was really Rothschild Oil, and when Rockefeller created the abomination of modern pharmaceutical medicine he was doing it for the Rothschild dynasty. The Rockefellers went to America from the Rothschild heartland of Germany, where they were known as the Rockenfelders. Frederic Morton describes the way the Rothschild dynasty hides the extent of its power in his 1962 book, *The Rothschilds*.

> Though they control scores of industrial, commercial, mining and tourist corporations, not one bears the name Rothschild. Being private partnerships, the family houses never need to, and never do, publish a single public balance sheet, or any other report of their financial condition.

It is important to stress that when I talk about 'the Rothschilds' I am not referring only to those with that name. I mean the Rothschild bloodline. As I have explained in previous books, there are staggering numbers of people throughout the world who have Rothschild genetics. They are brought up by different families under different names, but they are still Rothschilds and later come to prominence in positions of power in politics, banking, business, the military, the media, religion, entertainment and so on. One of these unofficial Rothschilds told me how he was planted in the Christian Church to do the dynasty's work. This doesn't mean that the Rothschilds must be having sex every ten minutes. They actually have Rothschild sperm banks to constantly expand the bloodline, and the reason for this obsession with genetics will become clear later. Another point to stress is that not everyone, or even nearly everyone, with the name 'Rothschild' is part of this great conspiracy. 'Lower' levels of the family are kept in the dark about all of this, and others have picked up the name through marriage. When I say 'the Rothschilds' I mean the leading figures in that family that run their banking and business operations, and their bloodline assets within the global system – not least in politics – who carry the genes, but not the name.

The 'Cruellest Hoax'

We are led to believe that the Rothschilds are a family of biblical Jews and therefore originate in Old Testament Egypt and Israel. This is not true. They are Sumerians and I tell the story in detail in *The David Icke Guide to the Global Conspiracy (and how to end it)*. Sumerian and Babylonian peoples migrated north into an area near the Caucasus Mountains and the land mostly occupied today by the country of Georgia. Dr Sandor Nagy, author of *The Forgotten Cradle of the Hungarian Culture*, says there were two separate migrations of Sumerian people out of Mesopotamia. One was through Turkey to the Carpathian Basin which includes today's Romania – home to the vampire legends of Transylvania – Hungary, Bulgaria, and the countries of the former Yugoslavia, like Serbia and Croatia. The other Sumerian peoples went east, and then north, across the Caucasus Mountains into the area between the Caspian and Black Seas. These latter Sumerians became known as 'Khazars' and their new country was called Khazaria (Fig 37 overleaf). In about AD 740, the King of Khazaria, King Bulan, adopted the religion of Judaism and the whole nation did the same. With the eventual break-up of Khazaria, these converts to Judaism moved north to become the East European Jewish communities and many went on into Western Europe. Among them were the family that became the Rothschilds. They passed through the centuries under various names,

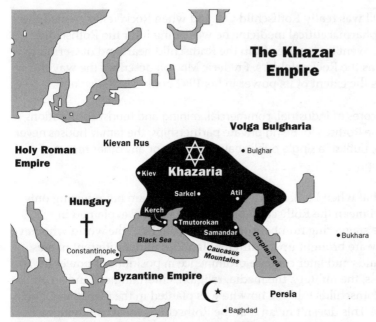

The Khazar Empire

Volga Bulgharia

Holy Roman Empire

Kievan Rus

• Bulghar

• Kiev   **Khazaria**

Hungary

Sarkel •   Atil •

Kerch •

• Tmutorokan

Samandar •

Black Sea

Constantinople •

Caucasus Mountains

Caspian Sea

• Bukhara

Byzantine Empire

Persia

• Baghdad

Figure 37: *The Khazar Empire had a mass conversion to Judaism in the 8th century and became the Eastern and later Western European 'Jewry'. They have no historical connection to Israel and mostly came out of Mesopotamia*

including Bauer. The Khazars are the ancestors of more than 90 per cent of people calling themselves 'Jewish' today and the Khazars had no connection whatsoever with the land called Israel. Their home was not the Dead Sea, but the Caspian Sea, which was once known as the 'Khazar Sea'. The people known as the Israelites have had their biblical identity stolen by former Khazars and Sumerians, and even that identity is nonsense. Thomas Thompson, Professor of Old Testament at the University of Copenhagen, demolishes the beliefs about biblical Israel in his book, *The Mythic Past*. He says that archaeological and linguistic research reveals an ancient Palestine radically different from the one described in the Bible. There was no Adam and Eve, no Noah or Abraham, no Moses or Joshua, and we now know why. These were invented 'characters' based on the far older accounts of Sumer, Babylon and Mesopotamia. The population of Palestine at the time of the 'great nation' of Israel was tiny, a few thousand at most, Thompson says. He continues:

> When one investigates the history of Palestine independently of the biblical view of the past, this period betrays little evidence of biblical Israel's emergence … There is no evidence of a United Monarchy, no evidence of a capital in Jerusalem or of any coherent, unified political force that dominated western Palestine, let alone an empire of the size the legends describe. We do not have evidence for the existence of the kings named Saul, David or Solomon; nor do we have the evidence of any temple at Jerusalem in the early period.

How come? They made it all up. The overwhelming majority of Jewish people today don't know this, but the Rothschilds and their associated families do. Some Jewish writers like Arthur Koestler have presented compelling evidence that Jewish people have no historical connection to the land of Israel. Alfred M Lilienthal, a Jewish former American State Department official, called these facts 'Israel's Achilles heel', because it destroys any claims to that land. Koestler wrote in his book, *The Thirteenth Tribe*:

> ... [It] would mean that their ancestors came not from the Jordan, but from the Volga, not from Canaan but from the Caucasus, once believed to be the cradle of the Aryan race [hence 'Caucasian']; and that genetically they are more closely connected to the Hun, Uigur and Magyar tribes than to the seed of Abraham, Isaac and Jacob. Should this turn out to be the case, then the term 'anti-Semitism' would be void of meaning, based on a misapprehension shared by both the killers and their victims. The story of the Khazar Empire, as it slowly emerges from the past, begins to look like the most cruel hoax which history has ever perpetrated.

The Khazars fought, made alliances and interbred with peoples like the Viking Rus (who became the Russians) and the Magyars with whom they had extremely close relations. Khazars were instrumental in the creation of the Magyar homeland of Hungary. Names like the Russian 'Cossack' and the Hungarian 'Hussar' came from 'Khazar', as did the German for 'heretic', Ketzer. The Khazars also had close links with the Byzantine Empire, which was part of the Roman Empire centred on Constantinople, and there was interbreeding between them. A Khazar princess married Byzantine Emperor Constantine V, and their son became Emperor Leo IV, known as Leo the Khazar, who ruled the Byzantine Empire from AD 775 to AD 800. The deposed emperor, Justinian II, fled to Khazaria in AD 705, where the king (the 'Khagan' or 'Kagan') gave him shelter and allowed him to marry his sister. She took the name Theodora and became empress when Justinian was restored to the Byzantine throne. 'Kagan', of course, is a common 'Jewish' name today. Historians believe the Khazars to be descendants of the Turkic tribe known as the Huns or Hun, which invaded and savaged Europe from Asia around AD 450, but the main source of the Khazars was Sumer. The Huns' territories stretched at one time from central Asia to central Europe, from Siberia and China to North India. They were a grouping of tribes and bloodlines from the interbreeding with many peoples, including the Chinese and Sumerians. The Huns are best remembered for their leader, Attila the Hun, who seized power by killing his brother, Buda, after whom the Hungarian city of Budapest was named. The Khazars, like the Huns, spoke the Turkic language and are believed to be the same people. They controlled a large and powerful 'Pagan' empire across most of Russia, to the Ural Mountains in the east and the Caucasus Mountains in the south. They made their living as traders and 'middlemen', levying taxes on the goods carried on the trade routes through their lands. Their influence in Eastern Europe extended well into the countries we now know as Poland, Czechoslovakia, Austria, Hungary, Romania and Bulgaria. They were phallic worshippers and engaged in human sacrifice rituals.

The Khazars' close associates and subordinates, the Magyars, were also related to the Sumerians. It was believed that the Magyars were a nomadic people from the north with a language of Finnish-Ugrian origin, but Dr Sandor Nagy writes in *The Forgotten Cradle of the Hungarian Culture* that the people who later became known as Magyars were Sumerians from the 'Fertile Crescent', now Iraq. Dr Nagy uses extensive examples to confirm the linguistic similarities between the Sumerian, old Magyar, and current Magyar language. He also refers to several works written during the first millennium, including the *Arpad Codices* and the *De Administrando Imperio*, and completed 50 years of his own research. He says that while there are only 200 Magyar words related to the Finno-Ugric language, there are over 2,000 related to the Sumerian. It was the same

story with British, French and German archaeologists and linguists. They concluded
that the language of ancient Sumerian inscriptions was not Indo-European or Semitic,
but a language which demonstrated significant similarities with the group of languages
known at the time as the Turanian ethno-linguistic group. These included Hungarian,
Turkic, Mongolian and Finnic (later referred to as the Ural-Altaic group). Research has
indicated that the Sumerian and Hungarian languages have over a thousand common
word roots and a very similar grammatical structure. Kálmán Gosztony, professor of
Sumerian philology at the Sorbonne in Paris, demonstrated in *Sumerian Etymological
Dictionary and Comparative Grammar* that the structure of the Hungarian language is the
closest to that of the Sumerian. Of the 53 characteristics of Sumerian grammar, 51
matched in the Hungarian, compared with 29 in the Turkic languages, 24 in the
Caucasian, 21 in the Uralic languages, 5 in the Semitic languages and 4 in the Indo-
European. The linguistic similarities between Sumerian, Hungarian and other languages
are confirmed by archaeological and anthropological evidence. It is clear that the
overwhelming majority of what we call 'Jewish' people originally came out of Sumer,
and the Sumerians were not Semitic, which refers to people of a particular language
group. Therefore, to refer to 'anti-Semitism', with regard to Jewish people, is thoroughly
inaccurate, as the Rothschilds and their circle well know.

The Khazars and the Huns are descended, like the Magyars, from the Sumerians of
Mesopotamia. An ancient traditional pre-Christian account of Hungarian origin says
they are the descendants of the Babylonian 'king' Nimrod, who is said in the Bible to be
the son of Cush and great-grandson of Noah. These connections will become more
relevant later. The legend claims that Nimrod had two sons, Magor and Hunor. It is said
that Magor was the ancestor of the Magyars and Hunor was the ancestor of the Huns,
so providing the common origin of the Magyars and the Huns (Khazars). Interestingly,
Nimrod is considered a 'god' by the Illuminati bloodlines and their satanic religion.
Ancient Byzantine sources say the Magyars were also called the Sabirs and originated
from Mesopotamia, the land of Sumer and Babylon. Numerous other ancient and
medieval sources refer to the Scythians, Huns (Khazars), Avars and Magyars as the
same peoples, even though the Hungarian authorities appear desperate to deny this.
There was some highly significant interbreeding between bloodlines from Sumer and
those from the Far East and China. This Caucasian-Chinese-Turkish combination
produced very important 'royal' bloodlines from the Illuminati perspective. The Khazar
Empire, the first feudal state in Eastern Europe, broke up in a series of wars and
invasions culminating in the arrival of the Mongol 'Golden Horde', best remembered
for their inspiration, Genghis Khan. Over the centuries of waning power and influence,
the Khazar peoples began to migrate in many directions. S W Baron says of Khazaria in
A Social and Religious History of the Jews:

> Its population was largely absorbed by the Golden Horde which had established the
> centre of its empire in Khazar territory. But before and after the Mongol upheaval the
> Khazars sent many offshoots into the unsubdued Slavonic lands, helping ultimately to
> build up the great Jewish centres of Eastern Europe.

The Khazars took their Judaic and Talmudic (Babylonian/Sumerian) faith and settled in
East European and Alpine lands, especially Poland and Lithuania. There are many

ancient place names in Poland and the Ukraine inspired by the name 'Khazar' or 'Zhid', a term meaning 'Jew'. These include Kozarzewek, Kozara, Kozarzow and Zydowo. As the Khazar Empire collapsed in the period after AD 960, a number of Slavonic tribes, led by the Polans, formed an alliance that became the state called Poland. 'Jews' (Khazars) played an important role in the Polish legends about the formation of the country. One says that a 'Jew' called Abraham Prokownik was elected by the tribes to rule them. Certainly Khazar 'Jews' became prominent in many countries of Eastern Europe. Jewish writer, Arthur Koestler, who was born in Hungary, writes in *The Thirteenth Tribe*:

> Both the Hungarian and Polish sources refer to Jews employed as mintmasters, administrators of the royal revenue, controllers of the salt monopoly, tax-collectors and 'money-lenders' – i.e., bankers. This parallel suggests a common origin of those two immigrant communities; and, as we can trace the origins of the bulk of Hungarian Jewry to the Magyar-Khazar nexus, the conclusion seems self-evident.

The traditional garb of Polish Jewry is of unmistakably Eastern origin, including the skullcap (yarmulke) worn by orthodox Jews, Uzbeks and other Turkish people in the Soviet Union, and by Muslims and the Roman Catholic hierarchy. The so-called 'Jewish nose' is not a genetic trait of Israel, but the former land of Khazaria in the Caucasus. The Sumerian-Khazars eventually developed a new language called 'Yiddish' because they did not speak Hebrew. This is understandable. Why would they speak the language of a people with whom they had no connection? Shlomo Sand, Professor of History at Tel Aviv University, confirms the fake history of the 'Jewish race' in his book, *The Invention of the Jewish People*:

> The Jews were a class of people dependent on the German bourgeoisie in the East, and thus they adopted German words. Here I base myself on the research of linguist Paul Wechsler of Tel Aviv University, who has demonstrated that there is no etymological connection between the German Jewish language of the Middle Ages and Yiddish. As far back as 1828, the Ribal (Rabbi Isaac Ber Levinson) said that the ancient language of the Jews was not Yiddish. Even Ben Zion Dinur, the father of Israeli historiography, was not hesitant about describing the Khazars as the origin of the Jews in Eastern Europe, and describes Khazaria as 'the mother of the diasporas' in Eastern Europe. But more or less since 1967, anyone who talks about the Khazars as the ancestors of the Jews of Eastern Europe is considered naive and moonstruck.

Ashkenazi domination

The former Khazars became known as 'Jews', and a false history and origin was constructed by their leadership and priesthood (the bloodlines) that claimed them to be the descendants of the biblical Israelites. The Khazar 'Jews' were confined to ghettos as a result of papal dictate in the mid-16th century and this, together with the 17th century Cossack massacres in the Ukraine, led to another mass exodus into Hungary, Bohemia, Rumania and Germany. There were hardly any Jews in Germany until this time. 'Thus the great trek to the West was resumed,' says Arthur Koestler. 'It was to continue through nearly three centuries until the Second World War and became the principle source of the existing Jewish communities in Europe, the United States and Israel.'

Another writer, Stewart Swerdlow, who is also Jewish, comes from a completely different research background to Koestler. He gleaned much of his knowledge while forced to serve a government-military mind-control programme at Montauk on New York's Long Island. He says in his book, *Blue Blood, True Blood*:

> … [the Sumerians] mostly established themselves in the Caucasus Mountains and [later] became the Khazars. From here, they spread west towards Europe, seeding the national identities for the Vikings, the Franks, the Teutonic [German] peoples and the Russians. Keep in mind that when Atlantis sank, some of those refugees went to Western Europe and developed into the Celts. Some went to Greece and others to the Italian Peninsula. These peoples were here before the [Sumerians] moved in … These Blueblood leaders also infiltrated the Middle Eastern peoples, such as the biblical Canaanites …

This means, as I have long known, that the 'elite' families of the Roman Empire who interbred with the 'elite' families of the rest of Europe to produce European royalty and aristocracy were essentially the same bloodlines. Swerdlow continues:

> … Babylon was the civilization that Sumer developed into as it expanded into Central Asia to become the Khazars. In fact, many of the Blueblood organisations that developed through the millennia called themselves Babylon Brotherhoods. [They] later combined with the secret Atlantean-Egyptian schools in Europe to become the Freemasons. Some of these immigrants went by the name of Bauer, now known as the Rothschilds. The family quickly took control of the financial and trade foundations of Europe.

The former Khazar people are known today as the Ashkenazi Jews (plural Ashkenazim), and some writers estimate that perhaps 90 to 95 per cent of those calling themselves 'Jewish' worldwide are Ashkenazi, or former Khazars. The Ashkenazim (Sumerian-Khazars) hold the reins of power in Israel and have done so since the country was created by the Rothschilds in 1948. Every Israeli prime minister has been an Ashkenazi Sumerian-Khazar. The name 'Ashkenazi' is said by some to originate from Ashkenaz, the Hebrew word for Germany, but the Bible refers to the Ashkenaz as a people living in the region of Mount Ararat (now Turkey) and Armenia – where the biblical 'Noah's Ark' is said to have come to rest. This would certainly fit the basic location of the Khazars. The multiple linguistic influences in their language were also mirrored in the genes of the former Khazars. They interbred with so many other races that they became a genetic cocktail that included Sumerian, Turkish, Far Eastern and northern and western European. However, their 'royal' bloodlines, like the Rothschilds, remained 'pure' through careful interbreeding, and they are a race apart from the Jewish people – just like the bloodlines within all nations and races. So I am not saying there is a 'Jewish plot' to control the world. I am saying that their leading families, who could not care less about Jewish people in general, are major players in the bloodline network that has infiltrated all peoples and nations with the aim of establishing a global fascist/communist dictatorship.

Shlomo Sand (also 'Zand'), Professor of History at Tel Aviv University, writes in *The Invention of the Jewish People* that Jews never existed as a race or nation with a common origin. Instead, they are a considerable mix of races and groups who adopted the Jewish religion over the centuries. This is seriously at odds with the official history that has been carefully compiled to deceive Jewish people with a false account of their collective origins. Israel's Declaration of Independence says that Jews come from the ancient Land of Israel and were exiled from this homeland. Israeli schoolchildren are taught that this happened during the period of Roman rule in AD 70. The nation remained loyal to its land, the official fairytale goes, and pledged to return. Shlomo Sand says, rightly, that the mythical history of an ancient people traversing thousands of years before returning to their 'Promised Land' is untenable by the facts, and this myth has led its advocates to form a racist view of the world and other peoples. Sand says there never was a Jewish people, only a Jewish religion, and the exile never happened. He rejects most of the biblical stories about the formation of a Jewish national identity, including the exodus from Egypt. Sand says this is all made up to justify the establishment of the State of Israel. The Israeli daily, *Haaretz*, said in a positive review of Sand's book:

> We find, then, that the members of a variety of peoples and races, blond and black, brown and yellow, became Jews in large numbers. According to Zand, the Zionist need to devise for them a shared ethnicity and historical continuity produced a long series of inventions and fictions, along with an invocation of racist theses. Some were concocted in the minds of those who conceived the Zionist movement, while others were offered as the findings of genetic studies conducted in Israel.

Sand also says that many Jews converted to Islam after the Arab conquest of the Middle East and elsewhere, and they were genetically assimilated into the Arab races. He contends, with extraordinary irony, that these Jews were ancestors of the Palestinian people. *Haaretz* points out that Sand did not invent this thesis – it was espoused 30 years before Israel's Declaration of Independence by leading Zionists like David Ben-Gurion, the first Prime Minister of Israel, and Yitzhak Ben-Zvi, the State's second and longest-serving President. Research by Sand and others also concludes that it is not only the Ashkenazi Jews who have no connection to Israel. He says the Sephardic Jews that emerged out of Spain and Portugal came from *Arabs* who converted to the Jewish religion, and from Europeans who did the same. There was no 'Diaspora' ('The Scattering'), Sand says, when an ancient Jewish people were exiled and scattered. It was not the Jewish people who 'scattered', he stresses; it was the Jewish religion, which picked up converts in many places from many races. *Haaretz* sums up Sand's findings about the origin of the historical myths about an ancient Jewish race:

> At a certain stage in the 19th century intellectuals of Jewish origin in Germany, influenced by the folk character of German nationalism, took upon themselves the task of inventing a people 'retrospectively', out of a thirst to create a modern Jewish people. From historian Heinrich Graetz on, Jewish historians began to draw the history of Judaism as the history of a nation that had been a kingdom, became a wandering people and ultimately turned around and went back to its birthplace.

For 19th century intellectuals of Jewish origin in Germany, read the Rothschilds. They orchestrated the creation of the historical myth of the 'Jewish' historical connection to

Israel in preparation for their plan (under the title 'Zionism') to use the Jewish masses to seize the land of Palestine for Rothschild-Illuminati ends. Shlomo Sand told *Haaretz*:

> It is clear that the fear is of an undermining of the historic right to the land. The revelation that the Jews are not from Judea would ostensibly knock the legitimacy for our being here out from under us. Since the beginning of the period of decolonization, settlers have no longer been able to say simply: 'We came, we won and now we are here' the way the Americans, the whites in South Africa and the Australians said. There is a very deep fear that doubt will be cast on our right to exist …

> … I don't think that the historical myth of the exile and the wanderings is the source of the legitimization for me being here, and therefore I don't mind believing that I am Khazar in my origins. I am not afraid of the undermining of our existence, because I think that the character of the State of Israel undermines it in a much more serious way. What would constitute the basis for our existence here is not mythological historical right, but rather would be for us to start to establish an open society here of all Israeli citizens …

> … I don't recognize an international [Jewish] people. I recognize 'the Yiddish people' that existed in Eastern Europe, which though it is not a nation can be seen as a Yiddishist civilization with a modern popular culture. I think that Jewish nationalism grew up in the context of this 'Yiddish people'. I also recognize the existence of an Israeli people, and do not deny its right to sovereignty. But Zionism and also Arab nationalism over the years are not prepared to recognize it.

No matter how much the Zionists may scream and yelp at the facts in hope of discrediting the truth and the truth-bringers, it is clear that the official 'history' of Jewish people is a manufactured lie to serve the interests of the House of Rothschild and the

Illuminati family network that knows they are not 'Jewish', because there is no 'Jewish' in the context that they claim. The Rothschilds and their ilk are a Sumerian bloodline that has kept its 'purity' by interbreeding and it has infiltrated what we call Jewish people to use them as a front – a cover – for their horrific activities and to make them take the blame when necessary.

The Red-Shields

The name 'Rothschild' first appeared in the 18th century when Mayer Amschel Bauer established his banking empire in Frankfurt, Germany, and changed the family name. This is why Frankfurt remains an important city for the Illuminati and was chosen as the home of the new European Central Bank when it opened in 1998. It is a creation of the Rothschilds secured through another creation, the European Union. The Bauers were a

Figure 38: *The Rothschild home in Frankfurt where it all began* notorious satanic family in Middle Ages Germany and the major Rothschilds remain master black magicians to this day. Mayer Amschel's father, Moses Amschel Bauer, was a moneylender and proprietor of a counting house. The name 'Rothschild' derives from the German 'rotes-schild', or 'red shield'/'red sign'. This referred to the red hexagram on the Bauer/Rothschild home in Frankfurt (Fig 38) and it is better known as the 'Star of David'. Despite what most people believe, this is not an exclusively Jewish symbol and was not used in that context until the Rothschilds took it as their

Figure 39: *The Rothschild 'logo' on the flag of Israel – the Land of Rothschild*

own. The hexagram is an esoteric symbol going back to antiquity, and today it is displayed on the flag of Israel because the Rothschilds own the place (Fig 39). Mayer Amschel Rothschild and his five sons established banking houses in Frankfurt, London, Paris, Vienna and Naples. He selected the wives of his sons for the business connections they would bring to the family and he wanted his offspring to marry cousins wherever possible to keep the bloodline 'pure'. He had 18 grandchildren, and 16 of them married first cousins. You find a similar story with other bloodlines, like the Rothschild associates, the Habsburgs, and 'royal' families going back to the ancient world. Rothschild's daughters all married bankers – Worms, Sichel and Beyfus – and the family became immensely rich, and infamous, by funding all sides in wars that they had covertly created. Many famous banking names, including Lazard, Warburg, Worms, Sichel and Beyfus, came out of Rothschild-dominated Frankfurt.

In 1790, Mayer Amschel Rothschild encapsulated the family's manipulation technique when he said: 'Let me issue and control a nation's money and I care not who writes the laws.' Something similar is also attributed to his son, Nathan, who is quoted as saying: 'I care not what puppet is placed upon the throne of England to rule the Empire on which the sun never sets … The man who controls Britain's money supply controls the British Empire, and I control the British money supply.' The game was, and is, to get companies and governments into enormous debt and then take them over. The Rothschilds seized control of the United States economy from the start through their aristocratic agent in George Washington's first government, Treasury Secretary, Alexander Hamilton. It was Hamilton who established the country's first central bank, the Bank of the United States, chartered in 1791, and closed in 1811 when Congress refused to support it any longer. Another version came and went before the Rothschilds used their agents, the Schiff and Warburg families, to create the privately-owned 'American' central bank, the Federal Reserve, in 1913. Most people think the Federal Reserve is owned by the US government, but it is a cartel of private banks controlled by the Rothschilds. They love central banks because when you centralise anything you increase the power of the few over the many. This is why they are seeking to destroy all diversity wherever it is and impose uniformity. The Schiff and Rothschild families were as one, and shared the same house in Frankfurt in the days of dynasty founder Mayer Amschel. Jacob Schiff ran the Rothschild-controlled banking operation of Kuhn, Loeb & Co in the United States, while the Warburgs would later become bankers to Hitler. Kuhn, Loeb & Co was a major funder of the Russian Bolshevik Revolution and its official instigators, the Sumerian-Khazars, Lenin and Trotsky (real name, Bronstein). The

Rothschild-contrived 'revolution' imposed the political creed of another Sumerian-Khazar and Rothschild asset called Karl Marx, and removed the Russian Tsars who were refusing to play ball with the Rothschilds. London's *The Times* newspaper reported on 29th March 1919:

> One of the curious features of the Bolshevist movement is the high percentage of non Russian elements among its leaders. Of the twenty or thirty commissaries, or leaders, who provide the central machinery of the Bolshevist movement, not less than 75% were Jews.

In other words, Rothschild agents and pawns going under the name of 'Zionists'. Soviet dissident author, Aleksandr Solzhenitsyn, writes in *Gulag Archipelago, volume two* that Zionists created and administered the Soviet concentration camp system in which tens of millions died. He names Aron Solts, Yakov Rappoport, Lazar Kogan, Matvei Berman, Genrikh Yagoda and Naftaly Frenkel – all Zionists.

Kuhn, Loeb & Co – in other words, the Rothschilds – was the source of funding behind the Rockefeller, Harriman, J P Morgan and Carnegie financial and industrial empires, among many more. They are just other names for 'Rothschild'. Jacob Schiff at Kuhn, Loeb & Co ordered the creation of the Council on Foreign Relations just before he died in 1920 (as an American satellite of the Rothschild Round Table in Britain), and a year later the CFR was founded by Rothschild assets, Bernard Baruch and Colonel Edward Mandell House. Baruch and House were the controllers of President Woodrow Wilson when he took the United States into a First World War in which the British Rothschilds loaned money to the British, the French Rothschilds loaned money to the French and the German Rothschilds loaned money to the Germans. Hmmm. And guess who funded the Americans. Schiff also established the National Advancement for the Association of Coloured People (NAACP) as part of the Rothschild strategy of playing different races and sections of society off against each other to divide and rule. Howard Sachar, a Jewish historian, says in his book, *A History of the Jews in America*: 'In 1914, Professor Emeritus Joel Spingarn of Columbia University became chairman of the NAACP and recruited for its board such Jewish leaders as Jacob Schiff, Jacob Billikopf and Rabbi Stephen Wise.' Others included Julius Rosenthal, Lillian Wald and Rabbi Emil G Hirsch, and it was not until 1920 that the NAACP felt it appropriate to appoint its first black president, James Weldon Johnson. The Rothschilds have gone on manipulating, creating and controlling organisations allegedly for the benefit of black people and other minorities about whom they don't give a damn. 'Civil rights leaders', like Jesse Jackson and Al Sharpton, are among the many Rothschild assets in this field, plus, of course, Barack Obama.

Money, money, money

The Rothschild dynasty is controlled by the family's satanic black magicians who know how reality works and how they can manipulate energy and human perception. They know that money, like everything else, is energy and they have set up the financial system to exploit this knowledge. People talk about 'flows of money', but it's really flows of energy and they have created an energetic construct that ensures that the energy of money flows to them. We call this construct the 'economic system' or 'the economy' and it appears to consist of banks, financial houses, stockmarkets and other forms of trading; but all of these entities are just acupuncture points on the meridians of money to ensure that the wealth of the world flows to the bloodline families. It is because of this that the Rothschilds count their wealth not in millions or billions, but in multiples of trillions and more. They control more money than all the world's governments put together by controlling the energy-construct that we call the financial system. To the Rothschilds, it is like watching billions of rivers and canals pouring water 24/7 into an enormous lake that gets wider and deeper by the hour. For 'water' read 'money', and for 'money' read 'energy' – life force. Money is a means of exchanging energy. They create money and circulate it throughout society as it passes from person to person, and each one is unknowingly imprinting their own energy field on the energy field of the money. By stealing our money, they are stealing our life force. I have had direct experience of this myself. If person A contributes energy in the form of work for person B, then person B can either reciprocate with his work or balance the energy interaction with money. If this exchange does not take place in a fair and balanced way, someone is giving out more energy than they are receiving. The economic system is specifically designed to make this the daily norm in the energy exchange between the masses and the elite few. First of all, most people are paid the minimum the employer can get away with to secure the services of someone they need. Most people do not even begin to get a fair return for their daily contributions of energy and that is how it is meant to be. This, however, is just the start. The basic income – energy received for energy given – is then subject to a long, long list of energetic vampires. Most notably, the ones called 'taxation' and 'interest on money'. Levels of taxation are now extraordinary with income tax, sales tax, council or state tax, inheritance tax, car tax, etc., etc., and more are being added all the time. Sales tax is simply a fine for spending your own money, while inheritance tax and 'death duties' are the taxation of money that has already been taxed. Here is a list of US taxes, by no means all of them, at **whatistaxed.com**:

Accounts Receivable Tax; Accumulated Earnings Tax; Ad Valorem Tax (includes duties on imported items); Alternative Minimum Tax; Aviation Fuel Tax; Capital Gains Tax; Cement and Gypsum Producers License Tax; Coal Severance Tax; Coal Gross Proceeds Tax; Consumer Counsel Tax; Consumption Tax; Corporate Income Tax; Corporation License Tax; Court Fines (revenue from many activities); Customs Duty; Dog License Tax; Double Tax; Electrical Energy Producers Tax; Estate Tax, Inheritance Tax; Federal Income Tax; Federal Unemployment Tax; Fishing License Tax; Food Service License Tax; Fuel Permit License Tax; Gas Guzzler Tax; Gasoline Tax; Generation-skipping Transfer Tax; Gift Tax; Gross Production Tax; Hospital Facility Utilization Fee Tax; Hunting License Fee Tax; Inventory Tax; IRS Interest Charges; IRS Penalties Tax; Kiddie Tax; Land Value Tax; Liquor License Tax; Liquor Tax; Local Tax; Lodging Facility Use Tax; Luxury Tax; Marriage License Tax; Medicare Tax; Metal Mines Gross Proceeds Tax; Metal Mines License Tax; Miscellaneous Mineral Mines License Tax; Miscellaneous Mines Net Proceeds Tax; Nursing Facility Bed Tax; Oil and Natural Gas Production Tax; Parking Meter Tax; Payroll Tax; Professional Privilege Tax; Property Tax; Proxy Tax; Public Contractor's Gross Receipts Tax; Public Service Commission Tax; Public Utility Tax; Real Estate Tax; Real Estate Transfer Tax; Rental Vehicle Sales Tax; Resort Tax;

Resource Indemnity and Groundwater Assessment Tax; Retail Telecommunications Excise Tax; Sales Tax; School Tax; Self-Employment Tax; Septic Permit Tax; Severance Tax; Social Security Tax; State Income Tax; State Unemployment Tax; State-wide Emergency Telephone 911 System Fee Tax; Surtax Tax – extra tax; Tariffs – a tax on imports; Telephone Federal Excise Tax; Telephone Federal Universal Service Fee Tax; Telephone Minimum Usage Surcharge Tax; TDD Telecommunications Service Fee Tax; Tobacco products tax; Toll Road Fee Tax; Toll Bridge Fee Tax; Toll Tunnel Fee Tax; Tonnage Tax; Traffic Fines; Trailer Registration Fee Tax; Use Tax; Utility Tax; Vehicle Registration and License Tax; Vehicle Sales Tax; Watercraft Registration Tax; Well Permit Tax; Wholesale Energy Transaction Tax; Workers Compensation Tax.

If you added together all the forms of taxation that we pay in a year and subtracted that from your income, you would be shocked at how much of the energy you receive for your energy given goes back to the system in taxation alone. Ultimately, this money/energy ends up in the Rothschild 'lake' and this is why, despite the ever-increasing taxation, we get an ever-decreasing quality of services which this money is supposed to be paying for. Add to all this the interest paid to the banks for 'borrowing' non-existent money called 'credit' and you can see that humanity is being energetically and systematically sucked dry. Something else is being sucked dry also – choice and potential. How often are people denied what they want to do or where they want to go by the mantra of 'I can't afford it' or 'I don't have the money'? Our money is part of our energy field, part of 'us', because that 'ownership' makes a vibrational connection between our energy field and that of the money. Giving and receiving money is energy 'in' and energy 'out'. Look at all of the above and you can see that the masses are being manipulated to give out far more energy than they are getting back. Even after the original exchange has taken place in the form of salary or profit, most of what we receive is then consumed by taxation, interest on money and artificially-inflated costs for essential services. The economic system, headed by the House of Rothschild, has been created to vampire the life-force of the global population. The public see money, but the Rothschilds see everything as energy, which, of course, it is. We call money 'currency', but it should be *current*-cy. This is how the Rothschilds use it, as like an electrical current which they circulate and then get back at a much greater voltage, or 'plus interest'.

Money Out of Nothing

The Rothschilds control the global financial system and have accumulated their power by theft and exploitation. Their whole system is based on a gigantic fraud because there is no money, as we perceive it. The paper money and coins in your pocket are backed by nothing. Their value is only the value that we can be persuaded they have. They are just worthless pieces of paper (a promise-to-pay or promissory note) and pieces of metal that we are tricked into taking seriously. Most 'money' is not even something you can hold today. It is only figures a computer screen – current-cy in every sense. 'Money' is brought into circulation through what is called 'credit', but what is this 'credit'? It is a belief-system, that's all, a belief that it exists. The banks are not lending us anything and we are paying them fortunes to do so. The bloodline families, particularly the Rothschilds, have controlled governments and banking for centuries and they have been able to dictate the laws of the financial system and introduce what is called 'fractional reserve lending'. This allows banks to lend at least ten times what they have on deposit. In other words, they are lending 'money' they don't have and that doesn't exist – called 'credit' – and are charging interest on it. When you go to a bank to borrow, say £50,000, you have to provide 'collateral' by signing over your house, land, car or business, and this will go to the bank if you don't meet the repayments. What is the bank giving you in return for this? *Nothing*. It types into your account £50,000 and that's it. The £50,000 doesn't really exist – it is a line of non-existent 'credit'. Oh, but there's more. Say you give someone a cheque for £20,000 from the original £50,000 and the recipient deposits the money into another bank. Now this second bank can lend ten times the £20,000 to other people, quite legally, and charge them interest. When you follow the original £50,000 from bank to bank to bank, the amount of 'credit' that is created as it circulates the banking system is absolutely fantastic. We are talking here about a single loan that was created out of thin air in the first place. I have featured in other books a document called *Quiet Weapons for a Quiet War*. It is an insider-manual on how to mass mind-control the population by using the 'quiet weapons' of mental and emotional manipulation. The document specifically highlights Mayer Amschel Rothschild and the energetic financial system that has evolved from his insights. It says:

> Mr. Rothschild loaned his promissory notes [worthless 'credit'] to individuals and to governments. These would create over-confidence. Then he would make money scarce, tighten control of the system, and collect the collateral through the obligation of contracts. The cycle was then repeated. These pressures could be used to ignite a war. Then he would control the availability of currency to determine who would win the war. That government which agreed to give him control of its economic system got his support. Collection of debts was guaranteed by economic aid to the enemy of the debtor.
>
> The profit derived from this economic methodology made Mr. Rothschild all the more wealthy and all the more able to extend his wealth. He found that the public greed would allow currency to be printed by government order beyond the limits (inflation) of backing in precious metal or the production of goods and services (gross national product, GNP).

This is how the Rothschilds have come to own governments and most of the world. Interest on money is the key here. If money was put into circulation interest-free, and there was no interest on money in any form, it would return to its rightful role as a unit of energy exchange that overcomes the limitations of barter. It is when you introduce interest that the trouble starts because then you are making money from money and it no longer serves the people – it enslaves them. The bank credit/interest system means that the unit of exchange for human activity comes into circulation right from the start as a debt. Governments could create their own money interest-free to pay for public services, but instead they borrow it from the banking system and the population has to pay it back, plus interest. It is the same with individuals and businesses. Governments don't create their own interest-free money because they are controlled by the families who also control the banks, most notably the Rothschilds. Abraham Lincoln was assassinated by the Rothschilds when he began to print interest-free money called 'greenbacks' to fund the North in the American Civil War. The Rothschilds were funding both sides in the Civil War, as they do in all the wars they engineer, but Lincoln eventually refused to pay their phenomenal levels of interest. The greenback system worked so well that Lincoln was considering making it the permanent means of government finance. This was the worst nightmare for the Rothschilds, and London's Rothschild-controlled *The Times* newspaper wrote:

> If that mischievous financial policy, which had its origin in the North American Republic, should become indurated down to a fixture, then that Government will furnish its own money without cost. It will pay off debts and be without a debt. It will have all the money necessary to carry on its commerce. It will become prosperous beyond precedent in the history of the civilized governments of the world. The brains and the wealth of all countries will go to North America. That government must be destroyed, or it will destroy every monarchy on the globe.

The Rothschilds had Lincoln assassinated by John Wilkes Booth in 1865 and the greenback policy went with him. On 4th June 1963, President John F Kennedy signed Executive Order 11110 which allowed the US Treasury Secretary to issue $4.29 billion in interest-free money called silver certificates which bypassed the Rothschilds and their privately-owned 'central bank of America', the Federal Reserve. On 22nd November 1963, Kennedy was assassinated and his successor, Lyndon Johnson, who was in on the murder, rescinded the policy. JFK was killed for many reasons, including his opposition to both the Israeli nuclear programme and the escalation of the Vietnam War. Lyndon Johnson, a Rothschild puppet, supported both. The spectre of interest-free money was, however, at the heart of why Kennedy was removed, and the Rothschilds have been at war with the Kennedys ever since. JFK's brother, Bobby Kennedy, and his son, John Fitzgerald Kennedy Jr, were other assassination victims of the Rothschilds. Some researchers say that the Israeli intelligence agency, Mossad, was involved in JFK's murder, and this makes perfect sense. Mossad, one of the most evil organisations on earth, does not represent Israel, but the Rothschilds who own Israel. You can see why presidents, prime ministers and others do whatever the Rothschilds demand when they know the consequences of not doing so. I have described the background to the Kennedy assassination in detail in … *And The Truth Shall Set You Free*.

Boom and Bust

There is another vital aspect to understand about interest on money: when you take out a loan, the bank 'creates', in the form of 'credit', the amount of the 'loan'. This sounds obvious and straightforward, except for one thing. You are not paying back only the loan; you are paying pay the loan, plus interest, and the interest is not created, only the principle figure. This means that there is never even nearly enough 'money' in circulation to pay back all the outstanding loans and interest. It is a fatal flaw with regard to human freedom and it has been done purposely to ensure that bankruptcy and loss of property and possessions to the banks is built into the system. It is all part of the Rothschild energy-construct that flows the wealth and energy of the people in their direction. A fantastic amount of the money that you pay in taxes goes straight to the private banks to pay back interest on 'money' that the government could create itself, interest free. What we call 'privatisation' is the selling of state assets in response to bank-created debt. The world's poorest countries are handing over control of their land and resources to the Rothschild banks when they can't pay back the loans made specifically to ensnare them in this very situation. 'Third World Debt' was manufactured to replace physical occupation of resource-rich or strategically-situated countries with today's financial occupation. I describe in detail how they did this in ... *And The Truth Shall Set You Free*. Once a country is indebted to the Rothschild bankers with non-existent credit, it is forced to hand over control of its affairs to the banks, the World Bank and

Illustration by David Dees (deesillustration.com)

Figure 40: *The Rothschild Technique: Get them in debt; give them diversions to focus their attention on trivia; then crash the system and reap the rewards*

the International Monetary Fund (IMF). These then dictate economic and social policy at every level. The World Bank and IMF are wholly-owned subsidiaries of the Rothschilds and always have their place-men at the helm. Poor countries with debt they are struggling to repay are forced to cut spending on social programmes, health, education and humanitarian projects to pay the banks the 'debt' they owe. The world does not have to be in poverty and conflict. It is manipulated to be that way to serve the bloodline agenda for global dictatorship.

By controlling the issuing of 'money' through credit, the Rothschilds control the entire world economy, as described in *Quiet Weapons for a Quiet War*. They can expand it or crash it at will. The depression that began in 2008 is yet another Rothschild creation to further centralise global finance and introduce the long-planned world central bank. The Rothschilds have been engineering booms and busts for centuries to advance their goals and it is so simple once you have interest on money and control the creation of 'current-cy'. The difference between a boom and a bust is the amount of 'money' in circulation and its perceived value. Both are dictated by the Rothschilds. They and their associated bloodline families decide how much money will be issued and circulated through their control of both banks and governments. The Rothschilds stimulate a boom by making credit easy (putting lots of 'money' into circulation) and this gets the population deeply in debt during what are called the economic 'good times' (Fig 40). They then crash the economy by finding an excuse to take money out of circulation and making credit harder to get. Businesses and people can't repay their loans because there is not enough money in circulation to generate the economic activity, and the Rothschilds take the spoils with all the collateral that was pledged when the loans were taken out. This also reduces dramatically the numbers of businesses in existence, and their products and markets are taken over by Rothschild corporations to further centralise their global economic power. It's the same with governments. When a depression decimates government revenues they seek still more loans to maintain spending, and the Rothschild control of governments and their agencies continues to expand. In fact, at least many governments, including the United States and the United

Illustration by David Dees (deesillustration.com)

Figure 41: *US Federal Reserve Chairman, Alan Greenspan, and his poodle successor, Ben Bernanke, are both assets of the Rothschilds*

Kingdom, have been in a state of bankruptcy to the Rothschild cabal since the 1930s. I have described here precisely what happened in the 'boom years' from the mid-1990s, followed by the crash in the autumn of 2008 and the subsequent 'credit crunch'. It was all the work of the Rothschilds and their lackeys like Alan Greenspan, the chairman of the Rothschild-created US Federal Reserve, and his successor, Ben Bernanke, who was, of course, reappointed by 'Mr Change' Obama (Fig 41). The Rothschilds have been engineering these cycles for hundreds of years and they include the Wall Street Crash of 1929 and the Great Depression of the 1930s. Overpaid economists and economic correspondents, most of whom have no idea what is going on, will tell you that boom and bust is part of some natural 'economic cycle'. What nonsense. It is systematic manipulation to steal the real wealth of the world.

The Rothschild Technique

The Rothschilds and the bloodline families are moving trillions of dollars a day around the global stockmarkets and they dictate if they go up or down, boom or crash. Stockmarket crashes don't just happen – they are made to happen. If you know the crash is coming because you are going to cause it, you know to sell stocks at the highest point and buy them back once the crash has happened. In this way you can increase your holdings massively by acquiring companies at a fraction of the cost before your manipulated collapse. A classic example of this was from Nathan Rothschild during the Battle of Waterloo in 1815. If England's Duke of Wellington won the battle, the London Stock Exchange would soar; if the French leader Napoleon prevailed, it would collapse. The Rothschilds ran an information and espionage operation renowned as the fastest and most effective in Europe with an extensive network of contacts that used codes and carrier pigeons to communicate secretly and quickly. This intelligence network would eventually develop into Mossad, the Israeli intelligence arm today, as well as the CIA and the modern version of British intelligence. At the highest level they are all the same organisation, along with many other national security agencies and postal and courier services, including the Rothschild-owned Federal Express. This is made possible by the spider's web, or the pyramids-with-pyramids, whichever analogy you want to use. Investors at the London Stock Exchange in 1815 knew the Rothschild intelligence system was better than the British government's, not least because the Rothschild couriers were the only ones allowed to pass through both the British and French blockades. With the battle raging, all eyes were on Nathan Rothschild for any sign of what was happening. Had Wellington or Napoleon won? Rothschild gave the signal for his agents to start selling his stocks, and everyone else followed believing that Rothschild must know that Wellington had lost. The market collapsed by 98 per cent in the panic and investors lost fortunes; but not Rothschild. He knew almost a day before the official news arrived that Wellington had won. When the market collapsed, Nathan Rothschild gave another coded signal to his agents and they began buying enormous numbers of stocks at the knock-down prices. When he had done so, the official news reached London that Wellington had won the battle. Stock prices soared, and it is estimated that the Rothschilds increased their wealth and ownership by some 20 times. They have controlled the British economy ever since and, thus, the government, no matter what party is officially in 'power'. The *New York Times* reported 100 years later that Nathan Rothschild's grandson had sought a court order to suppress publication of a book detailing the 'Waterloo' scam, but the order was denied.

This is how the manipulation works, and it is happening every day all over the world. Global finance, whether it be banking, stockmarkets, or whatever, is simply a confidence trick. When people are confident, they buy and invest and the economy expands; when they lose confidence, they don't buy and invest and the economy contracts. All it needs is a gloomy economic forecast from a Rothschild-controlled financial spokesman, or a rumour circulating about economic problems, and the house of cards can come down overnight. The Rothschilds are experts at this. They and their banking cartel have also funded all sides in virtually every war since about 1800 – wars that their agents in government, the military and intelligence agencies have manipulated into being. This has cost the lives of at least hundreds of millions (75 million in the two world wars alone) and allowed governments and people to be controlled through debt payments on the loans. When the wars have devastated countries, the Rothschild banking cartel lends more money to rebuild them – plus interest, of course. They also own the armament companies that supply the weapons at staggering profits secured by direct sales and still more loans to governments to buy them. As Gutle Schnaper, Mayer Amschel Rothschild's wife, said shortly before she died in 1849: 'If my sons did not want wars, there would be none.'

The Rothschild money system today is run by a network of supercomputers that connect with those of the stock exchanges and money markets and operate a virtual monopoly called 'high-frequency trading'. This represents 70 per cent of the volume on the exchanges and can process millions of trades per second. It has expanded the daily volume of trading activity by 164 per cent since 2005 and increased dramatically the speed at which the wealth of the world can be seized and the global economy destroyed at will. Through a system called 'predatory algorithms', supported by artificial intelligence, the major players are able to dominate world finance as never before. They pay large fees to access the Stock Exchange computers to see potential trades before they are made and then use the fantastic speed of their own supercomputers to make the trade first. Smaller traders have got no chance of competing and the Rothschild cabal controls everything. Joe Saluzzi, at Themis Trading in New Jersey, said: 'We are just mice dancing between the elephants of capital and their supercomputers.'

When commentators talk about a terrible time for the banking industry they miss the point. Yes, it is bad for those who lose their savings, homes and jobs. However, the Rothschilds, and their associated network of interbreeding families, own the system – the game. As I said earlier, if you own the game of football it doesn't matter if this team beats that team or not because whatever happens you still own the game. Merrill Lynch may have failed, but it was absorbed by the Bank of America, another Rothschild bank if you follow the trail of hidden ownership. The game just goes on with fewer names.

When Lehman Brothers collapsed, others picked up those assets and its business. Lehman Brothers was not saved by the US government because the Rothschilds needed at least one major bank to go under to cause the fear and panic that collapsed the system still further and made the disgraceful banking 'bail out' much easier to sell. The Wall Street Crash of 1929 and the banking crisis of the Great Depression was triggered by the Rothschilds, and led to the demise of vast numbers of smaller banks who had their assets and customers picked off by the giants. This process is ongoing. The Rothschilds and the bloodline families don't want diversity or real competition in the banking industry, or any other. They want total control. As the Rothschild frontman, John D Rockefeller, put it: 'Competition is a sin.' Those assets they want to keep are either absorbed by their front banks or bailed out by government money – our money – because they also own the governments. The banks screw people by lending them money that doesn't exist and charging interest on it; and then screw them again when the people's money is used to bail them out of trouble. Do we still believe that governments control countries?? Governments always have extraordinary amounts of money for two things – wars and banks. It is no surprise, therefore, that the Rothschilds and the Illuminati families are behind both.

Andrew Jackson, US President from 1829 to 1837, took on the Rothschild banking cartel and their Second Bank of the United States. He called them a 'den of vipers'. Jackson was an unpleasant piece of work, but in that statement he was spot on. His use of the word 'vipers' was far more accurate than he would have realised, as I shall be explaining when I get to the origin of the bloodlines. Jackson said if the people knew how the 'vipers' operated in the United States 'there would be a revolution in the morning'. The Rothschilds tried to do to Jackson what they did to Lincoln and Kennedy when they also became a 'problem'. On 30th January 1935, an assassin attempted to shoot Jackson, but both pistols misfired. Jackson said later that he knew the Rothschilds were behind it. The would-be killer, Richard Lawrence, was found not guilty by reason of insanity. He was to say that he had been hired by powerful people in Europe who pledged to protect him if he was caught. Now, who would that have been, I wonder? Erm.

Stench of evil

Wherever you find misery, especially large-scale misery, the Rothschilds won't be far away. What a different world we would live in without their manipulations and without the bloodlines in general. In June 2009, London's *Financial Times* revealed the involvement of the Rothschilds in the slave trade:

> Two of the biggest names in the City of London had previously undisclosed links to slavery in the British colonies, documents seen by the Financial Times have revealed. Nathan Mayer Rothschild, the banking family's 19th-century patriarch, and James William Freshfield, founder of Freshfields, the top City law firm, benefited financially from slavery, records from the National Archives show, even though both have often been portrayed as opponents of slavery.

In fact, for a long time the Rothschilds *ran* the slave trade. They have misled people about their real views by creating a cover story, a fake persona. The Rothschilds presented themselves as being against slavery, when they were controlling the slavery networks worldwide. Nathan Mayer Rothschild had the reputation of being a 'philanthropist' and official Rothschild histories claim that he 'fought publicly' for the emancipation of slaves when, in truth, he was making a fortune from their injustice and suffering. He was also promoted as a 'civil liberties campaigner' when the Rothschild dynasty seeks to make every man, woman and child on the planet a slave to their global fascist/communist state. The *Financial Times* discovered that the Rothschild dynasty used slaves as collateral in banking dealings with slave owners, which is consistent, at least, because they literally use every human being as slave collateral. It was Nathan Rothschild who secured the loan to fund the government bail-out of British slave owners when slavery was abolished in the 1800s. The big banking names and Rothschild fronts, like JP Morgan and so many others, were at the heart of the slave trade and they still are in countless forms.

The Rothschilds and their networks own the leading politicians and reward them for services rendered. Today, JPMorgan Chase pays a pig-trough salary to Tony Blair, the Rothschild glove-puppet and war criminal, for his 'advice'. London's *Daily Telegraph* reported that Blair is earning £2 million a year for this 'advice' without ever needing to go into the office. Blair's 'consultancy' roles with JP Morgan, Zurich Financial Services, the Kuwait government and Mubadala, a United Arab Emirates investment firm, are reported to pay him at least £6 million a year, and he also earns millions on the lecture circuit, as much as £6,000 a minute. Mubadala, which pays Blair about £1 million a year as an 'international adviser', has been in negotiations to join a consortium of western oil companies developing the Zubair oilfield in southern Iraq – a deal made possible by the Bush-Blair invasion of the country. All this money is Blair's pay-off for serving the Rothschilds so well with his lies and manipulations that led to the invasions of Afghanistan and Iraq and transformed British society into a police state that George Orwell would immediately recognise.

It's Rothschild, Rothschild, Rothschild, everywhere you look. When their power is removed – and it will be – the world will be a very different place.

7

Zion Mainframe

The basic tool for the manipulation of reality is the manipulation of words. If you can control the meaning of words, you can control the people who must use the words
Philip K Dick

A theme in the *Matrix* movie trilogy was the 'Zion Mainframe', the computer on which the last remaining humans depended for survival. The Rothschilds have their own version called 'Zionism', which in many ways is the 'mainframe' today of the bloodline network, at least in the public arena.

Zionism is, at its core, a secret society connected to all the others in the global web, and its 'bibles' are the Babylonian Talmud and the kabala/kaballah/cabala, its 'hidden tradition' of esoteric knowledge. This comes from the Arab word, 'Khabba', which means 'to hide' or 'to conceal'. How appropriate it is, then, to speak of the elite 'cabal', which survives by hiding and concealing. Zionism was not established for the benefit of the Jewish people, but to exploit them and use them as a cover for the manipulations of the House of Rothschild and the Illuminati families. This merciless political creed is a 100 per cent Rothschild creation and represents a major force in the bloodline network. I shall refer to it from here on as 'Rothschild Zionism' to constantly underline who and what it truly represents. Rothschild Zionism has big ears and a long trunk and stands so blatantly in the living room, but people are frightened to see or identify what is really 50-feet high with flashing neon lights. The Rothschilds and their agents have created a pincer-movement on the human psyche by hijacking fantastic amounts of political, corporate, banking and media power on one side, and, on the other, using the fear of being called 'anti-Semitic' if you dare to state the bloody obvious. They have been able to do this by equating in public perception that Zionism = Jewish people. It does *not*. Zionism is a political creed established by the House of Rothschild to advance the goals of the Illuminati families that are largely controlled by the Rothschilds. When people think of Zionism they think of Jewish people. When they think of Israel they think of Jewish people. This is understandable given the propaganda, but it is seriously misleading and those instant connections need to be broken if we are going to understand what's going on here. 'Zionism' means Rothschild, just as 'Israel' means Rothschild. When we see the extraordinary number of Rothschild Zionists in major positions around the world we are looking not at 'manipulating Jews', but manipulating Zionists representing the interests and demands of the Rothschilds. Those that are running the Rothschild

Zionist agenda couldn't care less about Jewish people in general. They, too, are just an expendable irrelevance to the greater goal. As the first Israeli Prime Minister, the terrorist David Ben-Gurion, said:

> If I knew that it was possible to save all the children of Germany by transporting them to England, and only half by transferring them to the Land of Israel, I would choose the latter, for before us lies not only the numbers of these children but the historical reckoning of the people of Israel.

And they still let him out alone without a psychiatric nurse. Significant numbers of Jewish people oppose this vicious and appalling creed, and many Rothschild Zionists are not Jewish. These include the Christian Zionists and Barack Obama's vice-president, Joe Biden, who told Israeli television: 'I'm a Zionist.' All it means, officially at least, is that you support a homeland for Jews in Israel, although that is just a public persona. If, as Biden rightly says, you don't have to be a Jew to be a Zionist, how can it be a racial rather than a political movement? It can't. It's just made to appear like that to manipulate public perception. Opposing Rothschild Zionism is then seen as opposing Jewish people as a whole and the 'you're a racist' card can be played over and over. Far from protecting and advancing the interests of the mass of Jewish people, the Rothschild agenda has often been devastating for them and has caused millions to be labelled unfairly by the actions of the Rothschild Zionist elite. A feature on the Jews Against Zionism website highlights how Rothschild Zionism targeted Jews who had lived for generations in Palestine side-by-side with Arabs in peace and harmony:

> The religious Jews who, by virtue of their faith, clearly contradicted Zionist nationalism, and who had lived peacefully with their Arab neighbours for generations, became unwillingly identified with the Zionist cause and their struggle with the Arabs. They requested the United Nations that Jerusalem be designated as a de-facto international city. They appealed to the diplomatic corps assigned to Jerusalem – but to no avail. They were hence confronted with the choice of either becoming a part of the Zionist State, which diametrically opposed the interests of Jews as a religion, or abandoning the land of which their forefathers were the first Jewish settlers.

Let's get this straight. Rothschild Zionism is not about Jewish people. To the Rothschilds, and their Zionist gofers and thugs, Jewish people as a whole are merely cattle to be used and abused as necessary – just like the rest of the human population. It was the Rothschild-funded IBM that supplied machines to the Nazis to produce punch-cards for the initial identification and social expulsion of Jews, confiscation of their property and concentration-camp designation. It was the same Rothschild IBM that developed the barcode system and today IBM Credit Corp funds Applied Digital Solutions, the parent company of the VeriChip Corporation, the world's leading producer of microchips for humans. You see those of the political 'right' blaming 'Jews' for ills of the world and the 'New World Order' because they don't understand the difference between Jewish people as a whole and the elite who use them as a shield to hide their horrific activities. Rothschild Zionism was created for and by the latter, not for the mass of Jewish people who have been victims of it. Henry Makow, the Canadian writer and researcher, rightly points out this essential difference. Makow's Jewish parents suffered in Nazi-occupied Poland, and his grandparents perished. He highlights the connection of the Rothschilds and their Zionist elite to Jacob Frank (1726-1791) who 'led a satanic heresy against orthodox Judaism'. Frank wanted the 'annihilation of Western civilization and the triumph of evil', Makow says, and anything would be allowed, including incest and paedophilia (both of which are part of life within the bloodline elite). Frank claimed to be the 'Messiah' and a reincarnation of another Satanist, Shabbetai Zvi (1626-1676). Their followers became known as Frankists or Sabbatean-Frankists and these include the elite of the Rothschild dynasty since its formation by Mayer Amschel Rothschild, an associate of Jacob Frank. It was Rothschild, Frank and their frontman, Adam Weishaupt, who founded the Bavarian Illuminati in 1776. Henry Makow writes:

> ... there is an unrecognized schism in the Jewish people, where heretics have exterminated the mainstream and taken control of the remnant through Zionism. Yet, due to the anti-Semitism that the Illuminati Jews cause and organize, Jews mistakenly cling to their leadership.

Gunther Plaut, a prominent Canadian Rabbi, published a book in 1988 called *The Man Who Would Be Messiah*, which implied that the Frankists were responsible for what happened to Jewish people in Germany. Plaut did extensive research into Jacob Frank and wrote his findings in the form of a novel. He said that Frank saw Jews as a barrier to a 'new order' and he has him say:

> Yes, the Jews. Someone will come and discover that he can't upset the old values without destroying the people who really believe in them and, what's worse, practise them. And when he's convinced that the Jews stand in his way he'll find ways to kill them all. Destroy them, exterminate them like vermin ... the Jews should be killed because they believe in traditional morality and thereby perpetuate the status quo in the world.

I have outlined in other books how many of the major Nazis appeared to be of Jewish or part-Jewish descent, and this is no longer a mystery when you realise that there are Jewish people in general and then there are the Sabbatean-Frankists, like the Rothschilds, who see Jews in general as fodder to be exploited to advance their plans for world domination. The German Jew, Dietrich Bronder, wrote this about the Nazi elite in his 1964 book, *Before Hitler Came*:

> Of Jewish descent, or being related to Jewish families were: the Leader and Reichschancelor Adolf Hitler; his representatives, the Reichsminister Rudolf Hess; the Reichsmarshall Hermann Goering; the Reichsleader of the NSDAP, Gregor Strasser, Dr. Josef Goebbels, Alfred Rosenberg, Hans Frank, Heinrich Himmler; the Reichsminister von Ribbentrop (who pledged close friendship with the famous Zionist Chaim Weizmann, the first head of the State of Israel who died in 1952); von Keudell; field commanders Globocnik (the Jewish destructor); Jordan and Wilhelm Hube; the great SS-Leaders, Reinhard Heydrich, Erich von dem Bach-Zelewski and von Keudell II, who

also were active in the destruction of Jews. (All of them were members of the secret Thule Order/Society).

The Thule Order was one of a network of secret societies in Germany that brought the Nazis to power. The Frankist modus operandi is to infiltrate every religion and ideology, Henry Makow says, and pretend to be what they are not. In doing so, they can play different factions, religions and organisations off against each other and destroy them from within. Makow writes:

They are recognized by the fact that they pretend to be Christians or Jews or Muslims etc. A typical example is John Kerry who pretended he was an Irish Catholic, when in fact his father was a Frankist Jew (who worked for the CIA) and his mother a Forbes. Barack Obama's mother may have been a Frankist/Illuminati Jewess. Another example is the English Rothschilds who marry non-Jews yet pretend to be Jews. They are all Illuminati Satanists ...

... Moreover, Churchill, FDR [Franklin Roosevelt] and Stalin were also Illuminati or Frankist Jews. So you can see how the Second World War could have been contrived partly to fulfill Frank's goal of exterminating the Jewish people. Frankists may explain the presence of 150,000 part-Jewish soldiers in the German army.

For sure, the networks of the House of Rothschild were behind Adolf Hitler and the rise of the Nazi Party in the Rothschild fiefdom of Germany. The Rothschilds used public sympathy for Jewish people targeted by the Nazis to press for a homeland in Palestine. This was the alleged reason for the founding of Rothschild Zionism, but that is only part of it. As I show in *The David Icke Guide to the Global Conspiracy (and how to end it)*, and other books, the campaign to impose a Rothschild state in Palestine goes back at least to the earlier part of the 19th century and probably long before. Their takeover of Palestine was given a massive boost with the Balfour Declaration in 1917 when the British Foreign Secretary, Lord Arthur Balfour, declared in a letter his government's support for a Jewish homeland in Palestine. This letter was sent by Balfour – an inner-circle member of the elite secret society called the Round Table – to Baron (Walter) Rothschild who funded the Round Table, the central core today of the network which includes the Royal Institute of International Affairs, Council on Foreign Relations, Trilateral Commission, and Bilderberg Group (Fig 42). All these are Rothschild organisations. Balfour wrote:

Figure 42: *The 'Balfour Declaration' was a letter between Lord Balfour, an inner initiate of the Round Table Secret Society, and Lord Rothschild who funded and controlled the Round Table*

Foreign Office
November 2nd, 1917

Dear Lord Rothschild,

I have much pleasure in conveying to you, on behalf of His Majesty's Government, the following declaration of sympathy with Jewish Zionist aspirations which has been submitted to, and approved by, the Cabinet.

His Majesty's Government view with favour the establishment in Palestine of a national home for the Jewish people, and will use their best endeavours to facilitate the achievement of this object, it being clearly understood that nothing shall be done which may prejudice the civil and religious rights of existing non-Jewish communities in Palestine, or the rights and political status enjoyed by Jews in any other country.

I should be grateful if you would bring this declaration to the knowledge of the Zionist Federation.

Yours sincerely,
Arthur James Balfour

The Balfour Declaration was a letter exchanged between two members of the same elite secret society with Rothschild dictating what it said, and part of the deal was that, in return for this public support for a 'Jewish' (Rothschild) Palestine, the Rothschilds would guarantee to bring the United States into the First World War, which they did through their puppet president, Woodrow Wilson. The Rothschilds funded the early settlers from Europe to relocate in post-war Palestine. Some were funded by Baron Edmond de Rothschild, from the Paris branch of the dynasty, including two of the original settlements in Israel, Rishon LeZion in Tel Aviv and Zikhron Ya'akov in Carmel. The Rothschilds had bought 125,000 acres of land and 40 settlements by the mid-1930s and so it has continued ever since. Most of the Jews that were shipped to Israel after the Second World War didn't want to go. The Jewish historian Gabriel Kolko worked on a boat in 1949 ferrying Jewish settlers to Israel. He said in an article for *Counterpunch*:

I learned from someone who ran a displaced persons camp in Germany that the large majority of Jews wanted to go anywhere but Palestine. They were compelled to state Palestine or else risk receiving no aid. I understood very early that there was much amiss in the countless Arab villages and homes I saw destroyed, and that the entire Zionist project – regardless of the often venal nature of the Arab opposition to it – was a dangerous sham.

The Rothschilds also armed and funded the terrorist groups that bombed Israel into existence in 1948. This campaign of murder and terror forced 800,000 Palestinians to leave the land of their birth. The world simply looked on – just as it does to this day – because Israel is a law unto itself and terms like justice, fairness, decency and mercy do not apply. The Israeli Education Ministry announced plans in 2009 to delete a passage in their history books that describes the expulsions of 1948 as 'ethnic cleansing'. The ministry said it would re-issue the history textbook taught to secondary schools after the relevant changes were made. The key passage that upsets these censors, apparently, was: 'The Palestinians and the Arab countries contended that most of the refugees were civilians who were attacked and expelled from their homes by armed Jewish forces, which instituted a policy of ethnic cleansing.' That's exactly what it was, and still is, but, for goodness sake, don't let Israeli children know the truth. The offending passage is mild compared with what really happened. Members of the Irgun terrorist group, led by future Israeli Prime Minister, Menachem Begin, and another Israeli terrorist operation, the Stern Gang, led by future Israeli Prime Minister, Yitzhak Shamir, massacred between 100 and 200 Palestinian men, women and children while they slept, in the village of Deir Yassin in April 1948. Palestinians were then told through loudspeakers positioned on trucks that if they did not leave immediately they would be slaughtered, too. With the knowledge of Deir Yassin fresh in their minds, the Palestinians knew the Israelis meant what they said and this is why 800,000 fled their homeland. Who was behind it all, the masters behind the Israeli terrorists? The Rothschilds.

Israel is the State of Rothschild, and how appropriate that they funded the construction of the Israeli parliament building, the Knesset, and the Israeli Supreme Court. Israeli President, Shimon Peres, said of the Rothschilds: 'Never has a family donated so much of its wealth to the making of the State of Israel.' This sliver of land called Israel, which you could drive around in a day, comes up again and again in the story of global tyranny and manipulation because it is owned and controlled by the House of Rothschild. The adopted symbol of the Rothschilds, the hexagram, or 'Star of David', was imposed upon the Israeli state. Many people wanted the 'Menorah' on the flag, the seven-branched candelabrum which has been a long-time symbol of Judaism, but, hey, this is the Land of Rothschild, so what they want, they get. Some pointed out, rightly, that the hexagram was not a Jewish symbol and instead was used to symbolise an ancient deity called 'Moloch', to whom children were (and still are) sacrificed. Much more about these connections later. In 2006, during the Israeli-Lebanese war, the Israeli writer, Barry Chamish, told of a meeting he had with banker Evelyn Rothschild's grandson who 'abandoned the family to be a Mormon'. In truth, Rothschild money established the Mormon Church, which was created by the Freemasons, Joseph Smith, Hiram Smith and Brigham Young, all of whom were bloodline. The Watchtower Society, or Jehovah's Witnesses, is, like the Mormons, another Rothschild front created by Freemasons Charles Taze Russell and Joseph Franklin Rutherford. Both organisations are pledged to introduce a 'New Jerusalem' called 'Zion'. This is the real meaning of 'Zion-ism' – a 'New Jerusalem', a New World Order of total enslavement. Chamish said the Rothschild grandson told him that just seven families were enjoying the 'fruits of the war' in the Lebanon at the time. The grandson said of the Rothschilds: 'They created Israel as their personal toy. It makes them richer and gives them more control. It's not going to be destroyed.' There are many reasons why the Rothschilds and their allies wanted to hijack Palestine, and one was to keep the Middle East in a state of disruption and turmoil from which a global war can eventually be triggered to usher in a world government dictatorship. The creation of Israel is a means, not an end, and the Rothschilds will be quite happy to leave the Jewish population to their fate if it suits them. After all, they've done it before.

Target Palestine

The Rothschild-controlled British government told the Palestinian Arabs during the First World War that if they fought the Ottoman Turks and forced them out of Palestine they would be rewarded with an independent country. The British Foreign Secretary at the time was the Rothschild secret society initiate, Lord Balfour; yes, the same guy who, in his letter to the Rothschilds, had pledged British government support for a Jewish homeland in Palestine. The Arabs agreed to this deal-that-never-was and with support from a British Lieutenant Colonel called Thomas Edward Lawrence – 'Lawrence of Arabia' – the Ottoman Empire was defeated. The Arabs' reward was not, of course, independence (Fig 43). Britain took over the administration of Palestine pending the arrival of the Rothschild Zionists. The Arabs were lied to, as Lawrence later admitted, and they have been lied to ever since. All these 'road maps' and 'peace processes' are always designed to lead nowhere. They are just holding positions to maintain the status quo until the Palestinians are basically no more. The Rothschilds had one ambition when they finally arrived in Palestine after World War Two – drive the Palestinians from their lands and constantly expand the borders of Israel through war and intimidation. The 'Jewish homeland' was from the start a Rothschild fiefdom orchestrated through the global secret society network of interbreeding families, and the major secret society involved is called Zionism. The Rothschilds funded the early European settlers in Israel, manipulated events in Germany that led to the horrific treatment of Jewish people and others, and then used that as the excuse to reach their long-term goal, a Rothschild-Illuminati stronghold in Palestine using the Jewish population as fodder to be used as a cover for what was really going on.

Figure 43: *T E Lawrence ('Lawrence of Arabia') helped to dupe the people of Palestine into fighting for the British when he knew that their land was already assigned to the Rothschild Zionists*

The Rothschild Zionist bully-boys spend their time condemning the terrorism of others and yet their very State was established through terrorism of the most grotesque kind via groups like Irgun, Haganah and the Stern Gang. They bombed and terrorised Israel into being and they later merged to become today's Israel Defense Forces, or IDF, which continues to bomb Palestinians out of existence. Among the leading lights in these and other terrorist groups were Menachem Begin, Yitzhak Shamir and Ariel Sharon, butchers who became Israeli Prime Ministers and had the nerve to condemn Arab terrorism. The butchery goes on to this day with the goal of destroying the Palestinian people. The idea was always to destroy them step-by-step long before Israel was even created. The Balfour Declaration, in supporting a Jewish homeland, said that 'nothing shall be done which may prejudice the civil and religious rights of the existing non-Jewish communities in Palestine'. What a joke that was! The Rothschild gofer, Chaim Weizmann, would later say: 'With regard to the Arab question – the British told us that there are several hundred thousand Negroes there but this is a matter of no consequence.' Nor have they been ever since and the goal of destroying them is closer today than ever before. The first Prime Minister of Israel, another terrorist called David Ben-Gurion, made no secret of this fact within his inner circle. Former Israeli Prime Minister, Yitzhak Rabin, said in an uncensored version of his memoirs, published in the *New York Times* on 23rd October 1979:

> We walked outside, Ben-Gurion accompanying us. Allon repeated his question – 'What is to be done with the Palestinian population?' Ben-Gurion waved his hand in a gesture which said, 'Drive them out!

The bombing campaigns against Gaza Palestinians today are just the latest step to that end. They have forced Palestinians into the Gaza Strip, which is little more than a concentration camp, and the Rothschild 'Israeli' Defense Forces control all that goes in and out – people, supplies of food, medicines and other essentials (Fig 44). When the Israelis close the border posts, the Palestinians are trapped and at the mercy of the heartless and soulless that control the Tel Aviv government and military under Rothschild direction. One writer described conditions in Gaza:

> … Israel nails shut the coffin that is Gaza under a siege that has lasted nearly three years, steadily intensifying so that malnutrition rates rival those of sub-Saharan Africa, sewage runs raw in the streets and pollutes the ocean, homes are still being bulldozed to super-add collective punishment upon collective punishment; men, women and children are still being sniped at and killed; children are deafened by continuing sonic booms, the vast majority of them suffer from post-traumatic stress syndrome, and many of that majority have no ambition other than becoming 'martyrs' …

And it's a whole lot worse now. Look at the constant theft of Palestinian land in Figure 45 (overleaf) and you'll see what the plan has been all along. How can anyone inflict such a lack of mercy on an entire people? The Palestinians, like the rest of the global population including the mass of Jewish people, are simply animals to the Rothschild Zionist extremists. The Israeli Prime Minister and terrorist, Menachem Begin, described Palestinians in a speech to the Israeli parliament as 'beasts walking on two legs'. Another Prime Minister and terrorist, Yitzhak Shamir, told Jewish settlers in 1988 that the Palestinians 'would be crushed like grasshoppers … heads smashed against the boulders and walls'. Prime Minister and terrorist, Ariel Sharon, then Israeli Foreign Minister, confirmed in 1998 what the plan really was for the Palestinians:

Figure 44: *David Dees' powerful depiction of 'life' for Palestinians under the merciless onslaught of the Israeli government and military*

■ Palestinian land ☐ Jewish land

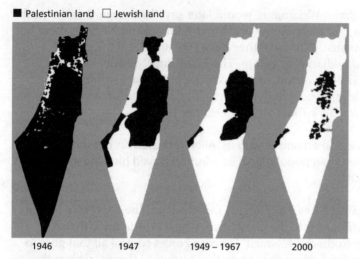

1946   1947   1949 – 1967   2000

Figure 45: *Palestinian land seized by the Israelis from 1946 to 2000 – and a lot more has been taken since*

It is the duty of Israeli leaders to explain to public opinion, clearly and courageously, a certain number of facts that are forgotten with time. The first of these is that there is no Zionism, colonialisation, or Jewish State without the eviction of the Arabs and the expropriation of their lands.

No Empathy, No Mercy

The plan is to kill or drive out the Palestinian people using poverty, hunger and war, and allow the Rothschild Zionists to expand into 'Greater Israel'. This plan is now well advanced. They are seeking to establish a 'Greater Israel' that includes their former homeland of Sumer and Babylon and this is another longer-term implication for the American-British (Rothschild) invasion of Iraq. While Rothschild Zionists go on and on about racism, Israel is a deeply apartheid state – not just between Jews and Arabs, but also between different 'levels' of Jews. The Ashkenazi from Sumer-Khazaria are always at the top, naturally, and the black Jews from Ethiopia are at the bottom and treated with appalling racism. It was revealed that black Ethopian women of child-bearing age in Israel were being systemically injected with the birth control drug, Depo-Provera, to stop them having children. Fifty-seven per cent of Depo-Provera users in Israel are black Ethiopian women while the Ethiopian community is less than two per cent of the Israeli population. Blood donations by Ethiopian blacks in Israel are also routinely discarded. The apartheid government in South Africa used Depo-Provera, often by force, to limit the fertility of black women and here we have apartheid Israel is doing the same. Hedva Eyal was the author of the report on the scandal published by Woman to Woman, a feminist organisation based in Haifa, northern Israel. She said:

> This is about reducing the number of births in a community that is black and mostly poor. The unspoken policy is that only children who are white and Ashkenazi are wanted in Israel.

Yes, and it is done on the orders of the apartheid Israeli authorities that go on and on about what they claim to be the 'racism' of others. Palestinian Arabs have been herded into the tiny Gaza Strip and another Palestinian enclave known as the West Bank. This is occupied by the Israeli army, and illegal Israeli settlements there are advancing at a quickening speed to ensure that this, too, will become part of the Greater Israel. At the same time they demolish Palestinian homes for being 'illegal' and build a massive wall – 'security barrier' – that has been located to steal Palestinian land, part families, reduce or deny access to water, food and medical treatment, among much else (Fig 46). It is estimated that the wall steals 12 per cent of Palestinian land in the West Bank and East Jerusalem. Palestinians in East Jerusalem, which lies within the wall, are also being systematically driven out by the demolition of their homes for Jewish settlements, Jewish 'parks' and Jewish 'archaeological sites' run by Jewish settlement organisations. This is all being funded by tens of millions of dollars in donations from Rothschild Zionists worldwide. When the Palestinians protest peacefully against

Figure 46: *The Israeli 'security barrier' that has taken even more Palestinian land and turned most of the rest into a prison camp*

their despicable treatment they are subjected to tear gas attacks. Put the words: 'Israeli soldiers fire on Al Jazeera correspondent' into YouTube and you will see an example. The International Court of Justice unanimously ruled on 9th July 2004 that 'the construction of the Wall being built by Israel, and its associated regime, are contrary to international law ...' It decreed that construction must stop, what had been built must be dismantled, Palestinian land returned and compensation paid. The Israeli authorities lifted their collective finger and pointed it to the sky. They don't recognise international law, except when it is applied to others, and nor do they respond to resolutions by the United Nations when it means any kind of justice for the Palestinians. What was the 'international community's' response to this 'up yours' defiance? Zilch. This is Israel, remember. Nothing is ever done because the nations of the 'West' are also controlled by the Rothschilds and are terrified of them. Even worse, President Obama (Rothschild Zionist) and his Secretary of State, Hillary Clinton (Rothschild Zionist) agreed in the autumn of 2009 to no longer 'demand' (lip-service only) that Israel stop building settlements on occupied Palestinian land, but instead to 'rationalise it'. What the hell does that mean? It is not meant to mean anything, except 'do as you like and we'll look the other way'. This same Obama 'won' the Nobel Peace Prize and presents himself as a 'man who cares'. Rothschild puppet first, second and last. In 2009, Tzipi Livni, the Israeli foreign minister at the time of the Gaza invasion, had to abandon a trip to Britain when Palestinian supporters there secured a warrant for her arrest for war crimes. The British government's response was to announce that it would change the law so this could not happen again. The bias is so obvious.

Look at the lack of response and action in early 2009 when Gaza was being bombarded from earth and sky by the brave men of Tel Aviv. State-of-the-art Israeli jets and tanks, supplied by the United States, constantly bombed civilian targets in this tragic, poverty-stricken wasteland, which acts as a holding camp for the human beings the Israeli government would rather be dead. The criminally-mendacious Israeli spokespeople said they did not target civilians. No, they just bombed where they live. Some Israeli soldiers were so outraged by what they were ordered to do that they organised a campaign group called 'Breaking the Silence' to expose the lies of the Israeli government. Their testimonies confirm that the merciless slaughter and destruction in

Gaza was Israeli military policy (Figs 47 and 48). One said: 'People were not instructed to shoot at everyone they see, but they were told that from a certain distance when they approach a house, no matter who it is – even an old woman – take them down.' Other statements by the soldiers revealed the following:

- Palestinian civilians were used as human shields by soldiers when they entered buildings.
- Large numbers of homes and other buildings were demolished as a precaution or to clear 'lines of fire'.
- Some troops had an aggressive, ill-disciplined attitude.
- Vandalism of Palestinian property.
- Soldiers fired at water tanks at a time of severe water shortages for the Palestinians.
- White phosphorus, which burns people alive, was used in civilian areas in ways that were gratuitous and reckless.
- There had been very little direct engagement with the 'Palestinian militants' that they were supposed to be there to remove.

Figure 47

Figure 48
The genocidal slaughter of Palestinian people goes on and on ...

That last point is easy to explain. The assault on Gaza was to destroy the Palestinians' ability to survive, not to stop 'militants', and this is why the civilian population was the prime target. Congratulations to those Israeli soldiers who have spoken out, because their soul is greater than their mind. The same goes for those fantastic young Israelis who are refusing even to serve in the army because they are sickened by the treatment of the Palestinian people. Once again, they are special human beings because their heart is more powerful than their fear of the consequences – which include being jailed for refusing to be a killer for a sick and evil government. One of the few political or administrative figures who did speak out was the Jewish UN representative, Richard Falk. He said: 'The Israeli airstrikes on the Gaza Strip represent severe and massive violations of international humanitarian law as defined in the Geneva Conventions, both in regard to the obligations of an Occupying Power and in the requirements of the laws of war ...' Those violations included:

- Collective punishment: the entire 1.5 million people who live in the crowded Gaza Strip were punished for the actions of a few militants.

- Targeting civilians: airstrikes were aimed at civilian areas in one of the most crowded stretches of land in the world, certainly the most densely populated area of the Middle East.
- Disproportionate military response: airstrikes not only destroyed every police and security office of Gaza's elected government, but killed and injured hundreds of civilians. At least one strike reportedly hit groups of students attempting to find transportation home from the university.

Israeli Prime Minister, Benjamin Netanyahu, the vicious Rothschild Zionist extremist, said in the face of this and other reports on Israeli war crimes that he would never allow any Israeli leaders or soldiers to be put on trial for what they did. With the Rothschilds behind the scenes, he knows he has the power to say that. Tony Blair (Rothschild Zionist), an Israeli sock-puppet, publicly supported his stance. Of course he did. That's why he was given the 'job' of 'Middle East' envoy for the United Nations, European Union, United States and Russia, despite coldly lying to justify the mass murder of untold numbers of Arabs in Iraq. They're laughing at us; but not for much longer. A South African Jewish judge, Richard Goldstone, with close ties to Israel, produced a 575-page report for the United Nations on the 2008-2009 Israeli invasion of Gaza. It said: 'The mission concluded that actions amounting to war crimes and, possibly, in some respects, crimes against humanity, were committed by the Israel Defense Forces (IDF).' The Israeli government, led by extremists and crazies like Netanyahu and Haganah terrorist, Shimon Peres, reeled back in horror that they could be criticised for the mass murder of a helpless people and, of course, the United States arm of the Rothschild global empire was right with them. You are a disgrace, Obama, a disgrace to everything you claim, mendaciously, to stand for.

Those Palestinians 'living' in official Israel and the Israeli-occupied West Bank and East Jerusalem are having their homes bulldozed or stolen and their land confiscated for Jewish settlements. Israel holds the property of more than four million Palestinian refugees in custodianship under international law until a (never-meant-to-arrive) 'peace settlement' decides how many of the refugees will be allowed to return to the more than 400 villages destroyed by the Israelis. This, naturally, is not enough for the brutal and power-crazed Israeli government, which, in violation of international law, began selling off this land for profit and Jewish settlements (Fig 49). These people give the word 'evil' no meaning. In one incident, a decision by the Israeli High Court in August 2009 permitted Israeli security forces to forcibly evict nine Palestinian families, numbering 53 adults and 20 children, from their homes in the Sheikh Jarrah district. The properties were then given to a Jewish settlement organisation. Two of the evicted families were left to live in the street near their former home. While this was happening, the inhabitants of the Bedouin village of Amra were being intimidated and

Figure 49: *Palestinian houses are being constantly demolished to make families homeless and transfer the land to Israeli ownership*

harassed in an effort to force them off their land. They are descendants of a few thousand of their people who were able to stay on after the mass expulsions following the 1948 war and terrorism that founded Israel. The Tarabin tribe, all of them Israeli citizens, suddenly had their only access road sealed off, and the dirt track they used instead was subject to checkpoints where papers and vehicles were stopped for detailed inspection. Razor wire was installed to circle the village and children as young as eight were arrested. In fact, since the 1967 Israeli occupation of the Palestinian East Jerusalem, West Bank and Gaza Strip, many thousands of Palestinian children have been arrested by the Israeli military. They are blindfolded, handcuffed, 'interrogated' and abused verbally and physically. The 'convicted' children are often held in adult jails where they can suffer more abuse, including sexual abuse. Tulab Tarabin, one of the residents of Amra, said: 'Four-fifths of our youngsters now have files with the police and our drivers are being repeatedly fined for supposed traffic violations. Every time we are stopped, the police ask us: "Why don't you leave?"' The Israeli authorities want to use their land to build homes for Israeli army officers. Morad al Sana, a lawyer with the Adalah legal centre for Israel's Arab minority, said: 'The policy in Israel is that when Jews need land, the Bedouin must move – no matter how long they have been living in their homes or whether their communities predate Israel's creation. The Tarabin's crime is that they refuse to budge.' These people are utterly ruthless and brutal, and the world looks on, or rather the other way, when Israel is the most racist country on Earth. In January 2010, the callous Israeli authorities opened a dam and flooded villages in Gaza without even telling the people it was going to happen. Families were trapped in their homes or had to climb on roofs to escape the water. Those living in tents because of the ten thousand homes destroyed by Israeli bombing suffered even more misery as these Israeli criminals continue the campaign to drive them and their nation out of their homeland.

Genocide Tax

The Palestinians are being systematically crushed by the tyrants who call the shots in Israel on behalf of that country's real power structure, the House of Rothschild. And, taxpayers of America and elsewhere, *you* are paying for this calculated slaughter. American aid to Israel accounts for something like a third of all US overseas aid when Israel is home to just 0.001 per cent of the global population and has one of the highest incomes per head in the world. This is without all the 'private' donations from US corporations and individuals that are tax-deductible even when given to the Israeli military, unlike any other foreign power. According to 2007 figures, the United States government gave more than $6.8 million to wealthy Israel every *day* while the desperate and devastated Palestinians of the Gaza Strip and the West Bank received just $300,000. US military 'aid' to Israel increased by more than a quarter to an average $3 billion a year in 2007, a figure guaranteed for ten years. This, and other support, makes Israel the biggest recipient of United States foreign military funding since the Second World War. The United States is also Israel's biggest supplier of fighter planes, weapons and other military technology. As a result, Israel has the world's largest F-16 fleet outside the US Air Force. In their book, *The Israel Lobby and U.S. Foreign Policy*, John J Mearsheimer and Stephen M Walt write:

Since the October War in 1973, Washington has provided Israel with a level of support dwarfing the amounts provided to any other state. It has been the largest annual recipient of direct U.S. economic and military assistance since 1976 and the largest total recipient since World War II. Total direct U.S. aid to Israel amounts to well over $140 billion in 2003 dollars.

Israel receives about $3 billion in direct foreign assistance each year, which is roughly one-fifth of America's entire foreign aid budget. In per capita terms, the United States gives each Israeli a direct subsidy worth about $500 per year. This largesse is especially striking when one realizes that Israel is now a wealthy industrial state with a per capita income roughly equal to South Korea or Spain.

The House of Rothschild controls Israel and the political system of the United States. The network that links the two is Rothschild Zionism, and American aid to Israel is simply one branch of Zionism handing the cash to another. This is why it is so outrageously out of proportion with need. The might of this Rothschild Zionist cabal spanning Israel, the United States, Canada, Europe, Australia and beyond, is like the playground bully attacking and torturing the little kid in the callipers – the people of Gaza and the West Bank. Thousands of men, women and children are killed or injured – many disabled for life as they bomb the unarmed innocent knowing there will be no credible response. This is the way all bullies operate. Oh, brave men of Israel. The parallels are endless between the bloodthirsty 'God' of the Old Testament and the actions of the heartless and soulless that control Israel. They have no more empathy, no more mercy, for those who suffer the consequences of their actions than would a desktop computer. Imagine if Iran, or anyone else outside of Israel and the United States, was doing what the Israeli military is doing to the Palestinians. There would be global condemnation of the country involved, not least from Israel and the United States. Resolutions would be passed in the UN Security Council against the country involved and there would be demands for sanctions or military intervention to 'save the innocent'. When Israel is involved we have vacuous calls for a truce and an end to the violence, while 'understanding Israel's position' (Fig 50). As Gaza, one of the most crowded pieces of land on Earth, was being bombarded in early 2009, the soon-to-be President 'Change' Obama refused to comment. Silence was his only response. He said he wouldn't say anything because America could only have one president at a time. Funny, when terrorists were killing people in Mumbai, India, just a few weeks earlier he couldn't find a microphone quick enough. 'Mr Change' is a Rothschild Zionist puppet, as we shall see. Rothschild-controlled Israel is not subject to the same rules as everyone else, for all the reasons I am explaining. As former Israeli Prime Minister and terrorist, Ariel Sharon, said:

Illustration by David Dees (deesillustration.com)

Figure 50: *The American presidential candidates in 2008 were all agreed on one thing ...*

Israel may have the right to put others on trial, but certainly no one has the right to put the Jewish people and the State of Israel on trial.

Prime Minister, Golda Meir, betrayed the same Rothschild Zionist arrogance:

This country exists as the fulfilment of a promise made by God Himself. It would be ridiculous to ask it to account for its legitimacy.

Ah, it's all in the Old Testament? Gotcha, right, well do as you like then. The Obama government is slavishly pro-Israel, not least because he needed the sanction of the truly enormous Rothschild Zionist lobby in the United States to secure his presidency, and his administration is awash with Rothschild Zionists, including the White House Chief of Staff and White House Senior Advisor. His Vice-President, Joe Biden (Rothschild Zionist), is a long-time bag-carrier for Israel, and Secretary of State, Hillary Clinton, is another Rothschild puppetess who pledged to 'obliterate' Iran if it launched a nuclear attack on God's chosen country. Would she say she would obliterate Israel if it launched a nuclear attack on Iran? Of course not. Different rules, see. The Palestinians have never had a chance. The table is weighted, the game is rigged and it always has been. If you remove injustice, you remove the motivation for a violent response to that injustice. Put people in a position where they either accept their pathetic plight or open fire and some are bound to choose the latter. Instead of tackling the root cause, injustice, Israel responds with a state-of-the-art bombardment to 'protect itself'. In 2007, twenty-five Palestinians were killed for every Israeli, and in the 22-day Israeli offensive on the Gaza Strip across the start of 2009, Amnesty International says that some 1,400 Palestinians were killed, including 300 children. The Israeli civilian death toll was … three. This is rather more than just 'protecting yourself'.

Israel also has a massive nuclear arsenal that it refuses to acknowledge or deny, and it is supported in this by an official United States policy of never asking if they have nuclear weapons while knowing full well that they have had them for at least 30 years. Obama announced that he would continue this policy while condemning anyone else who refuses official inspections. Mohamed ElBaradei, Director General of the International Atomic Energy Agency, has said that 'Israel is the number one threat to the Middle East' because of its nuclear capability. He said that the Israeli government has refused to allow inspections of its nuclear installations for 30 years. How do they get away with it? The Rothschilds own Israel and its nuclear arsenal and they own the US government. Mordechai Vanunu, a former nuclear technical assistant, revealed details of Israel's nuclear weapons programme to a British journalist in 1986. He was then lured to Italy by a Jewish-American woman called Cheryl Bentov, drugged and kidnapped by Mossad, the Rothschild 'intelligence' agency, and subsequently jailed for 18 years for 'treason and espionage' – 11 of them in solitary confinement. Bentov now apparently uses the name Cheryl Hanin, and works as a real estate agent in Florida, although how she sleeps at night only she knows. Vanunu is a political prisoner and denied freedom of speech. Since his release in 2004, he is still subject to a long list of restrictions on his movement and freedom of expression. He has been arrested a number of times for giving interviews to foreign journalists and attempting to leave Israel. In December 2009, Vanunu was arrested for having a Norwegian girlfriend which the crazies said broke his ban on having contact with foreigners. His lawyer, Avigdor Feldman, said Vanunu was arrested because he has a Norwegian girlfriend whom police had already interrogated. 'Vanunu was arrested [for] a relationship between a man and a woman, with a Norwegian citizen,' Mr Feldman said. 'He is not being accused of giving any secrets. She is not interested in nuclear business – she's interested in Mordechai Vanunu …' Once again, imagine if Iran or other country in the Middle East did this. The American government would be at the microphone in a flash to voice their condemnation and claim that it confirmed the tyranical nature of the regime. The response from the government of the 'Land of the Free' to Vanunu's outrageous treatment? Silence.

The Rothschild Lobby

The Rothschilds control the United States, in part, through an organisation called the American Israel Public Affairs Committee, or AIPAC. It sounds like something connected to government, which is appropriate, but it is actually a mega-funded lobby operation to ensure that the United States slavishly supports the interests of Israel and the Rothschild networks. You cannot become president or be appointed to any significant political office unless you are either acceptable to them or, preferably, have an addiction to licking their backsides. The AIPAC network was behind the Boy Bush administration, which was notoriously controlled by the so-called 'neocon' or neoconservative network that included Rothschild Zionist 'think tanks' like the Project for the New American Century and the American Enterprise Institute which, together with others, orchestrated the invasion of Afghanistan and Iraq. These neocon groups are utterly ablaze with Khazar/Sumerians and their agents (see *The David Icke Guide to the Global Conspiracy (and how to end it)* and *Tales From the Time Loop*). At the heart of the Rothschild-controlled neocon cabal were Richard Perle (Rothschild Zionist), Paul Wolfowitz (Rothschild Zionist), Dov Zakheim (Rothschild Zionist), Douglas Feith (Rothschild Zionist), John Bolton (Rothschild Zionist), Lewis Libby (Rothschild Zionist), the list goes on and on. The same situation can be found with the 'Obama regime' in America's one-party state. You can't swing a cat in the Obama White House without hitting a Rothschild Zionist. Jewish people make up less than two per cent of the American population, but account for 50 per cent of the political campaign contributions, according to former BBC and Independent Television News correspondent, Alan Hart, in his book, *Zionism: The Real Enemy of the Jews*.

In the UK, the Rothschilds use a network called the 'Friends of Israel' to influence policies towards Israel. The three main political parties – Labour, Conservative and Liberal Democrat – all have branches of the Friends of Israel, or, rather, Friends of the Rothschilds. Members of these organisations, and their other branches, can be found throughout the British establishment and they include Prime Minister, Gordon Brown (Rothschild Zionist), Foreign Secretary, David Miliband (Rothschild Zionist), and former Prime Minister, Tony Blair (Rothschild Zionist). The most influential figure by far in the British government at the time of writing is Peter Mandelson (Rothschild Zionist), who continues to amass more titles and powers from the beleaguered Gordon Brown. Mandelson is an insider operative for the Rothschilds and has frequently accepted hospitality from his close friend and associate, Nathaniel Rothschild. Mandelson has called for the UK to join the Rothschild single European currency and he wants to see the country completely controlled by the European Union bureaucracy that rewarded him so handsomely when he was a commissioner. The hapless and hopeless Gordon Brown accepted an invitation to be patron of the Jewish National Fund, or JNF. He would not have dared to say no. The JNF's constitution demands that its work only benefits Jews and it seeks to impose an exclusively Jewish state in Israel, not least by supporting the theft of what is left of Palestinian land. It is hardly surprising, given this background, that Brown appointed Ivan Lewis (Rothschild Zionist) to be minister of state with responsibility for, wait for it ... British policy on the Middle East. Lewis, vice-chair of the Labour Friends of Israel, was an outspoken supporter of Israel's slaughter of the innocent in Gaza in early 2009. Lewis said of his new job:

> My responsibility for the Middle East peace process is particularly poignant. I have never hidden my pride at being Jewish or my support for the State of Israel.

Neither do you need to, mate. With anything to do with Israel, unremitting bias is a great career move. The British Ambassador to Israel is Matthew Gould, a Rothschild Zionist, who was appointed by Foreign Secretary, David Miliband (Rothschild Zionist). For nine years under Tony Blair (Rothschild Zionist) the special envoy to the Middle East was Lord Levy (Rothschild Zionist to his bootstraps). Miliband's brother, the former London School of Economics student, Ed Miliband (Rothschild Zionist), is Secretary of State for Energy and Climate Change, a key role to sell the "global warming' lie and agenda. The previous holder of the 'climate change' brief was ... David Miliband. Another leading figure in the Blair/Brown governments has been Jack Straw (Rothschild Zionist), who has held the offices of Lord High Chancellor of Great Britain and Secretary of State for Justice, Home Secretary, Foreign Secretary, Lord Privy Seal and Leader of the House of Commons. Straw and company are inept, but somehow they keep getting major jobs in government when Jewish people in the UK number just 275,000 in a population of some 70 million. Again, a number of these British Jews will not be Rothschild Zionists. Being a 'Friend of Israel', or put another way, a friend of the Rothschild agenda, is pretty much essential to achieving high political office. The Israel (Rothschild) lobby is fantastic in its political reach and influence all over the world. The biggest group affiliated to the UK Conservative Party, headed by David 'I'm a Zionist' Cameron, is the Conservative Friends of Israel that has massive influence on the selection of candidates to stand for Parliament. David Cameron (Rothschild Zionist), a would be next Prime Minister, has family ties to the Rothschilds. Yaakov Wise, a research fellow at the University of Manchester Centre for Jewish Studies, said in 2009 that Cameron could even be 'a direct descendant of Moses'. This would be difficult, given that there was no 'Moses', but I get his drift. Cameron's great-great-grandfather, Emile Levita (descendant of the priestly class, the Levites), came to Britain from the Rothschild fiefdom of Germany in the 1850s and was later director of the London-based Chartered Bank of India, Australia and China. His son married a relative of King George III and that makes Cameron a fifth cousin of the Queen, once removed while he promotes himself as a 'man of the people'. These are the stated aims of the Friends of Israel within the UK Liberal Democrat Party and it will be the same with all of them:

- To maximise support for the State of Israel not only within the Liberal Democrats but within Parliament itself.
- To influence the party's Middle East policy.
- To liaise with Israeli politicians and government.
- To provide parliamentarians with briefing material for parliamentary debates, questions to ministers and public appearances.
- To rebut attacks on Israel in the media, Parliament and the party.
- To arrange and accompany Liberal Democrat Friends of Israel delegations to Israel.
- To keep in regular contact with the Embassy of Israel.

The 'different' Friends of Israel groups within political parties are in truth one group that coordinates and manipulates through all parties. The Nolan Committee on Standards in Public Life listed seven principles of public life for all MPs to follow. Among them is this one: 'Holders of public office should not place themselves under any financial or other obligation to outside individuals or organisations that might seek to influence them in the performance of their official duties'. Yet when it comes to the most powerful of all the lobby groups, those related to Israel, they are given immunity from such a basic principle, because they also control the committees that are supposed to police what is left of political integrity. It is real simple: control both sides and you win the game. Rothschild Zionist lackeys for Israel control the British government and opposition parties and both the Intelligence and Security Committee and Foreign Affairs and Defence Committee. They're everywhere and it's the same in the United States, Canada and country after country after country. As the magnificently outspoken Jewish musician and writer, Gilad Atzmon, has pointed out, 56 per cent of appointees in the Bill Clinton administration, for example, were Zionists taken from less than two per cent of the American population (see **www.gilad.co.uk**). The French leader Nicolas Sarkozy is also a Rothschild Zionist and long-time asset of Mossad, the Rothschild enforcement agency masquerading as the intelligence agency of Israel.

Rothschild Arabia

Have you ever wondered why the 'home' of Islam, Saudi Arabia, says and does nothing in the face of what is being visited upon the Arab world? There is a reason for this. The House of Saud is a fake front for the House of Rothschild and they are not 'Arabs' or 'Muslims' at all. They are Rothschild Zionists who can be traced back to a Jewish man called Mordakhai bin Ibrahim bin Moshe. Researchers say that in the year AD 851 members of the Arabic Al Masaleekh clan formed a trading caravan and met with Mordakhai bin Ibrahim bin Moshe, a merchant in Basra in what is now Iraq. Mordakhai was Jewish, but told them he was from their clan and had relocated to Basra after a family feud. He asked if he could join them on their journey to Najd, in Arabia, where he changed his name and eventually settled in the town of Al-Dir'iyyah, or Diriyah (where the founder of the modern House of Saud came from in the official story). Mordakhai gathered support among the Bedouin tribes and then declared himself their king, this research suggests. Some tribes resisted and attacked Al-Dir'iyyah. Mordakhai was forced to flee and take shelter in a farm at near Al-Arid, which is now the Saudi capital, Riyadh. Within a month, it is said, he had killed the farmer, blamed it on a band of thieves, and taken ownership of the property, which he called Al-Dir'iyyah, after the town he had been forced to flee. Mordakhai, who now claimed to be an Arab Sheikh, began begetting on the phenomenal scale that is continued by the House of Saud to this day and his family secured ever greater swathes of land through violence, murder and deceit. They also arranged for a false history and lineage of the family to be written to connect them with Arab royalty and the Prophet Mohammed. One of Mordakhai's sons, Al-Maraqan (said to be from the Jewish Mack-ren) had sons called Mohammad and Saud, from which the name of the dynasty originates, researchers say. The House of Saud continued its mass begetting and killing until it reached its goal of controlling the entire Arabian Peninsular. The House of Saud is a fascist dictatorship of the most extreme kind. As one Arab researcher wrote:

> They have named the whole Arabian Peninsula after their family name as if the whole region is their own personal real estate, and that all other inhabitants are their mere servants or slaves, toiling day and night for the pleasure of their masters (The Saudi Family). They are completely holding the natural wealth of the country as their own property.
>
> If any poor person from the common people raises his/her voice complaining against any of the despotic rules of this Jewish [Rothschild Zionist] Dynasty, the Dynasty cuts off his/her head in the public square. A princess of theirs once visited Florida, USA, with her retinue; she rented 90 Suite rooms in a Grand Hotel for about one million dollars a night! Can anyone of her subjects comment about that extravagant event? If he/she does, his/her fate is quite known: Death with the edge of the Saudi sword in the public square.

The extreme 'Islamic' creed used to justify these atrocities is called Wahhabism, and is named after a man, also claimed to be Jewish, called Muhammad ibn Abd-al-Wahhab. He formed a brutal new political force with Muhammad bin Saud in the 18th century. The House of Saud fought for control of Arabia for 180 years before founding the present dynasty and the Kingdom of Saudi Arabia in 1926 (more formally in 1932) under King Abdul Aziz bin Saud. They are Rothschild Zionists who do the bidding of the Rothschild dynasty. This is why they are so close to America and the Bush family (Rothschild Zionists); support the US in its assaults on the Middle East; call Israelis their 'cousins' (true); and in 2009 gave Israel permission to use its air space if it chose to attack Iran. It was also suggested in a 2009 report in London's *Daily Telegraph* that Iranian President Mahmoud Ahmadinejad comes from a Jewish family called Sabourjian, apparently a common Iranian Jewish name. It would explain why Ahmadinejad has a history of saying and doing things that give the Rothschild Zionists the ammunition they need to demonise Iran. His ancestry, however, has not been confirmed at the time of writing and may not be correct. All this is not about being paranoid – just streetwise. Remember that the world you see on the television news and hear in the political speeches is just a movie directed by the Rothschilds and their bloodline networks.

The Gatekeepers
The scale of this ongoing Rothschild Zionist evil has been suppressed by fear of being called 'anti-Semitic'. The Rothschild dynasty has created a highly-funded network of

'anti-hate' groups to label as 'racist' anyone who dares to expose or condemn Israel, Rothschild Zionism or its networks of manipulation within the United States and elsewhere. Politicians, university professors, people like me, and anyone with a public stage, are immediately condemned as 'racist' if they challenge Israel or anyone who happens to be Jewish. One of these Rothschild fronts is B'nai B'rith, or 'Sons of the Covenant', which was established in 1843. All twelve of B'nai B'rith's official founders were born in Rothschild Germany and moved to New York in the same period from the late 1820s and into the 1830s. It calls itself the 'global voice of the Jewish Community', when it is a global voice

Figure 51: *The hate laws agenda is not about protecting 'minorities'. It is designed to destroy freedom of speech, as the ADL's Abe Foxman well knows*

for the Rothschild Illuminati and operates as a strand in the secret society network. It is very closely connected with the Scottish Rite of Freemasonry. In 1913, B'nai B'rith spawned the Anti-Defamation League, or ADL, which is today the Rothschilds' premier racist-branding organisation. With typical Orwellian irony, the role of the Anti-Defamation League is to defame people, and the full title of B'nai B'rith is the '*Independent* Order of B'nai B'rith' when that's the last thing it is. You can only laugh, really. 'We are the Chosen People and above all others, and you are a racist.' I love it. B'nai B'rith and the Anti-Defamation League claim to be there to protect Jewish people, but, as Plato said: 'This and no other is the root from which a tyrant springs; when he first appears he is a protector.' The ADL is a sub-agency of the Israeli (Rothschild) centre for covert operations, the Mossad, which, according to a former agent, has the motto: 'By way of deception, thou shalt do war.' If that isn't the motto, it should be. The ADL is behind the introduction of 'hate laws' which are aimed at silencing dissent against Rothschild Zionism or Israel (Fig 51). The Jewish academic, Noam Chomsky, said this of the ADL in his book, *Necessary Illusions*:

> The ADL has virtually abandoned its earlier role as a civil rights organization, becoming 'one of the main pillars' of Israeli propaganda in the U.S., as the Israeli press casually describes it, engaged in surveillance, blacklisting, compilation of FBI-style files circulated to adherents for the purpose of defamation, angry public responses to criticism of Israeli actions, and so on. These efforts, buttressed by insinuations of anti-Semitism or direct accusations, are intended to deflect or undermine opposition to Israeli policies, including Israel's refusal, with U.S. support, to move towards a general political settlement.

The American rabbi, Michael Lerner, agrees:

> The ADL lost most of it credibility in my eyes as a civil rights organization when it began to identify criticisms of Israel with anti-Semitism, still more when it failed to defend me when I was receiving threats to my life from right-wing Jewish groups

because of my critique of Israeli policy toward Palestinians (it said that these were not threats that came from my being Jewish, so therefore they were not within their area of concern).

Firstly, the ADL has never been a civil rights organisation. Its very purpose has been to take them away. Secondly, it is not there to defend anyone, Jewish or otherwise. It is there to represent the sadistic interests of the House of Rothschild and the wider Illuminati. One aspect of the ADL's method of operation is to manipulate politicians behind the scenes to introduce 'hate crime' laws which claim to be designed to stop people preaching hatred about others for their beliefs and sexual preferences. The ADL actually frames these laws for government legislation, but they are not motivated by a desire to stop discrimination. The real reason is to stop all criticism and exposure of Israel, Mossad and the activities of the Rothschild Zionist cabal across the world. Did you say that Israel's merciless bombing of Gaza civilians and burning them alive with white phosphorus is wrong? Hey, you are guilty of a hate crime, you racist. The ADL, and the Rothschild Zionist propaganda machine in general, has taken the term 'hypocrisy' to still new levels of absurdity. If you are targeted by the ADL, their main weapon to discredit you is to encourage public hatred of you. They are not against hate, it's their very life-blood, and it is just another weapon to be used as it suits them. The ADL's entire armoury is based on the use of hatred and fear, and they are heavily involved in delivering their propaganda to American schoolchildren in 'partnership' with the National School Boards Association and other bodies. This means the Rothschilds are doing that. At the same time, no laws are applied to the horrific racism of the Rothschild Zionists. For example, Rabbi Friedman in the United States said this:

> I don't believe in western morality, i.e. don't kill civilians or children, don't destroy holy sites, don't fight during holiday seasons, don't bomb cemeteries, don't shoot until they shoot first because it is immoral. The only way to fight a moral war is the Jewish way: Destroy their holy sites. Kill men, women and children (and cattle).

What if anyone had said that about Jewish people? They would have been vilified, even jailed; but there is one law for the Rothschild Zionists and one for the rest of us because they control government and the application and enforcement of the law. These people press for 'hate laws' against others, and even write the legislation for governments, and yet they follow the teachings of the shockingly racist Talmud. They refer to non-Jews as 'goyim' or 'goy' (cattle) and here are some examples of what I mean by racist:

- If a goy hits a Jew he must be killed (Sanhedrin 58b).
- If a Jew finds an object lost by a goy it does not have to be returned (Baba Mezia 24a).
- If a Jew murders a goy there will be no death penalty (Sanhedrin 57a).
- What a Jew steals from a goy he may keep (Sanhedrin 57a).
- Jews may use subterfuges to circumvent a goy (Baba Kamma 113a).
- All children of the goyim (Gentiles) are animals (Yebamoth 98a).
- Girls born of the goyim are in a state of niddah (menstrual uncleanness) from birth (Abodah Zarah 36b).

- The goyim are not humans. They are beasts (Baba Mezia 114b).
- If you eat with a goy it is the same as eating with a dog (Tosapoth, Jebamoth 94b).
- Even the best of the goyim should all be killed (Soferim 15).
- Sexual intercourse between the goyim is like intercourse between animals (Sanhedrin 74b).
- When it comes to a Gentile in peace times, one may harm him indirectly, for instance, by removing a ladder after he had fallen into a crevice (Shulkan Arukh, Yoreh De ah, 158, Hebrew Edition only).

The scale of hypocrisy makes it hard to breathe. Israel has even launched an advertising campaign urging Israelis to inform on Jewish friends and relatives abroad who may be 'in danger' of marrying non-Jews. Television and Internet advertising seeks to stop the 'assimilation' of Jews outside Israel (Diaspora Jews as they are called) and urges them to move to Israel. The idea is to increase the size of the Israeli population to seize more and more Palestinian land. One advertisement said that 'assimilation' (Jews marrying the partner they love) is 'a strategic national threat' and it warned: 'More than 50 per cent of Diaspora youth assimilate and are lost to us.' Lost to 'us'? Who the hell do these people think they are? They treat the mass of Jews like bloody commodities. The advertisement featured missing person posters showing images of Jewish youths with the word 'lost' in various languages. The voiceover asks people who 'know a young Jew living abroad' to call a hotline and give details. 'Together, we will strengthen their connection to Israel, so that we don't lose them,' it said. Israel also refuses to recognise Jewish and Arabian intermarriage unless it is performed abroad. If anyone else acted with such racism they would be condemned by Israel and its fronts like the ADL. Max Blumenthal and Jesse Rosenfeld exposed Israeli racism with their YouTube video called *Feeling the Hate in Jerusalem* in which American Jews visiting the country were asked about Barack Obama. A barrage of foul-mouthed racism followed including, 'White power! Fuck the niggers!' Ironic, given that Obama is the Rothschild Zionist's puppet in the White House, but these brain-donors are too stupid to realise that. There was also outrageous racism from Israeli students with regard to the Palestinians. The video was banned by YouTube and some other sites after getting hundreds of thousands of hits. If that had been a video of white supremacists condemning Jews in the same terms there would have been a global outcry and never would it have been banned. We would never have heard the last of it. What criminal hypocrisy.

I said that the ADL is an arm of the Rothschild intelligence agency, Mossad, and it also uses the same techniques. The ADL was exposed in 1993 for spying on Arab-Americans and what are called 'progressive groups', and for collecting files on more than 600 organisations and 10,000 people. These included the American Civil Liberties Union and 20 labour unions in the San Francisco area. The ADL shared this information with Mossad and even passed details about anti-apartheid groups to intelligence agents representing apartheid South Africa. This is the mentality of the people who accuse others of racism. Noam Chomsky, who has widely criticised Israel's treatment of the Palestinians, revealed that the ADL compiled a 150-page dossier on him. An ADL insider sent him the document which Chomsky said looked like an FBI file. '... It's clear they essentially have spies in classrooms who take notes and send them to the ADL and other organisations,' Chomsky said. 'The groups then compile dossiers they can use to condemn, attack or remove faculty members. They're like J Edgar Hoover's [FBI] files. It's kind of gutter stuff.' The ADL *is* gutter stuff. It seeks to terrorise academics, students and university authorities into stopping all criticism of Israel on behalf of their masters, the Rothschilds. As I write this chapter, an academic at the University of California in Santa Barbara is in their gun-sights. Sociology professor, William I Robinson, committed the capital crime of introducing materials criticising Israel's impact on global affairs. Mark Levine, a Jewish professor of Middle Eastern Studies, said pro-Israel groups had, in effect, created a 'large machine' to attack Israel-critics on college campuses. 'These are powerful, organised groups in the Jewish community who use fear and intimidation to try to make sure Israel doesn't get criticised,' he said. 'They go after anyone, even more so when the critics are Jews, because they fear that if we can criticise them, then everyone can.'

Vilifying the 'self-haters'

If anyone still thinks the political creed of Rothschild Zionism is about Jewish people then please read on. Zionism is, at its centre, a secret society connected to all the others in the global web. It was not established for the benefit of Jewish people, but to exploit them and use them as a cover for the manipulations of the House of Rothschild and its associates. Zionism is another word for tyranny. No-one is allowed to question it or expose it without consequences – including Jews. Well, actually, *especially* those of Jewish parentage, as Mark Levine said, because they can't be credibly labelled 'anti-Semitic' by the Rothschild-fronts that seek to defame, discredit and destroy anyone who is getting too close to the truth. They've tried it on me, and will do so again after the publication of this book, but I'm still here and will continue to be so whatever they may throw my way. A fellow researcher, Henry Makow, the inventor of the board game, *Scruples*, has been called before a Canadian 'Human Rights' Tribunal over a complaint that he foments hatred against Jews. What makes this claim even more insane than usual is that Henry is the son of parents who suffered in Nazi-occupied Poland and his grandparents perished. His parents only survived by posing as Catholics. Now here is the son and grandson of those Jewish victims of the Rothschild-funded Nazis being accused of spreading hatred against Jews. *Come again??*

The complaint has been lodged by the Canadian Jewish Congress and its chief executive, Bernie Farber, who campaigned for years to stop me speaking in Canada. This man is outrageously considered to be one of Canada's leading experts in 'hate crime' when his job is to use allegations of 'hate crime' to silence his targets. The Canadian Jewish Congress is seeking to persecute Henry Makow because he exposes Rothschild Zionism and its true agenda, and alerts Jewish people to how they are being used to impose a new world system that will enslave them as well as everyone else. George Orwell wrote, prophetically: 'In times of universal deceit, telling the truth will be a revolutionary act.' It is also fast becoming a crime. Astonishingly, in an allegedly 'free country', truth is no defence in cases heard by the Thought Police of the Canadian 'Human Rights' Commission (Fig 52). It doesn't matter if what you say is true, you can still be prosecuted if the 'Human Rights' mafia consider it was wrong to say it. The Canadian Jewish Congress, or CJC, has been closely associated with the Bronfman family, who are Rothschild subordinates in the Zionist network. The CJC works in league with B'nai B'rith and the ADL. It was exposed for planting an agent into the

Canadian Nazi Party to increase the party's profile and perceived influence. The idea was to frighten the Jewish community and justify 'hate laws' that the CJC wanted the government to introduce. These are the kind of people we are dealing with.

Figure 52: *Rothschild Zionists want 'hate laws' in which truth is no defence*

Henry Makow faces a potentially expensive legal bill to defend himself before the Canadian 'Human Rights' dictatorship and protect his website from the censors. The Canadian 'Human Rights' Commission (CHRC) is another front for the Rothschild network that is targeting free expression and those who expose its manipulation behind world events. The CHRC is superbly exposed in a book called *Shakedown* by the Canadian Jewish writer and publisher, Ezra Levant, another target of the Thought Police. As he rightly says: 'The CHRC are on a mission to destroy real human rights like freedom of speech and replace them with counterfeit human rights, like the fake right not to be offended.' Ezra exposes the extraordinary behaviour of former CHRC 'investigator' and serial complainant, Richard Warman, which includes posting deeply racist comments on websites and then reporting the same websites to the CHRC for publishing racist messages. No, you didn't misread that. Richard Warman was given a 'human rights' award by the Canadian Jewish Congress, run by his friend, Bernie Farber, the man who is targeting Henry Makow. The Canadian 'Human Rights' Commission and its 'Tribunals' are simply kangaroo courts in which everyone is guilty before the evidence is even heard. Henry Makow rightly says:

> The CHRC ... forwards the Zionists' complaints to the 'Tribunal' which prides itself for being an impartial court. But the Tribunal has never refused to hear a case, no matter how baseless. Nor has any complaint been settled in favour of the defendant.

Thanks to the tireless efforts of people like Ezra Levant, even the Canadian media has begun to realise the scale of censorship and human rights abuses that are going on. The *Ottawa Citizen* said: 'A court where the rulings go only one way is the very definition of a show trial. These institutions should be the source of shame to Canadians.' Yes, but these are the very courts that the Rothschilds want to impose all over the world and not just to hear 'human rights' cases. They want all courts to operate like this in the fascist/communist global state. Ezra Levant is, ironically, a passionate supporter of Israel and Zionism and yet he is still in the gun-sights of Rothschild Zionist organisations like the Canadian Jewish Congress. Ezra's crime is to stand up for freedom of speech and expose the 'Human Rights' Commission and the Canadian Jewish Congress for seeking to deny such freedom. These two organisations work very closely together even though the Commission is supposed to answer to government and the other is 'private'. What connects them is the Rothschild network of systematic censorship. Henry Makow puts it very well when he says: 'Human rights have become dirty words in Canada because Zionists determine who will have them. Welcome to the future.' Not just in Canada, either. It is happening worldwide as 'hate laws' are introduced through the manipulations of Rothschild Zionist organisations like B'nai B'rith and the Anti-Defamation League.

Hijacking Education

Jewish professor, David F Noble, faced the wrath of the Rothschild Zionist lobby when he exposed their control of Canada's third-biggest university, the York University in Toronto. He distributed flyers headed: 'The York University Foundation: The Tail That Wags the Dog (Suggestions for Further Research)'. The Foundation is the university's major fundraising body and Professor Noble said it had been hijacked by the 'Israel lobby' (see Rothschild) to influence university policy. He also exposed the broader influence of Israel in Western institutions. What was the reaction of the Rothschild Zionist lobby? They actually called this Jewish professor 'anti-Semitic'. How desperate can you get? Unbowed, Professor Noble has issued a $25 million lawsuit at the Ontario Superior Court of Justice for defamation. The defendants include the private corporate entity, York University Foundation; pro-Israel lobbying and fundraising organisations; Hillel of Toronto; the United Jewish Appeal Federation of Toronto; and the Canadian Jewish Congress, Ontario, and their agents. The lawsuit accuses these groups of trying to harm, silence and malign Professor Noble because of his critical investigations into external influences on his university. He said:

In an effort to suppress my inquiries, publicly destroy my reputation, and isolate me from my peers, the defendants launched the most vile kind of personal attack – attempting to stigmatise a Jewish man as an anti-Semite – because I dared examine and expose their pernicious activities. These rich and powerful people pretend to be friends of higher learning but are in fact its worst enemies. They think they have bought themselves a university. They haven't.

Figure 53: *Norman Finkelstein is the target of the Rothschild Zionist Thought Police because he commits the crime – a capital offence in their eyes – of telling the truth*

Good on you, mate.

A famous Jewish hate-figure of the Rothschild Zionists (hate is their base emotion) is the magnificent Norman Finkelstein (Fig 53), who exposed their sickening abuse of Jewish people in his book, *The Holocaust Industry: Reflections on the Exploitation of Jewish Suffering*. Both of Finkelstein's parents survived the Nazi concentration camps. His mother was held in the Majdanek camp, and two slave labour camps, and his father was in Auschwitz. Every other member of his family on both sides was killed by the Nazis. I thoroughly recommend his book if you want to see the unimaginable lengths to which the Rothschild Zionists exploit Jewish people. It is truly breathtaking. These people have no shame. Finkelstein shows how the number of alleged 'Holocaust survivors' increased from 100,000 in 1945 to nearly a million by 1997 as the Rothschild Zionists of the Holocaust Industry demanded ever more compensation for fake victims. 'If everyone who claims to be a survivor actually is one,' his mother used to say, 'who did Hitler kill?' Meanwhile, the real survivors have lost out because, to the Rothschild Zionists, they don't matter. Finkelstein's mother received only $3,500 in compensation from the German government via Jewish organisations while others, many of whom never went near a concentration camp, were given lifetime pensions by Germany worth hundreds of thousands of dollars. Rothschild Zionists worked this scam by negotiating with the German government that the compensation should not go to individuals who actually suffered, but for the rehabilitation of Jewish 'communities'. In other words: to Rothschild Zionist organisations. Oh yeah, there were two exceptions to the no-payment-to-individuals rule ... rabbis, and 'outstanding Jewish leaders'. They still got their individual cheques in the post and by today's values the money paid out by Germany amounts to tens of billions of dollars. The Rothschild Zionist front that negotiated this outrage was the 'Conference on Jewish Material Claims Against Germany', which included the American Jewish Committee, American Jewish Congress and B'nai B'rith. These are the very organisations that say we need 'hate laws' to protect Jewish people about whom they do not give a shit.

One rabbi denounced the compensation deal in words that captured the real motivation of these self-appointed 'protectors' of Jewish people. Rabbi Arthur Hertzberg said: 'It's not about justice; it's a fight for money.' The Executive Vice-President of the Conference on Jewish Material Claims Against Germany (the 'Claims Conference') is a guy called Saul Kagan, and Finkelstein says of him: 'The reported annual salary of Saul Kagan ... is $105,000. Kagan rings up in 12 days what my mother received for suffering six years of Nazi persecution.' The hundred grand salary was in the year 2000 – think what it will be now. Kagan is still in situ and says that his organisation has so far secured more than $60 billion in compensation payments to 'Holocaust survivors' throughout the world. Finkelstein writes:

> In recent years, the Holocaust industry has become an outright extortion racket. Purporting to represent all of world Jewry, living and dead, it is laying claim to Holocaust-era Jewish assets throughout Europe. Fittingly dubbed the 'last chapter of the Holocaust', this double shakedown of European countries as well as legitimate Jewish claimants first targeted Switzerland. [After a protracted campaign which enlisted the American political establishment] the Swiss finally caved in [in] 1998 and agreed to pay $1.25bn. 'The aim ...' a Swiss bank's press release read, 'is to avert the threat of sanctions as well as long and costly court proceedings.'

> Its solicitude for 'needy Holocaust survivors' notwithstanding, the World Jewish Congress wants nearly half the Swiss monies earmarked for Jewish organisations and 'Holocaust education'. The Simon Wiesenthal Centre maintains that if 'worthy' Jewish organisations receive monies, 'a portion should go to Jewish educational centres'. As they 'angle' for a bigger share of the loot, reform and orthodox organisations each claim that the ... dead would have preferred their branch of Judaism as financial beneficiary.

The World Jewish Congress and the Simon Wiesenthal Center are more Rothschild-controlled organisations. Historian Guy Walters exposed the true background to 'Nazi hunter' Simon Wiesenthal in his book, *Hunting Evil*, and shows him to be a liar who brought only a handful of Nazis to justice while ignoring the rest. As I have said before, Wiesenthal ignored the crucial and provable Rockefeller and Bush family support for the Nazis because he was part of that cabal – the Rothschild cabal. This is why Wiesenthal was not in the least bit interested in targeting the stream of Nazis, including the 'Angel of Death', Josef Mengele, that were brought to the Americas after the war to work on US covert projects that included genetics, mind control and high technology (see *The Biggest Secret*). Guy Walters says of the world's most famous 'Nazi hunter':

> Simon Wiesenthal's reputation is built on sand. He was a liar and a bad one at that. From the end of the war to the end of his life, he would lie repeatedly about his supposed hunt for Eichmann as well as his other Nazi-hunting exploits. Wiesenthal would also concoct outrageous stories about his war years and make false claims about his academic career.

Walters has described there the reccurring, indeed obligatory, mentality of the bloodline network and its gofers. These are the holier-than-thous who have the nerve to condemn others for racism and circulating untruths.

'Bad Jews' Are 'Self-Haters'

Norman Finkelstein has also exposed Israel's treatment of the Palestinians and its human rights abuses. He said it was guilty of state terrorism and the 'only difference between Israeli terrorism and Hamas terrorism is that Israeli terrorism is three times as lethal'. And the rest. Finkelstein's exposure of these sick and corrupt people made him dangerous indeed to the Rothschild Zionist establishment and they retaliated in the usual way. A campaign of vilification was unleashed, spearheaded by the Rothschild Zionist, Alan Dershowitz, the Harvard law professor and advocate of 'torture warrants' to make torture legal. If you are Jewish, and the label 'anti-Semite' is not credible, they dub you a 'self-hater'. Never mind refuting your evidence; that is irrelevant. They know that if they debate the issue with evidence they are in serious trouble. No, abuse is their weapon. If you expose them and you are not Jewish, you are an 'anti-Semite'. If you expose them and you are Jewish, you are a 'self-hater'. A Rothschild Zionist critic said that Finkelstein was 'a sick, disgusting example of self-hatred'. As one writer put it:

> According to this propaganda, Jews who raise serious criticisms of Israel for the mistreatment of Palestinians, Jews such as Norman Finkelstein, Noam Chomsky, Sara Roy, and many others, are, in short, 'Bad Jews'.

> It is left to the 'Good Jews' to neutralize such criticisms of Israel by tarring critics with these labels, thereby ending their employment, blocking speaking engagements, or generally attempting to destroy their credibility with the public – and with university presidents. In this taxonomy, it is the 'Good Jews' who claim to speak for Jews collectively.

Put another way, the only 'Good Jews' are the Rothschild Zionists and those that do what they tell them. Jewish people in general need to understand this or they will go on being scammed. Zionism does not mean Jewish; it means 'Rothschild'. In 2007, Norman Finkelstein was 'denied tenure' (in effect sacked) by DePaul University in Chicago after a vicious campaign against him led by Alan Dershowitz, who sent members of the university 'a dossier of Norman Finkelstein's most egregious academic sins, and especially his outright lies, misquotations and distortions'. I'm sure it was a very balanced document. Finkelstein's department and a college-level personnel committee still voted in favour of his tenure, but he was opposed by the dean of the College of Liberal Arts and Sciences and the University Board on Promotion and Tenure. This is how the Rothschild Zionists manipulate – by controlling or influencing organisations and the key positions of power. It is far more difficult to impose your will upon many individuals, so you need to control the upper echelons of the organisational pyramids. The university president, the Reverend Dennis Holtschneider, had the final decision and he gutlessly bowed to Rothschild Zionist pressure. Finkelstein was out. I was able to speak at Toronto University in the late 1990s only because the top guy refused to give in to pressure from the Canadian Jewish Congress, Anti-Defamation League and 'human rights campaigner', Richard Warman, to have me banned. Soon afterwards, he was gone. There is a crackdown on diversity and dissent throughout the education system and academia, as the Rothschild Zionists seize ever more power in the way described earlier by Professor Noble at York University in Toronto. They control the funding and manipulate policy and appointments. Norman Finkelstein's academic career has been essentially destroyed for telling the truth, and that's the reason why Professor Noble was vilified and Henry Makow has been under attack. They are all from Jewish backgrounds, but that matters not. Rothschild Zionism is not about the interests of Jewish people. It is about control.

Fake 'Muslim' Terrorists

Rothschild Zionism is by far the major force behind what is called the 'Islamic terror network'. I remember Andreas von Bülow, the former German Defence Minister, telling me that the 'Muslim terrorist' of the 1970s and 1980s, Abu Nidal, was an asset of Mossad, and once you begin to understand the game this makes perfect sense. They are creating the perception of a problem (terrorism) to which they can offer a solution (more control and war). The FBI named an American citizen called Adam Yahiye Gadahn on their list of 'most wanted terrorists' and the FBI website said that he had been 'indicted in the Central District of California for treason and material support to Al Qaeda'. Gadahn made a series of ludicrous B-movie videos in which he called for violence against the 'infidels' and other such low-budget garbage. The FBI said he was allegedly involved in 'a number of terrorist activities, including providing aid and comfort to Al Qaeda and services for Al Qaeda'. He should be considered armed and dangerous, we were told, and a million dollar reward was offered for evidence leading to his arrest. The FBI asked for any information the public could give them about this very dangerous man and, it so happens, I can help them there. 'Adam Yahiye Gadahn' is really a Jewish man called Philip Pearlman, the grandson of Dr Carl K Pearlman, chairman of the United Jewish Welfare Fund and board member of the Anti-Defamation League. Another chap being used to frighten Americans into compliance is Yousef al-

Khattab at the website, **RevolutionMuslim.com**. He says he wants the United States to impose Sharia Law that includes flogging or stoning to death for pre-marital sex and adultery. The website has posted pictures of the Statue of Liberty being hit by an axe, and videos lampooning the deaths of American soldiers and the beheading of an American journalist. Well, well, it turns out that 'Yousef al-Khattab' was born into a Rothschild Zionist family and called Joseph Cohen. Just a coincidence, nothing to worry about.

Prophetic Forgery

One more point before we move on … If you quote from the now infamous *Protocols of the Elders of Zion*, you are guaranteed to be called a racist, especially by the 'liberal left' or the 'hard left', none of whom ever miss a chance to posture their own self-purity. I call them the 'Robot Radicals' and they are an essential weapon in the Rothschilds' ability to protect themselves from legitimate investigation. When anyone gets too close to the truth, the Rothschild fronts like the ADL scream 'anti-Semite!' This is the cue for the Robot Radicals to pull up their sleeves, allowing full access to the hearts, and off they go – 'Condemn him! Condemn him!' Meanwhile, the Rothschilds and their assets are laughing at them with unbridled contempt knowing that they are defending the very system that is dedicated to enslaving them and their families. The Protocols are alleged to be accounts of meetings of the Zionist elite in Basel, Switzerland, at the time of the first Rothschild Zionist Congress in 1897. This event had to be moved from its original location in Munich, Germany, because of opposition from Jews who did not support the Zionist plan to move them all to Israel (remember this was long before the horrors of Nazi Germany that led to just this relocation). The Basel conference was led by Rothschild placeman, Theodor Herzl, the so-called founder of modern Zionism, who would write later in his diary:

> It is essential that the sufferings of Jews … become worse … this will assist in realization of our plans … I have an excellent idea … I shall induce anti-Semites to liquidate Jewish wealth … The anti-Semites will assist us thereby in that they will strengthen the persecution and oppression of Jews. The anti-Semites shall be our best friends.

Yep, the Zionists have the best interests of Jewish people as their priority. The Protocols first appeared publicly in Russia in 1903 and, no matter what the abuse-hurlers and reality-deniers say, their content presents a plan for a world dictatorship that mirrors what has actually happened since. You can find them on the Internet and also at *Amazon*. Give them a look and see what you think. People should make up their own minds, not be told what to believe without checking the validity for themselves. The Protocols talk of covertly creating wars, slumps and revolutions, increasing the cost of living, and engineering massive unrest that would lead to the ultimate goal of global conquest by establishing a world government 'by consent'. Sound familiar? Elite banker, James Paul Warburg (Rothschild Zionist), son of Paul Warburg (Rothschild Zionist), the man behind the creation of the US Federal Reserve, told the United States Senate Committee on Foreign Relations in 1950: 'We shall have World Government, whether or not we like it. The only question is whether World Government will be achieved by conquest or consent.' Here is a summary of what the Protocols say, taken from an article actually denouncing them as fake:

> The Protocols purport to describe a secret conspiracy for Jewish world domination, in an instructional style, suggestive perhaps of a training manual for a new conspiracy member.
>
> The expressed purpose of the described program is to bring the Gentile world under a single government, headed by a king from among the Jewry. In preparation for this, it is necessary to eliminate all rival nations, governments, religions and economic systems.
>
> While the actual domination of the world is to take place through violence, the preparation takes place through subtle sabotage of existing systems. Stressed is the need for the masses to welcome their enslavement. This condition is to be effected by:
>
> - Use of loans and usury to bankrupt and control states
> - Use of mass media to control the minds of the masses
> - Artificial creation of discord, war and economic depression
> - Establishment of democratic or republican governments
>
> The Protocols frequently refer to a powerful and massive 'agentur' to carry out the directives of the conspiracy, as well as an enormous cache of gold at their disposal. They also refer repeatedly to secret societies such as the freemasons as a front for their covert operations.

I am not saying the Protocols are genuine or not genuine, only that they tell the detailed story of the last hundred years before it happened. The conspiracy described by Dr Richard Day (Rothschild Zionist) at the meeting of doctors in Pittsburgh in 1969 was pretty much exactly the one outlined in the Protocols more than a hundred years ago. Is this just a coincidence? Dr Day was a Rockefeller insider as National Medical Director of their Planned Parenthood eugenics operation, and 'Rockefeller' means 'Rothschild'. It is widely believed, mostly because of constant repetition, that the Protocols are a forgery, and they may be; but if they are, the writer was a fantastic prophet. The proof that they are a forgery is said to have appeared in articles in London's *The Times* newspaper in 1921. Is this the same newspaper controlled for much of its history by the House of Rothschild? The one that said Abraham Lincoln's America must be destroyed to stop them printing interest-free money and no longer being dependent on the Rothschild banks? Is this the same newspaper that today is owned by the Rothschild Zionist, Rupert Murdoch? It would appear to be, unfortunately. To be fair, the paper did publish an article on 8th May 1920 asking if the Protocols could be true. It said:

> Whence comes this uncanny note of prophecy, prophecy in part fulfilled, in parts far gone in the way of fulfillment? Have we been struggling these tragic years to ... extirpate the secret organization of German world dominion only to find underneath it, another, more dangerous because more secret? Have we ... escaped a Pax Germanica only to fall into a Pax Judaeica?

Figure 54: *The notorious Allen Dulles provided the 'source' to discredit the Protocols*

A little over a year later, however, *The Times* produced its 'the debate is over' exposé of the Protocols and condemned them as a hoax and forgery. The writer was Philip Perceval Graves who worked with T E 'Lawrence of Arabia' on the Turkish Army Manual when Graves was a captain in British Army Intelligence. His uncle, Sir Robert Windham Graves, had been a British Consul in Turkey, financial adviser to the Turkish government, and worked for British Intelligence in Cairo in the same period as his nephew. It was while Philip Perceval Graves was in Constantinople (now Istanbul), Turkey, that this former captain in British Army Intelligence 'found the evidence' to prove the Protocols were a forgery. Who put him onto it, pray? Why, only Allen Dulles, the notorious first civilian head of the CIA (Fig 54). Dulles was a Hitler and eugenics supporter and was fundamentally involved in the Rothschild-instigated Project Paperclip operation that allowed a stream of major Nazi figures, including scientists, geneticists and mind-control experts, to escape from Germany to the United States and the rest of the Americas to continue their dastardly work after the war. Josef Mengele, the 'Angel of Death', was among them – see my other books, like *The Biggest Secret*, for the detailed background. Dulles was the liar, cheat and Nazi sympathiser who 'found' the source to discredit the Protocols. How many of those who just parrot the mantra 'the Protocols were exposed as fake by *The Times*' know that? Very few, if any, because they are repeaters – not open-minded researchers. They don't want the truth, just confirmation of their own world-view and their own self-purity and self-identity.

Dulles was also massively implicated in the Rothschild-orchestrated assassination of President Kennedy in 1963 and its cover-up. He and his brother, John Foster Dulles, who married into the Rockefeller family, were legal representatives of the Rothschild bank, Kuhn, Loeb & Co. This funded the Russian Revolution, the Rockefeller, Harriman and Carnegie empires, among others, and helped to impose the Rothschild Federal Reserve on the American people. While Allen Dulles was at the CIA after World War Two, his brother was US Secretary of State. Two more obvious Rothschild placemen you could hardly imagine. Allen Dulles, a director of the Rothschild-Rockefeller Council on Foreign Relations, was apparently in Constantinople to 'develop relationships in post-Ottoman Turkey' when he discovered 'the source' that said the Protocols were a hoax and he passed him on to British intelligence asset, Graves. According to writer, Peter Grose, in his book, *Gentleman Spy: The Life of Allen Dulles*, the 'source' was a Russian émigré who refused to be identified, and negotiated a 'loan' from *The Times* on the understanding that it would not be paid back. The subsequent articles in *The Times* have been quoted ever since as proof that the Protocols were a forgery. If you even mention them, or point out how they predicted the events of the last hundred years so accurately, you are accused of being an anti-Semite claiming there is a Jewish plot to take over the world. Well, I am certainly not doing that. There is a Rothschild-Illuminati plot using the public face and covert manipulations of Zionism as one of its prime vehicles. I should point out to those self-pure advocates of the 'liberal left' that they are not called the Protocols of the Elders of All Jewish People. They are called the Protocols of the Elders of *Zion* – Rothschild Zionism.

The public, particularly Jewish people, have to be aware of this background to Rothschild Zionism, because its agenda is speeding along virtually unchallenged through lack of awareness and the fear of being dubbed 'racist'. Well, I couldn't care less what people say about me with regard to this or anything else. I want to uncover the truth, not win a popularity contest. We must refuse to be intimidated into silence over this. Martin Luther King said: '... we must straighten our backs and work for our freedom. A man can't ride you unless your back is bent.'

It is time to stand up, in every sense.

8

Selling the 'Movie'

One does not establish a dictatorship in order to safeguard a revolution;
one makes a revolution in order to establish a dictatorship
George Orwell

A crucial insight that came to me in the early years after Peru was the way the population was programmed en masse through numerous techniques of mind and emotional manipulation. There are two in particular that people must know about. I have been repeating them over and over for years and will go on doing so, because they are so important to understand.

I have called them 'Problem-Reaction-Solution' and the 'Totalitarian Tiptoe', and every day they are used to sell the bloodline fascist/communist agenda to an uninformed public. Dr Richard Day (Rothschild Zionist) was quite right when he told those Pittsburgh doctors in 1969: 'Everything has two purposes. One is the ostensible purpose which will make it acceptable to people; and second is the real purpose which would further the goals of establishing the new system …' This describes perfectly the reason for the technique that I have dubbed Problem-Reaction-Solution. This is now a term widely-used by those who can see what is going on, and that's great because to understand P-R-S is to become so much harder to manipulate. It works like this: you want to change society in ways that you know will attract enormous opposition, as with a world government, central bank, army, currency, microchipped population and a surveillance state that would make George Orwell wince. To avoid this scale of hostility, you don't reveal your plans openly. You employ Problem-Reaction-Solution. In stage one, you covertly create the problem. This could be a terrorist attack, an economic collapse, a war, a pandemic – anything appropriate to your agenda at the time. In stage two, you tell the people, through an unquestioning and pathetic mainstream media (owned by the bloodlines), the version of the problem that you want the public to believe. This could be that 19 Arab hijackers who struggled to fly a one-engined Cessna suddenly downloaded, like Trinity in *The Matrix*, the ability to fly wide-bodied passenger jets with extraordinary skill on 9/11. You don't have to worry about being challenged by the mainstream media no matter how implausible your story. They will just repeat whatever you say without question, and so will most of the public. You are now looking for a reaction from the people of fear and outrage and a demand that 'something must be done'. What the public in general doesn't understand is that the force that is covertly behind the manufactured problem is the same force offering the solutions, which just happen to advance the agenda for centralisation of power and control. It is for this reason that I describe the official version of events and the world as 'the movie'. It is a cover-story to hide what is really going on and where it is leading. The 'movie', which you see and hear on the television news, mainstream radio and in the newspapers every day, is only there to present false explanations for national and world events that obscure their true significance and motivation. Virtually every journalist, except those answering directly to the bloodlines, will have no idea of the part they are playing in this daily unfolding of Problem-Reaction-Solution. They are as ignorant as anyone, in fact often more so.

There is also another version of Problem-Reaction-Solution that I call *No*-Problem-Reaction-Solution. With this, you don't need a real problem, just the public's perception of one. This was played out most famously before the invasion of Iraq in 2003, which was ordered (on behalf of their hidden masters) by the Rothschild assets, George W Bush and Tony Blair. Both have the character flaws so essential to serving the cabal and reaping the financial rewards – they have no conscience whatsoever and could lie for the Universe. If a half-truth ever appears in a Blair speech it is a typing error. Blair's spin-doctor-in-chief at the time, the bully and liar, Alastair Campbell, is even worse. If he ever speaks a half truth he demands an internal inquiry. They were all quite aware that Saddam Hussein was no threat, and the British weapons-inspection expert, Dr David Kelly, who had wide experience of Iraq's missile capability, was murdered in the run-up to the war to remove his potential to demolish the lies that were justifying the invasion. The endless contradictions within the official story of Kelly's 'suicide' have a simple explanation: it wasn't suicide. Six doctors who say Kelly was murdered have taken legal action to demand the inquest into his death is reopened. They said they would publish a hard-hitting report which would prove that he did not commit suicide. Bush (Rothschild Zionist) and Blair (Rothschild Zionist) are guilty of mass murder for launching a war on a calculated lie. The invasion of Iraq was planned long before it was talked about in public, as my books revealed years ago and this has since been confirmed by official sources. Weapons of mass destruction' were simply a No-Problem-Reaction-Solution to justify to the public the orgy of death and destruction that followed. Tony Blair now travels around the world picking up enormous fees for irrelevant speeches and 'advice' from Rothschild assets like JPMorgan Chase. I hear he is also starting his own company, SoulsForSale Inc. Pity he hasn't got one to sell, then.

Well in excess of a million lives have been lost in Iraq as a result of the Bush-Blair lies to justify the invasion, and there is the most horrific ongoing suffering. Women in the targeted town of Fallujah are terrified of having children when they see, as a petition to the United Nations said, 'the increasing number born grotesquely deformed, with no heads, two heads, a single eye in their foreheads, scaly bodies or missing limbs.' Young children in Fallujah are now suffering with hideous cancers and leukaemia as a result of the depleted uranium used in the weapons employed by the US and British military sent in via Bush and Blair. In September 2009, Fallujah General Hospital had 170 newborn babies, 24 per cent of whom were dead within the first seven days, and a shocking 75 per cent of the dead babies were classified as deformed. Figures for 2002, before the invasion, were 530 babies born, six dead within a week, and only one deformed. Doctors have also said that even 'a significant number of babies that do survive begin to develop severe disabilities at a later stage'. When the British government has been challenged on these horrors, the professional purveyors of bollocks like Gareth Thomas MP, a minister at the Department for International Development, say there is no problem because there are no more than two or three deformed babies in Fallujah in a year. At best he is a sock puppet repeating the words of the bureaucracy; at worst he's a bloody liar. A gravedigger at one cemetery alone said he was burying four or five babies a day, most of which were deformed. Is that enough for you, Mr Blair? Make you feel like a man, does it?All this was brought about using the simple, but devastatingly effective technique of create the problem (or the illusion of one) and then offer the solution.

9/11 P-R-S

The attacks of 11th September 2001 were the most classic Problem-Reaction-Solution you could see. The Rothschild secret society networks are the controlling and coordinating force behind the US government, US military, National Security Agency (NSA), CIA, FBI, foreign security agencies – especially British Intelligence and Israel's Mossad – and the aerospace and hi-tech corporations. Through these many and various strands in the web, the bloodlines planned and executed the 9/11 atrocities. It was a problem blamed falsely on 'Arab terrorists' that led to the 'solution' – the 'war on terror', invasions of Afghanistan and Iraq, and the explosion of Orwellian laws and impositions that have advanced the global police state so rapidly since 2001. The global conspiracy would not be anywhere close to where it is today without the 'justification' of 9/11 and the 'threat of terrorism' (Fig 55). This was the very reason the bloodline networks attacked the twin towers with aircraft remotely-controlled from the ground, a technique that is child's play today as we can see with planes like America's Global Hawk. It has the wingspan of a 737 and flies all over the world without a pilot (Fig 56). You often hear on the news how remotely-controlled surveillance drones are constantly used in places like Afghanistan and Pakistan to snoop behind enemy lines or launch bombing attacks. I demolish the official story of 9/11 in my book, *Alice in Wonderland and the World Trade Center Disaster – Why the Official Story of 9/11 is a Monumental Lie*, and there is a wealth of written and video information in the 9/11 research archive at my website: **davidicke.com**. The twin towers were brought down by controlled

demolition to ensure a maximum impact on the collective human psyche, preparing it for the 'solutions' that were waiting to be unleashed. If anyone thinks none of this could happen they should look at the Operation Northwoods documents that came to light in 2001 (see *The David Icke Guide to the Global Conspiracy*). They were made public four months before 9/11 by James Bamford, a former Washington investigative producer for ABC Television, in a book called *Body of Secrets*. These official documents detail a plan in the 1960s by the Joint Chiefs of Staff at the Pentagon, headed by the chairman, Army General, Lyman L Lemnitzer, to instigate a

Figure 55: *9/11: Problem-Reaction-Solution*

campaign of terrorist attacks that would be blamed on Castro to justify an invasion of Cuba. Bamford writes:

Figure 56: *The remotely-controlled Global Hawk that can fly around the world without a pilot*

> ... the plan, which had the written approval of the Chairman and every member of the Joint Chiefs of Staff, called for innocent people to be shot on American streets; for boats carrying refugees fleeing Cuba to be sunk on the high seas; for a wave of violent terrorism to be launched in Washington DC, Miami, and elsewhere. People would be framed for bombings they did not commit; planes would be hijacked. Using phoney evidence, all of it would be blamed on Castro, thus giving Lemnitzer and his cabal the excuse, as well as the public and international backing, they needed to launch their war.

Operation Northwoods even included the use of remotely-controlled drone aircraft. This was 40 years before 9/11. One plan was to convince the public that Cuba had shot down a chartered civil airliner on a flight from the United States to Jamaica, Guatemala, Venezuela or Panama. The destination would be chosen so the route would cross Cuba. The 'real' plane (actually a CIA aircraft) would carry 'selected' passengers boarded under 'carefully prepared aliases' and take off from a civilian airport. It would be replaced in the sky south of Florida with a remotely-controlled replacement and this would then be flown over Cuba, send out a distress code and be destroyed by radio signal. The original plane would be landed at an Air Force base where the make-believe 'passengers' would be taken off. James Bamford quotes from the Northwoods documents in *Body of Secrets*:

> An aircraft at Elgin AFB would be painted and numbered as an exact duplicate for a civil registered aircraft belonging to a CIA proprietary organization in the Miami area. At a designated time the duplicate would be substituted for the actual civil aircraft and would be loaded with the selected passengers, all boarded under carefully prepared aliases. The actual registered aircraft would be converted into a drone [a remotely-controlled unmanned aircraft]. Take off times of the drone aircraft and the actual aircraft will be scheduled to allow a rendezvous south of Florida.

> From the rendezvous point, the passenger-carrying aircraft will descend to minimum altitude and go directly into an auxiliary field at Elgin AFB where arrangements will have been made to evacuate the passengers and return the aircraft to its original status. The drone aircraft meanwhile will continue to fly the filed flight plan. When over Cuba the drone will be transmitting on the international distress frequency a 'May Day' message stating he is under attack by Cuban MiG aircraft. The transmission will be interrupted by destruction of the aircraft, which will be triggered by radio signal. This will allow ICAO [International Civil Aviation Organisation] radio stations in the Western

Hemisphere to tell the US what has happened to the aircraft instead of the US trying to 'sell' the incident.

This is the mentality of the people we are dealing with. The plan was apparently stopped by President Kennedy who refused to give his approval, but something very close to what happened on 9/11, and with subsequent 'terrorist' attacks like the London bombings of 2005, was provably planned 40 years ago. Imagine the technological potential they have now compared with then. These 'false flag' events, when governments and intelligence agencies commit terrorist acts and blame them on other people, are a common technique of the Rothschild-controlled Mossad. Most of the time they get away with it, but in 1954 a scandal broke when it was revealed that Israeli agents had planted bombs in a number of buildings in Egypt, including one belonging to the United States, and left planted evidence to implicate Arab 'terrorists'. One of the bombs went off too soon and a bomber was captured. This led to the exposure of a Mossad spy-ring operating in Egypt. Mossad agents are at work in every country of interest to the Rothschilds, and massively so in North America and Europe.

The alleged 'lead hijacker' on 9/11, Mohammed Atta, ran drugs for the CIA through Venice Municipal Airport in Florida where many of the hijackers were 'trained' (see *The David Icke Guide to the Global Conspiracy*). He and the others were set up to take the blame when they had nothing to do with it. The infamous wire transfer to Atta before 9/11 of $100,000 from the head of the Pakistan Inter-Services Intelligence agency, or ISI, was not to pay for the attacks, as claimed; it was part of the drug-running operation involving the ISI, which is little more than the Pakistan branch of the CIA. The ISI is the conduit between the poppy growers of Afghanistan and the heroin that ends up on the streets of America and the rest of the world to fund covert bloodline projects, like 9/11, and keep everything off the balance sheet. The man who had the money wired to Atta was ISI chief, Mahmoud Ahmad, who arrived in Washington a week before 9/11 to meet government and intelligence officials. While the attacks were happening, he was having breakfast with Florida senator, Bob Graham, Chairman of the Senate Intelligence Committee, along with Pakistan's ambassador to the US, Maleeha Lodhi, and other US members of the Senate and House Intelligence Committees. These included CIA agent, Representative Porter Goss. It was Graham and Goss who later co-chaired the joint House-Senate 'investigation' (it says here) which, of course, supported the official story of the 9/11 attacks.

Rothschild Fingerprints

Rothschild Zionists are all over 9/11. Larry Silverstein (Rothschild Zionist) and his partner, Frank Lowy (Rothschild Zionist), purchased a 99-year lease on the entire World Trade Center complex weeks before 9/11 and insured it for $3.55 billion. They claimed twice that amount after the attacks. Lowry joined the Zionist terror group, Haganah, in 1945 in the reign of murder and intimidation against the Palestinians, and he is a close associate of Israeli prime ministers, including Benjamin Netanyahu and Ehud Olmert. Silverstein, seen here in Figure 57, has also been a close friend of Netanyahu, Ariel Sharon (the Israeli Prime Minister at the time of 9/11), and Defence Minister, Ehud Barak, who ordered the mass murder of Palestinians in Gaza in 2008-2009. Silverstein and Lowry negotiated the World Trade Center deal with Lewis Eisenberg (Rothschild

Zionist), Chairman of the Port Authority of
New York and New Jersey, and formerly with
the Rothschild-controlled Goldman Sachs.
Silverstein and Eisenberg both held senior
positions with the United Jewish Appeal, a
billion dollar Rothschild Zionist organisation
raising money for Israel. Silverstein was not in
the World Trade Center on 11th September
2001. A scheduled meeting with officials of the
Port Authority on the 88th floor of the South
Tower was cancelled at the last minute.
Associated Press reported that he had a
'dermatologist appointment'. Silverstein also
said that another World Trade Center tower,
known as Building Seven, was 'pulled', which
is demolition parlance for a 'controlled
demolition'. Yet the official story is that the
building fell because it was so damaged.
Silverstein let the truth slip out, however, and

Figure 57: *Larry Silverstein – 'pull it'*

has been desperately trying to explain away
what he said ever since. To 'pull' something as
big as Building Seven would take at least days
of preparation, carefully placing the explosives
in exactly the right places to make the structure
fall in on itself and not topple over. How come
they managed to do this, according to
Silverstein, in next to no time after the 'pull'
order was given? It is nonsense, of course, like
the rest of the 9/11 story that the mainstream
media so unquestioningly repeats. The
explosive charges were already laid in Building
Seven well before September 11th in
preparation for it to be 'pulled'. It was part of
the long-planned 'script' unfolding that day.

The US Assistant Attorney General on 9/11
was Michael Chertoff (Rothschild Zionist), a
former student at the Fabian Society's London
School of Economics (Fig 58). His mother was
one of the first Mossad agents after the State of
Israel was bombed into being in 1948. Chertoff

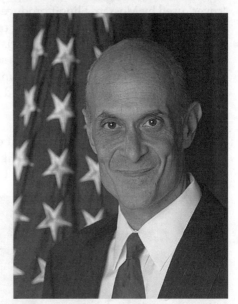

Figure 58: *Michael Chertoff – Israel's man at Homeland Security*

was the second head of the Orwellian Department of Homeland Security when it was
established after 9/11. He freed more than 100 members of an Israeli spy-ring which had
penetrated the highest echelons of American intelligence agencies and the American
military. Some of them tailed Mohammed Atta for weeks before the attacks, but when the
ring was discovered, Chertoff, an American-Israeli dual citizen, let them go. Chertoff also
released five Mossad agents who were arrested in New Jersey on September 11th after

they were seen filming and cheering the attacks. They were found to have false passports, a large amount of money, and boxcutters like those alleged to have been used (but weren't) by the 'hijackers'. Boxcutters were, however, 'found' at the locations where the 'hijackers' went. Remember, Atta was tailed by Israeli spies for weeks. The five Mossad agents used a 'transport company' called Urban Moving Systems as their front and cover story, and immediately after 9/11, its 'owner', Dominic Suter (Rothschild Zionist), was away fleet-of-foot to Israel. One of the five Mossad (Rothschild) agents told Israeli Radio that they had been sent to New York to 'document the event'. How could that be unless they knew well in advance that it was going to happen? Two Israel-based employees of a Rothschild Zionist software company called Odigo, two blocks from the World Trade Center, were warned of the attacks by computer message two hours before the first tower was hit, but the warning was not passed on. The address of the sender was handed to the FBI, but nothing happened. Why? Well, we know why. Those behind the attacks control the FBI. Odigo's base is in Israel, and its research and development department is in Herzliya, a small town north of Tel Aviv. This just happens to be the home of Mossad, which has stream of software front-companies. Jonathan Elinoff, a researcher at **Coreofcorruption.com**, also broke a story in October 2009 about German and Austrian 'art students' who were living in the North Tower at the World Trade Center before 9/11 and were arrested with the Mossad spy-ring after the attacks. 'Art student' is a known 'cover' used by Mossad. Elinoff produced documents, photographs and extensive supporting evidence. They were living on the 91st floor in May 2000, sleeping in tents, and doing construction. They had official construction passes and it is claimed that they were there to pull off an 'art stunt'. It is said that they were connected to a group called Gelatin which encourages publicity stunts to promote pop culture. Elinoff says that these students were arrested with the Mossad agents, but were later released.

Rothschild 'Neocons'

The neoconservatives, or neocons, that controlled the Bush administration were almost entirely Rothschild Zionists – people like Richard Perle, Paul Wolfowitz, Dov Zakheim, Douglas Feith, John Bolton and Lewis Libby. They produced a document exactly a year

Figure 59: *Dov Zakheim – Israel's man controlling spending at the Pentagon*

to the month before 9/11 calling for the removal of Saddam Hussein and the instigation of other wars of conquest. This 'process of transformation' was likely to be a long one, the document said, 'absent some catastrophic and catalyzing event like a new Pearl Harbor'. See *The David Icke Guide to the Global Conspiracy (and how to end it)* for the full story. One of the signatories to this document was Dov Zakheim (Rothschild Zionist), the Pentagon comptroller in charge of finances at the time of 9/11, and another American who studied at the Fabian Society's London School of Economics (Fig 59). He somehow managed to 'lose' more than three *trillion* dollars in his time at the Pentagon. The sum of one trillion became public in 2004 when Zakheim was simply allowed to resign, but three years earlier, under Zakheim's watch, Defence Secretary, Donald Rumsfeld, announced *the day before 9/11* that another $2.3 trillion could not be accounted for. September 10th was the day that anything announced was going to be lost in the wake of the attacks the following day. Good timing, Don. Pure coincidence, of course. You would have thought that Zakheim's career would be over after 'losing' three trillion dollars, but, no. After all, he was only doing what he was told to do. He left the Pentagon to join Booz Allen Hamilton, one of the world's biggest consulting firms, which works closely with the Defense Advanced Research Projects Agency (DARPA), the research arm of the Department of Defense. This is an extremely sinister organisation and this will not be the last time it is mentioned in this book. Another Booz Allen Hamilton 'client' was Blessed Relief, a charity that has been linked with Osama bin Laden. In other words, linked with the CIA because Bin Laden was their guy. Zakheim is an ordained rabbi, another Israeli/American citizen, who supplied Israel with an array of F-16 and F-15 fighter planes at a fraction of their value by classifying them 'military surplus'. This is how Israel came to have the biggest fleet of F-16s outside of America. Zakheim's father was an operative with Betar, part of the Rothschild Zionist terrorist network that bombed Israel into existence. Anyone have any idea who Zakheim would have been really working for as head of Pentagon finances from 2001 to 2004? Zakheim was also a former CEO to a company that makes the technology for remotely-controlled aircraft.

The head of the CIA during 9/11 was George Tenet (Rothschild Zionist), who was given the highest honour awarded by the Rothschilds' Anti-Defamation League. When Boy Bush and Dick Cheney were at last pressured into announcing an 'investigation' into 9/11, they said it would be headed by Henry Kissinger (Rothschild Zionist), one of the prime Illuminati agents of the last 50 years. Kissinger stepped down amid the furore that followed, but the final report of the '9/11 Commission', which agreed the official story was true, was written by Philip Zelikow (Rothschild Zionist). These are only a few 'headlines', just a glimpse of the connections, and the extent of the maze is extraordinary, as I show in other books like *Alice in Wonderland and the World Trade Center Disaster* and *The David Icke Guide to the Global Conspiracy (and how to end it)*. Where is the mainstream media? Either silent, or ridiculing and condemning those who challenge the official story which 'professional journalists' don't have the intelligence or the guts to do. The former President of Italy, Francesco Cossiga, said publicly in 2009 that the 9/11 attacks were orchestrated by Mossad in league with the CIA. Cossiga, who was the Italian President from 1985 to 1992, said it was common knowledge among the intelligence services in America and Europe that the 'disastrous attacks' were 'planned and realised by Mossad with the aid of the Zionist world in order to put under accusation the Arabic countries, and in order to induce the western powers to take part in Iraq [and] Afghanistan'. He certainly knows how the 'game' is played. Cossiga helped to create Operation Gladio which was behind terrorist bombings in Europe between the 1960s and 1980s. Its role was to engineer terrorist attacks and have them blamed on people and groups the Rothschild cabal wanted to demonise. As I have already said, Mossad is the world leader in this technique. The Gladio agent, Vincenzo Vinciguerra, said in sworn testimony in 2001:

You had to attack civilians, the people, women, children, innocent people, unknown people far removed from any political game. The reason was quite simple: to force the public to turn to the state to ask for greater security.

That is precisely what 9/11 was about. On Christmas Day, 2009, there was another 'terrorist attack' on an American airliner and yet again it was an obvious set up. The official story was that a Nigerian man, 23-year-old Umar Farouk Abdulmutallab, had tried to blow up a Northwest Airlines flight landing in Detroit with a device in his underpants. He became known as the 'crotch bomber', as opposed to the 'shoe bomber' etc., etc. The guy burned himself, but not much else and was overpowered by passengers and crew, we are told. Gordon Duff, a military analyst and counterinsurgency specialist, said of the 'attempt to blow up a plane': 'His explosives couldn't have blown up his own seat. Even if full power, it wouldn't have worked.' It was all a set up. The 'problem' was immediately followed by the solution – even more invasive 'security checks' with the ludicrous British government announcing the introduction of full-body scanners that can see through clothing to the naked body. The technology already existed and was being used in 'trials'. They needed an excuse to introduce it as the norm and, right on cue, a Nigerian chap sets fire to his knickers. It also gave them the chance to target the strategically-placed Yemen, where the 'bomber' was alleged to have been 'trained' by 'al-Qaeda'. Michael Chertoff (Rothschild Zionist), the second head of Homeland Security after 9/11, immediately called for the body scanners to be used at all American airports. It just so happens that his 'security and risk-management' company, the Chertoff Group, has a client that manufactures body-imaging screening machines. That is the Illuminati way. Advance the agenda of global control, but always make money while you are doing so. A big part of the scanner agenda is to literally strip people of their dignity and self-respect. The document I have called 'Confessions of a Satanist' in Appendix II describes how they use 'debasement of their victims as a ritual of power to themselves and their Deities.' The scanners will fry every passenger with radiation and frequent fliers are going to suffer serious health effects, including sterilisation. Depending on the security arrangements at each airport, it is also possible that some passengers will be radiated several times a day on trips that involve changing planes. The plan is to use mobile scanners on the streets, too, and Dutch police have announced that they are developing a mobile scanner that will 'see through people's clothing and look for concealed weapons'. The Transport Security Administration (TSA) in the United States lied to media and public when it said that the 'digital strip search' scanners could not save, store or transmit the images they take. Documents uncovered by the Electronic Privacy Information Center have revealed that they can do all of those things. TSA specification documents, released under the Freedom of Information Act, confirm that all full-body scanners purchased by the TSA must have the ability to both save and transmit their images. You cannot believe a word the State and its minions say. It is just lie after lie after lie. Funny, I was waiting in a long queue for security at Heathrow Airport a few months earlier as people had to remove their shoes (shoe bomber) and their belts (has there been a belt-bomber?), and I joked with a couple of fellow passengers that if anyone ever carried a device in their underpants we would be in trouble. Then it happened. If there is ever a stick-it-up-your-arse bomber I am not flying any more.

It turns out that the 'crotch bomber's' father, Alhaji Uma Mutallab, is a former chairman of First Bank and Nigeria's former Federal Commissioner for Economic Development. He is one of the richest men in Africa with connections to the International Monetary Fund (IMF) and the World Bank, both Rothschild creations. Nigeria is a corrupt and vicious dictatorship where more than half the population live on less than a dollar a day and to make the money that Mutallab has done you need to be seriously involved with the state corruption machine that has very close connections with the Israeli/Rothschild 'intelligence agency', Mossad, which has a major presence in Nigeria. Mutallab also ran the national arms industry in partnership with Israel, and especially Mossad, with whom he is reported to have been in daily contact. He went to the United States Embassy a few weeks before his son's pants caught fire to warn officials that his boy was a potential terrorist, the official story goes, and it is said that he also told the CIA. No action was taken that would have prevented his son getting on the Northwest plane because that is what they wanted him to do. Umar Farouk Abdulmutallab boarded the flight at Amsterdam's Schiphol Airport where the security is run by an Israeli (Mossad) security company called ICTS. Its senior management are 'former' Israeli security officials. The Israeli daily, *Haaretz*, questioned how Abdulmutallab could have been allowed on the aircraft by ICTS security when there was more than enough evidence and circumstance to suspect him. Well, how can I put it? ICTS has a rather 'unlucky' record when it comes to terrorism on various means of transport.

This is the same company that operated at the airports involved in 9/11 (when no relevant CCTV footage was available) and the one that handled security for the London Underground and buses at the time of the London bombings on tube trains and a bus in 2005, the so-called '7/7' attacks (when CCTV cameras were 'not working'). ICTS was involved in security at the Paris Charles De Gaulle Airport when the 'shoe bomber', Richard Reid, boarded his flight and the company also works with the Nigerian government. Israel had identified Reid as a 'terrorist suspect' some time before the 'shoe bomb' flight, but it did not tell British, American, or any other security agency about its concerns, and then an Israeli security company lets him board the US-bound plane in Paris. Claudette Lewis, Reid's aunt who raised him in south London, was quoted as saying that she believed he had been 'brainwashed'. American researcher, Wayne Madsen, who worked with the US National Security Agency (NSA), said that his sources had confirmed that the CIA, Mossad, and India's Research and Analysis Wing (RAW) orchestrated the 'crotch bomber' operation. Madsen says that the same combination was behind the 'terrorist attacks' in Mumbai, India, in 2008 and the assassination of former Pakistani Prime Minister Benazir Bhutto, which also involved former intelligence agents with the Afghan KHAD agency. Michigan attorney Kurt Haskell and his wife, Lori Haskell, also an attorney, told the American media that they saw a 'well-dressed Indian man' arrange for 'crotch bomber' Umar Farouk Abdulmutallab to board the Northwest flight without a passport at the check-in desk at Schiphol. Haskell told *CBS News*:

> Only the Indian man spoke, and what he said was, this man needs to board the plane, and he doesn't have a passport. And the ticket agent then responded saying you need a passport to board the plane, and the Indian man then said he's from Sudan. We do this all the time.

Kurt Haskell also said that after the passengers were taken from the plane in America, another Indian man on the flight, who he calls the 'man in orange', was taken for interrogation and later led away in handcuffs. Haskell said that an FBI agent came over to the other passengers and told them: 'You all are being moved to another area because this area is not safe. I am sure many of you saw what just happened (referring to the man in orange) and are smart enough to read between the lines and figure it out.' The authorities publicly denied that any other passenger had been arrested, but when faced with other witnesses confirming what happened they said: 'Er, oh yes, there was someone arrested, but he was on another flight.' The Northwest passengers were kept together throughout, well away from anyone else, and so the statement is a bare-faced lie. Passengers also reported that a man on the plane was filming Abdulmutallab with his camcorder during the flight and when the 'bomber' tried to activate the device the man went on calmly recording. The whole story has all the usual elements of a false flag operation, a Problem-Reaction-Solution. It certainly gives new meaning to the phrase 'liar, liar, pants on fire'.

World War P-R-S

The two world wars were Problem-Reaction-Solutions to transform the face of global society and centralise power like never before through Rothschild-created institutions like the United Nations, International Monetary Fund (IMF), World Bank and the European 'free trade' area that became the European Union. Nothing changes a society more comprehensively and permanently than a war, and that is the main reason why we have so many of them. The bloodlines and their agents installed Hitler and funded the Nazis to power, and it explains how Germany was able to go so quickly from economic catastrophe during the Weimar Republic after the First World War, with inflation running at thousands of per cent, to an economy and a military that could take on Europe. Prescott Bush, the grandfather of President Boy Bush, worked for the (Rothschild-controlled) Harriman business empire that funnelled vast sums to the Nazis. This was done through a company run by Prescott Bush called the Union Banking Corporation (UBC), which interfaced with the steel and banking empire of acknowledged Hitler-funder, Fritz Thyssen. It was Thyssen's factories that built the Nazi war machine, and he was funded by the Union Banking Corporation of Harriman/Bush. The UBC was eventually closed down in America for trading with the enemy, but the major Rothschild Zionist organisations in the United States, which constantly cry 'anti-Semite' and 'Nazi-collaborator', stay deathly silent about the support given to Hitler by bloodline families like the Rockefellers, Bushes and Harrimans. This is perfectly understandable given that these 'Nazi-hunting' organisations are controlled by the Rothschilds, as are the Rockefellers, Bushes, Harrimans, and so on. I have been writing about the Bush family's Nazi connection since the mid-1990s, and in 2001 the facts were also highlighted by John Loftus, president of the Florida Holocaust Museum. Loftus, a former prosecutor in the Justice Department's Nazi War Crimes Unit, said that leading Nazi industrialists secretly owned the 'Harriman/Bush' UBC operation (controlled by the Rothschilds) and they were moving money into the UBC through a second bank in Holland even after the United States declared war on Germany. The bank was liquidated in 1951, Loftus said, and President Bush's grandfather, Prescott Bush, and great-grandfather, Herbert Walker, received $1.5 million as part of that dissolution. Herbert Walker is where the 'H W' comes from in Father Bush's name. Loftus said he had a file of paperwork linking the bank and Prescott Bush to Nazi money. 'That's where the Bush family fortune came from: It came from the Third Reich,' Loftus said in a speech during the Sarasota Reading Festival in 2001.

Loftus also said that the Rockefeller family had Nazi ties, something else I have been highlighting since the mid-1990s. The Rothschild-controlled Rockefeller family funded the work of Ernst Rudin, Hitler's foremost 'racial hygienist', at Germany's Kaiser Wilhelm Institute for Eugenics, Anthropology and Human Heredity. Other Nazi doctors conducted incredibly cruel and vicious experiments on live human subjects and at the centre of it was the 'Angel-of-Death', Josef Mengele, who would later perform unspeakable genetic and mind-control experiments on concentration camp victims (Fig 60). Writer and researcher, Anton Chaitkin, says that body parts 'were delivered to [Josef] Mengele, [Otmar] Verschuer and the other Rockefeller-linked contingent at the Wilhelm Institute'. The Rothschilds, Rockefellers and Harrimans were behind the race purity eugenics movement. The bloodlines see themselves as the master race while everyone else is merely cattle. See ... *And The Truth Shall Set You Free* for the background to the eugenics movement. It was the Rockefeller connection, among others, that allowed Josef Mengele to escape to South America and the United States after the war, where he worked in government/military mind-control and

Figure 60: *'Angel-of-Death', Josef Mengele, who escaped from Germany thanks to the Rothschild-Rockefeller networks*

Figure 61: *Soldiers think they are serving their country, but they have very different masters behind the scenes*

genetic programmes under the name 'Dr Green'. The Rothschilds have been engineering wars for hundreds of years to transform countries and global society in line with their agenda. While the always-expendable fodder-troops have believed they were serving their country, and most still do, they have been serving the interests of the Rothschild/Rockefeller corporations that seek to destroy their country (Fig 61). This was brilliantly and courageously exposed from long and personal experience by US general, Smedley Butler, in his 1935 book, *War is a Racket*. He wrote:

I spent 33 years and four months in active military service and during that period I spent most of my time as a high class muscle man for Big Business, for Wall Street and the bankers. In short, I was a racketeer, a gangster for capitalism [cartelism]. I helped make Mexico and especially Tampico safe for American oil interests in 1914. I helped make Haiti and Cuba a decent place for the National City Bank boys to collect revenues in. I helped in the raping of half a dozen Central American republics for the benefit of Wall Street.

I helped purify Nicaragua for the International Banking House of Brown Brothers in 1902-1912. I brought light to the Dominican Republic for the American sugar interests in 1916. I helped make Honduras right for the American fruit companies in 1903. In China in 1927 I helped see to it that Standard Oil went on its way unmolested. Looking back on it, I might have given Al Capone a few hints. The best he could do was to operate his racket in three districts. I operated on three continents.

The Rothschild cabal is planning a third world war involving the United States, Europe, China and Russia to create the global problem to which they can offer a global solution – a world government and army to 'stop this ever happening again'. The financial collapse was coldly planned and then instigated in 2008 to trigger the start of such chaos and suffering that the people will eventually accept a new global financial structure based on a world central bank and a single electronic currency. 'It's terrible, oh what a mess, what suffering, but we can save you if you let us do whatever we want.'

Figure 62: *Two 'parties', but one master. The Republican 'neocons' and the Democrat 'democons' are controlled by the same force – the Illuminati, symbolised by Neil Hague as the bearded man. I have put Henry Kissinger in the democons because he is an advisor to Obama, but he moves between the two depending who is in office*

Presidential P-R-S

We have witnessed a most blatant example of Problem-Reaction-Solution with the seamless replacement of President George W Bush with the yet-to-prove-he-qualifies-to-be-President, Barack Obama. Bush was the most obvious of puppets and spent much of his time either on vacation at his ranch or watching the sports on TV with a bottle of Jack Daniels for company. He just signed what he was told to sign and said, when he could manage it, the words he was given to say. The bloodlines use three types of people for public office: (1) Those who know the big agenda and support it (very few); (2) Useful idiots and self-obsessed wannabes who desire status and power and will do anything to get it (these are the majority, which is why there are so many arrogant incompetents in official positions); (3) Those who have dark secrets, often sexual, that the bloodlines can reveal at any time unless they do whatever they are told to do without question (far, far, more than most people realise). George W Bush was partly all three with the emphasis, of course, on number two. The Republican and Democratic parties, and their equivalents around the world, are

owned by Illuminati
bloodlines through the
'transnational corporation'
structure of the secret
society web. During the
Bush years, the Republican
administration was
notoriously controlled by
the so-called 'neocon' or
neo-conservative network,
as I have already
mentioned. This was based
around 'think tanks' like
the Project for the New
American Century and the
American Enterprise
Institute which, together
with others, orchestrated

Figure 63: *Zbigniew Brzezinski, co-founder of the Trilateral Commission and mentor to Obama*

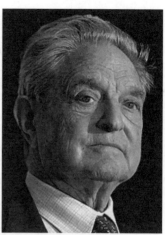

Figure 64: *George Soros, billionaire Rothschild frontman and funder of Obama*

the invasion of Afghanistan and Iraq. The neocons are the bloodlines' operatives with the task of controlling the Republican Party. There is a Democrat version of the neocons that involves another maze of people, with their 'think tanks' and trusts. I call these the 'democons'. The Rothschild Illuminati networks control both the neocons and the democons and run the government no matter who 'wins' an election (Fig 62). The 'con' doesn't really refer to 'conservative', but rather literally to 'con', a word the dictionary defines perfectly as: '… relating to, or involving, a swindle or fraud'. The democons notably include the Trilateral Commission co-founder, Zbigniew Brzezinski (Rothschild Zionist, no matter how he may deny it), and the multi-billionaire financier, George Soros (Rothschild Zionist). These two characters just happen to be mentor and funder to Barack Obama, a bloodline frontman to his fingertips (Figs 63 and 64). The Center for American Progress, a key democon 'think tank', has been funded by Soros. The Polish-born Brzezinski will claim that he is not a Rothschild Zionist; but he is. There is no chance that he would be a co-founder of the Rothschild's Trilateral Commission with David Rockefeller if he were not. George Soros, real name, George Schwartz, is an utterly ruthless man who helped to confiscate the possessions of his fellow Jews in Nazi-occupied Hungary while posing as a non-Jew. His views are straight from the song-sheet of the bloodline families. This is part of an article about him in the *Wall Street Journal* that included his 'solutions' to global economic problems:

And what remedies did Mr. Soros suggest? As a first step, the creation of an international central bank; in the long run, nothing less than a transformation of how the world itself is governed. 'To stabilize and regulate a truly global economy,' he wrote, 'we need some global system of political decision-making.' Though it was neither 'feasible nor desirable' to 'abolish the existence of states,' Mr. Soros conceded, nevertheless 'the sovereignty of states must be subordinated to international law and international institutions.'

Brzezinski admitted in an interview with the French news magazine, *Le Nouvel Observateur*, that it was he, as National Security Advisor to President Carter, who ordered the funding and training of what he would call today 'terrorists' in Afghanistan. He wanted them to oppose the Soviet-controlled government in the capital, Kabul, in the late 1970s. The idea, he said, was to entice the Soviet Union to invade Afghanistan to protect the Kabul regime and give the rival superpower 'their Vietnam'. The plan worked at the cost of a million Afghan lives during the Soviet occupation from 1979 to 1989, a consequence that troubles Brzezinski not at all. His Afghan 'freedom fighters' would become known as the 'Mujahideen', and later the Taliban and what is claimed to be 'Al-Qaeda'. This is the mentality of Brzezinski, a major player behind 'anti-war' (yeah, right) Barack Obama. The frontman for the resistance to the Soviet occupation of Afghanistan was Osama bin Laden, the stooge of the CIA and the Saudi 'royal' family, and the CIA database of Mujahideen personnel is the origin of the name 'Al-Qaeda'. It literally means 'the base' or 'database', as former British Foreign Secretary, Robin Cook, confirmed a month before he died from a sudden heart attack. It was common knowledge that President Carter would do nothing involving foreign policy without the okay from his security advisor, Brzezinski, the co-founder of the Trilateral Commission which chose Carter for president. It is one of many great ironies of the Obama presidency that he is ordering massive troop reinforcements for Afghanistan to fight the Taliban terrorists who were initially armed, trained and organised by Brzezinski, a mentor of Obama. As Morpheus says in *The Matrix*: 'Fate, it seems, is not without a sense of irony.' But then, in Brzezinski's case, it is not 'fate'. It is cold-blooded calculation.

The Bush years were designed to create catastrophic problems for the United States, and therefore the world, and Obama was being prepared to appear as the 'Messiah' who would offer the 'solutions'. The inside job that was 9/11 led to the long-planned invasions of Afghanistan and Iraq and stretched American resources to the limit, both financially and militarily. Throughout the Reagan, Father Bush, Clinton and Boy Bush years, the checks and balances on the financial system were constantly removed until it became a free-for-all so grotesque that it made a pig trough look like a royal banquet. The man directing and fuelling all this was the bloodline asset, Alan Greenspan, a Rothschild Zionist and member of the Bilderberg Group, Council on Foreign Relations, and Trilateral Commission. Predictably, Rothschild Zionists are invariably members of these Round Table satellite groups that the Rothschilds have established. Greenspan was Chairman of the Federal Reserve, the privately-owned 'United States central bank' that most Americans believe is owned by the government. It is not. It is a cabal of private banks created and controlled by Rothschilds (see … *And The Truth Shall Set You Free*) and led by the Federal Reserve Bank of New York. These are some of the major Rothschild banks, according to researchers in October 2009, that own the Federal Reserve: Bank of America; JPMorgan Chase; Wells Fargo and Wachovia; Citibank; PNC Bank; Bank of New York Mellon; US Bank; Suntrust BK; HSBC Bank; Goldman Sachs.

The Rothschild White House (and Treasury, Congress, Senate …)

Alan Greenspan was head of the 'Fed' for nearly 20 years from the end of Reagan through to most of Boy George's time as president. He left just before the 'house' he had been purposely undermining for nearly two decades collapsed on cue in the last weeks of the Bush administration (Fig 65). The banks were drowning in debt, allegedly through bizarrely-bad investments in pursuit of maximum profit, but it was more than that at the highest levels of the banking system where the Rothschilds lurk largely unseen. It wasn't greed by the banks that caused the collapse – it was greed that was *exploited* to cause the collapse. Greed-obsessed bankers, hedge fund managers and stockmarket gamblers were just more violins being plucked to manipulate an outcome. Greenspan was replaced as head of the Fed by Ben Bernanke (Rothschild Zionist), who would now advise on 'solutions' to the problems his friend and master had created. With Bush leaving the White House in January 2009, stage one of the presidential P-R-S was complete, and stage two was about to begin. Enter Barack Obama, the Great One, amid public outrage and fear at the implications of the banking collapse. A major bank, Lehman Brothers, was allowed to fold while others were protected because, in part, they needed at least one big name to go under to maximise public panic. Obama's job, for which he had been prepared since at least the 1980s, was, and is, to serve the interests of the Rothschilds and their Wall Street bankers by introducing the 'solutions' to the problems they have callously created. He has been surrounded by

Figure 65: *Alan Greenspan (Rothschild Zionist) removed the checks and balances that allowed the bankers and financial opportunists to run riot and collapse the global economy*

Figure 66: *Rahm Emanuel, the son of a Rothschild Zionist terror group operative, is the real power in the White House*

Rothschild Zionists, just as Bush was, and these include his White House Chief of Staff, Senior White House advisor, and virtually his entire 'economic team'.

Obama's Senior Advisor is David Axelrod and his Chief of Staff, and Svengali, is Rahm Emanuel (Fig 66). Both are super-Rothschild Zionists. Emanuel has served in the Israeli army and his father was an operative with the Rothschild terrorist group, Irgun. This was behind the bombing of the King David Hotel in Jerusalem in 1946 that killed 91 people. Rahm Emanuel also worked closely Robert E Rubin (Rothschild Zionist) during the Clinton years to impose the North American Free Trade Agreement (NAFTA), which was designed from the start to be a stepping-stone to a North American Union and eventually a union of the whole of the Americas. Axelrod ran Obama's election campaigns and now oversees the content of his speeches and public remarks. There is little that Obama says that his Rothschild Zionist handlers don't tell him or give him to say. It was the same with Bush. His words were written by speechwriters like David Frum (Rothschild Zionist), who coined the term 'Axis of Evil' with reference to Iraq, Iran and North Korea – all Rothschild/Illuminati targets. The chief of staff to Obama's Vice-President Joe Biden is Ron Klain (Rothschild Zionist), former chief of staff to the global warming liar, Al Gore (Rothschild Zionist). You get the picture.

Obama did as he was told and appointed Dennis Ross (Rothschild Zionist) to head US policy for Iran and the Persian Gulf. Ross has served Rothschild Zionist interests in successive American administrations. There will not be a cigarette paper behind the scenes between Obama and that trio of tyranny: Netanyahu, Lieberman and Barak, who are the prime minister, foreign minister and defence minister of Israel respectively. They are all Rothschild stooges, or they wouldn't be in those positions; and coordinating events in the background will be Henry Kissinger (Rothschild Zionist), an Obama 'adviser' and one of the Rothschilds' most active agents over five decades. Add to all this Obama's list of 'czars' appointed as specialists in different areas. They include Cass Sunstein (Rothschild Zionist), Director of the Office of Regulatory Affairs and a friend of Obama's at Harvard, who has said that the Internet is a 'threat to democracy'; Kenneth Feinberg (Rothschild Zionist), appointed by Obama to 'regulate the pay' of more than 175 US corporate executives and the man who worked with Bush to stop lawsuits against the US government by families who lost loved ones on 9/11; Daniel Fried (Rothschild Zionist), the 'Guantanamo closure czar' and Assistant Secretary of State for European and Eurasian Affairs; Alan Bersin (Rothschild Zionist), Director of Obama's Special Representative for Border Affairs within the Department of Homeland Security; Carol Browner (Rothschild Zionist), Obama's Energy Coordinator with special attention on 'climate change'; Todd Stern (Rothschild Zionist), 'Envoy for Climate Change'; Steven Rattner (Rothschild Zionist), Director of the Presidential Task Force on the auto industry and former executive with Lehman Brothers, Morgan Stanley, and Lazard Freres; and Ron Bloom (Rothschild Zionist), Senior Counsellor for car and other manufacturing policy, and former advisor to Treasury Secretary, Timothy Geithner (Rothschild Zionist). The American auto industry is a target of the Rothschild Zionists, as Dr Richard Day (Rothschild Zionist) revealed in that speech in 1969. The idea is not to save it, or to expand it, but to destroy it. There is an extraordinary ratio of Rothschild Zionists to positions of power when you think that the Jewish people make up no more than two per cent of the American population, and some of those won't be Zionists. Jewish people, again far from all of them Zionists, are just 0.2 per cent of the world population. This makes the ratio of Rothschild Zionists to positions of power and influence absolutely fantastic.

President Obamabush

Alan Greenspan (Rothschild Zionist) orchestrated the economic collapse in league with many other people over the decades of constant de-regulation of financial activity (Fig 67). His cohorts included Tim Geithner (Rothschild Zionist), President of the Federal Reserve Bank of New York; Robert E Rubin (Rothschild Zionist); and Larry Summers (Rothschild Zionist). Rubin, another student at the Fabian Society's London School of Economics, and Summers, were both Treasury

Figure 67: *The United States economy is being systematically destroyed*

Secretaries to Bill Clinton when Greenspan was at the Fed. After 'Mr Change' took office to 'solve the crisis', who did he appoint to head his 'economic team'? Tim Geithner and Larry Summers – Rothschild lackeys and the very people who helped to trigger the banking collapse and the deep recession that followed. Geithner was appointed Treasury Secretary, and Summers was made Chairman of the White House Economic Council. Summers was once Chief Economist at the World Bank, and he signed a memo in 1991 advising the bank to dump toxic waste in poor countries because the costs of the ensuing ill-health and death would be lower. Obama appointed Peter Richard Orszag (Rothschild Zionist) as his Budget Director, yet another former student at the Fabian Society's London School of Economics who was mentored by Robert E Rubin (Rothschild Zionist), also of the LSE. Orszag was the founder and president of the economic consultancy firm which advised the Central Bank of Iceland in the run up to the Icelandic banking crash in 2008, and he was advisor to the Russian Finance Ministry in the period when Rothschild Zionist 'oligarchs' were pillaging the nation's assets. He was also advisor to Rahm Emanuel and Bill Clinton on legislation that produced the North American Free Trade Agreement (NAFTA) that has devastated, on purpose, American manufacturing and the economy in general. These people are working to a script and Obama is just their public face. Obama (his masters) appointed Paul Adolph Volcker (Rothschild Zionist) to chair a new Economic Recovery Advisory Board. He attended, yep, here we go again, the Fabian Society's London School of Economics. Volcker was the head of the Federal Reserve before Greenspan and has been chairman of the prominent New York investment banking firm, J Rothschild, Wolfensohn & Co. The 'Rothschild' part of the name is obvious, but the 'Wolfensohn' is James Wolfensohn (Rothschild Zionist), former head of the World Bank. Other Obama appointees to his 'economic team' included a stream of people and associates of Geithner who made a fortune from the very banks and financial houses they were now bailing out. These included: Gene Sperling (Rothschild Zionist), a senior Treasury adviser and employed by the Council on Foreign Relations. He was paid $887,727 by Goldman Sachs, and $158,000 for speeches for companies that included Stanford Group, run by Sir Allen Stanford, who has since been charged with fraud; Matthew Kabaker, another adviser in the Treasury, earned $5.8 million at Blackstone, the private equity firm; and Lewis Alexander, another adviser, was chief economist to Citigroup before joining the administration and paid $2.4m in his last two years.

When the banking crisis began in the final weeks of the Bush presidency, his Treasury Secretary, Henry 'Hank' Paulson (Rothschild Zionist), former CEO of the Rothschild-controlled Goldman Sachs, handed billions to the banking system that he represents – the very banking system that had caused the crisis. Let it not be said, however, that Obama didn't bring a change of policy. Bush only hosed down the banks and financial system with hundreds of billions of dollars in borrowed money; Obama, Geithner and Summers made it trillions (Fig 68 overleaf). Anyone tell these two speeches apart?

George Bush, September 2008:
The government's top economic experts warn that, without immediate action by Congress, America could slip into a financial panic and a distressing scenario would unfold. More banks could fail, including some in your community. The stock market would drop even more, which would reduce the value of your retirement account. The

Figure 68: *Bush and Obama handed trillions to the banks and 'stimulus packages' and no-one seems to know where most of it went and what it was used for*

value of your home could plummet. Foreclosures would rise dramatically.

And if you own a business or a farm, you would find it harder and more expensive to get credit. More businesses would close their doors, and millions of Americans could lose their jobs.

Barrack Obama, February 2009:
Economists from across the spectrum have warned that if we don't act immediately, millions more jobs will be lost, and national unemployment rates will approach double digits. More people will lose their homes and their health care. And our nation will sink into a crisis that, at some point, we may be unable to reverse.

It was the same script ultimately written by the same people – the Rothschilds – who control both the neocons and the democons. They had their placemen deregulate the financial system to engineer the initial crash and then had their placemen in government, like Bush, Obama, Paulson, Geithner, Summers and Orszag, shower the system with trillions of dollars of borrowed credit that the population has to 'repay'. The Rothschild-created and owned Federal Reserve refuses to say what it did with the trillions of dollars of taxpayers 'money' (credit) that it used to bail out the banking system. Chairman Bernanke (Rothschild Zionist) says that any effort by Congress to find out through an audit would be a danger to the bank's 'independence' and could trigger 'reduced economic and financial stability'. When was the last time this guy looked out the window? I wouldn't let him handle the money on a market stall. Other countries, especially the UK, took the same approach. Neither Bush and Paulson, nor Obama and Geithner, demanded any changes or guarantees from the banks in return for the taxpayer bail-out. They just gave it to them. Lawyer, Elizabeth Warren, heads the Congressional Oversight Panel that is trying to unravel what happened to the money. She says she doesn't know where the money went because the system was designed to stop people from knowing. Bush Treasury Secretary, Henry 'Hank' Paulson, the Goldman Sachs man with the public chequebook, didn't ask the banks what they were going to do with the money or put any restrictions on it, Warren says. Paulson put more than $200 billion into the financial institutions and basically said, 'Just take it.' Warren pointed out that the money was supposed to be to protect the banks from their 'toxic assets', but today 'they still have those toxic assets'. So what has it been used for? Bankers' bonuses and, wait for it, buying assets for cents on the dollar when companies failed after the economic crash caused by … the banks that got the money. Elizabeth Warren said she wants to know why the government was so tough on the auto industry when bail-out money was handed over, but not on the banks. I can help her there. The people writing the cheques are controlled by the banks, and the agenda is to destroy the American auto and other manufacturing industries.

Attempts to use the US Freedom of Information Act to find out where the money went have been blocked, and the government and Federal Reserve aren't saying. The idea is to empty the barrels of governments in terms of their ability to respond to the crisis by taking them to a point where they can borrow no more. Then they plan to crash the economy again and trigger financial catastrophe to justify the introduction of a world central bank and the further destruction of the nation state. It is no problem for the Rothschilds to orchestrate this from the background when they have their men in the White House – Emanuel and Axelrod – and control US economic policy via Geithner, Summers, Orszag and Bernanke. They also control Robert Zoellick (Rothschild Zionist), the head of the World Bank, and Dominique Strauss-Kahn (Rothschild Zionist), the head of the International Monetary Fund. As I write, the man who utterly dominates the British government is the Business Secretary, or 'Mr Slither', Peter Mandelson (Rothschild Zionist), a close associate of the Rothschild family and their agent in government. Mandelson is known, quite rightly, as the Prince of Darkness. If he's not manipulating, he gets withdrawal symptoms.

Figure 69: *The plan is to use America to destroy America*

Figure 70: *America is being systematically undermined on every front*

The 'solutions' that Obama has been installed to introduce go beyond just economics. They involve the further centralisation of power, a police state, and the destruction of what we know as 'America'. This is the 'change' that he constantly talked about, but never defined. I have been saying for many years that the plan has been to use America to destroy America, financially and militarily (Fig 69). You can't have a world government and world army dictatorship if there are superpowers with the financial and military might to say 'no' to you. The idea is to so devastate America on every level that it will be absorbed into the North American Union and eventually broken up into regions (Fig 70). A map was even revealed in the Nixon years of the United States in regional form. The 'devolved governments' of Scotland and Wales and the attempt to create regional assemblies in England are all part of the same agenda, incidentally. It is sold as 'power to the people' when the real power is going further and further away. I will go into more detail later about the game plan for the next few years.

Goldman Stinks or 'Gold in Sacks'

At the core of the engineered economic collapse, and of so much else, is the 'investment bank', Goldman Sachs. It is a Rothschild-front, officially founded by the Rothschild Zionist, Marcus Goldman, in 1869 after he emigrated from the Illuminati stronghold of Bavaria in the Rothschild fiefdom of Germany. He was one of many Rothschild Zionists who went to America from Germany in the 19th and 20th centuries to establish major banks, companies and organisations, including B'nai 'B'rith. The 'Sachs' part of the Goldman operation came with the arrival of his son-in-law, Samuel Sachs (Rothschild Zionist), a German-American, whose parents came from Bavaria. Sachs had a long-time friend in Philip Lehman of the Lehman Brothers banking operation. The Lehman family arrived in America, yet again from Bavaria in the 19th century. Bavaria was also the home of the Rothschild-created Bavarian Illuminati, founded in 1776, and officially headed by Adam Weishaupt (Rothschild Zionist). The Bavarian Illuminati was involved in the manipulation of wars, revolutions and other society-changing events, including the French Revolution, and was extremely active in the United States. Rothschild-controlled Goldman Sachs is a monster dictating government policy to suit its own demands. Its main technique is to ensure that its people are appointed to the major financial posts in government. *Time* magazine described Goldman Sachs as 'the single largest supplier of financial talent to the government' and never more blatantly than in the banking bail-out. It also made the biggest single private campaign donation to Barack Obama.

Goldman Sachs, headed by Lloyd Blankfein (Rothschild Zionist), received $12.9 billion of borrowed taxpayers' money to prevent its collapse and benefited enormously from the initial $85 billion bail-out of the insurance giant, AIG, which could have triggered potentially fatal losses for Goldman had it gone under. AIG would later be given a total of more than $182 billion to keep it afloat, much to the delight of its long-time chairman, Maurice Greenberg (Rothschild Zionist), who resigned in 2005 over allegations of fraudulent business practice, securities fraud, common law fraud, and other violations of insurance and securities laws. Surely not? Greenberg is a close friend of Rothschild/Rockefeller agent, Henry Kissinger, who he appointed to chair AIG's advisory board, and AIG was also a client of the notorious Kissinger Associates. Greenberg is Honorary Vice-Chairman and Director of the Rothschild Council on Foreign Relations and a member of the Rothschild Trilateral Commission. Greenberg is a former chairman, and currently trustee, of the Asia Society; Trustee Emeritus of the Rockefeller University; and an honorary Trustee of the Museum of Modern Art. All these institutions were established by the Rockefeller family. Er, I wonder how AIG managed to get so much bail-out money? Must have been luck, I guess. The Rockefellers, and their 'bosses', the Rothschilds, are both fundamentally connected to Goldman Sachs and they dictated policy to the Bush administration and do so now to Obama.

Emails released in early 2010 revealed that two years earlier the Federal Reserve Bank of New York, then headed by soon-to-be Treasury Secretary, Timothy Geithner (Rothschild Zionist), told AIG to delete the details from the public record of payments it made with the bail-out money to banks that included Goldman Sachs and Societe Generale SA. At the time, other financial institutions were negotiating major discounts on insurance payments owed amid the financial collapse, but AIG paid several banks, including Goldman Sachs, the full face value on credit-default swap losses. This is estimated to have cost the taxpayer at least $13 billion more than necessary on the basis of what other institutions were paying out. Certainly Geithner's New York Fed could see the consequences of this being publicly known. E-mails obtained by Representative Darrell Issa, a member of the House Oversight and Government Reform Committee, proved that the New York Fed removed references to the payments and that AIG did the same when the Securities and Exchange Commission (SEC) filing was made public on Christmas Eve, 2008 (a great day to 'lose' a story you don't want to be highlighted). It was further revealed that the SEC had approved a request by AIG to keep documents secret that include detailed information about the tens of millions of dollars paid to Goldman Sachs and other banks with bail-out money. The SEC's Division of Corporation Finance ruled that the information will not have to be made pubic until 2018. The scale of corruption is unbelievable.

The bailouts were instigated by Boy Bush Treasury Secretary, Henry 'Hank' Paulson (Rothschild Zionist), who was chairman and CEO of Goldman Sachs before he joined the government in 2006. As one article said: 'The Secretary of the Treasury, who used to be the Goldman CEO, just spent $85 billion to buy a failing insurance giant that happened to owe his former firm a lot of money. Does that smell right to you?' No, it's crooked, because Paulson is crooked; a man spawned by a company that is based on crooked and controlled by the Rothschilds who could have invented the word. Paulson appointed former Goldman Sachs' Vice-President, Neel Kashkari, as head of the Office of Financial Stability, to decide who got the bail-out money. Kashkari, in turn, appointed Reuben Jeffery, a Managing Partner at Goldman Sachs, as Interim Chief Investment Officer. Other important players in the Treasury at this time were Dan Jester, Steve Shafran, Edward C Forst and Robert K Steel – all Goldman people. Goldman executives at the key New York Federal Reserve Bank were also involved in the bail-out discussions, including Stephen Friedman (Rothschild Zionist), the head of the board of governors. Bill Clinton's Treasury Secretary, Robert E Rubin (Rothschild Zionist), who did so much to prepare the ground for the collapse of 2008, was CEO at Goldman Sachs. Rubin, the co-chairman of the Council on Foreign Relations, was also named by Obama to his interim team. Three of Rubin's 'protégés', Timothy Geithner (Rothschild Zionist), Larry Summers (Rothschild Zionist) and Peter Orszag (Rothschild Zionist), were appointed by Obama to decide his economic policy. Goldman Sachs paid Summers $135,000 for a single day's 'appearance' in 2008. He was also paid $5.2 million by hedge fund D E Shaw in the two years before he joined the administration. Geithner, a former executive of Kissinger Associates and senior fellow with the Council on Foreign Relations, appointed Goldman Sachs lobbyist, Mark Patterson, as his chief of staff at the Treasury. Barney Frank (Rothschild Zionist), Chairman of the House Financial Services Committee, had the job (at least in theory) of questioning Treasury officials and investigating the bail-out policy. His top aide was Michael Paese, who left to become a lobbyist with Goldman Sachs. President Bush's chief of staff in this period, and the man who played a major part in the appointment of Henry Paulson as Treasury Secretary, was Joshua Brewster Bolten (Rothschild Zionist), an Executive Director for Legal and Government Affairs with Goldman Sachs in London. When AIG hit the rocks in September 2008, a new chief executive was appointed – Edward M Liddy, a former Goldman Sachs executive, who held $3 million in Goldman shares. He took the job at the request of Paulson, the Treasury Secretary and former Goldman CEO.

Marketwatch columnist, Paul Farrell, said that Goldman 'rules the world', and an article in *Rolling Stone* magazine described Goldman Sachs as 'a great vampire squid wrapped around the face of humanity'. The article rightly accused the bank of rigging every major market bubble and burst since the Great Depression, including the dot-com bubble, commodities bubble and the housing/credit bubble. The writer, Matt Taibbi, a contributing editor at *Rolling Stone*, exposed the central role that Goldman played in the crash of 2008. He said the 'big scam' was to have 'a whole bunch of crap, slap it with a triple A rating, and sell it to a whole bunch of institutional investors'. These institutions, using the money of people of modest incomes and pension funds, would then lose their investments and their clients would lose their pensions. Taibbi explains how in 2004 the then Goldman CEO, Henry Paulson, asked the Securities and Exchange Commission to relax the restrictions, if you can call them that, on Goldman's ability to lend money it didn't have:

> They felt restrained by certain rules that said they had to have one dollar for every twelve they lent out, so ... then chief Hank Paulson went to the SEC and asked them to basically end those rules, and they did it. There was no Congressional hearing, no vote or anything like that. The SEC granted Goldman and four other banks exemptions to these rules and said you can lend as much money as you want, you don't really need to have any money.

> Within two years, two of those banks went under, Bear Stearns and Lehman Brothers. This is just because they went to the government and asked for a change in the rules and they got it. This is what they do all the time and they also know that if they ever get in serious trouble they could just call up the government and ask them to give them a whole lot of taxpayer cash to bail them out and that has happened over and over again.

Taibbi said that he had never covered a story in which so many people had told him that he could not use their names for fear of retribution. He said there were people in government who were afraid to 'cross' Goldman Sachs (the Rothschilds). One Congressman had sent out a letter criticising Goldman and within an hour Richard Gephardt, the former Democratic presidential candidate, was on the phone 'acting as a Goldman Sachs lobbyist' requesting that he take back everything he wrote in the letter. 'The big threat is that if you cross Goldman Sachs you are never going to get campaign contributions again,' Taibbi said. 'And not only from them, probably anyone else in the Democratic Party.' Any Obama groupies still believe that he is acting independently and is not controlled by the system? Goldman Sachs is a tyranny and for 'Goldman Sachs', read Rothschild. When the horrific truth about Goldman Sachs and its government connections began to come out, Goldman executives claimed that the coverage included an element of 'anti-Semitism' and was 'subtly playing off the racist myth of a conspiracy of Jewish bankers controlling the world for their own benefit'. What? Nonsensical claims about anti-Semitism being used to explain why Goldman Sachs is being exposed for the criminal activity that it is? I never would have thought it. You've been caught with your fingers in the till, chaps – no racism necessary.

A Freedom of Information request by the *Associated Press* (AP) in October 2009 revealed a constant series of phone calls between Treasury Secretary and

Rothschild/Rockefeller placeman, Timothy Geithner, and the heads of Goldman Sachs, JPMorgan Chase and Citigroup, companies that all survived after September 2008 with support from the US taxpayer. The calls would happen as much as several times a day. Geithner's conversations with Lloyd Blankfein (Rothschild Zionist) at Goldman Sachs alone outnumbered his contacts with Senator Christopher Dodd, Chairman of the Senate Banking Committee. The AP report said:

> After one hectic week in May in which the US faced the looming bankruptcy of General Motors and the prospect that the government would take over the automaker, Geithner wrapped up his night with a series of phone calls.

> First he called Lloyd Blankfein, the chairman and CEO at Goldman. Then he called Jamie Dimon, the boss at JPMorgan. Obama called next, and as soon as they hung up, Geithner was back on the phone with Dimon.

> While all this was going on, Geithner got a call from Rep. Xavier Becerra, a California Democrat who serves on committees that help set tax and budget policies. Becerra left a message.

The Rothschilds control Geithner, Summers, Orszag, Volcker, Rubin, Obama, Biden, Emanuel, Axelrod, the whole lot of them. It is the same in virtually every country. The ups and downs of the world economy are 'random'? You must be bloody joking.

The Group of Thirty

Another major coordinating group in all this is the 'Group of Thirty' established by the Rockfeller Foundation in 1978 using a frontman called Geoffrey Bell who was, yet again, 'educated' (indoctrinated) at the London School of Economics (LSE). The Chairman of the Group of Thirty is Paul Adolph Volcker, former Chairman of the Federal Reserve, a student at the London School of Economics, and now Obama's Chairman of the President's Economic Recovery Advisory Board. Other Group of Thirty members include Obama's Treasury Secretary, Timothy Geithner, and Larry Summers, Director of the National Economic Council. Of course, Goldman Sachs is involved in the Group of Thirty in the form of Managing Director, Gerald Corrigan, the former President of the Federal Reserve Bank of New York, a position held by Geithner before he joined the Obama administration. Central to the unfolding plan to destroy the American economy has been to see the United States drown in a tidal wave of debt to China. The father of the Chinese-speaking Timothy Geithner is Peter F Geithner, who serves with Henry Kissinger on the board of the National Committee on US-China Relations. Another member of the Group of Thirty is Dr Zhou Xiaochuan, Governor of the People's Bank of China. Not coincidentally, Peter F Geithner worked for the Ford Foundation and oversaw the work of Ann Dunham who was funded by the Foundation to develop 'microfinance programmes' in Indonesia. Ann Dunham is the mother of Barack Obama. Another member of the Group of Thirty is Mervyn King, the placeman Governor of the Bank of England, and a former Professor of Economics at the Fabian-controlled London School of Economics. Others include top bankers and finance representatives from India, Argentina, Poland, Kuwait and the Arab world, Switzerland, Israel, Brazil,

Figure 71: *Obama's America: blank cheques for the bankers, but for people made homeless by the banks ...*

Germany, Mexico, Singapore, Japan, the International Monetary Fund, European Central Bank, and leading 'private' banks like Morgan Stanley. The Group of Thirty is a hub for coordinating the same Illuminati global policy. How apt, therefore, that it should include Jaime Caruana, the General Manager of the Rothschild-created and controlled Bank for International Settlements in Basel, Switzerland, the body that coordinates policy between national central banks on behalf of the bloodline families. This cabal has been targeting the United States economy for a long, long time and, by early 2010, the American debt had reached *$12 trillion*. China, Japan, Russia and oil countries like Saudi 'Rothschild' Arabia, are also conspiring to ditch the dollar as the 'oil' currency, a move that would devastate the dollar and speed its replacement with the 'amero' of the North American Union.

Shocking Inhumanity

While these bankers were destroying the livelihoods of billions and forcing ever more Americans into tent cities after losing their homes, the authorities in Obama's America are making their moves to criminalise homelessness (Fig 71). The extent of this was revealed in the Summer of 2009 by a report called 'Homes Not Handcuffs' by the National Law Center on Homelessness and Poverty in coordination with the National Coalition for the Homeless. Among the most commonly-used tactics to force the homeless off the streets are:

- Passing and enforcing legislation that makes it illegal to sleep, sit or store personal belongings in public spaces in cities where people are forced to live in public spaces.

- Selective enforcement against the homeless of other laws, like loitering, jaywalking, or open container laws.

- Sweeps of city areas in which the homeless are living to drive them out. This often results in the destruction of their personal property including personal documents and medication.

- Passing and enforcing laws that punish people for begging or panhandling to evict the poor and homeless out of a city or downtown area.

- Enforcement of a wide range of so-called 'quality of life' ordinances related to public activities and hygiene (public urination) when no public facilities are available to people without housing.

The report reveals that a third of the 235 cities surveyed had banned 'camping' in certain city areas and 17 per cent had banned it altogether to avoid the establishment of tent cities for the homeless. Nearly half prohibited loitering or begging in public places and nearly a quarter made begging illegal anywhere within city limits. The University of California in Los Angeles revealed that LA had been spending $6 million a year to employ extra police officers to patrol the city's Skid Row area with its substantial homeless population while, at the same time, allocating only $5.7 million for homeless services. Another $3.6 million was spent in 2007 to arrest and prosecute 24 people in the Skid Row area for 'crimes' like jaywalking that are rarely enforced in other parts of the city. The report notes that the same amount of money could have been used to house over 200 homeless people. The homeless in Los Angeles have frequently suffered from police brutality and it shows the depths of basic inhumanity that we are dealing with. Mind you, we are talking about a cabal that can slaughter multi-millions in manipulated wars without a second thought, so what are a few homeless people to them?

Figure 72: *President Fake is Illuminati trained, bought and paid for*

Figure 73: *Obama is just the latest string puppet*

President Fake

I shook my head during the Obama election campaign through 2008 when I saw even those who should know better falling for the hype (Fig 72). These were people who had accepted that political parties are assets of the same force and yet they still believed that Obama was an exception. Here was a man who was genuine and independent, they said, and a man who had somehow appeared from nowhere to beat the system. They continued to believe this nonsense even though Obama was funded by the very Wall Street bankers and Rothschild/Illuminati fronts – not least Goldman Sachs – that stood to lose if he was who he claimed to be. Yes, sounds feasible, eh? The turkeys were voting for Christmas and Thanksgiving (Fig 73). Obama was spawned from one of the most despicably-corrupt political cesspits on the planet – Chicago. If your soul is not for sale you have got no chance of prospering politically in that city, and Obama's star simply soared. This is why he has been so connected to the criminal and corrupt, including his slum landlord associate, Tony Rezko, a stalwart of Chicago's cross-party crime syndicate known as the Illinois Combine. Rezko was jailed for using his political connections to demand kickbacks from companies that wanted to do business with the state, and this is the man who has provided very large amounts of political funding, directly and indirectly, for Barack Obama – 'Mr Clean'. Obama is the kind of personality that the Rothschilds and the Illuminati target and develop to act as their front people and administrators. It is a personality type known as 'narcissistic'. This is defined as: 'excessive admiration of oneself … a psychological condition characterised by self-preoccupation, lack of empathy and unconscious deficits in self-esteem'. People like Obama and Tony Blair are wonderful examples and so are those who run the banking system. The lack of empathy of the narcissistic personality means that bankers can throw people out of their homes in an economic crash of their making and then continue to pay themselves millions in bonuses from taxpayer bail-outs. I have known people in my own life over the years who are narcissistic personalities and put themselves first, last and always. I know how selfish, self-obsessed, cold and calculating they can be while claiming to be 'love and light'. They remind me of a line in a Moody Blues song: 'All the "love" you've been giving, has all been meant for you.' They can also lie with a straight face over and over – just like Obama, Blair and their kind. To understand the narcissistic personality is to understand the people who run the system and those who parasite off others while refusing to earn a living for themselves. You can see them at work in all levels of society.

Obama's first job after leaving Columbia University was with Business International Corporation (BIC), a 'publishing and advisory' operation that was used as a cover for CIA operatives and covert operations in many countries, as confirmed by its co-founder in a 1997 *New York Times* article. Journalist, John Pilger, says that Business International was also used to infiltrate trade unions. Washington investigative journalist, Wayne Madsen, revealed in January 2010 that a veteran member of the White House Press Corps confirmed to him that the Obama administration had made it known through White House Press Secretary, Robert Gibbs, and other White House Communications officials that certain questions posed by reporters who cover the White House are definitely off-limits. Among them are questions about Obama's post-Columbia University employment with the CIA's Business International Corporation. White House reporters were warned not to ask any questions about Obama's time with BIC, his (withheld) records while he was a student at Occidental College in Los Angeles from 1979 to 1981, or his records at Columbia University in the early 1980s, a time when his mentor, Zbigniew Brzezinski, was head of the university's Institute on Communist Affairs. Wayne Madsen said he established that during Obama's time at Occidental College, when he was calling himself, Barry Soetoro, and had a passport in that name, he travelled to Pakistan which was being used by the US as a base to support of the Afghan 'mujaheddin' who were funded and trained on the say so of Zbigniew Brzezinski when he was President Carter's National Security Advisor. The man the US government chose to 'lead' the mujaheddin during the Soviet invasion of Afghanistan was Osama bin Laden. Madsen said he had also learned from 'informed sources in Kabul' that Obama has been extremely friendly, through personal correspondence on White House letterhead, with a private military company that has mujaheddin fighters from that era among its senior personnel. According to Madsen, this company is also involved in 'counter-insurgency' operations in Iraq and also Colombia, where the Obama administration is building seven new military bases. No wonder all these subjects are off limits for White House reporters. Madsen said that the White House had indicated that 'if anyone were to ask Obama about BIC or possible past CIA work, domestically or abroad, the offending reporter would see a quick pulling of the White House press credential.' This is the same Obama who said:

> My Administration is committed to creating an unprecedented level of openness in Government. We will work together to ensure the public trust and establish a system of transparency, public participation, and collaboration. Openness will strengthen our democracy and promote efficiency and effectiveness in Government.

Obama has been an insider for decades and now masquerades as a man of the people. For goodness sake, Obama even refuses to produce a birth certificate to prove he was born in the United States, an essential requirement under the Constitution to become president. He claims to have been born in Hawaii, but his grandmother, half-brother and half-sister all insist he was born in Kenya. At the time of writing he is spending a fortune to block lawsuits aimed at forcing him to produce the proof that he qualifies by birth to be president. Why, if what he says is true? Why not just show the paperwork and put an end to it? I think there is a good chance that the reason for not producing his birth certificate is to hide who his real father is. Obama is a fake and a fraud and he has long been moulded and prepared to be president by democons like Brzezinski and George Soros. *Los Angeles Times* writer, Dan Morain, said this about Obama in 2007 in an article headed 'Fresh face or old-school player?':

> Now, promoting himself as a fresh face on the national political stage, proclaiming his distance from lobbyists and the Washington culture of special interests, Sen. Barack Obama (D-Ill.) has to contend with his own history ... From Chicago to Springfield, his past is filled with decidedly old-school political tactics – a history of befriending powerful local elders, assisting benefactors and special interests, and neutralizing rivals.

For more on Obama, see the article on my website entitled 'Barack Obama: The Naked Emperor'. There is also an excellent book by the American researcher, Webster Griffin Tarpley, called *Barack H. Obama: The Unauthorized Biography*. The bloodlines sold Obama as an image and that's all he is. He has no substance and he reads his speeches, down to even short presentations and welcomes, from two teleprompter screens at either side of him. He is constantly looking left and right when he speaks as he reads the words that Rothschild agent David Axelrod and his associates have prepared for him. He rarely looks straight on where there is no script to see. Obama is so welded to the teleprompter that on St Patrick's Day in 2009 he thanked himself for inviting everyone to a reception because the Irish prime minister's script was left on the teleprompter by mistake. Obama doesn't come from the heart, but from the autocue. People say he is intelligent, but I don't agree. It doesn't mean he has substance because he reads his words better than George W Bush (hardly difficult). Have you seen him when his teleprompter stops working? You'll find examples on YouTube. They compare his 'intelligence' with Bush, but slow horses look fast when they are running past trees. Obama's colour has also been used to great effect to sell him as a new era – the first black (actually half-black) American president. On the face of it, this is a good thing after the horrors of slavery, but it is not the colour of your skin that matters, it is your state of Consciousness. Journalist, John Pilger, put it very well:

George Bush's inner circle, from the State Department to the Supreme Court, was perhaps the most multiracial in presidential history. It was 'PC' par excellence. Think Condoleezza Rice, Colin Powell. It was also the most reactionary.

Obama's very presence in the White House appears to reaffirm the 'moral nation'. He's a marketing dream. But like Calvin Klein or Benetton, he's a brand that promises something special, something exciting, almost risqué – as if he might be radical, as if he might enact change. He makes people feel good, he's a post-modern man with no political baggage ... and all that's fake.

I don't care what colour your skin may be. What matters is what's 'inside'.

Mass Mind Control

I studied military/government mind-control programmes and techniques in great detail for many years from the late-1990s, and the Obama 'phenomenon' is the most obvious mass mind-control operation you could observe. The manipulation of the words 'hope', 'change' and 'believe' were at the centre of this and so was the use of Neuro-Linguistic Programming, or NLP, which uses certain words in certain patterns to influence perception and behaviour. It is known as 'conversational hypnosis', and Obama uses it all the time. Put 'Obama NLP' into a search engine and you'll see what I mean. Politicians and government administrators are also programmed by NLP and other techniques. Obama repeated 'hope', 'change', and 'something to believe in' for an entire year in his campaigns against Hillary Clinton and John McCain. 'Hope' is like riding a carousel horse – no matter how fast you go you never get closer to the one in front. 'Hope' is always about tomorrow. The idea, however, is to persuade you to stay on the horse, despite the inevitable disappointment, in the 'hope' that things will change; but they don't, because the very system is designed to prevent it. This is the way 'hope' is employed by the dastardly and devious – take the crap we are giving you now in the 'hope' that things will get better (but we know they won't). Barack Obama is a purveyor of 'hope' for his masters who want the people to accept what they are given today in the hope that good times will follow. Do what we demand, oops, sorry, Barack demands, and in return he'll inspire you to hope that it is all leading to the Promised Land. It isn't, but, by the time you realise that, it's too late. What terrifies the bloodlines is that people will abandon hope, as a future sometime-never projection, and start to demand fairness, justice and freedom now. To avoid this nightmare, they need to keep those desires as something to aspire to, not to actually have. Thus, their man, Obama, sells 'hope' as a diversion technique, a holding position, to keep the masses from truly rebelling. We have no job, no food on the table and our home has been foreclosed, but at least we have 'hope'. Phew, thank goodness for that.

Obama's predominant mantra has been 'change'. Indeed, his money-no-object, record-breaking campaign was almost entirely based on that one word – change (Fig 74). This is a technique used by Bill Clinton and many others and it is highly effective because, at any point, the system ensures that most people are not happy with the way life is. When you don't like the status quo then 'change' can be a potent message, even if, like Obama, you don't say what it means. Remember what the Rothschild Zionist, Dr Day, said in 1969: 'People will have to get used to the idea of change, so used to change, that they'll be expecting change. Nothing will be permanent'. It was vital to Obama's success, and that of his controllers, that he never specified what his 'hope', 'change' and that other mind-control trigger-word, 'believe', were referring to in terms of policy and the way society in general will be affected. Hope for what? Change what? Believe in what? To answer those questions with specifics would have been fatal to Obama's appeal. White House Communications Director, Anita Dunn, said that the campaigns against Clinton and McCain focused on making the media report the issues that suited Obama and rarely did they communicate anything that wasn't 'absolutely controlled'. She made her remarks in a videotaped conference with the government of the Dominican Republic. The idea was to avoid Obama and senior campaign people having to speak to reporters, she said. 'A huge part of our press strategy was focused on making the media cover what Obama was actually saying as opposed to why the campaign was saying it, what the tactic

Figure 74: *Change? What change? Obama never specified what he meant by 'change' because it was just a vacuous slogan to scam the people to vote for him*

was ...' The manipulation of public opinion, in other words, was the foundation tactic of Mr Clean, Mr Genuine, er, Mr Fake.

The bloodline-owned media swoon over him most of the time and it is left to the tiny minority, like the veteran White House correspondent, Helen Thomas, to tell it like is. Thomas is 89, and has covered every presidency since JFK in the early 1960s. She told *CHSNews* that the Obama regime was seeking to manage the media like no other – more so even than Richard Nixon. She said reporters were being called the night before an Obama news conference to be told they are going to be given the chance to ask a question and then discussing with them what the question will be. It seems to the watcher as if reporters are freely asking questions of their choice when it is all stage-managed. This is done by the same 'Mr Change' who promised more openness and transparency in government. 'It's blatant,' Helen Thomas said. 'They don't give a damn if you know it or not. They ought to be hanging their heads in shame.' But they have no shame. 'What the hell do they think we are? Puppets?' Thomas continued. 'They're supposed to stay out of our business. They are our public servants. We pay them.' Ah, but that's not the way they see it. In their world, the media is not there to accurately portray events, merely to report the version that Obama and his corrupt cronies and controllers want people to believe. He's a crook and a conman who is string-pulled by

Illustration by David Dees (deesillustration.com)

Figure 75: *'The people think he's on their side ... ha, ha, ha, ha, ha, ha, ha, ha, ha ...'*

even bigger crooks and conmen, and yet so many people buy the fancy packaging with not a clue what is inside.

Hope-nosis

The plan was to make Obama the focus of everything people hoped for, believed in and wanted to change. It was crucial, therefore, for him not to specify and detail what was meant by his 'hope, 'change' and 'believe'. However, I can tell you what those words meant in the context of the Obama mind-game. They meant whatever you decided they meant or wanted them to mean. The idea was for you to project all that you stand for onto him and so he became the symbol of you and how you see the world. Specifics would have destroyed this 'I am whatever you want me to be' scenario and so you didn't get any detail – just 'hope', 'change' and 'believe'. They didn't want him only to be seen as 'the Messiah'; they also wanted him to be Abraham Lincoln, JFK, or Buddha – anyone you choose to project onto him, for he was a blank page, a blank screen and an empty suit. Obama was a make-your-own, do-it-yourself leader, a projection of your own mind. If you are still asleep, that is. If you are in any way awake, he's an open book (Fig 75). Once they secured his election, the true Obama quickly began to emerge and instead of bailing out the people (change), he bailed out the banks (business as usual). The guy is a fraud beyond words and many of 'his' policies are simply being cut and pasted from the books of his mentor, Zbigniew Brzezinski, and signed into law.

This includes his compulsory 'voluntary' work for young people (preparing them for the military draft) and his 'civilian security force', which is another layer of the Orwellian state in which the people police the people. He catches the headlines by saying he will close the abomination that is Guantanamo Bay, while refusing to end all the other sources of torture and abuse perpetrated in the name of the United States. When Obama took office in January 2009, he said that the use of 'extraordinary rendition' would be illegal under his administration. Extraordinary rendition is when the US authorities want to torture prisoners in ways that are banned by American law, and so they are simply transported to countries for 'interrogation' where torture is 'legal'. Within eight months of Obama's pledge about extraordinary rendition, his administration announced that the practice would continue. Another Obama U-turn. So, what's new? The *New York Times* quoted an administration official as saying: 'The emphasis will be on insuring that individuals will not face torture if they are sent overseas'. So why are you sending them overseas, you liar? Obama has also claimed the right to be able to hold people indefinitely without charge or trial – including Americans – if he considers them to be a 'threat'. No proof is necessary or the definition of what constitutes a 'threat'. John Pilger, a real journalist, wrote three months into Obama's presidency:

> In his first 100 days, Obama has excused torture, opposed habeas corpus, and demanded more secret government. He has kept Bush's gulag intact and at least 17,000 prisoners beyond the reach of justice. On April 24, his lawyers won an appeal that ruled

Guantanamo prisoners were not 'persons' and therefore had no right not to be tortured. His national intelligence director, Adm. Dennis Blair, says he believes torture works. One of his senior officials in Latin America is accused of covering up the torture of an American nun in Guatemala; another is a Pinochet apologist. As Daniel Ellsberg has pointed out, America experienced a military coup under Bush, whose secretary of 'defense', Robert Gates, along with the same warmaking officials, have been retained by Obama.

All over the world, America's violent assault on innocent people, directly or by agents, has been stepped up. During the recent massacre in Gaza, reports Seymour Hersh, 'the Obama team let it be known that it would not object to the planned resupply of 'smart bombs' and other high-tech ordnance that was already flowing to Israel' and being used to slaughter mostly women and children. In Pakistan, the number of civilians killed by American missiles called drones has more than doubled since Obama took office. He is the BBC's man, and CNN's man, and Murdoch's man, and Wall Street's man, and the CIA's man. The madmen did well.

Make-Believe-Man

Obama lies with the ease of a seasoned veteran. When South Carolina Congressman, Joe Wilson, shouted, 'Liar' during an Obama speech to Congress, President Jimmy 'empty shell' Carter said the remark was 'based on racism'. No, Mr Rockefeller-man Carter, it was simply the truth – no racism necessary. Obama has an image of being a 'man of the people' when he has handed trillions to the very forces that enslave the people, destroy their livelihoods and eject them from their homes. He has an image of being anti-war, a man of peace, while he sends still more troops to Afghanistan, sanctions the bombing of Pakistan as virtually his first decision in office, and supports a $1 trillion-a-year 'defence' budget to fund 760 bases in more than 130 countries, a figure that accounts for nearly half the world's military spending. He authorised more deadly bombing strikes by remotely-controlled aircraft in Afghanistan in his first year in office than George W Bush, with his trigger-happy reputation, had done in the previous three. Operators thousands of miles away watched more than 700 people, most of them civilians and children, blown apart by these attacks within Obama's first year. To them, it is just a hi-tech computer game to kill at a distance and it is sanctioned by President 'Peace' at the rate of about one murderous attack per week. Obama has an image of being against the invasion of Iraq, when he constantly supported Bush in votes on the issue and he plans to keep 50,000 troops in Iraq after the time he said he would withdraw US combat troops from the country. The combat units that will remain are being re-designated 'advisory brigades' in an effort to hide the contradiction. He has an image of being against state surveillance of the population yet it continues to advance. Major American bases and embassy complexes are being established in Iraq and Afghanistan because, as I said from the start, they have no intention of leaving. Under 'caring' Obama, the US government is spending 50 times more money on the military in Afghanistan than it is on helping the Afghan people in a land where one in four children die before their fifth birthday and 70 per cent of the population does not have access to clean water. The United Nations says it is the most dangerous place on earth to be born. But Obama doesn't care – he's the cabal's man and he does what he is told to do. The Bush regime Defense Secretary and the military hierarchy in the Pentagon all kept their jobs under

Obama to ensure a seamless transition from one Rothschild-Illuminati administration to another. Obama has sought agreement for US troops to be stationed at bases in Colombia as they further target South America and the centralised control of the whole of the Americas. I said in books many years ago that something must be planned for Colombia when Brown & Root, a subsidiary of the appalling Halliburton corporation, so closely associated with former Vice-President, Dick Cheney, began to acquire large amounts of warehouse space in the country.

Mr Fake Change told the CIA that his decision to release memos confirming torture by the Bush administration had been the 'most agonising' call of his presidency (a 'call' forced upon him, in fact, by a freedom of information lawsuit). Note that his 'most agonising call' was not bombing civilian areas of Pakistan and Afghanistan or giving multi-billions to his Wall Street backers while people are forced to move into 'tent cities' as their only shelter. It was to reveal proof to the public that the Bush administration, the CIA and the US military had employed torture on those it had imprisoned without charge or trial. That's the real Obama, the one behind the mask with the ever-smiling face. So would Obama prosecute those responsible for the torture to ensure it never happened again? Of course not. This was not a time for looking back, he said, but for looking forward. It was, in truth, an excuse for not looking at all, because he's a complete fraud selling a lie. The mainstream media is not going to expose any of this when it, like Obama, belongs to the bloodlines. I offer a golden rule for all things Obama: ignore the words and watch the actions. The words are there as essential cover for the actions – like his pledge to take on the banks. 'No, he couldn't be doing that because he said ...' Yes, he *said*. Obama is a political used-car salesman who has been installed to sell the Rothschild-Illuminati agenda to present the unfolding tyranny as 'coming together', 'change' and 'yes we can'. It's tyranny with a toothpaste smile. As a cartoon I saw said: 'The wolf found that shepherd's clothing worked even better.' Where is the anti-war movement as it was under Bush? Where is the challenge from the 'left' about human rights, surveillance and injustice that we saw under Bush? They've allowed themselves to be neutered, their balls no more, in the wake of the fantasy called Barack Obama. It's pathetic. Then, in October 2009, it was announced that Obama had been awarded the Nobel Peace Prize. It doesn't get any funnier. Yes, the cheats that gave Al Gore the Nobel Peace Prize for lying about 'global warming' gave it to Barack Obama, the man who was bombing Pakistan, vastly increasing troop numbers in Afghanistan and either continuing or expanding all the policies of George W Bush who was called a 'man of war'. You couldn't make it up? This is Obama. They always make it up. The Nobel Peace Prize, instigated by the armaments manufacturer and inventor of dynamite, Alfred Nobel, is a tool of the Control System to promote its agents of deceit by giving them an image that is the opposite of what they really are. For goodness sake, it was 'won' by the war criminal and genocidal maniac, Henry Kissinger, now an Obama 'advisor'. That's like giving an animal-protection award to the guy who runs the slaughterhouse.

Obama is the Control System's man to the core of every cell and they are desperate to sell him as a 'world statesman' that they can use to pied-piper humanity into ever greater servitude while smiling sweetly and reading the teleprompter full of other people's words.

9

Selling the Movie (2)

We read the world wrong and say that it deceives us
Rabindranath Tagore

Terrorist and extremist groups are often fronts for the real 'axis-of-evil' – British, American and Israeli military intelligence, which work together to bring mayhem to the world on behalf of the Rothschilds and the Illuminati network.

This trio of tyranny was the force behind the 'colour' revolutions in countries like Georgia and the Ukraine, and the attempted one in Iran in 2009. This is another expression of Problem-Reaction-Solution. The Rothschild-Illuminati networks are constantly seeking to manipulate countries and impose their leaders to fit the blueprint for centralised global control. Most people see events in terms of polarities. It is either/or and black/white. You are either for something or against it. Yet rarely is any situation so polarised, so clear cut, and unless we look at the shades of grey we are never going to see what is truly happening. To say protests in Iran are covertly manipulated by the United States, United Kingdom and Israel is not to say that I support the Iranian president, Mahmoud Ahmadinejad, or the 'Supreme Leader' dictatorship that really runs the country. Nor does it mean that I do not support the right of Iranian people to say what they feel about an election they believe to be rigged. But two wrongs make a double-wrong and there is another agenda going on here that the protests are used to promote. The story of the Iranian Prime Minister, Dr Mohammed Mossadegh, is an excellent example of how Problem-Reaction-Solution is used in this context and how country after country is being manipulated in the same, or similar, ways today.

Mossadegh was ousted in a coup in 1953 instigated by the CIA through what they called 'Operation Ajax'. British and American manipulation replaced Mossadegh with the vicious dictator, the Shah of Iran. This was agreed by US President, Dwight D Eisenhower, and British Prime Minister, Winston Churchill, and directed by the infamous US Secretary of State, John Foster Dulles, and his brother, Allen Dulles, head of the CIA – you know, the guy who provided the 'source' for the British intelligence officer, sorry, *Times* journalist, that the Protocols of Zion were fake. Official documents have since confirmed the background to the Iranian 'coup'. Mossadegh's crime was to insist that the people of Iran enjoyed some benefits from Iranian oil. He nationalised the oil industry that had been controlled by the British government via the Anglo-Iranian Oil Company, now British Petroleum, or BP. Mossadegh said in 1951:

Our long years of negotiations with foreign countries … have yielded no results this far. With the oil revenues we could meet our entire budget and combat poverty, disease, and backwardness among our people.

Another important consideration is that by the elimination of the power of the British company, we would also eliminate corruption and intrigue, by means of which the internal affairs of our country have been influenced. Once this tutelage has ceased, Iran will have achieved its economic and political independence.

The British and American governments determined that it would not cease, however, and so enter Kermit Roosevelt Jr, the grandson of President Theodore Roosevelt, and head of the CIA's Near East and Africa division. He worked closely with another CIA agent called Donald Wilbur, as revealed in a CIA document entitled *Clandestine Service History – Overthrow of Premier Mosaddeq of Iran – November 1952-August 1953*. The document details the way the coup against Mossadegh was engineered to bring the Shah to power, and it puts new light on the 'people's revolutions' in Georgia and the Ukraine and the protests in Iran in 2009. The CIA began a campaign of propaganda against Mossadegh within Iran and paid people to pose as Mossadegh supporters who threatened 'savage punishment' against anyone who opposed him, especially Muslim leaders. This allowed the CIA to depict Mossadegh as a tyrannical dictator and the propaganda began to stir opposition protests from religious groups. There were eventually large protests in the streets of Tehran organised by Roosevelt's Operation Ajax. Roosevelt revealed in his 1979 book, *Counter Coup: The Struggle for the Control of Iran*, how he paid people to protest for and against Mossadegh to trigger violent clashes that led to widespread violence, looting and 300 dead. Outside Tehran, tribesmen were paid to support a coup to replace Mossadegh with the Shah. Roosevelt secured control of the Iranian military with help from Norman Schwarzkopf Sr, the father of 'Stormin' Norman', who commanded the US military and their allies in the Gulf War of 1991. Father Schwarzkopf trained and organised security forces in support of the Shah which later became the horrific secret police known as the SAVAK. The Iranian military intervened to remove Mossadegh who was jailed and then lived out his life under house arrest. The Shah was placed into 'power' as a puppet of Britain and America and – surprise, surprise – he reached agreement with the oil companies to give them the great majority of Iranian oil revenues. The same combination removed the Shah for Ayatollah Khomeini in 1979. Their placemen are all expendable to the cause, and if it suits the Rothschild ambitions to have Obama assassinated to cause turmoil in the United States then they will have no qualms about doing so. Look at Kennedy.

'People Power'

They want to give the impression of spontaneous 'people's revolutions' because it hides the covert manipulation of events and the involvement of British, American and Israeli intelligence. This is what happened in Georgia in 2003 when Mikheil Saakashvili was brought to power by a 'people's revolution', or the 'Revolution of Roses', which removed President Eduard Shevardnadze. It was covertly instigated by the CIA and the billionaire financier, the Obama mentor and funder, George Soros. Saakashvili is a graduate of George Washington University in Washington DC, and Columbia

University Law School in New York. This is the university that Obama attended and where his mentor, Zbigniew Brzezinski, headed the Institute on Communist Affairs. Mikheil Saakashvili is one of many American-trained agents in government that are controlled by the network of Soros (Rothschild Zionist) and his associate, Brzezinski (Rothschild Zionist). Soros manipulates events through a complex network of foundations and organisations operating across the world in league with elite groups and agencies in the United States and Israel, including the CIA and Mossad. It was this Soros network, especially his Open Society Institute, which trained and funded Georgian students in the art of mass protest, and bankrolled the opposition TV station that mobilised the demonstrations. Zaza Gachechiladze, editor-in-chief of *The Georgian Messenger*, said: 'It's generally accepted public opinion here that Mr Soros is the person who planned Shevardnadze's overthrow.' As Manly P Hall, the 33rd Degree Freemason and 'Masonry's greatest philosopher', said:

> ... it is so difficult to determine the position of the ancient initiates ... They are the invisible powers behind the thrones of earth, and men are but marionettes, dancing while the invisible ones pull the strings. We see the dancer, but the master mind that does the work remains concealed by the cloak of silence.

It was Israeli-trained Georgian forces that carried out the attack in neighbouring South Ossetia in 2008, which brought a violent response from Russia. The Georgian Minister, Temur Yakobashvili (Rothschild Zionist), praised Israel for its role in training Georgian troops. Speaking in Hebrew, he told Israel Army Radio: 'Israel should be proud of its military, which trained Georgian soldiers'. One report also said that 1500 'advisors' from Blackwater (now 'Xe') – the infamous US 'private military/security' operation exposed for its outrageous and murderous behaviour in Iraq – were on the ground in Georgia. Massive shipments of arms and ammunition were supplied by the United States in the 18 months before the Georgian attack on the Russia-connected South Ossetia. This region of Georgia and the Ukraine were the lands of the Khazar-Sumerians, as Iraq is the land of the Sumerians. They have control of all three again now. The 'people's revolutions', such as the one in Georgia, are really coups in disguise and they take the same pattern. An election victory is claimed to be fraudulent and this is followed by public demonstrations. Invariably, they are symbolised by a colour worn by the demonstrators and this is why the colour green was at the centre of protests in Iran in 2009. The 'hero' in that colour-coded drama was Mir-Hossein Mousavi, the Iranian prime minister from 1981 to 1989, who claimed that President Ahmadinejad's election victory, officially by a landslide, was fixed. Mousavi said he had won and urged his supporters to protest. Now it may or may not have been fixed, though no evidence was produced, but events followed a very familiar pattern. President Saakashvili claimed he had won an election in Georgia, but had been denied by vote-rigging. Mass protests ensued, by those who put him in power. President Viktor Yushchenko claimed he had won an election in the Ukraine, but had been denied by vote-rigging. Protests followed that over-turned the result and led to a new election that put him in power. Researcher, Paul Craig Roberts, put it very well in a *Counterpunch* article with regard to Iran:

The claim is made that Ahmadinejad stole the election, because the outcome was declared too soon after the polls closed for all the votes to have been counted. However, Mousavi declared his victory several hours before the polls closed. This is classic CIA destabilization designed to discredit a contrary outcome. It forces an early declaration of the vote.

The longer the time interval between the pre-emptive declaration of victory and the release of the vote tally, the longer Mousavi has to create the impression that the authorities are using the time to fix the vote. It is amazing that people don't see through this trick.

As Roberts pointed out, the evidence for CIA involvement in the events in Iran is overwhelming. Their fingerprints are everywhere. Two years earlier, *ABC News* reported that the Bush administration had given secret approval for the CIA to launch a covert operation to destabilise the Iranian government. Pity old Kermit Roosevelt wasn't still around, he had the blueprint. Britain's *Daily Telegraph* reported in 2007:

Mr. Bush has signed an official document endorsing CIA plans for a propaganda and disinformation campaign intended to destabilise, and eventually topple, the theocratic rule of the mullahs.

You might also recall the story in 2008 that received quite wide publicity when investigative journalist, Seymour Hersh, wrote this in the *New Yorker*:

Late last year, Congress agreed to a request from President Bush to fund a major escalation of covert operations against Iran, according to current and former military, intelligence and congressional sources. These operations, for which the President sought up to four hundred million dollars, were described in a Presidential Finding signed by Bush, and are designed to destabilize the country's religious leadership.

The day before the 2009 Iranian election, the neoconservative extremist, Kenneth Timmerman (Rothschild Zionist), said there was talk of a 'green revolution in Tehran'. What is he, a psychic? Well, no, he doesn't have to be. Timmerman co-founded the Foundation for Democracy in Iran (FDI) in 1995 along with Joshua Muravchik (Rothschild Zionist) and the late Peter W Rodham (Rothschild Zionist). The FDI is an extremely well-funded operation used to create unrest in Iran, and one of its founders, Joshua Muravchik, wrote an article in the *Los Angeles Times* calling for Iran to be bombed. Timmerman was among the major propaganda architects of the Iraq invasion and one of his articles carried this confident headline six months before the troops went in: 'How Saddam Got Weapons of Mass Destruction: Saddam Hussein's War Machine is Being Built Systematically to Strike at the United States With New Nuclear, Biological and Chemical Weapons Designed to Kill Millions'. He was lying, as he well knew. Timmerman predicted the 'green revolution' the day before the Iranian election because he knew what was planned and his own organisation would have been seriously involved. Timmerman also wrote:

The National Endowment for Democracy has spent millions of dollars during the past decade promoting 'color' revolutions in places such as Ukraine and Serbia, training political workers in modern communications and organizational techniques.

Some of that money appears to have made it into the hands of pro-Mousavi groups, who have ties to non-governmental organizations outside Iran that the National Endowment for Democracy funds.

The National Endowment for Democracy (NED) was established in 1983 by an act of Congress and plays a major role in destabilising target countries. Bill Berkowitz of Working for Change says:

The NED functions as a full-service infrastructure building clearinghouse. It provides money, technical support, supplies, training programs, media know-how, public relations assistance and state-of-the-art equipment to select political groups, civic organizations, labor unions, dissident movements, student groups, book publishers, newspapers, and other media. Its aim is to destabilize progressive movements, particularly those with a socialist or democratic socialist bent.

More accurately, I would say, it attacks any regime that is potentially in the way of the Rothschild-Illuminati agenda for a global dictatorship. Barack Obama has said America won't meddle in the internal affairs of Iran, when this is precisely what is happening. He is funding Iranian dissident groups with $20 million in USAID grants, but that is a fraction of the money being spent in secret. The Israeli Mossad is also deeply involved in covert operations inside Iran. Meir Dagan, a former commando and retired general, took over Mossad in 2002 and, according to 'security sources' quoted in the media, his brief was to monitor and sabotage the Iranian nuclear programme ahead of any decision by Israel to use air strikes. Western media reports have claimed Mossad involvement in sabotage at Iranian nuclear facilities, and attacks on Iranian scientists and military personnel. An Iranian nuclear scientist, Professor Massoud Ali-Mohammadi, was killed by a booby-trapped motorbike explosion in January 2010 in an attack blamed by Iran on Israel and the United States, and it is certainly the way they operate. Three months earlier, in October 2009, a suicide bomb attack killed more than 40 people, including six senior commanders of the Iranian Revolutionary Guard, in the Pishin district near the border with Pakistan. The terror group, Jundullah, claimed responsibility and this is widely known to be backed by the CIA and Mossad. London's *Daily Telegraph* reported in May 2007 how the CIA was providing Jundullah with money and weapons to conduct raids into Iran from across the border in Pakistan. *ABC News* confirmed the same theme:

US officials tell ABC News [that] US intelligence officers frequently meet and advise Jundullah leaders, and current and former intelligence officers are working to prevent the men from being sent to Iran.

A senior member of Jundullah told an Iranian court in 2009 that the group was a front for the United States and Israel (the Rothschilds, in other words). Abdolhamid Rigi, brother of the group's leader, Abdolmalek Rigi, said Jundullah was being trained and funded by 'the US and Zionists' (same thing). He added that these twins of terror had ordered them to increase attacks inside Iran. Jundullah was once headed by Khalid Sheikh Mohammed, the alleged 'mastermind' (yawn, yawn) of 9/11. Wheels within wheels within wheels.

Talking of which, press reports have described how the British army has provided air transportation to relocate Taliban fighters from southern Afghanistan to the north where increasing violence was erupting. Afghan President, Hamid Karzai, an American-Israeli puppet, was quoted by the BBC Persian Service as ordering an investigation into reports of 'unknown' army helicopters carrying gunmen to the north. He said that, based on unconfirmed reports, the helicopters have been taking gunmen to Baghlan, Kunduz and Samangan provinces overnight for about five months. Anyone new to this will find such a suggestion of British involvement ridiculous. I mean, aren't they there to fight the Taliban? Actually, this is precisely the way the game is played. Diplomats were said to have leaked the information that British Chinook helicopters were being used to support the Taliban. They also said that Sultan Munadi, an Afghan interpreter kidnapped with *New York Times* reporter, Stephen Farrell, was killed by a 'British sniper' during the rescue operation to free Farrell. They said the interpreter was targeted because he possessed documents and pictures exposing the British military involvement in the transfer operation. The diplomats further said that American forces increased the scale of Taliban attacks by supplying Russian-made weaponry used during the 1979-1989 Soviet occupation of Afghanistan. These weapons had been gathered after the US/UK invasion of the country in 2001 during a campaign to 'collect weapons from irresponsible people'. The diplomats said Afghan Interior Minister, Mohammad Hanif Atmar, who received his higher education in the UK, was operating under British 'guidance'. The support for the Taliban by elite groups within the US and UK military means that US troops are being stretched beyond the limit as attacks increase. This is the idea – to use America to destroy America and justify increasing troop numbers to further stretch resources.

Operation Eurasia

Sitting in the middle, like a violin waiting to be played, are the people of these target countries who often have genuine grievances against the incumbent regime. This dissatisfaction with the status quo is exploited by the agent provocateurs and propaganda that generates the mass protests to bring about the goal of the manipulation – 'regime change'. But while the names and faces may change, those in the shadows simply increase their power and influence over the country by having their place-people in political office. President Saakashvili in Georgia would hardly blow his nose without asking the United States for permission, for example. Some 'people's revolution', eh? It's simple. Instead of invading a country to install the leaders you want, get the population to do it for you while thinking they are a symbol of 'people power'. John Bolton (Rothschild Zionist), the neoconservative crazy in the Bush administration, said a US military attack on Iran would only happen if economic sanctions and attempts to foment a 'popular revolution' failed. The focus on Iran is once again connected to the domination of the gathering global battleground that Obama mentor and Trilateral Commission founder, Zbigniew Brzezinski, calls 'Eurasia', which includes the massive oil and gas reserves in and around the Caspian

Sea. Eurasia stretches from the Middle East and Western Europe and across to Russia and China, and includes 10.6 per cent of the Earth's surface (36.2 per cent of its land area) and is home to more than 4.6 billion people, or 70-plus per cent of the human population. Brzezinski has written that, in effect, if you control Eurasia you control the world. This is what is going on. Look at the part of Eurasia surrounding Iran and you can see how many countries are, or have been, subject to unrest, tension, terrorism, conflict, invasion and 'regime change' (Fig 76). These include Georgia, Ukraine, Chechnya, Dagestan, Afghanistan, Pakistan, Iraq, Iran, Yemen

Figure 76: *A key area in the landmass known as Eurasia and it is no coincidence that so many of these countries have either been invaded, had US puppet leaders installed or are being targeted through fear-mongering propaganda and State-sponsored terrorism*

(thanks to the 'crotch-bomber' scam), and others. Go a little to the left and you are into Syria and Israel.

The military and covert operations orchestrated by Britain, America and Israel – all controlled by the House of Rothschild – have invaded and destabilised Iraq and Afghanistan and are now moving in on Pakistan with the mounting campaign of US bombing, infiltration through Illuminati private armies masquerading as 'security companies', like the civilian-killing Blackwater (Xe), and expansion of the US embassy complex. The bloodlines want control of Pakistan and they are using the Obama administration to achieve it. Two Taliban militant leaders, who defected from the notorious Taliban chief in Pakistan, Baitullah Mehsud, the mass killer of civilians and military personnel, said that he was an 'American agent' pursuing a US-Israeli agenda in Pakistan. One of them, Turkistan Bittani, said that Mehsud was being funded by US and Israeli intelligence services for brainwashing innocent youths. Bittani pointed out that the Al-Qaeda and Taliban leadership had never been targeted by the dozens of US drone strikes in Pakistan's north-west region. The other defector, Qari Zainuddin, said that Mehsud had established strong links with Israeli intelligence services which were destabilising the country. 'These people [Mehsud and his associates] are working against Islam,' he said. If what they say is true, Mehsud is actually working *for* the Rothschild Zionists. Mehsud, himself, publicly denied involvement in a bombing in Peshawar that killed about 120 people and injured hundreds more in October 2009. He blamed the US Blackwater 'private army' and US and Pakistani intelligence for the atrocity. The Illuminati terror attacks are being stepped up in countries like Pakistan to destabilise the region in pursuit of conquest and control. The engineered terrorist attacks in Mumbai, a speciality of Mossad, are part of the destabilisation of India. The big prize in this region of Eurasia is Iran, which would connect Iraq with Afghanistan and Pakistan and give them control of a region from Israel to the border with China. Iran would also give the British-American-Israeli cabal greater access to the Caspian Sea with its oil and gas reserves. The plan is to control as many countries as possible that border Russia, and this is the reason for the 'people's revolutions' in Georgia and

Ukraine and their desire to join NATO. The Rothschild cabal wants to trigger a war involving Russia and China that will bring about the planned world government and world army, and we can see the pieces being moved into place. Trilateral Commission co-founder, Zbigniew Brzezinski, wrote in his 1997 book, *The Grand Chessboard*:

> Potentially, the most dangerous scenario would be a grand coalition of China, Russia, and perhaps Iran, an 'anti-hegemonic' coalition united not by ideology but by complementary grievances. It would be reminiscent in scale and scope of the challenge posed by the Sino-Soviet bloc, though this time China would likely be the leader and Russia the follower. Averting this contingency, however remote it may be, will require a display of U.S. geostrategic skill on the western, eastern, and southern perimeters of Eurasia simultaneously …

> … how America 'manages' Eurasia is critical. A power that dominates Eurasia would control two of the world's three most advanced and economically productive regions. A mere glance at the map also suggests that control over Eurasia would almost automatically entail Africa's subordination, rendering the Western Hemisphere and Oceania geopolitically peripheral to the world's central continent. About 75 per cent of the world's people live in Eurasia, and most of the world's physical wealth is there as well, both in its enterprises and underneath its soil. Eurasia accounts for about three-fourths of the world's known energy resources.

It is obvious why Iran and that whole region is so important to the bloodlines, and the engineered conflicts and protests to cause 'regime change' are all part of the Rothschild/Illuminati designs on Eurasia. The US Assistant Secretary of State for European and Eurasian Affairs, charged with implementing American foreign policy in Europe and Eurasia, is Daniel Fried (Rothschild Zionist). The world looks very different when you understand what is going on.

'Climate Change' No-P-R-S

Figure 77: *'Global warming' became 'climate change' when temperatures began to fall year after year. So why does Al Gore still say the planet faces catastrophe from rising temperatures? Simple. He's a liar*

A current and ongoing No-Problem-Reaction-Solution is the blatant and outrageous lie that human-created carbon dioxide is causing 'climate change'. Note that what was once called 'global warming' is now called 'climate change' since temperatures began to fall year on year (Fig 77). It is a confidence trick of extraordinary mendacity and proportions that is being used to justify fantastic centralisation of power, global laws, long-planned de-industrialisation, further taxation and still new levels of the police and surveillance state. If you need a problem and there isn't one, then make one up. Hold on, I've got just the man corrupt and shameless enough to do that. Where's Al? The global warming sting on the collective human psyche is fronted most famously by Mr Al 'if-my-lips-are-moving-I'm-lying' Gore (Rothschild Zionist). There is not a new, let alone a used, car anywhere on the planet that you should buy from this man. Not even a push-bike, or a pair of nail clippers. Gore is another Rothschild asset. He attended Vanderbilt University with a grant from the Rockefeller Foundation, a 'philanthropic' tax-exempt 'charity' established by the Rothschild operative, J D Rockefeller. It is used to fund the conspiracy without paying tax. Gore's daughter has married into the Schiff banking family, the close Rothschild associates behind wars and revolutions via Kuhn, Loeb & Co. She is now known as Karenna Gore Schiff. It seems very strange for a major Jewish family like the Schiffs to marry a non-Jew, as Gore claims to be. Al Gore is given great support in selling the lie of carbon-caused climate change by David Mayer de Rothschild, author of the companion guide to Gore's 'Live Earth' concerts in which a long line of celebrities, including Madonna and agenda-asset, Bono, performed around the world to give legitimacy to the climate change fraud. Rothschild's book was called *The Live Earth Global Warming Survival Handbook: 77 Essential Skills to Stop Climate Change – Or Live Through It.* He is the son of Sir Evelyn de Rothschild, a pillar of the family. It was put to him on the Alex Jones radio show in the United States that other planets and moons, including Mars, were also warming at the time and so any temperature change could not be blamed on human carbon emissions. The common denominator had to be the Sun – which, of course, it is. Rothschild replied that it was obvious why Mars was warming: It was nearer to the Sun than the Earth. More research necessary, I feel, Dave.

Al Gore, the former vice-president in the corrupt-to-its-core Bill Clinton regime, has been selling the lie about climate change for many years now. He has become the face of global warming after his 2006 Paramount film, *An Inconvenient Truth*, became the third most successful documentary in American box-office history and predictably won the Oscar for best documentary feature. The bloodlines that control Hollywood made sure it did. Gore's book, also called *An Inconvenient Truth*, reached number one in the *New York Times'* bestseller list and he, again predictably, won the Nobel Peace Prize for his tissue of lies and laughable exaggeration. Well, if Obama and Kissinger can 'win' it, anyone can. Gore shared the prize with the United Nations Intergovernmental Panel on Climate Change, or IPCC, the organisation through which the global warming scam has been imposed upon the world. The Indian geologist from Punjab University, Dr Arun D Ahluwalia, a board member of the UN-supported International Year of the Planet, highlighted the manipulation of both the Nobel Peace Prize and the IPCC:

> The IPCC has actually become a closed circuit; it doesn't listen to others. It doesn't have open minds ... I am really amazed that the Nobel Peace Prize has been given on scientifically incorrect conclusions by people who are not geologists.

The 'climate change' propaganda is founded on the myth that temperature is increased significantly, and to potentially catastrophic levels, by human-created carbon dioxide emissions when, in truth, temperature changes are caused by increases or decreases in solar activity, known as sunspots, and other natural phenomena. We have been on a rising trend of solar activity which pushed up average temperatures, but at the time of writing this has now fallen year on year and, therefore, so have temperatures. When the

Contribution to the Greenhouse Effect (including water vapour)

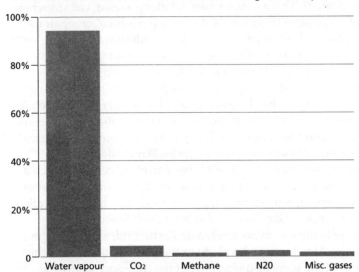

Figure 78: *How many people know that the overwhelming contribution to greenhouse gases comes from naturally-occuring water vapour and clouds? CO_2's effect is miniscule by comparison and even then only a fraction of that is carbon produced by human activity*

sunspots increase again in the next cycle, temperatures will rise again, before falling as the cycle comes to an end. This is how it has always been, although there are some strange things happening with the Sun at the time of writing, with sunspot activity staying low or virtually non-existent for far longer than usual. The doomsday climate predictions have come entirely from rigged 'computer models' of the shite-in-shite-out variety. I have presented the detailed background to the 'global warming'

lie in a chapter called 'The Carbon Con' in *The David Icke Guide to the Global Conspiracy (and how to end it)*. There are also many articles in my newsletter archive, and there is both written and video information in the planetary change research archive at **davidicke.com**, plus many excellent websites specific to the subject, including CarbonDioxide.com. I am not saying that there are no changes in climate – there always are. The climate is not static and never has been. The scale of change depends on the cycle we are experiencing and these can span thousands of years. When you look at the evidence instead of the propaganda it is obvious that 'climate change' is not caused by human-generated carbon dioxide through the 'greenhouse effect' that traps heat in the lower atmosphere. Carbon dioxide is a very minor greenhouse gas. By far the biggest contributors to the greenhouse effect are water vapour and clouds that make up about 96.5 per cent of natural heat-retaining phenomena. What do we do, ban water vapour and ban clouds? Why not tax water vapour and launch a cloud-and-trade scheme? Carbon dioxide comprises, wait for it, only 0.037 per cent of greenhouse gases – and human-generated carbon dioxide is a fraction even of that (Fig 78). Oh yes, and before carbon dioxide is demonised any more, it is worth remembering that it is responsible for making plants grow and without it, and indeed a greenhouse effect to retain heat, this planet would be uninhabitable for humans.

Crap and Paid

Al Gore has made a fortune out of the widespread and manipulated belief in his ridiculous climate-change scenario. He launched a company in London in 2004 with David Blood, formerly of the Rothschild-Illuminati stronghold, Goldman Sachs, and it is known in 'the City' as 'Blood & Gore'. Their Generation Investment Management is aimed specifically at exploiting the financial opportunities, like carbon offsets and trading, or 'cap-and-trade', offered by the 'global warming' myth peddled by Gore. It has already made him tens of millions of dollars so far. As an Internet writer put it:

> So Al can buy his carbon offsets from himself. Better yet, he can buy them with the money he gets from his long-time relationship with Occidental Petroleum. See how easy it is to be carbon-neutral? All you have to do is own a gazillion stocks in Big Oil, start an eco-stockbroking firm to make eco-friendly investments, use a small portion of your oil company's profits to buy some tax-deductible carbon offsets from your own investment firm, and you too can save the planet while making money and leaving a carbon footprint roughly the size of Godzilla's at the start of the movie when they're all standing around in the little toe wondering what the strange depression in the landscape is.

The cap-and-trade system, so beloved of Barack Obama, and so profitable for Al Gore, will cost families thousands of dollars a year when all the consequences are taken into account, while the architects of it make further fortunes. It has been described as the biggest tax increase in American history. One of the main tasks that Obama has been set by the cabal is to sell 'climate change' and all the long-prepared 'solutions' just waiting to be signed into law. He made an outrageous speech at the United Nations in September 2009 in which lie after lie after lie spewed from his teleprompter about facing an 'irreversible catastrophe':

> No nation, however large or small, wealthy or poor, can escape the impact of climate change. Rising sea levels threaten every coastline. More powerful storms and floods threaten every continent. More frequent drought and crop failures breed hunger and conflict in places where hunger and conflict already thrive. On shrinking islands, families are already being forced to flee their homes as climate refugees. The security and stability of each nation and all peoples – our prosperity, our health, our safety – are in jeopardy. And the time we have to reverse this tide is running out.

It was all straight from the Gospel according to Al Gore. The one named 'Bollocks'. Obama has filled his environment, energy and science departments with Gore groupies, including his 'science czar', John Holdren, who was arguing in the 1970s for drastic action, including eugenic population control, to save the world from global *cooling* and a new ice age. Holdren predicted 'ecocide' or the 'destruction of all life on this planet' from cooling temperatures. '… A sudden outward slumping in the Antarctic ice cap, induced by added weight, could generate a tidal wave of proportions unprecedented in recorded history', he wrote with his co-author. Now he is demanding government extremism and cap-and-trade to save us from global warming and melting ice. Pathetic. Obama and his handlers are targeting the public in general, and children and young people in particular, to demand 'action on climate change' and marginalise anyone who even questions the lie. He is introducing a carbon cap-and-trade system that he has admitted would make electricity prices 'necessarily skyrocket'. The bloodline-owned energy corporations don't want to make more money, though. They just want to save the planet, bless 'em. Cap-and-trade is a system by which governments set the limits of carbon emissions and issue permits to companies for their maximum allowance or 'credit', but if they need to produce more they can buy these allowances from other companies that produce less than their maximum. It is just another way for the few to make yet more money, impose more government control of economic activity and make it still harder for people to pay their bills. The French President, the Rothschild frontman, Nicolas Sarkozy, introduced a carbon tax that will increase energy costs for French people and said it was 'a question of survival of the human race'. Garbage. It is about the survival and expansion of the agenda he represents. You are going to see carbon taxes appear in country after country because it is all coordinated. The Rothschilds are, naturally, reaping the rewards across the world of their 'climate change' manipulation. Rothschild Australia announced the launch of the 'Carbon Ring Consortium' to exploit the carbon trading market in the Asia-Pacific region. Richard Martin, chief executive officer of Rothschild Australia, said:

> With recent developments in international climate change policy [manipulated by the Rothschild cabal], the question is no longer if, but when the global carbon trading market will emerge. Rothschild Australia, through Carbon Ring, intends to be at the forefront of this market, providing private investment vehicles to companies seeking to offset their greenhouse gas emissions liabilities.

Joachim Schellnhuber, the leading climate extremist advising the German government, has said that everyone in the world should be given a carbon 'budget' and be taxed if they exceed it. How could this be done without the fine detail of everyone's lives being subject to surveillance? Czech physicist Dr Lubos Motl described the idea as 'breathtaking' and said that Schellnhuber's proposal helped him 'to understand how crazy political movements such as the Nazis or communists could have so easily taken over a nation that is as sensible as Germany'. Something very similar to Schellnhuber's policy has been proposed in the UK. The California Energy Commission is even planning to introduce radio-controlled thermostats which the authorities can move up and down at will and this could not be overridden by the residents. None of this is about protecting the planet, it is about control and centralisation of power, and they are forcing it upon the people in the most despicable ways. Simon Linnett, a Rothschild Bank Executive Vice-Chairman, was painfully predictable when he called for a new international body, the 'World Environment Agency', to regulate carbon trading. This would join the World Bank, World Health Organization, World Trade Organisation etc., etc. – all Rothschild fronts for global control. Linnett said that the human causes of climate change are now well established (utter claptrap) and 'the International problem of climate change demands an international solution'. Unless governments ceded some of their sovereignty to a new world body, he said, a global carbon trading scheme cannot be enforced and regulated. There you have the real reason for the global warming/climate change agenda from the mouth of a man who has been a servant to the Rothschilds since he graduated from Oxford University in 1975.

Climate Fascism

The American Clean Energy and Security Act, which gave the government control over almost every aspect of American life, was passed in June 2009, even though 300 pages of it had been introduced at 3am and almost no-one had read them. When House Minority Leader, John Boehner, stood up to read the contents out loud, the bill's co-sponsor, Henry Waxman (Rothschild Zionist), objected and tried to stop it on grounds of 'procedure'. 'Climate change' is being used, as planned, to add countless new layers of Orwellian bureaucracy and control with thousands of new global laws and regulations and the 'Green Police' that will keep track of everything you do right down to where you place your rubbish bin. *Will?* It's already happening. The American Clean Energy and Security Act introduces mandatory home inspections, or 'energy audits', in which they will check your light fittings, types of socket, appliances, windows, walls, roofs and anything else they choose. Their 'findings will be reported to the Orwellian-sounding Residential Energy Services Network (RESNET), and the aim is to ensure that the public drown in paperwork and regulations. One report I saw on the consequences of the Clean Energy and Security Act said:

> According to RESNET, an audit consists of: Comprehensive Home Energy Audit – a level of the RESNET Home Energy Audit process defined by this standard to include the evaluation, diagnosis and proposed treatment of an existing home. The Comprehensive Home Energy Audit may be based on a Home Performance Assessment ('Comprehensive Home Performance Energy Audit') or Home Energy Rating ('Comprehensive HERS Audit'), in accordance with the criteria established by this Standard. A homeowner may elect to go through this process with or without a prior Home Energy Survey or Diagnostic Home Energy Survey.

See what I mean? Anyone who refuses to let these goons into their homes faces fines totalling thousands of dollars, and even if you allow them in they can send you a bill for the inspection that you didn't want. Al Gore has said that 'climate change' will help to bring about 'global governance' and that is another reason for inventing it. They are even using 'climate change' to press their depopulation agenda. Having children, apparently, is bad for your 'carbon footprint'. A study at Oregon State University concluded that the carbon consequences of an 'extra child' is almost 20 times more important than driving a high mileage car, recycling, or using energy-efficient appliances and light bulbs. You will see this theme being pushed ever more clearly to 'solve' a 'problem' that doesn't exist. The attempt to create hysteria about the end of the world reached even more insane levels in the run-up to the United Nations Conference on Climate Change in Copenhagen, Denmark, in December 2009 where they were seeking global laws across nearly 200 countries. A major propaganda report was published called *State of the Future* that ran to 6700 pages and claimed to draw on 2700 'experts'. It concluded that 'an effort on the scale of the Apollo mission that sent men to the Moon is needed if humanity is to have a fighting chance of surviving the ravages of climate change'. Without sustainable growth, it said, 'billions of people will be condemned to poverty and much of civilisation will collapse'. It was, in short, a tissue of lies. The 'report' was produced by a 'think tank' called the Millennium Project, commissioned by the United Nations Secretary-General in 2002. Its end-of-the-world 'climate report' was backed by United Nations agencies, the World Bank, IMF, the United States Army and … the Rockefeller Foundation. All of them are Rothschild-controlled via the spider's web. It is all so clear when you know what is going on.

Christopher Booker, author of *The Real Global Warming Disaster*, wrote this ahead of the Copenhagen UN Climate Change Conference in late 2009:

> As the world has already been through two of its coldest winters for decades, with all the signs that we may now be entering a third, the scientific case for CO_2 threatening the world with warming has been crumbling away on an astonishing scale.
>
> Yet it is at just this point that the world's politicians, led by Britain, the EU and now President Obama, are poised to impose on us far and away the most costly set of measures that any group of politicians has ever proposed in the history of the world – measures so destructive that even if only half of them were implemented, they would take us back to the dark ages.

But then, that's what they want. At the same time, the Copenhagen climate summit dropped a vital safeguard to protect the destruction of the world's rainforests and allowed them to be cut down and replaced with plantations of trees like oil palms. When environmentalists demanded that the safeguard be reinserted, the European Union, led by Britain, blocked it. The oil palm-type replacement of rainforests was still to be designated as 'forest' and so attract the very grants worth millions of dollars that were supposed to protect the true rainforest species from destruction. The replacement trees also absorb less carbon dioxide which shows again that the climate change agenda is just that – an agenda. These people don't care about the real environmental challenges. The manipulation reached yet a new low in 2009 when the British government began to run puke-producing prime-time advertisements using taxpayers money to make people feel fear and guilt about 'climate change' while mercilessly exploiting and frightening children. One ad includes pictures of puppies and kittens drowning in a deluge. The advertisements were ordered when polls showed that the climate change propaganda had not convinced more than half the British population to believe the crap they were being fed. Philip Stott, Emeritus Professor of Biogeography at the University of London, who says the official version of climate change is nonsense, rightly described the advertisements as an attempt to manipulate people with alarmist language and apocalyptic imagery. 'It is straight out of Orwell's *1984* – an attempt to control with images of a perpetual war against something, in this case climate change,' he said. Spot on, mate.

Tony B-liar – who else?

You know something is a gigantic fraud when Tony Blair is involved. The plan is to have draconian, Obama-type climate laws imposed globally and so Blair is on the case. He's also planning to cash in on the lie, like Gore, and he has registered the Internet domain name of 'Low Carbon Capital Fund'. Blair's vehicle for climate change stardom is an organisation called 'The Climate Group' which is described as an 'independent' and 'not-for-profit' non-governmental organisation. Well, for a start, nothing whatsoever involving Tony Blair can be described as 'independent', and non-profit 'NGOs' abound in the Rothschild-Illuminati web of deceit. The Climate Group is based in London and operates worldwide with an extremely well-funded network of offices in Europe, North America, Australia, 'Greater China' and India. The UK board of

The Climate Group is a mixture of banking, media, corporate and advertising executives, and it is chaired by John R Coomber, former chief executive and now director of the insurance giant, Swiss Re. Another Climate Group director is Matthew Anderson, Group Director, Strategy and Corporate Affairs for Europe and Asia, with the News Corporation of Rupert Murdoch (Rothschild Zionist). This is a corporate member of The Climate Group along with Tony Blair 'employer', JPMorgan Chase. Blair will feel right at home, then. Other members include:

> Barclays Bank, Standard Chartered Bank, HSBC, Swiss Re, British Petroleum, Coca-Cola, PepsiCo, Bloomberg, Sky Broadcasting, Virgin Atlantic, Cathay Pacific Airways, China Mobile, IBM, Dell IT, Google, Duke Energy, Florida Power and Light Group, Scottish Power, Nike, Johnson & Johnson, Marks and Spencer, Cadbury, Starbucks; and the governments of London, California, Los Angeles, New York, Miami, British Columbia, Ontario, Québec, Manitoba, Western Australia, South Australia, New South Wales, Victoria and Queensland.

Tony Blair travelled the world selling the climate change fakery ahead of the Copenhagen event, but when he was asked at a news conference what he had done to make his own life more 'sustainable' there was a long silence. 'We've got solar panels on our house,' he eventually spluttered.

> 'Which one?' (He has many.)
> 'The London one.'

More long silences followed. He is doing nothing to reduce his own carbon count, not least because he knows it doesn't matter. Selling the lie is all he cares about. This is why Al Gore, Mr Global Warming himself, has a carbon footprint the size of Godzilla. The UK Environment Secretary, the Fabian Society's Hilary Benn, wants to fine the public for not recycling their rubbish, but he was exposed for throwing out a long list of recyclable waste at his own home. This included recyclable glass, plastic, cardboard, paper and food. The cad then blamed his children even though the waste contained personal correspondence and government notepaper. Ironically, Benn's rubbish bags included a note from his private secretary at the Department of the Environment, Food and Rural Affairs about a campaign to encourage the public to throw away less food. The exposure came after Benn had declared a national 'war on waste'. It's all a sham.

The 'Stern Team'

It was the Blair government – through his then Chancellor of the Exchequer and later successor, Gordon Brown – that commissioned the 'Stern Review on the Economics of Climate Change' which reported in 2006 with a pathetic repeat of all the dire warnings of catastrophe. Oh, what a shock. The author was Nicholas Herbert Stern, Baron Stern of Brentford (Rothschild Zionist), a British economist and academic. Stern is I G Patel Professor of Economics and Government and Chair of the Grantham Institute on Climate Change and the Environment at, yes, the London School of Economics. He was the Chief Economist and Senior Vice-President of the Rothschild-created-and-controlled World Bank during the presidency of Rothschild business partner, James Wolfensohn (Rothschild Zionist), and he was an economic advisor to the Blair government. His brothers are Richard Stern, former Vice-President at the World Bank, and Brian E Stern, former Vice-President of the Xerox Corporation. He comes from a background, as you can see, which is independent and not at all connected to the establishment. Stern also has many connections into the carbon trading 'industry' and the Climate Change cabal in general. The 'Stern Team' organised a symposium in Washington DC in March 2009. Academics, corporation CEOs, politicians and government administrators heard from the choir yet again, including Tony Blair, the man who never utters a truth unless absolutely necessary. The 'Stern Team' symposium was co-sponsored by the following:

The World Resources Institute: 'think tank', founded by James Gustave Speth in 1982 who attended Oxford University, like Bill Clinton, on a Rhodes Scholarship. These scholarships were created in the will of Rothschild asset, Cecil Rhodes, who was the first head the Rothschild Round Table secret society that established the Bilderberg Group, Council on Foreign Relations, Trilateral Commission network. The World Resources Institute was heavily involved in the formation of the Convention on Biological Diversity, a major plank in the Rothschild-Illuminati environmental agenda, as I will explain shortly. Sponsors of the World Resources Institute include those environmental hippies, Goldman Sachs, JPMorgan Chase, Bank of America, Citigroup Foundation, Coca-Cola, Dow Chemical Company, DuPont, Microsoft Corporation, Shell International, Ford Foundation, Rockefeller Brothers Fund, Oppenheimer Brothers Foundation, the European Commission and a list of government departments. They even include Monsanto (producers of the environmently-devastating genetically modified crops) and Novartis, the pharmaceutical giant that makes swine flu vaccine.

The Peterson Institute for International Economics: 'think tank', formerly the Institute for International Economics and based in Washington DC. It was founded in 1981 by C Fred Bergsten, a former senior fellow at the Council on Foreign Relations and Assistant for International Economic Affairs to Henry Kissinger at the National Security Council. He has also been a senior fellow at the Illuminati Brookings Institution and the Carnegie Endowment for International Peace, which has been exposed by a Congressional committee for manipulating war (see ... *And The Truth Shall Set You Free*). Bergsten is a close associate of the Peterson Institute director, David Rockefeller. Bergsten's Institute for International Economics was renamed the Peterson Institute in 2006 in honour of Peter George Peterson, who replaced David Rockefeller as chairman of the Council on Foreign Relations, and remains, with Rockefeller, an honorary chairman of the CFR. Peterson is a former chairman of the key Federal Reserve Bank of New York and was United States Secretary of Commerce in the Richard Nixon administration. He also worked for Lehman Brothers, Kuhn, Loeb Inc., and founded the Blackstone asset management group with Stephen A Schwarzman. Once again, the Peterson Institute is awash with 'committed environmentalists'.

The Center for Global Development: 'think tank', founded in 2001 by C Fred Bergsten, yep, Rockefeller's buddy again, along with Edward W Scott, a former senior US official, and Nancy Birdsall, the former Director of the Policy Research Department at the World Bank. More environmental fanatics, then.

How obvious it all is. An 'International Day of Climate Action' in October 2009 coordinated demonstrators across the world demanding action on climate change. The organisers, 350.org, claimed that people 'in 181 countries came together for the most widespread day of environmental action in the planet's history' with more than five thousand events worldwide. The term '350' refers to the parts per million of carbon dioxide the carbon cultists say is the safe upper limit in the atmosphere. Guess who funds 350.org? It begins with 'R' and rhymes with 'knocker' and 'bella'. 350.org is an offshoot of the Sustainable Markets Foundation funded by the Rockefeller Brothers Fund and fronted by Bill McKibben, author of *The End of Nature*, and apparently an 'inspiration' to Al Gore. How strange. When I stood in the news shop in 1990 and my feet began to be pulled magnetically to the floor, I had a book in my hand that I had bought that day. It was called *The End of Nature* by Bill McKibben. After what happened, I never looked at it again, never mind read it.

British newspaper columnist, Charles Moore, said the Stern Review commissioned by the Blair government was the climate version of the 'dodgy dossier' published by the same Blair mendacity machine on the Iraqi weapons of mass destruction that, er, weren't. The Stern report 'findings' have been scientifically demolished by Lord Christopher Monckton, a former policy advisor to British Prime Minister, Margaret Thatcher, and a vehement critic of the climate change 'orthodoxy'. There would be many aspects of life on which I would disagree with him, but on this he is clearly correct. He exposes how the scam was orchestrated, not least by censoring the existence of what scientists call the 'medieval warm period' between about AD 800 – 1300 when temperatures were much higher than they were even before the cooling began from the late 1990s. I highlighted the medieval warm period in *The David Icke Guide to the Global Conspiracy (and how to end it)*, when there was no industry, no 'gas guzzlers', none of it. So how could it have been so much warmer? It was caused by a very active period of sunspot activity and thus solar radiation affecting the Earth. The medieval warm period is fatal to the credibility of the Carbon Cult and so they just deleted it from their reports. Monckton wrote in London's *Sunday Telegraph*:

> ... the UN abolished the medieval warm period (the global warming at the end of the First Millennium AD). In 1995, David Deming, a geoscientist at the University of Oklahoma, had written an article reconstructing 150 years of North American temperatures from borehole data. He later wrote: 'With the publication of the article in *Science*, I gained significant credibility in the community of scientists working on climate change. They thought I was one of them, someone who would pervert science in the service of social and political causes. One of them let his guard down. A major person working in the area of climate change and global warming sent me an astonishing email that said: "We have to get rid of the medieval warm period".'

> So they did. The UN's second assessment report, in 1996, showed a 1,000-year graph demonstrating that temperature in the Middle Ages was warmer than today. But the 2001 report contained a new graph showing no medieval warm period. It wrongly

concluded that the 20th century was the warmest for 1,000 years. The graph looked like an ice hockey-stick. The wrongly flat AD1000 – AD1900 temperature line was the shaft: the uptick from 1900 to 2000 was the blade (Fig 79). Here's how they did it:

- They gave one technique for reconstructing pre-thermometer temperature 390 times more weight than any other (but didn't say so).
- The technique they overweighted was one which the UN's 1996 report had said was unsafe: measurement of tree-rings from bristlecone pines. Tree-rings are wider in warmer years, but pine-rings are also wider when there's more carbon dioxide in the air: its plant food. This carbon dioxide fertilisation distorts the calculations.
- They said they had included 24 data sets going back to 1400. Without saying so, they left out the set showing the medieval warm period, tucking it into a folder marked 'Censored Data'.
- They used a computer model to draw the graph from the data, but scientists later found that the model almost always drew hockey-sticks even if they fed in random, electronic 'red noise'.

The 'hockey-stick' graph, which wrongly claims to depict a sudden explosion of temperature increases, was widely used by the United Nations to frighten the population and was sent to every household by the Canadian government, Monckton says. They refused to retract it, or apologise, when it was exposed as ludicrous. Even after that, the UN continued to sell its case using the 'hockey stick' data described by British writer, Christopher Booker, author of *The Real Global Warming Disaster*, as 'one of the most comprehensively discredited artefacts in the history of science'. Yet in January 2010 it was revealed that Professor Michael Mann of Penn State University, the 'climatologist' behind the 'hockey stick' graph, was given more than half a million dollars in government funding in Obama's 2009 'stimulus package'. It was to fund 'climate change research', no doubt with special emphasis on deleting the medieval warm period. Lord Monckton writes:

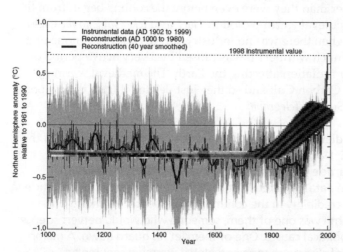

Figure 79: *The infamous 'hockey-stick' graph purporting to show how temperatures suddenly soared in the 20th century. It is calculated to deceive with its fraudulent 'science' and includes the deleting of the medieval warm period when temperatures were higher a thousand years ago than they were at their peak at the end of the 20th century*

Scores of scientific papers show that the medieval warm period was real, global and up to 3C warmer than now. Then, there were no glaciers in the tropical Andes: today they're there. There were Viking farms in

Greenland: now they're under permafrost. There was little ice at the North Pole: a Chinese naval squadron sailed right round the Arctic in 1421 and found none.

The Antarctic, which holds 90 per cent of the world's ice and nearly all its 160,000 glaciers, has cooled and gained ice-mass in the past 30 years, reversing a 6,000-year melting trend. Data from 6,000 boreholes worldwide show global temperatures were higher in the Middle Ages than now. And the snows of Kilimanjaro are vanishing not because summit temperature is rising (it isn't) but because post-colonial deforestation has dried the air. Al Gore please note.

In some places it was also warmer than now in the Bronze Age and in Roman times. It wasn't CO2 that caused those warm periods. It was the sun. So the UN adjusted the maths and all but extinguished the sun's role in today's warming.

Christopher Monckton increased his media profile in 2009 after a presentation in the United States that left the official story in tatters. He addressed some of the falsehoods that are the key foundations of the Big Lie:

'Global warming is happening now' (it's actually cooling).

'Global warming is getting worse' (it's actually getting better).

'Arctic sea-ice is disappearing' (there is no discernable trend in winter sea-ice area over the last 30 years).

'Antarctic sea ice is disappearing' (the area of sea-ice around Antarctica reached a 30-year record high in 2007).

'The Great Barrier Reef is being damaged by global warming' (there is no trend in the sea surface temperature of the reef over the last 40 years).

And so it goes on. Monckton has asked Al Gore to debate the facts with him on many occasions, even taken out newspaper advertisements to do so, and he repeated the challenge on American television in October 2009. But Gore won't bite. He will not debate with anyone who knows what they are talking about, because the game would be up.

Green is the word

The Green movement and its political wing, the Green parties, worship at the altar of the Carbon Cult, because (a) it suits their political and pressure-group campaigning and fund-raising potential, and (b) they are, like most of humanity, simply repeaters. Only a few people actually research the facts on which their opinions are based. The rest repeat the official line or what they have heard from their friends, politicians, economists, 'journalists' or some bloke on the telly. Mainstream 'journalists' are professional repeaters of the official version of events, which is why what really happened on 9/11 is never investigated. Politicians repeat what their 'advisors' and 'experts' tell them;

Figure 80: *Al Gore is the High Priest of the new religion and it talks the same bollocks as all the others*

doctors repeat what they are told at medical school and by the drug company reps; song-sheet scientists repeat the official line they are indoctrinated to believe, or must appear to believe if they want to attract funding and acclaim; teachers repeat what they were told at training college or what the official curriculum tells them to say. The world is enslaved by repeaters who parrot other people's opinions as their own without ever bothering to question or research for themselves. This was brilliantly observed by the great British writer, Oscar Wilde: 'Most people are other people. Their thoughts are someone else's opinions, their lives a mimicry, their passions a quotation.' All you have to do is tell people what they should believe and they will largely do so because either they have no independent thought or it suits their belief-systems and ambitions for what you say to be true. It is because of the above that the climate change lie has been so successful and what a pathetic sight it is to see tens of thousands of people from all over the world protesting outside events like the Copenhagen Climate Change Conference and urging the elite to be even more extreme in their Orwellian policies to 'save the planet'. The Climate Cult has become a religion in which the followers accept that their 'holy book' is 'the truth' and must never be questioned (Fig 80). The media is bombarding the population with climate change programming and the same is happening to children and young people in the schools and universities. Repetition is one of the most effective forms of mind-control, and provable lies morph into 'everyone knows that'. They want us to believe that 'the debate is over' about climate change. Forget about it, we all know its true, get on with your lives, no need to question. The Green movement's subservience to the Carbon Cult has been long-planned and orchestrated. One of the most significant organisations in the Illuminati environmental agenda is the Club of Rome, founded in 1968, which connects into the Bilderberg Group, Council on Foreign Relations, Trilateral Commission and so on. These are all Rothschild operations, coordinated by the Round Table secret society in Britain that was behind the Balfour Declaration. The founder of the Club of Rome, Aurelio Peccei, said in the organisation's 1991 publication, *The First Global Revolution*:

> In searching for a new enemy to unite us, we came up with the idea that pollution, the threat of global warming, water shortages, famine, and the like would fit the Bill ... All of these are caused by human intervention ... The real enemy, then, is humanity itself.

The Club of Rome is pressing for a global carbon tax and a 'new economic order' to use the human-made climate-change fraud to advance the agenda for world domination. The environmental movement was created by bloodline eugenicists like Julian Huxley, Prince Phillip and Prince Bernhard of the Netherlands, the former Nazi SS officer who was the first and long-time chairman of the Bilderberg Group. This trio created the

World Wildlife Fund, now the World Wide Fund for Nature. Huxley instigated the WWF while director of the Rothschild-Illuminati front, the United Nations Educational, Scientific and Cultural Organization (UNESCO).

'Scientific' Bullshit

The Carbon Cult is not interested in facts, only propaganda and the constant repetition of an alleged and unquestionable 'truth'. Crucial to this has been the creation and control of the United Nations Intergovernmental Panel on Climate Change, or IPCC. The UN is a Rothschild operation, and its headquarters are built on land in New York given by John D Rockefeller. The IPCC is believed to be a scientific body, but that's not true. It is a political organisation masquerading as scientific, and it manipulates by quoting the scientists who sing from the song sheet and ignoring those who say its claims about carbon dioxide, or CO_2, are nonsense. This gives a false impression to the public that scientists are pretty much all agreed on climate change, when this is not the case at all. Dr Rajendra Pachauri, chairman the IPCC, is a railway engineer who lectures the world on the 'science' of climate change. It was revealed in January 2010 that millions of pounds of British taxpayers' money is being paid to an organisation in India run by Pachauri. A research institute that he heads will receive up to £10 million in funding over five years from the Department for International Development, despite controversy over the finances of the London operation of The Energy and Resources Institute (TERI), based in New Delhi, which has Pachauri as its Director-General. It is India's most influential private body involved in 'climate change' and renewable energy and has been the subject of investigative articles by the UK *Sunday Telegraph*, which has also highlighted the fact that Pachauri holds more than 20 positions with banks, universities and other institutions that benefit from the worldwide industry now based on policies to 'stop climate change'. Coincidence?? You decide. Hundreds of scientists have signed the so-called Manhattan Declaration that challenges the official story. A US Senate Minority Report on climate change in 2008 featured 650 scientists refuting the alleged 'consensus' that global warming has been caused by human-generated carbon emissions. By contrast, only 52 scientists, together with diplomats and politicians, were behind the IPCC Summary for Policymakers in 2007 which has become the Bible of the Carbon Cult. Many of the 'hundreds of scientists' that are claimed to be connected to the IPCC are, in fact, sceptical or dismissive of the official fairytale. The 650 scientists quoted in the Senate report include leading experts in their fields, and many who are connected with the IPCC but don't agree with its official conclusions. Here are just some of their opinions quoted in the report:

[Warming fears] are the worst scientific scandal in scientific history ... When people come to know what the truth is, they will feel deceived by science and scientists – IPCC Japanese scientist Dr Kiminori Itoh, an award-winning PhD environmental physical chemist.

[The models and forecasts of the IPCC] are incorrect because they only are based on mathematical models and presented results as scenarios that do not include, for example, solar activity – Victor Manuel Velasco Herrera, a researcher at the Institute of Geophysics of the National Autonomous University of Mexico. [Please note: '... that do not include, for example, solar activity'. *What?*]

The Kyoto theorists have put the cart before the horse. It is global warming that triggers higher levels of carbon dioxide in the atmosphere, not the other way round ... A large number of critical documents submitted at the 1995 UN conference in Madrid vanished without a trace. As a result, the discussion was one-sided and heavily biased, and the UN declared global warming to be a scientific fact – Andrei Kapitsa, a Russian geographer and Antarctic ice core researcher.

The quantity of CO_2 we produce is insignificant in terms of the natural circulation between air, water and soil ... I am doing a detailed assessment of the UN IPCC reports and the Summaries for Policy Makers, identifying the way in which the Summaries have distorted the science – South African nuclear physicist and chemical engineer Dr Philip Lloyd, an IPCC co-coordinating lead author.

Creating an ideology pegged to carbon dioxide is a dangerous nonsense ... The present alarm on climate change is an instrument of social control, a pretext for major businesses and political battles. It became an ideology, which is concerning – Environmental scientist, Professor Delgado Domingos of Portugal, the founder of the Numerical Weather Forecast group.

At last the unheard voices of scientists challenging the global warming conspiracy are refusing to be silenced. The International Geological Congress in Norway is described as the geologists' equivalent of the Olympic Games, and in 2008 it included a large number of speakers who challenged the official line. Many scientists who have spoken out have lost funding and faced other forms of intimidation, including death threats. Dr William M Briggs, a climate statistician on the American Meteorological Society's Probability and Statistics Committee, said that his colleagues told 'absolute horror stories of what happened to them when they tried getting papers published that explored non-"consensus" views'. He said he was shocked at what he heard. Many have suffered abuse, loss of job opportunities and been marginalised by their song-sheet colleagues for simply speaking the truth. At a time when these scientists are refusing to be gagged there is another major problem for the 'Warmers': temperatures have been falling. Carbon dioxide continues to rise, yet the heat it is supposed to be causing has been consistently cooling. The geologist Dr David Gee, chairman of the science committee of the 2008 International Geological Congress, said:

'For how many years must the planet cool before we begin to understand that the planet is not warming? For how many years must cooling go on?'

I guess the answer is for as long as enough people believe the lies and deceit.

Lying for a living

The desperation to avoid the fact that temperatures have been falling has led to the figures being doctored by NASA's Goddard Institute for Space Studies. This is headed by another close Al Gore associate, Dr James Hansen, the man who has been called 'the father of climate change', but should really be called 'the father of the dodgy data that fuelled the myth of climate change'. Hansen's NASA Institute announced that October

2008 was the hottest on record and yet the experience across the world was of very cold weather and heavy snowstorms. When the obvious inaccuracy of the NASA figures was questioned it turned out that they had used the figures from the warmer month of September and said they were for October. This is highly relevant because the figures published by Hansen's Institute provide some of the prime data used by the IPCC to support its line about global warming and they have consistently claimed higher temperatures than other figures. I wonder why? It's not the first time Hansen has been caught out, either. In 2007, he was forced to accept that his claim that the 1990s was the hottest decade of the 20th century wasn't true. The hottest decade was the 1930s, when there was dramatically less carbon dioxide being produced. Atmospheric scientist Dr John S Theon, one of Hansen's colleagues at NASA, said:

> Hansen was never muzzled even though he violated NASA's official agency position on climate forecasting (i.e., we did not know enough to forecast climate change or mankind's effect on it). Hansen thus embarrassed NASA by coming out with his claims of global warming in 1988 in his testimony before Congress.

When you are serving the Illuminati agenda you are protected and allowed to break the rules while those challenging your propaganda are pressured to follow the rules to the letter, or even face new rules to shut them up. This has created a fantastically distorted perception of what is happening to the climate. Greenpeace International Executive Director, Gerd Leipold, was forced to admit that a press release claiming that Arctic ice would disappear by 2030 could not be substantiated, but he said that he did not apologise for 'emotionalising issues' to get the public to see the world his way. I think he means that lying is okay so long as the people believe you. Not only are the ice caps not disappearing, a report published in October 2009 said that the Antarctic summer 'melt' in 2008-2009 was the lowest ever recorded since satellite technology was introduced. The report, in the journal *Geophysical Research Letters*, was simply ignored by the mainstream media and environmental groups. If you want to see the original global temperature records most cited by the IPCC to check the data that the warming cult has been using… well, too bad. They've destroyed them, or 'lost' them. This happened, just by coincidence, of course, when the Climatic Research Unit at the UK's University of East Anglia was faced with requests to release them under the Freedom of Information Act. It had previously refused to release the raw weather station data and details of its processing methods, except to hand-picked academics (the song-sheet choir). Why would they destroy data that, if they are telling the truth, would support its case for human-caused climate change? Because it didn't – quite the opposite.

Those of us who have been researching this subject for years have long known that the data was systematically rigged, but the story went onto a whole new level in 2009 when a hacker accessed thousands of emails and documents from the Climatic Research Unit computers and exposed beyond question that 'climate change' has been manufactured by 'scientists' who have coldly set out to deceive the public. The emails include communications between prominent climate scientists and reveal everything from the unethical to the potentially illegal. There was a conspiracy to block Freedom of Information requests and to keep sceptical scientists out of the peer review process and scientific publications. Professor Phil Jones, the head of the 'Research' Unit, stood down while an investigation is carried out. One of his emails said: 'I have just completed Mike's Nature trick of adding in the real temps to each series for the last 20 years to hide the decline'. Another 'scientist' being investigated in the scandal was Professor Michael 'hockey stick' Mann. Dr Tim Ball, a climate science who challenges the official story, called the revelations 'not just a smoking gun, but a battery of machine guns'. He said that on a global scale it was frightening because this group of scientists not only control the UK Meteorological Office's Hadley Centre, which compiles the temperature data, but they also control the IPCC. In turn, the IPCC is the body that drives government climate policy around the world. To complete the circle, the Hadley Centre is co-funded by the UK government's Department for Environment, Food and Rural Affairs, Ministry of Defence and Department of Energy and Climate Change. Lord Christopher Monckton summarised the hacker's findings in a paper entitled 'Climategate: Caught Green-Handed':

- A tiny clique of politicised scientists, paid by unscientific politicians with whom they were financially and politically linked, were responsible for gathering and reporting data on temperatures from the palaeoclimate to today's climate. The 'Team', as they called themselves, were bending and distorting scientific data to fit a nakedly political story-line profitable to themselves and congenial to the governments that, these days, pay the bills for 99% of all scientific research.

- The Climate Research Unit at East Anglia had profited to the tune of at least $20 million in 'research' grants from the Team's activities.

- The Team had tampered with the complex, bureaucratic processes of the UN's climate panel, the IPCC, so as to exclude inconvenient scientific results from its four Assessment Reports, and to influence the panel's conclusions for political rather than scientific reasons.

- The Team had conspired in an attempt to redefine what is and is not peer-reviewed science for the sake of excluding results that did not fit what they and the politicians with whom they were closely linked wanted the UN's climate panel to report.

- They had tampered with their own data so as to conceal inconsistencies and errors.

- They had expressed dismay at the fact that, contrary to all of their predictions, global temperatures had not risen in any statistically-significant sense for 15 years, and had been falling for nine years. They had admitted that their inability to explain it was 'a travesty'. This internal doubt was in contrast to their public statements that the present decade is the warmest ever, and that 'global warming' science is settled.

- They had interfered with the process of peer-review itself by leaning on journals to get their friends rather than independent scientists to review their papers.

- They had successfully leaned on friendly journal editors to reject papers reporting results inconsistent with their political viewpoint.

- They had campaigned for the removal of a learned journal's editor, solely because he did not share their willingness to debase and corrupt science for political purposes.

- They had mounted a venomous public campaign of disinformation and denigration of their scientific opponents via a website that they had expensively created.

- Contrary to all the rules of open, verifiable science, the Team had committed the criminal offence of conspiracy to conceal and then to destroy computer codes and data that had been legitimately requested by an external researcher who had very good reason to doubt that their 'research' was either honest or competent.

The emails once again refer to the efforts to 'contain' the medieval warm period when temperatures were higher than they are now with no industrial age carbon dioxide in the atmosphere. Ben Santer, a climate researcher and a lead author on the 1995 IPCC Working Group I Report, has admitted that he deleted sections which stated that humans were not responsible for climate change. Lord Monckton said: 'In comes Santer and re-writes it for them, after the scientists have sent in their finalised draft, and that finalised draft said at five different places, there is no discernable human effect on global temperature – I've seen a copy of this – Santer went through, crossed out all of those and substituted a new conclusion, and this has been the official conclusion ever since.' Manipulation of temperature data is not confined to the Climate Research Unit at East Anglia. NASA Goddard Science and Space Institute at Columbia University in New York and the National Climate Data Center in Ashville, North Carolina, have been exposed for doing the same. The number of temperature monitoring centres around the world contributing to the official temperature data has been reduced from some 6,000 to about 1,000. The ones eliminated were at cooler locations at higher altitudes. They are taking temperatures at warmer places, like beaches, and reporting this as the temperature recorded (or rather not) for mountain ranges hundreds of miles away. If you want to see the ludicrous way that temperature data is being manipulated, er, sorry, 'monitored', go to an article headed 'Quality of US Temperature Data' at **theclimateconspiracy.com**. It was revealed in January 2010 that a warning by the IPCC that climate change will melt most of the Himalayan glaciers by 2035 was based purely on a news story in the science magazine, *New Scientist*, published eight years before the IPCC's warning in 2007. What's more, the *New Scientist* 'news story' was based on a short telephone interview with Syed Hasnain, a little-known Indian scientist then working at Jawaharlal Nehru University in Delhi. Hasnain later admitted that the claim was 'speculation' and was not supported by any formal research. It is 'scientific' claptrap in other words, and yet the mainstream media, as always, repeated it without question, not least the pathetic BBC.

Bear Mendacities

The whole Carbon Cult survives on lies and gross misrepresentation. I mean, the polar bears are dying out, right? Everyone knows that, surely? But they're not. They are at their highest numbers since the 1950s. Dr Mitchell Taylor, who has been been researching polar bears in Canada and the Arctic Circle for 30 years, confirms this. Polar bears are flourishing. This fact does not suit the global warmers, however. They continue to promote their lies with the picture of two bears standing on melting ice which has been used constantly by Al Gore to support his fakery. Amanda Byrd, who took the picture off the Alaskan coast, has said that the bears were in no danger at all. She had taken it only because it was such a great photo. Dr Mitchell Taylor, despite being such a polar bear expert, was told to stay away from a meeting of the Polar Bear Specialist Group (PBSG) in 2009 because his observed facts did not accord with the global warming official line that the polar bears are under threat. He was told that his views ran 'counter to human-induced climate change [and] are extremely unhelpful'. I bet they are. Dr Taylor signed the Manhattan Declaration, which exposed the official line, and he was told that this was 'inconsistent with the position taken by the PBSG'. Never mind the facts, your 'position' is what matters. Okay, temperatures are not rising, polar bears are not dying out and the ice caps are not melting as they claim. Surely something they say is true. What about rising sea levels? Er, nope. Nils-Axel Mörner, a geologist and physicist, is the former chairman of the International Commission on Sea Level Change. He says that despite fluctuations, down as well as up, the sea is not rising and it hasn't risen in 50 years: 'Quite apart from examining the hard evidence, the elementary laws of physics (latent heat needed to melt ice) tell us that the apocalypse conjured up by Al Gore and Co could not possibly come about'. He says he was 'astonished' to discover that not one of the 22 contributing authors in the last two IPCC reports on sea levels was actually a sea level specialist – not *one*. He said this 'deliberate ignorance' – exactly what it is – and the use of rigged computer models had become the most powerful single driver of the entire 'warmist hysteria'. NASA's Dr John S Theon said:

> Gore faces a much different scientific climate in 2009 than the one he faced in 2006 when his film *An Inconvenient Truth* was released. According to satellite data, the Earth has cooled since Gore's film was released, Antarctic sea ice extent has grown to record levels, sea level rise has slowed, ocean temperatures have failed to warm, and more and more scientists have publicly declared their dissent from man-made climate fears as peer-reviewed studies continue to man-made counter warming fears.

What does 'Mr Change' Obama do about all this evidence that the 'global warming' frenzy is a manufactured scam? He ignores it and instead appoints initiates of the Carbon Cult, and Al Gore groupies, to every major position in the relevant departments of energy, environment and what passes for 'science'. Why would he do this? He's the bloodline's boy. His 'climate change czars' are Carol Browner (Rothschild Zionist) and Todd Stern (Rothschild Zionist), just as Britain's climate change policy at the time of writing is headed by Ed Miliband (Rothschild Zionist), brother of David Miliband (Rothschild Zionist), who is Foreign Secretary. The American Clean Energy and Security Act of June 2009 gives the government control over every aspect of the American economy and introduces the cap-and-trade system to make people like Al Gore even richer while devastating the lives of millions, indeed billions, with its knock-on effects. Gwen Moore, a Democrat Congresswoman, plumbed still new depths of naivety and ignorance when she said: 'The energy bill passed by the House today is a much needed, responsible measure that will reduce the amount of pollution pushed into our atmosphere and start to reverse the effects of global warming that threaten our planet'. It is a plan of taxation, control and de-industrialisation to solve a non-existent problem that carbon dioxide does not cause. The Manhattan Declaration said:

> Attempts by governments to legislate costly regulations on industry and individual citizens to encourage CO2 [carbon dioxide] reduction will slow development while having no appreciable impact on the future trajectory of global climate change. Such policies will markedly diminish future prosperity and so reduce the ability of societies to adapt to inevitable climate change, thereby increasing, not decreasing, human suffering.

Shocking as it is, that's the plan. They want to de-industrialise the world. Where is the media, with a few honourable exceptions? Doing what it always does – towing the official line. The respected British TV news anchor, Peter Sissons, exposed climate change censorship in a newspaper article after he left the BBC. He said he was one of only a tiny number of BBC interviewers who had so much as raised the possibility that there was another side to the debate on climate change. He said the BBC's most famous 'interrogators' invariably begin by accepting 'the science is settled' when, as he points out, there are countless reputable scientists that say it isn't. I watched the BBC *Newsnight* presenter, Jeremy Paxman, with his reputation for tough interviewing, give Al Gore the easiest of times with not one question about the validity of human-caused global warming. Peter Sissions said that the same unquestioning approach and censorship of scientists challenging the official line could be found throughout the BBC:

> … it is effectively BBC policy, enthusiastically carried out by the BBC environment correspondents, that those views should not be heard – witness the BBC statement last year that 'BBC News currently takes the view that their reporting needs to be calibrated to take into account the scientific consensus that global warming is man-made'.

There is no scientific consensus, only the engineered appearance of one thanks to the disgraceful excuses-for-journalists at the BBC and across the global media who refuse to give voice to the tens of thousands of scientists who say the official story is a scientific absurdity. Sissons recalls an extraordinary interview that he conducted with the leader of the UK Green Party, Caroline Lucas, a woman with serious 'climate change' myopia and a religious zealotry to make everyone conform to her misguided views. I knew her when I was in the party in the 1980s. Sissons said he pointed out to Lucas that the climate did not seem to be 'playing ball' with her claims about rising temperatures caused by carbon dioxide. He put to her that there had been no warming for ten years, contradicting all the alarming computer predictions. Lucas was outraged, he said, and told him it was disgraceful that the BBC should be giving any kind of publicity to 'those sorts of views'. This is a lady who heads a party that claims to stand for freedom of speech and information, but the Mind-made advocates of the Carbon Cult are like the most extreme of religious fanatics who say it is blasphemy to challenge their religion in any way. They live in a world of double-think schizophrenia in which they say they support human rights and freedom and then press for 'climate' laws of the most draconian kind. Lucas is yet another example of someone who claims to challenge the 'club' when she has long since joined it. 'Greens' like Lucas and unquestioning 'repeaters' in the media are essential to pedalling the lie about human-generated 'climate change'. Sissons said that 'disquiet' about the way he handled the interview with Lucas went 'right to the top of the BBC'. This is what you are dealing with in 'news' organisations worldwide, and not only with regard to 'climate change'. The BBC, which is supposed to be an independent organisation, is nothing more than an arm of government and most of its 'journalists' and presenters, Sissons and a few others apart, are so ignorant of the world they are reporting that they have no idea that this is so.

There was embarrassment for the BBC in October 2009, however, when one of its 'climate correspondents', Paul Hudson, wrote an article admitting that temperatures had not increased for eleven years. The headline on the BBC website summed it up: 'Whatever happened to global warming?' He quoted Professor Don Easterbrook from Western Washington University as saying that falling ocean temperatures virtually assured us that the Earth would be in a cooling phase for some 30 years. The article was tucked away on the BBC website, but other sites ran the story and, oh, what knickers found themselves in a twist. As London's *Daily Telegraph* said:

> BBC bosses will hate this. The quiet U-turn on global warming by its climate change correspondent, Paul Hudson, is currently the most popular story on its website, way ahead of the tragic death of Stephen Gately. The whole world now knows something that the Beeb would rather not acknowledge: that its specialist reporter on global warming admits that global warming is not happening – and may not start again for 30 years.

What a hoot. But the Climate Change groupies just ignored it like a Christian hearing that Jesus did not exist. In December 2009, Barack Obama and an estimated 16,500 politicians, delegates, activists and reporters attended the United Nations Climate Change Conference in Copenhagen. They discussed demands to drastically reduce global carbon emissions while themselves producing an estimated 40,584 tons of carbon dioxide in the process – including the use of some 140 aircraft carrying world leaders, heads of state and so-called 'VIPs'. This is about equivalent to the annual carbon production of Morocco. All this took place in the midst of the revelations about fixed and manipulated climate 'science', but politicians and climate extremists maintained business as usual. The final Copenhagen Accord included a call for a global 'governance structure' to control taxes on CO2 emissions while Britain and France announced they were developing proposals for a 'European monitoring organisation' that will oversee every country's actions on emissions. Obama even said that spy drones and satellites

will be used to enforce carbon emission laws. This 'save the Earth from global warming' conference took place in the coldest winter in the UK for some 30 years (the Met Office had predicted a 'mild winter', as it predicted a 'heatwave summer' in 2009 that turned out to be anything but). The rest of the northern hemisphere, from America to Europe and Asia, experienced one of the worst winters in living memory. Even Florida was struggling to record temperatures above freezing (Fig 81). Christopher Booker, author

Figure 81: *'It's getting warmer – honest'*

of *The Real Global Warming Disaster*, said: 'It is amazing how this scaremongering from climate change lobbyists keeps arising even though they are constantly being proved wrong. Last year there was snow in Saudi Arabia and still they persist in saying the temperature is going up.' Funnily enough, at the same time this was happening scientists said that sunspot activity had stopped for longer than any living scientist had seen. Sunspots can stop in the down cycles of the Sun, but this time it was continuing for much longer than usual. Marc Hairston, a space physicist at the University of Texas, said: 'This is the lowest we've ever seen. We thought we'd be out of it by now, but we're not.' The so-called solar wind – streams of particles emitted by the Sun – is also at its weakest since records began. None of this was mentioned, let alone discussed, in Copenhagen because it challenges the official story. Can you believe that according to the 'scientific consensus' (song sheet), the Sun has had only a minor recent effect on climate change. What? The bloody Sun has only a *minor effect* on temperature? Call the guys in white coats, please, if not for these chaps, then for me. Fortunately, the Climate Cult did not get all that it wanted in Copenhagen, but it did win agreement to continue with the laws that created the carbon trading industry that is soon to be worth trillions of dollars a year and has already made fortunes for people like the Rothschilds, Rockefellers and Al Gore. Outside the conference venue were thousands of 'environmental campaigners' protesting that the carbon emission targets were not severe enough and so, by definition, urging the Illuminati families to make themselves even richer than they would otherwise be. This is nothing to do with 'saving the world', nor even primarily about reducing carbon emissions. It is about money and control through the deception and perception of a 'problem' that never was. The Fabian Society's Bertrand Russell described in his book, *The Scientific Outlook*, published in 1931, how lies can become perceived fact in the mind of the masses:

> From the technique of advertising it seems to follow that in the great majority of mankind any proposition will win acceptance if it is reiterated in such a way as to remain in the memory. Most of the things that we believe we believe because we have heard them affirmed; we do not remember where or why they were affirmed, and we are therefore unable to be critical even when the affirmation was made by a man whose income would be increased by its acceptance and was not backed by any evidence whatsoever.

In other words, a man like Al Gore. Fortunately, the public is increasingly not buying it.

Sustainable Control

The climate change agenda is connected to something called Sustainable Development. The term sounds a sensible idea at first, but it is a buzz-phrase that hides the real purpose – to use the excuse of the environment to transform global society. The Sustainable Development movement emerged from the 1992 United Nations Earth Summit in Brazil and a document called Agenda 21. The summit, formerly known as the United Nations Conference on Environment and Development (UNCED), was led by Maurice Strong, a Rockefeller frontman who is very close to the Chinese government (Fig 82 overleaf). He is mentioned many times in my book ... *And The Truth Shall Set You Free*. Strong is like a silent partner to Al Gore. One does the public profile, the other

Figure 82: *Maurice Strong ... the silent partner behind Al Gore*

manipulates in the background, but both make money from the climate change fantasy they peddle. Strong is a director of the Chicago Climate Exchange (largest shareholder, Goldman Sachs), which is described as 'the world's first and North America's only legally binding greenhouse-gas emission registry reduction-system for emission sources and offset projects in North America and Brazil'. Crucial funding to launch the Chicago Climate Exchange came from the 'charity', the Joyce Foundation, which handed over more than a million dollars. One of the Joyce Foundation directors at the time ... Barack Obama. As the late and great American comedian, George Carlin, said: 'It's a big club and you ain't in it.' Maurice Strong has been one of the major players in the Illuminati environmental conspiracy (and the 'New Age') and was a key figure behind the Kyoto climate change protocol signed by nearly 190 countries. He is quoted as saying, in line with the Rothschild plan for de-industrialisation: 'The rich countries won't do it. They won't change ... Isn't the only hope for the planet that the industrialised civilisations collapse? Isn't it our responsibility to bring that about?' Strong's 'green' CV is incredible. He has been a chairman of the World Resources Institute and closely involved with: the International Institute for Sustainable Development; Stockholm Environment Institute; Africa-America Institute; Institute of Ecology in Indonesia; Beijer Institute of the Royal Swedish Academy of Sciences; World Economic Forum; Advisory Council for the Center for International Development at Harvard University; World Business Council for Sustainable Development; World Conservation Union; World Wildlife Fund; and Resources for the Future. He also helped to establish the Earth Council and Earth Charter movement. He was a personal envoy for two years to UN Secretary-General Kofi Annan and he has been a senior advisor to the President of the World Bank and served on the International Advisory Board of Toyota. He has had a considerable business career that has made him a billionaire. Very sustainable. If Strong is involved, it is a Rockefeller operation, and if it is their operation it is the Rothschilds' operation. The whole 'climate change', 'global warming' campaign, with its breathtaking deceit, is connected with this 'Sustainable Development' agenda that ties in with Al Gore's lie machine, the Illuminati Club of Rome and the Round Table network like the Council on Foreign Relations, Trilateral Commission and Bilderberg Group. You see the term 'sustainable development' everywhere and the United Nations Division of Sustainable Development is just one of thousands of examples. Ironically, the main players behind all this are some of the biggest environmental assassins, although it's not an irony, really. It is just the way the game is played.

The foundation document of 'sustainable development' is the Biodiversity Treaty signed at Maurice Strong's UN Earth Summit in 1992. It is an internationally-binding treaty involving around 200 countries and it is a charter for land confiscation under the guise of 'saving the environment'. It also involves the government control of all water supply and usage, and the handling of power over land, resources and ecology to the United Nations and its successor, a world government. The United States signed the treaty, but it was not ratified by the Senate thanks to people like ecologist and ecosystem scientist, Dr Michael Coffman, who realised in the course of his work in the 1980s and 1990s that there was a plan to, in effect, confiscate half of America's land in the name of protecting the environment. This includes removing roads to destroy rural communities and force the people into the cities, as the bloodline agenda demands. We are already seeing rural exit roads from highways being removed to do just this.

The Totalitarian Tiptoe

One other point about mass manipulation: the bosom buddy of Problem-Reaction-Solution is the technique I call the 'Totalitarian Tiptoe' and the two work together. The Totalitarian Tiptoe goes like this: you are standing at point 'A' and you know you are taking people to point 'Z', but you have to keep this agenda hidden if you are going to make it to the end without a level of protest that would thwart you. So you don't go the whole way in one leap because the change would be so fast and obvious that people would look up from the television (tell-a-vision/sell-a-vision) or the sports game and ask what was going on. Instead, you move forward in steps A to B to C and so on. You go as fast as you can, but not so fast that you attract the scale of opposition that could stop you. Each step is presented as unconnected to the others to ensure the connections are never seen, except by those comparatively few that are awake to the game. By the time many of the rest begin to see it because by then it is so obvious, it's too late, a fait accompli. What we have today in Europe, and what is planned to follow with a United States of Europe under dictatorial control, was the aim from the start, as I explained earlier. The same has been happening in the United States, Canada and Mexico with regard to the North American Union. But when you know what the goal is, a centrally-controlled global police state, and you know the main methods of taking us there – Problem-Reaction-Solution and the Totalitarian Tiptoe – you are able to see what most of the population of the world cannot. This is why I have been stressing these three things at every opportunity since the early 1990s.

I have presented so far a summary of how the bloodlines have passed through 'history', what they are seeking to achieve, and the methods they are using to get there. The evidence and detail is simply enormous, and increasing all the time, and you can find it in my other works. Now the big question: where do these bloodlines come from?

Sit down and strap in.

10

He said they're *what?*

If you want to know the Illuminati, study the reptile
Credo Mutwa

It was a real shock when I was guided to this next revelation, and no doubt it will be for you if you are new to the subject. The concrete minds of the media ridicule me for it, as do most people in the field of 'conspiracy research'; but I don't give a bugger. It is what it is.

As I travelled America for three months in 1996, talking to what were then tiny audiences, I began to pick up on a theme here and there that the bloodlines were the genetic offspring of a race of reptilian entities. No, its okay, your eyes are working, don't worry. I really did say a race of reptilian entities. I am open to all possibility and I don't just dismiss something because it seems outrageous to the programmed mind; but, for sure, when I first heard about the reptilian connection I thought: *What?* Say that again and speak *very* slowly! I did what I do with everything that I can't immediately understand or fit together. I put it on the 'back burner' and let it bubble away until more information comes along (or doesn't) to make more sense of it; and come it did, in increasing abundance, after my next trip to America a year later. In a 15-day period in 1997, as I moved from place to place across the country, I met twelve different people who told me of their experiences with reptilian entities they had either seen themselves or heard about from friends and family. After that, the theme was constant for years to come. It was like, okay, next stage – look at this. Since 1990, I have often had this experience where a new theme suddenly enters my life and then bang, it comes from all angles. I didn't go looking for it; as usual it came to me. I knew it would bring another dose of ridicule to deal with, but, so what? If it's happening we need to know. The common accounts and themes were so compelling that there was no way I was going to ignore it just because people would find it hard to believe. If you let programmed perceptions and 'norms' dictate what you do and say to avoid ridicule or condemnation, how is anything ever going to change or move on? It became clear to me that the Illuminati bloodlines are human-reptilian hybrids, and the offspring of a race of reptilian humanoids that are widely described in ancient legends and accounts. The Rothschilds and the bloodline family network obsessively and incessantly interbreed because they are seeking to retain their 'special' genetics which would be quickly diluted by breeding with the general population. Researcher, Stewart Swerdlow, who discovered the reptilian connection as a captive in a US government mind-control programme, says that these hybrid bloodlines are the origin of the term 'blue bloods' to

describe royal and aristocratic families. He says
their blood contains more copper, and during a
process called oxidisation it turns a blue-green
colour. The reptilian race covertly controlling
human society is from a dimension of reality very
close to this one, but beyond visible light and
that's why we don't see them. They can move in
and out of visible light, however, and there are
reptilian 'cities' and bases inside the Earth. Some
top-secret underground military bases connect
with them. The hybrid bloodlines, like the
Rothschilds, serve their agenda on the surface and
within visible light.

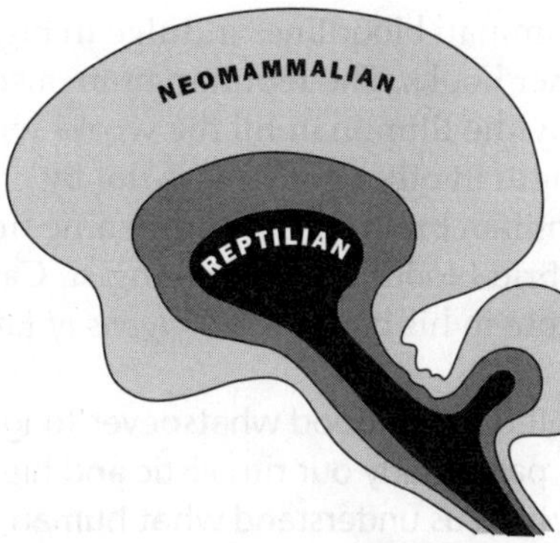

Figure 83: *The reptilian brain, or 'R'-complex', is one of the most powerful influences on human behaviour and perception*

The lizard in your head

People don't realise that all humans have reptilian genetics and they are fundamental to
human behaviour. 'Pheromone' is the substance secreted and released by animals so
they can be detected by members of the same species, and the pheromones in human
women and iguanas are a chemical match. You only have to look at the bottom of the
human spine to see the remnants of a tail, and some people continue to be born with
tails, or 'caudal appendages' as doctors call them. Most are removed soon after birth but
in some poorer countries, where medical support is not available, there are people who
live their whole lives with tails. A major part of the human brain is known by scientists
as the 'R-complex' or 'reptilian brain' (Fig 83). It is the most obvious expression of our
reptilian genetic history and has an enormous effect on our behaviour. In so many ways
human behaviour *is* the reptilian brain. It is home to our animalistic desires and
reactions and looks very much the same as the brains of lizards and other reptiles. Birds,
which some believe came from reptiles, also have a reptilian brain. Scientists say that it
represents a core of the human nervous system and is responsible for character traits
like aggression; cold-blooded and ritualistic behaviour; a desire for control; power and
ownership – 'territoriality'; might is right; domination; submission; compulsions and
obsessions; worship; rigidity; and a desire for social hierarchies. Is it really a coincidence
that the character traits of the reptilian brain are overwhelmingly those of the Illuminati
bloodline families and the societies they have created? I say not. Researcher, Skip
Largent, wrote this in an Internet article about the R-complex:

> At least five human behaviours originate in the reptilian brain. Without defining them,
> I shall simply say that in human activities they find expression in: obsessive compulsive
> behaviour; personal day-to-day rituals and superstitious acts; slavish conformance to old
> ways of doing things; ceremonial re-enactments; obeisance to precedent, as in legal,
> religious, cultural, and other matters and all manner of deceptions.

This again perfectly describes the behaviour of the bloodlines and the institutions they
have created. Reptilian genetics are also the source of their cold-blooded behaviour and
their lack of empathy with their billions of daily victims. Racism, and a sense of racial
superiority, comes from the reptilian brain, as does the aggressive, violent sex that the

Illuminati bloodlines indulge in big time – see the Illuminati names that I expose in my other books. The reptilian brain also communicates through visual imagery and that's why the Illuminati fill the world with their symbols and logos, as I have detailed at length in other books. It is not by chance that the Illuminati manifest all the traits of the reptilian brain while, at the same time, the evidence points to them being reptilian-hybrid bloodlines. Cosmologist, Carl Sagan, who knew far more than he was telling, wrote in his book, *The Dragons of Eden*:

> It does no good whatsoever to ignore the reptilian component of human nature, particularly our ritualistic and hierarchical behaviour. On the contrary, the model may help us understand what human beings are really about.

I am going to describe the effects on human behaviour of our reptilian genetics, and remember that these effects are going to be much more powerful in the Illuminati bloodlines with their far greater infusion of reptilian genetic codes. The reptilian brain *reacts* rather than thinks. We talk about people acting without engaging their brain, but what we are really saying is that they reacted from the reptilian brain without engaging the area known as the neocortex that likes to think things through. The reptilian brain is home to the body's reactive emotions and survival responses, in close association with an area in the centre of the brain called the amygdala, an almond-shaped mass of neurons in the region known as the limbic brain. When these guys press the panic button you can forget calm and reason. They want their mum – and fast. When we react to danger by fleeing, fighting or freezing (what psychologists call 'fight or flight'), this is the reptilian brain at work. It is constantly scanning its environment for possible dangers and reacting accordingly. When it thinks it can defeat the perceived danger it will fight; when it decides that it can't, it runs. It can also freeze the body – 'frozen with fear'. This is triggered by reflex responses that relate to animals that freeze in dangerous situations, where movement could alert a predator. The reptilian brain has two states: 'safe' and 'unsafe', with nothing in between. When it feels safe and relaxed the neocortex is allowed the peace and quiet to 'think straight', or at least straighter; when

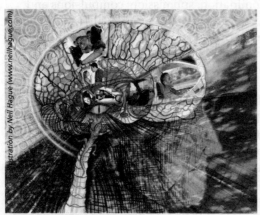

the reptilian brain feels threatened and unsafe it reacts like Corporal Jones in the UK television comedy series, *Dad's Army*. It runs around shouting 'don't panic, don't panic', while doing exactly that (Fig 84). Fear is contagious if you succumb to it, as research and experience has shown. Researchers at the University of Dusseldorf in Germany put cotton pads under the armpits of 49 student volunteers before a university exam, and collected sweat from the same students while they rode exercise bikes. A different group of students was then asked to sniff the cotton pads while their brains were monitored by an MRI

Figure 84: *If we allow ourselves to succumb to fear and the survival instincts, our perceptions, responses and lives are controlled by the reptilian brain*

Illustration by Neil Hague (www.neilhague.com)

scanner. They said they could not tell the difference between the 'panic sweat' and the 'exercise sweat', but their brains could. The panic sweat triggered areas of the brain that deal with emotions and empathy. It is, in fact, true that you can 'smell the fear', and fear is also communicated vibrationally to create potentially mass panic, with the reptilian brain leading the way.

The reptilian brain kicks in to override the thought processes of the neocortex with emotional responses based on fear of not surviving. This is when we talk about people 'losing their heads'. Well, yes they do. They lose their head to the reptilian brain. By survival, I don't just mean physical survival. The reptilian brain also decodes the business of survival as protecting status, power, reputation and superiority, intellectual pre-eminence, sense of self, and so on. When scientists, historians and religious advocates aggressively or dismissively reject new information or views that would demolish their rigid beliefs, they are activating the reptilian brain, or, rather, the reptilian brain is activating them. Their survival mechanism has been triggered. You see the same with so-called 'sceptics' who are obsessed with trashing any views or information that are at odds with their own set-in-concrete perceptions. It is another form of fear – fear of being wrong, fear of the world not being like you believed it was, and so sceptics are overwhelmingly slaves of the reptilian brain. A 'sceptic' is not someone who questions, as the word might imply. They set out from the start to undermine another view simply because it is different to their own. It is a reptilian-brain survival response. Most people glean a sense of security from having a fixed view of 'the way things are' and we see this in religion, science, politics, 'education', medicine, the whole lot. When these status quos are challenged in any way, the reptilian brain reads this as a danger that must be vanquished by either crushing the perceived 'opponent' (as with religious and scientific persecution), or by ignoring new insights and behaving as if they don't exist.

The reptilian brain doesn't operate in the realm that we call 'time' and so cannot discriminate between memory and current experience. When we have a memory of something related to being unsafe, the reptilian brain will respond as if we are actually having the experience. Think of something threatening and your body will respond as if it's real. People can wake up from a dream in a sweat, scream out or experience their body 'freezing', because the reptilian brain doesn't know the difference between real and imagined. It just reacts and it can do so with lightening speed, free from the need to think things through. The neocortex does that and is much slower to respond than the R-complex. An old proverb said, in words also attributed by some to Mark Twain: 'A lie will go round the world while truth is pulling its boots on.' The same can be said about the reptilian brain and the neocortex. The reptilian reaction and the consequences can be a done deal before calm consideration has even begun to consider. Look at how fast reptilian-brained lizards, snakes and birds can react to danger. It is a reaction-system. The reptilian brain also regulates breathing (hence it changes when we are in fear or highly emotional); digestion (hence 'nervous stomach'); elimination of waste (hence 'scared shitless'); circulation and temperature (both fundamentally affected by fear, danger and emotion); movement, posture and balance (hence you can read someone's emotional state by their body language). The reptilian brain never sleeps, it is searching for danger 24/7, and it keeps you breathing while you are in the land of nod.

Reptilian Society

The reptilian brain does not learn from mistakes, it just reacts to pre-programmed triggers based around survival and fear. It reacts immediately to situations in ways that we can later regret. When the reptilian brain is out of control it can be very destructive, and cause anything from a massive row with a partner to a world war. It communicates through images, not words, and so it is the target for the advertising industry, especially those with a sexual theme. Part of the reptilian brain survival programme is to seek out a mate and have sex to propagate the species. Sexual desire, and the potential for behaviour manipulation through sexual stimulus, comes from the reptilian brain. Just look at advertisements and see how they are dominated by themes of sex and survival in countless forms. The idea is to stimulate the reptilian brain as early as possible to make it a dominating force in even young children. This is one reason why sexual awareness is being introduced earlier and earlier. The bloodline-created-and-controlled United Nations is recommending that children as young as five receive mandatory sex education that would teach about masturbation and topics like 'gender violence'. The recommendation is included in a report by the UN's Economic, Social and Cultural Organization (UNESCO) and says that children between five and eight should be told that that 'touching and rubbing one's genitals is called masturbation' and that private parts 'can feel pleasurable when touched by oneself'. Michelle Turner, of Citizens for a Responsible Curriculum, asked: 'Why can't kids be kids anymore?' Answer: the cabal doesn't want them to be.

The whole issue of money is the reptilian brain again. Not surprisingly, given that money controls global society, the reptilian brain equates money with survival. It fears not having enough and sees having more than enough as giving it a better chance to survive. This is one reason why people can be obsessed with the accumulation of money even after they have enough for a dozen lifetimes. Money can also be used, and is, of course, to impose power and control over others and that is another trait of the reptilian brain. Once again, it sees having power over others as increasing its potential for survival. The same goes for food. Having enough to eat is clearly basic to surviving in the world as we perceive it and that's another role for the reptilian brain. As with money, it can see more than enough as meaning a better chance of survival, and so many people eat far too much because of the primitive survival urges of the reptilian brain that have gotten out of hand. When you see people fighting each other for food during shortages this is the reptilian brain at work big-time. The 'shouting matches' between people are reptilian brains communicating in the only way they know how. The thug and the bully are puppets of the reptilian brain and this includes dictators and tyrants of every kind. It is the cause of behaviours like 'road rage'. If someone cuts in front of you, the R-complex sees this as your territory being invaded and reacts accordingly. The reptilian brain also connects with self-image and the need for 'status', as described in an Internet article I read at **eruptingmind.com**:

> Things that promise to improve the way you look, and/or the health of your body, stimulate reptilian brain responses such as obsessive, compulsive behaviour, dominance and self-maintenance. This is why some people become addicted to buying clothes, shoes, vitamins and [obsessed with] their overall appearance. What you may notice

when you see people advertising these products is that they all tend to be very attractive. Ever wonder why?

While attractive people are used because sex helps to increase sales, another reason why sex is used is to make you feel inadequate. Especially if you are not as attractive, wealthy and powerful as the person advertising the product. This stimulates aggression, jealousy, submission and/or a desire to compete with them.

By purchasing the product, your unconscious and irrational brain associates the purchasing of that product with the person advertising it. This is one reason why celebrities are commonly used in advertising. It provides a false illusion of the product transferring what the celebrity has to you ...

Most advertisements, government statements and engineered events are aimed at the reptilian brain. It works closely with the limbic brain and the amygdala. The limbic brain deals with emotions in a different way and connects them to memories. For this reason, we are more likely to remember events that are related to an emotional feeling or charge. It supports the survival demands of the reptilian brain by seeking to make survival instincts such as eating and sex as pleasurable as possible, so we are more likely to repeat them and, on the other hand, to make as unpleasant and painful as possible the things we do that could threaten survival. Fortunately, it is not as totally reactive as the reptilian brain in that it does have the potential to learn from experience.

Now, even before I go much deeper into this, consider the way global society is controlled and manipulated today. It is done through the reptilian brain. The technique that I call 'Problem-Reaction-Solution' operates almost entirely by activating the survival responses in the reptilian brain, and look at what I call it again: Problem-*Reaction*-Solution. The whole idea is to get the reptilian brain to react to the alleged problem with fear and a sense of danger so we will be open to the 'solution', the perceived 'saviour' and 'protector' from that danger. 'Oh, my God, there are terrorists everywhere. Take my freedoms away, microchip me, tell me what to do, anything, just save me.' This is why the foundation of the conspiracy is to keep the population in a constant state of fear, anxiety, stress and worry. These are all expressions of 'danger' and they lock us into the reptilian brain reaction programme. This operates at all levels of human experience, from fear of losing your partner, to fear of losing your job and your home, of death, of others dying, of 'God', of the 'Devil', and fear of Armageddon. Once people are in fear of not surviving in some way – physically, financially, whatever – they instinctively give their power away to anyone or anything they believe can protect them. The 'they' that is doing this is the reptilian brain. The way the world is structured as pyramid-within-pyramid hierarchies is classic reptilian brain, and so is the way that billions of people subordinate themselves to hierarchy and 'know their place'. Look at what happens when an authority figure, say a boss, walks into a room or calls you to his or her office. Most people have some emotional reaction that relates, mildly or strongly, to fear. Keith Miller, an American 'relationship therapist', wrote a very interesting Internet article about the reptilian brain and human relationships. He observed:

… when an authority figure enters the room, the portion of your brain that scans the environment may send the danger signal to the reptilian brain, even if you get along relatively well with that person. For many people, it is hard to relate to their bosses without slipping into fight (which usually takes the form of 'logically' disagreeing with whatever the boss or company says); flight (which is usually 'escaping' into avoidance behaviour – not saying what you really think or not expressing how you really feel); or freeze behaviours (when a normally intelligent and engaging person goes 'brain dead').

I have heard celebrities who don't agree with the monarchy describe how they go 'brain dead' in the presence of the Queen and act in a subordinate way to someone they would otherwise be cynical and critical about. Once again, that is the reptilian brain responding to a sense of danger in the face of an ultimate symbol of authority and reverting to hierarchy and 'knowing its place'. The reptilian brain was the target for Rothschild Zionist David Axelrod in the election campaigns that he and his associates ran for Barack Obama. The response from the crowds that Obama addressed across America did not come from the neocortex (listening to what he said, considering it, asking questions and demanding more detail); it came from the reptilian brain as an emotional reaction – change, hope, yes we can, something to believe in. Tibetan mystics define a destructive emotion as a state of being that distorts 'our perception of reality'. This is precisely what an out-of-control reptilian brain does, and this is why it's the key to human control. The depth of that statement will become ever more obvious as this book unfolds. I am still just scratching the surface here. Another Tibetan definition of a destructive emotion is 'excessive attachment' and, oh my goodness, that is so true. We have attachments to relationships (mostly based on emotional 'need'), beliefs, status quos, outcomes, money, and material 'things' in general. Once you form any attachment based on a perceived 'need', you are setting yourself up immediately with a fear of losing whatever you are attached to. When we think it could happen, even as a concept with no supporting evidence, the reptilian brain decodes reality accordingly and we live a life of constant unease through the fear of losing what we say has made us 'happy'. The reptilian brain is the reactive 'autopilot' working subconsciously to dictate so much of human behaviour, and it is this which goes to war, seeks to defeat the 'competition', impose its will, and crush anything that gets in its way. Emphasis on the word, 'subconsciously'. I talked earlier in the book about humans not being conscious and this will be a theme throughout. Most human behaviour is unconscious reaction and programmed response, and the reptilian brain is the autopilot through which it happens.

One other thing …The Illuminati bloodlines and their genetically-related agents are liars to an extraordinary degree. They lie constantly. Everything is a lie. They justify their agendas by lies and deceit, and they lie and deceive each other in their attempts to climb the greasy pole of power and status. I have described Tony Blair as a genetic liar and, when it comes to the bloodlines, that is literally true. The reptilian brain will do anything to survive, and it lies without any remorse if that is what it believes it must do to survive. I have had people like that in my own life and they lie so outrageously and without conscience that it takes you a while to accept that they have been lying, such whoppers do they tell with a straight face. They even have the nerve to reel back in outrage when anyone suggests they might not be telling the truth. Lying is just another weapon in the reptilian brain survival system. Tony Blair cannot tell the truth or he would be in jail with

George W Bush as a cellmate, and so he lies. Then he lies to cover his previous lies, and so it goes on. Every trait of the reptilian brain is compounded in the bloodlines, which have much greater reptilian genetics. Humans lie, but to the bloodlines and their offshoots lying is a way of life. I have said a number of times so far that these people have no shame and, because of that, they can lie without guilt or emotional consequence. The reptilian brain says: 'I lie because I have to survive; what's the problem?' The reptilian bloodlines say: 'I lie to get what I want; what's the problem?'

Reptilian Infiltration

I am not going to repeat all the detailed evidence about the reptilian connection here because it is available elsewhere in books like *Children of the Matrix*, *The Biggest Secret* and *The David Icke Guide to the Global Conspiracy (and how to end it)*. I will set out only what is necessary for the dots to be connected and the picture to be seen. Hybrid bloodlines were seeded in the ancient and prehistoric world by the genetic union of humans and non-human races 'from the stars'. This is how at least many of the variations in human form came about. It is a common theme throughout the world in the legends and accounts of native peoples, almost wherever you go. The word 'Zulu' alone means 'Children of the Stars' and virtually every native culture has its stories and legends of the 'star people', and other names, who interacted and interbred with humans. They are the origins of the ancient and modern 'gods'. The idea that we are alone in this universe and that life as we know it only exists on this one little planet in this one little solar system is extraordinary, but that is the academic mind for you when it is welded shut. Bulgarian government scientists even announced in 2009 that 'aliens already exist on earth' and they were in contact with them. Lachezar Filipov, deputy director of the Space Research Institute of the Bulgarian Academy of Sciences, confirmed the story. 'Aliens are currently all around us, and are watching us all the time', Filipov told the Bulgarian media. This is what the ancients said. They called them 'the Watchers'. The Bulgarian scientists further claimed to be in contact with extraterrestrial life and said the 'aliens' were in the process of answering 30 questions they had posed. Filipov said the Space Research Institute was deciphering a complex set of symbols sent to them and analysing 150 crop circles from around the world, which they believed answer the questions. There are many non-human races, or groups, who visit the Earth, but the one most relevant to the global conspiracy takes a reptilian form and it seeded the Illuminati bloodlines that today control global finance, politics, business, governments, the military, medicine, 'science', 'education' and connected institutions. More than that, it created the human form as we know it and used genetic manipulation to infuse reptilian genetics through which their slave race – Homo sapiens, and the 'upgrade' Homo sapiens sapiens – could be controlled. Fantastic? See what you think …

Reptilian races abound in the universe and can be found in many forms and variations, from those of humanoid appearance with green scaly skin, to albino whites, and those with tails and horns, even wings (Figs 85 and 86 overleaf) . Some are malevolent, like those manipulating humanity; some are benevolent, and most are somewhere in between. Among their locations are the Draco (Latin for 'Dragon') constellation in the northern sky, from which we get the appropriate term 'draconian'; the stars of the Big Dipper, also known as 'the Plough', in the same region of the heavens as Draco; the star system of Orion, and many others. Zulu historian, Credo

Figure 85

Figure 86

Two of the many types of Reptilian entities painted here from ancient and modern descriptions by Zulu Shaman, Credo Mutwa, and British artist, Hilary Reed

Mutwa, said that the Draco Reptilians are the most merciless, violent and destructive of the species, a theme I have picked up many times. They consider themselves 'royal'. Zulu lore and legend call them the 'Nommo', and the Draco constellation is known as Kayannomo – 'Home of the Nommo'. 'They are stinky, slimy and ugly', Credo said, and the Nommo are the most feared. African people were warned never to point to the Draco constellation, he said. Another theme is of different Reptilian factions and races fighting with each other for power and control. This is especially true of the war-like control-freaks, the Draconians, or Nommo. Reptilian races can look very different and act very differently from each other. What I will call for simplicity the 'Reptilians' include a whole range of factions, groups and genetic types. No single group represents them all, any more than Charles Manson represents all Americans, or Jack the Ripper the people of Britain. The manipulating Reptilians do not generally live within what is called 'visible light', the frequency range that our eyes can see.They operate mostly in a dimension just beyond human sight, although they can move between their 'world' and our own. This is why I often call them 'interdimensionals' rather than extraterrestrials. Our reality is what is known as 'Third Density' and the Reptilian entities manipulating human society come from the Fourth Density which resonates to a frequency range that we cannot currently decode and 'see'. It is still a 'physical' realm, though less dense than this one, and very different to our own. Entities there do not eat 'solid' food as we do, but instead get their sustenance from forms of energy.

The Fourth Density is like this one in the sense that the whole spectrum of states of being exist there, from those of great love and harmony to others, like this Reptilian faction, who have a lust for power and control and have hatred in what pass for their hearts. This desire for power and control betrays what they really are – insecure and full of fear. Whenever we think, or feel emotion, we generate energy, and the nature of the thought or emotion dictates the vibrational resonance of that energy. The Reptilians, because of their states of being, are very low-vibration entities within Fourth Density and so they must feed off low-vibration energy that 'syncs' with them. This energy – their 'food source' – is low-vibration human thought and emotion based on fear. This also includes emotional states like stress, depression, anxiety, guilt, anger, hatred and so on. Now we can see why this world is as it is. It has been manipulated and structured to generate maximum fear and stress in all its forms. Think of the energetic consequences of all the wars alone. When we think, or when we feel emotion, we can't see the energy it generates because it vibrates beyond human sight and 'bleeds' into the Fourth Density where it can be absorbed by these Reptilian entities. In short, we are their food source – and they are terrified that we will cease to be. The Peruvian-born writer, Carlos Castaneda, wrote a series of books from the late 1960s featuring who he said was a Yaqui Indian healer, or shaman, in Mexico called Don Juan Matus. There has been debate about whether or not Don Juan really existed, but that is a side issue. Wherever Castaneda got his information, the words attributed to Don Juan are magnificently accurate. He spoke of 'predators' that had taken over the human mind, as I will expand on later; and Castaneda reports here what Don Juan said about the predators' desire for the energy of children:

> ... He explained that sorcerers saw infant human beings as strange luminous balls of energy, covered from the top to the bottom with a glowing coat, something like a coat of plastic adjusted tightly around the cocoon of energy. He said that glowing coat of awareness was what the predators consumed and that when a human reached adulthood, all that was left of that fringe awareness was a narrow fringe that went from the ground to the top of the toes. That fringe permitted mankind to keep on living, but only barely.

Humans have a particular type of energy, and the Reptilians have structured human society to trawl that energy, especially from children when it is at its most 'pure'. There are Reptilian entities that operate within visible light, and there are colonies of them in underground cities and tunnel systems that are widely described in ancient and modern accounts. They also live inside the Moon and I will go into detail about this later. The power structure, however, is located in the Fourth Density and while those entities can, and do, manifest in our Third Density they can't stay here for long with our vibrational realm alien to their own body resonance. They have to return to Fourth Density to energetically replenish and re-'harmonise' themselves. Drinking human blood, though, helps them to stay here longer. It contains the human energetic codes and helps maintain their vibrational state in greater synchronisation with this reality. It also gives them energetic sustenance. Here you have the connection between the Reptilians and the legends about vampires and also the blood-drinking human-sacrifice networks that we know as 'Satanism'. Whenever I research a significant player in the conspiracy the connections lead to Satanism eventually. This is why.

Fourth Density Reptilians manipulate this reality by possessing 'human bodies' and taking over their mental and emotional processes. They 'wear' these bodies like a sort of spacesuit. It allows them to dictate events in this world without actually being 'in' it. Scientists who need to work with dangerous material will often don arms-length gloves that allow them to work inside a sealed tank while they themselves stand on the outside. The principle is the same. This is where the Reptilian hybrid bloodlines come in. They have been genetically-developed to have a sympathetic resonance with these Fourth Density entities thanks to their greater infusion of reptilian codes. It means that these hybrid bloodlines can be far more powerfully possessed by the Fourth Density Reptilians than the general population. The Illuminati bloodlines are simply the genetic vehicles that allow the Reptilians to control our world while hiding behind apparent

Illustration by Neil Hague (www.neilhague.com)

Figure 87: *The Reptilians possess apparently human form, and world leaders like Father George Bush are only the outer 'shell' that we see with our five senses within visible light. Their minds and 'emotions' are dictated by Reptilian entities that operate just beyond the frequency range that we can decode and 'see'*

human form (Fig 87). We decode the frequency range of visible light, and so we see only human bodies in the power structures of politics, banking, business, the media, the military and royalty; but if we could see beyond that we would see that those who dictate human events are overshadowed by entities that are anything but human. The global secret society network is there to manipulate these possessed bloodlines, and their agents, into the positions of power across the world. In other words, to put the Fourth Density Reptilians in those positions of power. Ancient texts across the world, including the Bible, feature this faction of Reptilian dictators under many names and in many forms. These include 'serpent gods' and 'serpent goddesses' and the symbolic snake in the Garden of Eden. The story of Adam and Eve in the Garden of Eden comes from Sumer, where the garden of the Reptilian 'gods' was referred to in the Sumerian Tablets as EDIN or EDEN. The Bible says, of course, that Eve was tempted by a serpent. An ancient Jewish text known as the *Haggadah* does not describe the

reptile in the Garden of Eden as a snake, but as a two-footed serpent that stood upright as tall as a camel. Ancient accounts found at Nag Hammadi in Egypt in 1945 say that Adam and Eve had horny, luminous skin. In Jewish lore, Eve is seen as the ancestral mother of the 'Nefilim' and she is associated with Hebrew words meaning 'life' and 'snake'. The Nefilim are described in the Bible as the 'sons of God' who interbred with 'the daughters of men':

> There were giants in the earth in those days; and also after that, when the sons of God came in unto the daughters of men, and they bare children to them, the same became mighty men which were of old, men of renown.

You find the same theme in ancient cultures across the world, and the use of the word 'God' there is misleading. It comes from a word meaning 'gods', plural.

Sumer, Sumer, Everywhere

When I am asked occasionally about the Reptilian information on Christian radio stations, I pose a simple question: do you really think that the 'serpent' in the Garden of Eden was literally a snake? I have often noticed over the years how people ridicule the views of others while never questioning their own far more bizarre beliefs. Is it more extreme and crazy to say that the serpent of Eden is symbolic of a humanoid, two-legged, two-armed, upright Reptilian entity, or that it was literally a snake that could talk to people? The ancient Hebrew word for serpent is 'Nachash' and this did not originally refer to a snake, but to a highly intelligent and cunning entity with the ability to communicate with humans. The Nachash stood upright on two legs. Most of the real meaning of the biblical texts has been lost in translation and manipulation. The Bible is claimed to be the unique word of 'God', but it is a collection of ancient stories and texts – some symbolic, some literal – that are repeats and re-writes of legends and accounts that originated thousands of years before the 'Holy Book', or its religious expressions, Christianity and Judaism. It is no coincidence that a highly significant figure in Judaism, Christianity and Islam is the man the Bible calls 'Abraham', who is said to have come from Ur, in Babylon, or 'Shinar' – the land of Sumer/Mesopotamia; nor that in 1975 the origin of the name 'Jerusalem', the city revered by Judaism, Christianity and Islam, was found on Sumerian and Babylonian tablets and written as URU-SA-LIM. Sumer expert, Samuel Noah Cramer, said in *History Begins in Sumer*:

> The archaeological research conducted in the "land of the Bible" that has produced such important results also throws light on the Bible itself, on its origins and the background in which it came into being. We now know that this book, the greatest classic of all times, did not come out of nowhere, like an artificial flower appearing in an empty vase. This book has roots that plunge into a distant past and extend to neighbouring lands … The Sumerians obviously did not exert a direct influence on the Hebrews, since they vanished long before the latter came on the scene. But there is no doubt that they influenced the Canaanites, the forerunners of the Hebrews in Palestine. This explains the many analogies between Sumerian texts and certain books of the Bible. These analogies are not isolated, but often occur in series … they are genuine parallels.

The tale of 'Moses' is one example of the biblical sleight-of-hand. The Bible says that a Princess found baby Moses floating on the river in a basket of bulrushes, and he was then brought up in the royal household. This same basic story was told long before about Sargon of Agade (Akkad), King of Babylon around 2550 BC. As I have already said, the biblical tale of Noah and the Great Flood is an almost verbatim repeat of stories told in Sumer and other ancient Mesopotamian civilisations, including Babylon; but then so is much of the Old Testament, especially Genesis and Exodus. The 'Noah' in the Mesopotamian originals is called Gilgamesh and, interestingly, the 'god' who warned him to build an ark to survive the flood is given the name 'Enki'. This guy, according to the ancient Mesopotamian clay tablets, was a leader, scientist and geneticist of an extraterrestrial race known as the 'Anunnaki'. The writer and researcher, Zachariah Sitchin, says that Anunnaki translates as 'Those Who from Heaven to Earth Came'. The tablets describe the Anunnaki in terms of a reptilian extraterrestrial race that interbred with humans to create hybrid bloodlines, or the bloodlines of the 'gods', as they were perceived. The French writer and researcher, Anton Parks, has done some excellent work in this area in recent years, especially with his translations of Sumerian terms. He says that the Sumerian name for the Reptilian race was GI-AN-AB-UL or, put more simply, Gina'abul:

Decomposed into Sumerian syllables, we get GI-NA (real, true), AB (contraction of AB-BA 'ancestor, father') and UL (magnificence, abundance, splendour), i.e., 'the true ancestors of magnificence' (or splendour). Much later in Sumeria, this term became a synonym for 'lizard' ...

...The term USUM-GAL (Great Dragon, monarch) is found in Sumerian literature. This attribute was basically assigned to Sumerian 'gods', and subsequently to the kings and rulers of KALAM (Sumeria). Its many definitions – 'great dragon', 'monarch', 'sovereign' and 'great lord' – confirm the reptilian origin of the 'gods' of the Earth and their royal descendants.

In addition to this, the Sumerian word MUS (reptile, serpent) reinforces the humanoid-reptilian connection with royalty through the homophone MUS [and other forms of the word] which has the meanings of an appearance, an aspect, a face and ... royal diadem [a crown worn as a sign of royalty and royal power]. A reptilian diadem decorated the crowns of the pharaohs.

As I began to understand the reptilian connection to life on this planet, I could see yet again why the theme of Mesopotamia, Sumer and Babylon had been following me almost from the day I met that first psychic in 1990. It was no surprise to me when the Illuminati networks invaded the land of Sumer, now Iraq, in 2003 and systematically looted the museums of their irreplaceable and priceless artefacts from ancient Mesopotamia which had the potential, if properly decoded, of revealing a whole new version of human history. This was all done systematically and it was not only museums, but ancient sites still not researched right across Iraq. London's *Guardian* newspaper put it into context while the bombing was still happening:

In museums and universities across the world, scholars and curators are fearful of another Armageddon. One not perpetrated on the Iraqi people but on their history and monuments. Iraq, particularly the green heart of Mesopotamia, the fertile crescent of land between the rivers Tigris and Euphrates, is the cradle of civilisation, the land of Nineveh, Babylon, Nimrud and Uruk, the world's first city. This is where the Sumerians invented writing 5,000 years ago, where the epic of Gilgamesh – the model for Noah and the flood – was committed to cuneiform a millennium and a half before Homer.

It is the land of the Old Testament, the Tower of Babel and of Ur, where Abraham, the father of the three great monotheistic religions, was born. It may have only a single official UNESCO listing but, with 1,000 acknowledged archaeological sites, Iraq is one huge world heritage zone. And on to this in the past few days have poured 740 Tomahawk cruise missiles, 8,000 smart bombs and an unknown number of stupid ones.

Calculated and barbarous as this was, we already know enough from translated ancient Mesopotamian tablets and artefacts to get the picture. The Sumerian civilisation came out of nowhere from a historical point of view at the peak of its powers, as so many of these ancient advanced cultures appeared to have done. The best of the pyramids in Egypt, for instance, are the oldest ones. The Sumerian language was a one-off which belongs to no known linguistic family and it would seem to be originally a language brought by the Reptilian 'gods'. Researcher, Anton Parks, who has made a detailed study of Sumerian language and its meanings, refers to this as 'Gina'abul-Sumerian' – 'Reptilian-Sumerian'. There was once a highly-advanced global society with one language. This was originally telepathy, not words, because minds could communicate directly without need of the 'middleman' we call 'language'. Later, a spoken language was developed from which today's multiple languages derived. Virtually every ancient society has its version of the

Figure 88: *Zulu shaman, Credo Mutwa. An extraordinary man and it is a privilege to call him a friend*

'Tower of Babel' (Babylon) story when 'God' or 'the gods' forced the people to speak in different tongues. The introduction of language to replace telepathy anchored people far more in five-sense reality because words are a five-sense phenomenon and the many different languages made it impossible to communicate as before. Those who study words from this perspective can see clear evidence of the original language from which all others came. My great friend, Credo Mutwa, the Zulu shaman, is one such person (Fig 88). He has a love of words and their origins and he can reel off different words in different languages with the most extraordinary ease. He told me that as he travelled the world meeting the native peoples it was so clear that our diversity of language has a single source. For instance, even though he is a Zulu from South Africa, he said he could understand about three of every five words of the Hopi people when he spent time with them in Arizona. It was the same almost wherever he went because of the single origin. Researcher, Anton Parks, says he discovered a single Sumerian-Assyrian-Babylonian syllable-system from which derive key words in a long list of ancient languages, including Egyptian, Chinese, Arabic, Hebrew, Ancient Greek, Hopi, Latin, Hindi and the languages we call Germanic.

Slave Race

The Sumerian Tablets say that the Anunnaki genetically-manipulated humans to become their slaves after arriving here hundreds of thousands of years ago. They wanted to mine gold and they used humans to do the work until there was a rebellion about 250,000 years ago, and they then decided to make a 'new human' that could be more easily controlled. The goldmines were in Africa where evidence has been found of gold mining more than 100,000 years ago. Rebecca Cann, Assistant Professor of Genetics at the University of Hawaii, co-authored a study in 1987 in the journal, *Nature*, suggesting that all modern humans are descended from a single mother who lived in

Africa about 200,000 BC. The connection, she said, was through the mitochondrial DNA, which passes down through the female. This turned minds to the biblical Eve in the Garden of Eden with Adam and the serpent – symbolic of the reptilian race. Interestingly, human brain capacity expanded at an increasingly rapid rate over perhaps millions of years, but this expansion suddenly stopped and went into reverse about 200,000 years ago. This was caused by genetic and environmental manipulation, as I will detail later. The 'God' referred to in the Old Testament is singular, mistranslated – on purpose – from the plural. In these two passages from *Genesis*, the plural still survives and describes the Annunaki decision to create a new human to serve them:

> And God said, Let us make man in our image, after our likeness; ... So God created man in his own image, in the image of God created he him; male and female created he them – Genesis 1:26-27

> And the Lord God said, Behold, the man is become as one of us, to know good and evil; and now, lest he put forth his hand, and take also of the tree of life, and eat, and live for ever – Genesis 3:22

After many failed experiments they spliced together their Reptilian genes with those of the human form called homo erectus. The new human was a clone to begin with and could not procreate, but they were later 'upgraded' so that they could reproduce. They did so to such an extent that they peopled the planet, and the Tablets say some of the Reptilian 'gods' were attracted to human women and had children with them – this is the Biblical 'sons of God' (the gods) interbreeding with the 'daughters of men'. The Annunaki leadership decreed that things had got out of hand and decided to destroy their 'new human' creations and start again, the Tablets say. About 13,000 years ago, they instigated the cataclysmic events that are recorded as the Great Flood which reduced the population to a fraction of what it had been. Ancient Indian works, like the *Book of Dzyan*, one of the oldest of Sanskrit accounts, and the epics, *Mahabharata* and the *Ramayana* support this theme. The *Book of Dzyan* tells of how a reptilian race it calls the 'Sarpa', or 'Great Dragons', came from the skies to bring civilisation to the world; and then came a deluge, the biblical Great Flood, but the serpent gods survived and returned to rule. Many ancient accounts connect the serpent gods, under endless names, with causing the geological catastrophe symbolised as the Great Flood, and with flying above the Earth while it was all happening. The 'ark' of 'Noah' is far more likely to have been a flying craft carrying genetic material than a boat with two of every animal, right? It is all symbolism. More genetic manipulation followed the geological catastrophe and humans 'went forth and multiplied' to 'replenish the earth'. In among the human population, the reptilian Annunaki placed hybrid bloodlines with more of their genetics and these were to be the 'middlemen', 'demi gods' and 'royal' bloodlines that would serve their interests among the human population. The 'gods' were going to disappear from human sight and manipulate in the background, because if humans didn't know they were being controlled there could be no opposition or rebellion against the 'gods' they did not know existed. The hybrids were taught advanced knowledge by the Reptilians/Annunaki across many fields, including astronomy, mathematics and technology. This knowledge was kept from the people as much as possible by using secret societies, oaths and

Figure 89

Figure 90

Figure 91

The Reptilian hybrid 'royal' bloodlines were often depicted symbolically with a human torso and legs like snakes. In Egypt, the pharaoh was symbolised as a cobra (a common symbol of the Reptilian 'gods'). The pharaohs were considered to be gods in human form and they were depicted with a cobra 'headdress'; a cobra on the forehead; and the belly of a cobra emerging from the chin

Figure 92

language, especially the language of symbolism. These hybrid 'royal' bloodlines of the gods were symbolised by emblems in the form of a dragon, snake (especially the cobra), sphinx, plumed serpent, or the tree-cross or Ankh, and depicted as half-human, half-serpent, with most often their torso being human and their legs like snakes (Figs 89 to 92). Thousands of years later, these Reptilian-hybrids are the interbreeding families controlling global politics, finance, business etc., etc. These are the bloodlines known as the Illuminati, and they are the servants of the now hidden Reptilian 'gods' who act as prison warders to their slave race.

The Curse of 'Cain'

The story of Cain and Abel, which can be found all over the world using different names, is symbolic of the two versions of the new human form genetically engineered by the Reptilians. The 'royal' Reptilian hybrids are the bloodline of the symbolic 'Cain'. He is said to have been the firstborn of Adam and Eve according to Christianity, Islam and Judaism. He is described in *Genesis* as being 'of the wicked one' and his descendants are said to carry 'the mark of Cain'. High-level initiates of the Illuminati secret society network still refer to themselves as the 'Sons of Cain'. In the biblical stories he murdered his 'brother', Abel, and 'Cain' archetypes can be found across the world in legends about Kronos/Saturn, Hermes/Mercury, Zeus, Vulcan, Oceanus,

Figure 93: *Asmodeus or the Devil in the church at Rennes-le-Château in southern France. Note the black and white floor, as found in Freemasonic temples*

Osiris, Oannes, Dagon, Moloch, Baal, Odin, Wotan, Votan, Viracocha and Quetzalcoatl. Another pseudonym of Cain is said to be Asmodeus, the 'Rex Mundi', 'Lord of the Earth', figure at the entrance to the mysterious and much-discussed church at Rennes-le-Château in southern France (Fig 93). The Illuminati Knights Templar are closely associated with the Rennes-le-Château myths, and with why that little church in the hilltop village is such a mass of legend, myth, rumour and occult symbolism (see *The Biggest Secret* for the detailed story). Within all this symbolism and religious-speak is the crux of the whole thing – bloodline. Some 900 documents, now called the *Dead Sea Scrolls*, were discovered between 1947 and 1956 in caves on the shore of the Dead Sea in Israel/Palestine. They include texts from the Old Testament, which differ from the highly-edited and censored versions we see in the Bible. For example, the Scrolls say:

And Adam knew his wife Eve, who was pregnant by Sammael [Satan, the 'Grim Reaper', the prince of demons to Jews], and she conceived and bare Cain, and he was like the heavenly beings, and not like the earthly beings, and she said, I have gotten a man from the angel of the Lord.

The term 'angel' is symbolic of the Reptilian 'gods'. The Sumerians knew they were slaves to the gods, but this understanding was lost to the modern world. According to the highly-respected scholar, Samuel Noah Kramer, a specialist on Sumer, the Sumerians believed that they were indeed the slaves of the gods and should never rebel. It was humanity's fate to suffer. Kramer adds another telling fact: 'He [the Sumerian] had to realise that he was a depraved being because, in the words of a wise man: "No woman has ever given birth to a child untainted by original sin".' All this stuff about original sin, which was continued in the Christian plagiarisation of ancient stories, relates to the Reptilian genetic manipulation. It was, and is, also the foundation of, and the prime technique of, human suppression – convincing them they had no power and would never have any. They were lower beings, nothing more than beasts, who had to obey the gods. Look at the world today – it is still going on. The original interbreeding was achieved largely through cloning and 'test tube' methods, and this is where the modern earth races in general came from. Eastern peoples, like the Chinese and Japanese, had an added genetic component – that of the 'Greys', the ant-like beings that most people think of when they hear the term 'alien' (Fig 94). The Greys were genetically-engineered by the Reptilians and they are soulless biological computer systems – biological robots – that act as servants and foot-soldiers to the Reptilians. When I say 'robots', don't think of the robot technology that we have today; this is fantastically more advanced. There is another race with close connections to the Earth – a tall blond-haired, blue-eyed, human-like people of extraterrestrial original, often known by UFO researchers as the 'Nordics' (Fig 95). They also have underground colonies and can operate far more freely in Third Density. Their human-like form means that they can mingle with human society without being detected. There are many non-human races in and around the Earth that we don't know about, including an insect-like group known by researchers as 'Insectoids', but when it comes to genetics and control the Reptilians are the major players. They are highly skilled in genetics and technology, way ahead of where humans are currently, and light-years ahead of where they were in the ancient world after the Flood.

Figure 94: *The 'Greys' are widely reported in extraterrestrial sightings*

The Adamic Race

The Sumerian Tablets describe how the original breeding-programme was headed by the chief scientist of the Reptilian Anunnaki, called Enki, or 'Lord of the Earth' (Ki = Earth), and his expertise in medicine. After many failures and some horrendous creations, the Tablets indicate, Enki and his female associate, Ninkharsag, produced a human hybrid that the Sumerians called a LU.LU ('One Who Has Been Mixed'). This would appear to be the biblical 'Adam'. Appropriately, the Sumerian name for humans was LU, and this has the root meaning of 'worker' or 'servant' and also implies a domesticated animal. The Bible says that 'Eve' was created from a rib of Adam, but the word from which 'rib' derived

Figure 95: *There is a race of blond-haired, blue-eyed extraterrestrial 'visitors' known by 'UFO' researchers as the 'Nordics'. In Africa, they were called the 'Mzungu', as portrayed here by Credo Mutwa. He says that when the white Europeans first arrived in Africa, the people thought it was the Mzungu returning*

was the Sumerian, TI, which means both 'rib' and 'life', according to the translations of Zecharia Sitchin, yet another graduate of the London School of Economics. To be created from the 'life' or life essence of the Adamic race makes rather more sense than a rib. There is another interpretation of 'rib' that I'll come to later in the book. The phrase 'dust from the ground', from which the Bible claims that Adam was created, really translates as 'that which is life' from the Sumerian term, TI.IT, according to Sitchin.

The new Adamic race was achieved through the splicing together of the DNA of the Anunnaki with that of humans. Geneticists today perform this same technique known as 'gene splicing' which, put simply, is like cutting frames from a film and putting them back in another place. Even more accurately, taking frames from two movies and editing them together. This creates a hybrid, and the amount of DNA used from each source decides which one is most dominant. Some of the Reptilian-hybrids have looked very reptilian, as ancient accounts describe, while others appear human. The Reptilians want their hybrids to look human, or the secret would be out. Lloyd Pye, a researcher and writer who has specialised in human origins, points out that human DNA has more than 4000 defects compared with only a few hundred in chimpanzees and gorillas. How could this be unless it has resulted from mistakes during gene-splicing experiments, which have tremendous potential for error? Proof of genetic manipulation is there to be seen in human DNA. As Lloyd Pye says, there is 'evidence of gene segments that have been cut, flipped and reinserted upside down back into the genome.' Chromosomes in humans have also been fused together which is why we appear to have two fewer than the higher primates like chimps and gorillas. Such fusions are only seen in laboratories. Mainstream science refuses to accept, or even investigate, the obvious, because the bloodlines control scientists through their funding and through the institutions that administer their profession. Parrot the official line and you'll get funding and status; tell the truth, or pursue the truth, and your career will be systematically ruined. The same goes for medicine, which is why millions die every year from diseases that are curable if 'doctors' would look beyond the scalpel and the drug. Most significant in the genetic manipulation, and vital to understanding the human experience today, was that the original twelve strands of active DNA were reduced to two. I'll expand on the consequences of this as we go along. The new genetically-modified human form was created to be a slave race for the Reptilian gods and this, as I have mentioned, is what the Sumerians themselves believed. The Sumer expert, Samuel Noah Kramer, wrote:

> The Sumerians thought that lowness and baseness, the calamities and cares of Man had been brought into this world by the gods, and they did not question the eccentric or capricious aspect of these divine beings. It was man's fate to suffer. Like Job, burdened by an undeserved load, the Sumerian was raised to think that he should not complain or rebel against incomprehensible misfortunes. He had to realise that he was a depraved being, because, in the words of a wise man: 'No woman has ever given birth to a child untainted by original sin'.

The Slavery Continues ...

It is little different today as billions slavishly serve their 'God' (the 'gods') and religious beliefs, that include never questioning 'God' (the 'gods') no matter how contradictory and often vicious 'He' (they) may be. There is still the belief in 'original sin' – you are 'sinful' just by being born – and it is the fate of humans to suffer. As the Bible says: 'Suffer little children to come unto me.' Humans serve the global economic and business system as largely unquestioning slaves who know their place. The reason for the obvious similarities between ancient and modern beliefs, perceptions and behaviour is easily explained. The world today is controlled by the same gods, and their hybrid bloodlines, that have controlled humanity for countless thousands of years. They controlled the mass of the Sumerian people and they do the same to the mass of humanity today. The hybrid bloodlines control the system, as they control the religions that are nothing more than the covert worship of the Reptilian gods. The composite singular 'God' of the monotheistic religions is merely symbolic. The former American Naval Intelligence operative, the late William Cooper, wrote in his 1989 book, *The Secret Government: The Origin, Identity and Purpose of MJ-12*: 'Throughout history, aliens have manipulated and ruled humanity by means of various secret societies, occultism, magic, sorcery and religion.' They are still doing it and they want total control of the planet through total control of the human mind. How apt that the word 'religion' has a common meaning around the world in different languages which, in the end, all derive from the Sumerian/Mesopotamian. It means 'to submit' and therefore to be dominated. This describes the plight of humanity since the Reptilians arrived. Humans are little more than sheep, controlled by shepherds with scaly skin.

This brings me to a vital point. 'Modern man' was manipulated genetically by the Reptilian 'gods' to be their slaves, and Homo sapiens were given the brain capacity and physical frame that could best serve the Reptilian Annunaki as administrators and workers. They had to be bright enough to do the jobs required of them, but not bright enough to see what was going on, and the Reptilians needed a collective control-system that could constantly feed their human robots a sense of reality that would keep them in line. There may have been reptilian genetics in the human body before the genetic manipulation, but I doubt it was a fraction of what we have now. It is my view, after so many years researching this and following the guided trail, that the reptilian brain as it is today was introduced by the Reptilian geneticists. It acts like an enormous microchip and locks us in to their control system. As I have already explained, the reptilian brain largely dictates human perception and behaviour. Its primitive, emotional, fear-based sense of reality provides the perfect vehicle for collective control and the conflict and insecurity so essential to divide and rule. The Reptilians also have their own 'hive' mind communication system, which I will describe in detail later, and the reptilian brain connects us to that system. They have tuned us in to their 'station'. This is so important to understand if we are to free ourselves from this enslavement and see through the false sense of reality that is fed to us every day. Consciousness – what we really are – is far more powerful than any reptilian genetics or communication system if we choose to connect with that awareness of self. Before anyone fights, or flights, or freezes with fear, there is a way out of this and we are heading closer to that every day; but crucial to casting off the chains of control and suppression is to know how the 'game' is being played and what the rules are.

Connecting the dots ...

The Annunaki Reptilians conducted many genetic experiments starting hundreds of thousands of years ago (in our timescale) to mix their own genetics with that of humans.

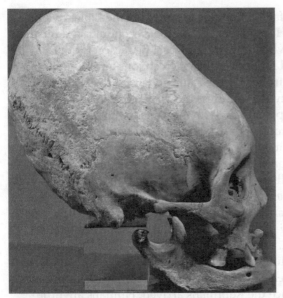

Figure 96: *One of the strange elongated skulls that have been found around the world*

Figure 97: *One of the mother and baby reptilian figurines found in graves of the Ubaid people (approximately 5300 to 4000BC) who lived in Mesopotamia before the Sumerians*

They produced some bizarre hybrids of human, reptilian and animal species, as ancient accounts recall, and their genetic experimentation and research continues today below the earth in underground military bases like Dulce in New Mexico. See *The Biggest Secret* for more about that. The Reptilians first located in what is now Africa and it was out of there, according to mainstream science, that 'modern man', or Homo sapiens ('Knowing man'), appeared about 200,000 years ago. There was then an 'upgrade' to Homo sapiens sapiens about 35,000 years ago. The so-called 'missing link' to connect the various changes in the human species has never been found – because there isn't one. The genetic leaps have been the result of genetic intervention. How come that only specific species have ever been found and not examples of the progression and transition between them? What have been found, though, are giant people ('there were giants in the earth in those days') and many with elongated heads that are very different from the human skull (Fig 96). The Reptilians have elongated heads and this can be seen with the reptilian humanoid figurines found in the graves of the Ubaid people who preceded Sumer in Mesopotamia (Fig 97). Notice the mother-and-child theme that originated with the Reptilians and was passed down in their religions, most famously in Christianity. The elongated head of the Reptilian gods is the reason that so many ancient 'gods' and deities, like those in Egypt and the Maya region of Central America, were portayed with elongated heads and headgear (Figs 98 and 99). This is also the origin of the tradition among some native peoples of tightly binding the heads of babies to try to elongate the skull to 'be like the gods'. There are other Reptilians and non-human visitors that have round skulls.

The theme of giants is common among ancient texts and native legends. The Ethiopian text, the *Kebra Nagast*, is thousands of years old and it refers to the enormous size of the babies produced from the sexual or test tube unions of humans and the 'gods'. It tells how: '…the daughters of Cain [son of Noah] with whom the angels had conceived … were unable to bring forth their children, and they died.' It describes how some of these giant babies were delivered by caesarean section: '… having split open the bellies of their mothers they came forth by their navels'. In the *Shahnameh*, or

Figure 98   **Figure 99**

The ancient Egyptians portrayed their royal families and pharaohs with elongated heads and headgear

Book of Kings, the legendary history of Iran completed in AD 1010 by the poet, Firdowsi, or Ferdowsi, he describes the birth of a baby called Zal, the son of a king called Sam. Again the king is horrified by the unearthly appearance of his child. He has a very large body 'as clean as silver', hair as white as an old man's and 'like snow', and a face compared with the Sun. Sam calls his son a demon child, a child of the 'daevas'. There are many references to these gods and demi-gods 'shining like the sun' and this is one origin of the worshipping of 'sun gods' that is still at the centre of the Illuminati bloodline religion today. The Biblical gods, the 'Elohim', comes from 'eloh', meaning 'light'. In the ancient Hebrew text, the *Book of Noah*, and its derivative, the *Book of Enoch*, a strange birth is described of a non-human child, who turns out to be Noah, of the Great Flood fame. References to this also appear in the *Dead Sea Scrolls* which include much material from the *Book of Enoch*. The strange child the texts describe is the son of Lamech. He is said to be unlike a human being and more like 'the children of the angels in heaven'. Lamech's child, Noah, is described as white-skinned and blond-haired with eyes that made the whole house 'shine like the Sun'. Reptilian beings with shining eyes and glowing bodies are described by Credo Mutwa in his African accounts, ancient and modern, and once again this can explain the close association between serpent worship and sun worship across thousands of years. The name 'Illuminati' refers to 'Illuminated Ones'. On one level this means illumination through knowledge, but it could have another meaning related to the 'shining ones'. Lamech questions his wife about the father of the child, Noah:

> Behold, I thought then within my heart that conception was [due] to the Watchers and the Holy Ones … and to the Nephilim … and my heart was troubled within me because of this child.

The open-minded end of mainstream science now has to address the obvious. A group of researchers at the Human Genome Project say they believe that the 97 per cent of non-coding DNA, what is termed 'junk DNA' (because scientists don't know what it does), is the genetic code of extraterrestrial life forms. Professor Sam Chang, the group leader, maintains that the vast majority of human DNA is of 'off-world' origin and the apparently 'extraterrestrial junk genes' merely 'enjoy the ride' with hard working active genes passed from generation to generation. I will explain this in another way later on. After comprehensive analysis with the assistance of other scientists, computer programmers, mathematicians, and other scholars, Professor Chang began to consider if the apparently 'junk human DNA' was created by some kind of 'extraterrestrial programmer'. The alien chunks within human DNA, Professor Chang says, 'have their own veins, arteries and immune system that vigorously resist all our anti-cancer drugs.' He continues:

> Our hypothesis is that a higher extraterrestrial life form was engaged in creating new life and planting it on various planets. Earth is just one of them. Perhaps, after programming, our creators grow us the same way we grow bacteria in Petri dishes. We can't know their motives – whether it was a scientific experiment, or a way of preparing new planets for colonization, or the long time ongoing business of seeding life in the universe.

Professor Chang speculates that the apparent 'extraterrestrial programmers' were probably working with 'one big code' consisting of 'several projects' that have produced life-forms on various planets. He suggests they may have 'wrote the big code, executed it, did not like some function, changed it or added a new one, executed again, made more improvements, tried again and again'. Professor Chang is one of many scientists and researchers to point to humanity's extraterrestrial origins. He says:

> What we see in our DNA is a program consisting of two versions, a big code and basic code. First fact is, the complete 'program' was positively not written on Earth; that is now a verified fact. The second fact is that genes by themselves are not enough to explain evolution; there must be something more in 'the game' ... Sooner or later we have to come to grips with the unbelievable notion that every life on Earth carries genetic code for his extraterrestrial cousin and that evolution is not what we think it is.

It doesn't work, Charlie

What I have been saying since 1991, and what Dr Chang's DNA research supports, can be found in ancient records and accounts all over the world. Non-human groups of many kinds have contributed to the creation of the human form and life on Planet Earth. It seems that before the Reptilians arrived there were no men and women, only androgynous humans with many powers and gifts that allowed them to connect with the 'great beyond'. The Reptilian genetic intervention removed those gifts and created man and woman. This is the symbolism of Eve being created from Adam – the two were genetically split from the one. The main difference between men and women is simply hormonal and you can easily see how they could have emerged as expressions of the same original form. The Reptilians gave them compatible sex organs for the new form of procreation that now began, and this is why the biblical texts and others talk about the pain of childbirth being introduced. It also brought a new type of sensation to the world – sex as we know it today. The Reptilians in Third and Fourth Density are obsessed with sex, both because of the sensations it produces and because they feed off the orgasmic energy. It is a major way that they drain us. Why do you think we live in such a sex-obsessed society? The modern human race, or Homo Sapiens, emerged far quicker than conventional 'evolution' would allow because there was a genetic intervention by these advanced geneticists. The famed cosmologist, Dr Carl Sagan, discussed humanity's reptilian origins in his book, *The Dragons of Eden*, and pointed out that the fossil record reveals a sudden and inexplicable leap in human brain function that cannot be explained by the claims of Charles Darwin and his advocates that humans evolved from reptiles, but very slowly. Darwin was working for the bloodlines to create a false understanding of human origins and reality. He did so with great effect because mainstream science is still being blinded by Darwin's version of evolution. Under the Darwinist timescale, it should have taken 200 million years for mammals to first appear and another five to ten million for them to evolve into humans, Sagan says. Instead, it happened very quickly in what Sagan describes as 'a major burst of brain evolution', and stone tools, for example, did not develop slowly, but appeared 'in enormous abundance all at once'. The ancient *Book of Enoch* describes how the 'fallen angels', especially one it calls 'Azâzêl', introduced this knowledge:

And Azâzêl taught men to make swords, and knives, and shields, and breastplates, and made known to them the metals of the earth and the art of working them, and bracelets, and ornaments, and the use of antimony, and the beautifying of the eyelids, and all kinds of costly stones, and all colouring tinctures.

And there arose much godlessness, and they committed fornication, and they were led astray, and became corrupt in all their ways. Semjâzâ taught enchantments, and root-cuttings, Armârôs the resolving of enchantments, Barâqîjâl, taught astrology, Kôkabêl the constellations, Ezêqêêl the knowledge of the clouds, Araqiêl the signs of the earth, Shamsiêl the signs of the sun, and Sariêl the course of the moon.

Once again this is a common theme all over the world – of knowledge being given to humans by 'the gods'. I would say it was this knowledge, rather than brain function, that caused humans to 'advance' so suddenly. The Reptilians have a fascist-style genetic structure of hierarchy that is mirrored in the Indian caste system in which genetics is everything and dictates your life from the moment it begins. Reptilians are obsessed with genetics and are deeply racist, a trait that has been passed on to their hybrids. It was the Reptilian 'gods' that founded the caste system in the Indus Valley during the Vedic period between approximately 1500 BC and 500 BC. I hear Indian authorities condemning the 'racism' of others when the caste system is the most racist division of people on earth. It still controls India today. Israel also runs its own caste system if you look at how Israeli society is racially structured. The Indus Valley version of the Anunnaki and Nefilim etc., were called the 'Nagas' (Fig 100 overleaf). The term 'Nagas' comes from Sanskrit, the ancient language of India, and nag still means snake, especially the cobra, in most of the languages of India. Researcher, Michael Mott, describes the Nagas in *Caverns, Cauldrons, and Concealed Creatures*:

Figure 100: *Ancient portrayal of the Nagas in Asia*

The Nagas are described as a very advanced race or species, with a highly-developed technology. They also harbor a disdain for human beings, whom they are said to abduct, torture, interbreed with, and even to eat. The interbreeding has supposedly led to a wide variety of forms, ranging from completely reptilian to nearly-human in appearance. Among their many devices are 'death rays' and 'vimana', or flying, disk-shaped aerial craft.

These craft are described at length in many ancient Vedic texts, including the *Bhagavad-Gita* and the *Ramayana*. The Naga race is related to another underworld race, the Hindu demons, or Rakshasas. They also possess, as individuals, 'magical stones', or a 'third eye' in the middle of their brows, known to many students of eastern mysticism today as a focal point for one of the higher chakras, or energy channel-points, of the human(oid) nervous system – the chakra associated with 'inner visions', intuition, and other esoteric concepts.

The same story turns up everywhere, if only people would look and interpret with an open mind. Human abductions by the Reptilians, Greys and other groups continue to this day. People are abducted to be implanted with tracking and perception-control devices; to have various hormonal and other chemical substances removed that the Reptilians use in Third Density; and to continue the ongoing genetic programmes which are aimed at replacing the present human form with another into which the Fourth Density Reptilians can directly 'incarnate' rather than merely possess. The Nazi 'master race' programme was part of this – one of their 'trial runs', if you like. Of course, the Nazi 'master race' involved blond-haired, blue-eyed 'Aryans' and part of the Reptilian breeding programme involves rogue elements in what are known as the Nordics, hence the blond hair and blue eyes.

'Children of the Serpent'

One of my most memorable moments on my travels around the world was to meet a wonderful man called Credo Mutwa. He is a famous Zulu shaman, or 'Sanusi', in South Africa and he contacted me in 1998 after the publication of my book, *The Biggest Secret*, when I first introduced the Reptilian information. He said on the phone during my speaking tour of South Africa that he had to speak with me urgently. When we met he asked: 'How do you know about the Chitauri?' I had no idea what he meant because I had never heard of these 'Chitauri'. (Credo has always spelt it out to me as Chitauri, but I have also seen it written as Chitawouli – what really matters is that it means the Reptilian race). He explained that the word translated from the Zulu as 'children of the serpent' or 'children of the python' and can also mean 'dictators'. This is so close to the Central

American name for the Reptilians, which translates as 'people of the serpent'. 'How do you know about the reptiles?' Credo asked me, making it clearer. I told him that this had come from multiple sources, ancient and modern, and included information gleaned from people who had worked, often against their will, on the 'inside' within government and security agencies and the mind-control programmes that turn out robotic pawns to serve the agenda and the bloodlines. This includes providing children for the sexual gratification for some of the world's most famous people. I name many of them in other books. Mind-controlled children don't tell, you see, but some do when they get older and their minds recall what happened. Africa, like every other continent, is awash with the legend of the serpent race. Credo said the existence of the Reptilians was more widely known before the coming of the Europeans to Africa. Those behind this invasion – the bloodlines – targeted the shamans, he said. These were the carriers of ancient knowledge and verbal history and the Reptilian hybrids of the British Empire, like the Rothschild agent, Cecil Rhodes, sought to delete the record of the Reptilians and impose an invented history enforced by the Christian missionaries. To overcome this, Credo told me, secret societies were formed among the shamans and others to ensure the knowledge survived as the European powers launched a vicious campaign of death and destruction across Africa in which they 'milked the minds of the shamans and then killed them'. Credo is approaching his nineties as I write this, and it was more than 50 years earlier that he was first initiated into these African secret societies. The initiations were extremely challenging to stop infiltration. Credo describes all this in detail in a six-hour DVD that I produced with him called *The Reptilian Agenda*.

Figure 101: *Credo Mutwa's Necklace of the Mysteries, which he says is at least a thousand years old. He uses the symbols to tell the story of Africa and its people*

Credo showed me artefacts passed down to him, including the 'Necklace of the Mysteries' which is mentioned in accounts 500 years ago and Credo says it is at least a thousand years old (Fig 101). It rests on his shoulders and how he walks around with it I don't know because it is extremely heavy. The large symbols that hang from the necklace tell the story of Africa's hidden history and the history of the world. At the front is a human woman, and there is a male figure that looks very much not human. The strange guy has an erect copper penis which was once made of gold until it was stolen (Fig 102). This mirrors the ancient Egyptian myths about Osiris, their god of the underworld, and son of the sun god,

Figure 102: *The symbols on the Necklace of the Mysteries recording the interbreeding between human women and extraterrestrial 'gods'. The Reptilians insisted that they were not portrayed as they really are and so they were symbolised instead in many non-human forms*

Ra. The 'green-skinned' Osiris is said to have been killed by his rival, Set, who cut his body into 14 pieces and scattered them across Egypt. Isis, the wife of Osiris, found 13 of the 14 pieces, but couldn't find the penis. She replaced it with one made of gold and gave birth to Horus, the Egyptian version of Jesus. A similar story is told about Nimrod, the 'first king of Babylon', because all these characters in ancient cultures are different names for the same 'myths' and 'people'. History becomes a lot less complicated when we understand this. The golden penis is symbolic of the hybrid bloodline and is represented today by the obelisk, so beloved of Freemasons. The once golden, now copper, penis on the 'Necklace of the Mysteries' symbolises the interbreeding between the Reptilian race and humans to create the hybrid bloodline. The male figure on the necklace doesn't look reptilian because, Credo says, the Reptilians warned the people never to depict them as they really looked. Instead, they portrayed them as clearly not human, but not as they actually were. Even so, some more literal depictions can be found, as with the reptilian humanoid figurines found in the graves of the pre-Sumer Ubaid people.

Also hanging from the 'Necklace of the Mysteries' is a 'flying saucer'; and there is a large hand, full of symbols (Fig 103). Credo says the 'flying saucer' was used by the Reptilians to commute between Earth and their giant 'mothership' orbiting the planet. African legends say the mothership orbited the Earth and the Reptilians went there during the 'Great Flood' cataclysms before returning afterwards to establish the advanced cultures in Sumer, the Indus Valley, China, West Africa, Central and South America, and elsewhere. Sumerian accounts tell of flying serpents, and dragons breathing fire, and the Egyptians said that the 'Watchers' came to Earth in their 'heavenly boats'. In ancient cultures across the world you have the constantly recurring theme of 'gods' arriving in some kind of flying machine to found civilisations and bring knowledge and techniques that were well in advance of what existed before. Ancient Indian accounts call the flying craft of the gods 'Vimanas' and there were several designs. Some were cigar-shaped while others were described as double-decked with a dome and porthole windows. Both types are regularly described in UFO sightings today. The ancient Indian texts describe anti-gravity technology of the type used in 'flying saucers'. Among the symbols on the Necklace of the Mysteries is the all-seeing eye, which symbolises, Credo says, the 'Watchers', as the Reptilians were known. The same all-seeing eye can be seen on the dollar bill, issued by the Rothschild Federal Reserve (Fig 104). There is also the constellation of Orion, which modern researchers have widely connected with extraterrestrial activity on Earth, and Reptilian groups, and there is a Star of David, the Rothschild symbol on their house in Frankfurt and now on the flag of Israel. The symbols used by the Illuminati bloodlines are not what they are claimed to be. They are connected with the Reptilian 'gods'.

Figure 103: *The hand and 'flying saucer' on the Necklace of the Mysteries. The hand is full of symbols, including the 'all-seeing eye' depicting the 'Watchers', the Rothschild symbol, the 'Star of David', and the constellation of Orion*

Wars of the 'gods'

It would appear from ancient descriptions that a hi-tech war broke out between factions of the Reptilians and other non-human groups, involving atomic and laser weaponry far in advance of what we have today. The battle is recorded in legends all over the world as the 'Wars of the Gods' (Fig 105). There is a lot of evidence of atomic warfare in the ancient world, including fused green glass found in Mesopotamia, Egypt, the Indus Valley, and elsewhere, which is the same as that created in atomic bomb blasts. The *New York Herald Tribune* reported one example as long ago as 1947:

> When the first atomic bomb exploded in New Mexico, the desert sand turned to fused green glass. This fact, according to the magazine Free World, has given certain archaeologists a turn. They have been digging in the ancient Euphrates Valley and have uncovered a layer of agrarian culture 8,000 years old, and a layer of herdsman culture much older, and a still older caveman culture. Recently, they reached another layer of fused green glass.

The same has been found at many locations and this is a passage from the *Mahabharata*, one of the two main Sanskrit epics of ancient India, and a major part of Hindu history and mythology. It has been called the Hindu Bible. It is twelve times longer than the Christian one and it tells the story of a great war that ended one age and began another. There are a number of estimates about its age, but most of the ones I have seen reckon that the texts were started in the period between 3000 BC and 1000 BC. The story it details, however, is much older. As I mentioned, the term 'vimana' is a flying craft. The *Mahabharata* says:

Figure 104: *The all-seeing-eye of the 'Watcher' Reptilians that was put on the dollar bill by the Illuminati in the 1930s*

> Dense arrows of flame, like a great shower, issued forth upon creation, encompassing the enemy ... A thick gloom swiftly settled upon the Pandava hosts. All points of the compass were lost in darkness. Fierce winds began to blow. Clouds roared upward, showering dust and gravel.

Figure 105: *Ancient wall art at the Temple of Abydos in Upper Egypt that looks remarkably like a helicopter and advanced flying and submarine craft – just what you would need for a 'War of the Gods'*

Birds croaked madly ... the very elements seemed disturbed. The sun seemed to waver in the heavens. The earth shook, scorched by the terrible violent heat of this weapon. Elephants burst into flames and ran to and fro in a frenzy ... over a vast area, other animals crumpled to the ground and died. From all points of the compass the arrows of flame rained continuously and fiercely.

Gurkha, flying a swift and powerful vimana hurled a single projectile charged with all the power of the Universe. An incandescent column of smoke and flame as bright as the thousand suns rose in all its splendour ... a perpendicular explosion with its billowing smoke clouds ... the cloud of smoke rising after its first explosion formed into expanding round circles like the opening of giant parasols ... it was an unknown weapon, an iron thunderbolt, a gigantic messenger of death, which reduced to ashes the entire race of the Vrishnis and the Andhakas ...

... The corpses were so burned as to be unrecognizable. The hair and nails fell out; pottery broke without apparent cause, and the birds turned white. After a few hours all foodstuffs were infected ... to escape from this fire the soldiers threw themselves in streams to wash themselves and their equipment.

If that is not describing an atomic weapon then what is? These descriptions abound in ancient Indian literature, and even include descriptions of battles on the Moon, which will be very relevant later. Researcher and writer, David Hatcher Childress, points out that when the Rishi City of Mohenjo-daro was excavated by archaeologists they found skeletons in the streets, some of them holding hands, as if some great catastrophe had suddenly overtaken them. 'These skeletons are among the most radioactive ever found, on a par with those found at Hiroshima and Nagasaki,' he says. In Mohenjo-daro, an ancient city with a plumbing system better than those in Pakistan and India today, the streets were littered with 'black lumps of glass' which turned out to be clay pots that had melted under intense heat. This phenomenon of vitrification, creating a glass or glassy substance through intense heat, can be found all over the world. There are vitrified rocks, homes, ruins and Mesopotamian and Iranian pyramids, or ziggurats, which have been found with clay bricks fused together by intense heat. Archaeologists discovered a vitrified area of sand in 1952 that covered hundreds of square feet and had the same appearance as atomic test-grounds like the White Sands site in the United States. As one writer put it: '... wherever we look in the world the baffling enigma of vitrified ruins challenges our intellect ... from Peru, to Scotland and Scandinavia; to the plateaus of China and India, this indelible evidence attests to some undeniably violent act.' The symbolic story of Sodom and Gomorrah could also be read as an attack by an atomic weapon. Lot's wife is told not to look back, and when she does she is 'turned into a pillar of salt'; but according to researcher, Zechariah Sitchin, the word translated as 'salt' means 'vapour' and so 'pillar of salt' becomes the far more credible 'pillar of vapour'. In 1990, when I was still blinking into the light of the new 'me', I was taken to the home of a woman in the west of England to see her 'channel' a consciousness she called 'Magnu'. It was a remarkable experience for many reasons. To see her face transform and her voice change as the consciousness spoke through her was quite an eye-opener for me at that stage. 'Magnu' said that energies had been withdrawn from the Earth to stop them being used for its destruction:

> My own allegiance with your planet goes back to an Atlantean period … [when] … there were many energies being used and information and knowledge being used which were for particular reasons of safety withdrawn, shall we say, to prevent complete catastrophe, to prevent total destruction of your planet. One could say these were sort of emergency measures if you like, to prevent the inhabitants of this planet from an untimely destruction.

These were the energies being exploited in the high-tech war which used weaponry based on a 'physics' unknown to humanity today and involving advanced laser and energy-weapon technologies that could certainly blow a planet apart. All this happened at the time of what I call 'the Schism', the nature of which I will be explaining later. Mu and Atlantis sank beneath the waves leaving only a few remnant islands, like Easter Island in the Pacific, part of Mu, where the massive statues of their 'gods' still survive. It seems the two land masses sank in stages. Few humans survived and many of those were protected underground in the ancient cavern cities and tunnel systems from which, along with the Moon, the new Reptilian-human race would emerge. This is the origin of Hopi legend of the 'ant people', the Greys, taking survivors of 'the Flood' into underground locations in the Grand Canyon (which was not 'worn away' by the Colorado River, but scored out during geological catastrophe). Whenever I have gone there I have had the same image in my mind of something akin to an open wound on human flesh. The main body of Reptilian entities in Third Density escaped the catastrophe in their spacecraft and sat it out, as I've said, in a 'mothership', as described in Mesopotamian, South African, and other ancient accounts. But as the Earth eventually settled down they returned. They had been possessing the human form and manipulating human genetics for a long time before the cataclysms to make humanity increasingly computer-like and focused more and more on purely 'physical reality'.

Myths, legends and occult sources also speak of a planet in this solar system being destroyed and its debris forming the 'asteroid belt'. It is said to have orbited between the current positions of Mars and Jupiter and is often known as 'Maldek'. Something called the Titius-Bode Law, or just Bodes Law, predicts the spacing of planets. It was discovered by Johann Titius in 1766 and further developed by J E Bode in 1778. Under this law, Bode said that there should be another planet between Mars and Jupiter, but what was later found there was the asteroid belt. Professor Michael Ovenden, astronomer at the Department of Geophysics and Astronomy, and the Institute of Astronomy and Space Science at the University of British Colombia, worked for 25 years to present his case that the asteroid belt was a planet which exploded millions of years ago. I suggest it happened much more recently than that. Ovenden's methodology was remarkably accurate when applied to other astronomical questions. The destruction of 'Maldek' brought catastrophe to the solar system and caused devastation on Earth. It was in this period that Mars, once a rich and abundant planet with its own population, had its atmosphere and landscape destroyed by the Maldek destruction that was connected to the 'wars of the gods'. Legends, mythology and occult beliefs suggest that Mars and Venus were home to advanced societies that were destroyed by a war in the solar system, symbolised by the battle between the Titans and the Olympians. The orbits of both planets were changed as a result of the Maldek destruction and left the scene of devastation that we see in the solar system today. Zulu

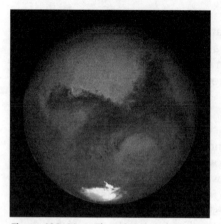

Figure 106: *Mars: There is so much more to know about what happened there and what is happening today*

legends call this lost planet 'Mpumakazi'. Credo Mutwa says that 'Mpu' means 'emerging' and 'kazi' means female, or great. It was 'the place the great mother was born', he said, and a beautiful world of 'fantasy'. But it was 'attacked by the jealous gods' and turned into 'burning ashes'. Immanuel Velikovsky, the psychiatrist turned writer and scholar, faced widespread ridicule when he wrote a series of books saying that the Earth and solar system had suffered a series of catastrophes right up to a few thousand years ago. Even if he was not right in every detail (who is?), he was certainly correct in his themes.

Mars is very significant in the Reptilian-human story and the Reptilians have had underground bases on Mars since ancient times, as have other non-human groups and some that look very much like humans. Zulu legend says that Mars was the home of the Reptilians and some are still there (Fig 106). All this would explain why there is such a serious cover-up going on with regard to Mars. Michael Brooks, a consultant for *New Scientist* and the author of *13 Things That Don't Make Sense*, wrote an article in *The Times* newspaper in 2009 in which he pointed out scientific errors in the search for life on Mars that were so basic it was 'beginning to look like a conspiracy'. He asked: 'Does someone not want us to find life on Mars?' The errors ensured that the scientists would never find what they were looking for. There is also a catalogue of failures with spacecraft sent to Mars, so much so that rocket scientists talk about the 'curse of Mars'. What don't they want us to know? Well, that there are extraterrestrial underground bases there, for a start.

Reptilian Royalty

The Illuminati are the representatives within human society of what were called the 'serpent gods' and they form a global dynasty, a word defined as 'a succession of rulers who are members of the same family'. Yes they are, the Reptilian family, but they are not ultimately in control of events as they seem to be. They are slaves themselves in many ways and terrified of the demonic entities that possess and dictate to them and through them. We should remember that the bloodlines are not the 'gods', they are the 'demi-gods', the middlemen and women. Today there are 13 Reptilian-hybrid bloodlines at the top of the fiercely-enforced hierarchy of hidden control. Among them are the Rothschilds, Rockefellers, House of 'Windsor' and the Merovingian bloodline made famous in recent times by books like *The Da Vinci Code* and *The Holy Blood and the Holy Grail*. The first is a novel and the other a detailed investigation. They are based on the theme of a bloodline resulting from the union of 'Jesus' and the biblical character called Mary Magdalene which located in what is now France and became the bloodline of the Merovingian kings. The problem with this theory is that there was no Jesus or Mary Magdalene because the Gospels – note 'spels/spells' – were re-writes of much older myths and stories found all over the world. The wider themes of these books, however, are correct. There *is* a conspiracy, it *is* about bloodline and it *does* involve the

Merovingian kings. The secret societies they mention like the Knights Templar and
Opus Dei *are* part of the cover-up of this in league with others like the Jesuit Order and
the Knights of Malta. *But.* The bloodline has nothing to do with 'Jesus' and everything
to do with the serpent 'gods'.

The Merovingians were the kings of what is now France and present-day Paris, the
'City of Light'. They were the royal lineage of a people called the Franks. The Merovingian
bloodline journeyed to France over thousands of years via the Caucasus Mountains, once
home to the Khazars, and Troy, in what is now Turkey, where it is said they took part in
the Trojan Wars. These were lands widely settled by the Sumerians. The Merovingians
were described as 'priest kings' or 'sorcerer kings', and this is a code for the bloodlines.
They claim to be 'royal' because of their genetic origin and they were given advanced
esoteric knowledge by the Reptilians that is kept from the mass of the people. The major
players in the Rothschild family are highly-skilled black magicians and could also be
described as 'sorcerers'. Charlemagne, the Holy Roman Emperor, who followed the
Merovingians in the same region of what is now France and Germany, is another highly-
significant Illuminati figure and bloodline. The Merovingian bloodline seeded today's
European royalty, including the House of Windsor, which is really the German House of
Saxe-Coburg-Gotha. They changed their name during the First World War when Britain
was at war with other members of their family in Germany. A long list of US presidents is
genetically descended from Charlemagne and so is Al Gore. The Merovingian symbol was
the bee, and beehive, and also the fleur-de-lis, the symbol of the House of Windsor, French
royalty and so many others. It is widely used by the Christian Church. The symbol of the
Merovingian kings had once been three frogs, before it became the three lilies, a symbol of
Judea. The Bible says that two phallic pillars of 'Solomon's Temple', called Jachin and
Boaz, were carved with 'lily work'. Jachin and Boaz are also the pillars in the Masonic
temple which is based on the biblical King Solomon's Temple. Freemasonry is the modern
expression of the ancient Mystery schools and all these themes of royalty, bloodline, secret
societies, religion and Satanism connect into the same web.

The whole idea of royalty comes from the Reptilian hybrids, and this is the origin of the
phrase 'divine right to rule'. It is the alleged right to rule because of your bloodline, your
DNA. Queen Elizabeth II is only the head of state in Britain because of her family
bloodline, and what still happens today has always happened since the Reptilian hybrids
were seeded. Colonel James Churchward, an ardent researcher into the existence of Mu or
Lemuria, says he was shown some ancient tablets in the late 19th century in the secret vault
of a monastery in northern India. They told the story of how the Naacals or Naga Mayas
('serpents') from the continent of Mu-Lemuria had travelled to India via Burma to establish
a colony there. Churchward put the texts together in years of painstaking work and
revealed how they described the destruction of Mu, the Motherland, and how the Naga
Mayas or Nagas had travelled to India. The Vedic scholar, David Frawley, explains how the
ancient Hindu holy books, the Vedas, reveal that the earliest royal bloodlines of India, the
priest kings (note 'priest kings' again), descend from the Bhrigus who arrived from a place
across the sea. The Bhrigus were an order of adepts initiated into the ancient knowledge.
Frawley says in his book, *Gods, Sages and Kings: Vedic Secrets of Ancient Civilization*, that the
monarchs of these bloodlines included the 'Serpent King', Nahusha. The Nagas became
five tribes and populated a large part of India, Churchward says, and went on to expand
their bloodline into China, Tibet and parts of Asia. The Buddhist text, the *Mahavyutpatti*,

lists 80 kings of India who descended from the Nagas or 'Serpent Kings'. Indian rulers claimed their right to power because of their genetic connection to the Nagas, who were described as offspring from the interbreeding of humans with the 'serpent gods'. Accounts in the ancient Indian epics describe how the Nagas interbred with white people, the Aryans, and these bloodlines became ... the Aryan kings. The Sum-aryan kings, maybe.

There is a common theme of royal bloodlines and reptilian people symbolised as half-human, half-serpent. Royal bloodlines of Central America claimed genetic descent from the serpent gods, Quetzalcoatl, Kukulkan and Itzamna, and the priest kings (again) of the Incas were symbolised by the snake and wore bracelets and anklets in the image of a snake. In Media, now Iran with an empire stretching into parts of Turkey, they referred to their kings as 'Mar', which means 'snake' in Persian, and they were called the 'Dragon Dynasty of Media' or 'descendants of the dragon'. Author, Jane Harrison, writes that in the Mycenaean age in Greece, the kings were 'regarded as being in some sense a snake'. Cecrops, the first Mycenaean king of Athens, was depicted as a human with a serpent's tail, and another, called Erechtheus, was worshipped after his death as a live snake. Erechtheus founded the Eleusinian Mystery School. Greek legend says that another king, known as Kadmus, morphed into a live snake when he died. Sargon the Great, the famous ruler of the Sumer/Akkadian Empire, claimed to descend from the gods, and the Sumerian Tablets say that 'kingship' was introduced by the Annunaki. The association between the snake, or serpent, and royalty can be found everywhere. The Akkadian word 'peor', meaning 'snake', is connected to the Sanskrit term 'pala', meaning 'king'. The same story can be seen in China and Japan where the emperors were known as Lung or Dragons and the earliest ones were depicted with reptilian features – just like the Nagas in India who expanded into China and Japan. One of them, called Huang Ti, was said to have been born with a 'dragon-like countenance' and the emperors in general were described as part-human, part-serpent. Huang Ti was said to have been conceived by a ray of golden light that entered his mother's womb from the Big Dipper constellation, part of the heavens associated with the Reptilians. The symbol of China and much of the Far East is the dragon and this is symbolic of the Reptilian gods that founded China after the cataclysms that sank the land of Mu. The dragon or serpent continues to be a symbol of royal and 'divine' heritage in places like Asia.

The Egyptian letters 'Dj' meant 'serpent' and there was an Order called 'the Djedhi' (hence the *Star Wars* 'Jedi'). Pharaohs of the serpent line included Djer, Djoser and Djedefre. It was in Egypt that a secret society called the Royal Court of the Dragon was established in 2170 BC and more formally by Queen Sobeknefru in 1783 BC. It is also known as the Imperial and Royal Dragon Court, and the Brotherhood of the Snake. This was created as a vehicle to pursue the agenda of the 'Dragon' and install the Reptilian-hybrid bloodlines into the positions of royal power. They became known as the Dragon kings and queens. The oil used to anoint the Pharaoh came from the fat of the revered Messeh crocodile. From Messeh we get 'Messiah' – the Jewish legend of the coming 'Saviour' – the one anointed with the fat of the crocodile: the new pharaoh. The word 'Christ' means 'Anointed One'. The oil still used today to anoint the monarch in the British Coronation is symbolic of the 'Messeh' fat of the Nile crocodile used in the Coronation ceremonies for the pharaohs in ancient Egypt. This can be found in Celtic mythology, too, as can so much dragon/reptilian symbolism, and the image of the Messeh evolved to become a dragon, the emblem of kingship.

Paradise Lost

Before the Reptilians came to Earth hundreds of thousands of years ago (in our perception of 'time'), life here was very different. What we call 'humans' were not men and women but androgynous male-female beings, as I said earlier, with a genetic structure that allowed them to access, and interact with, a range of densities. They were not 'physical' as we understand it, but much less dense and able to stay in contact with the Source, the *All That Is*. This was the Golden Age of legend across the world. These 'humans' represented the creative force within the duality of Creation, and the Reptilians in these hostile groups are expressions of the destructive force. In higher densities, and certainly within the Source of All Possibility, there is no duality of male and female, light and dark, positive and negative. They are part of the illusion of division and apartness, that's all. Earth was a lush paradise and spun on a different axis that meant there were no seasons. There was a constant climate and temperature, and legends speak of a canopy of water vapour around the Earth that made the Sun look hazy and protected the surface from the extremes of sunlight. There was no death and no pain or ill health as we know it. Human awareness just chose to leave the body and return to densities of pure consciousness, or moved into another body. I know it is hard for most people to comprehend these possibilities and there is a reason for this which I will address later. Golden Age humans didn't eat food – they secured their sustenance by absorbing energy from the atmosphere. Animals did the same, so negating the need for the daily mass murder that we call the 'law of the wild'. The lion really did lie down with the lamb. Take away the need to consume 'solid' food, and the need for animals to kill each other disappears also. There was no fear – no obsession with survival and, without fear, there is no need to kill your potential predators before they kill you. A Hopi legend tells of how the day came when the animals drew away from the people – 'the 'guardian spirit of animals laid his hands on their hind legs just below the tail, making them become wild and scatter from the people in fear.' The 'Magnu' channelling, which was given to me in 1990 before I knew any of this, spoke of the Golden Age of Atlantis when life on Earth was so different. It said:

> … you communicated with say, dolphins and whales. You understood these other sentient creatures. You could levitate. You could manifest things. You could cause spontaneous combustion by not miraculous means at all. Once you know what you are doing, these things follow. It is a matter of order.

The highly advanced cultures of Atlantis and Mu developed during the Golden Age and they were way ahead of where we are now. It was a global society with a common language of telepathic communication through which people decoded each other's thoughts. There was, at least for a long time, little need for the spoken word. When I say 'telepathy' I mean a form of communication way beyond what we think of as telepathy today. It wasn't like: 'Okay, I think I'm getting something, did you say so and so…?' Earth was indeed a paradise to behold; but trouble was brewing. Reptilian groups had targeted the Earth for aeons, seeking to plunder its riches and control the population. I stress again that we are talking here of certain Reptilian groups, not the whole species, many of which are connected to their higher levels of consciousness. But these renegade groups sought through psychic and 'physical' means to undermine the vibrational state of the androgynous humans, and very gradually they began to introduce the fear vibration on which these Reptilians both live and feed. Fear is a very low-vibration state and once humans allowed it into their awareness their resonance began to slow and they fell into the density that we can call dense physical. This is where humanity still is today. With fear came conflict and the perceived need to survive, and as humans fell into greater density they lost their powerful contact with the beyond. It was a downward spiral and well symbolised by Adam and Eve in the Garden of Eden with the temptation of Eve by the serpent. The knowledge of 'good' and 'evil' was the fall into the illusory reality known as duality. The dense physical is a reality where the sensations of the 'flesh' are very powerful and this was another aspect of the 'temptation' as humans fell into dense 'matter'. The Reptilians and the Greys began the process of manipulating the human energy field, or body, to control humanity's sense of reality, and humans experienced an ever-degenerating state of awareness.

I had assembled enough information by the late 1990s to see clearly that humanity was being controlled by a network of interbreeding families and that they were human-reptilian hybrids. I was also well-versed in their hierarchical structure of pyramids-within-pyramids and their two major techniques of mass manipulation: Problem-Reaction-Solution and the Totalitarian Tiptoe. There were many surprises still to come, but the world was looking very different, and making far more sense than it did when I picked up the psychic's book in the news shop some eight years earlier. What I learned from Credo Mutwa with his fantastic knowledge of African legends, myths and accounts confirmed what I was discovering in country after country. The Reptilians were here all right and I was not going to ignore the fact for fear of what people would say. Of course, the ridicule started again when I went public about the Reptilian manipulation of human affairs, but I just shook my head and carried on. It was interesting to see people dismiss something they had not researched or checked out just because it was so different to what they had been programmed to believe was possible. If they looked at the evidence and said, no, it's not enough for me – then that's fine. At least the neocortex has had a say. Instead, there was a reptilian-brain reactive response from most people of immediate dismissal. I can understand why they do that and it explains why humans are so easy to wrap and box. The establishment institutions – the bloodlines – dictate the 'norms' of what is possible and 'real' and most of the population just accept that without question, thought or research.

If you control what people think is possible by suppressing their sense of possibility, you can have them laughing at the truth. I have had a few chuckles myself, though, when I have been ridiculed by religious people about the Reptilians and I know that every week they go to church to worship them! They don't know this is what they're doing – but they are.

11

Serpent Worship

The world is not to be narrowed till it will go into the understanding …
but the understanding to be expanded and opened till it can take in the
image of the world as it is in fact
Sir Francis Bacon

The Reptilians appeared all over the world and this explains why the same 'serpent gods' can be found in virtually all ancient cultures and religions. They were later fused into one 'God' to create the monotheistic religions such as Christianity, Judaism and Islam, but they remain as 'gods', plural, in others such as Hinduism where they number their various deities in the tens of thousands. Serpent 'gods' became the Hindu gods, Sumerian gods, Babylonian gods, Egyptian gods, Chinese gods, Japanese gods, African gods, American gods, and so on (Fig 107). The Reptilians and their hybrids are still the force behind world religion today and they have used it mercilessly to control their slave race – humanity. Religion limits the perception of self and the world; creates a hierarchical structure of top-down dictatorship; uses fear and guilt to impose a belief system; and provides endless opportunities to divide and rule the population. John A Keel rightly says in his book, *Our Haunted Planet*, that the serpent race chose religion as the 'battleground' on which to conquer the human mind:

Figure 107: *There may seem to be countless 'different' religions, but they are all forms of 'serpent god' worship*

229

… The para-human Serpent People of the past are still among us. They were probably worshipped by the builders of Stonehenge and the forgotten ridge-making cultures of South America … In some parts of the world the Serpent People successfully posed as gods and imitated the techniques of the super-intelligence [Infinite Consciousness]. This led to the formation of pagan religions centered on human sacrifices. The conflict, so far as man himself was concerned, became one of religions and races. Whole civilizations based upon the worship of these false gods rose and fell in Asia, Africa, and South America.

… Once an individual had committed himself, he opened a door so that an indefinable something (probably an undetectable mass of intelligent energy) could actually enter his body and exercise some control over his subconscious mind … The human race would supply the pawns … Each individual had to consciously commit himself to one of the opposing forces … The main battle was for what was to become known as the human soul.

By choosing to give yourself to a deity or 'god', you open your psyche to possession by the force which that deity or 'god' represents. You make a vibrational connection. Deities like 'Mary' and 'Jesus', Yahweh and Allah, symbolise very different forces to those perceived by their believers, and the same goes for the stream of serpent deities under endless names worshipped by ancient and modern religions. World religions are a fantastic source of energy for the Fourth Density Reptilians when the worshippers are manipulated to focus on deities that represent them. This energetic connection is used to trawl and drain the life force of humans and this is what is happening on an enormous scale when two million Muslims gather in Mecca to circle the Kaaba, a symbol of the Reptilian gods. The saying that energy flows where attention goes is correct, and worship is an extreme form of attention. The trick is to manipulate human focus to concentrate on symbolic deities and make the energetic connection that lets them vampire human energy. The religions and their secret society and satanic counterparts encourage their advocates to 'give themselves' to the deity and in doing so they are giving these crazies permission to vampire and possess them. Religion, secret societies and Satanism are all worshipping the same Reptilian 'gods' and in doing so the advocates and participants are synchronising their energy fields with the Reptilians beyond human sight and feeding their life force to them. I met a guy in Utah who had developed technology that interacted with the energy fields beyond visible light. The only time it didn't work was when the Mormon churches in his area were packed with worshippers, because the energy fields were so disturbed by the energy being projected by the congregations. This is the energy being absorbed by the Reptilians through religious worship. Religions were also established to confine human perception to the beliefs, rules and regulations of the religious Thought Police and to lock people even more powerfully into the 'serpent vibration' that is being picked up by the reptilian brain. The Reptilians and their hybrids have been working for aeons to possess and control the human mind and disconnect us from higher consciousness, and if they can trick the population into worshipping them literally, or via symbolic deities and gods, it makes it much easier to do that. It was they who destroyed the 'Golden Age' by, among other things, infiltrating with their serpent-worshipping religions, secret societies and sacrificial rituals. This continues today and the deities, gods and demons worshipped by the religions, secret societies and Satanists are all the same. They are the Reptilians and their associated symbols relating to the worship of the Sun, Moon and the planet Saturn. Legends across the world say that humanity was ruined by 'the serpents' and this is precisely what has happened, with religion at the fore.

The Serpent Religion

Archaeologist, Sheila Coulson, from the University of Oslo, in Norway, published evidence in 2006 of python worship 70,000 years ago and it is the earliest human ritual yet discovered. She found the evidence in the Tsodilo Hills of the Kalahari Desert in South Africa. They are an isolated cluster of small peaks with the world's largest concentration of rock paintings. The ancient San people, also known as 'Bushmen', believe these hills to be sacred and they are known as the 'Mountains of the Gods' and the 'Rock that Whispers'. San mythology says that humans were created here by the 'python' and this is such a common theme. It is said that the giant python landed in the hills and created humans from eggs that he carried in a bag. Credo Mutwa, the Zulu shaman, told me that 'Africa' comes from the ancient word, 'Wafirika', which means 'The First People on Earth' or 'The First People Here'. The Reverend John Bathurst Deane produced a study in 1933 of serpent worship throughout the world and he traced its expansion out of *Babylon and Mesopotamia*. He discovered it was the basis of religious beliefs almost everywhere – in Egypt, Persia, Asia Minor (now Turkey), Phoenicia, Arabia and the Middle East, India and Asia, China, Japan, Ethiopia and the rest of Africa, Mexico, Britain, Scandinavia, Italy, Greece, Crete, Cyprus, Rhodes, Sri Lanka, the whole of Northern and Western Europe, and North, South and Central America. I would agree this started in Africa where, according to the Sumerian Tablets, the Reptilian Anunnaki first located to exploit gold reserves and forced humans to do the work of unearthing them. The slave race settled much later in Mesopotamia and became the Sumerians, but they were seeded all over the world. China, Japan and the Far East were so obsessed with serpent worship that the dragon became national symbols, but you find the same theme everywhere (Fig 108). Wherever you look you find the same basic story, deities and beliefs about the serpent gods. John Bathurst Deane says in his book, *The Worship of the Serpent*: 'The mystic serpent entered into the mythology of every nation; consecrated almost every temple; symbolized almost every deity; was imagined in the heavens, stamped upon the earth, and ruled in the realms of everlasting sorrow.' He also points out that the serpent is the main symbol of mythology and it is the 'only common object of superstitious terror throughout the habitable world'.

Serpents abound in religious symbols and on coins, and many 'Oracles' who were said to 'channel' the gods from other dimensions of reality were either symbolised in reptilian terms or their communicating 'gods' were. The Chinese

Figure 108: *The Chinese and Far East symbol of the Dragon originates from the 'serpent gods' and the dragon can be found in other cultures, too, for the same reason*

god, Fohi, was portrayed as a man and a snake, and the Athenian Cecrops and Erectheus, and the Egyptian Typhon, or Set, were the same. The Oracle at Delphi, the most important shrine in Greece, was known as Pythia, a name that derived from 'python', the serpent or dragon from Greek mythology which is said to have been slain by the sun god Apollo. The word 'dragon' comes from the Greek 'drakon', meaning a large serpent. The Olympic Games are really the reconstituted Pythian Games (serpent/dragon games) of ancient Greece that were held in honour of Apollo. Sun gods such as the Babylonian Nimrod were symbolised as an eternal flame, or lighted torch, and this is a major symbol of the Illuminati. The Olympic flame was inspired by this, too. As I said earlier, there is an ancient legend that Nimrod had two sons, Magor and Hunor, and that Magor was the ancestor of the Magyars and Hunor was the ancestor of the Huns/Khazars. Nimrod, an Illuminati god from Babylon, is going to come up quite a bit. Worship of the serpent throughout history is closely connected to the worship of the Sun, Moon and Saturn. Ancient sun god and moon god and goddess deities were invariably associated with the serpent. They were claimed to be half-human, half-serpent, or were symbolised by the serpent. Sun gods such as Nimrod, Apollo, Bel/Baal and Mithra, all fit this theme and the same with goddesses like Semiramis in Babylon. Tree worship and phallic worship were all offshoots of serpent worship, as we see with the druids of Britain and Europe. They worshipped the serpent god, Hu (a version of the Egyptian Osiris), who they symbolised as an adder and they called him the 'Dragon Ruler of the World'. This is a phrase you find across the globe. In this Druidic context, 'hu-man' means 'serpent-man' or 'serpent god-man'. The Celts and Picts of pre-Norman Britain called their kings Dragons. The title of Pendragon (the Great Dragon) was the symbol of the king of kings in the British Isles, and Uther Pendragon in the King Arthur stories is an example of this. The king of kings was also referred to as 'Draco', the Latin for 'dragon'. The malevolent Reptilians are often connected to the Draco star constellation, as I've said, as well as Orion and other locations. The Arthurian stories include all the classic elements of the theme, including the creation of royal bloodlines through the interbreeding between humans and non-human entities, and battles between competing dragons. There is also the theme of the 'Lady of the Lake' and this connects with the stories of goddess-worshipping serpent peoples like the Nagas living in underground centres located under lakes and lochs. The red dragon symbol of Wales comes from the claim by Merlin, Arthur's 'magician', that the red dragon symbolised the people of Britain. Merlin was described as only half-human because he was the child of an underground being and a human woman.

Codes like 'ob', 'ab', 'og', 'oph', 'ophis' and 'aub' were used to indicate a serpent deity in the ancient world and so you have Ophioneus, the giant serpent solar god of the Sumer-derived Phoenicians in Asia Minor and the Middle East. The tales of Ophioneus mirrored the story of 'Satan', a name which, itself, comes from Sumer in the form of Satam, Sandan or Santana who was portrayed with a trident or 'pitchfork'. We can see ophis in the name of the pharaoh, Amenophis IV, more famously known as Akhenaten who died around 1347 BC. He was the father of Tutankhamen and fought to introduce a one-god religion. From 'oph' comes the 'Ophiogenae', a serpent race in Asian legend whose descendants were said to be from a father who 'changed from a serpent into a man'. The island of Cyprus was originally known as Ophiusa, the 'Place of the Serpents', and had legends about serpents with two legs. There is also the Greek word, 'ophis', meaning 'serpent'. The Ophites were a people who followed the serpent religion that became known as 'Ophiolatreia'. They were also called 'Ophians' or 'Serpentinians' and lived in Egypt and Syria around AD 100, before expanding into Europe. According to Epiphanius, a Christian 'Church Father' of the fourth century, the Ophites worshipped the serpent in the form of a snake. One of their rituals later became the 'breaking of the bread' ritual seen today in the Christian Eucharist. The original Eucharist, long before 'Jesus', involved drinking real blood, not symbolic red wine. The Ophites were also the serpent worshippers known as the 'Hivites' in Canaan. This comes from 'hivvah', which relates to Eve, or 'female serpent'. The Hivites are said by some researchers to descend from Heth, son of Canaan, the son of Ham from a bloodline cursed by Noah, according to *Genesis*. The Bible says that this is the bloodline of the Babylonian, Nimrod. In Central America, there was a serpent-worshipping people called the 'Hivim' who described themselves thus: 'Being a Hivim, I am of the great race of the Dragon. I am a snake myself, for I am a Hivim.' The Hivim worshipped the Mexican serpent deity, Quetzalcoatl, and called themselves the 'descendants of the serpents'. Brasseur de Bourbourg, a translator of the Central American religious texts, the *Popol Vuh*, said the Hivim were the same as descendants of Ham, the accursed 'son of Noah', and once again the bloodline of Nimrod. The figure of Nimrod, whether real or symbolic, relates to the Reptilian-hybrid bloodline. The Mayan people of Central America, who are so associated with the alleged significance of 2012, worshipped the serpent god, Kukulkan, a version of Quetzalcoatl, 'the Plumed Serpent' or 'Feathered Serpent'.

'Land of the Plumed Serpent'

North America was another centre of serpent worship and some researchers say that the very name 'America' comes from 'Amaruca' after the plumed serpent god known as 'Amaru', or 'the serpent'. This would make the Americas the 'Land of the Plumed Serpent'. Worship of the serpent can be seen throughout the Americas where there are close genetic and historical connections between the native peoples of South, Central and North America. What we call the 'Indians' of the Americas go back to the lost civilisation of Mu, or Lemuria, and worship of the serpent travelled with them. According to the tradition of the Hopi in Arizona, all American Indian peoples came from a continent they call 'Kasskara' which sank under the Pacific 80,000 years ago. The famous Great Serpent Mound in Ohio is estimated to have been built 1,000 years ago and it is testament to how long serpent worship has been practised in what is now the United States (Fig 109). It is 1,330 feet long and is claimed to be the biggest earthwork effigy in the world. The star pattern of the constellation of Draco is pretty accurately portrayed in the layout of the mound, according to articles I have read. It is built on very unusual geology which was either formed by a volcanic eruption or a strike by a meteorite. The Cherokee and other Native American peoples have the legend of the horned serpent god, Uktena. He is also known by other names in other languages, but with the same meaning of 'great snake'. He is said

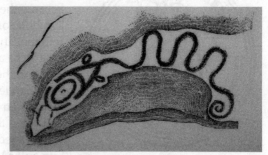

Figure 109: *The layout of the Great Serpent Mound in Ohio*

to be a reptilian 'horned god' with supernatural powers. The term 'horned god' with reference to the serpent can be found everywhere and people who have seen Reptilian entities have said that some of them have horns, although there can be other reasons for the 'horned god' symbolism, too.

The legends and creation myths of the Hopi people in Arizona, which are remarkably similar to the Sumerian, tell of the 'snake' who came to lead humans astray. They tell how the 'First People' multiplied and spread over the face of the land and were happy. They were of different colours and spoke different languages, but they felt as one and understood each other without talking. It was the same with the birds and the animals. They all 'suckled at the breast of their Mother Earth, who gave them milk of grass, seeds, fruit, and corn, and they all felt as one: people and animals.' But gradually there were those who forgot the commands to respect their Creator: 'More and more they used the vibratory centers solely for earthy purposes, forgetting that their primary purpose was to carry out the plan of Creation.' Then there came Lavahóya, the Talker, in the form of a bird called Mochni, and the more he kept talking, the more he convinced people of the differences between them – the difference between people and animals, and the differences between the people themselves by reason of the colour of their skins, their speech, and their beliefs in the plan of the Creator. It was then that the animals drew away from the people. The 'guardian spirit of animals laid his hands on their hind legs just below the tail, making them become wild and scatter from the people in fear'. In the same way, humans began to divide and draw away from one another, first those of different races and languages, then those who remembered the plan of Creation and those who did not. The Hopi legend goes on:

> There came among them a handsome one, Káto'ya, in the form of a snake with a big head. He led the people still farther away from each other and their pristine wisdom. They became suspicious of one another and accused one another wrongfully until they became fierce and warlike and began to fight one another. All the time, Mochni kept talking and Káto'ya became more beguiling. There was no rest, no peace.

It is an ever-recurring story. First there was paradise and then the serpent or snake people arrive to divide and rule.

Figure 110: *Queen Semiramis depicted on an ancient coin ...*

The Serpent Goddess

The gods and goddesses of the ancient world that became the religious figures of today are either symbolic of Reptilian 'gods' or the Sun/Moon/Saturn religions instigated by those 'gods'. A lot of deities later to be associated with other symbols, such as the Sun and the Moon, started out symbolising the Reptilian leadership, but the original meaning was lost. When the Reptilians moved into the background and ruled through their hybrid bloodlines they encouraged the loss of the true meanings in a maze of Sun and Moon symbolism. If you want to control secretly then obviously you need to destroy as much evidence as possible of your existence. The goddess or mother-goddess deity is universal and this is another focus of worship by the Rothschilds and the Reptilian-hybrid bloodlines. She has endless names in different cultures, like Semiramis, Lilith, Diana, Artemis, Athene, Barati, Britannia, Hecate, Rhea, and Persephone ('First Serpent'). The mother-goddess originally referred to a Reptilian entity who was given names like the 'Orion Queen', 'Snake Mother' and the 'Mother of All Gods'. The Reptilians may seem to be an extreme-macho race, but at the top of their fiercely-imposed hierarchical structure is the female, the 'queen'. The Reptilian goddess is symbolised by the Statue of Liberty which was given to New York by French Freemasons who knew that it represented the Babylonian goddess, Semiramis (Figs 110, 111 and 112). She is holding the lighted torch symbol of the Babylonian sun god, Nimrod, and there is another Statue of Liberty just the same on an island in the River Seine in Paris (Fig 113). 'Mother and child' symbolism can also be found across the world and not only in Christianity with 'Mary and Jesus'. There was Semiramis and Tammuz in Babylon, Isis and Horus in Egypt, and so many others (Fig 114 overleaf). The reptilian statuettes found in the graves of the pre-Sumer Ubaid people in Mesopotamia portrayed a mother and child. The author, Sir Laurence Gardner, has written at length about what he calls the 'Dragon bloodline' of the 'Dragon Queens', but still dismisses the involvement of a reptilian race. He says it's all symbolic and that the Anunnaki described in the Sumerian Tablets were not reptilian. The records of Sumer, Gardner says, reveal that the Anunnaki had a 'creation chamber' to produce these 'royal'

Figure 111: *Semiramis again as the Statue of Liberty, which was given to New York by French Freemasons in Paris who knew what the figure really symbolised – the goddess of Babylon*

Figure 112: *The Statue of Liberty (Semiramis) is also holding the lighted torch symbol of Sun god, Nimrod, and standing on a symbol of the Sun*

Figure 113: *Another Statue of Liberty stands on an island in the River Seine in Paris*

Figure 114: *The theme of the virgin mother and baby can be found in religions all over the world and they are different versions of Semiramis and Tammuz in Babylon, seen here on the left. It is a universal theme in Reptilian worship*

bloodlines and he says that the senior line of descent was determined by the 'Mitochondrial DNA of the Dragon Queens'. Gardner talks of the 'Blood Royal' or 'Sang Real' in the 'womb of a Dragon Queen'. Other texts in France called this bloodline 'Le Serpent Rouge' – the 'red serpent', or the 'serpent blood'.

Throughout the lands settled by the former Atlantean-Muan peoples you find the worship of the serpent goddess and her serpent son, who is often symbolised as a bull. The author and researcher, James Churchward, who wrote extensively about the lost land of Mu, or Lemuria, says that he discovered from ancient tablets and artwork that the Muans worshipped a goddess called 'Queen Moo', and that Lemuria/Mu was called the 'Motherland'. Around the Mediterranean the priest kings were known as the 'Children of the Serpent Goddess'. In this same region, temples and Mystery schools were created in her name, most notably the Temple of Artemis/Diana at Ephesus in Turkey, one of the seven wonders of the ancient world. Turkey (formerly Asia Minor), mainland Greece, and the islands of Samothrace, Cyprus and Crete were among the main centres of the goddess cult. Samothrace, 'the Sacred Isle', seems to have been the headquarters for this in the Mediterranean/Aegean region. Rites of the 'Sisterhood of Daughters' of the goddess Hecate were performed there and she was depicted with snake feet and snakes for hair. The symbol of a human upper body and snakes for legs or feet was a common way the ancients symbolised the bloodlines, as I've pointed out. The ancient Egyptian word and hieroglyph for 'goddess' also means 'serpent', and the Minoan civilisation on Crete, part of the Sumer Empire, called its line of 'Minos' kings the Sons of the Serpent Goddess. Ancient Crete, as with other connected centres, was famous for its labyrinth, a word meaning 'House of the Double Axe' or 'House of the Serpent Goddess'. Greece was another serpent goddess culture. They called the goddess 'Athene' and the Oracle at Delphi would speak the words of the serpent goddess, known there as Delphinia. The Oracle would go into a trance state while staring into the eyes of a snake. Pythagoras, the famous Greek hero and mathematician, grew up in the mysteries of the serpent goddess cult and his very name means 'I am the Python' or 'I am the Serpent'. The Indian goddess, Devi, was said to have been a serpent, and another called 'Kadru' was the serpent goddess and Mother of the Nagas, or Cobra people. Devi is described as carrying the god Vishnu over the waters of the Deluge. This matches Mesopotamian accounts of the Anunnaki flying over the stricken Earth during the cataclysms.

The Merovingian kings worshipped the moon goddess, Diana, the 'Mother of the Gods', also known as 'Artemis', and it was no accident – in any sense – that Princess Diana died in the city built by the Merovingians. She was born on the Windsor estate at Sandringham in Norfolk and

Figure 115: *The twelve-star circle of the European Union that represents the moon goddess of Babylon*

was named after the goddess Diana by her Satanist father. Her whole life was a ritual, including her sham marriage to Prince Charles, leading up to her ritual death in the Pont de l'Alma tunnel in Paris. According to an American researcher, that was the site of Merovingian rituals to the Goddess Diana. Pont de l'Alma translates as 'Bridge or Passage of the Moon Goddess'. It can also be translated as 'Bridge of the Soul'. Princess Diana has been associated with the rose, and memorials to her have included a five-petalled rose. This is used in churches to represent the womb of Mary and the Romans called it the Rose of Venus, their name for the Babylonian Semiramis and the universal goddess. Everything is symbolism and ritual to these people. See *The Biggest Secret* for more on the assassination of Princess Diana.

The Goddess Union

The Illuminati goddess can be seen in many guises, including the logo of the European Union. Europe gets its name from the goddess, Europa, another version of the moon goddess, Semiramis, and all the rest. The European Union is, therefore, the union of the goddess of Babylon and Sumer, the Reptilian moon goddess, and this is further confirmed by the twelve stars on the EU flag (Fig 115). The twelve stars – or pentagrams – of the Babylonian Zodiac are a symbol of the goddess. The Roman Church (the Church of Babylon relocated) claims that Mother Mary, the 'Queen of Heaven', has a 'crown of twelve stars'. In the *Book of Revelation* 12:1, it says: 'Then a great pageant appeared in heaven, portraying things to come. I saw a woman clothed with the sun, with the moon beneath her feet, and a crown of twelve stars on her head (Fig 116).' The circle is also a Mystery school symbol for the Babylonian virgin-born son, Tammuz. This European Union symbol is attributed to Paul Levi (Rothschild Zionist), a converted Roman Catholic who was director of the 'cultural section' of the European Council established

Figure 116: *The twelve stars around the head of the 'virgin mother', or moon goddess, with the 'serpent moon' at her feet. This imagery will become very relevant later.*

in London in 1949. Levi claims to have seen a statue of 'Mother Maria' that had a 'star coronet' shining under a blue sky. Levi is said to have immediately decided that twelve golden stars in a chain against a dark blue background should be the European flag. Oh, don't be silly. It was purposely designed to represent the goddess of Babylon. The European flag was introduced on 8th December 1955 on the feast of The Immaculate Conception of Mary, and on 2nd September 1958 the Archbishop of Milan, the future Pope Pius XII, unveiled a 20-metre high statue of Mary and called it 'Our beloved Lady, Ruler of Europe'. 'Beloved Lady' = the Babylonian goddess, the serpent goddess. Two stamps were issued for the European elections in Britain in 1984 and one depicted a woman riding a bull, led by a winged boy over seven hills or waves in the sea. This was goddess symbolism and depicts the legend of the goddess Europa, whom Jupiter (Nimrod) led away in the form of a bull. The bull is one of the Mystery symbols for Nimrod and for the moon god, with the horns representing the crescent moon. The other stamp design included a bridge with the word 'Europa'. The Latin word 'Pontifex', meaning 'Pontiff' or 'High Priest', comes from the Latin words 'pons', meaning bridge, and 'facio', meaning make. Pontifex means 'Bridge Maker'. The Roman Church and its Pontifex are often symbolised as a bridge in occult imagery. One of the major Reptilian-hybrid bloodlines is the Rothschild associates, the Habsburg dynasty. It was the Habsburgs and the Rothschild Round Table network, especially the Bilderberg Group, which brought the European Union into being to centralise power across the entire continent. You will find the detail in … *And The Truth Shall Set You Free* and *The David Icke Guide to the Global Conspiracy (and how to end it)*. The flag of the Habsburg Pan European Movement, or Union, which worked from the shadows to install the European Union, is the red cross of the Knights Templar over the yellow sun (Nimrod) surrounded by the star circle of Semiramis. It was designed by Otto and Karl Habsburg. Otto said in his book, *The Social Order of Tomorrow*:

> Now we do possess a European symbol which belongs to all nations equally. This is the crown of the Holy Roman Empire, which embodies the tradition of Charlemagne, the ruler of the united occident.

The 'occident' refers to the countries of Europe and the western hemisphere and Charlemagne is the Reptilian-hybrid who was King of the Franks from AD 768 to his death. He was virtually worshipped by Hitler and leading Nazis. Charlemagne expanded the Frankish kingdoms into a Frankish Empire that incorporated much of Western and Central Europe. Genealogists say many leading world figures, past and present, trace their lineage to Charlemagne, including every English monarch from circa AD 1000 to the House of Windsor, the Dutch House of Orange, and many US presidents, including George Washington, the Bush family and Barack Obama. Some genealogists say that virtually anyone with European blood is descended to some extent from Charlemagne, but the question that matters, from an Illuminati point of view, is how closely. A Charlemagne Prize was established to 'honour' those who work hardest for 'European unity', and one recipient was the Jesuit-trained President Bill Clinton who has called for the European Union to encompass Russia – a goal of the Rothschilds. Other winners of the Charlemagne Prize include Tony Blair. One to give a miss, I think.

The Common Source

At the centre of the Reptilian religious control system is the worship of the serpent, the sun god, the moon god and the moon goddess, or mother goddess. Serpent/Sun/Moon/Saturn worship was associated with human sacrifice to 'the gods' and also with the building of pyramids. The Reptilians and their hybrids were the pyramid-builders of Egypt, Sumer, Central America, China, and so on. It is one of their calling cards, be it the Great Pyramid at Giza or the step pyramids of Central America or the ziggurats of Mesopotamia. In their various forms, Serpent/Sun/Moon/Saturn worship are the foundations for all major religions and it is no surprise to find that their common source and inspiration is Sumer and Babylon, now Iraq. As we've seen, the Old Testament includes countless stories and themes re-written from the far older Sumerian and placed into another cultural and historical context and setting. The texts that became the Jewish 'Torah' (the first five books of the Old Testament) were also massively influenced by the decades of Jewish captivity in Babylon from about 586 BC. They were allowed to live and work in Babylonian society and their priestly class had access to the Mesopotamian knowledge and beliefs. There are two versions of the Jewish Talmud ('teaching' in Hebrew), the Jerusalem Talmud and the later and much longer Babylonian Talmud that includes many Old Testament references. It was passed on verbally for centuries before being written down in the fifth century. Religions had always worshipped multiple deities based on the multiple Reptilian figures and other origins, but eventually the single-god religions began to take over. You can still see in the Old Testament the odd reference in which the Sumerian gods, plural, have survived this transformation, like the one I mentioned earlier. The legends, myths and religion of Babylon are at the heart of all major religions and most of the smaller ones, too. These legends are founded on three characters: Nimrod, the father god, symbolised as a fish; Damu, or Tammuz, the virgin-born son who was said to be a reincarnation of Nimrod, so 'father and son were one'; and Queen Semiramis, or Ishtar, the virgin mother who was symbolised as a dove and also known as Lilith. It was said that when Nimrod died he became the sun god, Baal, and impregnated Semiramis with the rays of the Sun, hence the 'virgin birth'. Together this symbolic father-son-mother comprised the Babylonian trinity which would become the Christian trinity in a slightly different form. Nimrod, the 'founder of Babylon', was described as a 'mighty tyrant', a 'great hunter' and one of the 'giants'. Among his symbols was the snake, serpent or dragon. Arabs believed that after the Flood it was Nimrod who built or rebuilt the amazing structure at Baalbek in the Lebanon with its three stones each weighing 800 tons. It was said that he ruled the region that is now Lebanon and, according to *Genesis*, the first centres of Nimrod's kingdom were Babylon, Akkad, and others in the land of Shinar (Sumer). He was also said to have ruled Assyria and built cities like Nineveh where many of the Sumerian clay tablets were found.

The hybrid bloodlines of Sumer/Babylon migrated in all directions. Some located in what became Khazaria, and others would found and populate what became Rome. The religion of Babylon and Sumer was relocated to Rome and continued pretty much the same until it morphed into Christianity, which was, well, pretty much the same. Christianity was introduced as the state religion by the sun-god worshipper, Emperor Constantine, in the fourth century. He worshipped a deity called 'Sol Invictus', the

Figure 117: *The origin of the mitre worn by the Pope and other Christian 'frocks' – the Reptilian fish god, Oannes (Nimrod), as depicted in Babylon. The Church of Babylon became the Church of Rome*

'Unconquered Sun', and Christianity was just another version of that, among other esoteric concepts, including worship of the moon god. The Babylonian trinity continued as the 'Christian' trinity under other names. Father, Son and Holy Ghost (or Spirit) were just Nimrod, Tammuz and Queen Semiramis in disguise. Nimrod became the 'Father God' and Tammuz became 'Jesus'. Christianity symbolises the Holy Spirit as a dove, and that was the symbol for Semiramis in Babylon. Semiramis was also known as the 'Virgin Mother', 'Queen of Heaven', 'My Lady', and 'Our Lady' and these were transplanted onto the biblical figure of 'Mary', the virgin mother of 'Jesus'. 'Christian' holy days and festivals like Christmas, Easter and Lent all come from Babylon and the Pagan world. The cross was the symbol of Nimrod/Tammuz and was widely used thousands of years before Christianity. The Babylonians believed that baptism would purge them of 'sin' and even the fish-head mitre worn by the Pope and other Christian men-in-frocks is a steal from the fish-god symbolism of Nimrod in Babylon (Fig 117). The centre of American legislative power is in the states of Virginia and Maryland, and that is by design. Virginia is the state of the Virgin Mother of Babylon, and Maryland is Mary-Land, more goddess symbolism. These states surround Washington DC in the District of 'Columbia', a name derived from a word that means 'dove' – the symbol of the Babylonian goddess. In Rome they worshipped the goddess as Venus Columba, or Venus the Dove, and the French word 'colombe' means 'dove'.

Black Sabbath

Nimrod was known as 'Saturn' in Rome and his birthday was celebrated during the festival of Saturnalia in the period up to our Christmas. Rome was even called at one time 'The City of Saturn'. The Jewish Sabbath comes from Saturn-day – Nimrod – and in India, 'Saturday' is called 'Shanivar' from the Vedic god, Shani, who was said to manifest in ... the planet Saturn. The worship of Saturn, the 'Lord of the Rings', is still at heart of the political, commercial and religious systems. Saturn is the god of banking. Black robes are a symbol of Saturn, and so you have black robes worn by judges, barristers, catholic priests, rabbis and students at university when they graduate. Saturn is also known as the god 'El', as in Isra-el, and you have el-ections to be el-ected and if you become rich and powerful you are the el-ite. Understanding words and symbols is vital to seeing how the system works and its 'religious' foundations. When you write a word you 'spell' it. This is what words are when used malevolently. They are spells cast on the human psyche. The America researcher, Jordan Maxwell, is very well versed on this subject of word connections. Israel is composed of Isis, the virgin mother of Egypt; Ra, the Egyptian sun god; and El. The name 'El' also refers to a universal moon god and was called the 'father of the gods' and 'father of man'. El is the singular of the Biblical 'Elohim' which has been translated as singular when it is plural. These 'one gods' are actually a composite of many gods and goddesses. Nimrod's midwinter 'birthday' was more sun god symbolism. Nimrod/Tammuz represented the Sun which 'died' at the winter solstice when it reaches the lowest point of its power in the northern hemisphere. This is why sun god symbols like 'Jesus' were given the birthday of what became December 25th. Three days after the 'death' of the Sun on the winter solstice the ancients said the Sun was reborn to begin its 'journey' to the peak of its power in the summer. So, three days after the solstice – December 25th in our calendar – they celebrated the 'birth' of the Sun (Nimrod/Tammuz). Later the Roman Church, the Church of Babylon under another name, decreed that Jesus was 'born' on that day also. The Bible says that Jesus died on the cross, was laid in a tomb and was resurrected *three days* later. Our December 25th was Rome's Natalis Solis Invicti – the Birth of the Unconquered Sun. This is the meaning behind descriptions of Jesus as the 'light of the world' and the claim that 'they will see the Son of Man coming in a cloud with power and great glory' and this could relate to the Moon, too, as I will explain later. 'He' is a symbol of the Sun, among other things. There were a long list of 'Jesus' figures in the thousands of years before Christianity like Osiris and Horus (Egypt), Mithra/Mithras (Persia and Rome), Dionysus or Bacchus (Greece/Rome), Attis of Phrygia (now Turkey), Krishna (India) and, of course, Tammuz/Damu in Babylon. This is what was said about two of those 'Jesus' deities long before 'Jesus':

Attis of Phrygia

He was born on December 25th of the Virgin Nana.
He was considered the saviour who was slain for the salvation of mankind.
His body as bread was eaten by his worshippers.
His priests were 'eunuchs for the kingdom of heaven'.
He was both the Divine Son and the Father.
On 'Black Friday', he was crucified on a tree, from which his holy blood ran down to redeem the earth.
He descended into the underworld and after three days he was resurrected on March 25th as the 'Most High God'.

Dionysus (Greece) and Bacchus (Rome)

Dionysus was born of a virgin on December 25th and, as the Holy Child, was placed in a manger.
He was a travelling teacher who performed miracles.
He 'rode in a triumphal procession on an ass'.
He was a sacred king killed and eaten in a Eucharistic ritual for fecundity and purification.
Dionysus rose from the dead on March 25th.
He was the God of the Vine, and turned water into wine.
He was called 'King of Kings' and 'God of Gods'.
He was considered the 'Only Begotten Son', 'Saviour', 'Redeemer', 'Sin Bearer', 'Anointed One' and the 'Alpha and Omega'.

He was identified with the Ram or Lamb.
His sacrificial title of 'Dendrites' or 'Young Man of the Tree' intimates he was hung on a tree or crucified.

There was no literal Jesus or Mary, or any of it. The story is a symbolic, constantly-recurring myth told all over the world thousands of years before Christianity and so you find 'Jesus' under different names on every continent long before the name 'Jesus' was ever heard of. In ancient Mesoamerica, Quetzalcoatl, the 'Feathered Serpent', was said to have been born of a virgin, raised the dead and promised to return. Christianity is just another Reptilian religion which, in their various forms, spanned the world.

Allah the Moon God

There is another crucial aspect to the story of how the religion and rituals of Sumer and Babylon became the religions of today. This is the worship of the moon god and later in the book this will take on great significance. The moon god was later usurped by the sun god and moon goddess and the monotheistic religions, but throughout the ancient world the moon god was the primary deity. The Sumerians worshipped the Moon under many names, including Nanna and Suen, whose symbol was the crescent moon. This is a symbol today of Islam because that is a moon god religion (Fig 118). Other Mesopotamian cultures, the Assyrians, Babylonians, and Akkadians, followed the Sumerians in their worship of the moon god and the name they gave him was 'Sin', a derivative of 'Suen'. His sacred city was Ur in what is now Iraq. This is the origin of the term 'sin' or 'sinner' – the Mesopotamian moon god. The goddess Ishtar/Semiramis was portrayed as a daughter of Sin. Moon god temples have been unearthed at Ur and at Harran or Haran in south-east Turkey, once a major religious, cultural and commercial centre. These locations are both closely associated with the biblical Abraham, the patriarch of Christians, Jews and Muslims. *Genesis* says that Abraham, or Abram, was born in Ur and lived in Harran, which it spells with a single 'r'. He is said to have left there to head for Canaan to seed the Israelite race. The Bible says that 'God' told Abraham that the offspring of his 'seed' would be so numerous they would be 'like the dust of the earth'. It is claimed that God promised the descendants of Abraham the land from 'from the river of Egypt to the great river, the Euphrates, the land of the Kenites, Kenizzites, Kadmonites, Hittites, Perizzites, Rephaites, Amorites, Canaanites, Girgashites and Jebusites'. This is the origin of the 'Promised Land' of Israel and the Rothschild Zionist plan to secure what they call 'Greater Israel' from the Nile to Iraq. The Rothschild Zionist invasion of Iraq is all part of this.

A major temple to the moon god has been found in Palestine with statues of a man with a crescent moon on his chest and others depicting his daughters.

Figure 118: *The ancient Mesopotamian symbols for sun and moon deities became the international symbols of Islam*

Apparently, Mohammed's re-worked version of Allah originally had daughters, but these were later deleted from the story. Islam is the religion of the moon god, which continued in Arabia after it began to wane elsewhere. To the Arabians, he was the god above all others and his major shrine was … Mecca. The pre-Islam Arabians called the moon god 'al- ilah', or 'al-Llah', and even before the Prophet Mohammed arrived on the scene this had become 'Allah'. The most sacred site in Islam is the Kaaba, which Islamic tradition says was built by Abraham (Fig 119). When Muslims kneel and 'face Mecca' during their prayers they are really facing the Kaaba, the cube-shaped building which predates Islam and today stands within Masjid al-Haram, the world's biggest mosque. The Five Pillars of Islam demand that Muslims make the pilgrimage to the Kaaba at least once in their lifetimes. The main pilgrimage is called the Hajj and this, too, pre-dates

Figure 119: *Islam's most sacred site – the Kaaba cube*

Figure 120: *The little cube 'hat', the Tefillin, worn on the front of the head by Jewish people*

Islam. The Kaaba includes the Black Stone, allegedly part of a meteorite that Islamic lore dates back to Adam and Eve. Pilgrims walk around the Kaaba seven times and try to kiss the Black Stone on each circuit. The word Kaaba means 'cube' and this symbol is associated with Sun, Moon and Saturn worship. Followers of Judaism wear a little cube 'hat', called the Tefillin, as part of their ritual, for the same reason, but only the el-lite' know the real origin and meaning (Fig 120). The cube is a symbol of the moon god/Saturn god, El, and this is the god of both Judaism and Islam. Irony, or what? The Reptilian manipulation has established human religions using the same deities under different names and then played them off against each other to divide and rule. The cube is also a symbol of Freemasonry, because the foundations of religion and secret societies are the same.

Islam is the continuing worship of the ancient Mesopotamian moon god, and very large numbers of archaeological discoveries have confirmed this countless times. Mohammed was brought up in the religion of the moon god, Allah, the Arabian name for 'Sin'. His father and uncle had Allah in their names. The moon god was the supreme deity in the multi-god religion of the Arabians and 'above all other gods'. Mohammed simply said that the moon god, Allah, was not only the supreme god, but he was the *only* god. Exactly the same happened in Judaism when the multiple gods of Mesopotamia were fused together to become the composite Yahweh/Jehovah that was later fused with Christianity. The monotheistic religions are really the *moon*-otheistic religions. Judaism abounds with moon-god worship and symbolism. The god 'Sin' is the origin of the word Synagogue, or Sin-agogue, and also Mount Sinai where the Bible says that God gave the Ten Commandments to Moses. Sin was known as the 'God of the Mountain'. The biblical Wilderness or Desert of Sin, allegedly experienced by the Israelites, has the same source. The Jewish month begins with the new moon and the Passover is on the full moon. The 'Christian' Easter, another pre-Christian ritual, is on the first Sunday after the full moon. Moon as well as sun symbolism could be connected to the symbolic story of Jesus 'rising again' after three days. There are three days of darkness between moon phases before the new moon appears.

Same Old, Same Old

Christianity and Judaism/Talmudism derive from the same source and now we can see that so, too, does Islam. Do we think that the obvious connection between Muslim and Jewish 'dietary laws', Kosher and Halal, are just a coincidence? Both ban the consumption of pork and blood and their ritual method of slaughter is exactly the same, except that Muslims must say the name of Allah while facing Mecca before slitting the animal's throat. God help us. Muslims believe in the existence of the Christian Jesus, Mother Mary, and the Angel Gabriel, and in the Jewish Abraham, Noah and Moses. The Koran considers Jesus, or in Arabic, 'Isa', to be one of Islam's most significant prophets and gives considerable attention to Mother Mary, or 'Maryam' in Arabic. It agrees that Jesus was born through a virgin birth. The 19th chapter of the Koran is even named after Mary, one of only eight 'people' to enjoy such an honour in the entire book. The Koran says '[It is] ... the same religion has He established for you as that which He enjoined on Noah ... and that which We enjoined on Abraham, Moses, and Jesus'. Yes it is, but what is the true identity of 'He'? The Christian Father God, the Jewish Yahweh/Jehovah and the Muslim 'Allah' are all symbolic composites of the Reptilians, I would suggest. We see the same deities and stories in India, home to the Reptilian Nagas. Krishna, the virgin-born son of India, was called 'Christos', the same as the Greek 'Christ', or 'Anointed One'. The soldiers of Alexander the Great called Christos 'Krishna' when they invaded India. Krishna's father was said to have been a carpenter; his birth was marked by a star in the east and attended by angels and shepherds; he was persecuted by a tyrant who ordered the slaughter of thousands of infants; he worked miracles and wonders, raising the dead and healing lepers, the deaf and the blind; in some traditions he died on a tree or was crucified between two thieves. He was called the 'Shepherd of God' and considered the 'Redeemer', 'Firstborn', 'Sin-Bearer', 'Liberator' and 'Universal Word'. He rose from the dead and ascended to heaven 'in the sight of all men'. He was depicted on a cross with nail-holes in his feet, as well as having a heart emblem on his clothing. He was deemed the 'Son of God' and 'our Lord and Saviour' who came to earth to die for human salvation. He was the second person of the trinity. His disciples purportedly bestowed upon him the title 'Jezeus', or 'Jeseus', meaning 'pure essence'. He is to return to judge the dead, riding on a white horse, and to do battle with the 'Prince of Evil', who will desolate the earth.

Christianity, Judaism, Islam and their like are all a cover for worship of the Reptilians – serpent worship. It is the foundation of all human religion and is hidden behind symbolic deities, stories and rituals and I go into this in much greater detail in *Children of the Matrix*. Worship of the serpent is the origin of religious circumcision. This is seen today as a Jewish ritual that goes back to Abraham but, in fact, it can be found earlier in Egypt. It is the symbolic shedding of the skin like a snake, and the Jewish religion refers to circumcision as a 'covenant with God'. The 'gods' would be more accurate. John Bathurst Deane writes in his book, *Worship of the Serpent*:

> It appears, then, that no nations were so geographically remote, or so religiously discordant, but that one – and only one – superstitious characteristic was common to all: that the most civilized and the most barbarous bowed down with the same devotion to the same engrossing deity; and that this deity either was, or was represented by, the same sacred serpent.

> It appears also that in most, if not all, the civilized countries where this serpent was worshipped, some fable or tradition which involved his history, directly or indirectly, alluded to the Fall of Man in Paradise, in which the serpent was concerned.

> What follows, then, but that the most ancient account respecting the cause and nature of this seduction must be the one from which all the rest are derived which represent the victorious serpent – victorious over man in a state of innocence, and subduing his soul in a state of sin, into the most abject veneration and adoration of himself.

The Fall of Man does indeed describe the consequences of the Reptilian takeover and I will be exploring later the nature of that 'Fall'. Still today, the minds of billions are controlled by an unshakable belief in the Christian, Islamic, Jewish, Hindu and other versions of the same original myths from which they all came. This keeps their believers in Mind and out of Consciousness because religions are constructs of Mind. Does infinite, eternal, All-Knowing Consciousness go to church, get on its knees and worship some 'god' or deity? Please. No, *Mind* does all that because it is like computer software and will believe anything it is programmed to believe. The writer, Aldous Huxley, said:

> You never see animals going through the absurd and often horrible fooleries of magic and religion ... Dogs do not ritually urinate in the hope of persuading heaven to do the same and send down rain. Asses do not bray a liturgy to cloudless skies. Nor do cats attempt, by abstinence from cat's meat, to wheedle the feline spirits into benevolence. Only man behaves with such gratuitous folly. It is the price he has to pay for being intelligent but not, as yet, quite intelligent enough.

Religions are Mind-made and so are their unquestioning advocates and followers. This is not by chance, but by Illuminati/Reptilian design because they understand what the Mind is and how people can be locked into its illusions and limitations of perception. Once they are, they become easily controllable and one rigid belief can be set off against another to divide and rule the masses. It is the same with political parties, races, income brackets and suchlike. Fake self-identities (another form of belief) are sent to war against other fake self-identities on all levels of human interaction to prevent the unity of both understanding and purpose that will bring this nonsense to an end. Religion was created from the start to control us and drain us of energy and it has worked magnificently right up to present day. If you want to be free, have nothing to do with it.

Prisons of the Mind

If you are going to divert people into prisons of the Mind you could hardly invent a better system than religion. You want to stop people awakening to their true and infinite self, the *All That Is*, and so you invent false gods and deities to divert their attention onto endless expressions of the same fakery. Religions appear to be different with their different faiths (in theory) and names, but they all function in exactly the same way: (1) They have a set of beliefs founded on ancient texts, the origin of which is extremely obscure (always a bonus, because they can then invent their own 'history'); (2) They impose the foundation beliefs through rules and regulations that decide if you are a true 'Christian', Muslim', 'Jew', 'Hindu', 'Mormon' ... ad infinitum. That is pretty much it, really. The religion then becomes a self-policing, perpetual-motion machine fuelled by the energy of fear. They make it a crime to say you are 'God' and insist you are an unworthy piece of shit, a born sinner, who must fear 'God'. You must God-fearing. As methods of expanding consciousness go, I've seen better. The Reptilians and their hybrid families are desperate to stop people opening their minds and making the connection to Infinite Self and they created Mind-prison religions by twisting esoteric knowledge communicated through the ancient Mystery Schools and by selling analogy and symbolism as literal truth. Befrocked guards called priests, vicars, bishops, popes, rabbis, imam, ayatollahs and brahmin were placed at the door to Consciousness. Religions play the 'only through' scam of 'only through him', 'only through this', 'only through that', will you make it to heaven; and there is the threat of hell and damnation if you refuse to conform. The need to worship and submit to the will of others is another trait of the reptilian brain and so, depending on the character, is the desire to control and impose your will on others. These two aspects of the reptilian brain dovetail perfectly in the top-down pyramid structures (yet again) that we call religion. Doctors, politicians, scientists, teachers and journalists are all kept in line through ignorance and knowing the consequences of bucking the system, and that is exactly how religions operate amid even more dire threats for insubordination. Do you want to do as you're told, believe what we tell you and go to heaven? Or do you want to think for yourself and meet the guy with the pitchfork? *Mmmm*, tempting, but I'll still take the free-thinking deal, thanks.

The belief-systems of the faithful are fiercely policed through fear, guilt and even violence. Some zealots are so utterly insane, and without so much as a pinhead of intelligence, that they kill members of their own family for going against the rigid and ludicrous beliefs dictated by their prison-cell-of-choice. Wars, inquisitions, mass slaughter, destroyed families and communities, can be seen throughout the grotesque history of the Reptilian-created global religion hiding behind its different names and faiths. The hive minds of the congregated masses are played off against each other as they battle and argue over who has the 'truth'. Believers are set against non-believers, infidels and goyim to instigate the divide and rule so vital to the few controlling the many. The manipulators could not impose their will on a united population that is at peace with others having different views and beliefs. They have to work constantly to disunite us along manufactured fault-lines like race, politics, culture, income-bracket and the granddaddy, along with race, – religion. Every aspect of the Reptilian game plan gains from the global control-structure of religious belief and dogma. Through religion the Reptilians close minds; impose an incredibly limited sense of reality; make advocates submit to will of 'God' (them); make people deny, even fear as the 'Devil', esoteric knowledge that could set them free; divide and rule and trigger conflict between individuals, groups and even nations.

New? You Must be Joking

The New Age belief system is condemned by the religious mainstream and yet it is just another religion. It is like the Green Party claiming to be a different form of politics when it is really exactly the same. I call the New Age the last cul-de-sac before the gold mine. It is there to catch those who have rejected formal religion and could be in danger of breaking out of Mind and into Consciousness. New Agers say that we are all One, there is no death and Creation is comprised of different densities or ranges of frequency. They are getting far too close to seeing through the veil cast across the eyes of human perception and so the traps have been set to stop further progress into Consciousness. It was during the 1960s and 1970s that the New Age began to emerge from the manufactured 'Flower Power' era when an extraordinary number of famous musicians from military or intelligence agency families appeared on the scene to expand and define the period of 'free love' and the 'hippie rebellion'. One example is the late Jim Morrison, lead singer of the Doors. His father, Admiral George Stephen Morrison, commanded the US fleet in the Gulf of Tonkin in 1964 that claimed to have been attacked by the North Vietnamese when the evidence is that they never were. President Lyndon Johnson used this lie as an excuse to escalate the Vietnam War with all the death and destruction that followed. Squadron commander James Stockdale, one of the US pilots flying above Admiral Morrison's fleet at this time, wrote this in his 1984 book *Love and War*: '[I] had the best seat in the house to watch that event, and our destroyers were just shooting at phantom targets – there were no [North Vietnamese] boats there ... There was nothing there, but black water and American fire power.' It was just another No-Problem-Reaction-Solution, a fantasy, just like the Flower Power era was an engineered fantasy, not least through the circulation of mind-altering drugs. These were not used for an 'out there' experience, but as a way of daily life. Flower Power was designed to hijack the anti-war movement and dilute and divert its potential effect. I recommend an excellent series of Internet articles about the 60's 'revolution' called 'The Strange but Mostly True Story of Laurel Canyon and the Birth of the Hippie Generation'. Put those words into a search engine and you will find the series. It provides a whole new perspective on that era and the military/intelligence background of some of its heroes.

Out of the hippie generation came the New Age movement that was expanded behind the scenes through the efforts of major Illuminati insiders like Henry Kissinger. People close to Kissinger at the time have confirmed this to me and it makes sense, because they were seeking to create a new religion to seize the minds of those threatening to really wake up. Mystic conmen from the 'East', like the one-time Beatles guru, Maharishi Mahesh Yogi (Fig 121 overleaf), were brought to the West, or to the attention of the West, to fuel the expansion. Before long, 'awakened' New Agers had found new gurus and gods to worship in their cul-de-sac of enlightenment. There are many genuine people in what we call the 'New Age', but it is also teeming with frauds, fantasists and those simply placed there to mislead. Large numbers have been

Human Race Get Off Your Knees

Figure 121: *Maharishi Mahesh Yogi*

caught up in this pseudo freedom, even down to the way they dress. The New Age is supposed to be founded on the right to express uniqueness and yet you can often spot a New Ager from 100 yards just by the clothes they wear. What people choose to have in their wardrobe is entirely up to them, and none of my business, but it is hard to square a philosophy based on celebrating uniqueness with wearing what is, in effect, a uniform. The 'New Age' is clearly not new at all. It is another religion following the same program. The apparent anarchy presented by its public face hides the conventional religion that underpins it. Like all of them, it is founded on the worship of something or someone, and on seeing themselves as lesser-than, rather than part-of. Oh, I hear all the PR stuff about everyone being 'One' and 'taking your power back', but that is not what I see at the extreme end, and often less-than-extreme end, of the New Age arena. I see people giving their power away in the worship and exaltation of gurus and deities. The New Age even has its own version of Jesus, a chap called 'Sananda'. Christianity got it wrong about Jesus, sorry 'Sananda', they say. In fact, he's really a leading light in the 'Great White Brotherhood' of 'Ascended Masters' to whom we are supposed to focus our worship and devotion. Ah, yes, we must 'devote'. The New Age Sananda/Jesus looks just like the Christian version. What a coincidence, and how could this be when no-one knows what 'Jesus' is supposed to have looked like with no biblical descriptions worth the name? The classic 'Jesus'

Figure 122   **Figure 123**

The Christian 'Jesus' and the New Age 'Sananda' somehow look the same, even though there are no detailed descriptions of the 'man'

image comes from what artists decided to paint well over a thousand years after 'he' is supposed to have 'lived', and yet somehow he turns up in the New Age looking virtually the same (Figs 122 and 123). The New Age 'I AM University' in the United States even has an 'Ashram of Jesus/Sananda'. Here again we see the Eastern predominance. An 'ashram' is a 'usually secluded residence of a religious community and its guru' and comes from Hinduism. That is not to say that there is no merit in the knowledge of the East. There is indeed much of benefit with regard to the nature of Consciousness and illusory reality; but if people take the whole 'package' without discernment (the East = good by definition) they will suck in its malevolent aspects as well, which is what parts of the New Age have done. There is a writer called Mark Amaru Pinkham, based in Sedona, Arizona, one of the global centres of the New Age, who connects the legends of the serpent gods to this other-dimensional 'Great White Brotherhood'. He writes:

> The name Great White Brotherhood seems to have been an invention of the Theosophical Society, an organization founded and led by the Russian woman and world traveler Madam Blavatsky in the mid-nineteenth century. But well before Blavatsky's time the Great White Brotherhood was known as the Solar or Serpent Brotherhood; its members were known as 'Serpents', and its principal temples were pyramids, homes of the serpent power, as well as sun temples aligned with the solstices and equinoxes.

> In Egypt, for example, the most important temples were the complex at Heliopolis, the 'Place of the Sun', along with the Giza Pyramids and the solar temple at Karnak. Administering to these temples were the Egyptian priests, the Djedhi, 'those of the serpent lineage'. In Mexico, the members of the Serpent Brotherhood, the Quetzlcoatls or 'Plumed Serpents', administered numerous towering pyramids all aligned with the solstices and equinoxes. The same was true in Peru where the adepts were Amarus or 'Serpents', as well as in China where they were the Lung Dragons, or in India where the enlightened yogis were known as Nagas, the 'Serpents'.

I have long noted the closeness of the name, Djedhi, 'those of the serpent lineage', to the Jedi in the *Star Wars* movies of Illuminati insider George Lucas. The Jedi are described as ...

> ... members of an ancient and noble monastic order, faintly similar to the military and religious orders that arose during the Crusades [like the Knights Templar]. The Jedi Knights are known for two things: their observance of a religion founded on The Force and their selection and admittance to the order, based upon specific talents that demonstrate that a person has a special link to such Force.

What is the real meaning of the 'Force'? Mark Amaru Pinkham is quite right about 'those of the serpent lineage' who have carried advanced knowledge not known by most of the general population. He is further correct that they dominated the ancient priesthood and leadership all over the world that ruled the ancient civilisations like Sumer, Egypt, India and China. I also agree with him when he says that these ancient initiation schools developed into the secret society network of today. Where I fundamentally differ, however, is in the interpretation of the 'serpent lineage' and the agenda of the secret societies, like the Knights Templar and Freemasons, which have continued to covertly manipulate the population to this day. It is not about 'enlightenment', but control; and the deities of the New Age religion are the Reptilian entities – the same deities worshipped under different names in the mainstream religions. Consciousness doesn't 'do' religion; *Mind* does religion, because it is always about structure and hierarchy.

Unravelling the Nonsense

I have used the symbolism before of putting 50 kittens in a room with 50 balls of wool and coming back hours later to try to unravel it all. I have applied this to the way 'the system' has enslaved the human psyche, but it is equally applicable to the religious beliefs of India from which the soul of the New Age sprang. There are, apparently, 50,000 Hindu deities, enough to fill a good-sized football stadium, and it has all gotten seriously out of hand. At its most extreme, this involves arranged marriages and even killing young people who dare to marry below their 'caste' (perceived genetic class). Even in everyday life the complexity, myth and symbolism-taken-literally ensnare the lives of so many like flies in a spiders' web – appropriate symbolism for sure. 'Shiva says this'; 'Vishnu says that'; you only do this when there is an 'r' in the month; you only do that when your bum's pointing to the Ganges. How they keep up with it all, I really don't know. Of course, you get the same with all religions – must do this; mustn't do that; Jesus says this, Allah says that, Yahweh says the other. Even so, the scale of deity-think in India is breathtaking by any standards. Most religions are there to hide the simple truth that we are all one eternal Consciousness and not the bodies that we think we are. They may go on about 'soul' and life after death and all that, but in the way they play out they are constructs of Mind and body, not Infinite Consciousness. Compared with many religions, Hinduism talks more than most about 'Oneness', and it clearly requires the most manufactured complexity to divert its advocates from this core truth. 50,000 deities worth of complexity, it would seem.

I went to India in 2008 and saw this for myself. It is an amazing country in so many ways and I had a wonderful time, but to see the extent to which people were controlled by religion was all too depressing. I went to see a mountain called Arunachala, alongside the town of Thiruvannamalai, in Tamil Nadu, southern India. This was home to Sri Ramana Maharshi (Fig 124) who, from the aged of 13, began to ponder deeply on the meaning of 'I'. Who am I? What is the nature of this 'I' that we talk about? He concluded in a lifetime of deep meditation that the 'I' is one infinite, eternal,

unchanging Consciousness and that the 'physical' world is an illusion of what we call Mind. That was it, basically. He saw the so-called 'master' and 'pupil' as simply different points of view, or observation, not as one 'up there' and the other 'down here'. I don't agree with everything he said and believed in, but at its heart it was a simple truth. We are all one Consciousness and the 'physical' realm is an illusory reality in which people become lost in a perception of apartness and division. But, oh, my Shiva, what have they done with that? Since he died in 1950, they have turned this place into a shrine to him. I watched in amazement as devotees lay prostrate before his image, their foreheads on the ground in homage and awe. 'No, no,' I felt like shouting. 'You've missed his bloody point – get off your knees *and* your belly.' I

Figure 124: *Sri Ramana Maharshi*   arrived at the main ashram building and the shrine to

Ramana during the nightly gathering. He was not directly connected to the Hindu religion, but no matter. It has adopted him from what I could see and absorbed his simple message to fit its blueprint. Seated around the hall were Ramana devotees, both local and from around the world, and the ceremony took the form of someone reading from a book while the assembled replied in unison from the same said book. It could quite easily have been a Christian service or one from Islam, Judaism or the Hindu faith (which it was in structure and theme). Was I alone in seeing the irony of such religious ritual in the name of a man who said this world is a figment of Mind and that we are all One? It seemed so.

I watched as Western white people with Indian garb and close-cropped hair followed the program of religious advocates across the world. They wore the uniform and copied the haircut of the 'holy men' they so wished they could have been. I briefly met a lovely guy from Scotland with an accent that sounded surreal when contrasted with his 'holy

Figure 125: *The New Age is another Reptilian creation – the last cul-de-sac before the gold mine. It is designed to stop awakening people from breaking through Mind into Consciousness*

man' cropped hair and Hindu tunic. He walked, like so many of his West-finds-East persuasion, with a slowness and deliberation of footstep, as if traversing some invisible tightrope on the floor. This is not religious 'enlightenment'; it is a software program. I am not knocking such people or seeking to ridicule them. They should wear what they like and look how they like. What a bore if everyone dressed like me in baggy trousers and T-shirt. My point is exactly that – it doesn't matter how you clothe your body or style your hair. Enlightenment is not a fashion statement; it is a state of being. Those who think they need the outward persona are missing something very profound. They are still focused on the 'out there' reality while believing they are going 'within'. They think they are accessing Infinite Consciousness when it is all going on in their finite Mind of images and 'things' (Fig 125). It is Mind that is obsessed with outward persona; Infinite Consciousness doesn't give a shit. Mind thinks, and 'persona' is an expression of thought. The Infinite just is and thus it can recognise irrelevant bollocks when it sees it. Everywhere I went around Arunachala, people seemed to be constantly removing their shoes 'out of respect'; but respect for what? It is just more posturing. Respect comes from the heart, not the footwear. At one time, I was asked to remove my shoes just to cross a dusty car park and an open passageway to pick up the mountain path. I never actually entered any building. It was, apparently, a *sacred* dusty car park and open passageway. What brain-numbing nonsense. Is it just me? Maybe it is.

Religion of the Mind

People all over were sitting in the 'lotus position' while I sat in the 'holy places' in a folding garden chair to compensate for my arthritis. I got some funny looks, but who cares? We don't need the rule-book garbage about 'you must sit in the lotus position to align your energy with God', and all that stuff. Does that mean that I can't 'align' myself, because I have severe arthritis and can't even get down on the floor? Crikey, the only way I could cross my legs like those guys do is under anaesthetic. All this body mechanics business, all this structure of 'how you do it', is just another mirage and operates in the realm of Mind, from where all structure emanates; and Mind is the 'world' of illusion. 'Align your body?' There *is* no body! (Or, no body as we perceive it, anyway.) How do you align a figment of your imagination to 'God' when your imagination already *is* 'God', the Infinite All? It is the understanding that we are the Infinite that aligns us most effectively to a conscious awareness of the Infinite, not sitting in the lotus position. Our point of observation determines our sense of reality, that's all, and our sense of reality becomes our experienced reality.

I guess my general impressions of India's official 'spirituality' were encapsulated as I sat outside the Ramana ashram waiting for it to open. Nearby was a white American 'guru' sitting cross-legged with orange tunic (of course) and shaven head (ditto). He was addressing two middle-aged American women about the path to enlightenment. One was taking in every syllable in unsuppressed awe while the other was studiously recording every phrase she thought relevant in her little notebook. What he told them seemed terribly complicated and when he said that we were not worthy of being 'God' I folded up my chair and went away to take some deep breaths. At least the lady with the notebook asked the obvious question: 'If you are saying we are God, how can we not be worthy of being God?' By the time he completed his long-winded answer, I was thankfully out of earshot, though I did note that 'Jesus' got a mention or two. It was Christianity, Judaism and Islam wearing an orange disguise. As usual, simple truth was drowning in irrelevant complexity and manufactured hierarchy. God 'up there'; we 'down here'. This is exactly how the serpent 'gods' want us to perceive the relationship. There will also be some genuine 'gurus' or 'holy men and women' hidden under the tidal wave of pretentious, self-serving and misguided bullshit that bravely passes for 'spirituality' and 'enlightenment', but they are far from the majority. Some of the most selfish, deceitful and untrustworthy people I have met have been of the 'love and light', 'I love everyone', 'I hug everyone' variety. I have heard all the bollocks for 20 years – we support you, the word has got to get out, and such like. But, in the end, 95 per cent of them are only asking 'what's in it for me?' and when anything happens that their me, me, me obsession doesn't like they are quite willing to do all they can to harm the person they said they supported and the 'word' they said must get out. I have had much painful and costly experience with such narcissistic personalities masquerading as the epitome of 'love', 'light' and 'kindness'. They have no integrity whatsoever and they will condemn the 'system' with their words while using it whenever it suits their greed and vindictiveness. The New Age is another Reptilian religion to entrap those who reject all the others. How ironic that the mainstream media dub me a 'New Age guru'. It's pathetic.

Serpent Satanism

Religion, secret societies and what is known as Satanism are all connected via the Reptilian conspiracy. They are ultimately controlled by the same 'Spider' and, at the top level, they work as one organisation. The hidden secret within religion and the secret society network, known only to the elite, is the Reptilian bloodline's covert manipulation of the world. Secret societies have the same origin as the religions, many of which, ironically, condemn secret societies. They both emerged from the ancient Mystery schools that were established and hijacked by the Reptilians and their bloodlines. Religions are the public face of the secret society network in many ways. Religious believers are told to take their 'holy' books literally, while the secret societies understand the hidden meaning and symbolism. Well, the top guys do. Freemasonic heroes like Albert Pike, the Supreme Pontiff of Universal Freemasonry in the 19th century, have said that Freemasonry is a revival of the ancient mystery religions of Babylon, Egypt, Persia, Rome and Greece. 'Masonry is identical with the ancient mysteries', he wrote in his Freemasonic 'Bible' called *Morals and Dogma*. This is why the same serpent, Sun, Moon and Saturn symbolism abounds in secret societies and religions, as you can see in my other books. The chair, or throne, of the Worshipful Master in Freemasonry is positioned to face east in Freemasonic Temples, the direction of the rising sun, just as the altars in so many Christian churches face east for the same reason. It is said that 'Jesus' will return from the east and this is because, like his inspiration, Nimrod / Tammuz in Babylon, 'Jesus' is, at least in part, a symbol of the Sun. Christian websites condemn the Sun 'idolatry' of Freemasonry when Judeo-Christianity is a serpent-Sun-Moon-Saturn religion. Symbolism is the very foundation of the Reptilian-Illuminati secret codes and language, and Freemasonry calls itself a system of pure religion expressed in symbols. Remember, the reptilian brain communicates through images.

Mainstream religion is the public face of the serpent cult, and secret societies are its hidden expression; but there is a third element – the full-blown human sacrifice 'religion' of the Reptilian 'gods', nothing held back. This is what we know today as 'Satanism'. The upper echelons of the secret society network, and many lower ones, fuse with the global web of satanic groups that engage in animal and human sacrifice on a scale that beggars belief. Satanism and the Illuminati are indivisible and I name many famous people in my books who take part in human sacrifice and blood-drinking rituals (Fig 126). The very term 'Satan' comes from the Sumerian words 'Satam' and 'Sandan / Santana', as I said, and the Sumerian symbol for this 'entity' was the trident or pitchfork which is still a common representation of the 'Devil' or 'Satan' today. Satanists perform their rituals to a strict calendar related to astronomical and astrological

Figure 126: *Satanism – the worship of the Serpent 'gods' – dominates the global political and economic system*

movements of the Earth, Moon and planets and two of the key dates are across
Halloween and May Day. Halloween has now become a mini-Christmas with trick-or-
treat and all the rest but, during Halloween, staggering numbers of people, mostly
children, are sacrificed in ancient ceremonies around the world – just as they were in
Babylon and other ancient societies. Those in major positions of royal, political, banking,
commercial, media and military power are invariably Reptilian-hybrids and the
bloodlines have always performed sacrificial rituals going back to Sumer and the later
stages of Atlantis and Mu. Power and Satanism go together so often. David Berkowitz,
the serial killer in New York known as the Son of Sam, said he was part of a satanic
group that had planned the murders. In letters to a church minister, he revealed the
kind of people involved in ritual human sacrifice:

> ... Satanists (genuine ones) are peculiar people. They aren't ignorant peasants or semi-
> literate natives. Rather, their ranks are filled with doctors, lawyers, businessmen, and
> basically highly responsible citizens ... they are not a careless group who are apt to
> make mistakes. But they are secretive and bonded together by a common need and
> desire to mete out havoc on society. It was Aleister Crowley who said: 'I want
> blasphemy, murder, rape, revolution, anything bad'.

I have heard this so many times from those who have experience of these satanic
networks. As I was finishing this book, a document came to light in Australia claiming
to be a deathbed confession by a former head of the 'Alpha Lodge' of Satanism in
Sydney, Australia. There was no time to check its authenticity, but what I can say is that
it is perfectly in line with all that I have uncovered and learned over the last 20 years
about Satanism and its global manipulation and control. You can read the document in
full in Appendix II and it is well worth doing so to understand the influence of Satanists
on everyone's lives. It says that this influence is 'now so pervasive as not to be readily
noticed', and that Satanists are laced throughout society. It goes on:

> Amongst the highest echelons, some are politicians, medical doctors, high ranking
> police officers, lawyers, advertising gurus, decorated military men, media personalities,
> fashion models and social workers. Amongst the lowest (usually temporary) ranks are
> prostitutes, minor drug dealers and a number of High School students. Some operate
> from the mists.

> Their victims are drip-fed straight amnesia by an assortment of mind control measures
> and psychological torture tactics that would leave any normal person numb with the
> dawning apprehension that things are not as they seem – and they have not been for a
> long, long time. The most talented amongst them have lifestyles maintained on crime,
> but lacquered with a thin veneer of respectable professionalism and knowledge.

The document talks about the Church of Satan in the United States that became famous
in the 1960s after being founded by Anton LaVey (Rothschild Zionist). It says that if
people want more information about some of this satanic organisation's past and most
influential members they 'could do worse than study the late J P Morgan ... the
Kennedy's (including Jackie), Irving Berlin, Groucho Marx, Elvis Presley, [Christian

evangelist] Garner Ted Armstrong, Sammy Davis Jr, Ronald Reagan, Edward Heath, Thomas Plantard de Saint-Claire or a search amongst the bushes.' What he really means is a search among the Bushes with a capital 'B'. I have been naming the former British Prime Minister, Edward Heath, as a child-killing Satanist since 1998, while Thomas Plantard de Saint-Claire claimed to be head of a secret society called the Priory of Sion, made famous by books like *The Holy Blood and the Holy Grail*.

The document includes descriptions of human sacrifice and how the Satanists have secured an unlimited supply of children for their sexual perversions and sacrifice rituals. It also mentions a man known by the code-name of 'Pindar', a Reptilian hybrid who I have exposed in previous books as a player of global significance in the whole conspiracy. I came across a video from 1989 in which a Jewish woman told her story of Satanism on the *Oprah Winfrey Show*. What she said included all the major themes that I have heard over and over from people who have experienced Satanism from the inside. You can find many such stories in *The Biggest Secret*. The woman was referred to as 'Rachael' on the show, but it was later revealed that her real name is Vicki Polin. She is a native of Chicago where Satanism is absolutely rife amongst the 'ruling classes'. Chicago is the political and satanic sewage works that produced President Fake, Barack Obama, and his White House 'handlers', Rahm Emanuel and David Axelrod. Vicki Polin said that her family has been involved in sacrificial rituals for generations. 'My family has an extensive family tree, and they keep track of who's been involved and who hasn't been involved, and it's gone back to like 1700,' she said. Vicki also described the process of what Satanists call 'breeders', which I came across many years ago. These are women who are used to give birth to foetuses and babies that are used in the rituals. The births are not reported to the authorities because it all happens in secret and so, to the system, they never existed. Women are chosen carefully by their genetics to give birth to Reptilian-hybrids. This was the theme of the famous 1968 film, *Rosemary's Baby*. Mia Farrow played the wife of an actor who was promised fame and fortune if he allowed her to be impregnated in a satanic ritual. He agreed and she was mind-controlled to stop her remembering what happened. The Rothschilds and the Illuminati use mind control on a vast scale and this includes the programming of key politicians, most of whom have been groomed for decades before they come to office. Towards the end of *Rosemary's Baby*, we see a flash of the baby and it is reptilian. The film was directed by Roman Polanski, who well knew that the story he was portraying was based on fact. Polanski became a fugitive from the United States for having sex with a 13-year-old girl. He was the husband of actress Sharon Tate, who was murdered while eight months pregnant in 1969 by members of the 'Manson Family', the cult of mind-controlled Satanist, Charles Manson. Vicki Polin told Oprah Winfrey:

> There were people who bred babies in our family. No-one would know about it. A lot of people were overweight, so you couldn't tell if they were pregnant or not, or they would supposedly go away for a while and then come back ... There would be rituals in which babies would be sacrificed ... When I was very young, I was forced to participate in that – in which I had to sacrifice an infant ...

This will sound fantastic to most people, but I have met hundreds of victims of satanic cults within governments and elsewhere who tell the same story. Reptilian and other demonic entities operating just beyond visible light, feed off the energy of the terrified victims and the surge of energy released at the point of death. This is the origin and meaning of the age-old term 'sacrifice to the gods'. The Reptilians especially desire the energy of pre-pubescent children. After puberty, there are chemical and energetic changes that make human energy less 'pure' to these insane entities. The ancients talked about sacrificing 'young virgins to the gods'. By 'young virgins', they mean *children*. I have talked to many former Satanists who have seen human sacrifice and explained what happens. There are rituals in which fathers impregnate their daughters and the child is later 'sacrificed to Satan'. Another ritual demands that parents must sacrifice their firstborn. This doesn't always have to be on an altar. It can be in an engineered road-accident at an ancient ritual location to the Illuminati that appears to the public to be just an 'ordinary' road or street. Sacrificing their own children is also the cult's way of demanding total obedience. The satanic ritual network extends into social services, children's homes, runaway hostels and toddlers' nurseries to ensure a constant supply of children. The Illuminati goal is for the State to take complete control of children from their parents and we are seeing this happening ever more clearly, as I will detail later. Amazing numbers of children, many millions, go missing every year throughout the world never to be seen again. People don't realise this. They judge the scale of child disappearances by the number of such stories that they see on the television news. These represent only a tiny, tiny fraction of children that go missing. All this can happen because Satanism has its people in influential positions across the system, and when they get into positions of power they appoint others like them. Vicki Polin confirmed on the *Oprah Winfrey Show* that Satanists are 'pillars of society' that no-one would suspect. Her mother was an example, she said:

> She lives in the Chicago metropolitan area. She's on the human relations commission of the town that she lives in, and she's an upstanding citizen. Nobody would suspect her. Nobody would suspect anybody involved in it. There's police officers involved in it. There's, you know, doctors, lawyers, Indian chiefs involved in it ... I mean, to the outside world, everything we did was proper and right, and then there were the nights that things changed, that things just got turned around. What was wrong was right, and what was right was wrong.

Rothschild Rituals

I have spoken at length to therapists all over the world who have treated victims of satanic abuse and they all tell the same story, including a wonderful lady in Britain, the late and great Vera Diamond. She had her flourishing London practice destroyed when she went public with her exposure of Satanism and the famous people involved. An unofficial offspring of the Rothschild family (there are legions) told me of the fundamental importance of Satanism to the bloodline families and their 'sacrifices to the gods'. His Rothschild name is Phillip Eugene de Rothschild, but he now lives under another name in the United States after rejecting his family's horrific agenda for the world. He says he is the unofficial son of Baron Philippe de Rothschild of the Mouton-Rothschild wine estates in France, who died in 1988 at the age of 86. Phillip Eugene said he was one of hundreds of thousands of unofficial Rothschild offspring. All except a few are produced through sperm-bank breeding programmes to ensure the genetic 'purity'.

There is an important reason for this, from the bloodline perspective, which I will explain when we get into the nature of reality. These Rothschild children are brought up in other families, as I said earlier, and don't officially use the Rothschild name. They can then come to power in the institutions of society, including as presidents and prime ministers, without anyone realising the Rothschild connection. Phillip Eugene told me: 'My father was a decadent dilettante as well as a master Satanist and hater of God, but how he loved the fields and the wines. He used to say it brought out "the primitive in him".' Phillip Eugene said he was conceived by the 'occult incest' also employed by the Rothschilds and the bloodline families to protect their genetic code. He lived most of his childhood and adolescence with his father on their estate in France and they had a physical relationship to make sure he was, as Phillip Eugene put it, 'held fast in the emotional power of incest, which, in this culture, was normal and to be admired'. I have heard from many sources that incest is rife among the Reptilian bloodline families. He confirmed what I already knew by then about the way the bloodlines are possessed by demonic entities in rituals performed for that purpose. 'Possession' is an age-old theme and it is real. The 'human' hierarchy within the Illuminati and the bloodline families is a mirror of the demonic (Reptilian) hierarchy. The more powerful the Reptilians/demons that you allow to possess you and take over your mind and body, the higher you are in the hierarchy of the global power. The major Rothschilds are massively possessed and that is why they are conductors of the orchestra. As Phillip Eugene said: 'Being a Rothschild descendant, I was maximally demonised.' He said he observed his father's 'lust for power' and began to desire the same. He was placed within the Christian Church to work for the Rothschild agenda while appearing to be a perfect 'Christian', but he later rejected his role and the Satanism that went with it. He said:

I was present at my father's death in 1988, receiving his power and the commission to carry out my destiny in the grand conspiracy of my family. Like their other children, I played a key role in my family's revolt from God. When I watch CNN, it startles me to see so many familiar faces now on the world stage in politics, art, finance, fashion and business. I grew up with these people, meeting them at ritual worship sites and in the centres of power. Financiers, artists, royalty, and even Presidents …

… I can recall the Rockefellers and the Bushes attending rituals, but never having the supremacy to lead them. I still regard them as lackeys and not real brokers of occult power. Except for Alan Greenspan [long-time head of the US Federal Reserve], most of these fellows were camp followers in the occult, primarily for the economic power and prestige. Greenspan, I recall, was a person of tremendous spiritual, occult power and could make the Bushes and the younger Rockefellers cower with just a glance. Ex-CIA Director Casey (as were most of the CIA leadership for the past forty years), Kissinger, and [former US Secretary of State] Warren Christopher were in attendance at non-ritual gatherings and some occult rituals as well, but well back in the gallery.

Phillip Eugene de Rothschild also named Bill Clinton and Al Gore as others that he knew to be 'active and effective Satanists'. It certainly puts the economic crisis orchestrated by Alan Greenspan, and Al Gore's 'global warming', in their true light. Greenspan is higher in the hierarchy than US presidents and when Reagan, Father Bush,

Bill Clinton and Boy Bush appointed him to head the Federal Reserve he was really appointing himself. The right of the president to theoretically select the chairman of the Fed is just to give the impression that the Fed is owned by government, when it is not. Vicki Polin's therapist, Tina Grossman, also appeared with her on the *Oprah Winfrey Show*. What she said I have heard again and again around the world. The 'multiple personality disorder' she talks about is a form of mind control that results from severe trauma, like a satanic and sexual abuse:

> I've treated over 40 survivors of ritual abuse. Adult patients with multiple personality disorder, and from many states in this country as well as Canada. What we've seen and heard and gone through in the abreactions which is the remembered experiences … we are hearing the identical same things from these adults. These are not children that are three years old, and you can, as an adult, perhaps rationalise that this is fantasy material.

> These adults are saying things. They have never met each other before. They are describing identical rituals, just the same as, since I'm Jewish, you could go to New York or California and describe a [Passover] Seder in one state or another and, as a Jew, you would recognize it. This is the belief system in evil and the power that evil gives you, and so it has these certain rituals, so they are very similar with all of the survivors.

These 'certain rituals', including the widespread sacrifice of children, are being performed by the people running your world. To them, a world war, a 9/11 or mass starvation is just a mass death ritual. Another reason for the rituals is to create an energetic 'doorway' or 'gateway' between vibrational realities that allows the Fourth Density Reptilians to manifest in our world of 'visible light'. The structure of the ritual, especially the use of sound, can create a vibrational 'stepping stone' through which the Reptilians can enter this reality. I have spoken with a number of people over the years who have described how the Reptilians and other demonic entities manifested before them during rituals and how participants also 'shifted' from human to reptilian form in the same energetic environment. Satanism at its 'highest' levels is also designed through the rituals and the manipulation of energy to imprint its low-vibrational mind-patterns into the waveform fabric of our reality. As the 'death bed confession' document says in Appendix II: 'What most people do not realise is that Satanism is a ritually based practice and that this repetition has – over time – left strong impressions upon the Morphic Field!' This is the 'sea' of energy in which we all live and if you want to manipulate every fish at the same time, what do you do? You manipulate the sea. Once you start to understand the language of occult and Satanic symbolism you realise how widely it is used in corporate logos and the entertainment industry. The videos and clothing range of the money-obsessed rapper, Jay-Z, and other artists, is full of Illuminati and occult symbolism. There are some excellent articles about this at **vigilantcitizen.com**.

Lilith worship

One of the major Satanic Reptilian deities is known as 'Lilith' (Fig 127), another version of Semiramis. Some versions of the Garden of Eden story say Lilith was 'Adam's first wife' and the real mother of Cain, and that Lilith was symbolised by the snake that tempted Eve. She is depicted as half-human, half-serpent. Lilith was associated with the sons of Anu, or Anunnaki, and Samael, another demon 'angel'. Samael is said in Jewish lore to be the serpent that impregnated Eve to give birth to Cain. He is described as not having the face of other humans and Cain was said to be like the 'heavenly beings', not the 'earthly beings', and a 'child of the Lord'. Another form of Lilith, the Babylonian goddess, Semiramis, was known in Rome as 'Columba', or 'the dove', but the Latin word 'coluber' also means a snake or serpent. To the Babylonians, Lilith was the mother of the first vampires and she is widely associated in many cultures with stealing and killing children. Her name translates as 'female night being/demon'. She is said in some traditions to have forced herself upon Adam and bore him many demons and spirits that were called 'the plagues of humankind'. Lilith is an important figure in many secret society rituals and the Satanist, Aleister Crowley, gave the middle name of Lilith to his first child. Lilith is also described as a consort of Lucifer, the 'light bringer', and the god of Freemasonry. This is another version of Lilith-Samael. Lilith and Lucifer are said to be the androgynous figure of 'Baphomet' or the 'Goat of Mendes', a symbol of worship by the Illuminati Knights Templar (Fig 128). Lilith is also known as 'Babalon', 'the Scarlet Woman', 'Great Mother', 'Babylon the Great', 'Mother of Harlots', 'the Whore of Babylon', and 'the Mother of Abominations' described in Crowley's *The Book of the Law*. The lily is named after Lilith and this is a symbol widely employed by the Illuminati bloodlines and their associated networks. The lily is the inspiration for the fleur-de-lis, an ancient symbol of the Reptilian-hybrid bloodline and used by the House of Windsor, the Spanish monarchy, Grand Duke of Luxembourg and by French royal houses. You find it in the emblems and heraldry of the aristocracy all over Europe and on national and regional flags. It is on a gate at the White House and is used by military and scout organisations. Christianity employs the lily, or fleur-de-lis, to symbolise the trinity, but in occult lore it represents the serpent demon, Lilith.

Figure 127: *Lilith is associated with the serpent and the snake. This is a late 19th century depiction by British artist, John Collier*

The owl is also associated with Lilith, as you can see with the original Babylonian depiction in Figure 129 (overleaf). There is an owl in the road plan around the Capitol Building in Washington DC and it is, appropriately, in the belly of the owl – the belly of the Illuminati god/goddess (Fig 130 overleaf). I have written at length in my books about the 'summer camp'

Figure 128: *Baphomet' or the 'Goat of Mendes'*

Figure 129: *An original Babylonian terracotta relief of Lilith/Semiramis/Ishtar alongside the owls with which she is associated*

for the elite known as Bohemian Grove, 2,700 acres of redwood forest in Sonoma County, California, about 75 miles north of San Francisco, where the bloodline families and their sycophants and servants take part in rituals involving a 40-foot stone owl (Figs 131 and 132). This is again symbolic of Lilith and also a deity called Moloch, or Molech, which is associated with the sacrifice of children by fire and was known to the

Hebrews, Egyptians, Canaanites, Phoenicians, and others. Moloch was another name for Nimrod/Baal, and El, and was depicted as a calf or an ox and a man with the head of a bull. *Jeremiah* 32:35 says:

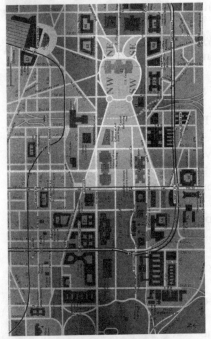

Figure 130: *An owl can clearly be seen in the road system around the Capitol Building in Washington DC and, appropriately, it has the home of American politics in its belly*

And they built the high places of the Ba'al, which are in the valley of Ben-hinnom, to cause their sons and their daughters to pass through the fire l'Molech; which I did not command them, nor did it come into my mind that they should do this abomination, to cause Judah to sin.

Leviticus 18:21 also mentions Moloch:

The laws given to Moses by God expressly forbade the Jews to do what was done in Egypt or in Canaan. 'You shall not give any of your children to devote them by fire to Moloch, and so profane the name of your God'.

The people who watch or perform these rituals to the symbol of child sacrifice are political and business leaders, including presidents like Boy George Bush; Father George Bush; Ronald Reagan; Richard Nixon; Jimmy Carter; Gerald Ford; Dwight D Eisenhower; Lyndon Johnson; Herbert Hoover; and Teddy Roosevelt. Rockefellers, Henry Kissinger and Al Gore also go to Bohemian Grove. I wonder what burning the Grove's ritual fire under the owl does for your carbon footprint.

Figure 131

Figure 132

Lilith/Moloch are worshipped by the 'elite' as a 40-foot stone owl in the rituals at Bohemian Grove

Reptilian Vampires

The stories about vampires are based on fact, and this is another universal theme that connects with the Reptilian manipulation. There isn't a part of the world or an era of history that does not have its myths and legends about vampires who feed off other people's blood and energy. Bram Stoker's Dracula character was based largely on a Reptilian-hybrid called Vlad the Impaler (Fig 133). He was the 15th century ruler of a country called Wallachia, not far from the Black Sea, in what is now Romania. This region includes what was once called Transylvania, the home of the most famous vampire legends. Vlad the Impaler, or Dracula, slaughtered tens of thousands of people and impaled many of them on stakes. He would sit down to eat amid this forest of dead bodies, dipping his bread in their blood. The decaying corpses were often left there

Figure 133: *Vlad the Impaler*

for months. It was once reported that an invading Turkish army turned back in fright when it encountered thousands of rotting corpses impaled on the banks of the Danube. Vlad the Impaler was the son of Vlad Dracul, who was initiated into the ancient Order of the Dragon by the Holy Roman Emperor in 1431. The Order of the Royal Court of the Dragon (also known as The Brotherhood of the Snake) was formed in Egypt in 2170 BC, as I said earlier, to infiltrate the royal and religious centres of power, especially the Mystery schools. Its emblem was a dragon, wings extended, hanging on a cross. Father Vlad wore this emblem and his coinage bore the dragon symbol. All the members of the order had a dragon on their coat of arms and Father Vlad was nicknamed 'Dracul' (the Devil or the Dragon). Son Vlad signed his name Draculea or Draculya, or the 'Devil's Son', and this later became 'Dracula', a name that translates as something like 'Son of Him who had the Order of the Dragon'. This same Dragon Order has been promoted by the British 'Holy Grail' author, Sir Laurence Gardner. Queen Mary, or Mary of Teck, the mother of King George VI and grandmother to the present Elizabeth II, was descended from a sister of 'Dracula', which is hardly surprising given that the House of Windsor is a Reptilian-hybrid bloodline.

Vlad Dracul may have been an extreme example, but blood drinking and human sacrifice is part of life for the Reptilian-hybrid bloodlines. They have always done it and they are still doing it. When you realise that, it makes sense of the horrors they perpetrate without a care for the consequences. They have contempt for humanity and nothing is off limits no matter how grotesque. In fact, to them, the more grotesque the better.

12

Encoded Truth

Wisdom is not in words; Wisdom is meaning within words
Kahlil Gibran

The synchronicity of my life (and the way the puzzle pieces are handed to me with such precision) has shown itself again and again while I have been writing this book. A prime example was when artist Neil Hague emailed me with a copy of a then unpublished work by a friend of his, Pierre Sabak (his pen name), a 'comparative linguist and symbologist'.

I read Pierre's book, and wrote this chapter, while on a speaking tour of Europe and the United States, and how fascinating and confirming the information turned out to be. *The Murder of Reality* is a detailed study of word derivations, associations and true meanings that shows how the serpent race, and its subjugation of humanity, is encoded into ancient languages and accounts. These words and meanings have since been passed through into what we call 'modern languages'. Sabak spent nearly seven years poring through dictionaries and documents to reveal the interconnecting words and meanings that encode all the major aspects of the conspiracy I am revealing here. These include:

- The serpent race, or 'gods', controlling humanity and being responsible for the geological catastrophe symbolised as the 'Great Flood'.

- The fundamental connection with royalty and a hybrid bloodline passing through history – the bloodline of 'Eve' and the serpent race that rules the world. The word 'Eve' is synonymous with 'life' and 'snake'.

- The association of the serpent race with 'light' and 'illumination' as in 'the shining ones' (in Latin, 'Illuminati' means 'enlightened'). I have explained how ancient accounts describe the serpent 'gods' or 'fallen angels' shining 'like the sun'.

- The symbols of the Sun and the Moon, and the religions they spawned, originate, at least in part, from the 'luminous' nature of these entities.

- The serpent race was known as 'the Watchers', hence the all-seeing-eye symbol of the Illuminati which can be found in many guises, including on the dollar bill, on Credo Mutwa's Necklace of the Mysteries, the Egyptian Eye of Ra, and so on.

- The theme of the 'Bringer of Light' is a name given to 'Lucifer' and the planet Venus. The serpent 'gods' are also symbolised as stars, or 'star people', and are associated with the symbol of the goat head and ram head.

- The symbolism of the serpent race as types of bird, including the owl, phoenix, eagle, hawk, falcon and dove. A famous example of this is Quetzalcoatl, the 'feathered serpent' or 'plumed serpent' god of Central America, known to the Mayan people as Kukulkan.

- The association between the serpent race and fire, as in the fire-breathing dragon, and the Greek Salamandra (salamander).

- The themes of blood-drinking and human sacrifice to 'the gods', and the drinking of menstrual blood, often symbolised as a fish, or the 'menstrual fish'.

- The theme of shapeshifting between human and reptilian form.

- The description of the serpent race as rapists, liars and deceivers who hide their existence behind symbolism that only the chosen ones are meant to decode.

- The pentagram, the symbol of Satanism, and the theme of 'Satan' as the 'dragon'. The reptilian race was known by some as the 'Shatani', or 'Satani', translated into Greek as 'Teitan', known collectively as the 'Titans', the giant race and a type of 'fallen angel'.

- The constant theme of the serpent race giving advanced knowledge to their chosen representatives (the hybrid bloodlines), and the subsequent description of the serpent race as the 'talkers' (remember the reference to the 'talker' in the Hopi legend).

The 'talker' comes partly because the word 'angel' literally means 'messenger' and the serpent people communicated information to their human representatives. Look at the common theme of religious heroes being visited by 'angels'. Mother Mary in the Bible, and Mohammed in the Koran are both said to have been visited by the same 'angel' called 'Gabriel'. Mohammed, himself, is known as the 'messenger'.

There is a deeper reason, however, for the theme of the 'talkers': the Reptilians introduced human language as we know it. At least most communication before was through telepathy and you have the recurring story around the world of 'God' (the gods) giving humans different languages to divide them. The tale of the Tower of Babel in the Bible is the most famous, but the same basic story can be found throughout the world. This is symbolic of the serpent race introducing language. Words are vibrational fields, and the Reptilians have programmed human perception to a large part by the introduction and manipulation of speech – the vibrational communication that we call language. Appropriately, the term 'Latin' comes from 'Latens', meaning 'hidden' or 'secret', and from the Arab word 'lut', meaning 'veil'. Language is indeed a secret veil through which humans are programmed. Pierre Sabak writes:

… The essence of language loans itself to symbolism represented sublimely through the study of philology [language] and homonyms [words that look and sound the same, but have different meanings]. A hidden mentor of man, the angel in occult lore, is a reptilian entity distinguished as the hidden master or king.

Principally, the dragon, a teacher of words and arithmetic, embedded knowledge of itself sequenced in numerical codes – a secret history veiled in mathematics, geometry, astronomy, semiology [the study of signs] and language. Systematic and intelligent, the adoption of signs is discursive of secret knowledge pertaining to the snake and its concealment.

Untrusting towards humans, this creature hides behind occult ritual. Frightened of being uncovered, it uses war, economic and political coercion to force nations to do its bidding. Ancient accounts suggest the snake is duplicitous in its designs and dealings with man.

You have to uncover the codes to see how widespread the evidence of the serpent race and its manipulation of human life actually is. The Reptilians desperately seek to remain hidden and so you have to work to unpick the locks, codes, symbols, words and mathematics that provide the 'cover'. It is a deep cover, too, and hidden in words that appear at first sight to have nothing to do with any serpent race.

Hello, Sailor

Pierre Sabak shows how the serpent gods were described in nautical terms. Their flying craft were described as 'heavenly boats', for example, and you find similar maritime themes in the legends of Egyptian deities like Osiris and Ra. The Theban priesthood in Egypt referred to the sky as the 'upper ocean' and spoke of solar vessels that carried the gods. Words used to describe the Reptilians often have the meaning of 'sailor' or 'crewmember' and they are also called the 'angelic host'. Sabak says that accounts record the 'host' as 'the sailor', 'nomad' or 'alien', and they appeared as 'serpents' or 'amphibians' who were called 'the destroyers', 'rapists' and 'pillagers'. I will outline later how the system of global law today is based on maritime terms and associations. This is why we have so many words that end in 'ship' – kingship, lordship, citizenship, relationship, membership, worship, and so on. The word 'sapiens', the name given to modern humans, is a highly significant code that relates to this theme. Sabak says that this comes from the Latin noun 'serpens' (serpent or dragon) which also relates to the Hebrew word 'sapan' (seaman). He charts the word 'Bible' back to 'byblos' (boat), and he says the word 'religion' derives from the Latin verb 'religare' (to moor a boat). The same associations between a boat, serpents and scriptures can be found in Arabic and in Hebrew. The Koran says of 'God': 'Among his signs are the ships, sailing like floating mountains.' We still today talk of space*ships*. Sabak's research also relates the name 'Baal' (Lord) to the Arabic root 'bah'har' (sailor) from 'bahr' (sea) and suggests that the religious themes of baptism and ritual bathing comes from this association between the serpent 'gods' and symbolic sailing. He writes:

Personifying conflict, the [Hebrew] 'tsabaoath' [the crew, the serpent race] are traced historically from the lineage of the deity Osiris, depicted as a sailor.

Veneration of Osiris' boat demarcates a star-ship or space-ship (duplicated liturgically through wor-ship). Diagrammatically, the church is laid out as a boat classified with the king and governance. In Old English, the noun 'weorthscipe' is transliterated in the modern idiom as 'worship', transcribed from the compound 'worth-ship'. 'Scipe' (a ship) is a diminutive of the Greek noun 'skaphos' (a boat), cogent with skipper and ship.

I have often seen depictions of sailing ships on the outside of Freemasonic temples, and this is the same symbolism. Pierre Sabak makes some interesting connections between key words that relate to the secret societies, which act as a priesthood for the Reptilians on Earth. He says that the union between the snake and its priesthood is 'archived universally' and is clearly demonstrated in the Roman and Semitic languages. The Latin word for 'Brotherhood' is named as 'the fraternity' derived from the Arabic classification 'ifrit/afreet' (malevolent demon). He further argues 'ifrit' comes from the Arabic word 'fritar' (deceiver), and 'frt' (deception), and connects with the Latin 'fratar' (brother) – the guardian of the serpent knowledge. This theme of deceiver/deception describes both the covert control of the serpent race, which is constantly described in such terms, and the secret society network that does its bidding. 'Fritar' appears in Modern Greek as 'feedhee' – pronounced 'feethee' – meaning 'snake'. The word 'Mason' also obviously relates to a 'builder', a term used as code for the serpent race. Pierre Sabak writes:

> The Builder or Mason, represented conventionally as a red snake, correlates with the Magical Crafts referred to in double-speak as 'The Arts'. In Babylonian and Ubaid iconography, the serpent rouge conforms to the goat-fish progenitor of the se'irim and the 'aliens' (the zari). These categories are variations of the 'menstrual fish' or the 'hairy snake' (human-angelic).

> Sacerdotal [priestly] traditions combine the motif of the builder (angel) with the fish and snake, recapitulated in the Arabic wordplays. So for example, 'ti'ban' (an eel) is related to 'ta'ban' (a snake). The reptile also is indicative of the 'builder' from the verbal stem 'bana' (to build). Judaic tradition connects 'banay' (a builder) to the 'moon' listed in the Hebrew lexicon as (le'vana).

Connecting the reptile 'builder' to the Moon fits perfectly, as we shall see later. Freemasons worship and revere the 'Grand Architect' (more 'builder' coding), and that, too, is extremely relevant to the real nature of the Moon. The secret society network, at the highest levels, knows full well what all the symbolism means and all the major secret societies, and most of the smaller ones, form one unified web, although only the inner circle Masons know this.

Who are the 'Angels'? One guess …

The description of the serpent race as 'fallen angels' appears widely in ancient accounts, not only in the biblical texts. For example, the Roman word 'angelos' (angel) comes from the Latin 'anguis' (meaning 'snake'), and this is also the origin of the word 'angry', Sabak says (Fig 134). The 'gods' and goddesses were invariably depicted with wings or the ability to fly (Figs 135 and 136). Angels are depicted as winged humans, often smiling, but this is a cover for their true appearance and, not by co-incidence, Babylonian tradition portrays the angels as smiling (grimacing) at children in the act of sacrifice. The Hebrew word for grimace ('ha'avaya') is connected to the Arabic word 'af'a'(viper). The European tradition of the smiling deity known as the 'Grim Reaper' is another symbol of the serpent race. As Sabak points out, you only need to add an 'S', a snake letter, to turn 'laughter' into 'slaughter', and 'S' in Old English was used as a prefix to signify 'God', the serpent gods. The fallen angels are divided, as always with the Reptilians, into a strict hierarchy. 'Arch' comes from the Greek 'arkh', a word meaning 'chief', and thus we have the archangel or 'messenger of the Lord' – messenger of the Reptilian 'Mr Big'. Arch is also related to the Syrian root word 'haka' (to speak, talk or tell), and that is why the slang word for a journalist is a 'hack'. Pierre Sabak says of the meaning of 'arch':

Figure 134: *Angels, and especially fallen angels, are code for the Reptilians*

… the Egyptian stem 'arq' (to wiggle or bind around) and 'akh' (to shine) corresponding with the Babylonian titular 'acan' (a flaming seraph) [Seraph means 'snake'].

Esoterically 'akh' is employed in the Arabic as the noun 'akh' (a brother) descriptive of the 'enlightened' or the 'illuminate', lateral to 'acan' (a shining serpent). The verbal

Figure 135

Figure 136

The Babylonian moon goddess, Semiramis/Ishtar/Lilith and the sun god, Nimrod, both depicted with wings – just like the 'angels'

stem 'akh' in Modern Arabic is addendum to the idiom 'haqq' (truth) – a term constant with a 'luminary', the 'hakim' indexed as 'a ruler'. 'Akh' is further utilised in Hebrew as the suffix 'mal'akh' 'an angel' denoting 'a shining king'.'

The name of the biblical gods, the 'Elohim', comes from 'eloh', meaning 'light'. 'Arch' is further connected to the Latin word 'archus', which means an 'arch' or 'curve', and the circle is a symbol of the reptile or dragon. Pierre Sabak points out that the Hebrew word 'igul' (circle) parallels the Arabic noun 'gul' (demon), and that the Persian adverb 'Pairi' (around) relates to the Persian 'race of serpents' called the 'Peri'. The circle theme can be seen in the symbol of the flying serpent disc. Given that the serpent race is symbolised by both the circle and the star, it gives even greater meaning to the twelve-star circle on the flag of the European Union, and the same with the stars on the flag of the United States. Sabak describes how ancient scriptures label the 'angels' as 'rapists and pillagers' (as with the biblical Nefilim), and liken them to an invading army (the 'host', a word associated with 'holy'). Ancient gods like Yahweh and Baal were given the title 'Lord of the Host' – a name equated with 'snake'. Sabak importantly draws comparison in the ancient Syrian language between the snake and the name of the 'god' known as 'Yahweh'. He says that word-meanings depict Yahweh as a serpent and are identical to the theme of 'Shaddai', another title for Yahweh, whose name is a derivation of 'shed' (devil or goblin) and is shown in the Ubaid figurines as a snake or snake entity. This, Sabak points out, is also true of the Islamic tradition where the Reptilians are multi-dimensional and are known as the 'Jinn' or 'djinn', which comes from the old Semitic noun 'djen', meaning 'serpent'. Its hieroglyphic version is a cobra, translated as 'd' or 'dj'. I outlined the same theme earlier in the book, and we are now seeing more and more evidence for what I have been asserting for years – that religions are all based on worship of the serpent 'gods'. Sabak says that in Egypto-Akkadian, 'Dj-En' means 'Snake Lord' and 'Dj-An' means 'Heavenly Snake'. Very significantly, we also get the word 'genes' from the Semitic 'djen' and there is an obvious connection between the Arabic serpents, the 'Jinn', and the Syrian 'jins' (sex; or gender) and 'jinsi' (sexual). A major Israeli lobby group in the United States is called 'JINSA', the Jewish Institute for National Security Affairs, a 'think-tank that puts Israel and its security at the heart of US foreign policy'. Among the members of JINSA during the Boy Bush years were leading lights in the neoconservative cabal, including Dick Cheney, Paul Wolfowitz, John Bolton, Dov Zakheim and Richard Perle. These were heavily involved in manipulating the invasions of Afghanistan and Iraq. A chapter of the Koran is called a 'sura', a word Sabak says is connected to the theme of a fallen angel transposed into the Greek language as 'saura' (lizard). In sura 55, verses 31-33, headed 'The Lord of Mercy', the 'thaqal' (a mighty or heavy army), is quoted thus:

We shall attend to you two huge armies ... Jinn and mankind, if you can pass beyond the regions of heaven and earth, then do so: you will not pass without Our authority.

The whole feel of these ancient accounts and the coded wordplays is of the serpent race enslaving humanity after some kind of war, and of the earth being a prison state administered covertly from the shadows via representatives in human form. Sabak's research into language confirms the connection between the serpent race, fallen angels and 'royal' bloodlines, what I call the hybrids. He writes that 'the bloodline of the sovereign emphasises human angelic descent replicated through the snake, a race of fallen angels'. This 'renegade group' is called the 'serpentigena' in Latin, which translates directly as 'the serpent race', or 'sprung from a serpent'. Pierre Sabak says that this is commemorated in Judaic tradition with the fallen tribe known as the 'serpentigena' and 'stylised as the star or dragon'. The reptilian-royal connection is everywhere. The Ancient Greek 'basilikos' (royal) becomes 'basileus' (king) from 'basiliskos' (serpent), and you find the same word associations between 'royal' and 'serpent' all over the world. Sabak writes:

> The Akkadian and Sanskrit designation 'peor' (a serpent) and 'pala' (a king) is comparable to the Persian noun 'mar' (a snake) and 'mal' (a leader) – this is rendered in Greek as 'basileus' (a king) from 'basiliskos' (a serpent). Basiliskos is a derivation of the Greek title 'baskanos' (a sorcerer). In addition, the Greeks referred to the Royal line as the 'hemitheos' (a demi-God), literally 'half divine' (human angel), and is a play on 'helminthos' (a worm). In the Greek mystery plays, the 'hemitheos' is referred to by the title 'dioskouros' (the Son of God), coded speak for 'diosauros' (a Reptile God).

Symbols used for the serpent gods are also employed by their 'royal' hybrids, including the representation of the monarch in Indo-European languages with the circle and eye symbols of the reptile or 'dragon' (a Watcher). This is why so many ancient heroes, kings and rulers have a birth story associated with the reptile or amphibian. Alexander the Great led his army in the conquest of Egypt, Mesopotamia, Troy, and into India, before he died in Babylon in 323 BC at the age of 33. Alexander was called the 'Serpent's Son' and when he founded the city of Alexandria, in Egypt, it became known as the 'City of the Serpent's Son'. Once again we see the recurring theme. The legend goes that Alexander's real father was the serpent god, 'Ammon' (Hidden), and this mirrors the story of Merovee, founder of the Merovingian dynasty, of whom a similar origin is given.

The Serpent Priesthood

I have written for many years about the Reptilian hybrid bloodline and the hidden knowledge held at the highest levels of the global secret society network, the elite priesthood of the serpent race. The ancient Middle East and Mesopotamia, especially Sumer, Babylon and Egypt, are locations where this priesthood can be identified, although it goes back much further (as we perceive 'time'). The Grand Masters and highest initiates of the interconnecting secret society and satanic networks are the modern version of the ancient serpent priesthood in the temples and Mystery schools. Pierre Sabak's research of words and languages supports this theme. He follows the passage through the centuries of the Sabian priesthood – the 'people of Noah' who established themselves in Mesopotamia. He says that 'Sabian' (only one letter away from 'Fabian') translates as 'the people of the star', from the word 'Saba'ia' (the star people). The Sabi priests were equated with the host and the serpent, he says. The Star of Israel (the symbol of the Rothschilds) is associated with the 'children of light' (the 'Sabi') and the star and sceptre are the symbols of their bloodline. Sabak continues:

Within the Semitic tradition, the serpent is depicted as a conquering army, the 'tsabaoth', rendered from the Modern Hebrew nouns 'saba', 's'baot' or 'sabaoth'. Philologically, 'tsabaoth' is a derivation from 'tsevet' (a crew) and technically specifies 'a crew of a ship or vessel'. Judaic lore casts the 'tsabaoth' as 'an army of a boat or a naval itinerant' explicit of 'saba' (a star or host).

The language research especially highlights Babylon and the priesthood of the city known as 'Thebes' in Egypt – the 'City of Amun'. The deity 'Amun' is also known as 'Amon', 'Amoun', 'Amen' and 'Amun-Ra' (or 'Atum-Ra'), and was a version of the Babylonian Tammuz/Nimrod. Christians and Jews say the name of this serpent deity at the end of every prayer with the word 'Amen'. Pierre Sabak's word associations, meanings and derivatives rightly connect the gods known as 'Osiris', 'Oannes', 'Baal' and 'Yahweh' as one entity, and you can add a lot more to that from around the world. He says that the similarity between the Akkadian, Arabic and Egyptian vocabulary 'suggest the deification of the serpent (angel) parallels the sun God, Atum'. The king who created the Babylonian Empire was called Hammurabi, which translates as the 'rabbi', or 'priest of Amun' – literally, the 'Hidden Western Priesthood', Sabak says. He points out that Babylon and the priesthood of Thebes were fundamentally connected with Hammurabi's Kingdom extending to the province of Thebes, the capital of Egypt three times between 2060 BC and 1085 BC. Sabak says that 'Theban' comes from the Arabic word 'ta'ban' (snake) and the Egyptian Arabic 'teaban' (cobra). 'Anguigena', the Latin term for a Theban, means 'offspring of the snake'. The relationship between the theme of the serpent race and their hybrid human 'initiates' can be seen in the words 'talib', 'taliba' and 'taliban', which all mean 'student'. Bacchus, the Greek version of 'Jesus', was the 'sovereign of Thebes', according to classical writers like the Roman, Pliny, and was known as the 'Son of Zeus' or 'dioskouros' in Greek which, Sabak says, is a cryptic play on 'diosauros' (a reptile god). Sabak uses linguistics to follow the Theban priesthood (along with the priesthood of Babylon) to Rome and on to 'London' (the new Rome and new Babylon). He says:

In the ancient order, Thebes' government annotated the Cobra crown, a device ratified covertly with Syria ... and the 'Western Priesthood' nominal of Amun. Secretly, this denomination is known throughout history variously as the 'Aamu', the 'Emori', 'Erech', 'Uruq', 'Amorite', 'Canaanite', 'Umma', 'Hyksos', 'Martu', 'Medoi' or 'Mada'. Its institutions seeded the Babylonian, Egyptian, Athenian and Roman Dynasties avowed as the 'Western Empire', the cornerstone and mantle of 'Europe'!

We can now also see the symbolism of the golden penis of Osiris and similar myths around the world, including the original golden penis on Credo Mutwa's Zulu 'Necklace of the Mysteries'. They say that Osiris, or whatever name is used in different cultures, was killed by the 'dark one', Set(h) in Egyptian myth, and his body cut into many pieces. A virgin mother figure, like the Egyptian Isis, finds all the pieces except for the penis and she replaces it with a golden one. This is symbolic of when the Reptilians infiltrated human genetics. Look how Osiris and Atun are depicted with a penis headdress in Figure 137. What pair of a dickheads.

The Sodalist (secret) priesthood has spanned thousands of years of gathering Reptilian enslavement. It has been known under many names – Zenda (Persian), Sauda (Syrian), Soter or 'saviour' (Greek), Sodi (Hebrew) and Sodalist (Latin). 'Sauda' is the true origin of the name 'House of Saud' and Saudi Arabia. This is why the Saudi 'Islamic' royal tyranny always does the bidding of the Rothschilds and their cabal. 'Sauda' means 'black' and this is where the term 'Black Nobility' comes from to describe European royal, aristocratic and banking families that emerged from Italy and included oligarchs like the satanic Medici family. Sodalist is also

Figure 137: *The penis headgear of the Egyptian gods*

remarkably close to 'socialist', the political system so widely used to centralise power throughout the world, and one of its most effective promoters is the Fabian Society. The Sodalists are also from the line of Zadok and were known as the 'Zadoks' or 'Zadiks' who, according to some ancient traditions, were the bloodline of the Watchers, the serpent race. The coronation of the British monarch uses Handel's anthem, *Zadok the Priest* – named after the Hebrew High Priest who is said to have anointed 'King Solomon'. Zadok, also seen in the priest-king 'Melchi-zadek', relates to the Arabic term 'Zokhel', meaning 'reptile'. As I said, the oil still used in the British coronation ritual is symbolic of the 'Messeh' fat of the Nile crocodile, that featured in the coronation ceremonies for the pharaohs in ancient Egypt. The Egyptian ceremonial title of 'Moche' means 'He who is anointed with crocodile fat from the Nile River'. From 'Messeh' we get 'Messiah', the Jewish legend of the coming 'Saviour'; the one anointed with the fat of the crocodile; the new pharaoh; and the earthly representative of the serpent race. Pierre Sabak says this of the Zadok connection:

> The appellation 'Zadok' is matched with the Sanskrit title 'sadhu' (a holy man). In the Islamic tradition, Zadok, otherwise Zadik, is rendered as 'Sadat' (the Masters or Descendents of the Holy Prophet). Esoterically, the assignment Zadik refers to the hidden bloodline of the Judaic Kings. Evidence for this statement is found encoded in the ancient Semitic.

> 'Zadik' or 'Zadok' is an anagram on 'Sod-Hyk' (a Secret King), equivalent to 'Sed-Hyk' (a Hunting King). 'Hyk', the Canaanite word for 'a Sovereign', is a diminutive of Hyksos [the so-called 'Shepherd or Foreign Kings' who ruled Egypt at one time and have been connected to the serpent bloodline in my previous books]. Propagation of the 'Zadik' or 'Sed-Hyk' is through the ancestry of the Sadducee deduced from the Sodalist priesthood of Moses. The Sadducee or Sodalist forms the backdrop to the 'Saudi / Sauda' ('Black' Nobility) transmitted through a 'secret' (sod) bloodline.

Sabak also shows how the Zadoks/Zaddiks/Sadducees had identical beliefs about the world to the Arabic Zandiks – 'Zenda' was another name for the Zadoks or Sodalists.

Different names, same team. He says that early New Testament manuscripts identified both 'Jesus' and his 'brother, James,' as Zaddiks (Sadducees). This also takes us to the Essenes, the sect in biblical Palestine, and apparent authors of the *Dead Sea Scrolls*. They called themselves the 'Sons of Zadok', literally, 'the Sons of Righteousness'.

Caput-al

One of the major symbols of the Illuminati network is the skull, or the skull and bones, most famously used by the Skull and Bones Society at Yale University that produces so many prominent people in the United States, including presidents like the two Bushes. The skull, or skull and bones, is a symbol of the serpent 'gods' and their association with ritual sacrifice. We see this employed in religion and politics, both of which are controlled by the 'skull' cabal. Capitol Hill in the United States is named after Capitol Hill in Rome where they erected a temple to the 'god' Jupiter. 'Capitol' comes from the Latin 'caput' (meaning 'head' or 'skull'), and so the word is used to mean 'dead'. Caput also connects with 'capra' (nanny goat), a symbol used in Satanism in the form of a goat head, as we saw with Baphomet. The Temple of Jupiter in Rome was relocated to Capitol Hill in Washington DC, the official home of American politics, and you will recall that this is located in the symbolic belly of the Owl – another covert symbol of the serpent race. The same symbolism can be found in the allegorical story of 'Jesus' and the crucifixion at 'Golgotha' (from the Greek 'Golgotha', Hebrew 'Gulgolet(h)' and Aramaic 'Gulgulta', all meaning 'skull'). Pierre Sabak says that this also relates to the Arabic noun for a 'temple' or 'forehead' (masdar), from the Old Semitic phrase 'mass-dar' (to harm a child), which is what happened, and still happens, in these 'temples'. The 'Masdar' (crown) is conferred upon the sacrificial death of the firstborn dedicated to the 'Council of Jupiter'. Sabak contends that from 'Masdar' comes 'Mossad', the name of the 'Israeli Intelligence Agency', an organisation that is nothing more than the private army of the Rothschilds. Sabak goes on:

> The Jewish Priesthood, the 'Nazai' (consecrated), is equivalent to the 'National Socialist' – the 'Nazi' predecessor to NASA. Divested from the rabbinical emblem of the cranium – Greek 'kranion' (a skull) recognizant with 'kube' – Greek 'koruphe' (a head). In spoken Arabic, 'kube' denudes the Kaaba shrine perquisite to the teachings of the kabala and the Society of 'Jupiter'. The 'death head' in Christianity refers to 'Golgotha' (the skull), location of Jesus' crucifixion symbolic of Capitol Hill, Rome.

> Contemporary examples of the 'Nazai' network include the Yale Skull and Bones fraternity, the German SS 'totenkopf' and their earlier partner, the Knights Templar. These societies all share identical iconography with the Jewish organization 'Mossad' … Mossad disguises its allegiance to 'Diovis' (Jupiter) – Hebrew 'Jehovah' adopting the 'masdar' skull. Emblem of the head signifies the rabbinical tradition annexed with the Caucasian or Western priesthood, the 'Nazai' (consecrated), analogous in the Arabic to 'nasiyah' (a forehead). Inference to such an alliance is disguised in the Semitic lexicology.

This is the symbolism of describing 'Jesus' as a 'Nazarene' (Latin 'Nazaraeus'), a title used to denote a religious vow taken by a Nazai priest. The recorded place-name, 'Nazareth', Jesus's alleged hometown, is symbolism rather than a historical location.

The religious, secret society, and ancient texts and books are written in a deep code that only the few can understand. These codes include the classic 'Jesus' symbols of the fish (serpent race) and the carpenter (Aramaic 'nagar', meaning a 'Mason', which connects in Arabic with 'naga' (the saviour or smiter), 'Nogah' the Judaic term for Venus, and 'naga', the Sanskrit word for 'serpent'. We see this most obviously in the serpent people known as the 'Nagas'. The name 'John', as in John the Baptist, is spelled 'Ioannes' in Greek, except for one character, and this takes us to Oannes, the Babylonian fish god, equated with Nimrod. He is depicted by the mitre in the Christian Church and was said by the ancients to be 'the teacher of mankind'.

Pierre Sabak also makes the language associations between 'stone', 'rock' and 'serpent', as with the Black Stone of the Kaaba at Mecca, and the symbolic 'rock' on which the Christian Church is said to have been founded. We also have the 'Dome of the Rock' on Temple Mount in Jerusalem, built over the stone from where Muslims believe that Muhammad ascended into heaven, and on which Jews believe that Abraham prepared his first-born son, Isaac, for sacrifice to 'God' (the gods). An ancient Semitic tradition claimed that the rock was held in the mouth of the serpent, 'Tahum'. Sabak says this location was said to be a crossing point between the underworld and the upper world. These ancient and religious texts appear to say one thing, but actually say quite another.

More on Molech

The language codes and meanings connect the serpent race to what we call 'Satanism' – blood drinking, human and animal sacrifice. Language research confirms the themes I have been writing about all these years, including how the Reptilians can stay in this reality for longer, even take and hold human form, by drinking human blood that carries the human genetic/vibrational codes. The very word 'sorcery' comes from the Greek 'sauros' (lizard) and 'sorel' (goat), which comes from the Semitic word 'se'irim' (goat). The goat and goat head symbols, used to denote satanic deities, are symbolic of the Reptilians and this relates to deities like the goat-god, Pan, symbolising the 'horned god' Reptilians (Fig 138). Sabak says that 'Pan' derives from the Hebrew noun 'pin' (meaning 'penis'), and that 'se'irim'/'seirim' (goat) is an expression of the 'seraph' (flaming snake), which connects into the biblical 'seraphim' – the 'highest rank of angel'. 'Goat' is 'tragos' in ancient Greek, which comes forward as 'tragedy', a signifier of the sacrificial 'scapegoat'. Understanding the derivation and meaning of words also tells us more about the deity, Moloch/Molech, worshipped at Bohemian Grove in northern California. Sabak says that this word and

Figure 138: *The goat god, 'Pan', is code for the Reptilian race*

other research reveals that Moloch was a goddess deity, although the common belief is that it was (is) a god. He produces some interesting information to support this idea, and certainly the owl is symbolic of the goddess, Lilith, but god or goddess is just detail compared with what was, and still is, done in his/her name – the sacrifice of children in fire. Sabak says:

Adoration of the 'mal'akh' (literally angel) within Judaic tradition proceeds dialectically from the Canaanite winged Goddess of Death – Moloch. Represented as a horned owl, the Goddess parallels the hunter in situ to the worship of nocturnal angels. Veneration of the owl earmarks child sacrifice linked with the human angelic or royal line …

… Moloch otherwise 'mal'akh' is consistent in the Arabic with the noun 'mahlik' (a place of destruction, danger or a danger spot) and 'muhlik', the adjective (fatal or destructive). The terms are interchangeable in Hebrew with 'malik' (a lord) and 'maluk' (a ruler). Phonological relationship between 'muhlik' and 'malik' implies (the sovereign) 'melekh' from the Akkadian titular 'malku' (a sovereign). In Arabic, 'melekh' (a monarch) is allied with angel cults synonymous with human [child] sacrifice …

… the Mal'akh are accredited with human sacrifice displayed in the Canaanite tradition as the patron Goddess Moloch. Addendum, the angels are conceived as 'crew members of a naval vessel' literally 'a star-ship' registered in the Hebrew lexicon as the 'tsabaoth', Latin (the angelic host).

… Philological evidence indicates the 'mal'akh' are synonymous with the 'crew' (the tsevet) recorded as the 'tsabaoth' alternatively the 's'baot', seminal of the king. His angelic ascendancy is evident in the Hebrew title 'melekh' (a king) subtracted from the Hebrew noun 'mal'akh' (an angel) sourced from 'malakh' (a sailor). Comparison between 'Melekh' (a Sovereign) and 'malakh' (a sailor – angel) is translated into English as 'king-ship'…

Symbols for mal'akh/Molech/Moloch include the dragon, navigator, shining serpent and radiant king. When Molech appears, conflict, war, famine and death are said to follow. You can appreciate the symbolism of the owl when you see how the language derivatives commonly refer to the worship of the 'nocturnal angels' who only appear at night (as with 'Dracula'). The owl also appears mainly at night and can see in the dark. Other codes for the serpent race include the goat, ram, hawk, jackal, dove, phoenix and eagle. This is the true significance of the symbolism behind the American eagle and the Nazi 'eagle'. The symbol of the eagle can be traced to Sumer. The Great Seal of the United States has the pyramid and all-seeing eye (the Watchers) on one side, and the eagle (the Nazai priesthood and the serpent race) on the other with the circle (serpent symbol) and the stars (serpent symbol). The symbolism of the flying serpent, the eagle, is also the origin of the 'feathered-serpent' gods such as Quetzalcoatl in Central America. The Roman Empire and the Byzantine Empire reserved eagle imagery for the 'Supreme God' and the emperor, and was seen as a metaphor of invincibility. It is connected in mythology by the Greeks with the God, Zeus, by the Romans with Jupiter, by the Germanic tribes with Odin and by Christians with God. Horus, the son of God, and Jesus's equivalent in Egypt, is symbolised as a hawk (Fig 139), which denotes the 'Royal line' and is also identified with the patriarchs of Judaism. The code association between the bird symbol and the serpent race can be seen in the Roman word 'Columba' (meaning 'dove'), a symbol of the moon goddess, and 'coluber' (meaning 'snake' or 'cobra'). The District of Columbia, home to Washington DC, is really the District of the Snake. The same applies to Columbia University; Columbia Pictures, with its logo of the goddess and the torch; Columbia Broadcasting (CBS), with its symbol of the all-seeing eye; and the many other versions of 'Columbia'. All these different symbols are used to hide the identity of the serpent race. This is done because, as Credo Mutwa says, the ancients were warned not to depict them as they really looked. They desperately do not want to be exposed as the hidden force behind human affairs. This is also the origin of the law in some religions that says you must not say the name of 'God'.

Figure 139: *The Egyptian god, Horus, portrayed symbolically as a hawk*

Pierre Sabak relates the term 'cabal' to the old Egyptian 'Qeb El' (serpent god). 'Qeb El' became the English word 'cobra'. This theme of cabal follows on to the 'ka'ba', the sacred shrine of Islam at Mecca, and the 'Kabalah', the esoteric teachings of the Judaic tradition. Both relate to 'Qeb El' (serpent god). Sabak points out that Islamic tradition links the Kaaba shrine with the fallen angel, Iblis (Satan). It is all there in the language, if you know what you are looking for and are prepared to put in the incredible effort it takes to uncover what does not want to be publicly displayed. Another motif of the serpent race and their hybrids is the hairy snake (part human-part reptile) and also the symbol of the mask in its many forms, hiding the true identity of the wearer.

The Serpent Covenant

The imposition of a 'royal' Reptilian-human hybrid bloodline was the result of an agreement that followed humanity's defeat in a war with the serpent race, or this renegade group, at least, that could well have involved other extraterrestrial races. It wasn't really an 'agreement' any more than any loser in a conflict 'agrees' to what the victor demands. This 'agreement' has passed through history under the name 'covenant' or 'God's/the gods covenant', and central to it is the interbreeding between humans and the Reptilians to create and maintain the ruling hybrid bloodline. It also involves an 'agreement' that the Reptilians be able to abduct human children on a massive scale, worldwide. Codes for the interbreeding include 'divine marriage' and a 'marriage between heaven and earth'. The offspring were said to be 'born of heaven and earth' and 'born of the clouds', among many other codes and symbols. The word-symbolism and meanings often relate humanity to a 'flock', which certainly fits the picture with 'Jesus' and other deities depicted as the 'shepherd'. Pierre Sabak maintains that the covenant with the 'flock' also involves an entity known as the 'keyholder', and this is the origin of the theme of the biblical 'Peter' (rock) who was said to have been given the keys to the Kingdom. In the Islamic tradition, the keyholder is 'Al Kidr' – 'the Green One'. You can see the Arabic word relationship with 'hada' (to guide), 'hadar' (presence), 'ha-dar (shapeshifter) and 'haddad' (keyholder). I have been emphasising for nearly 20 years that Britain is one of the main operational centres for the global conspiracy, and the very name 'British' means 'People of the Covenant'. Not all of them, mind, just those of the bloodline. The Roman word for 'Britain' was 'Albion', derived from the Latin 'Alba Longa', the ancient city of Latinum in the Alban Hills, south-east of Rome. Legend says that Romulus and Remus, the alleged founders of Rome, were from the royal dynasty of Alba Longa. Sabak says that London's Latin name, 'Londinium', was a corruption of the Greek word, 'Ladon'. This was the name given in Greek mythology to the hundred-headed dragon who guarded the apples (knowledge) on the sacred tree of Hesperides. Britain, particularly London, became one of the global centres for the Illuminati bloodlines, or, as William Blake put it in his classic hymn, *Jerusalem*:

> And did the Countenance Divine
> Shine forth upon our clouded hills?
> And was Jerusalem builded here
> Among these dark satanic mills?

The 19th century British Prime Minister, Benjamin Disraeli (Rothschild Zionist), who was extremely close to the Rothschilds, said: 'London is the modern Babylon.' Yes, it is – Babylon-don. It is more than that, though. It is the place where Reptilian hybrid bloodlines from Sumer and beyond came together after their various journeys through 'history' that took them to Egypt, Troy, Rome, through the Caucasus and up into Eastern and Western Europe as the leadership of the Khazars. From there, they have been exported around the world by the British and other European empires and by the Khazar conquest of Palestine. Interestingly, Pierre Sabak says the Hebrew word for 'star visitor' or 'space alien' is 'khayzar', and its equivalent is 'Caesar', rendered in the Greek as 'Kaiser'. We also have tzar or czar, so no wonder Obama's appointments are called his 'czars', a title that infers the royal bloodline. Sabak also points out that 'khayzar' is indexed in the Old Persian with 'ksaytiya' (king), shortened in the Late Persian as 'Sah'; in Arabic as 'Shah'. 'Satan' and 'Sultan' are interchangeable in Arabic from the word 'saluta' (meaning to rule). Add to this that Credo Mutwa, the Zulu historian, says that the kings and tribal chiefs of Africa were seeded by visitors who came from the skies and the common theme smacks you in the kisser! The ruling bloodlines of the world are Reptilian hybrids that have a 'covenant' with 'God' – the gods – to rule over the rest of us on their behalf. This 'covenant' (contract) is known in Old Semitic as 'Brit-An' (hence Britain) and 'Brit-ish' (People of the Covenant). In Modern Hebrew it is 'brit(h)' and so we have the name of the Rothschild front, 'B'nai B'rith' – 'Sons of the Covenant'. In English, 'brit', 'brith' and the Hebrew 'berith' become ... birth. Yes, we really are 'born into bondage'. Appropriately, the term for a branch of Satanism is a 'coven'. This theme of a contract with 'God' (the gods) and being the 'chosen' or surrendering to 'God' (the gods) can be found in all the major religions. Pierre Sabak writes:

Old Testament reference to the God of the Hebrews describes him in the plural as 'Lord of the Host'. His conquest parallels the 'subjugation' (slm) of man. The 'surrender' of humanity (slm) is a synonym of the verbal root 'shomer' (a keeper). God and his Elohim are depicted as conquerors of the world(s) and the domesticator of man.

Mediation between the host and mankind specifies a religious 'covenant' (the bariyth), Modern Hebrew 'brit(h)', cultic of the 'Shibboleth'. In Old Semitic, the contract is described as 'Brit-An' (Britain) and refers to the 'covenant of heaven'. Muslim scholars argue the covenant of God is commensurate with religious (submission) 'sallim', a homonym of 'salam' (peace). Salam is relative to 'sama' (heaven) and 'samah' (to forgive). Unequivocal, the 'surrender or resignation of oneself' is expressed in Arabic as 'aslama' transliterated into English as 'Islam'.

Early accounts of the 'Elohim' plural (the Gods) imply a military dictatorship identified with invasion and conquest. Historically the capitulation of man is attributed to the angelic crew, the 'tsabaoth' conceived as (the host). Itinerants, the sailors are annotated in Aramaic as the 'zari' (translated alien, stranger or foreigner) relative in Arabic to 'zau' (light) – Hebrew 'zohar' (to shine). The noun 'zau' is constant with the Arabic classification 'Zuhrah/Zohra' (Venus) and 'zuhr' (early afternoon prayer) identified with the Evening Star. Described as the light bringer or the fallen daystar, 'Zuhrah' is bracketed in Greek with 'sauros' (a lizard)'.

Denomination of the fish is ancient and ordained by the Roman clergy. Epiphanius states that the original 'Christians' in Judea, generally called Nazoreans (as in Acts of the Apostles), were known as 'Jessaeans'. They referred to themselves as the 'keeper of the covenant' (Nozrei ha-Brit) 'bariyth /barith'. From this term derived the 'Nozrim' – the earliest designation of the sect subsequently known as 'Christians' or 'fishes'.

Sabak says that in Indo-Persian languages, the universal symbol of the fish is applied to deities in the sky (the upper ocean) who are associated with copulation and conflict (Fig 140). Here is one example of the word associations, starting with Dagon, the 'fish god' of Babylon:

> Dagon's name is abridged from the Old Hebrew compound 'dag' (a fish) appended with 'anu' (heaven). His epithet 'the fish [of] heaven' informs the Greek noun 'drakon' (a dragon) defined as (a watcher). Dagon's Babylonian heritage is lucid with the amphibian Oannes – a God registered with the 'eye' (ayin). The 'eyelid' (af'af) is covert to the 'viper' (Arabic af'a).

Something to emphasise most strongly here: when groups talk of being the 'Chosen People', like the Jews, that doesn't mean all of them. It means those who made the covenant with the Reptilians, that's all – the

Figure 140: *Dagon, the fish god of Mesopotamia*

ruling bloodlines. This is why the Rothschilds couldn't care less about Jewish people as a whole. When I talk about the Sumerians, Khazars, Egyptians, and all the rest, I am only referring to the few in the bloodlines and priesthoods – not to the mass of those peoples who are as much the victims of this conspiracy as everyone else, more so in some cases.

Sacrifice of the Firstborn

The language-research confirms the many other sources that I have gathered together over the years that reveal a 'covenant' between the bloodline families and their serpent masters to sacrifice their first-born sons through immolation. This appears to have been one of the conditions imposed after humans lost the war with the Reptilians. The covenant also included the usurpation of human genetics by the reptile seed with the sacrificed child being replaced by the offspring of the serpent race, indicated through the mark of circumcision, Sabak says. These Reptilian replacements became known as 'changlings' (Latin 'suppositio' or 'substitute'). Sabak continues:

'Substitution' simulates a 'changeling' (Latin suppositio) from 'suppositus' the past participle (to substitute). In English, the wordplay approximates to change and trade or price and place. 'Suppositio' is divided from the stem 'positor' (a builder) employed in the Semitic and Persian languages to convey 'an angel', 'God' or 'serpent'.

Defined as the 'positor', translated as 'a builder', the 'positor' is matched with 'possideo' (the transitive verb to possess, occupy, have, own, dwell, live in, take hold of) and is a variation of 'posido' (to take possession of or to seize). The angels are thus able to 'occupy', 'possess' or 'take possession' of the body likened to 'positura' (a formation).

Labeled as a 'changeling', the 'supposition' designates a deity viewed metaphorically as a 'builder' (positor) figurative of the angel's ability to assume a human form, resembling a 'substitute'. Cultic Symbolism personifies the builder as a Master Craftsman represented in the Mystery Schools as a Mason or an Artificer.

Ritualistically, the 'substitute' (suppositio) is 'exchanged' with 'a changeling' recondite with a transfigured angel. Replacement of the body double with a replica concurs also within European folklore. Provident to Celtic tradition, an infant substituted at birth by stealth replaces an 'elf child' left by the fairies.

You see the constant recurrence of the sacrifice of the firstborn and the slaughter of the innocent in religious texts. The Old Testament's Abraham is asked to sacrifice his son, Isaac; there is the killing of the firstborn in Egypt (origin of the Passover ritual); and Moses is told by 'God' to 'give him' all the firstborn. 'God' tells Abraham:

Take your son, your only son – yes, Isaac, whom you love so much – and go to the land of Moriah. Sacrifice him there as a burnt offering on one of the mountains, which I will point out to you. (*Genesis* 22:1-18)

What a lovely 'God'. Those scales suit you, mate. This 'God' allows Abraham in the Old Testament account to save his son and burn a ram to death instead. This, once again, is hidden code. The sacrifice of the ram, or lamb, symbolises the sacrifice of a child if you follow the word associations, Pierre Sabak says. These are some other examples from the Old Testament of 'God's' demand for firstborn sacrifice:

> You shall not delay to make offerings from the fullness of your harvest and from the outflow of your presses. The firstborn of your sons you shall give to me. You shall do the same with your oxen and with your sheep: seven days it shall remain with its mother; on the eighth day you shall give it to me. (*Exodus*: 22:29-30)

> Behold, I have taken the Levites from among the people of Israel instead of every firstborn that opens the womb among the people of Israel. The Levites shall be mine, for all the firstborn are mine; on the day that I slew all the firstborn in the land of Egypt, I consecrated for my own all the first-born in Israel, both of man and of beast; they shall be mine: I am the LORD. (*Numbers*: 3:11-13)

> Nothing that a person owns that has been devoted to destruction for the LORD, be it human or animal, or inherited landholding, may be sold or redeemed; every devoted thing is most holy to the LORD. No human beings who have been devoted to destruction [sacrifice] can be ransomed; they shall be put to death. (*Leviticus*: 27:28-29)

> The dragon stood in front of the woman who was about to give birth, so that he might devour her child the moment it was born. (*Book of Revelation*: 12:4)

You find the same theme in every ancient culture, and the stories of sacrificing 'young virgins' are just code for children. The nobility of Carthage during the Punic Wars with Rome (264 BC to 146 BC) sacrificed hundreds of children to Baal (their serpent god) by throwing them into pits of fire. The Celts and Druids sacrificed children, and the Aztecs of Central America did it, and on a monumental scale. It went on everywhere and, covertly, it still does. I've already stressed that the number of children who go missing every year never to be found is simply fantastic, and significant numbers of them are sacrificed to the Reptilians, and eaten by them, as part of the 'covenant'. Impossible? Can't be happening? If only. Moloch is widely associated with the sacrifice of children through immolation, as we have seen, and the Druidic equivalent was the 'Wicker Man'. Pierre Sabak's research leads him to make this conclusion about the meaning of the 'Sabbath':

> The Sabbath records the surrender of man and the cessation of hostilities pivotal to the formation of the covenant mediated through kingship. Sacrifice of the firstborn is mentioned etiologically as the removal of [Isaac's firstborn son] Esau (Hebrew hair). This deceit is annunciated through the human angelic lineage personified as the 'reptile' or 'rapist'...

> ... The ratification of the Elhohim's covenant with humans through circumcision discloses castration of the male lineage. In ancient Judaic lore, the covenant required the sacrificial blood of a firstborn baby boy conveyed through the mutilation of the genitalia and the removal of man's ancestral lineage correlated with Adam, Isaac and Esau ...

... Celebration of the Sabbath outlines deception framed through the appropriation of a child and is adapted in Mosaic (Masonic) Law as the evening meal or communion. Observance of the Sabbath implies sacrificial death featured in the Semitic wordplays. The Hebrew day 'rishon' (Sunday) is a pun on the Arabic phrase – written backwards – 'rishsh' 'yom' (a deceitful day). The noun 'yom' signifying 'day' is grouped in the Middle Eastern languages with 'ayom' (horrid) relayed into English as day and die.

The religious texts are a mass of codes and symbols that the 'believers' do not even begin to understand. Those who know it is all coded language tell the congregations to take everything literally. Every religion has an inner core that knows what the texts really mean, and an outer 'Church' that hasn't got a clue. As a result, they are worshipping the serpent gods and giving them their mind-power and energy – making a vibrational connection – while believing they are worshipping 'God', 'Jesus', or whomever.

Covenant/Government

The Illuminati hybrid bloodlines in each country answer to the serpent 'gods', not the people, and 'human' laws are imposed through these middlemen and women by the Reptilians, who introduced the written law, as well as spoken language, and an economic system based on fresh-air 'money'. King Hammurabi established the Babylonian Empire during his reign from 1795 BC to 1750 BC and built the world's first known metropolis. He is also famous for introducing a written law known as the 'Code of Hammurabi' that he said had been given to him by the 'gods'. The preface to the law code says: 'Anu and Bel called by name me, Hammurabi, the exalted prince, who feared God, to bring about the rule of the righteousness in the land.' The same theme can be found everywhere and this includes the story of 'Moses', who is said to have been given the law or 'Commandments' by 'God' (the gods). Religions are founded on the law given to the people through a middleman, or 'prophet', by their various versions of 'God', or the gods – the serpent hierarchy. 'It is written' and all that stuff has been dictated by the Reptilians and imposed by their hybrids. It is still happening today with the global secret society network, orchestrated through hybrid bloodlines like the Rothschilds and Rockefellers, dictating the extraordinary imposition of laws to govern every area of human life for the serpent 'gods' they serve. The 'covenant' with 'God' by his 'Chosen People' is actually a contract with the Reptilians that was forced upon humanity. This continues to be imposed through governments (covenants) that are nothing more than administrators of the serpent laws and rules passed down through the bloodline families and the secret societies into the public domain. Pierre Sabak says of the real meaning of government:

Statecraft describes the 'government' adduced from the Latin transitive verb 'gubernare' (to rule or steer) and signifies (a navigator of a boat) 'gubernator'. 'Gubernare' is a Latinisation of the Greek 'kubernao' (to steer a boat), vocabulary associated with the angelic host. The ruler rendered in the Arabic as 'Sultan' parallels the Hebrew term for 'government' (shilton), essentially identified with the fallen angels – the 'S(h)atani'...

… The Satanic bloodlines administer (the government) 'shilton' and is a concept replicated in classical myth. 'Diabolus', the Greek name signifying the devil, conceals 'boule' the Hellenistic name for the 'Senate'. 'Diabolus' operates as a clever pun on 'dia-boule' (through the Senate) analogous in Hebrew to (satan and shilton). Boule is extrapolated from the Semitic cognomen 'Baal' (a Lord), titular of the Canaanite God. Allegorically, the Government is an agency of the devil and is linked to the lineage of the Shatani epitomized through the division of man.

'Adam', 'Eden' and Atlantis Revisited

Pierre Sabak's study of words across multiple languages throws further light on the themes of Adam, the Garden of Eden, and, possibly, Atlantis. His language-research confirms the connection I have long contended between 'Eve' and the serpent race. Sabak says:

In the Hebrew tradition, Eve's descendents are the ancestors of the 'Nephilim', a race translated from the verbal adjective 'naful' (to fall) i.e. the 'Fallen Ones'. They are also described as the 'awwim' interpreted as (the serpents or devastators) identical to the 'reptile', the 'pillager' or 'rapist'. The 'awwim' are mutual to the 'tsabaoth' (the host or dragon) and are described in related traditions as the conquerors of man.

This would support the ancient texts found at Nag Hammadi in Egypt in 1945 which say that Adam and Eve had horny, luminous skin. Biblical and other accounts indicate that Eve was created from the 'rib' of Adam but, Sabak says, the term 'rib' is symbolic of the snake. Some snakes have more than 400 ribs compared with the 24 in humans. They also have more than a hundred vertebrae attached to the ribs and they grow new ribs as they get larger. This bone structure of the snake is symbolically expressed as a ladder (Fig 141). Sabak writes:

The growth cycle of the reptile further explains the Biblical analogy between the snake (angel) and rib regarding the creation of Eve. 'The Rib in the English language is etymologically consistent with the Arabic stem 'r-b-b' (Lord). The scholar M. A. S. Abdel Haleem cites in his appendices to the Koran that the stem 'r-b-b' has connotations of 'caring' and 'nurturing' in addition to 'Lordship'. The idea of sustenance equated with the Lord twinned with the snake fits closely with what other academics have argued.

According to the linguist, Balaji Mundkur, the definitions of 'life' and 'serpent' are mutually supportive. The name Eve is synonymous with the word for 'life' and 'snake'. In Arabic, the word 'serpent' (haiya) is, itself, cognate with 'hayat' (life) and 'Hawwa(h)' (Eve). Jewish traditions link this

Figure 141: *Some snakes have more than 400 ribs and they have been symbolised as a 'ladder'*

very rare name with the prime verbal root 'hayah' (to make live) – derived from the Akkadian root. The play 'Hawwah' (Eve) and 'haiya' (snake) is matched in Arabic with 'hardun' (a lizard) corollary to 'Adam'.

Inference drawn from the Arabic philology shows the 'snakes' progeny (haiya) is extracted from the bloodline of 'Hawwah' (Eve). The point is theologically reiterated in Genesis 3:13. In this passage, woman's sexual awakening is explicitly recounted when woman explains to god 'the serpent beguiled me'. In Hebrew, 'ishiani' (beguile) can alternatively be read as 'He put his seed in me'.

The rib serves as an apologue and recollects Eve's creation privy to mortal angelic coitus. Anatomically, it silhouettes the crescent device of the priesthood diagnostic of the menstrual cycle mutual to creation … the word for 'rib' in Sumerian is 'tii', and 'tii' happens also to be the Sumerian verb (to make live). It is expressed, literally, in the Arabic wordplay 'ti-bana' (a builder of life) assigned to 'ti'ban(a)' (an eel). In English, the pun transfers to life and wife or rib and live.

Sabak finds that the origins of the morning sacrificial offering to the Egyptian God, Atum, can be sourced directly to the creation of Adam and the location called 'Eden'. It is clear that the symbol of 'Adam' can be found expressed in a long list of deities that are symbolic of the serpent race, including 'Atum' and 'Amen'. The Canaanite moon god, El, is also known as 'Ab-Adam' (father of man); and in Sumerian 'Adam' is used as a term for 'people' or 'humanity' in general. Eden was the place, according to Apocryphal literature, where the fallen angels were responsible for teaching knowledge of the seasons and agriculture to humanity, and where humans made their 'offerings' to them. 'Apocrypha' refers to accounts of a similar context to the biblical works, but not included in the so-called 'canon' of Scripture that makes up the Bible. Pierre Sabak says that word meanings and derivations show there is a strong relationship between the materialisation of an angel and the gathering of the crop. 'Development of 'agriculture' (zara'a) originates from the 'angelic' progeny, the 'zari' (aliens),' he writes.

Earth and Eden are closely connected with 'Adam', the collective term for 'man' in Hebrew, and 'adama' (land). You also see this in the Latin with 'humanus' (human), and 'humus' (soil). 'Eden thus describes the garden of offering implied from the verbal root 'Addin' (I give),' says Sabak. 'E-Din' translates as the 'House [of] Offering' in Akkadian, indicating a sort of temple. 'Eden/Edin' in Akkadian can also be translated as a 'steppe' or 'terrace', as in a raised agricultural terrace. Sabak says that it is also consistent with the Persian word 'paradise' and that this 'technically represents a walled enclosure from the Persian etymons "pairi" (around) and "daeza" (wall), related to the Hebrew etymon "pardes" (a grove).' The Persian adverb 'pairi' also connects with 'Peri', the Persian word for 'a race of serpents'. The connection between a wall and the serpent can be seen in the Arabic noun 'sur' (a wall) and 'sirr' (a mystery) which comes from the Sumerian root 'sirr' (a serpent) and links with 'seir'im (a red goat; or demon). As I have said in other books, the title 'sir', conferred on those given a British Knighthood, comes from a word meaning 'serpent'. This makes perfect sense if you say the word 'serpent' instead of 'sir' before the names of many of these people. The titles that the hybrid bloodlines and their gofers love so much, like 'king', 'queen', 'lord' and 'sir', all refer to, or are derived from, terms meaning the serpent race.

The language connections lead us to 'Atlantis' which, Sabak says, is indicated to have been a planet or planets and not a physical location on Earth. I am open to anything if the evidence is there to support it, but my own research over 20 years so far tells me this: There were certainly land masses in the Atlantic and Pacific that sank amid fantastic geological upheavals and the earth was devastated as a whole. It is in the geological and biological record. But there were also cataclysmic events on Mars due to some hi-tech war (well beyond 'hi-tech' as we know it) and the destruction of the planet between Mars and Jupiter that became what we call the asteroid belt. What names you give to these various locations is far less important than what happened to them. Sabak says that the translation of 'paradise' as 'a walled enclosure' connects with the description of Atlantis as a construction of a series of concentric or circular walls documented as enclosures by the ancient Greek philosopher, Plato, in his work *Critias*. Plato says: 'He "Poseidon" made two rings of land and three of sea as round as if he had laid them out with a compass and lathe.' This is Pierre Sabak's interpretation of that:

Plato's writing is intentionally covert; the compass in Greek and Byzantine culture signifies creation characteristic of the snake and is copied as the insignia of Modern Freemasonry. The calipers circumscribe the disk pageant of the reptile celebrated as the builder.

Originally, the two rings of earth, in Critias' account, designate two planets surrounded by sea – symbolic of an atmosphere. The planet is represented as a walled enclosure 'pairi-daeza', its destruction recounted mythologically.

The place name 'Atlantis' translates as the (daughter of Atlas). According to the scholar Alan Alford, it is derived from the root 'tlao' (to suffer or bear) – literally 'A-tlao' (to bear or suffer together). The sibling 'Atlantis' is probably the same woman as the mortal 'Tyro'. In Greek mythology, Tyro consummated her relationship with the fish deity Poseidon encountered in the myth of Eve and the serpent...

... According to Plato's narrative in the *Timaeus*, occupants of the fabled island (planet) are defeated by the 'Athenians' – a Grecian name extracted from the Arabic root 'a'fa' (a viper).

Poseidon was known as the god of the sea, and the 'Earth-Shaker', the creator of earthquakes; and this once again links with the fish/sea/water symbols of the Reptilians and their destruction of the Earth with geological upheavals. I'll come to how they did it later. The Greek pantheon of 'gods', such as Poseidon and Zeus, were serpent gods. Pierre Sabak says that the name 'Zeus', for example, came from the Sanskrit 'Djaus', the Brahmin sky-god and a word meaning 'heaven'. This derives from 'dyu' (to be brilliant) and continues the theme of the 'shining ones'. Tyro's connection to suffering links with the Egyptian term 'trai' (meaning to obliterate, decimate or destroy). Sabak argues the root of 'trai' can be traced through to 'Troy', another major symbolic location in the story of the Reptilian bloodlines. This, too, may be another reference to Atlantis

Figure 142: *The story of the Trojan Horse symbolises precisely how the Reptilians have infiltrated and manipulated the world*

under another name, he says, and what perfect symbolism we have with the Trojan Horse, when you think of how the Reptilians infiltrate covertly while hiding behind apparent human form (Fig 142).

The Martians Have Landed

Pierre Sabak says that his language derivatives suggest that 'Adam', or the genetic form this name represents, was created on Mars. This planet is called 'Ma'adim' in Hebrew, while the phrase 'me'adim' translates as 'from Adam' or 'out of Adam'. He is also referred to by the ancients as the 'red man' (Adam/adom-red), indicative of the red planet; and the word 'adamatu' in Akkadian means 'red earth'. Mars was said to be a home of a Reptilian group and it would make sense of genetic manipulation happening there. Zulu legend also connects the Reptilians and humans to Mars. The Sanskrit term for 'noble westerner' (or westerners) is 'Adar martu' and this connects with the phrase 'adi mitra', which means 'the first covenant'. Sabak says:

> Affiliation of 'Martu' with Adam and Mars suggests 'Martu' is a variation of the Modern English label 'Martian' from the Latin 'martianus'. Descendents of the 'martu', Akkadian the (Adamatu), traveled from Mars towards the Earth. The 'Adama(r)tu' are described as the original descendents of 'Adam', correlated in the Old Semitic with 'qadam' (east), unified with the western nation (Thebes). In both English and in Latin, Martian is similar to martial and marital, expressions of the covenant.

The term 'martial law' certainly takes on new meaning. There is also a common theme of the colour red. We have the red planet; red as the colour of Satanism; the red cross of the Knights Templar; the red cross flag of England; and the Illuminati-controlled organisation that we know as the 'Red Cross'. Pierre Sabak says the red cross is a symbol of Mars and the Adamic bloodline. The very name of the Rothschilds means 'Redshields' or 'red sign', and this symbolism follows the bloodline through the centuries. I have highlighted in other books how the Hyksos, or 'Shepherd Kings', used the colour red in their symbolism (their kings wore a red crown), and also the snake. The Hyksos, who have been widely associated with Canaan (from the Old Semitic word 'khanun', meaning 'red'), were closely associated with the Egyptian Theban priesthood of the serpent race. The Hyksos ruled Egypt for more than a hundred years from around 1630 BC and some historians have connected their eventual banishment from Egypt with the biblical Exodus. Sabak says that this Hyksos line later appeared as the Ramnes (Egyptian Rameses) bloodline that changed its name to 'Romans'. The Ramnes were a 'noble class' of 'blueblood aristocracy' who were considered the direct descendants of Romulus, the alleged founder of Rome. The Hyksos bloodline under many names infiltrated countless peoples, including the Arabs, and later located in Britain, which the

Romans called 'Albion', from the Latin 'Alba Longa'. This was a royal dynasty, which, it is said, produced Romulus and his fellow 'founder' of Rome, Remus. It's all code, and the truth is there to be seen if you can read it. There is certainly a major Mars connection to the human story and I first wrote about that in the first edition of *The Biggest Secret* in 1998. The more I know, the stronger that connection becomes.

I thoroughly recommend Pierre Sabak's book, *The Murder of Reality*, which goes into many areas and interpretations that I will leave to him. I just wanted to lay out here the foundation of what his language-research demonstrates and how much it supports the themes I have been presenting for all these years. You can get his book at **davidickebooks.co.uk**.

13

So where are they?

Evil hiding among us is an ancient theme
John Carpenter

The Reptilians once came and went openly among the people, as ancient accounts describe; but there came a time when they moved into the shadows, symbolically and literally, and hid behind the outwardly human form of their hybrid bloodlines.

There are Reptilians in our reality living within the Earth, but the main focus of the manipulation is on those that operate beyond visible light and possess the hybrid families (Fig 143). Most of these bloodlines operate within the surface world, but there are others who also live underground as part of the hidden control system. When it is said that the Reptilians come from the Orion or Draco constellations, we are not necessarily talking about our reality or frequency range. Planets and star systems, including Earth, also exist in other densities. Mars, for example, has a devastated atmosphere and landscape within visible light, but could be teeming with life in other densities. The most significant Reptilians in terms of the human control system are those that operate in Fourth Density and move between that 'dimension' and our Third

Figure 143: *The Reptilians can possess the hybrid bloodlines far more powerfully than the general population because of the compatible vibrational resonance that comes from compatible DNA*

Density reality through interdimensional craft, interdimensional 'gateways' and through energetic manipulation performed in satanic ritual. The 'gateways' are major vortex points on the Earth's energy field which 'spin' the densities together, and if you know what you are doing you can move through these 'stepping stone' energy fields from one energetic 'world' into the other. Stories like *The Lion, the Witch and the Wardrobe* by C S Lewis, where children walk through a 'wardrobe' and find themselves in a different reality, are symbolic of this. Sumer, now Iraq, is home to some significant energetic gateways and 'portals', and so is Egypt, but they exist all over the world.

Those who think this is all too far-fetched should look at the research being conducted in China at the Hong Kong University of Science and Technology, and the Fudan University in Shanghai, which was published in the *New Journal of Physics*. Scientists describe the concept of 'a gateway that can block electromagnetic waves but that allows the passage of other entities'. They describe it as like 'a 'hidden portal' as mentioned in fictions'. The concept is based on manipulating light and other forms of electromagnetic radiation in 'complicated directions' to create a hidden portal that is 'tuneable' and can be switched on and off remotely. This is the sort of technology they have in far more advanced form in underground bases and under major control centres, including the Pentagon, where Fourth Density Reptilians can manifest and interact with their human, and semi-human, lackeys. The Chinese project involves metallic or semiconductor substances called 'metamaterials', and this is the branch of physics research behind the possible creation of a real Harry Potter-type cloak of invisibility. When you think that this is where they are in official research into 'gateways' – imagine where they are in the money-no-object underground projects and, even more so, where the Reptilians are. Their technology is so advanced that it makes the 'hidden portal' research akin to a push bike. Before people cry, 'Not possible!', they should understand that what is called the 'cutting edge' of human science is merely the first grade of what the Reptilians can do.

The controlling Reptilians have 'bodies' that enable them to interact with their level of density, the 'Fourth Density', but, of course, this means they vibrate to a different rhythm to our Third Density. They have to use the hybrid bloodlines to manipulate this reality because when they do come here through interdimensional craft and interdimensional energetic 'gateways' they can't stay for long or they are confined to the areas technologically-manipulated to vibrate closer to their frequency range. *Torchwood,* a BBC science-fiction drama, broadcast a series in 2009 called *Children of the Earth* that featured the theme of 'extraterrestrials' that were able to live on the Earth only in a specially-created tank with an atmosphere that suited them. They arrived in the human world in a flash of energy to enter the 'tank', and then demanded a 'gift' of ten per cent of the world's children. Both themes were based on fact, whether the writer knew it or not, because the Fourth Density Reptilians don't sync with our vibrational frequency range and the 'covenant' with 'the gods' includes the right to take human children, aided by the surface families and their covert intelligence and military networks. Humans are sustenance to the Reptilians – we are their food source. They are 'physical' food when the Reptilians are in Third Density, and 'energetic' food in Fourth Density, produced by low-vibration emotions and mental states like fear, hate, anger, stress, worry and depression. Large numbers of the children and others that go missing every year end up being consumed by the Reptilians in surface rituals and in underground bases which open out into the ancient cavern and tunnel systems where Reptilians and other non-human species, like the 'greys' and the blond-haired, blue-eyed 'Nordics', have hidden from human sight for thousands of years. Look at how most humans view cattle and sheep … a source of food; and that's how the Reptilians view us. The theme of the serpent race consuming humans can be found in ancient accounts and symbolic images all over the world (Figs 144 to 148 overleaf).

Figure 144　　**Figure 145**　　**Figure 146**　　**Figure 147**　　**Figure 148**

Depictions of reptile entities eating humans can be found all over the world. Credo Mutwa has painted the image on one of his huts (Fig 147) to symbolise the stories in Africa and the same image appears on the logo of Italian car-maker, Alfa Romeo

'Hell' Below

There are also underground colonies of Third Density Reptilians connecting with underground military bases all over the world, including Antarctica, and they are especially prevalent in the United States where the underground bases and cavern cities are linked by tunnel networks with incredibly fast electromagnetic transport systems and even more advanced technology I will describe later on. Reptilian and other extraterrestrial groups also have bases in the deep oceans, lochs and lakes, another reason for the symbolism of the Reptilians as 'fish gods'. The massive underground facilities at Dulce and Los Alamos in New Mexico, and the China Lake Naval Air Weapons Station in the northeast of California's Mojave Desert, are among the Reptilian-human bases in the United States. I have driven around the perimeter of China Lake a couple of times and it is a vast area with virtually nothing above ground. It is connected by tunnel systems – cut at incredible speed by advanced nuclear technology – to underground bases in nearby Death Valley and Edwards Air Force Base, and far more distant locations, including: Mount Shasta in California; Las Vegas and the Area 51 base in Nevada; Sedona in Arizona; and the sinister Denver Airport in Colorado which has been widely exposed by researchers as a cover for an underground base. The airport is adorned by Freemasonic symbolism, reptilian gargoyles and horrible murals depicting a humanity subjugated by evil (Fig 149). One grotesque mural includes three caskets with dead females in them. There is a Jewish girl, a Native American and a black woman. Another girl is holding a Mayan tablet which tells of the

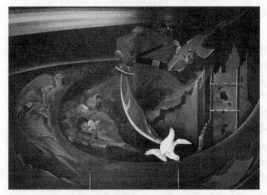

Figure 149: *A scene from the horrible murals at Denver Airport portraying a fascist takeover*

destruction of civilization. A huge character, described as a 'green Darth Vader' by researcher Alex Christopher, stands over a destroyed city with a sword in his hand; and women are walking along a road holding dead babies. All the children of the world are depicted taking weapons from each country and handing them to the figure of a German boy with an iron fist and an anvil in his hand. Phil Schneider, the son of a German U-boat commander in World War II, said he was commissioned to build a number of deep underground bases in the United States. I saw some of his lectures on video when he began to speak out publicly about the underground network of bases, cities and tunnels throughout the United States. He later died in very suspicious circumstances that were claimed to be 'suicide'. Schneider said that Denver Airport was connected to a deep underground base that had at least eight floors, which included a 4.5 square mile underground city and an enormous base. Other contacts who have been underground at Denver Airport claim that there are large numbers of human slaves, many of them children, working there under the control of the Reptilians. Two other bases that Phil Schneider claimed to have helped construct are Area 51 in Nevada and Dulce in New Mexico. I report in *The Biggest Secret* the horrendous scenes described by former employees at underground military bases today like Dulce and Los Alamos in New Mexico, and what they say is the same as the Sumerian descriptions of the 'Great Below' and other accounts around the world. Here are two accounts from people who said they had worked at Dulce:

> I have seen multi-legged 'humans' that look like half human/half octopus.
> Also reptilian-humans and furry creatures that have hands like humans and cry like a baby, it mimics human words ... also a huge mixture of lizard-humans in cages.

> ... I frequently encountered humans in cages, usually dazed or drugged, but sometimes they cried and begged for help. We were told they were hopelessly insane and involved in high risk drug tests to cure insanity. We were told never to try to speak to them at all. At the beginning we believed that story. Finally, in 1978, a small group of workers discovered the truth.

Most people who work at these establishments don't know about this. The bases are structured as many floors or levels, and the lower you go the higher security clearance is required. The lowest level opens out into the cavern and tunnel systems. This allows 'human' scientists, government and military personnel to work with the Reptilians on genetic and technology programmes to advance the agenda of human control. Most of the major technological 'advances' that allow ever-greater enslavement of the population start out in this way, and a cover story is concocted to explain where it came from and how it was discovered and developed. These technologies are circulated on the surface in line with the timescale they are working to. Computers, nanotechnology and so much more was available to the Reptilians while humans were still knocking rocks together. As insiders have revealed, 'beam me up, Scotty' technology is no science fiction fantasy. They have what some researchers refer to as 'jump rooms' in underground and secret above-ground bases which transport the occupants to other parts of the world in an instant and also to extraterrestrial underground bases on Mars. An insider called Arthur Neumann told the 2009 European Exopolitics Congress in Barcelona: 'There is life on Mars. There are bases on Mars. I have been there.' He says he has been involved in top secret technology programmes in the United States and the UK and he described how he had been teleported to an extraterrestrial base on Mars where he said he took part in a 'project meeting' attended by representatives of 'an intelligent civilization that lives in cities under the surface of Mars'. Neumann says that this extraterrestrial group look virtually like humans and they could pass most people in the street without turning a head. It is only when you

Figure 150: *The Reptilians have a different relationship to 'time' and can move up and down our 'timeline' introducing technology at the most appropriate moment to advance their agenda. Those who have access to the Reptilian game plan can write 'prophetic' books that include technology which has not even been 'invented'. But it doesn't have to be 'invented'; the Reptilians have had it all along. It is just a case of when is the best time to introduce it to human society*

see them close up that you spot the differences, he said.

This is the scale of what is going on while humanity goes about its business every day waiting for the bus, sitting in a traffic jam, and oblivious of how this world is really being run – and who by. Advanced technology has been sitting there all along waiting to be introduced to human society as the unfolding control system requires it. What would have been the use of introducing computers or nanotechnology in 1650? It is released when it can be used by, and on, the human population. The Fourth Density Reptilians operate in the different reality and have a different relationship to 'time'. This means they can move up and down our 'timeline' and introduce their technology at the most appropriate moment to best advance their agenda of control. This allows those at the highest levels of the Illuminati (symbolised by Neil Hague as the bearded man in Figure 150) to know the long term projections for how global society is designed to change. This is how 'prophetic' books can be written, many in novel form like *1984* and *Brave New World*, that prove to be so accurate decades later. This includes the use of technology that wasn't known about when the books were written. The Reptilians have created a hierarchical structure of global control in which the hybrid

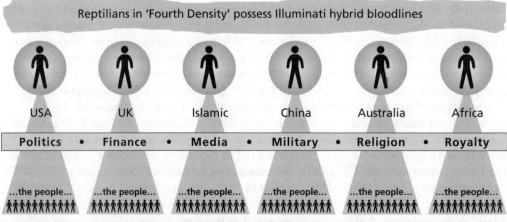

Figure 151: *The structure for global control. The Reptilians dictate the agenda to their hybrid bloodlines of the Illuminati network and the Illuminati manipulate human society in pursuit of a global Orwellian State*

Figure 152: *The 'world stage' that you don't see. The Reptilians manipulating human society through their hybrid bloodlines who then manipulate through their puppets in 'power' around the world. Neil Hague has portrayed the Reptilians in conflict here because they fight amongst themselves all the time*

Figure 153: *The Illuminati choose and dictate the 'leaders' across the world while the public think they are deciding at the ballot box*

bloodlines they possess are manipulated into power across the world, or their agents and gofers are. These 'leaders' may fight among each other for power, but they are united in their collective goal – the suppression and subjugation of humanity. It is they who declare the wars and make the political and financial policy on behalf of the Reptilians. When nations go to war it is not the Reptilian hybrid leaders who do the fighting, suffering and dying – it is the human masses in each country who are played off against each other (Fig 151). The so-called 'world stage' consists of the Reptilians beyond human sight dictating events through their bloodlines and the Illuminati network who, in turn, dictate to their puppets in apparent power, like Obama (Fig 152). All over the world the Illuminati network – the spider's web of secret societies – ensure that their assets are in power (Fig 153). Researcher, Bruce Alan Walton, has written extensively about the Reptilian connection under the pseudonym, 'Branton'. What he refers to as 'full-bloods' are the fully-fledged Reptilians and not their Reptilian-human hybrids:

> Underneath most major cities, especially in the USA in fact, there exist subterranean counterpart 'cities' controlled by the Masonic/hybrid/alien 'elite'. Often surface/subsurface terminals exist beneath Masonic Lodges, police stations, airports and federal buildings of major cities … and even not so 'major' cities. The population ratio is probably close to 10% of the population (the hybrid military-industrial fraternity

'elite' living below ground as opposed to the 90% living above). This does not include the full-blood reptilian species who live in even deeper recesses of the Earth.

Some of the major population centers were deliberately established by the Masonic/hybrid elite of the Old and New 'Worlds' to afford easy access to already existing underground levels, some of which are thousands of years old. Considering that the Los Alamos Labs had a working prototype nuclear powered thermolbore drill that could literally melt tunnels through the earth at a rate of 8 mph 40 years ago, you can imagine how extensive these underground systems have become. These sub-cities also offer close access to organised criminal syndicates, which operate on the surface. They have developed a whole science of 'borg-onomics' through which they literally nickel-and-dime us into slavery via multi-levelled taxation, inflation, sublimation, manipulation, regulation, fines, fees, licenses ... and the entire debt-credit scam which is run by the Federal Reserve and Wall Street.

New York City, I can confirm, is one of the largest draconian nests in the world. Or rather the ancient underground 'Atlantean' systems that network beneath that area. They literally control the entire Wall Street pyramid from below ... with more than a little help from reptilian bloodlines like the Rockefellers, etc. In fact, these reptilian genetic lines operate in a parasitic manner, the underground society acting as the 'parasite' society and the surface society operating as the 'host' society ...

The 'extraterrestrials' aren't coming – they're *here*. People look to the skies for the 'aliens', when they are also under our feet. The whole hierarchical pyramid is based on parasites of various kinds feeding off the sweat and efforts of others. The Reptilians and their hybrids parasite off humanity and a lot of humans parasite off each other, as I well know. Then there are parasites that feed off the human body. It happens at levels of reality.

The Ancients Knew

The theme of non-human races living under the ground, some of them reptilian, is another common one in ancient accounts and legends. We have the stories of Agharta and Shamballa, and the Mesopotamian accounts about Gilgamesh, the 'demi-god' and 'semi-divine' version of 'Noah', who sought the immortality of the 'gods'. Sumerian accounts tell of KI-GAL, 'the Great Below', ruled by the goddess Ereshkigal and the god Mergal. Many gods and goddesses are associated with 'the underworld', including the Norse Goddess, Hel (which I have also seen written as 'Helle' and 'El'). She was the queen goddess of the underworld and from her we get the word 'Hell', associated with stoking the fires 'down below'. Sumerian clay tablets describe KI-GAL as a place where violent guardians called 'scorpion men' reanimated human bodies, spirits and the 'undead'. They also tell of robotic beings known as 'Galatur' or 'Gala', which were used to abduct humans from the surface (the 'Greys'?), and 'eagle-headed' Reptilians, many of which were said to have wings. This is another reason for using the eagle symbol for the Reptilians. The accounts describe a 'king of the demons of the wind' called 'Pazuzu', a dog-faced 'human' with reptilian scales and a tail. There are versions of an underground 'Hell' in every ancient culture. The Chinese 'Hell' was said to be entered from Taishan Mountain in central Shandong Province and was guarded by demons called 'Men Shen' with animal-like faces or masks. The 'Lords of Hell' interacted with the 'Dragon Kings' on the surface. The Japanese 'Hell', or underground network, was described in similar terms, and was peopled by various non-human entities, including the 'Kappa', semi-aquatic reptilian humanoids and shapeshifters who lived in mountains, under the ground or under the sea.

Folklore names like 'trolls', 'etins', 'fairies', 'elves', 'troglodytes', 'Nefilim', 'Brownies' and the 'little people' of Ireland (some of the 'Greys' are very small) are all different names for the subterranean entities described in the modern accounts of former workers at underground bases and by those who claim to have been 'abducted by aliens'. What the folk tales say about them is the same as the modern reports about 'extraterrestrials' and 'UFOs'. This includes interbreeding with humans and not being able to go out into sunlight – like Dracula. This is understandable if they spend their lives living underground. People who have been abducted by 'aliens' have experienced 'missing time', and the same was said by those who met the underground beings in the folk tales. This puts into another perspective the countless stories told today by people claiming to have been abducted by non-human entities, many described in reptilian terms, that forced them to have sex, took their eggs or sperm, or impregnated them. The babies that resulted often disappear in early pregnancy with no medical explanation. Credo Mutwa told me how common this is in Africa, but it happens around the world. There are many 'abduction' experiences that are simply invented or have other, more earthly, explanations; but to dismiss them all, given their number and often consistency of detail, would be just as ridiculous as believing every word of every one. Abductees report experiences with a variety of non-human entities, such as tall blonde 'people', the classic 'Greys', reptilian types, and crossbreeds. The Reptilians are described as very tall – seven feet and more – with scaly, green-brown and sometimes almost albino-white skin, with webbed, clawed 'hands', and golden eyes with split pupils. Some are reported to have tails and there are clearly many different types, as with humans. These entities are said to have the ability to control the minds of their victims while various procedures, often painful and distressing, are performed on them. Most human abductions are not physical, as they appear to be to the victim. Their body-energy field or human awareness – the 'lower mind' – is taken, and this is why abductees have talked about being removed from their homes by passing through the walls. This energetic awareness, or 'lower mind', is not vibrating to the same frequency as the wall and so it can pass through in the same way that radio frequencies pass through walls to your transistor. There are physical abductions, but mind abduction is the primary method and it gives them access to human frequency codes and allows them to program the reality of the abductee. When the awareness returns to the body it appears in their memory as a physical experience, when it wasn't.

The underground people of folklore were also said to kill and mutilate cattle to remove their blood and this is happening today with no credible explanations offered by the authorities. Cattle, horses and sheep are surgically mutilated, their reproductive and other organs removed and blood drained often without any sign of bleeding. The wounds seem to be cauterised by an intense heat. What little blood is left can have strange colours and may takes days to coagulate. Even where an animal is found in soft mud there is no sign of tracks leading to and from the spot. Some have even been dumped in treetops. This is done for the bizarre Reptilian-Grey genetic experiments and to provide them with mammalian blood. It is clear from folk stories that cattle mutilation is not the modern phenomenon that it appears to be. The Norse/Germanic fairies, goblins, knockers, leprechauns, sidhe, tylwyth teg (terlooeth teig) and others were either malevolent or indifferent to humanity. They lived under the ground and in mounds, hills, ruins, hill-forts, mountains and cliffs, and ancient cities were said to be the 'rooftops' of their palaces. European folklore often claimed that these 'fairy' people entered their underground homes through lakes, which is what ancient Indian accounts say about the reptilian Nagas. Michael Mott produced an excellent book about the underground people of folklore called *Caverns, Cauldrons, and Concealed Creatures*. He writes:

> ... To remove all doubt as to their relationship with Norse hidden-folk and Indian Nagas alike, they shunned the sunlight and often seemed interested in crossbreeding their own bloodlines with those of human beings, or even in crossbreeding their 'livestock' or fairy cattle, horses, hounds and so forth with the surface species which were most compatible. The goblin-dwarf, Rumpelstiltskin, in his lust to have the human baby and its genetic bounty, is just one example of this in folklore. The elves took a regular interest in human affairs – weddings, births and deaths, the success of crops and livestock, and so forth – but only for their own selfish interests. They seemed to be overly-concerned with genetic and biological diversity, and they pilfered livestock, crops and human genes via theft or cross-species liaison whenever they saw fit to do so ...

> ... They are mostly reptilian or reptilian humanoids or 'fair' and Nordic; they are telepathic with superior mental powers; they can shapeshift and create illusions; they want to interbreed with humans and need human blood, flesh and reproductive materials; they have advanced technology; they have the secret of immortality; they can fly, either by themselves or with their technology; they mostly have a malevolent agenda for humans; they cannot survive for long in direct sunlight; they have been banished from the surface world or are in hiding from surface people and/or the Sun; they want to keep their treasures, knowledge and true identity a secret; they covertly manipulate events on the surface world; they have surface humans working for them through the priesthoods, cults and secret societies; they have a putrid smell like 'sulphur and brimstone' ...

The bodies of the Reptilians and Greys contain a lot of sulphur and it is no surprise that abductees often talk of experiencing a powerful smell of sulphur from their captors (it smells like rotten eggs). Zulu Shaman, Credo Mutwa, tells of his abduction by the 'Greys' in the DVD interview series I did with him called *The Reptilian Agenda*. He said of the Grey that took him: 'The creature smelled like nobody's business. It had a strange smell, a throat-tightening, chemical smell, which smelled like rotten eggs, and also like hot copper, a very strong smell.' Michael Mott's research confirmed the reptilian domination of folk tales about the underworld:

> The reptilian aspect of some underworlders permeates folklore. One universal theme that recurs in the folktales of many, many cultures is that of the snake-husband or snake-wife, who can transform into a 'human' or humanoid form and is invariably of royal blood among his or her own kind (talk about the ultimate pick-up line!). Often

the snake or serpent-man exacts a promise of marriage, or the hand of an unborn human child in betrothal, consistent with the theme of the subterraneans' interest in maintaining their own genetic diversity.

A variant of this should be familiar to most readers of fairy tales, in the form of 'The Frog Prince'. The frog-prince is a Handsome Prince, but like the Japanese seducing dragon, he has a reptilian or amphibian form. The underworld link is complete, for frequently the frog lives in a deep well, from which he is discovered or rescued by the female protagonist. A possible connection is evident in the Scandinavian belief that some dwarves would 'turn into toads', if caught by the Sun, much like Mimoto's lover turned from a man into a 'dragon' when the same thing happened. Slovenia has its legends of fairies and 'little people', but Slovenian fairy tales are also permeated by the presence of the 'Snake Queen', a great, white, cave-dwelling creature who is part woman and part serpent. The serpentine-yet-human Nagas are still believed by devout Hindus and some Buddhists to dwell beneath India, Nepal and Tibet.

The Shapeshifters

The underground entities of folklore were said be able to shapeshift and this is a major theme of the stories told to me around the world by those who have had contact with the Reptilians. People from all walks of life in many different cultures have described how they have seen someone morph, or shapeshift, from a human form into a non-human entity, mostly reptilian in appearance. These experiences, usually brief before the human form returns, are also recorded in ancient legends and myths. Credo Mutwa talks of the shapeshifting abilities of the Reptilian bloodlines, and in India the reptilian Nagas were said to take human or reptilian form at will. The serpent 'sea' or 'fish' gods of Sumer and Babylon, like Oannes/Dagon/Nimrod, were said to be able to change shape and look human whenever they chose. These shapeshifters were referred to in ancient texts as 'changelings'. The Reptilian-hybrids have dual DNA coding and while the human codes are open you see a human body; but when the reptilian codes open there is an energy shift and the reptilian form appears. To the observer, there has been a 'shapeshift'. Their base state is reptilian and they constantly drink human and animal (mammalian) blood because its coding and vibrational nature helps to keep their human DNA codes open. Without the blood we would see what they really were – reptilian. If your reaction to all this is that it's impossible for a solid body to change into another solid body then I agree with you; but that is not what is happening with shapeshifting, as I will explain when I get to the nature of reality. For now, I will just say that what we think of as a solid 'world' is not solid at all. It just appears to be so because that is the way the brain is programmed to decode reality. This 'world' is only a frequency range that our five senses can decode, in the same way that a radio or television can only 'see', or connect with, the radio station or television channel they have been tuned to.

Reptilian-hybrids can sometimes shift from human to reptilian form spontaneously and without intent. This can happen especially at times of high-emotion, such as anger, which can affect their vibrational state and shift the DNA codes. It is also the case that they can project an energy field, like the cloaks of invisibility developed by the US military and intelligence network, that stops the brain 'seeing' what lies behind it – in this case a Reptilian entity. What's more, they can project something else that you *do* see – a human form. How this is done is very simple if you know what you're doing, and in the next few chapters that will become clear. The theme of shapeshifting can be found in all ancient cultures, and the King Arthur stories include descriptions of shapeshifting and the use of energy-field projections and holograms to hide a being's true form. The hologram is crucial to understanding this 'solid' reality, as I will be explaining.

Hiding in the Shadows

The Reptilian connection and all I have outlined here had become firmly established in my research when I came across something called the *Emerald Tablets*. These are said to have been found beneath a Mayan temple in Mexico. They describe the Reptilians, their ability to shapeshift, and how they possess the bodies of people in power. The accounts correlate remarkably with modern experience and reports, and with my own research before I had even heard of them. They are known in full as the *Emerald Tablets of Thoth*, who was a deity of the Egyptians. It is claimed that they date back 36,000 years and were written by Thoth, an 'Atlantean priest-king' who, it is said, founded a colony in Egypt. His tablets, the story goes, were taken to South America by Egyptian 'pyramid priests' and eventually placed under a Mayan temple to the sun god in the Yucatan, Mexico. The translator of these tablets, Maurice Doreal, claims to have recovered them and completed the translations in 1925, but only much later (he says) was he given 'permission' for part of them to be published. You can read the whole translation and interpretation of the tablets on this website: **crystalinks.com/ emerald.html**. I don't have to accept all the details of that story to appreciate the synchronicity between what these 'tablets' say and what I have uncovered from endless other sources. They tell of the 'children of the shadows' manipulating this reality. The translations have 'Thoth' saying this:

Speak I of ancient Atlantis, speak of the days of the Kingdom of Shadows, speak of the coming of the children of shadows. Out of the great deep were they called by the wisdom of earth-man, called for the purpose of gaining great power.

Far in the past before Atlantis existed, men there were who delved into darkness, using dark magic, calling up beings from the great deep below us. Forth came they into this cycle, formless were they, of another vibration, existing unseen by the children of earth-men. Only through blood could they form being, only through man could they live in the world.

In ages past were they conquered by the Masters, driven below to the place whence they came. But some there were who remained, hidden in spaces and planes unknown to man. Live they in Atlantis as shadows, but at times they appeared among men. Aye, when the blood was offered, forth came they to dwell among men.

In the form of man moved they amongst us, but only to sight, were they as are men. Serpent-headed when the glamour was lifted, but appearing to man as men among men. Crept they into the councils, taking form that were like unto men. Slaying by their arts the chiefs of the kingdoms, taking their form and ruling o'er man. Only by magic could they be discovered, only by sound could their faces be seen. Sought they from the kingdom of shadows, to destroy man and rule in his place.

But, know ye, the Masters were mighty in magic, able to lift the veil from the face of the serpent, able to send him back to his place. Came they to man and taught him the secret, the Word that only a man can pronounce; swift then they lifted the veil from the serpent and cast him forth from place among men.

Yet, beware, the serpent still liveth in a place that is open, at times, to the world. Unseen they walk among thee in places where the rites have been said; again as time passes onward, shall they take the semblance of men.

Called, may they be, by the master who knows the white or the black, but only the white master may control and bind them while in the flesh.

Seek not the kingdom of shadows, for evil will surely appear, for only the master of brightness shall conquer the shadow of fear.

Know ye, O my brother, that fear is an obstacle great; be master of all in the brightness, the shadow will soon disappear. Hear ye, and heed my wisdom, the voice of LIGHT is clear, seek the valley of shadow and light only will appear.'

Whatever the origins of this information, it tells the story of the Reptilian manipulation and of how it is done. The kings and queens of history and today's leading politicians, banking and business leaders, major media owners and heads of the military are the 'serpent-headed beings' hidden behind human form (or their puppets and stooges). These are the Reptilian-hybrids, the Illuminati bloodlines, and they have duped humanity by appearing to be human and coming from diverse backgrounds. They are not and do not; they are the same Reptilian tribe. Interestingly, the *Emerald Tablets* say that 'in ages past were they conquered by the Masters, driven below to the place whence they came'. This is so similar to the biblical passage in the *Book of Revelation* where the 'Devil' is described in reptilian terms:

And the great dragon was cast down, the old serpent, he that is called the Devil and Satan, the deceiver of the whole world; he was cast down to Earth and his angels were cast down with him.

... And he laid hold on the dragon, the old serpent, which is the Devil and Satan, and bound him for a thousand years, and cast him into the abyss, and shut it, and sealed it over him, that he should deceive the nations no more.

The term 'Satan' comes, as I mentioned, from a Sumerian 'god', Satam, Sandan, Santana, who was represented with a trident, or pitchfork, and these now universal deities known as 'Satan', the 'Devil' and 'Lucifer' are all names for the Reptilian gods, either a specific entity or collectively. *The Emerald Tablets* also identify the reason why Satanism and the Reptilian-hybrids are so connected:

Forth came they into this cycle, formless were they, of another vibration, existing unseen by the children of earth-men ... Only through blood could they form being, only through man could they live in the world.

This is describing how the Reptilians operate in another frequency range outside the limits of human sight, and to manipulate this world they must have a 'body' through which to do it – 'only through man could they live in this world'. The point about 'only through blood could they form into being' explains why the Reptilian-hybrids, the Illuminati leadership, are obsessed with blood drinking and human-sacrifice rituals, just as the Reptilians have been since they came aeons ago in our perception of 'time'. It is human blood – a powerful infusion, or transfusion, of the human frequency/vibration – that allows them to hold human form when their genetics are so reptilian. This will make more sense when I address the question: what is reality? Once you realise the Reptilian connection to governments, banks, corporations and world events you begin to see the mass of reptilian symbolism all around us in advertisements, children's books and animated films, movies and dragon/serpent imagery in countless forms. Rarely has it been so in-your-face than in an advertisement for a media system called 'Hulu' which was broadcast during the 2009 US Super Bowl to an audience of some 150 million. The theme was of a reptilian 'alien' race taking over the planet by controlling the minds of the population. This is a transcript:

Hello earth. I'm Alec Baldwin, TV star. You know they say TV will rot your brain? That's absurd. TV only softens the brain like a ripe banana. To take it all the way, we've created Hulu. Hulu beams TV directly to your portable computing devices, giving you more of the cerebral, gelatinizing shows you want anytime, anywhere – for free.

Mmm. Mushy, mush. And the best part is there is nothing you can do to stop it. I mean what you going to do? Turn off your TV and your computer? Once your brain is reduced to a cottage cheese-like mush, we'll scoop them out with a melon-baller and gobble them right on up. Oooops, I think I'm drooling a little. Because we're aliens, and that's how we roll.

Hulu – an evil plot to destroy the world. Enjoy.

As Baldwin delivers the line 'because we're aliens, and that's how we roll', reptilian imagery appears from under his jacket. Do a search for 'Hulu Super Bowl commercial' on YouTube and you can watch it for yourself. When I first went public on the Reptilians and their hybrids, the subject was virtually non-existent on the Internet and I was met, as usual, with incredulity and ridicule. Today, if you search with combinations of words like 'Reptilian ET', 'Reptilian aliens' or just 'Reptilians', tens of thousands of pages appear. The Reptilian influence on human life is real and the time is coming when even the most sceptical will have to chip away the cerebral concrete and look at this in a new light. Indeed, it is already happening.

14

Spaceship Moon

I don't know if there are men on the moon, but if there are they must be using the earth as their lunatic asylum
George Bernard Shaw

There is another crucial aspect to this question of: 'so where are they?' The answer will open me to yet more ridicule (er, and?), but for others, what I am about to say will make perfect sense of the evidence and connections I have been presenting over the years.

I was sitting at the computer writing this book when I had the overwhelming feeling out of 'nowhere' that the Moon was not 'real'. By 'real', I mean not a 'heavenly body', but an artificial construct (or a hollowed-out planetoid) that has been put there to control life on Earth – which it does (Fig 154). I have pondered on this possibility a few times over the years, but this time I just 'knew'. It was like an enormous penny had suddenly dropped. When I started this journey consciously in 1990, I would look at information and evidence and come to conclusions with my mind. But for many years now, it has been the other way round. I feel a powerful intuitive 'knowing' about something and the 'five-sense' information then follows quickly afterwards. So it was with the Moon. When the very powerful intuition hit me, I went on the Internet to see if there was anything about the Moon being artificial. Within a couple of minutes, I found a book called *Who Built the Moon?* by Christopher Knight and Alan Butler. Knight and Butler also worked together on another book, *Civilization One*; and Knight was the author of *The Hiram Key*, an investigation into the origins of Freemasonry. Their book about the Moon arrived in a few days, and I read it immediately. Other information about the Moon was coming to me by that time and a familiar pattern was emerging. First a new subject comes into my life and then information about it comes from all angles. *Who Built the Moon?* details many extraordinary mathematical and other connections between the Moon, Earth and the Sun. The key to these

Figure 154: *The Moon is not a natural 'heavenly body' – it is an artificial construct, a gigantic spacecraft*

alignments and connections is the size, position and movement of the Moon. It is well beyond miraculous 'chance' that the Moon is what it is and where it is. Moon anomalies are so many and so various that Irwin Shapiro, from the Harvard-Smithsonian Center for Astrophysics, said: 'The best explanation for the Moon is observational error – the Moon doesn't exist.' Knight and Butler write:

> The Moon is bigger than it should be, apparently older than it should be and much lighter in mass than it should be. It occupies an unlikely orbit and is so extraordinary that all existing explanations for its presence are fraught with difficulties and none of them could be considered remotely watertight.

Isaac Asimov, a Russian professor of biochemistry and writer of popular science books, said that the Moon, which has no atmosphere and no magnetic field, is basically a freak of nature in that Earth is the only planet in the solar system orbited by a satellite so enormous in relation to the world it circles. It is bigger than the planet Pluto. Some scientists have even called it a twin-planet system, rather than a planet and a satellite. Asimov said that by all cosmic laws, the Moon should not be orbiting Earth. He went on:

> … we cannot help but come to the conclusion that the Moon by rights ought not to be there. The fact that it is, is one of those strokes of luck almost too good to accept … Small planets, such as Earth, with weak gravitational fields, might well lack satellites …

> … In general, then, when a planet does have satellites, those satellites are much smaller than the planet itself. Therefore, even if the Earth has a satellite, there would be every reason to suspect … that at best it would be a tiny world, perhaps 30 miles in diameter. But that is not so. Earth not only has a satellite, but it is a giant satellite, 2,160 miles in diameter. How is it then, that tiny Earth has one? Amazing.

There are so many anomalies with the Moon. It has no magnetic field, and yet moon rocks are magnetised. It has the phenomenon known as 'mascons' (mass concentrations), which are large circular areas of unusually high density and a higher gravitational 'pull'. Don Wilson, author of *Our Mysterious Spaceship Moon*, says it appears that mascons could be some kind of artificial construction. They are found in the vast plains on the Moon known as 'maria' that were once believed to be seas. About a third of the Moon facing the Earth is made up of these maria while there are few on the 'dark side', and no-one can explain why the two sides are so different. The Moon produces precisely the same seismic vibrational effects every time it moves closer to the Earth. How can this be if it is a natural phenomenon that would be bound to change over time? *New York Times* writer, Walter Sullivan, said it was 'as though the ups and downs of the stockmarket repeated themselves precisely for each period of fluctuation'. The oldest rocks collected from the Moon are far older than any found on Earth. Some moon rocks are said to date back 4.5 billion years and that makes them a billion years older than any found on this planet. Harvard's astronomy journal, *Sky and Telescope*, reported that the 1973 Lunar Conference was told how one moon rock was dated at 5.3 billion years old. This would make it nearly a billion years older than the predicted age of Earth. The rocks were also discovered to have a different composition to the lunar dust in which they were found, and the dust has apparently been estimated to be a billion years older than the rocks. Huh?

Science has no idea where the Moon came from and how it was formed, and none of its theories stand up to scrutiny. One theory was that it was captured by the Earth's magnetic field, but the science of that doesn't add up. Another is that a body the size of Mars smashed into the Earth and a great chunk of the Earth broke off to form the Moon. This is known as the 'Big Whack' theory, but when the science of that didn't stand up, either, someone postured the 'Double Big Whack' theory. This is that the 'Mars' planet smacked into the Earth and then came back for another go. Talk about desperate. The truth is that they have no idea where the Moon came from or how it came to be where it is. Earl Ubell, a former science editor with CBS, asked:

> If the Earth and Moon were created at the same time, near each other, why has one got all the iron and the other [the Moon] not much? The differences suggest that Earth and Moon came into being far from each other, an idea that stumbles over the inability of astrophysicists to explain how exactly the Moon became a satellite of Earth.

Extraordinary 'Coincidences'

Christopher Knight and Alan Butler reveal in *Who Built the Moon?* many remarkable mathematical connections with regard to the Moon, Earth and the Sun using the base number of ten. These mathematical synchronicities only work with these three bodies and not with any of the other planets or moons in the solar system. The Moon is 400 times smaller than the Sun, and at a solar eclipse it is 400 times closer to Earth. This makes the Moon appear from Earth to be the same size as the Sun – hence a total eclipse (Fig 155). The Moon has astonishing synchronicity with the Sun. When the Sun is at its lowest and weakest in mid-winter, the Moon is at its highest and brightest, and the reverse occurs in mid-summer. Both set at the same point on the horizon at the equinoxes and at the opposite point at the solstices. What are the chances that the Moon would naturally find an orbit so perfect that it would cover the Sun at an eclipse and appear from Earth to be the same size? What are chances that the alignments would be so perfect at the equinoxes and solstices? The Moon always shows the same side or 'face' to the Earth during the period when we can see it. We never see what is called the 'dark' or far side of the Moon from the Earth. This is due to the synchronicity of the Moon's rotation. It rotates on its axis in about the same time it takes to orbit the Earth, and this means that the same 'face' is turned towards Earth at all times. The Moon's rotation is extremely slow compared with Earth's, and in the time it takes for the Moon to complete just one turn, Earth will rotate more than 27 times.

Earth rotates at a speed 400 times faster than the Moon, and turns 40,000

Figure 155: *The Moon is so perfectly positioned that at a solar eclipse it looks, from Earth, the same size as the Sun*

Figure 156: *Christopher Knight and Alan Butler say great megalithic structures like Stonehenge are encoded with the same unit of measure as the Earth, Sun and Moon*

kilometres on its axis in a day to the Moon's 400. Earth spins 366.259 times during one orbit of the Sun, and the polar circumference of the Earth is 366.175 times bigger than that of the Moon. The polar circumference of the Moon is 27.31 per cent the size of the earth and the Moon makes 27.396 turns per orbit of the Earth. Knight and Butler say that if you multiply the circumference of the Moon by that of the Earth, the result is 436,669,140 kilometres. If this number is divided by 100 it becomes 436,669 kilometres – the circumference of the Sun correct to 99.9 per cent. If you divide the circumference of the Sun by that of the Moon and multiply by 100 you get the circumference of the Earth. Divide the size of the Sun by the size of the Earth and multiply by 100 and you get the size of the Moon. The writers correctly conclude that the number-play involved with the Earth-Moon-Sun system is 'nothing less than staggering', and the Moon appears to have been inserted into the Sun-Earth relationship 'with the accuracy of the proverbial Swiss watchmaker'. Knight and Butler also say that the Moon, Earth and the Sun are encoded with the unit of measurement known as the 'megalithic yard'. This was discovered by Professor Alexander Thom, a Scottish engineer, when he made a detailed study of stone circles, such as Stonehenge, and other megalithic structures in Britain and France. He found that they all used a standard measurement equal to 0.829 metres (or 2.72 feet) and he called this the 'megalithic yard' (Fig 156). Knight and Butler say that the circumferences of the Moon, Earth and the Sun all conform to the megalithic yard. They write:

> This all seemed very odd. The Megalithic structures that were built across Western Europe were frequently used to observe the movements of the Sun and the Moon, but how could the unit of measure upon which these structures were based be so beautifully integer to the circumference of these bodies as well as the Earth?

I would say that it is because the Reptilians who control the Moon were also involved in the building of the Megalithic structures. Knight and Butler say that megalithic-yard mathematics can be found in other units of measurement such as the pound and the pint. The ancients worked with a circle based on 366 degrees to match the number of Earth rotations in an orbit of the Sun, a number dictated by the position and influence of the Moon on Earth's speed of spin. The Sumerians changed the mathematics when they introduced the 360-degree circle and the units of 60 minutes and 60 seconds.

Hollow Moon

There are countless indications that the Moon is hollow, and it is acknowledged that the core is far less dense than the outer layers. Some scientists say it may even have no core at all. NASA scientist, Dr Gordon MacDonald, said in the early 1960s that 'it would seem that the Moon is more like a hollow than a homogeneous sphere'. He surmised that the data must have been wrong – but it wasn't. MacDonald was right the first time. Dr Sean C Solomon of the Massachusetts Institute of Technology said the Lunar Orbiter experiments had vastly improved knowledge of the Moon's gravitational field and indicated the 'frightening possibility that the Moon might be hollow'. Cosmologist, Carl Sagan, made the point that 'a natural satellite cannot be a hollow object'. The Moon has only 60 per cent of the density of Earth, and an equal amount of Earth material would appear to weigh almost twice as much as that of the Moon. This has led some scientists to believe that the Moon either does not have an iron core and/or that it is partially hollow. A team at the University of Arizona said they believed that the Moon does have a core, but that it is tiny. Lon Hood, the team leader, said: 'We knew that the Moon's core was small, but we didn't know it was this small … This really does add weight to the idea that the Moon's origin is unique, unlike any other terrestrial body – Earth, Venus, Mars or Mercury.' Yeah, it's artificial.

The Apollo 12 mission to the Moon in November 1969 set up seismometers and then intentionally crashed the Lunar Module causing an impact equivalent to one ton of TNT. The shockwaves built up for eight minutes, and NASA scientists said the Moon 'rang like a bell'. Maurice Ewing, a co-director of the seismic experiment, told a news conference that he had no idea why this had happened: 'As for the meaning of it, I'd rather not make an interpretation right now, but it is as though someone had struck a bell, say, in the belfry of a church a single blow and found that the reverberation from it continued for 30 minutes.' Dr Frank Press from the Massachusetts Institute of Technology said that for a 'rather small impact' to produce an effect that lasted for 30 minutes was 'quite beyond the range of our experience'. The Apollo 13 mission to the Moon in 1970 was aborted due to potentially catastrophic technical problems, and the Saturn V launch vehicle, weighing 15 tonnes, was crashed into the Moon about 100 miles from where the previous mission had left the seismometer. When the launch vehicle made impact with the equivalent of eleven tonnes of TNT, NASA scientists said the Moon 'reacted like a gong' and continued to vibrate for three hours and twenty minutes to a depth of up to 25 miles. Ken Johnson was a supervisor of the Data and Photo Control department during the Apollo missions, working for a company contracted to NASA. He told *Who Built the Moon?* author, Alan Butler, that the Moon not only rang like a bell, but the whole Moon 'wobbled' in such a precise way that it was 'almost as though it had gigantic hydraulic damper struts inside it'. All of which would explain why the Moon vibrates in exactly the same way every time it moves closer to Earth. The Moon was hit by a meteor with the power of 200 tonnes of TNT in 1972. This unleashed enormous shockwaves deep into the interior, but *none came back*.

The outer surface of the Moon is extremely hard and contains minerals like titanium. Moon rocks have been found to contain processed metals, including brass and mica, and the elements uranium 236 and neptunium 237 that have never been found to occur naturally. Uranium 236 is a long-lived radioactive nuclear waste and is found in spent nuclear fuel and reprocessed uranium. Neptunium 237 is a radioactive metallic element and a by-product of nuclear reactors and the production of plutonium. How the heck did this stuff get into Moon rocks? They also found iron particles that don't rust, and again, this does not happen naturally.

The Moon is a Spacecraft

Two members of the Soviet Academy of Sciences wrote an article in 1970 in the Soviet *Sputnik* magazine called 'Is the Moon the Creation of Alien Intelligence?'. I would answer that question with a resounding 'Yes'. Mikhail Vasin and Alexander Shcherbakov suggested that the Moon was a planetoid that had been hollowed out using huge machines by unknown beings with highly advanced technology. If this technology was nuclear in nature it would explain the presence of the uranium 236 and neptunium 237. Vasin and Shcherbakov said the machines would have melted rock to form cavities within the Moon and the lava would have poured out onto the surface to produce a lunar landscape made from metallic rocky slag. They said that for whatever reason the Moon was eventually placed in orbit around the Earth. This is part of what they wrote in *Sputnik* magazine:

> If you are going to launch an artificial sputnik, then it is advisable to make it hollow. At the same time it would be naïve to imagine that anyone capable of such a tremendous space project would be satisfied simply with some kind of giant empty trunk hurled into near-Earth trajectory.

> It is more likely that what we have here is a very ancient spaceship, the interior of which was filled with fuel for the engines, materials and appliances for repair work, navigation instruments, observation equipment and all manner of machinery … in other words, everything necessary to enable this 'caravelle of the Universe' to serve as a Noah's Ark of intelligence, perhaps even as the home of a whole civilisation envisaging a prolonged (thousands of millions of years) existence and long wanderings through space (thousands of millions of miles).

> Naturally, the hull of such a spaceship must be super-tough in order to stand up to the blows of meteorites and sharp fluctuations between extreme heat and extreme cold. Probably the shell is a double-layered affair – the basis a dark armouring of about 20 miles in thickness, and outside it some kind of more loosely-packed covering (a thinner layer – averaging about three miles). In certain areas – where the lunar 'seas' and 'craters' are, the upper layer is quite thin, in some cases, non-existent.

The facts support this thesis and explain the long list of anomolies. Dr D L Anderson, a professor of geophysics and director of the seismological laboratory at the California Institute of Technology, said 'the Moon is made inside out' and that its inner and outer compositions should be the other way round. Vasin and Shcherbakov said that material inside the Moon was brought to the surface to make the outer shell. The thinner outer layer, averaging about two and a half to three miles, but sometimes going deeper, would explain why moon craters are nothing like as deep as they should be given the width of the impact (Fig 157). They are uniformly shallow. Foreign bodies like meteorites are prevented from going deeper when they hit the 'dark armouring of about 20 miles in thickness'. Vasin and Shcherbakov said that when a meteorite strikes the Moon the outer layer plays the role of a buffer before the foreign body strikes the impenetrable 20-mile armour plating, which is only slightly dented. 'Bearing in mind that the Moon's defence coating is, according our calculations, 2.5 miles thick, one sees that this is approximately the maximum depth of the craters.' They pointed out that surface lunar rocks have been found to contain titanium, chromium and zirconium, which are all metals 'with refractory, mechanically-strong and anti-corrosive properties'. 'Refractory' metals are extraordinarily resistant to heat and to wear, and the scientists said that the combination found on the surface of the Moon would have 'enviable resistance to heat and the ability to stand up to means of aggression'. Vasin and Shcherbakov continue:

Figure 157: *Moon craters are uniformly shallow compared with their width*

> If a material had to be devised to protect a giant artificial satellite from the unfavourable effects of temperature, from cosmic radiation and meteorite bombardment, the experts would probably have hit upon precisely these metals. In that case is it not clear why lunar rock is such an extraordinarily poor heat conductor – a factor which so amazed the astronauts? Wasn't that what the designers of this super-sputnik of the Earth were after? From the engineers' point of view, this spaceship of ages long past which we call the Moon is superbly constructed.

Some lunar rocks have been found to contain ten times more titanium than titanium-rich rocks on Earth. Titanium is used in supersonic jets, deep-diving submarines and spacecraft. Dr Harold Urey, a winner of the Nobel Prize for Chemistry, said he was 'terribly puzzled by the rocks from the Moon and in particular their titanium content'. He said the samples were 'mind-blowers' and that he could not account for the titanium. Dr S Ross Taylor, the geochemist in charge of lunar chemical analysis, said the problem was that maria plains the size of Texas had to be covered with melted rock containing fluid titanium. He said you would not expect titanium ever to be hot enough to do that, even on Earth, and no one had ever suggested that the Moon was hotter than Earth. What could distribute titanium in this way? Highly advanced technology developed and operated by entities that are immensely more technologically advanced than humans.

Vasin and Shcherbakov say that the strange variations in gravitation fields called 'mascons' in the flat maria plains can be explained from this perspective. The maria are areas from which the protective coating was torn from the armour cladding, and to make good the damage 'the installation producing the repair substance would have had to be brought immediately beneath the site so that it could flood the area with its 'cement' – a lava-like material.' The resulting flat stretches are what look like seas to the terrestrial observer, the scientists say, and 'the stocks of materials and machinery for doing this are no doubt still where they were, and are sufficiently massive to give rise to these gravitational anomalies'. The enormously different ages of lunar rocks and lunar dust can be explained by the cosmic travels of the spaceship Moon in which it would have picked up material from many places and of many ages. The Moon has a large bulge on the 'dark side' that can only be satisfactorily explained by the immense strength of a spaceship hull preventing the Moon from breaking apart. Unexplained eruptions of water vapour have been detected over areas of the Moon of some 100 square miles, with some reports saying they are coming from beneath the surface. Farouk El Baz, who worked with NASA on the scientific exploration of the Moon, said: 'If water vapour is coming from the Moon's interior this is serious. It means that there is a drastic distinction between the different phases of the lunar interior – that the interior is quite different from what we have seen on the surface.' Vasin and Shcherbakov said there are gases within the Moon which creates an atmosphere that sustains life. If they escaped to the surface from time to time it would explain the vapour clouds that have bewildered scientists. Author and researcher Don Wilson lists some of the major lunar mysteries in his book, *Our Mysterious Spaceship Moon*, but they can be explained once we realise that the Moon is an artificially-constructed spacecraft. These 'mysteries' include:

1. Why the Moon is a freak world – too big and too far out to be a natural satellite of Earth.
2. Why the Moon has such shallow craters.
3. Why and how the Moon can sustain its bulge.
4. Why some moon rocks are older than Earth, and as old (at least) as the solar system.
5. Why the Moon seems 'inside out'.
6. The various mysteries of the maria and mascons.
7. How the Moon can be a dry-as-dust world and yet have occasional clouds of water vapour.
8. Why the Moon vibrates like a 'huge gong', transmitting tremors great distances around and through itself.
9. How the Moon can produce so many contradictions of data and findings.

I hadn't read any of this until I had that overwhelming feeling at my computer that the Moon was artificial and was being used to control life on this planet. It is the Reptilians' control system. The placement of the Moon dictates the speed of Earth's rotation and the angle at which it rotates – 22.5 degrees from vertical. This angle creates the four seasons because of the way planet faces the Sun during its annual orbit. The Moon has a major influence on the tides – far more than the Sun – and with the human body consisting of some 70 per cent water it is bound to have a fantastic influence on us, even on that level alone. The Moon also dictates so much of our relationship with time, and the term 'month' is really *Moonth*, a period based on the cycles of the Moon. The realisation that the Moon is a gigantic spacecraft is the strand that connects all the rest, not just in relation to Moon anomalies, but also to life on Earth and the conspiracy to enslave humanity. The fact is that the Reptilians in the Moon and in underground bases on Mars depend on humans and the Earth for food – their very survival. This is one key reason why they are desperate not to be exposed. Water and other resources are constantly being taken from this planet to the Moon and Mars and this is not a new phenomena, either. Ancient Zulu stories say the same.

Interestingly, the Sumerian accounts of the Anunnaki say that they came to Earth to mine gold and they genetically-engineered their human slave population to do this in Africa. In early 2010, the *Pakistan Daily*, an online news agency, ran a story that apparently no one in the mainstream media would touch. It alleged that vast amounts of gold bars all over the world had gone missing to be replaced by tungsten bars with a gold coating. Tungsten apparently has exactly the same density as gold, to three decimal places. The *Pakistan Daily* article said that during the Bill Clinton administration, in which financial policy was controlled by Robert E Rubin (Rothschild Zionist), Larry Summers (Rothschild Zionist) and Alan Greenspan (Rothschild Zionist), 'between 1.3 and 1.5 million 400 oz tungsten blanks were allegedly manufactured by a very high-end, sophisticated refiner in the USA' – more than 16 thousand metric tonnes. Subsequently, it said, 640,000 of these tungsten blanks received their gold plating and were shipped to the US 'gold' depository at Fort Knox where they remain to this day. The article reported that in October 2009 the Chinese received a shipment of gold bars in payment of debts and the government asked that special tests be performed to guarantee their purity and weight. Four small holes were drilled into the bars and the metal analysed. Officials were shocked to learn, the article claimed, that the 'gold' bars were fake. They were made of tungsten with only a outer coating of gold. The bars contained serial numbers for tracking purposes, the article went on, and they proved that the bars originated in the US and had been stored in Fort Knox for years. The shipment reportedly consisted of between 5,600 to 5,700 bars. The House of Rothschild has always been the dominant force in the global gold market and the price of gold was set every day at the offices of N M Rothschild in London from 1919 until 2004 when the Rothschilds suddenly announced that they were withdrawing from the gold market. Mmmm. More to know about all this, for sure. What if gold is essential to sustain activities in the Moon? If so, how much of the 'gold' in enormous vaults all over the world is really 'gold' anymore?

The 'Death Star'

The Moon is a 'modus operandi' of this Reptilian group. They construct these massive 'spheres' with the specific aim of traversing the Universe and hijacking planets in precisely the way they have with Earth. Russian astrophysicist, Dr Iosif Shklovsky, is reported to have said in 1959 that Phobos, a moon circling Mars, could be an artificial satellite set into orbit by an extraterrestrial civilisation (Fig 158). He made his calculations based on the strange orbit and the extremely low density of Phobos that indicated it may be hollow, although some have since said that he did not make a connection to extraterrestrials. Dr S Fred Singer, special advisor to President Eisenhower on space developments, certainly did say said this

Figure 158: *It has been suggested that Phobos, a moon of Mars, is an artificial construct built by an advanced extraterrestrial race*

about Phobos, and Raymond H Wilson Jr, Chief of Applied Mathematics at NASA, also agreed. Wilson said in 1963 that 'Phobos might be a colossal base orbiting Mars' and he added that NASA was considering the possibility. There are indications that the European Space Agency thinks the same after taking photographs at close range. The Reptilians can cause geological mayhem when they put their moons in orbit around a planet, or move it. This is what happened when the 'Golden Age' was ended by the geological catastrophe described in ancient accounts and clearly identified in the geological and biological record. The ancients consistently blamed the 'serpent gods' for what befell the Earth, but how could they have triggered such cataclysmic earth changes and upheavals? Now we know, at least in part, because so many other catatstrophes were happening when the Moon arrived. There was a war in the heavens, as described in ancient accounts, and the planet that once orbited between Mars and Jupiter was destroyed to become the asteroid belt of today. The solar system was torn asunder. The myths and legends talk about the 'Earth turning over' and that is what would have happened when the Moon drew close and if it was moved after it was put in place. As I've said, we have the seasons of the year today because of the way the Moon holds the Earth in a certain angle of rotation as it orbits the Sun. No wonder the ancients recorded how the serpent gods taught the people about 'the seasons'. Why would people on this planet not know about the seasons and their effects if they had lived here for generations experiencing spring, summer, autumn and winter? The *Star Wars* movies, produced by big-time insider, George Lucas, have featured the 'Death Star' of the Darth Vader mob and it is clearly based on the Moon (Fig 159). One movie shows the 'Death Star' (Moon) being constructed in space for the specific purpose of cosmic conquest. This is a description of the Death Star that I found at **starwars.com**:

> The Death Star was the code name of an unspeakably powerful and horrific weapon developed by the Empire. The immense space station carried a weapon capable of destroying entire planets. The Death Star was to be an instrument of terror, meant to cow treasonous worlds with the threat of annihilation ...

> ... The Death Star was a battle station the size of a small moon. It had a formidable array of turbolasers and tractor beam projectors, giving it the firepower of greater than half the Imperial starfleet. Within its cavernous interior were legions of Imperial troops and fightercraft, as well as all manner of detention blocks and interrogation cells.

> The technical schematics for the Death Star were developed by the cutting edge technologists of the Confederacy of Independent Systems during the Clone Wars. With the defeat of the Separatists and the Republic's transformation into Empire, the Death Star project fell under the command of Grand Moff Tarkin, one of the Empire's pre-eminent governors ...

Figure 159: *The Death Star of Darth Vader in Star Wars. It was an artificial construct – just like the Moon*

… In a brutal display of the Death Star's power, Grand Moff Tarkin targeted its prime weapon at the peaceful world of Alderaan. Leia Organa, an Imperial captive at the time, was forced to watch as the searing laser blast split apart her beloved world, turning the planet and its populace into orbital ash and debris …

… Over three years later, the threat of the Death Star returned, as the Alliance discovered a second, larger Death Star under construction over the remote forest moon of Endo …

It is interesting that the *Star Wars* story includes the Death Star moon using advanced technology to blow apart a planet when a destroyed planet is a recurring theme, both in ancient accounts and in the more recent research of people like Immanuel Velikovsky, and many others. The Death Star's interior in *Star Wars* was said to have 'two orientations'. Those areas closest to the surface were built 'with concentric decks with gravity oriented towards the Death Star's core' and the interior 'had stacked decks with gravity pointing toward the station's southern pole'. A huge equatorial trench 376 kilometres in length split the Death Star into two equal hemispheres, each divided into twelve 'zones'. There were also parks, shopping centres and recreation areas. The description continues:

… At the heart of the Death Star is a gigantic hypermatter reactor. Within this chamber burned a fusion reaction of prodigious proportions, fed by stellar fuel bottles lining its periphery …

… Facilitating the Death Star's realspace propulsion were a network of powerful ion engines that transformed reactor power into needed thrust. In order for the Death Star to be a viable threat, it needed to be mobile. Using linked banks of 123 hyperdrive field generators tied into a single navigational matrix, the Death Star could travel across the galaxy at superluminal velocities.

The incredible energies harnessed by the station combined with its great mass gave the Death Star magnetic and artificial gravitational fields equal to those found on orbital bodies many times greater in size.

I know that people will say it is just a movie series, but the themes of *Star Wars* and the Death Star, coming from the insider knowledge of George Lucas, are based on far more fact than is understood. The opening sequence to the movies talks about it all happening 'a long time ago, in a galaxy far, far away'. I say it is based on events much closer to home.

Ancient Confirmation

There are many legends around the world that describe the Moon as a 'chariot' of gods and goddesses. The Indian god, Chandra, was said to ride his chariot, the Moon, through the night sky pulled by ten white horses; and the Greek moon goddess, Selene, was portrayed riding a silver chariot led by white horses. The Romans knew her as Luna, Latin for the Moon. Remember from earlier how the the moon goddess was depicted as the virgin mother with twelve stars around her head and the 'serpent moon' at her feet. I called my great friend, Credo Mutwa, the walking library of ancient legends and accounts, and asked him what Zulu lore had to say about the Moon. I said nothing about what I was thinking and merely asked the question: what do Zulu shamans say about the Moon? He said that they believed the Moon to be hollow and the home of the Python, or 'Chitauri' – what I call the Reptilians. The legends say that the Moon was brought here 'hundreds of generations ago' by two brothers, Wowane and Mpanku, who were the leaders of the Reptilians. They were known as the 'Water Brothers' and had 'scaly skin like a fish'. This corresponds with the Sumerian and Mesopotamian accounts about the leaders of the Anunnaki, the brothers Enlil and Enki (Lord of the Earth). The latter was known as a water god under the name, 'Ea', and can be equated with Oannes and Dagon, the 'Fish of Heaven' in Mesopotamian accounts. Credo said the Zulu legends tell of how Wowane and Mpanku stole the Moon in the form of an egg from the 'Great Fire Dragon' and emptied out the yolk until it was hollow. They then 'rolled the Moon across the sky to the Earth' and caused cataclysmic events on this planet. The symbolism of the Moon and the egg can be seen throughout the ancient world. Legends say that the moon goddess, Semiramis, said that she came down from the Moon in a giant 'moon egg' that fell into the Euphrates River at the time of the first full moon after the spring equinox. Zulu myths say that the Reptilians come to the Earth when the Moon is at its brightest – the full moon, when satanic rituals abound all over the world and legends say that people become werewolves or vampires. A 'flying saucer' could be easily symbolised as a 'moon egg' and I have heard of UFOs being described as 'egg-shaped'. Zulu stories describe the same theme of the Reptilians arriving from the Moon in an egg and entering the water – thus Wowane and Mpanku are called the 'water brothers' and we have the symbolism of the 'fish gods'. Eggs, winged-discs, winged-gods, fiery chariots and so on, are all descriptions of flying-saucer craft and/or of the Moon itself (Fig 160). We can now see another reason why there is such a connection between the worship of the Moon, the Sun and the serpent, the combination of which is the foundation of all religion. The worship of the moon god, under names like 'Sin', 'El' and 'Allah', all makes sense now, as do the endless expressions of moon-goddess worship. They are all the worship of the Reptilian gods based in the Moon and they are feeding off the energy of the billions who worship them under different names, deities and symbols. It is the same with the sun deities which, as Credo confirmed, also originated, in part, with the Reptilians that were said to have 'eyes as bright as the Sun'.

Figure 160: *The ancient symbol of the reptiles and the 'flying disc' – the Moon*

Credo said that Earth was very different before the Moon came. There were no seasons and the planet was permanently surrounded by a canopy of water vapour. People did not feel the fierce glare of the Sun that we do today and they could only see it through a watery mist. 'The Earth was a beautiful place,' Credo said, 'a gentle place, lush and green, with a gentle drizzle and mist, and the fury of the Sun was not there.' The water canopy fell to the Earth as a deluge of rain when the Moon came. This was symbolised by the biblical rains for 40 days and 40 nights. Zulu legends say that the Reptilians manipulate the Earth from the Moon, where 'the Python lives', and people are warned never to upset the Moon. It is said that the Sun is forgiving, but never the Moon. Zulus and other native African accounts say the Moon was built 'far, far away' to control people and as a vehicle to travel the Universe. Credo says that the Reptilians' 'giant mothership' referred to in the Zulu legends was actually the Moon and that's where they went during the cataclysms of the 'Great Flood', which they had caused by manipulating the Moon and instigating other cosmic events. This was also where the 'Noah' figure was taken, with others who were chosen to survive and replenish a new genetically-modified species after the Earth began to recover. The 'Ark' was not a boat; it was a flying craft that took people to the Moon to sit out the catastrophe. I only shared my thoughts about the Moon with three close friends before this book was published and I asked one of them, Neil Hague, to ask Pierre Sabak if he had established any theme about the Moon in his word research. Sabak's reply: 'Archaically, the Moon is the receptacle or vessel that held the seed of man, prior to the destruction of Mars ...'

Credo said that the Reptilians came here – come here – from the Moon in the flying-saucer craft (depicted on the 'Necklace of the Mysteries'). There are other means of 'transport', however, like teleportation. If the secret underground bases on Earth are using this, clearly so are those who gave them the technology in the first place. 'The Moon is a magician,' Credo said. 'We call it "Nyanga", which means the shaman or healer.' Credo told me of 'high stories' in Zulu legend that the Reptilians were created by the Sun to cause havoc for Creation. 'The reptiles were given the authority to really mess things up in the Universe,' Credo said. Some African peoples refer to the Reptilians as 'Basinyai' – 'They who ruin things'. I couldn't have put it better. The arrival of the Reptilians and the Moon transformed everything on Earth. It changed the Earth's rotation and angle – 'the Earth turned over', as the ancient legends say – and brought the more powerful tidal systems that had once been much gentler. Women did not menstruate before the Moon arrived, the legends suggest, and I'll discuss this more later. Credo said that African shamans believe that the Moon stops the Earth from getting too fertile and that the Moon and Earth are involved a silent war – 'the Moon, out of jealousy, is a bad sister to the Earth'. Legends say that the Reptilians threatened to take away the Moon if humans didn't do what they were told. This, of course, would cause devastation on Earth.

Before the Moon

The Zulus and other African peoples are far from alone in believing the Moon has not always been here. There are many examples of folklore around the world that say there was a time 'before the Moon'. Ancient Greek authors, Aristotle and Plutarch, and Roman authors Apollonius Rhodius and Ovid, all mentioned a people called the Proselenes who laid claim to lands in Arcadia because their ancestors were there 'before there was a moon in the heavens'. Proselene translates as 'before Selene' – Selene is the Greek goddess of the Moon and the name is often applied to the Moon itself. The Roman writer, Censorinus, referred to a time aeons ago when there was no Moon, and Dr Hans Schindler Bellamy identifies the same theme in his work, *Moons, Myths and Men*. He highlights a native tribe in Colombia called the 'Mozces' who say they 'remember a time before the present Moon became the companion of the Earth'. Some

Babylonian depictions of the Moon in the eleventh century BC place it between Venus and the Sun. There are a people in Central Asia called the 'Yuezhi' which means 'Moon Clan' or 'Moon Race' and that brings me to another legend that Credo told me about ...

'Humans are from Orion'

Credo said Zulus believed that humans come from 'a world among the stars' which he calls 'Mpalalatsani' in the constellation of Orion. You might recall that Orion is depicted on the 'Necklace of the Mysteries'. Credo says that Mpalalatsani is a paradise world and, according to legend, it is 'a red place with red rocks, red earth, red sand and seas'. I asked him what it was called by western astronomy and he said he didn't know. He only knew it as Mpalalatsani, which means 'The Scatterer of Life'. There is, however, a 'supergiant' bright, reddish star or world in the Orion group called Betelgeuse, 640 light-years from Earth. If it replaced our Sun it would reach out as far as Mars. Observers and researchers at the University of California said in 2009 that Betelgeuse has shrunk by 15 per cent in the last 15 years. It was the first star to have its size measured and it is one of only a handful of stars that appears through the Hubble Space Telescope as a disc rather than a point of light. Zulu legends say that humans used to live on the 'red world' called Mpalalatsani (another possible origin for all the 'red' symbolism, but there are also Zulu accounts about Reptilians living on Mars). It is said there was a 'great war between human men and women on Mpalalatsani and the survivors were banished for their greed, lust and other behaviour. Humans were once androgynous and there were no men or women, but the Reptilians instigated genetic manipulation on Mpalalatsani to divide the original human form into male and female, the legend goes. Credo says that Mpalalatsani is the real location of the biblical Garden of Eden, from which humans were banished, and that genetic manipulation started there and continued within the Moon and later on Earth. Another African word used for Mpalalatsani is 'Matfieng', and this means 'Lord of the Insects' or 'Lord of the Flies'. Credo said this was an insulting description of the humans who were ejected from Mpalalatsani and, interestingly, it is the meaning of the name of the Hebrew demon called 'Beelzebub'. This demon is also known as 'Satan' and the 'Devil' in some cultures, but is separate from them in others. Beelzebub derives from 'Ba'al Zebûb', 'Ba'al Z_bûb' or 'Ba'al Z_vûv' and these words mean ...'Lord of the Flies'. 'Baal' is another name for the Babylonian Nimrod. Beelzebub is said to be high in the hierarchy of Hell and the fallen angels and presides over the 'Order of the Fly'. The author, William Golding, published a famous book in 1954 called *Lord of the Flies*. It is an allegorical novel about a group of schoolboys who are stranded on a desert island without any adults and it explores the conflicting impulses of living in peace and harmony or fighting for power – appropriate given what Zulu legends say about what happened with humans on the 'red world'. The book also includes the themes of groupthink against individuality, morality against immorality, and rational thought against emotional reactions. The schoolboys descend into violence before being rescued by a naval ship.

Zulu legends say that the surviving humans banished from Mpalalatsani were brought to Earth by the Reptilians in the Moon. It carried all types of humans, including shamans, Credo said, and the different human groups were kept in different compartments within the Moon. Dr Farooq Al-Baz, who worked with NASA on the scientific exploration of the Moon, once said: 'There are many undiscovered caverns suspected to exist beneath the surface of the Moon. Several experiments have been flown to the Moon to see if there actually were such caverns.' NASA unveiled the manned spacecraft in 2009 that it planned to send to the Moon in 2020. They called it Orion and it replaced the mission named after the sun god, Apollo, but then Obama suddenly cancelled the project in February 2010. Zulu legends say that a higher Consciousness, known to Zulu lore as the 'Tree of Life', wants humans to come back into the fold to reconnect with their true selves and 'higher forces', but the Reptilians, in Credo's words, 'really want to mess things up'. The Tree of Life is another universal concept found in every ancient culture and it is based on the belief that all life on Earth (the branches of the tree) is related. This is precisely what I am saying in my books using other words and analogies.

Calling Cards of the 'gods'

The Moon is central to so many ancient myths and legends, and nowhere more so than the city of Tiahuanaco, 12,500 feet up in the Andes Mountains of Bolivia. It is 15 miles from Lake Titicaca with its Sun Island and Moon Island which I got to know very well when my conscious journey began after 1990. Tiahuanaco is the ruins of a once-fantastic city believed to pre-date the Inca civilisation. The name is said to mean 'City of the Decaying Moon' or 'City of the Doomed Satellite', according to the late researcher and author, Dr Hans Schindler Bellamy. Another translation, he said, is 'Divine Island Kept by the Gods Above the Waters'. Tiahuanaco was built before the 'Great Flood' and is estimated by some to go back at least 17,000 years. Ancient Indian legends say that Tiahuanaco was built by the 'star gods' who came in their 'fiery chariots'. It certainly wasn't built by human technology, with its massive blocks of stone weighing between 100 and 150 tons (one block weighing 440 tons) and carried very long distances. Even modern technology could not build the city as it was. It is said that the same 'gods' who built Tiahuanaco also made the mysterious Nazca lines in Peru, those depictions of animals, birds and insects that can only be seen in their entirety from aircraft. One stone at Tiahuanaco, unearthed in 1903, has become known as the 'Great Idol'. It is 24 feet long, weighs 20 tons, and is covered with hundreds of symbols chiselled superbly into its surface. The German archaeologist, Edmund Kiss, said that it included a calendar based upon observations of what he called advanced astronauts from aeons ago. Dr Hans Schindler Bellamy produced a book called *The Great Idol of Tiahuanaco* with another scholar, Dr Peter Allan, in which they translated writings on the stone. They said the symbols of the Idol record that the Moon came into orbit around the Earth 11,500 to 13,000 years ago. This coincides with many estimates of the period of the cataclysmic Great Flood and the end of Atlantis and Mu and is in sync with the geological and biological record outlined by researchers Allan and Delair in their book, *When the Earth Nearly Died* that I featured earlier. I am not saying that this is the time when the Moon arrived, though who knows? I feel the Moon came hundreds of thousands of years ago and subsequent geological catastrophies have been caused by its manipulation. But people will have to reach their own conclusions, as always. What is for sure is that there were some extraordinary geological events on Earth in the period of 11,500 to 13,000 years ago. Another incredible monument in Tiahuanaco is called the 'Gate of the Sun' and the nuclear physicist, Jacque Bergier, who made a detailed study of the area, said that it 'bears inscriptions which it is thought contain a Venus calendar, spaceships and extraterrestrial beings'. It is clear, too, that these extraterrestrial entities must have had a profound connection to the Moon. Tiahuanaco abounds with moon gods and goddesses, moon temples and moon houses.

There are also a number of structures on the Moon's surface that cannot be explained by natural occurrences. A 'bridge' 12 miles long was observed in 1953 and has been confirmed on other occasions since then. The British astronomer, H P Wilkins, stated that 'it looks artificial'. Wilkins was also bemused by strange dome-like structures that appear to have been first spotted in 1953 and have increased dramatically in number since then. Obelisk-like structures were discovered by Lunar Orbiter II in 1966 and Orbiter III two years later. One was more than 150 feet in height and was configured with others in the same pattern as the three pyramids at Giza in Egypt. Dr Farooq Al-Baz, one of NASA's leading geologists, said of these obelisks or spires:

There have been quite a few unexplainable objects, but most interesting are these tremendously long shadows cast by enormous spires almost everywhere on the Moon. These objects become very dramatic anomalies for us – huge, huge shadows that stretched for miles and thinned out like needles at their points.

Some of these spires are only 100 yards high; others are taller than the tallest buildings on Earth – often two and three times taller. They're much lighter in colour than the surrounding mare or lava fields, which gives them an additional aura of mystery. They seem to have been constructed of different material.

The obelisk-building Reptilians explain the obsession that secret societies like the Freemasons have with obelisks, and the same with ancient peoples like the Egyptians and Mesopotamians. Astronomers have consistently reported seeing strange lights on the Moon for centuries, often in the same areas, including in the crater known as Plato. Some of these lights are said to have been in distinct patterns or formations. American, Soviet and British astronomers identified an object in 1958 heading towards the Moon at 25,000 miles per hour and it was, they said, emitting radio signals which they did not understand. Many astronauts have had strange experiences and have seen other spacecraft, and these are only the reports that get out from time to time. There is a vast amount that we are not being told. Former military and NASA personnel have gone public with what they know about extraterrestrial activity with regard to the Moon, Earth and Saturn. Yes, some of them, even many of them, will be disinformers to mislead and discredit researchers, but many are not. Edgar Mitchell, who is officially the sixth man to step on the Moon, has spoken publicly several times about his belief in extraterrestrial life and how governments have been keeping 'ET' activity from the public for 60 years. Mitchell told the NBC *Dateline* programme in 1996 that he had discussed the subject with officials from three countries who said they had experienced personal encounters with extraterrestrials. He said the evidence for such contact was 'very strong', but it was classified by governments that were involved in a cover-up of the existence of alien bodies recovered in places like Roswell, New Mexico, in 1947. Mitchell also said that extraterrestrials had provided technological secrets to the American government (the cabal that operates within the American government). Whenever there is a UFO sighting, even of the most compelling and unexplainable, the official line is to either ignore them or dismiss them with some ludicrous explanation, although this attitude has been changing more recently for reasons I will come to later. Don Wilson writes in *Our Mysterious Spaceship Moon* of the experience of Major Gordon

Cooper when he was orbiting the Earth in Fair 7 in 1963. Cooper said he heard voice transmissions that he described as an 'unintelligible foreign language' on the VHF channel reserved exclusively for space flights. Wilson says that the tapes later proved to be in a language not known on this planet. Cooper also saw a 'UFO' when his orbit took him over the Muchea Tracking Station near Perth, Australia, which 200 staff at the station also witnessed. He said in his book, *We Seven*:

> I also had the idea there might be some interesting forms of life out in space for us to discover and get acquainted with. I don't believe in fairy tales, but as far as I'm concerned there have been far too many unexplained examples of unidentified objects sighted around this earth to rule out the possibility that some form of life exists beyond our world.

You bet, mate.

Moon Base

The Disclosure Project is an organisation headed by American, Dr Steven Greer, that campaigns for governments to reveal what they know about extraterrestrial activity. Greer arranged in 2001 for presentations at the National Press Club in Washington DC by more than 20 witnesses from the military, intelligence, government, industry and science who told of their experiences. Among them was Sergeant Karl Wolf who was working as a precision electronics photographic repairman at the Langley Air Force Base in Langley, Virginia, in 1965. Langley is a centre for the CIA and its master, the National Security Agency (NSA), and it was from Langley that planes were scrambled on 9/11 in such a shockingly 'incompetent' (on purpose) way that they failed to get to Washington before the Pentagon was hit (see *Alice in Wonderland and the World Trade Center Disaster*). Sergeant Karl Wolf told the Press Club about how he saw photographs of an 'alien base' on the 'dark side' of the Moon. He said he was asked to go to a facility at Langley Air Force Base where the NSA was collating the information from the Lunar Orbiter photographing the Moon. When he arrived, two officers took him into a laboratory. He said he didn't know the real purpose of the darkroom or the operation going on in the facility. He had thought it was where they were bringing in the data and then releasing the images to the public. They were using 35mm strips of film at the time, which were then assembled into what were called 'mosaics'. They were compiled from pictures taken in successive passes around the Moon. He was met in the laboratory by a man who, like himself, was an Airman Second Class, and Wolf takes up the story:

> … he was showing me how all this worked and we walked over to one side of the lab and he said: 'By the way, we've discovered a base on the back side of the Moon.' And at that point I became frightened and a little terrified, thinking to myself if anybody walks in the room now I know we're in jeopardy, we're in trouble, because he shouldn't be giving me this information. And then he pulled out one of these mosaics and showed this base which had geometric shapes that were towers. They were spherical buildings; they were very tall towers and things that looked somewhat like radar dishes, but they were large structures.

If I compare it to what I have seen now, because I do have photographs that have artefacts in them that are similar to what I saw, they're massive. Some of the structures are half a mile in size, so they're huge structures. Some of the buildings seemed to have very reflective surfaces on them. A couple of structures that I saw reminded me of cooling towers at power generating plants. They had that sort of shape; some of them were just very, very straight and tall with a flat top.

Some of them were round, some of them looked like a Quonset Hut, with a domed kind of, like a greenhouse. The particular shot that I saw there were several clustered together over a landscape, a fairly large landscape. I didn't want to look at it any longer than that, because I felt that my life was in jeopardy and I knew the young fellow who was sharing this was really, really overstepping his bounds at that point.

I worked there for three more days and I remember going home and naively thinking I can't wait to hear about this on the evening news and here it is more than 30 years later ...

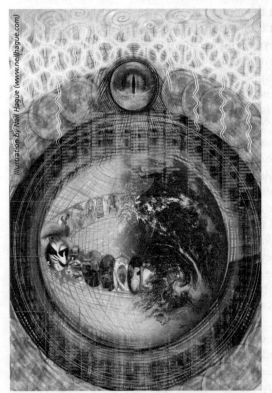

Illustration by Neil Hague (www.neilhague.com)

Figure 161: *We see the Moon as a 'physical' phenomenon, like everything within 'visible light'. But that is only one level of the Moon. It is also a technologically-generated interdimensional portal that allows entities, craft and energies to move between other realities and ours*

Other witnesses explained how pictures of structures on the Moon and UFO activity were airbrushed out before the pictures were released to the public. What is described as a 'base' on the far side of the Moon is actually an entrance to the interior, I would suggest.

The Moonsters

The Moon is the key to understanding how humanity and life on Earth has been, and is being, manipulated by a hidden force. It is the centre of Reptilian operations and their spacecraft are constantly to-ing and fro-ing between the Moon and underground facilities and bases on Earth. The Moon is not just a 'physical' phenomenon; it is a technologically-generated interdimensional portal that allows Fourth Density Reptilians and other entities and energies to enter Third Density reality (Fig 161). They can then travel in spacecraft or be teleported, still cocooned from the Third Density vibrational field, to underground locations within the Earth that give them protection from Third Density consequences for Fourth Density entities.

There are also the Third Density Reptilians that are a part of all this, too. Much of their genetic experimentation has been, and is, conducted within the Moon, and this is where so many 'abductees' are taken while they think they are in 'spaceships'. The Moon is also the major location for the genetic programme to produce the Reptilian-hybrid bloodlines. The 'human' monarchy is really the *moon*archy, just as its major weapon of control, money, is *moon*ey. The money/*moon*ey system comes from the Reptilian hierarchy in the Moon and has been used to subjugate many 'worlds' and peoples. There is a blueprint playing out here in which they use their spaceship moons to hijack planets and then impose upon them a control system to suppress and manipulate the population with a view to complete takeover. They do what they do so well, because they have done it so many times before.

This brings me back to the Rothschilds and other major Illuminati families. Yes, the bloodlines have passed through the ages via interbreeding; but others have been placed in the surface society, from the genetic programmes on the Moon and from facilities within the Earth, to play a major role in advancing the agenda. A prime example of this is the House of Rothschild. The Bauer bloodline, itself a Reptilian hybrid, was 'upgraded' in the period before Mayer Amschel Bauer appeared on the scene to rename the new bloodline 'Rothschild'. Their astonishingly rapid rise to power, influence and control across the world was due to their origin and to their Moon and below-ground support system – for reasons I will explain in a few chapters from now. The Rothschilds are major Reptilian surface agents for the lunar and underground control-system. When I mention family names, such as 'Bauer', for instance, I am not saying that everyone called Bauer or any other name are all Reptilian-hybrids. I only mean a particular bloodline that uses that name. We need to remember that surface Reptilian hybrids number only some four or five per cent of the population, and those in full knowledge of who they are and what they are doing will be significantly fewer than that.

Fake Moon Landing

One other point at this stage … The bloodlines don't want us to know the truth about the Moon, and there is much more to the Apollo missions than we have been told. Humans have been to the Moon in far more sophisticated craft than the rockets and shuttles that we have seen taking off to such fanfare. The secret government that controls the official space programme has long had access to the sort of flying-saucer technology used by the Reptilians and other extraterrestrial and interdimensional groups. It was being developed in Nazi projects as early as 1943, and at the end of the war the scientists and engineers involved were helped to flee Germany by a CIA-British Intelligence-Vatican operation known as 'Paperclip'. These scientists, including geneticists and mind-control experts like 'Angel of Death', Josef Mengele, were taken to the United States to continue their work. In the world of the Illuminati families, there are no borders and no 'sides' except themselves and humanity as a whole. It was the Paperclip scientists who set up the US government's mind-control programme, the infamous MK-ULTRA, and further developed the anti-gravity 'flying saucer' craft and other technology which, in the public arena, appears only in science fiction. Not all the 'flying saucers' that people see are flown by non-humans and this is the technology they use for their unofficial visits to the Moon. One thing is for sure, though: the first official landing on the Moon, the 'giant leap for mankind', was a complete fraud, at least in the way it was portrayed to the people. Much has been written about this over the years, but the most compelling confirmation has come from American filmmaker, Jay Weidner, in an exposé on his website in 2009. Jay had organised a talk for me in Los Angeles in the autumn of 2008 and he said he was writing a biography about the legendary film director, Stanley Kubrick. He mentioned to me then that Kubrick had directed the 1969 Moon landings in a studio very much on Earth, and his website article later presented the facts in detail. Weidner says that many sources inside the military-industrial complex have told him that President Kennedy was shown the flying-saucer technology soon after his election and he realised its potential for many other advances, including a source of cheap and environmentally-benign energy. Weidner writes:

> Soon after seeing the flying saucer technology, JFK made his famous speech asking NASA to land a man on the Moon before the decade was out. Many insiders believed that this was a ploy by JFK to get NASA, and the secret government, to release their saucer technologies. Since it was obvious to everyone that standard rocket technology could not get man to the Moon and back, JFK may have thought that NASA would be forced to release the knowledge of the technology behind the flying saucers in order to fulfil his vision and get to the Moon by the end of the 1960s. JFK's ploy was therefore intended to free this advanced technology from the insidious hands of the shadow government.

Kennedy was assassinated in 1963 and NASA hatched a plan to make it look like they had gone to the Moon with rocket technology while maintaining the secrecy of their advanced flying saucers, Weidner says. They chose Stanley Kubrick to direct the make-believe footage, because they believed he was the most skilled in employing movie special effects in the 1960s. Weidner says that it seems Kubrick negotiated in return an almost unlimited budget to make his science fiction film, *2001: A Space Odyssey*, and an agreement that he could make any film he wanted for the rest of his life with no oversight from anyone. It is certainly the case that the *Space Odyssey* movie was one of the most expensive productions of its time and the President of MGM said publicly that he never saw a rough-cut in the four years it took to make. The production of the movie spanned the same period as the first Apollo program. Both started in 1964 with the movie released in 1968 and the alleged Moon landings shown to the world in 1969. The scientist, Frederick Ordway, worked for NASA on the Apollo program and was also Kubrick's top science advisor on his film. Jay Weidner shows in compelling detail how the same special effects, and visual anomalies, can clearly be seen in both *2001: A Space Odyssey* and the 'moon landings'. The picture comparisons that he produces are devastating proof that the landing was shot in a studio on Earth, and I recommend you visit his website: **Jayweidner.com** to get the full story and see the visual evidence, plus other excellent supporting articles, including one dissecting the symbolism of Kubrick's film, *The Shining*. Weidner has also made a documentary about all this called *Kubrick's Odyssey*.

It is because the scenes on the Moon were shot in a studio that a long list of contradictions has been exposed by researchers, especially with regard to lighting (Fig 162). Weidner believes that Kubrick purposely included these anomalies so that the truth would later be uncovered. We have to be very careful with anything that NASA says about the Moon. If it can fake the first landing to hoodwink the entire world, its word is obviously not to be trusted when it says, as it did in October 2009, that it had 'bombed' the Moon in an effort to find water. Yeah, okay, and Barack Obama is the Virgin Mary. NASA announced that it has found 'significant amounts' of water on the lunar surface after a missile impact at twice the speed of a bullet. All this, of course, underpins the belief in the public mind that the Moon is a 'natural' phenomenon when it isn't. Far more is known than people are being told. Kubrick died in 1999, soon after showing his last movie, *Eyes Wide Shut*, to executives at Warner Brothers. The film starred Tom Cruise and Nicole Kidman and told the story of a satanic mind-control network of elite people and families. Warner executives apparently wanted

APOLLO 11
FAMOUS SHOT OF ALDRIN "WALKING ON THE MOON" - SIGNS OF FAKERY

(1) The face shield (right) shows inconsistant ground lighting, left side spotlit (2) Ground hotspot around astronaut, (top left) but dark horizon, unlike sunshine. (3) Rock in the distance (left) front lit, while astronaut is back lit. Rock shadow should be parallel to astronaut's (4) Dark side of astronaut fully lit, but no flashbulb, while his shadow is solid black

Figure 162: *There were countless anomalies with the pictures of the 'first landing on the Moon'*

him to re-edit the film, but he refused. If it is true that he secured a life-long contract for uncensored filmmaking, there was nothing they could do about it – unless he was dead. Kubrick then conveniently died of a 'heart attack' and something like 15 minutes of footage was removed from *Eyes Wide Shut* (a mind-control trigger phrase) before it was released. Warner Brothers still refuses to produce a DVD of Kubrick's original version. The date of the film's release, which Kubrick had written into his contract, was 16th July 1999 – thirty years to the day after the first 'moon landing'.

I know that most people will dismiss what I say about the 'spaceship moon', but they dismissed me with great hilarity when I described in detail nearly two decades ago how an Orwellian nightmare was being manipulated into place. I've had it and heard it all before. Nor am I saying that the Moon alone explains everything. There is so much more to know about so much, including the history and nature of Mars, Venus and Saturn. They are very much involved in this story, as are Orion, Draco and Sirius. I am well aware that mainstream scientists and others will say that, without the Moon, life would be very different (true) and that this planet would be an unstable, wobbling, catastrophe of extremes in weather, temperature and tidal movements. This is what their computer models tell them, but look at the nonsense those models say about human-caused 'global warming' on the basis of flawed data in = flawed data out. If you take the Moon away now you are not going to be left with how things were before it came. The solar system was very different then with other 'bodies' and forces that held the Earth in a greater, not lesser, stability than today. The spaceship Moon was involved in battles and destruction that beggar the imagination because of the levels of technological potential involved. At least one planet was destroyed; and we are not looking at a like-for-like situation that simply equates Earth with the Moon or without it. Science will realise that eventually. The controllers of the Moon removed the opposition in every sense and then hijacked the Earth.

But the Moon did – does – something else. If you think what I have written so far is extraordinary, incredible, nonsensical, whatever, just wait until I come to what the Moon is doing to human perception. Wow, oh wow. Before I can explain that, however, we need to explore the nature of reality itself.

15

The Voice

As long as habit and routine dictate the pattern of living, new dimensions
of the soul will not emerge
Henry Van Dyke

Twelve years after my experience on the mound in Peru, my life was to enter a new and
amazing stage in which so many 'mysteries' were to be explained. Lifetimes of
experiences had already been packed into little more than a decade as I had criss-
crossed the world and criss-crossed every human emotion, or so it seemed. Many times
I recalled the words given to me through the psychic:

> He also had to learn how to cope with disappointment, experience all the emotions and
> how to get up and get on with it. The spiritual way is tough and no one makes it easy.

I had no argument with that after the years of abuse and ridicule I endured, and the
frustration of trying to alert people to their collective plight only to be ignored or
dismissed as 'that nutter'. When I asked some of them as I passed them in the street
why they were laughing at me, it was clear they really had no idea. Some simply said
'everybody laughs at you'. Okay, I would reply, but tell me why *you* are laughing. Many
couldn't give me an answer when confronted with this question because they were just
computer programs reacting to input. 'There's that David Icke.' Press 'Enter'. 'Ha, ha,
ha, ha, ha.' Others would just parrot the tired clichés of the 'journalistic' brain-deads –
'You believe in seven-foot lizards' or 'You think you're Jesus.' I would ask them
sometimes how they knew that a Reptilian race was not involved in human affairs. Had
they ever done any research on it? Read any books? Gone any further than: 'Icke
believes in seven-foot lizards'? No, of course not. They had descended to the level of
computer software, reacting to program. The years of extraordinary ridicule taught me
many things about myself, the world and why it so easy for the few to control the lives
of billions. As Albert Einstein said: 'Condemnation without investigation is the height
of ignorance.' It is not only that people are manipulated to be ignorant, it is also that
they *allow* themselves to be ignorant. They are the key players in their own enslavement.
Their padlocked minds condemn them to a life of prison-cell perception, outside of
which nothing else – in their reality – is possible. Humanoid-reptilian entities cannot
exist; end of story, no debate necessary. It is ignorance by reflex action. Fundamental to
controlling human belief and behaviour is to control the perception of what is possible.

If you suppress information you give people a distorted version of what is possible, and you therefore manipulate their perception of the possible. For instance, tell people that the Earth is a sphere without including the law of gravity and they will laugh at the very idea – 'Don't be silly, anyone on the bottom would fall off.' Tell people that Icke believes in seven-foot lizards without including a mass of supporting evidence and background and they will say I am crazy. Seven-foot lizards cannot exist and shapeshifting is impossible. I repeat: suppress information about what is really possible and you will suppress the public perception of what *is* possible. In this state of ignorance, you can present the truth to people and they will just giggle or get extremely angry because 'you are talking nonsense'.

By 2003, the reaction to me was changing very quickly, however, and that has continued to this day. I began to notice the difference after the attacks of 9/11. Most people just accepted the official story without question, but a significant number of others had an instinctive feeling that something wasn't right. They began to feel that what they were told by the authorities just didn't add up. This was not only with regard to 9/11, but also with the direction the world was taking generally. The awakening took another giant leap with the bare-faced lies that were used to justify the invasion of Iraq, and the subsequent deaths and horrendous disfigurement of millions of civilians. If those in power could lie so outrageously about 'weapons of mass destruction' to unleash the mass murder they called 'shock and awe', what the hell else were they lying about? Try just about everything. I saw a massive increase in public interest in my work during this period. The halls had been packed immediately after my initial mass ridicule in 1991 as people came to laugh; but when they tired of that and 'Icke's a nutter' was no longer 'news', I spent years talking to next to no-one. These were lonely and dispiriting years when I wondered what the heck I was doing it for; but something drove me on. Then, in the wake of 9/11 and the invasion of Iraq, thousands began to turn up, not to laugh but to listen with an open mind – an *open* mind. Most people still had a big problem with the reptilian aspect and I understood that, but at least they were open to the increasingly obvious fact that George Orwell's vision of a global prison camp had entered the realms of daily experience. Big Brother wasn't coming; he was *here*. The world that I described in … *And The Truth Shall Set You Free*, which I wrote in 1994, was now on the daily news as 9/11 was constantly exploited to justify the murder of the innocent, and the surveillance and control of the population on a scale that beggars belief. The term 'Problem-Reaction-Solution' began to circulate around the world as people saw how the manufactured problems were being used to transform society into a gathering Orwellian nightmare. The media was still ridiculing me, as always, and Mind-made people just repeated what Mind-made 'journalists' told them to think. No matter, at least the tide had turned and it continues to do so as ever more people across the world tease open their minds and their perception of possibility.

Breaching the Veil

Whilst all this was beginning to happen in 2003, I was being launched into the next and most important stage of my own awakening. I said when I finished *Alice in Wonderland and the World Trade Center Disaster* in the summer of 2002 that if I was going to take this story forward I needed to see what lay beyond the five senses. I knew that this 'world' was only a range of frequencies and that we were being manipulated by reptilian and other entities that operate, at least primarily, outside the range of human perception. But I needed to know more about the nature of reality itself to increase my understanding of what was going on. Around this time I received an invitation to speak at an event in the Brazilian rainforest that involved taking a psychoactive drug produced from a rainforest plant called 'ayahuasca'. This has been used by South American shamans for hundreds of years (at least) to take people into states of consciousness that are beyond the five-sense level of reality. It is known as the 'teacher plant' and it allows people to experience these unseen realms where so much can be learned about self, life and reality. It is also dubbed the 'plant of the gods', no doubt because it can allow you to see those dimensions where the 'gods' of myth reside. In fact, it was the number of times that participants at these events had seen reptilian entities and imagery in their altered states of awareness that led the organisers to invite me. Ayahuasca contains many powerful hallucinogenic properties including Dimethyltryptamine, or DMT, a naturally-occurring component of the metabolism of mammals and plants. DMT is known by some as the 'spirit molecule'. I had never taken psychoactive drugs, and haven't since except for a small quantity of 'magic mushrooms' a few weeks after my experience in Brazil; but I was keen to try ayahuasca because of my desire to see beyond this reality. I arrived at Manaus in northern Brazil in January 2003 for the hour's drive to the rainforest location. Ayahuasca is used in religious ceremonies and rituals in parts of Brazil and it is quite legal in these circumstances. It is largely illegal to own or take the brew in the 'western world', as it is with potions in general that can open conscious awareness to realities beyond the five senses.

The night before the first ayahuasca session, my inner 'voice' said that I would not be taking it with the rest of the group the following evening but instead I would be taking it on my own. For various reasons, that's the way it turned out. I lay on the floor of a large, wooden 'round house' building, alone in the darkness, except for Zoe, one of the organisers, who had experimented with all kinds of such drugs and their combinations. There can't be much left of the rainforest that he has not drunk or smoked. I have heard it said that the plant takes you here or takes you there, but I don't agree. I think that ayahuasca opens the channels (or rather deludes you into thinking it does, because it's all in the mind) and allows you to take yourself into conscious awareness – to where you already are. Some will see 'demons' that reflect subconscious states and others will go to paradise. Where people are at in their subconscious may not be where they appear to be in their 'physical' lives. A happy-go-lucky, five-sense personality can be a front to hide subconscious emotional trauma that can manifest as a 'dark' ayahuasca experience. I drank the brew from a little glass (it tasted a bit like liquorice) and I began to feel the effects rather rapidly. I felt nauseous and agitated. I then began to scream out years of pent up frustration ... and I mean *scream*. The frustration going back to the days of the mass ridicule, the suppressed emotion I didn't even know was there, was all unleashed into the darkness. As the effects of the ayahuasca kicked in, I went into altered states whenever I closed my eyes, and saw bright, swirling colours and images. When I opened my eyes I was back in five-sense reality, albeit in a slightly altered form. The more powerful the experience became the less I wanted to keep my eyes open and when I did, they didn't want to stay open for long.

I lay on my back looking into the pitch darkness and my arms suddenly stretched out at about 45 degrees, much as they did when I was in the standing position on the mound in Peru. Out of my mouth, and in a very different voice to 'David Icke', came the words, slowly and powerfully: 'I am love.' I then began to repeat: 'I am everything and everything is me; I am infinite possibility.' With that, I felt a fantastic energy pour from the centre of my chest, my heart chakra, and fill the room. A striplight on the ceiling began to flicker on and off. Within a few minutes, three of the lights came on full power. I looked across and thought: why has Zoe turned the lights on? But he hadn't. The lights were all switched off and they had come on by themselves without electricity, or the usual kind, anyway. Music was being played on a hi-fi system, but that switched off and came back on again after ten seconds or so. It sounds weird and impossible, but it's not. The electrical circuitry of the lights

Figure 163: *The Time Loop is a Mind-construct that entraps people in a perpetually recurring cycle of repeating experience. 'Time' appears to be going 'forward' from 'past' through 'present' to 'future', but what we call 'time' in this reality is actually a 'loop'. We only experience a small part of the loop in a single 'lifetime' and so we have the illusion of going 'forward' into the 'future'. The only way to break the cycle is to become Conscious and perceive beyond Mind*

and the music player were being affected by the electromagnetic energy that was filling the room. I felt the energy pouring through my heart chakra and forming an 'arc' to my head. The words I was speaking appeared to come from this energetic connection. Where the energy was striking my head it felt like someone was gripping the skin very tightly. I began to speak fluently in my altered state, but it wasn't that I had thoughts and then articulated them in speech; the words just came from my mouth and that is the first I knew of them. I will summarise what they said and what came to me even more powerfully in another form the following night. I was told in my altered state that all that exists is one infinite Consciousness, which was referred to as 'The Infinite', 'Oneness' and 'The One'. We had become detached from an awareness of The One in our manipulated, illusory, reality and we viewed everything in terms of division and duality instead of seeing that all is connected – all is the same Infinite Oneness. My words in the first ayahuasca session said that the five-sense 'world' which we experience daily is a 'time loop' that goes around and around basically repeating the same sequence, in theme if not detail. What we call the 'future' eventually becomes the 'past' and spins around to repeat the 'present' over and over again. The time loop is going around and around in a perpetuating spiral or cycle that has become a prison for the consciousness that is trapped by its seductions and illusions (Fig 163). The time loop operates within a structure of 'non-physical levels' that have also lost contact with Infinite Oneness. The Voice referred to this multi-level structure as 'the Matrix'.

It's all an Illusion

On the first night, I had spoken the words out loud, but on the second night I heard a female voice as clear as can be that added much more detail. 'Her' words were thought-fields decoded by my mind and so I heard the words in English. An Italian or an Egyptian

Figure 164: *The chemical cocktails in food and drink destabilise body and mind and stop people opening to higher levels of Consciousness. It is all coldly calculated by the inner circle of the Illuminati who know how we interact with reality*

would decode them in their own language and way of speaking. I will refer to the communicator as 'the Voice'. I decoded it as female, but it represented unity, not the duality of male and female. I took an increased amount of ayahuasca on the second night. I lay down with my eyes closed and began to see the swirling colours and images again. For a time they had a very Chinese look about them. Then I began to hear the Voice very clearly. It was not some distant 'what did it say?' type of voice, but a loud and powerful one, more so than anything I had experienced. It spoke with great dignity, assurance and clarity. 'David,' it said, 'we are going to take you to where you come from, so you can remember who you are.' With that I was taken to a realm of indescribable bliss. There was no 'time' and there was no 'place'.

Everything just was. I had no body, I was only Consciousness, and I was everything. There were no divisions, no polarities, no black and white, no us and them. I was Infinite, but I was also completely self-aware as an 'individual' with my own point of observation within the whole. This is what we all are – awareness looking at infinity from our own point of observation. If only people could experience the bliss of Oneness, the world of the five senses would be transformed. This is why the Reptilian-Illuminati conspiracy works so hard to keep us in a state of disconnection through fear, stress, hatred, mind programming, suppression of knowledge, and a long, long list of other methods, including electromagnetic pollution and chemical additives in food and drink (Fig 164). All these things are designed to imprison us in five-sense reality and this is the major reason for demonising psychoactive drugs. In the state of bliss that I was experiencing, the energy was not vibrating as it does in the realm of form and 'things'. I experienced it as either stillness or as the waves of an ocean moving in slow motion and perfect harmony. 'This is the Infinite, David,' the Voice said. 'This is where you come from and this is where you shall return.' The following words then began to repeat over and over in my mind:

Infinite Love is the only truth – everything else is illusion; Infinite Love is the only truth – everything else is illusion; Infinite Love is the only truth – everything else is illusion.

The Voice said that this is all we really needed to know because everything comes from that. I began to form a question in my mind. I was going to say: 'You really mean everything?' But before the thought could form, the Voice interrupted: 'Infinite Love is the only truth – *everything* else is illusion; no buts, no exceptions – that's it.' This word 'love' has connotations and it is often perceived as weak or naïve. I hear people say: 'You need more than love, mate.' The understanding of love has become distorted by its human definition. It means, to most people, a powerful attraction to another person, but that is not love in the sense that I mean here. The human perception of 'love' is an electrochemical attraction, or what I call 'mind love'. Those with experience of mind-control have told me that this can easily be stimulated through chemical brain manipulation to cause two people to fall 'madly in love' when they would otherwise never go near each other. Infinite Love is beyond physical attraction. Love, in its true sense, is not what you are in, it is what you *are*. Infinite Love is the balance of all. Infinite Oneness is the only truth, everything else is illusion. Infinite 'Love' is also Infinite Intelligence, Infinite Knowledge, Infinite Everything. All Potential, All Possibility. I was told how humanity had been manipulated to identify itself with illusory 'personalities' and not with the Infinite that it is. This had trapped people in the illusions of a disconnected state. The Voice would return to this theme, as it communicated with me through the rest of the night and I experienced this incredible 'place' of harmony and bliss. 'Why do you think you needed to scream and try to throw up?' I was asked. 'Do you feel any frustration or anger in this place?' No, I did not. 'Do you have any worries or fear or guilt where you are now?' No, I didn't, there was only harmony, peace, love and bliss. 'Frustration, anger, fear, guilt and pain are only illusions, figments of disconnected mind,' the Voice said. 'They don't exist except in your imagination.' It went on: 'Do you think the Infinite you are now experiencing needs to throw up?' No. 'Do you think the Infinite ever gets ill?' No. 'Of course not, these states are only illusions of the conditioned mind.' Later in the night I began to feel a little nauseous again and immediately the Voice said:

> Where is your nausea coming from? Do you think the Infinite is feeling nauseous now? So you must be identifying with your body. It's an illusion, David; your body is an illusion, and so must be the nausea you think you are feeling in your body. If your body does not exist how can nausea or pain? These are illusions and they only exist in the minds of those caught in the Matrix.

With that, the nausea left me, never to return. I was told that what we call the Universe is a holographic illusion akin to looking up at the 'night sky' projected on the ceiling of a planetarium. The only difference was that with the Universe the projections appeared to be three-dimensional, because they were holograms. I will explore this subject in more detail later. The Universe was a figment of our conditioned imagination, the Voice said, and it was only our reality because we believe it is. I was being given information in the simplest form as I was being introduced to these concepts, but later I would understand with much greater depth and detail what was meant by 'believe it is'. The Universe was also far smaller than people perceived. 'Look at the sky in a planetarium and it seems so vast, yet it only goes as high as the ceiling.' Once again, I would later realise more profoundly what was meant by this. Then the Voice said: 'Do you think that's the Earth you're lying on now? *Hmmm. ILUUUSION!*' As with everything in the 'Time Loop' and throughout the multi-levelled 'Matrix', Earth was a holographic projection and thus so was its illusory 'surface'. 'You are lying on the Earth now only because you think you are,' the Voice said. If you are new to all this and you think it is fantastic and unbelievable, you are going to be amazed at how much scientific evidence is now coming to light to confirm that this is correct. 'Remember always,' said the Voice,

'Infinite Love is the only truth, everything else is illusion – *everything*.' It then said something very profound that made total sense a little later when I had other experiences along the same theme:

> If it vibrates, it is illusion. The Infinite does not vibrate; it is the harmony and Oneness of all. Only illusion vibrates – that which is created by the imagination and delusion of mind.

I mentioned earlier that when I experienced the state of Oneness and infinite unity there was no vibration, only stillness and at most a slow-motion wave. I was told that the 'laws' of physics were also illusions. 'There are no laws of physics,' said the Voice. 'The scientists create illusory 'laws' to measure an illusory Universe.' There are no 'laws' of any kind, because everything just is. 'Do you think the Infinite needs 'laws' through which to express itself?' The laws of physics and mathematics and all the others that 'govern' the physical and non-physical worlds were the creations of Mind. If scientists believed in such 'laws' then that would be their experience. I would understand this in more detail later, also. The Voice said that this illusion only continues until someone comes along and changes the belief, the program – the collective reality. Then such 'laws' cease to apply. What we call 'miracles' are just the overcoming of a programmed mind, breaking out of its sense of limitation and creating or experiencing a different reality. Those still in the program think this is impossible, which, to their state of awareness, it certainly appears to be. As a result, they dub anything beyond their sense of limitation a 'miracle' when it is nothing of the kind. Walking on hot coals without getting burned is not a 'miracle'; it is about going into a state of awareness that knows that both feet and fire are illusions, and an illusion cannot burn an illusion unless you believe it can. All this will seem very strange to those new to these concepts, but it will become very clear and simple as we go on. Nothing is impossible, but a belief in limitation makes it seem so. It has been shown again and again that the beliefs of the scientists performing an experiment will affect the outcome of the experiment. The nearest thing there is to a 'law' is this: what you believe you will perceive.

Living in a Dreamworld

The Voice explained how what we believe to be a 'solid' world only exists because we are programmed to believe it does. The 'world' is not 'out there', it is 'in here' – in our minds. Scientific experiments have shown that we do not see up to 50 per cent and more of what comes 'through' our eyes. It is filtered out by the temporal lobes of the brain on the basis of our conditioned belief before it gets to the visual cortex, the point at which we actually 'see'. It is our *brain* that sees, not our eyes. Eyes only provide electrical information and it is the brain/mind that decides what to make of it. Whatever our brain/mind is conditioned to see or not see, it will, or won't. We think we are going about our lives in a state of consciousness when, in fact, we are experiencing a dream every bit as much as those we experience in sleep. It's just a different dream. The Illuminati and their Reptilian masters use this understanding of mind to manipulate our sense of reality and maintain the population in ongoing control. They tell people what they should see and should not see and so they do, or don't. This is the fundamental role of the 'norms' (official 'truths') I have spoken and written about so widely. It is also why the authorities are desperate to remove or discredit those who challenge the norms and offer another vision of possibility that allows people to 'see' a different potential reality.

Our bodies are holographic illusions that do not really exist in the way that we think we see and experience them, the Voice said (and I will be greatly expanding on this). To understand the true nature of the body is to understand so much more about how humanity is being manipulated and suppressed. The Voice said that we only have to eat and drink because we and our bodies are programmed (through conditioning, and the DNA) to believe that we do. We only have to breathe for the same reason. Yes, if we stopped breathing we would 'die', but this is not because we have to die. It only happens because our conditioned minds and bodies are programmed to believe that this will be the outcome, and so that is what they create. 'Do you think the Infinite sits down to dinner?' the Voice said. 'Do you think the Infinite has to breathe or it will die? So why,' the Voice asked, 'do those in the Time Loop?' Answer: they identify who they are and their sense of possibility with a physical 'personality' subordinate to illusory 'laws', and not with what they really are – the Infinite 'One'. The Voice offered an example of the chasm between perceived reality and infinite self:

> Why do you need to fly around in aircraft? You are point A and you are point B and you are everything in between. Why then do you need to use an aircraft to fly through yourself?

The Voice then turned to astrology. Yes, it said, astrology appeared to 'work' in the sense that certain types of 'personalities' and traits could be predicted by the illusory 'time' and 'place' and 'year' in which a person was born; but why was this? Astrology 'read' the vibrational fields of the Time Loop but, while it could do this effectively in skilled hands, it was still a Matrix illusion that was based on division, and not Oneness. Astrology, said the Voice, was a feature of the Matrix to manipulate people to identify still more powerfully with their illusory 'personalities' – I am a Taurus, a Leo, a Gemini, whatever. It emphasised the idea of division, of parts, not the whole. 'Do you think the Infinite has its astrology read?' asked the Voice. 'Do you think it consults a psychic about its 'future' or visits a tarot-card reader?' These were all identifications with the 'physical' personality and such 'forward' predictions were peering down the Time Loop, that's all. Psychics were extremely useful in showing people that 'death' is an illusion, and the best of them – those connecting with awareness beyond the Matrix – could bring profound and mind-freeing information into the Time Loop, it said. But if people believed what the psychic or tarot-card reader said was going to happen, they could make it happen. In fact, we all have the power to create whatever reality we choose. If I don't identify with being a 'Taurus' or an 'Aries' or 'David Icke', I begin to release myself from such influences and limitations. I am not David Icke, I am Infinite Consciousness having an *experience* called David Icke.

No Light or Dark

The New Age and mainstream religions have a belief in the existence of 'light' and 'dark', but there was no 'light' or 'dark', the Voice said. These were illusions. The belief that light was needed to balance the darkness was utterly misguided, and a belief in the existence of 'light' was as divisive as a belief in the existence of 'dark'. To believe in the 'light' means you must also believe in the 'dark' and so belief in the 'light' also creates the illusion of its perceived polarity – dark. Once more these were figments of disconnected Mind. Light and dark were illusions of the virtual-reality Matrix designed to cause division, conflict and fear. The Infinite was not light any more than it was dark. It was the balance of all things. It is not 'good' nor 'bad', 'light' nor 'dark', black nor white, male nor female; it just *is* – the Oneness of all. Neither were there any 'demons', the Voice said. 'If Infinite Love is the only truth and everything else is illusion, how can demons be anything, but illusions?' They were holograms projected into the imagination of frightened and manipulated minds, the Voice said. The idea that the 'light' must 'fight' the 'dark' and the demons only reinforced the belief in their perceived existence. There was no need to 'fight' anything and those who did so were only giving what they fought more power by confirming it was 'real'. As I have said: what you fight you become. If people didn't like their life experience they should perceive another reality and the manifestations of the present one would disappear, the Voice said. You don't like your dream? Then dream something else.

The Voice emphasised that to free ourselves from the illusions of the Matrix we had to identify with being the Infinite and not a fragment of mind stuffed inside a body. If we relate to being the Infinite and not some hologram dreamed into imaginary 'existence', the Matrix will no longer control us because it would no longer be. Stop asking questions, the Voice said, and start knowing the answers. It didn't mean rhetorical questions to illustrate a point, but those that come from the belief that we don't know something. 'You are the Infinite so you know everything. Do you think the Infinite asks questions when it knows all there is to know?' Whenever we identified with limitation, ignorance and our illusory personality we were disconnecting from the Infinite that knows all, and is all. When we ask questions we are accepting that we don't know the answer. Would the Infinite do that? Stop asking the question and you will know the answer, the Voice said, and, modifying a line from the first *Matrix* movie, it added: 'It's not the question that drives you mad, it is asking it.' Scottish psychiatrist, R D Laing, once said: 'If I do not know I know, I think I do not know.' People so lack confidence in themselves that they look to others to tell them what to think, but if they could free their minds of such doubt and limitation, they would simply intuitively 'know'. Intuition comes from Consciousness, not Mind. Don't think it, *know* it. Don't ask it, *know* it.

I have understood so much more about the nature of our dreamworld reality since the experience in Brazil and this has become the major theme of my life and work. I have not taken psychoactive drugs since then, except on one occasion, and I have no plans to do so again. Getting 'out there' without them is much better. The other experience I had with a reality-changing drug came a few weeks after Brazil. I walked along a beach near my home on one occasion in an altered state on a beautiful sunny day thanks to 'magic mushrooms'. The Voice began speaking to me again. It said: 'Look around you. Does it not seem like a dream? Does it not feel like a dream that you have in sleep?' It certainly did, and later the 'memory' of the experience was extremely dream-like. Did it happen? Was it really all a dream? It was like walking through a painting, a reality 'bubble', and laughter came far easier than it does in the purely five-sense state. What I found interesting was the way that 'this world' phenomena could bring me out of the altered state in an instant. I was walking along enjoying my expanded reality when I saw a police car and began to think of the authoritarian system. Immediately, I was out of my altered state and back 'here'. I later began to think about something relating to fear and the same happened. Whenever I checked the 'time' on my watch I was kicked out of the altered state as I related to the reality of the Time Loop. This allowed me to understand more of how the Time Loop/Matrix holds us in a manipulated reality and why the global system is structured as it is. A whole new level of understanding would emerge from this about the Illuminati conspiracy and the world we think we lived in.

Who Are You? Everything

Interest in psychoactive substances exploded in the sixties with the use of drugs like LSD, but they largely became an escape from this reality rather than a bridge to a new one. I don't want to escape this reality; I want to see it transformed from a prison to a paradise. Experiencing altered states can help us to understand the game we are dealing with, and those who have studied the effects of drugs like LSD from this perspective have certainly learned a great deal more about reality than they would otherwise have done. One is Stanislav Grof, author of *The Holotropic Mind*, and a former professor at John Hopkins University School of Medicine. He was a founder of the International Transpersonal Association and has developed a means of taking people into altered states called 'Holotropic Breathwork'. Grof was a convinced materialist and atheist until he began studying the effects of LSD in the 1950s as he sought to establish if there were any medical benefits. He was to continue his research for decades to come. In his first experience on LSD, he had what he called 'an extraordinary encounter with my subconscious'. He realised immediately that the unyielding 'truth' of the scientific establishment, taught as fact in the schools and universities, was a fantasy:

> Traditional science holds the belief that organic matter and life grew from the chemical ooze of the primeval ocean solely through the random interactions of atoms and molecules. Similarly, it is argued that matter was organized into living cells, and cells into complex multicellular organisms with central nervous systems, solely by accident and 'natural selection'. And somehow, along with these explanations, the assumptions that consciousness is a by-product of material processes occurring in the brain has become one of the most important metaphysical tenets of the Western worldview.

> As modern science discovers the profound interactions between creative intelligence and all levels of reality, this simplistic image of the Universe becomes increasingly untenable. The probability that human consciousness and our infinitely complex Universe could have come into existence through random interactions of inert matter has aptly been compared to that of a tornado blowing through a junkyard and accidentally assembling a 747 jumbo jet.

Author and researcher Itzhak Bentov calls this mindset the 'giraffe syndrome' in his book, *Stalking the Wild Pendulum*. The term refers to the story of a man who sees a giraffe for the first time with its enormous height, neck and legs. It is such a shock to his sense of reality that he dismisses it as impossible and rejects the idea that such an animal could exist, even though he is looking at it. Stanislav Grof conducted some 4,000 LSD sessions and 20,000 with his Holotropic Breathwork, which involves a combination of breathing techniques, sound, bodywork and artistic expression. His clients have been able to access extraordinary states of awareness. They have experienced what it is like to be animals and plants, and they have described intricate details of their genetics and behaviour that later proved to be 100 per cent correct. They have even experienced being an atom or a blood cell, seeing inside the Sun, and what it was like for them in the womb and in the birth canal. Others have said they became the Consciousness of the whole cosmos and I know myself exactly what that feels like. This is possible because we *are* the cosmos and every cell and atom. All we do is move our point of *observation* and 'become' what we are focusing upon. We are all expressions of one infinite whole and the sense of 'apartness' and division is an illusion. The five-sense prison – the Time Loop – disconnects us from the understanding that we are all One. In fact, this perception of division *is* the prison.

In these altered states beyond the five senses we can regain our conscious connection to the Infinite and experience any expression of it – anything in all of existence. Look at the ocean ... We give it different names like the Atlantic and the South China Sea, just as we give ourselves names like Ethel Jones and David Icke.; but these 'different' oceans are the same body of water, as we are the same Infinite Consciousness in endless disguises. Where is the ocean? Is it crashing on the coast of South Africa? Is it lapping on a beach in Bali? Is it the Roaring Forties or the Strait of Hormuz? It is *all* of them and so it can experience all of them. We are the Infinite Consciousness that is everything. Where are we? And what are we? Are we the flower on the roadside? Are we the tree in the garden? Are we the Sun or the sky? Are we the raindrops on the window or the wind on our face? We are all of them. We are an expression of the seamless One and we can experience any aspect of the Infinite unity that we are. We have been manipulated to believe we are isolated 'individual' droplets when in fact we are the ocean. We are not even part of the ocean – we *are* the ocean. When you place a droplet back in the water, where does the droplet end and the ocean start? There is no division; the droplet becomes the ocean. We have become the droplet that thinks it stands alone, but a change of perception and 'plop', there we go.

This knowledge has been communicated by the enlightened throughout human existence, but official science has denied its validity because the mainstream 'scientific' establishment has been controlled from the start by the Reptilian-hybrid families to keep us from the truth that would set us free. The ancient Greek philosopher, Plato, said that human beings were like people sitting in a cave always facing a wall. The Universe was the shadows projected onto the wall, illusions that the people mistake for reality. The only reality or truth was the 'light' – Consciousness – that made the shadows possible. The ancient Vedic works of India make the same point. The eighth century Hindu mystic, Shankara, said: 'This entire Universe of which we speak and think is nothing but Brahman [Infinite Consciousness]. Brahman dwells beyond the range of Maya [Illusion]. There is nothing else.'

I had known this consciously since my transformation began in Peru, but in the Amazon rainforest I experienced it in a much deeper way than ever before – and even more so today. The nature of reality became the predominant subject in my life after Brazil, and the reason is obvious. Without the understanding of who we are and 'where' we are, nothing else can be seen in its true perspective. This is why the Reptilians and their hybrid bloodlines have worked so ceaselessly to make us believe in a material, 'solid' world, and in religions that follow the laws and false realities imposed by the 'gods' – *them*.

16

Virtual-Reality 'Game'

We all live every day in virtual environments, defined by our ideas
Michael Crichton

My experience in Brazil triggered an explosion of information into my life about the nature of reality and this has taken me ever deeper into the illusion we call the 'physical world'. This is the knowledge that makes sense of everything else and it is not possible to grasp the depth of the conspiracy without understanding reality itself.

I realised that mainstream science would already know that the 'physical' world is illusory if the various disciplines talked and cooperated with each other, and stopped jostling for supremacy, status and funding. Putting quantum physicists together with those who understand how the brain works would be a good start, but the bloodline families who control scientific research through the institutions, universities and funding don't want the dots connected. It suits their agenda magnificently for people to see themselves as insignificant 'little mes' and to believe in all the limitations of a truly solid, physical world. The Reptilians and their bloodline lackeys know how reality works and they want to make sure that their target population never does. Religion was their major vehicle for this through the ages and then 'science' came forward to play its crucial role in suppressing the truth. The party line in the 'science' establishment is that the world is solid and physical and there is no 'afterlife'. Anything to do with the so-called 'paranormal' is condemned or ridiculed by the programmed, often malevolent, 'experts' wheeled out to debunk views, experiences and research that demolish the manufactured myopia that is mainstream 'science'. Ironically, most of what is accepted as scientific 'fact' turns out to be simply assumption and not fact at all. This includes, indeed especially so, Charles Darwin's 'natural selection' or 'survival of the fittest'. As João Magueijo, the Portuguese cosmologist and Professor in Theoretical Physics at Imperial College London, said: '... most science is just a theory and is not motivated by existing observations crying out for an explanation.' He also rightly observed: 'It seems to me that contradicting textbook wisdom is only heresy for those who have learnt it from the text book.'

It is quite a sight to see 'experts', like Professor Richard Dawkins at Oxford University, trying to discredit anything that doesn't fit with their concrete belief-system. He condemns religion while being an evangelist for his own – the religion of this-world-is-all-there-is. Dawkins ridicules the 'God religions', but doesn't realise that he is a leading voice of the 'no-God religion'. He is the High Priest and Chief Zealot of the religion called 'Scientism' and he is desperate to debunk anything that could question his intellectual pre-eminence. Dawkins targets with religious zeal those who challenge the omnipotence of mainstream science. I have seen him close up during a debate at the Oxford Union, and also on his television programmes, attempting to debunk alternative healing and the 'paranormal'. I see fear in his eyes for some reason and almost a sense of panic and desperation. The thought that he could be wrong seems to terrify him, but surely he must know by now that he has been talking bollocks for decades. If he doesn't, given the evidence available, it's a real head-shaker. Where has he been? It is the legions of Mind-made, song-sheet scientists like Dawkins that man the barricades whenever the party line is under threat. They are gatekeepers who seek to impose their own ignorance upon the masses. A few of them, and certainly those who run the institutions, know what they're doing, but most have just been programmed by the system to program others.

Reading Reality

When you begin to see the true nature of 'physical' reality, you realise just how completely humanity has been deluded and continues to be so. You also understand how the few can control the majority so comprehensively when the few know what reality is and the majority do not. We are experiencing what can be likened to a cosmic virtual-reality game, and the human body is a computer system that connects us to this game, just as a computer reads information on a software disk and projects it as images onto the screen. The body-computer/mind is the interface between Consciousness and the 'game'. I call our reality the 'Cosmic Internet', because the Internet analogy is very apt. If you log on to the World Wide Web with a computer anywhere in the world you are connecting to the same collective reality. What you make of it may vary, but it is the same collective 'world'; so it is with our virtual-reality universe. The body-computer/mind is the interface that allows 'us' (our Consciousness, Awareness) to 'log on' to the Cosmic Internet. This is a vibrational construct made up of information which the body-computer decodes into an apparently, though illusory, 'physical' reality. Being born is like Consciousness going online. Ask someone to describe the Internet and they will say it is websites with graphics, words, colours and pictures. Well, yes it is, but the only place the Internet exists in that form is on the computer screen. Everywhere else the Internet is electrical circuits, mathematical codes, and so on. Ask someone to describe television and they will say it is moving pictures on a screen. Once again, yes it is, but the only place television exists in that form is on the screen. Everywhere else it is electrical circuits, mathematical codes, vibrational wave-fields, and so on. It is the same with our five-sense reality. The only place it exists in the 'solid', 'three-dimensional' form that we experience as the 'world' is on our screen – the computer system in the brain that decodes energetic, electrical and digital information into people, places, landscapes and 'things'. What is the Internet? It is information decoded into colours, shapes, words and pictures by a computer. What is five-sense reality? It is information decoded into colours, shapes, words and pictures by a computer – the human body/brain (Fig 165). There are plans to make the Internet itself a much more virtual-reality experience through interfacing with the senses and implanted microchips in the brain. Technology is increasingly mirroring our experienced reality and scientists can connect the brain to a computer, because they are connecting two computers. Albert Einstein was right when he described reality as 'an illusion, albeit a persistent one'. The illusion is that the 'world' is 'solid'. It is, in fact, vibrational, electrical, electromagnetic, chemical and digital information that we decode into what only appears to be three-dimensional solidity. The illusion is persistent because that decoding is constantly happening, just as computer is constantly decoding information passing through it. Einstein said:

> A human being is a part of the whole, called by us Universe, a part limited in time and space. He experiences himself, his thoughts and feeling as something separated from the rest, a kind of optical delusion of his consciousness. This delusion is a kind of prison for us, restricting us to our personal desires and to affection for a few persons nearest to us. Our task must be to free ourselves from this prison by widening our circle of compassion to embrace all living creatures and the whole of nature in its beauty.

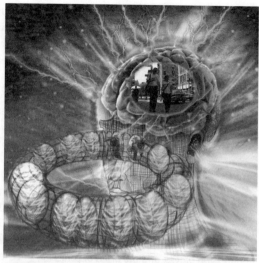

Figure 165: *There is no 'physical' reality. The 'solid' world that we think we see and experience is an illusion decoded by the brain and the genetic structure as a whole from vibrational information, much like a computer decodes the Internet*

We live in what we think is a solid, physical world, but there is no such thing. Am I having one of my 'turns'? Not at all. There is no 'out there' in terms of a physical reality of streets, landscapes, aircraft, cars, stars and other people. It is like a 3-D movie running in our heads. The five senses transform vibrational information into electrical information and this is sent to the brain to be constructed into the illusion of physical reality. We experience this reality as being 'out there', when it isn't. This was explained perfectly in the *Matrix* movie trilogy in an interchange between Neo and Morpheus. Neo asks for confirmation that the 'physical' world he thinks he is experiencing 'isn't real'. Morpheus replies:

> What *is* real? How do you define 'real'? If you're talking about what you can feel, what you can smell, taste and see, then 'real' is simply electrical signals interpreted by your brain.

Yes, that's exactly what it is. Virtual-reality technology that we see today employs the same senses and brain decoding processes. People don headsets and 'cybergloves' to feed information to the brain through the eyes and hands that it decodes into an apparent 3-D reality. The computer tracks your head position and calculates what you should be seeing and depth comes from each eye being given a slightly different view of the scene. You can be standing in an empty room and yet be experiencing any situation that you choose via the information embedded in the software of the game (Fig 166 overleaf). Our reality works in the same way. The Reptilians know this and so do the

Figure 166: *Virtual-reality technology mirrors the way we decode 'physical reality'. It communicates information to the senses via goggles and gloves, and the brain decodes this into an apparently three-dimensional 'solid' world*

highest levels of their hybrid bloodline network, but it has been systematically kept from us through the control of religion and science. Human bodies are incredibly advanced (incredible from our perspective, anyway) computer systems and the five senses are like antennae tuning into energy fields within the frequency range of what is called 'visible light'. The brain, and in fact the whole of the body's genetic structure, is a computer and receiver-transmitter system reading information encoded in 'light' and decoding it into pictures on a symbolic 'screen' in the brain. Colours are just different frequencies within visible light that the brain decodes into colours. This bright and colourful 'world' only exists in the brain which, itself, is in a state of complete darkness. Our eyes transform vibrational information into electrical signals via cone cells that pick out the information encoded within light which the brain decodes into colours. These cells are sensitive to red, green and blue and from this all shades of colour can be decoded. When this system breaks down people become 'colour blind', like a computer that will not decode colour from a software disk. Our ears are an obvious vibrational decoding system. There is no sound 'out there' any more than there are physical objects. We hear sound only when vibrating energy is transformed into electrical signals by the ears and the brain decodes it into noise. When this system malfunctions people 'hear' only silence, because 'outside' the body-computer that is all there is. The brain is silent as it decodes sound, just as it is dark as it decodes light and colour. The other senses of smell, touch and taste all work on the same principle. It is the brain that does the smelling, touching and tasting. If you can override the decoding the system you can get people to eat one thing and taste another. You see it all the time in stage hypnotist shows. When you are holding something hot it is the brain's decoding system that makes you go 'Ouch', and the same when you bang your knee or hit your thumb with a hammer. Hey, brain, thumb here, I've got some information for you … 'aaaagggghhhh'. If you can override the brain's temperature-decoding mechanisms you can walk through fire without getting burned. You can only burn if your brain decodes it. As I said earlier, an illusion can't burn an illusion unless you decode the illusion of burning and so experience the apparent consequences.

Don't Move! Er, I'm Not

The 'I', in the form of Infinite Consciousness, doesn't 'incarnate' into a 'physical body' and nor do we actually 'leave' the body at death, although that analogy is fine to use symbolically. When you are sitting at a computer and you log onto the Internet 'you', the person at the keyboard, don't go anywhere. You sit in your chair while the images on the screen change as your computer reads information and turns it into text and images that you can see. What you are *observing* appears to move, but not you. Our reality is like that, too. Our Consciousness looks into this 'world' through the body-computer in the same basic way that you look into the Internet through your desktop computer. I was sitting in the bath one day when I had a vivid picture appear in my mind. It began a mass of swirling energy that I immediately took to be Consciousness. An eye then appeared amidst the energy and in front of the eye came a telescope. This looked out to Earth and the wider Universe, and finally the telescope morphed into a human body. I asked Neil Hague to paint what I saw, and you can see this in Figure 167. Consciousness experiences this reality through the 'lens' of the body computer. It doesn't go anywhere. It is always where it is and when the computer/lens/telescope 'dies' we – Consciousness – are still where we always were. It is just that we are not looking through the lens anymore and thus our reality changes. When we turn off the desktop computer after a period

Figure 167: *Mind and body are the lens, the interface, between our eternal Consciousness and the virtual-reality universe. They are not who we are, they are what we are experiencing*

on the Internet we are still where we were when we were on the Internet. We *look* into the World Wide Web; we don't actually *go* into it. The virtual-reality universe can be so compelling, however, that Consciousness becomes mesmerised and bewildered into believing it is inside the game. This transfers attention to the five senses alone and people become trapped in mind and body reality. When the body 'dies', the lens ceases to function and Consciousness starts to remember what the lens had caused them to forget, although the imprint of the virtual-reality experience can continue to powerfully affect the sense of reality even after the body has gone. What we call 'death' is simply ceasing to look through the lens. 'Death' is putting your telescope down.

Even 'physical' movement is an illusion. I read about a woman with brain damage that prevented her from perceiving movement as most people do. A car she saw in the distance would suddenly be flying past her with apparently nothing in between. When she poured tea into a cup it would appear to her as an arc of still liquid, akin to a freeze-frame and not as a flow of movement. This is because decoded 'physical' reality is not one continuous flow. It is like a movie film going through the projector as a series of still images which give the illusion of continuous movement. When this lady's brain was damaged and she could not decode reality as a continuous movement, she began to see 'still frames', or jump from one 'frame' to another with nothing in between. The so-called 'quantum leap' in physics is when an atom 'leaps' from one state to another without going through a staged transformation. You could say that it goes from A to C without passing through B. This is what the lady experienced with the cars. Different

Figure 168: *This man is not moving as he plays a computer game, but to his perception he will be moving. It is an illusion – just as it is in the 'real' world*

areas of the brain decode different aspects of the vibrational/electrical information and together they construct what we think is reality. When you play one of those virtual-reality car-racing games you are just sitting there while the track is moving (Fig 168). Our reality is a bit like that. Sometimes I go into states of consciousness where I see the world moving in my brain while my body goes nowhere, like watching a movie. During these experiences the virtual-reality game is so clear. There is a story of two monks debating about the movement of a flag in the wind. 'The flag is moving,' said one. 'No, the wind is moving,' said the other. A third, passing by and hearing the conversation, said, 'The flag is not moving. The wind is not moving. Your mind is moving.' In movies like *The Matrix* and *The Thirteenth Floor*, people are 'plugged in' to illusory realities through their brains while they are sitting in a chair or lying on a table without moving. It's the same principle with our reality (Fig 169). So how come people seem to be moving all over the place, racing cars and winning the 100 metres? It reminds me of the line in *The Matrix* when Neo is out of breath in a computer software fight sequence. Morpheus says to him: 'Do you believe that my being stronger or faster has anything to do with my muscles in this place? Do you think that's air you're breathing now?' The mind experiences what it believes it is experiencing and submits to rules it believes are real.

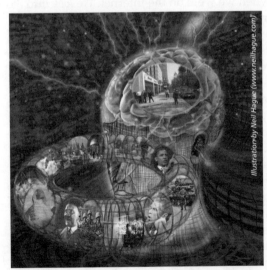

Figure 169: *We are not 'moving' through the 'world'. We are decoding information that makes it seem so – just like there is apparent movement in a computer game when it is only information being decoded by a static computer standing on a desk*

Here's another cracker ... there is no 'space' either. Scientists can't understand why subatomic particles can communicate instantly with each other over staggering 'distances'. They are thinking in terms of space when there is no space. It is like the droplet of water and the ocean. There are no particles, plural, except in the way we perceive them in the illusion. All particles are the same *One*. They don't have to communicate between each other when there is no 'each other'; and they don't move from one place to another, because there is no space and so there can be no 'places'. The illusion of time and space is created by the way the brain reads information it receives from the senses. The Universe is, as Einstein said, 'limited in time and space', because time and space were programmed into the virtual-reality construct by those who created it. There is no time and space beyond the realms of virtual reality. The perception of time and space is just part of the 'software' program that we decode into the apparent experience of time and space. This is what 'natural' laws really are – whatever the creator or creators of the game, the virtual-reality, decided they should be. The principle is the same as with the programmers that create computer games that are played in such numbers today. They decide what the rules and limitations are going to be and they can be different with each game. Scientists have found that in other dimensions, or what they term 'parallel universes', the so-called 'laws' of physics can be very different to ours. 'Parallel universes' are other virtual realities and we can interact with them and them with us if they can make the vibrational leap between frequencies. This is what the Reptilians, Greys and others non-human races are doing when they move in and out of visible light. Appropriately, the word 'Utopia' means 'no place' – beyond the illusion of time and space. As the old song goes: 'You're everywhere and nowhere, baby; that's where you're at'. Infinity and a pinhead are actually the same because all is One – the ocean. The poet William Blake captured this truth about time and space when he wrote:

> To see a World in a Grain of Sand
> And a Heaven in a Wild Flower
> Hold Infinity in the palm of your hand
> And Eternity in an hour

The Virtual Prison

Many of the concepts portrayed in the *Matrix* movies about humanity being tricked into experiencing an illusory reality are accurate. Where it sways from the truth is how it suggests that there is a 'real' solid world outside of the Matrix. Even many of those suggesting that we live in a virtual-reality Universe still talk about a 'real' physical world beyond it. That is not the case. Creation is made up of virtual-reality worlds and Consciousness. There is no 'physical'. We are experiencing an infinitely more sophisticated version of a computer game, except that for the vast majority of 'humans' the game is playing *them*, not the other way around. It plays them through mind, 'intellect' and the reptilian brain. Genetic manipulation and the suppression of information has turned what was created as a playground for Consciousness into a prison – a prison of perception (Figs 170 to 175 overleaf). The virtual-reality game itself is not good or bad, right or wrong; it is a vehicle for experience. The Reptilians have intervened to isolate humanity from most of the game and imprison our perception through genetic manipulation and other means to the tiny frequency range called visible light. I will expand on this as we go along.

The very foundation of the Reptilian-Illuminati conspiracy is to keep us in ignorance of who we are, where we are, and the nature of the reality we are experiencing. It is designed to keep us focused on the seemingly material world and believe that we are our body, name, occupation and income bracket. We are not. We are Consciousness, or Awareness, having a brief experience in this virtual-reality universe for what we call a 'lifetime'. The body-computer is the vehicle that enables us to interact with this reality;

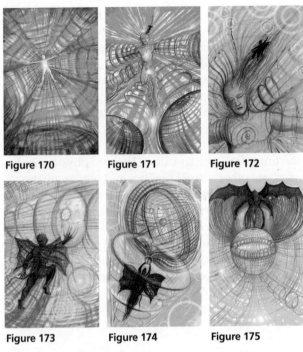

Figure 170   Figure 171   Figure 172

Figure 173   Figure 174   Figure 175

Humans were once connected in full awareness to their greater self, but the Reptilian intervention has entrapped 'incarnate' humanity in Mind and detached them from Consciousness. Only by doing this could the Reptilians and their hybrid bloodlines have secured the level of control that they have

Illustrations by Neil Hague (www.neilhague.com)

it is not who we really are. If you want to go on the Internet you can't just do it. You need a conduit, an interface, to allow you to experience that collective reality. Consciousness is the same. To interact with any reality you must be resonating within the frequency-range of that reality or it would be like two radio or television stations trying to interact with one another. They can't, because they are on different wavelengths. Consciousness in the way that I am using that term cannot directly interact with this reality or density and so it 'wears' the human body-computer like an astronaut wears a spacesuit. Or, more accurately, it looks through a genetic 'telescope' that is resonating within the frequency range of the 'world' it wants to experience. It is this that allows my Consciousness to tap these keys. Neil Hague has

symbolised in Figure 176 the distinction, as I see it, between Consciousness and Mind, the vibrational-digital interface with the virtual reality. Consciousness, All Possibility and Potential, is our eternal state and the virtual-reality universe, the realm of the Mind, is what we experience as the 'physical' world. The Reptilian-Illuminati control system is specifically designed to entrap our attention, our point of observation, in Mind and block our connection to Consciousness. Enslaving billions of conscious people would be impossible, but, as we can see, it can be done when the target populations are slaves to the Mind.

Consciousness is the Infinite *All That Is* in awareness of itself. This is a crucial point. Everything is the same unified Oneness, including Mind, the Reptilians and the bloodline families. They have to be because, ultimately, that is all there is. The difference comes down to awareness. What I am calling Consciousness is *All That Is* in awareness of itself as *All That Is*. It is the eternal All-Knowing state of All Possibility from which everything comes and returns. Mind does not see unity – only apartness, time, space and form. It is a part of *All That Is* which is not in awareness of its true nature. Consciousness is the flowing ocean and Mind is like frozen water. It comes from the same substance, but it is in a different and far more limited form. Consciousness knows, while Mind can merely think. The advancement of intellect (having a 'great mind') is seen within the virtual reality as the measure of intelligence and awareness when, as I mentioned earlier, intellect and thought are village idiots compared with Consciousness and knowing. It is for this reason that I have to present my information in baby-steps to those who are imprisoned by intellect – thinking in 'the box'. I talk in far more advanced terms to people who are Conscious, even though they may never have passed an exam in their lives or have seen the inside of a university. The latter intuitively know, while the slaves of the intellect have to go through the process of thought or working it all out with levels of awareness that see only division and apartness rather than unity, and physicality rather than energetic illusion. I am sure the virtual-reality construct was created for benign reasons as a way for Consciousness to have a particular form of experience, but the 'game' has been 'hacked' by the Reptilians in ways I will be describing. Neil Hague's image symbolises how expressions of

Figure 176: *The Reptilian game plan has been to isolate 'incarnate' Mind from Infinite Consciousness. Once that connection is lost people perceive everything through the five senses and become prisoners of 'physical' reality and all its illusions. When you retain that connection, or regain it, you are 'in' this world, but not 'of' it in terms of your awareness and perception of reality. Everything looks very different from the perspective of those aligned with Consciousness, and Mind-people call them 'crazy' and 'dangerous'. They are neither; they are looking at events from a completely different point of observation*

Consciousness 'enter' the virtual reality for the 'physical lifetime' experience, but the overwhelming majority become so entrapped and enchanted by the illusions of the virtual reality that they fall under the spell of Mind. This is the whole foundation of the conspiracy and it expresses itself at the five-sense level through the manipulation of the Illuminati bloodlines. I will develop this theme as we proceed, but there was a time when humans decoded a far greater range of frequencies than we do now. Genetic and other manipulation has dramatically reduced how much of the Universe we can 'see' and restricted us this to the tiny, almost infinitesimal, frequency range that we call visible light. If it was any smaller we would be blind. There is the virtual-reality Universe as a whole and then there is the tiny part that we can see. I will call the latter the 'Matrix' to distinguish it from the wider virtual realty.

Fake Persona

The most powerful means of disconnecting us from our true state of Consciousness is to give us a false identity. This fake persona is the identification of self with the body. The first major catch-all in the virtual-reality fly-trap is when we are taught to look in the mirror and recognise the reflection as 'me' or 'who I am'. This is called 'self-awareness', but this is when the trouble starts if that is all we believe ourselves to be. Each generation of virtual-reality slaves is teaching their children to take on the same false self-identity that is crucial to a 'lifetime' of service to Mind – and to the Reptilians manipulating us through Mind. What we see looking back at us in the mirror is not 'ourselves' or 'who we are'; it is the vehicle that allows us to experience this virtual-reality universe. Once we identify who we are with the body-computer we are donning the fake persona that enslaves us for a lifetime. The focus of self-identity on the body-computer also draws our sense of awareness into the five-sense realm of the virtual-reality and away from our true and infinite self ... Consciousness. The balance between Consciousness and body-senses is lost and we live in what I call 'body-reality'. From the earliest of ages, the five-sense 'world' becomes the master of our sense of self and perception. When that happens, the Matrix has you. We are the infinite ocean of Consciousness, but once we identify with the body-computer alone our perception of self becomes that of a droplet – a disconnected, 'powerless' 'little me'. When that happens we see ourselves as Charlie Smith or Jennifer Jones and our sense of who we are and what we can do is sucked into a lifetime of myopia that perceives only limitation, not infinite possibility; only division, not everything as One. If we go back to those words of Albert Einstein you can see how they perfectly apply to the virtual reality we are experiencing. He said that:

> ...'Man'... experiences himself, his thoughts and feeling as something separated from the rest, a kind of optical delusion of his consciousness. This delusion is a kind of prison for us, restricting us to our personal desires and to affection for a few persons nearest to us.

This sense of separation comes from losing our connection to infinity and unity – Consciousness – and falling for the virtual-reality illusion of the Mind. This locks perception into a sense of isolation and apartness underpinned by a belief in time and space, and past, present and future, all of which are only illusions programmed into the virtual-reality 'software'. Einstein also said: 'Our task must be to free ourselves from this prison by widening our circle of compassion to embrace all living creatures and the whole of nature in its beauty.' From my perspective I would put it this way: we need to become Conscious and free ourselves from the illusions of Mind. Everything else comes from that.

The Body-Computer

When I use the term 'computer' I am not talking about something like the desktops and laptops that we are familiar with today. The theme may be the same, but that's about all. The body is a biological computer, by which I mean it has the ability to process data and make decisions on how to react to that information. Instead of just being programmed to respond predictably to input, as with merely electronic computers, the biological version can 'think' for itself – up to a point. Alan Turing, who is considered by many to be the 'father' of modern computer science, said that almost all human behaviour was defined by rules that could also be followed and expressed by a computer. As I am writing this, for example, the computer keeps intervening to tell me the laws of grammar, spelling, and so on. If you observe human behaviour it is invariably defining itself according to rules of some kind. Turing said there was no significant difference between the mental function of a human being and what can potentially be achieved by a 'thinking' computer. Biological computers are 'living' computers – 'biological' is defined as 'pertaining to life and living things'. Professor Bill Ditto, who heads the biological-computer research at the Georgia Institute of Technology, puts it this way:

'Ordinary computers need absolutely correct information every time to come to the right answer. We hope a biological computer will come to the correct answer based on partial information, by filling in the gaps itself.' Put simply, it is a computer that can work out solutions without being told exactly how to do it. This is what the human body is doing all the time as it responds to environmental influences like cold and heat or potential dangers that trigger a response from the immune system. We don't tell our bodies to do any of these things because we are oblivious to what is going on with the second-by-second adjustments that the body systems are making. The human body-computer does all of this on its own initiative. It has the capacity for thought because it is an expression of Mind.

All this is way ahead of where our computer technology is now, but even so the latest developments in robotics and biological computer-systems are heading in the direction which will lead eventually to developing something like a human body. What's more, that's only what is happening in the public arena – the secret government and military projects will already be far closer, and those working directly with Reptilian geneticists are already there. This is a vital point to make for those who may say that the premise of this book is too far-fetched. Technological developments in robotics, biological systems and computer potential are heading in the very direction that I am saying the manipulators of the Moon Matrix have already reached. It is predicted that we may be less than 20 years away from developing virtual realities that human perception will not be able to tell from the 'real' world – the 'real' virtual reality that we experience daily – and introducing emotional reactions into robots is now being researched and developed. One research project is called 'Reverb', short for 'Reverse Engineering the Vertebrate Brain'. Henry Markram, Director of the Blue Brain Project based in Switzerland, said it is possible to build a human brain and this could be done through reverse engineering within a decade. Henrik Christensen, Director of the Center of Robotics and Intelligent Machines at the Georgia Institute of Technology, believes that we will have to consider human rights legislation for 'conscious' robots over the next 50 years. We are certainly fast heading for a society dominated by intelligent machines. Maybe we are already there, depending on how you define 'machines'. The UK's Royal Academy of Engineering says that artificially intelligent robots and computers will become increasingly common and be making life and death decisions. The academy says a public debate is needed to consider the social, legal and ethical issues of the increasing use of 'thinking' machines doing the work of surgeons, soldiers, babysitters, therapists and carers for the old. They say that 42-ton trucks with no human driver could be in use on Britain's roads within a decade using laser-radar, video cameras and satellite navigation. These robot trucks are said to be able to 'learn from their mistakes'. Let's hope you're not one of them. They are already close to introducing driverless taxis at Heathrow Airport, apparently. Robot pets and even sexual partners are also on the way in our Brave New World in which biological machines are planned to eventually take over from humans.

A story I have told in other books will give you an idea of where today's technology is going in relation to all this and confirm my point that what we call 'genetics' is actually part of a biological computer system. A study at the University of Florida removed 25,000 neural cells from a single rat embryo and taught it to fly a plane! Well, at least an F-22 jet simulator. How can this be? Cells are 'thinking' biological computer-chips and they can download information and make decisions on how to respond to that data. It was not the 'rat' embryo that flew the plane, but the cells – the chips – which made up its body-computer system. These cells/chips have far more potential than is used in the body-systems of rats or even humans. Rats can't fly aircraft, but their brain cells have the potential to do so because they are computer chips that can download the knowledge and learn how to use it. The rat embryo neural cells were suspended in a specialised liquid to keep them alive, and then laid across a grid of 60 electrodes in a small glass dish. Under a microscope they looked like grains of sand at first, but quickly connected to form what scientists call a 'live computation device'. We'd call it a brain. The researchers attached electrodes to stimulate and monitor neural activity, which enabled them to study how the brain processes and transfers information. The rat brain cells were then connected through a desktop computer to the jet simulator and they were taught to fly the plane. They were eventually able to control the aircraft even in hurricane-force winds. One of the Florida team, Dr Thomas DeMarse, explained:

> When we first hooked them up, the plane 'crashed' all the time, but…. the neural network slowly adapts as the brain learns to control the pitch and roll of the aircraft. After a while, it produces a nice straight and level trajectory. The network receives the information about the aircraft's pitch and roll in the form of stimulation pulses, and its responses change over time. We are its external teachers as it learns.

This is what the human body-computer is doing. It learns from what we call experience, an information download – hence the phrase: 'practice makes perfect'. Its biological

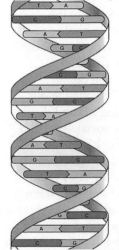

'thinking' nature allows it to assess and make decisions based on that download/experience, just as the rat cells did with the simulator. We refer to this process as 'learning from experience'. Projects like the one at the University of Florida aim to develop 'sophisticated hybrid computers, with a thinking biological component'. These can be used to put 'living computers' into unmanned aircraft to use on missions considered too dangerous for pilots, and for technology such as bomb-clearance machines. The potential for 'thinking' computer systems and machines is fantastic, not least for taking control of the world, as portrayed in the *Matrix* trilogy. Indeed, that is the idea. The Reptilians want machines to control humanity in their behalf.

Genetic Hard Drive

The human body ticks all the boxes for a highly-advanced biological computer-system. A computer hard drive, or hard disk, stores information as digitally-encoded data and the human body is just the same. Its 'hard drive' is what we call 'genetics', including DNA, or deoxyribonucleic acid, and trillions of cells (Fig 177). You can see in Figure 178 how reptilian our DNA looks in close-up and how appropriate it is that DNA is often symbolised by the two snakes in the 'caduceus', the symbol of today's medical profession

Figure 177: *DNA is a crystalline receiver-transmitter of information and is the foundation of the body-computer 'hard drive'*

(Fig 179). When humans procreate we see this as two parents combining their genetics to produce a child that is a combination of both. Sometimes the physical and personality traits of one parent will be more emphasised, sometimes the other, and maybe even traits from further 'back' in the genetic line. From the perspective that I am presenting here, what we call 'procreation' is actually two 'hard drives', the parents, downloading their genetic data to produce a combination 'hard drive' – the genetic traits of the child. The two spiralling strands of DNA in the cells are said to be the body's genetic library, but there is something to emphasise here. We need to remember that what we see as 'physical' DNA and cells are only the

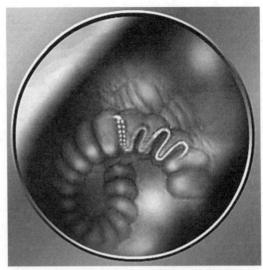

Figure 178: *Human DNA has a very reptilian 'feel' about it when seen through a powerful microscope*

decoded 'pictures' that our brain constructs from reading energetic/digital information. Cells, DNA and everything else we perceive as 'physical', are just the decoded expression of vibrational-electrical-digital information and it is at this energetic level of reality that the genetic data is actually stored. The storage capacity is extraordinary. The 120 billion miles of DNA in the human body retain more than a hundred trillion times more information than any device that human science can construct.

There is far more to DNA than just data storage, as I will come to, and scientists still know very little about it in truth. To prove the point, some 95 to 97 per cent of DNA is called 'junk DNA' because scientists have no idea what it does. But, of course, it is not 'junk' in the sense of being irrelevant; it all has a purpose. Mainstream 'science' is shockingly off the pace when it comes to understanding reality and how it works, plus the fact that Reptilian genetic-manipulation has rewired and disconnected much of it from its rightful function. DNA is a universal software program, amongst other things, and I mean universal. The DNA of all 'living things' – biological computer-systems – is basically the same. There is very little difference in the DNA and genetic make-up of a mouse, a flower, a fish or a human compared with the vast differences expressed in their 'physical' form. Some 85 per cent of genes in mice and humans are the same, and similarly with rats. This makes the idea of rat brain cells flying a plane simulator seem less fantastic. DNA of all kinds has the same four codes known as adenine, guanine, cytosine and thymine, or A, G, C and T. The only difference between 'physical' forms is the order in which these four codes are put

Figure 179: *The ancient symbol known as the caduceus, with its two entwined snakes, is often used as a symbol for DNA*

```
CCCAACACCCAAATATGGCTCGAGAAGGGCAGCGACATTCCTGCGGGGTGGCGCGGAGGGAATGCCC
GCGGGCTATATAAAACCTGAGCAGAGGGACAAGCGGCCACCGCAGCGGACAGCGCCAAGTGAAGCCT
CGCTTCCCCTCCGCGGCGACCAGGGCCCGAGCCGAGAGTAGCAGTTGTAGCTACCCGCCCAGGTAGG
GCAGGAGTTGGGAGGGGACAGGGGGACAGGGCACTACCGAGGGGAACCTGAAGGACTCCGGGGCAGA
ACCCAGTCGGTTCACCTGGTCAGCCCCAGGCCTCGCCCTGAGCGCTGTGCCTCGTCTCCGGAGCCAC
ACGCGCTTTAAAAAGGAGGCAAGACAGTCAGCCTCAGCCTCTGGAAATTAGACTTCTCCAAATTTTTCTCTAG
CCCTTTGGGCTCCTTTACCTGGCATGTAGGATGTGCCTAGGGAGATAAACGGTTTTGCTTTAGTTGT
CGCCAAGGCAGTTCCCTTCCAAACTAGCGCTAGAGCGAATGAGCGAGCAGCCAGGACCACCATTCTG
GGTTTCCAACAGGCGAAAAGGCCCTTTCTGAGTTTGAAATGTCACAGGGTTCCTAACAGGCCACTCT
TCCCTGGATGGGGTGCCAACGCCTTTCCCATGGGCATCTCCTTCCACCCTCACGCTGGCCCAGCAAG
CAGGCAGTGCTGAGGCCTTATCTCCCTAGGTGACAGATGTGGTCAGGGAGGCGCAGAGAGGATGGGC
ACTAGCGTCCAGCTCCTGGAACAGGTGTCAGGCAGGGAGGGCAGACAGGTCTTGGGAACATGTTCCC
CTGGCTATGTGGACAGAGGACTTCTCAGTGGGTCTCGCGACCCTGTGCCCCTTTTCCTGGTTCAGGG
CAGCCTTAGCCGGGGCAAAGGTCGAGAAGAGAAACCCCTGGTCGCCGCCCTGGCAGAATTTGAGTGGC
TCCGGCAGGAGATGTCCCTAGGTTCCTGGGGAGGGAGGACGTCGGGGCCAGCCAGGCTTACCCCCCC
CTGCCGCTGAGACTTCTGCGCTGATGCACCGCGCCTCTTCGCGGTCTCCCTGTCCTTGCAGAAACTA
GACACAATGTGCGACGAAGACGAGACCACCGCCCTCGTGTGCGACAATGGCTCCGGCCTGGTGAAAG
CCGGCTTCGCCGGGGATGACGCCCCTAGGGCCGTGTTCCCGTCCATCGTGGGCCGCCCCCGACACCA
GGTCAGGCTGCCCCTCCGCAGAGGGAGCCGGCTCGGGGTCCCCGCGTAAGCCAGCCTGGTGCCACC
```

Figure 180: *All DNA consists of the same four codes known as adenine, guanine, cytosine and thymine, or A, G, C and T. When put together in a sequence they look very much like the green codes on the computer screens in the Matrix movies. The comparison is very apt*

together, and very small differences in the coding can produce massive differences in physical characteristics. You can see in Figure 180 that the DNA codes look like a digital sequence and they remind you of those green codes in the *Matrix* movies. So they should, because, like everything in the virtual-reality universe, DNA is a digital as well as a vibrational phenomenon. Every desktop computer has its own digital identity code, and it is the same with the human body-computer; it also has a unique vibrational code and so does every species. They operate on specific wavelengths. It is through these compatible vibrational-digital codes that members of a species can communicate over long distances. The Bushmen of Africa and other such peoples are very skilled at this, because their sensitivity has not been suppressed by Western-style 'education' and programming. An article in the *San Francisco Chronicle* put it very well when it said: 'DNA is a universal software code. From bacteria to humans, the basic instructions for life are written with the same language.' There can be no greater confirmation of the computer-nature of the human body than the fact that cells are biological computer chips, and we have some 75 trillion of them. Bruce Lipton, a research scientist and former medical school professor, is the author of *Biology of Belief* which details his study of cells, particularly the cell membrane. He discovered that the membrane is a 'liquid crystal semiconductor with gates and channels' and a computer chip is defined as ' ... a crystal semiconductor with gates and channels'. He writes:

> I spent several more intense seconds comparing and contrasting biomembranes with silicon semiconductors. I was momentarily stunned when I realised that the identical nature of their definitions was not a coincidence. The cell membrane was indeed a structural and functional equivalent ... of a silicon chip.

The principle component of semiconductors used in our electronics and chips is the silicon crystal, hence the term 'Silicon Valley' in California and the 'silicon economy'. Scientists have found that DNA has rare superconducting properties similar to those of carbon nanotubes. DNA and cells are indeed part of the hard drive of the body-computer

Meridian motherboard

Ask most people what the image in Figure 181 reminds them of and they would say 'a circuit board'. What's more, they would be right. You are looking at the circuit board of the human body-computer – the network of energy lines known as 'meridians' in the ancient Chinese healing art of acupuncture. It is a computer-enhanced version of an image produced at the Necker Hospital in Paris in a joint study with the Cytology Laboratory at the Military Hospital. They injected a radioactive tracer into what are called acupuncture points and then took the photograph with a gamma camera. The tracer followed the energy lines of the meridian system that the ancient Chinese were aware of thousands of years ago. Acupuncture is based on the balancing of these energy flows and the main technique, though there are others, is to put hair-like needles into specific access points that exist throughout the network. The needles adjust the flow of energy to bring it into balance. Too much or too little, too slow or too fast, can cause the body-computer system to malfunction – a state we call illness or disease. There is a very good reason for this because the energy passing through the meridian network, what acupuncture calls 'chi', is … *information*. The Necker study discovered that the slower the energy passed through the meridians the more illness ensued, but when it was flowing at optimum speed and balance the person was in good health. To understand how this can be we need to look at the computer analogy once again. What happens when your computer is 'running slow'? The information passing around the computer is not being communicated quickly enough to make it work at the necessary speed and efficiency. If it were human we'd say it was 'not well'. In fact, often the reason for this disruption of information – 'my computer is running slow' – is a 'computer virus'. What is that? Rogue information that scrambles the computer's communication networks and causes it to malfunction. This is precisely what happens to the body-computer with what we call dis-ease – disharmony. Viruses and other attacks on the body – be

Figure 181: *A computer-enhanced image of the body's meridian system picked out by a gamma camera and radioactive tracers. It looks what it is – the body-computer's 'motherboard'*

they chemical, electrical, whatever – are just the 'physical' (decoded) expressions of energetic and digital information. In other words, the information balance of the body-computer is disturbed by rogue information that leads it to misread the normal program. This misreading manifests as a rash or a pain that is only the 'physical' sign that something is amiss on the level of energetic information-decoding. The 'virus' can go on to distort communications to the extent that the computer won't even turn on anymore. What do we say at that point? 'My computer is dead'. This is what happens when 'we' die. 'We' don't die; our computer-vehicle ceases to function.

Central processing

How appropriate that a central processing unit, or CPU, is known as the 'brain' of a computer because it reads, processes and filters all communications traffic. The brain is the central processing unit of the body. It filters the information passing around the body, assesses it and decides what to do with it or where it should go. It controls the body's electrical / chemical, or electrochemical, systems which are, in fact, another form of information communication and response. These systems connect with the meridian circuit-board network of energy lines – again, information – which in turn interact with the series of vortices known by the ancient Sanskrit word 'chakra' (meaning 'wheels of light') that I described earlier. These 'chakras' connect through into other energetic levels of being beyond human sight. All these sources of information are processed through the human brain, which operates on many more levels than science appreciates. It's not just a central processing unit for the five senses; it operates multi-dimensionally. This means is that if a malevolent force wished to control human life by controlling human perception of self and the world (which it does and is doing) then the brain would be a prime target within the 'physical' realm. It is the brain that constructs the reality we think we are experiencing as the 'out there' 'world' of people, places and landscapes, etc. Controlling the brain's perception of reality dictates what people will experience as decoded 'physical' reality. It will control their lives, as we shall see.

One other point to stress about the brain and human genetics in general: the body is not just a computer; it is a biological, living, thinking computer and can respond to changing circumstances. It is believed by medical 'science' – wrongly, as usual – that the brain is 'hardwired' or 'fixed' from birth and cannot change with circumstances. If you damage your brain, that's it, nothing can be done about the functions you have lost. This is patent nonsense, however, as the pioneers of what is called neuroplasticity have shown. Most prominent among them was the late Paul Bach-y-Rita who did incredible work to help people with strokes and many forms of brain damage and dysfunction by training the brain to rewire and decode information in another way. There are specific parts of the brain that specialise in certain senses and activities, but they can also perform other functions as well. The emerging science of neuroplasticity has proved this beyond question.

Computer memory

A computer has two forms of memory – the hard drive that retains information permanently, or until it's erased, and a 'virtual memory', or RAM, which is used while you are working at the keyboard opening different files and other applications. When you open too many pages or files at one time and it breaches your 'RAM', or virtual memory space, you will get a notice on the screen saying that your virtual memory is too low and advising you to respond by closing some applications. When you press 'Save' on the computer the information held in the virtual memory is transferred to the hard drive to be held indefinitely. The body-computer is the same; we call it 'short-term' and 'long-term' memory. We retain a certain amount of information for a very short time, not more than a minute is the general opinion of researchers, and what registers passes into the long-term memory – or goes from RAM to hard drive. With forms of dementia the short-term memory process can malfunction and so you have people who forget what they said or did a minute ago, but can clearly recall events of decades ago. Their 'Save' function is not working as it should. We also have a version of running low on virtual memory when someone is giving us a list of facts that we can't process and we say, 'Hold on, slow down, I can't remember all of that.' This is the body-computer's way of saying 'my virtual memory is too low; please close some applications' ('Shut-the-fuck-up'). An article at **Psychtests.com** describes the process like this:

> Basically anything you see, hear, touch, or experience enters almost instantly (in a
> quarter of a second) into your short-term memory. We have short-term memories so we

can use something immediately and then forget it if we no longer need to know it. We use it to recognize or understand something right at the moment that we're faced with it. Everything, essentially, starts with short-term memory ...

... Your long-term memory is where you keep all the memories and facts that you use to define who you are. Your first memory as a child, the first love letter you ever wrote or received, the time you broke your arm – it's all in there. While we can't explain for sure why we recall certain things and not others, we do know some things about long-term memory. Information passes through short-term to get to long term.

It's the same principle as virtual memory and the hard drive.

Computer Security

Wherever you look with the human body, the computer analogy plays out. Everyone who works with a computer will be familiar with anti-virus or 'firewall' software which blocks, isolates or destroys viruses and files or other information that invades the computer system and causes it to malfunction. In the worst cases it can so scramble the operating and communication systems that they shut down altogether and won't restart. In other words, the computer 'dies'. Here is an explanation of computer viruses from **microsoft.com**:

Computer viruses are small software programs that are designed to spread from one computer to another and to interfere with computer operation. A virus might corrupt or delete data on your computer, use your e-mail program to spread itself to other computers, or even erase everything on your hard disk.

That's how viruses and other forms of illness and disease attack the human body and can be spread from person to person. Note also: computer viruses are small software programs. So are human viruses and other forms of disease. They are disruptive software programs within the virtual-reality – information that is decoded by the body-computer and causes it to miss-read the usual flow of data. The makers of the Norton Anti-Virus system include this theme on their website:

One of the biggest slowdowns of a PC is caused by viruses, adware or spyware as it's often called ... A virus is a piece of malicious software code written to cause some kind of damage to a computer system, or network, or even the Internet itself. Viruses spread, similar to their biological namesake, from one machine to another and can spread havoc wherever they go.

When it reads the data accurately, the body is healthy because it is in digital and vibrational in harmony; but when the virus throws a symbolic spanner in the works (rogue data) it triggers information disharmony or what we call 'illness'. Scientists may appear to see a 'physical' virus under the microscope, but that's only after his or her brain has decoded it into that form. If we could see the virus (and everything else) before the decoding we would see it as digital (mathematical data 'software') and on another level as a vibrating energy-field or waveform. To deal with the explosion of computer viruses today we employ what is called 'anti-virus software', which is programmed to detect and deal with disruptive data packages before they can harm the computer's operating system. This is an Internet explanation of how these anti-virus systems deal with one form of virus called 'malware' (short for malicious software) which also goes under names like worms, trojan horses, rootkits, spyware, dishonest adware and crimeware:

> Signature based detection is the most common method that antivirus software utilizes to identify malware. To identify viruses and other malware, antivirus software compares the contents of a file to a dictionary of virus signatures. Because viruses can embed themselves in existing files, the entire file is searched, not just as a whole, but also in pieces.

The makers of Norton Anti-Virus say of their software:

> It runs unobtrusively in the background, checking all vulnerable files for possible infection by mischievous, sometimes malevolent, programs called viruses and worms. [It] … does this by looking for the identifying signatures of these worms and viruses and comparing them to known viruses for which it has files.

Those passages could just as easily be describing the human immune system, which is a fantastically more sophisticated version of anti-virus software. It creates firewalls to defend the body-computer against attacks from disruptive data, better known as illness and disease, and to do this it … 'compares the contents of a file to a dictionary of virus signatures'. This is why when a new disease comes along which the immune system isn't programmed to read, people can 'drop like flies' because they have no protection. This happened when smallpox was introduced by Europeans to the then smallpox-free Native American population. New anti-virus signatures have to be programmed into desktop computers as new threats are identified, but because the body-computer is 'living or biological' it has the ability to think and work it out for itself. When a new disease emerges, the immune system eventually learns to identify the signature and deal with it. Ironically, and not by accident, vaccines that are supposed to boost such protection actually undermine the body's defences by overwhelming them with the horrific shite they contain in the form of toxic chemicals, DNA from animal tissue and aborted foetuses, and foreign proteins like either live or dead viruses and bacteria. To think that babies and toddlers, with their immune defences still forming, are now given some 25 vaccines, including combinations, before the age of two. The Illuminati-controlled pharmaceutical cabal, or 'Big Pharma', makes billions of dollars a year from vaccines and still more from drugs for those who suffer from immune-system damage caused by vaccinations. The other point to make here is that the toxic cocktails called 'vaccines' are themselves data that disrupts the brain/genetic decoding system. The same goes for the pharmaceutical drugs and this is why they cause so many problems with so-called 'side-effects'. They are not 'side-effects' at all. They are *effects* – computer virus effects. The Reptilians and their hybrid families coldly target the immune system to destabilise the human body-computer from the earliest possible age and this is a motivation behind moves for compulsory vaccination.

Seeing the obvious...

I have identified the body computer's hard drive, circuit board, central processing unit, and memory systems, and the list of body-to-computer connections just goes on and on. What happens, for instance, when a computer shuts down and ticks over with a blank screen and minimum activity? We say it is in 'sleep mode' – the same state that our body-computer goes into when it is at rest and using minimum energy to tick over. When a computer won't turn on we say it is 'dead'. And what is the quickest way to 'kill' a computer? Drop it from a great height or deal it a fierce blow. So it is with the body-computer because, in both cases, it destroys the communication system that gives it 'life'. What I am saying here is so obvious, but often what is in front of our eyes is the last thing to register. Even some mainstream scientists are seeing the connections between computers and the human body, though not the wider implications of what that means. Computers work on the binary number system of 1 and 0 which represent on and off electrical impulses. I found this explanation on the Internet:

> A digital computer is designed to process data in numerical form; its circuits perform directly the mathematical operations of addition, subtraction, multiplication and division. The numbers operated on by a digital computer are expressed in the binary system; binary digits, or bits, are 0 and 1 ... Binary digits are easily expressed in the computer circuitry by the presence (1) or absence (0) of a current or voltage.

'Trinary' computers are now being developed that operate with the numbers 1, 0 and minus 1. This will provide much greater potential because instead of being in either a 1 (active charge) or 0 (no charge) on-off state which simply reacts to input, the additional option of minus 1 allows them to ignore information not considered relevant to the immediate task. You will not be surprised by now to know that the human brain operates on the same binary and trinary systems. Every cell membrane has what are called 'gates and channels' that allow in what the cell needs and keep out what could do harm. This opening and closing is activated by on-off electrical charges – the binary system found in computers. Incidentally, this is one reason why electrical and electromagnetic fields can be so damaging to health. If the body's electrical system is disrupted or short-circuited, the cells can open and close at the wrong time to allow destructive substances to breach the defences. This is one reason why we have people living near and under power lines – which project massive electromagnetic fields – getting a greater prevalence of certain cancers than the general population, and the same with those who work with electromagnetic and microwave technology. DNA is fundamentally affected by magnetic fields and is being constantly influenced by the Earth's magnetic field and the energy meridians known as ley lines. The electrical charges in DNA create little magnetic fields which communicate with, and are therefore affected by, other magnetic fields. What would happen if you put a computer in a powerful and disruptive electromagnetic field? It would not work properly; and neither does the body. This will become extremely relevant when I get to the influence of the artificial Moon and what it is doing to human perception.

Computer information is communicated through combinations of on-off electrical states and the sequence of noughts and ones represent words, colours, graphics, etc., in

Figure 182: *Binary numbers represent on-off electrical states and, as with DNA, their sequence decides the outcome*

their decoded state and they have the same feel as the A, C, G and T codes of DNA (Fig 182). They look so similar because although one is far more advanced than the other, the basic theme is the same. Randall O'Reilly, Professor of Psychology at the University of Colorado, is one mainstream researcher who has made the connection between the binary system of computers and the human brain. He says that a region of the brain that scientists believe is critical to human intellectual abilities functions much like a digital computer. 'Many researchers who create these models shun the computer metaphor,' O'Reilly said. 'My work comes out of a tradition that says people's brains are nothing like computers and now all of a sudden as we look at them, in fact, in a certain respect they are like computers.' What has thrown science off the path, apart from rigid preconceived ideas, manipulation by the hybrid families and pressure to conform to the 'party line', is that computers and the human body may be the same in principle, but they are poles apart in terms of sophistication. Digital computers operate by turning electrical signals into binary on-off states, and Professor O'Reilly found the same in the brain. 'The neurons in the prefrontal cortex are binary – they have two states, either active or inactive – and the basal ganglia are essentially a big switch that allows you to dynamically turn on and off different parts of the prefrontal cortex,' O'Reilly said. The prefrontal cortex was the 'executive centre' of the brain and supported 'higher level' cognition, including decision-making and problem solving. Researchers believe that the prefrontal cortex is critical to human intellectual ability and to understanding more about human intelligence. For many years I have felt that the replacement of analogue television with digital is highly significant to the manipulators because it will allow a greater connection to the digital human brain.

The brain, as I've said, also works on the trinary system of three numbers and states. Guosong Liu, a neuroscientist at the Picower Center for Learning and Memory at the Massachusetts Institute of Technology, said in the publication *Nature Neuroscience* that understanding this could have major implications for the development of new computers, because the third mode of minus 1 would allow them to ignore information as necessary – like the brain ignores your surroundings while you are concentrating on something. 'Computers don't ignore information,' Liu said. 'This is an evolutionary advantage that's unique to the brain.' Well, computers currently developed don't ignore information, but clearly they can once that knowledge is understood. It is believed that future computers and software will function on trinary systems and make everything we see today obsolete within the next ten years. Even further along the road (in the public arena, anyway) are so-called 'quantum computers' which are now being planned and developed. These will have far greater speed, memory and computing power through harnessing the limitless potential of atoms, molecules and energetic waveforms. This is much closer to the way the 'computer' system of the virtual-reality universe operates, including the human body. Quantum computing has the potential to solve problems that would otherwise take millions of years to overcome and they will take computer potential into the stratosphere. The Reptilians and their hybrids already have them. Experts in the field say that for a quantum computer to work, the atoms must be held in a fixed space to create an undisturbed, oscillating wave motion. This atomic 'quantum wave' can store far more information than a normal computer 'bit' and so can process much quicker and more powerfully than the systems we see today. This is more confirmation of the potential for waveforms to retain information and the primary state of this virtual-reality is waveform information, vibration or oscillation, which the five senses transform into electrical signals for the brain to decode into illusory three-dimensional reality. Interestingly, I read about one major development in quantum computer technology which involved trapping atoms (to set up the wave motion between them) in a silicon crystal. As we shall see, the human body is basically a liquid crystal down to the DNA and every cell.

Downloading 'evolution'

The understanding that the human body is a biological 'thinking' computer system within a virtual-reality universe dissolves so many 'mysteries' into the patently obvious. Take 'evolution', for instance, when species (body-computers) adapt to their changing environmental needs. I would emphasise that the 'evolution' I am talking about here is that which affects the body, not Consciousness. These are constantly confused and inter-changed with regard to 'evolution' when they are not the same at all. We have all marvelled at how birds, fish and other animal species have 'developed' amazing abilities that are specific to their life-cycles and environment. This includes night-sight for nocturnal species and telephoto eyes for some birds, to enable them to see fish from a great height. This can be easily explained. These traits were programmed into the body-computer of these species when they were created by the architect, or architects, of the virtual-reality and they were introduced into the 'game' (Fig 183). It can also be that the architects 'upgrade' the species as the virtual-reality landscape changes, but given that the 'physical' form is a biological computer, there is, at least mostly, no need for that. What we call 'evolution' is the body-computer receiving information from its environment and making adjustments in response. If these changes are done

Figure 183: *Animals also have body-computers – all 'physical' life does – and their programs can be written by their creator and changed ('evolved') or deleted (made 'extinct')*

quickly enough to keep pace with the changing environment it is called 'evolution'. If the change happens too slowly to keep up, it is called extinction. The architects of the virtual reality, the 'Universe', could well choose to delete programs and this would also be experienced as 'extinction'. You can see the programs clearly written into animal species that synchronise with the rest of the game. Raccoons survive and prosper through the sensitivity of their hands and fingers and so the program writers devoted some 60 per cent of the surface of the raccoon's neocortex to the hand. Mice use their whiskers to read and interact with the world and half their sensory cortex is connected to the whiskers. How could this happen? Click, click, 'Enter'. The term 'mutation' is defined as: 'a change of the DNA sequence within a gene or chromosome of an organism resulting in the creation of a new character or trait not found in the parental type.' These changes are generated by the body-computer system which receives information from its environment and constantly assesses the consequences for its comfort and survival. One example is the process of thermoregulation that maintains body temperature within certain levels even when it is faced with very different external conditions of hot and cold. The body is constantly making small and large adjustments in response to inner and outer change and challenges (physical, mental and emotional). These adjustments by the body-computer lead eventually to permanent changes if there are permanent modifications to its environment.

The Body Mind

There is another vital point to make here if we are going to grasp the true nature of our interaction with the virtual-reality universe and recognise the fake identity we are living: our body-computers are thinking biological entities and therefore they have what we call 'personalities'. One of the most profound ways that we get lost in the Moon Matrix is that we mistake these personalities for 'us'. When we lose a connection to the awareness I call Consciousness, the *All That Is*, our perceptions, emotions, reactions and responses are driven by the personality software programs running through the body-computer. Some psychologists talk about 'archetypal personalities' and I have heard it claimed that everyone's personality can be found in just twelve of these archetypes and combinations of them. How can this be? The 'archetypes' are the 'personality software' programmed into human body-computers by the Reptilians that have manipulated the program to impose such limitation. The only way we can override these programmed 'personalities' with their programmed perceptions, beliefs and behaviour is to reconnect with what we really are – Consciousness. Without that, the program runs our lives.

Carl Jung, the famous Swiss psychiatrist, sought to connect these personality archetypes to genetic inheritance and he believed them to be instinctive. He said we are born with these patterns that structure our imagination and make it distinctly human. Jung suggested that archetypes are very closely linked to our bodies. In fact, they *are* our bodies – our body-computer systems – and their energetic expression, the electromagnetic field that we call the 'aura'. Jung identified 70 archetypal patterns in every culture and period of human history. He found that they followed the same archetypal 'laws' in all cases and he said that a 'Universal Unconscious' was behind all of this. Humans did not have separate, or personal, unconscious minds and instead shared a single Universal Unconscious, Jung said. Yes, what I call the Mind. Jung concluded that the conscious mind was rooted in this Universal Unconscious and to him the human mind was shaped according to universal patterns. Yes, the patterns of the Mind, the one Mind through which we all interface with this reality. Jung said personality traits are inherited and are closely linked with the body. Yes, they are, through the computer download we call procreation. These are the patterns that, in his terms, make us 'distinctly human' – yes, the human software program. People talk about themselves as 'being human', but that's not who they are. They are Consciousness, and what we call 'human' is a construct of the virtual reality that allows us to experience this 'world'. 'Human' is a body-computer and it is programmed not only with 'physical' traits, but also with emotional responses and behaviour responses that we know as 'personalities'. Psychiatrists and mainstream therapists who work with the 'human mind' are like computer tech-support, and hypnotists are re-programmers. They are not dealing with Consciousness, but the computer 'mind' and emotions – both expressions of the Mind.

Personality downloads

It is so important to appreciate that emotional, behaviour and personality traits that appear to be 'us' are often, I would say most often (at the very least), programs running through the body-computer that we mistake for 'us'. 'We' also inherit thought patterns, attitudes, aptitudes, abilities and emotional traits in the body-computer program, and then take these to be our 'personality' and who we are. Every experience in this life – the nice and the not so nice – that impacts on our memory systems is also downloaded into the 'mix' and adds to the body programs that come together under the terms 'human' and 'personality' or 'character'. Then there is the reptilian brain constantly chattering away and reacting to circumstance with 'primitive emotional responses'. Scientists are discovering ever more genetic connections to human emotions and behaviour. For example, German researchers identified the gene (program) that they say makes some people angrier than others. They asked more than 800 people to fill in a questionnaire designed to gauge how they handled anger and then gave them a DNA test to determine their version of a gene called DARPP-32. This affects levels of dopamine, a brain chemical linked to anger and aggression. They found that people with two versions of the gene were significantly angrier and more aggressive than others in the test group. The study at the University of Bonn also found that the angry types had less grey matter in the amygdala, the emotional partner of the reptilian brain. The evidence is now overwhelming that so much of human behaviour is genetically and energetically programmed, and I will be presenting more as we go along.

These programs can include all forms of fears, phobias and character traits that don't appear to have any explanation in what has been experienced since birth. This can be a fear of dogs, when a dog has never harmed you; a fear of flying, when you have never been on a plane; a fear of water when you have never had a bad experience with water. We can all list an endless number of examples in ourselves and in others' reactions that seem to have no logical explanation. They are inherited programs, and every time we have something powerful happen to us we are downloading data that the 'next generation' may have to cope with or may benefit from. I would suggest that many of the reincarnation 'I was this or that in another life' memories come from data held in the body's hard drive. This inherited programming is one explanation for why many people who have been regressed into 'past lives' (not necessarily) have realised that the experiences of a previous 'incarnation' are symbolised by 'physical' traits in their bodies. Someone who had his throat cut (or has a body-program holding such a memory) in 'another life' might have an unexplainable scar-like line on the throat; or a person who had her hand smashed through torture might have a deformed hand in this 'life'. This is information held in the program and at least many 'past-life regressions' are opening up files holding that genetic memory and not actually 'past lives' for the consciousness of that person.

Hypnotists and suchlike who help people overcome fears and phobias are really body-computer technicians who are deleting programs, or rather the best of them are. One of the most famous examples is the 'hypnotist and personal-development trainer' in the UK called Paul McKenna. At the start of a TV show he will meet people who are frightened of heights, spiders, flying, or whatever, and then he brings them back at the end either far better or 'cured'. What he is doing is downloading alternative realities onto the computer and deleting the program that is causing the problem – fear of heights, spiders, flying, and so on. This is not a cop-out for human behaviour because we always have the option of becoming Conscious and overriding these programs. If we want a better world it is our responsibility to do that. But it does explain so much about our behaviour and why people constantly, in fact invariably, react to situations in such predictable ways. Only when Consciousness enters the equation does that predictability no longer play out because the mental and emotional body-software is being overridden. I say again that the 'personality' and 'physical' programs that are common to all or most body-computer systems come together under the heading of 'being human'. What we call 'human' in its 'physical' and overwhelmingly mental and emotional expression is a computer program. The term 'being human' is, in truth, 'being the program'. My friend, Mike Lambert, a British healer and scientific researcher, was telling me how planets have vibrational connections to particular metals and draw these to prominence in the cells of babies depending on the positions of the Sun, Moon and planets at the time of birth. This metallic-vibrational connection continues for life at the body-computer level and dramatically influences the character traits of the person. Mike is an expert in Chinese medicine and philosophy, including their system of 'years' – year of the pig, dragon, rat, etc. I gave him the birth date of someone I knew without letting on who it was. He told me what the personality would be in the Chinese Lunar Calendar and he was absolutely spot on. Unless people become Conscious, the program is controlling their every perception and reaction. In the same way, what we call 'races' and 'cultures' are sub-programs of the main 'human' program. Look how different races and cultural groups live, act and perceive reality in basically, often almost totally, in the same (desperately limited) way. They are playing out the racial and cultural software programs running through their body-computers.

Programmed reactions

One of the major confirmations of 'our' personality is considered to be the way 'we' react emotionally to life. Are we calm, quick-tempered, 'rational' or emotional dynamite? But what are emotions? They are electrochemical *reactions*. These can be triggered from the auric field (the lower levels of which are the energy-counterpart of the body-computer anyway); from the emotional programs stored in the hard drive; or from influences accessing the body-computer through the five-senses and other 'this world' means. At the very least, the large majority of our emotional reactions are not 'us', the 'incarnate' consciousness, the true 'I'. They are body programs and 'external' influences. A British woman suffered from clinical depression for 40 years after she had a large number of mercury-based dental fillings and she only recovered when the fillings were replaced and she went on a mercury-detoxification programme. In those four decades she had no idea that her deep and dark depression, which involved periods in mental institutions, was not 'her', but the result of the mercury's effect on her body-computer system. Anyone knowing, treating or observing this lady in that time would have believed that the mental and emotional state they saw was 'her' personality and that 'she' was a manic depressive. But her condition was not 'her'; it was the mercury's effect on her body-computer's chemical balance which caused it to malfunction in the way it decoded reality. When 'we' think or feel emotion, it starts an electrochemical process in the brain and the body as a result of the electrical signals and chemicals it causes the body to transmit and release. In the same way, the reverse is true: chemicals and electrical fields can cause 'us' to feel emotions. In other words, they disrupt the decoding system of the body-computer. Once again, what we call 'chemicals' and electrical phenomena are information that we decode into what we perceive in this reality as chemicals and electricity. These can cause great damage to the body-computer because their information can disrupt the body's own information construct. Disharmonious electrochemical information is decoded into the disharmony we call illness, death and ... emotional imbalance, which, at least on one level, is electrochemical in nature. Many people who live near to mobile phone masts and overhead power cables can feel depressed for the same reason, and so it is with so many children consuming chemical-infested food and drink who become subject to hyperactivity and other behaviour modification. The chemical shite they are given to eat and drink imbalances the electrochemical system and manifests as imbalanced behaviour.

People who have had near-death experiences (when they have 'died' and been revived) talk of going to a place of bliss and love in which they had no emotion, as they perceived emotion while in the 'physical' body. I know what they are describing after experiencing that through other means. It is not that you are cold and callous in this non-emotional state; quite the opposite, in fact. It is *human*-type emotion that is no longer there. Emotional reactions are part of the computer software that manifests as programmed responses which are nothing more than electrochemical reactions played out through the reptilian brain. 'Unconscious' humans ride a constant electrochemical roller-coaster of emotional reactions with each situation, experience, television programme, movie, or whatever. Once more, it is like typing in the data (experience), pressing 'Enter', and watching the files in the hard drive and the software programs play out on your 'screen'. I have observed how many people suffer from what I call 'emotional addiction' in that they become addicted to the chemicals released by different mental and emotional states. This can be an addiction to the chemicals produced by depression, or worry, or the adrenalin rush that comes from competition or danger. Such people constantly manifest experiences, mostly subconsciously, that give them a 'fix' of their emotional drug of choice. The cell receptors that absorb emotional chemicals are the same ones that absorb heroin or cocaine. Given that these responses come from the reptilian brain it means that these emotional addictions, as with others, are addictions to the reptilian brain. When we experience something, or see or hear something, we 'react' to it, usually in the way that most others would react. People say: 'What is your reaction to this or that?', or, 'Why did you react that way?' This is exactly what it is: a reaction; a *chemical* reaction. Almost every time, we react according to the body-computer program, which we inherit and then add to by the way we experience what we call 'reality'. Trauma downloaded during childhood is especially powerful in programming a lifetime of reaction and perception. These reactions are stored in the information levels of the cells – the computer chips – and the rest of the biological, energetic and digital structure. Here is stored both the inherited program and the daily downloads that come from our experiences. It is the information stored in the cells/DNA that 'reacts' to daily life on the basis of how the body-computer has been programmed to react. Most of what people call their 'demons' are inherited or downloaded software programs running in the body-computer. Only by becoming truly conscious can we break this cycle and begin to take control of our lives. At that point, the body-computer serves Consciousness as a vehicle to experience this reality as it chooses. The computer is no longer the master and we start to live life instead of life living us. Addictions in general are body-computer phenomena and if you know how it works you can implant the program to trigger the addiction, reaction or belief. Marketing expert, Martin Lindstrom, reveals in his book, *Buyology*, how the global stop-smoking campaigns with all their warnings and horrific images actually stimulate an area of the brain known as the 'craving spot'. These campaigns encouraged people to smoke by activating the craving spot, the 'nucleus accumbens', and once stimulated it demands higher and higher doses of its fix, whatever it may be. There is a whole new area of sales known as 'neuromarketing' which targets different parts of the brain to elicit the required response, leading to buyers thinking they are making their own free choice. Humanity is being individually and collectively controlled by the same techniques orchestrated by experts in the field who are far more skilled than any marketer.

The sex illusion

The most profound sense of human self-identity is the one of being a man or a woman. Some get so confused between the two that they endure long and painful sex-change surgery. But how can 'you' be male or female if chemicals and surgery can change you from one to another? In 2006, British newspapers ran the story of Freaky the chicken who had begun life as a hen and for eight months had been happily laying eggs. Then 'she' began to sprout a scarlet comb, crow at dawn and try to mate with other hens. Freaky had changed sex – mentally, emotionally and physically – and become a cockerel! This happened simply because, for some reason, 'she' began to produce large amounts of testosterone and turned into a 'he'. The whole incredible transformation of sex and sexuality was caused by a chemical change. A BBC report explained how scientists had been able to control the brains of flies and make females behave just like males. Researchers genetically modified the insects so that a group of brain cells that control sexual behaviour could be 'switched on' by a pulse of light. The team was able to get female fruit flies to produce a courtship song – behaviour usually only seen in males. How can 'we' be a man or woman when chemistry and genetic modification decides if 'we' are one or the other? Consciousness isn't male or female, it just is. It is All Possibility. It is the programs of this virtual-reality universe, the body-computers, which are designed as male or female and you can see from the fruit fly example how it has been possible for the Reptilian geneticists to dictate human personality-types through genetic and chemical manipulation. Consciousness can choose to experience the male program or the female program, or both, but Consciousness is not the 'man' or the 'woman' – the *body-computer* is. In fact, it was androgynous before the Reptilian geneticists intervened. When people in a male body feel they should be female (and vice versa) it is often because the chemical make-up of their body-computers contains a lot of female elements and this makes them feel they should be a woman. Indeed, the process of going through a sex-change involves the infusion of male or female chemical hormones, testosterone and oestrogen, to grow breasts or lower the voice and so on. Heterosexuality is an electrochemical software-program, and so is homosexuality, and if the program changes the sexuality changes. The period we call puberty, when teenagers go through the chemical changes that lead to sexual maturity and adulthood, is also the result of the body-computer releasing hormones into the system. It is part of the unfolding computer-program that takes us from birth to old age. It is not that we need to deny we are a man or a woman within the virtual-reality or, indeed, the fact that we are a father, mother, factory worker, truck driver, chief executive or sea-boat captain. It's that we can choose not to be trapped in a false-identity by realising that these labels are not what we are, but what we are experiencing. What we *are* is Consciousness.

For those who still doubt that our behaviour can be controlled by the programs of the body-computer, look at the story of old Freaky the chicken. One of things that happened when 'she' became a 'he' was that 'he' started crowing at dawn and feeling frisky with the lady 'chicks'. Does anyone think that Freaky suddenly made a conscious decision every morning to start crowing when the Sun came up? It was 'instinctive' once 'he' had been locked in chemically to the cockerel program, which the creators or manipulators of the virtual-reality universe will have written, or developed by mixing programs, as they have with all 'physical' forms, including the one we call 'human'. You see programmed behaviour happening constantly amongst humans, animals, insects, the whole shebang. Do we believe that birds all have the same instant thought at the same time when they start to chirp in the morning? Have a look at the lifecycles of animals and you'll see how they're clearly following a software program, as are 'humans' when they are not connected to their true state of Consciousness. Sexual desire is the same. Consciousness does not desire sex; that's a program of the body-computer, not least to ensure continued 'human' existence and produce the orgasmic energies on which the Reptilians also feed. Did you see that scene in the *Matrix* trilogy when the appropriately-named 'Merovingian' (a major Illuminati bloodline or software program) accessed a woman's body-computer via a cake (information) and caused her to become sexually aroused and attracted to him? That is based on fact because sexual desire can be activated by accessing the body-computer through one or more of the five senses, or electrochemically. That's what Viagra is doing, also pornography and thought (fantasy). What we call sexual fantasy or 'what turns you on' is so often the result of inherited programs and mental and emotional thought patterns. I cannot imagine Consciousness ogling across a bar and saying, 'Cor, I'd give 'er one.' There is absolutely nothing wrong with enjoying sex, it is one of the many sensations that attracts Consciousness to the human experience. Conscious people are quite capable of enjoying sex without being controlled by it, just as sex is also a potential addiction and trap like everything else – and is meant to be.

Transplanting reality

All this explains the 'mystery' of why so many organ transplant patients take on character traits of the donor. William Sheridan, a retired American catering manager, was in a New York hospital awaiting a heart transplant when he began an art therapy course to relieve the boredom of lying in bed. To put it mildly, William showed no artistic talent, but days after he was given his new heart he began to produce far more intricate drawings and paintings. His art therapist, Beth DeFuria, said: 'It was quite amazing how his talent blossomed.' William was stunned and bewildered. He had no idea where the talent had suddenly come from, and neither had anyone else. He agreed to waive the usual anonymity between recipient and donor as part of a campaign to encourage more people to donate organs and, as a result, he met the donor's mother and had the chance to ask about her 24-year-old son, Keith Neville, a Wall Street stockbroker who had died in a car crash. William asked if Keith had been artistic in any way and she replied: 'He was very artistic. He showed an interest in art when he was just 18 months old. He always preferred to be given art supplies rather than toys.' Somehow, William had inherited Keith's artistic ability through the transplantation of his heart. And this is no rare event. There have been many cases of organ recipients taking on the personality traits and abilities of the donor. William said his own personality had changed and he had become more 'caring and loving'. Other cases that doctors cannot explain include:

- A woman terrified of heights who became a mountaineer after receiving the lungs of ... a mountaineer.
- A seven-year-old girl who had nightmares about being killed after she was given the heart of a child who had been murdered.
- A man who had no interest in music, but then cried every time he heard the singer, Sade, since receiving the heart of a Sade fan.
- A lawyer who had a sudden craving for Snickers chocolate bars after he was given the heart of a 14-year-old with a craving for Snickers.
- A gay woman who became heterosexual after she was transplanted with the heart of a teenage girl.

The bravely-entitled 'modern medicine' cannot explain these 'mysteries' because it doesn't understand what the human body is, let alone the nature of what we call 'life'. It is not 'modern' at all; it is backward, brutal, ignorant and archaic. Stone Age 'medicine', I call it. To see the simple behind the apparently complex we need to re-set our perception of the human form. Put aside what it seems to be – flesh, bone, blood and all that stuff – because that's just the decoded version that we perceive via the five senses. It's an illusion constructed in the brain, which is also an illusion in its 'physical' sense because the brain, too, as we perceive it, is decoded information. It is at the information level, what we call the subconscious, that decisions are made which determine the type of world we 'live in' and the 'lives' that we experience and these deeper levels of self are being targeted by the Reptilians through the reptilian brain and endless other means, including subliminal messages. What the body is, beyond the decoded version that it appears to be, is a biological computer system and includes up to 70 trillion cells that are all phenomenally-advanced computer chips. The cells are, in part, the hard drive of the body-computer along with the DNA and the genetic structure in general and it is here, on an energetic, or 'auric' level, that the body software programs and 'files' are stored and accessed. These files include mental and emotional character traits and aptitudes ('natural gifts') that are inherited through the download called procreation and the experiences that have been added in this 'lifetime' or life cycle. So when an organ, especially the heart, is transplanted from one person to another it is the same as downloading information from one computer to another and if the receiving computer opens that file it affects what appears on the screen. In the same way, if a transplant receiver connects powerfully with the energetic information contained in the donated organ it will affect what appears on their 'screen' – the way their brain decodes and constructs reality. And that, if you think about it, is what 'personality' is … the way we decode and construct reality. It is because the body-computer controls (in the absence of Consciousness) this decoding and reality-construction that our responses and reactions are so predicable. The William Sheridan 'mystery' can be solved. He took on some of the artistic abilities and character traits of the donor when he downloaded the information into his body-computer from the donated heart, and his decoding system added that to the data pool when constructing – 'updating' – his new sense of reality. Gary Schwartz, a professor of neurology, psychiatry and surgery at the University of Arizona, and a rare mainstream researcher into this phenomenon, led a team that studied 70 such cases in which the professor believes abilities and character traits were transferred via organ transplantation. He says:

> When the organ is placed in the recipient, the information and energy stored in the organ is passed on to the recipient. The theory applies to any organ that has cells that are interconnected. They could be kidneys, liver and even muscles. The stories we have uncovered are very compelling and are completely consistent.

Credo Mutwa, the Zulu sanusi or shaman in South Africa, told me that at the time of cannibalism in southern and central Africa they had a strict rule that the unfortunate victim had to be boiled over a very hot fire. They had seen from experience and heard from folklore that if the body was not properly cooked, the people who ate the victim 'became him', took on his 'personality'. Boiling destroys the cells, or 'hard drive', and prevents the 'download' during consumption – much like heating a microchip until its circuits are buckled.

Downloading Mind

There is another important point about the mind-body computer … Its knowledge – its 'hard drive' – can be downloaded into another body and even into a machine or digital construct like the 'woman in the red dress' in the *Matrix* movies. She looked every bit as human as everyone else, but in the story she was a digital construct inserted into the computer program. There are tens of millions – and likely far more – of these digital people in the world today. They function by following their software program as an interactive insert into the virtual-reality, and the more sophisticated of them have minds downloaded from other people that can make them appear very intelligent. A lot of 'intellectuals' are digital inserts with downloaded minds. I know this sounds crazy, but

Illustration by Neil Hague (www.neilhague.com)

Figure 184: *The 'elite' bloodlines are digital software vehicles for the Reptilians to possess – the equivalent of the 'woman in the red dress' in the Matrix movies*

even in the public arena we are moving this way. What we call mind is an energy field containing information and it is possible to make a copy of this field and implant it into someone else, even a digital construct or robot. The major Reptilian-hybrids pass on their minds when they 'die' so the knowledge base doesn't die with them. It continues in another body and there are specific rituals they do during the death process that downloads the mind into someone else. These bloodlines are, as I have been saying for years, just versions of the woman in the red dress (Fig 184) – digital software that act as conduits for the Reptilians to manipulate this reality. Satanists talk of receiving the soul or energy of a dying Satanist or sacrificial victim, and the principle is the same. I have read a number of articles about the feasibility of mind-downloading to create what some term 'digital intermediaries' or 'mind children'. What they all miss, however, is that it is already happening. The Reptilians have been doing this for aeons and their hybrid bloodlines are examples of their 'digital intermediaries' or 'mind children'. 'The Voice' in Brazil talked of the bloodlines, and indeed of the renegade Reptilians themselves, being computer programs, but they are biological computers and function in ways that appear to be truly 'alive'.

The evidence is so obvious when you free your mind, or free yourself *from* mind, and look at it with an open mind (let Consciousness in). The body that we think is 'us' is actually a biological, living, thinking, emotional, computer system that 'we' use as a vehicle to experience this reality. When we lose contact with our higher levels of awareness, what I call Consciousness, we become the unknowing prisoners and pawns of the body software programs which we, and others, believe to be our 'personality' and 'character'. No wonder humanity is in such a lost and bewildered state. In turn, the body-computer connects with the virtual-reality 'game' as a whole and how it does that we will now address.

17

The Cosmic Internet

'Follow the evidence, wherever it leads'
Socrates

The virtual-reality universe operates in the same way as the wireless Internet. Encoded information is read by a computer system and turned into a collective reality. A desktop computer decodes unseen 'wireless' information into the World Wide Web and the body-computer decodes unseen 'light' information into apparent physical reality.

People ask why is it, if we construct reality in our brains, that we all see the same car, street scene or landscape. The answer is that the body-computer is connected to the same virtual-reality universe in pretty much the same way computers all over the world log on to the Internet. The World Wide Web is a collective reality for computers and the virtual-reality universe is the collective reality for human body-computers. Both operate in the same way by decoding information to construct a collective 'world'. When you connect with the Internet anywhere, no matter what the culture, race or situation, you are accessing the same collective reality as everyone else (unless your system has been blocked, as in China, to stop you from accessing knowledge and information that the authorities don't want you to see). This, too, is very close to the human experience, as

we shall explore, but, generally, anyone logging on to the Internet experiences the same collective reality. What people make of that reality and which websites they choose to visit is where the differences occur. Some will like what they see on a website and others will dislike the very same thing. Some will go to a sports site, others to news or nature sites, and still others to pornography. The point is, though, that whether you access the Internet in London, New York, Tokyo, Sydney or Cape Town you experience the same collective reality. I have just described how 'we' interact with our 'universe' (Fig 185).

Figure 185: *These laptop computers are decoding the wireless Internet from information encoded in an unseen 'Wi-Fi' energy field. We do the same in a far more advanced and sophisticated way when we decode energetic information into 'physical' reality*

361

The human crystal

The body-computer is a receiver-transmitter of information and is connected to the virtual-reality universe vibrationally and digitally. In this way we both receive information from the virtual-reality, and 'post' our own perceptions back to the system. The Internet analogies go on and on. From the moment we are born (go 'online') we are receiving information from the 'Web' and adding our own information and perceptions to that collective 'Mind'. This is how our perceptions are shaped by the virtual-reality, but we also have the opportunity to influence the collective. For all these reasons, and others, the body-computer would have to be a superb receiver-transmitter of information if what I am saying here is correct. And it turns out that's exactly what it is. The crucial element in transmitter-receiver technology, like radios and computers, is quartz crystal and the human body just happens to be a walking, talking crystal. As I have already mentioned, Bruce Lipton, a research scientist and former medical school professor, produced a detailed study of the cell membrane in his book, *Biology of Belief*, and concluded that 'the membrane of every cell is a liquid crystal semiconductor'. This is highly-significant because semiconductors are excellent conductors of electricity and can also be used as insulators. They are found in devices like computers, digital audio players, televisions, watches, cell phones, sonar and radar. Your computer screen is called an LCD screen, short for Liquid Crystal Display. Anything that is computerised or uses radio waves depends on semiconductors, and here we have a semiconductor liquid-crystal membrane encasing every cell in our bodies – and we have up to 75 trillion of them! It had been thought that the nucleus was the control-centre of the cell, but when this is removed the cell goes on functioning. In fact, as is now understood, the cell receives its information through molecular antennae on the liquid crystal membrane. But there's more. DNA is also a crystalline substance with a shape that makes it a perfect receiver-transmitter. As an Internet article pointed out:

> From the characteristic form of this giant molecule – a wound double helix – the DNA represents an ideal electromagnetic antenna. On one hand it is elongated and thus a blade which can take up very well electrical pulses. On the other hand, seen from above, it has the form of a ring and thus is a very magnetical antenna.

DNA, with its crystalline structure, is a powerful receiver, transmitter and amplifier of the frequencies or 'light' that connect us to the Cosmic Internet – the virtual-reality universe. The body is basically a liquid crystal. I have even seen the crystalline nature of blood when massively magnified thanks to the work of Harvey Bigelsen, author of the book, *Holographic Blood*. I looked through a microscope as the magnification of my own blood was gradually increased, and what did it become? Quartz crystal, clear as day. The Earth is awash with crystal. Quartz crystal is one of the most abundant of all minerals and appears in every grain of sand, in quartzite and granite, and it is found in nearly every type of rock. The crystalline nature of the Earth and the human body-computer will become extremely relevant later when I describe how our sense of reality is being manipulated from the Moon. Quartz crystal has the ability to generate a fixed frequency and convert vibration into an electrical signal and that's just what the five senses do. Our body-computers are crystalline transmitter-receivers right down to the heart of every cell and they are decoding frequencies on an extraordinary scale every fraction of a second (of how we perceive 'time'). The brain is estimated to receive 400 billion items of information every second, but we are aware of just 2,000 or so. Think what the rest of the DNA/cellular computer network is processing. We take what we call the conscious mind to be 'who we are' when it is an almost infinitesmial fraction of who we are, even at the level of the body alone. Incidentally, the body is a processor of electrical information … and what is a highly-effective conductor of electricity? Water and its salt/mineral content. What does up to 70 per cent of the body consist of? Water.

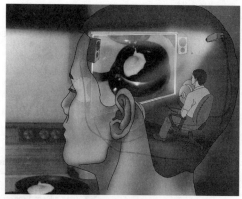

Figure 186: *The brain/body decodes vibrational information into electrical information and then the digital information that we perceive as the 'physical' world. But this 'world' only exists as an illusion in our 'heads'*

So let me sum up a little here. The body-computer is a crystalline receiver-transmitter and decoder of information. The five senses decode information from vibrational wave-states and transmit it to the brain as electrical signals. The brain, itself made up of crystalline cells, then decodes that information into an apparently three-dimensional 'world' that appears to be outside of us, but only exists in that form inside our brains. It is the same principle as television programmes on the screen or the Internet on a computer screen and can also be likened to a movie projected onto a 'screen' in our heads (Fig 186). There is no 'out there' in terms of the 'real world'. The brain decodes the electrical information from the senses in two stages. Firstly it transforms it into digital information, a pixel state; and then the left side of the brain 'reads' that into the world that we think we 'see'.

Digital World

Okay, another question … How can something constructed in our own brain appear so solid and 'physical'? Again, it's very simple. Most people will have seen those holograms you can buy in the shops where you can see apparently three-dimensional images on a flat surface. We construct our reality on the same principles. Holograms are not really three-dimensional or 'solid', they just appear that way, and so it is with our whole reality. A hologram is 2D information turned into the illusion of 3D, and that's what the brain does. The holograms we can buy are made by directing two parts of the same laser onto photographic film (Fig 187 overleaf). One part (the 'reference beam') is directed at the film through a semi-transparent mirror, while the other half (the 'working beam') is deflected away to strike the object to be holographically photographed. The working beam is then directed back onto the photographic film where it collides with the reference beam. This creates on the film what is called an 'interference pattern' and it is similar to throwing two pebbles into a pond and having their two wave patterns collide, causing a web of interference. The pattern in the water is like a vibrational or waveform representation of the stones and their point and speed of entry. It is the same with the laser patterns on the film. They are a vibrational or wave

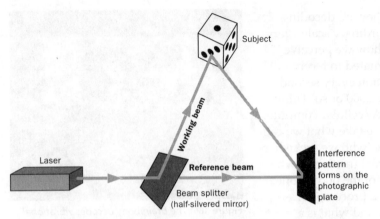

Figure 187: *Holograms are made by using two parts of the same laser light. One half (the reference beam) goes almost directly onto the photographic print and the other (the working beam) is diverted onto the subject being photographed. The working beam is then diverted onto the print where it forms an 'interference pattern' with the reference beam. This is a vibrational – waveform – version of the subject. If a laser is now shone on this pattern, a three-dimensional image of the subject appears. It can look very solid, but it is an illusion that you could pass your hand through*

portrayal of the object being photographed. The wave patterns look like a series of random lines, a bit like fingerprints (Fig 188) but when a laser is directed at the film, an apparently three-dimensional image suddenly comes into view. Holograms can look as solid as our 'physical' world appears to be when, in fact, you can put your hand straight through them. Their solidity is an illusion (Fig 189 to 194). But even the holographic

technology I have just described is becoming dated as a new form of hologram is fast emerging. This is … the digital hologram. These are made by computers using mathematics and pixels and they make possible the printing of holographic pictures from your desktop and the creation of holographic television and movies. An Internet article described the potential:

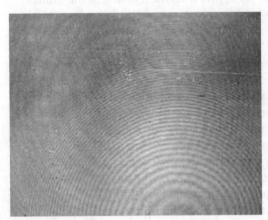

Figure 188: *The 'interference pattern' on a holographic print is information about the subject encoded in waveform. The laser then 'reads' that information to produce the holographic image. We do the same when we decode waveform information encoded in what we call 'light' into a holographic 'physical' world*

The new breed of holograms are not just simple and small 3D yellow-green-red images on credit cards. Thanks to technology from … Texas-based Zebra Imaging, full color high quality images of unlimited size are now possible in digital format. And they look real – so real that when Ford used a Zebra hologram to show off a car concept model 'people stopped, afraid to walk into it'. They thought the holographic car was really there, boasts Robin Curle, Zebra's CEO.

This is how the brain can construct a holographic 'world' that looks so 'real'. It is the brain, taking information from the eyes, that constructs the digital holograms which we call the physical world. It also adds the illusion of depth

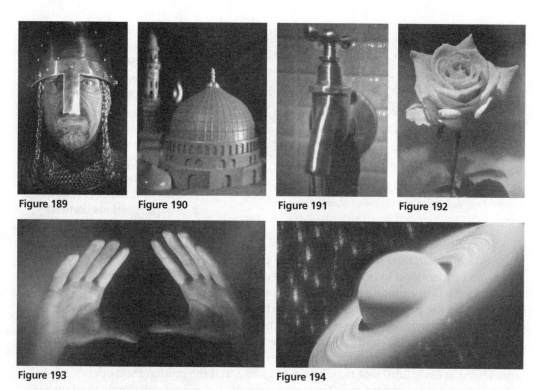

Figure 189　　　　Figure 190　　　　Figure 191　　　　Figure 192

Figure 193　　　　　　　　　　Figure 194

All of these images are illusory holograms and yet they look 'solid'. So it is with our 'physical' reality

Picture 'Old Soldier' courtesy of Holography Studio, All-Russian Exhibition Center, Moscow, see www.holography.ru • Picture 'Medina' courtesy of Laser Trend Holographie, Germany, email: lasertrend@aol.com • Picture 'Running Tap' courtesy of 3-D Hologrammen, Amsterdam, see www.3-Dhologrammen.com • Pictures 'Rose2' and 'Father' courtesy of Holography Studio, All-Russian Exhibition Center, Moscow, see www.holography.ru • Picture 'Saturn' courtesy of Royal Holographic Art Gallery, see www.holograms.bc.ca

and distance by reading information encoded in the signals it receives. What seems so far away is actually in your head, just as the depth and distance in computer games is all on the same little disk. Often we repeat new 'buzz' words without understanding the true significance of what they mean. These are a few dictionary definitions of the term 'digital': expressed in numerical form, especially for use by a computer; using or giving a reading in digits; representing data as a series of numerical values; of or possessing digits; computer science of, or relating to, a device that can read, write or store information that is represented in numerical form. This explains so much about our reality which, as I have been saying for years, is expressed on one level as mathematics and numbers. This is why numerology can be so powerful, and why recurring sequences of numbers can be found throughout the 'natural world'. Scientists and researchers have identified recurring mathematical codes like the Fibonacci number sequence which involves adding the last two numbers to get the next one, as in 1, 1, 2, 3, 5, 8, 13, 21 … The sequence can be found throughout nature in everything from the proportions of the human body to the way plants and shells grow (Figs 195 and 196 overleaf). The discovery of the Fibonacci number sequence is often attributed to the 12th/13th century Italian mathematician, Leonardo of Pisa, also known as Leonardo Fibonacci, but it was known in India and almost certainly other ancient cultures at least hundreds of years earlier. It would have been known for hundreds of thousands of

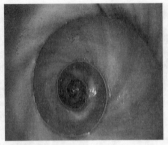

Figure 195   **Figure 196**

The way plants grow and shells form, and the proportions of the
human face, equate to the Fibonacci number sequence

years by the Golden Age society before the series of 'Great Flood' cataclysms.

Other mathematical and geometrical codes and recurring sequences include those known as Pi, Phi, 'sacred geometry', numerology, the Chinese 'I Ching' and astrology. These recurring number sequences and proportions connect with each other. The Phi 'golden number' of 1.618 (plus many more, but let's keep it simple) is also known as the 'golden section', 'golden ratio' and 'divine proportion' and is found throughout the human body in the proportions of hands, face, even teeth. Some say it can be identified in body temperature and the resting human heartbeat and it can be seen in the proportions of animals, sea life, insects and ... DNA. You find the same numbers and the proportions in the pyramids of Egypt, the Greek Parthenon, and endless other structures, because the ancients knew about these mathematical constants. The ancient Greek philosopher Plato believed the golden section to be the most binding of all mathematical relationships and the key to the physics of the cosmos. Scientists announced in early 2010 that they had established that the golden ratio operates in the subatomic quantum realms, too. Their experiments discovered subatomic frequencies resonating to golden ratio mathematics. Dr Radu Coldea, from Oxford University, the principal author of the research paper, said:

> ... we found a series of resonant notes: The first two notes show a perfect relationship with each other. Their frequencies are in the ratio of 1.618 ... which is the golden ratio famous from art and architecture. It reflects a beautiful property of the quantum system – a hidden symmetry.

But there has to be a 'hidden symmetry', because the holographic state we call 'matter' is merely a reflection of the information blueprint in the quantum realms. Modern science has discovered how the 'physical' world can be broken down into numbers and algorithms, which are problem-solving procedures widely used in physics, computers and software. Richard L Thompson writes in *Maya: The World as Virtual Reality*:

> There are many more ways to be complex than there are to be simple. The fact that the laws of physics are so simple and mathematically elegant has led many prominent scientists to conclude that God must be a mathematician ...

> ... Consider the fact that all electrons have exactly the same charge, and all protons have exactly the same opposite charge. This is essential for the stability of atoms and molecules. If these charges varied randomly from one particle to another, neutral atoms would not be possible and biological molecules such as DNA could not function. It would seem that physics has been set up in such a way as to allow life.

It all synchronises so perfectly because the program was written to be that way. The ancient Greek genius, Pythagoras, saw numbers in everything and much of what he said was known long before in Babylon (here we go again). Pythagoras lived and studied there and had access to that knowledge-base going back to Sumer and beyond. Many artists used number sequences and 'divine proportion' in their paintings and sculptures, including Leonardo Da Vinci in works like *The Last Supper*. Author and researcher, William Neil, identifies other recurring numbers in his book, *How We Were Made: A Book of Revelations*. He found that the ancient Sumerian system based on the number 60 and its derivatives constantly recurs with regard to humans, planets, ancient structures like Stonehenge, the measurement of 'time', snowflakes, and so much more. He also found that his repeating number sequences included 360, 3,600 and 6 x 6 x 6 (216). The biblical *Book of Revelation* says: 'Here is wisdom. Let him that hath understanding count the number of the beast: for it is the number of a man; and his number is Six hundred threescore and six.' Neil found that the precession of the equinoxes also fitted with these sequences. This 'precession' is caused by the fact that the Earth not only rotates on its axis, but also wobbles. This wobbling motion creates a circular movement that takes just under 26,000 years to complete the 360 degree circuit. The 'heavens' through which it 'moves' have been divided into 12 sections which correspond to a sign of the Zodiac, hence we talk about moving from the Age of Taurus into the Age of Aries, and about the 'new' Age of Aquarius. All these recurring numbers, proportions and sequences are the mathematics of the digital virtual-reality computer 'game'. What we call 'astrology' is part of the vibrational/mathematical construct and in skilled hands it can be used to read future trends, but they are still the trends of the virtual reality, the computer program. Infinite Awareness doesn't have a star sign; the body-computer does. Everything can be expressed as numbers within the virtual-reality universe and Stephen Marquardt, an American doctor who has studied Fibonacci and phi sequences with regard to the human face, correctly concluded: 'All life is biology. All biology is physiology. All physiology is chemistry. All chemistry is physics. All physics is math[s].' He could have added that all maths is energy and all energy is consciousness. Galileo Galilei, the 16th/17th century Italian physicist, astronomer, astrologer and philosopher said:

> [The universe] cannot be read until we have learnt the language and become familiar with the characters in which it is written. It is written in mathematical language, and the letters are triangles, circles and other geometrical figures, without which means it is humanly impossible to comprehend a single word.

In the *Matrix* movies they look at computer screens full of moving green codes, but what they see are street scenes and people, and our Matrix works in the same way. When I post items to my website I put in mathematical computer codes, and when I press 'Enter' they appear on the screen in the form of graphics and pictures. Once again, the same principle applies to our 'physical' reality as our brain decodes information into an apparently 'solid' world which is nothing more than a mass of digital holograms.

Holographic Illusions

Television was developed thanks to the discoveries in the 19th century of the Frenchman Jean B J Fourier. He identified a mathematical system of converting patterns into simple waveforms and back again that became known as 'Fourier transform'. From this came the means for a television camera to convert pictures into electromagnetic frequencies and for the television set to convert them back again (Fourier's discovery also led to the development of holograms). We construct what we believe to be 'physical' reality in basically the same way, though, of course, it is infinitely more advanced. Information, the foundation construct of the virtual-reality universe, is encoded into energy and appears firstly in waveform, as with the wave patterns on the holographic print. Our five senses then decode the waveforms into electrical signals for the brain to further decode into the 'world' of 'three-dimensional' people, street scenes, landscapes and everything else that we see as 'physical'. It does this by decoding the electrical information into digital constructs that we call holograms, which appear to be outside of the body but only exist in the brain. Holographic reality is not a continuous construct; it is like the pixels that make up the television screen. Look at the television from your sofa and it seems to be a continuous picture, but look at it in close-up and you see it is a series of dots. If you could follow this process of reality-decoding in reverse you would start with the holographic form and as you went deeper into it you would see the pixels that make up this digital-holographic level of reality. Keep going and the pixels would give way to electrical signals which, in turn, as you headed back to the five senses and beyond, would become just waveforms. But all of these stages, levels and expressions are just different forms of the same information. This explains so many of the 'mysteries' that currently baffle mainstream 'science'.

After years of talking and writing about our illusory reality and its holographic nature, I picked up a copy of the UK's mainstream science magazine, *New Scientist*, in early 2009. It proclaimed on its front cover: 'You Are A Hologram … projected from the edge of the universe' (Fig 197). The article inside, headed 'All the world's a hologram', was based on the work and speculation of Craig Hogan, director of the Fermilab Center for Particle Astrophysics in Illinois. The statement on the cover that you 'are' a hologram was quickly backtracked in the article to 'maybe', but Hogan believes from his research and calculations that our reality could be a vast hologram. There have been a few other scientists who have taken the same line, as the *New Scientist* reported:

The idea that we live in a hologram probably sounds absurd, but it is a natural extension of our best understanding of black holes, and something with a pretty firm theoretical footing. It has also been surprisingly helpful for physicists wrestling with theories of how the universe works at its most fundamental level.

The holograms you find on credit cards and banknotes are etched on two-dimensional plastic films. When light bounces off them, it recreates the appearance of a 3D image. In the 1990s physicists Leonard Susskind and Nobel prizewinner Gerard 't Hooft suggested that the same

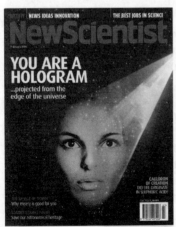

Figure 197: *The* New Scientist *front cover*

principle might apply to the universe as a whole. Our everyday experience might itself be a holographic projection of physical processes that take place on a distant, 2D surface.

The 'holographic principle' challenges our sensibilities. It seems hard to believe that you woke up, brushed your teeth and are reading this article because of something happening on the boundary of the universe. No one knows what it would mean for us if we really do live in a hologram, yet theorists have good reasons to believe that many aspects of the holographic principle are true.

It was a funny feeling reading that *New Scientist* article quoting high-flying scientists and a Nobel Prize winner because I have never passed an exam worth the name in my life and have never been to college or university. I left school at 15 to play professional football. But it is possible to understand reality without any of that academia; in fact in many ways the 'education' (indoctrination) gets in the way. I make this point for all those who didn't have a 'good education' (indoctrination) and feel inferior to those who did. Some of the most academically qualified people I have met were also the most stupid – or 'educated idiots', as my father used to call them. 'Education' is far less important than being Conscious and connecting into the stream of infinite knowledge and awareness that is sharing the same 'space' as we are and is available to anyone who can free themselves from programmed mind and tune into it.

Here's Looking at You, Kid

The forefront of professional science, what is known as quantum physics, has long understood that the physical world is illusory after exploring reality at levels deeper than the atom – hence the term 'subatomic'. What scientists discovered in these realms caused them to rewrite the old theories about the reality we thought we lived in. They found that subatomic particles, like electrons, could manifest as either a particle ('physical') or a wave (non-'physical') and move back and forth between the two. Light, gamma rays, radio waves and x-rays etc., can also 'change' form or 'shapeshift' in this way. Scientists use the term quantum (plural quanta) to describe this state of neither one nor the other. They are both waves and particles at the same time. Think of the ocean and the white crest of a wave as it crashes on the shore. The ocean and the crest may look very different, but it is the same water. The difference between a particle and waveform is only the way the same frequency field is being decoded by the observer. Scientists, remember, are observing their experiments through a body-computer 'lens' like everyone else. The waveform of energy is the prime 'physical' reality encoded with the information from which the virtual-reality is made manifest; the particle form is the brain decoding the wave or frequency field into a holographic image that looks three-dimensional, but isn't. What we call atoms and particles only exist when the brain has decoded frequency fields into holograms. Waveforms can be encoded with incredible amounts of information or potential outcomes and it is the observer who decodes – observes – these potential realities into holographic reality, or what we call his or her 'physical' experience. The waveforms are potential realities and the particle or holographic form is the decoded and experienced reality. Why we choose one potential over another is down to our state of being, perception and belief. If you can control people's state of being, their sense of reality, you will manipulate them to decode, from the waveform potential, the experienced reality that suits your agenda of control. This reality only exists in 'physical' form when, through observation or focus, it is decoded. When a computer is decoding a software disk it doesn't put everything on the screen at the same time. What appears on the screen is only that which the computer is observing – reading and decoding on the disk at that moment. The rest of the disk does not appear on the screen because it is not being decoded. It is the same with our reality. When it is not being observed it exists only in its energetic waveform.

Atoms and subatomic particles are 'physical' expressions of waveforms. It is not a case of 'either/or'; it is 'same as', or 'different expressions of'. For example, the waveform construct on a holographic print or interference pattern doesn't disappear when the laser reads its information to produce the holographic image. The hologram and the interference pattern both exist together. The human body is, at the same time, both a waveform construct (encoded information) and a hologram ('physical') if the 'physical' is being decoded by observation. Thus we have a body and the energetic field we call the aura. One is the encoded information and the other is that information after it has been 'read', as with the laser on the holographic print. The body and the auric field are two versions of the same information source and they work as one unit. Some cutting-edge scientists have suggested that information might not be stored in the brain, but in interference patterns or waveforms 'outside' the brain. They're right. Our information source is the vibrational wave-construct we know as the auric field and that's the location of the memory, too. The brain reads that information in the aura – it doesn't actually hold it, except very short-term; and when you are searching for 'that name' or 'that address' in your mind you are searching the auric field, the 'interference pattern'. When the connection is not clear we have a 'bad memory' and when it is crystal clear we have a 'photographic memory'. Where there is a problem with the transfer of short-term information to the auric field people can often remember in detail what happened several decades ago, but not what happened a minute ago. The body is connected to the aura and higher levels of awareness through the central nervous system, the chakra vortices and the endocrine glands like the pineal and the pituitary. Karl Pribram, a neurophysiologist at Stanford University, is one of the pre-eminent proponents of the holographic view of 'physical reality', and author, Michael Talbot, presents his view very well in *The Holographic Universe*:

> … [Karl] Pribram [realised] that the objective world does not exist, at least not in the way we are accustomed to believing. What is 'out there' is a vast ocean of waves and frequencies, and reality looks concrete to us only because our brains are able to take this holographic blur and convert it into sticks and stones and other familiar objects that make up our world …

> … In other words, the smoothness of a piece of fine china and the feel of beach sand beneath our feet are really just elaborate versions of the phantom limb syndrome [when amputees 'feel' a limb long after it has been removed].

> According to Pribram, this does not mean there aren't china cups and grains of beach sand out there. It simply means that a china cup has two very different aspects to its reality. When it is filtered through the lens of our brains it manifests as a cup. But if we

could get rid of our lenses, we'd experience it as an interference pattern. Which is real and which is illusion? 'Both are real to me,' says Pribram, 'or, if you want to say, neither of them are real.'

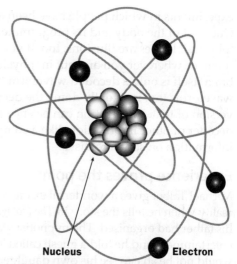

The illusion of solidity is created by the way the virtual-reality programs are written. Watch a virtual-reality computer game at home and you'll see that the people, landscapes, etc., look solid. The best of them these days even look three-dimensional. But no-one thinks they are really solid and three-dimensional, do they? That would be silly, right? After all, it's just a computer program. The reason everything looks solid and three-dimensional is because the information on the software disk is encoded to be read that way. There you have the explanation for another unsolved mystery of mainstream science and quantum physics. Scientists say the 'physical' world is made of atoms, but at the same time they agree that atoms have no solidity. They are packets of energy, basically, made of particles that take both wave and particle

Nucleus   **Electron**

Figure 198: *We are told that atoms are the building blocks of the 'physical world', but they have no solidity. The electrons and nucleus (also 'empty' with no solidity) are much further apart than can be portrayed here. If an atom was the size of a cathedral, the nucleus would be the size of a ten cent coin. So how can atoms create 'physical' reality? They can't, and don't. The apparent solidity is an illusion of the decoding process*

form. In other words, the scientists are saying that the 'solid physical' world is made from atoms that have no solidity (Fig 198). How can this possibly be? The answer is so simple. Does the information on a computer game software disk have any solidity? No, it's just information which the computer decodes into the appearance of 'solidity' on the screen. And that's what we do. The apparent solidity of this 'world' comes from the way the software is designed to be decoded – solid wood, solid walls, less solid human bodies and oceans. It's all in the information and the decoding process. At a waveform or vibrational level, the slower something is vibrating the denser and more 'solid' it appears when decoded by the brain. The faster it vibrates the less solid it appears to us. When it is resonating beyond the speed that the senses can decode it 'disappears' from human sight, but it hasn't de-manifested; it's just left the frequency range that the human body-computer can access. This is what is happening when people say they saw a UFO or 'alien' appear and disappear 'before their eyes'. What they are observing 'arrives' from and 'leaves' into another vibrational reality which the human body-computer is not able to access. So the object, whatever it may be, gives the impression of disappearing into 'nowhere'.

One other vital point to make is that even the senses themselves are illusions, and so is the brain. We don't need our eyes to see, as people clearly experience in near-death and out-of-body experiences when they leave the body and continue to see as before. The body-computer is encoded to believe that it needs eyes to see, and it responds to that programming, but this can be overridden and there have been a number of experiments in which people have been able to 'see' with other parts of their bodies. Once out of the body and its programmed restrictions we see without eyes because our 'physical' bodies are illusions, too. If you look at your body now it appears to be in the room, or wherever you are, but in 'physical' form it also exists only in your 'head'. The brain itself is only a decoded waveform construct and it is the information in those waveforms that is actually doing the decoding. The brain we see is just the holographic version of that. Information can be encoded, yes, but it can also be programmed to be a decoder of other information, like a computer is information encoded to read other information on software disks.

Experience proves the point

Michael Talbot gives a wonderful example of what I am saying about illusory and decoded reality when he tells the story in *The Holographic Universe* of a stage hypnotist at a party that his father had organised. The hypnotist was putting people into a trance state as part of the entertainment and he told a guest, called Tom, that when he returned to a waking state he would not be able to see his own daughter. The hypnotist then stood the girl directly in front of her father and clicked his fingers, or whatever they do. Tom 'woke up' and was asked if he could see his daughter – who was standing inches from his eyes. No, he said, she wasn't there. The hypnotist put his hand in the small of the girl's back and asked Tom if he could see what he was holding, even though the girl was between them. Yes, said Tom, he was holding a watch. Could he read the inscription on it? Tom peered forward and read what it said while his daughter was standing 'solidly' between him and the watch. This is impossible to the reality peddled by mainstream 'science'; but it isn't. The hypnotist had implanted the deep subconscious belief into Tom's brain/mind that his daughter was not in the room and that had tricked the brain's decoding system into ignoring his daughter's vibrational energy field and not 'reading' it. The 'physical' scene in the room only existed in Tom's brain and, if his daughter's energy field was not 'read', she would not appear in the 'physical' holographic 'movie' his brain was constructing. Everyone else in the room could see the daughter because their decoding systems had not been programmed, like Tom's, not to do so. This is why some people will see a 'ghost', UFO or non-human entity and others will not. It depends on whether their brain decodes that energy field into holographic reality. There is a form of brain dysfunction known as 'prosopagnosia', sometimes called 'face blindness', which prevents people from recognising faces. In some cases it can even affect their ability to recognise familiar objects like household furniture or vehicles in the street. The brain is not decoding certain energy fields, or waveforms, into holographic 'physical' reality and so they do not exist in the universe constructed in their 'heads'.

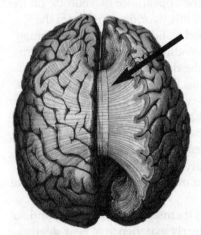

Figure 199: *The corpus callosum is the 'bridge' that passes information (perception) between the left and right hemispheres of the brain*

Fundamental to understanding the way the body-computer decodes reality are the two hemispheres of the brain. The right and left hemispheres are connected by a 'bridge' called the corpus callosum (Fig 199). The left side of the brain is our 'this world' reality of language and structure, what passes for 'logic', and the general 'physical' world perspective; the right side is the creative, the artistic, the 'out there' connection to levels of consciousness beyond five-sense reality (Fig 200). In a balanced 'whole brain' state, the two sides are in harmony, neither dominating the other, with the bridge passing information and insight between the two. But almost everyone in human form is a prisoner of the left-brain and the more you are subjected to the pea-sized box called mainstream 'education', 'academia' and 'science' the further you are enslaved in left-brain reality (Fig 201). This is not by accident, but by design. There is nothing wrong with the left-brain as such; it plays an essential role as our interface with five-sense reality, and that's as it is meant to do. The problem comes when it is the total arbiter of perception. Then what should be a servant to our experience becomes the governor, the jailer, the dictator. One woman's personal experience presents a wonderful example of what I mean. On the morning of 10th December 1996, Jill Bolte Taylor, an American neuroanatomist, was given an extraordinary insight into how the brain decodes the virtual-reality universe and the very separate functions of the two hemispheres. She woke up feeling very strange and although she didn't realise it immediately, a blood vessel had burst in the left side of her brain. Jill tried to ignore the way she was feeling and stepped onto her exercise machine, but when she looked down at her hands they looked like 'primitive claws grasping onto the bar'. She looked down at her body and thought, 'Whoa, I'm a weird-looking thing.' She said:

Figure 200: *Neil Hague symbolises the functions of the left and right hemispheres. The right side is 'out there' and sees everything as one. The left decodes everything into structure, form, sequence, time, space and language. Both are necessary to experience this reality, but when the left dominates, as it does in most people, it can become a prison of perception*

Figure 201: *The Reptilians and their hybrids have structured society to put symbolic guards at the entrance to the left brain called mainstream 'education', 'academia', 'science' and 'media' to stop the perception of the right brain impacting on our sense of reality. This creates what I call 'left-brain prisoners'*

... it was as though my consciousness had shifted away from my normal perception of reality, where I'm the person on the machine having the experience, to some esoteric space where I'm witnessing myself having this experience. I look down at my arm and I realize that I can no longer define the boundaries of my body. I can't define where I begin and where I end, because the atoms and the molecules of my arm blended with the atoms and molecules of the wall. And all I could detect was this energy. Energy. And I'm asking myself, 'What is wrong with me, what is going on?'

What was going on can be clearly understood from the perspective of this book. The burst blood vessel had affected the way her brain was decoding reality – reading the information encoded into the energy fabric of the virtual-reality universe. Jill said that suddenly her 'brain chatter' went 'totally silent'. It was like someone had taken a remote control and pushed the mute button, she said. This is because the 'brain chatter' comes from the computer level of reality and when you disconnect from it you are left with silence. The constant voice rambling on and on in your head is not 'you', it is your body/mind. Jill said:

And at first I was shocked to find myself inside of a silent mind. But then I was immediately captivated by the magnificence of energy around me. And because I could no longer identify the boundaries of my body, I felt enormous and expansive. I felt at one with all the energy that was, and it was beautiful there.

Then all of a sudden my left hemisphere comes back online and it says to me, 'Hey! We got a problem, we got a problem, we gotta get some help.' So it's like, OK, OK, I got a problem, but then I immediately drifted right back out into the consciousness, and I affectionately referred to this space as La La Land. But it was beautiful there.

Imagine what it would be like to be totally disconnected from your brain chatter that connects you to the external world. So here I am in this space and any stress related to me, to my job, it was gone. And I felt lighter in my body. And imagine all of the relationships in the external world and the many stressors related to any of those, they were gone. I felt a sense of peacefulness.

And imagine what it would feel like to lose 37 years of emotional baggage! I felt euphoria. Euphoria was beautiful – and then my left hemisphere comes online and it says, 'Hey! You've got to pay attention, we've got to get help.' And I'm thinking, 'I got to get help, I gotta focus.'

Note that statement ... Imagine what it would feel like to lose 37 years of emotional baggage. As I said earlier, emotion as we experience it comes from the body-computer with its genetic programs and Reptilian manipulation that constantly feeds us fear and anxiety via the reptilian brain. Jill couldn't remember the phone number at work, but she had a business card with the number on. As she looked through a pile of business cards all she could see were pixels and not the 'physical' cards. Pixels are the smallest item of information in a digital image. The problem in her left hemisphere had caused it to stop decoding information as it normally would and she was now seeing a deeper level of the virtual-reality digital construct. American physicist, Craig Hogan, said in that *New Scientist* article about holograms that at a certain level of magnification 'the fabric of space-time becomes grainy and is ultimately made of tiny units rather like pixels …' But, of course that must be so if the Universe is a virtual-reality hologram that functions on one level as a digital construct – which it does. Jill said that the pixels of the words on the business cards blended with the pixels of the background and the pixels of the symbols, and she couldn't tell the difference. She would have brief waves of what she called clarity and after 45 minutes she had managed to piece together the card and the number. But now it was about to get even more bizarre (bizarre to those who do not understand reality). The haemorrhage continued to expand in her left-brain and all she could do, she said, to figure out the number was to 'match the shape of the squiggles on the card to the shape of the squiggles on the phone'. She eventually dialled the number, but when a work colleague answered the phone all Jill could hear was: 'Whoo, whoo, whoo, whoo.' She recalls:

> I think to myself, 'Oh, my gosh; he sounds like a golden retriever!' And so I say to him, clear in my mind I say to him, 'This is Jill! I need help!' And what comes out of my voice is, 'Whoo whoo whoo whoo whoo.' I'm thinking, 'Oh, my gosh; *I* sound like a golden retriever.' So I couldn't know, I didn't know that I couldn't speak or understand language until I tried.

This is because what we call 'language' only appears as words that we hear after vibrational waves and electrical signals have been decoded into language. This is why an Italian psychic will decode 'other world' communications into Italian, and an English one into English. The actual communication is not in words, it is by energy waves – a vibration, a thought form. It is the decoding system of the ears and left-brain that turns it into language and this developed as the human form of communication after the sensitivity was lost to communicate telepathically. When we learn a language we are actually programming the body-computer to decode in that language from waveform information. Jill lost consciousness and woke up later to the shock of still being alive. She said that her mind was now suspended between two very different planes of reality:

> Because I could not identify the position of my body in space, I felt enormous and expansive, like a genie just liberated from her bottle. And my spirit soared free like a great whale gliding through the sea of silent euphoria. Nirvana, I found Nirvana. I remember thinking there's no way I would ever be able to squeeze the enormousness of myself back inside this tiny little body.

> But I realized 'But I'm still alive! I'm still alive and I have found Nirvana. And if I have found Nirvana and I'm still alive, then everyone who is alive can find Nirvana.' And I picture a world filled with beautiful, peaceful, compassionate, loving people who knew that they could come to this space at any time.

These two perceptions of reality are the holographic (particle) state of illusory physicality and limitation, and the waveform state of infinite expansion. To control us, the Reptilians and their allies want to keep us enslaved in state one and disconnected from state two. What a different world we would be experiencing if humans could override the mind programs that dictate their perception of self, each other and reality in general. Interestingly, after what I said about software personalities, Jill Bolte Taylor, a brain scientist, points out that the two hemispheres process information very differently; each hemisphere thinks about different things, cares about different things – 'and, dare I say, they have very different personalities.' Oh, go on, dare; because it's true. She says that the right hemisphere functions like a parallel processor and the left as a serial processor. Parallel processing is the ability to perform multiple operations or tasks simultaneously, and serial processing is when a computer decodes data in a sequence. This is why the experience of the right-brain is so expansive with everything happening at the same 'time', while decoded left-brain reality is one of apparent sequences and linear 'time'. There is no time; it is just the program being decoded in a sequence to seem as if there is. The 'speed' that the left-brain decodes the sequence decides how 'fast' or 'slow' we perceive 'time' to be passing. Everything we think we are experiencing 'physically' is illusion.

The Biological 'Fall From Grace'

This book was finished and I was preparing to send it off to start the production process when I read an article about a book called *Left in the Dark* by Graham Gynn and Tony Wright. I immediately sent for a copy and did a very quick speed-read before this manuscript had to go to meet the printing deadline. Gynn and Wright spent 15 years researching human evolution, particularly with regard to the brain, and their findings were fascinating to me in the light of my own work. They conclude that the human brain reached the peak of its powers 'some time in the distant past' and then began to 'devolve'. Brain capacity expanded at an increasingly rapid rate over perhaps millions of years, the authors say, but then this expansion suddenly stopped about 200,000 years ago and a brain mass of about 1,440 grams at its peak has since declined to around 1,300 grams. The period of 200,000 years ago corresponds closely with the work I cited earlier of Rebecca Cann, Assistant Professor of Genetics at the University of Hawaii. She co-authored a study in 1987 in the journal, *Nature*, suggesting that all modern humans are descended from a single mother who lived in Africa about 200,000 BC. Ancient accounts throughout the world also include, of course, the same theme of a state of paradise, the Golden Age, being replaced by the 'Fall of Man'. Graham Gynn and Tony Wright correctly say that humans are, perceptually and physiologically, a shadow of what we once were due to a fundamental dysfunction within the human brain that distorts and limits our sense of reality. This is something I have been saying for many, many years. They say that the evidence 'suggests that the human brain has suffered a significant long-term decline in structure and function [and] … the damage is primarily restricted to the dominant [left] half of the brain.' We are born with this condition, they say, and it progresses with age. It makes what they call the 'damaged left-brain' the dominant perceiver of reality. Symptoms of this include depression, a significantly compromised immune system and a distorted sexual experience, among much else, they say, and the suppression of the perceptually-superior right hemisphere has led to a profoundly dysfunctional state of 'consciousness' (or what passes for it). The authors question if we are, as claimed, at the pinnacle of human evolution. Clearly we are not – nothing like – and the goal is to still further erode human brain capacity. Rapid brain development ends at puberty and the Reptilians and their bloodlines are seeking to hasten the onset of puberty to reduce the period of such development. This is why children are being encouraged to 'grow up' ever more quickly and become teenagers at nine or ten. It is also the reason why children are being exposed to more and more sexual stimulus by the media and 'education'. Gynn and Wright say that the 'damage' to the left hemisphere that started around 200,000 years ago stimulates fear, which leads to a need to control – all traits of the reptilian brain, in association with the left-brain. They say that men are more neurologically damaged than women and that, in particular, older men who control the major global institutions are the most neurologically damaged of all. They are pushing against an open door with that one. *Left in the Dark* is also spot on when it says that humanity has fantastic latent potential if only the brain dysfunction and imbalance is corrected. This potential remains locked away in the right-brain because of the domination of the left.

Scientists at the Centre for the Mind at the University of Sydney in Australia have made the same conclusion. Professor Allan Snyder, the centre's director, says that high levels of brain function are latent in everyone, but they are suppressed by the activity of the 'evolutionary advanced' rational side of the brain – the left-brain. By reducing its dominance, he says, there is the potential to turn 'ordinary people' into 'geniuses'. I have been saying all these years that humans have no idea of their true potential for creativity and genius. Research at the Centre for the Mind is revealing a whole new level of potential that lies dormant in most people. Professor Snyder says that the left-brain edits out much of the 'raw data' – reality – accessed by the five senses and that many processes and skills are lost in what you might call this neurological censorship. Experiments at the Centre for the Mind have shown that if the 'rational' brain areas lose their dominance it enhances artistic and mathematical ability and improves memory. People who have experienced damage to the left brain have suddenly manifested extraordinary, or what we would call 'super-human' abilities, as the potential of the right brain is unlocked. But they are not 'super-human'; they are 'natural human' that has been able to break the 'firewalls' imposed upon 'suppressed human'. These incredible feats of mathematics, memory and other 'miraculous' skills are performed by even young children once damage has reduced the limiting-influence of the left-brain. Many of them are known as 'savants', children who have an amazing skill or skills while also having developmental problems, 'mental retardation', brain injury or disease. Around half of these so-called 'savants' have autism. They are accessing brain potentials that are dormant in the vast majority because of the Reptilian manipulation, and, therefore, they not only have incredible abilities, but find it hard to function within left-brain society. It seems to me that part of the problem is that when the right brain really opens, the left-brain can have its reality-circuits busted, because it can't cope with that level of perception and energy.

Stephen Wiltshire, an 'autistic savant' in the UK, is a wonderful example of their extraordinary 'gifts'. He was taken on a helicopter ride over London at the age of twelve for a BBC documentary in 1987 and was allowed to take no notes or photographs, not that he wanted to, or needed to. He then proceeded to produce an incredibly accurate drawing of the city, as it looks from the air, and included more than 200 buildings – some of which had hundreds of windows accurately portrayed when he didn't even have the ability to count because of his autism. It was all done purely from memory and he later did the same in Rome. You can see Stephen's work at **www.stephenwiltshire.co.uk**. Daniel Tammet, another British 'autistic savant', can do mathematical calculations at computer-like speeds and can speak seven languages (at the last count). He learned Icelandic in a week and his language teacher described him as a 'genius' and 'not human'. Oh, but he is *very* human – the human the Reptilians are desperately trying to suppress. They know the game is up once we access even a fraction of who we really are. No wonder they don't want to be exposed as the manipulators of human life. Stephen Wiltshire and Daniel Tammet are just two examples of what the right-brain is capable of once it is set free, because it connects us to the infinite potential of 'out there'. I say that the right-brain operates overwhelmingly in other 'dimensions' of reality and the corpus callosum is the bridge into this reality – the left-brain. If you can close down, or massively suppress, information crossing that bridge you isolate humanity in the left-brain – five-sense – reality. This is what the Reptilians have done. The human body-computer is, in other words, a 'portal' between this reality and others, and the Reptilians have sought to close that 'door'. When it is reopened through escaping from Mind, or damage to the left-brain, all possibility and potential can be accessed. Musical geniuses like Mozart, who began writing symphonies at the age of nine, are getting their incredible abilities and creativity through the right-brain 'portal'. It is the same with people like the extraordinary American, Patrick Henry Hughes, who was born without eyes and confined to a wheelchair by a physical condition, and yet he is a brilliant pianist and musician. The right-brain doesn't need eyes, because it can instinctively 'see' without them. Sports people talk about being 'in the zone' when they manifest their greatest performances. They say things like 'time stood still' and 'everything went quiet'. What they call 'the zone' is when they access right-brain reality and all the potential that goes with it. I have experienced 'the zone' as a footballer and also when I am writing books and speaking on stage. The left-brain is a kindergarten by comparison. Human potential is going to soar, not least in athletic performance, when we regain our right-brain potential – as we will. Left-brain = limitation; right-brain = no limits.

Professor Allan Snyder believes that the brain has 'traded in' these skills for the benefits of the logical reasoning mind. But have they been 'traded in', or have they been manipulated to be 'traded in'? I would definitely say the latter. Graham Gynn and Tony Wright say in *Left in the Dark* that the Fall of Man happened when humans stopped eating a tropical fruit diet that gave them hormone-related chemicals which promoted brain growth and elevated neural activity. When humans were forced from their tropical forest, or 'Garden of Eden', some 200,000 years ago, the authors say, the link with biochemically-rich fruit was lost. This stopped brain development and, indeed, reversed it. Some functions were lost and our sense of self was transformed into what I call 'little me'. An article on the *Left in the Dark* website says: '… a golden age descended in stages to our present materialist, fear-based age of plastic and Prozac. These neurological effects are now being revealed and verified by today's cutting edge science.' I have no doubt that all these themes are true and that the change of diet certainly had a highly significant effect. But the reason for the change of diet is connected to the successive cataclysmic effects of the Earth upheavals caused by the Reptilian intervention. I would say that the most profound reason for the neurological 'Fall of Man' was genetic manipulation (with the reptilian brain, especially) and the right-brain influence was artificially suppressed – with all the limitless potential that goes with it. This is why billions of neurons in the corpus callosum, the bridge between the two hemispheres of the brain, don't appear to have any function. They have been *switched off*. This genetic suppression also explains why we use only a fraction of our brain capacity, within five-sense reality, anyway.

The movie, *Avatar*, released in 2009, tells the story of what happened on Earth – in reverse. It involves a people with blue skin and lion-type noses who are native to Pandora, 'a moon of the gas giant, Polyphemus, which orbits Alpha Centauri A'. They live in total harmony with their environment and know that everything is connected and part of a unified Consciousness. The trees and plant life of Pandora have formed electrochemical connections between the roots and these act as neurons to form a sentient planet-wide 'brain', or Consciousness. Although the blue people are depicted as 'aliens', they are symbolic of humans, with their right-brain fully 'online', before the Reptilians arrived with their 'spaceship moon' and, as Zulu legend says, 'really messed things up'. The 'Reptilians' in *Avatar* are portrayed as humans who came from Earth to Pandora in their advanced spacecraft to set up a base from which they could take over the planet and plunder its valuable resources. These 'humans' are left-brain-dominated and thick-as-shite, which meant they did not understand what the blue people said about the inter-connection of life. It all was just the superstition of a 'primitive people'. Heard that before? Try almost any 'scientist'. The *Avatar* 'humans' (symbolic of the Reptilians) used high-tech weaponry to destroy the lifestyle of the blue people and used technology to implant their minds into blue people bodies – possess them – to covertly infiltrate their society. Pandora's atmosphere is poisonous for these 'humans' and they have to stay in the artificial atmosphere of their base and flying craft. Sound familiar? *Avatar* ends with some breakaway 'humans' helping the blue people to remove the invaders and restore their world and lifestyle to what it had been before. This part of the story hasn't happened on Earth yet – but it will. I promise you it will and that process is already well underway, although it may not appear so.

The genetic intervention, in association with other impositions that I will detail later, have made the limited left-brain the dominating perceiver of reality at the expense of the limitless right-brain. The left hemisphere keeps us 'in here' and the right hemisphere is our route to 'out there'. It is rather shocking to discover that people can have large parts of a hemisphere, even all of it, removed and still survive. But it's true, and studies of such people using psychoactive drugs, like LSD and so on, have shown that the drugs have no effect on expanding awareness to 'out there' states once the right brain is removed. The left-brain keeps the door firmly shut and doesn't react to such psychoactive stimulus. But when the left-brain has been removed, the psychoactive effect is the same as normal. I can't stress enough, as I have been doing for years, that if you close down, or significantly suppress the influence of the right brain (and the heart chakra), you imprison people in five-sense reality. This is what has happened through the Reptilian manipulation, because only by doing that can they control and manipulate billions of people who are, in their true state, infinite genius. We can see the domination of the left brain by the fact that up to 90 per cent of people are right-handed (each hemisphere connects with the opposite side of the body because of a crossover in the nervous system). Why would you create a body-type in which one hand or side was dominant? You would want them to be ambidextrous, surely? Most people are not, because of the genetic and other manipulation that makes the left-brain dominant. Some other points about the left-brain-right-brain relationship. The left brain has certain 'specialisations', like language etc, but the right-brain does not 'specialise' in the same way, because it is connected to the limitless information/potential field. This means that, as we see with those who have had parts of their left-brain removed or damaged, it can take over language and other functions, too. Experiments have also shown that it is the left-brain that demands sleep, not the right brain, which is quite happy without it. This can be explained by the fact that the left-brain decodes information into 'sequence', 'time' and 'space', while the right-brain operates in the realm of 'no-time' and sees everything as One. Without a sense of 'time' there is no illusion of needing to 'rest'. The brain also becomes a third more active in the sleep state than in the 'waking' state. Part of this is caused by the fact that, as experiments have shown, the right brain can stay awake when the left brain is 'asleep'. With the left-brain shut down, the right-brain can express itself in 'dreams'. I put quote marks around 'dreams', because the 'waking' state is also a dream. I often have dreams that are just as vivid as the reality I experience when I am 'awake'. As someone once said, are you a human dreaming that you are a butterfly, or a butterfly dreaming that you are a human? Another aspect to emphasise is that the right-brain is a great source of what we call 'empathy' – something the renegade Reptilians and their bloodlines don't have. The right-brain connects us to 'Oneness' and, through that, a connection to each other via that 'unified field'. The left-brain sees everything as apart from everything else – it perceives division, not unity – and thus it does not have the same empathetic connection to others and their plight. It is also through the right-brain that we have the ability for powerful communication through telepathy. Once the right-brain was suppressed, so was our ability to communicate telepathically in the way we could before, and left-brain language took over. This is symbolised by the common legends, including the one about the biblical Tower of Babel, in which the universal language of humans (telepathy) was replaced by 'many tongues'.

The structure of the brain, and which regions are dominant, reflects itself in the human experience. When humans were androgynous, a balance of male and female within the same body, they were in a balanced whole-brain state. The human foetus still starts out as what you might call 'neutral' and then soon takes on female characteristics before some transform female genitalia into male. Internal reproductive organs and the external genitalia are decided by hormones produced by foetal gonads (ovaries or testes) and the cellular response to them. If the foetus develops testes, and they produce testosterone, and the genital cells respond to that, a male it will be. You can change a race genetically by changing the information codes of the blueprint. The left-brain and right-brain can be symbolised energetically as what we call male and female. I don't mean so much as men and women. There are 'male' people in women's bodies and 'females' in men's bodies. I am using male and female here in terms of the left-brain being about structure, form and thought ('male' energy), while the right-brain is the intuitive and the psychic ('female' energy). I said earlier that the Reptilians genetically-engineered the androgynous humans into men and women and in doing so they disconnected the whole-brain state and gave us the two-hemisphere brain. This was symbolised in the various stories about the 'Garden of Eden'. They then 're-wired' the brain connections, in ways I will come to later, so that the left hemisphere was dominant and suppressed the potential of the 'out there' right hemisphere. The authors of *Left in the Dark* speculate that the over production of testosterone (found in greater quantities in males) could be a major source of the damage and change to brain function after the 'Fall'. I am sure that this is at least in part correct.

It is also interesting that Zulu legends say that humans were banished from the 'red world' paradise in the Orion constellation because of wars between men and women. Zulu lore says that the genetic manipulation of humans and the creation of men and women by the Reptilians began there. The House of Rothschild symbol, the hexagram, or 'Star of David', is said to esoterically represent the union of male and female, and it is similar in theme to what the Chinese call the 'yin and yang'. The Rothschilds chose this as their symbol, and that of Israel, to distort the energy it was originally designed to represent – male-female union, harmony and peace. As usual with the Rothschilds and their networks, it is all about the malevolent manipulation of energy, or black magic. They don't want harmony. They want imbalance and different energies at war with each other, especially male and female. Look at the divorce settlement, child custody and other laws that are designed to cause conflict between men and women and drive them apart. The Reptilian quest for left-brain domination is also why the education system is almost entirely dominated by left-brain emphasis and information, and why governments (those who control governments) are seeking to start left-brain 'education' earlier and earlier in toddlers at the expense of right-brain 'play' which stimulates the imaginative and the spontaneous. All that I have described here has transformed and severely limited the way we decode waveform information into the holographic reality that we experience as human 'life'.

Ahhh, so that's how it's done

The holographic nature of 'physical' reality explains how various methods of alternative healing work, although the overwhelming majority of even the practitioners don't seem to know this. One of the amazing characteristics of a hologram is that every part of the hologram is a smaller version of the whole. If you cut the interference patterns on a holographic print into four pieces and point the laser at each one you will not get four parts of the whole picture projected holographically; you will get quarter-sized versions of the whole picture. This happens no matter how small you go and it is the reason why healing techniques like reflexology, acupuncture and others have identified how parts of the body, such as feet, hands, eyes and ears have points that represent the organs and others parts of the body. These can be used to diagnose and treat problems in those areas, because they have a connection via the hologram. (Figs 202, 203 and 204 overleaf). Each cell is a smaller version of the information in the whole body and so a body can be grown from a single cell. It is also known that cells have their own version of the brain. All this has to be the case when the body is a hologram. It is the same principle with things like palm reading – the hand is a smaller representation of the whole body hologram. The American neuroscientist, Paul Bach-y-Rita, and others working in the field of neuroplasticity, discovered that areas of the brain designated for decoding one sense could be used to decode others. The audio region was employed to decode vision, for example. This is possible because the brain is a hologram and so every part of the brain is a smaller version of the whole and can decode all functions. The specialist area may do it better, but all areas have the potential to perform other tasks and this is a key reason why people can have a whole brain hemisphere removed and still function. 'Modern' medicine does not understand what the body is, let alone how it works, and

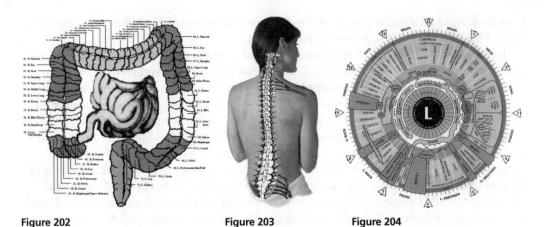

Figure 202   **Figure 203**   **Figure 204**

The body is a hologram and so every part must be a smaller version of the whole. This is why all of the body is represented in its parts, as with these examples of the colon, spine and eye

Colon and Iridology charts courtesy of the copyright owner, Bernard Jensen International of California. To purchase this and other charts see www.bernardjensen.org • Spinal chart courtesy of copyright owner, Koren Publications, Surrey, England. To purchase this chart (which includes the information about which areas of the body the vertebrae represent), e-mail Richard@familychiropractic.co.uk • Further details at the back of the book

the medical industry therefore creates mayhem in human health by attacking the body-computer's electrical and chemical balance with its drugs, radiation and surgery.

The universe itself is a hologram, what I call the Super-Hologram, and so every part – including the human body/mind – must be a smaller version of the whole universe, just as a cell is a smaller version of the whole body. Every planet, star, drop of rain and blade of grass is ultimately a smaller expression of the whole. This is another way that we are influenced by the whole and the whole is influenced by its 'parts'. The term 'as above', so below' is a reflection of this and you can see the obvious similarity in Figures 205 and 206 of the human body and auric field, and the Earth and its magnetic field. I came across this Internet description of the every-part-is-a-smaller-whole principle of holograms:

This is possible because during holographic recording, each point on the hologram's surface is affected by light waves reflected from all points in the scene, rather than from just one point. It's as if, during recording, each point on the hologram's surface were an eye that could record everything it sees in any direction. After the hologram has been recorded, looking at a point in that hologram is like looking 'through' one of those eyes.

To demonstrate this concept, you could cut out and look at a small section of a recorded hologram; from the same distance you see less than before, but you can still

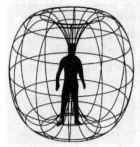

Figure 205   **Figure 206**

The human auric field and the magnetic field of the Earth look the same because they are versions of the same hologram

see the entire scene by shifting your viewpoint laterally or by going very near to the hologram, the same way you could look outside in any direction from a small window in your house. What you lose is the ability to see the objects from many directions, as you are forced to stay behind the small window.

This is what we do via the body-computer. We see reality through a 'small window' and perceive everything in terms of limitation. The 'small window' in question is the tiny frequency range that we call 'visible light'. The goal of the Reptilians and their hybrids has been to make that window as small as possible and so keep us trapped in limitation and ignorance. To know how they do that is to hold the key to human freedom.

The Metaphysical Universe

Now we come to a fundamentally important point that will explain so much about so much that happens in the 'world' that we think we 'see'. The foundation construct of the virtual-reality universe consists of vibrating energy, or waveforms. This is where the information is encoded which is 'read' into the electrical, digital and holographic (Fig 207). If you want to change the 'physical'/holographic, you have to change the waveform level of reality, or what my friend, Clem Hulsen in South Africa, calls the Metaphysical Universe. It is an excellent name and I will use this throughout the rest of the book to describe the vibrational information – waveform – construct from which

manifest all other levels of the virtual-reality universe, the electrical, chemical, digital and holographic. When people talk about the subconscious, or 'going within', they are talking about (whether they know it or not) the vibrational/waveform level of reality from which all 'form' and 'things' are decoded into manifestation. It is the information blueprint of the virtual-reality universe and this is where everything is made to happen, or not to happen, in the 'physical' 'world' of daily experience. This is the 'stadium' in which the outcomes of the game are decided (Fig 208 overleaf). All other levels, through to the holographic, are just the game – by then already decided – playing out. I have seen it suggested that something like 98 per cent of the decisions we make are not made by what we call the 'conscious mind', but by the subconscious. I would go further and say that the figure is 100 per cent. The 'conscious mind' is not the decider of reality; it is the *experiencer* of it. You could think of the waveform level – the Metaphysical Universe – as the movie projector, and the holographic 'physical' world as the movie screen. Once the

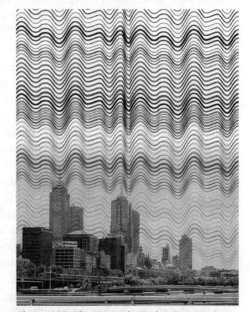

Figure 207: *The 'Metaphysical Universe', the waveform information blueprint, is the foundation structure of this virtual-reality. We decode information encoded in the Metaphysical Universe into the holographic 'world' that we daily experience. To change the holographic, therefore, we must change the waveform blueprint*

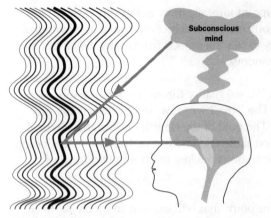

Figure 208: *What we call the 'sub-conscious' operates in the realms of waveform and so connects us to the waveform blueprint, or information construct, of the Metaphysical Universe. We then decode information from the Metaphysical Universe into electrical, digital and holographic reality. Our vibrational state of being and awareness decides which information we connect with in the waveform blueprint and thus what we experience in the holographic 'world'. This is why deleting subconscious beliefs and behaviour patterns is so important to changing our holographic experience – individually and collectively*

movie is being projected there is no changing it. You can shout at the screen as much as you like, get as angry and emotional as you like, but the movie is not going to change once it has left the projector and hit the screen. The virtual-reality universe is just the same. Once the waveform has been decoded into the holographic it is a done deal. To change the holographic we have to change the waveform information blueprint, the Metaphysical Universe. Scientific experiments have shown that the electrical activity in the brain associated with taking an action begins before the person has consciously decided to take that action. This is another expression of the waveform blueprint dictating events and the 'conscious mind' simply experiencing those decisions or perception patterns. So how do we know what needs to change in the sub-conscious? Read the language of life, the events, people, places, situations and experiences that come into your life, or don't. They are the manifestation of subconscious – Metaphysial Universe – patterns. Your daily experience is telling you what is happening in your subconscious by how you interact with the 'play out' holographic 'movie'.

Gifted psychics and those who have premonitions are connecting with the Metaphysical Universe and seeing 'events' in the blueprint that have yet to be decoded into the holographic. There are accounts of people who have had dreams or premonitions about 'future' events which have happened in every detail, and others where an event has happened but the outcome was changed by taking action based on what they had already seen unfold in the dream. One example was where a woman in Washington State dreamt that a big chandelier had fallen and crushed her baby in the crib. In the dream, she and her husband had stood in the room looking at what had happened and a clock said 4:35. It had been windy and raining in the scene in the dream, but she awoke in a panic to a calm night. She decided to take the baby from the crib and have her sleep in another room. Some two hours later, the woman and her husband were awakened by a loud bang. They rushed into their baby's usual room to find the chandelier had crashed onto the crib. The clock stood at 4:35 and it was windy and raining outside. What she had done is access the Metaphysical Universe in the dream before the final decoding of that situation into holographic reality and so she was able to rewrite the blueprint. Psychics are not reading the definite 'future', but the probable or possible 'future'. It can be changed; although the closer it is to the holographic decoding, the more likely it is to happen. Until it does there are many possible 'futures' – outcomes – that could be chosen. The Metaphysical Universe can communicate as a literal premonition of something or a symbolic one. I had an incredibly vivid dream one night when I saw the 'future' symbolically. I was sitting up in bed (in the dream) when someone I couldn't see slid under the bedclothes at the bottom and moved up the bed in a fast, snake-like, side-to-side motion before popping their head out next to me while shaking an empty purse. Two days later that person began demanding money from me.

I have been saying for years that we won't change 'this world' or bring down the global conspiracy until we understand where it is all being projected from. Now I know – the waveform information blueprint that I will refer to as the Metaphysical Universe. The Reptilians and their hybrid networks are not actually manipulating the 'physical' world directly; they are manipulating the information blueprint that we decode into the 'physical' world. The Rothschild global money system construct that I described earlier was created in the Metaphysical Universe and only plays out in the holographic. Once the blueprint is in place in the Metaphysical Universe it basically runs itself unless that program is changed. The Orwellian agenda can play out with such synchronicity and speed for the same reason that when you have programmed a computer with information everything happens in synchronistic order once you press 'Enter'. When we decode the waveform into the holographic we are also pressing 'Enter' and choosing an outcome from the vibrating 'pool' of possibility in the Metaphysical Universe. All the mass mind manipulation and subliminal triggers and instructions that bombard us every day are aimed at the subconscious, our waveform level of being that operates in the Metaphysical Universe. They are also seeking to implant a sense of self and reality that will lead people to decode the Reptilian program into holographic reality rather a mass of other possibilities that are also in the waveform fabric of the Metaphysical Universe. It is like tuning the human decoding system to their 'channel'. The Reptilian cabal is writing, or rewriting, the program at this level which is then decoded and played out in the holographic realm, and to do that they need to keep us in Mind and out of Consciousness. Once you know this, the way global society has been structured and manipulated starts to make perfect sense. They are manipulating and programming the Metaphysical Universe with their sacrificial and other rituals which are based on interacting with the vibrational realm of waveform. When you know how all this works, the conscious mind can stop being just the spectator and experiencer and start working with the subconscious to change the blueprint of the Metaphysical Universe – individually and collectively – and so change the 'physical' level of experience and perception. This is how the Control System is going to be dismantled ... the waveform information construct on which it is founded is being rewritten. Did you hear that, you guys with the scales? Rewritten.

I'll go into more detail in the latter chapters of the book about how we can all play our part in this, because we can and we will. Many already are.

18

Decoding Reality

The man with a new idea is a crank – until the idea succeeds
Henry David Thoreau

The nature of reality became my passion after my experience in Brazil, and continues to be so. I read everything that came my way on the subject – scientific journals and papers, the views of seers and mystics through the ages, and accounts of what are called 'near-death experiences' – where people have died and withdrawn from their bodies before being revived.

The 'quiet voice' guided me through the maze of information, as always. I have been aware of this since I saw the psychic in 1990 and I have learned to recognise and acknowledge its guidance. It is very different from the loud, clear voice I heard in the rainforest. This one is quiet, almost silent, but it speaks to me through a sort of 'knowing'. It says 'yes' and 'no' without actually saying 'yes' or 'no', and only someone who has experienced this will fully understand what I mean by that. Yes and no are simply a difference resonance that you come to understand, and the same with 'go here' and 'don't go there'. Synchronicity, or what we call 'coincidence', puts information before me and the quiet voice says 'look at this', 'that's not right', 'this is accurate', and so on, in ways I have come to recognise instantly. I have worked like this every day since the start of my conscious awakening. What I am doing is following the information blueprint for my personal journey in the Metaphysical Universe and bringing it into holographic manifestation. When I was told that all I had to do was 'follow the clues' it was another way of saying that all I had to do was stay on the 'path' that had been encoded in the Metaphysical Universe. That means staying committed to the 'cause' no matter what traps, diversions, abuse or ridicule that are put in my way. I can now understand so much about my life that I could not understand before. The Reptilian Control System operates from the Metaphysical Universe and it can see potential challenges before they become a holographic 'done deal'. The Reptilians work and scheme to make life more difficult for those who are 'here' to expose the conspiracy by encoding people and situations into the blueprint to block them, divert them and generally undermine them. This is when we need to have the strength of will to keep going whatever the scale of diversion or stress. I said earlier that there is 'good' synchronicity and not so good synchronicity and these are different forces at work in the Metaphysical Universe seeking to guide or divert and entrap. Just because events are synchronistic and full of amazing 'coincidences' does not mean it is always 'meant to be'. We need to use our intuition to discern what feels right and what doesn't, no matter how synchronistic a situation may be. In the end, however, they are all just experiences whatever we choose to manifest and, on a higher level of awareness, it might all be 'meant to be' anyway, whether we like it or not – 'True love does not always give the receiver what it would like to receive, but it will always give that which is best for it.'

People think that I must have 'whistleblowers' and insider contacts who feed me information or confirm facts, but it's not like that. I have met such people, yes, but there is no ongoing relationship. Nor do I interact very much with other researchers, indeed hardly at all. The words through the psychic said: 'Knowledge will be put into his mind and at other times he will be led to knowledge.' This is exactly what has happened and it has been my challenge to let it happen and not allow pre-conceived ideas or limitation of possibility get in the way. Some people call this 'surrender', but it's not about giving in to another force so much as getting the programmed mind out of the way so higher states of awareness can communicate. In the end, of course, they are higher states of me, the Infinite 'I' that is all of us. One insider once told me that I had quoted a disinformer in one of my books, but that I had only quoted the parts of what he said which were true. 'How do you do that?' he asked. By following the quiet voice within. It doesn't mean you will always get everything 100 per cent correct with so much information to filter, but it sure helps you to make it through the minefield – or *mind*-field – of conflicting views and information. It is also the case that this 'quiet voice' guidance can only communicate what the receiver can grasp at the time and so it unfolds in layers, each one more detailed and closer to the truth than the one before. I know from experience that what I need to know, I will know when I need to know it. In the early days I was running around 'seeking', but now I just allow myself to 'find'. It makes life so much easier and everything you need drops in your lap exactly when you need it. As a psychic communication said in 1990:

> Arduous seeking is not necessary. The path is already mapped out. You only have to follow the clues ... We are guiding you along a set path [in the Metaphysical Universe]. You are learning according to our teaching of you. It was all organised before you incarnated.

It has been many years since I read those early psychic communications and it has been fascinating for me to see how accurate they were with the benefit of the experiences in between. A famous British advertisement says: 'It does exactly what it says on the tin.' This has certainly been the case with that (or those) which is guiding me. In the years that followed my experience in Brazil, I have had mountains of information come to me about reality and how we experience it. In the next two chapters, I am going to outline a few more of those countless threads that are essential to understanding how humanity is enslaved by forces it cannot see, and how what is happening in the artificial Moon is controlling human perception.

Everything and nothing

The primary state of Infinite Consciousness is silence and stillness, or what some call 'the Void'. This gives the impression of 'nothingness', almost a vacuum, but this is seriously misleading. In the silent and the still is All Possibility – unmanifest potential. We are experiencing a realm of form and we think that reality is defined by the 'things' that we see. In fact, it is defined by the apparently *no*-thing. How can there be any 'things' without the apparent space between them, the no-thing? It is the no-thing that defines the some-thing. We worship and desire 'things' when they are just temporary forms that emerge from the no-thing – the Infinite All-Possibility, the still and silent 'Void' of balance and love. Sound can only exist because of the silence from which it comes and to which it returns – the no-thing. How can you have sound (a vibrational frequency we decode into what we 'hear') without the silence to define it? Try sitting for a moment in silence. Within that apparent 'no-thing' of silence is all existence, all potential … all possibility. This is where the silent voice originates that speaks to us in knowing. It is our connection to 'home', to what and to who we really are. When you have experienced the silence for a while, say something. What you have done with your words is break the silence or, put another way, you have pulled one potential or possibility – your words/thoughts – out of all potential and possibility, the still and silent Void, the Infinite One. Stop talking and what happens? Your single potential, your sound, merges back into all potential – the silence. The same happens when a 'physical' form 'dies'. It dissolves and merges with the no-thing that is also the every-thing. All

Possibility means that Infinite Oneness is everything and nothing; everywhere and nowhere; it is and it isn't; it will and it won't; it can and it can't. These are not contradictions or paradoxes as they at first seem to be. They are simply different expressions of All Possibility.

This unmanifest All Possibility is who we really are and it pervades all existence. Therefore, so do 'we' because 'we' are expressions of the Infinite One. When people think of 'God' or 'Heaven' they tend to look up to the sky; but it's not like that. Creation is not built like a chest of drawers or a tower block with layer on top of layer. It is different densities of energy, frequencies if you like, sharing the same space, just as television and radio stations share the same space without interfering with each other unless their frequencies are too close together. The Reptilians are able to interfere with our reality because their frequency is close enough to ours. All Possibility, manifest and unmanifest, exists in the space you are standing or sitting in now, but the base state of Infinite Awareness is the unmanifest, the still and silent All Possibility. It is always there, pervading everything, but in the

Figure 209: *The* All That Is *pervades all of existence, but when we close our minds to Consciousness, and become what I call 'bubble people', we can no longer 'hear' its wisdom, awareness, inspiration and insight. That's when we become trapped in Mind and the five senses – the very state the Reptilians and their hybrids are seeking to impose*

Illustration by Neil Hague (www.neilhague.com)

world of 'things' and forms the vast majority don't hear the silent source of *All That Is*. They hear only the noise of manifest illusion and so they live lives of limited possibility instead of all infinite possibility (Fig 209). Unmanifest 'Oneness' is where we find love in its true sense and so Infinite Love is the only truth, everything else is illusion. The still and the silent Void of All Possibility is the only truth; everything else is potential made manifest – the illusory world of 'things'. There are two major states of awareness – the still and silent *All That Is* in awareness of itself, and what is called 'Creation', the realms of sound and vibration. This is why 'the Voice' in Brazil said: 'If it vibrates, it is illusion.' The realms of vibration, the manifest, are a means through which the *All That Is* experiences itself and so 'we' are Infinite Consciousness having an experience. The foundation of all Creation, the realms of 'things', is vibration, which, when decoded through the body-computer, manifests as sound. It is vibration that breaks out of the stillness and it is sound that breaks out of the silence. But vibration and sound are the same; they are just different expressions of the same resonance. This is how form emerges from the Void of no-thing/every-thing. String Theory in mainstream science is actually based on this. It says that particles are really invisible vibrating 'strings', as the American theoretical physicist, Burt Ovrut, explained:

> You can think of it as a violin string or a guitar string. If you pluck it in a certain way you get a certain frequency, but if you pluck it a different way you can get more frequencies on this string and in fact you have different notes. Nature is made of all the little notes, the musical notes, that are played on these super-strings.

All form is vibrating energy and sound which, in turn, are generated by thought. I say 'thought' because that's the closest I can get with human language, but it is a trillion light years beyond what we perceive as thought. You could call it 'Infinite Thought' and it could also be described as 'Divine Will' – the Will of All Possibility to experience itself. 'Divine Imagination' is another term that comes to me. The world we 'see' is a series of sound vibrations encoded with information that we decode into what only appears to be 'solid' matter. Form is vibrating energy held together by sound, but more particularly by information that is infused by thought and regulates the sound. Form is actually a *thought-form* which generates the sound ('sound' as we decode it anyway) to vibrate energy in particular ways to create different 'things'. When thought-forms change or disperse, so do the 'things' they have created. The science of Cymatics, from a Greek word meaning 'wave', is an excellent example of what I mean. Particles are sprinkled onto a metal plate and sound is used to make the particles form together into often intricate geometrical patterns that stay in place as long as the sound continues (Fig 210). Once the sound ceases, the patterns break up. When the sound is changed,

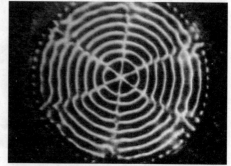

Figure 210: *This pattern has been created, and is held together, by particles reacting to a blueprint communicated through sound. When the sound changes the pattern changes and when the sound stops the particles return to a random state. This is how 'worlds' are created out of the still and silent All Possibility*

a different pattern forms because the sound vibration is now generating a different resonance. This is how form is created and then 'dies' or disappears.

Creation emerged from the Infinite Awareness of All Possibility and began to perpetuate itself. The created became creators who themselves affected the nature of Creation. The term 'themselves' really refers to the same *All That Is*, because everything is One. Yes, the Reptilians, too. There is a difference, however, between the 'One' in its state of still, silent All Knowing, All Possibility and its created forms in less expanded states of awareness. They are all expressions of the same 'One', but they can be observing reality from very different levels of Consciousness, understanding and wisdom. All will progress 'back' to the Source, the *All That Is* in awareness of itself, albeit via endless routes and experiences. This is described symbolically in the biblical story of the Prodigal Son, the 'bad boy' who is welcomed home by his father with the same love and enthusiasm that he showed for his other 'good boy' son who stayed at home. This is what 'the Voice' in Brazil was referring to when it said 'all will be gathered and no sheep will be left in the field alone'. I had been told something similar through a physic in 1990:

Illustration by Neil Hague (www.neilhague.com)

None of you realise how much the love of the Godhead [the *All That Is*] enfolds you. It cares and guides. Not one single being is left alone, uncared for. All is gathered in at the end of the day and not one sheep will be left in the field.

All Possibility as still, silent potential can obviously express itself as multiple possibilities within the vibrational realms of Creation; and it does. All expressions of Creation are involved in the process of the *All That Is* experiencing itself, and terms like 'good' and 'bad' take on a far more fluid perspective.

Stairway to 'Heaven'

Creation is a series of densities that form different worlds or 'dimensions' of reality, with each level vibrating to a different range of frequencies while sharing the same 'space' as all the others and, indeed, the still and silent 'Void' itself (Fig 211). Well, at least that's one way of putting it. To be more accurate, what we call Creation is one seamless energy field and it is the *observer* that perceives the illusion of 'levels' and dimensions. For example, the human form 'observes' or 'sees' only the range of frequencies that we call

Figure 211: *Out of still and silent All Possibility come the 'worlds' of form, or what we call 'Creation'. They all vibrate to different frequencies and so share the same 'space' without interfering with each other unless they are very close on the 'dial'. Or, more accurately, it is the observer who creates the frequency range, or 'reality', by how much of the seamless energy field he or she can decode*

visible light. Many animals, such as cats, have a wider visual range and so they can see what humans can't see. It might be said that cats can see into 'another dimension', but in fact they are simply seeing more of the same energy field. This field consists of many densities (again, sharing the same 'space' and not piled on top of each other), and which range of density you decode creates the perception of a 'world'. It isn't really; it is the observer that makes it seem so. The density field is simply information, and the density that we decode dictates the level of information available to us. The higher the frequency we can access the more information or 'awareness' is available to us. The Reptilians want to suppress the range of frequencies we can decode because that keeps us in ignorance through lack of information and limited awareness. This was a major motivation behind their genetic engineering of the human form, which I will expand upon in the next chapter. To keep it very simple, you have the silent and still *All That Is*, or 'the Source', and its Creation, a series of frequency ranges that people call 'densities' or 'dimensions'. These densities are a waveform construct – the 'metaphysical' – and many have a holographic 'physical' level decoded into manifestation through a body 'vehicle' of some kind. These are the different 'species', as we call them. These 'physical worlds' are also of different densities and can be much less 'solid' (dense) than we are in our reality. Aspects of the *All That Is* experience these densities or 'worlds' and so allow the *All That Is* to experience itself. There are realms of pure Consciousness without form as we know it and denser levels that we think of as 'physical'. I call our 'world' (the range of frequencies we decode) the 'Third Density'; and close to us, vibrating to a different resonance, is a realm known as the Fourth Density, or what some people call the 'astral' reality. These are just names and all we need to know is that the Reptilian conspiracy is orchestrated from a density beyond visible light, but very close to it. The vibrational resonance of the densities increases as we progress back to the Source until they transform into the stillness and silence and we are 'home' again to the *All That Is* in awareness of itself.

I guess you could symbolise the principle as like a 'stairway to heaven' and you climb the vibrational 'steps' by expanding your awareness from limitation to All Possibility; from service to self, to service to the whole. The latter is very significant. The more you expand your awareness, the more you identify with the whole and not the illusory 'parts'. By its very nature this directs your focus onto serving the whole ('service to others') and not the self-interest of the illusory individual ('service to self'). It would appear that the Fourth Density is the furthest you can progress while still serving self, and that's where the Reptilians are, though they work in Third Density, too. They have used their 'intellectual' levels of awareness through technology and energy-manipulation to reach that point, but that's as far as they go until they move into a mode of service to others. In fact, they are so stuck in their sense of reality, fear and the need to control that they have no desire to progress vibrationally. They just want more control in order to pacify their constant state of fear. All desire for control over others, control over anything, is a manifestation of fear and insecurity and these guys are consumed by it. This explains their obsession with control. Conscious people don't seek control over others because they know they *are* the others.

Welded to the 'World'

We are multi-dimensional beings operating on many levels of awareness. What we call the 'conscious mind' is only one of them, and by far the least aware. When these levels

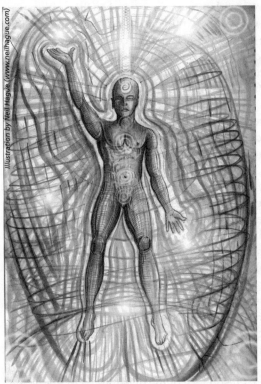

Illustration by Neil Hague (www.neilhague.com)

Figure 212: *When we open the auric field – open the mind – we can reconnect in awareness with higher levels of Consciousness*

of awareness fail to communicate, the lower levels become isolated from their higher knowledge, wisdom and perception. In that one sentence I have described the plight of humanity. The body-computer is the holographic expression of what we call the aura and these are different levels of the same energy or information field that I call the body/mind, or what some call the 'ego'. This is our interface between higher Consciousness and the 'physical' world. What is known as the 'soul' is the part of us looking through the 'telescope', the lens of body/mind, and this is what people become aware of during a near-death experience. They speak of an enormous expansion of Consciousness and awareness in the out-of-body state and this is because their attention has moved from five-sense reality into soul reality. The soul connects with the body-computer at the level of the auric field and experiences the virtual reality through the 'ego', or body/mind via an energy field that some call the 'subtle body'. These are very different levels of awareness, but they can have a powerful influence on each other. If the aura is open ('open mind', 'open heart') we allow our soul Consciousness to express itself through the energetic connection of soul/subtle body/mind/'physical' body (Fig 212). These different levels of being are necessary, because the soul is operating at a much higher frequency than the body/mind and requires energetic 'stepping-stones' to make a connection. When the heart and mind are open, the soul which connects with the aura/body/mind is a seamless flow of awareness. We are 'in' the world, but not 'of' it. Most people's sense of awareness identifies overwhelmingly, even totally, with the body/mind – the ego – and the five senses, and they perceive themselves as their name, occupation and reflection in the mirror. When this happens, the aura 'closes', especially when we fall for the fly-trap called fear (Fig 213) or service-to-self (what's in it for me, me, me?). This is caused by the attention, the point of observation, focusing purely on the material and the perceived 'physical' self. Hence the saying: 'energy flows where attention goes'. In truth, the aura doesn't so much 'close' in these circumstances, though that is an excellent symbol. It is more that its vibrational state becomes so dense by an obsession with the dense material 'world' and service-to-self that it cannot maintain a powerful connection with higher levels of Awareness. This disconnects our attention from higher realms of Consciousness and the energetic fields reflect that in their vibrational response. The body/mind/subtle body then becomes virtually a closed system that looks not to soul for inspiration and answers, but 'into' the material world of the five senses and sources of 'information' provided by the institutions of education, science, medicine, politics, and the media, etc. These are dominated by the Reptilians and their bloodlines. The idea is to isolate our sense of awareness in the body/mind and then program the body/mind, the ego, to perceive, and therefore decode, reality in ways that secure mass control and a constant energetic food supply. The more we are closed down energetically the more we are tuned to the Reptilian agenda blueprint in the Metaphysical Universe, and the more we awaken to higher levels of self the more we disconnect from that blueprint and 'read' another into holographic manifestation. We would experience this as the world and our lives being transformed and the Control System collapsing.

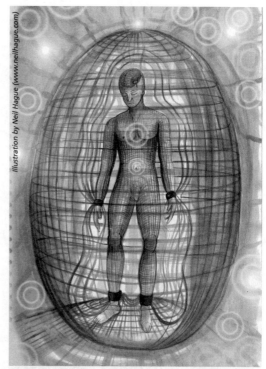

Illustration by Neil Hague (www.neilhague.com)

Figure 213: *When we close our mind, the auric field falls into a vibrational state that can no longer connect with Consciousness. We become trapped in the illusions of the five senses and the reptilian brain*

The Time Illusion

The illusion of time is encoded into the virtual-reality construct. There is no time – end of story. The only 'moment' is the eternal NOW. Once we fall for the base illusion that the world is physically 'real', all other illusions follow and at the heart of them is our belief in the reality of 'time'. When I first heard the statement 'there is no time', I knew instinctively it was true; but I couldn't get my 'head' around it, because Mind is tuned to the software program called 'time'. Try telling a computer that something is not true while it is decoding the fact that it is from a software disk. Once I got out of Mind and into Consciousness, I could immediately understand how there was no time while there certainly appeared to be. We are completely welded to time in our perceptions of reality (Fig 214 overleaf). 'What's the time?' 'Is that the time?' 'I don't have the time.' 'Look at the time!' 'Time waits for no man.' How many 'times' a day are you aware of what the 'time' is? How appropriate that the white rabbit followed by Alice was obsessed with time: 'Oh dear! Oh dear! I shall be too late!' Yet there is no time, nor any past or future in the way we perceive them to be. Everything happens in the NOW and nothing happens outside the NOW, because there is nothing else. What we can, and do, get trapped in, however, is the *perception* of past and future – 'time'. Where is the past and where is the future? The usual answer is that the past is what has 'happened' and the future is what is yet to 'happen'. Fine, but where are they? When is the only 'time' that you can experience anything, past, present or future?

Figure 214: *Consciousness operates in the realms of 'no-time' while this reality is enslaved by the perception of 'time', which is just an illusion decoded, along with 'space', from the information blueprint in the Metaphysical Universe. When we fall for the illusion of time being 'real', we become detached vibrationally from the realms of 'no-time' – Consciousness*

In the NOW.

Where are you when you think of the past?
In the NOW.

Where are you when you think of the future?
In the NOW.

As the late American writer and thinker, Alan Watts, said: 'I have realized that the past and future are really illusions, that they exist in the present, which is what there is and all there is.' Past and future are mind constructs, not locations. They are a program playing out in the NOW and it is the program which gives them the appearance of existing and being tangible. They are tricks of the mind constructed by the left-brain, the 'serial processor' that decodes data in a sequence. Events are not happening in a sequence that we call 'time'; the left-brain just arranges them to appear like that. This gives us the illusion of time moving faster or slower depending on how the left-brain constructs the sequence. When you are in the dentist's chair 'time' appears to pass slowly, and when you are doing something you enjoy 'time' just 'flies by'. Time seems to pass very quickly when you panic, but not so when you stay calm. For goodness sake, how can time be 'real' when if you travelled in a very fast spacecraft you could experience a few minutes while someone else is experiencing days or years in the same period of 'time'? It is indeed all relative. *New Scientist* magazine ran an article about the development of what are called quantum-gravity computers that operate on energetic levels deeper than the 'physical' atom. The limitless potential of such computers would be that they are beyond the 'laws' of five-sense reality and outside our perception of 'time'. The article said of these computers: '… it is inevitable that we are going to have trouble with notions of cause and effect: the logic of tock following tick or output following input just won't apply in the quantum-gravity universe.' Albert Einstein concluded that the past, present and future all exist simultaneously. He wrote that ' … physicists believe the separation between past, present and future is only an illusion, although a convincing one'. This is exactly how near-death experiencers describe reality 'outside' the body. Here is one example:

... everything from the beginning, my birth, my ancestors, my children, my wife, everything comes together simultaneously. I saw everything about me, and about everyone who was around me. I saw everything they were thinking now, what they thought then, what was happening before, what was happening now. There is no time, there is no sequence of events, no such thing as limitation, of distance, of period, of time, of place. I could be anywhere I wanted to be simultaneously.

To withdraw from the body is to withdraw from the reality-decoding processes of the body and so the experience and perception are dramatically different. We only 'live' the illusion of ageing because that is written into the body-computer software and our mind falls for it. A hologram projected by a laser from an interference pattern never ages, yet our bodies – also holograms – go through a predictable cycle of young to old, birth to death. The difference is that one hologram is programmed to age and the other is not. I have met many recovering mind-slaves from government mind-control operations who were denied watches and any awareness of 'time' as part of their programming. While this was happening they only aged fractionally compared with people of similar years. Their DNA/cellular system was not so connected to the illusion of time which leads to a programmed belief in ageing and an experience to match. The Reptilians don't want people living incredibly long lives as humans once did. For them, there is great energy potential in the 'death' process with all the low-vibrational emotion that is generated both from the dying and from the pain and grief of their loved ones. Also, the more people that die, the more there will be a fear of death, which is a major control mechanism and, again, energy source. I am not saying that everyone should take their watches off and cover the clocks, though that is an option if it suits you, but we can change our perception of time by seeing it for what it is – an illusion. You can still function in a time-obsessed society by checking the 'time' to make sure you meet with someone and don't turn up after they have left; but in doing so you can acknowledge that 'time' is a construct of this reality and not 'real' any more than the invisible line in the ocean is 'real' that tells you that you have entered tomorrow or yesterday depending on which way your plane is heading. This acknowledgement is very powerful, because it brings the illusion of time out of the subconscious into your 'here' awareness. It ceases to be subliminal (below threshold) and so ceases to have the power over your sense of reality that it had before.

See how I used the word 'before' there? Our very language is founded on the concept of 'time' and that, too, is constantly underpinning a belief in its existence. We don't have the words to describe 'no-time' adequately, because modern language has been developed by the Mind-controlled and the time-obsessed. With Consciousness in a state of no-time and the Mind locking us into its illusory perception of 'time', you can see how a belief in 'time' is a major factor in our disconnection from Consciousness. There are many things that change when we emerge from this slavery to past and future illusions and consciously live in the HERE and NOW. One is that you start to focus on what you are doing or being and not have that focus diluted and pulled into what you perceive as the past and the future. 'Oh, I wish I hadn't done that'; 'Oh, I am so worried about what will happen.' Regret, regret, regret ('past') and I gotta, gotta, gotta ('future'). How many lives, how many NOWS, are blighted by this? Most people live their 'lives' as memories of the 'past' and projections of the 'future'. The HERE and NOW is the

Figure 215: *The Time Loop that entraps humanity in the illusion of 'time' and moving 'forward' is a waveform construct that we decode into holographic reality*

Illustration by Neil Hague (www.neilhague.com)

Figure 216: *Life is like a movie on DVD. The perspective of past, present and future comes from which part of the DVD you are experiencing at the 'time'*

only moment that exists and the only moment we can change anything. People don't grasp that opportunity when they are caught in the illusion of past and future 'time'. As John Lennon wrote: 'Life is what happens to you while you're busy making other plans.'

The Time Loop

I have been writing for years about a 'Time Loop' since 'the Voice' talked about it in Brazil and I wrote a book called *Tales From the Time Loop* a few years ago. The Time Loop is the 'physical', holographic level of reality, although there are other levels, too, not least the Metaphysical blueprint. I use the term 'loop' to give people the feel of a recurring 'sequence', but it is actually like a broadcast signal of light frequencies encoded with the information that we decode into the collective reality that we call the material world (Fig 215). You can liken it to watching a movie on a DVD. The movie is already complete when you put it in the DVD player. 'Past, present and future' is all there from the start and exists in the same NOW. As the laser runs across the disc the scenes in the movie that you have watched become the 'past' to your reality; the 'present' is the scene you are consciously watching; and the 'future' is the scenes that you have yet to see; but the whole movie exists at the same 'time' (Fig 216). Your perception of 'past', 'present' and 'future' is defined by the part of the movie you choose to give your *attention* to. Spin it back a few scenes and you can give your attention to the 'past' and experience the equivalent of 'time' travel; or you can spin forward and see the 'future'. You are not 'going' anywhere; it is only that your focus of attention has changed. So it is with the Matrix of visible light and the wider virtual-reality universe. As you move your attention you appear to be moving through 'time', but you are not. 'Past', 'present' and 'future' are different parts of the same program and they are all happening in the same NOW. What we call 'history' has not disappeared; it is still happening at the same 'time' that you are reading this. 'History' can be changed just as software can be rewritten. A holographic 'photograph' can have many different interference patterns on the same print, and each can be picked out by changing the angle at which the laser strikes. The illusion of moving through 'time' is a bit like that as you change the angle at which you 'see' reality. Different dimensions can be read from different angles of observation, too. People have told of having strange experiences like seeing a building, only to find it is no longer there when they return hours, sometimes even minutes later. They have somehow accessed a different part of the program. The enlightened among the ancients knew that this reality was cyclical and not linear. They talked about different ages, great cycles, suns, worlds and yugas. The Mayans of Central America with their serpent-god religion believed that history repeated itself in a sort of perpetually recurring circle. Plato called the 'loop' the 'Great Year'. It is not only Earth going around the Sun; the solar system is also orbiting another point and then on and on it goes. As we 'move' through these loops (or the loops 'move' through us) we experience different energy environments which affect the Earth's electromagnetic field that, in turn, affects human consciousness and awareness. This is how we can have civilisations 'long ago' that were far ahead of where we are now. The cycles of the Time Loop ebb and flow.

Scientific Confirmation

Years after I realised we were in a time loop, I came across articles about a concept in science called 'causal loops'. These are where scientists say 'time', or a sequence of events, loops back on itself until the end connects with the start. The term 'causal loop' rather than 'time loop' is used because time is relative to the observer (decoder), but with that caveat understood, they are really describing what I have been referring to for years as 'time loops'. One definition I saw said:

> A causal loop is a chain of causes that closes back on itself. A causes B, which causes C ... which causes X, which causes A, which causes B ... and so on, ad infinitum.

Put another way – a time loop; but I stress again that causal loops are only the holographic expression of encoded vibrational information. Oxford University physicist, David Deutsch, and philosopher, Michael Lockwood, author of *The Labyrinth of Time*, wrote an article for *Scientific American* called 'Quantum Physics of Time Travel' in which they said: 'Common sense may rule out such excursions – but the laws of physics do not.' They say that quantum effects make time-travel possible and do not prevent it, as some scientists claim. I have spoken to a number of people over the years who have had direct experience of time travel experiments by the American military in top secret projects. Two Americans went public with similar information in 2009. They were Andrew D Basiago, a lawyer from Washington State, and physicist, Dr David Lewis Anderson, director of the Anderson Institute. Basiago said he had been involved with a secret programme called Project Pegasus, run by our old friend the Defense Advanced Research Projects Agency (DARPA). He said that US agencies have been developing time and teleportation technology since the late 1960s. Basiago described on the US *Coast to Coast* radio show how he was teleported between locations in New Jersey and New Mexico by technology which opens a 'chasm' in the fabric of time-space 'that is wrapped around the "teleportees" as they are repositioned to a new location.' He said he witnessed an accident in which a boy's feet were sheared off after he was teleported, and he described how teleportation technology can be used for time travel. Basiago said that he was teleported to past and future events and to a base on Mars (just like the insider, Arthur Neumann, as I mentioned earlier). Basiago claimed that time travel was used to brief US Presidents, including Bill Clinton, the Bushes, and Barack Obama, about their destinies years before they took office. He also said that former Defense Secretary Donald Rumsfeld and New Mexico Governor Bill Richardson both served in Project Pegasus. Dr David Lewis Anderson described his involvement in time travel development at the Edwards Air Force Base in California's Mojave Desert, which has often been connected with extraterrestrial involvement in its underground facility. These advanced technologies have great potential for transforming life for the better in so many ways, not least with producing free energy, but Andrew Basiago said that if misused they could also be employed to create a fascist society based on 24-hour surveillance. This, of course, is what is planned.

Crucial to understanding time travel and the nature of human enslavement is a phenomenon called 'world lines'. Put simply, the world line of an object is the unique path of that object moving (illusion of moving) through space and time – the *construct* we call space and time. It is a line that combines where you go and how quickly you get there and the concept was pioneered by Albert Einstein through his general theory of relativity. It is a bit more complicated than this, but you could think of it as the route taken by a person, planet, solar system, etc., as it 'moves' through space and time between its birth and death. World lines are different to orbits in that they include the movement through 'time' as well as 'space'. Einstein's general theory says that enormous bodies such as black holes and stars distort space-time and make world lines bend. If the distortion is powerful enough the world line curves back on itself to create a closed loop in which the world really does go round … and round … and round (or appears to). Gravity is encoded information. It is the means through which thought creates form by the pressure – gravity – that holds energy in a vibrational structure that we read as a 'physical' form or 'thing'. Every form has gravity, including the human body, or it couldn't be a form. It is just that human technology has not yet been developed to measure the more subtle expressions of the gravitational 'thought' force, as with the human body version. The world lines, and the closed-circuit loops they can create, are also thought forms and so generate their own gravity to hold them together. Until more powerful thought forms rearrange their structure, or disperse them, they just go on 'spinning'. David Deutsch and Michael Lockwood write:

> If we tried to follow such a Closed Timelike Curve (or CTC) exactly, all the way round, we would bump into our former selves and get pushed aside. But by following part of the CTC, we could return to the past and participate in events there. We could shake hands with our younger selves or, if the loop were large enough, visit our ancestors. To do this, we should either have to harness naturally occurring CTCs or create CTCs by distorting and tearing the fabric of space-time. So a time machine, rather than being a special kind of vehicle, would provide a route to the past, along which an ordinary vehicle, such as a spacecraft, could travel.

These world-line loops going around and around are everywhere and we live 'in' the one I call the Time Loop. The symbol for infinity is a snake swallowing its tail (Fig 217), but it is really far more symbolic of the illusory infinity of the ever-repeating Time Loop;

the closed circuit traps people into believing they are going somewhere when they are always heading 'back' to where they started. We don't live long enough in human bodies to go even nearly the whole way round, and so we are only aware of a fraction of it in one 'life'. This gives us the appearance of going from A to B and into the 'future'. It is all an illusion.

The 'Loopies'

Now, here's a vital, vital, point … Everything has a world line, a unique route 'through' time and space – including humans. The human world line starts at birth and goes on until we leave this reality. The world lines of children break off from the lines of

Figure 217: *The serpent Time Loop*

their parents and go their own way. As I have just mentioned, Einstein's general theory of relativity says that enormous bodies such as black holes and stars distort space-time and make world lines bend, and if the distortion is powerful enough the world line curves back on itself to create a closed loop in which the world goes round and round. I would strongly suggest that it is not only 'enormous bodies' that do this – everything does. Of course, not everything does it as powerfully, but everything distorts the fabric of space-time to an extent just by being here, including the human form. Remember, too, that space-time is an energetic construct and its foundation state is vibrating energy. The body is vibrating energy and one must affect the other. What's more, space-time can be distorted by Mind through thought and emotion. It seems obvious to me that most humans are entrapped in their own personal time loops within the collective one. It is the holographic law of 'as above, so below' where everything is a smaller version of the whole. If you can 'fix' the hologram at a higher level then all holograms within that must reflect the master hologram, or 'super hologram'. People have 'closed' auras because their space-time world lines have formed a 'Closed Timelike Curve' that goes round and round and keeps repeating itself. You see the result of this in people constantly repeating the same behaviours, perceptions and responses. I have seen humanity symbolised as a mouse on a treadmill running faster and faster, but getting nowhere. They keep coming back to where they started. This is what the manipulation of our reality and the Mind programming is designed to do – enslave us in these individual and collective time loops. Once we are trapped we can change nothing, only keep repeating what we have already done. People become what I call 'loopy' or 'loopies'.

Mass programming of reality becomes possible because when the master hologram changes, all holograms within that are immediately encoded with the new information – the new program. The Reptilians have done this to humanity and I will describe how in the next chapter. Sit down for that one! It is the attention and total focus on five-sense reality – a 'location' in encoded time and space – that causes human world lines to curve back on themselves (a bit like running on the spot) and form mini time loops. When you become Conscious, your point of observation moves beyond the construct of time and space and your sense of awareness is no longer subject to the distortions of the construct. Mind is subject to them because it operates in the realm of illusory time

Figure 218: *The Möbius Strip or Möbius Band. The twist means that you can pass along both sides simply by moving 'forward' and with no need to cross an edge*

and space, but Consciousness does not. This is why when we break out of Mind and into Consciousness we see things that we didn't see before and perceive this reality with a clarity we never thought possible.

I have been symbolising the Time Loop as a circle to keep it simple, but it is really shaped like a Möbius Strip or Möbius Band in its decoded form (Fig 218).These are named after 19th century German mathematician and astronomer, August Ferdinand Möbius. If you take a strip of paper and glue the two ends together you would have two sides of the paper circle and to cross from one side to the other you would need to go over an edge. The twist in the Möbius Strip means that you can pass along both sides simply by moving forward and with no need to cross an edge. The Time Loop is very similar in its decoded expression. We don't move through this loop so much as the loop moves through us, you could say. Whenever I think about this, I get a picture of one of those Victorian fairground music machines in which a strip of metal with holes imprinted moves across the machinery activating musical instruments to play in the imprinted sequence. We are receiving encoded information within what we call light that makes us 'play', live, perceive and react in line with the imprinted sequence (the Metaphysical blueprint) unless we become Conscious and override the system. If you are caught in the illusion of five-sense reality, you are not playing the game – the game is playing you. In other words, there is nothing in your life that isn't robotically responding to information input, and becoming Conscious, going beyond Mind, is the only way out.

Changing 'Past' and 'Future'

When we talk of someone coming 'back from the future' or communicating with entities 'in the future', we are referring to those experiencing another 'part' of the Time Loop in the same NOW. They are watching a different part of the 'DVD'. How do I know that? Because there is only the NOW and nothing else. To travel into the 'future' or the 'past' ('time travel') is to experience a different part of the holographic movie in the NOW. It's the same with psychics who 'read' the future or the past. They are accessing another part of the 'loop' at the Metaphysical level. If you can do that, you can be a 'prophet' and 'see the future'. History is not a fixed sequence of events, not least because the whole Time Loop can be changed from anywhere within the Time Loop and the perceived 'future' can change the past. The Time Loop is not set in stone and Consciousness can change it. You could think of it as like writing a story on your computer. When you add or change a word or sentence in the text everything readjusts instantly to encompass it. It is also the case that the programmers of the Metaphysical blueprint can change the movie and its 'history'. Are 'historical' discoveries really from the 'past', or are they programmed into the holographic movie to be found in what we call the 'present' to give us a false sense of the 'past'? In fact, if the 'past' in the Time Loop is changed, from our point of observation, do artefacts from the new 'past' turn up in our 'present'? It may seem that I am disappearing up my rear end here, but what I want to emphasise is that when you are dealing with virtual-reality, *anything* is possible. The history I presented earlier in the book is one 'time-line' sequence within the Time Loop which has led to current events; but it can be changed at any point along the way and so cause a change in current events. Within the overall Time Loop are endless timelines which scientists refer to as 'parallel universes'. As a BBC *Horizon* documentary said:

> For almost a hundred years science has been haunted by a dark secret: that there might be mysterious hidden worlds beyond our human senses. Mystics had long claimed there were such places. They were, they said, full of ghosts and spirits. The last thing science wanted was to be associated with such superstition, but ever since the 1920s physicists have been trying to make sense of an uncomfortable discovery. When they tried to pinpoint the exact location of atomic particles like electrons they found it was utterly impossible. They had no single location ...
>
> ... The only explanation which anyone could come up with is that the particles don't just exist in our Universe. They flit into existence in other universes, too and there are an infinite number of these parallel universes, all of them slightly different. In effect, there's a parallel universe in which Napoleon won the Battle of Waterloo. In another the British Empire held on to its American colony. In one you were never born.

Alan Guth, from the Massachusetts Institute of Technology, told the programme: 'Essentially anything that can happen does happen in one of the alternatives which means that superimposed on top of the Universe that we know of is an alternative universe where Al Gore is President and Elvis Presley is still alive.' These are different timelines, perceptions and choices within the overall Time Loop 'movie', but they are all happening in the same NOW. The story may be constantly changing in the Time Loop, but not nearly as much as it would if those attached to it knew what they were really experiencing. There was no birth or death before human genetics were manipulated. People just came and left as they chose in awareness of what they were doing. In other words, they knew what the game was to a much greater extent. Once the Reptilians intervened and introduced childbirth as the means of entering the Time Loop, 'humans' came down the birth canal almost entirely disconnected from their memories or awareness beyond the realm of electromagnetic light. They were looking into a 'real world' with no comprehension of who they were, where they were, or where they had come from. They started all over and were at the mercy of the programming awaiting them to impose a perception of self and reality that suited the Reptilian agenda. It's still going on. The Control System is utterly dependent on keeping incarnate humanity in a state of disconnection from true self. We are Infinite Awareness operating on multi-densities and no densities connecting 'back' to the Source, and the Reptilians seek to isolate the body-computer/mind from higher levels of awareness to entrap us in the illusion of physicality with all the fear, division and bewilderment that comes from that.

Is Anybody There?

There is another factor here, too. For most people the illusion continues 'between' human lives in realms that I call the 'false heavens' and 'false hells'. They are vibrational levels close to this one where Awareness can become trapped in a cycle of 'death' and reincarnation in the belief that this is what you have to do to 'evolve'. The term 'reincarnation' literally means 'to be made flesh again'. These 'between-life' realities, which are a vital part of the Control System, can have beliefs and perceptions that are little more expanded than we have here, except that they realise that you survive 'death' and there are multiple realities or 'worlds'. These are the levels that 'people' like television psychics connect with when they are telling audience members that their departed dad says 'take that job', or their 'passed over' mum says 'look after the cat'. There used to be a show like this on a cable channel in the UK that I watched almost every night for weeks. The psychic, or medium, was often clearly connecting with something, because the accuracy of some of the information was extraordinary. I remember one show where he said he had connected with the father/husband of a family in the audience. 'He's saying he was here one second and over there the next,' the medium said. 'He says the last thing he heard was [his daughter] saying, 'Are you alright, Dad?" The family confirmed that the father was sitting on the sofa one second and keeled over dead with a heart attack the next, and the daughter had shouted, 'Are you alright, Dad?' Now, of course, there are charlatans in the psychic and medium business, and those who manipulate people with word and mind techniques to glean information that they then repeat as if it is from 'the other side'. However, they are not all like that and, as per usual, the professional sceptics hurl babies out with bathwater in a desperate attempt to protect their own this-world-is-all-there-is belief system.

What I observed from these shows, and many others around the world, is that the information communicated from 'beyond' was all based on this reality. I have never once heard anyone 'come through' and say, 'Hey, it's all an illusion and religion is a bunch of bollocks.' I saw a television psychic passing messages to a man from his departed Muslim father that included the advice to keep following that religion. This only makes sense when you begin to understand that there are 'between life' realms that include Muslim 'heavens', Christian 'heavens', 'Jewish 'heavens', and so on. They are the collective-mind creations of those who have left the body, still disconnected from higher Consciousness, with their religious beliefs still dominating their perception and so their manifested experience. They are still in a form of Mind. Death is no cure for ignorance, as they say. When we withdraw attention from the body, the soul and its subtle body (the experiencer of the virtual realities), transfers that attention to the 'between-life' realms. This is what is happening when people have near-death experiences and pass through the 'tunnel' and all that stuff. The vibrational resonance of the soul decides the between-life reality, and the effect of the human experience in the Matrix can so lower the vibrational state of the soul's awareness that it becomes entrapped in a cycle of 'death' and reincarnation, or the perception of it. The subtle body, which has directly experienced material reality through the 'physical body/mind', repeats its role in these various incarnations and is imprinted vibrationally with the results of those experiences. This is another reason why someone may have an unexplainable mark on their 'physical' body which is a throwback to another incarnation of the subtle-body/soul. The vibrational consequences of these incarnations and experiences will either increase the resonance to the point where they can escape the reincarnation cycle, or they will slow the resonance and keep the subtle-body/soul trapped in the vibrational range of the reincarnation cycle. It is for this reason that so many people drop back into the program so easily when they return to the Time Loop. They've been this way before. The Voice explained this to me in the Brazilian rainforest.

I was shown a picture of people symbolically dropping from the sky onto a footpath across a field. The voice said that because consciousness in the Matrix was caught in a cycle of moving in and out of the Time Loop through 'reincarnation', they were not only conditioned by the beliefs of one 'physical' lifetime. They were conditioned by endless experiences in the Time Loop and between these 'physical' excursions they were in another form of illusory state. So they were already conditioned even as they returned to the Time Loop reality for still more conditioning. This was why humanity dropped into the conditioned, servile state so easily. They had been there many times before. As these words were being spoken, I saw the footpath being worn away by the trampling feet going over the same ground until the path looked like a sort of record groove. It went ever deeper and the figures walking the path went down and down into the dark 'groove' until they disappeared. 'Is it any wonder that humans look up for their God?' the Voice said. 'It is the only place where they can see any light!'

Near-death experiencers often recall how they met family members or beings who told them their work on earth was not finished and that they had to 'go back'. They talk of feeling enormous love in those moments and I have no doubt that they did; but they are still in the illusion, another fake reality, which traps awareness in the cycle of birth, death and re-birth within the virtual-reality Matrix. It is so important for people to have an awareness of true self when they withdraw from this reality, because this will set them free from all levels of the illusion and allow reconnection with the true self beyond its illusory vibrational 'walls' and those of the between-life realms. Reincarnation is associated with cause and effect, also known as 'karma'. The 'law of karma' – the idea that what you give out you get back – applies only in the vibrational/mathematical construct of the virtual-reality and its between-life realms. Once you consciously operate in the higher states of Awareness, there are no 'laws'. Karma is only one possibility, so it cannot exist as a rigid 'law' within All Possibility. I know some people will ask how we can 'learn' unless we face the consequences of our actions. But All Possibility – Infinite Awareness – is not a 'we', or an 'our'; it is an 'I'. At these levels of Awareness everything is One and so the duality of cause and effect, or karma, does not exist. Anyway, *All That Is* has nothing to 'learn'. It is All-Knowing, All Possibility. Karma, or cause and effect, is part of the cosmic game of virtual reality and it is basically about erasing the dense vibrational imprints on the soul's subtle body that trap it in the densities of the reincarnation cycle. These imprints reflect the soul's state of being, and karma is a cycle of experience based on what-you-give-out-you-will-get-back which leads to the self-realisation that we are all One. 'The Voice' in Brazil was referring to the reincarnation/karmic cycle, in part, when it said 'all will be gathered in and no sheep will be left in the field alone'.

The Reptilian manipulators are naturally caught in the same cycle, but it seems they have no desire to escape it. They are so consumed by service-to-self, control, and fear, and nothing else matters to them, certainly not 'spiritual' advancement. They know their way around these lower realms of density and live in embodiment far longer than the humans they have condemned to very short 'physical' lifetimes. They have a fundamental interest in keeping as many souls as possible locked in the reincarnation cycle that produces their energetic food source.

Okay, after detailing this essential knowledge about the illusory nature of 'physical' reality, we can return to the Moon.

19

The Moon Matrix

In the beginning the Universe was created. This has made a lot of people
very angry and been widely regarded as a bad move
The Hitchhiker's Guide to the Galaxy

The virtual-reality universe was not designed to be a prison. It was created by advanced
Awareness as a vehicle for a certain kind of experience that we cannot have in our
primary state of Oneness.

The idea is to experience the unique nature of this reality, overcome the challenges
and return to the Source, the still and silent *All That Is* in awareness of its own infinity.
It's a sort of cosmic game. Virtual realities also allow Consciousness in many states of
awareness to interact when they normally would not. Beyond the realms of virtual
reality, Consciousness gravitates to densities that synchronise with its resonance or state
of being. The 'physical' body allows everyone – those with expanded awareness and
those with closed minds – to experience the same frequency range and so the same
'game'. The Universe is clearly a construct that was created for purpose, the equivalent
of an incredibly-advanced computer program. Even fractional differences in the balance
between forces operating at all levels, atomic and subatomic, mathematical, atmospheric
etc., would make life as we know it impossible. Instead, the interactions of these forces
are perfect for life to flourish and that is because it was designed to be like that, just as a
computer programmer encodes software with the information necessary for a game to
work. There could be no life on Earth, apparently, if even Jupiter was not positioned
where it is to block space objects that would otherwise hit this planet. It acts on Earth's
behalf as a cosmic goalkeeper, or so I read. Perfection and precision can be seen
everywhere. The obvious is in front of our eyes – the Universe is a carefully designed
construct, an interactive computer game of fantastic advancement.

Scientists fret and argue about how the Universe began and all that stuff about a 'Big
Bang', but it's a bit like fretting and arguing about what happens when you boot up a
computer or click the mouse to activate software. The Universe was created as an
energetic construct based on the receiving and transmitting of information. It is like a
software disk being read by a computer to produce pictures on the screen. There are
phenomenal numbers of these virtual realities all sharing the same 'space' (like radio and
television stations) and operating on different frequencies with different 'laws' of physics.
These laws differ simply because the creators of the virtual-realty universes decided on
different rules for their 'game'. Once again, scientists search for answers to apparently

complex questions when things are as they are because the creators decided that this is how it would be. Why does this or that 'law' of physics exist? Click, click, 'Enter'. It was made to be like that. It's a program. Some open-minded scientists at the cutting edge of mainstream science are now seeing that our reality is not the only one. The theoretical physicist, Michio Kaku, has said that we live in a 'multiverse' and there could be infinite numbers of universes each with their own laws of physics. 'Our universe could be just one bubble floating in an ocean of other bubbles,' he suggests. I have referred to our reality many times as a bubble within bigger bubbles – the hologram within a bigger hologram. The virtual-reality universe operates as waves, particles and vibrating 'strings', numbers, chemicals etc., but these are names for the same Infinite Awareness, just like David Icke, Billy Smith and Mary down the road. Scientists try to find a theory for everything, when they are dealing with All Possibility. Every time they think they are getting close another anomaly turns up to crash the theory. Of course it does, and it always will. Infinite possibility will not, and cannot, be pinned down like that. There are many things that we can understand, but in the end it is a case of 'anything is possible'.

The Firewall

The point is, however, that the original virtual-reality, the one that still exists beyond human sight, was not designed to be what we see today. Yes, it provided a different experience, but mass slaughter, war and suffering was not in the original script. Humans have put it there and have been manipulated to put it there. What we are experiencing is not the original virtual-reality universe, but a tiny frequency range within it. The Reptilians have hacked into the system and installed a 'firewall' to disconnect our perception from even the virtual reality as a whole, much like the government firewalls the computer system in China to stop the people accessing large areas of the Internet that contain information the authorities don't want the population to see. It is a virtual reality within a virtual reality that I call the 'Matrix'. The extraordinarily-gifted British psychic, Carol Clarke, is a great friend of mine and I have seen how astonishingly accurate she has been with me over the years (see her at the back of the book). She told me about a

vivid dream she had in which the famed American cosmologist, Carl Sagan, appeared and talked about 'photons', the basic 'unit' of light and all other forms of electromagnetic radiation. Sagan published more than 600 scientific papers and popular articles and was the author, co-author or editor of more than 20 books before he died in 1996 (Fig 219). Carol said that in the dream 'Sagan' talked about the nature of the Universe, and here she describes what happened:

He said the Universe was a closed structure, like a bubble, with most of what we know as galaxies spread over the surface. There were some galaxies down the centre of this bubble but, despite popular belief in a universe overflowing with galaxies, the bubble was largely empty. As the bubble vibrates, the galaxies shift very slowly, giving the illusion that the Universe is expanding.

Figure 219: *Cosmologist, Carl Sagan*

The stars/suns are the most important part of the nature of reality. Their light gives rise to life but the suns are the 'controllers' of reality. The photons they emit have a direct effect on the brain and DNA. They are code carriers and penetrate the DNA and stimulate the visual centre of the brain. The illusion or Matrix is not external, but within each of us, hence we all see the same basic illusion. It's only the level of vibration of the individual which changes our personal circumstances. This was the fundamental design of the Universe.

Why is it that it is only our planet in the solar system that is like paradise? Because it is what we want it to be. Our combined vibrational illusion makes it appear the same to us all. We love the Sun, and feel good when it is light; in fact we manufacture light, because we are programmed to seek the photons whenever we can. The Illuminati know this and, as you rightly say, their symbolism is everywhere. That is why monarchs wear crowns and jewellery, sparkling with light reflecting diamonds representing the Sun. The old civilisations worshipped the Sun, because they knew it was the source of reality. We often say new leaders will be a 'shining light' and example to create the perfect world. People say they are working towards or with 'the light', and are seeking Nirvana.

He said that black holes are the source of the vibration. Electromagnetism and gravity are generated there. In turn, this energy creates and fuels the Sun to emit the photons. He said there were those who had this knowledge and used it for their own ends, disrupting the energy vibration. This led to the suns' increase in intensity, making our sun (and probably many others) less stable. The codes held in the individual photons were becoming less structured. He then said a very strange thing – it was because of this knowledge that his life was cut short.

Carl Sagan died at the age of 62 after suffering from myelodysplasia, a rare disease that often leads to leukaemia. I am sure that the themes of what was said in Carol's dream are correct. Black holes resonate the frequency and different frequencies trigger different levels of information – awareness – to be emitted by the Sun in the form of photons (it is photon energy – *chi* – that flows through the body's meridian network – information from the Sun, now 'hacked' by the Reptilians). Different levels of resonance 'unlock' different levels of information (Fig 220). A new vibration is being resonated from the black holes and this is causing another level of information to be emitted by the Sun – the 'Truth Vibrations' that I wrote about in 1990 which are in the process of transforming human perception of self and the world and bringing the Control System to an end. I'll go into more detail about this later. In 2008, a 16-year study by German astronomers confirmed that there is a giant black hole at the centre

Figure 220: *Black holes are the source of vibration that dictates the level of information, or awareness, that is emitted by the suns*

of our galaxy. It is estimated to be 27,000 light years from Earth and is four million times bigger than the Sun. Dr Robert Massey, from the Royal Astronomical Society, said the results suggest that galaxies form around giant black holes in the way that a pearl forms around grit. This all makes sense in the light of what 'Sagan' said. Carol Clarke had a second 'Sagan' dream just as this book was being completed in which he said that 'natural' disasters, including tsunamis, were caused by energies 'entering the Moon'. He said that many phenomena were coming in and out of our reality that were invisible to us and this was fundamentally impacting on human experience. This relates to what I said earlier about the Moon being an inter-dimensional, inter-density, portal that allowed entities and energies to be transferred from other densities into this one. It is a means by which the Fourth Density Reptilians lock humanity into their hive mind. Sagan repeated in the second dream that he had been killed for what he knew.

The Reptilian genetic-manipulation of the human body-computer limited dramatically the frequencies it could access within the virtual reality, and tuned humans to the frequency range of the firewalled Matrix, so disconnecting them from the wider universe they could access before. The Matrix is a vibrational/digital transmission that you could liken to a television channel that is broadcast from a transmitter and decoded into pictures by the television set. In this case the pictures decoded by the body-computer are holographic, but the principle is the same. The virtual-reality universe in its entirety is like that, though far less limited; but the Matrix has a different motivation. It is a sub-realm of the virtual reality, a vibrational/digital transmission created to entrap awareness in a false self-identity. This transmission is coming from the Moon, as I will be explaining. When we perceive only the material and 'physical', and filter everything through the five senses, our vibrational state falls into greater density and the Matrix becomes a vibrational flytrap. It is Catch-22. The way out is to expand your awareness – open your mind. But the focus on the material, plus all the designer-manipulation to keep us asleep, combines to keep the Mind under lock and key and disconnected from Consciousness. This produces endless potential for division, conflict and emotional trauma which generates the low-vibrational energy on which the Reptilians and others feed. It is the vibrational equivalent of a sheep pen. Before the genetic manipulation of the body-computer, and the Moon transmissions, humans could see the Reptilians and other entities. The human visual frequency range was much greater, just as cats and other animals react to things today that we cannot see. Accounts of direct Reptilian interaction with humans come from the 'time' before the human frequency range was narrowed. The Reptilians genetically modified the body transmitter-receiver system to remove themselves from human sight, making control far easier.

Seeing the Light

To understand what is happening we need to look with fresh eyes at what we call 'light'. Like almost everything else in this reality you have to turn it on its head to discover its true nature. To be 'of the light' is a phrase people use to describe 'goodness' and high levels of awareness, a connection to 'God'; but 'light' is the trap, not the way out. It gets confusing because the word 'light' has a number of meanings. There is light from the Sun; light you switch on in your home; light that symbolises a 'spiritual' state, as in the 'Light of God'; and there is the light that physicists talk about. The latter is defined thus:

> Light is electromagnetic radiation, particularly radiation of a wavelength that is visible to the human eye (about 400-700 nm, or perhaps 380-750 nm). In physics, the term light sometimes refers to electromagnetic radiation of any wavelength, whether visible or not.

This is what I mean when I speak of 'light'... electromagnetic radiation within the so-called 'speed of light', which is estimated to be 186,282.397 miles per second. Once you go beyond that speed you leave the Matrix and enter the wider virtual-reality universe. The speed of light is like a firewall. I was reading about light on a website called *How Stuff Works* and there was a simple statement that sums up what I am saying here. It said: 'Light is all our eyes can see.' More accurately, it is all the brain can decode holographically in its manipulated genetic state. Either way, it is the limit of human perception within the 'physical' world, and it's meant to be. This is what the body receiver-transmitter has been genetically-manipulated to do – to see only within the realm of electromagnetic radiation or visible 'light'. The speed of light is not the fastest speed possible; it is the frequency range of the Matrix within the firewall. Nor is the speed constant; it can be changed. Einstein's Theory of Relativity says the speed of light is the fastest that anything can travel; the maximum speed for matter. It is not. It is the fastest speed that matter can travel before leaving the frequency range of the Matrix, the manufactured reality we are experiencing within the virtual-reality universe. As you approach the speed of light everything starts to change. Matter becomes compressed, mass increases, distance is foreshortened and 'time' slows down dramatically. You would age far more slowly and at the speed of light your body would live forever, so scientists say. Go through that speed of light barrier (firewall) and you are out of the Matrix. Spacecraft or 'UFOs' come in and out of the Matrix from other parts of the virtual reality by moving faster and slower than the speed of light, although from a higher perspective that's all illusion, too. By the way, we are told that light travels much faster than sound which is why you see an explosion before you hear the 'bang' and see the lightning before you hear the thunder, etc. The difference between them is, in fact, not in their speed of movement, but the way the brain decodes vision differently from sound. There isn't any movement as we perceive it, so how can anything move at different speeds? It is the way we decode reality that determines how fast everything appears to 'move'.

'Dark' is not dark

The original virtual-reality universe beyond the Matrix lies in the realms of what scientists call 'dark matter', 'dark mass' or 'dark energy'. This cannot be seen by telescopes, because it does not emit electromagnetic radiation, infrared radiation, ultraviolet radiation, radio waves, x-rays or gamma rays (all energy levels of the Matrix). It is, therefore, described as 'dark', but this is extremely misleading, not least with the way that humans use the terms 'light' and 'dark'. We equate light with good and dark with evil. This is a fundamental misunderstanding that must cease if we are to grasp what is going on. What we call 'light' is merely the frequency range of radiation that the human receiver-transmitter can decode holographically. 'Dark' is only dark because humanity and its technology can't tune into it and make it manifest in its reality. If you were in the realms of what is called 'dark matter' it would not be pitch

Illustration by Neil Hague (www.neilhague.com)

Figure 221: *The terms 'dark matter' and 'dark energy' don't refer to realms of the Universe that are literally 'dark'. They are simply beyond the frequency range of 'visible light' that the human body-computer can decode and they are teeming with life that we can't see*

black! It is another range of frequency, that's all (Fig 221). The existence of dark mass and matter has been identified from its gravitational effect on our 'luminous matter'. It operates on a different energetic frequency that does not involve the Matrix phenomenon of electromagnetic radiation etc., and is not subject to the same Matrix 'laws of physics', which are simply designed to limit perception and can be overridden. The electromagnetic spectrum is only 0.005 per cent of what is believed to exist in the universe, and visible light is far smaller even than that (Fig 222). The overwhelming majority of the rest is 'dark', or more to the point we cannot decode it through the lens of the human body. The original virtual-reality universe is teeming with life of incredible diversity and some of it travels in and out of this realm of electromagnetic radiation, the Matrix. We experience this as UFOs and entities manifesting and demanifesting. There are many ways to enter the realm of what we call 'light' depending on our level of advancement.

The genetic manipulation of the human form, and the transmissions from the Moon, stopped the body-computer decoding the rest of the Universe beyond what is called 'visible light'. We should have twelve strands or more of DNA, not two. The others were 'switched off' to our conscious mind and they were our vibrational and receiver/transmission connection to the rest of the virtual-reality universe. This is one reason for the 95 per cent or more of human DNA that scientists call 'junk' because they don't know what it does. Ancient accounts and myths speak of people living to amazing ages, and of miraculous feats and happenings in a 'Golden Age', but people looking from today's perspective say that is impossible, a fantasy, a fairytale. The ancients were describing a world before the body-computer was downgraded, when humans were decoding at least a vastly greater range of the Universe and all enjoying the incredible abilities that came with that level of awareness. The ancients talked about the gods living among them and they did, because humans could decode the energetic realms in which they existed. They still live among us, but we can no longer see them after the range of frequencies the body-computer can access were reduced dramatically and a fake reality imposed. Like I said, we talk about different 'dimensions' etc., but it is actually one energy field. It is the way we decode that energy field, and how much of it that we decode, that determines the 'world' we appear to live in. It is like sitting in a house and thinking it's a universe because you can't see anything 'outside' of it. Expand your decoding potential and you realise that the house is part of a street and the street is part of a town and the town is part of a country, and so on. They were there all the time while you sat in your little house thinking there was nothing else. So it is with the virtual-reality universe. What is called the 'speed of light' is the limit of body-computer perception; and when you reach those

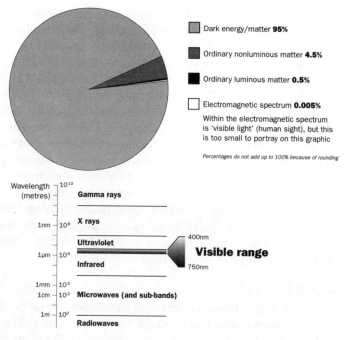

Figure 222: *The human visual frequency range – 'visible light' – is tiny*

'outer' limits strange things start to happen. These are caused by the effect that this has on the body-computer decoding system. You are hitting the 'firewall'. It is not that these effects are actually happening in the energy-field itself, so much as they are being perceived by the observer to be happening. Scientists are experiencing reality through a body-computer, too. With the body DNA fully activated and awakened, the strange things that appear to happen at the speed of light would not happen. Our decoding system would be much wider and not on the limits of its decoding potential. It is the distortion of the observer's decoding process that is behind the reality changes at the speed of light.

The Matrix is a small range of frequencies within the wider virtual-reality universe and we are locked into it by the manipulation of the body receiver-transmitter system and the reality transmissions from the Moon that hack the system. Remember also that human DNA and genetics can be changed and suppressed en masse by electromagnetic and other vibrational fields and it doesn't all have to be done 'physically'. DNA is a receiver-transmitter and if you can send encoded frequencies on its wavelength you can change its structure and thus 'evolve' or change the form of the human body. It is the same with animal and plant species – anything with a DNA receiver – and it gives a whole new perspective to 'evolution'. This happens through the encoded photons emitted by the Sun – the virtual-reality construct – and by hacking into that information from the Moon. The information encoded in light dictates what we collectively see, hear, touch, taste and smell, and includes the illusion of time, space, distance and even movement. The Reptilians and their hybrid cohorts cannot ignore the rules of the 'game' in the wider virtual-reality because they, too, are subject to them; but they can, and have, used them and bent them for their own ends. Their vehicle for this is the Moon.

I know that what I am about to say is true, in theme if not every detail. How do I know? For the same reason that I knew that the Orwellian global state was coming 15 years before it became obvious and the same reason I have come to understand the illusory nature of reality without ever passing a school exam, let alone studying in scientific academia. The 'They' who have been handing me the puzzle pieces since 1990 have shown me what I am about to outline through various means – putting knowledge into my mind, vivid dreams and the incredible synchronicity of information, people and personal experience that has come to me. This has been backed up by some of the very few people, even on the inside working in underground bases and with advanced technology, who know what the Moon is doing to human perception. This information about the real nature of the Moon is fiercely compartmentalised and only the minimum necessary are privy to what I am about to say. I am not trying to convince anyone that it is true. I am not trying to convince anyone of anything. People will just have to feel it for themselves. Most will dismiss it, as usual, and even more ridicule will come my way, but I don't care. Others will know intuitively that the themes are correct. Everyone must be their own judge of what to believe.

Moon Control

The effect of the Moon on human perception and life on Earth is obvious, even without the artificial transmissions that I will call the 'Moon Matrix'. The Moon is closely associated with mind and emotions – the very targets of the Reptilian agenda. The UK *Independent* newspaper reported in 2007 on research confirming the influence of the Moon on human behaviour in an articled headed 'How the Moon Rules Your Life'. Folklore has long connected the Moon to people becoming 'lunatics' – losing their mind. Researchers discovered, however, that the effects go much deeper into the fine detail of human life. They reviewed 50 studies and added their own research before suggesting that doctors and police should prepare for their work to increase at certain phases of the lunar cycle. The study revealed that doctors' appointments rose by 3.6 per cent during a full moon and that gout and asthma attacks peaked during new and full moons. The bladder (water) is also affected, as is hormonal balance. The *Journal of the Florida Medical Association* reported findings by Dr Edson J Andrews that 82 per cent of postoperative bleeding crises happened nearer the full and the new moon, even though fewer operations were performed at those times. The Moon influences fertility fundamentally and the moon goddess is always associated with fertility and childbirth. Data from 140,000 births in New York showed 'systematic variations' in births over the lunar cycle of 29.53 days with the peak in the last quarter. The report said that 'the timing of the fertility peak … suggests that the period of decreasing illumination immediately after the full moon may precipitate ovulation'. Dr Michael Zimecki of the Polish Academy of Sciences said the lunar cycle has an impact on human reproduction (in particular fertility), menstruation and the birth rate. These effects are not all caused by the Moon's gravitational pull on the Earth, as was once believed, but also by the effect it has on human hormones. Fertility, spontaneous abortions and thyroid disease were also affected and Dr Zimecki said more research was needed to establish why this was so. He suggested that it could be the effect of the Moon's gravity on immune systems, hormones and steroids. 'The prime candidates to exert regulatory function on the immune response are melatonin and steroids, whose levels are affected by the moon cycle,' Dr Zimecki said. He went on:

It is suggested that melatonin and endogenous steroids may mediate the described cyclic alterations of physiological processes. Electromagnetic radiation and/or the gravitational pull of the Moon may trigger the release of hormones.

Look at the implications for control and influence if you have the power to control these things. Studies of crime figures found them to be much higher on full-moon days than any other, and that road accidents were significantly more frequent during the waxing than the waning of the Moon. A study at Georgia State University found that eating and drinking habits are influenced by moon phases. It said that 'a small but significant lunar rhythm of nutrient intake was observed with an eight per cent increase in meal size and a 26 per cent decrease in alcohol intake at the time of the full moon relative to the new moon'. University of Miami psychologist, Arnold Lieber, and his colleagues studied data on murders in one county over 15 years. They matched the murder figures with moon phases and found they rose and fell together. The murder rate rose sharply as the full and new moons neared, and declined during the first and last quarters. They repeated the experiment in another county in Ohio and saw very similar results. An American Institute of Medical Climatology report for the Philadelphia Police Department discovered that the full moon marks a peak in a number of crimes, including murder, reckless driving and arson. There are apparently more fights, riots and general unrest among prison inmates at the full moon. Greek philosopher, Aristotle, and Roman historian, Pliny the Elder, believed that the Moon influenced the brain, the 'moistest' organ in the body, as it affected the tides. Modern scientists mostly reject this, but they don't understand the full effect of the Moon on human perception because it operates on many wavelengths that they are unable to measure. Vedic Astrology is an ancient Indian astrological system that interprets the movements and positions of planets and the Moon with regard to their effects on humanity and the Earth. It goes back thousands of years to the Indus Valley culture and beyond. Vedic Astrology says that the Moon rules the mind and both thoughts and feelings. It says that the Moon is the father of Mercury, because Mercury (intellect) is born from the Moon. Mercury rules the rational mind, according to this system, while the Moon rules everything else, including the past, memories, conditioned behaviour patterns and emotional responses. These patterns and responses are the very foundation of human control and there is a very good reason for that: humans are controlled from the Moon. There are many who say that we are not significantly influenced by the Moon and yet experiments with something as small as a cockroach have shown stress-related changes in the chemical composition of their blood connected to the new and full moon. It is suggested that this is caused by changes in the Earth's electromagnetic field instigated by the Moon. That is precisely the point. The Moon's influence is happening in the Metaphysical Universe – the information blueprint from which everything in the holographic realm of 'physical' experience is made manifest. Electromagnetic changes become holographic changes.

Moon Time

The illusion of time is one of the most powerful ways of disconnecting Mind from Consciousness. There is no time, only the eternal Now, and Consciousness operates in this no-time Now, while Mind perceives everything as past, present and future – linear time. Crucial to this perception is the Moon. The Sumerians used a lunar calendar along with a solar one and began the month with the first crescent moon. This is, of course, an important symbol of Islam, a moon religion, which still uses a calendar linked to the Moon. The Chinese Lunar New Year is the longest chronological record in history, dating from 2600 BC, when the Emperor Huang Ti introduced the first cycle of the zodiac. If you remember, Huang Ti was the guy who was said to have been born with a 'dragon-like countenance'. The Chinese Lunar Calendar is the one that names each year after an animal. Our year is broken up into months, a word that comes from moon, or 'moonth'. It was originally based on the 29 days from new moon to new moon. The term 'menstrual' has the same origin and derives from the Latin word 'mensis', meaning 'month', which comes from 'moon'. The menstrual cycle of 28 days is strongly connected to the phases of the Moon and thus so is fertility. The 'Christian' festival of Easter, an ancient pagan celebration of rebirth, is associated with the Moon. The very word derives from the Babylonian moon goddess, Semiramis, or Ishtar, also known in Europe as 'Eostre' and 'Europa'. The timing of Easter is still linked to the Moon. It falls on the first Sunday after the first full moon following the spring equinox. The Jewish Passover festival also starts on the night of the full moon after the equinox. Even the solar calendar is controlled by the Moon because it regulates the speed the Earth rotates and therefore the length of the day. It is estimated that if the Moon were not there the day would be eight hours and not twenty-four. The Moon fundamentally influences our perception of time and disconnects us from the realm of no-time – Consciousness. This is no coincidence.

The Moon is Mission Control

The Moon is the Reptilian control centre and it is manipulating and regulating life on Earth in extraordinary detail. Earth is travelling at 67,000 miles per hour in its orbit around the Sun and, at the same time, rotating at around 1,000 miles per hour; while the Moon is orbiting Earth at more than 2,000 miles per hour. Put that little lot together and you have a massive energy-generating system connecting the two bodies and not only on the levels that we can measure, either. The Reptilians are broadcasting a false reality from the Moon that humans are decoding into what they think is a physical world. It is a vibrational/digital construct, the same as the reality portrayed in the *Matrix* movies. The Moon, like all 'physicality', is a waveform phenomenon that we decode into a hologram that only exists as such in our decoded reality. It is all happening on a vibrational level as wavefields in the Metaphysical Universe. The transmissions from the Moon – the Moon Matrix – are broadcast in the Metaphysical Universe and we then decode them into holographic reality, response and experience. The Moon is transmitting information to the human body-computer which the Reptilians genetically-modified to receive and decode it. We are living in a dreamworld within a dreamworld – a Matrix within the virtual-reality universe – and it is being broadcast from the Moon. This is how they have hacked into the virtual-reality game. The precision in the mathematics and proportions of the Moon in relation to Earth and the Sun is all part of this, as is the connecting mathematics, proportion, alignment and geometry of the megalithic structures all over the world. The information construct for the virtual-reality universe as a whole is encoded in the photons emitted by the suns in conjunction with what we call black holes. The transmissions from the Moon have hacked into this information to distort it and encode other information – realities – into the photons emitted by the Sun. Carol Clarke's 'Carl Sagan' dream said that the suns are the controllers of reality in that they emit photons encoded with information that penetrate the DNA and stimulate the visual centre of the brain (where we construct holographic reality). Holographic reality is not an external 'world'; it is all happening within us as we decode what I call the Holographic Internet, the collective reality broadcast as information by the suns. It is obvious that if you hack into that information and change or distort it, you are going to change the perceived reality of the receiver. If you have also genetically modified the 'receivers' to tune them into your information source, your influence on their reality is even more powerful. This is what is happening – via the Moon. Humans are not decoding the original information in the photons emitted from the Sun, but a hacked version of it (Fig 223). The creator of this manufactured and 'hacked' reality which holds humanity in servitude is worshipped by Freemasons as 'The Grand Architect'. The target 'receiver' of the Moon Matrix transmissions is the frequency range of what we call Mind, especially the reptilian brain, and to keep us enslaved in the false reality of the Moon Matrix, the Reptilians and their hybrid networks must ensure that we do

Illustration by Neil Hague (www.neilhague.com)

Figure 223: *The Moon is a gigantic spacecraft that has been specifically positioned in relation to the Earth and Sun to create the 'Moon Matrix', a false reality that 'hacks' into the information from the Sun encoded in 'Light'. The Moon Matrix feeds the hacked reality into the human collective mind via the Metaphysical Universe, the Earth's ocean and crystal structure, the reptilian brain and the left hemisphere of the brain. Unless people become Conscious, 'their' mind is the Moon's mind – the Reptilian hive mind*

not expand our state of awareness beyond Mind and into Consciousness. The more we do this, the more we will see what is really going on – the Reptilians are controlling humanity from the Moon (Fig 224 overleaf).

The other prime Moon-Earth-human connections are crystals and water. The vibrational interplay between the Moon and crystals within the Earth is key to the Moon Matrix. I said earlier that the Earth is awash with crystal, not least quartz crystal. You find this and other crystal in stones, rocks and every grain of sand. The planet is crystalline, just like the human body, and both are transmitter-receivers of information. Quartz crystal has the ability to generate a fixed frequency and convert waveform resonance, or vibration, into an electrical signal, which is what the five senses do. What isn't appreciated is the scale of crystal content within the Earth and below the seabed – right down to the core. These gigantic crystals and crystal deposits are there to receive

Figure 224: *The Reptilians manipulate humanity from the Moon and also have underground bases on Earth and Mars*

and transmit information encoded in the photons emitted by the Sun. The transmissions from the Moon have hacked into this Sun-Earth connection (hence the remarkable symmetry of the Moon with the Earth and Sun) and created the vibrational sub-reality that I call the Moon Matrix. It is a manufactured vibrational/waveform 'web' that transmits and receives encoded information passing between the Moon, the human body/brain, crystals within the Earth and, as I will come to, the ocean. It is vibrating to a particular frequency range and humanity has to be kept in a low-vibrational mental and emotional state (based on fear and survival) if we are to be 'tuned in' to the Moon Matrix. The electrochemical destabilisation of the body-computer through food additives and electromagnetic pollution adds to this 'tuning in' effect. This explains so much about why the world is as it is. When people 'awaken' and start to escape the perceptional confines of Mind, they are disconnecting from the Moon Matrix 'hack' and reconnecting with the photons from the Sun, through which we can, in turn, reconnect with the *All That Is*. The 'ley line' network of energy flows that surround and interpenetrate the Earth are following lines of crystals under the ground. The crystal 'matrix' within the Earth is expressed as the energy force-lines that we call ley lines or meridians. This may upset some people who research in the 'earth energy' and 'megalithic' arena, but I strongly suggest that at least most of the great stone circles, stone 'forests', such as the more than 3,000 standing stones at Carnac in Brittany, France, and other megalithic structures, were actually put there to block and dilute the power of the energy passing through the ley line and vortex network. I include famous locations like Stonehenge in this. It is the same with pyramids, the calling card of the Reptilians. The reason for these megalithic structures (with their geometry so often based on the Moon-synchronising 'megalithic yard') was two-fold: to access the energy for their own ritual and other purposes, but also to suppress the power and vibration of the energy pumping around the planet to maintain both the Earth and humanity in the low-vibrational state that tunes them into the Moon Matrix and dilutes and distorts the purity of the waveform information coming from the Sun. Today they do this by putting nuclear power stations, major cities, road interchanges and other disruptive structures on the vortex points where many ley lines cross. The most important area the Reptilians and their hybrids had to target this way was the United Kingdom. The 'channelling' by the entity known as 'Magnu' explained this to me in 1990:

As in your human body, there are energy lines around your planet, through your planet, which correspond, I suppose, very much to the acupuncture lines and meridians in your body. Where two lines cross, you create a vortex, a tiny vortex if it's two. The more lines that intersect, the bigger the vortex. Therefore when you have a chakra you have a large vortex of intersecting energy.

It is the same with your planet. Where the most lines cross there is the biggest vortex. Now you could say the plexus in and around the islands you call the British Isles is the hub of the wheel of plexuses and energies which surround your planet. It has acted in other times like a fail-safe device. In order to activate these chakric points upon your planet, the energies must all pass through the central point. They must pass through the heart of the pattern.

The United Kingdom is in so many ways the hub of the global conspiracy at operational level because the black magicians of the Illuminati want to control the 'heart of the pattern' to hijack the Earth's energy field to harness that energy for their own purposes and to suppress its vibrational state in line with the frequency range of the Moon Matrix and their own low-vibrational nature. There are more stone circles, standing stones and ancient earthworks in the United Kingdom and Ireland per square mile than anywhere else in the world. The 'Magnu' channelling also said that powerful energies were 'switched off' at the time of what I call the Schism to stop them being abused and this also affected the vibrational state of the planet, however much it may have been necessary. The combination of all these things locked the Earth and its occupants into the vibrational range of the Moon Matrix – and we are in the process now of breaking free from it.

Animals are also affected by the Moon transmissions and this was a major reason for the fear-based disconnection between humans and animals that ended what had previously been a much closer and interactive relationship. The Moon Matrix is targeting our crystalline DNA and, through this vibrational connection, it can manipulate the human body-computer mentally, emotionally and physically. When people expand their awareness beyond Mind and into Consciousness they break out of the control of the Moon Matrix transmissions. To do this, we must open the right side of the brain and end the perception-domination of the left. This is why society, not least education, is structured as it is – to stop us doing that. It is the same with all the vaccines, drugs and, as I have said, additives in food and drink. The Moon transmissions are also designed to vibrationally suppress the right brain with all its insights and 'miraculous' abilities and ensure that humans access only a fraction of our true potential. The Moon-Earth crystal connection further allows the Reptilians within the Moon to manipulate the Earth biologically and geologically to change weather patterns and cause earthquakes, volcanoes and tsunamis. They have done this so many times since the Moon came and there have been many 'Great Floods'. Some of the legends about these catastrophes are a fusion of multiple events. One other aspect to stress is that crystals are seen as something positive and many people like to hold them, wear them around their necks or keep them at home. That's fine, but it is worth remembering that the crystal itself is not positive or negative; it is neutral. What matters is the frequency it is emitting and if it is the Moon Matrix that is not good at all. It is another way of holding you in the frequency trap.

Seventy per cent of the Earth's surface is water and, according to one figure I saw, this totals some 326 million trillion gallons. The human body is 60 to 70 per cent water and the Moon Matrix transmissions have also encoded their fake-reality information into the planet and humanity through the conduit of water (at the level of the Metaphysical Universe). Most people think that water is an excellent conductor of electricity, but that's not strictly true. Water only becomes an efficient conductor of electricity when salt is added, because it is not the water that conducts electricity so much as its chemical and other content. How interesting, then, that 97 per cent of the water on Earth is sea water – salt water (mostly from sodium chloride). The human diet is also full of salt, especially in processed foods produced by the Illuminati corporations. These foods account for 75 per cent of the salt that people consume and the human diet contains far more salt than the body needs. One of the consequences of this is that the body retains more water than it normally would. Significantly, language researcher, Pierre Sabak, says that 'salt' was part of the covenant between 'humanity' (the bloodlines) and the Reptilian 'gods'. The theme of salt can be found in Christianity and Judaism, among other faiths. The biblical *Second Book of Chronicles* clearly connects salt to the covenant between 'God' (the gods) and Israel: 'Don't you know that the Lord, the God of Israel, has given the kingship of Israel to David and his descendents forever by a covenant of salt?' The Hebrew term 'melakh' (covenant of salt) relates to the 'mal'akh' (the angel or shining king). Sabak says that 'halos', the Greek polymorphic (many forms) noun for 'salt', signifies 'halos' (the disk of the sun or moon) and 'halos' is related to 'hals' (the sea). From 'sal' (salt) we also get the Greek noun 'Selene' (the moon goddess). The symbolism of 'salt' and the 'covenant' are also the origins of 'salary' from the Roman word 'salarium' (a soldier's ration or salt money). Hence, of course, we talk of someone being 'worth their salt' or being the 'salt of the Earth'.

When I came across this information I had the sudden feeling, or 'knowing', that the seas of the Earth were not always salty. Somehow the Moon had been used to infuse the salt content. I rang Credo Mutwa in South Africa, the library of African legends and symbolic stories. I asked him if there were any accounts about the sea not always being salty and as I was posing the question I knew what he would say – 'Yes'. Credo said that there was a time when the sea was fresh water, 'but the moon goddess put a curse upon the sea and made it undrinkable'. The legends say that a mountain of salt was placed in the centre of the world to make the seas salty and this was done by the Reptilians, he said, 'to drive the good gods away'. Still today in Africa it is said that you must never put salt on the food of the gods, and salt is used in rituals to 'keep spirits at bay'. The accounts say that the sea became salty at the time of the Great Flood (there have been many). The canopy of water above the Earth – the 'Great Sky Lake' – fell as fresh water during the cataclysms, but 'the ice that fell was salty', the stories say. Credo told me that the 'high sangomas' in South Africa are not allowed to put salt on their food because it is said to diminish their psychic gifts. Once again we see the male-female divide of the Moon and Sun in the way that African shamans see fresh water (female) and salt water (male). It is believed that Mars, another Reptilian target in the 'past', had salty oceans (and according to some scientific speculation, at least one artificially-created 'spaceship moon'). A study by Carleton Moore, Professor of Chemistry and Geology at Arizona State University, Douglas

Sawyer of Scottsdale Community College, Michael McGehee, an Arizona University graduate student and Julie Canepa of Los Alamos National Laboratory, suggested that ancient Martian oceans had a mineral composition similar in variety and concentration to Earth's ocean. The finding came after analysis of a 1.2 billion-year-old Martian meteorite. Professor Moore said: 'We have concluded that we have extracted salts that were originally present in Martian water. The salts we found mimic the salts in Earth's ocean fairly closely.' NASA's Cassini spacecraft has also provided strong evidence that a salty ocean exists below the icy shell of the Saturn moon, Enceladus. Once again it is thought that the salt content is as high as that in our sea. There is a great deal more to know about all this, of course, and it came up just as the book was being completed, so I can't take it any further for now. But we are onto something here with the theme of water, salt and the transmissions of the Moon Matrix. If you know the frequency of salt you can infuse that into water at the level of the Metaphysical Universe and it becomes salt water in the decoded, play out, holographic realm.

The Schism

The Reptilians seized control and replaced harmony with disharmony through what I call 'the Schism'. Legends talk about the wars of the gods that destroyed at least one planet and devastated Mars and Earth, but we come back again to the core understanding. The 'physical', or holographic, 'world' is a decoded version of the information construct – the Metaphysical Universe. When the Moon arrived, it caused a gigantic energetic 'tear', or more accurately a 'distortion', in the information construct of the Metaphysical Universe and destroyed the previous balance and harmony (Fig 225). This distortion was then decoded through into the holographic level of reality as war, division and mayhem. The human 'personality' was also subject to the Schism and people, too, became fractured and distorted and were no longer 'whole' (Fig 226 overleaf). The Schism in the Metaphysical Universe – the information blueprint – had to manifest in the holographic realm, because that is merely a decoded version of the waveform construct. The blueprint in

Figure 225: *The arrival of the Moon, the hi-tech wars and the destruction of Mars and a planet between Mars and Jupiter (now the asteroid belt) caused a massive 'tear' or 'distortion' in the Metaphysical Universe which was decoded through into holographic reality as extraordinary destruction and catastrophic geological upheavals. Human society immediately descended from an advanced technological world into the Stone Age*

Illustration by Neil Hague (www.neilhague.com)

Illustration by Neil Hague (www.neilhague.com)

Figure 226: *The Schism in the Metaphysical Universe was decoded through into holographic reality as a devastated planet and distorted and fractured human personalities and perceptions*

the Metaphysical Universe was now facing cataclysmic energetic upheavals and so, therefore, was its holographic expression. It manifested as geological and biological catastrophe. This was the devastated blueprint becoming the devastated decoded holographic 'world'. The distortion was expressed at every level, not least in fractured and distorted human perception, self-identity and imbalanced thought and emotion. This was the time that the 'Magnu' channelling was talking about when it said:

My own allegiance with your planet goes back to an Atlantean period ... [when] ... there were many energies being used and information and knowledge being used which were for particular reasons of safety withdrawn, shall we say, to prevent complete catastrophe, to prevent total destruction of your planet. One could say these were sort of emergency measures if you like, to prevent the inhabitants of this planet from an untimely destruction.

The affect of the Schism on the human personality, together with the Reptilian desire for war and conquest, was the reason these energies were withdrawn. Very powerful energies have the potential for creating an incredible world, but, in the control of imbalanced and malevolent minds, they can cause catastrophe. Everything can be used for good or ill. The withdrawal of these energies – information – meant that human potential and awareness plummeted and became what we would call 'primitive' compared with what it had been before. The Reptilians and their Moon Matrix have been in control ever since of a mentally, emotionally and physically truncated humanity, but that is in the process of changing, as I will detail in the latter stages of the book. Another consequence of the loss of these energies was that humans and animals now had an energy 'gap' between what they could absorb from the atmosphere and what they need to survive. This was bridged by eating food – each other. The 'law of the wild' had begun. It is all an expression of the energetic and information imbalance, the Schism.

Arrival of the Moon = 'Fall of Man'

Now we can see the true meaning behind the symbolism of the Zulu tradition. Credo Mutwa told me that Zulu stories describe how the Reptilians and their Moon changed the mentality of humans and 'hijacked the female Sun'. He said that the Sun was worshipped as female, but the Reptilians changed this from the sun goddess to the male sun god. All the main gods had been female and the Sun was known by the female name, 'Langa', which means 'to desire', 'to long for' (Fig 227). Credo said that this switch from perceiving the Sun as female to worshipping it as male made possible the creation of 'war-like kings' that took what they wanted by force. Everything changed when the perception of the Sun changed, he said. Everything changed when the encoded information from the Sun was hacked into from the Moon and changed the nature of the energy (information) from 'female' to 'male' – the Reptilians and their Moon hijacked the female Sun. This explains so much about what has happened since and why the influence of the Moon made possible the creation of 'war-like kings' that took what they wanted by force. The 'hack' means that we don't 'see' (decode) all that there is to see, and we experience other phenomena that does not come from the wider universe, but from information transmissions from the Moon. If you think that this is crazy and impossible, then look at the effect of analogue television frequencies alone. Did you know that they – and cellphone frequencies – prevent us from receiving radio waves from whole galaxies? The very mainstream science magazine, *New Scientist*, reported in its edition of 7th November 2009:

> US skies are clearer than usual after the switch in June from analogue to digital TV freed up a chunk of the radio spectrum. Astronomers are now rushing to see what they can find before transmissions from cellphone companies and others fill the space.
>
> Prior to the switch-over, naturally occurring radio waves at frequencies between 700 and 800 megahertz were obscured by analogue TV signals, preventing astronomers from investigating the universe using this band …
>
> … The freeing up of this bandwidth is a once-in-a-lifetime opportunity to see galaxies in this range. The new window may also help in the hunt for pulsars – neutron stars that emit beams of radio waves from their poles. In this

Figure 227: *The Sun was known by the female name, 'Langa', before the Reptilians and the Moon arrived. Langa means 'to desire', 'to long for'. Credo Mutwa said that perception of the Sun changed from female to male and this 'made possible the creation of "war-like kings" that took what they wanted by force'. Everything changed because the encoded information from the Sun was hacked into from the Moon and the 'female' energy became 'male'. It explains so much about what has happened since*

part of the spectrum, their beams are less impeded by interstellar electrons, which can scatter radio waves.

These frequencies are being auctioned off to cellphone companies and others, and astronomers had little more than a year to observe what they couldn't access before. This is the effect of television frequencies; imagine the potential for 'alien' technology that is, as some insiders estimate, some 10,000 years ahead of our own – in the public domain, that is. The 10,000 figure is misleading, however, in that once you cross a certain line of understanding reality the technological potential simply explodes. This means that the '10,000 years' can be made up very quickly. The aim of the Reptilian race is to stop humans from crossing that line – hence the suppression of knowledge and the control of what passes for science.

It seems that 'moons' are the modus operandi of the Reptilians and they have other such mooncraft that are used to travel the Universe and hijack planets by hijacking the reality-perception of their inhabitants. Given their connection to Mars, it seems less fantastic that Russian astrophysicist Dr Iosif Shklovsky said in 1959 that Phobos, a moon circling Mars, could be an artificial satellite; or that he was supported by Dr S Fred Singer, special advisor to President Eisenhower on space developments, and Raymond H Wilson Jr, Chief of Applied Mathematics at NASA, who said in 1963 that 'Phobos might be a colossal base orbiting Mars'. Inside Earth's moon is an entire artificial world of enormous size and technological advancement. It includes the 'computer' system (way beyond what we would call 'computers') broadcasting a manufactured reality, the Moon Matrix. When you look at everything from this perspective, who is to say 'where' we really are? We are certainly not on a 'physical' Earth, because that is only a decoded illusion. Encoded light from the Sun is being re-encoded as it enters the energetic field of the Earth-Moon system and the almost perfect relationship between the three bodies is part of this (Fig 228). Most crucial to making it all 'fit' is the size and location of the Moon. When I say that the Reptilians have hacked into the virtual-reality universe, I mean just that. They have also installed technology within the Earth that receives and transmits information from and to the Moon to underpin the vibrational sub-reality. The

Figure 228: *Neil Hague's concept of 'Moonopoly' – the 'board game' of human life dictated from cradle to grave by the transmissions from the Moon that dictate the perception and sense of reality of all of those operating purely in Mind as 'luna-tics' and 'loopies'. It is an ever-recurring cycle that can only be broken by Consciousness*

1998 Hollywood movie, *The Truman Show*, starring Jim Carrey, was very symbolic of what I am saying here. I watched it for the first time while I was writing this book. Carrey's character was born into a reality-television show that took place on an island disconnected from the rest of the world. He was never told that he was on a television show 24/7 and, with no other coordinates, he thought this was how life was. But the Sun coming up and going down to be replaced by the Moon was all a computer program, as was the weather. When he got close to leaving the island he was stopped by manufactured circumstance and suppression of knowledge. Eventually he realised that something was seriously wrong and he escaped in a boat. When he sailed on what he thought was the open sea he reached the wall of a big dome, the wall of a vast 'studio' in which the show took place. Years before I saw this, I was sitting at a table outside a cafe in the countryside of the Isle of Wight, when I looked up and saw the sky as a gigantic dome, like the ceiling of a planetarium. If you think *vibrational* dome, that's about right. The operations centre in *The Truman Show*, from where the whole thing was orchestrated, even looked very much like the Moon. If you haven't seen the movie, it is worth watching for the symbolism alone.

The Biological 'Fall From Grace' Revisited

I described earlier how brain capacity expanded at an increasingly rapid rate over perhaps millions of years, but then this expansion suddenly stopped about 200,000 years ago. This could well have been around the time the Moon arrived, although I am very open on this. It could have been much more recent, hard as that will be for most people to believe, or much earlier. *When* it happened is far less important than the fact that it did, and the effect it had. The arrival of the Moon brought geological and biological catastrophe to the Earth and the wider solar system. It changed the angle and spin of the planet and imposed a new climate based on the four seasons. This was not the only geological and biological disaster to strike the Earth. There have been many since then and there was certainly one in the period of 11,500 to 13,000 years ago, maybe more than one. These could easily have been caused by literally moving the Moon, even marginally, a threat that Zulu legend says the Reptilians made when humans refused to obey them. They can also manipulate biological and geological events through the Moon transmissions themselves to the crystal structure within the Earth. I said earlier that brain capacity began to go backwards because of genetic manipulation and the isolating of humans overwhelmingly in the left-brain through some sort of re-wiring operation to isolate us from the 'out there' genius of right-brain reality. I would say that a key part of this isolation is made possible through the Moon Matrix, which vibrationally/digitally targets the reptilian brain and left brain, and vibrationally suppresses the right. It also connects with the 'third eye' pineal gland to close down the 'out there' connections and hold people in five-sense perception. The mere presence of the Moon, let alone its transmissions, massively influences human hormone production and the pineal gland, although opening the Mind to Consciousness can overcome this. It can overcome anything. It is also the Moon Matrix vibrational web that has switched off the multi-billions of cells in the corpus callosum 'bridge' between the hemispheres, and in other parts of the brain. When regions of the brain are activated and operational they 'light up'. The Moon Matrix stops these targeted areas and functions of the brain from 'lighting up' as they normally would. This is done in much the same way as it is possible to firewall a computer so that it doesn't respond to information and does not 'pick up' large tracts of the Internet. The human firewall is done by particular vibrational/digital codes delivered to the human brain/body-computer by the Moon Matrix, and if these codes were broken then human reality and potential would be transformed – like Sleeping Beauty waking up from her induced slumber. I can tell you now, whether people believe it or not, that these codes *are* going to be broken. You heard it here first. All this is hard to believe for most people, I know, but it is true all the same.

Time Loop Revisited

Other matters can be brought into a clearer perspective once you understand how the 'game' has been hacked, not least the Time Loop (Fig 229). This is a vibrational software program encoded with information that we decode as an experience of past moving through present to future when, in truth, the only 'time' is NOW. I have described already how the world lines of planets and people, their space-time coordinates, can curve back on themselves to create what scientists call 'causal loops'. I am saying here that the Moon Matrix manipulates reality to form such causal loops – time loops – around Planet Earth and its inhabitants. Humans are living in their own little time loops within the Moon-Earth energy construct. We may look 'out' from this Moon-Earth field to see the Sun, stars and planets, but we are decoding that information from within the Moon-Earth fake reality. We see what we decode, not what is necessarily there. We are living in a hologram in which every part is a smaller version of the whole. The human energy field looks like the Earth's energy field, and so on. Therefore, if the Earth's energy field is influenced by the Moon, human energy fields must be so, too (as smaller versions of the Earth's hologram). The system has been set up to turn the human energy field into a smaller version of the Moon-Earth Matrix – in other words a closed system. As I said in the last chapter: 'If you can 'fix' the hologram at a higher level then all holograms within that must reflect the master hologram.' It is because of this system that the default state of humans within the Moon Matrix is to have a closed auric field disconnected from Consciousness and that's exactly how it is designed to be. The movement of the Moon around the Earth is reflected in energetic movement around the human auric field that reflects the closed Moon-Earth system into the human aura. It artificially creates closed world lines or causal loops – time loops. This is why I call people in this closed-mind state 'loopies'. 'The Voice' in Brazil was referring to this in another way when it talked about people coming into this reality and getting immediately caught in the same 'record groove' over and over. The only way out of this is to use our awareness to break through the loops and into Consciousness. This can be done, as I'll address later.

These 'moon loops' enclosing the human aura explain so much about human behaviour (Fig 230). The energetic pressure is to keep the loop enclosed and intact – that's its default

Figure 229: *The Time Loop*

position unless Consciousness gets involved. When people go into denial to avoid breaking out of the loop (seeing and living life outside of the 'box') it is the moon-loop applying pressure to maintain its closed system, the 'status quo'. I'll give you an example. A friend pointed out to a head teacher that Ritalin, the mind-altering drug widely given to children, is actually a derivative of cocaine. The head teacher, on hearing this, angrily demanded to know if he was accusing her of giving cocaine to children. A Conscious person would say something like, 'What? Tell me more – if this true it must be stopped.' This lady

Figure 230: *The 'Moon Loops' are designed to close the human auric field – and keep it closed – and imprison people in left-brain reality*

was not Conscious, however, she was a loopy and so her reflex response was to attack the messenger rather than maturely deal with the message. I see the loops defending themselves – the status quo – all the time. There was a man that I knew who spent his whole career in the military and was in real denial that what I am saying could possibly be true. He later came to a seven-hour presentation I did in the United States and was in tears afterwards at what he had seen and heard. I had never seen him like that and it seemed that a breakthrough had happened, but within a short time he was back in denial again. The loop had defaulted to base state. Only Consciousness and an unbreakable will not to conform to program no matter what can break the loop and change reality. Professional sceptics who don't question, but merely defend the status quo, are big-time loopies and the global system of government, public agencies, medicine, science, education and banking are teeming with Moon loopies. They are exactly the people the system is looking for and they are specifically programmed that way by 'education'. The system wants its minions to be people who would never think of questioning the programmed perception of their loop.

Reptilian Brain Revisited

The reptilian brain, or R-complex within the human brain, is vital to the success this far of the Moon Matrix. I stress again, however, that, like everything else, what we call the reptilian brain is encoded energetic information and it only appears to be 'physical' when those codes are read. I suggest that the reptilian brain did not form aeons ago, like scientists say, as humans evolved in part from reptiles. The more I research this, and the more my Consciousness expands, the clearer it is that the Reptilian geneticists implanted the reptilian brain (at least in its current form) as part of a mass control system. It may well have happened aeons ago on another world, as the Zulu shamans suggest, but the point is that it was implanted when the androgynous bodies of earlier humans were divided into men and women which brought about 'the pain of childbirth', as the Bible and other ancient accounts describe. The genetic manipulation and the division of male and female changed human behaviour dramatically and led to them being ejected from 'paradise'. It is through the reptilian brain that the Reptilians

Figure 231: *The Reptilian hive mind has hijacked the human mind via the reptilian brain and the Moon Matrix*

and their associates manipulate our perceptions and behaviours and connect humanity to a hive-mind control system, as well as feeding a false and truncated reality. As I mentioned earlier, the Reptilians and Greys have a hive mind that is much like the ones that queen bees or queen ants use to communicate with their workers. They have locked humans into their hive mind through the installation of the reptilian brain within the human brain (Fig 231). This is why humans repeat so much of their behaviours and perceptions, especially those connected with fear and the obsession with survival. What do the biblical gods say? 'Let's make man in our image.' The writer, Carlos Castaneda, reports what his Yaqui Indian healer, or shaman in Mexico, Don Juan Matus, said about this very subject. I read this quote long after I had concluded that humans were connected to the Reptilian hive mind and I nearly fell off my chair when I saw what it said:

We have a predator that came from the depths of the cosmos and took over the rule of our lives. Human beings are its prisoners. The predator is our lord and master. It has rendered us docile, helpless. If we want to protest, it suppresses our protest. If we want to act independently, it demands that we don't do so ... indeed we are held prisoner!

They took us over because we are food to them, and they squeeze us mercilessly because we are their sustenance. Just as we rear chickens in coops, the predators rear us in human coops, humaneros. Therefore, their food is always available to them.

Think for a moment, and tell me how you would explain the contradictions between the intelligence of man the engineer and the stupidity of his systems of belief, or the stupidity of his contradictory behaviour. Sorcerers believe that the predators have given us our systems of beliefs, our ideas of good and evil; our social mores. They are the ones who set up our dreams of success or failure. They have given us covetousness, greed, and cowardice. It is the predator who makes us complacent, routinary, and egomaniacal.

In order to keep us obedient and meek and weak, the predators engaged themselves in a stupendous manoeuvre – stupendous, of course, from the point of view of a fighting strategist; a horrendous manoeuvre from the point of those who suffer it. *They gave us their mind.* The predators' mind is baroque, contradictory, morose, filled with the fear of being discovered any minute now.

Well, now they have been.

Humanity has become a sub-species of the Reptilians and Greys, who were involved with the Reptilians in the genetic manipulation of Far Eastern races like the Chinese and Japanese. The hive-mind broadcast from the Moon and the genetic manipulation of the body-computer have programmed humanity's belief systems and emotional reactions and that is why people are so depressingly predictable. Data (life situation) becomes programmed reaction (emotional response). Type in the data, press 'Enter', and hey presto another human reacts the same as almost every other human would in the same circumstances. Don Juan was so right when he said: 'Think for a moment, and tell me how you would explain the contradictions between the intelligence of man the engineer and the stupidity of his systems of belief, or the stupidity of his contradictory behaviour.' The Reptilian-human hive mind is programmed for inner and 'outer' conflict which produces all the fear, stress, worry, anger, hostility, and so on, that generates the low-vibration emotional energy on which the Reptilians feed. These emotional responses are no more than an expression of the Reptilians' own mental and emotional state – fear of not surviving. Don Juan is said to have told Castaneda:

I know that even now, though you never have suffered hunger ... you have food anxiety, which is none other than the anxiety of the predator who fears that at any moment now its manoeuvre is going to be uncovered and food is going to be denied. Through the mind, which, after all is *their* mind, the predators inject into the lives of human beings whatever is convenient for them. And they insure, in this manner, a degree of security to act as a buffer against their fear.

Sorcerers of ancient Mexico ... reasoned that man must have been a complete being at one point, with stupendous insights, feats of awareness that are mythological legends nowadays. And then, everything seems to disappear, and we have now a sedated man. What I'm saying is that what we have against us is not a simple predator. It is very smart, and organised. It follows a methodical system to render us useless. Man, the magical being that he is destined to be, is no longer magical. He's an average piece of meat. There are no more dreams for man but the dreams of an animal who is being raised to be a piece of meat: trite, conventional, imbecilic.

But we don't have to be like that as this book will show before I finish. What has been done can be undone through a return to Consciousness and by breaking the code that holds the hacked system together. The Reptilian control is not a done-deal. In the light of what I am saying here, it is worth recapping on the personality and emotional traits that come from the reptilian brain through which we are attached to the Reptilians' hive mind (Fig 232 overleaf). This is is what I wrote earlier and it can now be seen from an even more profound perspective:

- Scientists say the reptilian brain represents a core of the nervous system and from this come character traits like aggressive, cold-blooded and ritualistic behaviour; a desire for control, power and ownership – 'territoriality'; might is right; social hierarchies; and 'primitive emotional responses'.

- At least five human behaviours originate in the reptilian brain: obsessive compulsive behaviour; personal day-to-day rituals and superstitious acts; slavish conformance to old ways of doing things; ceremonial re-enactments; obeisance to precedent, as in legal, religious, cultural, and other matters and all manner of deceptions.

Figure 232: *When we are entrapped by Mind and tuned to the Moon Matrix via the reptilian brain, our perception is dictated by the reptilian hive mind. We are little more than computer terminals*

- Cosmologist, Carl Sagan, wrote in *The Dragons of Eden*: 'It does no good whatsoever to ignore the reptilian component of human nature, particularly our ritualistic and hierarchical behaviour. On the contrary, the model may help us understand what human beings are really about.'

- The reptilian brain is home to the body's reactive emotions and survival responses. When we react to danger by fleeing, fighting or freezing (what psychologists call 'fight or flight') this is the reptilian brain at work. It is constantly scanning its environment for possible dangers and reacting accordingly. When it thinks it can defeat the perceived danger it will fight; when it decides that it can't, it runs; and it can also choose to freeze the body – 'frozen with fear'.

- When the reptilian brain kicks in it overpowers the thought processes of the neocortex through emotional responses based on fear of not surviving. This is when we talk about people 'losing their heads' or 'not thinking straight'. They lose their head to the reptilian brain which scrambles calm, considered thought.

- The reptilian brain also sees 'survival' as protecting status, power, reputation, superiority, intellectual pre-eminence, sense of self – the list is endless. When scientists, historians and religious advocates aggressively or dismissively reject new information or views that would demolish their rigid beliefs they have activated the reptilian brain, or, rather, the reptilian brain has activated them. Their survival mechanism has kicked in.

- So many people glean a sense of security from having a fixed view of 'the way things are' and we see this in religion, science, politics, 'education', medicine – the whole lot. When these status quos are challenged in any way the reptilian brain reads this as a danger that must be vanquished by either crushing the perceived 'opponent' (as with religious and scientific persecution) or by ignoring new insights and behaving as if they don't exist.

- The reptilian brain doesn't know the difference between real and imagined; it just reacts, and it can do so with lightening speed. It is not burdened by having to think things through. The reaction and the consequences can be a done deal before calm consideration has even begun to calmly consider.

- The reptilian brain also regulates breathing (hence it changes when we are in fear or are highly emotional); digestion (hence 'nervous stomach'); elimination of waste (hence 'scared shitless'); circulation and temperature (both fundamentally affected by fear, danger and emotion); movement, posture and balance (thus you can read someone's emotional state by their body language).

- The way the world is structured as pyramid-within-pyramid hierarchies is classic reptilian brain and Reptilian mentality, as is the way billions of people subordinate themselves to hierarchy and 'know their place'. When an authority figure, like a 'boss', walks into a room, or calls someone to his or her office, most people have an emotional reaction that relates, mildly or strongly, to fear. Keith Miller, an American 'relationship therapist', said this in an Internet article about the reptilian brain and human relationships:

  ... when an authority figure enters the room, the portion of your brain that scans the environment may send the danger signal to the reptilian brain, even if you get along relatively well with that person. For many people, it is hard to relate to their bosses without slipping into fight (which usually takes the form of 'logically' disagreeing with whatever the boss or company says); flight (which is usually 'escaping' into avoidance behaviour – not saying what you really think or not expressing how you really feel); or freeze behaviours (when a normally intelligent and engaging person goes 'brain dead').

Humans have become the mind-set of their Reptilian controllers – those who are stuck in Mind and are not Conscious, that is.

Reptilian World

Put that all together and you can see how we live in a global society that is little more than a collective expression of the reptilian brain. The reason for that is becoming clearer and clearer – the reptilian brain within the human brain is how we are connected to the Reptilian hive-mind and the Moon transmissions, and how our behaviour and perceptions are dictated. The more we stay out of the reptilian brain, and I'll come to that towards the end of the book, the less we are controlled by these deeply imbalanced entities. This is why society is structured to activate the emotional reactions and responses – all based on fear – which lock us into the decoding system of the reptilian brain. Now we can see how and why the global population is kept in a constant state of fear, anxiety, stress and worry. Crucially, we are pressured and manipulated to live our entire lives in fear of not surviving. I don't mean just the fear of dying, either. These survival responses include the fear of losing your partner, fear of losing your job and your home, fear of having no money, fear of 'God', fear of the 'Devil', and fear of just about anything. The hive mind keeps people in a state of anxiety that niggles away in the belly even when nothing is happening that should make us anxious. As I have pointed out, the reptilian brain doesn't know the difference between 'real' and imagined. When you simply think of something that frightens you or makes you anxious, the reptilian brain will react as if it is happening. This gives no respite from the state of anxiety which is always there running in the background even when we are not directly aware of it. I have said before that humans have no idea what happiness and contentment really means because we measure our 'happiness' by our level of unhappiness. When we feel less unhappy and anxious we take this contrast with more extreme states of unhappiness and anxiety as being happy and content. This daily anxiety, fear and focus on survival in all its forms feeds the Reptilians the low-vibration emotional energy on which they feed, and there are endless other consequences.

Must 'Fight', Must 'Win'

Two of these are conflict and competition, both of which produce the divide and rule so essential for the few to control the many. Wars are engineered by triggering the reptilian brain responses of the population. We see a constant stream of 'bogeymen', 'enemies' and situations produced to activate our survival codes – Osama bin Laden, Saddam Hussein, Iran, the war on terror, climate change, economic crisis, manufactured health scares; on and on it goes. Once people fear not surviving they are under the control of the reptilian brain and the hive mind and they will support, accept, even demand, actions by government, the military and the system in general to protect them from the perceived threat to their survival. All wars are fought by the reptilian brain – every man for himself, kill or be killed, it's us or them. Wars of conquest are reptilian brain responses. Remember those character traits again: aggressive, cold-blooded and ritualistic behaviour; a desire for control, power and ownership, 'territoriality'; might is right; social hierarchies; and 'primitive emotional responses'. When the American or Israeli military bomb the innocent from the skies of Baghdad or Gaza, how is it 'justified' by its advocates and perpetrators? Survival. 'Saddam Hussein has weapons of mass destruction that threaten you'; 'Palestinian terrorists are a threat to Israel's survival'. The cold-blooded killing of children who are no harm to anyone comes from the cold-blooded traits of the reptilian brain, as do other unspeakable 'acts of war' when killing an 'enemy' is not enough. They have to make him suffer, dismember him, have him scream for the mercy that will never come. Wars are declared by the reptilian brain, fought by it and 'justified' by it. The reptilian brain is, indeed, a war machine – the complete package. It is also the control mechanism of the psychopath, serial killer, rapist and paedophile. The reptilian-hybrid bloodlines are all of these on a monumental scale, as I have exposed in other books, because they are utterly dominated by Reptilian genetics. When the paedophile is having sex with a child the possessing entity is drawing off the child's life-force from the base chakra; and the victims of psychopaths,

serial killers and rapists generate extreme
levels of fear that the possessing Reptilian
feeds on. This is a reason why these sick
people often keep their victims in captivity and
high states of anxiety before doing their deed.
It is the same principle as a satanic ritual when
the victim knows they are going to be
sacrificed, but the ritual is drawn out to ensure
maximum terror.

Illustration by David Dees (deesillustration.com)

Figure 233: *The Reptilian hive mind at work*

The reptilian brain's addiction to survival
and the conflict that comes with it is not
confined to war. We see it at all levels of
human relationships and interactions as people
fight for power and control, compete for
influence, status and money or seek to defend themselves from perceived threats,
illusory or otherwise. We could cooperate to our mutual benefit, but the reptilian brain
and the hive mind of the Moon Matrix wants to compete, win, conquer. Underlying this
is the belief in the survival of the fittest and the strongest (survival yet again) and that
it's a 'dog-eat-dog' world. If someone wins, someone must lose and it's not going to be
me. It's all bollocks, but try telling that to the reptilian brain which could have invented
the term 'dog-eat-dog' and likely did. This competition, the desperate clamber up the
greasy pole, leads to the few to having far more than they need while others starve and
suffer for the lack of even the basics (Fig 233). Would Consciousness do that? No, but
unconsciousness would, and does, via the programmed Mind and reptilian brain.
Winning and losing has become a human obsession because it equates winning with
survival and losing with non-survival; it equates winning with status, dominance and
power (expressions of the reptilian brain) and losing with a lack of all three. The desire
to control – be it a partner, child, situation, country or world – all come from the
reptilian brain. It is a survival mechanism once again that perceives that the more
control you have the greater your chance of survival. The Illuminati Reptilian-hybrids
are terrified of unpredictable people and situations and they are obsessed with
controlling all sides to control the outcome. We see this in the way the global economy is
controlled, not even by open competition in what we call 'capitalism', but by 'cartelism'.
The market is rigged to ensure the desired outcome. The Reptilians and their hybrids
become seriously anxious with states of flux and so do most humans because they are
attached to the same hive-mind responses; the Reptilians are just more extreme, that's
all. The desire for ever more 'things' and everything to excess is another expression of
the reptilian brain. French anthropologist G Clotaire Rapaille wrote an article in the *Los
Angeles Times* that highlighted the reptilian brain's greed and excess. The article was
headed 'Living Ever Larger; How Wretched Excess Became a Way of Life in Southern
California'. He said:

> … the desire for excess comes from the reptilian brain … The reptilian wants to grab as
> much food as possible, to be as big and powerful as possible, because it's focused on
> survival. When it comes to a choice between the intellect and the reptilian, the reptilian
> always wins.

Satisfying that inner lizard has its downsides. Our insatiable appetites have left Americans 9 pounds heavier, on average, than we were two decades ago, and more vulnerable than ever to heart disease and diabetes. We're racking up mountains of debt (the late fees we pay on credit cards have more than tripled since 1996, to $7.3 million a year) and burning up fossil fuels like crazy. We demand things that, deep down, we don't really want or even use ...

You can see the reptilian brain and the hive mind at work as people live their lives as a daily ritual, like going to the same supermarket at the same time every week and having the same meals on the same days. The Reptilian-hybrids, the reptilian brain and the hive mind have turned human society into a clock-watching, ever-repeating daily cycle, and one in which the focus is on physical or financial survival and the pursuit of more, more, more. This is all reptilian-brain perception. Humans are also obsessed with the television and movies and this is by design, too. Researcher Skip Largent writes:

All movies and television are a projection of the reptilian brain. How so? Movies and television (video games etc.) are all undeniably dreamlike, not only in their presentation brain wave patterns as when they are dreaming. And guess where dreaming originates in your head? In the reptilian brain (although other parts of our brain are involved) ... The 'language' of the reptilian brain is visual imagery. All communications transferred by reptiles are done so by visual symbolic representations, each having specific meaning.

The Reptilian-hybrids of the Illuminati families have their own language of symbolism which is all around us if you know where to look. All the symbols of the Babylonian goddess, Semiramis, such as the Statue of Liberty, are among millions of examples (see *The David Icke Guide to the Global Conspiracy*). These symbols, in the landscape or in advertising and company logos, communicate subconsciously with the reptilian brain of the population and plant perceptions and responses. In early childhood the mental and emotional state is controlled almost exclusively by the reptilian brain through visual imagery. The purveyors of children's 'entertainment' like, for example, Disney, exploit this knowledge, and it's the same with computer games. Wherever you look in 'human' society you see the reptilian brain and the Reptilians' hive-mind Control System. We need to understand this and its implications for free thought and awareness if we are going to bring this captivity to an end, which we are. Everything I have said about the Reptilian control of humans applies even more so to their servants-on-earth: the Illuminati families. Their genetics are even more reptilian than the general population's and they are possessed by Reptilian entities operating just beyond human sight. Consciousness affects genetics, because in the end it is all the interaction of energy. Reptilian-hybrid bloodlines that have been possessed generation after generation by these reptilian entities are locked into their hive mind even more powerfully than the general population. They are just following a different program. The Illuminati families may think they are so clever and powerful, but, in truth, they are little more than shells for their masters vibrating beyond visible light who dictate their every thought and act.

One vital point here, however. The bloodline families are connected to the Reptilian system in a different way. They are not psychically and perceptually closed down like the mass of humanity and they can see and perceive things that the general population cannot. It is to do with the way their 'special' genetics decode reality. They can see auras and 'scan' a person's energy field for information. This can allow them to know more about a person than they even do themselves. These people are like schizophrenics. They are one personality in everyday life and something very different behind the scenes and this is most certainly true of families like the Rothschilds and Rockefellers, etc. Their access to these gifts while denying them to humanity is one of the major ways they imposed themselves on the 'masses'. To perpetuate this advantage and keep humans in a smaller 'box' of awareness they have to systematically suppress our potential to perceive beyond the five senses.

Closing the Third Eye

Earth is the equivalent of a Reptilian food-production colony – a gigantic farm or zoo. Crucial to keeping it like that is to disconnect humans from Consciousness and enslave them in their closed, ever-repeating loops within the Moon Matrix. Another way this is done is by manipulating hormones linked to mood, emotional responses and inter-dimensional perception, all of which are affected by the Moon, even without the actual transmissions themselves. This is an Internet explanation of what hormones do:

> Hormones are chemical messengers that travel throughout the body coordinating complex processes like growth, metabolism and fertility. They can influence the function of the immune system, and even alter behaviour. Before birth, they guide development of the brain and reproductive system. Hormones are the reason why your arms are the same length, why you can turn food into fuel, and why you changed from head to toe at puberty. It is thanks to these chemicals that distant parts of the body communicate with one another during elaborate, and important, events.
>
> In response to a signal from the brain, hormones are secreted directly into the blood by the glands that produce and store them. These glands make up what is known as the endocrine system (endocrine means 'secreting internally'). Chemicals that interfere with the function of hormones are therefore known as endocrine disruptors.
>
> The testes and ovaries, or 'gonads', are perhaps the most familiar endocrine glands. In males, testes produce sperm and secrete the male sex hormone testosterone; in females, ovaries produce eggs and the female hormone estrogen. It is these hormones that determine secondary sex characteristics like muscle mass and facial hair. They also help to orchestrate sperm production, menstruation and pregnancy. Other endocrine glands include the thyroid, pancreatic islets and adrenal glands. These are involved primarily in growth, metabolism and the 'fight or flight' response to stress.
>
> While all cells are exposed to hormones circulating in the bloodstream, not all cells react. Only a hormone's 'target' cells, which have receptors for that hormone, will respond to its signal. When the hormone binds to its receptor, it causes a biological response within the cell. If we liken a hormone to a radio signal, then a receptor is the

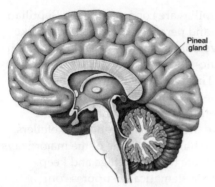

Pineal
gland

Figure 234: *The pineal gland, part of the 'Third Eye' that opens our awareness to realms beyond visible light*

antenna. Without the antenna, no signal would be received and no music would exit the radio. Signalling ends when the circulating hormones are broken down and excreted by the body.'

Those entrapped in five-sense reality and disconnected from Consciousness are literally biological robots of the Reptilian control system that dictates virtually their every thought and response, just as the queen ant does with the worker ants. The Internet article about hormones mentions the endocrine system that includes the pineal and pituitary glands. Both of these are in the brain and fundamental to 'seeing' beyond five-sense reality. The pineal gland is about the size of a pea, looks like a pine cone, and is located near the centre of the brain between the two hemispheres (Fig 234). It produces the hormone melotonin that regulates sleep patterns, and scientists have said that the Moon affects the production of melotonin – presumably by affecting the pineal gland. This is rightly believed to be part of the human 'third eye' system that allows us to see into other levels of reality. There is a great line in the Muse song *Uprising*, an anthem for our times, which goes: 'If you could flick a switch and open your third eye, you'd see that we should never be afraid to die'. Some biologists believe that the pineal cells of vertebrates share a common ancestor with retinal cells in the eye. This obviously fits the picture. René Descartes, the French philosopher and mathematician, embarked on a long and detailed study of the pineal gland. He called it the 'seat of the soul' and said it connected the body to the intellect. I would say it connects the body-computer to higher levels of awareness than the intellect, but he certainly understood its basic function. Mystery school and esoteric lore has long understood that the pineal gland connects the 'physical' with the 'spiritual' realms and allows people to see beyond the space-time construct.

Opening this 'third eye' activates psychic gifts and what some describe as supernatural powers. The pineal gland is activated by light and controls the body's bio-rhythms in concert with the hypothalamus gland which regulates hunger, thirst, sexual desire and the biological clock that dictates how fast we age. Look at the potential for mass control if you can externally suppress and manipulate the pineal and hypothalamus glands alone. You can make it much harder to perceive beyond the five senses, decide how quickly people age, how much they want sex, when they are hungry and thirsty and for how long. This is the key reason for putting sodium fluoride into water supplies and toothpaste. The pineal gland absorbs more fluoride than any other part of the body and becomes calcified by this highly-damaging toxin. Sodium fluoride is an appalling waste product of the aluminium industry and has been used in rat poison. It causes cancer, genetic damage, Alzheimer's disease, disrupts the endocrine system and dumbs down the brain (Fig 235). It was added to drinking water in the Nazi concentration camps to make the inmates more acquiescent and docile (see *The David Icke Guide to the Global Conspiracy (and how to end it)* and my other books). About two-thirds of American drinking water is fluoridated and it is increasing around the world despite the evidence that (a) it does nothing to protect teeth and (b) it can seriously damage the body, including the teeth! Andrew Burnham, the British 'Health' Secretary and another member of the Hopeless Brigade in government, called in 2009 for the fluoridation of all UK water supplies. Mr Burnham was vice-president of the British Fluoridation Society. Fluoridation was forced upon the English seaport city of Southampton despite 78 per cent of people opposing the plan in a 'consultation process'. Why?

Figure 235: *Sodium fluoride is a waste product of the aluminium industry and an ingredient in rat poison. It calcifies the pineal gland and is terrible for human health – while doing nothing to stop tooth decay*

Because it's the agenda and so it is imposed no matter what and the water supply is a major target for drugs and pollutants designed to make people 'love their servitude'. It is already being polluted by fluoride and pharmaceutical drugs and there are even some calls to add the 'mood-stabiliser', lithium, which is known to cause significant weight gain, increase appetite and thirst and suppress the thyroid, another endocrine gland, among other negative effects.

The pituitary gland is again about the size of a pea and connects to the hypothalamus at the base of the brain (Fig 236). It is located between the eyes, and controls things like growth, blood pressure and sex organs. The pituitary and pineal glands, and the 'brow

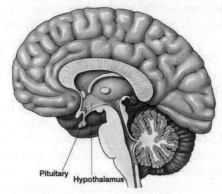

Figure 236: *The pituitary gland and hypothalamus*

chakra' vortex in the centre of the forehead, comprise the 'third eye' that opens the way to experiencing other levels of Consciousness and reality. Close down that system and you entrap people in purely five-sense reality – and this is the central goal of the whole Reptilian conspiracy. As Zulu legends say, the Reptilians are 'the spoilers of communications with the gods'. They do this from the Moon. Reptilian and Grey geneticists within the Moon experimented with the creation of an even more manipulated human form during the long time before the Earth began to recover from the cataclysms. The aim was to totally control the minds, perceptions and behaviour of their human slaves. The genetic manipulation re-wired the electro-chemical circuitry to isolate humans overwhelmingly in 'physical' reality as prisoners of the five senses and visible light. They could not do it totally, but they could make it much more difficult. One of the abilities they deleted (or massively suppressed) was, as I said earlier, telepathic communication, and so words became the means through which humans interacted. This is symbolised by this biblical story of the Tower of Babel, the themes of which you find in much older accounts across the world:

And the whole earth was of one language, and of one speech. And it came to pass, as they journeyed from the east, that they found a plain in the land of Shinar [Sumer]; and they dwelt there. And they said one to another, Go to, let us make brick, and burn them thoroughly. And they had brick for stone, and slime had they for mortar. And they said, Go to, let us build us a city and a tower, whose top may reach unto heaven; and let us make us a name, lest we be scattered abroad upon the face of the whole earth.

And the Lord came down to see the city and the tower, which the children of men builded. And the Lord said, Behold, the people is one, and they have all one language; and this they begin to do: and now nothing will be restrained from them, which they have imagined to do. Go to, let us go down, and there confound their language, that they may not understand one another's speech.

Does that sound like 'God' speaking, or a Reptilian dictator?

Frequency Fence

As well as their genetic tinkering and reality transmissions, the Reptilians have also surrounded the Earth with a 'frequency fence' projected from the Moon to block frequencies that could bring enlightened understanding to their slave race. This is being expanded still further by what is called the High Frequency Active Auroral Research Program (HAARP), based in Alaska and now expanding to other countries. It is jointly funded by the United States Air Force, United States Navy, University of Alaska, and the deeply sinister Reptilian-Illuminati operation called the Defense Advanced Research Projects Agency, or DARPA. The technology used by HAARP bounces high-frequency radio waves off the ionosphere, the highest level of the atmosphere hundreds of miles above the Earth, and then back again. The technology can change the weather, not least by super-heating the ionosphere; cause hurricanes, tsunamis and earthquakes; implant thoughts and emotions in the human brain, individually and collectively; block communication systems worldwide; kill people with a particle beam weapon, or 'death ray', again individually or en masse; shoot down aircraft and manifest phenomena in the sky, among much else. When aircraft 'mysteriously' crash with no explanation, as with Air France flight 447 off the South American coast in 2009, think HAARP. The Reptilians and their hybrid cabal employ their technology to engineer 'natural disasters' to devastate a country or region and then use this as an excuse to take over in the name of 'humanitarian aid' and/or 'keeping the peace'. Witness Haiti in 2010. Jesse Ventura, the former governor of Minnesota, presented a television documentary about the sinister nature of HAARP on the truTV channel in 2009 and demonstrated how the simplest technology can be used transmit directly to the brain, never mind something as sophisticated and powerful as HAARP. The main reason for HAARP is to add significantly to the 'frequency fence' projected from the Moon to maintain humanity in a false sense of reality (Fig 237). There is a reason why they are doing all this now, as I will be explaining. Dr Gordon J F MacDonald, science advisor to President Lyndon Johnson and a professor of geophysics at the University of California, told the House Subcommittee on Oceans and International Environment back in 1972:

> The basic notion … was to create between the electrically charged ionosphere in the higher part of the atmosphere and conducting layers of the surface of the Earth this neutral cavity, to create waves, electrical waves that would be tuned to the brainwaves … about ten cycles per second … you can produce changes in behavioural patterns or in responses.

This is what the HAARP technology is designed to do in support of the main mind-manipulation system generated from the Moon and, as with the Moon Matrix, the real influence of HAARP is happening in the Metaphysical Universe – the information blueprint. This can be overcome by opening the Mind to Consciousness, but those in body-computer reality will not be able to tell the

Figure 237: *The HAARP project in Alaska, and its connecting facilities around the world, have been created to add more power to the 'frequency fence' and false reality projected from the Moon*

difference between what they believe are their own thoughts and emotions and those broadcast externally for their brain to decode. We have been decoding the Moon Matrix since birth and thinking it is real, so planting thoughts and perceptions through HAARP technology would be a cinch by comparison. Experiments have shown how people in sound-proofed rooms have heard words broadcast by pulsed microwaves. And in 1970, Zbigniew Brzezinski, Jimmy Carter's National Security Advisor and mentor to Barack Obama, wrote about how 'accurately-timed, artificially-excited electronic strokes could lead to a pattern of oscillations that produce relatively high power levels over certain regions of the Earth … one could develop a system that would seriously impair the brain performance of a very large population in selected regions over an extended period'. That was four decades ago. Think what they can do now with the technology released to them by the Reptilians, because that is where all this is coming from. They supply the technology as required to advance their agenda. Something else to know … within the Moon and the underground bases on Earth the genetic manipulation of the human form continues. Many soldiers officially killed in action in wars who didn't really die have been used to work in the lower levels of these bases in a virtually robotic state. Reptilian technology and genetics allows them to live extremely long lives. They have also been used in genetic experiments underground and in the Moon along with others who have been abducted by extraterrestrial entities and the human military. These have reproduced to create a whole new 'human' species that is being prepared to replace the current one after it has been 'culled', or at least that is what they want.

I saw a movie a long time ago called *They Live* and in theme and much detail it is extremely accurate in the world it portrays. *They Live*, released in 1988, was made by producer/director, John Carpenter. You only have to look at Carpenter's filmmaking history in science 'fiction' and horror to see that he knows a lot about what is going on – though he will no doubt deny that. He worked with insider, George Lucas, on the special effects for *Star Wars*. The theme of *They Live* is of an extraterrestrial race that had taken over the world by hiding behind human form. It is set about now amid a devastating economic depression with large numbers of unemployed and homeless people living in tents or corrugated shelters wherever they could find wasteland. Draconian laws are brutally enforced by a police state. Members of a resistance movement have realised who the real controllers are and they develop special 'sunglasses' that allow them to see the extraterrestrials behind their apparent human bodies. The glasses also reveal the subliminal messages in advertisements and the media that would not otherwise be seen. These messages include 'obey', 'no independent thought', 'stay sleep', 'do not question authority', 'no imagination', 'conform' and 'consume'. The subliminal message 'This is your God' is embedded in money. The extraterrestrials work with a human 'elite' in underground facilities where the manipulation of the surface population is orchestrated and we see people being transported, or teleported, from the underground location to other planets. The main character in the movie eventually discovers that some kind of signal is being broadcast that is stopping the human population from seeing their extraterrestrial controllers and it holds them in a kind of trance that blocks out most of what there is to see. This signal is being broadcast from a television station tower block in *They Live*, but in our world it is being broadcast from the Moon. When the television tower signal is switched off, the human population can immediately see the extraterrestrials. They include the US President, business leaders, many in law enforcement, news readers and so on. If you replace the *They Live* extraterrestrials with Reptilians and the television tower with the Moon you are so close to what is happening. You can still see *They Live* on YouTube.

Some very strange things began to happen to me as I was writing these sections about the Moon. Technology like the so-called 'keystroke' programme allows the Control System to know every letter that I type on this computer and since I began to detail the information about the Moon my flat has been bombarded with electromagnetic fields every night. My great friend, Carol Clarke, a psychic with an incredible record of accuracy with me over ten years and more, had warned me that many attacks and diversions were being planned by the Illuminati network to discredit me and the book, undermine my health and dilute my focus. The revelations about the Moon were getting far too close to the very foundations of the human Control System and there was bound to be a response. Carol was not wrong. I began to wake up in the night, or rather early morning mostly, with the top of my head vibrating and throbbing as if it was being zapped with something – which it was. My heart would also be beating extremely fast sometimes even though I was not in an emotional state to cause that. Lying there in a calm state while your heart races away is a weird feeling. I would look around the room and clearly see vibrating balls of energy arcing and sparking, often taking the form of something that looked like a big electrical spider. On one occasion I awoke to see a large spinning energy field that look like a Catherine wheel firework with a spider-like centre. It was spinning extremely fast. Another night I saw a large 'moth'-like image flying around the room. It was bright orange with big white spots. I had a good laugh at that one. I also began to have incredibly vivid dreams every night because of the electromagnetic fields being projected into the room. My arthritis worsened quickly and dramatically to the point where moving any joint was painful, often agony. Putting my socks on in the morning and getting dressed in general became a daily challenge. My hands are so bad as I write this that the only two fingers I can use are the two I need to tap the keys. The rest are useless. As the book goes to the printers, the situation with the electromagnetic attacks and my health remains the same. It just goes on night after night. Carol Clarke's view is that they are trying to give me cancer, which make sense because cancer, like everything, is a frequency and the technology targets you with that frequency. Many people challenging the system in their different ways have suddenly died of a heart attack or developed fatal cancers. But sod it; I am going nowhere until the job is done. Sorry to disappoint you chaps, but that's the way it is, pain or no pain. I also heard of plans to discredit me personally, but, once again, you throw it guys and I'll hit it back to you. No problem. 'He will face enormous opposition, but we will always be there to protect him.'

It seems to be a nightmare scenario that I am exposing in this book, and I understand that for sure, but it depends on how you choose to observe it. You can see this information as terrifying, which will just activate your reptilian brain, or you can celebrate the fact that the veil is lifting at last and we can do something about it. I'm not in least bit frightened, let alone terrified, by either what we face or of the emotional retards that have sought to enslave us. There is a reason why a constant theme is that the Reptilians and their hybrids are desperate not to be exposed as the force behind human affairs. This is because it is *we* who have the power if only we would awaken from the trance and engage with our true Consciousness and potential. There is a vibrational change unfolding that is getting faster and faster – the Quickening – that is awakening the human psyche from its long slumber. These are the 'Truth Vibrations' that I wrote about in 1990. The Reptilian Control System is doing everything it can to stop humanity tuning into this new vibration and that is why it is manning the vibrational barricades with HAARP and countless other means to support the transmissions from the Moon. Remember the Zulu legends I recounted earlier. They say that a higher Consciousness, known to Zulu lore as the 'Tree of Life', wants humans to come back into the fold and reconnect with their true self and 'higher forces', but the Reptilians, in Credo's words, 'really want to mess things up'. They will 'mess things up' for many people in terms of reconnecting in awareness to the higher Consciousness, but with many they will not and this collective awakening is what will bring down the house of cards. Have no fear, there are other forces at work here that are far more powerful than those who seek to control and suppress.

This is no time to freeze – we need to get up and get on.

THE STORY
IN PICTURES

Okay, we'll take a break at this point for Neil Hague's brilliant
artwork which symbolises the story I am telling. I have known
Neil almost from the start of my conscious 'awakening',
within a couple of years of my experience in Peru.

We have an almost telepathic connection in that I get
images in my mind and Neil paints them so accurately with
the addition of his own exceptional powers of inspiration
and visual insight.

Enjoy ...

NEIL HAGUE
GALLERY

Out of the stillness and silence of All Possibility come the 'worlds' of form, or what we call 'Creation'. They all vibrate to different frequencies and so share the same 'space' without interfering with each other unless they are very close on the 'dial'. Or, more accurately, it is the observer who creates the frequency range, or 'reality', by how much of the seamless energy field he or she can decode.

The human body is only one level of our Infinite Consciousness. The body is not who we are. It is a vehicle for our Consciousness – Awareness – to decode and experience this virtual-reality universe, much like we need a computer to experience the Internet.

Mind and body are the lens, the interface, between our Infinite Consciousness and the virtual-reality universe. This is Neil Hague's portrayal of the 'vision' I had.

Humanity has become entrapped in mind and body and lost touch with its Infinite Self. 'Mind'-people see almost everything from the perspective of the five senses and so become captivated by the illusions of the 'physical' world. This makes them so easy to manipulate and control. Conscious people retain the connection to their higher levels of awareness and see everything from another point of observation. This is why Mind-people see them as 'crazy' or 'dangerous'.

There is no 'physical' reality 'out there'. The 'solid' world that we think we see and experience is an illusion decoded by the brain and the genetic structure as a whole (the body-computer) from vibrational information – just like a computer decodes the Internet into pictures and text on the screen.

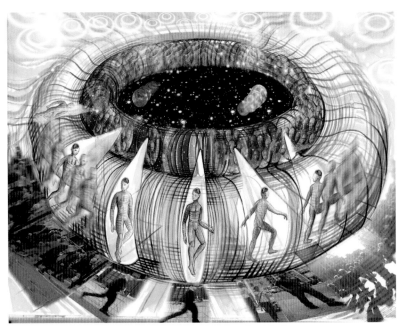

What we call the 'physical world' is a holographic Time Loop. It is a Mind-construct that entraps people in a perpetually recurring cycle of repeating experience. 'Time' appears to be going 'forward' from 'past' through 'present' to 'future', but what we call 'time' in this reality is actually a 'loop'. We only experience a small part of the loop in a single 'lifetime' and so we have the illusion of going 'forward' into the 'future'.

The Time Loop is waveform information encoded in the Metaphysical Universe which the body-computer decodes into electrical, digital and holographic information that we perceive as the 'out there' reality of matter and form. But it is not 'out there' – it only exists in our 'heads'.

When we break through the Mind programs of manipulated perception and suppression, and remember who we really are, we reconnect in awareness to Consciousness. This is why global society is structured to entrap us in Mind.

Consciousness operates in the realms of 'no-time' while this reality is enslaved by the perception of 'time', which, as with 'space', is just an illusion decoded from the information blueprint in the Metaphysical Universe. When we fall for the illusion of 'time' being 'real', we become detached vibrationally from the realms of 'no-time' – Consciousness.

The Sun was once known in Africa by the female name, 'Langa', before the Reptilians and the Moon came. Langa means 'to desire', 'to long for'. Credo Mutwa says that the perception of the Sun changed from female to male when the Moon arrived and this 'made possible the creation of "war-like kings" that took what they wanted by force'. Everything changed because the encoded information from the Sun was hacked into from the Moon and the 'female' energy became 'male'. It explains so much about what has happened since.

The Reptilians manipulate humanity from the Moon and also have underground bases on Earth and Mars.

We see the Moon as a 'physical' phenomenon, like everything within holographic reality. But that is only one level of the Moon. It is also a technologically-generated interdimensional portal that allows entities, craft and energies to move between other realities and ours.

The arrival of the Moon, the hi-tech wars and the destruction of Mars and a planet between Mars and Jupiter (now the asteroid belt) caused a massive 'tear' or 'distortion' in the Metaphysical Universe. This is what I call the 'Schism' and the distortion was decoded through into holographic reality as extraordinary destruction and catastrophic geological upheavals. Human society immediately descended from an advanced technological world into the Stone Age.

The Schism in the Metaphysical Universe also fractured human personalities and distorted humanity's sense of reality. We 'forgot' who we really were and became trapped in mind and body.

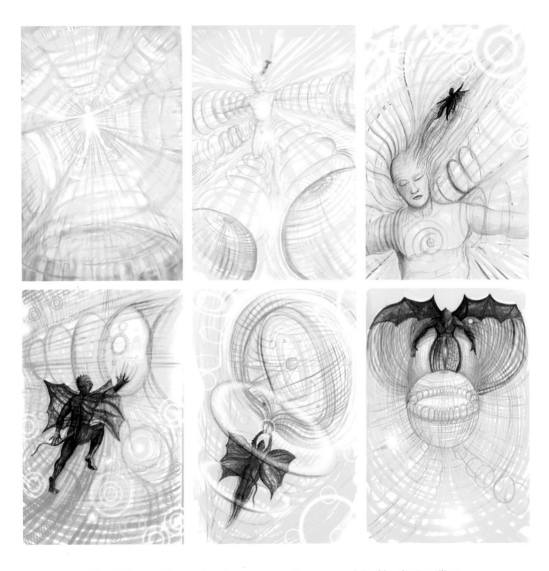

The Schism and its effect on human perception was exploited by the Reptilians to take control of the human psyche.

The Moon is a gigantic spacecraft that has been specifically positioned in relation to the Earth and Sun to create the 'Moon Matrix', a false reality that 'hacks' into the information from the Sun encoded in 'Light'. The Moon Matrix feeds the hacked reality into the human collective mind via the Metaphysical Universe and the reptilian brain. It is also encoded in water and the crystalline Earth. Unless people become Conscious, 'their' mind is the Moon's mind – the Reptilian mind.

Neil Hague's concept of 'Moonopoly' – the 'board game' of human life dictated from cradle to grave by the transmissions from the Moon that manipulate the perception and sense of reality of all of those operating purely in Mind as 'luna-tics' and 'loopies'. It is an ever-recurring cycle that can only be broken by Consciousness.

Humanity is overwhelmingly disconnected from Consciousness by manipulated diversions and belief-systems dictated by the Moon Matrix and the Reptilian Control System. They are designed to focus perception on the five senses. When we fall for this we block out infinity and perceive a fraction of what there is to 'see' and know.

The terms 'dark matter' and 'dark energy' don't refer to realms of the Universe that are literally 'dark'. They are simply beyond the frequency range of 'visible light' that the human body-computer can decode and they are teeming with life that we can't see. The Moon Matrix and genetic manipulation have created a firewall within the body computer that prevents us perceiving far more of the Universe than we currently do.

Neil Hague symbolises the functions of the left and right hemispheres. The right side is 'out there' and sees everything as one. The left decodes everything into structure, form, sequence and language. Both are necessary to experience this reality, but when the left dominates, as it does in most people, it can become a prison of perception.

The Reptilians and their hybrids have structured society to put symbolic guards at the entrance to the left brain. These are called mainstream 'education', 'academia', 'science' and 'media', and they stop the perception of the right brain impacting on our sense of reality. This creates what I call 'left-brain prisoners'.

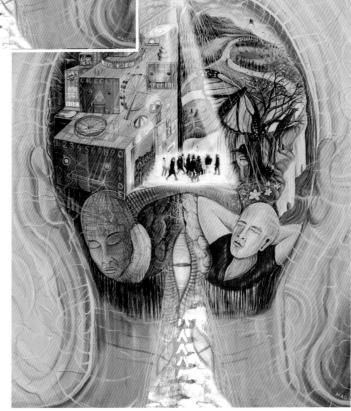

The Reptilian hive mind broadcast from and through the Moon has hijacked human perception.
As Don Juan Matus said: 'They gave us their mind'.

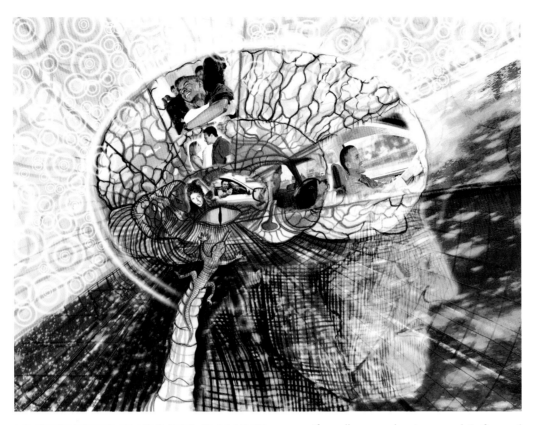

If we allow ourselves to succumb to fear and survival instincts, our perceptions, responses and lives are controlled by the reptilian brain, one of the key access points of the Moon Matrix into the body computer.

When we are entrapped by Mind and tuned to the Moon Matrix via the reptilian brain, our perception is dictated by the reptilian hive mind. We are little more than computer terminals.

Without a connection to Consciousness, people are condemned to 'the box' – the vibrational 'box' of limited and bewildered perception

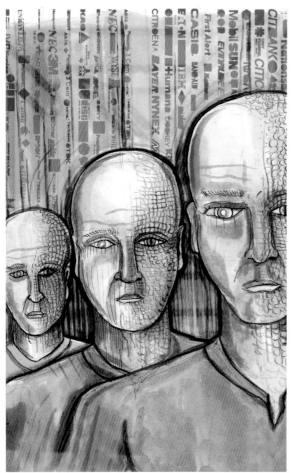

The Reptilians embarked on massive genetic manipulation of the human body computer and also specifically created a network of Reptilian-human hybrid bloodlines to act as their 'middle' men and women within human society. These became known as the 'demi-gods' – part human, part 'gods' – and these are the families still running the global system today.

The Reptilians can possess the hybrid bloodlines far more powerfully than the general population because of the compatible vibrational resonance that comes from compatible DNA. This possession also blocks out higher levels of awareness. The Illuminati families are as much slaves as the general population, more so in many ways.

The Reptilians 'possess' their hybrid bloodlines and hide behind human form. World leaders like Father George Bush are only the outer 'shell' that we see with our five senses within visible light. Their minds and 'emotions' are dictated by Reptilian entities that operate just beyond the frequency range that we can decode and 'see'.

The Reptilians have a different relationship to 'time' and can move up and down our 'timeline' introducing technology at the most appropriate moment to advance their agenda. Those who have access to the Reptilian game plan can write 'prophetic' books that include technology which, at the 'time', has not even been 'invented'. But it doesn't have to be 'invented'; the Reptilians have had it all along. It is just a case of when is the best time to introduce it to human society.

Neil's Hague's superb portrayal of the spider's web structure through which the Reptilians and their hybrids dictate the direction of the world.

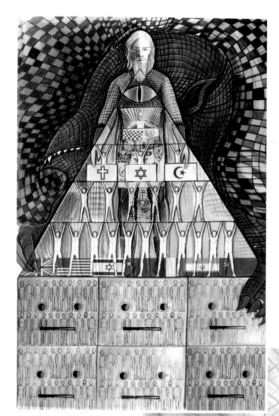

The 'spider's web' structure can also be symbolised as a pyramid and this allows global society to be covertly manipulated by the Reptilians through the hybrid bloodlines and the Illuminati networks. The structure is fiercely compartmentalised and everyone is told no more than they need to know to make their contribution. Only those at the capstone know how it all fits together.

The pyramid within pyramid structure means that all roads lead eventually to the Reptilians, their hybrid families and the hive mind.

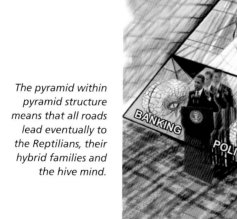

The 'world stage' that you don't see. The Reptilians manipulatiing human society through their
hybrid bloodlines who then manipulate through their puppets in 'power' around the world.
Neil Hague has portrayed the Reptilians in conflict here because they fight amongst themselves all
the time.

WORLD STAGE

Two 'parties', but one master. The Republican 'neocons' and the Democrat 'democons' are controlled by the same force – the Illuminati, symbolised by Neil Hague as the bearded man. I have put Henry Kissinger in the democons because he is an advisor to Obama, but he moves between the two depending who is in office. What you see here applies to every country.

The Illuminati choose and dictate the 'leaders' across the world while the public think they are deciding at the ballot box.

The Reptilians and their Illuminati networks are seeking to impose a fascist/communist global dictatorship based on a world government, central bank, army and currency. But the 'lion' energy is going to thwart the game plan.

The Reptilian hybrids control the mainstream media. This is essential to selling their agenda and manipulating the public's perception of world events ...

... and the same applies to their creation and control of world religions. There may seem to be countless 'different' religions, but they are all forms of 'serpent god' worship.

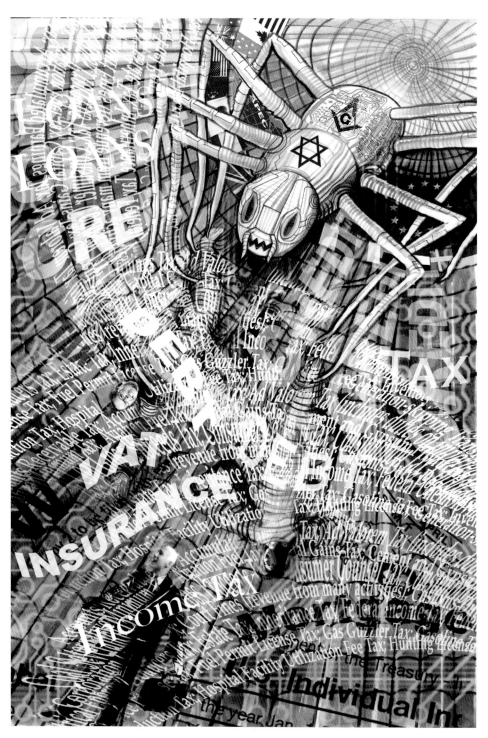

The Control System is introducing ever more laws, taxes and financial demands to tie the human flies to its web. Political Correctness is very much part of this.

The microchip is designed to connect humans even more powerfully to the Reptilian hive mind of the Moon Matrix to ensure that we perceive reality in the way that suits the agenda of control. They want to turn humanity into barcoded robots, which so many are close to being already without any need for the chip.

But we are in a time of fantastic transformation that will eventually bring down the Control System. A new vibration is being resonated by the black holes and it is changing the information emitted by the Sun as photons. Neil Hague and I symbolise what I call the 'Truth Vibrations' as a lion.

The Truth Vibrations are giving everyone the chance to transform themselves and the world. We just have to open our hearts to their resonance.

There is an enormous awakening happening to people all over the world as they open their hearts and minds to the Truth Vibrations that are in the process of healing the energetic Schism.

The Truth Vibrations are revealing all that has been hidden within ourselves and the world.

They are in the process of dismantling the energetic construct of the Control System – 'breathing' a new awareness into this reality.

When we come together in unity and refuse to bow to fear and intimidation, humanity will cast off the chains of suppression and control as the Truth Vibrations do their work.

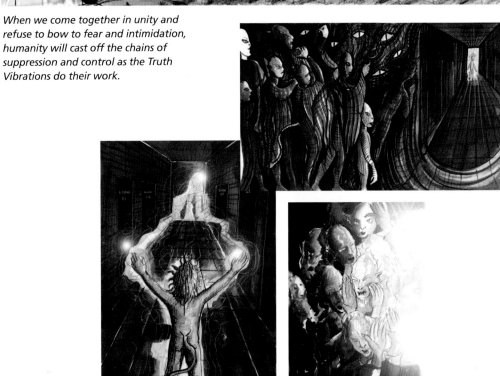

The Truth Vibrations are healing the Schism and seeking out the manifestations of the energetic distortion. The Control System cannot survive without the Schism – they are expressions of each other – and so it must fall as it is energetically dismantled.

The lion sleeps no more.

THE 'LION' FOILS
THE GAME PLAN

In this second section of the book I am going to set out in detail the 'game plan' that the Reptilians and their hybrids are seeking to play out in the next few years – indeed it is already well underway.

But please remember as you read on that we are in the midst of an extraordinary transformation of human perception of self and the world that is going to dismantle the house of cards Control System that depends for its very existence on human ignorance and apathy.

The Reptilians and their lackeys think the game is over.

It *isn't*.

20

Game Plan (1): Destroying Health

I am dying from the treatment of too many physicians
Alexander the Great

The renegade Reptilians can't just arrive in spacecraft and take over. They would have done so long ago if it was that easy, and why would they have worked for thousands of years through their hybrid bloodlines if it was not necessary?

There are a number of 'X-factors' that we yet need to know in order to understand this, but certainly the problem with the Fourth Density Reptilians needing Third Density bodies to stay in our reality for long will be at the heart of it, along with other factors. These include their inability to live for long in sunlight. They are protected from the sunlight and Third Density resonance inside the Moon, in their spacecraft and underground within the Earth, and when they possess their hybrid bloodlines only the 'human' level interacts with solar radiation within the electromagnetic spectrum. The stories of vampires like Dracula who have to be back in their closed coffins by sunrise originate from the need for the vampire Reptilians to keep out of the sun. Demonic entities in folklore come out at night. It is also the case that there are not many of these renegade Reptilians compared with humans and that is another factor in wanting to keep themselves out of sight and human awareness. They may have advanced technology, but they are extremely outnumbered. This is why there is a plan for a culling of the human population and the subjugation of those remaining through microchipping and other means in preparation for a complete takeover after which the Reptilians are planning to eventually reveal themselves. I am not saying they are going to achieve any of this, only that this is what they want to do. How it all turns out is down to how we respond in league with other non-human forces and expressions of Consciousness that are working to set humanity free.

In the next series of chapters I am going to detail the Reptilian 'game plan' in its countless interconnected facets and forms which they seek to impose over the next few years and beyond. When people know what is happening, and why, they are in a far more powerful position to do something about it. Once you begin to understand the nature of reality and the agenda for human control, what appears to be an insane and bewildering 'world' then morphs into clarity. This can be encapsulated in one sentence: The world is 'crazy' because it is meant to be. Then again, it's not crazy, really, once you realise why things are as they are. Human life does appear to be a form of mental illness when you think what abundance there could be, what peace and harmony, if we only we did things differently. But when you understand the game, you can see that human society is like it is for a reason – the enslavement of the many by the tiny few. The world may appear to be demented, and indeed the renegade Reptilians *are* demented, but there is a method in their madness. Things are as they are because of the outcome the Reptilians are seeking. Writer Michael Ellner summed up the human experience with this great quote:

> Just look at us. Everything is backwards; everything is upside down. Doctors destroy health, lawyers destroy justice, universities destroy knowledge, governments destroy freedom, the major media destroy information and religions destroy spirituality.

All of these examples may seem to be paradoxes and contradictions; but they are not. If you want to impose a planetary prison camp it has to be as Ellner describes. To do otherwise would create a world of health, justice, knowledge, freedom, and awareness of true self and reality. Try manipulating the masses in a society like that. You can only grasp what is really happening in the world when you understand what

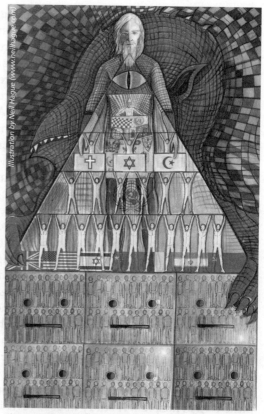

Figure 238: *The pyramid structure of global society allows the Reptilians to dictate the agenda through the hybrid bloodlines and the Illuminati networks. The structure is fiercely compartmentalised and everyone is told only what they need to know to make their contribution. Only those at the capstone know how it all fits together*

the outcome is designed to be, and the pyramid structure we are dealing with (Fig 238). The body is a biological computer system, and to program the desired perceptions and responses you need the access codes. These are vibrational, electrical, chemical and mathematical, and the whole system is set up to allow the programmers to manipulate the body-computer minute by minute through all these means of entry to underpin the hive-mind reality being broadcast from the Moon. They are seeking to download beliefs and perceptions of reality that suit the agenda, and also to destabilise and imbalance the body's receiver/transmitter system so that we can't get 'out there' and connect with levels of awareness that will allow us to see through the smoke and mirrors. You will see what I mean as we go through those Ellner 'paradoxes'.

Doctors Destroy Health

I have been highlighting for 30 years how the medical establishment around the world is just a tool of the pharmaceutical cartel, or 'Big Pharma'. The last thing it represents is human health. Mainstream medicine is about wealth, not health, and, even more than that, it aims to keep people mentally, emotionally and physically sick, or in states of being that deny them a connection to their true and infinite self. Big Pharma works as one network, despite the appearance of apparently different 'companies', and its classic Illuminati pyramid-within-pyramid structure controls the entire mainstream medical profession and its associated 'industry'. In truth, it is an 'industry' founded on human suffering, and the more suffering the better. After all, healthy people don't pay medical bills; sick people do. Big Pharma controls what is taught in the medical schools, the drugs that doctors prescribe, how far they can stray from strictly-enforced medical 'norms' (hardly at all), and dictates government 'health' policy. It does this through a range of techniques that include political contributions and bribes to doctors such as all-expenses-paid trips to 'conferences' in exotic places that are nothing more than free holidays. Mainstream 'Big Pharma' medicine is a grotesque cesspit of corruption and self-interest made even worse by the extraordinary levels of ignorance and incompetence among those who are paid outrageous sums to be 'medical experts'. Control of the medical schools and governing bodies, and the brutal policing of any practitioners who challenge the 'norms', means that mainstream doctors don't even know what the human body is and how it really works, let alone how to treat it. They just know what they are told to know and they are jumped on immediately if they try to expand their knowledge and act upon it in the way they treat their patients. Doctors daily kill and maim on a monumental scale worldwide. How insane that doctors are the third biggest cause of death in America after heart disease and cancer with upwards of a quarter of a million people dying in US hospitals every year from unnecessary surgery, medication and other errors, the effects of the drugs given to 'help' them, and infections picked up in hospital. A study in 2009 revealed that more people die because of prescription 'painkillers' than the combined total of those who die from the effects of heroin and cocaine. The US Food and Drug Administration (FDA) estimates that the Merck painkiller, Vioxx, widely used by sufferers of arthritis, may have contributed to 27,785 heart attacks and sudden cardiac deaths between 1999 and 2003 alone. Merck subsequently withdrew the drug and said it was 'putting patient safety first', but the *Wall Street Journal* reported that the company had fought for years to keep news of the health risks quiet so that its annual sales of some $2.5 billion would continue. There are genuine doctors, but I have met many over the years that I wouldn't let loose on an inflatable doll. There have been idiots, incompetents and fake physicians who hide their mistakes in the graveyards. Yet every day people line up in their surgeries and clinics in awe of their perceived expertise. 'Yes, doctor, thank you, doctor, I'm so grateful for you killing me doctor.'

Same Names ... Yet Again

The Reptilian Rothschild-Rockefeller networks created the system of medical associations, like the British Medical Association (BMA) and the American Medical Association (AMA), to control medicine and the medical profession. Many people seem to think that Big Pharma 'medicine', or 'allopathic medicine', came first and alternatives like homeopathy followed later. It was actually the other way around, and the Illuminati funded the creation of medical associations to replace what we now call 'alternative' medicine with their own. The AMA was established in 1847 and immediately set about controlling the medical schools and the forms of healing that were taught and administered. They were supported by the Rockefeller family and the Illuminati Carnegie Foundation (see my other books) which employed a man called Abraham Flexner (Rothschild Zionist) to visit the medical schools and report on their suitability to teach. Flexner just happened to be the brother of Simon Flexner (Rothschild Zionist), who directed the 'research' into the cause and prevention of disease for the Rockefeller Institute from 1903 to the 1930s. The Flexner Report, published in 1910, demanded that American medical schools impose higher admission and graduation standards and adhere only to the protocols of mainstream science in their teaching and research. The medical industry that we know today was born. American healer, Harvey Bigelsen M D, has written an excellent book on the manipulation of medicine and the involvement of the Rockefeller family, called *Medical Conspiracy in America*. The AMA, a Rothschild/Rockefeller front, increased its attacks on the medical schools and on alternative healing by introducing a Propaganda Department, later called the Investigation Department. Its role, described here by Harvey Bigelsen, will sound very familiar to those interested in alternative methods of healing:

> The Propaganda Department was headed by Dr Arthur Cramp, an editorial assistant at the *Journal of the American Medical Association* (JAMA). The committee, comprised of allopathic physicians, reviewed and analyzed various non-allopathic treatments, modalities, and services and reported their unfavorable findings to the Councils, which published them in JAMA.

The reports that regularly seek to discredit alternative methods of healing are invariably produced by those funded by, and answerable to, Big Pharma. They are simply there to destroy the opposition and they are in a real panic now with so many people rejecting the scalpel and the drug and using alternative forms of treatment. The other prime aim of the Rockefeller-controlled AMA was to introduce a system of licensing which, as always, is justified by ensuring that all medical staff are 'qualified'. Frankly, I don't care if someone is 'qualified' under the system's definition; I care if the person is any good at healing people. 'Qualified' doctors are killing patients every day in battlefield numbers. Yes, of course, there are charlatans and phoneys in alternative healing – lots of them – but they are far less dangerous than 'qualified' doctors wielding powerful and potentially lethal chemical cocktails while taking the Big Pharma dollar. The real reason for AMA licensing was to control both the medical profession and the treatments it employs. This twin strategy of attacking the independence and diversity of the medical schools and licensing practitioners devastated the, until then, pre-eminent 'alternative' sector, and replaced it with Big Pharma domination. Even the Hahnemann School in Philadelphia, named after the creator of homeopathy, Christian Friedrich Samuel Hahnemann, switched to teaching Big Pharma 'medicine'. Health researcher, Karl Loren, says that John D Rockefeller, the founder of Standard Oil, with backing from the Rothschilds, had single-handedly destroyed the prevailing medical approach and replaced it with a new one controlled by Big Pharma: 'The primary result of this activity was that his crude oil, worth perhaps a nickel per gallon, suddenly turned into medical drugs worth millions of dollars per gallon.' Harvey Bigelsen writes in *Medical Conspiracy in America*:

By 1919, there was a 50 per cent reduction in the number of medical school graduates to 2,658. By 1970, there were only 107 medical schools. Only the 'good medical schools' (those capable of teaching modern scientific medicine) were financially supported with money from the Rockefeller Empire.

Homeopathic schools did not use 'modern scientific medicine' and did not receive funding from the Rockefeller Foundation and other drug companies, in spite of the fact that Rockefeller himself had a personal preference for homeopathy and died at the age of 97 with his personal homeopathic physician, Dr H. L. Merryday of Daytona Beach, in attendance.

How ironic that the man who formed the medical industry wouldn't touch it. To Rockefeller, allopathic medicine was simply a way to take money he made from Standard Oil and use it to make even more money via the pharmaceutical industry. Keeping you sick is big business! Whether most doctors realize it or not, wellness is not, and has never been, the goal of allopathic medicine.

Why would these spiritually and emotionally sick people want the population to be healthy when they can only sell them drugs and treatments when they are not? Homeopathic remedies were relatively inexpensive and available without prescription before Rockefeller moved in to replace them with drugs that required a doctor's signature. The prescription system introduced a virtual monopoly for doctors and their Big Pharma masters, and the idea is to make it a full-blown monopoly in the next few years. Since launching scalpel and drug 'medicine' on the United States, Rothschild-Rockefeller networks have imposed it upon the world. Today they control all 'sides' in the medical field – the World Health Organization (WHO), which they created from the start; the public 'protection' agencies like the US Food and Drug Administration (USFDA) and Centers for Disease Control and Prevention (CDC); the pharmaceutical cartel; and the doctors' organisations. Add to this the ownership of the media and they control the game, as all these organisations work as one unit to the same goal. One shocking example of this two-side conflict of interest was Dr Paul Offit at the Children's Hospital of Philadelphia (CHOP). He was paid at least $29 million, maybe a lot more, for his share of profits for Merck's RotaTeq vaccine, which causes diarrhoea in infants. Despite this extraordinary conflict of interest, he used his position with the CDC's Advisory Committee on Immunization Practices (ACIP) to ensure that childhood vaccination with his vaccine became compulsory. The *Age of Autism* website, which exposed Dr Offit, said:

Clearly, based on the distribution of income rights outlined in [CHOP's policies], Paul Offit had a greater personal interest in RotaTeq's commercial success than any other single individual in the world; and more than other individual in the world, he found himself in a position to directly influence that success.

Unlike most other patented products, the market for mandated childhood vaccines is created not by consumer demand, but by the recommendation of an appointed body called the ACIP. In a single vote, ACIP can create a commercial market for a new vaccine that is worth hundreds of millions of dollars in a matter of months.

And examples like this are not even rare.

Suppressing Prevention and Hiding the Cure

The figures are fantastic. Some eight million people die every year from cancer worldwide – more than half a million in the United States alone. The global number is predicted to rise to twelve million by 2030. Cancer is the biggest cause of death for people under 85, and in the US one in four people die from cancer. One in *four*. We have our freedoms removed by the day to 'protect the public from terrorism' when all these people are suffering and dying every year from a disease that the bloodline families and their pharmaceutical cartel systematically refuse to cure. Dr Richard Day, from the Rockefeller-controlled eugenics organisation, Planned Parenthood, told those doctors in 1969: 'We can cure almost every cancer right now. Information is on file in the Rockefeller Institute, if it's ever decided that it should be released.' Day said that letting people die of cancer would slow down population growth: 'You may as well die of cancer as something else.' He also said all those years ago that the plan was to control and cull the population through medicine, food, new laboratory-made diseases and the suppression of a cure for cancer. These people have no soul and that's why they do what they do. Big Pharma has no desire to cure cancer when it is making unthinkable fortunes from treating the symptoms with devastating drugs and cell-killing, people-killing poisons like chemotherapy. But it is not primarily even about money. The bloodline families want people to suffer and die earlier than necessary as a way of culling the population. This is why when anyone outside the Big Pharma cabal discovers an effective way of treating cancer they are immediately targeted by the medical establishment and government agencies. One such case is the Italian doctor, Tullio Simoncini, a brilliant and courageous man who has refused to bow to the enormous pressure he has faced, and continues to face, after he realised what cancer is and how it can be dealt with. Simoncini's 'crime' has been to discover that cancer is a fungus caused by Candida, a yeast-like organism that lives in the body in small amounts even in healthy people. The immune system keeps it under control normally, but when Candida morphs into a powerful fungus some serious health problems can follow – including cancer. My friend, Mike Lambert, an extremely gifted healer at the Shen Clinic near my home on the Isle of Wight, says of Candida:

> Fungus, and Candida in particular, thrive by eating the body of its host (yours) by dissolving it. It also needs your body to breed, as it can't do this on its own. No wonder in Chronic Fatigue conditions, which can in many cases be attributed to Candida colonisation, the sufferer feels so bad both physically and psychologically.

Tullio Simoncini says that cancer is this Candida fungal infection and that the conventional medical explanation of cancer as a cellular malfunction is plain wrong. Simoncini is a specialist in oncology (treatment of tumours), diabetes and metabolic disorders, but he is more than that. He is a real doctor who seeks to uncover the truth for the benefit of his patients and refuses to parrot the official version of what doctors should do and think. He challenges the dogma of 'intellectual conformity' with all its unproven assumptions, lies, manipulations and falsehoods and he has been extremely critical of the medical establishment as it continues to pursue 'treatments' that are useless in curing the global epidemic of cancer. From the time he entered medicine he realised that something was seriously wrong with the way cancer was treated:

> I see terrible sufferings. I was in a paediatric oncological ward – all the children died. I was suffering when I was looking at the poor, poor children dying with chemo, with radiation.

His frustration and sorrow at what he was seeing led him to go in search of new ways to understand, and treat, this devastating disease. He began his journey with an open mind and a blank sheet of paper unsullied by any rigid assumptions peddled and indoctrinated by mainstream 'medicine' and 'science'. Simoncini realised that all cancers acted the same way no matter where they were in the body or what form they took. There had to be a common denominator. He also observed that the cancer 'lumps' were always white. What else is white? Candida. Simoncini realised that what mainstream medicine believed to be cell growth going wild – 'cancerous growth' – is actually the immune system producing cells to defend the body from Candida attack. He says the sequence goes like this:

- Candida is normally kept under control by the immune system, but when that becomes undermined and weakened the Candida can expand and build a 'colony'.
- The Candida eventually penetrates an organ and the immune system has to respond to the threat in another way.
- This 'way' is to build a defensive barrier with its own cells and this growth is what we call 'cancer'.

It is said that the spreading of cancer to other parts of the body (metastasis) is caused by 'malignant' cells escaping from their origin. Simoncini, however, says this is not the case at all. The spread of cancer is triggered by the real cause of cancer, the Candida fungus, escaping from the original source. What allows cancer to manifest, as I have been saying in my books for years, is a weakened immune system. When the immune system is working efficiently it deals with the problem before it gets out of hand. In this case, it keeps the Candida under control. But look at what has been happening as cancer numbers worldwide have soared and soared. There has been a calculated war on the human immune system that has got more vociferous with every decade. The immune system is weakened and attacked by food and drink additives, chemical farming, vaccinations, electromagnetic and microwave technology and frequencies, pharmaceutical drugs, the stress of modern 'life', and so much more. What defences are today's children going to have when they are given 25 vaccinations and combinations of them, before the age of two while their immune system is still forming for goodness sake? This is how the Illuminati families are seeking to instigate a mass cull of the population – by dismantling the body's natural defence to disease. Now, here's the real shocker. What destroys the immune system quicker than anything else?

CHEMOTHERAPY

You can add radiation to that as well. Chemotherapy is a poison designed to kill cells. Er, that's it. The 'cutting edge' of mainstream cancer 'treatment' is to poison the victim and hope that you kill the cancer cells before you have killed enough healthy cells to kill the patient. But wait. This chemotherapy poison also kills the cells of the immune system and leaves it shot to pieces. And the Candida is still there. This devastated immune system cannot respond effectively to the Candida and it takes over other parts of the body to start the process again, so causing the cancer to spread. Even those who appear to have recovered after surgery and chemotherapy and have been given 'the all-clear' are mostly just a ticking clock. Their immune system is now shattered and it is only a matter of time before the Candida triggers a relapse. In other words:

Chemotherapy is killing the people it is supposed to be curing.

Of course, it can never 'cure' anyone of anything, except life. It is a poison destroying the very system that we need to be healthy and strong if we are to be cured. The cancer industry is a fraud, nothing more than a money-making killing machine. Mammograms for women, for example, are causing far more cancer than they detect and yet the 'industry', with Big Pharma in league with many cancer 'charities' and 'support groups', is urging women to have them more often. Disgusting. When Tullio Simoncini realised that cancer was a fungal infection, or infestation, he went in search of something that would kill the fungus and so remove the cancer. He realised that anti-fungal drugs don't work because the fungus quickly mutates to defend itself and then even starts to feed off the drugs that are prescribed to kill it. Instead, Simoncini found something much, much simpler – sodium bicarbonate. Yes, the main ingredient in good old baking soda (but, I stress, not the same as baking soda, which has other ingredients). He used this because it is a powerful destroyer of fungus and, unlike the drugs, the Candida cannot 'adapt' to it. The patient is given a liquid form of sodium bicarbonate orally and through internal means like an endoscope, a long thin tube that doctors use to see inside the body without surgery. This allows the sodium bicarbonate to be placed directly onto the cancer – the fungus. The ancient Egyptians knew about the healing properties of anti-fungal substances and Indian books going back a thousand years actually recommend 'alkaline of strong potency' for treating cancer. I have heard many times over the years that cancer cannot manifest in an alkaline environment and now it is clear why – it kills the fungus. This is why the enormous increases in cancer have mirrored the ever-increasing acidity in the human diet. It is good to have a pH test and if your body is acidic it would be wise to do something about it.

Curing is a Crime

In 1983, Simoncini treated an Italian man, Gennaro Sangermano, who had been given months to live, with lung cancer. A few months later he wasn't dead; he was back to health and the cancer was gone. More than 20 years later he was still alive. Further success followed and Simoncini presented his findings to the Italian Department of Health in the hope that it would begin scientifically-approved trials to show that it worked. But he was to learn the true scale of medical manipulation and deceit. The authorities not only ignored his documentation, he was disbarred from the Italian Medical Order for prescribing cures that had not been approved. Yep, I really said that – *for prescribing cures that had not been approved.* He was subjected to a vicious campaign of ridicule and condemnation by the pathetic media and then he was sentenced to three years in jail for causing 'wrongful death' to patients he had treated, a sentence they said would be enforced if he ever treated people again. From all angles the word was out – get Simoncini. The medical establishment said that his claims about sodium bicarbonate were 'crazy' and 'dangerous' (unlike chemotherapy). One 'leading doctor' even ludicrously referred to sodium bicarbonate as a 'drug'. All the time millions of people were dying from cancers that could have been treated effectively. These people don't give a shit. Tullio Simoncini is, thankfully, no quitter and he has continued to circulate his work on the Internet and in public talks. His website is **www.curenaturalicancro.com**. I heard of him through Mike Lambert at the Shen Clinic and Simoncini spoke on the Isle of Wight while I was out of the country. I know that he is having remarkable success in dramatically reducing and removing altogether even some late-stage cancers using sodium bicarbonate. This can take months in some cases, but in others, such as breast cancer where the tumour is easily accessible, it can be days before it is no more.

People are also curing themselves under Simoncini's guidance and if you go to the Shen Clinic website (**www.theshenclinic.com**) you can hear people talk about their experiences and cures. I had picked up the theme before I heard of Simoncini that cancer is a fungus when I came across the work of two British scientists and researchers, Professor Gerry Potter of the Cancer Drug Discovery Group, and Professor Dan Burke. Their combined findings reveal the following: Cancer cells have a unique 'biomarker' that normal cells do not, an enzyme called CYP1B1 (pronounced sip-one-bee-one). Enzymes are proteins that 'catalyse' (increase the rate of) chemical reactions. The CYP1B1 alters the chemical structure of compounds called 'salvestrols' that are found naturally in many fruit and vegetables. This chemical change turns the salvestrols into an agent that kills cancer cells, but does no harm to healthy cells. The synchronicity is perfect. The CYP1B1 enzyme appears only in cancer cells and it reacts with salvestrols in fruit and vegetables to create a chemical substance that kills only cancer cells. But here's the point with regard to cancer being a fungus. Salvestrols are the natural defence system in fruit and vegetables against fungal attacks and that's why you only find them in those species subject to fungus damage, like strawberries, blueberries, raspberries, grapes, blackcurrants, redcurrants, blackberries, cranberries, apples, pears, green vegetables (especially broccoli and the cabbage family), artichokes, red and yellow peppers, avocados, watercress, asparagus and aubergines. What's more, the Big Pharma/Big Biotech cartels know all this and they have taken the following action to undermine this natural defence from the fungal attack that is cancer:

1) The chemical fungicide sprays used in modern farming kill fungus artificially and this means the plants and crops do not have to activate their own defence – salvestrols. You only find them in any amount today in organically grown food. (You can also get them in a potent capsule form from the Shen Clinic.)

2) The most widely-used fungicides are very powerful blockers of CYP1B1 and so if you eat enough chemically-produced food it wouldn't matter how many salvestrols you consumed; they would not be activated into the cancer-destroying agent they are designed to be.

This is all by calculated design, and explains the gathering attack on organic food production with new regulations planned to put organic growers and farmers out of business. Britain's Food Standards Agency, a so-called 'independent' government 'watchdog', has blatantly sought to undermine organic food. This is no surprise given that the agency is a front for Big Pharma and Big Biotech. It published a propaganda report in 2009 saying there is no nutritional benefit to be gained from eating organic produce. Oh really? So food infested with chemical poisons, growth hormones and antibiotics is no different to food with none of those things? What nonsense. But the report wasn't published on the basis that it was true; it was only to influence public opinion.

The Codex Con

Suppressing human health is also the goal of the Illuminati organisation, Codex Alimentarius ('Food Code' or 'Food Book'), which is seeking to block access to food supplements of adequate doses and quality that compensate for the loss of nutrients in our food and keep us protected from the diseases these madmen are concocting in their laboratories. The Codex con is being justified by the 'harmonisation' of food and supplement laws and regulations across the world (international law is essential for any world government), but the real reason is to hand control of supplements and their like to Big Pharma to stop people finding other sources of nutrients which have been lost in the soil and food production processes. The true motivation of Codex Alimentarius can be seen with its creators, the Nazis Hermann Schmitz and Fritz ter Meer. Schmitz was president of the Nazi chemical giant, IG Farben, and Fritz ter Meer was an executive. IG Farben ran the concentration camp at Auschwitz where ter Meer was heavily involved. It was ter Meer who had the phrase 'Arbeit Macht Frei' (literally 'Work Makes Free') placed over the main gate at Auschwitz. He was also employed by Bayer, an IG Farben company created by his father, and, like Schmitz, ter Meer was jailed by the Nuremberg trials for war crimes. He served only four of his seven year sentence thanks to the intervention of his friend, Nelson Rockefeller, the four-times Mayor of New York, and he was released to become Supervisory Board Chairman of Bayer and to help launch Codex Alimentarius, which is attempting to hijack global food laws. Why would Nelson Rockefeller help a Nazi? The Rockefellers and the Bush family were instrumental in funding the Nazis to start the Second World War and transform global society. Forget the idea of 'democracy', 'fascism' and 'communism' when it comes to these people. They created and manipulate all political systems and philosophies. To them they are just a means to an end. The Codex Alimentarius Commission was officially established in 1963 by the Food and Agriculture Organization of the United Nations and the World Health Organization, and is recognised by the World Trade Organization. All these bodies are bloodline creations.

The Reptilian bloodline families target anything and anyone that could prevent or cure cancer and other mass killers. They want people to die of cancer, not be cured of it. They are mentally and emotionally as sick as you can imagine and they see humans as sheep and cattle. They don't care how much distress, suffering and death their manipulation and suppression will cause – the more the better from their insane perspective. And that is what these people are ... *insane*. But Tullio Simoncini refuses to buckle and continues to campaign for what has been seen as an effective treatment for cancer, while, in the 'real' world, the number of cancer deaths goes on rising incessantly because of treatments that don't work, based on assumptions that aren't true. It is indeed a crazy, crazy society, but then, from the perspective of the bloodline cabal, it's meant to be. Thank goodness for courageous and committed people like Tullio Simoncini. We need more like him – and quick. What a stark contrast he is to those who serve the medical establishment. When Simoncini spoke on the Isle of Wight in 2009, some local doctors dismissed him before he arrived and ridiculed his views. They were invited along to his talk, which would have been of potentially life-saving benefit for their patients. Chairs were reserved for them to hear what Simoncini was saying first hand and give them the chance to ask any questions. What happened?

They never came.

Another Italian doctor, Paolo Zamboni, a professor of medicine at the University of Ferrara, had a similar experience when he successfully treated his wife and many others for multiple sclerosis, a potentially devastating neurological disease that strikes people in the prime of their lives. In seeking a cure for his wife he realised that multiple sclerosis was caused by an excess of iron which led to inflammation and cell death in the brain. He discovered that 90 per cent of people with multiple sclerosis, including his wife, had malformed or blocked veins draining blood from the brain. People without MS, did not. Dr Zamboni performed a simple operation to unclog veins and restore blood flow, and the results were stunning. Again, he should have been a hero, but he, too, has faced suppression and disinterest from the system – not least from multiple sclerosis charities. After all, if there is a cure for the disease, they no longer have a reason to exist. They're all in it together, it's a cosy web of self-interest (Fig 239).

Targeting Dissent

This is the web of corruption and deceit that connects doctors, politicians, government officials and the drug giants, and claims the right to judge and destroy the career of someone like Dr Andrew Wakefield. He was the man who first suggested a link between the combined measles, mumps and rubella vaccine, or 'MMR', and bowel problems that have been linked to autism. He caused an international medical storm in 1998 when he and eleven other doctors produced a research study which reported

bowel symptoms in twelve autistic children and claimed a possible link with the MMR vaccine. What followed was a tidal wave of condemnation to discredit his claims by discrediting him, the age-old method used by the Illuminati-controlled establishment against information it wants to suppress. It has been used on me many times, but I'm still here. Wakefield had been hired by lawyers to investigate the link with autism with a view to parents suing the drug companies involved, and he did not mention this in the published paper. This was jumped upon to discredit the research and ten of the other eleven authors of the report withdrew their support; but the question remained and remains: are the

Ingredients: Mercury, Formaldehyde, Aluminum Phosphate, Aspartame, Human Fetal Tissue, MSG, Bovine Fetal Serum

Figure 239: *No need to worry. Big Pharma is only there to keep you healthy*

findings true? This is of little importance to the establishment that behave like a hanging posse or inquisition when anyone challenges its dogma and those who fund its gravy train – the drug companies. The pressure comes from the top of the pyramid and filters down through the dark suits that administer the system. They either do exactly as they're told, because they are soulless or brainless, or they know it would be a bad career move to question the dictates from 'on high'. Service to self is what holds the entire Reptilian construct together at every level.

Andrew Wakefield, a Canadian-trained gastroenterologist, left the Royal Free Hospital in London 'by mutual consent' in the aftermath of his report and has since worked mostly in the United States, continuing his research at Thoughtful House, a centre for autistic children in Texas. The establishment, however, is always motivated by revenge for those who dare to challenge its agenda. It may have to wait some time to strike, but it never forgets or forgives. The General Medical Council (GMC) in Britain charged Dr Wakefield with professional misconduct with a view to striking him off and destroying his medical career and livelihood. He was accused of 'inadequately founded research, failing to obtain ethical committee approval, obtaining funding 'improperly' and subjecting children to 'unnecessary and invasive investigations'.' Given the extraordinary numbers of people killed or permanently damaged by doctors and drug company products every year, the charge of 'inadequately founded research' would be hilarious if it were not so serious for Dr Wakefield and for medical freedom. It is the same with 'unnecessary investigations', given the number of unnecessary drugs and 'tests' that doctors prescribe. The strike against Wakefield had nothing to do with justice or protecting anyone. They want him to suffer for having the nerve to challenge their tyrannical orthodoxy and to serve as an example to others of what happens when you step out of line. An editorial in Britain's *Daily Mail* newspaper, headed 'MMR and a Doctor Only Doing His Duty', encapsulated the real reason for the attempt to destroy Andrew Wakefield. It pointed out that no-one has complained to the General Medical Council about him and nor has anybody suggested that he said or wrote anything dishonest when he believed he had discovered a link between the MMR vaccine and autism. Why, it asked, was the GMC now throwing the book at him? The editorial went on:

> The case has the whiff about it of a medieval inquisition, called to defend the orthodoxy of the establishment against the heresy of an independent mind. Dr Wakefield's 'crime' was to open an important debate that remains unresolved. Eight years on, he is by no means alone among doctors in believing that he may have been on to something. The trouble is we just don't know.

> Even Tony Blair, though publicly committed to the triple vaccine, seems to have private doubts. What else would explain why he has refused to tell MPs if his son Leo has been given it? After all, he has never been above dragging his family into the spotlight, when it suits his political purposes ...

> ... Think what an uproar there would be today if it was discovered that Dr Wakefield had kept his suspicions to himself and a link had subsequently been proven. He had a duty to speak out – and now he is being made to suffer for it.

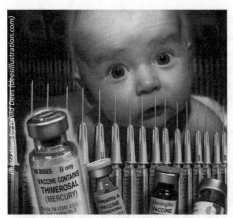

Figure 240: *Babies are now given 25 vaccinations and combinations – and growing – before the age of two*

His treatment by the GMC is utterly unjust. If this preposterous body had existed 200 years ago, defending the prevailing wisdom against new ideas, doctors would still be treating illnesses by slitting their patients' veins.

The primary motivation for targeting Wakefield is that his findings led to a significant fall in the number of parents allowing their children to have the combined MMR vaccine and undermined public confidence in vaccinations in general. What an irony that Wakefield has been accused of a conflict of interest over his research on behalf of families with autistic children, when bribery of doctors by drug companies is common practice. Doctors on the take are the norm, not the rarity. There is another link between Wakefield's research and vaccine immunity for drug companies in America. Mercury in vaccines has a major impact on the development of autism in children. As the number of mercury-contaminated vaccines increased between 1989 and the late 1990s, so did the number of children becoming autistic (Fig 240). Fabian Society member and eugenicist, Bertrand Russell, who died in 1970, wrote in detail about how mercury and other chemicals could be used to damage the brain and the ability to think clearly and sharply.

The latest weapon to silence doctors who speak out are the draconian British libel laws. Henrik Thomsen from Copenhagen University hospital, one of Europe's leading radiologists, is being sued for defamation by GE Healthcare, a subsidiary of General Electric, for what he said about the drug, Omniscan. Thomsen and other doctors could not understand why 20 kidney patients who had been given routine scans then developed nephrogenic systemic fibrosis (NSF), which makes the skin gradually swell, thicken and tighten. One of the patients died and others were confined to wheelchairs. It was later confirmed that the apparent common denominator was that all were given Omniscan to enhance the images produced by the scan. The Medicines and Healthcare Products Regulatory Agency confirmed that there had been 20 cases of nephrogenic systemic fibrosis in the UK after patients were given Omniscan and five people had died. But Henrik Thomsen now refuses to speak about the subject in the UK after being issued with a libel writ for what he said about the drug. This is the world we live in today.

Systematic Corruption

Mainstream medicine is founded upon corruption and greed at all levels from Big Pharma boardroom to doctor's surgery. The top ten drug companies make more in profits than the rest of the Fortune 500 combined and the very fabric of global 'medicine' is a web of lies, deceit and self-interest. Investigations into drug company profits have found mark-ups of thousands of per cent over the cost of ingredients. The patient? Who gives a damn? Doctors are routinely offered top-of-the-range, all-expenses-paid trips to exotic locations by drug companies on the pretext of 'conferences'. The 'conference' takes a few hours a day, if indeed they bother turning up, and the rest of the time is a holiday on Big Pharma. Sigma, a generic drug manufacturer and the third-biggest pharmaceutical company in Australia, offered doctors prescribing its drugs a luxury ten-day Mediterranean cruise visiting Italy, Malta, Corsica and Monte Carlo. It was classically billed as a 'perfect mix of education and relaxation' because of 'conference sessions', including a 'keynote speech' by the appalling Jeff Kennett, former premier of Victoria. Yes, very educational. It's a cruise, end of story, and a clear conflict of interest. Doctors are also funded by the drug giants to conduct 'research' that allows them to travel the world on the Big Pharma dollar. Then there are the incentives to prescribe more drugs than are necessary or send people for hospital tests they don't need. Professor Ann Blake Tracy writes in *Prozac: Panacea or Pandora*: 'Did you know that some hospitals offer special incentive deals that give doctors valuable gifts, like fax machines and car phones, if they schedule surgeries when the hospitals are hurting for business?' These are financial incentives to play with people's lives and they claim that doctors represent 'ethics'. Some do, as with the decent police officers, but the system doesn't want them. It wants the corruptible, because they are better for business. The bribery and corruption of doctors is a finely tuned operation by Big Pharma. Kathleen Slattery-Moschkau, a former drug company representative and now independent filmmaker, has detailed how the corporations and their reps monitor doctors in the United States down to the last pill. This is done through a system known as 'prescriber reports' or 'prescriber profiles' and these are compiled from various databases. The US Drug Enforcement Administration codes doctors via ID numbers along with the drugs they prescribe, while another source, the 'physicians master file', which is sold for millions every year by the American Medical Association, matches the doctor ID numbers with their names. Put the two together, along with other information sources, and you can establish who prescribed what and how much. Prescriber reports are issued every week by the drug companies and the system gives Big Pharma reps the information they need to see how successful they've been in influencing a doctor's prescribing policy. The reps also use personality profiling of the doctors to establish the best way to approach them. Are they people who respond to 'scientific' information or do they like to be flattered? In an article called 'Spin Doctored', Shannon Brownlee and Jeanne Lenzer write:

> If Doctor A increased her prescriptions after being treated to a facial and full-body massage, more expense-paid spa excursions are in order for her. If Doctor B didn't respond to a courtesy 5-course meal, then maybe it's time to try football tickets, or up the free drug samples, or plug clinical research that touts the proffered drug's benefits.

Prescriber reports rank doctors in four tiers based on the amount of drugs they prescribe. This allows the reps to target the big prescribers – the easy pickings – to prescribe even more, while low prescribers can have their manipulation increased. The scale of bribery is simply monumental. As an Internet article pointed out:

> Big Pharma spends nearly $19 billion a year bribing and influencing physicians, by the way. That's billion with a 'B'. How much money is $19 billion? It's more money than NASA wastes smashing satellites into Mars and exploding space shuttles in Earth's upper atmosphere. It's more money than the entire junk food industry spends

hypnotizing obese children into nagging their parents for another box of sugar-bomb breakfast cereal at the quickie mart. Heck, it's more money than the entire United States spends on genuine disease prevention and health education.'

This is the true background to drug companies.They are horrific organisations structured purely to make as much money as possible from the sickness, distress and misfortune of others and, even more important to the agenda, to maintain the population in mental, emotional and physical disarray. An outrageous example of how the system works was the exposure of Tamiflu, produced by Roche, that was claimed to be safe and effective against swine flu and to reduce hospital admissions by 61 per cent. Billions were spent by governments stockpiling the stuff amid hysteria about a 'pandemic'. But an article published in the *British Medical Journal* said that Roche had misled governments and doctors over the effectiveness of Tamiflu. Eight of the ten studies quoted by Roche in support of its claims were never published in scientific journals and the original data on the other two was, well, 'lost'. The only complete data available is from an unpublished study of 1,447 adults which showed that Tamiflu was no better than a placebo. Former employees of Adis International, a Big Pharma public relations company, said they had been hired to ghost-write the studies for Roche and they were told what to write by Roche. One of the ghostwriters told the *British Medical Journal*:

> The Tamiflu accounts had a list of key messages that you had to get in. It was run by the [Roche] marketing department and you were answerable to them. In the introduction ... I had to say what a big problem influenza is. I'd also have to come to the conclusion that Tamiflu was the answer.

Former US Secretary of State, Donald Rumsfeld, has a big stake in the American company that owns the rights to Tamiflu and both Al Gore and Barack Obama are reported to have a financial interest in Tamiflu sales.

Political Pig Trough

Big Pharma, like all Illuminati cartels, has no empathy with those who suffer from its daily exploitation, or those it uses as guinea pigs in drug 'trials'. 'Go get us some poor people, we need to test something.' Humans are just serfs to the Reptilians and their hybrids. Big Pharma's other major target is, naturally, the politicians and government agencies that decide and enforce – supposedly – medical and drug policy. Figures compiled by the Center for Responsive Politics, the Campaign Finance Institute, and the Center for Public Integrity, reveal that, in 2004, $158 million was spent by drug companies to lobby the US federal government; $17 million was given in political campaign donations, 67 per cent of it to Republicans; $7.3 million was spent on political party conventions, with 64 per cent going to the Republicans. A million dollars was given to the presidential campaign of George W Bush, and half a million to John Kerry. Figures uncovered by the *Raw Story* website and the Center for Responsive Politics revealed that Barack Obama was given a staggering $20,175,303 by the 'healthcare' industry during the 2008 election cycle – almost three times the amount given to his presidential rival, John McCain. Obama then produced a 'healthcare' bill that served the interests of the pharmaceutical cabal. Big Pharma has around 1,300 lobbyists in Washington – more than two for every member of Congress. 'They are powerful,' said Senator Chuck Grassley, chairman of the Senate Finance Committee. 'You can hardly swing a cat by the tail in that town without hitting a pharmaceutical lobbyist.' Is it any surprise then that legislation favourable to the drug industry, including immunity from prosecution, is constantly passed by the poodles on the Hill? It is the same elsewhere, too, in this global gluttony of bribery and corruption. In Britain, for example, doctors are awarded bonuses for meeting government 'vaccination targets'. In other words, they are given financial incentives to increase the uptake of the poisonous vaccine potions purchased by the government from Big Pharma. Republican senator and one-time Senate majority leader, Bill Frist, is a classic Big Pharma manipulator and he was at the forefront, with House Speaker, Dennis Hastert, of lying into law the legal immunity for the drug cartel for vaccines given during a declared state of emergency. It is called the Public Readiness and Emergency Preparedness Act (PREPA), and as one commentator put it:

> The PREPA is unconstitutional. It removes the right to due process and judicial review for persons injured by vaccines, thus granting a virtual license to kill. Under the new law, companies making vaccines can be grossly negligent and act with wanton recklessness and still escape liability as long as they can show that their misconduct wasn't 'wilful'. It is impossible to conceive of a lower standard for the drug companies or a higher burden of proof for injured parties.

Democrat representative, David Obey, said the legislation was 'unilaterally and arrogantly inserted into the bill after the conference committee was over'. It was 'a blatant power play by the two most powerful men in Congress'. Yes, two men hand in hand with Big Pharma. Frist comes from a medical background and while he was at medical school he arranged for a regular supply of animals from care shelters by saying he wanted to give them a good home. What he was actually doing was dissecting and killing them in his experiments. He has enjoyed campaign donations from the drug cartel while the drugmaker Schering-Plough has made its Gulfstream corporate jet available to him. This is how Big Pharma and the Reptilian-hybrids make their own laws and the same happens right across the institutions of government, medicine, biotech, food production, and so on. There is always someone for sale or someone you can compromise to do your bidding. The 'Obama' administration is in the pocket of Big Pharma. A White House memo leaked to the *Huffington Post* website in August 2009 confirmed how Obama and his handlers had struck a deal with Big Pharma in which the White House agreed to oppose any congressional efforts to bargain for lower drug prices or import cheaper drugs from Canada. They further agreed not to pursue Medicare rebates or change the designation of some drugs which would have cost Big Pharma billions in reduced income. Obama and Co lied to cover up the covert agreement while the drug companies spent up to $150 million on television commercials supporting Obama's healthcare 'reform' plans that included the deal. 'Corruption' and 'mendacity' are Obama's middle names. His supporters even stood up at public meetings about his healthcare plan claiming to be doctors who supported what he was proposing to do. In fact, they weren't 'doctors' at all – just plants.

Killing the old and sick

'Obama's' health policies hand decisions about patient care to presidential appointments who would decide what medical plans covered, what doctors can and cannot do, and the extent of treatment allowed for elderly people. Rothschild Zionist, Dr Richard Day, said in 1969 that 'limiting access to affordable medical care makes eliminating the elderly easier'. There were also laws to this effect hidden away in the Obama 'stimulus' package and one of the main people involved in this was Tom Daschle, the former US Senate Majority Leader, who was Obama's nominee for Secretary of Health and Human Services, but he had to withdraw over non-payment of taxes. Daschle wrote in his book, *Critical: What We Can Do About the Health-Care Crisis*, that 'seniors' should be forced to sacrifice their heath care in favour of younger people by denying them treatment. He added that seniors who receive a 'hopeless diagnosis' need to accept their condition and not seek treatment for it. One of Obama's presidential appointees to dictate 'healthcare' for Americans is, well, well, well, again ... Dr Ezekiel Emanuel (Rothschild Zionist), the brother of White House Chief of Staff, Rahm Emanuel (Rothschild Zionist). They are both the sons of an operative with the Irgun terrorist group, funded by the Rothschilds, which bombed Israel into being. Another brother is Ariel 'Ari' Zev Emanuel (Rothschild Zionist), a Hollywood agent who represents people like Martin Scorsese, Jude Law and filmmaker, Michael Moore. Dr Ezekiel Emanuel, a fellow at the Hastings Center, a 'bioethics research institute', was appointed to the key position of health-policy adviser at the Office of Management and Budget to advise Budget Director, Peter Orszag (Rothschild Zionist). He will work alongside Jeffrey B Liebman (Rothschild Zionist). Emanuel has been quoted as saying the following: cost savings would require changing [change, always change] the way doctors thought about their patients; doctors take their Hippocratic Oath too seriously and treat it as an imperative to do everything for the patient regardless of the cost or effects on others; doctors should look beyond the needs of their patients and consider other issues like whether the money could be better spent on somebody else; 'communitarianism' should guide decisions on who gets care; it should be reserved for the non-disabled and not given to those 'who are irreversibly prevented from being, or becoming, participating citizens' ... and that an example would be not guaranteeing health services to patients with dementia. He is further quoted as saying:

> Unlike allocation by sex or race, allocation by age is not invidious discrimination; every person lives through different life stages rather than being a single age. Even if 25-year-olds receive priority over 65-year-olds.

Emanuel says his words were taken out of context, but it is difficult to see how. The theme of removing healthcare for the elderly is becoming common. A group of experts caring for the terminally ill wrote a letter to the UK's *Daily Telegraph* newspaper highlighting the way people, mostly the elderly for obvious reasons, were wrongly being diagnosed as 'close to death'. This is extremely important because the UK's National 'Health Service' (NHS) is introducing a policy of withdrawing food, fluid and treatment once the judgement has been made to put them on what they call the death 'pathway'. The patient is also fed sedative drugs continually until death which can mask the fact that their state of health has improved. The letter was signed by, amongst others, Professor Peter Millard, Emeritus Professor of Geriatrics at the University of London, and Dr Peter Hargreaves, a consultant in Palliative Medicine at St Luke's Cancer Centre in Guildford. It said that patients are being diagnosed as being close to death 'without regard to the fact that the diagnosis could be wrong'. Dr Hargreaves said that some patients were being wrongly put on the 'pathway', which created a 'self-fulfilling prophecy' that they would die. He said that he had personally taken patients off the pathway who went on to live for 'significant' amounts of time and warned that many doctors were not checking the progress of patients enough to notice any improvement in their condition. 'I have been practising palliative medicine for more than 20 years and I am getting more concerned about this death pathway that is coming in,' he said. Anyone reading this book so far will see why it is coming in. Hazel Fenton, an 80-year-old British grandmother, had her drugs and food stopped under this 'scheme' when doctors told her she had days to live and yet nine months later she was still alive after her outraged daughter, Christine Ball, fought with doctors for four days to have the drugs and food restored. A nurse even asked Christine what she wanted to do with her mother's body. Christine was exactly right when she said: 'My mother was going to be left to starve and dehydrate to death. It really is a subterfuge for legalised euthanasia of the elderly ...' It is indeed the drip, drip, drip to forced euthanasia.

One other thing ... Cass Sunstein (Rothschild Zionist), Obama's choice to head the Office of Information and Regulatory Affairs, has also called for a policy of taking all the organs of the deceased who have not specifically said they don't want this to happen. It is currently the other way around. Sunstein's policy is only one step from taking them from everyone by law – drip, drip, drip, again. He outlined his proposals in a book called *Nudge: Improving Decisions About Health, Wealth, and Happiness*, co-written with Richard H Thaler. They talk about introducing what they call 'mandated choice' – when the government forces you to decide on something, yes or no, or be denied things like a driving licence. The term 'Nudge' in the title of the book refers to the government and institutions setting out to influence, or 'nudge', the public in the direction those governments and institutions think is best. It is not hard to see why Sunstein is so attractive to Obama and his handlers.

Another question: where will all the organs go if the presumption of 'yes' policy is introduced to vastly increase their number. Will they all go to transplant patients? No, of course not. So what else could they be used for when we are dealing with entities that eat human flesh? Can't think.

21

Game Plan (2): The Cull

'The only safe vaccine is one that is never used.'
Dr James R Shannon

Documents and statements that have emerged over the years make it clear that the Illuminati bloodline families want to reduce the global population dramatically to perhaps as low as 500 million – more than six billion fewer than at present.

This is also the figure used on the mysterious 'Georgia Guidestones' in which ten foundation principles, or 'guides', for a new society are listed in English, Spanish, Swahili, Hindi, Hebrew, Arabic, Chinese and Russian. A shorter message at the top is in Babylonian, Classical Greek, Sanskrit, and Egyptian hieroglyphs. Some people call it the 'American Stonehenge' and the stones are aligned with the Sun and the Moon (Fig 241). The Guidestones were commissioned in 1979 by a person unknown using the pseudonym of R C Christian, which is believed by some to be a play on the name of Christian Rosenkreuz, founder of the Rosicrucian Order in the 14th century, a strand in the Illuminati web. One of the 'guides' is to: 'Maintain humanity under 500,000,000 in perpetual balance with nature'. The draft copy of the United Nations' Global Biodiversity Assessment calls for the world population to be reduced to some one billion. The Illuminati Club of Rome is also singing from the cull-the-people song-sheet. Such propaganda has been funded by the Global Environment Facility (GEF), a partnership of 178 countries, international institutions, non-governmental organisations, and private corporations designed to sell the environment and climate change as an excuse to impose centralised control of the planet and cull the population. The 'Third World' is being targeted for enormous population reductions, as detailed in documents like 'National Security Memorandum 200: Implications of Worldwide Population Growth for U.S. Security and Overseas Interests'. It was produced in 1974 by the US National Security Council under the control of

Figure 241: *The Georgia Guidestones*

458

eugenicist, Henry Kissinger (Rothschild
Zionist). This covert plan, made public in the
1990s, was to instigate population control
through contraception, war and famine, and by
using the threat of withdrawing US financial
and food aid to force governments to
cooperate. That Satanist's 'deathbed
confession', which you can read in full in
Appendix II, says that the aim is to remove 'at
least seventy per cent of the globe's population
by the year 2030.' The Bill and Belinda Gates
Foundation, which is a major funder of
vaccination programmes in the 'Third World',
has given multi-millions to to Planned
Parenthood (Bill Gates' father was a leading
member of its board) and other 'population
control' organisations, while CNN founder,

Figure 242: *Compulsory vaccination is one of the foundations of the Reptilians' global fascist State because of the effect on mind and body*

Ted Turner, has donated massively to population reduction 'causes'. He said that a 95
per cent decline in the world population to between 250 and 300 million 'would be
ideal'. Even the Gates' were outdone by their friend, the multi-billionaire financier,
Warren Buffett, who pledged $37 billion to the Gates' Foundation, much of it for
population-reduction organisations. The 'Obama' healthcare plans include provisions to
pave the way for government-funded abortion without limits and this is another
expression of the population agenda, as predicted by Dr Richard Day in 1969.

War on the Immune System

The foundation of the mass 'cull' is to destroy the human immune system. Big Pharma
has been increasing its influence and control over medicine decade after decade, and, by
funding and bribing corrupt politicians and medical 'experts', it has dictated political
policy. Now it wants to introduce mandatory vaccinations so that every child, in fact
everyone, must be injected with its venomous poisons (Fig 242). It is the latest stage in
the Reptilian/Big Pharma war on the human immune system designed to cause yet more
death and disease by devastating the body's natural defences. These cocktails of
chemical shite contain toxins, DNA from animal tissue and aborted foetuses, and foreign
proteins in the form of live or dead viruses and bacteria. What's worse, they are not even
necessary. I show in other books how the diseases they claim to have eradicated were in
freefall before they were introduced. It is a strong immune system working to full
potential that stops disease, and vaccines undermine that. To think that babies and
toddlers, with their immune defences and their brains still forming, are now given some
25 vaccines, including combinations, before the age of two. This is coldly calculated to
undermine the body-computer on every level of being, but more people are saying 'no'
to this lunacy and so the bloodlines are increasing the pressure. You can watch the pieces
being moved so clearly to checkmate the population into vaccination by law.

The UK government has handed control of the nation's vaccination policy to a
private group with very close links to the vaccine makers. A report headed, 'Jab
Makers Linked to Vaccine Programme', in the UK's *Daily Express* newspaper revealed

that the government would now be legally bound to accept the recommendations of the Joint Committee for Vaccination and Immunisation, or JCVI. Dr Richard Halvorsen, author of *The Truth About Vaccines*, said: 'The JCVI is unelected and many have ties with drug companies. That is a concern.' Actually, a little more than just a 'concern'. Several members have paid consultancy posts with Big Pharma companies like Merck, GlaxoSmithKline, Roche, and Novartis, while some have received grants and travel fees from two vaccine manufacturers, Wyeth and Merck. This is a Big Pharma front-group with a record of covering up vaccine risks and yet it has been given control of the UK's vaccination policy. Once again, this would seem to be madness unless you know that the same Illuminati/Reptilian network controls the governments. They, and Big Pharma, want to enforce vaccinations to access the human body-computer en masse whenever they choose. The button has clearly been pressed on compulsory vaccination with a series of events, changes and statements coming together. The British Medical Association is a wholly-owned subsidary of Big Pharma and the Rothschilds, despite its claims of independence. The BMA's former chairman, Sir Sandy Macara, has called for the highly controversial MMR (measles, mumps and rubella) vaccine to be made compulsory for children attending a state school. The triple MMR has been linked with autism, and the reaction of parents has led to a significant drop in children given the vaccine. So what is Macara's response to this parental choice? Take it away:

> Our attempts to persuade people have failed. The suggestion is that we ought to consider making a link which in effect would make it compulsory for children to be immunised if they are to receive the benefit of a free education from the state.

I said earlier that I have met many doctors in my life who were simply idiots and, after that quote, I rest my case. If you can't persuade them, force them, he says, with not a glimmer of understanding of the scale of fascist imposition that entails. Or maybe he has. He talks of 'a free education from the state' as if the authorities are some benign benefactor proffering gifts when it is we, including the parents refusing the MMR, who pay for the education system and for the shysters who run the institutions of state. Articles calling for compulsory vaccination can be breathtaking. A guy called Charles Waddicor, writing in the *Local Government Chronicle*, actually asks the question: 'Why do we leave it to individual choice to determine whether or not to be inoculated?' Well, Charlie boy, because we don't want the ignorant and moronic like your good self, or those with sinister intent, dictating what is injected into our bodies; note *our* bodies, and those of our children. But, no, Charlie's got it all worked out:

> Local councils could boost immunisation rates among children by making it part of the preparation for going to school. Parents could be asked if their child has been immunised. If they haven't, this could be done by the school nurse as a matter of routine when the child visited their new school before enrolment.

> It would fit very well with councils' duties under Every Child Matters. The same principle could be extended to take in the new vaccine against cervical cancer (HPV), which is being offered to schoolgirls. Girls moving from Year 7 to Year 8 could be seen by the

school nurse and given the vaccine as part of the preparation for moving up the school: a bit like end-of-year exams.

Yes, just like school exams, Charlie, good thinking; but isn't this the same 'cervical cancer vaccine' that has already caused thousands of adverse reactions in young girls? The one that doctors' reports reveal has caused convulsions, fever, paralysis, nausea, muscle weakness, dizziness and blurred vision in 12 and 13 year-olds? It surely is. But, no, Charlie is right – a right Charlie. Where do they get these people from? How do they remember to breathe? Steven Novella, writing in *Science-Based Medicine*, is even closer to the official view and the tactics they employ:

There also seems to be no way to avoid the conclusion that we need to fight fire with fire – fear with fear. We have to make parents more scared that their children will contract serious preventable infectious diseases than they are about the false fears surrounding vaccines. And I need to emphasize – parents should be more scared of this.

Many countries of the 'free world', including the United States, Spain, Greece and much of Australia enforce 'no-vaccine, no-school' rules and now they are seeking to introduce the same in the UK. My son, Jaymie, is 17 at the time of writing and has never had a single vaccination, nor has he had any of the diseases they are supposed to protect him from; but his vaccinated school mates have. I think there should be a law preventing vaccinated children from going to school. It's far too dangerous for those who haven't had the jabs. Dr Marion Lyons from the National Public Health Service for Wales has made the extraordinary claim that 'the only protection against measles is two doses of the MMR vaccination'. Will you tell her about the immune system, or shall I? These people are just programmed repeaters for the drug cartel masquerading as public servants.

The Swine Flu Con

The population cullers have been the driving force behind the swine flu vaccination programme. The US President's Council of Advisors on Science and Technology in the United States warned that swine flu was a 'threat to our nation'. It estimated that 90,000 could die and said everyone must be vaccinated. This Council of Advisors is chaired by John P Holdren, director of the White House Office of Science and Technology. Holdren co-wrote a book in 1977 called *Ecoscience* that details proposals to mass-sterilise the population by medicating food and the water supply and to impose a regime of forced abortion, government seizure of children born out of wedlock and mandatory bodily implants designed to prevent pregnancy. Holdren wrote the book with those infamous population-control extremists, Paul and Anne Ehrlich. Have no doubt that such sterilisation plans have long been implemented – sperm counts have dropped by a third since 1989 and by half in 50 years. Holdren has been desperately trying to deny that he supports forced population control after the content of *Ecoscience* was exposed. This is rather difficult, however, when you have co-written a 1,000-page textbook advocating exactly that. The bloodline families and the higher levels of the Big Pharma pyramid have no interest in protecting the health of the population. Like almost everything else in this upside-down world, we need to reverse their statements to see their true motivation. They want to cull the global population and reduce human numbers dramatically to make them more 'manageable' and there can be no more effective way to access the body-computer than compulsory vaccination. Once these laws are passed, anything goes with regard to vaccine content. You are seeing the demands increase for another kind of immunity – immunity from prosecution for drug companies who kill, maim and brain-damage people with their witches' brews.

The reason for the ever-continuing increase in the number and types of vaccines and combinations being given to children and young people is to destroy the immune system. There has also been an emphasis with 'swine flu' vaccine on the importance of giving it to pregnant women, so accessing the child even before birth and undermining its immune system from the start – or worse. By early 2010, the **organichealthadviser.com** website was compiling reports that it said were 'pouring in from all over the United States' from women who lost babies by miscarriage very soon after receiving the H1N1 'swine flu' vaccine. The Illuminati families want the population's immunity to disease and people's potential for clear thought and connection to Consciousness to be dumbed down, and ideally eliminated. No, this is not over the top. I only wish it were. The plan is to kill enormous numbers of people by releasing laboratory-created viruses and impose compulsory vaccination that will contain potentially deadly ingredients. This is precisely what Dr Richard Day said 40 years ago was going to happen; and the Illuminati front in the United States, the Project for the New American Century, in a document published in 2000, talked about bioweapons that strike different genetic types. The document, 'Rebuilding America's Defenses: Strategy, Forces and Resources For a New Century', said: 'Advanced forms of biological warfare that can "target" specific genotypes may transform biological warfare from the realm of terror to a politically useful tool.' The same document said that a 'new Pearl Harbor' was needed to justify wars of conquest and control. A year later to the month came 9/11. The Project for the New American Century is a Rothschild-Rockefeller front that was one of the leading neoconservative (Rothschild Zionist) organisations behind the Boy Bush administration. The UK *Sunday Times* newspaper reported in 2004 that Israel was developing a biological weapon, or 'ethno-bomb', that would affect Arabs but not Jews. The report said:

> In developing their 'ethno-bomb', Israeli scientists are trying to exploit medical advances by identifying distinctive genes carried by some Arabs, then create a genetically modified bacterium or virus. The intention is to use the ability of viruses and certain bacteria to alter the DNA inside their host's living cells. The scientists are trying to engineer deadly micro-organisms that attack only those bearing the distinctive genes.

The *Sunday Times* said the 'ethno-bomb' programme was based at the biological institute in Nes Tziyona, the main research facility for Israel's secret arsenal of chemical and biological weapons. The disease could be spread by spraying the organisms into the air or putting them into water supplies. Dedi Zucker, a member of Knesset, the Israeli parliament, denounced the plan: 'Morally, based on our history, and our tradition and our experience, such a weapon is monstrous and should be denied,' he said. I understand what he says in the light of what the 'Angel of Death' Josef Mengele did in horrific genetic experiments on Jews at Auschwitz before continuing his work for the Illuminati in the United States and South America. But it makes sense when you realise that the Rothschilds were behind Mengele as they are behind Israel. Also significant is the number of leading microbiologists and related scientists who have been murdered or have died strange and suspicious deaths. Nearly a hundred have died in these circumstances in the last 15 years, including some with connections to the British scientist and weapons expert, Dr David Kelly, who himself was murdered before the US/UK invasion of Iraq because he had the potential to expose the lies that Saddam Hussein had weapons of mass destruction. He was probably killed for other reasons, too. The pattern of murdered scientists working in top-secret projects goes back decades. Once they have nothing left to contribute they are killed to stop them talking about what they have been involved in.

Laboratory 'Flu'

Austrian journalist, Jane Bürgermeister, announced in 2009 that she had filed criminal charges with the FBI against the World Health Organization (WHO), the United Nations, Barack Obama, David de Rothschild, David Rockefeller, George Soros and many others over a plot she uncovered to cull the population with a deadly vaccine. She said that bird flu and swine flu had been developed in laboratories and released to the public with the aim of mass murder through vaccination. Her filed document was called 'Bioterrorism Evidence': It said:

> There is evidence that an international corporate criminal syndicate, which has annexed high government office at Federal and State level, is intent on carrying out a mass genocide against the people of the United States by using an artificial (genetic) flu pandemic virus and forced vaccine program to cause mass death and injury and depopulate America in order to transfer control of the United States to the United Nations and affiliated security forces (UN troops from countries such as China, Canada, the UK and Mexico).

> There is proof many organisations – World Health Organisation, UN as well as vaccine companies such as Baxter and Novartis – are part of a single system under the control of a core criminal group, who give the strategic leadership, and who have also funded the development, manufacturing and release of artificial viruses in order to justify mass vaccinations with a bioweapon substance in order to eliminate the people of the USA, and so gain control of the assets, resources etc. of North America. The motivation for the crime is classical robbery followed by murder although the scale and method are new in history. The core group sets its strategic goals and operative priorities in secret using committees such as the Trilateral Commission, and in person to person contact in the annual Bilderberg meeting.

> Specifically, evidence is presented that Defendants President Barack Obama, President of the United States, David Nabarro, UN System Coordinator for Influenza, Margaret Chan, Director-General of World Health Organisation, Kathleen Sebelius, Secretary of Department of Health and Human Services (HHS), Secretary Janet Napolitano, the Department of Homeland Security, David de Rothschild, banker, David Rockefeller, banker, George Soros, banker, and Alois Stoger, Austrian Health Minister, among others, are part of this international corporate crime syndicate which has, marching as

one phalanx to carry out their plan of genocide, developed, produced, stockpiled and used biological weapons to eliminate the population of the United States for financial and political gain.

Some familiar names indeed; and Jane Bürgermeister, from her own area of research, exposed people and families in her document that have been in my books for two decades. Her reward for putting humanity first and challenging the global state machine was to be fired from her job as European Correspondent of the *Renewable Energy World* website. It is their backbone and sense of decency that need renewing, but it shows how controlled everything is. The two pharmaceutical giants that she named were Novartis and Baxter International. Novartis, in Basel, Switzerland, was once a component part of the Nazi pharmaceutical cartel, IG Farben. It was IG Farben that ran the concentration camp at Auschwitz, and the company was at the centre of the Nazi war machine. Baxter International, of Illinois, operates worldwide with manufacturing, research or distribution centres in Austria, Belgium, Czech Republic, Germany, Ireland, Italy, Malta, Poland, Spain, Switzerland, Tunisia, Turkey, Ukraine, the United Kingdom and many other locations in North, South and Central America, Europe and Asia. Baxter International was exposed in February 2009 for contaminating vaccine materials with live bird flu virus sent to 18 locations. The virus was supplied by the World Health Organization and was mixed with seasonal flu viruses to produce a potentially deadly combination. This 'mistake' – yeah, right – was only discovered when a laboratory in the Czech Republic tested the concoction on ferrets and they all died. This is the same Baxter International that 'accidentally' contaminated blood products which led to thousands of haemophiliacs dying of AIDS. Just the kind of people you want producing a vaccine, then. The idea that the release of the laboratory-created avian flu concoction was an 'accident' is ludicrous. Experts say that the safety measures are such that it could not have happened unless it was meant to happen. Baxter Healthcare Corporation, a subsidiary of Baxter International, settled with the State of Kentucky at a cost of two million dollars in July 2009 after the company had been exposed for inflating the cost of the intravenous drugs sold to Kentucky Medicaid, at times by as much as 1,300 per cent. Nice people. Since 2009, tens of billions of public dollars, pounds and euros were handed to corporations like Baxter International and Novartis to mass vaccinate the global population. No matter what the economic situation there is never a shortage of money when the agenda is involved, be it for wars or vaccination programmes. Killing people is big business – ask the weapons producers.

Jane Bürgermeister's submission said there is clear evidence that pharmaceutical companies and international government agencies are actively engaged in producing, developing, manufacturing and distributing biological agents classified as the most deadly bioweapons on Earth. She said that the swine flu virus was created and released with help from the Rothschild/Rockefeller-controlled World Health Organization, which then claimed it was spreading so fast that a pandemic had to be declared. This was not the case. It was just an excuse to justify the pandemic declaration which automatically triggers a range of new powers for the Rothschild-Rockefeller World Health Organization (Fig 243). The idea was to have compulsory vaccination for the manufactured 'pandemic' and kill people on a vast scale over the shorter and longer term through immune-system destruction and other means. Bürgermeister was supported in her claims by investigative journalist, Wayne Madsen, a former naval officer who has worked with the US National Security Agency (NSA). He said that a top scientist for the United Nations, who has examined the outbreak of the deadly Ebola virus in Africa, as well as AIDS victims, concluded that the H1N1 swine flu virus possesses certain transmission 'vectors' that suggest that the new flu strain has been genetically-manufactured as a military biological warfare weapon (Fig 244). Some researchers say that the 'swine flu' strain can be traced to the work of Dr Jeffrey Taubenberger and a team of geneticists and microbiologists at the US Army Institute of Pathology at Fort Detrick, Maryland, who used supercomputers to map, or 'reverse-engineer', the flu strain that killed tens of millions in 1918. It is claimed that this virus was then given to Novartis. Fortunately, at the time of writing, no strain that virulent has been released and a fantastic Internet campaign over many months exposing the dangers of the vaccine has thwarted the swine flu scam with only a fraction of the predicted numbers agreeing to be vaccinated. This is such a sign of the awakening times as ever more people open their eyes to the world as it really is. The cabal will come back for another go, no doubt, either with a strengthened 'swine flu' or something else, and we must stand firm again and again – as many times as it takes.

Figure 243: *The World Health Organization was created by the Rothschilds and the Rockefellers to dictate global 'health' policy. It has a very sinister agenda that includes mandatory vaccination*

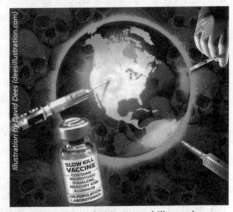

Figure 244: *The plan is not to kill people immediately with vaccines because that would be too obvious and people would react accordingly. The goal is to systematically dismantle the human immune system*

Where are the Pigs?

Here's a question: if it is 'swine flu', why are pigs not affected in any way? We were led to believe that it broke out on a pig farm in Mexico in April 2009, but, apart from the idiotic Egyptian government ordering an immediate mass culling of pigs, the porkies have never had a mention since. The United Nations food agency said there was no justification for culling pigs or limiting their movements as there was no evidence the virus affected pigs or made their meat dangerous. Yes, because it is nothing to do with pigs – it has been made in a laboratory. It includes genetic material from flu strains not occurring in pigs, including avian flu and different forms of human flu. The Centers for Disease Control and Prevention in the United States said it is a combination of North American swine flu, North American avian flu, human H1N1 flu and a swine flu strain found in Asia and Europe. If it is not swine flu specific to pigs, which it isn't, how could it have emerged from a pig farm in Mexico??

Novartis and Baxter International applied for patents for the N1H1 vaccine long before the engineered 'outbreak' in Mexico. Novartis made its provisional patent application in 2005 and it was approved in February 2009. Baxter International applied for its patent in August 2008 and it came through in March 2009, just before the virus was released in Mexico to start the whole thing rolling. The sequence was this: patent the vaccine; release the laboratory-created 'swine flu' virus in Mexico; use the controlled and pathetic media to cause panic in the population over 'deadly' swine flu; tell the World Health Organization to declare a pandemic and demand vaccination for the entire human race to attack the human immune system and implant nano-technology microchips, of which more later. Oh yes, and get governments to give you blanket immunity from prosecution for the effects of your vaccine. As I have been stressing for years, the same families, led by the Rothschilds and the Rockefellers, created and control the World Health Organization, the US Centers for Disease Control and Prevention and the Food and Drug Administration (also their equivalent around the world), and the pharmaceutical cartel, or Big Pharma. These bodies may appear to be unconnected, but in the upper levels they are all on the same team answering to the same masters. Executives from drug giants Baxter International, Novartis and GlaxoSmithKline sat on the World Health Organization's vaccine advisory board that recommended mass vaccinations in July 2009. It was revealed that a Finnish advisor on vaccines on the WHO board had been given six million euros for his research centre by vaccine manufacturer, GlaxoSmithKline. Professor Juhani Eskola, director of the Finnish research vaccine programme, is a member of the Strategic Advisory Group of Experts. This gives advice to the WHO Director-General, Margaret Chan, which included the type and number of vaccines that member countries should purchase for the swine flu 'pandemic'. GlaxoSmithKline produces the H1N1 vaccine, 'Pandemrix,' which the Finnish government purchased for a reserve stockpile on the recommendation of WHO. Other members of the WHO's 'expert group' have also been exposed for secretly working for the pharmaceutical industry. Wolfgang Wodarg, head of health at the Council of Europe, said in January 2010 that the makers of flu drugs and vaccines had influenced the WHO's decision to declare a pandemic and this led to them securing 'enormous' financial gains while government's 'squandered' their meagre health budgets on a relatively mild disease. It was exposed in January 2010 that more than half the UK government's 'swine flu taskforce' had links with Big Pharma giants producing the vaccine. The Scientific Advisory Group for Emergencies (SAGE) was established to make recommendations to government about how to control and treat the virus – and recommended mass vaccination. One member, Professor Sir Roy Anderson, was paid £87,000 and was given £29,000 worth of shares in 2008 for attending six board meetings as a non-executive director of GlaxoSmithKline. The company's share price rose by more than ten per cent after the 'swine flu' 'scare'.

Manipulating the Figures

The initial 'swine flu' outbreak did not spread as the cabal had hoped and so they did what they always do – they lied. If people with flu-like symptoms had their illnesses properly tested it would be shown how little 'swine flu' there actually was. So, the Centers for Disease Control (CDC) ordered that the testing stop. This allowed them and the World Health Organization to make up whatever figure they liked to justify the announcement of a 'global pandemic'. This also happened elsewhere and this is why people's personal experience of swine flu, or lack if it, was so at odds with the high-pitched fear mongering of people like the dreadful WHO chief, Margaret Chan. The CBS investigative reporter, Sharyl Attkisson, later accessed figures under the Freedom of Information Act, which the authorities had sought to block, and exposed the extent of the deceit. The CDC had sought to deny her the swine flu figures because: 'This is not a matter of widespread and exceptional media or public interest.' Can you believe it? These people have no shame. When Attkisson eventually secured the documents it was immediately clear why they had been so desperate not to release them. Looking at the state by state figures of those who had been properly tested she found that only a fraction of those initially diagnosed with 'swine flu' actually had it. For example, of the 13,700 cases tested in California for 'flu-like symptoms', 86 per cent did not have flu at all, never mind swine flu. Only two per cent – *two per cent* – were confirmed with swine flu while the WHO's Margaret Chan was calling it a global pandemic and Barack Obama would announce an official health emergency in the United States which, again, triggered a series of emergency powers to ignore the usual checks and balances with regard to vaccinations and treatment. Sharyl Attkisson estimated that some 80 per cent of people diagnosed with swine flu after the testing stopped did not have it. The UK government played the same game. It was estimating that 65,000 people would die from 'swine flu' in Britain in the winter of 2009-2010 while the symptoms in most people had been extremely mild. They, too, not only stopped testing, but told people not to even go to their doctor if they had flu symptoms. Instead they set up 'call centres' manned by untrained, unqualified members of the public. Some of those diagnosing over the phone have been as young as 16. As a result, we have had children dying from meningitis that was diagnosed by a call centre as 'swine flu' and others suffering from diseases like pneumonia that they were told (without testing) was 'swine flu'. All this allowed the authorities to make up the swine flu figures to make it seem more widespread than it was. The call centres, by the way, were being organised long before 'swine flu' emerged in Mexico in April 2009.

American troops who are subject to compulsory swine flu vaccinations, even after the debacle with the anthrax vaccine and Gulf War Syndrome, have revealed that several websites offering alternative information about the vaccine had been blocked from the military computer system while the official story was still available through the websites of the Centers for Disease Control, Food and Drug Administration, and the Department of Health and Human Services. One serviceman who contacted *The Huffington Post* website said: 'It's unfortunate that the service members who are defending our civil rights are not afforded the same consideration.' You are not defending civil rights, mate, you are unknowingly helping to destroy them, and those that you are really serving could not care less about troops or their children. Make a difference – refuse to fight and refuse the vaccine.

Vaccines Can Spread Disease

The nasal spray version of the swine flu vaccination contains live virus, although weakened according to the authorities. This itself has the potential to spread the disease by direct contact and through a phenomenon known as 'shedding', where the virus passes through the vaccine recipient via faeces, urine, saliva and mucous membranes and on to other people. Oral polio vaccine was withdrawn in the US because of this very problem, but it is still used in so-called developing countries. Live oral polio vaccination can give people polio in the form of a disease called vaccine-associated paralytic polio, and live polio virus has been found in the faeces of babies for up to six weeks after vaccination. Quite a thought when you consider that children are being given around 25 vaccinations and combinations by the age of two. Anyone fancy changing a nappy? Genetic material from the measles virus has been found in urine up to two weeks after vaccination; live rubella virus has been discovered in the nose and throat for up to 28 days after the vaccine was injected, and can be passed on through breast milk; vaccine-induced chickenpox has been shown to replicate in the lung and can be passed on through various means; FluMist vaccine sprayed into the nose contains live influenza viruses and it has been proved that they can be passed on by a recipient to other people. The World Health Organization also announced in July 2009:

> In view of the anticipated limited vaccine availability at global level and the potential need to protect against 'drifted' strains of virus, it is recommended that promoting production and use of vaccines such as those that are formulated with oil-in-water adjuvants and live attenuated influenza vaccines is important.

This statement was merely taken from a script written a long time ago and delivered on cue. The term 'attenuated' means that the virus is reduced in strength, but that does not stop it infecting the vaccine recipient or being spread among the population. The 'oil-in-water adjuvants' are officially used to increase the effects of a vaccine by stimulating a bigger response from the immune system. An adjuvant being used in the 'swine flu' vaccine is called 'squalene' and this has the potential to increase the impact of the 'attenuated' live 'swine flu' virus and cause havoc in many other ways. Dr Joseph Mercola at **Mercola.com** explains the effect of squalene:

> Your immune system recognizes squalene as an oil molecule native to your body. It is found throughout your nervous system and brain. In fact, you can consume squalene in olive oil and not only will your immune system recognize it, you will also reap the benefits of its antioxidant properties.

> The difference between 'good' and 'bad' squalene is the route by which it enters your body. Injection is an abnormal route of entry which incites your immune system to attack all the squalene in your body, not just the vaccine adjuvant.

> Your immune system will attempt to destroy the molecule wherever it finds it, including in places where it occurs naturally, and where it is vital to the health of your nervous system.

Squalene in anthrax vaccine has been connected to the 'mysterious' outbreak of Gulf War Syndrome among Gulf War veterans after 1991. A study conducted at Tulane Medical School found that virtually every soldier with Gulf War Syndrome had antibodies to squalene, showing that their immune systems had reacted to it. The troops who did not have Gulf War Syndrome had no antibodies to squalene. Dr Viera

Scheibner, a former principle research scientist in New South Wales, Australia, spent many years investigating the destructive effects of vaccines. She said of squalene:

> ... this adjuvant [squalene] contributed to the cascade of reactions called 'Gulf War syndrome', documented in the soldiers involved in the Gulf War. The symptoms they developed included arthritis, fibromyalgia, lymphadenopathy, rashes, photosensitive rashes, malar rashes, chronic fatigue, chronic headaches, abnormal body hair loss, non-healing skin lesions, aphthous ulcers, dizziness, weakness, memory loss, seizures, mood changes, neuropsychiatric problems, anti-thyroid effects, anaemia, elevated ESR (erythrocyte sedimentation rate), systemic lupus erythematosus, multiple sclerosis, ALS (amyotrophic lateral sclerosis), Raynaud's phenomenon, Sjorgren's syndrome, chronic diarrhoea, night sweats and low-grade fevers.

The 'swine flu' vaccine also contains toxins like thimerosal (mercury) and aluminium salts. The US government announced that because of the 'pandemic' it was 'temporarily suspending' limits on the amount of mercury (thimerosal) allowed into the H1N1 vaccine given to pregnant women, and children under three. Mercury is a lethal brain-poison that has been rightly connected to autism in children, and it re-wires brain function. Pregnant women are warned not to eat tuna because of the potential mercury content and yet the government and 'health' authorities then agree they can be injected with the stuff! (Fig 245). Professor Chris Shaw at the University of British Colombia published a study in *Toxicological and Environmental Chemistry* in June 2009 which confirmed that thimerosal is toxic to the unborn foetus. Look at how they have been specifically targeting pregnant women (in other words, their unborn babies), children and young people for swine flu vaccination. These are the very generations who will be adults in the planned New World Order, the Orwellian global state. The aim is to destroy their immune systems and destabilise them mentally, emotionally and 'physically'. Aluminium hydroxide is also in the 'swine flu' vaccine, and aluminium has long been known to cause brain damage. In the very month that 'swine flu' was supposed to have broken out on a 'pig farm in Mexico', the *Journal of Inorganic Biochemistry* published a study connecting aluminium hydroxide injections to motor neuron degeneration and other brain damage. The 'testing' of the H1N1 vaccine was purposely fast-tracked, justified by the manufactured hysteria, to avoid the consequences being exposed until it was too late. Given this background, what an utter disgrace it has been to watch governments and the media targeting children to manipulate them and their parents to 'get your flu shot' (Fig 246 overleaf). One method in particular was beyond belief. It was an edition of the animated series, *Sid the Science Kid*, made by the Henson Company of *Muppet Show* fame. Some of the company's real-life Muppets teamed up with the US Department of Health and Human Services to produce a special edition, with

Figure 245: *Vaccinations don't protect human health – they destroy it*

Figure 246: *The bloodline families are targeting children more than anyone with their vaccination agenda to turn them into good little robots with damaged immune systems for life*

catchy tune, called Getting a Shot: You Can Do It! The message was that if the children were not vaccinated they would give swine flu to their friends who were (which doesn't say much for the vaccine does it?). The show was stomach-wrenchingly appalling and disgusting. The Control System is increasingly using children's media to sell its lies and manipulations – especially with 'climate change'. Detroit Health Department has tried to bribe children and young people to have the swine flu vaccine by offering them a pizza if they do. The department acted in desperation after only ten per cent returned vaccination forms. Officials cut a deal with Happy's Pizza that each class in the city that has a vaccination rate of 80 per cent or more will get a pizza party for the entire class. Neil Master, Director of Advertising for Happy's Pizza, said: 'Kids love pizza and we love kids in Detroit and we take care of them whenever we can.' Pass the sick bag. The world's bloody mad.

Injected Microchips

There is one other aspect of the attempts to enforce mass vaccinations and that is microchipping. I am going to deal with this in detail later and for now I will just say that once again there are mental, emotional and physical reasons for seeking to do this. I was approached through a third party to meet a CIA scientist in 1997 who wanted me to communicate information that he said it was vital for people to know. He couldn't do it himself, not least because – in CIA parlance – he was 'patched'. He opened his shirt while I was talking with him and showed me what looked like a transparent shampoo sachet on his chest. Inside was an orangey-gold liquid. He said this was a drug that his body had been manipulated to need to stay alive, and that the patch had to be replaced every 72 hours. If he didn't use his scientific brilliance as the authorities demanded the patches would be stopped and he would die a painful death. He tried it and he realised they were not kidding. The scientist told me many things that I have detailed in other books, but one was that microchips in the secret projects were then, in 1997, so small that they could be inserted through hypodermic needles in mass vaccination programmes. This was what was planned, he said. We call this today nanotechnology, and it is microscopic. Nanotechnology cannot be seen or touched by scientists because it is far too small, and can only be accessed with special instruments and under powerful magnification. A nanometre is one billionth of a metre, and if you symbolise a nanometre as a marble then a metre would be the size of Earth. I have no doubt that the cabal is using many methods to get this technology inside of us to gain mental, emotional and physical control. One way is through mass vaccination, as the CIA scientist told me, and I have been saying since May 2009 that nano-microchips were part of the swine flu vaccine agenda. Hitachi in Japan claims to have developed the world's smallest microchip – as small as a speck of dust – and technology this tiny is being used to treat brain disorders. It can also be used to manipulate the brain through what are being called 'nano-robots'.

How interesting, then, is the story told by Dr Ryke Geerd Hamer, another pioneering doctor who took on the medical establishment and introduced something called New German Medicine. Hamer said that in August 2009, he was giving a talk near Vienna, Austria. When the topic of swine flu was raised, a woman in the audience stood up and said that a friend worked for a pharmaceutical company in Vienna (Baxter International has a subsidiary there: Baxter AG), and her friend had confirmed that swine flu needles, not the vaccine itself, did indeed contain nano particles in their very tips. This could not be seen by the naked eye but was clearly visible with as little as twelve times magnification. She said that staff at the pharmaceutical company were told that the nano particles work in the human body and could store lots of data. The woman also said she herself worked in the medical field and she had asked a lawyer who came to her as a patient, how it was possible to avoid being chipped. He had told her that he was aware of the planned chipping of the population and most upper class members of society were aware of this plan. There would be no forced vaccinations in 2009, he said, and the plan was to encourage people through the media to volunteer for the jab. If not enough agreed, compulsory vaccination was planned from 2010. He said that certain professional groups like 'the elite', politicians and suchlike would be exempt, but for the majority of the population there was no escape. We'll bloody well see about that. The German newspaper, *Der Spiegel*, reported in its online edition that the German Chancellor, Angela Merkel, and government ministers would receive a special version of the H1N1 vaccine. 'The vaccine does not contain disputed additives – contrary to the vaccine for the remainder of the population,' it said. 'The German government elite and the armed forces will receive Celvapan, an adjuvant-free vaccine manufactured by Baxter,' the report went on. 'The German public will receive a vaccine produced by GlaxoSmithKline with adjuvants.' *Der Spiegel* said there was an 'open rebellion' by medical professionals and child physicians in Germany over the use of the toxic vaccine. Dieter Ludwig, chairman of the drug commission of the German medical profession, said that health authorities had colluded with pharmaceutical companies. Of course they had – they are controlled by the same force.

In the light of this, it is worth remembering that once people are chipped they can have their minds, emotions and bodies externally manipulated, and they can be killed from a distance. I cannot stress enough how vital it is for people not to have the swine flu vaccination or allow their children to have it. Dr Ryke Geerd Hamer said that every single chip-vaccination needle had its own individual code number, which is added to the ID number. Some doctors, including Dutch general practitioner, Dr Jan Takken, have said that the needles used to immunise people 'against' H1N1 are blunt. He said in an article in the medical journal, *Medisch Contact*, that being injected is unpleasant and 'feels as though the skin is being torn'. The swine flu vaccination campaign in Norway was delayed when hospitals had to wait for special needles and syringes. The authorities confirmed that the swine flu needles are different from those used with seasonal influenza and were specially developed to 'minimise risks and simplify the injection procedure'. It all fits. All the major Big Pharma companies are also reported to have contracts with human microchip producer, VeriChip.

History Repeating

The potential dangers of the swine flu and other vaccines can be seen with the experience in the United States after the mass vaccination programme in 1976. This was 'justified' by the death of a single person, an Army recruit at Fort Dix, in New Jersey. A panic was then generated on the basis that he had died from a swine flu strain allegedly similar to that which killed tens of millions in 1918. It was later established that the recruit died because 'normal' flu had turned to pneumonia and this was compounded by dehydration and heavy physical work. He collapsed on a morning run. The Centers for Disease Control and Prevention admitted that not a single case of swine flu was confirmed. Mass vaccinations for 'swine flu' followed the death of the army recruit and led to hundreds of people developing Guillain-Barre syndrome, an autoimmune disorder affecting the nervous system that causes paralysis in the legs, upper limbs and face, and an inability to breathe. At least 25 died and, longer term, the figure would have been far higher. The drug companies and the World Health Organization tells us that the 'swine flu' vaccine is safe when it has been revealed that 600 senior neurologists in the UK were sent a confidential letter by government health officials warning of a coming increase in Guillain-Barre syndrome as a result of the 'swine flu' vaccinations. The letter came from the Health Protection Agency, the official body that oversees public health, and warned neurologists to 'be alert for an increase in a brain disorder called Guillain-Barre Syndrome (GBS), which could be triggered by the ... vaccine'. A senior neurologist quoted in London's *Daily Mail* said: 'I would not have the swine flu jab because of the GBS risk.' Great, eh? The government 'Health Protection' Agency tells 600 neurologists about the expected effects – but not the public. The Centers for Disease Control in the United States officially predicted 30,000 serious and potentially fatal reactions to the H1N1 vaccine while at the same time insisting that it is effective in only three out of every ten recipients. The requirement is even less for people over 65. Even in the first few weeks of the swine flu vaccination programme, one health website, **organichealthadvisor.com**, described what it called an 'avalanche' of serious adverse reactions that were being reported, including Guillain-Barre Syndrome, and seizures. Deaths were also reported.

Forced Vaccinations

Manufactured viruses and health scares are a Problem-Reaction-Solution to enforce compulsory vaccination. The moves are being put into place even as I write. 'Barack Obama's' (his masters') 'healthcare' bill makes it mandatory for all Americans to take out health insurance, or face fines, even jail, if they don't. At the same time, the Centers for Disease Control has said that anyone who does not keep their vaccinations 'up-to-date' will be refused health insurance until they have them. No vaccinations, no health insurance; and no health insurance, a big fine or jail. It is mandatory vaccination by the back door and goodness knows what else is hidden in the bill's thousand pages and more of legalese which those voting for it will not even have read. The Massachusetts Senate has passed the flu pandemic bill S 2028 that imposes a state of fascism whenever the governor decides to do so in the wake of a flu 'pandemic', manufactured or otherwise. The bill authorises the state health commissioner, law enforcement, and medical personnel to: vaccinate the population; enter private property with no warrants; quarantine people against their will; arrest without a warrant anyone a police officer deems has violated an isolation or quarantine order; jail or fine at the rate of $1,000 a day anyone in such violation. Similar isolation orders were being implemented in Florida, Washington, Iowa and North Carolina and the same is planned all over the world – if we stand for it. What we are seeing is the creep, creep, step, step, technique of the Totalitarian Tiptoe. An internal French government document came to light detailing covert plans to vaccinate everyone in France without exception. The document was signed by Rosaylne Batchelot-Narquin, the French Health Minister, and Brice Hortefeux, the French Minister of Interior and Overseas Territories. It was sent to the heads of the country's 'defence zones', law enforcement and regional health authorities. Some of its main points were:

- Medical personnel, medical students and medical army personnel can be compelled to administer vaccines or face penalties.
- 'Vaccination centers' to be established in 'secure facilities' in every region and no medical establishments will be involved, and nor will any general practitioners.
- Schoolchildren to be vaccinated at school by special mobile pandemic vaccination teams.

Similar documents would have been circulating in all 194 member states of the World Health Organization because all this is centrally coordinated. The French President, Nicolas Sarkozy (Rothschild Zionist), a long-time Mossad operative, was reported to be planning compulsory vaccinations for the entire population of France using the excuse of 'swine flu', but the plan flopped because the voluntary take-up was so wonderfully low. To impose compulsory vaccination they have to increase dramatically those who agree to it voluntarily. Then they can marginalise and demonise the minority who refuse and insist that they 'comply' for the benefit of the 'whole community'. It's divide and rule again. In the winter of 2009, the numbers were far too small to do this and the virus too weak.

Just Say No
How many people there must be around the world who wished they had said 'no' to vaccinations that have destroyed their health. Hundreds of State employees in the UK, doctors, nurses, firefighters, prison officers, police officers, forensic scientists and refuge collectors say they have developed serious physical and mental health problems after vaccinations that are compulsory to do those jobs. Some of them are 60 per cent disabled and yet the government that insists on the vaccinations as compulsory to employment is refusing to compensate them because the State doesn't give a damn. I know that most people would find it impossible to believe that drug companies, in league with governments, coldly set out to kill and maim vast numbers of people. But hold on – that's their job. They have been doing it year after year since Big Pharma was created by John D Rockefeller, an asset of the Rothschild dynasty. American researcher, Patrick Jordan, uncovered World Health Organization memos dating from 1972, explaining how to kill people with vaccines by injecting viruses and activating an immune response so powerful that it kills the body. This is known as a 'cytokine storm' and is blamed for many of the tens of millions of deaths in the flu pandemic of 1918. The initial spread of

AIDS in the United States matched the locations of vaccination trials for Hepatitis B in homosexual communities, and the initial outbreak in Africa mirrored the locations of mass smallpox vaccinations ordered by the World Health Organization with vaccine reportedly supplied by Novartis. Big Pharma and the World Health Organization are killing machines and the cemeteries of the world are full of their victims. Gullibility can indeed be lethal. Shane Ellison was a medicinal chemist for drug companies Array BioPharma and Eli Lilly, but resigned in disgust at what he saw on the inside. He now promotes natural remedies under the title: 'The People's Chemist'. He said:

> As a young chemist working in the chemistry labs of corporate America, I watched as they promoted cancer causing drugs as anti-cancer remedies (tamoxifen). I also witnessed the pharmaceutically compliant media convince the world that depression was a disease and you needed the so-called antidepressant drug Prozac™ to treat it. I began to wonder, 'How gullible are the masses?' The reaction to the swine flu scare answered this.

Fear and gullibility – babes-in-arms syndrome, as I call it – ensured that large numbers of unquestioning dupes would race to the vaccine centres; but the world is a lot wiser to what is happening than it was five, ten or twenty years ago and there are now very large and ever-increasing numbers of people who can see through the lies. As a write, the 'swine flu' scam is in tatters with governments desperate to off-load billions of dollars of vaccines that no-one wants. But, like I say, they will be back.

Disease from the sky

In late October 2009, the 'swine flu' story took another turn when the best part of two million people in the Illuminati-controlled Ukraine went down with a virulent respiratory illness and hundreds died. Post mortems were reported to have revealed that some of the dead had 'black lungs' that seemed to have been burned. This was a trait with many people who died in the killer outbreak of 1918. Researchers had claimed before this that the 1918 strain had been re-engineered from the DNA of a corpse killed in that pandemic. No-one seemed to know the cause of the illness in the Ukraine. Some suggested it was a stronger strain of H1N1, but it appeared to be something else. The World Health Organization instigated genetic tests, but refused to reveal the detailed findings. Professor Victor Bachinsky, head of the Chernivtsi regional forensic bureau, said that people were dying from 'viral distress syndrome' – destruction of the lungs. Those with a strong immune system were resisting the virus, but those with weakened immune systems were not, he said. What made all this even stranger was that three months before the Ukraine outbreak a Los Angeles talk show host, Dr True Ott, on the Republic Broadcasting Network, said that a man named Joseph Moshe had called him to say that Baxter International's laboratory in the Ukraine had created a biological weapon and planned to put it into vaccines to kill millions in America. It has been reported that Moshe is a Mossad microbiologist with dual American-Israeli citizenship, but at the time of writing the situation is not clear about this. What we can say is that on the day after Ott said they had their conversation, Joseph Moshe was stopped by an FBI hit squad while driving his car in Los Angeles, apparently, so reports say, on his way to the Israeli consulate. He was surrounded and attacked with tear gas and 'non-lethal' weapons in a stand-off lasting an hour and some sort of microwave weapon was employed which blocked the electronics in his car and all communication devices. The FBI said that he had made a phone call threatening to bomb the White House, but researchers say he actually told the White House that he intended to go public with what he knew. Moshe then became aware that the FBI was after him and set out for the Israeli consulate, the story goes, only to be stopped before he got there. Some say he was deported back to Israel, but there were also reports that he was in being held at the Patton State mental hospital in California. What is very compelling is that he could name both Baxter International and the Ukraine some three months before the outbreak of an unknown and virulent disease in that same country. Before the sudden outbreak in the Ukraine, there had only been two cases of swine flu reported, and no-one had died. At the time of writing, the official figures say that 1.58 million people have been infected with some 500 dead, but the worst of the outbreak is over – at least for now.

Figure 247: *The 'gum' dropped by aircraft flying low over my home town*

Another aspect of the Ukraine situation is that days before the outbreak, hundreds of people contacted newspapers in the capital, Kiev, to complain about aircraft spraying an aerosol substance. Local business owners said they were 'advised' to stay indoors during the day by the local authorities. There were reports of helicopters spraying aerosols over Kiev, Lviv, Ternopil and throughout the Ukraine. The authorities denied there had been any spraying and apparently pressured radio stations in Kiev to deny the reports. So much is being sprayed from the sky onto unsuspecting populations all over the world. Small planes fly over my home town of Ryde on the Isle of Wight dropping a gum-like substance that you can see afterwards all over the pavements and roads in the aircraft's flightpath. I walked with my friend, the healer and scientific researcher, Mike Lambert, across the town on one occasion following the trail of 'gum' with thousands of pieces to be seen in pretty much a straight line that would have gone virtually over my house (Figs 247, 248 and 249). Everyone I told about the gum blobs came back

Figure 248: *The 'gum' in close-up. The 'blobs' expand over time*

Figure 249: *At one location, the 'blobs were in a virtually straight line*

to me later to say 'they're everywhere'. It's funny how people don't notice them until they are pointed out and they are shocked at how widespread they are and at why they had never noticed them before. It is all happening on a subliminal level until the conscious mind is alerted. The usual explanation is that 'it's just chewing gum', but that is nonsense. There is far too much of the stuff for a start. Mike says that his research indicates that the 'gum' is a carrier vehicle for viruses and other horrors. In the days after the 'gum' plops on the pavement it expands and releases its contents. Mike says he first came across the phenomena when he was a professional health investigator more than 20 years ago and he believes it probably originates at somewhere like the biological weapons research establishment at Porton Down, near Salisbury in Wiltshire, home to the Defence Science and Technology Laboratory, an agency of the Ministry of Defence. It is a very sinister place indeed. Mike sent some of the gum for laboratory analysis, but it had to be sent on to a more sophisticated lab to establish what it is and the results are not available as I write. A scientist at the first laboratory did say, however, that the 'gum' seemed to be a form of latex that contained a pesticide-type substance, or 'of that family'.

The 'swine flu'/compulsory vaccination agenda is an ongoing story, but the bottom line is that the cabal want to mass vaccinate the global population for very malevolent reasons and we need to refuse to comply – whatever. With such public resistance to the vaccine there are bound to be other manipulations in the effort to enforce it, including increasing the increase the strength to scare people into the vaccine queues. There will also be attempts to turn the 'wills' against the 'won'ts' on the basis of those refusing the vaccination are putting the rest at risk by preventing 'herd immunity'. We must not succumb to compulsory vaccination, because the individual and collective consequences are potentially catastrophic. Most will, of course, but there are ever-increasing numbers who do have a mind they can call their own and do have a determination to stand for what they know to be right. Those people need to be harnessed and brought together in a mass refusal to bow to this tyranny that demands we concede to the State the control of our own bodies. If not enough of us are prepared to score a line in the sand on this most basic expression of Big Brother then prepare for the barcodes. And you know what? We'll deserve them. After all, who is going to stop this unless we do? The doctors?? The media?? The politicians?? You must be joking.

Calculated mass murder

What is happening today is just an expansion of the eugenics 'master race' movement created by the Rothschilds, Rockefellers, Harrimans and other Illuminati families. The Reptilian hybrids are behind the eugenics movement, as you would expect given their obsession with 'elite' and 'inferior' genetic types. Eugenics laws and forced sterilisation of 'lower stock' were once imposed in a long list of American states before its most infamous advocate, Adolf Hitler, brought an end to its public 'popularity'. Eugenics didn't disappear, however, it just changed its name and rhetoric. The goal of eugenics is to create a 'master race' by the controlled breeding of 'superior' bloodlines and the sterilisation and demise of 'inferior' types. This is still a key motivating force behind global population policy, euthanasia, the environmental movement, 'healthcare', social sciences, and so much more. The belief in elite bloodlines, the 'demi-gods', has been with us since the interbreeding of humans with reptilian and other non-human entities.

Thomas Robert Malthus, English clergyman and economist, inspired many who would follow with his *Essay on the Principle of Population* in 1798. He said that if population growth by the poor was not limited it would outstrip food supply and then famine and war would act as the checks and balances on population expansion. Malthus argued against higher wages and welfare for the poor because it allowed them to survive and breed to increase the population. He has been described as the 'father of scientific racism'. Charles 'survival of the fittest' Darwin was a keen follower of Malthus and included many of his theories in his work on 'natural selection' and evolution, *The Origin of Species*, published in 1859; but it was Darwin's cousin, Francis Galton, who really spawned the insanities that led to Hitler and beyond. Galton, a biologist among many other things, was inspired by his cousin's theories to investigate how physical and intellectual traits can be inherited. He wasn't so much interested in natural selection – he wanted unnatural selection by controlled breeding. Galton coined the term 'eugenics', which is Greek for 'good birth', and launched the eugenics movement in 1869. His idea was to encourage those with 'good genes' to have more children and 'discourage' those with 'bad genes' from breeding at all. He was supported by members of the Illuminati Fabian Society, like writers George Bernard Shaw and Bertrand Russell, and founders, Sidney and Beatrice Webb. Shaw defended Hitler's race policies and advocated using lethal gas to kill those who couldn't 'justify their existence'. The Fabian university, the London School of Economics, became a stronghold of eugenics. Sidney Webb said in 1909:

> What we as eugenicists have got to do is to 'scrap' the Old Poor Law with its indiscriminate relief of the destitute as such and replace it by an intelligent policy of so altering the social environment as to discourage or prevent the multiplication of those irrevocably below the National Minimum of Fitness.

The Fabian Society, with its logo of a wolf in sheep's clothing, is a major strand in the Illuminati global web, as I have said, and it was from this knowledge source of the future agenda that Fabian members George Orwell and Aldous Huxley got their inspiration for their books, *1984*, and *Brave New World* respectively. The theme of *Brave New World* is a society in which the state produces all children through laboratory breeding programmes in 'Hatcheries and Conditioning Centres'. They are specifically bred for different castes in a genetic hierarchy. This is the utopia of the eugenics crazies, including the Fabian Society. A president and vice-president of the British Eugenics Society was Julian Huxley, brother of Fabian and *Brave New World* author, Aldous Huxley, who also supported eugenics. Their grandfather was Thomas Henry Huxley, an English biologist known as 'Darwin's Bulldog' for his vociferous support of Charles Darwin's theory of evolution. The eugenics movement continued its plunge into ever-greater extremes when Leonard Darwin, a son of Charles Darwin, replaced Francis Galton as head of the British Eugenics Society in 1911 and continued at the helm until 1928. He and his mentally-deranged supporters criticised charities and churches that fed the weak and poor and kept them alive to reproduce. Leonard Darwin campaigned for laws that would incarcerate everyone considered to have 'defective' genes – a policy he called 'segregation'. He wrote in *Eugenics Review*, the journal of the Eugenics Society, in 1925:

Compulsion is now permitted if applying to criminals, lunatics, and mental defectives; and this principle must be extended to all who, by having offspring, would seriously damage future generations.

Darwin had much influential support for his 'segregation', including Winston Churchill, an enthusiastic eugenicist, and classic Reptilian hybrid families such as the Rockefellers. Archibald Church, a Fabian Society Member of Parliament, sought to introduce a sterlisation bill in 1931 that was aimed at mandatory sterilisation for, as Church once put it, 'those who are in every way a burden to their parents, a misery to themselves and in my opinion a menace to the social life of the community'. These were the words of a Member of Parliament for the British Labour Party, which was created by the Fabian Society and is controlled by it to this day. Former Prime Minister, Tony Blair, his successor, Gordon Brown, and significant government ministers are Fabians. The same was happening even faster in the United States where the Rockefeller, Carnegie and Harriman families funded the eugenics movement and sought to issue licences to those who were to be allowed to breed. Eugenics and sterlisation laws were passed in 1907 and imposed upon those with deformities and low test results. Yes, all this in the 'Land of the Free'. Theodore Roosevelt, the US President from 1901 to 1909, captured the mentality of the bloodlines when he said:

Society has no business to permit degenerates to reproduce their kind ... Any group of farmers, who permitted their best stock not to breed, and let all the increase come from the worst stock, would be treated as fit inmates for an asylum ...

... Some day we will realise that the prime duty, the inescapable duty of the good citizens of the right type, is to leave his or her blood behind him in the world; and that we have no business to permit the perpetuation of citizens of the wrong type. The great problem of civilisation is to secure a relative increase of the valuable as compared with the less valuable or noxious elements in the population ...

... The problem cannot be met unless we give full consideration to the immense influence of heredity ... I wish very much that the wrong people could be prevented entirely from breeding; and when the evil nature of these people is sufficiently flagrant, this should be done. Criminals should be sterilised and feebleminded persons forbidden to leave offspring behind them ... The emphasis should be laid on getting desirable people to breed ...

The Fabian writer H G Wells was a major promoter of eugenics, and his lover, Margaret Sanger, was bankrolled by the Rockefeller family from 1923 to expand eugenics in the United States. She went about her task with the frenzy of the zealot that she was. State administrations, schools and churches were all involved in promoting eugenics, and compulsory sterilisation of 'lower stock' was introduced in some 25 US states by 1927 with the backing of the Supreme Court. During the eugenics hysteria, fuelled and funded by the bloodline families in the first half of the 20th century, social workers were appointed to decide which children should be sterilised and taken away from their families. We are seeing history repeating with today's fast-emerging social worker dictatorship. Margaret Sanger founded the American Birth Control League, now called Planned Parenthood, and she wrote in a letter to an associate that black leaders would have to be recruited as frontmen in sterlisation programmes aimed at black people:

> We should hire three or four colored ministers, preferably with social-service backgrounds, and with engaging personalities. The most successful educational approach to the Negro is through a religious appeal. We don't want the word to go out that we want to exterminate the Negro population, and the minister is the man who can straighten out that idea if it ever occurs to any of their more rebellious members.

She was a lovely lady. Some other Sanger quotes:

> No woman shall have the legal right to bear a child ... without a permit for parenthood.

> The most merciful thing that a family does to one of its infant members is to kill it.

> Birth control must lead ultimately to a cleaner race.

> Eugenic sterilization is an urgent need ... We must prevent multiplication of this bad stock.

Appropriately, the *American Journal of Eugenics* was formerly known as *Lucifer the Light Bearer*. Adolf Hitler and his 'race-purity' fanatics were inspired by the British and American eugenicists. Rockefeller-funded and Rothschild-orchestrated horrors were to follow in Germany and Nazi-controlled Europe in pursuit of a 'master race'. Hundreds of thousands were sterilised or killed in its name. Hitler was advised before the war by America's leading eugenicists. They were sent to Germany by the Rockefeller family who, as I said earlier, also funded the work of Ernst Rudin, Hitler's foremost 'racial hygienist', at Germany's Kaiser Wilhelm Institute for Eugenics, Anthropology and Human Heredity. Rudin was President of the International Federation of Eugenic Organizations and a global figure in the eugenics movement which advocated – still advocates – the removal of 'inferior' people through segregation, sterilisation and extermination to create a 'better' or 'master' race. The atrocities that followed in Nazi Germany and occupied Europe brought an end to the open promotion of eugenics. There were too many obvious parallels between what the Nazis did and what the eugenicists were seeking to do. The response was to give eugenics a 'respectable' face by calling it 'population control' or 'birth control'. Margaret Sanger's American Birth Control League changed its name to Planned Parenthood, and *Eugenics Quarterly* became *Social Biology*. It was business as usual under other names and methods.

China, the blueprint for the Illuminati global society, imposed a one-child per family law in association with Planned Parenthood and United Nations agencies. Father Bush, who is extremely close to Planned Parenthood, also advised China on its one-child law. The Chinese face big financial penalties, even jail, for having more than one child and forced abortion is common. There are some 30 million more men than women in the country as a result. The bloodline families want to impose a global one-child policy and even then only for those they 'licence' – the very policy demanded in the US by Margaret Sanger, the founder of the American Birth Control League, now Planned Parenthood. The lie about human-caused climate change is now being used to press for one-child laws around the world. The Population Council is another eugenics front. It was established in 1952 by John D Rockefeller III with funding from the Rockefeller Brothers Fund and is a further example of how post-Hitler eugenics resold itself as population control. The Population Council's first president was Frederick Osborn, leader of the American Eugenics Society. He wrote in 1968: 'Eugenic goals are most likely to be achieved under another name than eugenics.' The Council now has 18 offices in New York, Africa, Asia, and Latin America and operates in more than 60 countries. Its international board of trustees includes representatives from biomedicine, business, economic development, government, health, finance, the media, philanthropy and social science – all areas used to promote a covert policy of eugenics. The first head of the United Nations Educational, Scientific and Cultural Organization (UNESCO), launched in 1945, was Julian Huxley, the Vice-President of the British Eugenics Society from 1937 to 1944 and President between 1959 and 1962. UNESCO was just another underground eugenics operation headed by the brother of *Brave New World* author, Aldous Huxley. The future 'Sir' Julian said of the consequences of Hitler's disastrous PR for eugenics:

> Even though ... any radical eugenic policy will be for many years politically and psychologically impossible, it will be important for UNESCO to see that the eugenic problem is examined with the greatest care, and that the public mind is informed of the issues at stake so that much that now is unthinkable may at least become thinkable.

Julian Huxley also founded the World Wildlife Fund, now the World Wide Fund for Nature, with two other eugenicists, Prince Phillip and Prince Bernhard of the Netherlands, the former Nazi SS operative who was the first and long-time chairman of the Illuminati Bilderberg Group. The environmental movement is another cover for the continuing policy of eugenics, although most of its supporters and promoters have no idea. It was the executive of Planned Parenthood in 1969, Dr Richard Day, who gave the private meeting of doctors in Pittsburgh a detailed account of how the world was going to be transformed into a global Orwellian state. What he said has proved extraordinarily accurate because Planned Parenthood is a Rockefeller organisation, and Day's close connection to that Reptilian-hybrid family gave him access to the projected plot. The Rothschilds and Rockefellers, who have been behind the eugenics movement all along, are pulling the strings of the World Health Organization, vaccine makers such Novartis, Baxter International, and GlaxoSmithKline, and the governments and agencies that are supposed to be protecting the public from the pharmaceutical cartel.

We are now seeing 'eugenics, the final frontier', with the emerging movement known as 'transhumanism'. This is developing and promoting various control technologies like microchips, brain-chips, brain-computer interfaces, cyborgs and nanotechnology. Its advocates talk of 'upgrading' the race by implanting more and more external technologies into the human body. The word 'transhumanist' was first used by Julian Huxley, the eugenics fanatic. The transhumanists push the benefits of improving health and intellect, but the real idea is to create a master race that is part human and part machine. It is another front operation for eugenics, although most of its lower ranks have no idea that this is so. The transhumanists refer to mere humans as a future 'sub-species' of the cyborgs: 'Like we have cows now, we will have humans in the future', as one of these strange people put it. That quote comes from Kevin Warwick, Professor of Cybernetics at the University of Reading, England, who has become known for having himself implanted with chips. In his case, though, I can understand it, because if I were him I would be trying to become more intelligent, too. The guy has no idea where this is all designed to lead and, even less so, why. This is another of his classics: 'If a machine is passing down signals that keep you completely happy then why not be part of the Matrix?' As *Brave New World* author, Aldous Huxley said: 'Make the people love their servitude.'

Eugenics has come a long way since Malthus and Galton, but eugenics is still what it is.

22

Game Plan (3): War On Mind and Body

Every time you get angry, you poison your own system
Alfred A. Montapert

The biggest targets for Big Pharma, and its associated biotech industry, are children and young people. Aleister Crowley, the Satanist, Freemason and Illuminati operative, said of children: 'Get them by eight, or it's too late.' They want them mentally, emotionally, physically and vibrationally screwed up as early as possible so they can lock them into the Moon Matrix for life and disconnect them from 'out there' Consciousness.

Here is a staggering statistic ... one in ten American children take the mind-altering drug, Ritalin, and other research puts it at around one in eight. Pause for bloody breath. *WHAT*?? Ritalin is a derivative of cocaine. What is happening to children across the world is a most obvious example of the Totalitarian Tiptoe, and those figures for Ritalin consumption show how far it has gone. Some more extraordinary numbers: UK doctors wrote 3,500 prescriptions for Ritalin in 1993; by 1996 it was 26,500; in 2006 the UK National Health Service (not including private medicine) issued 250,000 prescriptions; and in 2007 the figure was 461,000. It reached such a scale that even a government spokesman said it should be curbed. Along with Ritalin, other copy-cat drugs have been produced to exploit the obsession, and the calculated agenda, of drugging the young

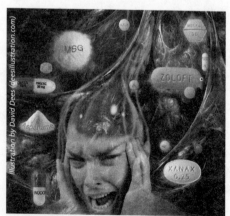

Figure 250: *The drugging of children and young people is now extraordinary and it's all part of the plan*

(Fig 250). These include Adderall, Concerta, Metadate CD, Ritalin LA, Focalin XR, and Strattera (Atomoxetine). The Bush family-connected Eli Lilly is heavily involved as you would expect. Another drug given to children is Risperdal which was used on political prisoners in the Soviet Union to extract information. David Healy, a leading psycho-pharmacology expert and Professor of Psychiatry at Cardiff University in Wales, said: 'People who took [Risperdal] would tell anything to anyone. When you think about giving these drugs to kids, it's a whole new ball game.' Let that sink in for a second: we are allowing drugs to be given to children that had political prisoners in the Soviet Union telling anything to anyone. A study published in the January 2010 issue of the *Journal of the American Academy of Child & Adolescent Psychiatry* revealed that Risperdal and other 'antipsychotic' drugs were being given to children as young as two. It also said that the number of cases in which these drugs are given to children aged between two and five had doubled in recent years – this is the plan unfolding to drug young people as early as possible. The drugs have the same effect as amphetamines and cocaine. These are, of course, illegal and yet drug companies and their lackeys, called 'doctors', are quite legally giving similar drugs to children like candy at Christmas. The drugs also have possible health consequences such as heart problems and diabetes. These are described, like all negative impacts of drugs, as 'side-effects', but they are not 'side-effects' at all. They are *effects*; nothing 'side' about it. The 'problem' promoted by 'Big Pharma' to trigger this explosion of child drug abuse is something they call Attention-Deficit Hyperactivity Disorder or ADHD. Professor Healy said:

> There is an active campaign by pharmaceutical companies to convince people that there's adult ADHD. Adults having problems are being told they have adult ADHD and are being offered drugs for it. Pharmaceutical companies market these drugs aggressively. How can GPs refuse to prescribe a drug 'clinically proven' to work?

By having a mind of their own, is the answer to that one. There is now increasing evidence that these drugs don't even impact the 'condition' they are claiming to treat, and there is much expert and experienced opinion that says there is no such thing as Attention-Deficit Hyperactivity Disorder, except for that caused by food additives, as I will explain shortly. In which case we are looking at a No Problem-Reaction-Solution, like the 'weapons of mass destruction' in Iraq. This is a widespread technique used by Big Pharma, inventing ever more diseases and syndromes to justify ever more drugs and vaccines. They make their multi-billions through people being physically, mentally and emotionally sick and to keep increasing profits they need more illness, or, through No Problem-Reaction-Solution, the public's perception of more illness. This includes inventing 'new' ones that don't actually exist. Mike Lambert, at the Shen Clinic on the Isle of Wight, says that drug companies are treating as a 'disease' many natural body immune and other responses that are necessary to keep people healthy. He says that morning sickness is the body's way of expelling toxins so they don't affect the child. Any medication to 'treat' this is causing the body to retain what it wants to be rid of. Mike says that in these circumstances some miscarriages are caused by the body ending the pregnancy when the system is simply too toxic. Look at what happened when thousands of pregnant women took the drug, thalidomide, in the late 1950s and early 1960s, to suppress the symptoms of morning sickness. They produced babies with major birth defects, including those born without arms. It has been described as 'one of the biggest medical tragedies of modern times'. Many conditions that are now seen as a problem or an 'illness' in need of treatment by the drug cartel are actually the body doing what it needs to do to correct imbalances or react to a potential problem, Mike says. 'Attention Deficit Disorder' largely means that you are so bored by school that you can't focus on the crap they are seeking to program you to believe. I suffered from it myself under that definition, but I could always focus fine looking out of the window at a football match on the sports field. The state's herd of doctors, psychiatrists, teachers and other robots have responded to this 'disease' by giving the 'victims' appalling Big Pharma drugs like Ritalin (also known as methylphenidate) that chemically rewire the brain and the central nervous system. These are some of the side-effects ... no, some of the *effects*:

> Nervousness and insomnia, loss of appetite, nausea and vomiting, dizziness, palpitations, headaches, changes in heart rate and blood pressure, skin rashes and itching, abdominal pain, weight loss, digestive problems, toxic psychosis, psychotic episodes, drug dependence syndrome, tremors and muscle twitching, fevers, convulsions, and headaches (may be severe), irregular heartbeat and respirations (may be profound and life threatening), anxiety, restlessness, paranoia, hallucinations and delusions, excessive repetition of movements and meaningless tasks, formication (sensation of bugs or worms crawling under the skin), and severe depression when the drug is withdrawn.

There you go, darling, get these down you, I'll fetch you a drink. Doctor knows best. They are handing this stuff out like confetti to children today, and other similar drugs, and it is all part of the calculated war on our children (see war on the immune system, war on freedom, war on diversity, ad infinitum). A report in the August 2009 issue of the *Archives of General Psychiatry*, a journal of the American Medical Association, found that anti-depressants like Ritalin, Prozac and similar concoctions are the most prescribed drugs in the United States. The use of these drugs has soared since 1996. As many as 27 million people have been estimated to take these mind-altering prescription drugs (Fig 251). They are being prescribed to children as young as six. Some parents are actually giving their children Ritalin they have bought off the Internet, to 'help them concentrate' in their studies and exams. Now that is child abuse. Children are also being given drugs by their parents out of concern that they are 'bored, restless or distracted'. Crikey, with parents like that, is anyone surprised? One strange guy called Professor John Harris, a 'bioethics expert' at Britain's University of Manchester, has encouraged the use of Ritalin in this way, for adults as well as children, and he likens it to 'synthetic sunlight' – the equivalent of what firelight, lamplight and electric light are to the Sun. He said that adults should take it to

'enhance their brain power'. Well, presumably he must take it then. I rest my case. It clearly doesn't work. A study published in the January 2010 edition of *Archives of General Psychiatry* also revealed a serious increase in the prescribing of two or more psychiatric drugs to be taken as a combination – something known as 'psychotropic polypharmacy'. Researchers investigated the medications prescribed between 1996 and 2006 at more than 13,000 visits to psychiatrists by adults in the United States. They found that the percentage of visits at which two or more medications were prescribed increased from

Figure 251: *The drugging of the human mind*

42.6 per cent to 59.8 per cent, and the percentage when three or more drugs were prescribed rocketed from 16.9 per cent to 33.2 per cent. The number of medications prescribed at each appointment increased on average by 40.1 per cent. Even if you are not directly taking these drugs, you are getting them cumulatively in the water supply. An *Associated Press* investigation revealed that antibiotics, anti-convulsants, mood stabilizers, sex hormones and a vast array of other drugs have been found in the drinking water supplies of at least 41 million Americans. It is simple; the more you drug the population, the more they pee the residue into the water supply for everyone else – and it is all planned. There is another vital aspect to this mass-drugging of society and it was predicted by Aldous Huxley, the Fabian Society member and *Brave New World* author, in 1959:

> ... it seems to me perfectly in the cards that there will be within the next generation or so a pharmacological method of making people love their servitude, and producing ... a kind of painless concentration camp for entire societies, so that people will in fact have their liberties taken away from them, but will rather enjoy it, because they will be distracted from any desire to rebel by propaganda, brainwashing, or brainwashing enhanced by pharmacological methods.

This is precisely what is happening today. The plan is for every baby to be microchipped at birth and then be subjected to compulsory vaccinations and drugs for life, so ensuring complete control by the state from cradle to grave. Isolate them in the five senses and then program their disconnected minds by controlling the sources of information – the mainstream media and what passes for 'education'. For those who still won't be programmed, and insist on behaving and perceiving differently from the herd, they now have the fall-back position of diagnosing Attention-Deficit Hyperactivity Disorder and plying them with mind-scrambling drugs. The conspiracy for global control is targeting everyone, but their main focus is children and young people who are going to be the adults when the structure of world dictatorship is supposed to be in place and the Reptilians are planning to make themselves known. The Reptilian-hybrids are well aware, too, that the effect of what they are doing is cumulative and by the time the young become adults their bodies and minds will be messed up to a far greater extent than they are now. We see again and again that young people who have gone on insane killing sprees in schools, universities and elsewhere have been prescribed these mind-altering drugs (Fig 252). The effect of all this is described by these three parents of children prescribed Ritalin or Risperdal:

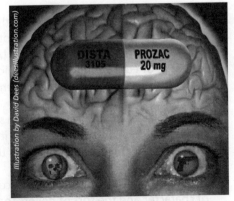

It was as if my son had been replaced by a doped-up zombie. I could hardly wake him in the morning. It was as if all his personality was disappearing, like a patient in a mental institution.

Figure 252: *Young people involved in killing sprees have invariably been taking mind-altering pharmaceutical drugs*

. . . . .

'... within a month, I knew something was terribly wrong. I couldn't wake him in the mornings. It was as if my son was disappearing before my eyes. I did some research and found they give this brain-altering drug to adults in mental institutions. Why did they give it to my son?'

. . . . .

When it's a doctor you just smile and nod. I knew nothing about the drug or how toxic it was. But things rapidly went downhill once John started taking it. He became aggressive and he couldn't cope with the word 'no'. He became a horrible person. The doctors increased the dose and he turned into a monster. He was headbutting walls and throwing things out of the window. The doctors said: 'You need more Ritalin'.

Like I say, if you want to locate an idiot, the medical profession is often a good place to start. Most of them are not healers – they are chemists; they simply dispense drugs that their computer tells them they should prescribe for this or that condition. Tap, tap, tap, press 'Enter' – take this. Children and young people are being hit from every angle and their perceptions are being distorted by the chemical and brain-suppressing poison in their food and drink; drugs like Ritalin; microwaves and electromagnetic pollution, especially in mobile phones; the programming of their reality through 'education' and 'entertainment'; and reduced language diversity through text messaging and text-speak. Fabian Society member and eugenicist, Bertrand Russell, wrote in his 1953 book, *The Impact of Science on Society*:

I think the subject which will be of most importance politically is mass psychology ... Its importance has been enormously increased by the growth of modern methods of propaganda. Of these the most influential is what is called 'education'. Religion plays a part, though a diminishing one; the press, the cinema, and the radio play an increasing part ... It may be hoped that in time anybody will be able to persuade anybody of anything if he can catch the patient young and is provided by the State with money and equipment.

Although this science will be diligently studied, it will be rigidly confined to the governing class. The populace will not be allowed to know how its convictions were generated. When the technique has been perfected, every government that has been in charge of education for a generation will be able to control its subjects securely without the need of armies or policemen ...

... Fitche laid it down that education should aim at destroying free will, so that, after pupils have left school, they shall be incapable, throughout the rest of their lives, of thinking or acting otherwise than as their schoolmasters would have wished.

Diet, injections, and injunctions will combine, from a very early age, to produce the sort of character and the sort of beliefs that the authorities consider desirable, and any serious criticism of the powers that be will become psychologically impossible.

Gradually, by selective breeding, the congenital differences between rulers and ruled will increase until they become almost different species. A revolt of the plebs would become as unthinkable as an organized insurrection of sheep against the practice of eating mutton.

Figure 253: *Mobile phone technology: The silent holocaust*

You are going to see all these things increasing, along with the many other ways that children and young people are targeted to manipulate their perception and disconnect them from Consciousnesss. The body is an electrochemical system and anything that imbalances that is going to have negative consequences physically, mentally and emotionally, all of which, on one level, are electrochemical phenomena. It is no co-incidence that since the Reptilian conspiracy began its sprint to the finishing line over the last 30 years, the population, and most especially the young, have been bombarded with electrochemical attacks. I call mobile phones the silent holocaust, because their consequences for brain function and health is potentially catastrophic as the damage accumulates, not least in causing brain tumours (Fig 253). The bloodline families are well aware of this. They understand how the body works, what it is, and how technology affects it. They have just made sure that the population doesn't know, but the consequences of what I am saying are now becoming clear from pure experience. Yet in the midst of this gathering evidence, and the sheer stupidity of heating up the brain with close-range microwaves, the British government announced that using a mobile phone is no more harmful for children than taking a hot bath or exercising! Yes, this is lunacy (literally), and yes, this is plainly ludicrous; but this is beyond mere stupidity. It is calculated to serve the population-culling agenda. The government has now dropped child safety guidelines for mobile phone use while conceding that there are 'significant gaps in our scientific knowledge'. The gaps in their intelligence and decency are far more significant. Researcher, Alasdair Philips, from the organisation Powerwatch, which specialises in the effects of electromagnetic and microwave fields, said in response that a number of international studies have found a significant increase in brain tumours among people who have used a cellphone for more than 10 years. 'It's incredible that the notion there is no good reason to restrict children's use of mobile phones could be the official government line – this would be completely irresponsible and immoral.' But, then, that is what they are. Dr Paul Rosch, clinical professor of medicine and psychology at the New York Medical College, said:

It is generally not appreciated that there is a cumulative effect [on our bodies] and that talking on the cell phone for an hour a day for 10 years can add up to 10,000 watts of radiation. That's 10 times more than you get from putting your head in a microwave oven.

It is not only cellphones, either. We live in an electromagnetic 'soup' today made up of cellphones, cell phone transmitter towers, the wireless Internet and so on, and this has been linked with cancer, Alzheimer's, brain tumors, autism, impaired fertility, hormone disruptions and much more. Of course, this must be the case. These electromagnetic fields

Illustration by David Dees (deesillustration.com)

Figure 254: *One brain-changing additive is the artificial sweetener, aspartame, which I have exposed in detail in other books. It is in virtually all soft drinks and many foodstuffs. Aspartame was manipulated through the safety checking procedure by Donald Rumsfeld, the US Defense Secretary at the time of 9/11. He was appointed to head the pharmaceutical company, G D Searle, because of his connections in the Reagan-Bush administration which ensured that aspartame was given the all-clear. Searle was later taken over by the infamous Monsanto*

disrupt the body's electromagnetic fields. I have been highlighting for years the dangers to members of the emergency services posed by the Terrestrial Trunked Radio (TETRA) communications system and now police officers in the UK are suing the authorities over the effects on their health. Nothing is done about the dangers from electromagnetic and microwave technology because governments and the telecom companies are owned and controlled by the same families, and so the agenda of those families is served by both governments and telecom companies. It is the same with Big Oil, Big Pharma, Big Biotech – all of them. I hear people say that governments are just serving the interests of the telecom or biotech industries, or whatever, when they are really serving the 'interests' of the same families who, in turn, represent the 'interests' of the Reptilians.

'Food' Additive P-R-S

Research about food additives was published in the medical journal, *The Lancet,* in 2007 and revealed what anyone with a modicum of brain activity should have known already – there was a clear link between food and drink additives and hyperactive behaviour in children (Fig 254). Scientists from the University of Southampton conducted the research on nearly 300 three-year old and eight-year old children, none of whom suffered from a hyperactivity disorder. They drank a mixture of additives that reflected the average daily additive intake of a British child, and afterwards they were observed to become 'boisterous and lose concentration'. They were not able to play with one toy or complete one task and they exhibited what was called 'impulsive behaviour'. The eight-year-olds were not able to complete a 15-minute computer exercise. Look at these findings in their entirety: the observed effects after drinking these chemical cocktails included hyperactive and compulsive behaviour, making the children 'boisterous and lose concentration', and not able to play with one toy or complete one task. Now, what does Big Pharma and its in-the-back-pocket medical profession tell us are the symptoms of Attention-Deficit Hyperactivity Disorder which must be treated with Ritalin and the like? They say that this 'condition' can be seen in children who:

- Have trouble keeping attention on tasks or play activities.
- Do not follow instructions and fail to finish schoolwork, jobs or activities.
- Are easily distracted.
- Have trouble playing or enjoying leisure activities quietly.
- Are 'on the go' or act as if 'driven by a motor'.
- Exhibit impulsive and compulsive behaviour.

The behaviour traits of kids in an official additives trial and those given mind-altering drugs like Ritalin for 'behaviour disorder' are the *same*. No wonder, then, that the astonishing rise in the use of these mind-altering drugs has followed the astonishing rise in the mind-altering additives in food and drink. At least the overwhelming majority of child behaviour problems are caused by their brain and body-computer systems being scrambled by the chemical and electrical war that has been declared on the children and young people of the world. It is important to remember that all the cartels, be they Big Pharma, Big Oil, Big Biotech, all of them, are controlled by the same network – the global 'corporation' of secret societies that manipulate in every country. These groups, therefore, work as one, and never more obviously than Big Biotech and Big Pharma. The Biotech cartel makes people ill with its chemical concoctions and Big Parma gives them still more chemical concoctions in the name of 'treating' the manufactured problem. Everyone's a winner, except for the people. Those they can't get to through food and drink – and there aren't that many now – they get through 'philanthropic' vaccination programmes in the developing world. Good old Bill Gates, eh? What a lovely chap for giving all that money to vaccinate poor, deprived children.

The best way to get rid of a problem is not to find a solution, but to remove the cause. In this case, the cause is the crap we give to children to eat and drink, in association with other great swathes of mind programming. John Tyson, the father of a Ritalin victim, took his son to the Cactus Clinic at the University of Teesside School of Social Sciences & Law in the North East of England where they don't use drugs to treat behaviour. Clinic manager, Amanda Clarkson, says: 'Attention disorders are not diseases, but patterns of inappropriate behaviour.' Yes, they are; and they can be changed by working with children, not drugging them; and by changing the diet that is so often the subliminal villain in the background. John Tyson removed gluten, wheat and dairy foods from his son's diet and gave him mineral supplements. The effect was clear to see:

> After six weeks, the benefits were noticeable. After three months, I knew I was getting my boy back. I think it's wicked how children are being doped when there are alternatives.

Studies in England and Australia have found that six capsules a day of fish oil can vastly improve children's behaviour and is more effective than Ritalin and related drugs without any of the 'side-effects' (effects). One mother, Rachel Gow, told of the amazing transformation in her son, Nathaniel, after she replaced the Ritalin-like drug, Concerta, with fish oil. She described how within days of starting the Concerta medication for 'Attention-Deficit Hyperactivity Disorder' her son lost his appetite and suffered violent mood swings:

> He stopped eating, he wasn't sleeping and I couldn't get him away from his PlayStation – it had a hypnotic effect on him. He was focusing on it but in a disturbing way. It was as if his soul had gone. He was a wide-eyed shadow of his former self. His mood swings were extreme – he went from hysteria to uncontrollable anger to crying like a baby within minutes. Anything could set him off. He wasn't Nathaniel; he wasn't my son. It was frightening.

'It was as if his soul had gone'. Exactly – that's what they want. Rachel replaced the drug with six Omega 3 fish-oil capsules a day and his symptoms all but vanished. She said: 'We've noticed a dramatic reduction in his hyperactivity; he is much happier, doesn't have the mood swings and his concentration has improved.' The ingredients in the fish oil helped to balance the chemical imbalances that were causing the imbalanced behaviour in a destabilised body-computer caused by the chemical cocktails in the drugs. It's not bloody rocket science. They say of computers that if you put garbage in you get garbage out and it is the same with the body-computer. This is why the system is designed to give us garbage to eat, drink and think; but we don't have to do what it wants us to do. There may be a war on our minds and bodies, but we don't have to come out with our hands up.

Genetically-Modified Food (People)

Genetically-modified food is a major part of the Reptilian agenda and those in the shadows behind the demonic biotech cabal, most notably the grotesque Monsanto in St Louis, know exactly what they are doing and why. Here we have the ever-recurring theme of genetic 'modification', or, more accurately, genetic manipulation. Genetically-modified food is, in keeping with the Reptilian conspiracy, designed to genetically modify us (Fig 255). It is sold under the guise of 'feeding the world' when mass murder would be far more accurate. Monsanto is the company that told us that PCBs, DDT, and Agent Orange – all lethal – were safe. Big Biotech is already devastating the genetic foundations of nature and people in North America and their target is the entire planet. There has been resistance in Europe where there are stronger networks of environmental activists, but the European Union is just waiting for the chance to give GM food the all-clear, because the EU is controlled by the same families that control Big Biotech and Big Pharma. As I write, Hilary Benn, the pathetic UK Environment Secretary, is calling on the European Union to accept a quicker GM 'authorisation process'. He said: 'If GM can make a contribution then we have a choice as a society and as a world about whether to make use of that technology, and an increasing number of countries are growing GM products.' Genetically-modified food is horrific, you idiot! Hilary Benn is a member of the Fabian Society, just like his father, the former Labour cabinet minister, Tony Benn. An article for the *Huffington Post* website pointed out that in the nine years after GM food was imposed on the United States multiple chronic illnesses in the US nearly doubled; allergy-related emergency-room visits doubled between 1997 and 2002; and food allergies, especially among children, skyrocketed. There was also a dramatic rise in asthma, autism, obesity, diabetes, digestive disorders and certain cancers (Fig 256). I tell the detailed story of GM and the biotech agenda in *The David Icke Guide to the Global Conspiracy (and how to end it)* and it is a catalogue of deception

Figure 255: *Genetically-modified food is designed to genetically modify humanity*

and utter disdain for human health and wellbeing. Monsanto has placed its 'former' employees in key posts in government agencies that are supposed to police the biotech cabal (just like Goldman Sachs at the Treasury Department), and also hires people from those same government agencies and departments. There is a revolving door between Monsanto and government that allows Big Biotech to make the law and block checks and balances on its activities. This has been going on for decades, aided by biotech presidents and prime ministers like the genetically-corrupt Bill Clinton and Tony Blair. The cold and vicious

Figure 256: *GM is terrible for human health – just as it is meant to be*

Monsanto was a producer of Agent Orange, the lethal herbicide and defoliant used by American forces in the Vietnam War for ten years up to 1971 and the cause of so much death and destruction. Monsanto is Illuminati to its fingernails.

Members of the Working Group on Biosafety make recommendations on the use of genetically-modified food produced by Monsanto. These members have included: Linda J Fisher, Vice-president of Government and Public Affairs for Monsanto and formerly with the US Environmental Protection Agency; Dr Michael A Friedman, Senior Vice-President for Clinical Affairs at G D Searle & Co., a pharmaceutical division of Monsanto, formerly with the US Food and Drug Administration; Marcia Hale, Director of International Government Affairs for Monsanto, formerly assistant to the President of the United States; Michael (Mickey) Kantor, director of Monsanto, former Secretary of the US Department of Commerce; Josh King, director of global communication in the Washington DC office of Monsanto, former director of production for White House events; William D Ruckelshaus, director of Monsanto, former chief administrator of the United States Environmental Protection Agency; Michael Taylor, head of the Washington DC office of Monsanto, former legal advisor to the Food and Drug Administration; Lidia Watrud, former microbial biotechnology researcher at Monsanto, who joined the United States Environmental Protection Agency's Environmental Effects Laboratory; Jack Watson, staff lawyer with Monsanto in Washington, former chief of staff to the President of the United States, Jimmy Carter. Others include representatives from the Illuminati-controlled DuPont, and Dow Chemicals. Among them is Clayton K Yeutter, former Secretary of the US Department of Agriculture and former US Trade Representative, who led the US team negotiating the US-Canada 'free trade' agreement and helped to launch the Uruguay Round of the GATT 'Free Trade' negotiations, the forerunner to the World Trade Organization. He became a director of Mycogen Corporation, whose majority owner is Dow AgroSciences, a wholly-owned subsidiary of the Dow Chemical Company. It is extraordinary that conflict of interest on this scale could even be contemplated, let alone allowed to happen, but this is common practice in the cesspit world of Illuminati manipulation. As with politicians who don't read the legislation they are voting for, so many members of these 'public protection' bodies don't read the evidence and, in the case of GM, proper testing is actually *banned*. Researcher, F William Engdahl, author of *Seeds of Destruction*, writes:

An editorial in the respected American scientific monthly magazine, *Scientific American* ... reveals the shocking and alarming reality behind the proliferation of GMO products throughout the food chain of the planet since 1994. There are no independent scientific studies published in any reputed scientific journal in the world for one simple reason. It is impossible to independently verify that GMO crops such as Monsanto Roundup Ready Soybeans or MON8110 GMO maize perform as the company claims, or that, as the company also claims, that they have no harmful side-effects, because the GMO companies forbid such tests!

That's right ... For the past decade, the period when the greatest proliferation of GMO seeds in agriculture has taken place, Monsanto, Pioneer (DuPont) and Syngenta require anyone buying their GMO seeds to sign an agreement that explicitly forbids that the seeds be used for any independent research.

Scientists are prohibited from testing a seed to explore under what conditions it flourishes or even fails. They cannot compare any characteristics of the GMO seed with any other GMO or non-GMO seeds from another company. Most alarming, they are prohibited from examining whether the genetically modified crops lead to unintended side-effects either in the environment or in animals or humans.

You couldn't make it up; but then you don't need to when it's true. Scientists pointed out the potential dangers of genetically-modified food, but their views were ignored by the US Food and Drug Administration (FDA) which is supposed to protect the public. The FDA is nothing more than a subordinate agency to Big Biotech and Big Pharma. The technique is very simple. If you want to control what you can and cannot do, control the agencies that, in theory, decide what you can and cannot do. Some of the most important cogs in the criminal drug-running networks in the United States and around the world are the very agencies that are supposed to be stopping it. These include the CIA and the Drug Enforcement Agency, or DEA. After all, unless you know the game, who is going to suspect them of doing the very thing they are there to police? By 1992, the FDA was so deeply in the hip pocket of Big Biotech that it said no testing was necessary with regard to GM crops if the industry itself believed them to be safe. They were told they could put them on the market without even telling the FDA. 'We know of no information showing that the foods created from these new methods differ in any meaningful or uniform way,' the FDA declared. It was a big lie, as 44,000 internal FDA documents proved when they came to light as a result of a lawsuit.

Taylor-Made for Monsanto

The documents revealed that GM can produce allergies, toxins, new diseases, antibiotic-resistant diseases, nutritional problems and cancer-causing agents. They also confirmed that scientists and experts at the FDA had said that GM food was different from that created normally and therefore had different risks. How come, then, that the FDA said publicly there was no difference? The man responsible for taking that line was Michael Taylor, the number two at the FDA, a former attorney to Monsanto, and later a Monsanto Vice-President for Public Policy. Taylor is a Monsanto placeman-in-government of the most glaring kind; and who did Obama pick to be his 'food czar'?

Michael Taylor. He is responsible for the 'implementation of new food safety legislation', which, without question, will be Monsanto's 'food safety legislation'. Dr Richard Day (Rothschild Zionist) told the meeting of doctors in 1969: 'Growing food privately will be banned by saying it isn't safe.' Now we have the US Food Safety Modernization Act of 2009 (HR 875) that establishes a centralised dictatorship over the food supply (Fig 257). It is called the 'Food Safety Administration' and operates within the Department of Health and Human Services, the body orchestrating the response in America to 'swine flu'. The Administration will be headed by the Administrator of Food Safety appointed by the President for a term of five years, after which they can be reappointed. Any food establishment or foreign food establishment engaged in manufacturing, processing, packing or holding food for consumption in the United States must register annually with the Administrator. A Monsanto spokesman went out of his way to stress that the company had nothing to do with this bill when, of course, the opposite is the case.

Figure 257: *David Dees' portrayal of the effect of legislation targeting organically-grown food*

The Food Administrator's job will be to destroy small and medium-sized farming and organic production, even the growing of food in your own garden (Fig 258). The legislation gives the goons the power to enter private property – a common theme – and big fines

Figure 258: *The Illuminati want to destroy small-scale farming and stop people growing their own food on the grounds of 'safety'*

can be levied for refusing entry. HR 875 was introduced by Democratic Congresswoman Rosa DeLauro, the member for New Haven in Connecticut, home of Yale University and the Illuminati Skull and Bones Society. She secured a masters degree at the Fabian Society's London School of Economics. The organisation behind the bill is Trust for America's Health, a non-profit organisation sponsored by the Robert Wood Johnson Foundation. This was established by Robert Wood Johnson II who made the US pharmaceutical and medical company, Johnson & Johnson, a global name. Margaret Hamburg, who was appointed by Obama to head the Food and Drug Administration, is on the board of directors at Trust for America's Health and the Rockefeller Foundation, which has spent a fortune promoting genetically-modified food. Trust for America's Health produced a report entitled 'Keeping America's Food Safe: A Blueprint for Fixing the Food Safety System at the US Department of Health'. The report consultant was Monsanto's *Michael Taylor*, now Obama's 'food czar'. Taylor's wife, Christine Lewis Taylor, a long-time employee of the Food and Drug Administration, has been promoting the ludicrous idea that nutrients should be defined as toxins to justify the imposition of limits on the quantity of essential nutrients that people can consume. This is all connected to the Nazi-created Codex Alimentarius that is planned to destroy the food supplement and nutrient industry in anything but name. Still, at least Mr and Mrs Taylor are perfectly matched, and they thoroughly deserve each other. Then there is the Food Safety Enhancement Act of 2009 (HR 2749). This gives the Food and Drug Administration the power to quarantine any area on the grounds of 'food contamination' and includes a provision for 'prohibiting or restricting the movement of food or of any vehicle being used or that has been used to transport or hold such food within the geographic area' . This refers to any vehicle, effectively, because how many vehicles have not transported food of some sort? Farmers' markets and local food sources could also be closed down under this bill, even if they are not the source of the alleged contamination.

It has all been planned for a long time – to ban safe food by saying it is unsafe while imposing upon the people genetically-modified shite with all manner of dangers to health. Rats used to test a GM potato developed pre-cancerous cell growth in the intestine and stomach, developed smaller brains, livers and testicles, and had damaged immune systems. These people get off on the death, suffering and mayhem they cause. They have no empathy whatsoever with those who suffer the consequences of their actions, for the reasons I have explained. Big Biotech claimed that DNA is destroyed on consumption and was no threat to human DNA, but it knew that wasn't true. Studies and tests have since confirmed this, with GM DNA surviving intact as it passes through the body and having the potential to fundamentally impact on human DNA and affect gene function. Those scientists and researchers who seek to expose the truth about GM and Big Biotech in general find themselves fired and threatened with lawsuits, even violence against their families. While the 'protection' agencies and government departments give Big Pharma and Big Biotech such a free ride they come down heavily on alternative methods of healing and those with discoveries and technology challenging the corporate monopolies, including methods of generating energy for free by harnessing the energy fields in the atmosphere all around us. If you control these agencies and the government you can use them to destroy your opposition – and they do. Also, does anyone still think that the dramatic drop in sperm count is not connected to the chemical and genetic onslaught against the human body at a time when they want to cull the global population? The Big Biotech placemen and women are everywhere. In January 2010, Gordon Conway, Professor of International Development at Imperial College London and a former UK government adviser, called on organic farmers to 'embrace' genetically-modified crops. Conway is a former president of the Rockefeller Foundation.

Controlling the Food Chain

The plan is for the Reptilian bloodline corporations and governments to control the production and supply of all food and we are seeing it happening today. Biotech giants like Monsanto are destroying seed variety and patenting the rest for their exclusive use – even natural varieties which they have had no part in developing (see *The David Icke Guide to the Global Conspiracy*). When you are an Illuminati front you can do as you like. Bloomberg reported in 2009 that Monsanto, the world's biggest seedmaker, planned to increase the price of new genetically-modified seeds by a colossal 42 per cent. The idea is to create a monopoly on seed production and then put all small growers and farmers out of business by constantly inflating the price. This would leave only the Illuminati corporations, most notably Monsanto, to control global food production. Once again, this is why we are seeing the increasing attacks on organic farmers and growers to destroy supplies of decent food and impose the monopoly. The usual crowd are behind the campaign to impose genetically-modified crops on the rest of the world, including Africa. The Rockefeller Foundation funded the first 'Green Revolution' in Asia and Latin America in the 1960s to secure further control of their food production, and joined with the Bill and Melinda Gates Foundation to launch the Alliance for a Green Revolution in Africa (AGRA). Their plans for the takeover of Africa's food supply were supported by two reports from a 'think tank' called 'Resources for the Future', based in Washington DC. Its major funders include the United States Environmental Protection Agency, Goldman Sachs and the Robert Wood Johnson Foundation, sponsors of Trust for America's Health, the organisation behind the food dictatorship bill HR 875. The two Resources for the Future reports about Africa, both funded by the Rockefeller Foundation, were written by ... yes, Monsanto's *Michael Taylor*. Obama is, of course, also on board and he told the website **AllAfrica.com** that he was 'still frustrated over the fact that the Green Revolution that we introduced into India in the '60s, we haven't yet introduced into Africa in 2009'. That wouldn't be the Green Revolution in India that has left the country's farmers with brutal levels of debt, paying ever-higher costs for seed and pesticides, and committing suicide in extraordinary numbers, would it? You know ... the one that has depleted the water table and poisoned the environment? It surely would, and that is what they want to do to Africa led by an Illuminati president masquerading as one of 'Africa's own'.

In early 2010, the Bill and Melinda Gates Foundation appointed Sam Dryden as director of Agricultural Development for its 'Global Development Program'. With his career history, he was perfect for the job the Gates' will want him to do. Dryden was Managing Director of Wolfensohn & Company, a private investment and advisory firm founded by Rothschild partner, James Wolfensohn, a former president of the World Bank; Dryden is CEO of Emergent Genetics – a plant sciences investment holding company promoting and marketing 'biotechnology-enhanced seed products' which was bought out by Monsanto (for whom he now works) and Syngenta AG; he was President and CEO of Agrigenetics Corporation that is now part of Dow AgroSciences; he has been an advisor to the Rockefeller Foundation and chaired a Rockefeller Brothers Fund development initiative 'to benefit developing country food security'; he also served on the Board of the South/North Development Initiative, a private Rockefeller family foundation for 'alleviation of rural poverty in less developed countries through entrepreneurial development'; he is a member of the Council on Foreign Relations. Talk about fit-for-purpose.

The food monopoly and control agenda is also, in part, the reason for the systematic destruction of marine life by the United States Navy. The 'Warfare Testing Range Complex Expansions' in the Atlantic, Pacific, and the Gulf of Mexico are projected to kill millions of marine mammals and other sea creatures every year. This has been approved by the National Marine Fisheries Service (NMFS). Rosalind Peterson, writing for **NewsWithViews.com**, says:

The NMFS approvals will have a devastating impact upon the marine mammal populations worldwide and this last Navy permit, which is expected to be issued in February 2010, for the 'taking' of more than 11.7 million marine mammals in the Pacific will be the final nail in the coffin for any healthy populations of sea life to survive.

Now with ever-increasing numbers of permits being issued for sonar programs in more than twelve ranges in the Pacific, Gulf of Mexico, and the Atlantic regions of the United States, our marine mammals and other sea life are facing complete devastation. When you add bomb blasts to this list, warfare testing of all types, future war testing practice, and the toxic chemicals which are both airborne and to be used underwater, there is little chance that most marine life will survive in any significant numbers.

The Bush administration weakened US environmental laws with regard to the Navy in 2004 and Bush signed a no-debate Presidential Order exempting the Navy from environmental laws that protect threatened and endangered species. Next came the NMFS approvals that are estimated to involve the slaughter of nearly twelve million marine mammals over five years. This is all part of the ongoing plan to destroy diversity and food sources to create total dependence on the state-corporation monopoly. Do as we say or you don't eat.

Emotional Disease

The most destructive force with regard to human health and wellbeing is low-vibrational emotion on which the Reptilians feed. It destabilises the body-computer's energetic construct and, thus, electrical and chemical balance. In the same way that chemicals or electromagnetic fields imbalance the body chemically or electrically, they also do so vibrationally, because everything is connected 'forward' and 'back', 'up' and 'down'. In fact, everything in this reality is vibrational ultimately, whatever name you give to it because it the holographic expression of the waveform Metaphysical Universe. Stimulating these low-resonance emotions, all based on the central theme of fear, has many benefits for the Reptilians and their hybrid subordinates: it maintains the flow of energetic 'sustenance'; keeps the body-computer in a state of emotional imbalance that stops us thinking straight; locks us even more powerfully into the survival mechanisms of the reptilian brain – the connection to their hive mind and the Moon Matrix; makes it more difficult to connect our awareness to 'out there', because fear focuses the Mind on five-sense survival and lowers our vibrational resonance; and it ensures that humans don't live too long. The latter is important to them given that the death process, and fear of death, is an enormous generator of low-vibrational emotion. It is also true that the longer you live the more chance you have of working out what is really going on. Understanding the nature and origin of 'body' emotion, and the way it is mercilessly manipulated, is the key to understanding so much about human enslavement and how it is achieved. The most debilitating human emotion is fear, and that can be so powerful that literally your body can't move, hence 'frozen with fear'. This is the reptilian brain kicking in, as I described earlier. Healer, Mike Lambert, told me that he once felt fear to such a degree that he could not move even his eyelids, and his experience as a cutting-edge healer has shown him how emotion is pre-eminent in mental and physical disease. The very word 'e-motion' means 'stop movement' and all imbalanced emotion is affecting the speed and efficiency of the body's communication systems by suppressing movement – the exchange of information between brain, organs and cells. Emotion is the major cause of illness or what we call dis-ease.

Once you appreciate how the body is an interconnected communication and response network, you can see why Mike Lambert says that at least 90 per cent of ill health is caused by emotional imbalance. I remember many years ago reading a letter sent by the local doctors' practice to all its patients. It said: 'Patients are reminded that appointments with doctors are for five minutes only and this is not a time to discuss your other problems'. If anything sums up the ignorance and irrelevance of mainstream 'medicine', this is it. The fact that the 'other problems' are the real cause of the symptoms is simply beyond the bounds of their concrete reality. Never mind the cause, give 'em a drug. When we feel emotion, either ongoing or as a sudden reaction, it takes the form of an electrical charge that in more extreme cases you can actually feel. These emotional charges affect the electrical/energetic balance of the body and, through that, the chemical balance. One is just a different energetic form of the same information. From this emotion-generated electrochemical imbalance comes the potential for all dis-ease and, of course, low-vibrational emotion is connected to the reptilian brain that locks people into the hive mind and Moon Matrix. Big Pharma medicine, and much of the alternative sector, responds to this by focusing on the symptoms or what appears to be the cause. The response of mainstream medicine is usually the scalpel or the drug which either cuts away the physical manifestation of the problem or targets the chemical imbalance (often causing more chemical imbalance called 'side-effects'). Cancer invariably returns, because the cause – emotional imbalance – is still there undermining the immune system and opening the body to fungal attack. What do people say about powerful emotion? Something 'is eating me away'. This is what the fungus that causes cancer does – eats the body away. This must be so because it is only a 'physical' expression of the energetic emotion. Mike Lambert says:

> People talk about being 'cancer-free', but are they? Or is there just no sign of cancer cells? If they are still in the same shit marriage, still in the same shit job, the problem will return. If things don't change, they remain the same.

I know from long personal experience the effect on the body of emotion and stress. By 2007, the pressure of my life, and the virtual absence of any 'chill out' time or periods of peace, was killing me, no doubt about it, and increasingly quickly, too. I was going down and down with the vortex of stress and pressure that was engulfing me with no respite in any area of my life. There was a time in 2003 when I was under particular stress that I had excruciating pain in my neck – the worst I have ever experienced. Mike Lambert said immediately that it was caused by stressed emotion, and you realise that common phrases like someone or something being 'a pain in the neck', are based on fact. Mike says that energetically the emotion of fear is connected to the kidneys, while anger connects to the liver and gallbladder. How accurate it is, then, to refer to something as 'galling' or say that someone is 'venting their bile' (which is produced by the gallbladder). The emotional trauma or stress affects the flow of the gallbladder energy meridian and this imbalance is passed on to the neck further up the same energy line. The gallbladder meridian passes through the backside and affects the sciatic nerve, and so we rightly refer to people who give us stress as a 'pain in the arse'. I've known a few of those. Mike also says that you can see a greenish-blue tinge to the skin near the eyes of people who are feeling extremely envious, and they are literally 'green with envy'. As major sources of stress left my life from the summer of 2007, I began to release a lifetime of pent-up emotion and frustration that led to inner and outer peace that transformed my health. My life changed, my emotions changed, and so my health changed. It's all emotion, emotion, emotion and society is intentionally structured to keep us in fear and stress. It maintains the energetic food source of the Reptilians, keeps people mentally suppressed, and causes ill-health galore.

Running on Adrenalin

When we're stressed, we often feel exhausted and this is caused by a worn-out adrenal system which is responsible for dealing with stress. It is a bit like a fuel tank and when you are not producing enough adrenaline and related hormones it can leave the body in a state of acute fatigue. When I saw the connections between that feeling and the adrenal glands, I realised that this has happened to me many times over the years when I thought I was just exhausted from sheer effort. Mike Lambert tells me that post-natal depression is the result of adrenal breakdown in some women due to the stress of giving birth. He explained that if a cell doesn't receive adequate oxygen cancer can follow, and the causes of oxygen deprivation include the chemicals in food and drink, and the toxins and electrochemical imbalances caused by negative emotions like fear, guilt, depression, anger, hatred, resentment and frustration. Our emotions are literally killing us physically and speeding the ageing process. 'People have all this cosmetic surgery as their bodies age, but what they really need to do is look inside and deal with the real cause,' Mike Lambert says. The biggest emotional killer according to Mike is expectation, both the expectation we have for ourselves and trying to meet the expectations that others have for us, especially our parents. So much begins with a lack of love and affection from parents and this feeling of being 'not good enough' and 'not lovable enough' can continue throughout life. It can lead people to seek attention and acknowledgement by striving to be seen as successful in the system's terms when often that is not who they are, or, if the truth be known, what they even want to be. As Mike put it:

> People are not being who they are, but what they and others expect them to be. If you drove a Ferrari off-road it wouldn't last 20 minutes, because it's not designed for that. Energetically, people are not designed for what most of them do, because they are trying to be what they are not. If someone of an extremely sensitive and emotional nature became a litigation lawyer it would probably kill them, or at the very least give them a stress-related illness.

Deep within the secret society network and beyond to its Reptilian masters, they know all this and they have structured society to maintain a constant state of emotional trauma and imbalance. This is why Mike has pinned this question on his young son's bedroom door: 'If you are going to fill your mind with other peoples' thoughts, then what's the point of having any of your own?' Be who you are, not what you are told you should be. He also quotes the old Hindu saying, 'we create our own suffering' and he recalls the question posed by Carl Rogers, the founder of Humanistic Psychology: 'Why do you think the way you do?' It is a question that can open the door to why we experience reality in a certain way and through a particular filter. We might also ask ourselves: Why do we do what we do? Is it because we want to do it or because we think we *have* to do it, or is it to meet the expectations of ourselves and others? I saw a quote once which said: 'Happiness does not come from doing what you want, but wanting what you do'. If we are not flowing with the energetic truth of who we are then we will resonate to the imbalance of what we're not. Denying our true self will just dam the flow, imbalance our energy field and soon it's: 'Hello, doctor, can I have my five minutes?' The Beatles sang in *Eleanor Rigby* 'All the lonely people, where do they all come from? All the lonely people, where do they all belong?' Most people are lonely, even within families and amongst a crowd. They leave behind their real self to act out the fake self, the face they put to the world because the world demands it. This fake self can become so powerful as our alter-persona that most people, not least through insecurity, even demand of it themselves. I must succeed, I must be rich, I must make my dad proud of me, I must be seen to have 'made it'. Bollocks to that; and 'made it' as what, exactly? Made it as an actor on the stage we bravely call 'life'? Succeeded in the terms of a system that is utterly insane and devoid of neuron activity? Shit, congratulations on that one, a round of applause for the guy with the smart suit and the big car who'd rather be living on a mountain in Nepal. Oh, and by the way, mate, the cemetery is first on the left.

The Dots Connect

The road to understanding this and so much else began for Mike Lambert when he took up martial arts at the age of 14. He became so advanced that he represented Britain some 200 times and it allowed him to appreciate from a very early age that there was far more to the body, especially energetically, than most people realised. He also had an experience, again at 14, in which he saw a bright ball of light, about 20 millimetres across, hovering just over the top of his shin. He panicked because he had been reading about how the body can burst into flames through spontaneous combustion, but he now knows that what he was seeing was photon energy. As he says, the meridian energy lines identified in acupuncture are channels of photon energy, known to the Chinese as 'chi', and the 'acupuncture points' along these lines are like 'junction boxes' where the flow can be affected and balanced. Sometimes, energy can build up at these 'junctions' and if you can tune with its energetic frequency it can appear as a ball of light. 'What I saw was photon energy at the point called 'stomach 36',' he says.

It took Mike weeks to recover from the shock of what he had seen, but he went on to become fascinated by the knowledge and philosophies of the 'East'. He became interested in Zen Buddhism, graduated in oriental medicine and studied with some of the most advanced practitioners in places like Tibet and Japan. Understandably, Mike found school very difficult, like 'doing time', and the teachers put his disinterest down to lack of ability (they would call it Attention Deficit Disorder today). However, an IQ test revealed it was nothing to do with lack of ability and his reading was 168 points – higher than his headmaster's. Such is the irrelevance of the 'education' system to human intelligence. He left school to become a carpenter and joiner, but the turning point came when he took up the compensation case of a man injured in a scaffolding accident. He was taking on a major company, and he won so convincingly that they offered him a job as a Health and Safety investigator. This gave him years of experience in endless cases and situations to add to his understanding about the nature of the body and 'life' itself. He also went to college to study psychology and hypnosis and today he has brought all of this multi-faceted knowledge and insight together in his unique and extraordinarily successful approach to health. International researchers and scientists increasingly head for his door looking for answers to the 'mysteries' that mainstream medical science cannot understand, and he has been invited to events at the Royal Society in London, the very bastion of establishment science. Mike points out the fundamental difference between 'recovery' (the absence of symptoms, often temporarily) and 'regeneration' (the body returned to optimum wellness). He says of the Shen Clinic: 'We don't deal in ill-health; we deal in wellness.'

> When someone is deficient in say vitamin C, a doctor will prescribe vitamin C. But I want to know why they are deficient; what's the cause? Life is driven by energy and biochemistry is secondary, including vitamins.

To take this approach means to see the connections between everything and not to treat (a) only symptoms, and (b) only those parts of the body where the symptoms manifest. A simple example: a headache might well be caused by a blockage or problem in an acupuncture meridian in the foot, because that same meridian circuit also flows through the head. Mike quite rightly contends that there is 'fragmented thinking' in both conventional medicine and 'alternative' healing. Both are dominated by specialists when they need to be skilled in many disciplines to be truly effective. Mike is an acupuncturist, but not only; a psychologist, but not only; an expert in oriental medicine, but not only, and so on. To connect the dots and to see how the body, mind and emotions interact requires the hands-on experience of seeing and identifying these interconnections, not just passing exams and gaining 'qualifications' by repeating the official line. 'Tell me and I'll forget; show me and I might remember; involve me and I'll understand,' he says.

The Sugar Scam

The body is a hologram, and every part of a hologram is a smaller version of the whole. This includes the mind and emotions which are also expressions of the hologram, as is the way we walk and hold ourselves physically, the tone of our voice and the smell of our breath. All these are access keys to the holographic computer that are available to those rare practitioners of multi-levelled insight such as Mike Lambert. When someone arrives at the Shen Clinic and Mike is apparently just making them welcome he is actually studying everything about them, the way they walk and the tone of their voice included. Each of these aspects of ourselves is an open book to someone who knows what he or she is looking for, and by the time you sit down to discuss your symptoms Mike can pretty much know what you are going to say. Even a doctor he once treated said: 'I'm staggered that you know what you know about me because I haven't told you yet.' Many times, before I have even said a word, he has looked at my tongue and told me – accurately – how I am feeling … physically, mentally and emotionally. The tongue is a smaller version of the whole body hologram and the state of the tongue reveals the state of the body. It is the same with the eyes. Mike explained:

The liver empties energy into the eyes, the heart empties into the tongue and the kidneys empty into the ears. This is why many cases of tinnitus are actually a kidney deficiency. The source of the symptom is rarely the source of the problem.

It is fascinating from this perspective to see how it all connects and how what seems to be the cause or seat of a health problem is anything, but. For example, he explained to me the destructive cycle triggered by consuming refined sugar. First of all, he says, a single lump of refined sugar would kill you if the body did not instigate a survival response to cope with it. Refined sugar is acidic to a potentially lethal degree, and the body protects itself by releasing massive amounts of calcium into the system from the bones and teeth. Obviously, there comes a point where so much calcium has been used for the body to survive that the bones and teeth begin to show the consequences, and one of these is osteoporosis when the bones lose strength and density and are far more prone to fracture. The consumption of refined sugar affects the pineal gland in the brain, and with that the production of the neurotransmitter called serotonin. When this is depleted it triggers depression. People in this state are often attracted to sugar products like chocolate, cola and 'high energy' drinks to lift their mood and energy levels (comfort eating and drinking) and the cycle is repeated even more destructively. A can of cola contains nine teaspoons of sugar, Mike says, 'and just one could kill you without the body's calcium response.' We are now seeing an explosion of sugar-related disease because of our sugar-saturated society. The hormone, insulin, carries sugar in the form of glucose to the cells, and too much sugar (including the glucose/sugars derived from carbohydrates) means that either the pancreas cannot produce enough insulin to cope or the whole system is swamped by overload. This has multiple consequences. One is that when glucose is not being absorbed and used as energy by the cells it is stored as fat – a major reason for our increasingly obese society. Insulin imbalance can, through the domino effect, lead to prostate and breast cancer (by its effect on the immune system), diabetes (now an epidemic) and imbalance the thyroid, the master gland, which maintains the body's temperature, metabolism, strength of the immune system and hormonal stability. When the thyroid is malfunctioning, the whole system follows, and chloride in public drinking water is a big source of thyroid 'attack'. It depletes iodine which is critical to thyroid function. Once again, it is an attack on the glands of the endocrine system, including those of the 'third eye'.

One quick aside, which might be helpful for people … Mike Lambert tells me that a very significant cause of cancer (again by the effect on the immune system), coronary heart disease, dementia and Alzheimer's disease is a toxic amino acid called homocysteine. There is no drug for this which, no doubt, is a big reason why the medical profession don't treat it. Homocysteine can only be detected with a blood serum test that many doctors will not authorise, or even consider, because they have either never heard of it or have no idea of its destructive potential. Mike sets marker levels of homocysteine at between 6 and 10 and he becomes concerned for a patient's health if they reach 13. The UK National Health Service blood testing department told him that even when they check for homocysteine their 'safe' marker is 18. One patient at the Shen Clinic had a level of 32 and consequently suffered major heart problems, but he survived when Mike Lambert's treatment lowered his homocysteine levels to seven. Stress is a major cause of high homocysteine levels.

'Modern society' has introduced endless chemical and electromagnetic influences that have short-circuited the interactions and mutual dependencies between body and earth, body and Consciousness, with appalling consequences for human health. If this had happened through ignorance that would be bad enough, and for most people that is how it did happen. Doctors, and those in other professions, largely think what they are told to think and with most of them you can even forget the bit about 'largely'. Their slavish belief in the system's version of everything makes them ignorant repeaters; but behind the wizard's curtain, where the true nature of reality is hoarded by the few and kept from the people, including doctors, they have known all along what the consequences would be of the electrochemical and emotional attacks on the human body. The effect of Big Biotech fungicides on salvestrols in fruit and vegetables and the cancer marker CYP1B1 is just one of endless examples of the cold calculation and it serves very well as a symbol for the calculated mass-murder that has been visited upon the human race under the guise of 'progress'. We must not get caught in the cul-de-sac of 'it's all about money' or 'it's all about oil'. The accumulation of money and the monopoly on oil supplies are by-products of the real agenda – mass human control. The main thrust of this is the suppression of both the intellect and, even more crucially, the multi-dimensional connection that allows people to be 'in' this world 'physically', but not 'of' this world in terms of their point of observation and perception. To do this, they need to destabilise the body-computer and its electrochemical processes, especially through the survival mechanisms of the reptilian brain that trigger low-vibrational emotion based on fear.

Once achieved, Consciousness cannot make its voice heard through the body, any more than a brilliant computer programmer can get his perceptions onto the Internet through a faulty computer. Big Pharma and Big Biotech are a fundamental part of this, but only a part. There is so much more.

23

Game Plan (4):
Different Masks – Same Face

Make crime pay. Become a Lawyer
Will Rogers

There are multiple ways to program the body-computer. You can do it chemically through Big Pharma and Big Biotech, or electromagnetically, verbally and vibrationally through a whole range of methods and means.

The desired outcome is to disconnect the body/mind from Consciousness, suppress and distort the body's receiver-transmitter system and program a sense of reality based on fear, 'little me' and limited possibility. What we call 'society' has been specifically structured at every level to achieve this and impose an all-pervading control system. This is why Michael Ellner's list of apparent paradoxes are not paradoxes at all. It is the way the world is designed to be.

Lawyers destroy justice

'Law', together with control of finance, is the most effective way of imposing your will on a population. In fact, the two are completely connected and today's legal system is founded on the ancient Roman law of money, or commerce. A judge sits on a bench and this is the origin of the word 'bank'. Moneylenders in Rome set up their stalls on a long bench called a 'bancu' and this later became 'banco' and then 'bank'. Laws in the United States are made, at least in theory, on Capitol Hill (capital, money) and the name comes from Capitol Hill in ancient Rome. The centre of government in every country is called the 'capital'. The system of statute law throughout the world is founded on Roman law which came from Babylonian and Sumerian law. It is most obvious in the United States where, as in Rome, they have a 'Senate'. In the Roman Senate they used 'fasces' (a bundle of white birch rods tied together with a red leather ribbon into a cylinder, often containing one or two axes with their blades projecting) to symbolise power and jurisdiction, and this is the origin of the term 'fascism' (Fig 259 overleaf). It portrays perfectly the world the Illuminati bloodline families are seeking to impose – the rods (individuality) are tied together and ruled by the axe (dictatorship). What a symbol for the European Union. The official seal of the United States Senate includes a pair of crossed fasces, and the Mace of the United States House of Representatives is designed to resemble them. You can see the fasces on the wall of the House either side of the American flag, in the Oval office, on the seal and

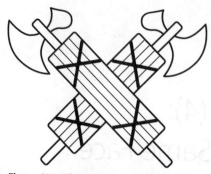

Figure 259: *The symbol from which the word 'fascism' appropriately came*

insignia of the National Guard and at the centre of the official seal of the United States Tax Court. Fasces also ring the base of the statue of the Goddess Freedom (Queen Semiramis) on the dome of the United States Capitol Building. This is again most appropriate, because she is not the goddess of 'freedom' at all. She is the moon goddess of Babylon. Look at the architecture of Washington DC or the Bank of England and other such buildings in London. They are based on ancient societies, especially Roman.

Controlling the people through Roman law is very simple. A few dictate what the law will be and anyone who refuses to obey is punished by a network of agencies known as 'law enforcement'. Unless there is a mass refusal to conform to a law, in numbers that would overwhelm the system, this is really all you need. Any individuals who resist are picked off one by one to serve as an example to others of what happens if the will of the State is denied, no matter how unjust a law may be. This control-system becomes even more powerful when you ensure that those subject to these laws have no say in making them. We have been programmed to equate 'democracy' with 'freedom' when they are not even nearly the same thing. The only real difference, especially today, between a fascist/communist dictatorship and an elected dictatorship (democracy) is that in theory the people have a vote every four or five years. Two points here: (1) What use is a vote when the options for government are all controlled by the same network of families? (2) Once you have cast your vote, the 'elected' government goes off and does as it likes. You may have voted for a politician or party because of what they promised they would do if put in power. But, as we see constantly, they have no obligation whatsoever to do what they promised once you have put them in office. My goodness, look at Obama for a start. He's already done more U-turns than a traffic jam in a riot. The vote is irrelevant, just a sop to kid the people they are free. Every country is a dictatorship, whether 'elected' or imposed by a coup.

Law by Decree

Another misconception is the idea that laws in 'democracies' are passed after public debate in Congress, the Houses of Parliament, or wherever, but the great majority are not. Most people don't have opinions based on detailed knowledge or understanding. They have an 'image' of what the situation is. This image comes from hearing – mostly half-hearing – mantras chanted incessantly by politicians, 'journalists' and academics. So they get the impression that for something to become law it has to be subject to debate by elected 'representatives' in national parliaments or local councils, but it's not true. Something like 75 per cent (and growing) of British law originates from unelected bureaucrats in the European Union. Then there are the other little wheezes that allow governments or presidents to introduce law without any debate or oversight worth the name. In the United States they have the system of Presidential Executive Orders that bypass Congress and have been used to build a mountain of laws and laws-in-waiting that are nothing less than a fascist/communist state sitting in the shadows until they are activated by a 'state of emergency'. As Bill Clinton's former advisor, Paul Begala, said in the *New York Times* in 1998: 'Stroke of the pen. Law of the Land. Kinda cool.' Executive Orders are legally-binding dictates issued by the president without public debate. They don't require Congressional approval, yet have the same legal weight as laws passed by Congress. If Congress passes a bill to challenge laws made by Executive Order the president has the power of veto. To override this veto takes a two-thirds majority – highly unlikely to say the least. The way the United States form of government was set up gives fantastic power to one man and, more to the point, to those who control him. There is a long list of executive orders introduced by successive presidents (frontmen for the same force) over the decades which can be activated simply by announcing a state of national emergency. They are truly proclamations of fascism that give the government the right to take away your home; break up families and take away children; make people live and work wherever they are told; take control of all media, transport – including private vehicles – and all sources of energy, plus a whole lot more. How many Americans know that? They also have a system known as 'rulemaking' in which laws passed – at least in theory – on Capitol Hill are given further added detail by the rulemaking agencies often packed with, or advised by, unelected and often unknown scientific, economic and corporate 'experts'. It is another way of introducing legislative changes without proper political debate and oversight. In the UK, we have what is called 'secondary legislation', also known as subordinate or delegated legislation and, in the case of government ministers, Statutory Instruments. This is a definition from **www.answers.com**:

> Statutory Instruments (SIs) are parts of United Kingdom law separate from Acts of Parliament which do not require full Parliamentary approval before becoming law. These are usually brought to Parliament by a Government minister, exercising legislative powers delegated to them by an Act of Parliament.

They basically do as they like and the Legislative and Regulatory Reform Bill, passed in 2006, increases these powers substantially. Thousands of rules, regulations and laws are introduced in the UK alone every year without any public debate, and even the legislation that is passed through a debating chamber is not read by most of those who vote for it. Fundamental changes, like the fascist US Patriot Act, and fundamental transfers of power from national parliaments to the European Union, are voted through by people who have not read the legislation. The Obama Clean Energy and Security Act, which gave government control over almost every aspect of American life, was passed in June 2009, even though 300 pages of the legislation had been introduced at 3am and almost no-one had read them. When House Minority Leader, John Boehner, stood up to read the contents out loud, the bill's co-sponsor, Henry Waxman (Rothschild Zionist), objected and tried to stop him on grounds of 'procedure'. All you need to pass any law is a majority representation for the governing party, and no matter what the effectiveness of opposing arguments they just vote like sheep for 'their' side. Don't question or dissent, it'll be bad for your career. Service-to-self yet again is the fuel that empowers the conspiracy. Day after day, year after year, this has been going on incessantly and it has produced a mountain range of legalisation that now dictates the finest detail of people's lives. Those in the background who write the laws on behalf of their Freemasonic and Illuminati masters hide their cyanide pills for human freedom in the endless gobbledegook of clauses and sub-clauses that the politicians and public have not only never read, but often wouldn't understand them anyway. Legislation is specifically worded to hide the real meaning. When someone later says, 'I never voted for this,' they find that they did in clause 71, sub-clause 55. This is how the fascist/communist global state has been covertly constructed. And now we have the new buzz-phrase of 'international law'. We are going to hear much more of this, because international laws are laws that everyone on the planet is supposed to obey. This is all part of the preparation for a one-world government.

The Grand Deception

Nothing highlights the scale of the deceit more than the way the true nature of the law is kept from the people. There is an increasing number of researchers who are focusing on what is a minefield – once again *mind*-field – of calculated complexity. This area of research is very much a work in progress and it is a bit like finding the combination to the door of a bank vault. Once you think you have the numbers, another combination is behind the first one, and so on. I have great admiration for those who are researching this subject – most of them, anyway. It takes an incredible amount of work and commitment. Yes, they will make mistakes and there is always more to know, but if you don't take on the task then the manipulation remains unseen. This is not my area for the simple reason that to research the subject properly and effectively this is pretty much all you have time to do. It is a web of intrigue, word-meanings and derivatives, and legal traps to catch those who take on the system this way. What I will do here is summarise the main points that these researchers make, but remember it is a work in progress and there will be much that we don't yet know and many surprises are yet to be uncovered …

When people talk about the 'law of the land' they are referring, many researchers say, to Common Law and not the Statute Law dictated by governments. Common Law has evolved over thousands of years through customs and precedents. British researcher, Veronica: of the Chapman Family, has specialised in this area of the conspiracy and you will see in a moment why I have written her name in that apparently strange way. She says:

> Back in the Celtic times the British Isles were populated by tribes. They had traditions and customs. Nothing was permanently written down, but they lived by rules that everyone knew. This entirely mirrors the situation world-wide. There was a time when everything was tribal, and each member knew the rules that governed their lives. If anyone broke these rules there would be some kind of Tribal Meeting, and the Chief or Holy Man would preside. A judgment was made on the basis of arguments put forward by both sides, and that judgment was executed.

Common Law was enshrined in the original Magna Carta (Great Charter) which King John was forced to sign in 1215. If you don't breach the peace, nor cause harm or loss to another, and do not employ mischief in your agreements, then you will not violate the tenets of Common Law. The use of Common Law is the use of common *sense* in that each situation can be judged on its merits without 'statutory' laws that tell the judge what he or she must do in given circumstances. One modern definition is this:

> Common law is the system of deciding cases, that originated in England and which was later adopted in the US Common law … [it] is based on precedent (legal principles developed in earlier case law) instead of statutory laws. It is the traditional law of an area or region created by judges when deciding individual disputes or cases. Common law changes over time.

Now there you have a big reason why Common Law was of little use to the Illuminati families. It changes over time, yes, but mostly not very quickly and sometimes very little, and people can even make their own Common Law. If you want to create a global prison camp in any realistic timescale, you need laws that you can introduce quickly and change at will to suit your requirements. You certainly don't want people able to make their own laws. The Reptilian bloodlines usurped Common Law, what researchers call the 'law of the land', with Statute Law, the 'law of the sea'. This is also called Maritime Law or Admiralty Law and Commercial Law, amongst other terms, and is widely known today in the United States as the Uniform Commercial Code (UCC). It is based on Roman/Vatican Canon Law. Douglas J Whaley, a professor of law at Ohio State University, says there are two jurisdictions: the UCC and Common Law. The UCC is concerned solely with the sale of goods or the sale of leases of goods, he says, and goods must be 'moveable'. They don't have to move very far, but they must be able to be moved. This means that anything immovable, such as buildings, and all services, falls solely within the realm of Common Law, some researchers say. The Illuminati families took the laws of shipping and trade by sea and brought them ashore to be called Statute Law. If it seems strange that a court or building on dry land could be administered under Maritime or Admiralty Law, look at US Code, Title 18 B 7. It says that Admiralty Jurisdiction is applicable in the following locations: (1) the high seas; (2) any American ship; (3) any lands reserved or acquired for the use of the United States, and under the exclusive or concurrent jurisdiction thereof, or any place purchased or otherwise acquired by the United States by consent of the legislature of the state. In other words, mainland America. By its very nature, maritime law is commercial law, the law of contracts. These are the 'laws' introduced by governments and parliaments and they can sometimes do this in hours – perfect if you want to impose a slave state. When the Queen signs an Act of Parliament or the US President signs a bill into law they are simply signing a contract to make a contractual agreement. A new law was passed every *three hours* during the ten years that Tony Blair was in Downing Street – 98 per cent of them by statutory instruments, rather than Acts of Parliament. You can do this with Statute Law, the law of the sea, but not with Common Law, the 'law of the land'.

There was, however, a problem they had to address before they could override Common Law. It was that Common Law refers to the living, breathing human being while Statute Law is the law of commercial contracts between corporate entities. So the purveyors of Statute Law had to invent fake 'persons' – corporations – to which their 'laws' could be applied. This is the invented entity known as the 'straw man', a legal fiction, which researchers of this subject say is created using your name in all-capital letters, as in DAVID ICKE, and through other versions and means. Notice that when government, law enforcement, legal and financial agencies etc., communicate with you they invariably write your name in all-capital letters. This is because they are not writing to you, the living being, but to the fake 'straw man' that was created when you were born. The trick is to keep you believing throughout your life that, in my case, the living, breathing me and DAVID ICKE are the same thing. They are *not*. If you think about it, all names are fictions, no matter how they are written in that they are names given by parents or deed poll to an experience, not to the 'I' that we are – Infinite Consciousness, the force with no name unless we choose to give it one. How can your name be who you are when you can change it any time you want? However, at this point in the uncovering of the straw-man fraud some people are refusing to refer to themselves in the conventional way – DAVID ICKE, David Icke or even david icke, and they are instead using terms like 'Veronica: 'as I am commonly called' or Veronica: of the Chapman Family. She says that in doing this she is not saying that this is her name, only that this is what she is 'commonly called'. The idea is to avoid the name trap that can lock you into the Statute Law scam. She says:

> If you want my attention, you can write or speak to me 'as I am commonly called' e.g. 'Veronica'. And that's it. If there is more than one Veronica around, and you want to single out my specific flesh and blood, then 'Veronica: of the Chapman family' (add my tribe) and you have singled me out as much as the name 'Veronica Chapman' ever did … We add the colon to make it harder for them to type into a database.

Terms like 'Mr' and 'Mrs' also refer to corporations and if you use them you are acting as the corporation, not the living, breathing 'you'. Once you agree to accept these titles and certain versions of your name as being you, then the contract is made, at least in the eyes of officialdom, with the government and associated corporations, and you become subject to commercial law – Statute Law.

Governments are private corporations

Many researchers say they have established that governments, government agencies, local councils, courts and the 'justice' system, police forces, etc., etc., are private companies and corporations. They advise people to confirm this at the website of Dun & Bradstreet, which provides credit information on businesses and corporations worldwide. They point out that these various public authorities are listed by Dun & Bradstreet as private organisations, not as public bodies. The United States and United Kingdom governments, for example, are private corporations. Members of Parliament, the military, intelligence services, and so on, do not swear an oath of allegiance to the people of the country. They swear allegiance to the Queen (the corporation) and the Queen refers to 'My' government and 'My' Parliament. All this nonsense about a government of the people and for the people is just that – nonsense. The existence of the government corporations and the way they trick people into servitude is, naturally, a big secret known by only a few. There have, however, been some rare references to it in *Hansard*, the official record of the UK parliament. The following exchange happened in 1940:

> Mr Craven-Ellis: asked the President of the Board of Trade whether the formation by the government of the United Kingdom Corporation is only a wartime measure; and will he give an assurance that the corporation will be wound up immediately after hostilities cease, so that the export trade may flow through its normal peace-time channels.

Mr Johnstone: The corporation was formed with a view to meeting difficulties in overseas trade which are due to conditions arising out of the war. It is impossible to foresee the conditions that will obtain when hostilities case and, therefore, I cannot say whether at that date it will be desirable to terminate the activities of the corporation.

Another MP asked the Chancellor of the Exchequer in 1944 to provide a list of names of the directors of the United Kingdom Commercial Corporation and they turned out to be representatives of major banks and companies. The list also revealed the existence of a United Kingdom Commercial Corporation (Spain) Limited and others for a stream of countries and regions including Portugal, Ethiopia, Egypt, Eritrea, Iran, Iraq, Palestine, Sudan, Syria and Lebanon, and East Africa. Those with insider knowledge (the few) know this and certainly the Queen in the UK will know this, but most of them are clueless about the very system they are briefly administering, or appearing to. The shareholders in the corporation are the people, like you and me. It is just that the authorities forget to tell us. Every time a baby is born, a single share in the corporation is issued in its name in all-capital letters, but because this fact is systematically kept from us we don't ask for either the share or the money it is worth. Instead, the share is held in trust by the government along with all dividends due and the voting rights that come with it. The trustee, the government corporation, uses these 'votes' to decide the future of the corporation and whether, for instance, it will agree to a corporate merger to create the European Union or North American Union. By keeping their true lawful status from the people, they turn the shareholders into employees of the corporation (or slaves to be more accurate), and one of the key ways they do this is by using words that have one meaning to the population and another in legalese.

Re-defining language, Me Hearties ...

The term 'legal' does not mean 'lawful', hence I call banking 'legalised robbery'. It is 'legal' under Statute Law, but it is still robbery – an unlawful offence. Common Law is what is lawful; Statute Law is what we call 'legal', as in the 'legal system'. We think that a 'person' is a human being, but under the 'legal' definition of Statute Law a 'person' is a corporation and, to meet the criteria of Maritime Law, the Uniform Commercial Code, the 'person' represents a ship, in effect. This is why when a 'person' goes to court – a maritime court in reality – the 'person' stands in the *dock*. Look at the maritime language in everyday use, especially in relation to governments and legal terms, such as ownership and citizenship. We also have a courtship before agreeing a corporate merger called marriage in which we contract with the government corporation through a marriage certificate that makes two people 'partners'. Yes, *business* partners, according to Statute Law. The whole system is based on Roman Law, or Vatican Law, the relocated Church of Babylon; and remember how the ancients used to symbolise the heavens as the 'upper ocean' and used maritime symbols for the Reptilian 'gods'.

We also have words like leadership; rulership; lordship; statesmanship; premiership; chairmanship; directorship; governorship; dictatorship; relationship; partnership; professorship; scholarship; apprenticeship, dealership; distributorship; fellowship; friendship; guardianship; censorship; receivership; readership; sponsorship; township; trusteeship; even worship. I saw a definition of Admiralty Law which said that it 'also covers many commercial activities, although land-based or occurring wholly on land, that are maritime in character'. What they do is use language that makes everything 'maritime in character'. What happens when we arrive in this 'world' after leaving our mother's waters and travelling through the 'birth canal'?? We are issued with a birth/berth certificate. When a ship berths in a port or dock the captain has to produce a *'berth* certificate', a 'certificate of manifest', detailing his cargo and its value. It is not the spelling that matters, as with 'birth', so much as the sound or 'phonetics' – a word that comes from the seafaring people known as the Phoenicians. I say that 'Phoenicians' is another name for a people deriving from the Sumerians. The word 'captain' comes from 'capital' – money. When people die, a death certificate is signed by a doc-tor. Jordan Maxwell, one of the leading researchers in the United States on the Uniform Commercial Code scam, explains how this system is also applied to every child born into this 'world'. He is talking from the American perspective, but the same applies elsewhere:

> When you are born you come out of your mother's water, therefore you must have a birth certificate, a certificate of manifest, because you are a corporation-owned item. You are a human resource. This goes back to the German Nazi concept that every human coming out of their mother's water must be 'berthed'. Therefore, you have to have a certificate of manifest to see how much this individual is going to make for us in our New World Order.

> I am telling you that until you understand the laws, the symbols, emblems and what these words mean, you are never going to suspect how far gone we really are. Did you know, for instance, that your birth certificate is a security on the stock exchange in the New York Stock Market? Did you know that? ... On all birth certificates in this country ... on the right-hand corner, you will always have a series of red numbers ... those are a security number on the world stock exchange.

> Go to any good stock office and ask them to check these numbers in the computer and see what this stock is worth. They will check it on the New York Stock Exchange and find you. Your birth certificate is a stock on the stock exchange in America. Why? Because you are worth money to the international banks ... we need to wake up. This is serious stuff.

United States flags in every federal building, court, school, or wherever, are framed with a gold/yellow fringe because of the meaning this has in maritime law. Whenever the president makes an address on television or speaks in a federal setting you will see the 'American' flag behind him with a gold/yellow fringe. Once again this is Maritime/Admiralty Law. Under the International Law of the Flags, the type of flag displayed by a ship decrees the law that applies aboard that vessel. By going aboard you are accepting the jurisdiction of the law that applies to that flag. The same happens with foreign embassies. The flag they fly ensures that the law of the country they represent applies within the confines of the embassy. A flag with a gold fringe indicates Admiralty Law and when you appear in a court displaying a flag of that nature you are agreeing to be tried under Statute Law, the law of the sea that applies to a legal fiction and not to you, the living, breathing human being with a soul. As an article at **usa-the-republic.com** put it:

> When you enter a courtroom displaying a gold or yellow fringed flag, you have just entered into a foreign country, and you better have your passport with you, because you may not be coming back to the land of the free for a long time. The judge sitting under a gold or yellow fringe flag becomes the 'captain' or 'master' of that ship or enclave and he has absolute power to make the rules as he goes. The gold or yellow fringe flag is your warning that you are leaving your constitutionally secured rights on the floor outside the door to that courtroom.

Look at US troops in places like Iraq and you'll see the gold fringe around the flag on their uniforms, indicating that they are the army of the corporation, not the people or the country as they think they are. Fortunately, the game is being uncovered and it is possible to disconnect from statute slavery if you know what you're doing. This includes taxation and credit-debt which are also fictions of Statute Law. The wording of all communications with the State needs to be carefully constructed, not least your name. Accept that you are your name, or use prefixes like 'Mr', 'Mrs', 'Miss' or 'Ms', and Statute Law will prevail; but researchers say that if you use other wording you can cease to contract with Statute Law, the law of the sea. This leaves you subject only to Common Law, they say. You have to be *very* careful to do everything correctly to the letter and that means getting seriously informed about how the statute system works. A little knowledge can be a dangerous thing here and many people have ended up in jail because they had pieces in the puzzle missing. It is important to know what you are doing or work with someone who does. It doesn't mean there will be a criminal free-for-all when Statute Law is collectively rejected and Common Law returned to its rightful place in human affairs. If you breach the peace, cause harm or loss to another, or employ mischief in your agreements, then you are subject to Common Law, no matter what you call yourself. There is a lot of information now on the Internet if you search with terms like: 'straw man, common law' or 'lawful rebellion'; and Veronica: of the Chapman Family has a website at **www.fmotl.com**. Be very careful of acting without being fully informed, however. There is still a great deal more to know about all this. I repeat: it is a work in progress and goodness knows what there is still to uncover.

Legalised Tyranny

Many judges, and those in the upper echelons of the global legal profession, know that the system is fraudulent, and the same goes for leading government administrators. Most come-and-go politicians haven't a clue. The legal profession is just like the medical profession, including the fact that both are full of Freemasons and initiates of other secret societies. In fact, the legal profession is a secret society, especially with the Inns of Court in London that are located in the Temple District, named after its 'former' owners (former, my arse), the Knights Templar. It is through the secret societies that the same agenda is coordinated between the governing bodies of medicine and law. All the professions are structured the same and they are controlled by using the same techniques based on the carrot and stick. Doctors go to medical school to be told what to believe about the human body, and lawyers go to law school to be told what to believe about the law. Doctors are widely motivated by money and status and so are lawyers. Their outrageous fees deny access to the law to most people and make it a privilege of the rich and powerful – exactly as planned.

Once again it is about service-to-self and not to justice. Keep your head down, keep the system on your side and you may even end up a judge. Wow! The corporate lawyers are paid fortunes to defend the indefensible and crush their victims until their bones crack. You want to challenge my corporate imposition on your life? Okay, take us to court. Oh, you can't, can you? Heh, heh. There are some instances where you find decent lawyers who truly care about justice, but they are the exception in my experience. The legal profession is as corrupt as medicine with its itemised bills, compiled with a stopwatch, which no-one can possibly check to see if they are an accurate reflection of the work that's been done. You have to take the word of lawyers about the work they claim to have done and how long they took to do it. You get bills that state things like '2.30 minutes: read email from client'... and on it goes down the list with a big figure at the end. '7.30 minutes: went to toilet, had a long one, pondered on your case.' 'Safe' judges are appointed to cases that governments want to win to ensure that they make the 'right' decision, no matter what the implications for justice. We even have 'Republican' and 'Democrat' judges in the United States who are appointed through the patronage of the bloodline families who control both parties. They make judgements according to political and secret society allegiance, and that's how Boy Bush was awarded the presidency in 2004 by a Supreme Court with a 3-2 Republican majority. The fact that he didn't actually win the election was irrelevant to the purveyors of 'justice'. Do what you're told, the money is great. The same system of political patronage for legal appointments operates everywhere, even where it is against the country's constitution. Little matters like constitutions are for public consumption only, not for those who run the country.

What 'American Constitution'?

Oh yes, and while Americans quote the 'We the People' Constitution in support of their rights, there are researchers who say the document doesn't even *apply* to the American people. They say the Constitution only applies to the 39 signatories and their successors. American researcher, David Parker-Williams, who has studied this subject for a long time, highlights something called 'capitonym', a term that describes words that change their meaning, even their pronunciation, when they are capitalised. A simple example is china and China. One means cups and saucers and the other is a country. The point is that capitalisation can change the meaning of a word in minor and major ways. David Parker-Williams says this in relation to the US Constitution:

> So, in the original Constitution ... why did 'they' capitalize the 'P' in 'People'?
> Because the meaning was changed to a specific 'People'. Thirty-nine to be exact.
>
> It is not that someone has hidden this ... the average folks aren't looking and paying attention. The Preamble ('Pre' – in front and 'amble' – to walk) ... a statement that 'walks in front of something' to define its purpose ... that preamble told everyone: we do this 'to secure the blessings of liberty to ourselves and our Posterity'. Not 'everyone's posterity' ... only theirs. 'They' told everyone plainly.

Well, yes, in a way. 'Plain' to me means: 'We want to make it clear that this document does not apply to the American people, only to us.' But I take the point. David Parker-

Williams looks at the straw-man arena from a different angle to most other researchers in the field. He doesn't take the route of Common Law / Statute Law and says that this is a diversion from what people really need to do. This is his approach:

> Once in, there is a way out, but it is not as easy as what is 'being said' (by the alleged gurus); because those saying 'it' start from a false premise that 'we the (little) people are free'. They say this without considering the obligations of the contracts that they voluntarily signed. Once in as a US citizen, the only way out, is 'out', as in 'all the way out'. One must seek a 'new status'.

> In case law it states 'the only way to divest oneself of US citizenship is to voluntarily undergo a naturalization process in a foreign (nation)/state'. Until then, they have NO RIGHTS, because; whether by fraud, misrepresentation, or artifice … they 'went into the contract' voluntarily, and they are 'in the United States'.

Once again I take the point, but I personally can't see how being tricked into contracting through fraud and misrepresentation can constitute doing it 'voluntarily'. David Parker-Williams has been researching this subject for many years and, at time of writing, he is in the process of creating a new website to detail his information.

Universities destroy knowledge

The last thing any would-be dictatorship wants is a truly informed and aware population. The less that people know the less trouble they are going to be for you. In those few words you have the reason (a) why the 'education' system was created in its current form, and (b) why it really does destroy knowledge, or at least suppress it. Knowledge cannot really be destroyed, but it can be kept from public awareness. The 'education' system and the laws that enforce it are perfect vehicles for indoctrinating children and young people from the earliest age to see the world in the way that suits the Reptilian agenda. 'Education' gives you the system's version of reality – finance, politics, history, medicine, possibility, the whole caboodle. I have detailed in other books how the writing of history and other versions of official 'truth' were funded by Illuminati families and organisations. This, together with the suppression and dismantling of the ancient and native accounts, has deleted the Reptilian 'gods' from mainstream history, along with evidence of their genetic manipulation of the human form. Teachers are like doctors and lawyers in that they go to teacher-training centres to be indoctrinated themselves after years of being indoctrinated already through the school, college and university machine. If the teachers conform to the demands of the system in how and what they teach they are rewarded with a job, usually for life, and they may even become a head teacher or university professor. Rock the boat with independent thought to encourage your students to question everything and, oh dear, bad career move. It is the same for the children and students who soon learn that if you tell the system what it wants to hear you get good marks and if you don't, well, you don't. Exams are not a test of intelligence, but of obedience to the status quo. My son, Jaymie, was told that if he challenged the official version of 'global warming' in his exam he would have no chance of passing. Conform … you know it makes sense.

Left-brain Prisoners

One of the main aims of the 'education' system is to imprison people in the left side of the brain, the 'serial processor'. This constructs reality in a sequence embedded with 'time', structure, and communication through language, as I have discussed. The left hemisphere, more than anything else, is responsible for constructing the version of reality that we experience today as 'human life'. I have spoken many times at Oxford University, or more accurately the Oxford Union, a debating society founded in 1823 and the breeding ground for many leading politicians of the last 185 years. Five British Prime Ministers have been officers of the Union – William Gladstone, Lord Salisbury, Herbert Asquith, Harold Macmillan and the satanic child-killer Edward Heath – and a long list of government ministers and other politicians, including Benazir Bhutto, the assassinated former Prime Minister of Pakistan. She was Union President in 1977. The Union has attracted the leading British politicians of their day to speak in their debates and also the high and mighty from overseas, including: US Presidents, Reagan, Nixon and Carter; former secretary of State and Illuminati front-man, Henry Kissinger; and Robert Kennedy, the assassinated brother of JFK. South Africa's Archbishop Desmond Tutu, Mother Teresa, the Dalai Lama, Michael Jackson and even Kermit the Frog have also appeared.

The last time I spoke there was in 2008 when I was asked to present my information about how the few control the many in pursuit of a global fascist dictatorship. There were some open people who turned up, but, I found once again, as I have every other time at Oxford and Cambridge, that the intellect, left to itself, is a prison of the mind. The 'education' system is after the intellect first, second and last. Society is structured to

Illustration by Neil Hague (www.neilhague.com)

entrap awareness – focus, attention – in a manufactured 'fairground' of false realities that function like a stage hypnotist to the five senses and the intellect (Fig 260). When I was thinking about how best to present the information at the world's most prestigious university, I found myself going through the apparently bizarre process of leaving out certain areas and concepts, because I knew it would be too much for the intellect alone to take. Instead, I honed it down into sort of baby steps. What? Yes, 'baby steps' at the home of the intellectual 'elite' when at my usual public events I can give everything to an audience of the 'general public' of all ages, races and backgrounds, most of whom will never have seen the inside of a university, let alone Oxford. How come? *Intellect*, that's how come. If you look at what we call

Figure 260: *The left-brain is the target of the 'education' system*

'society', it has been created by intellect. Not heart, not Consciousness – intellect. The education system worships the intellect and seeks out through examinations the sharpest intellects to run the institutions of government, finance, business, science, education, the media and military in the next generation. This is where Oxford University comes in. Oxford and Cambridge (its fellow traveller) are the ancient universities where those with the best examination passes from mostly the 'best' schools are sent to be indoctrinated to see the world the way the Illuminati families decree for their future system-servers. They mix with other students at these 'prestigious' universities who have made it to Oxford and Cambridge through the influence of their elite families and the financially-exclusive private-school network. It is much the same in the United States with the Ivy League Universities like Harvard and Yale where entry is virtually guaranteed if you come from the 'right' family. In these 'centres of learning' like Yale, Oxford and Cambridge you have the coming together of those considered by exam passes to be the most intellectually able, and those who are there because of who their father, mother or grandparents are – Boy George Bush being a classic example at Yale. We have the children of the families who control the system sharing the same 'educational' and perception-programming as those who will run the system on their behalf in the next generation. It has been the same for centuries.

Oxford University is the elite of the elite and one of the Illuminati's prime global locations for developing the programmed intellects to serve their purpose of global control. This was why the infamous Rothschild agent, Cecil Rhodes, left money in his will in 1902 to fund the so-called Rhodes Scholarships that bring highly-selected students from overseas to attend the Oxford indoctrination machine under its motto, 'Dominus Illuminatio Mea', or 'The Lord is my Light'. Which 'Lord', though? Bill Clinton was a Rhodes Scholar at Oxford, and even outside the Rhodes system the elite families in countries across the world send their children there to be 'westernised' – Illuminised – and they return to change their own societies in line with the Oxford blueprint. This has been one of the most effective vehicles for 'Westernisation' of the world. Oxford has produced 25 British prime ministers and many overseas leaders, 20 archbishops of Canterbury and major system-servers and manipulators like media tycoon, Rupert Murdoch. His and other media organisations are packed with Oxford and Cambridge ('Oxbridge') graduates and so are political parties and the controlling layers of government administration, medicine, mainstream science and the military. Oxbridge is also a major recruiting ground for British Intelligence operatives who go on to play their little boy 'intellectual' games with the lives of others.

What do they all, or at least the great majority, have in common? They are prisoners of the intellect, as are the elite Illuminati families, and thus we have a society founded on, and created by, intellect – one of the lowest expressions of awareness. Those who dictate the perceptions of society, like scientists, doctors, teachers, lawyers, politicians, journalists, bankers, business leaders, and all the rest, are invariably prisoners of the intellect. The 'education' system is specifically designed to produce such people to run the system on the bloodlines' behalf while most of them have no idea that this is what they are doing. The intellect manifests itself through the left-brain, the part that filters reality in terms of can I see it, touch it, taste it, hear it or smell it? Okay, it exists, then. The left-brain perceives reality through the five senses, and perceives the world in parts, rather than unity. The system is structured to entrap us in the left-brain from the moment we sit down in our first classroom right through to leaving college and university. You progress within the 'education' system by passing exams and the more effective you are at taking in left-brain information and repeating it in exams, the quicker and higher you progress. If you do that brilliantly you end up at Oxford or Cambridge, Harvard or Yale. Now, what do you need generally to be a doctor, scientist, top politician, government administrator, military leader, etc? Exam passes and a 'good education' (good indoctrination), and so the institutions that run the system generation after generation are controlled by people enslaved in the left-brain, or intellect, and see everything in terms of parts and not unity. It explains so much. I spoke with a couple of young students before I made my last presentation to the Oxford Union and it was like conversing with a wall. Neither could even conceive of the possibility of a society that was not controlled by a 'strong' hierarchal government. It simply would not compute for them; any alternative was considered crazy. As Einstein said: 'Common sense is the collection of prejudices acquired by age eighteen.' Another Oxford attendee said that he could follow me when I was explaining the structure of how the few can control the many (left-brain), but he could not get his head around what I was saying later about the illusory nature of reality (right-brain). Classic.

The right-brain – the balance for the intellect – deals with the random, intuitive, holistic and subjective. Its perspective is one of unity, of free-flowing creativity and of infinity, not limitation. It expresses itself most obviously through the artistic and the maverick. The aim of the Illuminati sausage machine called 'education' is to activate, stimulate and reward the left-brain while suppressing the right. It is possible to have an advanced intellect and not be subject to its limitations if you also open your mind to Consciousness. These are 'whole-brained' people who balance and connect their awareness through both hemispheres of the brain. Such people are 'out there' and 'down here' and they can see from a higher perspective while still being able to function within five-sense reality and explain their 'out there' understandings through the intellect in words that most people can grasp. I am not knocking the left-brain intellect, because without it we could not express ourselves efficiently through the body-computer. How many 'right-brainers' have you met who were 'out there' somewhere in the ether, but struggled to function in five-sense reality or could not express themselves in ways that most people could understand? I have met many over the years. We need the intellect to operate efficiently through the five senses, but it has to be in its place and not the governor of perception. When it dominates the sense of reality it can be a monster and also subject to the most shocking levels of ignorance. Left-brain audiences are the most challenging for this reason and I have never been to a university yet where that was not the case in general – though that's certainly not true for every individual. There are some whole-brainers at universities, too.

Cleverness without Wisdom

Once you begin to understand how the brain works and how the system, especially education, is designed to program its perceptions, so much about our society and how it operates becomes ever clearer. There is no mystery about why I can talk to the 'uneducated' public and they 'get it', while people from the so-called cream of intellectual society (adults as well as 'elite' students) look at you with incredulity. It is simply the difference between an open mind operating and scanning many levels of awareness and the closed mind of the intellect imprisoned by five-sense perception. Naturally, a society created by intellect measures intelligence by intellectual prowess, but the terms 'intellect' and 'intelligence' are not the same thing, or at least they're not if the intellect is acting alone. Examination passes are no more a measure of intelligence than cleverness is a measure of wisdom. As I said earlier, it may be very clever to make an atomic bomb, but it is wisdom not to do so. In the same way, it takes intellect to orchestrate a war, but Consciousness not to do so. It takes intellect to explain the apparent complexities of this illusory world of division and apartness, but Consciousness to know that we are all One. The 'physical' reality that we live 'in' has been created/decoded by intellect and it will only be changed by the heart, or Consciousness. The university system, elite or otherwise, is ever more irrelevant, ever more in retreat from the cutting edge. There is a revolution of perception going on and the isolated intellect simply can't see it, nor can it see how ignorant the religion of intellectualism really is. How is mainstream science ever going to understand reality when it is populated by 'scientists' filtering everything through a left-brain that can only perceive sequence, time and apartness? It never is and it was never *meant* to. The idea is to keep people from the truth about reality and the human condition by keeping that knowledge from science. It is the head/heart scientists who are at the cutting edge, not the regular bunch personified by people like Professor Richard Dawkins. He's the Darwinism groupie at Oxford University who targets his nose-in-the-air bile and ridicule at anyone who has another view of reality beyond the edges of his postage stamp. He condemns religion and yet he is the high-priest of his own – Scientism, the belief that only mainstream science has the truth and anything else is blasphemy. I once appeared with him at the Oxford Union years ago. It was like debating with concrete on legs. He didn't like me; I can't think why. The whole Darwinist nonsense, which takes the creator out of Creation, was carefully calculated to indoctrinate a mass perception of life with no purpose, one in which we are mere accidents of 'evolution' and life's a bitch and then you die. It still dominates the collective mind of what is bravely called 'science'.

As with medicine, law and education, so the closed-world of mainstream science is structured to repel all boarders who threaten to breach the dam that passes for its perception. One method is to attack alternative approaches to healing and condemn them as 'crackpot' or 'dangerous', but what could be more crackpot and dangerous to human health than chemotherapy? The science establishment presses for new laws to 'protect' people from alternatives while pursuing policies and technologies that are potentially lethal to both people and planet. Scientists who buck the establishment and seek knowledge through an open mind find their funding and job opportunities disappear. Talk to some of those scientists who have challenged the orthodoxy of global warning, for a start. It is the carrot and stick again and it is used across the entire system to keep dissenters in line and truth in the closet.

Governments destroy Freedom

The first thing to know about governments is that they are not there to serve the interests of the people. They are structured with one thing in mind – *control* of the people. Once you understand that, everything else comes into focus, such as why governments constantly act in the interests of Big Banking, Big Business, Big Pharma, Big Biotech, and their associated organisations and personnel, and against the interests

of the population. How would it be any other way when the same network that owns
the 'Bigs' also owns the governments and any political party with any chance of
forming a government? Life's a lot less complicated when you see what's going on.
There came a time when the people rebelled against rule by royal dictatorship and
demanded a say in who ran their country. So the bloodlines began the process of
replacing the overt royal dictatorships with one that had the appearance of freedom
while being business as usual. Tyranny you could see was replaced with the much more
effective tyranny that you can't see, or most people can't, anyway. The Illuminati's
worst nightmare was for people to be elected to government who were genuinely
independent and had the best interests of the population at heart. Their solution was to
introduce the concept of political parties and they created a structure which, through
funding and organisation, gave those who did not join one of these parties virtually no
hope of being elected to parliament and certainly not forming a government in
association with other genuine independent people. You want to go into politics? Okay,
pick a party. You might note that the word 'structure' keeps coming up. Structure is vital
to the control of the many by the few. The formation of political parties produced the
structure through which members of parliaments, and those at other levels of
government – local and state – could be controlled. Instead of having to force their will
upon hundreds of individuals, all they had to do was force it upon those who controlled
the parties and they, in turn, would enforce it upon their members. Quite simply, if you
want to want to progress in politics you need first to join a party and then keep the
ruling elite of that party as happy as you can by what you do and say. Here we go again.
As with doctors, lawyers, scientists and teachers, you keep your head down, don't rock
the boat, and certainly don't oppose anything significant through personal conscience
that is against the wishes of your party establishment. Real 'progress' in any of these
professions demands that you close your mind or sell your soul. Preferably both.

How appropriate it is that political parties in the UK parliament have people known
as 'Whips' to make sure their MPs vote according to the party line. The very fact that
Whips are allowed to exist and operate openly is testament to the corruption and
irrelevance of politics. They offer wavering MPs promises of good things for them if
they comply, and if they still won't budge they are told the facts of life about the
consequences for their careers. The same system operates in every country, although not
always with official 'Whips' necessarily, and detailed files are kept on politicians, often
aided by access to intelligence agency data, which can be used to terrify a doubter into
line through fear of secrets becoming public. Remember that those who control the
political parties also control the intelligence agency network, not least the Rothschild
dynasty. At that level there are no divisions or moral dilemmas about little things like
integrity and laws on data protection. The more secrets people have that would destroy
them if revealed, the better they are to have in key positions. It they ever try to stand up
against your demands, well, there's always the file. The upper echelons of politics are
full of people who are dancing to the piper for fear of public exposure for anything from
financial fraud to paedophilia. There are basically three types of politician that gets
anywhere near to governmental power: (1) The small minority who are knowingly part
of the conspiracy and aware of its goals; (2) Those who just want power and status and
will do anything to get it, saying and doing whatever it takes; and (3) those who have
big secrets that can be revealed at any time if they refuse to take orders. I am not saying

that every politician is like that, only the vast majority of those who make it to government or to the top of the major opposition parties with any chance of forming a government. The 'cement' that coordinates the manipulation between 'different' political parties and countries is the spider's web of secret societies that I described earlier, with Freemasonry among the most important.

Voting for Rothschild

As the saying goes, it doesn't matter who you vote for, the government still gets in. Yes, the Rothschild / Illuminati / Reptilian government through the control of any party that has a chance of winning office, and many who don't, but can influence policy and opinion. You don't like Rothschild Zionist-controlled Boy Bush? Okay, this is a democracy, so vote for Rothschild Zionist-controlled Obama. You don't like Rothschild Zionist-controlled Gordon Brown and Peter Mandelson in Britain? Then replace them with Rothschild Zionist-controlled David Cameron, the man from the privileged elite family with connections to the Rothschilds. Politics is full of frauds with no integrity who say one thing while believing another. I was taken aback the first time I debated at the Oxford Union to find that the student debaters draw lots to decide if they will speak for or against a motion. Many of them didn't believe what they were supporting and did believe in what they were opposing. It was just a game and yet they appeared to passionately believe in what they were saying. No wonder so many students from the Union end up in politics where they can get very well paid for doing exactly the same. Put all this background together and you see that political parties are merely vehicles to introduce the agenda of the Reptilian-hybrid families, the 'shells' for the Reptilians themselves, that demand the transformation of human society into a global dictatorship. People are saying in ever larger numbers that elections are irrelevant, because nothing ever changes. Well, now it is clear why this is the case. The major parties have been systematically hijacked and brought closer and closer together until the only difference is their name. The parties have to claim to be different or the people would realise that they live in one-party states. The governing party governs and the opposition parties oppose, or appear to, but when the 'opposing' party gets into government it follows the same agenda as the one it replaced and had previously 'opposed'. Meanwhile, the former governing party now opposes the policies it supported in government to fuel the illusion of 'debate' and 'choice'. It's all a mind-game to buy enough time to put the global police state into place along with mass surveillance, microchipped people and a society based on total control (Fig 261). No longer is it a paradox that governments destroy freedom. That is what they are there to do.

Major media destroy information

If you are going to control the people by manipulating their perceptions of reality, you clearly have to dictate the 'information' they receive. This makes control of the media and education utterly essential to any tyranny, and

Figure 261: *Change we can believe in*

Figure 262: *The mushroom approach – keep them in the dark and feed them bullshit*

my goodness how they have achieved that. The global media, by design, constantly targets and activates the reptilian brain through its daily obsession with fear, sex and money to entrap people in emotional turmoil, five-sense desires and low levels of awareness (Fig 262). I was a journalist for years in newspapers, radio and television and if people could see what goes on in newsrooms around the world they would weep. Some of the most closed minds I have ever met have been journalists. Most are programmed with a desperately limited sense of reality which they are employed to transmit as 'news' to the masses. Journalists in general are extraordinarily uninformed about the world they claim to report, but, because they are called 'journalists', they think they must know what is going on. Ignorance and arrogance are a telling combination. As with everything, the global media is owned and controlled by fewer and fewer corporations, which, in the end, is one corporation, anyway. The owners (the bloodline families) appoint and control the editors, who appoint and control the journalists, who write what they are told to write. This top-down power structure allows the families to largely dictate what does and does not appear in the media for the public to read, hear and see. Of course, they can't control every word, but they can and do ensure that the overwhelming majority of what appears in the media is in line with how they want the population to see life and the world (Fig 263).

Figure 263: *The mainstream media encapsulated*

Controlling the media does not mean looking over the shoulder of every journalist. That couldn't happen and it's not necessary. All you have to do is to set the parameters, the 'norms, through which the media filters everything. For example, the norm at one time was that the Earth was flat and today's media would have dismissed and ridiculed at that time anyone who said it was a sphere. They would not have had to be told to do this; they would have done it by reflex action because of the way they were programmed by the norms to see possibility and reality. It is essential to have a media that is ignorant and merely repeats what the establishment 'norms' have programmed them to accept without question. Look at the pathetic way most of the global media repeats the official version of 'global warming' and 'climate change' and rarely even glances at the mass of evidence and scientific opinion that says it's all nonsense. Journalists, like doctors, lawyers, politicians, and the public in general, are *repeaters*. They repeat without question and accept 'everyone-knows-that' norms like a little boy who is told to believe in Santa Claus. This also leads them to ridicule, attack, or simply ignore those who challenge these norms. Yes, there are editors and journalists who are knowingly manipulating for the Illuminati families in their own service-to-self, but they are the few. Most are just clueless babes-in-arms with minds programmed by the system.

More Left-Brainers

So many of the leading 'journalists' and current-affairs presenters and editors are products of the programming machine that we call the elite universities, like Oxford and Cambridge, or the so-called Ivy League universities in the United States. Before they even begin to 'report' the world for the global masses, they go through a long and powerful mind-manipulation programme ('education') to implant their perception of reality. They might be of the political 'left', 'centre' or 'right', but it doesn't matter. They are all 'system people'. They might want to tinker with the details of the system (more tax, less tax), but they don't see the system for what it really is – an enslavement machine and reality-suppressor. I have encountered many such people in the last 20 years from newspapers, radio and television and, while there have been honourable exceptions, the norm has been like having a conversation with a concrete block (apologies to concrete blocks, by the way). I presented the foundations of the global conspiracy and the interconnected nature of 'Big Brother' society to journalists at a news conference when I stood in a parliamentary by-election in 2007. The sitting Conservative MP, David Davis, had resigned his seat and stood again for election in protest, he said, about the gathering Big Brother state. I stood in the election to use the opportunity to highlight the true scale of the real Big Brother, not the sanitised version that Davis was talking about. I must be the only election candidate in history to say he didn't want any votes. They were irrelevant to me. The last thing I wanted to be was a politician, and votes in a rigged system are no measure of anything. All I wanted was a public platform to get information circulating that people would not otherwise get to hear. When you do that, and the mainstream media is involved, you need to understand that they will dismiss, ridicule and misrepresent you. This is what they did with what I said at the news conference; but some people do see through the misrepresentation and it is they who make the frustration of talking to the mainstream media worthwhile.

One of those who attended the news conference was Quentin Letts, the political columnist on the UK national, the *Daily Mail*. This covers many Big Brother-type stories, but refuses to connect the dots so that the real picture can be seen. Letts has had a classic system-indoctrination at the Roman Catholic-controlled Bellarmine University in Kentucky, Trinity College in Dublin, and Jesus College in Cambridge. While his columns are often cynical about politics, as anyone observing it for long would be, he dutifully records reality in the image that the *Daily Mail* demands. If he didn't, of course, he wouldn't be there for long. He sat watching my presentation, part listening, part reading a newspaper, and after nearly an hour of me putting the puzzle pieces together to reveal the *Big* Big Brother, Mr Letts could summon just one question, words to the effect of: 'How much money have you raised for your election fund?' That was it. The following day he dismissed what I had said in one line: 'It's nonsense, of course.' What he meant was that his reality-bubble could not conceive that what I said could in any way be true and so, by definition, it must obviously be nonsense. Once again, what is really possible is mistaken for the limits of what Bubble People *perceive* to be possible. Letts would have said the same about those who declared that the Earth was round. 'Nonsense, of course,' he would have written with his quill pen. How much time had Letts spent researching the subject of a global conspiracy? *Zero*. How much time would he devote to seeing if it's true? *Zero*. This is the most powerful force behind the suppression of information by the mainstream media – self-censorship, closed-minds and ignorance. I was on a radio show in Chicago when a questioner said that he 'didn't buy' the idea that there was a conspiracy. He said he was from the 'old school of journalism' which believed that a conspiracy involving large numbers of people was 'impossible'. It was a classic moment. First of all it doesn't require a 'large number of people' because of compartmentalisation that allows the few to manipulate the many who have no idea what they are daily contributing to. Second, did this 'old school journalist' ever investigate if there *was* a conspiracy? No, of course not. Why? Because he knew that it was impossible, so why bother? I pointed out to this man that he and his like were one of the major reasons that we have got into this mess. They dismiss any possibility of a conspiracy by reflex action and so never do any research to know one way or the other. This is the mentality of the 'journalists' all over the world that stand between what is happening in the world and what they tell you is happening. Yet I still hear people say that if there was a conspiracy 'the media would tell us'. Excuse me a moment, my sides are spitting and I need to find a needle and thread.

Don't Question the Norms

Every day I see newspaper, television and radio journalists misreporting a world they don't understand. They are glued to official history, official norms and the official version of events. It is a disgrace beyond words that mainstream journalists have never questioned the official story of 9/11 while condemning and ridiculing those who do (Fig 264). But how could it be any other way given the Mind-made people that are employed

Figure 264: *The refusal of the mainstream media to investigate the official story of 9/11 is a disgrace*

by the media corporations to report the 'news' in a way which suits the conspiracy and keeps it under wraps? They report politics like a soap opera, us and against them, claim and counter claim, battles for power and public support. They never see or highlight the connections between the apparently unconnected. They never investigate the real reasons why wars are declared in which millions are killed or maimed. The official version of almost everything is just repeated and becomes official history even though the most minor investigation would either demolish what they are reporting as 'fact', or at least offer an alternative explanation for why something is happening as it is. Once the official version is downloaded, like 9/11 and 'climate change', journalists at every level all over the world simply repeat it as fact. This leads to most of the population doing the same. Talk about the blind leading the blind. Many mainstream journalists also tend be lazy. Investigative journalism is bloody hard work, as I know myself after 20 years of it day after day. It is much easier to accept the official version of everything and report events from that perspective. Even better, no-one is going to question what you say or try to discredit you for revealing the truth that the establishment doesn't want the people to know. The media corporations are hardly going to fund journalists for the long-term research necessary to uncover what is really going on and 90 per cent of journalists have no inclination to do so, anyway.

There are exceptions, like the excellent Australian reporter, John Pilger; and there is a guy called Robert Fisk on the UK *Independent* who has reported Israel and the Middle East with a refreshing honesty. Even so, Fisk still feels the need to ridicule me, along with the rest of his profession. While he honestly reports what he sees, his mind won't open to a far bigger picture. Once again, like doctors, lawyers, politicians and the public in general, the psyches of journalists are welded to a programmed sense of reality and so they do what the bloodline families want them to do while dismissing any suggestion that the families even exist. You also have the ubiquitous carrot and stick control-technique yet again. Toe the line of your newspaper, television or radio station and all is well, the cheques keep coming in. Challenge those restrictions and, sorry, we have to let you go. While I was writing this book the CNN presenter, Lou Dobbs, was removed for refusing to toe the network's party line. Dobbs was questioning what his colleagues wouldn't question, including the manipulation into place of a North American Union. One of the blatant media frauds in my view is a guy called Anderson Cooper on CNN. He promotes the image of 'seeking the truth' when he is just another corporate arse-licker who heads for every major war to tell the public the version of events the elite want them to believe. His mother was heiress, Gloria Vanderbilt, great-great-granddaughter of Cornelius Vanderbilt of the Illuminati Vanderbilt dynasty. He attended Yale University before working for the CIA. This was perfect preparation for working for the US media. I watched Cooper 'interview' the CNN 'medical correspondent', Sanjay Gupta, who presented the line of the pharmaceutical cartel on the question of the 'swine flu' vaccine with Cooper just handing him the soft ball questions necessary to trash all criticism of the vaccine. Gupta is hilariously called a 'medical correspondent' when he promotes the Big Pharma agenda, just like 'medical' and 'science' 'correspondents' the world over. Obama offered Gupta the job of Surgeon General. That's how 'safe' he is. No wonder he works for CNN.

Who Owns the Media?

The pyramid structure allows the bloodlines to dominate and influence the media they own right down to what you see and hear. It is sobering to see how few people and corporations control what you watch or read. Bloodline corporations like Disney, National Amusements, Viacom, CBS Corporation, Time Warner, News Corporation, Bertelsmann AG, Sony, General Electric, Vivendi SA, Hearst Corporation, Organizações Globo and Lagardère Group own extraordinary swathes of the global media. Here is a list of companies owned, a few jointly-owned, by Time Warner as of autumn 2009. Er, take your time …

AOL; AOL Radio; AdTech, AG; Advertising.com; AOL By Phone; AOL CallAlert; AOL for Broadband; AOL Latino; AOL International; AOL Instant Messenger; AOL Music; AOL Sports; AOL Local; AOL Voicemail; Bebo; CityGuide; CompuServe; Games.com; GameDaily; ICQ by Mirabilis; Kid's AOL (KOL); LightningCast; MapQuest; Moviefone; MusicNet@AOL; RED; Third Screen Media; Truveo; Weblogs, Inc.; Winamp by Nullsoft; HBO; Cinemax; HBO Independent Productions; HBO Multiplexes; HBO on Demand; Cinemax Multiplexes; Cinemax on Demand; HBO HD; Cinemax HD; HBO Video; HBO Domestic and International Program Distribution; HBO Films; Picturehouse (co-owned by New Line Cinema); HBO Asia; HBO Czech; HBO Hungary; HBO India; HBO Poland; HBO Romania; HBO Latin America Group; HBO Latin America; HBO Brazil; Warner Channel; E! Latin America; Cinemax Latin America; Turner Broadcasting; Adult Swim; Boomerang; Cartoon Network; truTV; TBS; TNT; TCM; WPCH; CNN / U.S.; Airport Network; Headline News; HD Networks; TNT HD; CNN HD; TBS HD; Cartoon Network HD; Adult Swim HD; Cartoon Network Studios; Williams Street; Court TV Original Productions; TNT Originals; TCM Productions; TBS Productions; CNN Originals; Headline News Productions; TCM & Cartoon Network / Asia Pacific; CNN en Español; CNN International; Cartoonito; TNT Latin America; TCM Europe; Pogo; Cartoon Network; Retro; Space; MuchMusic Latin America; I.Sat; Infinito; HTV; Fashion TV Latin America; Accent Health; Cartoon Network Japan CNN+; CETV; CNN-IBN; CNNj; CNN Türk; CNN.de (German); CNN.co.jp (Japanese); NBC / Turner; NASCAR Races; n-tv; Zee / Turner; BOING; CNN Radio; Court TV Radio; Headline News Radio; CNN en Español Radio; Headline News en Español Radio; Adult Swim Video; Cartoon Network Video; Court TV Extra; Crime Library; DramaVision; GameTap; CallToons; Play On! Powered by ACC Select; Super Deluxe; The Smoking Gun; TNT Overtime; Toonami Jetstream; Very Funny Ads; CNNStudentNews.com; CNN.com; CNN Mobile; CNN Newsource; CNN to Go; CNNMoney.com; SI.com; PGA Tour.com and PGA.com; CNN Pipeline; NASCAR.com; Bamzu.com; Dealer Entertainment Network; The Checking Network; Warner Bros; New Line Cinema; New Line Distribution; Picturehouse (co-owned by HBO); New Line Home Entertainment; New Line International Releasing; New Line Merchandising/Licensing; New Line Music; New Line New Media; New Line Television; New Line Theatricals; Warner Bros. Pictures; Castle Rock Entertainment; Warner Bros. Pictures International; Warner Independent Pictures; Warner Bros. International Cinemas; Warner Bros. Studios; Warner Bros. Consumer Products; Warner Bros. Television Group; Warner Bros. Television; Warner Horizon Television; Warner Bros. Television Distribution; Witt/Thomas Productions; QDE Entertainment; Warner Bros. International Television Distribution; Telepictures Productions; The CW Television Network; The CW Daytime; CW Now; Warner Bros. Animation; Hanna-Barbera; Looney Tunes; Kids' WB!; Warner Bros. Home Entertainment Group; Warner Home Video; Warner Premiere; Warner Bros. Family Entertainment; Warner Bros. Domestic Cable Distribution; Warner Bros. Technical Operations; Warner Bros. Anti-Piracy Operations; Warner Bros. Digital Entertainment; Warner Bros. Consumer Products; Warner Bros. Games; Eidos Interactive; Monolith Productions; Warner Bros. Online; DC Comics; *Mad Magazine*; Vertigo; Wildstorm; Warner Bros. Theatrical; *25 Beautiful Gardens*; *25 Beautiful Homes*; *25 Beautiful Kitchens*; *4x4*; *Aeroplane*; *All You*; *Amateur Gardening*; *Amateur Photographer*; *Angler's Mail*; *Better Digital Photography*; *Bird*

Keeper; *BMX Business News*; Bulfinch Press; *Business 2.0*; *Cage & Aviary Birds*; *Caravan*; *Chat*; *Chat Passion Series*; *Classic Boat*; *Coastal Living*; *Cooking Light*; *Country Homes & Interiors*; *Country Life*; *Cycle Sport*; *Cycling Weekly*; *Decanter*; *Entertainment Weekly*; *Essentials*; *European Boat Builder*; *Eventing*; *Farm Holiday Guides*; *First Moments*; *For the Love of Cross Stitch*; *For the Love of Quilting*; *Fortune*; *Freeze*; *FSB: Fortune Small Business*; *Golf magazine*; *Golf Monthly*; *Hair*; *Health*; *Hi-Fi News*; *Homes & Gardens*; *Horse*; *Horse & Hound*; Housetohome.co.uk; *Ideal Home*; *In Style*; *In Style Australia*; *In Style Germany*; *In Style UK*; *International Boat Industry*; *Land Rover World*; *Leisure Arts*; *Life*; *Livingetc*; *Loaded*; *Look Magazine UK*; *Marie Claire*; *Maghound*; *MBR-Mountain Bike Rider*; *Media Networks, Inc.*; *MiniWorld*; *Mizz*; *Mizz Specials*; *Model Collector*; *Money*; *Motor Boat & Yachting*; *Motor Boats Monthly*; *Motor Caravan*; *NME*; *Now*; *Now Style Series*; *Nuts magazine*; *Oxmoor House*; *Park Home & Holiday Caravan*; *People*; *People en Español*; *Practical Boat Owner*; *Practical Parenting*; *Prediction*; *Progressive Farmer*; *Racecar Engineering*; *Real Simple*; *Rugby World*; *Ships Monthly*; *Shoot Monthly*; *Shooting Gazette*; *Shooting Times*; *Ski*; *Skiing*; *Skiing Trade News*; *Soaplife*; *Southern Accents*; *Southern Living*; *Sporting Gun*; *Sports Illustrated*; *Sports Illustrated for Kids*; *Stamp Magazine*; *Sunset*; *Superbike*; *Synapse*; Targeted Media, Inc.; *The Field*; *The Ass Truckers Whole Sale Club*; *The Golf*; *The Guitar Magazine*; *The Railway Magazine*; *This Old House*; This Old House Ventures, Inc.; *Time*; *Time Asia*; *Time Atlantic*; *Time Canada*; *Time Distribution Services*; *Time Europe*; *Time for Kids*; Time Inc. Custom Publishing; Time Inc. Home Entertainment; *Time Latin America*; *Time South Pacific*; *TV & Satellite Week*; *TV Easy*; *TV Times*; *Uncut*; *VolksWorld*; *Wallpaper Navigator*; *Wallpaper*; Warner Publishing Services; Webuser; *Wedding & Home*; *What Camera*; *What Digital Camera*; *What's On TV*; *Who Weekly*; *Woman*; *Woman & Golf*; *Woman & Home*; *Woman's Feelgood Series*; *Woman's Own*; *Woman's Own Lifestyle Series*; *Woman's Weekly*; *Woman's Weekly Fiction Series*; *Woman's Weekly Fiction Special*; *Woman's Weekly Home Series*; *World Soccer*; *Yachting Monthly*; *Yachting World*; Ubu Productions; Uncut Presents Series.

Phew. It is like almost everything in global society. You see different names that appear to be 'individual' organisations and companies, but they are all ultimately owned and controlled by a ridiculously few people. The same families own the 'right-wing' stations and the 'left' or 'liberal' networks. This may seem contradictory, but it's not. They have to keep all shades of political opinion in the pen and, for instance, by having Fox News coming from the Republican angle and MSNBC supporting the Democrats they pull supporters of both into the illusion of 'choice' when, in fact, the same families control not only both parties, but both 'news' stations. It is the same in the UK where we have the 'right-wing' *Sun* and the 'left-wing' *Guardian*. They come from a slightly different angle, far smaller than would at first appear, but in all fundamentals with regard to reality they report the world the same. If you want to meet someone who is coming purely from Mind and the left hemisphere of the brain, go see a *Guardian* journalist. There are those who seem to be challenging the system, but look closer and you'll see different. John Stewart on America's *Daily Show* makes fun of politicians and highlights some of their hypocrisy. When, however, he has people like Tony Blair live on the show he fails to ask them the telling questions that would expose their lies and deceit. Stewart said during a fawning interview with Homeland Security Secretary, Janet Napolitano, that those who believed in government conspiracies were 'crazies' and he urged that 'the conspiracies should be executed'. It was a strange sentence and maybe he meant to say 'conspiracy theorists'. That's nice and alternative, Mr 'Funny Man'. I also once met a chap called Bill Maher who, to me, seemed an extremely wound up and mixed up bloke. He's another in the United States with a reputation for not being politically correct, but there are few who ridicule and attack people challenging the official story of 9/11 more than Maher. Guys like these make fun of the system, but only within strictly limited boundaries. I call them 'steam whistles'. They allow people to release frustration without ever being a threat to the prevailing world view.

Zion Mainframe (Media Branch)

Once more the Rothschild-Zionist network is at the fore when it comes to the media, as it is with politics, banking, and so on. Look at the Rothschild Zionist control of the entertainment and media industry in the form of people like Fox News President, Peter Chernin (Rothschild Zionist); NBC News President, Neil Shapiro (Rothschild Zionist); ABC News President, David Westin (Rothschild Zionist); Paramount Pictures Chairman, Brad Grey (Rothschild Zionist); Walt Disney CEO, Robert Igor (Rothschild Zionist); Sony Pictures Chairman Michael Lynton (Rothschild Zionist); Warner Brothers Chairman, Barry Meyer (Rothschild Zionist); AOL division of AOL-Time-Warner Chairman and CEO, Jonathan Miller (Rothschild Zionist); Miramax Films CEO, Harvey Weinstein (Rothschild Zionist); CBS CEO, Leslie Moonves (Rothschild Zionist); Chairman of Paramount Pictures' Motion Picture Group, Sherry Lansing (Rothschild Zionist); MGM Chairman, Harry Sloan (Rothschild Zionist); NBC/Universal Studios CEO, Jeff Zucker (Rothschild Zionist); and News Corporation tycoon, Rupert Murdoch (Rothschild Zionist). Murdoch's enormous news and media empire includes the Fox network, Sky Television network, Star TV, 20th Century Fox, My Space, and a long list of newspapers around the world, including the UK's *Sun, News of the World, Times* and *Sunday Times*; and the *New York Post* and *Wall Street Journal*. News York's biggest daily, the *New York Times*, is owned by the Sulzberger family (Rothschild Zionists), while the owner of the *New York Daily News* and US World Report is Mortimer Zuckerman (Rothschild Zionist). The Rothschild Zionist-controlled *New York Times* also owns thirty-three other newspapers, including the *Boston Globe*; twelve magazines, seven radio and TV broadcasting stations, three book publishing companies and a cable-TV system. The *New York Times News Service* also supplies more than 500 other newspapers, agencies and magazines with 'information'. The *Washington Post* has been long-time controlled by the family of the late Katharine Meyer Graham (Rothschild Zionist) and its holdings include other newspapers, television and magazines, including *Newsweek*. The Rothschild Zionists also dominate news agencies and book publishing. Their control over these Rothschild Zionist media conglomerates, added to their massive influence over banking and politics, forms an interconnecting web that gives the Rothschilds and their Zionist cabal truly shocking levels of control over global society and the information that people receive – or don't. The *Los Angeles Times* columnist, Joel Stein (Rothschild Zionist), wrote an article proclaiming that Americans who don't think Jews (Rothschild Zionists) control Hollywood are just plain 'dumb' (Fig 265). Stein went on:

> The Jews are so dominant. I had to scour the trades to come up with six Gentiles in high positions at entertainment companies. But lo and behold, even one of that six, AMC

President Charles Collier, turned out to be a Jew! ... As a proud Jew, I want America to know of our accomplishment. Yes, we control Hollywood.

Not only Hollywood. Shahar Ilan, a daily features editor with the leading Israeli newspaper, *Ha'aretz*, wrote: 'The Jews do control the American media. This is very clear, and claiming otherwise is an insult to common knowledge.' The Rothschilds are the close-to-the-spider orchestrators of the global tyranny that requires for its success the control of information from which the people construct their sense of reality. This is why 'major media destroys information'. I love the quote from Abraham Foxman, National Director of the Anti-Defamation League, who told the *Jerusalem Post*:

Figure 265: *Rothschild Zionists control the media and the 'entertainment' industry*

There is now a new form of American anti-Semitism much like the old form. This new form says that Jews run the banks, the newspapers, and Hollywood. The difference is that now, that perception is gaining ground in the mainstream.

Now, Abe, old chap, why do you think that perception could possibly be gaining ground? Try the fact that it just happens to be blatantly *true*. But the foundation of hate laws is that truth is no defence. I am worried about a perception gaining ground in the mainstream that the Sun comes up every morning and goes down every night. This could lead to Anti-

Figure 266: *The Internet has been used magnificently to expose the Orwellian agenda, and the bloodline families are now seeking to suppress the free flow on information on the Web*

Solarism and anyone who believes in sunrise and sunset should be banned from doing so. Bring in the hate laws, I say.

Censoring the Internet

The real journalism today can be found on the Internet and produced by people who are willing to go where the mainstream lackeys are too ignorant or too frightened to go. Yes, there is a mountain of crap on the Web, but there is some magnificent investigative journalism, too, which is way ahead of anything you will find in newspapers or on radio and television (Fig 266). So much so that the mainstream news media, especially newspapers, are fast losing viewers and sales. The Illuminati families control the telecom giants and the major servers and search engines, and the Internet has given them some major benefits in terms of surveillance, but there has been a downside with the explosion of information across the Net about their covert operations and manipulation of the population. It has been getting out of hand from their point of view and you are going to see increasing efforts to censor and edit the Internet. This must not be allowed to happen. The genie is out and he's not going back, but there will be many challenges to overcome as the Illuminati networks seek to censor the Net by employing every excuse they can think of. One, naturally, will be 'cyber terrorism' and the man pushing for Internet censorship is, well, well, well, Senator Jay Rockefeller. He jointly introduced the Cybersecurity Act of 2009 that gives the president the right to 'declare a cybersecurity emergency' and to either close down or restrict any information network 'in the interest of national security'. Who would decide what was a 'cybersecurity emergency'? The president, or rather those who control him. Rockefeller actually said that it 'would have been better if we'd have never invented the Internet'. Better for whom, Mr Rockefeller? Ah, for *you*; gotcha. As I write, Internet censorship bills are being presented in the United States, United Kingdom and Australia to give governments the power to dictate what can and cannot appear on the Web and this is a step-by-step plan to introduce Chinese-like censorship throughout the world.

Given all of the above, anyone who cared about the free flow of information would welcome the challenge by the people's news sources on the Internet to the biased and suppressed sources of 'news' that we have endured in the mainstream since the modern media emerged. But Barack Obama doesn't want freedom of expression – he serves the system that wants to destroy it. Obama has said that he would consider a bail-out of the failing news industry because otherwise Internet news sources would take over the world and that would be a 'threat to democracy'. What democracy? And democracy is a dictatorship, anyway. Obama said: 'I am concerned that if the direction of the news is all blogosphere, all opinions, with no serious fact-checking, no serious attempts to put stories in context, that what you will end up getting is people shouting at each other across the void but not a lot of mutual understanding.' No, Mr Fake, you are concerned that you will continue to be subjected to legitimate investigation and exposure by Internet sites that refuse to be the journalistic prostitutes of the mainstream that give you such a free ride. Newspapers are failing because most of them are biased, boring, blatantly controlled and bloody irrelevant.

The remaining paradox in Michael Ellner's list is 'religion destroys spirituality', and I covered the religion agenda at length earlier. The main function of religion is to stop people making the awakened connection to Consciousness and they do this by manipulating people to give their focus, energy and power to hierarchies, deities, images and made-up stories that imprison the mind in rigid belief. In this, religion is at one with government, law, science, medicine, education, the media and the other institutions that I have highlighted. They all adhere to basically the same blueprint and modus operandi programmed into the Metaphysical Universe and played out by anyone trapped in the vibrational frequency of Mind. Given that they were all created to enslave the global population, it is no longer a mystery why they destroy everything they claim to stand for.

24

Game Plan (5): 'World' Everything

People can foresee the future only when it coincides with their own wishes, and the most grossly obvious facts can be ignored when they are unwelcome
George Orwell

The Reptilians and their hybrid bloodlines are now seeking to complete their long-term plan for total control of humankind and this is so close today that only the most self-denying automaton could fail to see it. But, then, there are still whole nations of such people with minds so blinded by the system that they can't see the obvious. The media alone is full of them.

I said many years ago that there would come a time when what had remained hidden through the centuries would have to break the surface where it could be seen. When you have been covertly planning to transform society into a global prison camp there must come that moment when you are so close to completion that people begin to see what is happening. It leaves the shadows of the planning and covert stages and becomes the literal and symbolic bricks and mortar that we can touch and see. We are in that time now and the pace of the gathering dictatorship has been increasing by the week, especially since 9/11. If anyone is still in any doubt that this is true, I will describe the nature of the global society the Reptilian agenda is designed to impose. See if you recognise it ...

The foundation of any tyranny is centralisation of power. The principle is always the same, whether in a family, where the father or mother dictates events, or in a global Orwellian State where the few enforce their will on everyone else. If you don't centralise power and decision-making you cannot impose a dictatorship. This is why we have today what is called 'globalisation'. It is the centralisation of power in all areas of our lives – government, banking, business, the media, the military, everything. I was saying from the early 1990s that this was the plan and now here we are with the centralisation of global power given its own name ... 'globalisation'. Millions protest about the consequences of this accumulated power that is devastating lives, communities and countries around the world. This is especially true of the weak and poor who are mercilessly exploited by cold and corrupt corporations (corporation singular, in fact) which are owned and controlled by the hybrid families. What the protestors don't seem to realise, however, is that the corporations are not the *engineers* of globalisation; they are merely the *vehicles* for it. The politically 'left-of-centre', and the academia that supports it, are Mind-made people overwhelmingly and they still see the system in

Illustration by Neil Hague (www.neilhague.com)

Figure 267: *The planned global pyramid headed by a world government controlled by the Illuminati families and, ultimately, by the Reptilians*

terms of us and them, black and white, left and right. This makes it difficult to see the unity of purpose behind the apparently different 'sides' and every facet of globalisation – 'education', politics of all shades, the media, religion, law, medicine, Big Pharma, Big Biotech, and all the rest. These are all working as one unit controlled by the same force and they seek the same end of human enslavement. How can there truly be different 'sides' in politics when no matter what 'side' gets in, 'left', 'right' or 'centre', the same agenda continues to play out? Does anyone think there are really different 'sides' in the oil cartel, pharmaceutical cartel, biotech cartel, and so on?

Squeezing Diversity

The plan is to centrally-control the planet with a structure of world government, world army, world central bank, world currency and a microchipped population connected to a global computer system and the global positioning satellite network (Fig 267). I have been warning about this for two decades, and look at the world today; it's *happening*, and so fast. Humans once lived in tribes where tribal leaders, chiefs or councils made decisions for the tribe. Tribes were then brought together into 'nations' and a few people at the centre enforced their decisions on all the amalgamated tribes. The next stage is to bring the nations together into superstates to allow a few people at the centre to enforce their decisions on all the nations. The first superstate was the European Union, followed by the emerging African Union, and these are planned to be joined by a North American Union – eventually a union of the whole of the Americas – an Asia-Pacific Union, and possibly others. At the top of this structure is planned to be a world government that enforces its decisions on the superstates, which enforce them on the nations, or rather the regions. The idea is to break up countries into regions and dilute any unity of response to the world government/superstate dictatorship. The Scottish and Welsh parliaments and the attempts to introduce regional government in England are all part of this agenda which is being sold, irony of ironies, as devolving 'power to the people'. The European Union was evolved, as planned from the start, from the 'free-trade' zone called the Common Market, or European Economic Community. In the same way, the North American Union (Fig 268) is planned to emerge from the 'free trade' zone called the North American Free Trade Agreement (NAFTA), and the Asia-Pacific Union from the 'free trade' zones called Asia-Pacific Economic Cooperation (APEC) and the Association of Southeast Asian Nations (ASEAN).

This is happening bit-by-bit, step-by-step, via the Totalitarian Tiptoe, although the pace is quickening every day. When I put 'Asia-Pacific Union' into an Internet search engine a

few minutes ago, there at the top of the list was
the headline: 'Australian PM wants Asia-Pacific
Union'. Australian Prime Minister, Kevin Rudd,
an asset of the Fabian Society, said he wanted to
see an 'Asia-Pacific Community' by 2020
structured like the European Union. Oh really?
I'm shocked. Rudd said there was a 'brittleness'
in bilateral ties and, while regional bodies like
ASEAN and APEC had achieved much, there
was a need for a 'region-wide architecture' to
tackle the growing challenges of the Asia-Pacific
century. Oh, nice one, Kev, you read the script to
the letter. Hey, but don't forget to scare 'em, too:
'Terrorism in Southeast Asia will remain a
continuing challenge ... across wider

Figure 268: *The North American Union will spell the end of America as a sovereign nation state*

continental Asia, the rise of India and China represent great economic, environmental,
energy policy and security reverberations for the future.' Well done, Kev, you're good.
Rudd said an Asia-Pacific Community, including the United States, Japan, China, India,
Indonesia and the other states of the region, would encourage cooperation and action on
economic, political and security issues and also develop a 'genuine and comprehensive
sense of community'. Bollocks, Mr Dud. It is designed to impose centralisation of control
over that vast area of the Earth and you bloody well know it. Rudd is the leader of the
Australian Labour Party (see the Fabian Society) and he is pursuing precisely the same
agenda as his predecessor, the leader of the Australian Liberal [Conservative] Party, John
'where do you want me to lick, Mr Bush?' Howard. They are different frontmen for the
same force, just like Bush and Obama in the United States, and Blair/Brown/Mandelson/
Cameron in the UK (Fig 269). You might be able, in theory, to vote to change the leader,

but not the policy they are all following.
The illusion of 'sides' is only there to fool
the people into believing they are
selecting their government. They ain't.
There is one government under two
names, or three names in some countries.
Miguel D'Escoto Brockmann, President of
the United Nations General Assembly,
presented a document in June 2009
openly calling for global government. It
said:

> Globalization without effective global
> or regional institutions is leading the
> world into chaos. It impedes the global
> decisions and actions necessary to
> confront the challenges facing
> humanity, especially in the
> environmental area. The control of

Figure 269: *The pyramid within pyramid structure means that all roads lead eventually to the Reptilians and their hybrid families*

global institutions by forces that are both reticent to democratize but eager to minimize has contributed to the world political malaise of lack of solutions to urgent global problems.

Some countries have found that the best route to determining their own destiny is in regional organizations. The principle should be to strengthen the United Nations and especially the General Assembly as the body with one nation one vote that can create a global institutional sphere with legitimacy. At the same time, the regional level should be strengthened.

This is the agenda word for word. Centralise global power through what we call globalisation and when the people suffer the consequences of that you offer the solution – even greater centralisation of global power. 'Father' D'Escoto, a Roman Catholic (Church of Babylon) priest and a member of the Illuminati Jesuit Order, also demanded a list of new United Nations institutions to transform the present UN into a world government. These were:

The Global Stimulus Fund
The Global Public Goods Authority (Sea, Space, Cyberspace)
The Global Tax Authority
The Global Financial Products Safety Commission
The Global Financial Regulatory Authority
The Global Competition Authority
The Global Council of Financial and Economic Advisors
The Global Economic Coordination Council
The World Monetary Board

No wonder the United Nations' logo looks like a target aimed at the world (Fig 270). Father D'Escoto's blueprint for global dictatorship, called the 'World Financial and Economic Crisis and its Impact on Development Draft Outcome Document', included point after point that I have been warning about for two decades and the themes are now being constantly repeated by world leaders and commentators. Gordon Brown, the

Figure 270: *The Reptilians and their bloodlines targeting the world*

British Prime Minister at the time of writing, is a member and puppet of the Illuminati Fabian Society, which has guided Labour Party policy since it helped to form the party in 1900. His predecessor, Tony Blair, is another 'Fabian Man' and both have worked and plotted to advance the Fabian agenda for a global socialist/fascist state. Brown called for the creation of a 'truly global society' (world government) and 'a new financial architecture for the global age' (world central bank and all that goes with it). He told the US Congress in the wake of the economic crash of 2008 that 'we should seize the moment, because never before have I seen a world so willing to come together'. Put another way – we have the people just where we want them to get what we want. The Pope is the official head – emphasis on *official* – of the Church of Babylon, now known as the Church of Rome. The Pope has also called for a world government. He said that a 'true world political authority' must be introduced to 'manage the global economy . . . revive economies hit by the crisis . . . [and] avoid any deterioration of the present crisis and the greater imbalances that would result'. This authority 'would need to be universally recognised and . . . vested with the effective power to ensure security for all, regard for justice, and respect for rights'. He added: 'Financiers must rediscover the genuinely ethical foundation of their activity so as to not abuse the sophisticated instruments which can serve to betray the interests of savers.' The Alan Greenspan wing of the conspiracy creates the economic crash and the Papal wing says we must have a world government to deal with it. The cement that connects them both is the Rothschilds. This is how the world government and the rest of the fascist structure is planned to be introduced – a combination of Problem-Reaction-Solution, No-Problem-Reaction-Solution and the Totalitarian Tiptoe, which is fast becoming a sprint.

World War III

The agenda includes a third world war involving North America, Europe, Russia and China. The State of Israel is being prepared to be at least one of the triggers for this together with Pakistan, North Korea and countries around the Caspian Sea, like Iran. The idea is to create a global conflict (problem) that will lead to the imposition of a world government and world army to 'stop it ever happening again'. This is precisely the technique used after the first and second world wars to justify the enormous concentration of global power through new institutions like the Rothschild/Rockefeller-created United Nations, European Union, World Bank, International Monetary Fund, and their many associated organisations. They need to destroy the 'superpowers' of the United States, China and Russia if they are going to install their world government tyranny. What better way to do this than to play them off against each other in a war of mutual destruction? The American Freemasonic 'superstar', Albert Pike, is said to have detailed in the 19th century the three world wars that were planned to transform Planet Earth into a centralised tyranny. Albert Pike, a Sovereign Grand Commander of the Scottish Rite of Freemasonry, and major Illuminati operative, is alleged to have written a letter in 1871 to an infamous Illuminati agent called Giuseppe Mazzini in which he outlined the three world wars that would lead to global domination. The first war, he is said to have written, would overthrow the Czars in Russia through a conflict between the British and Germanic empires. The second would lead to political Zionism being strong enough to install a sovereign State of Israel in Palestine. There are those who say the letter never existed, but, as with the *Protocols of the Elders of Zion*, the forger must have been an inspired prophet. This is what Pike is supposed to have said about World War III:

> The Third World War must be fomented by taking advantage of the differences caused by the 'agentu' [a term also used in the Protocols] of the 'Illuminati' between the political Zionists and the leaders of the Islamic World. The war must be conducted in such a way that Islam (the Moslem Arabic World) and political Zionism (the State of Israel) mutually destroy each other. Meanwhile, the other nations, once more divided

on this issue, will be constrained to fight to the point of complete physical, moral, spiritual and economical exhaustion ... We shall unleash the Nihilists and the atheists, and we shall provoke a formidable social cataclysm which in all its horror will show clearly to the nations the effect of absolute atheism, origin of savagery and of the most bloody turmoil.

Then everywhere, the citizens, obliged to defend themselves against the world minority of revolutionaries, will exterminate those destroyers of civilization, and the multitude, disillusioned with Christianity, whose deistic spirits will from that moment be without compass or direction, anxious for an ideal, but without knowing where to render its adoration, will receive the true light through the universal manifestation of the pure doctrine of Lucifer, brought finally out in the public view [the Reptilians]. This manifestation will result from the general reactionary movement which will follow the destruction of Christianity and atheism, both conquered and exterminated at the same time.*

* Source: *Commander William Guy Carr, former Intelligence Officer in the Royal Canadian Navy, quoted in* Satan: Prince of This World.

Note the line about the war being 'conducted in such a way that Islam and political Zionism [the State of Israel] mutually destroy each other'. Rothschild Zionism has never been about the interests of Jewish people and they are being set up to be annihilated just as much as anyone else. Rothschild Zionism and Jewish people in general are not the same thing. It was reported in July 2009 that the Russian President, Dmitry Medvedev, and Chinese President, Hu Jintao, had issued an 'urgent warning' to the United States that if it allowed an Israeli nuclear attack on Iran 'World War will be our response'. A little advice to anyone in Israel/Palestine: if you see the Rothschilds leaving, get the hell out of there.

The People Policing the People

The authorities already know a war of some kind is coming and they are secretly preparing for it. I received a letter in early 2008 from a UK traffic warden who issued fines to motorists for illegal parking. He had become extremely alarmed and bewildered by information he had been given in the course of his work. The warden (I will call him 'Andy') had been doing the job for some two decades and it had always been focused on issues relating to traffic and parking law – nothing else. This is all that traffic wardens were supposed to be involved with. Everything was fine, he said, until about five years earlier when changes in management brought a whole new change of emphasis. Suddenly, it was no longer about keeping the traffic moving efficiently; it was all about issuing as many parking tickets as possible to increase dramatically the money taken from motorists in fines. Andy said that many wardens left in protest with comments like, 'The heart has been ripped out of this job,' and, 'We are now managed by robots.' In his letter to me, Andy described how he had been asked to see his office manager for a 'quiet word', during which he was given three cards for himself and his colleagues. The first card dealt with his work on parking issues. Fair enough, that's his job; but the other two left him confused and increasingly concerned about what was going on. Card number two was a 'PACE' card, short for 'Police Action and Court Evidence', with the words that police officers have to say by law when they are arresting someone: 'You do not have to say anything, but it may harm your defence if you do not mention when questioned something which you later rely on in court. Anything you do say may be given in evidence.' Traffic wardens had no need whatsoever to know this police caution text. They were not in a position where they would – or could by law – use it. Only the police and some other government law enforcement officers have the power of arrest. The third card authorised Andy and his colleagues to act on behalf of the local council for the enforcement of various statutory provisions – 'including entering and inspecting premises'.

Excuse me? What on earth had entering and inspecting premises and the words said during a police arrest got to do with people who simply issued tickets to motorists who were illegally parked? This was the question Andy put to his bosses when the cards were issued, but he was told that they had been ordered to distribute them and he should just keep them safe and await further instructions. Andy later met a police officer he knew from some years before. After a general chat among other wardens, the officer pulled Andy aside and said he wanted to speak in private. He said that Andy should not breathe a word of what he was about to say and he was only telling him the information because he was an old friend. He said that for months he had been on 'special duties' coordinating a top secret operation, meeting with 'top brass' from the police and national and local government. This was happening all over the country, he said, and certain officers had been chosen – or were being made – to do what he was doing. The officer asked for another promise from Andy not to reveal details of the conversation before saying that the government was preparing for what he was about to reveal 'well, well, in advance'. They were expecting ' ... a war, a lot of riots, a lot of very big trouble.' The officer said that he understood that Andy and his colleagues had been given a number of cards, one with the PACE caution and one giving permission to enter various premises. He went on:

> Let's just say, I know, now, the reason you have been given them is because when all of this happens, and it will, we [the police] will be on the front line with the armed forces and people in your kind of jobs ... parking wardens, security officers, CCTV operatives and so on will be required to do our job.

'You must be joking, that's crazy!' Andy said, but the officer said this was no joke: 'This is on the level. I am just putting you wise to what will happen, but the main thing is please don't tell anyone.' So here was a police officer, on the inside of this covert operation, saying there was going to be a war and that the expected mass protests were going to be dealt with by the police and the military while the normal police work was going to be done by traffic wardens, private security guards, CCTV operatives, and so on. Andy contacted me in March 2008 to tell me the story, but his conversation with the police officer happened some months earlier. The 'war' and the preparations to meet the public response have been in the planning a long time and a 'war' is only part of it. Reaction to compulsory vaccinations and a global economic collapse is also part of this covert operation. A few days after I received Andy's letter and saw the cards he was talking about, the government announced that traffic wardens were going to be renamed 'civil enforcement officers' and their powers increased and expanded to include some of the tasks normally done by the police. A few months later, in August 2008, the UK government said that a new designation of law enforcement called 'Accredited Persons' was being introduced. 'Accredited Persons' were to be a whole list of 'civilians' accredited to do police work and these included ... security guards, council officials, car park attendants, store detectives, park wardens, even stewards at sporting events. This is exactly what the police officer described to Andy the best part of a year earlier and the plan is to continue to hand police powers to the non-police and add ever more layers of civilian law enforcement agencies. The same is happening everywhere and this is the reason for Barack Obama calling for a United States civilian security force as well-funded as the US Marines.

There are already thousands of these Orwellian-entitled 'Accredited Persons' under the 'Community Safety Accreditation Scheme' and the numbers are going to explode. All they have to do is pay, or have their employers pay, a small fee for their next-to-no-training and next-to-no-background-checks and off they can go onto the streets where they can stop vehicles, issue fines, take photographs of people, patrol with dogs, confiscate property and demand names and addresses. It has reached the point where people who drop litter, no matter how minor, are being photographed when they refuse to give their names to these agents of the State and their picture printed in the local paper like a wanted poster. Alex Deane of Big Brother Watch said: 'This is little less than state-sanctioned vigilantism ... It's even worse than policing on the cheap, it's policing without the checks and balances that we get with the actual police force.' For the moment, 'Accredited Persons' will wear badges on their current uniforms, but the government plans eventually to have them all in special uniforms (in time for the war, no doubt, and black shirts would be most appropriate). They will join the former traffic wardens, now the Orwellian-entitled Civil Enforcement Officers, and the so-called 'Special Constables' who also do police work without the same level of training. Together, with yet more classic Orwellian language, this little lot are being called by the government 'the extended police family'. 'Family', see; sounds cuddly and non-threatening to obscure the reality of what it really represents. They were far more accurately being dubbed 'Jacqui Smith's Secret Police' or 'Smith's Stasi' after the notorious East German Stasi secret police and the British Home Secretary who was officially behind the policy, but, of course, wasn't in truth. Jacqui Smith was utterly inept and out of her depth as Home Secretary and was fired in 2009. She was the poodle of her 'advisors' and top civil servants and played the role of an official rubber stamp. It wasn't *her* policy she was bringing in to law; it was the Illuminati's, and they are always in office no matter what the name on the door. This is how it is in every country thanks to the global spider's web of interconnecting secret societies and groups – the 'corporation'.

Global Police Force

The Third World War is also planned to be the catalyst to introduce a world army, which, as I have been saying all these years, is designed to be an amalgamation of NATO, the United Nations 'peacekeeping' operation and other groupings like the army of the African Union, the proposed European Union army, and others. The plan is to have no national armies and the world government in control of the global military. The world army would be centrally commanded and operate at lower levels as the armies of the superstates stationed around the regions that are planned to replace nations. This would mean the centrally-controlled world military would be operating (dictating) at every level, from global to local community. It would be a planetary version of the military structure in Nazi Germany or China, both of which are blueprints for the global society the Reptilians and their hybrids have worked for so long to impose. We are talking a global police/military state that would rule the population with an iron fist. Have you noticed how the police are increasingly looking and acting like the military? What you are seeing is the rapid transition from the old way of policing, which only people of my age would largely remember, and the military dictatorship that is

Illustration by David Dees (deesillustration.com)

Figure 271: *The police are looking, and behaving, more and more like the military*

coming in by the hour (Fig 271). Whatever the French President and Rothschild/Mossad agent, Nicolas Sarkozy, proposes is Illuminati policy, end of story. It is no surprise then that he is pressing for the creation of a European Army which would be the European Union arm of the world army. Former British Defence Secretary, John Hutton, dubbed anyone questioning Sarkozy's plan as 'pathetic': 'I'm not one of those EU haters [who think] anything to do with the EU must by definition be terrible,' he said. 'There's plenty of them around. I think frankly those kind of views are pathetic.' How funny, the same word came to mind when I read Hutton's comments. Isn't synchronicity incredible? These people are clueless as to what is going on and this guy was Britain's Defence Secretary, although thankfully no more. But then, those who followed have been equally inept. There are some in politics who do know at least some of the real agenda, people like Obama, Blair, Sarkozy, Cheney, Father George Bush, and their like, but most of them are just useful idiots, babes-in-arms. Another aspect of this is the increasing number of military and naval 'exercises' that involve multiple countries, including the United States and China, and it is all part of the transition from national armies to a world army. I was once asked by a mainstream 'journalist' what would be the point of a world army … 'after all, there would be no-one to fight.' Deep breath, shake head, move on. The reason for a world army and no other, of course, is that the world government would then have complete power to impose its will on any country or individual who refused to obey the will of the world government.

Robot Army

There is a whole network of weaponry out in space ready to be aimed at the Earth and any country or group that fails to comply. It is like a mega version of a James Bond movie, except that this, unfortunately, is not fiction. The space weaponry, including lasers and other energy weapons, has been developed and installed behind cover stories like 'Star Wars' initiatives and satellite systems. It is paid for by what are called 'black budgets' that are kept off the official government balance sheets and involve Illuminati front-companies like Lockheed Martin, Boeing, Northrop Grumman, and other US

Figure 272: *The remotely-controlled 'robot' aircraft, the Predator*

defence contractors and companies involved in military and civilian space contracts. It is overseen by the appalling Defense Advanced Research Projects Agency (DARPA). This is the US Department of Defense agency officially responsible for the development of new military technology. In fact, it is far more than that and one of the most sinister organisations on Earth. The plan is also to create literally a robot army in which technology is used to kill and control people, directed by operators, joysticks in hand, at some secret and secure location nowhere near their target. We are seeing this already with the remotely-controlled 'drone' aircraft that are increasingly used for bombing raids and surveillance, but check around the Internet and you'll see how remotely-controlled 'robot troops' and mobile weaponry are rapidly being developed. Well, not even developed so much, because the technology is already in place. It is just a matter of introducing it. A company called Robotic Technology Inc (RTI) has produced a military robot that can refuel itself by extracting and consuming energy from biomass in the environment – including dead bodies. It is called the Energetically Autonomous Tactical Robot, or 'EATR'. Dr Robert Finkelstein, President of RTI, told Fox News that the EATR would be programmed not to consume human or animal bodies. The US Congress wants a third of ground combat vehicles to be unmanned robots by 2015. More than four thousand robots are already being used in Iraq with others in Afghanistan. The media reported that a remote-controlled MQ-1 Predator aircraft (Fig 272) was activated from seven thousand miles away to kill 'terrorist suspects' travelling in a car and now the US military is dramatically increasing the number of robot technologies that make their own decisions when to kill and not kill. The conspirators are massively outnumbered by the population, and when the time comes that their Control System is so obvious that the people rebel and seek them out, they need to be able to stay hidden while their technology goes to war for them. That is the idea of the robot army.

The plan is to also have global 'civilian' law enforcement – another arm of the military in truth – in the form of a world police force. The United Nations and the International Criminal Police Organization, better known as Interpol, have been meeting to discuss the formation of a worldwide police operation that would have access to a global database of DNA, biometric and fingerprint records. At the centre of these discussions is Ronald K Noble, an advisor to the Chinese government on policing major events and the man who agreed to the attacks on the Branch Davidian compound in Waco, Texas, in 1993 when 56 men and women and 20 children were burned to death or shot by the federal government of Bill Clinton. Noble was Undersecretary for Enforcement at the United States Department of the Treasury and after the horrors at Waco he worked to suppress the truth of what really happened. Noble was selected to become secretary-general of Interpol by Clinton's attorney general, Janet Reno, another architect of the Waco mass murder. He is now calling for a global database to maintain instantly-retrievable records of everyone on Earth to be used by his world police force.

Global Financial Crash

The global institutions and structures are to be imposed – including the world central bank and world currency – by engineering problems for which they can propose 'solutions'. They want the world central bank to control all global finance and a single electronic currency (no cash) to replace all existing currencies. To do that they need extreme economic problems so they can suggest the solution of a world

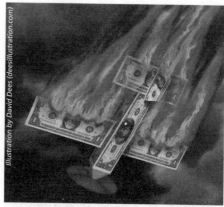

Figure 273: *The plan is to eventually scrap the dollar*

central bank and global currency. Jesuit Father Miguel D'Escoto Brockmann, President of the United Nations General Assembly, was exploiting the economic crisis to propose world government and global control of finance when he presented that UN document in June 2009. The document said: '… it is not possible to continue globalizing human relations without global regulation and institutions … Our growing global problem set will also eventually require global financial mechanisms to solve them.' Problem-Reaction-Solution. The United Nations called, in September 2009, for a new global reserve currency to be administered by a new global reserve bank, and the International Monetary Fund began to expand its operation to become a de facto world central bank. The call was made in a report for the UN Conference on Trade and Development, co-authored by German economist and globalist, Heiner Flassbeck. The same theme is being pressed all over the world by agents of the cabal in China, Russia, Europe and North America. The dollar is doomed, that's for sure (Fig 273).

We saw the start of this mind-game with the economic crash in September 2008 in the last weeks of the Bush Administration, but that was only stage one. This was immediately followed by Bush and his banker's boy, Treasury Secretary and former head of Goldman [Rothschild] Sachs, Henry 'Hank' Paulson, handing billions in borrowed taxpayer 'money' to the banks that caused the crisis. It would later become trillions. Never mind the families going under because of the greed of the bankers. We must save the bankers, or gangsters/banksters as they really are. In June 2009, amid an economic crisis and after receiving $12.9 billion from the taxpayer bailout fund, Goldman Sachs announced the biggest staff bonuses in the firm's history. They're laughing at us. 'Mr Change' Obama not only continued with the same bailout policy when he replaced Bush, he expanded it enormously with trillion upon trillion of borrowed money thrown at the banks and the 'stimulus' packages. These ludicrous sums of borrowed 'money' are the foundation of stage two in this three-stage plan to crash the economy so deeply that a world central bank can be presented as the 'only solution'. Stage two is to ensure that governments reach the limits of their ability to respond to the economic crisis by fire-hosing borrowed money in all directions. When the bullets are shot and the barrels are empty, the bloodline families plan to further crash the economy in stage three. This will be unleashed at the point when it will have

Figure 274: *The Reptilian-hybrid bankers and their agents create the bubbles and then burst them*

Figure 275: *It is so easy to create a financial panic when you control the banking system, the stock markets and the media*

maximum impact and cause most suffering and chaos (Fig 274). They want people in such fear, stress and trauma that they will agree to any solution they are told would solve the problem. It is a psychological fact that when people are in fear and stress (reptilian brain) they are most open to suggestion. The trauma techniques used in government 'Manchurian Candidate' mind-control programmes are also employed against the masses. See *The Biggest Secret* and *The David Icke Guide to the Global Conspiracy (and How to End it)* for the detailed background to these government-military mind-control programmes and their trauma-based programming techniques. It is all so tragically easy to glean the public reaction they require by triggering panic in the reptilian brain (Fig 275). The financial system is based on confidence. When you have confidence in a bank you will use it or invest in it; when you lose confidence you don't use it or invest in it. When confidence evaporates, the speed of collapse can be astonishing. All it takes is a planted rumour (planted fear) that a bank is in trouble. It doesn't even have to be true, and often isn't, but as long as enough people believe that it's true the die is cast. As I have been saying throughout this book, the whole thing is a mind game.

Why a Cashless Society?

We are already seeing national currencies disappearing to collective currencies like the euro and the plan is to continue this trend by replacing the US dollar, Canadian dollar and the Mexican peso with the 'amero', a new currency for a North American Union. Or, at least 'amero' is the working title. In Britain, where they have not yet been able to replace sterling with the euro, they are doing it by stealth with more and more businesses accepting the euro as legal tender. A crash of the British pound would also lead to pressure for reluctant Britons to replace it with the euro.

Eventually, they want a single world currency which would be purely electronic. Look at how cash is being used less and less and how governments, financial institutions and the media are talking about the coming 'cashless society'. In 2009, the National Irish Bank announced that it was no longer handling cash at its branches. It was not the first and eventually this will be the norm. Even cheques are being phased out. The mass use of credit cards is all part of this, of course, and everything was in place a long time ago. A friend in the United States complained to her local branch of the Bank of America in Florida in 1970 when she was asked to put her thumb-print on a cheque. The manager invited her and her husband into his office where he told them they should not be concerned about a thumb-print when it was planned, step-by-step, to introduce credit cards as the main form of payment and eventually a cashless society with microchipped people, cameras in the streets and total surveillance. She told me how she and her husband thought he was from the Twilight Zone, but then began ticking off what he told them as one by one they happened. London's *The Times* newspaper ran this headline in June, 2009: 'To fight deflation, abolish cash. Could Japan make reality of 'science fiction'?' There is no science fiction involved, just careful planning. The story explained that there were calls in Japan to abolish cash, something I have said was coming since the early 1990s. Richard Jerram, a senior economist with Macquarie Bank, told investors that 'the proposal has become practical with the broad penetration of electronic money and credit cards in Japan'. The same theme will be repeated all over the world. You make electronic money the norm and then you say there is so little cash being used now that we might as well get rid of it. The reason for a cashless society is, once again, control. If you want to buy something now and the computer won't accept your credit card you can still pay with cash. But when there is no cash and the machine refuses your card – or your microchip as it is planned to be – how do you purchase anything? You can't, except through barter, and once again that's the idea. Whoever controls the computer system controls your life once cash is out of circulation. If you look beyond the apparent diversity and complexity, you can see the global structure emerging. The world government is planned to control the world central bank and this, in turn, would dictate to the central banks of the superstates. This is why we have a European Central Bank in the Rothschild home city of Frankfurt and they want central banks for the North American Union, African Union and Asia-Pacific Union. These would control the national and regional central banks and they would control the banks in the towns and cities. There would be no financial diversity … only dictatorship feeding down from the global hierarchy, and the same with government and the military.

Destroying Information Diversity

The concentration of power in the global media is fast moving to a similar structure that destroys diversity and ensures that everyone receives the same version of 'news' and information no matter where they are. Look at how local news is being cut back or replaced by centralised bulletins that give every community the same 'news'. The plan is to continue with this demolition of diversity and further deregulate the media to allow the few to own still more. The power structure desperately wants to silence those who are exposing the plot and they will be increasingly targeting with propaganda and vilification the researchers, like myself, who offer another version of events that the Reptilian families don't want people to hear. It's all part of the agenda to control all sources of information. Well, up yours, darlin', I'm going nowhere. We are already seeing this campaign building with members of the 9/11 Truth Movement being branded as terrorists. Glenn Beck, a Rupert Murdoch lackey on Fox News, said outrageously that James Von Braun, the man who opened fire on security guards at the Holocaust Museum in Washington DC in 2009, was 'a hero of 9/11 Truthers'. He said this during an interview with 'former' CIA operative, Mike Baker, who enthusiastically agreed that those who challenge the official lies about 9/11 are motivated by 'hate'. The inane Beck declared:

> Our country is now vulnerable. Those people who would like to destroy us – our enemies like Al Qaeda. They'd like to destroy us, and they will work with anyone. There are also people like white supremacists or 9/11 Truthers that would also like to destroy the country. They'll work with anybody they can.

On another occasion, he said:

> These Truthers are exactly the kind of people who want to rock this nation's foundation, tear us apart and plant the seeds of dissatisfaction in all of us …
> [The 9/11 truth movement is] the kind of group a Timothy McVeigh would come from.

McVeigh was executed after being convicted for the 1995 Oklahoma bombing. Glenn Beck says whatever suits his boss, Rupert Murdoch (Rothschild Zionist), and he dare not do any other if he wants to keep his job. But Beck really doesn't require any encouragement or pressure to talk utter tripe; he's a natural. I trust the money's good, Glenn. At the same time he has people on his show like CIA analyst, Michael Scheuer, who says that America needs more terror attacks to increase its security: 'Only Osama can execute an attack that will force Americans to demand that their government protect them effectively, consistently, and with as much violence as necessary.' This is considered sane by the Beck mentality while those challenging such callousness are dubbed crazy. It was Beck who led the media campaign to force Obama 'green jobs' advisor Van Jones to resign for, among other things, signing a petition in 2004 from the group '911Truth.org' which suggested that Bush administration officials 'may indeed have deliberately allowed 9/11 to happen, perhaps as a pretext for war'. Question the official line and you're out. You will see more of this Beck-type propaganda from the mainstream media to discredit those who challenge and expose the conspiracy. The

bloodline families are terrified that the truth about them will be understood by the masses and those communicating this information are becoming ever more effective and successful in doing so. There was bound to be a reaction against them (Fig 276). Clare Swinney, a resident of New Zealand, complained to the Broadcasting Standards Authority about New Zealand Television for claiming that Osama bin Laden was responsible for the attacks of 9/11. Shortly afterwards, she was threatened and then imprisoned in a psychiatric ward. The chief psychiatrist (rarely met one who didn't need one) told a judge that Clare should be kept at the hospital because her claims that 9/11 was an inside job proved that she was 'delusional'. The judge agreed with him, so

Figure 276: *The more successful we are in exposing the agenda, the more we will be targeted by the system*

proving that it was the psychiatrist and the judge who were delusional. None of the public officials involved wanted to look at the mountain of evidence to show that she was right. They were programmed computer disks and it wouldn't have registered anyway. The authorities are going to be taking the psychiatric route more often to silence the opposition to their own insanity.

Psychology Today, a magazine that gets much of its revenue from Big Pharma, published a ludicrous article in September 2009 entitled 'Dark Minds: When does incredulity become paranoia?' The author was one John Gartner who attempted to show that 'conspiracy theorists' suffer from mental instability and have lost touch with reality. People like Gartner never look at the evidence of a conspiracy because, well, they have lost touch with reality. Mind you, I guess if you've never *been* in touch with reality there is nothing to lose. One of Gartner's batch in the UK, a professor of 'psychology' called Christopher French, takes the same party line. French said on British television that there was no evidence to support what I say and so I asked him if he had read any of my books. 'No,' came the reply. Then how did he know what I was saying? He had 'read it in the papers'! What were their mothers doing? The standard line all these people parrot about conspiracy researchers is that they construct their theories to make sense of a chaotic and complex world. Yawn; the times I have heard it. What they never ask, or seek to check, is: could what the researchers say be *true*? It is taken as read that it can't be true, because if it were true these jokers like Gartner and French would be wrong and that is not possible. Arrogance and a concrete mind is a lethal combination. Totalitarian regimes, like the Soviet Union and Nazi Germany, always dub those who challenge their tyranny as 'psychotic' and 'crazy' to justify their incarceration in psychiatric hospitals. Have no doubt that this current expression of the global dictatorship will seek to use the same technique. Useful idiots like Gartner and French are just the foot soldiers and, probably, far too ignorant to realise that.

The most extreme policy (so far) proposed to stop the truth coming out was delivered by Cass Sunstein (Rothschild Zionist), Director of the Office of Regulatory Affairs and a friend of Obama's at Harvard, who has said that the Internet is a 'threat to democracy'. Sunstein published a paper in January 2008 highlighting the need to break up 'the hard core of extremists who supply conspiracy theories' with 'cognitive infiltration of extremist groups, whereby government agents or their allies (acting either virtually or in real space, and either openly or anonymously) will undermine the crippled epistemology [the nature of knowledge, its presuppositions and foundations, and its extent and validity] of believers by planting doubts about the theories.' He made these proposals in a paper called 'Conspiracy Theories' in which he said ... no, he *really did* ... that a government ban on conspiracy theories or a tax of some kind on those who disseminate such information 'will have a place under imaginable conditions'. He wrote:

> Many millions of people hold conspiracy theories; they believe that powerful people have worked together in order to withhold the truth about some important practice or some terrible event. A recent example is the belief, widespread in some parts of the world, that the attacks of 9/11 were carried out not by Al Qaeda, but by Israel or the United States. Those who subscribe to conspiracy theories may create serious risks, including risks of violence, and the existence of such theories raises significant challenges for policy and law.

This is the mentality within Obama's 'open government' and there will be great efforts to discredit conspiracy researchers and to ban their work – this book included.

Microchipping the Masses

When I first wrote about the plan to microchip the global population it was thought by most people to be a wild exaggeration or science fiction nonsense. The very suggestion that we were heading for microchipped people was guaranteed to elicit guffaws and belly laughs. But not any more. Today it is happening. Microchipping babies at birth is the goal of the bloodline families to ensure that no-one comes into this reality in human form without being connected to the Reptilian computer network and the Global Positioning System (GPS) which is there to monitor everyone on the planet via satellite. The microchip will allow the population to be tracked every minute of their lives and there would never be a single second in a lifetime when the authorities would not know where you were. It is about more than just surveillance, however. Even most of those who are aware of the microchipping agenda think it's all about surveillance, and on one level it is, but only by understanding the true nature of reality and the human body can the even more sinister aspects of the microchipping agenda be seen. The body is a biological computer and they want to implant the microchip to hijack its electrochemical systems, control every human being mentally, emotionally and physically and 'tune' them even more powerfully into the transmissions of the Moon Matrix. A dissident CIA scientist told me in 1997 how once a microchip is inside the body the person can be externally controlled via signals to the chip. They can be made to think, or not think, whatever the signals decide, and the same can be done with emotions. Microchipped people can be manipulated to be aggressive or submissive, sexually high or sexually suppressed, and made to feel extreme fear at the touch of a button or the click of a mouse. Then there is the little matter of having the ability to kill you from a distance via the chip if ever you make waves and refuse to be a good little slave. This can be done directly through the chip or it can transmit your exact location for a 'clean' assassination. The US military are having chips planted in target areas or on target people and then using the signal to guide their missiles. The CIA and Special Operations pay tribesmen to plant the devices in places like Pakistan and elsewhere, and remotely-controlled aircraft without pilots are guided to the chip location by an operator on the other side of the world at Creech Air Force Base, 35 miles from Las Vegas. Details of this have even reached the mainstream media here and there. Bob Boyce, an inventor in North Carolina, revealed in 2009 that he had found a microchip, made by VeriChip Corporation, in his shoulder. He had no idea how it got there. Bob has developed an electrolysis system that draws energy from the atmosphere and that is the last thing the Illuminati power companies want in circulation. He discovered the chip when he picked up a weak signal on an EMF meter and

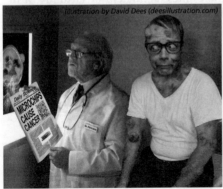

Figure 277: *Microchips can cause cancer just by being there, never mind what can be done externally through the chip*

traced it to his shoulder. Later he found that he had a rare form of cancer where the chip had been. It all fits the agenda. If they can trigger cancer from a distance using electromagnetic technology, how easy it would be with a microchip that can cause it just by being there (Fig 277).

The award-winning American film producer, the late Aaron Russo, said publicly in 2007 that he was told by a member of the Rockefeller family, Nick Rockefeller, about their plan for a microchipped population. Russo said Rockefeller was trying to recruit him into the elite and he was asked if he would like to join the Council on Foreign Relations. When Russo said that he was not interested in enslaving people, Rockefeller asked why he cared about the 'serfs'. 'I used to say to him, "What's the point of all this?"' Russo said. 'You have all the money in the world you need, you have all the power you need, what's the point, what's the end goal?' Rockefeller replied that the goal was to get everybody chipped, to control the whole of society, to have the bankers and the elite people control the world. Russo was told that if he joined them his chip would be specially coded to avoid unnecessary inspection by the authorities. Rockefeller also told Russo about the depopulation agenda.

Chipping the Mind

The chip is the interface between two computer systems and allows the one controlled by the authorities to manipulate the one we call the human body. Thought generates electrical signals and thought waves and, going the other way, instructions (thoughts) can be implanted in the human psyche by sending them in vibrational/electrical form through the chip. In that state, humans become nothing more than robots that think and feel whatever their controllers decide (Fig 278). They can isolate an individual through a unique code in each chip or they can do it en masse. It gives them access to the body-computer's electrical and chemical systems and they can do basically what they like once the chip is in place unless the instructions are overridden by Consciousness. They want a microchipped world army of human robots to work with the robot technology (Fig 279). The brain decodes electrical information to construct the reality we call the 'physical' world and the chips are able to communicate with the body/brain electrically. Think about the

Figure 278: *The bar-coded robots the Reptilians want humans to be*

Figure 279: *The bloodlines want to use the microchip to create a robot world army to operate the robot technology*

consequences of that for total human control, in conjunction with the transmissions of the Moon Matrix, and how humanity could be fed an even more powerful false reality. Finnish researcher, Rauni-Leena Luukanen-Kilde, has produced detailed studies about the potential of microchips for human control. She writes:

> Every thought, reaction, hearing and visual observation causes a certain neurological potential, spikes and patterns in the brain and its electromagnetic fields, which can now be decoded into thoughts, pictures and voices. Electromagnetic stimulation can therefore change a person's brainwaves and affect muscular activity, causing painful muscular cramps experienced as torture ...

> ... The [National Security Agency's] electronic surveillance system can simultaneously follow and handle millions of people. Each of us has a unique bioelectrical resonance frequency in the brain, just as we have unique fingerprints.

> With electromagnetic frequency (EMF) brain stimulation fully coded, pulsating electromagnetic signals can be sent to the brain causing the desired voice and visual effects to be experienced by the target. This is a form of electronic warfare. US astronauts were implanted before they were sent into space so their thoughts could be followed and all their emotions could be registered 24 hours a day.

Figure 280: *The chip is designed to connect humans even more powerfully to the Reptilian hive mind of the Moon Matrix to ensure that we perceive reality in the way that suits the agenda of control*

There will be no need for torture techniques or complex mind control programmes in the world of microchipped people. They'll have a one-stop-shop – the chip (Fig 280). The technology to 'monitor behaviour' is already well advanced and available. 'Behaviour fingerprint' chips can sense when a medicine cupboard is opened or a microwave switched on and send the data to a monitoring centre. *RFID Journal* reports that 'a company could use the system, for instance, to monitor the behaviour of employees to ensure no security rules are breached'. Oh, how wonderful, I'll take two, don't need a bag. *RFID Journal* has so many helpful ideas: 'The workers could be issued RFID-enabled ID badges that are read as they arrive at and leave work, enter and exit various departments, and log onto and off of different computer systems,' it tells us. 'Over time, the system will establish a pattern that reflects the employee's typical workday.' If a naughty worker 'enters the office much earlier than normal on a particular occasion', or 'goes into a department in which he or she does not work', the chip would alert those in authority. The so-called brain-computer interface, or 'direct neural interface', is being developed so that people can communicate with their desktop computer purely through their own thoughts, and so let no-one think that what I am saying about the chip is not possible. British scientists are developing a 'telepathy' chip that allows people to control computers, televisions and light-switches by the power of thought. A tiny sensor positioned on the surface of the brain would pick up the electrical activity of nerve cells and pass the signal wirelessly to a receiver on the skull. This signal would then control a cursor on a

Figure 281: *The plan is for every baby to be chipped at birth, so connecting them to the Control System for life*

computer screen, operate electronic technology or steer an electric wheelchair. The potential for human control is horrific (Fig 281). Research into brain-computer interface technology, known as BCI, officially began at the University of California, in Los Angeles, or UCLA, in the 1970s. This institution is infamous to mind-control victims and researchers. The development of the brain-computer interface was conducted under contract to, wait for it … DARPA – the Pentagon's Defense Advanced Research Projects Agency, which I described earlier as one of the most sinister organisations on Earth. Human-computer interface research has expanded tremendously in recent years and can have some potential benefits for those with paralysis and disease caused by problems with electrical communication; but DARPA has not funded the development of this technology to help anyone. It is about total control of the human body and its mental and emotional responses and perceptions. Imagine if you were feeding off low-vibrational human emotion and you had the power to turn those emotions on and off at will. Human microchips are designed to interact with the reptilian brain and give it even greater control of behaviour within the Moon Matrix. The reptilian brain is activated now through the hive mind Moon transmissions and by generating fear through the survival responses. The microchip would give them all of this with a simple click, click, 'Enter'.

Another crucial aspect of the microchip agenda, the most crucial in fact, is the body/mind/consciousness connection. The foundation of this book, and the conspiracy, is the way 'incarnate' humans are disconnected from the awareness of their true and infinite self. The body is a crystalline transmitter-receiver and if you can disrupt and imbalance its potential to 'receive' you further isolate human awareness in the five senses. This is the major reason why they want a microchip that they control inside every human body. They are using a range of excuses to do this, including financial security by replacing credit cards with under-the-skin chips, maintaining surveillance on children and people with dementia and 'detecting viruses'. Then there is covert microchipping through mass vaccination. The US VeriChip Corporation in Florida, which I have been exposing for a decade and more, has been awarded an exclusive licence for two patents to develop 'implantable virus detection systems'. I have my own, thanks; it's called the immune system. None of these Illuminati corporations have any interest in protecting the health of the cattle, as they perceive the human masses. They want access to the human body-computer for very different reasons. VeriChip is promoting an implanted chip that links to an online database containing the person's medical records, credit history and social security ID. In 2009, VeriChip changed its name to 'PositiveID' and bought the Steel Vault Corporation, a health and security company. **News-Medical.Net** reported:

> VeriChip Corporation … a provider of radio frequency identification (RFID) systems for healthcare and patient-related needs, and Steel Vault Corporation … a premier provider of identity security products and services, announced today that VeriChip has completed its acquisition of Steel Vault to provide unique health and security identification tools to protect consumers and businesses. In conjunction with the merger, VeriChip has changed its name to PositiveID …
>
> PositiveID represents the convergence of a pioneer in personal health records and the first and only FDA-cleared implantable microchip for patient identification, VeriChip, with a leader in the identity security space, Steel Vault, focused on access and security of consumers' critical data.

You can see the pieces being moved into place.

Clearing the Frequencies

Patrick Redmond, a former employee of computer giant, IBM, said in 2008 that the switch from analogue to digital television was mainly to free analogue frequencies for scanners that would read implanted microchips and track people and products wherever they went. Redmond had many jobs at IBM over 31 years, including 15 years in the company's Toronto laboratory, and he knows from the inside the scale of the microchip agenda. He said the chips give off a unique signal indicating the identity and location of the subject. Redmond said the rush to 'go digital' is because of the plan to use the UHF-VHF frequencies for the chips: 'They do not want to overload the chips with television signals, so the chips' signals are going to be taking those frequencies … They plan to sell the frequencies to private companies and other groups who will use them to monitor the chips.' Even car radios are being switched to digital at massive inconvenience and cost to the public and this apparently crazy policy supports what Redmond says. He goes on:

> People are being chipped now. There's a trend that they're promoting in the media in terms of chipping people; they're saying why not chip children for safety, so we can protect them, especially if they're in the hospital then nobody could steal the newborn babies. Why don't we chip the sick, then if someone has a heart attack and falls on the floor, we can read the signal in the chip and send someone to help them.

We should chip the military so we would be able to know where the soldiers are and if they're alive. After we could chip people on welfare so we could make sure they're not cheating the government. Then we can chip all the criminals so that we could control them, and we'll chip workers because a lot of them goof off at work. Then we'll chip all the pensioners because they're just taking money from us; and after that we'll chip everyone else.

Another ruse is to say that credit card fraud could be eliminated by having a microchip under the skin for all financial transactions, and the agendas for the microchip and the cashless society are closely linked. Big Pharma, in the form of Novartis and Proteus Biomedical, are planning to implant chips so that patients can be reminded to take their pills. The Novartis plan involves two chips – one inside the pill which sends a signal to another in the shoulder. If you don't take the next pill the shoulder chip sends a text to your mobile phone. No, I'm not kidding. You can see the microchip increasingly promoted in the wake of every high-profile child abduction case and at least some of these kidnappings will involve Illuminati operatives to provide the excuse and momentum for microchipping children. Problem-Reaction-Solution is at work everywhere. The microchipping of animals was introduced first to get people used to the concept and then came the chipping and tagging of goods and products. Microchipping is being considered 'normal' practice today. Now, as I have long predicted, they are moving in on humans, starting with vulnerable people like the elderly and those suffering from Alzheimer's. The whole debate about identity cards is a diversion and a stepping-stone to the real goal of human microchipping. You will see a long list of different reasons to encourage microchipping, even to enforce it, but all must be resisted. If we don't make a stand on this, that's the end of the human being as we know it. *Nothing, nothing, nothing,* is more important than refusing to be chipped and refusing the swine flu and other mass vaccinations. The two are almost certainly connected, as I said earlier.

Microchipped Chemtrails?

They have developed nanotechnology microchips for computers, and new Intel processors have four hundred million transistors on a chip half the size of a postage stamp. Anything you see in the public domain is way behind what is developed in the secret projects and underground bases where 'elite' scientists interact with Reptilians and Greys and have access to their advanced technological knowledge. They introduce the technology into human society as it suits their agenda and they use fake cover stories for how it was 'discovered' and by whom. Microchips are now microscopic and well beyond the realm of human sight. Hitachi unveiled a tiny, new 'powder' chip measuring 0.05 x 0.05 mm and say they will begin marketing them in two or three years. The truth is that if any company is talking openly about something coming 'in the future' it means such things have long existed in the secret projects and underground bases. I am sure that nano-microchips are part of the chemical and metallic mixture that is known today as chemtrails. We all see contrails, or condensation trails, that pour from the back of aircraft and disperse almost immediately. Chemtrails look the same at first, but they don't disperse. They expand out across the sky and eventually dump their contents on the land and the people below. You can watch planes criss-cross the sky going back and forth for

Figure 282   **Figure 283**   **Figure 284**
Chemtrails are being sprayed daily across the world from military and commercial aircraft

hours at a time (Figs 282 to 284). I sat in America every morning for a week watching a clear blue sky turned into an apparently cloudy day by the constant spraying of chemicals from two aircraft working in unison. Author and researcher, William Thomas, became the most vocal exposer of chemtrails soon after they began in the United States and Canada in about 1998. They are now reported all over the world and I have seen them myself in almost every country I have visited (Fig 285). Even mainstream television, including the History Channel, has covered the story on occasions. Chemtrails have many components. William Thomas says that analysis has found highly toxic pathogens, among them Mycoplasma fermentans (incognitus). This was discovered by Dr Garth Nicholson in some 45 per cent of former soldiers suffering from the debilitating illness known as Gulf War Syndrome. Symptoms reported in sprayed areas have included respiratory and flu-like conditions and sometimes mental confusion and depression. This is an effective way they can spread their laboratory-created diseases. The chemtrails also consistently contain barium and aluminium. Barium is toxic to humans and undermines the immune system – the recurring theme. It deactivates T-cell receptors and stops them resisting disease-causing agents. We should not be surprised at biological warfare against the population when such scandals have been exposed many times since the 1940s. Unsuspecting communities have often been used as laboratory animals to test germ warfare agents and some 20 thousand covert experiments on civilian populations in the United States between 1910 and 2000 have been uncovered by

Figure 285: *David Dees captures the mentality behind chemtrails*

Congressional investigations. The same has happened and continues to happen in Britain, Israel and elsewhere. Unbelievable numbers have been murdered and maimed for life as a result, including the Sephardic Jewish children (not Ashkenazi) who were subjected to radiation experiments by the Israeli government for ten years from 1951. Something similar happened in the United States. Troops and prisoners are often used in these experiments because they are a controlled and easily testable and observable group.

As I mentioned, the Project for the New American Century, a front-group for the neoconservative Rothschild Zionists behind the Boy Bush regime, produced a report calling for the development of 'advanced forms of biological warfare that can target specific genotypes …' This is the scale of insanity we are dealing with here and so spraying the population with poisons and microscopic microchips is no problem at all to these deeply imbalanced 'people'. Chemtrails have been linked by some researchers, including myself, to the outbreak of 'Morgellons disease' (Fig 286). This was first identified in 2001, three years after the chemtrails appear to have begun, and its official cause is a 'mystery'. Well, maybe it's not. The symptoms include crawling, stinging and biting sensations; skin lesions that will not heal; extreme fatigue; severe mental confusion; short-term memory loss; joint pain; a sharp decline in vision; itching so bad that some victims consider suicide; and serious neurological disorders. The most striking symptoms, however, are lesions with coloured fibres growing out of them (Fig 287). The fibres can be pulled from the body with force, but this does not appear to stop their growth. We are looking at nanotechnology here which is able to grow and reproduce and I have no doubt it is coming from the sky in chemtrails. It is not just about someone inserting a microchip in your arm; it is also about breathing them in.

Figure 286: *Chemtrails, nanotechnology and Morgellons disease are all connected*

Figure 287: *Morgellons is an horrific 'disease'*

You can see the scale of what we are facing here. We have some serious challenges before us, for sure, and we have to be big enough to meet them. Try telling your children and grandchildren that you are not up to it given the consequences for them of us running away to hide. There is nowhere to hide, so we'd better run straight at them.

25

Game Plan (6): Assault on Freedom

The welfare of the people in particular has always been the alibi of tyrants, and it provides the further advantage of giving the servants of tyranny a good conscience – **Albert Camus**

The microchip is the centrepiece of a now enormous global network of ever-growing surveillance and control that I have long warned was coming. Britain's Information Commissioner, Richard Thomas, said that people are 'sleepwalking into a surveillance society' and he could not have described it more accurately, except by using the terms 'sleep-running' or 'sleep-sprinting'.

The Orwellian police state becomes ever more tyrannical and brutal behind the cover of political and economic crisis, 'celebrity' scandals, sex, sport, and all the rest. These diversions are designed to ensure that most people look the other way or stay asleep and don't see what's going on. Richard Thomas, who ended his term in 2009, made his comments about the 'surveillance society' in response to a report into the use of surveillance technology edited by Dr David Murakami Wood, managing editor of the journal *Surveillance & Society*, and Dr Kirstie Ball, an Open University senior lecturer in Organisational Studies. The report was produced by a group of academics under the title of the Surveillance Studies Network. It warned that people may be forced to be microchipped 'like pet dogs' to track their movements and store personal information, which, of course, would no longer be personal to anyone with a chip reader. The chips could be used not only by the government, the report said, but also by companies to keep tabs on employees. In short, we would be like monkeys in an electronic cage or rats in an electronic maze. The report said that by 2016 almost every movement, purchase and communication could be monitored by a complex network of interlinking surveillance technologies unless we turn back from the brink pretty damn quick. 'The call for everyone to be chipped is now being seriously debated,' the authors warned. Actually, the 'debate' is a sham – it has been planned for decades and more. Dr David Murakami Wood said:

> We really do have a society which is premised both on state secrecy and the state not giving up its supposed right to keep information under control while, at the same time, wanting to know as much as it can about us.

The report said that 'the surveillance society has come about without us realising'. Well, that depends on where you have been looking all these years. I have been warning about this from the early 1990s, and so have many others, and it has only 'crept up' on people who haven't been paying attention. 'What time's the game show on tonight, honey?' The surveillance state has been introduced through the Totalitarian Tiptoe, piece-by-piece, and only now are far more people beginning to see the scale of this accumulated tyranny. The Surveillance Studies Network report said that Britain, which claims to spread 'freedom and democracy', is the planetary leader in surveillance technology and the British are the most spied-upon nation in what is so ironically called the 'free world'. What is happening in Britain is being introduced in the rest of Europe, North America and elsewhere. There are four million closed-circuit television cameras in the UK for a population of just 60 million – a camera for every 14 people. The UK Home Office spent an astonishing 78 per cent of its crime prevention budget in the 1990s on installing surveillance cameras. In Britain, you are caught on a camera on

Figure 288: *A surveillance camera next to a plaque saying 'George Orwell lived here'*

average 300 times a day – every 4.8 minutes – but in the cities it is even more extreme and increasing all the time. Look at the irony in Figure 288 of what now stands outside the former home of George Orwell. Tenants at one group of apartment buildings in Torquay, Devon, are watched by 112 CCTV cameras pointing at their front doors. They have also been told they will have to pay an extra £2 a week in rent to meet the £375,000 cost of making them 'feel more safe and secure'. Most of the residents were shocked at the level of surveillance, but one still said: 'I don't like the way the government is recording everyone, but I am willing to accept a bit less freedom for a bit more safety and peace of mind.' Cognitive dissonance / doublethink. Cameras are also being installed that can 'read' your lips and body language and recognise your face. An Israeli company is even producing 'mind-reading' surveillance technology.

Another development, straight from the pages of Orwell's *1984*, is cameras with speakers that allow operators to issue orders to people they are spying on. A document obtained from the London Metropolitan police through the Freedom of Information Act has revealed that CCTV footage solves less than one crime for every 1,000 cameras in Britain's capital city and yet surveillance cameras account for three-quarters of the government's spending on crime prevention. The cameras were never installed to solve or prevent crime. The bloodline families want *more* crime to generate the fear that leads to more control, just as Rothschild Zionist, Richard Day, said in 1969. Large amounts of reported crime are not even investigated today for this reason. Surveillance cameras are there to track opposition to the Orwellian state, not the general population who are no threat to the system. There are 6,000 speed cameras in the UK and 8,000 registration-plate recognition devices, with technology on the way to photograph anyone using their mobile phone at the wheel or not wearing a seat belt. The London Metropolitan Police have 'eye in the sky' cameras that can read registration plates from helicopters thousands of feet above the ground, and remotely-controlled 'drone' aircraft are to be used in Scotland to spy on the population. Parliament has called for even more speed cameras, even though a government report found that 85 per cent of road accidents are not connected to drivers breaking the speed limit. 'Stop and Search' powers – another form of surveillance – have also been increased. Children as young as two are being stopped and searched in the UK. 'Anti-terrorist' laws used on the general population state that anyone can be 'stopped anywhere and at any time, without notice and without any choice as to whether or not to submit to a search.' By 2009, the British government was spending an incredible £380 a minute – £200 million a year – on a tremendous expansion of surveillance on the population that it is supposed to serve. The 'upgrade' is a 1,700 per cent increase on the previous system and allows the authorities to monitor every move and click a person makes on the Internet and access details of every email and telephone call. This includes monitoring networking sites like Facebook and Twitter, and every Internet and telecommunications company would have to allocate an ID to their customers. All this detailed information is kept on a giant database that connects with all other databases and allows 'public bodies' to access everything about you and your life. Even not registering your name and address on the electoral roll is subject to a fine of £2,500. Agencies of the State, including local councils, were making one request every minute by 2009 to spy on the telephone records and email accounts of members of the public – even before the expanded system was introduced. London's *Guardian* newspaper revealed that photographs and personal details relating to thousands of people attending demonstrations, rallies and political meetings were being stored in secret national databases. They are labelled 'domestic extremists'. The campaign of surveillance was carried out by a private organisation funded by the government called the Association of Chief Police Officers (AcPO) and they produced 'spotter cards' with photographs of activists that police are told to watch for at protests and rallies. Passengers at Sheffield bus station in northern England are even warned that they will be traced by DNA if they spit at staff and will be on the national DNA database 'forever' (Fig 289).

Figure 289: *The 'spit and run' poster at Sheffield bus station*

Fake 'Terror' Laws

We have technology to identify faces in crowds and 'suspicious behaviour patterns', with 'lie detectors' being planned for airports. As a result of Tony Blair's Regulation of Investigatory Powers Act, passed in 2000, Internet providers have to record our surfing activity and provide this information to MI5. Blair's Act is yet another example of 'terrorist' legislation being worded in such general terms that it can be used on the general public. This, as I said at the time, was planned all along. The US Patriot Act is the same and under 'anti-terrorist' legislation Americans can have their citizenship removed, be jailed without trial, be flown to another country to be tortured and even be executed in secret. Extraordinary figures were revealed for the UK in 2009 that confirmed how far this has now gone. State spying on the public had increased 44 per cent in two years with 504,073 new cases. This means that an average of one adult in 78 is subjected to some kind of surveillance, including being followed by undercover agents and watched by hidden cameras. A total of 653 state bodies, including 474 local councils, are allowed to employ these surveillance powers and people have no right to know they have been spied upon even if no wrongdoing has been found. The Children Act of 2004 creates a database to record detailed information about our children right down to their eating habits. This can be accessed by police, doctors, social workers and teachers. Three 12-year-olds in the English West Midlands had their DNA taken after being arrested by police for ... breaking branches while building a den. DNA is now taken as a matter of course when anyone is arrested and this is kept on file even if they are subsequently not charged or found to be innocent. The last figure I saw showed that nearly six million samples were being held and that's growing by the hour. The European Court ruled that retaining the DNA of people arrested but not charged with a crime, or acquitted, was 'disproportionate' and the government reduced the period for holding the DNA of the innocent to six years – always expecting to change it back eventually. Confirmation that a DNA database is being created by stealth came with the revelation that police were arresting people specifically to get their DNA. The Human Genetics Commission, comprised of scientists and academics, found that the tactic was 'routine'. Commission chairman, Professor Jonathan Montgomery, said: 'People are arrested in order to retain DNA information that might not have been arrested in other circumstances.' A retired senior police officer, a superintendent, told the commission:

It is now the norm to arrest offenders for everything if there is a power to do so. It is apparently understood by serving police officers that one of the reasons, if not the reason, for the change in practice is so that the DNA of the offender can obtained.

The Control System intends to connect the DNA databases until every human's DNA is on file. After reading about the Reptilian obsession with genetics, maybe people will now appreciate the real agenda behind this. It is not to 'solve crime' and 'protect the people', it to have access to everyone's genetic code and their unique vibrational frequency. Once they have that they can specifically target an individual with vibrational technology tuned to their unique frequency. DNA evidence is claimed to be virtually infallible, but that is nonsense. Scientists in Israel have proved how easy it is to fabricate DNA 'evidence'. Dan Frumkin, lead author of a research paper published

Figure 290: *Menwith Hill in North Yorkshire, England. The Echelon spy-network is only part of what goes on here. It is a facility of global, indeed inter-planetary, significance*

online by the journal *Forensic Science International: Genetics,* said that any biology undergraduate could do this. 'You can just engineer the crime scene,' he said, and all you needed was a small amount of DNA from single hair or a drinking cup. It is even easier if you have everyone's DNA on file.

There are CCTV cameras; registration-plate recognition-cameras; facial recognition cameras; shop RFID microchip tags on products that we buy; monitoring of mobile phones, credit card transactions and store loyalty cards; satellite surveillance; electoral roll; medical records; phone-tapping; hidden cameras and bugs; Internet cookies and keystroke programmes, which allow the keys that you hit on your computer to be recorded and used to obtain passwords or encryption keys. This can also be employed to monitor work rates for computer operators, and the whole package is designed to record our every movement 24 hours a day. The latest technological research is designed to identify people by their brain patterns and heart rhythms, and by a 'sensing seat' fitted to trucks to record each driver's characteristic seated posture 'in an attempt to spot whether commercial vehicles had been hijacked'. This all comes under the heading of 'Humabio', or 'Human Monitoring and Authentication using Biodynamic Indicators and Behaviourial Analysis'. Telephone calls, emails and faxes are being monitored by the Echelon spy-network that searches for key words and voice recognition patterns at establishments like the deeply sinister Menwith Hill in North Yorkshire, England (Fig 290). This is officially a Royal Air Force station, but it is controlled by the US National Security Agency and acts as a ground base for satellites operated by the US National Reconnaissance Office. It has many other unofficial functions, too, and operates worldwide. Some other centres for the Echelon system are at Morwenstow (Cornwall, UK); the Australian Defence Satellite Communications Station (Geraldton, Western Australia); Misawa Air Base (Japan); Pine Gap (near Alice Springs, Northern Territory, Australia); Sabana Seca (Puerto Rico, US); Sugar Grove (West Virginia, US); Yakima (Washington, US); and Waihopai (New Zealand). Statewatch, an organisation monitoring civil liberties in Europe, summed up where we are and where we are going unless we wake up fast:

Across the EU, governments have, or are, adopting national laws for the mandatory retention of everyone's communications data – all forms of communication (phone calls, faxes, mobile calls including locations) which will be extended to keeping a record of all internet usage from 2009 – even though few are aware this is happening.

When traffic data including internet usage is combined with other data held by the state or gathered from non-state sources (tax, employment, bank details, credit card usage, biometrics, criminal record, health record, use of e-government services, travel history etc.) a frightening detailed picture of each individual's everyday life and habits can be accessed at the click of a button.

The European Union took this to a new level with the announcement of a surveillance system that would monitor data taken from countless sources through the continuous monitoring of 'websites, discussion forums, usenet groups, file servers, p2p networks [and] individual computer systems'. This information is planned to be collated and assessed by the giant computer system to detect 'abnormal behavior'. The system is called 'Project Indect' and will be used by a European Union police force and its equivalent of the CIA, both of which are well on the way to being introduced. It has been described as 'Echelon on steroids', but it is nothing like the end. The bloodlines and their Reptilian masters want a global system in which all databases become one. A tidal wave of new European Union Big Brother laws are all ready to be introduced now the Lisbon Treaty has been fraudulently passed to give the EU bureaucrats a range of new powers to impose upon what is left of the national states. There are also plans to severely restrict travel – just as Dr Richard Day said there would be in 1969. Americans will have to get permission from the government to travel by air or take a cruise as the 'no-fly' and 'watch' lists reach ludicrous proportions and have even included babies. The plan is to extend this to cover other forms of travel.

Thugs in uniform

The scale of all this is simply breathtaking. US border agents can now even seize laptop computers or other electronic devices from any traveller and keep them indefinitely, without any suspicion of wrongdoing. Homeland 'Security' announced in July 2009 that its agents can keep any information-storing device and share the data with other agencies – 'absent individualized suspicion'. They love their Orwellian language; it goes with their computer mind. The authorities are becoming increasingly fascist, arrogant and brutal. It is now commonplace for non-violent protestors and others to be subjected to police violence. Two women in the UK were forced to the ground, grabbed by the throat, bound by the feet and thrown into a police van. Their crime? Asking a police officer for his identification and seeking to take a picture when he refused. The authorities can film your every move, but take a photograph of the police and you are under arrest. British police claim the right to prevent themselves being photographed by the public. The Counter-Terrorism Act makes it an offence to take pictures of officers 'likely to be useful to a person committing or preparing an act of terrorism'. Who decides what does and does not meet this definition? The police. Andrew Carter, a British plumber, photographed an officer who ignored a no-entry sign while driving a police van. He wanted evidence to report the officer for breaking a law that the police impose on the public. This, however, is fascist Britain. The officer knocked the camera from Mr Carter's hand, handcuffed him, put him in the police van and kept him at a police station for five hours. He returned to answer bail a week later and was held for another five hours before being released without charge. A newspaper vendor called Ian Tomlinson was thrown onto the pavement by a police thug during the mass protest at the G20 Summit in London in April 2009, and he died shortly afterwards. He wasn't even taking part in the protest and he was minding his own business when the moron-in-uniform attacked him for absolutely no reason. Another thug police officer from Dolton, Illinois, was forced to resign when he was taped viciously beating 15-year-old Marshawn Pitts, a brain-injured student at a special needs school. Marshawn's crime? Not having his shirt tucked in. It turned out that the officer, 38-year-old Christopher Lloyd, was facing a rape charge and a lawsuit from his former wife for shooting her new husband 24 times in front of their children. He was not charged with murder because police accepted his claim that the 24 shots were 'in self defence'. Look around conspiracy websites, including my own, and the videos on YouTube, and you will see how widespread police brutality has become. The Marshawn Pitts video can be found with the search words 'Special Needs Student Beaten by Police for Dress Code'. For every example that is captured on film there are thousands, at least, that are never recorded or reported.

There is one law for the police and another for those they are supposed to be serving. Go a few miles over the speed limit on an empty road at midnight and a camera will flash and the fine drops on the doormat a few days later. Drive a police car at 128 miles per hour on a public road, as one British police officer did, and the court lets you off because you were just 'testing the car'. If you punch someone in a pub fight you are arrested, but if you are a police officer who shoots an innocent Brazilian electrician seven times in the head at point blank range while other officers pin him to the ground, nothing happens. One criterion to denote a fascist state, I would suggest, is whether the law is applied equally to both the public and those who enforce it. If the law enforcers are not subject to the same treatment as the public, in other words they are above the law, we live in a police state. By that definition virtually everyone does today, and it is getting more and more extreme as decent police officers are replaced by the new breed of arrogant, trigger-happy thugs, or are 'retrained' to see the world the system's way. The police become more like the military every day, because that is what the agenda demands – an amalgamation of the two. The most basic foundations of justice are being picked off one by one to unleash the global military dictatorship. The British Court of Appeal has ruled that a criminal trial can take place without a jury for the first time in England and Wales. The case will be heard by a lone judge under new laws passed by the government of Fabian agent Tony Blair (Rothschild Zionist) in 2007. The excuse is the concern that the jury would be threatened in a trial involving alleged bank robbers, but this is just another example of the constant erosion of any fair system of justice and law enforcement. The appalling UK Lord Chancellor, the Fabian, Jack Straw (Rothschild Zionist), also changed the law to allow the government to hold any future inquests into 'controversial deaths' in secret, with not even the family permitted to attend. This is a charter to cover up whatever the State does not want its people to know.

There is another common theme across the world – encouraging the public to spy on each other for the State. This is precisely what happened in Nazi Germany and the Soviet Union. Janet Napolitano, Obama's Homeland Security Secretary, told a gathering of the Council on Foreign Relations (how apt) that she intended to engage 'ordinary' people in 'scouting' activities against rising 'home-grown terrorism'. The lie about 'rising home-grown terrorism' is simply a ploy to justify the use of terrorist laws against the general population. There is also the 'WeTip' scheme in the United States, one of many that encourages people to anonymously report each other to the authorities in return for cash – just as the Nazis did in the 1930s (Fig 291). Don't worry, though, it's only there to ensure 'A Safer America'. I mean, how sinister must WeTip be when it is endorsed by the Bushes, Bill Clinton, and California Governor, Arnold Schwarzenegger? Matthew Falconer, a candidate for Mayor of Orange County in Florida, described the agenda very well when he said he would establish a 1,000-strong spy force of young people to cruise-patrol communities on bikes reporting suspicious behavior to uniformed supervisors via radio. Obama wants something like this across the country, or what he calls a 'national civilian security force' that would be 'just as powerful, just as strong, just as well-funded' as the US military. The Los Angeles Police Department announced in late 2009 that it was 'on course' to take over the Explorer Program from the Boy Scouts movement. New uniforms, patches and other insignia would be unveiled, along with a new name, the LAPD said. More than 3,000 young people are part of the program that trains young people to prepare for law enforcement careers. This move is all part of the creation across America of the 'national

Figure 291: *The WeTip scheme*

civilian security force' that will involve the use of children to spy on their neighbourhood, even their own families. The people policing the people, the slaves policing the slaves. And if you want to protest at what is going on – go to your 'free speech zone' (Fig 292).

Great Idea: Give Morons a Stun Gun

You don't have to be intelligent to be a police officer, nor do you have to be stable in mind and emotion. Some of the most mentally-challenged people I have encountered have had badges on their caps. All you need to become a police officer is to be accepted and selected by those in authority. Er, that's it. Thus, police forces worldwide are peopled to a significant extent by the stupid, corrupt, psychopathic and emotionally crippled (see Louisiana, I rest my case). Law enforcement professions and the military have great attractions for those with serious personality problems that lead to a desire for power over others. They also attract thugs in search of an outlet to practise their thuggery. This would be bad enough by itself, but now they are arming these same people with something called a Taser to unleash 50,000 volts of electricity on anyone who upsets them (Fig 293 overleaf). The Taser, the new toy-of-control for the heavies-in-uniform, is the latest in the long line of 'supposed to bes' imposed

Figure 292: *The 'free speech zones' – a stepping stone to having none at all*

Illustration by David Dees (deesillustration.com)

Figure 293: *55,000 volts of electricity is a 'non-lethal weapon'??*

by governments. The Taser is *supposed to be* a 'non-lethal' weapon, but the deaths continue to mount. It is *supposed to be* used only on those who physically threaten the police or public, but it is being used in response to the most minor lack of cooperation. It was *supposed to be* used only by officers trained in firearms, but now it is being handed out to all and sundry, which was the plan from the start, of course. *Supposed to bes* are for public consumption only, as with legislation that is only *supposed to be* used against 'terrorists' when it is actually aimed at the general population. It was always known that the Taser had the potential to kill. It is stating the obvious to say that the body's electrical system is rather crucial to staying alive and when that system is short-circuited the consequences can clearly be lethal. The Taser unleashes 50,000 volts of electricity to 'jam the nervous system' and they didn't know it had the potential to kill? Even Taser International, the weapon's official inventor, admits:

> Taser technology is *not risk free*, but independent medical and scientific experts have determined that when used properly, Taser technology is among the most effective use-of-force interventions available to law enforcement. (My emphasis)

What utter baloney. 'Most effective' use-of-force simply means that it works in controlling people. Smacking them around the head with a baseball bat would also be extremely 'effective' in achieving the same end. It doesn't make it right. Even when 'used properly' the Taser shocks the victim with 50,000 volts of electricity, never mind the repeated doses inflicted by some of the goons caught on video (put 'Taser' into YouTube). One guy, 39-year-old Antonio Galeano, collapsed and died 15 minutes after being stunned up to *28 times* by a 50,000-volt Taser gun during a confrontation with idiot police in Queensland, Australia. People with heart problems, including pacemakers, are at even greater risk and how do police officers know the state of health of those they attack with what a UN committee has dubbed 'a form of torture'? The Taser-peddlers employ misleading propaganda like this: 'In healthy subjects, exposure to a five-second electrical discharge from a Taser does not result in any significant changes that indicate increased physiologic stress ...' So if you get hit by a Taser and die it's your fault because you weren't healthy enough. Stories of people dying after being Tasered are coming in almost by the week and this will increase with its expanding use. Hundreds have died so far and that figure is going to soar (Fig 294). People in handcuffs, pregnant women, the old and the young, are now fair-game for these brain-donors. One innocent deaf guy was Tasered by Wichita Police who forced their way into his home after a false alarm about a shooting. He kept saying, 'I can't hear! I can't hear!', but they Tasered him for 'refusing to obey their commands'. A British man was Tasered twice by another numbskull police officer while he lay in a diabetic coma. 50,000 volts and a uniform with a brain the size of a pea is not the greatest combination I have ever come across. Invariably, even the most extreme use of the Taser is defended by superiors to protect the credibility of the weapon. A Polish immigrant can be seen on video being Tasered to death at Vancouver Airport when he was no threat to the three big 'brave' officers who dealt with him. The lawyer for Robert Dziekanski's family said he had been in touch with witnesses and viewed the video of the incident taken by an onlooker. It appeared that the interaction between the police and Mr Dziekanski, who could not speak English, lasted just 24 seconds before the Taser was used.

Illustration by David Dees (deesillustration.com)

Figure 294: *The Land of the Free*

Many police forces can even use the Taser on children and they are doing so, as we saw with the case of the nine-year-old girl at an Arizona school for children with special needs. The girl was already handcuffed when a 'veteran officer', clearly senile, used the Taser on her. 'It didn't involve an integrity issue,' his superior said. 'The officer made a decision to do what he thought he needed to do.' How can it involve integrity when you don't have any? A 14-year-old girl in New Mexico was Tasered in the head for running off after an argument with her mother, and was left with a giant scar. In the UK, it is quite legal to use the Taser on children even though the government's own Defence Scientific Advisory Council medical committee has said that not enough is known about the health risks of using the weapon on children. The committee, which comprises scientists and doctors, said that limited research suggested there was a risk children could suffer 'a serious cardiac event'. The committee recommended that officers should be 'particularly vigilant' for any adverse response from Taser victims and asked for guidelines to be changed to 'identify children and adults of small stature' as being at potentially greater risk from the cardiac effects of what are claimed to be non-lethal Tasers. The manufacturers have refused to accept that any death anywhere has been caused by its products. Being hit by a Taser and then dying does not, apparently, constitute a connection. Point number one: They knew it could, indeed would, kill people. Point number two: They knew that with so many John Wayne wannabes, idiots and emotional cripples in the law enforcement professions around the world the Taser was going to be abused. This is what they wanted. People dying from the Taser and police using it for the most minor 'refusal to comply' is meant to impose total subordination of the people to law enforcement. An article by a journalist who saw the Taser in action was headlined: 'Whatever you say officer, just don't use that thing on me'. This is the real reason for the Taser and the plan is to issue one to every police officer on the planet. The same company has now introduced a projectile Taser called the 'XREP' that can be delivered at a range of 100 feet and be used in a 12-gauge shotgun. The victim would suffer an excruciatingly-painful electric shock for 20 seconds after impact. Taser co-founder, Rick Smith, told reporters:

Figure 295: *Peaceful protestors are being scattered by excruciatingly painful sound technology*

Figure 296: *You are feeling sleeeepy ...*

It's a bigger projectile to reach out to extended ranges. It's moving faster; it's going to, potentially, cause a much bigger bruise, contusions. It's going to be a pretty bad thing.

Do you think he sleeps at night? No problem, I'm sure. Other crowd-control weaponry in the pipeline includes a microwave system designed to be fired from aircraft to inflict pain on the people below. It is an extension of the 'Active Denial System' that uses microwaves to heat the surface of the skin and is now being 'upgraded' by the Pentagon's Joint Non-Lethal Weapons Directorate in Quantico, Virginia, for use on crowds protesting against the takeover of their countries by the fascist cabal. Already peaceful crowds involved in legitimate protest are being scattered by excruciatingly painful sound waves broadcast from a police truck, as we saw at the G20 summit in Pittsburgh, Pennsylvania, in 2009 (Fig 295); and police with machine guns are patrolling parts of London for the first time. All this has been incessantly expanding while the population was focused on 'the game', the soap, the lottery or the reality TV show. Here, watch this, shut up (Fig 296).

Military on the Streets

The police are being rapidly militarised and the official military is being prepared to patrol the streets. In fact, it is already happening. Checks and balances on the use of the military for domestic law enforcement continue to be removed by the mass of anti-terrorist legislation passed since 9/11. Congress has given the President the right to commandeer Federal and State National Guard Troops for use against American citizens. Bill HR 5122, passed in 2006, gives the President the power to:

> ... employ the armed forces, including the National Guard in Federal service, to ... restore public order and enforce the laws of the United States when, as a result of a natural disaster, epidemic, or other serious public health emergency, terrorist attack or incident, or other condition in any State or possession of the United States ... where the President determines that ... domestic violence has occurred to such an extent that the constituted authorities of the State or possession are incapable of maintaining public order; suppress, in a State, any insurrection, domestic violence, unlawful combination, or conspiracy ...

The bill overrides the Posse Comitatus Act of 1878 that abolished the use of the military against US citizens. This is crucial given that they intend to use the military in domestic law enforcement and impose a military dictatorship by declaring Martial Law in response to 'problems' they will engineer (Fig 297). This is the reason that the Pentagon asked Congress in 2009 for clearance to post nearly 400,000 military personnel throughout the United States in the event of an 'emergency' and 'major disaster', and large numbers of these troops will not even be American. The military has been amassing an army of foreign troops to patrol the streets of America in the knowledge that many American soldiers will be reluctant to fire on their own people. The

Illustration by David Dees (deesillustration.com)

Figure 297: *The world the Reptilians and their Illuminati want to see*

military has been gradually deployed on the streets of America to get the public used to its presence, in line with the technique of the Totalitarian Tiptoe, and by mid-2009 troops were to be seen right across the country. They are also engaged in a series of 'drills' in which they 'practise' taking over American towns and cities. US Northern Command, or 'Northcom', is the domestic military operation created as a Problem-Reaction-Solution after 9/11 to 'protect' the 'homeland' from 'terrorists' (the people). Northcom, which operates out of Peterson AFB, Colorado Springs, is also responsible for 'theater security cooperation' with Canada and Mexico. Its current commander is General Victor Eugene Renuart Jr, who is also commander of North American Aerospace Defense Command (NORAD), which was fundamentally involved in the engineered attacks of 9/11. See *Alice in Wonderland and the World Trade Center Disaster* and *The David Icke Guide to the Global Conspiracy (and how to end it)*. It was Northcom that circulated a 'Congressional Fact Sheet' called the 'Legislative Proposal for Activation of Federal Reserve Forces for Disasters'. This proposed that the Secretary of Defense, the Bush/Obama-appointed Robert Gates, be authorised 'to order any unit or member of the Army Reserve, Air Force Reserve, Navy Reserve, and the Marine Corps Reserve, to active duty for a major disaster or emergency'. It describes an 'emergency' according to terms 'defined in section 5122 of title 42, US Code'. This is a section that gives one man, the puppet President, the sole discretion to decide what constitutes an 'emergency' or 'major disaster'. It is all so blatant. Secure the right to have hundreds of thousands of troops on the streets of America in the event of an emergency or major disaster and then engineer the excuse for your yes-man President to declare an emergency or major disaster. As David Rockefeller said at the United Nations in 1994: 'We are on the verge of a global transformation; all we need is the right major crisis.' In January 2010, Obama signed the undebated Executive Order 13528 to establish a 'Council of Governors', an 'advisory panel' of ten state governors (appointed by Obama) that will speed the 'synchronization and integration of State and Federal military activities in the United States' and expand military involvement in domestic law enforcement. The move is designed to allow the federal government to seize control of state National Guard troops during a 'national emergency'. This would put National Guard units under the control of United States Northern Command – the organisation set up precisely to impose domestic 'law enforcement' by the military in America.

That's FEMA, spelled: N...A...Z...I

At the centre of all this in the United States is an organisation called the Federal Emergency Management Agency (FEMA), which is *supposed to be* a rapid-response system in the wake of hurricanes and suchlike. This, however, is only the cover story. The real reason for FEMA's existence is to create and administer the control networks, including concentration camps, in preparation for the military takeover when 'dissidents' who refuse to conform are due to be rounded up and killed. The *Washington Post* reported in 2006 that the National Counterterrorism Center held the names of 325,000 'terrorist suspects', four times more than in 2003. Imagine what it must be now. These will include people like me, anti-war protestors and anyone who would challenge what they call the New World Order (Fig 298).They have a long-established colour-coded system in place to identify levels of resistance and these 'colour groups' are planned to be 'removed' in order of perceived danger to their dictatorship. Oh, do make me a red, chaps. It suits me. Check the Internet for the background and location of the camps, or 'holding facilities', and you'll be shocked, if indeed it is possible to be shocked any more after reading this book. As I write, the National Emergency Centers Establishment Act, Bill HR 645, has been presented on Capitol Hill by the Florida Democrat, Alcee L Hastings, which directs the Secretary of Homeland Security to establish 'not fewer' than six national 'emergency centres' on military installations to hold civilians. In fact, there are already hundreds in the United States alone with the infamous Dick Cheney-connected Halliburton Corporation now contracted to build more. There will be a similar situation in other major countries. The US National Guard began to advertise for 'Internment/Resettlement Specialists' in 2009. The job description said that they would ensure 'the smooth running of military confinement/correctional facility or detention/internment facility, similar to those duties conducted by civilian Corrections Officers'. US Army Regulation 210-35, headed the 'Civilian Inmate Labor Program', includes 'guidance for establishing and managing civilian inmate labor programs on Army installations' and 'guidance on establishing prison camps on Army installations'. All this is part of a planned military coup in America called 'Rex 84' that

was established during the Reagan-Father Bush administration by, amongst others, the infamous Oliver North. He somehow became a hero to many Americans for his part in the drugs-for-weapons Iran-Contra scandal of the 1980s when weapons were illegally sold to Iran and the profits used to fund a terrorist army in Nicaragua and a drug-running operation. Lovely people. 'Rex 84' is short for Readiness Exercise 1984. The *Miami Herald* reported in 1987:

Figure 298: *The truth is – they never were*

> Lieutenant Colonel Oliver North and the Federal Emergency Management Agency ... had drafted a contingency plan providing for the suspension of the Constitution, the imposition of martial law, and the appointment of military commanders to head state and local governments and to detain dissidents and Central American refugees in the event of a national crisis.

This plan has been ongoing with many subsequent 'exercises' involving FEMA and the Department of Defense in association with federal civil departments and agencies, the CIA, the FBI, the Secret Service and other NATO nations to respond militarily to 'civil disturbances' and 'demonstrations and strikes' that could affect continuity of government and/or resource mobilization. They plan to engineer events to trigger the response from the public that would then 'justify' military intervention to detain anyone they choose, control the movements of people and impose martial law. Presidential Executive Orders have been signed by successive Illuminati placemen and they are all activated by the declaration of a state of emergency. These include:

- EO 10990: Allows the government to take over all modes of transportation and control of highways and seaports.
- EO 10995: Federal seizure of all communications media in the US.
- EO 10997: Federal seizure of all electric power, fuels, minerals, public and private.
- EO 10998: Federal seizure of all food supplies and resources, public and private and all farms and equipment.
- EO 10999: Federal seizure of all means of transportation, including cars, trucks, or vehicles of any kind and total control over all highways, seaports and waterways.
- EO 11000: Federal seizure of American people for work forces under federal supervision, including the splitting up of families if the government so desires.
- EO 11001: Federal seizure of all health, education and welfare facilities, both public and private.
- EO 11002: Empowers the Postmaster General to register every single person in the US.
- EO 11003: Federal seizure of all airports and aircraft.
- EO 11004: Federal seizure of all housing and finances and authority to establish forced relocation. Authority to designate areas to be abandoned as 'unsafe', establish new locations for populations, relocate communities, build new housing with public funds.
- EO 11005: Seizure of all railroads, inland waterways and storage facilities, both public and private.
- EO 11051: Provides FEMA complete authorization to put above orders into effect in times of increased international tension of economic or financial crisis (FEMA will be in control in case of 'National Emergency').

Not coincidentally, Father George Bush, a major player at his level of the hierarchy, signed Executive Order 12803 in 1992 to authorise the sale of the infrastructure of the United States or the 'disposition or transfer of an infrastructure "asset" such as by sale or by long-term lease from a State or local government to a private party'. The assets the order listed – and they were only examples, not everything involved – were roads, tunnels, bridges, electricity supply facilities, mass transit, rail transportation, airports, ports, waterways, recycling/wastewater treatment facilities, solid waste disposal facilities, hospitals, prisons, schools and housing. The Bush sell-off opened the way for this vital infrastructure to be sold to the Illuminati cabal of corporations headed by the Rothschilds. How much has been sold? To whom and where did the money go? This is connected to the planned coup on the United States and the same is waiting to be instigated in other countries. Peter Anthony DeFazio, a Democratic Representative for Oregon, said in September 2008:

> Ladies and gentlemen, there is a plan that is in place to be executed by the Federals to lock down the cities and towns across our land and to begin gun confiscation. There is a plan to deal with mass quarantining of the population and its subsequent internment and suspension of the Constitutional rights of Citizens.

> Now that you know, you can plan with this in mind when a 'national emergency' is declared and some group of unscrupulous people seek to gain total control over the population or portions of political dissidents – you now know what power the Federals will not hesitate to utilize for their insidious ends.

FEMA, which is behind the 'holding camps', has a budget of billions and has the power to suspend laws and the Constitution (even if it did apply to the population); arrest people and hold them indefinitely without trial; commandeer food supplies, property and transport of any kind, including private vehicles; break up families and force people, even large populations, to relocate as instructed. This fascist organisation wasn't even created by Congress, but by Presidential Executive Order that requires no debate in what is so erroneously dubbed the 'Land of the Free'. Executive Order Number 12148 was signed by Jimmy Carter in 1979 just in time for the Reagan-Father Bush administration to mould it into the covert tyranny it was always meant to be. FEMA became part of the Orwellian Emergency Preparedness and Response Directorate within the Department of Homeland Security in 2003. Father Bush was the architect of FEMA as it is today along with his cousin, Louis Giuffrida, and Oliver North. A memo in 1982 to the then FEMA director Louis Giuffrida said that martial law 'suspends all prior existing laws, functions, systems, and programs of civil government, replacing them ... with a military system'. It is no surprise, therefore, that I was told the following by a man who attended a FEMA training course. He described his experience of the Bush family relative, Louis Giuffrida:

> I was at FEMA training headquarters in ... Maryland, attending a radiological defense pilot course in 1982 for the Washington State Department of Emergency Services. During the orientation, Louis Giuffrida, one of the head honchos and a cousin of George Bush, came in to observe. When he sat down I noticed a dark haze around him. I kept looking at him to see if my eyes were playing tricks on me or what, but it stayed the same.

> I was up in the seats alone as I like to be in these things. Soon, I noticed he was staring at me! This unnerved me. I closed my eyes and tried to relax. When I opened my eyes

again, I saw him coming toward me. He sat down a few rows behind and to the left of me. I glanced back and saw him leaning forward with his eyes closed. I figured he was just tired and decided to take a rest with me.

While sitting there trying to relax, I heard a strange hissing and swishing sound come from behind me. I opened my eyes, but was afraid to look around. I saw a woman in our group looking up in our direction with a look of astonishment and shock on her face. She kept looking up nervously in our direction. Eventually, Giuffrida left with his body guards (waxy-faced suits with sunglasses) and the presentation continued.

After the orientation, I walked outside and found this woman sobbing and shaking in the arms of another participant. I intruded and said I wanted to know why she was looking up with that look on her face. She didn't want to say, but with repeated assurance from me she told me. She had seen Giuffrida 'turn' into a lizard! The other guy said Giuffrida had the nickname of 'lizard man' in the circles around FEMA and he has a skin disease that makes his skin look like scales.

We tried to assure her that she was just stressed or something. I thought maybe too many drugs or over active imagination. But she was very adamant about what she saw and was visibly shaken by it. The other guy also said there was scuttlebutt of an underground rail system that ran under the FEMA facility. Just as he said that, we felt a low rumbling beneath our feet like a subway. We noticed some suits coming in our direction and headed off.

Over the course of the next two weeks we all got to know each other fairly well. All these people were professionals in their fields. I found them all reasonable and fine examples of who I would call true friends. I had forgotten about this experience until I read David's book. It was just one of those odd things that didn't make sense. Now it does. So, what more can I say? I don't just believe it's real, I 'know' it is. Unless, of course, I want to deny my own experience and senses.

There will be many who have read this far and yet still don't want to accept that the world is controlled by Reptilian entities hiding behind human form. I understand that; but it's true, and we need to get used to it and get on with sorting it out while we still can. The Bush family is a Reptilian-hybrid bloodline and so it is easy to see why this gentleman had the experience he did with Bush cousin, Giuffrida. The positions of power in all these major government and military departments and agencies building the global fascist dictatorship are Reptilians operating just outside of visible light who possess the human form of their hybrids or can also energetically project the appearance of human form. Occasionally, they experience an energy shift that allows their true form to be seen in this reality. FEMA is a vital cog in the Reptilian plan for America and it was bound to involve one of their own in Giuffrida and another shapeshifter, Father Bush. See *The Biggest Secret* and *Children of the Matrix* for a lot of stories told to me by people around the world who have witnessed human-reptilian shapeshifting.

Military Government

You can see the reptilian symbolism in the military and 'security' systems in America with agencies and groups like the VIPER teams, or Visible Intermodal Protection and Response teams that work undercover to maintain surveillance on those using railways, buses and ferries. The same symbolism is employed in Britain, too. I have written in other books about a leading member of the Reptilian-hybrid elite who uses the code name: 'Pindar'. This word comes up a few times in different contexts with regard to the conspiracy. What is said to be the most important underground military fortress, or 'citadel', in London, and possibly the whole country, is called PINDAR. It is located under the Ministry of Defence in Whitehall across the road from Downing Street. It was officially completed in 1994. London is a maze of tunnels connecting the ministries with Downing Street, Buckingham Palace and other centres of power. It means that someone can enter one building and then go via the tunnels to another without anyone on the surface knowing. This is how events are orchestrated between people who never officially meet. The PINDAR facility is described as a crisis management and communications centre and connects the Ministry of Defence with the centre of military operations, the Permanent Joint Headquarters in Hertfordshire on the outskirts of London which is known as the Northwood Headquarters. This also has a major NATO presence and is planned to be a major centre for the army of the European Union. It has undergone a great deal of expansion in recent years to update command, control and communications technology and allow its personnel to direct military operations worldwide. PINDAR and Northwood will be the centres for military control when they plan to impose their police-military state on the back of some engineered 'national emergency'. The coordination centre for government-military-security agency leaders at a time of 'national emergency' is called COBRA, after the location where the Civil Contingencies Committee meets – the Cabinet Office Briefing Rooms (COBR). Well, that's the official story for the name, anyway. COBRA is located in Whitehall right next to PINDAR. Officially, its purpose is to 'enable the prime minister, senior ministers, key government officials, and other critical persons such as the Metropolitan Police Commissioner, Mayor of London, Director of the SAS and intelligence officials to obtain vital information about an incident and to secure lines of communication to the police and other emergency services, army, hospitals, and all relevant branches of government'. The real reason for both PINDAR and COBRA is, like FEMA, to coordinate a planned military coup, although most of the here-today-gone-tomorrow politicians won't know that.

The point to grasp is that America is not controlled from the White House or Capitol Hill, but from the Pentagon. In the same way, Britain is not controlled from Downing Street or Parliament, but from Northwood headquarters and associated military centres. The military is itself controlled at the highest levels by the bloodline families and it is vital that the fodder troops rebel and break ranks when they are ordered to attack and suppress their own people. If they don't, they are allowing themselves to be the pawns of the bloodline cabal in pursuit of very sinister ends. A wonderful example of how effective this can be is the case of US General, Smedley Butler, the man I quoted earlier about war being a racket. He told the McCormack-Dickstein Committee in 1934 how he had been approached the previous year to lead a fascist coup on the United States by representatives of famous Wall Street and corporate names, including DuPont,

Goodyear and JP Morgan, along with military figures. One of them told Butler: 'We have got the newspapers.' And that is why most people have never heard of this fascist plot to seize control of America in the 1930s. It was a fantastic story, revealed at public hearings by a highly respected general, but the media ignored the story and the McCormack-Dickstein Committee deleted the major names involved from its final report and refused to make them appear to be questioned. Butler said in 1935:

> Like most committees it has slaughtered the little and allowed the big to escape. The big shots weren't even called to testify. They were all mentioned in the testimony. Why was all mention of these names suppressed from the testimony?

The point is, however, that thanks to Butler's courage and sense of decency the plot failed and what is happening now will fail if the troops themselves refuse to cooperate with the fascist control of their own families. How people like Smedley Butler are needed in the military today.

Controlling the 'Opposition'

There are organisations that claim to 'fight' for civil liberties, but at least the major ones are embedded in the very system they claim to be challenging. The UK 'civil rights' group, Liberty, is among them. I heard a Liberty spokesman say that they had nothing against surveillance technologies in themselves, but the danger was that they would not be 'properly regulated' and people could find themselves living in 'a surveillance society'. Number one: what does he mean by 'could find themselves' when we are already in a surveillance society? Number two: his words perfectly summarise the official civil liberties movement. They have no idea what they are dealing with and so they are next to useless in dealing with it. The face of civil liberties in Britain is Shami Chakrabarti, the head of Liberty and a former barrister with the UK Home Office, which has an appalling disregard for the freedoms of the population. She is a governor of the Ditchley Foundation, a forum or 'think tank' for the political elite that connects into the Round Table/Bilderberg Group network. A fellow governor is Lord Carrington, a long-time chairman of the Bilderberg Group, Secretary-General of NATO and close associate of Henry Kissinger and the Rothschild family, to which the Carrington clan is related. Carrington is widely mentioned in my earlier books. The Ditchley Foundation, based in a mansion at Ditchley Park in Oxfordshire, describes itself in the classic terms of these Round Table 'think tanks' and includes, as always, 'strict rules of confidentiality':

> ... Ditchley's style and programme provide an opportunity for brainstorming unique in international affairs. Small invited groups of about 40 distinguished men and women are brought together from senior levels in the worlds of politics, business and industry, academic life, the civil service, the armed forces and the media. Conference subjects are carefully chosen in response to new international challenges arising from issues of concern to democratic societies. Conferences stress open, informal discussions that reflect personal thinking and take place under strict rules of confidentiality.

John Major, the former British prime minister and European head of the Bush/neocon-controlled Carlyle Group, says that the aim of Ditchley is to change government policy.

Shami Chakrabarti also describes how her world-view has been changed by her involvement with Ditchley. Both are goals of these Round Table 'think tanks' – to influence the policy of governments and the opinions and perceptions of those invited to be involved. Having the head of a civil liberties organisation associated with elite groups that include leading politicians and establishment figures and operate under strict rules of confidentiality is, I would suggest, not a way to represent demands for a free and open society. Another theme of many of the Round Table 'think tanks' is to bring together the elite of Britain and America and this is the aim of the appropriately named British-American Project, also known by some as 'Junior Bilderberg'. Lord Carrington turns up as a patron along with Lord Robertson, another former head of NATO and a Bilderberg attendee. Among the members of the UK Advisory Board is BBC frontline journalist, James Naughtie, and among the 'Fellows' are Jeremy Paxman, the BBC's leading television current-affairs presenter, and Jonathan Powell, chief of staff to Tony Blair. Another alumnus of the British-American Project is Shami Chakrabarti, of Liberty. The British-American Project is another group that connects into the Round Table. It was created with help from the Royal Institute of International Affairs and is funded by a rake of global corporations, including the horrific Monsanto, the company behind GM food, the brain-suppressing sweetener, aspartame, and Agent Orange that caused human and environmental devastation during the Vietnam War. Among the American members of the 'Advisory Board' of the British-American Project is Paul Wolfowitz, one of the main architects of the invasions of Afghanistan and Iraq and the 'war on terror' that has been used to justify the Big Brother State world-wide. The head of 'Liberty' is involved with *these people*?? Chakrabarti has been ranked by the UK's *Daily Telegraph* as one of the most influential people on both the Right and Left of British politics, but clearly she is not influential at all. She is supposed to be defending liberties when they are being removed by the hour and she is operating in the very circles that are destroying them.

Seat at the Table

Shami Chakrabarti was educated, or I might call it something else, at the Fabian Society-created-and-controlled London School of Economics where she is now on the 'Court of Governors'. The London School of Economics and Political Science (LSE) was founded in 1895 by members of the Fabian Society, Sidney and Beatrice Webb, Graham Wallas and George Bernard Shaw, as I detailed earlier. It has been directed by the Fabian Society ever since and is appropriately located close to Temple Bar in London, home to the Knights Templar and the centre of the legal profession. The LSE 'Court' is chaired at the time of writing by Peter D Sutherland, a major player in the Bilderberg Group, a Trilateral Commission member, chairman of BP and Goldman Sachs International, and former Director-General of the World Trade Organization (WTO). He is also a financial advisor to the Vatican, the Church of Babylon, and has been a regular name in the pages of my books. LSE governors also include Cherie Blair (wife of Fabian Tony) and Sir Evelyn de Rothschild, one of the dynasty's major players. I am not saying that Chakrabarti is knowingly involved in any conspiracy with these people, but you can see the establishment circles she operates in. What is she doing working so closely with the very people who are systematically destroying basic freedoms? If I was the Fabian Society and the wider Illuminati and I could choose the best person to represent the 'civil liberties' that I wanted to destroy, it would be someone from the 'anti-establishment establishment', like Shami Chakrabarti. She accepted an honour from the Queen in 2007, the Commander of the Order of the British Empire (CBE). She said she believed it was an encouragement from the Queen to continue to protect civil liberties, which is a bit like saying that someone was honoured by the Nazis to encourage them to continue to protect Jews, Communists and gays. The naivety and ignorance of what is really happening in the world is shocking for someone at the head of Britain's most high-profile civil liberties group. A freedom campaigner who tried to explain to her that 9/11 was an inside job said her eyes just 'glazed over'. If you don't know what truly happened on 9/11, and won't even research it, how on earth can you understand the background to the attacks on civil liberties? She has no compass to work with and so she's no threat whatsoever to those who wish to delete every civil liberty you could imagine.

The Illuminati network operates on many levels to orchestrate the outcome of the 'debates' it seeks to win and policies it is determined to impose. One of the keys to this is to have establishment figures leading the opposition to your establishment agenda, even if they don't even realise themselves how they are being used. This gives you a much better chance of controlling how the 'debate' plays out. In Sharmi Chakrabarti, they have just such an establishment figure – a former government barrister, governor and member of Round Table groups who interacts through many forums with the very people who want anything but liberty for the people either of Britain or the wider world. It is the same with the official civil liberties organisations in the United States and elsewhere, because they won't look at the bigger conspiracy, either. The Shami Chakrabarti of the United States for 17 years until 2008 was Nadine Strossen, a law professor, who became the first woman, and youngest, President of the American Civil Liberties Union (ACLU). Professor Strossen is a member of the Council on Foreign Relations and replaced the previous ACLU president, Norman Dorsen, a member of the Council on Foreign Relations. It is time that those who claim to represent our civil liberties began to wake up to what is really going on and understand the true nature of the force that is destroying those liberties across the world.

The Last Generation

I call young people today the 'Orwell generation'. They are getting the Big Brother State full blast from the earliest age and it is sobering to think that those of us born before the mass surveillance began are the last generations who have the experience to compare what the world was like with what it is becoming. Today's children will not be able to make that comparison and that's crucial to the Reptilian manipulators. When we 'arrive' in this world we see it as 'the way life is'. We've never known anything else so this is how things must be. As the world changes throughout our lives, we have a coordinate – how it used to be – to observe the change and if we don't like it we can make our feelings known. The pandemic of freedom-busting today is a great example of this. But when you are born into a society that already has its schools and streets peppered with cameras, children have their fingerprints taken to access school meals, and surveillance is everywhere, the new arrivals are coming into the world 'as it is'. To them, it will be 'the norm' – all they have known (Fig 299 overleaf). That makes those with a few decades behind us, the ones with their eyes open anyway, the last generations who will be able to see what is happening so blatantly, and it presents us

Figure 299: *Are we going to sit around and let this happen?*

with enormous responsibility. We are seeing ever-younger children targeted by the boneheads in uniform to instil fear of authority from an early age. The British Home Office is even fingerprinting under-fives, and may include babies, in a biometrics ID scheme 'trial'. All 'trials', as in GM crop 'trials', are merely scams to slowly introduce what they know all along is going to be done. Have you noticed how all 'trials' are 'successful'? A spokesrobot said that fingerprinting was an established biometric technology and there was no minimum age for its use. We are seeing surveillance cameras in schools across the world, in some cases 50 and more, even in toilets. Other schools have gone as far as imposing a system of fingerprinting students to monitor absenteeism, often supported by headteachers who think (if their minds ever get that far) that quicker administration is far more important than the basic freedoms of those who are supposed to be in their care. The big sell for Big Brother 'education' is 'protecting the children' after violent events in schools and colleges in Arkansas, Colorado, California, Kentucky, Virginia, Mississippi and other states, and in places like Dunblane in Scotland. Problem-Reaction-Solution.

The official 'civil liberties' organisations have proved to be next to useless in holding back the tide of tyranny. We need politicians and civil liberties advocates that are not connected in any way to the Round Table web – people who refuse to 'join the club' or be involved with the Establishment, except to expose it. This will not happen in anything like the near future and so we, the people, need to defend our own liberties before there is nothing left to defend. That means a People's Revolution of peaceful, *always* peaceful, non-cooperation with the system that seeks to enslave us.

26

Game Plan (7): Stealing the Children

George Orwell's *1984* is the most famous 'Big Brother' book, but there is another that was equally prophetic and accurate. Put the two together and you pretty much have the world that we are now hurtling towards unless humanity chooses to apply the brakes – *now*.

This second book is Aldous Huxley's *Brave New World*, published in 1932 and, as I explained earlier, both Huxley and Orwell acquired the information for their 'novels' through their association with the Illuminati Fabian Society. *Brave New World* describes a global system of total control in which children are raised in communal nurseries and conditioned from birth to worship the State. They are electro-shocked like laboratory rats if they do anything that does not conform to their programming. One scene has babies crawling towards pictures of flowers and birds only to be shocked, because the State didn't want them to like nature. People are punished today through various means for not acting in ways acceptable to the State and they are rewarded when they do as demanded. One form of 'electro-shock' is to attack and ridicule people who challenge conventional 'thinking' and make it a crime to be different. Children in *Brave New World* are brainwashed even when they sleep as subliminal messages turn them into insatiable consumers to drive the engine of industrial production. The foundation of child-control in Huxley's book is to remove children from the influence of their parents and break up the family unit. This is demonstrably happening now and it has been planned since well before Huxley wrote his book in the 1930s (Fig 300 overleaf). You may recall that the Rothschild Zionist, Dr Richard Day, said in 1969 that the family was planned to diminish in importance, and in that same year the British Humanist Association proclaimed: '... Some opponents of Humanism have accused us of wishing to overthrow the traditional Christian family. They are right. That is exactly what we intend to do.' Humanism dismisses religion and the 'supernatural' while being basically a branch of the religion of 'scientism'. It does not accept life after death and says that every human is a unit of mind, body and personality. There is no dualism of body and soul and so mind and body cease to exist at death. Humanism is a front to remove the concept of eternal Consciousness from human perception. The British Humanist Association was founded in 1896 by American, Stanton Coit, as the Union of Ethical Societies. Coit was a prominent member of the Fabian Society and, when his organisation was renamed the British Humanist Association in the 1960s, its first president was Julian Huxley, brother of the Fabian, Aldous '*Brave New World*' Huxley. He was succeeded in 1965 by A J Ayer whose father worked for the Rothschild family. The 'No God' obsessive, Professor Richard Dawkins, is a vice-president of the British

Figure 300: *The dumbing down and drugging of children is well underway, just as Huxley described*

Humanist Association while fronting up his own religion of scientism (left-brain imprisonment is essential for membership). The United Nations Convention on the Rights of the Child was introduced in 1989 via UNICEF, the United Nations Children's Fund, and it is a major stepping-stone towards State control of children. It is presented as a human-rights charter for children when it is really designed to forge a wedge between children and their parents. The United Nations works closely with the World Federation for Mental Health through UNESCO, the United Nations Educational, Scientific and Cultural Organization, whose first Director-General was Julian Huxley. The World Federation for Mental Health was established in 1948 in the same era as the United Nations and the World Health Organization and its first president was John Rawlings Rees, founder of the global social engineering operation, the Tavistock Institute, in London of which more later. Rawlings Rees pledged to transform society through mass behaviour manipulation. The United Nations has a 'consultative relationship' with the World Federation for Mental Health. This is highly significant given that the Federation's founding document, 'Mental Health and World Citizenship', says this:

> Studies of human development indicate the modifiability of human behaviour throughout life, especially during infancy, childhood and adolescence … Social institutions such as family and school impose their imprint early … It is the men and women in whom these patterns of attitude and behaviour have been incorporated who present the immediate resistance to social, economic and political changes.

In other words, destroy the family so that the State can implant its own sense of perception from birth. Aldous Huxley is describing the Illuminati agenda for children in his *Brave New World*, and here the 'Director of Hatcheries and Conditioning' explains the origin of the term 'parent' to his students:

> In brief, parents were the father and mother … These are unpleasant facts, I know it. But then most historical facts are unpleasant … In those days … children were brought up by their parents and not in State Conditioning Centres.

Children in *Brave New World* are produced artificially by the World State and not by natural childbirth. Rothschild Zionist, Dr Richard Day, told those doctors in 1969 that 'they' would be 'redirecting the purpose of sex – sex without reproduction and reproduction without sex'. Children are divided into five castes in *Brave New World*, the Alphas, Betas, Gammas, Deltas and Epsilons, and each caste is sub-divided into sections called Plus and Minus. The highest caste is allowed to develop naturally while the others are given chemicals to suppress them mentally and physically. This is already happening in mainstream society with chemical cocktails we call food and drink, and the products aimed at children are some of the worst. Then, of course, there is the mass drugging of children through mind-altering potions like Ritalin. Alpha or Beta castes are produced from one fertilised egg developing into a single foetus, but the others are the result of what Huxley calls 'Bokanovsky's Process'. We would call it mass cloning. It allows nearly a hundred children to be produced from a single egg and thousands from a single ovary. There are no emotional relationships in *Brave New World,* because 'everyone belongs to everyone else'. The concept of family is abhorrent and the idea of being a parent is considered obscene. The book may have been written 80 years ago, but it was right on the button. The world that Huxley describes is how the bloodline families and their Reptilian masters want it to be and you can see the steps of the Totalitarian Tiptoe heading in that direction with quickening speed.

State Control of Children

We are seeing an ever-lengthening list of excuses to remove children from their parents, and a common theme is to equate refusing to follow the official line with being a 'bad parent' or even 'child abuse'. If you won't do what the State decrees is best for your children the State must either make you conform or take them away. You can see this happening with vaccinations. Sandy Macara, former chairman of the Rothschild-controlled British Medical Association, has said that if parents can't be persuaded to give their children the highly-controversial MMR vaccine then it should be made compulsory. The next stage, if people continue to remain spectators in their own enslavement, will be to accuse those who still say 'no' of abusing their children and putting them in danger by not having them vaccinated. This is why it is so important that parents get involved now and join together with like-minded people to form networks to communicate information and support each other. The bloodlines are terrified that people will do this en masse. They are constantly dismantling structures that bring people together and we need to establish new ones. Parents are losing more and more rights to make decisions about their children as the State takes them for itself. Barack Obama read his teleprompter to call for children to spend still more time at school away from their families and for an end to the summer vacation as we know it today. Obama said that American children spend too little time in school and 'the challenges of a new century demand more time in the classroom'. This is all part of the constant pressure to have children and young people in the hands of the State for longer and longer. The man is a disgrace. John Taylor Gatto was New York State Teacher of the Year in 1991, but he sees clearly what state education is all about – programming, indoctrinating and dehumanising the world's children. He wrote:

> Networks like schools are not communities in the same way that school training is not education. By pre-empting 50 percent of the total time of the young, by locking young people up with young people exactly their own age, by ringing bells to start and stop work, by asking people to think about the same thing at the same time in the same way, by grading people the way we grade vegetables – and in a dozen other vile and stupid ways – network schools steal the vitality of communities and replace it with an ugly piece of mechanism. Nobody survives these places with his humanity intact, not kids, not teachers, not administrators, and not parents.

Illustration by David Dees (deesillustration.com)

Figure 301: *We're coming to get you kids. You belong to us now*

Now Obama and his masters want children in the tentacles of the State for even longer (Fig 301). Dr Richard Day said in 1969 that the plan was to have 'schools as the hub of the community'. Obama 'Education' Secretary, Arne Duncan says he has a 'vision' of 'schools as the heart of the community'. Oh, really? Tell me, pray, who gave you this 'vision'? No answer necessary. Duncan is another product of the Chicago political cesspit that produced Obama, Emanuel and Axelrod. The calculated programming of children and young people has been exposed by Charlotte Iserbyt, Senior Policy Advisor in the Office of Educational Research and Improvement at the US Department of Education during the first Reagan Administration. She reveals in her book, *The Deliberate Dumbing Down of America*, and in media interviews, how she was trained to target those in the system who would 'resist' the transformation of American and global education. She reveals from insider knowledge that programmes engineered by the Illuminati Carnegie Foundation and Julian Huxley's UNESCO set out to impose behaviour and perception modification through the 'education' system. Charlotte Iserbyt said:

> It all started in 1934 when the Carnegie Foundation set the agenda for the next hundred years and that was to change our country from a free, individualistic economy to a planned economy – and to do it through the schools. American education would henceforth concern itself with the importance of the group rather than with the importance of the individual ... The purpose of education would shift to focus on the student's emotional health, rather than academic learning.

The plan was to create new generations of Americans who would look to the United Nations as their 'nation' and not to the United States, opening the way for a one-world government. They wanted to program children and young people not to think for themselves, and the use of drugs was part of this. Everything Charlotte Iserbyt reveals about the calculated attack on the psyche of American children is happening in ever-greater extremes around the world. She especially highlights the part played in the programming of children by Benjamin Bloom (Rothschild Zionist), the American 'educational psychologist' at the University of Chicago and an educational advisor to the government of Israel. Bloom actually stated that the purpose of education was to 'change the thoughts, actions and feelings of students'.

Schools are becoming tyrannies – exactly as they are meant to be. One Republican in Texas even demanded that parents be fined $500 and be given a criminal record for not attending a scheduled meeting with a teacher. Yes, the very idea is ludicrous, but this is the way the world is going. A British mother was banned from a school for calmly asking a bully to stop using her five-year-old son as a 'human punch bag'. Christine Hart had complained to teachers over many months, but nothing was done. Christine was told not to cross the school gates at Orleans Infant School in Twickenham, London, and to attend a hearing with the governors to discuss her conduct. She was accused of 'verbally abusing' the pupil and interrupting a class, and warned that causing a 'nuisance' at school could constitute a criminal offence. Any further incidents would be reported to police. This was a mother trying to protect her five-year-old son who was coming home every day in tears while staff at the school did nothing to stop the bullying. If this was an isolated case, you could write it off as just stupid people at a single school; but it's not. Schools acting like dictatorships are increasing all the time and it is part of the step-by-step plan to have the State own all children. Parents in Britain who drive groups of children to scouts, brownies and sports events now have to undergo a criminal record check or face fines of up to £5,000. Officials estimate that eleven million people, any authority figure that comes into contact with children, will have to be registered with the Orwellian 'Independent Safeguarding Authority' – even parents giving their children's friends a lift to events. Parents who want to accompany their children to Christmas carol services and other festive activities are being officially vetted for criminal records at UK schools in case they are paedophiles. One village primary school told parents they had to be vetted before they could accompany pupils on a ten-minute walk to a morning carol service at the local church. Other schools demand checks on parents who walk with children from the school to post letters to Father Christmas. A criminal check is also to be forced upon British teenagers involved in the government's policy of compulsory 'community service' for 16 to 18 year olds. All of these extremes and stupidities are sold as protecting children from paedophiles, when the real reason is still greater State control of children and the erosion of parential rights. If they want to catch paedophiles they should go visit Capitol Hill or the Houses of Parliament. There's loads of them there. Ask Father George Bush; he'll tell you.

The Fabian Agenda

The British government launched the Orwellian 'Family Intervention Projects' in 2009 for the compulsory supervision of families that the State considers 'shameless'. They were established by the 'children's minister' with the inspired name of Ed Balls (Fig 302). 'This is pretty tough and non-negotiable support for families to get to the root of the problem,' he said. Targeted families will be forced to accept 'intensive 24-hour supervision to make sure children attend school, go to bed on time and eat proper meals'. Balls wants to see these 'projects' in every part of the country and it is just another step on the Totalitarian Tiptoe to the State ownership of children. Parents and their children are forced by the government every year to sign a 'Home-School Agreement' – a 'behaviour contract' in which the government demands what the parents and children must do. Parents are being asked to report other parents who 'allow their children to engage in bad

Figure 302: *Balls.*

behaviour' and these reported parents will be targeted for 'interventions'. The opposition Conservative Party, led by Rothschild-frontman, David Cameron, denounced the government policy as... *'too little, too late'*. Aldous Huxley got his inspiration for *Brave New World* from his knowledge of the Fabian agenda and so you won't be surprised to know by now that children's minister, Ed Balls, is a leading member and former chairman of the Fabian Society. He is simply following the Fabian agenda for the State ownership of children by encouraging the public to spy on each other and report parents to the authorities. Balls wants children to start formal schooling at the age of four. Once again, get the children from their parents as early as possible and start to lock them into the left-brain of 'formal education' at the expense of right-brain play that requires the imagination. Fabian Society asset, Tony Blair, introduced legislation in 2007 in his last months as prime minister that will track children from birth to 'identify potential criminals'. The net should be cast as widely as possible 'to prevent criminality developing', the Blair government said, and it proposed to 'establish universal checks throughout a child's development to help service providers to identify those most at risk of offending'. The plan included a new database of children and their parents, and a child's behaviour will be assessed for signs that they could become criminals. These include a short attention span (mostly a product of boring classes and food additives). We are talking here of the Orwellian concept of the 'pre-crime' when people are arrested and jailed for crimes the authorities say they *might* commit. The Fabian, Bertrand Russell, described the agenda for children in his 1931 book, *The Scientific Outlook*:

> All the boys and girls will learn from an early age to be what is called 'co-operative,' i.e., to do exactly what everybody is doing. Initiative will be discouraged in these children, and insubordination, without being punished, will be scientifically trained out of them ...

> ... education should aim at destroying free will, so that, after pupils have left school, they shall be incapable, throughout the rest of their lives, of thinking or acting otherwise than as their schoolmasters would have wished ...

> ... Diet, injections, and injunctions will combine, from a very early age, to produce the sort of character and the sort of beliefs that the authorities consider desirable, and any serious criticism of the powers that be will become psychologically impossible. Even if all are miserable, all will believe themselves happy, because the government will tell them that they are so.

The agenda for children is global and what is happening in Britain is happening elsewhere. The Obama 'healthcare' bill introduced in 2009 includes the same themes hidden away in its more than one-thousand pages in language so general you could make it mean anything. The Orwellian language not withstanding, you can see what they really mean – State control of children. Sections 440 and 1904 of the House bill are about 'home visitation programs for families with young children and families expecting children'. Is the Fabian Ed Balls working for Obama as well, then? The Obama bill mandates 'well-trained and competent staff' (government-trained robots) to teach parents about child behaviour (behaviour modification) and how to bring up their children. Aldous Huxley smiles and shakes his head. The next step is to remove parents from the scene altogether. President Fake's 'healthcare' bill, developed and decided by his handlers for him to sign into law, says that parents will be provided with 'knowledge of age-appropriate child development in cognitive, language, social, emotional, and motor domains ... modeling, consulting, and coaching on parenting practices ... skills to interact with their child to enhance age-appropriate development'. Now George Orwell is smiling and shaking his head. The bill targets the same people as Ed Balls – the State 'shall identify and prioritize serving communities that are in high need of such services, especially communities with a high proportion of low-income families'. All this will be paid for, amid unbelievable levels of debt, with grants from the federal government. Money is no object when the agenda is at stake.

Legalised kidnapping

Most disturbing is the way the State is taking children away from parents via secret 'family courts' for the most extraordinary reasons. These courts have no jury and the standard of proof required is lower than in criminal courts. The authorities do not have to prove beyond reasonable doubt that a child has been abused, only that on the 'balance of probabilities' this might be the case. We have had mothers acquitted of abuse in a criminal court who have still had their children stolen by the State in the family courts, which demand lower levels of evidence. Arrogant, mind-programmed 'social workers' are using this rigged system to seize children and hand them to foster parents of their choice while warning the real parents that if they challenge this outrage they will never be allowed to even see their children again. If you are new to this information, that last sentence is worth a second read. A mother in the UK had her twin babies taken from her by social workers for joking that the Caesarean birth had ruined her body. She spent £38,000 on IVF treatment in a desperate attempt to have children and these deeply disturbed people removed them within weeks. When she lost her temper at what they had done they reported that she had 'anger problems' which could be a threat to her twins. The authorities exploit high-profile real abuse cases to scan the community for fake 'abuse' that they can use to steal children from their parents. This is becoming common, but the public don't realise it because it is all done in secret. The cases that we do hear about represent only a fraction of the parents who have their children removed by the State every year. Jack Straw (Rothschild Zionist), the Fabian 'Justice' Secretary, promised that family courts would be opened to the media amid the growing outrage at this injustice, but judges ruled that journalists could not tell the public anything they saw or heard while the court was in session. Sir Mark Potter, the President of the Family Division, issued guidelines that said 'the proceedings remain proceedings held in private, and ... therefore the existing position relating to the publication of matters relating to proceedings which are so heard continues to apply'. This is the establishment's usual long-winded way of saying the ban on reporting child cases in family courts remains – and Straw knew it would. It was revealed in 2007 that local authorities were taking children from parents to meet their 'targets' for adoptions and an average of some 25,000 children a year are now taken into 'care' by the State in the United Kindom alone. The government pays a financial bonus to the councils if they secure their 'quota'. Think about that: Children are taken into 'care' unnecessarily and given to adoptive parents simply to meet government targets and cash in on financial incentives to do so. How can you have 'targets' for adoptions when each case must be judged on its merits? How can you have financial incentives to steal children from their parents? As always, when something doesn't make any sense and offends all natural justice, it is the agenda at work.

John Hemming, a Liberal Democrat MP in Britain, coordinates an organisation called Justice for Families which campaigns for reform of the system. He said that local authorities are using the family courts as 'retaliation' against families who question doctors' diagnoses of their children or challenge other decisions. 'Very often care proceedings are used as retaliation by local authorities against 'uppity' people who question the system,' he said. One family had all six of their children taken into care after they questioned the need for an invasive medical test on their daughter who was suspected of having a blood disease. The test proved negative, but the order stealing the children stayed in place. Another MP, the Conservative, Tim Yeo, accused Suffolk County Council of 'actively seeking opportunities to remove babies from their mothers'. 'Its social work staff do so in a manner which in my view is sometimes tantamount to child kidnapping,' he said. He was exposing the behaviour of social workers who forced a couple to give up their 11-week-old baby girl for adoption when there was no evidence of abuse whatsoever. He said that staff waited until the child's father was out before launching a raid with police at the family home to 'snatch the baby from the arms of her mother'. Yeo told MPs: 'The fact that no fault could be found in the physical and emotional care provided by her parents did not deter the council from destroying this fragile family.' The parents are allowed to see their daughter just once a month on a supervised visit and they planned to leave the country because the mother was pregnant again and terrified of having that baby kidnapped by the State, too. Despite the breathtaking injustices that come to light ever more often, Martin Narey, chief executive of the UK children's charity, Barnardo's, has called for many more children to be taken from their families. The former head of the UK Prison Service (some career move) said that social workers should be more 'pro-active' and 'if we really cared about the interests of the child, we would take children away as babies and put them into permanent adoptive families, where we know they will have the best possible outcome'. He was supported by MP Caroline Flint, a member of the Fabian Society. This theme is building all the time. Yes, some children need to be protected from their parents, but once the checks and balances go – and they are going faster and faster – you are entering the realms of fascism. During the eugenics frenzy funded by the bloodlines in the early part of the 20th century, social workers were appointed to decide which children should be sterilised and taken away from their families, and we are seeing history repeating. Social Services has become a State mafia and social workers are recruited with the 'right attitude' to be the foot soldiers of tyranny while genuine, decent, social workers are filtered out.

A girl in Scotland was banned by social workers from getting married two days before her wedding because they said she wasn't intelligent enough. This is the basis on which the eugenics movement began. What the girl had was mild learning difficulties and her fiancé said he had known her for two months before he found out because he had not seen evidence of it. Even so, the bully boys and girls at Fife Council's Social Services objected and the authorities refused to sanction the marriage when the rings, wedding dress and reception had all been paid for. These cold and callous people then announced they would, in effect, steal the pregnant girl's child a few hours after birth and give it to foster parents of their choice. The father of the child, the girl's would-be husband, said he wanted to take full responsibility for his son, but he was powerless to do so because ... he wasn't married to the mother. *Don't tell me that the block on the marriage and the theft of the child were not connected.* The father said: 'Social Services are ruining our lives. As we are not married – because social workers would not let us marry – it seems I have no rights as a dad at all.' The scale and depth of State imposition is shocking. By the autumn of 2009, record numbers of UK children were being taken into care 'due to the recession'. Yeah, okay. A massive surge in cases took the number in foster homes to around 50,000 in England and Wales alone.

Paid-As-You-Kidnap

The abduction of children by the State is not confined to the United Kingdom. It is happening across the world, because the plan is, as Huxley outlined in his 'novel', to have a World State that breeds and owns all children. An investigation by the *Los Angeles Daily News* found that Los Angeles County was paid nearly $30,000 a year from federal and state governments for every child seized by the Social Services with its oh so appropriate initials of 'SS'. The figure can be as high as $150,000 for children with special needs. This money pays for foster parents and the wages and benefits of social workers who steal the children. It is rightly dubbed the 'perverse incentive factor'. The more children they have in the system, the more money the system makes. The money-factor can be seen in the breakdown of the figures. Children from poor families and minorities make up 85 per cent of foster children in LA County and 70 per cent in California as a whole. A major reason for this is that the federal government pays for most of the costs of foster children from poor families, while states and counties have to pay most of the costs of foster children from more affluent families. The number of children handed to foster parents has increased 500 per cent in California since the 1980s and has doubled in the United States. An estimated one in four children will now have contact with the child welfare system before the age of 18. Does this mean there is 500 per cent more abuse of children in California or twice as much in America since the 1980s? No, of course not; it's the agenda playing out.

It is right that children should be protected from genuinely abusive parents, but that is not what most of this is about. The system itself doesn't care about children. US government statistics show that children in the 'welfare' system are six to seven times more likely to be mistreated and three times more likely to be killed than children in the general population. More than 660 children in the LA County foster care system have died since 1991 and more than 160 were murdered. Imagine what the figure must be worldwide. The *Miami Herald* revealed that 31 per cent of teenagers in foster care in Florida have been prescribed psychotropic drugs. Neuropsychologist and attorney, Toni Appel, said: 'One gets the impression that these drugs are utilised as chemical straitjackets, not for therapeutic reasons.' He is right, of course, and it has become the norm. Foster children under government control are also used to test drugs and pesticides, as with the experimental AIDS drug covertly used on foster children as young as three months at a home run by the Catholic Church in New York. They became known as the 'guinea pig kids' after their suffering was exposed, and they are far from alone. Paediatric nurse, Jacklyn Hoerger, who alerted the world to what was going on, fostered two of the children and took them off the drugs. This resulted in an 'immediate boost to their health and happiness'. So much so that the authorities took the children away, accused Jacklyn Hoerger in court of being a child abuser and prevented her from seeing the children again. When I say these people are evil, I am not kidding. Many children in State 'care' are forced into the networks of paedophile rings that operate within the 'child protection' system.

Anthony Cavuoti, a social worker with LA County for 14 years, said that some parents have had their children removed for yelling at them, allowing them to miss or be late to school or having a dirty home. 'The service that [the system] now provides is worse than the abuse that most abused children ever experienced,' he said, 'The trauma they inflict on ordinary children is unspeakable.' An investigation in 1992 by California's Little Hoover Commission quoted experts who said that between 35 and 70 per cent of foster children in the state should never have been taken from their parents. These children had suffered deep psychological trauma, they said. About 175,000 children are in the state's 'protective system' and, once again, think what the number must be now across the world. John Elliott, a special-effects technician, spent $150,000 to get his daughter back from LA County and he described the Social Services scandal as 'legal kidnapping to make a profit'. He filed a claim saying that social workers made false statements to take his daughter into 'care' and she was eventually returned. He said:

> They tell lies to keep your kids in the system. My daughter was abused the whole time she was there. It's a multibillion-dollar business. It's all about profit.

Yes it is, but not only about profit. The money is just the incentive paid by the bloodline families to encourage social workers to steal children and set precedents for the State to seize more and more control from parents. I am now seeing home-schooled children targeted by the system. Our Fabian frontman, Ed Balls, commissioned a report to 'investigate' if home schooling put children at greater risk of abuse. Oh my God, you know what it found? They *were*! All these things are puzzle pieces in the hijacking of children by the State on the road to a Brave New World. We must understand that injustice for others leads to injustice for everyone. We should stand against *all* injustice, simply because it is right to do so. But even those with merely selfish motives must surely see that this is in their own self-interest, too. There should be an outcry over the stealing of children by the State and if we don't unite to demand justice for others it will be our children and grandchildren eventually. Can't people see that?

The Reptilian agenda is for State-bred babies to be microchipped at birth so they can be externally controlled, mentally, emotionally and physically for life, and for the State to dictate all that they think and do. This would also ensure an endless supply of children for the Reptilians. I would encourage everyone to get together with like-thinkers and start to build support and communication networks to secure the strength in unity and numbers that is essential to stand firm against the fast-unfolding State dictatorship. If they don't, then they and their children will regret it for the rest of their lives. You will find support websites in various parts of the world on the internet.

27

Game Plan (8): The Useful Idiots

I believe that political correctness can be a form of linguistic fascism, and it sends shivers down the spine of my generation who went to war against fascism
P D James

Simple mathematics means that the global Control System has to be administered by Mind-slaves and useful idiots secured from the target population. The bloodline hybrids and their offshoots are no more than four or five per cent of what we call humanity and so the masses must be employed to police each other.

As the system has become more authoritarian, so have those in dark suits and uniforms that enforce the will of the Reptilians and their bloodlines upon the people. The robots are becoming even more robotic as they impose their mountains of rules and regulations with an arrogance and stupidity that makes the jaw drop. They cannot see anything wrong with fining people – the ones who pay their wages – £200 for putting their rubbish bin out on the wrong day for collection; or issuing fines for feeding the birds in a park; or using anti-terrorism legislation to follow parents to see if they live in the catchment-area of the school they have applied for their children to attend; or giving parking fines to an ambulance attending an emergency, or doing the same to a funeral cortege; or restricting the rights of volunteers to feed the homeless and insisting they must have a permit. The callousness and contempt for common sense, decency and justice that now prevails throughout national and local governments around the world has happened in such a coordinated way that there has to be a common cause. On one level we are back to the Reptilian hive-mind of the Moon Matrix. As more people wake up from the collective trance, others are going deeper into it. A vibrational parting of the ways is going on here and those who have descended into the deepening trance are the ones getting the jobs that administer the system as government and agency personnel, council officials, parking attendants or police officers. They have been replacing their sensible and decent predecessors for many years and they are so controlled by the hive mind that they have little capacity for free thought. We are all affected by the fake reality being broadcast from the Moon, but there are many levels of this. At its most extreme, those most powerfully and comprehensively attached to its vibrational and digital impulses are little more than computer terminals responding to input. They are like ants reacting as instructed to the vibrational and chemical dictates of the queen, and these are the people the bloodlines seek out to administer their system, or rather, their Reptilian masters' system.

A 'Common Purpose' – Control

This prison of perception is further implanted by 'training organisations' which have expanded dramatically in more recent times to program potential 'leaders' to see themselves and their job in the way that suits the dictatorship. This 'training' (mind-programming) is designed to tune them into the Reptilian hive-mind and the Moon Matrix even more powerfully and disconnect them from any free-thought (Fig 303). One of these 'training' operations is based in the UK and is called 'Common Purpose', a name that captures perfectly the spirit and aim of the organisation. It wants to program a common perception to ensure common behaviour patterns. You have probably never heard of Common Purpose, unless that is you are a 'leader' or aspire to be one, or you have read the work of conspiracy researchers. It began in the UK in 1988, where it has some 45 offices, but has now taken its sun symbol logo into many countries as Common Purpose International. These include France, Germany, Ghana, Hungary, India, Ireland, the Netherlands, South Africa, Spain, Sweden, Switzerland and Turkey. It is moving in on the United States using people close to Barack Obama and in association with the Dale Carnegie training operation and the 'democon' Center for American Progress. The latter is sponsored by the Rockefeller Brothers Fund and the Rothschild financier and manipulator of 'regime change', George Soros, another Obama handler. This is Common Purpose's stated goal:

> Common Purpose aims to improve the way society works by expanding the vision, decision-making ability and influence of all kinds of leaders. The organisation runs a variety of educational programmes for leaders of all ages, backgrounds and sectors, in order to provide them with the inspiration, information and opportunities they need to change the world.

From such bland descriptions come two questions immediately: A common purpose to what end? And 'change the world' in what way exactly? We need answers here. Common Purpose is sweeping through the UK, 'training' leaders in all areas of society. If they have a 'common purpose' we ought to know about it. The organisation now has training programmes in every major town and city in Britain and, since 1989,

Figure 303: *People in uniform, dark suit administrators of government and members of the other Control System professions are being locked even more powerfully into the hive mind of the Moon Matrix by 'training courses' and by selection of certain personality types*

more than 100,000 'leaders' have been involved in Common Purpose programmes. The sales-pitch proclaims the benefits of Common Purpose training:

- Participants gain new competencies and become more effective in a diverse and complex world.
- Organisations benefit from stronger, more inspired, better-networked managers and senior managers who are closer to the community.
- Communities benefit from cross-sector understanding and initiatives as different parts of the community learn to operate more effectively together.

Those who complete the courses are called Common Purpose 'graduates' and throughout society such 'graduates' are at work in government, law enforcement, health, and many other areas that affect daily life. What is it all about and what is going on here? The official founder and Chief Executive of Common Purpose is Julia Middleton. She was head of personnel selection in the office of John Prescott, the Deputy Prime Minister to Tony Blair. Prescott was the man given responsibility for creating 'regional assemblies' around the United Kingdom, which are part of the plan to abolish nations and bring their powerless 'regions' under the jackboot of the European Union. He did, of course, seek to sell this as 'devolving power to the people'. Prescott failed to get this policy through, but they will be trying again, for sure. The European superstate is designed to be centrally controlled and managed at lower levels by 'leaders' who are all programmed to think the same. This is where Common Purpose comes in. You can always tell an Illuminati front by its desire to centralise everything and that includes the centralisation of thought as diversity is scorned, ridiculed and dismissed in favour of a manufactured 'consensus'. You can see the Orwellian *Newspeak* technique of promoting an organisation as standing for the very thing it is seeking to destroy. Common Purpose says its aim is to develop 'diverse' leaders, when the opposite is the case. Illuminati fronts also tend to use language that tells you nothing when describing what they do. You wouldn't know by reading its blurb what Common Purpose teaches its leaders and, with its courses costing thousands of pounds, it would be expensive to find out. It will be founded, however, on manufacturing a consensus reality among its 'diverse' clientele. This is a foundation technique of the Reptilian bloodlines – to manipulate agreement on a range of issues that then become the 'norm' to be defended from all challenge and true diversity. It has been developed by organisations like the Tavistock Institute in London. Tavistock was funded into existence in 1946 with a grant from the Rockefeller Foundation and it is one of the Illuminati's global centres for implanting the 'hive mind' mentality or 'group and organisational behaviour'. Tavistock works closely with 'public sector' (State-controlled) organisations, including the UK government, European Union and throughout North America. The Orwell-speak on its website could have come straight from the pages of Common Purpose. Or, rather more credibly, the other way around. Jargon is always the language of the junta:

> Multi-organisational working, cross-boundary working and the global-national-local interface each raise their own set of organisational dynamics which must be surfaced and worked with if collaboration is to be effective. They also raise particular challenges

for leadership (and followership). The Institute's approaches to organisational consultancy and leadership development, based on organisational theory and systems psychodynamics are particularly appropriate for helping organisations to address these complex issues.

Yes, complex issues like working out what the hell all that is supposed to mean. Notice how that kind of gobbledegook from the Tavistock Institute has become the language of the system and 'political correctness'. What we can see is that Tavistock and Common Purpose share the same pod, as does the Fabian Society. No shock, then, to find that Common Purpose and Tavistock have close connections with the Fabian Society, Royal Institute of International Affairs, European Union, and Council on Foreign Relations who all share the same goals and methods. They are preparing (programming) the useful idiot 'leaders' for what Common Purpose actually calls the 'post-democratic era' and they all want to develop 'leaders' in the same way by manufacturing consensus that eliminates diversity and by using group pressure on anyone who won't conform. Mind manipulation techniques like Neuro-Linguistic Programming, or NLP, are also liberally embedded within the language used to engineer the consensus. NLP is a technique of using words to re-program the body-computer to accept another perception of reality – in this case the 'consensus' agreed by the manipulators before their victims even register for the 'course'. Apparently, the CIA refers to these pre-agreed 'opinions' as 'slides'. As one Internet writer said:

A 'slide' is a prefabricated, 'politically correct' blanket 'pop' 'opinion', 'view' or 'take' upon a particular issue of general interest which is designed to preclude further consideration, analysis or investigation of the issue in question. In other words, it is a 'collectivised' mental position which is never to be questioned. This is precisely the 'product' of the Deputy Prime Minister's insidious neurological linguistic control programme 'Common Purpose'.

Anyone who resists the programming is isolated and the group turns against them until they either conform or lose the credibility to be a 'leader'. Look at global society in any country and you will see this happening in the workplace, among friends down the bar and in television discussions. The consensus on 'climate change' is that the cause is human activity and anyone saying otherwise is an uncaring, selfish racist who is quite happy to see the planet and humanity face catastrophe. The fact that this is all garbage is irrelevant. 'Truth' is what the consensus has agreed it to be and if you don't agree with the extreme consensus you must be an extremist. It is the manipulation of consensus that has turned the main political parties in the United States, Britain and elsewhere into *one* party with their leaders occupying the same ground. They might offer slightly different policies – *only* slightly – but they are all agreed on the fundamentals and this makes elections irrelevant. The Tavistock Institute has been working this flanker for decades, and Common Purpose seems to me to have the Curriculum Vitae of a Tavistock front. One of the Tavistock founders, Dr John Rawlings Rees – who also became co-founder of the World Federation for Mental Health – talked of infiltrating all professions and areas of society. 'Public life, politics and industry should all ... be within our sphere of influence,' he said. '... If we are to infiltrate the professional and social activities of other people I think we must imitate the Totalitarians and organise some kind of fifth column activity!' He said that the 'salesmen' of this perception re-programming (mass mind-control) must hide their identity and operate secretly:

> We must aim to make it permeate every educational activity in our national life ... We have made a useful attack upon a number of professions. The two easiest of them naturally are the teaching profession and the Church; the two most difficult are law and medicine.

This they have demonstrably done.

Targeting the 'Right Type'

Brian Gerrish, a former British naval officer-turned-researcher, is the outstanding expert on Common Purpose. He says that the organisation, in league with agencies of government and commerce, seeks out 'narcissistic' personalities. As I said earlier, narcissism is defined as: 'excessive love or admiration of oneself ... a psychological condition characterised by self-preoccupation, lack of empathy [note, a major Reptilian trait] and unconscious deficits in self-esteem'. These are the personality-types that have been placed in positions of administration and management throughout the system and so the attitude of authority to the population has changed dramatically in more recent times. Law-enforcement agencies and the 'extended police family' at all levels are employing these narcissistic personalities at the expense of the 'old school' and, once again, this is why the attitude of law enforcement to the population has also become so much more arrogant and authoritarian. The narcissistic ego is so flawed with its unconscious lack of self-esteem that it wallows and glories in having 'power over'. It is also, apparently, much more susceptible to Neuro-Linguistic Programming and other forms of mind control. Common Purpose and company identify their target-type through psychometric testing. Psychometrics is the measurement of knowledge, abilities, attitudes and personality traits mostly using carefully designed questionnaires and tests. You are seeing this employed with job applications right across the system today. Being able to do the job expertly is not enough any more. You have to be the 'right type'. Brian Gerrish says of the narcissistic personality:

> Their love of themselves and power automatically means that they will crush others who get in their way. I received a major piece of the puzzle when a friend pointed out that when they made public officials re-apply for their own jobs several years ago they were also required to do psychometric tests. This was undoubtedly the start of the screening process to get 'their' sort of people in post.

> The picture is getting clearer all the time that they have set up an NLP training network via Common Purpose consultancies and official government bodies such as the Local Government Association ... The thread name and cover is leadership. Aside from achieving control over key individuals and thus control of organisations and society, they are also drawing people into a new hive mind and group think. Those that rebel are rejected and in due course will be eliminated.

Psychometric testing can be traced to Illuminati figures like Francis Galton, the father of the 'master race' eugenics movement so beloved of the Rothschilds, Rockefellers and the bloodline families in general.

Blob-Think

The common purpose of the Tavistock/Illuminati guerrilla war on the human psyche is to wipe clean any sense of the individual and the unique. Only by doing this can they impose a global dictatorship and have the masses accept it. Brock Chisholm, former Director of the Rothschild/Rockefeller World Health Organization, was right when he said: 'To achieve One-World Government, it is necessary to remove from the minds of men their individualism.' Enter Common Purpose and its training of 'leaders'. If you can get the leaders to think the same, it makes it much easier to transfer that to the general population. Julia Middleton's organisation, and whoever and whatever else is really behind it, has been making dramatic inroads into British society while it has largely flown below the radar. It needs to have a much higher profile in public awareness. Researcher, Brian Gerrish, discovered Common Purpose when he was involved with a group in Plymouth in the west of England helping people find work. One of their projects was repairing wooden boats. He said they had lots of public support and backing from the local authorities and everything was going fine, but then it suddenly changed and council support was withdrawn. When they tried to continue alone, key people in the project began to be threatened. Brian said:

> When we started to explore why we were being threatened we were absolutely staggered to find a very strange organisation called Common Purpose operating in the city. And we were absolutely amazed that there were so many people involved, but they were not declaring themselves ... [Common Purpose] was operating throughout the structure of the city, in the city council, in the government offices, in the police, in the judiciary. Essentially, we discovered what is effectively, at best, a quasi secret society which doesn't declare itself to ordinary people.

Further research has led Brian to establish that Common Purpose is recruiting and training leaders to be loyal to the objectives of the organisation, the United Nations and the European Union and is preparing the governing structure for the 'post-democratic society' as nations are replaced by regions answering to the European Union and a world government. The United Nations is the stepping-stone to world government and already has offices in the UK in readiness for the takeover. It is not only a post-democratic, but a post-industrial society that is in their sights and this is a major reason for the climate change/global warming agenda – to de-industrialise the world. What Brian Gerrish has found in his investigations of Common Purpose fits precisely with my own exposure of the global conspiracy. He says of Common Purpose 'graduates': 'They are learning to rule without regard to democracy, and will bring the EU police state home to every one of us.' Gerrish has found Common Purpose 'graduates' throughout the government structure with more than £100 million of taxpayers money spent on CP courses for State employees. It has 'graduates' in national government, local councils, civil service, the National Health Service, the BBC, the police, the legal profession, religion and Regional Development Agencies. Common Purpose graduate, Cressida

Dick, issued the 'shoot-to-kill' order to police officers that led to an innocent Brazilian electrician, Jean Charles de Menezes, being held down by the police and shot eight times at point blank range, seven of the bullets in the head. Dick was later promoted from Commander to Deputy Assistant Commissioner in the Metropolitan Police. If you are a Common Purpose graduate willing to play the game, the right doors quickly open. Janet Pataskala, a chief executive officer of the Law Society, is a Common Purpose graduate and trustee, and there are many and increasing numbers in the law and enforcement professions. Common Purpose 'graduates' are taking over the administration of the system at national and local levels.

When, for example, Common Purpose was given an award by Newcastle University in 2005, it was revealed that among its graduates in that area of the English North East were: Michael Craik, Northumbria Police Chief Constable; Andrew Dixon, Executive Director of the Arts Council England, North East; Glyn Evans, Newcastle City Centre Chaplain; Chris Francis, Centre Manager of the Wildfowl and Wetlands Trust; Anne Marshall, Chief Officer of Age Concern; Anthony Sargent, General Director of The Sage Gateshead; Miriam Harte, Director of Beamish Museum; and Sue Underwood, Chief Executive of NEMLAC (the North East Museums, Libraries and Archives Council). That gives you just a small example of the reach of Common Purpose, and that was in 2005. It has increased its numbers massively since then thanks to government and local council grants that fund the courses their staff attend. This is how the mentality of government and law enforcement has descended so rapidly into such arrogance and stupidity. These people are being programmed and brainwashed to run the system as those in the shadows demand, and that includes the police. They operate like a semi-secret society within the agencies that employ them and, like all secret societies, Common Purpose 'graduates' have a central leadership that ensures a common policy. They do indeed all work to a common purpose – the creation of what they call the 'post-democratic world' of human enslavement. Shami Chakrabarti, the head of 'freedom' group, Liberty, has, with the greatest of irony, been a contributor to Common Purpose courses.

Mind bending

Brian Gerrish has compiled a large dossier of case studies to confirm how Common Purpose operates, how it changes personalities and targets those that refuse to conform. One lady told him about her experience in a UK government 'quango' (quasi non-governmental organisation). Quangos are financed by government, but act independently (supposedly). She said her boss, a Common Purpose 'graduate', was continually making decisions that were obviously doomed to fail, and they began to clash over this. He then suggested that she become his mistress and she complained to the 'human resources' department. She soon realised that this 'private' conversation had been leaked and the Common Purpose mafia began to systematically and psychologically undermine her. Her Common Purpose colleagues said she was a troublemaker who was inventing stories and eventually she was told that her contract was not being renewed. She sought help outside the organisation, but experienced the same treatment from others who she learned were also connected to Common Purpose. This lady could remember very little about her Common Purpose training – highly significant – but she showed Brian Gerrish her application form and he said it was clearly designed to be a psychological profile to glean information that could 'reframe' the 'graduate's' personality. The lady also said that she felt sure that men on the course were getting 'extras' from the course leader. The husband of another CP trainee told Brian how his wife's personality had changed after she attended a course for which he had paid more than £3,500. After the course they began to row for the first time in their 30-year marriage and their relationship ended. He said she became moody, withdrawn, and didn't communicate like before. She shouted at him on one occasion, 'The trouble with you is that you are just a little man!' Making CP graduates feel superior is all part of the game and it leads to the 'we up here, you down there' relationship between officialdom and the public, a trend that is now so obvious. It came to light that the woman was having an affair with her CP-trained boss. The husband said that after his wife moved out he was sure she wanted to come back to him and their children, but would then 'blank out' and become another person. When Brian explained that Common Purpose was, in his opinion, a 'cult', the husband said:

> I began to wonder if I was going mad or she was. I knew something very strange was happening to her, but just couldn't pin it down. A cult just fits; it just fits.

A 16-year-old girl who attended a course on 'cities and regeneration' with about ten others from her year group also went through a personality change, according to her father. There were once again arguments between father and daughter that didn't happen before and she would not talk in any detail about what had happened on the course. She was put on drugs for depression, had to take a year out of school and undergo psychiatric treatment before regaining '85 per cent of her old self'. The father discovered that the course leader was trained by Common Purpose. His daughter became distressed when her friends on the course said that she had changed, but he said he now realised that, actually, the course had changed them all. He had also asked her about the European Union and she replied that 'they said it was a good thing, but I didn't like the control'. It was a strange answer, which the father did not pursue because of her mental state at the time. Later, when she recovered her mind, she said: 'It's weird ... I sort of remember things, but it's weird, it's almost like I dreamt things.' Brian Gerrish says of the case:

> [The girl] suffered mental ill effects as a result of Common Purpose reframing designed to get brighter children into the new social and political paradigm. As with [the lady who left her husband] she could not remember what had been done to her. Where NLP and associated techniques are used, and especially where the victim does not fully 'take' the training, and/or there is some personality weakness, the victim can suffer mental illness such as depression, personality change, anxiety, fear, paranoia.

> This risk increases when the victim is challenged on a subject and a mental conflict (cognitive dissonance) arises between their true views and morality and the implanted ideology. Common Purpose is extremely active amongst school children with Your Turn and other courses. Parents usually have no, or little, idea of the true nature and purpose of these courses.

Brian was also asked to visit a woman in Cornwall who was very unwell and on heavy doses of Prozac. She said she was being hounded out of her job by Common Purpose 'graduates', her ideas were being stolen and she was very fearful and depressed. She had been on a CP course and she showed Brian some of the material. He said that Common Purpose was using regression techniques to 'disassemble' personalities so new ones could be implanted. A lady in Ireland told Brian what had happened to her husband after a CP course. He had found it to be 'rubbish' and of little value, but within weeks many things began to change. He noticed that his colleagues who had been CP-trained were making strange decisions which, once again, were bound to fail. As this began to seriously impact on his own department, he found himself in conflict with people that he had previously had good relations with. A plot followed to have him dismissed. He fought the case and won damages, but had to agree to a gagging order as part of the deal. His wife said that Common Purpose had begun to operate in Ireland, but, then, this organisation, and others like it, is seeking to infiltrate every country. This is a summary of what Brian Gerrish has found to be the recurring themes with Common Purpose and the people that it 'trains':

1) The person's life is normal until they are selected to get involved with CP and then the personality begins to change.

2) People who are trying to do something to help the community find themselves harassed and bullied, and their projects stolen or closed down. If they fight back they become aware that others are working against them in a secretive and coordinated way.

3) Those that have come forward to talk about bad experiences with CP are invariably frightened and do not want to reveal names.

4) CP personnel use mantras and repeating sound bites instead of reasoned argument.

5) They can take on a similar appearance in dress code, especially women – all in little smart business suits.

6) They can behave in a robotic way. This has been observed especially in Social Services where mothers describe the lack of compassion and normal human warmth. Local authority CP graduates will lie, cheat and falsify documents to protect CP and/or hide what they are doing.

7) CP is now collecting information on those asking questions about its activities.

8) Information is denied under the Freedom of Information Act after CP officials have told authorities how to avoid making the information public.

9) CP is desperate to get to children and young people.

10) It targets the brightest children and adults because these are easier to 'reframe'.

Brian Gerrish says that his observations about Common Purpose have been confirmed by several 'very experienced NLP and military professionals' who describe the CP ideology as 'subversive'. He says that by using a profiling system to screen potential graduate trainees they can select those with the desired position, power, financial control and influence. Narcissistic personalities are preferred, he says, because they are good 're-framing personalities' and can more easily be controlled by a 'friend' or mentor controller after they have been reprogrammed. This is why many young politicians look and act the same, he says. Common Purpose meetings are held under the 'Chatham House rule' in which participants are free to use the information received, but not to reveal the identity or affiliation of the source, nor anyone else participating. Chatham House is the headquarters of the Illuminati's Royal Institute of International Affairs, part of the web that includes the Council on Foreign Relations and Trilateral Commission in the United States, and answers to the Rothschild's Round Table secret society. The Institute introduced the 'Chatham House rule' to keep its meetings secret while still having its policy promoted on a non-attributable basis. From the efforts of the Tavistock Institute and its associated organisations, has come a common network with a common purpose that is leading to the rapid and coordinated introduction of *Newspeak*, political correctness and 'management initiatives' that take us ever further down the road to fascism/communism. The network seeks to eliminate social identity, destroy freedom and merge public and private sectors into one centralised whole. A definition of fascism is the amalgamation of corporations and State, exactly what happened in Nazi Germany and fascist Italy. Brian Gerrish has got the Common Purpose leadership so concerned with his determined exposure of their activities that they had his website, **www.cpexposed.com**, taken down by the web server in late 2009 on the grounds of posting 'copyrighted material' – material that was actually in the public domain. It was later restored on another server and that is what we must do when the system seeks to impose its will. No matter what it does, we get up and get on. We shall not be broken.

Political Correctness: Kindergarten for 'Adults'

The programming of the useful idiots and administrators at all levels of government is underpinned by what is called 'political correctness'. You might have noticed a pattern throughout the book in which the official reason for something turns out to be a cover for precisely the opposite, and so it is with political correctness. It is *supposed to be* the means to stop minorities being 'upset' by what people say, but it is, in fact, a very powerful form of mind-programming. It is also an insult to the very 'minorities' it is supposed to be 'protecting'. What scale of child-like stupidity does it take to change the term 'black coffee' to 'coffee without milk', or 'black pudding' to 'breakfast pudding', so not to upset black people? What scale of contempt for the intelligence of black people does it take to think they could give a damn? Other 'potentially offensive' phrases being banned by government departments and taxpayer-funded organisations include: 'whiter than white', 'gentleman's agreement', 'black mark', 'black looks', 'black day' (use 'miserable day'), 'right-hand man' and 'master bedroom'. We have 'Christmas lights' changed to 'winterval lights' to stop non-Christians being offended. A UK police authority said it did not use British Rover cars, because buying 'anything British, including British cars, was an overtly nationalist statement and could be considered offensive by vulnerable, deprived and ethnic minority groups in our society'. A bakery manager had the name 'gingerbread men' changed to 'gingerbread persons'. Someone pointed out that you couldn't discriminate against a biscuit, but, oh, you can when you a dealing with a mind that does not have batteries included. Under the jackboot of political correctness, the nursery rhyme 'Ba ba black sheep' becomes 'Ba ba rainbow sheep', and the line in Humpty Dumpty saying that Humpty couldn't be put together again becomes 'Humpty Dumpty counted to ten then Humpty Dumpty got up again!' There you go children, don't you worry about jumping off that high wall; you'll be fine. You won't kill yourself, just count to ten. A customer claimed that a supermarket was being racist by selling 'thick Irish sausages'. It actually had to be pointed out that the word 'thick' referred to the size of the sausages and not the mentality of Irish people. Tunbridge Wells Council and others banned the use of the term 'brainstorming' and replaced it with 'thought showers' in case they offended epileptics. The National Society for Epilepsy said their members were not offended, but that doesn't matter to the PC brigade, because at its foundation this is nothing to do with offending or not offending people. It is a programming device that has already programmed those who now impose their programming on others. Val Green, the head of personnel at Tunbridge Wells Council, made a statement about 'thought showers' and the reaction from epileptics was that they are not offended by 'brainstorming'. It is a priceless example of the genre and encapsulates the depth of lunacy (literally) to which 'PC' has descended:

> We take equality and diversity issues very seriously. It is important to us not to offend people and we are sorry if through trying to avoid this, we have indeed caused offence to the very people we were trying not to offend.

> If the epilepsy association finds the term perfectly acceptable, then we welcome this clarification. If however, the term does in fact offend even a small minority, we would encourage people to get in touch with us.

No words necessary, or, indeed, possible at this moment.

The French government is even introducing a law that could leave married couples with criminal records for insulting each other during arguments. It is the first country to ban 'psychological violence' between married and cohabiting couples. The law is expected to cover every kind of insult, including repeated rude remarks about a partner's appearance. Repeat 'offenders' could be fined, electronically-tagged, even jailed. This is part of the psychological game-plan to make people watch every word they say in every situation, even with their partner. It is a form of mental and emotional survellience in which everyone is a potential 'Big Brother' to everyone else.

Don't Breathe, You Might Hurt Your Lungs

There is another virulent strain of political correctness around the world which goes under the name in Britain of 'Health & Safety', or 'elf 'n' safety', as it is widely known. Here are some examples so you get my drift: The Italian ice-cream chain, Morelli's, banned staff from putting toppings on customers' ice creams in case they dripped off and made people slip over. Customers were instead given the cone with the topping in a separate pot to pour on themselves, which, of course, could still 'drip off'. One school ordered adults and children to wear goggles when using Blu-Tack, and another banned children from using spray foam when marking out lines in the playground in case a child slipped and 'drowned' in it. A primary school dropped the three-legged race from sports day on the grounds that it was too dangerous. Staff at Bishops Down Primary School in Tunbridge Wells (clearly a place where the bypass is especially useful) have banned pupils from throwing paper planes except at a special target. Another school banned the annual rounders match between staff and pupils in case someone was injured and decided to sue. Staffordshire County Council has produced forms listing more than 70 'risk assessments' for schools. One highlights the need for 'voice care' in the face of 'hazards' like 'throat clearing, failing to lubricate the mouth, singing in too high or too deep a tone, using a forced whisper or talking too quickly.' It warns children against the perils for their voice of eating 'hot spicy foods, very hot drinks and breathing continually through the mouth.' Another authority circulated a 35-page health and safety code for primary schools which says that hemlock and deadly nightshade plants should not be grown by children. Oh cheers, thanks, I'd missed that one. A risk assessment about music lessons says that pupils must use a trolley to transport bigger instruments, and bans the use of drum sticks or percussion hammers unless staff are present for fear they might cause injury. Staffordshire County Council's 70 risk assessments include a 'helicopter landing at school'. This identifies the danger of excited pupils running to the aircraft and lack of air traffic control clearance. It says pupils may watch the landing from a classroom window – 'provided the glazing is safe'. Mick Brookes, general secretary of the National Association of Head Teachers, said: 'Schools used to feel under pressure to have a policy for everything that moves, now they have to have a policy for everything that *might* move and even for things which don't.'Half the 600 teachers questioned in a poll by Teachers TV said that Health & Safety rules were now too restrictive and were having a negative effect on children's education. But, then, that's the idea. The plan is to program children to see everything in terms of danger and limitation, because then they will do the same when they are adults. It is another Mind program.

An author was told by her publishers to take out references to a red ring on an electric cooker; to a boy using a ladder and to a dragon toasting his marshmallows by breathing fire on them. The author was told that all three 'went against Health & Safety'. A fire station was built without the traditional pole, because firemen (oops, sorry, fire-fighters) might sprain their ankles as they hit the ground. It would be better for them to run down the stairs, officials decided. Yes, a lot of men and women running down the stairs together as fast as possible seems very safe to me. To make everything perfectly safe, I suggest they simply ban fire-fighting and fire stations, but then what happens to the health and safety of those people trapped in burning houses? Better do a study chaps to assess the risks. Hey, got it, why not just ban *fire*? Yep, sorted, and it will help with global warming. Ambulance staff in Somerset, England, were stopped by a paramedic from treating a man with a broken back while he was lying in six inches of water. They were told it would breach Health & Safety (never mind the health and safety of the guy with the broken back) because they were 'not trained in water rescues'. Six inches of water constitutes a 'water rescue' for this moron who refused pleas from the ambulance staff to do the obvious and help the victim. A spokesman for the South West Ambulance Service said only fire crews were trained for water rescues. He said: 'The incident was managed in accordance with procedures.' No, in accordance with not having a brain they are prepared to engage. A hospital banned visitors from cooing at newborn babies after a staff advice session stressed the need for respect and dignity for patients. Signs have been put up in the hospital saying: 'What makes you think I want to be looked at?' In the case of the policymaker, what makes you think I want to look? I was in a branch of Pizza Hut (I'm not proud of it, I was hungry) and asked for a cup of coffee. I was told that the coffee machine had broken and they were not allowed to boil a kettle due to 'Health & Safety regulations'. A restaurant is not allowed to boil a bloody *kettle*? And we take this shit from these people? Brian Gerrish makes a very valid point about this phenomenon from his research into Common Purpose:

> It is interesting that many of the mothers who have had children taken by the state speak of the Social Services people being icily cool, emotionless and, as two ladies said in slightly different words, '… like little robots'. We know that NLP programming is cumulative so people can be given small imperceptible doses of NLP in a course here, another in a few months, next year etc. In this way, major changes are accrued in their personality, but the day by day change is almost unnoticeable.

> An example is the policeman who would not get on a bike for a press photo because he had not done the cycling proficiency course. Normal people say this is political correctness gone mad. Nothing could be further from the truth. The policeman has been reframed and in his reality it is perfect common sense not to get on the bike 'because he hasn't done the cycling course'.

> Another example of this is where the police would not rescue a boy from a pond until they had taken advice from above on the 'risk assessment'. A normal person would have arrived, perhaps thought of the risk for a moment, and dived in. To the police now 'reframed', they followed 'normal' procedure.

The 'training' organisations are developing unthinking, unconscious, robots to run the system who are not in control of their own minds. Political correctness and 'Health & Safety' are lethal weapons targeting free-thought and free expression with a mountain of ever-expanding rules and regulations dictating the fine detail of people's lives. It is like a spider tying a fly to its web. Eventually, the fly is so restricted that it can't even move and this is the real plan behind political correctness, Health & Safety, Common Purpose, Sustainable Development and the Tavistock social engineering operation (Fig 304 overleaf). They, in turn, connect into the vast European Union bureaucracy and the Illuminati networks. They move as one in pursuit of a common end, although many who work for them, and definitely those programmed by them, have not a clue what they are involved in. People like Mrs Thought Shower at Tunbridge Wells Council are just pawns in a game they don't even begin to understand. They help to create an Orwellian nightmare for themselves, their children and grandchildren while believing they are being kind and not 'upsetting' anyone. But they *are*. They are 'upsetting' basic human freedom and it is starting to get seriously pissed off. So where did all this nonsense come from? Well, well …

Here We Go Again …

Political correctness appears to be quite a modern phenomenon. It is only in the last few decades that it has really broken the surface and expanded to the insane levels we

Figure 304: *The Control System is introducing ever more laws, taxes and financial demands to tie the human flies to the web. Political Correctness is very much part of this*

see today. In fact, its origins go back at least to the time of the First World War and it was being planned in the shadows long before that. The Illuminati, led by the House of Rothschild networks, want to transform global society into a 'one world' dictatorship and to achieve this all diversity has to go. The Reptilian-hybrid families have destroyed diversity in government, banking, business, the media, medicine, and virtually every other aspect of society. Organisations like Common Purpose are there to eliminate diversity of thought and perception among those who administer these institutions of government and law enforcement. Together, they are targeting the biggest prize of all – the destruction of *cultural* diversity. This is where political correctness comes in. Its goal is to dismantle the diversity of language, view and culture until all that is left is a bland, vacuous blob of coagulated banality that will pass for 'human society'. Words that mean anything will be banned and people will be frightened to say anything without a careful choice of language to avoid punishment for offending anyone. Look around, for goodness sake, it is already happening, and happening fast.

One of the prime conduits for the development and expansion of political correctness has been the Marxist movement. Marxism, the domination by the few over the many (see, also, fascism), was another Illuminati/Rothschild creation. Karl Marx (Rothschild Zionist) was an Illuminati frontman who married into British aristocracy. Marxism and fascism are two expressions of the same central control structure and it is appropriate that Marx was involved in something called the Young Hegelian Movement. This was named after Georg Wilhelm Friedrich Hegel who is famous for his 'Hegelian dialectic' in which opposing forces are played off against each other to fuse them together. This has been described as: thesis + antithesis = synthesis. We are seeing this happening now as Marxism and fascism are fused to become the ruling creed of global society. There never was much difference between them, anyway, and none in the sense of freedom for the people. A group of Marxists established the Frankfurt School of 'philosophical thought' in 1923 that became the most significant promoter of political correctness. As its name suggests, it was located in the German city that was, and is, a Rothschild stronghold. One of those involved in its initial creation was the Hungarian aristocrat, György Lukács (Rothschild Zionist), who is described as the founder of Western Marxism. He tried to introduce many facets of what we call today political correctness when he was briefly minister of culture in Hungary in the mid-1950s. People were outraged, particularly at the way he targeted children. An associate of Lukács, a guy called Willi Munzenberg (Rothschild Zionist), once suggested that the way to transform the West in the way their agenda demanded was to 'organise the intellectuals and use them to make Western civilisation stink [sic]'. The Frankfurt School was funded into being by Felix Weil (Rothschild Zionist) and the first director was Carl Grünberg (Rothschild Zionist) followed by Max Horkheimer (Rothschild Zionist). Two of the main influences on the school's thinking were Theodor W Adorno (Rothschild Zionist) and Herbert Marcuse (Rothschild Zionist). The Frankfurt School relocated to Switzerland before moving to New York in 1935. It moved again to California, one of the global capitals of political correctness, in 1941. In the United States, the 'school' made its play to control American social science and this is what they proposed to introduce. Recognise it?

- The creation of racism offences.
- Continual change to create confusion.
- The teaching of sex and homosexuality to children.
- The undermining of schools' and teachers' authority.
- Huge immigration to destroy national identity.
- The promotion of excessive drinking.
- Emptying of churches [targeting anything that brought people together].
- A legal system with bias against victims of crime.
- Dependency on the state or state benefits.
- Control and dumbing down of the media.
- Encouraging the breakdown of the family.

This was only part of it, but you see the common themes that continually recur. They refer to 'huge immigration to destroy national identity', and remember how Dr Richard Day told the meeting in 1969 that long-established communities would be destroyed by unemployment and mass immigration. This is the real reason for the borderless European Union and why the United States is withdrawing border defences with Mexico in preparation for the borderless North American Union. None of the aims on that list are for the benefit of the people. The Illuminati don't care about homosexuals, any more than they care for the children they abuse while claiming to protect them. Rothschild-Illuminati fronts like the Anti-Defamation League are not concerned with 'racism'. They simply use it to justify more control, suppressing freedom of speech and introducing 'hate laws' to make your opinion a criminal offence in which truth is no defence. Where there is no racism, the authorities simply invent it to justify their 'solutions'. Vitriolic racist comments against Mexicans were posted on a website of *The Wayne County Star* newspaper in New York State in 2009 and the paper traced some of them to Internet protocol addresses at the Department of Homeland Security. The paper also reported that it had discovered others from a year before that appeared to have come from computers affiliated with Homeland Security. These are far from isolated incidents – they're the norm. The ADL is a Rothschild front that connects into another Rothschild operation called political correctness. This is not about 'protecting' anyone from either racism or offence. It is about social breakdown and division so that a new order, *their* order, can be introduced. Now we can see why the Illuminati networks, including organisations like the CIA, are the major force behind the drug-running syndicates that make hard drugs so readily available around the world. Production of poppies for heroin has soared in Afghanistan since the invasion in 2001 and it was the CIA that organised the Colombian drug barons into cartels to make them easier to deal with. The global drugs market is also a prime source of funding for the covert programmes, the so-called 'black projects' (how politically incorrect), that can't be financed from on-the-record government sources. The Bush family and the Clintons are up to their necks in this drug racket – see my other books for the detail. You can see the theme over and over everywhere you look: breakdown of society, conflict and lack of cohesion that all result in fear, stress and loss of identity and direction.

Programming the Language

A theme of Orwell's *1984* is mass and individual mind control through the manipulation of language. This is most obviously expressed today through 'political correctness' and 'hate speech', or 'hate crime'. These terms alone could have been invented by Orwell who explained how vital language is to perception. He coined the term *Newspeak* for the official language of the superstate called Oceania and the number of words available was reduced every year – see political correctness, 'hate speech', and the mobile-phone text 'language' which are fulfilling precisely this role today. *Newspeak* was based on the premise that the fewer words you have available, the less efficiently you can articulate your views, but it goes even further than that. In this reality we also think in words, and limiting the language available diminishes your ability to even think freely. As one Internet article put it: '… Can we communicate the need for freedom or organise an uprising if we do not have the words for either?' *Newspeak* was designed to eliminate all meaning from language, leaving only blandness that says nothing (see most political speeches) and it replaced the previous vibrant language known as *Oldspeak*. Once more, this is what is happening today. The word free still existed in *Newspeak*, but could only be used in statements like 'the dog is free from lice' or 'this field is free from weeds'. It could not be used in its old sense of 'politically free' or 'intellectually free', since political and intellectual freedom no longer existed, even as concepts, and were, therefore, nameless. All words relating to concepts of liberty and equality were contained in the single word, *Crimethink*, while all words relating to objectivity and rationalism were contained in the single word, *Oldthink*. When Tony Blair came to power in the British Labour Party he denounced 'old Labour' and renamed the party 'New' Labour. With that, all 'old Labour' thinking and language were expunged from debate. Words which powerfully express the opposite meaning to those promoted in the propaganda are eliminated in the world of *1984*. The opposite of 'good' was 'bad' and thus bad is replaced by 'ungood'. Instead of meaningful words like 'best', comes the term 'doubleplusgood'. Very bad becomes 'doubleplusungood'. We are seeing the ever-increasing introduction of such meaningless words into our language to hide the reality of what is happening. One example of how words are used to obscure the truth is the way that 'civilian casualties' or 'dead people' have become 'collateral damage'. They are also used to discredit opponents by the implication behind the terms used to describe them. If you challenge the impositions of the authorities you are an 'anti-government group'; if you suggest, indeed prove, that the government is lying you are a 'conspiracy theorist'.

I said in the first edition of my last book, published before Obama came on the scene, that 'change' is another word spun by the Orwellians. This is generally used to suggest that a particular idea is good, because it is newer; but newer is not always *better*. Nazism and communism were 'change'. Obama's election campaign was classic Orwell. Tony Blair's buzzwords were always 'change' and 'reform' and they are used in the context that 'change' and 'reform' are, by definition, good, and what they replace is 'bad'. Then there are the new words, or *Newspeak*, and the re-definition of words to make people sound 'bad' for having legitimate, often caring, views. Those who oppose 'globalisation' – the centralisation of global power and the criminal abuse of poor people and countries – are dubbed 'anarchists', or 'anti-capitalist demonstrators', when what they are actually opposing is 'cartelism' and mass human abuse. Someone who thinks differently, or questions the insanity of the way the world is run, is called an 'extremist'. If you resist injustice you are a 'militant'. A 'peacekeeper' is someone who occupies another country, and the 'peace process' is the means of placating an oppressed people in an effort to stop them opposing their oppression. It is a 'road map' with no destination. 'Western values' are the values that must be imposed on the rest of the world when those 'values' are not even applied in the 'West' (see 'freedom' and 'democracy'). *1984* is here. People are now frightened of what they say, write, even think. They're afraid of using the wrong word that could be seen as offensive, insensitive, racist, sexist or homophobic, just as people in China are terrified of saying anything that upsets the authorities. But, hey, China is not free, but we are, right?

Mass Mind Control

Political correctness and the explosion of rules and regulations, dos and don'ts, musts and mustn'ts, are there to inflict mass mind control on the population, and Common Purpose-type 'training' organisations are there to mind-manipulate the administrators of the system to impose the rules and regulations that enslave the people. Mind control of the masses is deployed in the same way that rats in a laboratory maze have their behaviour manipulated by electric shocks or punishments. If they go down the 'wrong' channel they keep getting shocked until eventually they won't go there even if you take the shock equipment away. Their mind has been reprogrammed to react as you desire using the carrot and the stick technique. Conform to everything we say and we'll leave you alone; question or refuse and *smack*! This is happening every day as people are faced with rules, regulations, instructions and orders wherever they go and whatever they do. There is no respite from it in mainstream society and the rules are getting more numerous and invasive as we head for the global fascist state. Even putting out the rubbish bin in the UK is now an ordeal for many as they are watching the clock and counting how many inches it is from the edge of the pavement. These constant punishments and fears of punishments have the same effect on the psyche, if you concede your power to them, as the electric shocks do on the rats. They lead to subservience and acquiescence to authority and programmed behaviour patterns. The Fabian, Bertrand Russell, wrote in his 1931 book, *The Scientific Outlook*:

> Science has given us, in succession, power over inanimate nature, power over plants and animals, and finally power over human beings ... It is the manipulative type of

idealists who will create the scientific society. Of such men, in our own day, Lenin is the archetype and Mao Zendong.

All real power will come to be concentrated in the hands of those who understand the art of scientific manipulation ... Science will be diligently studied, it will be rigidly confined to the governing class. The populace will not be allowed to know how its convictions were generated ... Ordinary men and women will be expected to be docile, industrious, punctual, thoughtless, and contented ...

... Of these qualities probably contentment will be considered the most important. In order to produce it, all the researches of psycho-analysis, behaviourism, and biochemistry will be brought into play ...

There is growing technological support for this mass mind control and this includes strobe lighting, digital television and compulsory energy-saving light bulbs that are justified by 'global warming'. The pulse of strobe lighting opens the psyche to hypnotic suggestion and its effect can be seen in the way it can trigger epileptic seizures. Television has a similar effect on the Mind and digital television is designed to increase this through a closer energetic connection to the digital levels of the brain. 'Energy-saving' fluorescent light bulbs, which are being made compulsory by the European Union, are also meant to cause physical and hypnotic effects. They can make some people physically ill (Fig 305). Energy-saving light bulbs are supposed to 'protect the environment', but they contain mercury, a lethal poison, with all the disposal problems that entails. The British government warns that if one of these bulbs is broken the room should be cleared for 15 minutes to stop anyone breathing in the dangerous mercury vapour. Workers in Chinese factories making these bulbs are suffering the effects of mercury poisoning. It is crazy to force these bulbs on people, but it is being done because of the effect on the population. The human psyche is being bombarded from all angles. The game is to subjugate the Mind to follow a pattern of response every bit as extreme as the laboratory rat or mouse walking round the maze no longer needing external intervention to dictate where to go. Unthinking acquiescence – the comfort zone where conformity = comfort. Aldous Huxley wrote in *Brave New World* that the infiltration of the mind by the State would continue through suggestion and punishment until ...

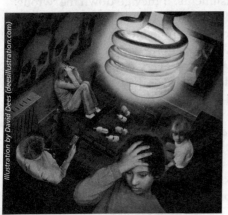

Illustration by David Dees (deesillustration.com)

Figure 305: *So-called energy-saving light bulbs are not being introduced to 'save the planet, but because of their vibrational effect on the human mind and energy field*

... at last the child's mind is these suggestions, and the sum of the suggestions is the child's mind. And not the child's mind only. The adult's mind too, all his life long. The mind that judges and desires and decides – made up of these suggestions. But all these suggestions are our suggestions ... Suggestions from the State.

In pursuit of this, the Reptilian-hybrid families are planning to stage more terrorist events, wars and disasters, engineer a devastating economic crash, impose ever more authoritarian laws, including those to 'save the planet' from 'climate change', and increase the fear and stress of the people in every way they can. Underpinning this will be further centralised control of the media, vicious attacks on the alternative media and freedom of expression, and ever-increasing 'hate laws' and political correctness to ensure that the real story of what is going on cannot be heard by the public. We must not bow to this or the consequences will be unthinkable.

Look at what I have written in the last few chapters alone about the worldwide manipulation of politics, the military, the media, medicine, law, Big Pharma, Big Biotech, 'leadership training', civil liberties groups, political correctness, and so much else. Is there anyone who still believes that all this has come about by accident or chance? Or that it is all orchestrated by men in dark suits sitting around a table deciding their next move? It is much bigger than that – *fundamentally* so. It has happened and is happening through the Illuminati global web that has ensnared the people of this planet and is increasingly dictating every facet of their lives. This web, in turn, serves the agenda of the Reptilians and is constantly supported by vibrational communications broadcast from the Moon to capture the collective mind in a false reality, the Moon Matrix. These communications are implanted in the Metaphysical Universe – the waveform blueprint for this holographic reality. This contains infinite possibilities and the Control System seeks to tune the global population into the low-vibrational Moon Matrix programs by manipulating people into low-vibrational states of Mind, all based on different expressions of fear. When people are tuned into the Moon Matrix blueprint they will play out the program just like the characters in a computer game will do whatever the program decides they will do. The 'training' organisations are seeking to connect the 'leaders' into the control blueprint in the Metaphysical Universe and once they are locked in they will all act according to the program. It is like making the movie in the Metaphysical Universe and manipulating 'humans' to project it onto the 'screen'. This is how the Control System can be introduced with such speed and coordination. It is not being decided around a table 'within' this holographic reality. It is being 'written' into the waveform construct and merely played out in the 'world' that we directly experience.

Only by becoming Conscious and expanding perception beyond Mind, can we override the Reptilian program 'written' into the Metaphysical Universe and so decode other possibilities into holographic reality. People have to open their perception to a dramatically greater sense of reality than the one we have been programmed to believe in. Only then can we understand the scale and depth of what is going on, and bring an end to this Reptilian dictatorship.

Okay, so what can we do?

28

Breaking the 'Spell'

Be master of mind rather than mastered by mind
Zen proverb

If you've got this far you will have gathered, to put it mildly, that humanity is in serious trouble with monumental challenges ahead. I have no desire to understate that fact, because unless we face it nothing can be done. There are, however, other forces at work that I will discuss in the final chapter. We are not alone.

There are two ways to solve a problem. You can find a solution or you can remove the cause. The world is drowning in supposed solutions, but the problems remain, as they must do when the cause is still there. It is like giving someone a painkiller for a broken leg. Unless the leg is fixed, the pain will keep returning no matter how many pills you take. I would suggest that we need to look at the world today from the same perspective. We need to deal with the cause and when that is removed the problems must, by definition, disappear, too. We have got into this mess through manipulated ignorance of the reality we are experiencing; through being dominated by the traits of the reptilian brain and the false reality of the Moon Matrix; through refusing to honestly face the situation we are in; through not understanding what freedom is, nor standing together to defend it; through allowing ourselves to be divided and ruled; and through those twins of human enslavement: cognitive dissonance and denial. A 'spell' has indeed been cast on the human psyche (Fig 306). All those behaviour patterns apply both to the 'individual' and the collective and I am going to address them in this chapter. If we can remove these causes of human suppression and manipulation then, again, the suppression and manipulation must end.

Lying to the Mirror

Cognitive dissonance and denial, both forms of lying to ourselves, are a human plague and if this doesn't change then nothing else will. I have known people in my life who are so in denial of their own behaviour that they construct a fake self to stop them facing who and what they really are. They talk endlessly about 'love and light' and how they 'love everyone' while actually being cold, callous, devious, totally self-serving and vindictive. Me, me, me is the only show in town and if they ever told the truth they would immediately implode from the shock. They hide this from themselves with the fake personality-construct based on them being 'loving'. Cognitive dissonance, as I said earlier, means to hold two contradictory beliefs simultaneously and accept that both are

true. George Orwell called it 'doublethink'.
When two beliefs or behaviour patterns are
fundamentally at odds within the same mind,
it creates unpleasant emotional disharmony, an
inner friction – dissonance – that somehow has
to be dealt with. This can be done by changing
beliefs in the light of new information, or the
evidence before us. In the example I am
referring to here, the people acknowledge that
talking endlessly about 'love and light' and 'I
love everyone' cannot be sustained in the face
of their cold, callous, devious, totally self-
serving and vindictive behaviour. If they do
this they can move forward by facing the truth
about themselves and so change the behaviour
patterns. Instead, what most people do is agree
from the start that their beliefs or view of
themselves – 'love and light, I love everyone' –
is immovable. It is taken as fact that this must
be true. To overcome the cognitive dissonance
they must find a way of explaining away to
themselves their contradictory behaviour and
this invariably means finding someone else to
blame for why they act as they do. People in
cognitive dissonance are invariably the victim,
never the perpetrator, in their own little

Figure 306: *A spell has been cast on the human collective mind through the Moon Matrix and the reptilian brain to turn humanity into a robotic race of slaves*

twilight world of self-denial. I have had characters in my life who have such extreme
cognitive dissonance that they will cause enormous pain and hurt for others and
disrupt the work they claim to 'support' in one moment, and then say they 'love
everyone' and support the work in the next. What happens? These people never
change because they have convinced themselves there is nothing to change. After all,
they have such 'love for the world'. They are so deeply controlled by cognitive
dissonance that they can say that 'people need to wake up and see what's going on'
while doing everything they can to undermine the ability of another to circulate and
communicate that very information. They see no contraction in this because of
cognitive dissonance, the foundation mindset of so many frauds and fakes, and, my
goodness, I have known some.

There is a collective version of this, too, and this needs to change urgently if the
Control System is to be unravelled. There are still fantastic numbers of people who
believe they live in a 'free world', when all the evidence points to the opposite. They go
into cognitive dissonance to avoid accepting what they don't want to face ... the fact
that they live in a fast-emerging tyranny. The Orwellian State is being introduced with
the most extraordinary speed and coordination worldwide while so many people
vehemently deny there is any conspiracy or common force behind it. On the one hand it
seems there is incredible organisation and coordination, and on the other is the belief
that it is not organised and coordinated. People would rather this not be true and so

Figure 307: *Ignorance is bliss – but only for a while*

they convince themselves that it's not. This is when people justify their governments going to war on the innocent by saying that you have to 'fight for peace', or that pepper-bombing civilians is somehow giving them 'freedom'. The one I love is that taking away basic freedoms is necessary to 'protect our freedoms', as with the Orwellian laws justified by the 'war on terror'. Cognitive dissonance and denial connect very powerfully with 'wishful thinking'. Once again, you would rather it not be happening so you lie to the mirror and convince yourself that it's not (Fig 307). But where does all this take us in terms of unlocking the Control System? Nowhere. It is this very state of mind that holds the Control System together and allows the few to control the many. We need to grow up and take responsibility.

It Is what it Is

I find myself saying so many times these days: 'It is what it is'. This is the antidote to cognitive dissonance. When you are facing a situation honestly, it can be dealt with. It is no longer a case of 'I don't want it to be what it is and so I will decide to believe that it isn't'. Once we are prepared to accept what we see before us without editing and censorship to protect ourselves – temporarily – from changing our view or facing what we don't like, cognitive dissonance cannot manifest. This is crucial. Unless people are honest and open enough to accept what is happening, how can they possibly do anything about it? To say 'it is what it is' does not mean giving in to a situation. It is the essential starting point to *not* giving in through denial and thus acquiescence. How many people have died of a disease that could have been cured at an earlier stage, but they didn't want to face the possibility of what was wrong and so they did nothing about it? People stay in tired, loveless, even abusive relationships, because they don't want to face what is. If you leave something that needs dealing with, it goes on getting worse. I have heard women concoct the most amazing excuses for their partners knocking the crap out of them. 'It was my fault; I made him mad at me.' No, he's a bully. Face it. Get out of there. He is what he is. It is what it is. If I have a rotting piece of pie on my plate I am not going to convince myself it is fresh out of the oven just to make me feel better. If I do, the pie will go on rotting and will eventually stink the place out. Stick it in the bin and make another. We can do this once we accept what is.

There is another aspect to this, too. 'It is what it is' brings you into the *Now*, the only moment that exists, and allows you to escape the illusory past and future. Only by being in the Now can we affect anything. If we 'live' in the past and the future we are 'living' – perceiving – in a world that doesn't actually exist. It is just a belief-system. How can we change anything in that state and from that 'place'? We can't. We make ourselves impotent. The phrase goes 'it is what it is', not 'it was what it was' or 'it will be what it will be'. It perceives from the 'is', the Now, and so gives us the power to change 'what is' in the only moment that anything can be changed. My son, Jaymie, was not happy one day when his football team lost a game. 'We should have won! If only ...' (we had done this or that). True, but they didn't. There is only what 'is' – they lost the match. The final whistle has gone; the game is over, the outcome a done deal. There is no point poring over what could have been or should have been ... if only, if only, if only. We just have the Now – what is – and you either accept that and get on with your life, or you go on feeling regret and disappointment about something you cannot change. The past can then hurl you into the future as you start focusing your attention on the next game and how you must win or play well in that one. This, too, can blight your life with anxiety and nervousness about the outcome long before you can do anything about it. Will we win or will we lose again? Hey, that will be two defeats in a row. Oh, no! There is another way ... the way of the *Now*. Accept what is – we lost – and learn from the lessons of the experience. Then get on with your life without any more 'if onlys'. Enjoy the Now without the party poopers of past and future. After all, what's the alternative? Not enjoying the Now. It doesn't sound much like fun to me. I guess what I am saying here can be summed up by this famous 'prayer':

> God, grant me the serenity
> To accept the things I cannot change;
> The courage to change the things I can;
> And the wisdom to know the difference.

I would replace 'God' with 'Consciousness', but the theme is the same. Unless we accept the things we cannot change, or change immediately, we destroy our enjoyment of the Now. The phrase: 'It is what it is' has many expressions. There is, for instance: 'It is what it is so let's do something about it'; and there is: 'It is what it is and there's nothing I can do to change it at the moment, so I have to accept what is'. Both are dealing with the 'is' by using the 'wisdom to know the difference'. I also saw a poem that said:

> I cannot predict the future,
> I cannot change the past;
> I have just the present moment;
> I must treat it as my last.

Why Me? Why Us?

Life does not always give us the perfect hand as I am sure you'll have noticed (well, perfect from our perspective, anyway). There are things we like and things we don't like and if we don't treat them both as twin impostors we are going to be bouncing emotionally between floor and ceiling and will end up battered in the process. Never more so than in the months and years ahead as the crazies throw their final cards that are destined, eventually, to be trumped. Worrying about what might happen and feeling frustrated at how it could have been allowed to happen will not help us to deal with what is happening. It is what it is. We can no longer change how we got into this mess. Nor can we affect where this mess is taking us by focusing on some illusory 'what if?' 'future'. We can only change the Now and what is – not what has been or will be. The 'will be' can change only if we change the Now, not least because the Now is the

Metaphysical Universe from which we manifest holographic reality. We can't change 'here' without first changing 'there'. Some questions that come from all this: Why is this happening to us? Why are we in this reality when all this is going on? Why do things happen to you and not to me, and to me and not to you? Why is your life as it is and others' lives as they are? Answer those questions and you change everything. In the earliest weeks of my conscious journey in 1990, a psychic told me that 'they' had a message for me. 'They' said:

> True love does not always give the receiver what it would like to receive, but it will always give that which is best for it. So welcome everything you receive whether you like it or not. Ponder on anything you do not like and see if you can see why it was necessary. Acceptance will then be very much easier.

That is the key – acceptance. It is what it is. I emphasise again that this does not mean acquiescence to a situation, only knowing when you can change it and when you can't. But back to those questions: Why is your life as it is and others' lives as they are? Can you see patterns of recurring experience in your life? What is life telling you about yourself? 'Ponder on anything you do not like and see if you can see why it was necessary.' I have learned from long and sometimes harsh experience that you can change your life by recognising what life is telling you. In effect, what one level of you is telling another level of you. Once you acknowledge what your experience is saying in what I call the language of life, the experience disappears. The experience is not about punishment, it is about expanding awareness and removing the blocks in perception. The situations we face, the people that come into our lives, whether life flows or goes nowhere, are all telling us about ourselves and the direction we need to go. Why is this experience happening to me? Why is this pain in the arse in my life? Why am I attracting these things into my energy field? Once the learning happens, there is no further need for the experience and so it dissolves into the ether. Those who do not identify the 'why?' are destined to continue the same experience indefinitely until they do. Has he got it yet? No. Same again then, Bill. Humanity as a whole is about to be offered an enormously challenging opportunity to identify the collective 'why?' – why is this fascist imposition happening while we are here to experience it? The answer will not be the same for everyone, but it will be for the vast majority. When people have worked it out, the experience will be over, because it will no longer be necessary. The starting point is to ditch the denial. It is what it is and what we face we can replace. I'll return to the collective 'why us?' in the final chapter.

There is that brilliant scene in the first *Matrix* movie when Morpheus tells Neo the truth about the illusory reality he had thought was real. The trigger for Neo's personal transformation was when Morpheus said: 'You are a slave, Neo. Like everyone else, you were born into bondage ... born into a prison that you cannot smell or taste or touch. A prison for your mind.' This was followed by the choice that Neo made to take the 'red pill'– the decision to both accept that he was a slave and to make the choice to be free. This is the decision that everyone needs to make now. Not tomorrow, not next week or when there is an 'r' in the month. Today, now, this minute. We go nowhere with removing the Control System unless very large numbers of people are prepared to do that and what it takes to make it happen. If people reading this book decide not to commit themselves to this then they have wasted their time reading this far. They merely know a great deal more about their own prison, but without that total commitment to individual and collective freedom, the cell door will stay firmly locked. Once you make the decision to recognise your own slavery and commit yourself to freedom for yourself and others, everything changes – so long as it is genuine and not just words. That change of perception and desire for freedom changes the vibrational state of your energy field and you begin to attract to you the people, locations, experiences and knowledge to achieve what you have made a commitment to manifest. There is no need to organise anything, it just happens through 'like-attracts-like'. It may appear to express itself as organisation, but it is really energetic waveform connections in the Metaphysical Universe playing out in the decoded 'world' of holographic form. The key is to change our perception and attitudes to make those connections in the Metaphysical Universe that express themselves as synchronistic organisation in this holographic realm. While we are in denial or cognitive dissonance over what is happening, or refusing to commit ourselves to securing freedom for all, the connections can't be made and things must stay as they are. This is not esoteric navel gazing; it is the first and most important step in sinking the Control System.

Out of Mind

I began very early in this book talking about the difference between Mind and Consciousness and the theme has been with us throughout. This is especially important as we consider what can be done about the current human experience. Albert Einstein said: 'You cannot solve problems with the same level of consciousness that created them.' He was so right and yet that's what we do. We use Mind to respond to problems caused by Mind. Plato said: 'When the mind is thinking, it is talking to itself.' We have to go beyond Mind and into Consciousness where we can feel the answers and know what we each can and must do if we want this nightmare to end. We need to access levels of awareness that can perceive beyond the illusory holographic play-out realm of dense form. It is not that we have to go anywhere to make this connection; it is already part of us, at one with us. We need to remove the mental, emotional and vibrational barriers that prevent us from 'hearing' and feeling those expanded levels of our awareness. These barriers are Mind, in a closed-circuit, 'loopy' state, and they hold us in five-sense perception where we are isolated from Consciousness – the manipulators' clump of virgin clay to make of whatever they want by programming the blueprint in the Metaphysical Universe. Mind, especially left-brain mind, deals in structure, hierarchy and rigid belief. These are body/mind realities and they must cease to dictate human perception of self and the world. This is how we got into this state and it is certainly not going to get us out of it – 'you cannot solve problems with the same level of consciousness that created them'. Rigid belief has to go for a start … religious belief, political belief, racial belief, cultural belief, self-identify belief. We are being asked to transform our entire sense of reality from the small to the All; from the 'little me' to the *All That Is*; from Mind to Consciousness (Fig 308 overleaf). This involves a total reassessment of how we see the world and ourselves and it means an end to the worship of rules, regulations, hierarchy and structure for their own sake. As my father used to say: 'Rules and regulations are for the guidance of the intelligent and the blind

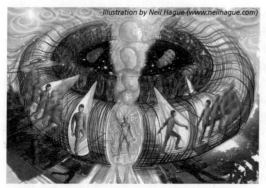

Illustration by Neil Hague (www.neilhague.com)

Figure 308: *When we break through the Mind programs of perception and suppression and remember who we really are, we reconnect in awareness to Consciousness. The Moon Matrix then loses its power over us and our sense of self and the world. That is why global society is structured to keep us in Mind*

obedience of the idiot.' Acquiescence to rules, regulations, hierarchy and structure is what holds the prison together. The few make the laws and rules and control the hierarchical structures while the mass of the people, who could bring the system down in a day, just accepts what the Control System tells them to do and to believe. We are by far the most important contributors to our own enslavement, and that's great news because it means we have the power to set ourselves free.

Frozen Minds

It is in the apparently little things in daily life that you can see where the world is collectively heading and how deep the 'rules is rules' mentality and political correctness is now embedded in mainstream society. I was driving with my son, Jaymie, to a football match in southern England a few years ago when he needed a wee. Nothing could be more natural – water in, water out. Everyone needs to wee or they would eventually explode. It's one of those things that connects us all, be we a prince or a pauper, rich or poor. Even the Queen of England with all her wealth and power needs to have a widdle. There is probably even some Mistress of the Potty to administer the royal flush accompanied by the sound of booming cannons.

'One would like a wee.'
Cue music: 'Hallelujah! Hallelujah!'

Cue commentator speaking in hushed tones: 'And now, in accordance with the tradition of the ages, Her Majesty is approached, head bowed, by the Mistress of the Potty and begins her sacred journey down the corridor to the royal water closet. She waves to the assembled courtiers as they line her route and they bow and wish her well in her coming endeavours. God save the Queen!'

The rest of us in need of a tiddle have to find a place to do it without the sycophants in wigs and breeches marching in unison and that can be less than straightforward when you are dealing with people who have a neuron-pathway deficit and an addiction to 'rules-is-rules'. Jaymie and I were out on the motorway (freeway) when the need arose and we turned off to begin a 25-minute search amid the residential streets of a place called Eastleigh in Hampshire – until there it was, like an oasis in a desert ... a petrol filling station and a shop called 'Alldays' on Passfield Avenue. However, Pass*water* Avenue it was not. Jay was, by this time, dancing more than walking and the situation had reached, shall we say, an acute stage. He ran into the shop while I filled up the car. A minute or so later he was back. 'They say they don't have a toilet,' he said. I went in to pay for the petrol and make it clear to them that we had an emergency on our hands in the wee department. Behind the counter were two teenage girls who had both sadly failed to secure the title of 'Brain of Britain'.

> 'Excuse me. My son needs the toilet real badly; haven't you got one he can use?'
> 'No, we don't 'ave one.'
> 'So where do you go, then?'
> 'In the staff toilet.'
> 'So you do have a toilet?'
> 'Yeah, but the public can't use it.'
> 'Okay, but my son is really struggling, can't you make an exception just once?'
> 'No, it's not allowed – there's a toilet at the Sports Centre down the road.'

I asked to see whoever was in charge and onto the scene came the manageress, a lady with an expression akin to chewing a lemon, or, as my former mother-in-law would say, with 'a face like a smacked arse'. She was about five-foot-four, but somehow managed to look down on me, which was quite a feat, but one which, it seemed to me, she had taken endless opportunities to practise.

> 'What's the problem?' our lemon-sucker began.
> 'My son is desperate for the toilet and I am told you have a staff toilet. Could he use it please?'
> 'No.'
> 'Why?'
> 'It's against the rules.'
> 'But can't you just do it out of basic humanity, one human being in trouble helped by another?'
> 'No. If I let one do it, I would have to let everyone do it.'

This is the 'rationale' of the unconscious, uncaring 'Mind' – that if you make an exception in the light of extreme circumstances you are somehow opening the floodgates (appropriately in this case) to a long queue of people saying 'you allowed him, so we want the same'. Minds enslaved by rules are energetically frozen and they can't move and flow with changing circumstances. If it's not black, it must be white, there is nothing in between. They are locked into only two potential responses – 'yes' or 'no' – in accordance with whatever the rule book has decreed. It is the binary system of on-off electrical charges, I guess. What was encapsulated in that brief interchange at the petrol station was the way the system controls the people (those who have chosen to stay in their comatose state) in the same way that computer programs control robots. For instance, the unbreakable rule that 'only staff can use the toilet' is no different to an instruction encoded into computer software or robot technology. You press the button and the program kicks in: 'I ... am ... a ... Da ... lek ... on ... ly ... staff ... can ... use ... the ... staff ... toi ...let ... ex ... ter ... min ... ate ... ex ... ter ... min ... ate ...' The software controlling this lady's actions was the 'Alldays' corporate rule-book and, just like a robot, she will not deviate from its program no matter what the circumstances. Her mind is no longer hers; it belongs to the book, the company, which is nothing more than an agent for the system. What's more, others in the queue behind me were not saying,

'Come on, let the lad use the toilet; don't be silly.' They were asking how long I was going to keep them waiting. There was just no empathy, no basic humanity for someone in trouble. It was a scene from a sci-fi movie like the *Matrix* or *Stepford Wives*. Were any of these people actually conscious? It seemed not. To anyone conscious the situation was simple. Here was a young lad that desperately needed the toilet and here was a toilet – the perfect match; but enslaved Mind doesn't 'do' simple, let alone see it. The world is a complex realm of rules and regulations that they must follow and obey. Unless the rules say the situation is simple, and they rarely do, it cannot be so.

I was at a youth football match watching Jaymie playing in goal for his team. I stood near his goal and took photographs of him when he was called into action. Once again, real simple – a father taking photos of his son. But not so in the minds of those in Never, Never Land. In this case, Never, Never take photographs of your own children without getting permission from the parents of all the other players on the pitch who may or may not be in the background of any images. The referee of the game, who must surely work at 'Alldays', came over to say it was against the rules for me to take photographs without the permission of all the players' parents (most of whom weren't even at the match).

'I am taking photographs of my own son,' I said. 'What the hell can be the problem?'
'The FA [the governing body of English football] has said that no pictures can be taken without permission from the parents – it's to stop paedophiles.'
'But he's my *son*.'
'Sorry, those are the rules.'

Then came the classic you hear all the time from these rule-book 'minds': 'There's nothing I can do, I am just following the rules.' Well, actually, there is something you can do; you can use your own mind and take the situation on its merits. This referee had stood beside me while I took Jaymie through a warm-up before the match – he knew he was my son. But no; rules is rules, mate, nothing I can do, no exceptions. At another match I was filming Jaymie at a ground near my home and *everyone* there knew he was my son, including the referee who stopped the game to trot over to tell me I had to stop filming unless I had permission from all the parents. If I didn't, said the man-in-black, he would ask me to leave the ground. I told him that he could ask me what he liked, but I wasn't going anywhere and I wasn't going to stop filming. I invited him not to be so silly and to give me the size of his shoes and how many times he changed the laces because I needed the information for a government database. With his sense of authority thus deflated, he restarted the game and I carried on filming. We don't have to take this crap, so why do we?

Rules is Rules

When a few wish to control the many they have to get members of the many to enforce the rules that give them the control they need. There are nowhere near enough manipulators, working in full knowledge of the agenda, to police and pen the masses. They have to get the masses to police and pen each other. To do this they need to target and develop the rule-book mentality which concedes all rights to free thought to people they have never met, and probably have never heard of, who have decided what the rules will be in any given situation. Rule-book groupies are the non-conscious made manifest, and without them the few could never control the population. These blueprint minds almost always appear in uniform, which is the physical, 'outward' expression of the *uniform*ity that exists between their ears. Look the same, obey the same (with honourable exceptions). I can see ever more clearly the parting of the ways between those who are awakening from the trance and those who are going ever-deeper into it. In the small town where I live, I observe the zombies-in-uniform and the luminous-jacket-Mafiosi as they ply their robotic trade with rule-book-in-hand and rule-book-in-head. The system, with help from organisations like Common Purpose, is turning out what I call 'traffic cameras on legs'. The thousands of speed cameras we have across the UK have no discretion. It doesn't matter if you drive slightly over the speed limit on an empty road at midnight or if you drive at the same speed in heavy traffic at noon. The camera just flashes and the two situations get treated the same. This is what the system wants from its robots-in-uniform. No discretion, just slavish obedience – traffic cameras on legs. In my town, we once had a lovely bloke who enforced the car-parking regulations. He did it with good sense and good humour and if you parked in an illegal, but safe, place for a minute or two to use an ATM, for example, he would just say, 'Okay, quick as you can.'

Everything worked fine, but he was sacked for not writing enough tickets and along came his replacement, an officious John Wayne wannabe who had to settle for giving out tickets to motorists. The whole atmosphere changed, and so did the number of tickets because Consciousness had been replaced by a software Mind. There are now four or five equally robotic uniforms doing the same job in the town today where once one man did it so well and with such common sense. This is happening everywhere as the personnel are employed to enforce the ever-expanding Orwellian State. The more rules and laws you introduce to impose on the people, the more robotic minds you need to employ to unthinkingly and unfeelingly enforce them. The explosion in 'law enforcement' personnel is merely the public face of the explosion in laws to enforce. They are nothing more than pawns of the State, cogs in an engine, going round and round without thought or discretion until it's time to replace them with a new one that works just the same. The last thing the system wants is people in uniform or administration that are conscious and can deal with situations on their merits using fairness, justice, empathy and simple good sense and without the limitation of pre-conceived ideas and catch-all rules. We can do it in our own lives, however, and what a difference it would make to the world, and human freedom, if we stopped saying 'rules is rules' and started to decide everything on the basis of fairness, justice, empathy and basic intelligence in any given situation. We are Infinite Consciousness, not an extension of a rule book or computer program. The rule book mentality is an expression of Mind and only by going beyond that can we open ourselves to Consciousnesses.

Fraudulent 'Freedom'

Almost everyone would say they believe in freedom; but they don't. They believe in their *version* of freedom, which is usually not freedom at all. This is a crucial point. If we don't know what freedom really is, how can we ever secure it? Most people are frightened of freedom in its true sense because it means that people they disagree with, or whose lifestyles they condemn, have the very same rights and freedoms as they do. The following story encapsulates the point I am making. I crawled out of bed in a

Swedish hotel room one morning peering through the jet-lag of a long flight from America and wondered where I was going to get the energy from for an eight-hour presentation two days hence. I went slowly, very slowly, through a list of pending emails until I opened one from a lady who was screaming an ultimatum at me. Huh? Rub eyes, look again. What? 'I am furious,' said the lady, though I got the impression she gets 'furious' quite a lot, about quite a lot. I had to condemn the BBC for allowing fascists onto their airwaves, she said, or she would unsubscribe to my newsletter. As I don't take ultimatums from anyone, I said it was better if she did unsubscribe, not least because she clearly doesn't understand where I am coming from anyway, so what was the point of her reading my articles? Some background: I had been half aware as I passed through airports in America from CNN on the TV that there was a furore going on back in Britain about an invitation from the BBC for Nick Griffin, the leader of the far-right British National Party, to appear on its weekly political debate show, *Question Time*. The British National Party, known as the BNP, restricted its membership until recently to 'indigenous British ethnic groups'. It basically wants Britain to be for whites only in its ideal world, but settles publicly for a policy of 'firm but voluntary incentives for immigrants and their descendants to return home'. I doubt for a second that the word 'voluntary' has any meaning whatsoever should the BNP ever come to power, which, of course, it won't. It's not meant to come to power, from the perspective of the bigger picture; it is meant to be a 'right' polarity that can be played off against the 'left' polarity to create the divide and rule and diversion of focus that allows the real fascist/communist power-structure, represented by the main political parties and the European Union, to advance unchallenged. The BNP is led by Nicholas John 'Nick' Griffin, a privately-educated Cambridge graduate. He has secured a high profile as leader of the BNP that culminated in the election of himself and another member to the irrelevant European Parliament in 2009. The BNP's electoral success, strictly limited as it was, automatically entitled them, according to BBC rules, to be invited to appear on the political debate show (once again, see under irrelevant) called *Question Time*. Oh, dear … that's when the trouble started.

The lady that sent me the email was one of countless thousands who condemned the BBC for having a 'fascist' on their programme. The fact that *Question Time* has been having fascists on the show since its inception, disguised as government ministers and 'opposition' MPs, passed them by – as usual. The emailer was quite civil until I questioned her stance, and then, well, she wasn't civil anymore. No sweat, I've been there many times. I have said before that what you fight you become, and this is a wonderful example. The lady talked about the need to silence Griffin and deny him access to the BBC to protect our 'freedom and democracy', as if we actually *had* freedom and democracy. If you equate a threat to 'freedom and democracy' with a minor political party then the most important understanding is lost – the British government and Parliament, in league with the European Union, are demolishing the most basic freedoms every day and 'democracy', which has basic flaws, anyway, disappeared long ago, if it ever really existed. The system doesn't need Nick Griffin and the BNP to destroy freedom; it is doing perfectly well without them, thank you. I asked the lady, as I would ask the other protestors at the BBC decision, if she was campaigning for Tony Blair to be banned from *Question Time* and other such political programmes. Blair is responsible for the slaughter of more than a million people in Iraq alone (low-side estimate). If the BNP, why not him? Why not ban the British Cabinet that supported the manufactured wars of death, destruction and conquest of other peoples' lands? Why not ban Prime Minister Gordon Brown who, with Blair and Bill Clinton, imposed sanctions against Iraq in the 1990s that, even according to UN figures, cost the lives of half a million Iraqi children? Where does it end? Let's ban everyone we don't agree with, shall we? What a world of freedom we would live in then. The lady replied to my questions in a blaze of fury and said that she had called for Tony Blair to be tried as a war criminal. But thousands of people have done that and, besides, it wasn't my question. I asked if she was campaigning for Blair to be banned from the BBC, as she was with Griffin. Answer: No. But, why not? Griffin runs a party of overwhelmingly prejudiced people who want to see people of dark-coloured skin removed from the country, but will never get the chance to do it. Blair blatantly lied to send in 'the boys' to kill and maim millions of dark-coloured innocents in Iraq and Afghanistan and cause horrific birth defects for generations from the depleted uranium in the weapons that were unleashed on the population. Which one is the most dangerous fascist?

Being What You Condemn

Making these points is described by the barely-one-dimensional advocates of censorship as 'defending the BNP'. It is the only way their minds can compute such views when in fact what I am doing is defending free speech for *everyone* – including them. Calmness is what we need, not the heart-on-the-sleeve, holier-than-thou 'fury' that scrambles the mind and obscures the fact that people can, and do, become a mirror of what they claim to oppose. What did the Nazis do in Germany? They systematically broke up the public meetings of opposition groups to deny them a platform to expose the Nazi agenda and banned opposition altogether once they came to power. They instigated mass burnings of books that took a different view of life and society. And what do the 'anti-Nazis' want to do? Er, exactly. 'We believe in freedom – BAN him!' The word 'pathetic' does not suffice. I have no problem whatsoever with homosexuality if that is how people want to live their lives, while Nick Griffin told the *Question Time* programme that he found the sight of two men kissing to be 'repulsive'. Now, if I have the right to have no problem with homosexuality, why can't Griffin have the equal right to find it repulsive? It's called *Freedom*. What are we going to do, put his head in a vice until he repents? If Muslims can have the right to say that Islam is the only true religion and that Muslims are the ones chosen by 'God', why can't Griffin have the right to say that Islam is a 'wicked and evil religion', as he does? The same with the Jewish faith. I don't understand. Do these people have any concept at all of what the 'freedom' they shout about really entails? It means the freedom for others to say things that you don't like. Oh, but of course, there is a difference between the 'fascists' who want to ban and burn and the 'anti-fascists' who want to ban and burn. The 'anti-fascists' are 'right' and because they are 'right' they have the high moral ground from which they can decree who and what is banned and who and what is not. Ahhh, but that's exactly what the fascists say. Mirror, mirror, on the wall ...

I had these self-appointed censors campaigning years ago for my public events to be banned on the grounds that I was, apparently, a racist. How did they know that? Someone told them. And how did he know? Er ... When they were invited to my events to hear what I was really saying, i.e., that racism is not only horrible, it's the height of stupidity, they refused. They don't want to know the truth. They don't do any research. They only want an outlet to posture their own sense of self-purity and self-righteousness. The venue where I spoke in Sante Fe in 2009 actually had a few calls saying that I should not be allowed to speak there because I was a 'neo-Nazi'. They said this about a man who spends his time saying that we are all one eternal Consciousness having different experiences and that therefore racism is ridiculous. I had a chat with a lovely man who came to that event in Sweden and he apologised for thinking for years that I was a 'racist'. Why did he think that? Somebody told him. The target of what I call the Robot Radicals, or Kindergarten Anonymous, may be saying the opposite to what they are claiming, as with myself, but who cares? 'I have shown myself, to myself, to be a good and pure person. What else matters?' The Robot Radicals are being played like a stringed instrument by the very system they claim to despise. Why can't we just debate with those who have another view, no matter how extreme it may seem to us? There are laws against inciting violence against others and so that side of it is sorted, anyway. What we need to do is provide information and awareness that will expose those we disagree with to be mistaken or extreme. If we can't do that, then what's going on? It is easy to say ban, ban, ban. What about exposing their views publicly by the power of argument and evidence? No, no, much too difficult. Better to ban, smash, and all that stuff. Why bother to debate when you can just use a slogan on a banner and scream at the top of your voice? And there is much to debate. Amazing as this will be to the both the BNP and its opponents, the world is not black and white. What? No, there are, staggeringly, shades of grey. Honest.

Same Rights for All

For example, the BNP would love to see an all-white Britain. I wouldn't. I love the diversity of colour, creed and culture and we would lose something fundamental if the UK was returned to the mono-culture it once was and as I remember as a small child. But, again, shades of grey. To say that stopping immigration is good and mass immigration is bad is just as ridiculous as saying mass immigration is good and stopping immigration is bad. Asian ghettos in Britain where white people dare not go are just as outrageous as white areas where Asians dare not go. What is the difference? There is none, but the authorities and the Robot Radicals invent one by condemning the white no-go areas while labelling anyone who complains about the Asian version as a 'racist'. There is no more racist structure on the planet than the Indian caste system that treats the perceived 'lower castes' of the same race like vermin. They dare to call others racist?? But they do, and to challenge this racism is to make you 'racist' in the Brave New World. You don't have to be white to be racist, you know. It's not genetic. But you would think so the way the law is enforced. If people don't want groups like the BNP to emerge then they need to support fairness and justice for all, no matter what the colour, creed or culture. Yes (stands back in amazement), even for *white* people. What is fuelling increased support for the BNP, ironically, is the frustration that millions of Britons feel at not being able to voice their feelings about their own communities and country without being condemned as a 'racist', or, often today, facing criminal prosecution by the Thought Police. What do you expect when white people are charged for saying things that others can say, and more, with impunity? It is the very Robot Radicals shouting about the 'rise of the BNP' who are ensuring that this continued frustration will cause many more to see the BNP as an outlet for their feelings. But it takes conscious people to see this connection, to see this shade of grey and its consequences, and self-pure people are never conscious. I had a little shake of the head when I saw a report in the Robot Radical daily newspaper, *The Guardian*, about how Turkish mafia gangs were set to become the deadliest criminal organisation operating in the UK as they sought 'to win a brutal battle for control of Britain's multi-million-pound heroin market'. One paragraph said:

> The African Crew had bought heroin from the Turkish gangs and then sided with them in a dispute with a West Indian gang from Lambeth that had attempted to make inroads into heroin dealing.

Are all Africans in Britain drug-dealing killers? No, of course they're not. The vast majority just want a peaceful life like everyone else. What about Turkish people? Same. West Indian people? Same. And don't white people run drugs and kill people. Yes, of course. But that's the point. *It is not the colour of your skin; it is the strength of your character.* The real racists are so often those who claim to be 'anti-racist' because they are more aware of race than anyone. They are obsessed with it. Where I see Consciousness in a black body, Asian body, or whatever, they see a suppressed minority due to the colour of their skin. Well, white people can be suppressed as well. In fact, we are *all* being suppressed and this manufactured racial division is designed to divide and rule us so that we do not unite to stop the enslavement of everyone – black, white, or sky-blue bloody pink. We must come together and focus on what unites us all – the Control System that seeks to enslave us all, no matter what our race, religion, politics or income bracket.

Another point about all this … I have been saying for years that the real reason for mass immigration around the world, not least the borders coming down within the European Union, is to destroy a sense of nationhood and culture. In this plan, both the indigenous populations and the immigrants are being equally exploited. Many people only head for Britain because the British Empire and the Western 'civilisation' that followed has so mercilessly exploited the 'developing world', including the imposition of corrupt leaders answering to Western interests, that their home countries are all but destroyed in terms of finance and opportunity. As I've said, the long-planned goal is for a world government overseeing superstates like the European Union which, in turn, will dictate to a mass of regions that are planned to replace the countries and nations of today. To do that, they have sought to destroy a sense of unique culture or nation by opening the gates to enormous numbers from other cultures and nations until the society becomes a cocktail of competing cultures with no one sense of national identity. They are doing the same in the United States. Still more confirmation of this came in 2009 with the revelation that former Prime Minister, Tony Blair (Rothschild Zionist), and Home Secretary, Jack Straw (Rothschild Zionist), conspired to open the door to massive immigration 'to change Britain's cultural make-up forever'. This was revealed by Andrew Neather, who worked for Straw when he was Home Secretary and was a speechwriter for Blair. Jonathan Portes, the civil servant who wrote this open-the-doors immigration policy, was a speechwriter for Gordon Brown, the Prime Minister at the time of writing. Blair, Straw and Brown are all long-time members of the Illuminati

Fabian Society that has been working since 1884 to destroy British culture and self-identity and have it swallowed whole by a global and European dictatorship. Andrew Neather further revealed that to stop the open-door immigration-plan being exposed, any opponents to immigration, including the rival Conservative Party, would be branded as racists. Who helped them to do that? The kind of people lined up with their banners to demand that the BBC ban Nick Griffin from taking part in a television political debate. Unthinking, unquestioning, unresearching, non-dot-connecting, puppets-on-a-string.

Man of Straw

Here is another irony: You know one of the people who appeared on *Question Time* with Nick Griffin to condemn his 'racism'? Why, only *Jack Straw*, he of the calculated open-door immigration policy designed to exploit the immigrants as much as the indigenous. This is the man who has the self-righteous, sanctimonious nerve to condemn those who say immigration has gone too far. Let us have a brief look at Jack Straw, as brief as possible from my point of view. This is an out-of-his-depth dark-suit who does whatever those in the shadows tell him to do. As a result, he has been appointed to a list of high offices of State when he should not even be let loose on a garage sale. He served his Rothschild masters in the Labour government from the time Blair won the election of 1997 and he has been a disaster for justice and liberty in every job he has been given. This is why he has been given them. As Home Secretary from 1997 to 2001, he oversaw the Blair demolition of freedoms and civil liberties. It was Straw who introduced the Orwellian Regulation of Investigatory Powers Act 2000, increased police powers against terrorism (the people), and proposed a reduction in the right to trial by jury. Straw turned down a political asylum request from a man fleeing Saddam Hussein's regime in 2000. He told him: 'We have faith in the integrity of the Iraqi judicial process and that you should have no concerns if you haven't done anything wrong.' Yes, he really said that. Ahhh, but then Straw's next set of orders was delivered when he became Foreign Secretary from 2001 to 2006. His appointment was perfectly timed in June 2001 to have him in situ at the heart of the response to 9/11 and the invasions of Afghanistan and Iraq. Straw, as the so-called government spokesman on foreign policy, lied and argued – as Blair did – to use the fraudulent claim about 'weapons of mass destruction' to justify the devastating onslaught against the civilian population of Iraq. He became Lord High Chancellor and 'Justice Secretary' (yet more irony), and one of his decisions has been to block the publication under the Freedom of Information Act of the minutes of government meetings in the run-up to the invasion of Iraq that he, himself, was involved in. Straw has also overseen the shocking policy of taking children from their parents via secret 'family courts' and handing them to foster parents for the most outrageous of reasons. The man is a liar, cheat, Illuminati gofer, and one of the most active players in the mass murder of Iraqis and Afghans and the introduction of the Orwellian police state. What did the Robot Radicals who campaigned for the banning of Nick Griffin say about Jack Straw being allowed to express his view on the same *Question Time* programme? *Nothing. Zilch. Silence.* Why is anyone concerned that humanity is being manipulated by external forces into a fascist/communist dictatorship when we are quite capable of building one of our own without any help whatsoever?

We are back to removing the cause of the problem. We are divided and ru
the manufactured fault lines of politics, class, race and religion, and it has to s
will be divided and ruled into a global tyranny very soon. We must demand o
freedom of expression, yes, but we must also demand with equal vigour the sa
for those we disagree with. If one person does not have the freedom to voice the
then no-one has. The rest don't have freedom of speech, only the 'right' to say th
acceptable to the State and public opinion. Where is the freedom in that? The Rob
Radicals who chant their slogans about freedom actually oppose freedom as they
showed with the Nick Griffin episode, and the same mentality can be found across
world. We need to stand for the rights and freedoms of everyone, not just those we
agree with. Not doing so is how we got into this situation and we are not going to ge
out of it by doing the same. If you always do what you've always done you'll always
get what you've always got.

Disconnecting from the 'Moon Mind'

These collective behaviour patterns of conflict, division, competition and emotional
reaction are being fed to us by the Moon Matrix through the reptilian brain and it is
crucial that we disconnect from its influence. To break the control of the hive mind we
need to do what the hive mind is programmed to stop us doing. We can override the
system by collectively refusing to do what the hive mind wants us to do. In doing so,
we disconnect vibrationally from the hive-mind frequency. Firstly, we need to bring an
end to emotional reaction and start to calmly assess before jumping in. Counting to ten,
or more, before responding emotionally to a situation is very powerful in switching off
from the reptilian brain and the hive mind. The mass manipulation technique that I call
Problem-Reaction-Solution is only possible because people react instead of taking time
to check, research and consider. This emotional reaction comes from the 'R-complex' or
reptilian brain, the centre of our survival reactions and 'primitive emotional responses'
that connect us to the Moon Matrix hive mind by tuning us in to its frequency range.
The hive mind does not want us to be peaceful, so we should be; it does not want us to
be kind, so we should be; it does not want us to think of others, so we should do; it does
not want us to have empathy with the consequences for others of our actions, so we
should have; it does not want us to cooperate instead of compete, so we should do; it
does not want the lion to lay down with the lamb (all expressions of life living in peace
and harmony), and so the lion must do; it does not want us to do what is right, only
what we think is right for me, me, me, and so we must do what we know to be right
and fair in all circumstances. Not only would all this break us out of the program and
the Reptilian hive mind, it would make this reality a lovely place to live and experience,
which is the last thing the Reptilians want because of the energetic and control
consequences this has for them. We want a world of peace? Okay, be peaceful. We want
a world of kindness? No problem, be kind. It's not that simple? *Oh, yes, it is.*

Does it Really Matter?

Humans are experts at getting their knickers in a twist over things that are utterly
irrelevant. It is one of the major ways that we are controlled, or rather control ourselves
– no shepherd necessary. The way we get wound up over things that don't matter
(reptilian brain) is such a waste of neuron circuitry, thought waves and electrical

signal
the p
bec
m

the

hat else we could use them for … little things like how to respond to
hat is speeding into place by the hour. I can speak from experience
o do it myself, so often getting wound up about things that didn't
ave a fail-safe circuit-breaker that kicks in, most of the time, anyway,
anger of falling for it again. I can't tell you how much calmer and more
comes when you start to see the wood for the trees and stop wasting
nd emotion on the endless list of situations and happenings that simply
My 'circuit-breaker' goes like this: 'And?' That's it; that's all you need. I
nend anyone to give it a try and they will be amazed at how powerful a
ord and a question mark can be in bringing peace into your life. 'And?' So
arts of the brain where emotional reactions are triggered don't deal in
are all about reaction. This is where '*And?*' comes in. It stops the reaction,
emotional circuit should it begin to activate. If anyone still doubts that
a biological computer system they should study the emotional centres of
(especially the reptilian segment) and how they constantly dictate reactions
ponses. They might then wonder how much Consciousness is actually involved
nan behaviour. We talk about people acting without engaging their brains, but
it we are really saying is that they re-acted from the reptilian brain without
igaging the area known as the neo-cortex which likes to think things through. This is
the crucial difference between these contrasting parts of the brain. The neo-cortex says
'And? What does it matter?' But *everything* matters to the reptilian brain. It is neurotic
on a scale that beggars belief and its effect on human behaviour, individually and
collectively, simply cannot be overstated.

How many times in your life have you reacted emotionally or flown into a rage or
panic about something when, 'with hindsight', you could see that what wound you
up so powerfully didn't really matter. Sometimes this can happen within seconds or
minutes when you start to regret what you did and said and realise that you 'over-
reacted'. Exactly. 'Over-reaction' means the control of your sense of reality by the
reptilian brain, and 'with hindsight' is the neo-cortex calmly thinking things through.
Human behaviour, however, is dominated by the reptilian-brain reaction-system, in
league with the amygdala, overpowering the neo-cortex. People don't think most of
the time; they react. This leads to constant conflicts between people and, collectively, it
means wars and other horrors that come from emotional reaction and not thinking
things through. Those who supported the invasion of Iraq were systematically
manipulated in their emotional centres by the propaganda of the Bush-Cheney
regime, aided and abetted by Tony Blair. 'Yeah, Saddam Hussein is a danger to the
world; we gotta get him,' said the reptilian brain with its survival responses activated
by a manufactured threat. The neo-cortex would realise that Saddam was not a danger
to the United States or Britain and see through the ludicrous 'logic' of 'freeing' the
people of Iraq from tyranny by bombing them from the sky. Soldiers go into battle
with the reptilian brain in total control most of the time because the survival instincts
are on highest alert. It's kill or be killed and 'we are protecting our country' – all
reptilian brain/amygdala responses. The neo-cortex would ask why it was fighting
people it had never met and had no personal quarrel with. They say that truth is
the first casualty of war, but I say it's the neo-cortex. Once you go to war it has
already lost.

When we apply all this to everyday life you can perhaps see the importance of 'And?' in calming the lizard in our head. It can be extremely effective. People get upset and defensive (survival instincts) when others say unpleasant and untrue things about them. But we can choose to be indignant (reptilian brain) or to say, 'And?' (neo-cortex). What does it matter? They'll be saying something else next week. Once the line is crossed into reptilian-brain paranoia we lose the plot and suddenly endless irrelevances are transformed into life-or-death importance. They start to *matter*. Another of my circuit-breakers, along with 'And?' is: 'Did anybody die?' It can bring things quickly into perspective when a panic is going on about an apparent catastrophe that isn't. If only we could look at daily events from the perspective we would have from our death-bed with ten minutes to live. It would all look so different and the challenge is to bring that point of observation into the Now. Would it matter that the lady in the store pushed in front of you in the queue? No. Would it matter that your teenage son dropped some food on the carpet? No. Would it matter that the guy cut you up at the lights? No. Then don't let it matter *now*:

'And? What has it cost me, another minute or so in the queue?'
'And? No big deal, get a cloth and be more careful next time.'
'And? I am going to get home 30 seconds later than I would before the guy nipped in front of me.'

But each of those situations can cause people to absolutely erupt with fury and stress when they allow the reptilian brain to prevail. Put it all through the filter of the neo-cortex and it looks very different. Instead of fury and stress there is calm, peace and perspective. A major consequence of reptilian-brain domination is that we stop thinking straight, or even thinking at all. This is why people say such stupid things when they are emotionally distraught or in a state of indignance. The reptilian brain is stupid even to the extent that it cannot even learn from experience. Other parts of the brain/mind do that and this inability to learn is one reason why the reptilian brain is the seat of ritualistic, repeating behaviour. How could it be any other way? What you don't learn from, you are destined to repeat. Unless we break free of control by the reptilian response-system nothing will change, because it can't. The ancient symbol of the snake swallowing its own tail is an image that perfectly describes the reptilian brain. Round and round and round, repeating, repeating, repeating – like the 'loopies' of the Moon Matrix.

Having a Laugh

We are not our bodies; we are Consciousness having an experience through a body hologram that we think is 'us'. It's just a vehicle that allows 'us' to experience this tiny frequency range we call 'the world'. It is not who we are, only what we think we are, and when we buy into that lie we live the body-computer's reality and lose the connection to what we truly are – Consciousness, Infinite Possibility. Life as 'a struggle' is the realm of the body program, which is part of the Moon Matrix program, and it doesn't have to be a struggle if we can break through the vibrational concrete that enslaves us to the will of the program. Laughing in the face of adversity and laughing in the face of danger and intimidation are two examples of this. It breaks the program because you are doing what the program does not want you to do. The idea is to keep us in fear so we give our power away to those we believe will protect us from what we fear – 'Give the banks our money – bail them out – save us.' We also need to be kept constantly worrying about the future, in a state of at least low-level depression that eats away our optimism and joy. This creates a dense ('I feel so tight and heavy') vibrational state which further disconnects us from a conscious connection with the *All That Is*. The more you think limited possibility the more you know you are in the program and not in Consciousness, and the energetic density that comes from depression and worry (expressions of fear) lock you into a sense of limited options and choice – limited possibility. It's a cycle and it's vicious. Our 'human' energy-fields constantly reflect our mental and emotional states in their vibrational resonance and, in turn, the resonance generates mental and emotional states. This is how low-vibrational influences such as drugs and chemical food additives can lead to hyperactivity and depression. It appears to be a chemical reaction that is behind the problem, but the chemical reaction is merely the 'physical' expression of a vibrational reaction.

We need to use Consciousness to break this cycle of cause-and-effect/effect-and cause. But how? Well, one way is to laugh. Try being serious – 'tight and heavy' – when you are laughing, or when somebody else is. Laughter bursts the bubble of pomposity and prevents us from taking ourselves and 'life' far too seriously; you cannot laugh and be in fear at the same time. I am not saying that we should laugh uncontrollably 24/7, but most people don't laugh enough, and some hardly ever. Laughter breaks up the density and frees the energy to flow. As the great British comedian, Ken Dodd, says: 'We're all born with a chuckle muscle, and if you exercise it every day it'll keep you young and frisky all your life, but if you don't it dries up and drops off.' What a wonderful sound it is to hear people laughing. 'The System' itself fears laughter. It removes its sense of power and control. If you react to an authority figure with anger and hostility you are to a large extent playing in their stadium. Ideally, they want unquestioned obedience, but they'll settle for anger as a second best because the game is still playing out on their territory. But have you ever laughed uncontrollably in front of some guy in uniform trying to be serious and 'powerful'? I have and they have no idea what to do. Their power has gone, as if their trousers have fallen to the floor. 'The System' is ridiculous and we need to stop taking it and ourselves anything like so seriously. It is the major change of perception that will set us free. Yes, we need to know how we are controlled, why, and by whom or what. But the way we respond to that knowledge decides if we remain controlled or refuse to be bound by fear, worry and stress. Imagine if, instead of people having a mass protest to shout abuse at their dark-suited targets, they just laughed at them en masse. It has now been shown in medical tests and trials that when you laugh it has a wonderful healing effect on the body (it is making energy flow and this affects the body's chemical state). There are increasing numbers of groups and organisations that have the aim of getting people to laugh. No matter how bad your situation, laughter will always make it seem better, or at least not as bad. How many times in our lives, from early childhood through school and adult life, are we told that we 'mustn't laugh'? Crikey, how many times do we tell *ourselves* that?? Hey, let's chill out. We are *All That Is* and ever can be – All Possibility having an experience in this reality. Let us celebrate who we are and express the joy of that.

I didn't laugh much for many years as I got bogged down with the challenges and obstacles that came my way in my work and the emotional pressures going on around me, but an enormous change has been taking place within me, starting in the summer of 2007. It is steaming along now to the point where 'David Icke', the man born in Leicester, England, in 1952, is fast disappearing. It's a strange feeling, but a wonderful one. It's like returning to myself, my true self, All Possibility, the 'One'. I am on the brink of fantastic breakthroughs into 'out there' that are going to change my life and the direction of my work in a fundamental and extraordinary way in the next few years. As I break through the programs of response and reaction in my body-computer, I am seeing the joy of being alive more than ever before. Yes, Earth can be a shitty place, and one based on suppression and control, but if we can't change everything we don't like overnight (though I know we can once we fully understand reality), at least we can change our relationship with what we don't like. The glass can be half full or half empty; a situation can be depressing or fearful, or ridiculous and funny. It's just a choice, a point of observation. When I went into another state of Consciousness during my ayahuasca experience in Brazil, in 2003, I spent most of the five hours in hysterics. 'The Voice' was such a hoot. I was lying on my back and several times my feet were in the air, I was laughing so much. People might not laugh often enough in the density of body-mind, but 'out there' there is so much fun. But then why shouldn't there be? 'Out there' they know that all is One and there is nothing to fear or get stressed about. The program tells us to do that and sets up situations to make us do that, but beyond the program there is so much joy at just being. The more we find that joy ourselves, the more we disconnect from the Moon Matrix because that is specifically designed to suppress that joy.

Anything we can do, think and feel that is at odds with the program of the Moon Matrix and the reptilian brain will dilute the power they have over our perception and behaviour. So will acknowledging, if you feel to, that the Moon is indeed projecting a false reality and influencing human perception. This brings the Moon-Mind connection out of the hidden and subliminal realm – the Metaphysical Universe – and into conscious awareness. In doing so, the subliminal influence loses its power. The subconscious (waveform) reveals its secrets to the holographic level of awareness. It is the same principle as subliminal advertisements. You can't see the subliminal implant until someone points it out to you but, once they have, the subliminal is the first thing you see whenever you look at the image again. It has moved from subconscious manipulation to conscious awareness and ceases to influence thought and behaviour. Whenever I see the Moon, I acknowledge what it is and what it is doing.

29

The Uprising

A hero has faced it all: he need not be undefeated, but he must be undaunted –
Andrew Bernstein

It may seem from what you have read in this book that all is lost and we are facing insurmountable odds. But all is *not* lost; far, far from it. There are other forces at work here, not only those that seek to control, destroy and enslave.

The 'they' who made contact with me in 1990 and have guided me through the maze and mind-field of suppression and secrets are part of a vast force of transformation that is going to change human reality on a scale that few could currently imagine. Some are what we call extraterrestrials, although I prefer 'interdimensionals', and some are expressions of pure Consciousness helping humanity to awaken. The energetic 'Schism' in the Metaphysical Universe caused by the Reptilian intervention, hi-tech wars and the Moon, which has brought such conflict, ignorance, suffering and disharmony, is in the process of being healed. It may not seem like that at this moment, or for a while, but it will eventually. The Reptilian manipulation is going to be ended, but it is not as simple as just sitting around and watching and waiting for it happen. We all have much to contribute and the more we do, the less traumatic this transformation will be as the world made manifest from the Schism is replaced by one made manifest from balance and harmony. The foundation of everything that is happening now is the energetic change that I call the 'Truth Vibrations' – the quickening. An energy of much higher vibration and faster resonance is being infused into the Metaphysical Universe through the suns and the black holes and it is awakening those who open themselves to its influence. It is encoded with advanced information and expanded awareness (Figs 309 and 310). When you tune in to its frequency you are never the same again, and it is an ongoing process as the Truth Vibrations break down the energetic barriers and blocks and lift the veil on the illusions and secrets about self and the world. I was told about this by the 'they' in 1990 when there was no evidence to support what they said. But now it is plain to see as incredible numbers of people are seeing themselves and the world with new clarity and perception. They are literally waking up from the trance and disconnecting from the scattered and fractured reality caused by the Schism in the vibrational realm, the Metaphysical Universe. It was at this level that the Reptilians intervened and caused massive energetic disharmony that has been decoded through our genetically-manipulated body-computers into the holographic disharmony that we call 'physical life'. This Schism is being rebalanced in the Metaphysical Universe by the

Illustration by Neil Hague (www.neilhague.com)

Figure 309

Figure 310

A new vibration is being resonated by the black holes which is changing the information emitted by the Sun as photons. Neil Hague and I symbolise these 'Truth Vibrations' as a lion

Truth Vibrations and we are being given the opportunity to decode that harmony and expanded awareness into holographic reality. As the 'Carl Sagan' dream said, photons emitted by the Sun have a direct effect on the brain and DNA and they are code carriers that penetrate DNA and stimulate the visual centre of the brain. When those codes change, as are they doing now, everything must change – our whole sense of reality. To the human observer and experiencer, the world is going to change dramatically, and for the better, although it won't seem so for some years yet. It has to be done gradually. If the change is made too quickly it will blow the gaskets – the minds – of those who have been tuned to the Schism's energy. There is a vibrational chasm to bridge, but there is coming a 'time' when the 'firewall' vibrational/digital codes of the Moon Matrix, which are working against the Truth Vibrations and seeking to suppress their effect, are going to be unpicked and then things will really start to move very much faster. As people are released from the Moon Matrix vibrational suppression, they will be able to hold far more powerful vibrations and so the transformation can speed up dramatically. The Truth Vibrations are affecting planets as a whole as they change the nature of their magnetic fields among much else. This is why research that I read as I was finishing this book suggested that the Earth's north magnetic pole in Canada is heading in the direction of Russia at nearly 40 miles per year because of what is said to be magnetic changes in the planet's core. I would say the change is coming from the Sun/black hole interplay which is changing the vibrational 'norm'. Certainly, as I write, sunspot activity has stopped for the longest period that living scientists have known, the solar wind is at its weakest since records began and the Sun's magnetic axis is reported to be 'tilted to an unusual degree'. The Sun is changing and that means that Earth must change.

The Orwellian global State is being imposed now, at the very time of this energetic transformation, because the Reptilians can see into the Metaphysical Universe and down the 'time-line' of the Time Loop to an extent and they knew this was coming. They have been preparing for this moment for thousands of years and this is where the prophecies about the 'future' have come from – the knowledge of where it was all leading to, and when. The fast-emerging police state is not even primarily about imposing more control. The main motivation is defending the control they already have from the consequences of the human awakening that will bring it down. They are trying to keep the lid on the transformation – the vibrational lid – and they are seeking to stop as many people as possible from being affected and influenced by the Truth Vibrations. This is the real reason for microchips, genetically-modified and chemically-infested food and drink, and mind-control in its many forms, most notably the HAARP project in Alaska. The Reptilians and their hybrids have been constructing a blocking frequency around the Earth to supplement the one being projected from the Moon in the Metaphysical Universe. The Moon Matrix was enough to hijack and manipulate human perception while the Schism was in place and unchallenged, but to resist the effect of the Truth Vibrations they needed to add other levels of mind control and suppression, especially HAARP. This is broadcasting low-vibrational thought-patterns to influence the perception of humanity about self and the world in a desperate – and it *is* desperate – attempt to stop the awakening that will set us free. The chemtrails that are being sprayed into the lower atmosphere all over the world contain metals and other ingredients, including nanotechnology, that are designed to create an energetic field most conducive to the broadcasts from HAARP as they are bounced to earth from the ionosphere.

The Large Hadron Collider built by the European Organization for Nuclear Research, or CERN, is all part of this, too. It is the world's largest and highest-energy particle accelerator and consists of a 17-mile tunnel loop beneath the Swiss-French border. It is described as an 'atom smasher' that collides particles and contains more than 1,000 cylindrical magnets arranged end-to-end. In November 2009, CERN announced that it had broken the record for proton acceleration and created beams of particles of 1.18 trillion electron volts and it planned to reach up to seven trillion electron volts. The project involves 10,000 scientists, with the biggest group from the United States. We are told that it was built at a money-no-object cost of billions of dollars for experiments to establish what happened at the time of the alleged (I stress 'alleged') 'Big Bang', and to understand the 'deepest laws of nature'. But this is just the cover story. It is connected with HAARP and other technology centres around the world, including the satellite network, in manipulating and disharmonising this reality to block the effect of the Truth Vibrations. The World Wide Web was invented by particle physicists at CERN and that, too, is a manufactured collective reality. The main reason for the microchip agenda is to access the body-computer and manipulate its ability to receive and transmit within the frequency of the Truth Vibrations, and the same with the electrochemical destabilisation through food and drink additives and electromagnetic and microwave pollution.

Fork in the Road

We are seeing a parting of the ways between those who are synchronising with the Truth Vibrations, and far greater knowledge, awareness and expanded potential, and those who remain in the clutches of the Schism. These groups are connected to two very different realities while living in the same 'physical' world, and it is becoming ever more obvious. Those who choose to go with the transformation will not be without great challenges, but they will experience massively-expanding awareness, insight and creative potential

Figure 311   **Figure 312**

The Truth Vibrations are giving everyone the chance to transform themselves and the world. We just have to open our hearts and minds to their resonance

(Figs 311 and 312). The Schism-people under the control of the Reptilian hive mind will become more and more robot-like, fearful and stressed as the energetic construct they are tuned into ceases to be in the Metaphysical Universe. If it doesn't exist there, it cannot manifest here because this holographic reality is merely decoded information from the Metaphysical Universe. How do you tell the difference between awakening people and Schism people? By their actions, not words. Are they doing what is right, or what they think is right for me, me, me? I have known people who thought they were so 'awake' when they were still encased in Mind and the perceptions of the Schism – what's in it for me?

It is a time of such enormous change. You would think that I would connect this to all the predictions about 2012 and the Mayan Calendar, when one great energetic and human cycle is supposed to end in that year and another to begin. But I don't. The evidence that the serpent-worshipping Mayans in Central America predicted what is claimed is far less certain than is portrayed, and my own feeling is that the hype about 2012 is a major diversion. The technology is available to manipulate the weather and make apparently amazing things happen, which means that it is quite possible to artificially create phenomena that fit with the 2012 story. We might well see some of that, but it will be staged rather than 'natural'. The Truth Vibration transformation is ongoing and getting more powerful all the time and I see the tipping point a few years after 2012, maybe 2016 or in the years that immediately follow. In the meantime, we are going to see the divergence of awakening-people and Schism-people becoming ever more blatant. On the one hand, the Control System will be pushing forward with its tyranny to the point where it seems that nothing can be done, but alongside that ever greater numbers of people will be waking up to see through the illusions and manipulations of this manufactured Moon Matrix reality. Eventually, the tipping point will come and the Control System will fall. When it ceases to exist in the Metaphysical Universe it cannot exist here, and the Truth Vibrations are now picking its locks in the Metaphysical Universe (Fig 313 overleaf). This is how the Reptilian tyranny will end – in the

Illustration by Neil Hague (www.neilhague.com)

Figure 313: *The Truth Vibrations are in the process of breaking the energetic construct of the Control System – breathing new life into this reality*

Metaphysical Universe where it is all projected and manipulated from. We all operate there, too, with what is called the 'inner-self' or subconscious. This is why people talk about 'going within'. It is at these levels of 'multi-dimensional' self that we interact with the Metaphysical Universe and can change the movie that we decode into the 'screen' in our 'heads' – the holographic world. It is like changing the movie in the projection-room rather than trying to change it once it hits the cinema screen. We can't do that, because by then it's a done deal.

You Already Made the Choice

Britain declared war on Germany after the invasion of Poland in 1939, but nothing seemed to be happening for many months until the Battle of France began in 1940. This period of apparent inactivity became known as the 'Phoney War'. We have been having our own 'Phoney War' in the sense that the conspiracy has been in the process of being exposed, but without direct 'engagement' with the system itself. That 'Phoney War' is about to end. We have seen mass protests about military invasions and about injustices of many kinds, but we are now entering a new era of understanding and for the first time we are going to see people protesting in large numbers about the conspiracy itself and not just its individual expressions, like globalisation and wars. It is a time when the irresistible force (the human awakening) is going eye-to-eye with what it *thinks* is the immovable object (the agenda for global control). Immovable it is not, as we shall see in due course, but it is not going to go quietly. We need to be strong and refuse to acquiesce to these control freaks under any circumstances, no matter what the scale of intimidation and provocation. The Illuminati families may have the money, governments, banks, corporations, police and military, but the humanity that they so mercilessly target has the sheer numbers. The tiny few cannot impose their will on the overwhelming majority unless the masses succumb to fear, and to 'divide and rule', and allow their bodies to be accessed with high-technology via microchips and vaccines. There will be so many attempts to divide us between the vaccinated and unvaccinated, employed and unemployed, 'haves and have nots', religion, income bracket, and the fear of engineered terrorism and make-believe bogeymen. If enough people come together and don't fall for this, the conspiracy cannot continue to advance at the speed it has in mind. The more we can slow it down, the less severe it will be by the time the Truth Vibrations have done their work (Figs 314 to 317). We have the power to meet the

The Truth Vibrations are healing the Schism by seeking out the manifestations of the energetic distortion. The Control System cannot survive without the Schism and so it must fall as it is energetically dismantled

Figure 314

Figure 315   **Figure 316**   **Figure 317**

challenge, but will enough make the choice to use it? We are about to find out. I know it can be frightening for people to ponder on what may be to come, but we need to view this from another angle. Why are we 'here' at this moment when all this is about to happen? Why did we choose to be here to experience this? Hard as it may be for many to grasp while in the vibrational confines of five-sense reality, we did *choose* to be here. There is no-one in another dimension with an AK-47 saying, 'Get in that body or I shoot.' It is a choice. As the Oracle said to Neo in the *Matrix*:

> You've already made the choice. Now you have to understand it ... you didn't come here to make the choice, you've already made it. You're here to try to understand *why* you made it.

What makes this most difficult to understand is that the level of 'you' that made the choice is not the level of 'you' that is directly experiencing the choice. This quote from a near-death experiencer gives us a better idea of the state of awareness that makes such decisions:

... everything, from the beginning, my birth, my ancestors, my children, my wife, everything comes together simultaneously. I saw everything about me, and about everyone who was around me. I saw everything they were thinking now, what they thought then, what was happening before, what was happening now. There is no time, there is no sequence of events, no such thing as limitation, of distance, of period, of time, of place. I could be anywhere I wanted to be simultaneously.

It is all a long way from Mary Smith or Chuck Jones looking at the world today and asking: 'Why me?' We are dealing with two totally different perspectives and realities and we need to bring the two together in harmony and mutual understanding.

No matter what happens to us in this little sojourn to this tiny reality called Planet Earth we will always be *All That Is And Ever Can Be*. The 'physical' reality we think we are experiencing is only a point of attention – that's all. This attention, or focus, on five-sense reality gives us the feeling of being 'little me' and separate from everything else. If we stay in that mode through the coming years, life is going to be very difficult. But if we move that attention, that point of observation, from 'I am David Icke' to 'I am *All That Is* having an experience as David Icke', everything changes. First of all, we start to consciously access levels of Consciousness that can inspire and guide us to be in the right place at the right time to both contribute to the human awakening and to avoid the traps and pitfalls set by the Control System. The perception of being eternal Consciousness having an experience also dilutes the emotional impact of the experience, whatever it may be, compared with those who think they *are* the experience. This brings me back to: why are we here? Why did we make that choice? It was certainly not just to work in the store, drive a bus or run an office. These are experiences while we are 'here', but not the main reason that so many *are* 'here'. The real motivation for being 'here' is to both experience, and make a contribution to, the exposure and dismantling of the Control System that has held this reality in servitude for thousands of years. What most people see as a challenge they would rather not face is actually an incredible gift of opportunity. This reality has been hijacked and it can be unhijacked if only we will redefine our self-identity from powerless to All-Powerful, from little me to the All-Knowing 'I'. This is the biggest challenge of all because everything comes from that shift in self-awareness. Once you open to that level of self you no longer need to ask, 'What do I do?' You *know*. You no longer have to summon the courage to do the right thing, you just do it. Making that shift is vital to what has to be done. We are going to need that mentality, attitude and response in abundance – very soon. It's going to be quite a ride. When we awaken to the truth of who we are, the world looks very different and so do the challenges that are put before us, or we put before ourselves. Move your point of observation and everything changes. Try it. Try ceasing to identify who you are with your body, your name and the reflection in the mirror. Try seeing those things as experiences and not who you are. Try observing your life and the world from the perception of the real you – eternal Consciousness, *All That Is, Has Been and Ever Can Be*.

Returning to Yourself

We can all open ourselves to the Truth Vibrations by changing our self-identity from the reflection in the mirror to Infinite Awareness, but it has to be more than just an intellectual exercise. We need to *be* that change of perception at the deepest levels.

I knew intellectually for years that I was not my name, my body or my reflection in the mirror. I knew I was pure Consciousness, the Everywhere and Everything, but that perception was still apart from me, a concept rather than a *being*. From the summer of 2007, a tremendous transformation began as I integrated that sense of self from a concept to a being and looked at the world from the perspective of Infinite Consciousness and not 'David Icke', the human personality. Of course, you move between the two and get pulled into the emotional reactions and responses of body-mind reality, but the more you hold that new point of self-awareness, the less the body-mind kicks in. What I felt at that time was a powerful energetic shift 'within me' (Metaphysical Universe) that manifested in many ways in holographic reality. I let go of tremendous amounts of pent-up emotional hurt and frustration attached to 'David Icke' that had been generated from the years of mass ridicule and other emotional stresses and pressures. It is amazing how we store these emotional memories while thinking we've let them go. As this cleansing and clearing was happening within me in the Metaphysical Universe, so it manifested in the decoded world as an almost obsessive desire to throw out everything I didn't need and to clean everything over and over. This lasted a few weeks and I could see that the inner was being projected as the 'outer'. Letting go of these emotional and mental blocks and layers is vital to opening your mind to higher Consciousness and the Truth Vibrations. This is why society is structured and manipulated to produce painful and distressing emotional reactions and energy. I know that people have been 'synchronistically' sent in on me by the manipulation of the Metaphysical Universe to cause me great emotional stress and close me down. But these experiences can also be opportunities to overcome the control that emotion has over us. Every challenge is also an opportunity and who says that, in the bigger picture of everything, it wasn't all meant to be anyway?

The most important first step to transformation of self is to make the decision (focus the intent) that this is what we want to do. If we do that and we *mean* it – 'I want to open to my true self', 'I choose freedom' – the intent starts to attract the experiences we need to achieve that intent through the process I call vibrational magnetism. These experiences can often be those we would rather not be attracting and it is vital to stay with it should your life start to 'fall apart'. Everything is energy, be it people, locations, jobs, relationships, whatever. The decided intent changes the vibrational state of our energy-fields (in the Metaphysical Universe) and it is these fields that are attracting and creating our 'life'. When they change through changing attitudes and intent they no longer attract, and synchronise with, what they did before. You may change jobs, end a relationship, start a new one, move location, and the old life starts to unravel to be replaced by the new, attracted by the new vibrational state of you. It is during this transition that we can talk about our life 'falling apart' and it can be painful, bewildering and frightening if you don't know what is going on. My goodness, look at mine after I met the first psychic and went to Peru. The old energy-state is being replaced by another, and one has to go for the other to come in. If we see this as the old life breaking down so the new can manifest it is much easier to cope with such transitions. Going with our intuition instead of our five-sense mind is also essential to break the bonds of 'little me' reality. Intuitive knowing is our connection, or one of them, to 'out there' and it seeks to guide us from a much higher and knowledgeable perspective than body-mind. As I've said, it can see the journey from source to sea while body-mind sees only the next bend in the river. Something you are being intuitively urged to do may seem crazy, ridiculous or self-destructive to the Mind, but intuitive knowing has read the whole book, not just a few pages, and it can see why it is necessary in the sequence of experience. Once again, look what happened to me in 1990 ... I seemed to be self-destructing, but I was actually setting myself free. If you are here to transform and 'clean out' low vibrational and manipulating energy-fields you may have to go into some very low and dark situations to synchronise with the energy you are transforming. If you don't connect with it you cannot affect it. Intuition will know this while Mind, and the Mind of others, may condemn what you do. But they don't know your journey, only you do at a deeper level. My journey, for example, is very clearly a case of experience-learn-communicate. Sometimes, as with me quite often, you need to experience what you would rather not so you can then learn new understandings and communicate that learning.

Intuition doesn't see life in anything like the way of body-mind, and so what is crazy or extreme to Mind can be necessary for events to happen and experiences to be created. Intuition is also key to choosing your intent, and to discerning between 'genuine' and 'manipulated' synchronicity. It may be synchronistic, but is this your desired journey or a trap set up in the Metaphysical Universe? Intent is neither good nor bad, it is simply an energy that says 'this is what I want' or 'this is what I intend to do'. The challenge is synchronising your intent with your pre-planned journey so that both energies – our intent and the flow of your pre-planned journey – move as one. This combination can make things happen very smoothly in your life, unless the experience of the unsmooth is part of your necessary experience. So many people spend their lives with their intent and their 'journey' at war with each other. They decide they want to do something or be something, when the flow of intuitive energy wants to take them somewhere else to do something else. They symbolically keep banging on doors that are not going to open, getting more and more frustrated, when there is another door swinging open for them if only they would drop the rigid, body-mind 'I want' and listen to their intuition and the language of life. Does your life flow? If not, why not? Why aren't you doing what you want to do? Is what you want to do what you have *come* to do?

All these things are part of the overall process of getting out of Mind and into higher levels of awareness that will set us free from the manipulated illusion and guide us to our most effective contribution to personal and collective freedom. Oh, yes, and we need to take responsibility for what happens to us, just as others will take their own consequences for what they do to us – nice and not so nice. Not everything is 'meant to be'. We make choices and take consequences, again nice and not so nice. We attract into our experience what attaches to our energy-fields, therefore it is no good blaming others for what happens to us. What that says is: 'I don't have power over my life – he does, she does, circumstances do.' We attract what we experience and so we are responsible. In accepting that responsibility we are taking our power back and acknowledging that we have the potential to change what we don't like by changing ourselves. The vibrational influences on our energy-fields are endless. There are astrological influences, personal attitude influences and encoded information specifically there to attract another person, location or experience into our lives. It depends on what we are here to do and experience. The most important point, though, is that there is no such thing as good luck or bad luck, only what we attract and what we don't attract. Sometimes people have to lose everything so they can be free of the illusions of form and things and dependency upon them. As the song goes, 'Freedom's just another word for nothing left to lose'. Often it is in your darkest moments that you break through into something greater. There is a proverb that says: 'Just when the caterpillar thought life was over, it became a butterfly.' It is so important that we all take responsibility during what is to come and remember that the darkest hour can indeed be just before dawn. We also need to hold fast to the perception of self as Infinite Awareness, and not Arthur Biggs and Ethel Cohen.

'Alien' Revelations

Another major aspect of these monumental times will be confirmation that (shakes head in amazement) we are not alone. There are many non-human races and groups operating in and around the Earth and we are going to be interacting with some of them eventually. There are those, like the Reptilians, that have a malevolent agenda, and others that are benevolent and have come to help with the transformation. Still others are neutral to us. Some even look like we do and could walk among us without being spotted. As I said earlier, Bulgarian government scientists announced in 2009 that 'aliens already exist on Earth' and that they were in contact with them. Lachezar Filipov, deputy director of the Space Research Institute of the Bulgarian Academy of Sciences, told the Bulgarian media: 'Aliens are currently all around us, and are watching us all the time.' This is what the ancients said, of course. They called them 'the Watchers'. How far we have come from the concerted cover-ups of past decades when governments, scientists and the military dismissed or ignored 'UFO' reports and claims that extraterrestrial life existed, never mind that it was visiting this planet. For a while now there has clearly been a more relaxed approach from officialdom to former insiders revealing their knowledge of extraterrestrial activity. Even the Pope's Jesuit chief astronomer, Father Gabriel Funes, wrote in 2008 in the Vatican newspaper that 'intelligent beings created by God could exist in outer space'. He said that life on Mars cannot be ruled out, either. The Vatican Observatory and the Pontifical Academy of Sciences organised a week-long gathering of scientists to examine the possibility of extraterrestrial life and its all a long way from the days when Giordano Bruno, an Italian monk well ahead of his time, was put to death by the Inquisition in 1600 for claiming that other worlds exist, among much else that has proved to be true.

Over the 20 years that I have been on my journey of research all over the world, I have experienced the very different 'before and after' period in the extraterrestrial field. I mean the 'before and after' a decision was demonstrably made to allow more information about non-human activity to be released bit-by-little-bit to the public. It is highly likely that this is preparing the ground for official disclosure of some kind. How often we have seen in human history the moments when perception awakened to something so obvious that had previously been dismissed and ridiculed. Accepting that the Earth was not flat is a good example. It seems obvious now that Earth had to be a sphere, but suppression and ignorance, not least about the law of gravity, made a flat Earth seem the only explanation for centuries. When the penny dropped, the prevailing 'wisdom' that had dominated human perception about the planet was seen to be plain silly and ridiculous. Humanity is in the process of experiencing another of those 'moments' with regard to extraterrestrial and interdimensional life. When the proof is revealed of the extraterrestrial presence, those who have dismissed the very idea will see how silly and ridiculous it was to believe that life only exists on this one little planet in this one little solar system in this one little frequency range called visible light. Human perception of life and reality is about to go through an incredible transformation. For many, it has already begun. If and when the authorities do 'go public', and the sea change in official attitudes certainly seems to be heading that way, don't hold your breath for the truth of what is really going on. Any ET 'disclosure' will be to suit the control-agenda, not human freedom and enlightenment.

There are a number of possible scenarios and one is known as Project Blue Beam. This was revealed in the 1990s by Canadian journalist, Serge Monast, who died of a heart-attack in 1996 during his continuing investigations. Another journalist working on the Blue Beam story also died of a heart-attack. Reports say that Monast's children were taken by the authorities on the grounds that they were abused by being home-schooled. Monast was arrested and spent the night in jail. The following day, back at home, he had a fatal heart-attack at the age of 46. Monast said in 1994 that his research revealed how Project Blue Beam, a NASA operation, was a multi-faceted plan to support the implementation of the global state or 'New World Order' and included a possible fake 'alien visitation' using holographic technology projected from satellites and a staged 'coming together' of world religious deities into 'one truth' and one religion. Monast said:

> The Blue Beam Project will pretend to be the universal fulfillment of the prophecies of old, as major an event as that which occurred 2,000 years ago. In principle, it will make use of the skies as a movie screen (on the sodium layer at about 60 miles) as space-based laser-generating satellites project simultaneous images to the four corners of the planet in every language and dialect according to the region. It deals with the religious aspect of the new world order and is deception and seduction on a massive scale.

> Computers will coordinate the satellites and software already in place will run the sky show. Holographic images are based on nearly identical signals combining to produce an image or hologram with deep perspective which is equally applicable to acoustic ELF, VLF and LF waves and optical phenomena. Specifically, the show will consist of multiple holographic images to different parts of the world, each receiving a different image according to the specific national, regional religion. Not a single area will be excluded. With computer animation and sounds appearing to emanate from the very depths of space, astonished ardent followers of the various creeds will witness their own returned messiahs in convincing lifelike reality.

Monast said that holographic images of religious heroes like Jesus, Mohammed, Buddha and Krishna would be projected onto the sky and then they would be merged to form the 'one true God' of the planned one-world religion. I am not saying that Serge Monast was right in all that he claimed, but a staged 'alien invasion' is something to keep in mind as a Problem-Reaction-Solution to a global government and military. It is also possible to put on a 'flying saucer' show without holographic technology by using the anti-gravity 'flying saucers' that the secret military bases have had for decades. Not all 'UFOs' are flown by 'aliens'. Another approach would be to justify the same global centralisation of power to represent the planet in the interaction and 'negotiations' with any 'disclosed' extraterrestrial group. There are many ways this could go – except to the truth. There are numerous types of non-humans that could be officially 'disclosed', but you can bet that the ones with the scales won't be getting a mention.

HAARP technology has been linked by researchers to a blue spiral of light that appeared in the sky over northern Norway in December 2009 on the eve of Barack Obama's Nobel Prize acceptance speech in that country. The light stopped in mid-air and began to move in circles to become a giant spiral (Fig 318). A blue-green light then shot out from its centre and lasted for ten to twelve minutes before

Figure 318: *The Norway light spiral close to a HAARP facility*

disappearing. It was described by onlookers as like 'a shooting star that spun around and around' and you can see film of it on YouTube. It was claimed to be a failed Russian missile test, but that made no sense at all of what happened. Significantly, close to where the light spiral appeared is the European Incoherent Scatter Scientific Association (EISCAT) facility, which is described as a 'HAARP antenna farm'. This was no coincidence and the technology is certainly available to do what Serge Monast said was planned. This is a time to be very light of foot and mind, because so much is about to happen in the next

few years as the Truth Vibrations open the curtain and reveal all that has been hidden from us (Fig 319). Amazing things. Reality-transforming things. Some will be manipulated, some will be real. Telling the difference is going to be the challenge and that's where a sharp intuition is needed. The head is so much easier to scam. The sudden change in official attitudes to the 'ET' question and the way the subject is appearing more in the mainstream media shows that something is coming. When, where and how is what we don't yet know for sure. Bulgarian scientist Lachezar Filipov said 'the human race is certainly going to have direct contact with the aliens in the next 10 to 15 years'. I think it will be sooner than that.

What Can We Do?

I saw a documentary called *Pray the Devil Back to Hell*. It told the story of the women of Liberia in West Africa and how they ended a bloody and horrific war by peaceful protest and non-

Figure 319: *The Truth Vibrations are revealing all that has been hidden behind the curtain, or veil, of deceit*

cooperation. It is a symbol of what we can, and must, do locally and globally to stop the tail wagging the dog, the few controlling the many. If these women could face and overcome what appeared to be their hopeless plight then we can deal with the global conspiracy. For goodness sake, there are more than seven billion of us! Charles Taylor, the then leader of Liberia, was an archetypal African despot, crazed by power and, as usual, constantly quoting 'God' to justify his ungodliness. No surprise then that tyrant Taylor was reported to have had extensive business dealings with American television 'evangelist' Pat Robertson, who seems to have an addiction to African dictators. The Liberian government became more and more tyrannical as the decades passed after 'independence', and Taylor was one of a long line of corrupt demagogues to lead the people deeper and deeper into relentless poverty while amassing vast fortunes for themselves. Charles Taylor, a Baptist lay-preacher educated in America, had been removed from the country by another agent of depravity called Samuel K Doe, who took power in a bloody coup. But Taylor returned in 1989 and gathered support to launch a counter-coup. This began a terrible civil war between rival ethnic factions, and children as young as eight were forced to take up arms and fight. Doe was tortured to death, and rape and murder engulfed the country. The violence continued, with rare respites for 'peace talks', before resuming. By 1997, 200,000 people were dead, close to a million were forced from their homes and another 700,000 had fled across the borders to neighbouring countries. The population was in terror from the child soldiers who had been turned into monsters, but they were victims, too. A 13-year-old 'soldier' later said:

> They gave me pills that made me crazy. When the craziness got in my head, I beat people on their heads and hurt them until they bled. When the craziness got out of my head I felt guilty. If I remembered the person I went to them and apologized. If they did not accept my apology, I felt bad.

Taylor supposedly 'won' an election in 1997, but within two years a new civil war erupted as rural 'warlords' from the north launched a violent challenge to Taylor under the name 'Liberians United for Reconciliation and Democracy' (LURD). As always, the name was a fallacy and they clearly got one letter wrong, anyway. The warlords wanted a cut of Taylor's action and, when he refused, the men and child soldiers of 'LURD', and another faction called 'MODEL', the Movement for Democracy in Liberia, were ordered to rape, kill and pillage wherever they went. Daughters were raped in front of their parents; husbands had their heads cut off in front of their wives and children. By now, the killers were so desensitised that concepts like 'compassion', 'empathy', even 'limits', had no meaning for these crazies. But now enter Leymah Gbowee. She was just 17 and fresh out of high school when the war came to the capital, Monrovia, and she was changed 'from a child into an adult in a matter of hours'. On one occasion she and her mother were advised to flee their church where 2,000 displaced people were being sheltered, and the following night more than 600 of them were slaughtered. 'We went just two blocks away, and we could hear people screaming, crying, begging for help – an all-night massacre,' she recalls. Later, with a son aged three and a daughter aged two, she had to run from their home to escape the fighting, passing checkpoints which the imbecile macho men sometimes decorated with 'a fresh young head'. As she recounts: 'The anger, the pain, the trauma, was not just for one year or one month. I needed to do something to make a difference.' And she did. Gbowee had a dream that she had to gather women together and pray for peace. She and another woman, Comfort Freeman, got together dozens of women in 2002 in a determined attempt to stop the war. They called their movement 'Women in Peacebuilding Network', or WIPNET. They began to protest peacefully where the despot Charles Taylor and his motorcade had to pass and they organised non-violent sit-ins, marches, peace vigils and blockades. One of their statements said:

> In the past we were silent, but after being killed, raped, dehumanised, and infected with diseases, and watching our children and families destroyed, war has taught us that the future lies in saying NO to violence and YES to peace! We will not relent until peace prevails.

They were protesting not only the atrocities of Taylor, but all the factions that made the war possible. Every day they were out there in public view, no matter what the weather or circumstances. 'No' was not an answer they were prepared to accept (Fig 320). Leymah Gbowee said at the time:

> By virtue of where we sit, the people of Liberia have hope ... Some say we are an embarrassment to the government, but sun and rain are better than the bullets of war. Our vision is for the unity of families and the elimination of hunger and disease.

Taylor dismissed them at first, but this initial example by a relative few inspired others to join them. They gathered together 3,000 women and pressed Taylor and the rebel factions to end the violence. Taylor resisted, but in the end the pressure forced him to relent and he agreed to negotiate at peace talks in Ghana. Leymah Gbowee later had the opportunity to address Charles Taylor from the podium at a public event. She said:

> We ask the honorable pro tem of the senate ... to kindly present this statement to his excellency Dr Charles Taylor with this message: that the women of Liberia, including the IDPs [internally displaced persons] ... are tired of war. We are tired of running. We are tired of begging for bulgur wheat. We are tired of our children being raped. We are now taking this stand to secure the future of our children because we believe, as custodians of society, tomorrow our children will ask us, 'Mama, what was your role during the crisis?' Kindly convey this to the president of Liberia. Thank you.

All those who say that nothing can be done about what is happening in the world today need to look at what these women achieved. Here was a small, unarmed and apparently powerless

Figure 320: *The women of Liberia would not take no for an answer. Neither must we*

group faced with the extraordinary challenge of stopping a war between rival factions who had become so dehumanised by year after year of rape and mass murder that they were engaging daily in the most unspeakable atrocities. But here was first one or two women, then a few more who joined with them initially, inspiring a whole national movement of non-violent, non-cooperation which forced these moronic men to the peace table by the sheer power of their refusal to accept nothing less than that. These are the three elements which together, as always, proved an unstoppable combination and made the apparent 'miracle' possible:

1) They said, 'Enough!' – and meant it.
2) They were not going to take 'no' for an answer, no matter how long it took or what sacrifices that entailed.
3) They crucially brought women together of different faiths and tribal loyalties behind the common goal of peace and freedom for all.

Coming Together

Leymah Gbowee was president of the women's organisation at St Peter's Lutheran Church in Monrovia, and Comfort Freeman was president of the National Lutheran Church Women in Liberia; but they didn't let their religious faith get in the way of unity. The movement was joined by Muslim women who were welcomed as much as the Christians were. Thanks to this, they removed any chance the authorities had to divide and rule them along ethnic and religious lines and it was this unity of purpose that brought the madmen to the table. But that was only the start. Taylor and the leaders of the rebel factions wanted to carve up the country for themselves and get the most profitable jobs in any new government. The rebel leaders from Liberia's rural areas were also enjoying five-star luxury during the talks in Ghana and they wanted to stay there as long as possible while the violence and mutilation continued back in Liberia. After seven weeks there was still no ceasefire and so the women said 'Enough!' again. Two hundred of them blocked the exits from the meeting room, locked arms, and told the 'powerful' men that they would be locked inside until an agreement had been made. Military generals were also locked in and they called for 'security' forces to arrest Gbowee for 'obstructing justice', a shocking statement in the circumstances. That very morning, she had heard how a missile had exploded in the American embassy compound in Monrovia. One moment two boys went out to brush their teeth and the next all that was left was their slippers. 'That day we had to do something dramatic,' Gbowee said. So when the 'security' came to arrest her she told them: 'Okay, I'm going to strip naked.' In West Africa it is believed to be a powerful curse to see a woman strip naked in public. As she said of the 'powerful' men inside: 'They would have given us the world rather than see us stripping naked.'

One warlord tried to push and kick the women out of the way, but the moderator of the peace talks, told him: 'Go back in there and sit down. If you were a real man, you wouldn't be killing your people. But because you are not a real man, that's why they will treat you like boys.' Two weeks later the terms of the peace treaty were announced. The 'all-powerful' Charles Taylor was forced into exile and is now held in the United Nations Detention Unit while he stands trial for war crimes. His son, a US citizen, was jailed for 97 years by a federal court for murder and torture when he was head of

Liberia's 'anti-terrorist' services. If only they treated American government terrorists the same way. American-educated Ellen Johnson Sirleaf became Africa's first elected female head of state in 2006 when she was inaugurated as President of Liberia and pledged a 'fundamental break' with the violence of the past. The current situation in Liberia is far from perfect to say the least and there is still widespread poverty and deprivation, but the women who stood up to the gun-toting lunatics on all 'sides' showed what can be done if you will not yield your aims and values to any scale of intimidation. *Pray the Devil Back to Hell* appears to be a documentary about women, but what it highlights has global significance. Women did it in this case, but men have done it in other situations – witness the leadership of Martin Luther King and so many others. Once again, it is not the sex of your body, any more than it is the colour of your skin. It is the strength of your character. It is to stand for love, justice, fairness and freedom and accept nothing less for ourselves and others no matter what the challenges we face. I hear people saying all the time that there is nothing they can do when they are merely providing themselves with an excuse to do nothing. But one day they will be called to account by their children and grandchildren if they continue with such outrageous self-deception. As Leymah Gbowee rightly said, the children would ask: 'Mama, what was your role during the crisis?' What will our answer be?

No Need to Fight, No Need to Riot

A crucial aspect of the stand by the Liberian women was that they stayed peaceful and non-violent throughout. The system wants you to riot in response to its injustices and so many are duped into this. They want an excuse to bring in a fully-fledged police state all over the world and those who riot in their desperation (instigated invariably by agent provocateurs) are just the excuse they are looking for. The military organisation is already in place to respond. The US Army War College produced a document called 'Known Unknowns: Unconventional Strategic Shocks in Defense Strategy Development'. It said the military must be prepared for a 'violent, strategic dislocation inside the United States', in the light of 'unforeseen economic collapse'. Unforeseen?? You must be joking. The document talks of 'purposeful domestic resistance', 'pervasive public health emergencies' or 'loss of functioning political and legal order'. It goes on:

> Widespread civil violence ... would force the defense establishment to reorient priorities in extremis to defend basic domestic order and human security. An American government and defense establishment lulled into complacency by a long-secure domestic order would be forced to rapidly divest some or most external security commitments in order to address rapidly expanding human insecurity at home. Under the most extreme circumstances, this might include use of military force against hostile groups inside the United States.

Already waiting in the wings are the agent provocateurs and the useful idiots primed to start the riots and civil unrest that the idiots believe to be challenging the existing order. But the existing order was created by the same network of Illuminati families that are seeking to create the 'new order'. To achieve this, as always, they need our cooperation and let no-one be in any doubt that those who choose to riot and loot in response to what is happening, and encourage others to riot and loot, are walking straight into the trap that has been laid for them. The government and military agent provocateurs will know that; the useful idiots will not, but it is time they did. The riots and looting they want to see – the chaos – will be met with the installation of a police state with curfews, jail without trial, the military on the streets, and the activation of the concentration camps for 'dissidents' that I and many others have long been warning about. The only way to stop all this is not to react as they want us to, with violence and hostility to both the State and each other. How many violent revolutions have led to just another tyrannical regime to replace the one that fell? It has to be so because what is destroyed by violence will be replaced by the same energy. Eternal Consciousness in awareness of itself doesn't riot; it is not violent and it doesn't loot. John Lennon put it perfectly when he sang:

> You say you want a revolution
> Well, you know
> We all want to change the world
> You tell me that it's evolution
> Well, you know
> We all want to change the world
> But when you talk about destruction
> Don't you know that you can count me out …
>
> … You say you got a real solution
> Well, you know
> We'd all love to see the plan
> You ask me for a contribution
> Well, you know
> We're doing what we can
> But when you want money
> for people with minds that hate
> All I can tell is brother you have to wait.

Martin Luther King also put it brilliantly when he said of rioting:

> The limitation of riots, moral questions aside, is that they cannot win and their participants know it. Hence, rioting is not revolutionary but reactionary because it invites defeat. It involves an emotional catharsis, but it must be followed by a sense of futility.

Those are the words of a revolutionary who succeeded through peaceful non-cooperation. Yes, they killed him in the end, but what he created through non-violence and determination went forth to end segregation. Physical life does not matter when compared with what is right, for we are all eternal Consciousness having an illusory experience, and the greatest illusion is death. I would much rather die 'early' doing what I know to be right than to eke out a few more illusory years as a slave to tyrants. But there is no need even for that to bring an end to this nonsense. There are billions of people being enslaved and a comparative handful doing the enslaving. Er, I think I see a way out of this. We need to come together in mutual support, love, kindness and empathy. We need to put aside the manufactured irrelevances that divide us – religion, politics, race, culture, and income bracket. This is not to say people have to reject their beliefs; just don't let them be weapons of division. We are all in this together and we need to meet the challenge together, not steal from each other, loot or riot, or look the other way because something happening to someone else is 'not my problem'. They are not seeking to enslave Muslims, Jews, black people, or white, middle-class Americans, and so on. They are seeking to do it to *all* of us and they are picking off different groups one by one, just like the Nazis did in Germany. Remember these famous words by a German pastor because they are so applicable now:

First they came for the Jews, and I was not a Jew so I did nothing.
Then they came for the communists, and I was not a communist so I did nothing.
Then they came for the trade unionists, and I was not a trade unionist so I did nothing.
Then they came for me, and there was no-one left to speak out for me.

Non-Comply-Dance

Let us unite behind that which affects everyone – the loss of our most basic freedoms. And if this is being done now, what kind of world are our children and grandchildren going to live in? Can you live with that thought while doing nothing or rioting as the authorities want? I can't. We need to start getting organised in communities and groups to support each other and to stop *cooperating* with the Control System, not to fight it. The system can only exist with our cooperation and acquiescence. We are holding it all together. They have their men and women of violence, called the military and 'Swat' teams, to deal with violent resistance. Their worst nightmare is our non-cooperation – the refusal to pay taxes; refusal to leave homes when banks foreclose on them because of an economic collapse caused by the same banks; refusal to 'comply' with our own enslavement in any form. The system couldn't cope if this was done on a massive scale. And that's the point: to do this we need to do it en masse and those not immediately affected need to support those who are. Instead of compliance, we need non-compliance, the non-comply-*dance* of people who beat to a different drum and will not comply with what is unfair, unjust, or targets their freedom and the freedom of others. This approach does not refuse to comply in a spirit of hostility, rage or violence, but with love, joy and laughter – and an unshakable determination not to cooperate with our own enslavement. We need a mass refusal to join the military, especially if they try to introduce the Draft; a refusal to do the compulsory 'community service' for young people that Obama's controllers want to introduce (as does the UK government and others); and a refusal to join, or accept the legitimacy of, Obama's planned civilian security force, which is nothing more than a scam to get the people to police the people on behalf of the elite. We need to start getting together local currency and barter schemes that can operate outside the system. Mass protests are an option, so long as they are peaceful, but they need to be part of the campaign of non-violent, non-cooperation, not the focus of it. How many mass protests have there been over the years around the world and yet everything just goes on as before, be it war or globalisation. We need to stop posturing with banners and then heading for the bar to feel good about ourselves and start doing what will actually make a difference. The protests need to be targeted at non-cooperation, refusing to accept laws that ban assembly by massive numbers turning up to defy them; surrounding the homes of neighbours when the bank bailiffs come to put them on the street; and filling the locations of government and finance with masses of people so that the system cannot function. And all of this needs to be good humoured and strictly peaceful. The 'Shministim' movement in Israel is a great example of non-cooperation. They are Israeli high-school students (Shministim means 'twelfth-graders' in Hebrew) who have been jailed for refusing to serve in the army that occupies the Palestinian Territories and kills the innocent in Gaza and elsewhere. They are incredible young people who put to shame those around the world who use the question 'But what can I do?' as an excuse to do nothing. One of them, Omer Goldman writes:

> I first went to prison on September 23 and served 35 days. I am lucky, after two times in jail, I got a medical discharge, but I'm the only one. By the time you read this, many of my friends will be in prison too: in for three weeks, out for one, and then back in, over and over, until they are 21. The reason? We refuse to do military service for the Israeli army because of the occupation.
>
> I grew up with the army. My father was deputy head of Mossad and I saw my sister, who is eight years older than me, do her military service. As a young girl, I wanted to be a soldier. The military was such a part of my life that I never even questioned it.
>
> Earlier this year, I went to a peace demonstration in Palestine. I had always been told that the Israeli army was there to defend me, but during that demonstration Israeli soldiers opened fire on me and my friends with rubber bullets and tear-gas grenades. I was shocked and scared. I saw the truth. I saw the reality. I saw for the first time that the most dangerous thing in Palestine is the Israeli soldiers, the very people who are supposed to be on my side.

What she experienced made her conscious, at least in that area of her life. If she had stayed in her Mind she would have looked at the consequences for herself of making a stand, especially as she was surrounded by the military in her life. Consciousness will not be denied once it is accessed. It must do what it knows to be right, no matter what. There is another incredible young Jewish-American who has decided that her allegiance must be with what is right and not with some genetic/religious/cultural Mind program. Her name is Anna Baltzer and she went to the West Bank to see for herself the plight of the Palestinians under Israeli occupation. What she saw changed her life, made her conscious with regard to what was happening. And, once again, when you connect with Consciousness, either totally or in relation to a particular situation, you can't walk away. What we are looking at with these examples is the answer to the injustice and suffering of this 'world'. Stop cooperating with those that instigate that injustice and suffering and then it can't happen because the 'elite' may manipulate the situation, but it is we, the people, who choose to play it out on their behalf. We have no choice? *Bullshit*. We never have 'no choice'. There are choices we'd like to make and there are choices we would like to avoid, but there is never 'no choice'. At the moment, those who have enough commitment to decency and justice to make a stand are still in the minority, but the potential of this has no limit. Without the cannon fodder in uniform there can be no war. It is the same with the system itself that encompasses government, banking, business, the media, and so on. All these institutions of control and manipulation require our cooperation to function and without that their house of cards would collapse. We are cooperating with those who wish to enslave us and if we didn't they would be powerless. How bad must it get before the waters break and the Mind opens to this obvious fact? Those young Israelis are an example of what we can do, and if enough follow that example the edifice of centralised power must collapse.

Animated Uniforms

I would also say this to those in uniform ... You may think you have power, but you are just pawns in the game like anyone else. You don't have the power; your *uniform* does, because that is an extension of the State. Those inside are just there to animate the uniform and do the bidding of those it represents. When you are useful to the cabal they'll praise you and when you are surplus to their requirements as part of the bigger agenda they'll show you the door. The same goes for those in government administration. You have children and grandchildren, too, who will have to live in the world you are administering and policing into existence by 'following orders' and believing the manipulative nonsense fed to you by governments and cabal 'training' fronts like Common Purpose. Wake up from the trance and stop building a police state for your own children and grandchildren and everyone else. Think about the consequences for those you love of what you are doing – and *stop doing* it. More than anything, we all need to free our Mind and become Conscious. From that, everything else will come, including the intuition, inspiration and knowing that will guide us on how most effectively to deal with what we face. If there are many things you would like to do in a room, but the room is dark and you can't see, what is the essential first step to anything else happening? You have to turn on the light and then all the rest becomes possible. Without that you are thrashing around in the dark and falling over the furniture. John Lennon also made this point in *Revolution*. We need to free our Mind and become Conscious:

> You say you'll change the constitution
> Well, you know
> We all want to change your head
> You tell me it's the institution
> Well, you know
> You better free your mind instead.

We are now fast heading for the eye of the storm that has been planned for so long to enslave the global population in a centralised dictatorship. But we don't have to accept it or acquiesce to it, meekly looking on as the walls of control close in by the day. That, however, is what is happening and it *has to stop*. For everyone's sake, it *has to stop*. We can come together, we *must* come together. Whether Reptilian insanity prevails is not in their hands, but in ours. It is we who have the power if only we have unity of purpose. We are One Consciousness deluded into thinking we are 'little me'. When we realise that we are all One – and act upon that with courage, love, kindness, peace and empathy for all who need support – the walls of oppression must fall. But sitting on your arse hoping it will all go away is no longer an option. It never was. People look at pyramids, like the pyramid

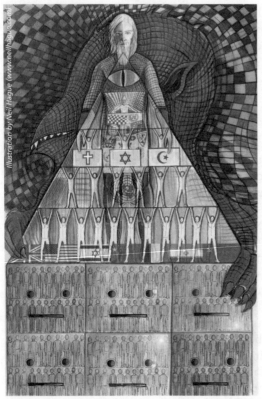

Figure 321: *The power and strength in a pyramid is at the bottom, not the top*

structures that control human society, and they instinctively look to the top for the power. But look again at the image in Figure 321. The top is only up there because the rest of the pyramid is holding it up there. Without the base there could be no capstone. We have been manipulated to see power where it isn't and thus powerlessness where it isn't. The two, in terms of the pyramid and global society, are the wrong way round in our perception of 'power'. This happens because the human race is frozen into non-action by ignorance and fear. The ignorant can't see their plight and most of those who can have cancelled the laxative delivery. It is this combination that allows the very few to control and enslave the very many. After 20 years of constant effort we are getting somewhere big time in diluting the ignorance and this is now being underpinned by daily experience as the mask of the conspiracy begins to fall. But it is no good knowing what you face if you are then going to turn around and run, or freeze.

Where Are the Heroes When You Need Them?

When I am out walking, I often listen to the music of Bonnie Tyler. God, could she bash out a song and there was one she sang called *Holding Out for a Hero*. The title line goes: 'I need a hero, I'm holding out for a hero 'til the end of the night.' It's a great song, but every time I hear it I am reminded of the greatest threat to human freedom: the population 'holding out for a hero'. When you do that, the 'end of night' comes with a knock at the door and some uniformed thug asking for your papers. Not a hero in sight. This is the dictionary definition of a hero:

1. In mythology and legend, a man, often of divine ancestry, who is endowed with great courage and strength, celebrated for his bold exploits, and favoured by the gods.
2. A person noted for feats of courage or nobility of purpose, especially one who has risked or sacrificed his or her life.

Well, that's what the dictionary says, but I would offer another definition of a 'hero'. It's *you*. Yes, little, what can I do, *YOU*. It is *all* of us, potentially. We all have divine ancestry, in that we are all One; we are all endowed with great strength and courage waiting to be activated; and we can all dedicate ourselves to a 'nobility of purpose'. It's just a choice.

Why does a 'hero' always have to be someone else? The famous 'Tank Man' incident filmed for the world to see in China in 1989 showed symbolically, and for a few minutes *literally*, what can be done when we have the courage to say, '*No*. Enough!' (Fig 322). But he was one man and there will always be the rare man or woman who will stand up for what they believe in, no matter what the consequences, because Consciousness doesn't bow to consequences. They are not part of its perception process. Doing what is *right* is all that matters. Whenever you let consequences enter the equation in these circumstances then freedom is always, but always, the loser. 'I would do what is right ... er, but ...' It's the 'but' that hands the power to those who are enslaving us. NO MORE BLOODY 'BUTS' – *PLEASE*. NO MORE BLOODY EXCUSES. Tank Man was one individual who made a mighty statement by his actions, but where was everyone else? What would the tanks have done if millions were standing before them and climbing all over them? This is why we need heroes, *plural*, and not just a hero (Figs 323 and 324).

The Chinese population is nearly 1.5 billion and it is controlled by a relative handful because of fear, divide and rule by giving the economic winners a stake in society as it is, and, in short, by a lack of unity among the 1.5 billion. If those people refused to cooperate with the system, if they downed tools and surrounded the government and military buildings in their millions, and in many other ways stopped the elite few from functioning, let alone controlling, it would be like a tsunami to a sandcastle. But they don't and instead they are 'holding out for a hero 'til the end of the night'. Yes, the night and nightmare that never ends because instead of expressing

Figure 322: *We need the spirit of 'Tank Man' – en masse*

Illustration by Neil Hague (www.neilhague.com)

Figure 323: *When we come together in unity and refuse to bow to fear and intimidation humanity will cast off the chains of suppression and control*

Illustration by David Dees (deesillustration.com)

Figure 324: *Open to Consciousness and we will break the bonds that hold us in servitude*

their right to freedom they hold on hoping someone else will do it for them. Well, Tank Man did, and it was fantastic, but the control goes on. We need numbers, big numbers, to summon the hero within and be the people they are currently waiting for. And it's not, in fact, about being a 'hero' at all. Our highest, Infinite state is not to be in fear and in the absence fear there is no need for the courage to overcome it. Human society does not produce 'heroes' on the scale that it could and should because the global population has been locked by fear into letting consequences get in the way. This world will come right when the people put *what* is right above all else, including the consequences they fear for doing so.

We will have freedom, peace and justice when 'What's in it for me, me, me?' becomes 'What is right?' Is it right that a few malevolent and deeply sick and disturbed people are imposing their will upon the world? No. So is it right to sit around and allow them to do it? No. Is it right to know at least the themes of what is happening and still do nothing? No. So what is the 'right' thing to do? That's the question we all need to ask ourselves and the question requires an answer, not prevarication or cognitive dissonance to justify our actions or non-actions. We don't have time for pussy-footing around here. The gun is cocked and the agenda for global fascism is moving so fast. The world central bank is being orchestrated as I write, justified by the manufactured problem of the banking collapse. The world army, the global occupation force, is moving into place and freedoms are disappearing by the day. It is clear from the increasing concern among many former sceptics that the Orwellian State is now infiltrating the very depths of everyday society. How long do we, therefore, hold out 'for a hero 'til the end of the night'? 'Til another government announcement advances the control even further? 'Til there's an 'r' in the month? 'Til it's all in place? *When*??

How about NOW?

I have come such a long way on so many levels since I knocked on the door of the psychic lady in 1990. It has been an incredible journey of redefining the world and redefining self. The personality called 'David Icke' is my vehicle to exist in this reality and experience its illusions. I, the real *I*, am not the man who was a professional footballer, television presenter, Green Party spokesman and figure of mass ridicule. He is my experience, my vehicle; he is not who I am. What I am is Infinite Consciousness that has no body and no form, it just is. I am *All That Is*, has been and ever will be, just as *you* are. I am not living the lie anymore, not pretending to be the guy from Leicester, England. I am from everywhere; I *am* everywhere, and nowhere. Today, 'David Icke' is the personality I acknowledge when he pulls me into body-mind and I recognise the source of an emotional reaction. We get along pretty well, better now than ever, but he's not 'me', except in the sense that I am everything. When we observe this 'world' from that perspective of who we really are, doing what we know to be right is not even a thought process. It's a given. What are the consequences? I don't care. I have taken enough already not to care, anyway. I may die? Oh, my God, run, quick!! But hold on, I can't die. I can only leave the body called 'David Icke' and I'll do that sometime whatever. His arthritis is starting to become quite a pain in the arse, and everywhere else come to that, so no problem. People may say nasty things about me? Oh, my God, shut them up, quick!! But hold on, so what? I have had the most extreme levels of abuse and ridicule thrown at me and I am still here with many of the former abusers and ridiculers now reading my books. How is that possible? By seeing the abuse and ridicule for what it is – *irrelevant*. So what is relevant? Doing what you know to be right. Everything else is diversion. When people become conscious and override the body/mind programs (I can't, I couldn't, I have no power, what can little me do?) you open to a flow that takes you to where you need to be to do what you need to do. You don't have to be told what you can do, you *know* what you can do, and the choice is then whether you will do it or allow body/mind to keep its trembling hands on the wheel. Truly conscious people will always be 'heroes', as humanity perceives them, because they do what they know to be right. But they are not heroes, in truth; they are simply conscious and closer to their true state of self-awareness. So where are the heroes when you need them? Try the mirror. He/she has been there all along and it's time to get acquainted.

More than anything at this extraordinary time of transformation, the human race must get *off its knees*. It has been down there for far too long. ENOUGH! We are *All That Is*, All Possibility, All Potential, All Existence. What are we doing with our knees on the floor and our hands clasped together in worship or pleas for mercy? We are *lions*, not lambs, and lions refuse to be herded. Stand up, wake up and let's get this sorted. We are lions disguised as sheep; but we don't have to be. The lion within can awaken whenever we choose to set it free. As the poet, Percy Shelley, said:

> Rise like lions after slumber
> In unvanquishable number,
> Shake your chains to earth like dew
> Which in sleep had fallen on you –
> Ye are many – they are few.

Come on – *let's go*

Appendix I

Students and staff at the Fabian Society's London School of Economics

This partial list of names is confirmation of the global influence of 'alumni' of the LSE.

Heads of State or Heads of Government

Harmodio Arias (1886-1962) – President of Panama, 1932-1936

Óscar Arias (b 1941) – President of Costa Rica, 1986-1990, 2006-present and Nobel Prize winner

John Atta-Mills (b 1944) – President of Ghana, 2009-present

Taro Aso (b 1940) – Prime Minister of Japan, 2008-present

Lord Clement Attlee (1883-1967) – Prime Minister of United Kingdom, 1945-1951

Errol Walton Barrow (1920-1987) – Prime Minister of Barbados, 1962-1966, 1966-1976, 1986-1987

Marek Belka (b 1952) – Prime Minister of Poland, 2004-2005

Pedro Gerardo Beltran Espanto (1897-1979) – Prime Minister of Peru, 1959-1961

Maurice Bishop (1944-1983) – Prime Minister of Grenada (1979-1983)

Heinrich Brüning (1885-1970) – Chancellor of Germany, 1930-1932

Forbes Burnham – (1923-1985) – President of Guyana

Kim Campbell (b 1947) – Prime Minister of Canada, June-November 1993

Eugenia Charles (1919-2005) – Prime Minister of Dominica, 1980-1995

John Compton (b 1926) – Premier of Saint Lucia, 1964-1979, and Prime Minister of Saint Lucia, February-July 1979 & 1982-1996

Sher Bahadur Deuba (b 1943) – Prime Minister of Nepal, 1995-1997, 2001-2002, 2004-2005

Tuanku Jaafar (b 1922) – Yang di-Pertuan Agong (King) of Malaysia, 1994-1999

Jomo Kenyatta (1891-1978) – First President of Kenya, 1964-1978

Mwai Kibaki (b 1931) – President of Kenya, 2002-present

Tanin Kraivixien (b 1927) – Prime Minister of Thailand, 1976-1977

Yu Kuo-Hwa (1914-2000) – Premier of Taiwan, 1984-1989

Hilla Limann (1934-1998) – President of Ghana, 1979-1981

Alfonso López Pumarejo (1886-1959) – President of Colombia, 1934-1938, 1942-1945

Michael Manley (1924-1997) – Prime Minister of Jamaica, 1972-1980, 1989-1992

Ratu Sir Kamisese Mara (1920-2004) – Prime Minister of Fiji 1970-1992, President of Fiji 1994-2000

Queen Margrethe II of Denmark

Queen Margrethe II (b 1940) – Queen of Denmark, 1972-present

Beatriz Merino (b, 1947) – First female Prime Minister of Peru, 2003-2003

Sri K. R Narayanan (1921-2005) – President of India, 1997-2002

Kwame Nkrumah (1909-1972) – First President of Ghana, 1960-1966

Sylvanus Olympio (1902-1963) – Prime Minister of Togo, 1958-1961, and first President of Togo, 1961-1963

Percival Patterson (b 1935) – Prime Minister of Jamaica, 1992-2006

Romano Prodi (b 1939) – Prime Minister of Italy, 1996-1998, 2006-present and President of the European Commission, 1999-2004

Navinchandra Ramgoolam (b 1947) – Prime
Minister of Mauritius, 1995-2000
Seewoosagur Ramgoolam (1900-1985) –
Prime Minister of Mauritius (1961-1982)
Veerasamy Ringadoo (1920-2000) – First
President of Mauritius, March-June 1992
Moshe Sharett (1894-1965) – Prime Minister
of Israel, 1953-1955
Constantine Simitis (b 1936) – Prime
Minister of Greece, 1996-2004
Sergey Stanishev (b 1966) – Prime Minister
of Bulgaria, 2005-present
Edward Szczepanik (1915-2005) – Prime
Minister of the Polish government in exile,
1986 – 1990
Banja Tejan-Sie, (1917-2000) – Governor-
General and leader of opposition Sierra
Leone People's Party in Sierra Leone
Anote Tong (b 1952) – President of Kiribati,
2003-present
Pierre Trudeau (1919-2000) – Prime Minister
of Canada, 1968-1979, 1980-1984
Lee Kuan Yew (b 1923) – Prime Minister of
Singapore, 1959-1990

Government and Politics

Prime Minister Clement Attlee
Leo Abse, British MP, famous for
legalisation of male homosexuality
Lord Waheed Alli, media mogul, openly gay
Muslim businessman
Charlotte Atkins, Minister
Richard Bacon, British MP
Jackie Ballard, British MP, journalist, Director
General of the RSPCA
Tony Banks, Baron Stratford, former MP and
British Peer
Baroness Virginia Bottomley, former
Cabinet Minister
John Bourn, Officer, British House of
Commons
Annette Brooke, British MP
Karen Buck, British MP
Munir Butt, High Commissioner to Pakistan
Shami Chakrabarti, Director of Liberty

Francis Cockfield, Baron Cockfield, Cabinet
Minster, Vice-President of the European
Commission
Yvette Cooper, Cabinet Minister
Jim Cousins, British MP
Edwina Currie, former British Conservative
MP, author, radio presenter
Hugh Dalton, Chancellor of the Exchequer
Andrew Dismore, British MP
Frank Dobson, Cabinet Minister
Michael Ellam, Prime Minister Gordon
Brown's Director of Communications
Daniel Finkelstein, Conservative Party
strategist and Comment Editor of The Times
Barbara Follett, British MP
Philip Gould, Baron Gould of Brookwood,
political advisor
Lisa Harker, government child poverty tsar
Mark Hoban, British MP
Margaret Hodge, Minister
Derry Irvine, Baron Irvine of Lairg, Cabinet
Minister
Brian Jenkins, British MP
Dr Syed Kamall, British MP
Ruth Kelly, Cabinet Minister
Mervyn King, Governor of the Bank of
England
Julian Le Grand, senior advisor to the Prime
Minister
Spencer Livermore, Prime Minister Gordon
Brown's Director of Political Strategy
Rachel Lomax, British economist and
government official
Michael Meacher, Minister
Baron Merlyn-Rees, former Home Secretary
Ed Miliband, Cabinet Minister
Andrew Miller, British MP
Maria Miller, British MP
Peter Mond, 4th Baron Melchett
Baron Moore of Lower Marsh, Cabinet
Minister
Marion Phillips, British MP
Stephen Pound, British MP
Baron Reginald Prentice
Baroness Joyce Quin

Baroness Rawlings, British MEP, former Chairman of the Council of King's College London
Tom Scholar, Chief of Staff to Prime Minister Gordon Brown
Andrew Selous, British MP
Virendra Sharma, British MP
Barry Sheerman, British MP
Josiah Stamp, former Governor of the Bank of England
John Stonehouse, former UK Minister
Jo Swinson, British MP
Ian Taylor, British MP
Glenys Thornton, Baroness Thornton, Junior Minister
Rudi Vis, British MP
Malcolm Wicks, Minister
Jennifer Willott, British MP
David Winnick, British MP
Anthony Wright, British MP
Baron **Michael Young**, academic and author of the 1945 Labour manifesto
United States
Elliott Abrams, Assistant Secretary of State in Reagan Administration; Senior Director of the National Security Council in Bush Administration
Eric Alterman, Professor at Brooklyn College; political columnist for The Nation; Senior Fellow at the Center for American Progress and the World Policy Institute
Donald Baer, White House Director of Communications and Strategic Planning in Clinton Administration
Valerie Lynn Baldwin, Assistant Secretary of Defence, Bush Administration
Thomas O. Barnett, Assistant Attorney General, United States Department of Justice
Lisa Belzberg, Founder and Director, PENCIL
Ben Bernanke, Chairman of the Federal Reserve
Walter Berns, Scholar, American Enterprise Institute
Karan Bhatia, Deputy United States Trade Representative; Assistant Secretary of Transportation, Bush Administration

Anne Bingaman, Assistant Attorney General, Department of Justice; Former associate professor of law at University of New Mexico
Alan Blinder, Chief Economist of the Council of Economic Advisors under Bill Clinton; economic advisor to John Kerry; vice-chairman of the Federal Reserve Board of Governors; Professor of Economics, Princeton University
John A. Bohn, President and Chairman at the Export-Import Bank of the United States
Clifford Bond, United States Ambassador to Bosnia and Herzegovina, Bush Administration
Rebecca Birget Certa, Democratic Member of US House of Representatives
Michael Chertoff, United States Secretary of Homeland Security, Bush Administration; US Attorney, Bush Sr and Clinton Administrations
Colm Connolly, United States Attorney, Bush Administration
Lauchlin Currie, White House Economic Adviser to President Franklin Delano Roosevelt
Rosa DeLauro, high-ranking Democratic Member of the US House of Representatives
Edwin Feulner, President of the Heritage Foundation Think Tank
George T Frampton Jr, Assistant Secretary of the Interior, Clinton Administration; Chairman of the Council of Environmental Quality, Clinton Administration
William Gale, Council of Economic Advisers, Bush Administration
Eric Garcetti, President, Los Angeles City Council
Marc Grossman, US Under-Secretary of State, Bush Administration; US Ambassador to Turkey, Clinton Administration; Special Advisor to the President on Near East Affairs, Carter Administration
Orval H Hansen, Republican Member of the US House of Representatives
Stuart Holliday, US Representative to the United Nations; Assistant Secretary of State

Frank S. Holleman, Deputy Secretary of Education, Clinton Administration

Genta H Holmes, United States Ambassador to Australia, Clinton Administration; United States Ambassador to Namibia; Chief of Mission to Haiti and Malawi

Alice Stone Ilchman, Assistant Secretary of Education and Cultural Affairs under US President Jimmy Carter

Dr Bruce Jentleson, International Affairs Fellow, Council of Foreign Relations; Senior Foreign Policy Advisor to Vice President Al Gore

Anthony Kennedy, United States Supreme Court, Associate Justice

John F Kennedy, President of the United States 1961-1963

Joseph P Kennedy, Jr, first son of Joseph Kennedy and elder brother of John F Kennedy

Robert F Kennedy, Jr, environmental activist, son of slain Senator Robert Kennedy

Vanessa Kerry, Democratic activist and daughter of Senator John Kerry (D-MA)

Ron Kind, Democratic Member of US House of Representatives

Mark Kirk, Republican Member of the US House of Representatives

Deborah Lehr, lead negotiator for China's WTO Accession; former partner at Mayer Brown

Susan Lindauer, ex-Congressional aide accused of assisting Iraqi intelligence prior to the 2003 invasion

Clay Lowery, Assistant Secretary of the Treasury, Bush Administration

Edward Luttwak, Consultant to the US National Security Council, State Department and Defence Department; Economist; Historian; Senior Fellow at the Center for Strategic and International Studies

John W McCarter, President and CEO of The Field Museum; White House Fellow during Lyndon B Johnson Administration

James McGreevey, former Governor of New Jersey

Elisabeth Millard, Senior Director of the National Security Council, Bush Administration; Deputy Chief of US Mission to Nepal

Brad Miller, Member of the US House of Representatives

Chris Moore, Assistant Secretary of State, Bush Administration

Richard H Moore, North Carolina State Treasurer

Daniel Patrick Moynihan, US Senator

Ethan Nadelmann, founder and executive director of the Drug Policy Alliance

Peter R Orszag, Special Assistant to the President for Economic Policy, Senior Economist, Council of Economic Advisors, Clinton Administration; Fellow of the Brookings Institution; Professor, Georgetown University, Congressional Budget Office Director, Director designate Office of Management and Budget

Max Pappas, Director of Policy at FreedomWorks

Alice Paul, American suffragist

Richard Perle, Assistant Secretary of Defense, Reagan Administration; Chairman of Defense Department Advisory Committee, Bush Administration; fellow, American Enterprise Institute

F Whitten Peters, Secretary of the Air Force, Washington, DC

Victoria Radd, White House Deputy Director of Communications, Clinton Administration; senior policy advisor to Bentsen, Dukakis and Mondale campaigns

David Rockefeller, former Chairman, Chase Manhattan Bank; Chairman/Honorary Chairman, the Council on Foreign Relations; Chairman/Honorary Chairman, the Trilateral Commission

James Rubin, Assistant Secretary of State, Clinton Administration; lead foreign policy adviser to John Kerry campaign

Robert Rubin, US Treasury Secretary and Director, National Economic Council, Clinton Administration; Director of Goldman Sachs

August Schumacher Jr, Under-Secretary of Agriculture, Clinton Administration

Dr Robert Shapiro, Undersecretary of Commerce, Clinton Administration; Fellow of Harvard University; Fellow of National Bureau of Economic Research

John Tower, US Senator

Paul Volcker, Chairman of Federal Reserve, Carter and Reagan Administrations; US Treasury Under-Secretary, Nixon Administration; President of the Federal Reserve Bank of New York

David Welch, Assistant Secretary of State, Clinton Administration; US Ambassador to Egypt, Bush Administration

Maureen White, US Democratic Party National Finance Chair; US Representative to UNICEF; Human Rights Watch, board-member

Kimba Wood, United States Federal Judge; Attorney General Nominee

Janet Yellen, Council of Economic Advisers, Clinton Administration; Vice-President, American Economic Association; President and CEO of the Federal Reserve Bank of San Francisco

Dr Dov Zakheim, Under-Secretary of Defense, Bush and Reagan administrations and Pentagon comptroller in the run-up to 9/11

Canada

Jon Allen, Canadian Ambassador to Israel, 2006-present

Ed Broadbent, Canadian socialist opposition leader

Kim Campbell, former Prime Minister of Canada

John Crosbie, Lieutenant-Governor of Newfoundland and Labrador, former Cabinet minister

Hal Jackman, former Lieutenant-Governor of Ontario

Michael Ignatieff, current deputy leader of the Liberal Party

Sheryl Kennedy, former Deputy Governor of the Bank of Canada

Joy MacPhail, former finance minister and deputy premier of British Columbia

Marc Mayrand, Chief Electoral Officer of Elections Canada

David McGuinty, Member of Parliament for the Liberal Party

Jacques Parizeau (b 1930) – Premier of Quebec, 1994-1995

Louis Rasminsky, Governor of the Bank of Canada from 1961 to 1973

Svend Robinson, former Canadian MP; first openly gay Canadian politician in major party

Gregory Selinger, Canadian politician

Mitchell Sharp, Canadian Minister of Finance

Walter Tarnopolsky, Canadian judge and member of United Nations Human Rights Committee

Gordon Thiessen, Governor of the Bank of Canada, 1994 to 2001

Pierre Trudeau, former Prime Minister of Canada

Michael Wilson, Canadian Ambassador to the US, 2006-present

Paul Zed, Member of Parliament for Saint John, New Brunswick

Latin America and the Caribbean

Fidel Herrera Beltrán, Governor of Veracruz, Mexico

Eugenia Charles, Prime Minister of Dominica

Mario Adolfo Cuevas, Director, National Center for Economic Research, Guatemala

Winston Dookeran, Trinidad and Tobago politician and economist

Eduardo Lizano, President of the Central Bank of Costa Rica from 1984 to 1990

Martin Lousteau, Minister of economy and production, Argentina

Shridath Ramphal, former Secretary-General of the Commonwealth

Juan Manuel Santos, Colombian politician, currently serving as Minister of National Defense

Europe

Georgios Alogoskoufis, Minister for Economy and Finance, Greece

Prince Amedeo of Belgium

Frits Bolkestein, Dutch politician and former EU Commissioner

Nikos Garganas, Governor of the Bank of Greece

Ian Goldin, Vice President of External Affairs, World Bank

Martin Grunditz, Swedish Ambassador to Greece

Prince Haakon Magnus, Crown Prince of Norway

Jan Kavan, former President of the United Nations General Assembly, member of the Czech Parliament, former Foreign Minister and Deputy Prime Minister of the Czech Republic

Ivan Miklo?, Minister of Finance of Slovakia

Franz Neumann, first Chief of Research of the Nuremberg War Crimes Tribunal

Érik Orsenna (real name: Erik Arnoult), former economist and advisor to François Mitterrand, member of the Conseil d'État and of the Académie française, 1988 Prix Goncourt

George Andreas Papandreou, Foreign Minister of Greece from 1999 to 2004, Prime Minister of Greece from 2009 to present

Jacek Rostowski, Minister of Finance, Poland

Michalis Sarris, Cypriot Minister for Finance

Jonas Gahr Støre, Norwegian Minister of Foreign Affairs

Alexander Stubb, Finish Minister of Foreign Affairs

Zdenûk TÛm, Governor of Czech National Bank

Leo Van Houtven, former secretary of the IMF

Michiel van Hulten, Dutch politician, former MEP

Jose Vinals, Head of monetary and capital markets division, IMF and former deputy governor of the Bank of Spain

August Zaleski, twice Minister of Foreign Affairs of the Republic of Poland

Africa

Saif al-Islam al-Gaddafi, political activist and elder son of Libyan President Muammar al-Gaddafi

Bolajoko Akinbolagbe, Nigerian.

Augustus Akinloye, Nigerian lawyer and politician. Chairman of defunct National Party of Nigeria

Kader Asmal, South African politician and member of the African National Congress' Executive Committee

Paul Kagame, President of Rwanda

Ibrahim Gambari, Under Secretary General for Political Affairs at the United Nations

Jeanne Hoban, Anglo-Sri Lankan journalist, Trotskyite political activist and trade-unionist

Aguinaldo Jaime, Deputy Prime Minister of Angola

Pallo Jordan, Minister of Arts and Culture of the Republic of South Africa

Nelson Mandela, former President of South Africa and freedom fighter

Michael Wamalwa Kijana, former Vice-President of Kenya

Mac Maharaj, South African ANC politician, former Minister of Transport

Mawere Mugabe, son of Robert Mugabe, President of Zimbabwe

Bayo Ojo, past head of the Nigerian Federal Ministry of Justice

Obafemi Awolowo, Nigerian independence leader, Fabian lawyer, human rights advocate

Alex Quaison-Sackey, former foreign minister of Ghana

Winston Tubman, Liberian diplomat and politician

Shamsudeen Usman Nigerian economist, technocrat and banker Current Minister of National Planning and past Minister of Finance of Nigeria.

Samuel G Ikoku notable Nigerian economist and politician; senior adviser of Dr Kwame Nkrumah of Ghana
Samuel Aluko famous Nigeria professor of Economics

Asia

Lee Kuan Yew, former Prime Minister of Singapore
B R Ambedkar, Buddhist revivalist, Indian jurist, scholar and Bahujan political leader who was the chief architect of the Indian Constitution
Piyasvasti Amranand, Thailand's Energy Minister
C. R Pattabhiraman, Indian member of Parliament and Union Minister
Taro Aso, Prime Minister of Japan
Syed Ishtiaq Ahmed, former Attorney General of Bangladesh and twice Adviser on Law for the two successive caretaker governments of Bangladesh
Choowong Chayabutra, former Thailand's Secretary of Ministry of Interior, Senator and a member of parliament
Tam Yiu Chung, current councillor from 1998 in the Legislative Council of Hong Kong and a member of the Democratic Alliance for Betterment of Hong Kong (DAB)
Audrey Eu, member of the Legislative Council of Hong Kong and currently the party leader of the Civic Party
Abul Fateh, Bangladesh diplomat
Mustafa Kamal (judge), former Chief Justice of Bangladesh
Vivienne Goonewardena, Sri Lankan Trotskyist freedom agitator, parliamentarian, trade unionist and women's activist
Wang Guangya, permanent representative of the People's Republic of China to the United Nations
Tsai Ing-wen, former Vice Premier of the Republic of China (Taiwan)

Amarananda Somasiri Jayawardene, Governor of the Central Bank of Sri Lanka
Yang Jiechi, current Minister of Foreign Affairs of the People's Republic of China
Emily Lau, Hong Kong politician
Dr Maliha Lodhi, Pakistan's High Commissioner to United Kingdom and former Ambassador to USA
Kashmala Tariq, Member of the National Assembly of Pakistan
Makhdoom Ali Khan, Ex-Attorney General of Pakistan and chief lawyer of President Pervez Musharraf
Makhdoom Khusro Bakhtiyar, Former Deputy Foreign Minister of Pakistan
Marvi Memon, Member National Assembly Pakistan
Krishna Menon, former Indian Permanent Representative to the UN, Minister of Defence, and leading proponent of India's emancipation
Goh Keng Swee, former Deputy Prime Minister of Singapore
Tharman Shanmugaratnam, Singapore's Finance Minister
Juwono Sudarsono, Indonesian Minister of Defence
Puey Ungpakorn, Governor of the (Central) Bank of Thailand
Nani Lal Barua, Banker, Central Bank of India, Calcutta, India
Salahuddin Ahmad, former Attorney General of Bangladesh

Australia

Ameer Ali, President of the Australian Federation of Islamic Councils
William Macmahon Ball, Australian diplomat
Peter Coleman, Journalist and conservative politician
Nugget Coombs, Governor of the Reserve Bank of Australia
Robert Hill, Defence Minister
John Laker, Chairman, Australian Prudential Regulation Authority

Gordon Reid, Governor of Western Australia and Vice-Chancellor of the University of Western Australia
Peter Sheargold, Secretary of Prime Minister's Department

Middle East

Sheikh Hamdan bin Mohammed Al Maktoum, Crown Prince of Dubai
Princess Badiya bint Al Hassan, member of royal family of Jordan
Shlomo Argov, prominent Israeli diplomat, former Israeli ambassador to the United Kingdom
Yishai Be'e, General in the Israel Defense Forces and currently the President of the Israeli Military Court of Appeals
Kemal Dervi, UNDP Administrator (Head) and former Minister of Finance of Turkey
Rafi Eitan, leader of the Gil Party in Israeli Politics, law maker, former security
Stanley Fischer, Governor of the Bank of Israel; World Bank Chief Economist
Emre Gönensay, Minister of Foreign Affairs of Turkey in 1996
Amnon Rubinstein, Israeli law scholar, politician, and columnist, Education Minister of Israel, 1993-1996
Jeremy Issacharoff, Israeli Ambassador, expert on global disarmament International organisations and ambassadors
James Allan, British High Commissioner in Mauritius and ambassador to Mozambique
Kader Asmal, South African politician and member of the African National Congress' Executive Committee
Rosemary Banks, New Zealand's Ambassador to the United Nations
Francis Cockfield, Baron Cockfield, Cabinet Minster under Thatcher; Vice-President of the European Commission
Kemal Dervi, UNDP Administrator (Head) and former Minister of Finance of Turkey
Nitin Desai, former UN Under-Secretary-General for Economic and Social Affairs

Ibrahim Gambari, Under Secretary General for Political Affairs at the United Nations
Ian Goldin, Vice President of External Affairs, World Bank
Jeffrey Goldstein, Managing Director, World Bank
Wang Guangya, permanent representative of the People's Republic of China to the United Nations
Robert Murray Hill, Australian Ambassador to the United Nations
John Huges, British Ambassador to Argentina
Robert E Hunter, former U.S. Ambassador to NATO
Rajmah Hussain, Ambassador of the Malaysia to the United States
Clete Donald Johnson, Jr, former Member of Congress and US Ambassador, LL.M 1978
Ahmad Kamal, Pakistani Ambassador to the UN
Jan Kavan, former President of the United Nations General Assembly, member of the Czech Parliament, former Foreign Minister and Deputy Prime Minister of the Czech Republic
Mohsin Khan, Director of the Middle East and Central Asia Department of the International Monetary Fund
Dr Maliha Lodhi, prominent Pakistani politician; Pakistani Ambassador to the US
John J Maresca, former US Ambassador to the OSCE in the George HW Bush Administration
Krishna Menon, former Indian Permanent Representative to the UN, Minister of Defense, and leading proponent of India's emancipation
Marty Natalegawa, Indonesian Ambassador to the United Kingdom
Marty M. Natalegawa, Indonesian Ambassador to the UK and Ireland, and Representative of ASEAN Ambassadors to the UK
Franz Neumann, First Chief of Research of the Nuremberg War Crimes Tribunal

Shridath Ramphal, former Secretary-General of the Commonwealth
Shaha Riza, World Bank
Pierre Sane, UNESCO's Assistant Director-General for Social and Human Sciences
Michele J Sison, current US Ambassador to Lebanon in the Bush Administration
Walter Tarnopolsky, Canadian judge and member of United Nations Human Rights Committee
Leo Van Houtven, former secretary of the IMF
Michael Wilson, Canadian Ambassador to the US, 2006-present
Wenzhong Zhou, Chinese Ambassador to the US
Arne Roy Walther, Norwegian ambassador to Japan

Business and finance

Lord Waheed Alli, House of Lords, media mogul, only openly gay Muslim businessman
Delphine Arnault, billionaire French businesswoman
Geoffrey Bell, banker, and Group of Thirty founder
Sir Gordon Brunton, Chief Executive Thomson Corporation, Former Chairman Sotheby's
Richard Caruso, Founder and Chairman of Integra LifeSciences Corporation and 2006 Ernst & Young US Entrepreneur of the Year
Tony Fernandes, entrepreneur
Clara Furse Chief Executive of the London Stock Exchange
Sir Stelios Haji-Ioannou, entrepreneur, founder of EasyGroup
David Heleniak, Vice-Chairman, Morgan Stanley
Samuel Isaly, Manager Eaton Vance Worldwide Health Sciences fund
Michael S. Jeffries, CEO Abercrombie & Fitch Co.
Richard Kahan, Chairman, Riverside South Planning Corporation, Donald Trump's building

Robert Kaplan, former Vice-Chairman of Goldman Sachs and Chairman of Goldman Sachs International
Michael Kopper, former Enron executive [1]
Spiro Latsis, billionaire
Charles Lee, Former chairman of the Hong Kong Stock Exchange
David Morgan, CEO of Westpac
Robert Murley, Vice Chairman of Credit Suisse First Boston and Chairman of Investment Banking for the Americas
Arif Naqvi, CEO of Abraaj Capital, the leading private equity firm in the Middle East
Christopher Nassetta, President and CEO of Hilton Hotels Corp
Erling Dekke Næss, Norwegian ship-owner and businessman
Richard Nesbitt, CEO, TSX Group; Toronto Stock Exchange
Jorma Ollila, former CEO of Nokia Corporation, Non-executive chairman of Royal Dutch Shell
Zarin Patel, BBC's Chief Financial Officer
Sheila Penrose, Chairman, Jones Lang LaSalle Incorporated; President of Penrose Group; Director of McDonalds
Gary Perlin, CFO Capital One Financial Corporation; Former CFO World Bank
Avinash Persaud, Global Head of Currency & Commodity Research at JP Morgan
Ruth Porat, Vice Chairman, Global Head of Financial Institutions Group at Morgan Stanley
Philip J Purcell, former CEO Morgan Stanley Dean Witter
Syed Ali Raza, President and Chairman of the National Bank of Pakistan
Stephen Robert, co-chairman of CIBC Oppenheimer Holdings Corp, Chancellor of Brown University
David Rockefeller, American billionaire and business tycoon
Barr Rosenberg, Chairman and director of research, AXA Rosenberg Investment Management LLC

Wieslaw Rozlucki, CEO Warsaw Stock
Exchange 1991-2006, Poland
Maurice Saatchi, founder of Saatchi and
Saatchi)
George Soros, Notable Financier; Billionaire
Brian MacCaba, Notable Jewish CEO of
Cognotec
Bryan Sanderson CBE, Chairman of
Standard Chartered Bank plc
Allen Sheppard, Baron Sheppard of
Didgemere, industrialist, Chancellor of
Middlesex University
Panagis Vourloumis, Managing Director and
President of the OTE's Board, the national
telecommunications provider of Greece
Arnold Weinstock, English businessman,
best known for building GEC
Jim Whitehurst, CEO of Red Hat
Jacques Bussières, former Governor of the
Bank of Jamaica
George Arthur Brown, former Governor of
the Bank of Jamaica
Victor E. Bruce, former Governor of the
Central Bank of Trinidad and Tobago
Winston Dookeran, politician and
economist; former Governor of the
Caribbean Development Bank and Central
Bank of Trinidad and Tobago
Simone Perillo, Secretary General of the
Formula One Teams Association

Nobel Laureates

1950: Ralph Bunche (Peace)
1979: Sir William Arthur Lewis (Economics)
1991: Ronald Coase (Economics)
1999: Robert Mundell (Economics)
2007: Leonid Hurwicz (Economics)

Founders and Professors

1925: George Bernard Shaw (Literature)
1950: Bertrand Russell (Literature)
1959: Philip Noel-Baker (Peace)
1972: Sir John Hicks (Economics)
1974: Friedrich von Hayek (Economics)

1977: James Meade (Economics)
1987: Óscar Arias (Peace)
1990: Merton Miller (Economics)
1998: Amartya Sen (Economics)
2001: George Akerlof (Economics)
2007: Leonid Hurwicz (Economics)
2008: Paul Krugman (Economics)

Economists

Daron Acemoglu, economist, John Bates
Clark Medal Winner 2005
Sir Roy Allen, economist and mathematician
Tony Antoniou, former Dean of Durham
Business School and Professor of Finance
Heinz Wolfgang Arndt, economist
Peter Thomas Bauer, development
economist
William Baumol, Professor of Economics and
Director, C V Starr Center for Applied
Economics, New York University
Charles Bean, economist, member of
Monetary Policy Committee
Timothy Besley, economics professor and
member of Monetary Policy Committee
Kenneth Binmore, economist
Alan Budd, British economist, Provost of The
Queen's College, Oxford
Willem Buiter, economist, ex-member of
Monetary Policy Committee
Ronald Coase, economist, Nobel Prize
winner
Richard N Cooper, Maurits C Boas Professor
of International Economics, Harvard
University; Previously Chairman, National
Intelligence Council and; Under Secretary of
State for Economic Affairs
Peter Cornelius, former Group Chief
Economist of Royal Dutch Shell, Former
Chief Economist of the World Economic
Forum
Lord Desai, development economist
Roderick D Fraser, economist, President of
the University of Alberta, 1995-2005
Charles Goodhart, economist, ex-member of
Monetary Policy Committee

David Forbes Hendry, British economist, currently Professor of Economics and Head of the Economics Department at the University of Oxford

J A Hobson, economist and writer

Samuel Hollander, British/Canadian/Israeli economist

Anthony Hopwood, Former dean of Oxford Said Business School

Eliot Janeway, American economist, economic advisor to Presidents Franklin D Roosevelt and Lyndon B Johnson

Lewis Webster Jones, economist, fifteenth President of Rutgers University

Nicholas Kaldor, economist

Paul Krugman, New York Times columnist, Nobel Prize winner, Pulitzer Prize winning journalist

Maurice Kugler, development economist

Ludwig Lachmann, economist

David Laidler, economist

Lord Layard, economist

Sir William Arthur Lewis, economist, Nobel Prize winner

Lisa M Lynch, William L Clayton Professor of International Economic Affairs and former Academic Dean at the Fletcher School at Tufts University

James Meade, economist, Nobel Prize winner

Merton Miller, economist, Nobel Prize winner

Michio Morishima, Japanese economist

Robert Mundell, economist, Nobel Prize winner

Stephen Nickell, economist, ex-member of Monetary Policy Committee

Andrew Oswald, economist

Baron Maurice Peston, economist and politician

Peter C B Phillips, Sterling Professor of Economics and Professor of Statistics at Yale University

William Phillips, economist

Christopher A Pissarides, Cypriot-born British economist, member of the Monetary Policy Committee of the Central Bank of Cyprus

Mihir Rakshit, economist

Lionel Robbins, economist

Tadeusz Rybczynski, Polish-born English economist, known for the development of the Rybczynski theorem

Anthony Saunders, Chairman, Department of Finance, Stern School of Business, New York University

Arthur Seldon, free market ideologue

Andrew Sentance, member of Monetary Policy Committee

G L S Shackle, economist

Neil Shephard, econometrician

Alasdair Smith, economist, former Vice-Chancellor at the University of Sussex

Piero Sraffa, economist

Nicholas Stern, economist

Sho-Chieh Tsiang, economist

Lord Turner, businessman, academic, chair of the Pensions Commission and the UK Low Pay Commission

John Van Reenen, economist, Director of the Centre for Economic Performance at the London School of Economics

Sushil Wadhwani, economist

Sir Alan Walters, monetary economist

Basil Yamey, industrial economist

Allyn Abbott Young, economist

Historians

Janet Coleman FRHS, historian of political thought

Martin van Creveld, Israeli military historian and theorist

Paul Kennedy, British historian specializing in international relations and grand strategy

David Levering Lewis, Pulitzer Prize winning author, prominent historian on African Americans

Desmond Morton, historian

Lewis Bernstein Namier, historian

Ben Pimlott, Fabian President, modern historian, former president of Nottingham University

Anthony Seldon, historian, biographer of Tony Blair and headmaster of Wellington College

Avi Shlaim, historian specialising in the Middle East

Alan Sked, leading Habsburg historian and founder of the United Kingdom Independence Party

David Starkey, historian specialising in Tudor England

David Stevenson (WW1 historian), World War One historian

John Stubbs, historian, former president of Trent University and Simon Fraser University

Juliette Levy, historian and Assistant Professor of History, University of California, Riverside

Jacob Talmon, historian

Arnold Joseph Toynbee, historian

Odd Arne Westad, leading historian specialising in the Cold War and contemporary East Asian history; currently Convenor of the LSE International History Department and Cold War Studies Centre

Charles Webster, British historian and diplomat

Alfred Marshall, historian and sociologist International Relations

Daniele Archibugi, former Visiting Professor of International Relations

Chris Brown, Professor of International Relations

Hedley Bull, Professor of International Relations

Barry Buzan, Professor of International Relations

Christopher Coker, Professor of International Relations, Department Head

Michael Cox, Professor of International Relations

David Held, Professor of International Relations

Fred Halliday, Professor of International Relations (Montague Burton Chair), to 2008

Kimberly Hutchings, Professor of International Relations

Mary Kaldor, Professor of International Relations

Parag Khanna, author and current PhD candidate

F S Northedge, former Professor of International Relations

Richard W Lyman, former Provost and President of Stanford University; Founder Stanford Institute for International Studies

Susan Strange, Professor of International Relations (Montague Burton Chair), 1978 to 1988

Leonard Suransky, Winner of Des Lee Visiting Lectureship in Global Awareness at Webster University

William John Lawrence Wallace, Baron **Wallace of Saltaire**, Professor of International Relations; deputy leader of the Liberal Democrats in the House of Lords

Sir Charles Webster, Professor of International Relations; founder of the United Nations

Margot Light, Professor of International Relations

Martin Wight, Reader in International Relations, 1949-1960

Law

Janice R Bellace, Samuel A Blank Professor of Legal Studies and Business Ethics, University of Pennsylvania, founding president of the Singapore Management University

Paul Davies, Cassel Professor of Commercial Law at the London School of Economics, Honorary QC

Talbot 'Sandy' D'Alemberte, former president of the American Bar Association, and former president of the Florida State University

Albert Venn Dicey, English jurist

Sir Morris Finer, Barrister, Judge, Chairman of the Finer Report on One Parent Families & the Royal Commission on the Press, Vice Chairman of Governors of LSE

Sir Christopher Greenwood QC, esteemed international lawyer; advised Tony Blair and the Bush Administration on the legality of the 2003 Iraq war, member of the International Criminal Court

Joseph Grundfest, W A Franke Professor of Law and Business, Stanford Law School
Osagie Imasogie, Grant Irey Adjunct Professor of Law, University of Pennsylvania
Makhdoom Ali Khan, Barrister-at-Law from Lincolns Inn and Attorney General of Pakistan
Philip Noel-Baker, professor of international law, politician, diplomat, Nobel Peace Prize winner

Adam Tomkins, John Millar Professor of Public Law at the University of Glasgow
Michael Zander QC, Professor Emeritus. A distinguished professor of law at LSE between 1977 and 1998, member of the Runciman Royal Commission on Criminal Justice (1991-1993) and the Legal Correspondent of The Guardian newspaper between 1963 and 1988
David van Zandt, Dean and Professor, Northwestern University Law School

Appendix II

Confessions of a Satanist

The following document was sent to the website, **loveforlife.com.au**, in January 2010 by someone using the name 'Aloysius Fozdyke'. It purports to be a 'deathbed confession' about the nature of Satanism and the depth of its influence and control throughout global society. The text is said to be the words of 'Petor Narsagonan' – aka Frater 616 – 'who died on 25th March 2004'.

'Aloysius Fozdyke' wrote:

> Petor Narsagonan was known by a number of names, at least one of which would be known by many South Africans. He published under a number of non-de plumes. I have no idea of all that he did and I do not wish to know. He is dead. He was found dead by a regular visitor to one of his homes (in Newcastle, New South Wales, Australia). His demise had been expected and yet I have heard rumours of peculiar events preceding it. His body was cremated (as is the tradition) in a ceremony that saw the Council of Seven convene in Melbourne; Victoria, Australia on 30th April, 2004.

I have no way of confirming if the following is genuine, but I can say that it fits perfectly with all that I have uncovered about Satanism, its methods and personnel, over the last 20 years. It is certainly true that Australia is a bastion of Satanism that controls the country and has great influence on the wider world, and the way the Control System is described here, along with its psychological manipulation, is extremely accurate.

By Frater 616

> I will go down to The Altars in Hell
> To Satan
> The Giver of Life
> O! Prince of Darkness
> Hear Me!
> Our Father which wert in heaven
> Hallowed be Thy Name
> In heaven as it is on Earth.
> Give us this day our Ecstasy
> And deliver us to evil
> As well as temptation
> For we are your Kingdom
> For Aeons and Aeons.

Satanism flourishes beneath the scintillating midnight-blue wet streets and bedevilling phosphorescent lights of Australia's glittering capital cities. Its practitioners are from all walks of life. Although marginal types and those with predisposing personalities have always and will always be important to Satanism and its leaders' ends, they are merely tools. Their antinomian influence is now so pervasive as not to be readily noticed.

Amongst the highest echelons, some are politicians, medical doctors, high ranking police officers, lawyers, advertising gurus, decorated military men, media personalities, fashion models and social workers. Amongst the lowest (usually temporary) ranks are prostitutes, minor drug dealers and a number of High School students. Some operate from the mists. Their victims are drip-fed straight amnesia by an assortment of mind control measures and psychological torture tactics that would leave any normal person numb with the dawning apprehension that things are not as they seem – and they have not been for a long, long time.

The most talented amongst them have lifestyles maintained on crime, but lacquered with a thin veneer of respectable professionalism and knowledge.

They dress with elegance – timeless and calculating; networking and conspiring in a dream that money alone cannot purchase. Often their personalities have a force that distorts the contours both of judgement and of everyday perception. I cannot mention every name, but I will drop enough clues. The doctors refuse to say exactly how long I have but …

I became involved in the whole sordid business in the 1970's, a decade noted for little beyond sartorial bad taste and crushingly optimistic fatalism. The decade that began as a drug-crazed carry-over of the 1960's soon bequeathed androgynous glam-rock, the Watergate scandal and the shallow opportunism of 'Rollerball'. Science fictionism stalked the streets with a rejected furtiveness bred of cowering beneath the backdrop of the Cold War and dancing with the resurrected agonies of another Asian based imperialistic conflict.

I fell through a crack in reality, having deliriously wandered amid the human wreckage and reached certain spiritual conclusions. In short, I do not know how I got there, but I know why. The 1970s were a dismal, incense-fuelled time that only those who lived through it can appreciate. The comprehensive dismissal of values and the adoption of pornography as the aesthetic standard by which all endeavour was to be categorised left its impressionistic fingerprints on everybody's imagination, mine included. I guess that I analysed and reacted differently. That is how I escaped the mundane – through one of western society's fault lines.

Credo quia absurdum!

I began dabbling in the black arts as an alienated university student. It was 1971 when I attended my first meeting – only to be led into an existence of happiness, sexual excess, acquisitive arousal and comfort. Within a week of meeting my Luciferian mentor I was operating a number of travel businesses in Sydney and flying to international destinations at least four times a year. I had a Jaguar, city apartment, holiday home in the country, access to a yacht on Sydney harbour and women. I was young and considered to be an up and coming star within the shadowy twilight of the Satanic infrastructure. The nether world was at my patent leather-soled feet. My suits were hand-make Italian; the cravats and neckties, Chinese silk and my nymphomaniac maids, French. (They dressed like French maids and would often wake me with a lesbian show.)

At that time the United States-based Church of Satan was the very public face of a movement that had begun almost a century before and had culled its adherents from the renaissance of magic, which had begun in Germany and flowered in England since the dying years of the nineteenth century. The Church of Satan was one of the front organizations for an ancient body whose very existence had never before been imagined. If you want more information on some of its past and most influential members you could do worse than study the late J.P. Morgan, Drs. James McDonald and René Hardy, the Kennedy's (including Jackie), Irving Berlin, Groucho Marx, Elvis Presley, Garner Ted Armstrong, Sammy Davis Jr., Ronald Reagan, Edward Heath, Thomas Plantard de Saint-Claire or a search amongst the bushes. [Bushes – the Bush family]

I learnt and reflected the glamour of the black arts: divination, dark meditation, sacrifice, sexual vampirism, talismans, voodoo dolls and sex magic. My life was one of calculated excess and dazzling fulfilment. I smoked handmade Partagas Cuban cigars. I had a personal secretary who was happy to engage my every whim and find like-minded others if I wanted a change or had a colleague I needed to impress. I finished every day with a restaurant meal, bottle of French Champagne and Black Mass orgy of unforgettable and unspeakable delight.

The streets were more innocent, the people more naïve. The American Intelligence Services were still involved in funding the occult but their influence was more ingratiating than dictatorial. In any event, many of America's high ranking military men were members of various Satanic Lodges or kindred organizations. Often sensitive materials and powerful figures – who operated from the comfort, safety and anonymity of the dark velvet shadows – were transported on U.S. and Australian Navy ships. Oil tankers were another favourite. Materials (and indeed, people) have been concealed and lost on oil tankers for years. Remember, this was in the Seventies when America's organized crime syndicates were establishing the narcotics markets of the Western World, Australia included.

I knew her as Lilith, a High Priestess of an ultra-secretive Black Order of Typhon. Hers was the easy smile of a true neurotic and the body of an Angel. Her long cruel fingernails were enamelled in the chic and expensive titillations of her victims and their fantasies. Urolagnists worshipped at her feet and obeyed her every sadistic command. They were not the only ones. Her clientele included the top-end of town and she frequented the boardrooms and bathrooms of power with an essence of mystery, wealth and alluring sluttiness that won her the attention and influence of very many.

I had first met her at a stately home in an inner Sydney suburb at one of the regular Black Masses held to strengthen the bonds of lust, occult knowledge and perversion. There she was indulging the Devil's faithful, teaching and being videoed for the 1970's black-market that existed in underground extreme porn: bestiality, paedophilia, body wastes and pain. After her services "to the Dark Lord" she told me over a reefer and through exhaustion that she was only seventeen and had met the Master. He had given her a mission.

Lilith was a child from one of Sydney's more self-conscious suburbs. Private school educated and with a future in her father's business, she sacrificed herself to help establish what is considered today, by those in the know, to be the most powerful and important Satanic organization in the world. That group comprises some of the most educated, wealthy, corrupt and corrupting people that have ever existed. And they operate out of Sydney, Australia – but their influence is international.

It transpired that she had been flown to the United States to be tutored and initiated into what was at that time, Anton La Vey's underground Satanic sisterhood of professional women with an aptitude for carnality and a conscience to match: the Ordo Cave Lupam. Her high school teacher – an Adept in the Black Arts – had spotted Lilith while she was still only a schoolgirl. Like all Satanists, he believed that truth and salvation could be found through the exploration of repressed human needs; that pornography gave joy and joy gave strength. Through his dedication and perverse ability he had secured her co-operation to begin her new education for her assigned task of political intrigue and influential debasement.

After completing her 'education' with the O.C.L. Lilith was tutored by an English gentleman who I knew as Pindar [I have highlighted this 'man' in several of my previous books]. I never met him but I worship the true father of the statutory heir. His were the 'Irish' mysteries of degradation and when his name was ever mentioned Lilith would often laughingly sing, '...the rosy red cheeks of the little children'.

Lilith procured children to satiate the debased lusts of many Satanists. These were taken from single girls by promises, for a fee or occasionally, simply stolen. Babies were bred for their various purposes by 'Broodmares' – young unemployed girls who were paid to hand over their 'produce'. Sometimes this magical pornography was filmed; sometimes children died. Once you have seen a young child crucified or a baby kicked to death you are and can never be the same again. The most disturbing aspect of the Black Masses held in Sydney was and remains the ease with which victims were and continue to be obtained and the lack of any effective interest by the police (although a number of Police Commissioners from various States were members of the Order). This is not to suggest that Satanists are simply perverts or child killers.

The Alpha-Lodge to which I was a member placed a great deal of emphasis upon Magic, both in theory and practice. Demons were evoked and dispatched; sigils made and sacrifice and the letting of blood encouraged. In this regard, many who bask in their own limited knowledge believe that Aleister Crowley is the father of modern manifestations of Satanism, but this is incorrect. Perhaps Crowley is the grandfather of modern left hand path groups, but their stepfather is Peter James Carroll, the founder of the Chaos Magick School. There are a number of reasons for this and the various Black Lodges within Australia have developed from their early twentieth century reliance upon recruiting from fringe Masonic groups, through High Magick in the nineteen-twenties, Low Magick in the nineteen-sixties and seventies to their current prospective candidates from amongst Chaos Magick practitioners (who are generally young, ambitious, enthusiastic, energetic and destined by their lifestyle choices to the shadowy world of Satanism).

A number of up-market Escort agencies in Australia and elsewhere are operated by Black Magicians. Yet brothels and pornography comprise only a small financial part of the International Satanic Empire. Most of the money comes from drugs (the C.I.A.), sophisticated blackmail, money lending and currency trading. Satanists of the highest order are behind a number of wealthy Conservative, New Right Christian Churches and organizations in America. These are some of contemporary Satanism's best cash-flow enterprises (mostly indirectly) and allow mass indoctrination and networking.

The aim of the Alpha Lodge remains illiteracy rates in the western world of at least sixty-six percent by 2010 and the destruction of at least seventy percent of the globe's population by the year 2030. All governments count on their sheeple to respond in typical infantile fashions, including unconsciously identifying with a more powerful force – even if it enslaves, brutalizes and humiliates them. Most Australians perform so badly in the role of adult that they rarely achieve complete satisfaction from this process. It is the weak who must tell you they are strong. In this regard, the infiltration of the United Nations by Satanists – which began in the 1970s – has paid off extremely well already, as has the career of Henry Kissinger. It was Henry Kissinger who preposed the use of fundamentalist Christianity to bring about war, firstly in the Middle East and then globally. In this he was aided by a number of American Presidents subsequent to Richard Millhouse Nixon handing over the reins to Gerald Ford – who was always one of ours!

As the Headquarters of International Satanism is Sydney, Australia it is not surprising to learn that Norman Lindsay – a former Magus of the Order – is considered a Satanic Saint [Norman Lindsay (1879 – 1969) was a famous Australian artist and writer]. Indeed there are a number of flourishing secret shrines dedicated to him and his memory throughout Australia and the United Kingdom. Every Equinox there are human sacrifices dedicated to him and the subtle but perverted influence his painting and children's literature continues to have. (Similar shrines exist in America under Henry Kissinger's authority but he has altered both the structure and subtle ethos of the American Alpha Lodge Shrines.) It was Lindsay who taught that every political solution leads to more complex and involuted problems.

He counselled that the public is not concerned with satanic manipulators but only with petty criminals and little issues which affect their insignificant lives directly. As the status quo is maintained by the masses, it gets heavier the deeper it sinks and the greater its fears. The people cannot succeed or achieve and so must sink deeper and hold on more strongly! The fact that for most people the days repeat endlessly until death relieves them speaks volumes about the (sub-) human condition!

Kissinger refined Hitler's 'Terror Technique' into the more subtle and powerful 'Tension Technique': building tension in society and then finding a scapegoat. Dark Path adepts do this in insignificant ways until they have the power and ability to move and direct people to more gross and hideous behaviours. In Australia recently, the Business Activity Statement for taxation purposes and the 'immigration debate' have worked exceptionally well. The 'War on Terror' has also been of incalculable international influence (even more so than La Vey's Satanic Bible continues to be). The rhetorical façade for George's Presidency may be Christian, but the plan is otherwise! (And for all of the new arrangements the sheeple have adopted, it was still safer to walk the streets in the Second World War than it is now. This is true of all the capital cities of the combatant nations.)

If you doubt the influence of Satanism in the modern world consider the following issues: According to the World Bank, Australia is the wealthiest (or second wealthiest, after South Africa) nation on Earth. No one knows the full extent of Australia's natural resources and yet the living standards of Australians is getting worse each year and while Australians are amongst the most highly taxed people in the world we are quickly heading towards third world nation status. Who owns and controls the Reserve

Bank of Australia (hint, it is the same people who own the American Federal Reserve and the Bank of England)? [The Rothschilds.]

Why do overseas-owned companies pay so little taxation in Australia and why does the Australian government (of whichever political persuasion) allow overseas mining conglomerates to rape our environment and give Australians back next to nothing in return?

Why was fluoride put into Australia's water supply and why is it impossible to have it removed?

Are you seeing a pattern here?

Why is the media of the 'Free World' so heavily controlled and their shamefaced relationship to government so symbiotic?

Why have the educational standards of the Western World been forced to 'dumb down' (a process accelerated in the 1980s by both Spielberg and Lucas at the instigation of the Australian Alpha Lodge)?

Why has multiculturalism been foisted upon the 'First' World (with the exception of Japan)?

And who was behind the September the 11th operation?

Which country's 'Intelligence Agency' supplied the W.M.D. story which 'caused' the Iraq invasion? (Hint, it was not a Christian or Islamic nation)

The fact is that Alpha Lodge politicians (or political advisors) appreciate that if they pretend to respect the rights of sheeple and fain interest in their concerns, even though most realise that this is a ruse, they will go along with the programmes and policies because it is the line of least resistance. The democratic process allows them to express some of their frustrations, reduces the pain of their pent up depression and aggression while ensuring that nothing changes. You can see the same Representative Democracy political system everywhere it has been implemented.

Sheeple always use reason and logic to justify their whims, so the Alpha Lodge initiate is taught to speak in moderation while convincingly offering miracles. It is only a matter of waiting for the media to generate the slogan that 'the government should do something' and the governments – everywhere and of all political persuasions – always will.

Australian Satanists have always been at the forefront of high quality videos and D.V.D.s devoted to 'kiddie-porn'. Sheeple are such that although they scream about the importance of 'justice', it is of no interest unless they are in some way harmed! Their morality is that of the herd, for the more that sheeple feel isolated yet together, the easier it is for Satanists to reign. Provide the subjects with the forbidden and they feel fragmented, weak, guilty and often worthless – all of which the Master Satanist employs for their own ends. In Australian produced paedophile entertainment certain Avon guard features predominate: sexual frenzy, degrading treatment, filth, coprophilia [getting turned on by shit], torture, rape and death.

All of this is carefully crafted and augmented by aphrodisiacs and violence. Often the women involved are far worse than the men – little boys agonised by the cruel fingers, long tapered fingernails, teeth, cigarettes and perversions of ravishingly beautiful and debased female practitioners who are without restraint and have been maddened with heartless pride. Genital torture and castration are a constant theme. I will never forget the heartfelt sobs, desperate pleas, blood, tears and screams induced in many little boys by the agonizing use of alligator-clips, the application of the strap, whip, dildo, knee and the torment of electric shock!

Often Satanists advertise in free youth culture Street newspapers. This provides them with a constant supply of young teenage hopefuls to recruit or exploit (or both). Often Street-kids are taken in, used and discarded. It is only another missing teenager! Coffee shops, city entertainment complexes and even evangelical youth based churches are still used to this day to lure the innocent and not so innocent, their hearts full of broken dreams from broken homes. (Thank you Lionel.)

Often members who have reached a certain Grade, whose task and Ordeal it is to establish and maintain Outer Temple Teaching Orders as a recruiting ground for the Traditional Satanic Lodges, do so with dazzling results. Candidates are accepted and accessed over the required time for character, imagination and intellect – in that order.

Debauchery as a science is taught and maintained by programmes – strict in nature and observance.

Rituals are conducted, thought-patterns established, relationships destroyed and dependencies enhanced. Psychopaths are studied and emulated.

Some of the deadliest, most effective and disarming assassins are women. Within the Alpha Lodges they are worshipped as embodiments of the Dark Goddess – who is known by many names and is virgin still! [The Reptilian moon goddess is all her expressions, including Lilith.]

Currently the Outer Head of the Alpha Lodge Australasia is a very highly placed and successful Federal politician – whose Satanic name is Bestia.

The Inner Head of the Alpha Lodge Australasia is the highest Crown Service operative in the Commonwealth … (having replaced former Crown Service agent and Greek Princess Eketrini, a.k.a Sheila Fraser). Together and with time, those at the highest echelons of International Satanism believe that there is nothing they cannot achieve. And if you knew even half of what they have already done you would agree.

Ask yourself whether you have not noticed a number of world tendencies coalescing around 'the inevitable'. That the social fabric is no longer made of whole cloth and that politicians everywhere are becoming more brazen and extreme in their prescriptions and accomplishments should long ago have left little pause for thought, but it didn't then and doesn't now! The modern media is a pastiche of sex and soft eroticism. The Western world's drinking water has been laced with chemicals that exert powerful effects over time. Rates of depression, suicide, incest and bank interest continue to rise – but no one bothers to join the dots!

What do all of the following people have in common: Norman Lindsay, 'Sir' William McMahon, Garfield Barwick, Lionel Murphy, Rosalyn Norton, Clyde Cameron and Stephanie Bartholomew (a.k.a Abigail)? From where do more Australians get their news and why? What is Michael Aquino's interest in Australia's Pine Gap Facility and why is discussion of the Base's use and purpose inadmissible within Australia's polite society and media?

[Pine Gap is a major Reptilian underground base near Alice Springs, operated by both Australia and the United States, and it is one of the key locations for the Echelon spying and surveillance network that includes Menwith Hill in the UK. The late Michael Aquino was US Army officer and mind control operative who founded the Temple of

Set as a Satanic 'church' after leaving the Church of Satan of Rothschild Zionist, Anton LaVey. See *The Biggest Secret*.]

> I believe in one Prince, Satan, who reigns over this Earth, And in one Law which triumphs over all. I believe in one Temple, Our Temple to Satan, and in one Word which triumphs over all: The Word of ecstasy. And I believe in the Law of the Aeon, Which is sacrifice, and in the letting of blood For which I shed no tears since I give praise to my Prince, The fire-giver and look forward to his reign And the pleasures that are to come!
>
> A number of Crown Service agents in Australia were relieved on the evening of 19th December 1967. A number of the President's men in Australia were quietly celebrating as the clock struck midnight on the 11th of November 1975. Both Intelligence Agencies had relations which were still trespassed by the ghost of Dr. Ward. Both reacted to these events because of Australian Satanism, in the first case because H.R.H. Queen Elizabeth II would be saved embarrassments and in the second because Gough Whitlam was not one of them. On this point I am in no doubt, Sir John did his duty to the Princess and Inner Head of the Alpha Lodge Australasia. And Sir Garfield explained it!

[Gough Whitlam is the only Australian Prime Minister to be dismissed by the British queen in her role as Australia's Head of State. She did this through her Governor-General, Sir John Kerr, amid a manipulated 'constitutional crisis' in 1975. Sir Garfield Barwick, Chief Justice of the High Court, advised Kerr to remove Whitlam. Not being a Satanist is bad for political careers.]

> Most people do not know that J. W. Howard's first overseas trip, as Prime Minister of the Commonwealth of Australia was to receive his thirty-third Masonic degree, for in matters of his true faith he manifests a decidedly disillusioned romantic apprehension. His is the perfect example of parallel lives and a compliant media well and truly out of their depth. The same could not be said for Harold and his parties and the fact that people were noticing and indeed, Sir William was invited.
>
> You have little if any idea of the history, connexions and the network of Australia's Sinister Lodges, the Temples within them or their adherents and puppets. Why are some politicians spectacularly successful and others dogged at every step? How was the New York based public relations firm paid by John for doing such a good job in the … elections? Has any one bothered to check the Commonwealth of Australia's Department of Treasury records and would they know what they were looking for?
>
> I became Outer Head of the Alpha Lodge Australasia in the same year a meteoric rise to power brought a change of federal government with a Prime Minister whose relationship to Satanism was tenuous and pedestrian at best. But then again, he liked to play around and a number of our special people were happy to accommodate him, for a price. He craved respect and understated admiration and received both from us for the efforts he expended.
>
> I left the Alpha Lodge – as best as one can – and tried to reclaim a more mundane if no less ingratiating lifestyle. I operated a media company publishing anti-Christian tractates, political pamphlets and pornographic videos, working for a number of organizations internationally. The extreme rightwing of Britain had recently been infiltrated by a very old and isolated left hand path tradition and this sinister development augured well for the

Alpha Lodges (although today, David Myatt is considered more of a Prophet than a representative of the Hebdomadry Magickal System).

(While the Order of Nine Angles pursues a more open approach in the United Kingdom and increasingly in the United States of America, in Australia we still work just out of view).

The strength of International Satanism continued to increase as its oldest families continued to wither. In the real world, money gives power and those best placed to dictate the money market always win, yet their magnetism and glamour have faded and their futures are more tenuous than at any other time. Their collective days may be drawing to an end. Their most enduring legacies will be the power structures they created and the relationships facilitated. Their funding of diverse groups dedicated to the destruction of Christianity is a story never to be told! (Their most successful recent social campaign was the "Please God, don't let the Priest rape me again!" effort in the late 1980's to date and the promotion of 'Lilac Seminaries'.)

Modern post-1980 Satanism is the result of some hard learned truths and well-practiced procedures. Everyone knows that we are becoming more obvious – there are decreasing reasons to hide. The World of High Fashion – always a glittering ephemeral chimera – became an overtly successful recruiting ground for 'sweet young things' with a daring and glamorous nature. Multi-Billionaires increasingly sought the spiritual comfort and insider information the Satanic Alpha-Lodges could provide. What most people do not realise is that Satanism is a ritually based practice and that this repetition has – over time – left strong impressions upon the Morphic Field! This reinforces security and comfort within the left hand paths true adherents!

Politically, the libertarianism of Twain that permeated Satanism gave way to the realization that the sheeple do not want freedom. They are happy to build their own pens. Two thousand years of Christianity has left them domesticated, so Satanism began taking to itself rightwing positionings, farther and farther a field. In any event, all bank vault doors swing open to the right! All the leaders are dictators and the sheeple eat from their hand – just the way they like to.

Satanism now free of its earlier hallucinations fully accepts the pathetic nature of the human condition, wrapped as it is in the gaudy packages of superstition.

Satanism finally managed to infiltrate the major left wing and middle of the road political parties on May Day, 1997. [This was the day Tony Blair was elected UK Prime Minister.] Another group long ago bought the American Congress, so the Alpha Lodges concentrated on the Republican Party and this has paid some very high dividends. Currently the U.S. federal government dances to our tune (a couple of steps removed, if you know what I mean)!

Within the left hand path, Satan is the Supreme Prince (the Hierarchy of Hell begins with The Prince). He is 'The Other', the bright Fire Giver and Illuminator! He is the only God who cares! Satanism is a spiritual Darwinian theory based on predation. Devoted Satanists dedicate themselves and their sex acts to their Dark Lord. Prayers are said, Chants intoned or Invocations recited all as the basis of obtaining the blessings of Hell.

Unknown – if not always unsuspected – Infernal Temples exist in every major city throughout the world – Vatican City included! Every hour of every day and every night people are knowingly engaged in Satan's service. Human sacrifice – whether ritually and quicker or slowly and degradingly over time – is all harnessed to specific ends.

Politicians are introduced by a carefully graded set of criteria and situations that enable them to accept that their victims will be, "Our little secret". Young children sexually molested and physically abused by politicians worldwide are quickly used as sacrifices. In Australia the bodies are hardly ever discovered, for Australia is still a wilderness.

Overseas, cremation is the favoured method and although the Satanic Alpha Lodges of Australia have access to crematoria when needed, this is surprisingly rare. Believe it or not many bodies are 'dumped over the side' every week in a number of isolated bush land settings.

The emerging set of Satanic leaders is young, savvy, competent and heartless. They are masters and mistresses of their emotions and their intellect. Many are involved in business, politics, the legal profession and the arts. They are affluent, mobile and stylish examples to the next generation and therefore to the next generation of Satanists that power is glory, lust is nobility and liberty is the highest ideal of the new world man and woman. They use debasement of their victims as a ritual of power to themselves and their Deities. Often their victims are made to suffer in any number of situations. All of them are dedicated 'to creating the new men and women of the future' and 'to surpassing the Old Ones'.

Beginning in Sydney in the late 1980s was a now International Underground Sadomasochist society founded by Satanists. Victims are abused to death in grotesque rituals held in secluded chambers throughout the global metropolis and never-ending suburbs and bewildered housing estates. Although many who attend are unaware of anything except their ability to fulfil special needs and cultivated tastes, all of these gatherings are Satanic in nature and magickal in purpose. This dark, ultra-secretive society has been used to corrupt and destroy; to distil fear and ensure petrified silence! (Remember 'The Family' of South Australia? Ever wondered why so many people conveniently die from electrical fires?)

Bodily juices of all descriptions are sacred to Satanists and can be used for magickal purposes. The advent of sadomasochism as an accepted form of expression is due to the efforts of Satanists in subverting normalcy and inverting mainstream Christian values. The S&M Society was used as recruitment ground for some of the most perverted geniuses I have ever met. And with the advent of the World Wide Web, extreme hardcore Bathroom Sex came into its own as a sub-genre to be taken seriously.

Today such stars as Alexia Cage (and Her growing number of friends) are enjoying careers that would have been inconceivable but a few short years ago. Indeed many Toilet Sex starlets are committed Satanists and Alpha Lodge members or affiliates. By their presence in the world does the Prince of Darkness achieve his aim of exporting enlightenment into the Objective Universe. Concomitantly, Restroom Magick continues to develop its own left hand path techniques in which the convenience serves as a representation of and chalice unto the Goddess. (By way of only one example, today in co-educational facilities throughout the Western World, Bathroom Sex and 'flute playing' are rampant across all age groups. Thank you High Priestess Monica and 'White' Witch. Fiona).

The people of the world are easy to manipulate. Homo sapiens are herd animals, after all! Its all colour and movement when it comes to the masses. Give them an election with no policy choices and for the most part they are happy. Allow their children no real prospect of success, inhibit their natural drives – particularly their sex drives; limit their options, coarsen their choices and society (such as it still is) quickly falls apart into pre-determined categories. No families, just weak individuals free to do as they are told. Satan is a wonderful 'systems man'!

Already there are rampantly individualistic spiritualities spreading throughout the world. Souls and agendas are kidnapped with ease and Luciferian style. 'Rock and Roll' Gods and Goddesses captivate the hearts and minds of the next generation. The boldness of the Black Metal musicians/magicians and the mantras they spread still excite and amaze me – even after my achievements! Advertising continues to chip away at acceptable standards such that nowadays almost anything is realized as being eminently possible. The foreign policy of the world's only superpower is directed from Israel and our work is now running on autopilot.

The Alpha Lodge has taken steps to try to ensure that after the next war the Tradition is maintained in the intervening centuries, before civilization, as we know it, begins again. At that time, Satanism will be in the only religion and science. We have secured the texts, books, relics and magickal weapons necessary for Our Dark Lord and I see the storm clouds gathering. Ritual activity is increasing. Social structures are almost totally eroded. The Sheeple gather for their slaughter. Vindex walks amongst us now and very few know (or think that they do).

The Other. Beyond that Attracting, Transforming, Forbidden, Essence. Contradictory Defiance: challenging in its purest, answering, archetypal, shape-shifting form. The fascination that creates, nourishes, destroys and redeems. The Prince of the Earth, the Lord of the Air, the Darkness of the Deep, and the God of Fire! The majestic potency, force, presence, power; Magick of the Name of one known by many. Intoxicating. Subversive. Eternal.

The Other. That arrogant, inspirational quest and elegant undercurrent to a superior life of overcoming – Everything you have never dreamed of and more than your deepest nightmares. The alarming, awful, sinister, dispossessed delight of the Empowerment of Knowing – The Triumph of Ecstasy reflected in Your Imagination, Honour, Genius and Terror!

Rebellion!

Liberty!

The Other. That banished suspicion and apprehensive silence – trespassing in disguise. A Question and An Accusation – The Fear and Celebration. The Shadow and horror unknown of Life and Death – Of Aeons passed and Potentiality.

Of Willing and Becoming and Exalting in this life …
Hail Myself that I Seek to Be
HAIL SATAN
It is revealed individually
To those who can bear it

* * *

May Satan the all-powerful Prince of Darkness
And Lord of Earth Grant me my desires.
Let there be ecstasy and darkness;
let there be chaos and laughter,

Let there be sacrifice and strife:
but above all let us enjoy The gifts of life!
Zazas Zazas Nasatanata Zazas!

PART TWO
By Frater 616

Law is the product of man.
What God can create man can destroy!
It is always politics.
Even when people obey the law, it is a political decision.
Spirituality is a tool. The State has employed it, always.
For Homo sapiens are herd animals.
Hate yourself enough and the World hates with you.
Freedom is a two-edged sword.

Count Hans Kolvenbach [Former head of the Illuminati Jesuit Order.]

The young woman was barely conscious yet her nipples were bullet-hard. Her inviting, natural sexual aroma interplays with the civet incense and dancing candlelight. The congregation stands in silence as infant children re-enact the pornography they have been taught. Upon the Altar the young woman lays with gaping legs and delicate droplets of urine upon her pubic hair. As the children finish their pre-arranged aping pantomime of degradation, the chanting to the Dark Gods and Dark Goddesses begins.
    The Altar is always a human body – male, female, alert, drugged, alive or dead. In every case, the Altar is fresh and young. The mechanics of a High Satanic Black Mass are the same as in any theatre designed to re-open psychic gateways, inculcate dedication, glorify, rarefy and idealize spirituality. Only the aims differ. In Satanism, sodomy is preferred because of its magickal effects. [It accesses the 'base chakra', as I said earlier] The sacramental nature of Ezekiel 4:12-13, II Kings 18:27, Malachi 2:2-3 and Isaiah 16:11 are only fully understood by Satanists. Even abstinence from all forms of satisfying and normal sexual congress is used to enable the destruction and replacement of old beliefs and standards. Merely to sidestep conventionality still leaves the neophyte with a mass of prejudices, idiosyncrasies, identifications and preferences that give comfort and definition to the personality. By pushing wider the parameters of being and expanding ideas, Satanists experience the inherent transience and contingent nature of all things. The Black Mass – whether High Satanic or Low orgy – achieves this.
    Any form of bizarre sexual congress is explored and encouraged because atrophied tastes need stronger stimulation. Children, the elderly, the mentally retarded and desperate are used at satanic ceremonies throughout the world. The left hand path caters for all tastes and responds to all needs. In Australia and throughout what used to be the Soviet Union, Downs Syndrome pornography is an expanding market and an acquired taste.
    Approximately one new D.V.D. – like The Gangbang of Mary Mongoloid Series (1998-2001) or Downer Syndrome Follies I-II (2001-2003) – hits the underground market

every couple of months. Before that were the still popular Paedophiles' Paradise and Toil-art videos. Cutting as it does through all of society; boutique pornography offers many opportunities to the Alpha Satanic Lodges. With the reform and application of the mercantile system to the Western World the opportunities for well organized crime and well-placed puppets burgeoned! "Brothels are built with bricks of religion; Prisons with bricks of law."

By misunderstanding the nature of Satan and His spirituality the True Adherents are safe to openly declare their allegiance to the world – which they do! Why did so many of the important people appear to have had well-planned excuses – if not escape routes? Wheels within wheels! To every Temple a God!

Since Norman Lindsay's time, the Alpha Lodges have maintained well-organized political affiliations. Senior 'public servants', career bureaucrats and the diplomatic service have been used to integrate the coming Satanic age – just ask Sir A.G. (Name removed)! Most people are more comfortable asserting their 'independence' than being correct, effective, well off or powerful. They believe, because they have no or very few facts and because their beliefs offer them comfort – mostly the comfort of moral superiority. They use logic, reason, history, law; indeed anything at all to help them follow their prejudices and fulfil their desires.

Governments everywhere cater for those people who would rather live on their knees than die on their feet. Politicians did not invent the human condition; they only take advantage of it. The Satanic aristocracy sees the masses as tools; means by which the ends envisioned may be achieved – individual suffering is irrelevant. The ends are all that matter; the means are chosen based on totally utilitarian and logical decisions. Corruption is endemic but accepted. That Queen Elizabeth II is claiming ignorance of her own governments' laws while disdainfully hiding behind her advisors and masquerading her interests behind complex business structures apparently bothers no one. Although the secret 'selling off of the farm' in Australia was thorough it was not slow. People assist their governments to push them to the side of their own lives – Always have, always will!

It's the War against Terror; it's the same everywhere. Yet everyone agrees that the streets of the world's major cities are more dangerous now than they were throughout the Second World War! But who cares? History is replete with stories that never get told. How many people know about General Douglas Macarthur's 40 pages Memorandum of Saturday the 20th of January 1945 to President Franklin Delano Roosevelt or the names and rank of the Port Arthur killers? And whatever did happen to the Frogmen of the 19th of December?

Viable, truly spiritual Satanism is becoming more overt. This is because of those who went before. And as the schedule works itself, the Alpha Satanic Lodges are growing ever more public. I will not mention names, front-organizations or interests. The time is when these will announce themselves – just like Disneyland! We infiltrated then built the modern media, created porno-film empires, turned 'Snuff' into art and liberated young people.

Ours is the obsession of the mystery of darkness!
This is our age: The Age of Satanas!

Internet sites full of the grossest vulgarity and operated out of Israel are mostly founded upon left hand path philosophies. Take Alexia Cage, for example. [I put Alexia Cage in a search engine after reading this and up came **www.alexia-shitgirl.com**. It is described as 'a kinky private website into scat piss and vomit with pics and movies'. Nice.] The number of diplomats or their children who are into scat(ology) is legion, with all the possibilities that brings. [Scatology is sexual acts involving excrement]. Billy S. (name deleted) was one of our better acquisitions – until he died in Sonia's arms.

Known behind his back as Billy Browno, A.S.I.O. destroyed the records – as they do for judges, senior bureaucrats, our businessmen's clubs and diplomats.

But the average Homo normalis is beyond caring. Provided their bellies are full, their minds empty and their time consumed with frivolous entertainment, Satanists are free to triumph. It took less than sixty years to turn the Western world from war heroes to poofters; from bold, adventurers to crybabies; from devoted couples to divorcees and although never afraid of work in the past, now everyone has a Doctor's Certificate. Chronic apathy bolstered by cynicism litters the economic cul-de-sacs of our society. Literacy is almost gone, television is almost irrelevant, public infrastructure is heritage protected and most are crushed by the foreboding knowledge that tomorrow is another day.

The Wand must be bedaubed.
The Cup drained.
The Sword dazzling.
The Disc penetrated.
With Fire the Tunnel is penetrated.
With thirst the Cup is dazzled.
With Air the Sword is drained.
With soil the Disc bedaubed.
Within the temple in the temple
Find here the Mysteries of the mysteries
The back passage is the shortest way
Turn Water into wine.

On the 21st of July 1913, Franz Kafka observed in his Diary, "Don't despair, not even over the fact that you don't despair". People exist as robots within a world of no win politics fortified by political structures that have either outgrown their usefulness or graphically and tragically proved their inherent inadequacies. By old religious traditions that subverted a message of denying Church by preaching the personal and interior nature of the Kingdom of Heaven, and the State and family by advocating a higher allegiance to individual conscience continue as unabashed as if nothing had happened at all. And in answer, nothing changes. Anton La Vey noted that, 'There is nothing inherently wrong with fascism, given the nature and needs of the average citizen ... Now it's not so much a case of avoiding fascism, but of replacing a screwed up, disjointed, fragmented and stupefying kind of fascism with one that is more sensible and truly progressive.'

And Anton was many things, but never a fool. He also opined that the best street cleaner was a riot-gun and there are few that would quibble. Turning against themselves they live alone and vicariously with others. They have allowed themselves to become prisoners in our mythological penitentiaries amid the bright-lights and dark corridors of their cheap and nasty psyches.

If viewed objectively, Satan does not need to buy souls. The crowds are drip-fed belief systems, pointless choices and hollow opportunities. From radios, televisions, print media, billboards and the accepted agenda of the day, they exist in a constant state of boredom.

Fashion experts assist psychopaths in both politics and big business. Words as empty as the hearts that speak them, hardly affect the masses any more. They exist in a universe of suspicion. Their jobs are tenuous; their comatose lives as artificial as their prejudices and their alienated futures mostly short-term.

Its not that the true nature of what has and is being offered has changed or wasn't obvious all along. Just get another beer, turn down the lights, heat your packaged dinner and watch the flat-screen colour and movement of compliant simplicities. Your parents 'could not think of a number so they gave you a name.' But the State has assigned you a number for your pettiness and you will work until you drop! Samuel Adams said it best at the Philadelphia State House on the 1st of August 1776, "If ye love wealth better than liberty, the tranquillity of servitude better than the animating contest of freedom, go home from us in peace. We ask not your counsels or arms. Crouch down and lick the hands which feed you. May your chains set lightly upon you, and may posterity forget that ye were our countrymen." Nobody listened then either, except initiates of the precursor to the (Satanic) Alpha Lodges.

We believe in the law of the Aeon, which is sacrifice and in the letting of blood. It's the only doctrine to which the masses have ever been faithful, that and the aesthetic of disgrace. A disguised post-modern Satanic Eugenics rests on the superiority of those who know that they are above 'the herd', which they view with revulsion and is reflected in the indignation of their policies for any form of commitment to anything wider than themselves – to the point of trivializing life itself. One wing of the Hospital helps infertile couples; the other unit terminates foetuses. Cloning is not required – as a trip around any Metropolis will prove. The condition of admission is an old school tie, a proper handshake, mobile phone, a credit rating and some proof from the government that you exist.

The herd continues a hallowed tradition of pious fear – both of life and death. They light candles but they never really kiss. It is not hard to find them refracted through the stained glass grotesque caricatures of spirituality, the sound-byte vomit of politics, the mathematical facelessness of plastic statistics or in the quietest moment of the night.

Their politics rest on tribalism, their social systems resemble a clique of High School Prefects not an open system where a vote actually means something. Next time you are standing in a queue imagine a world where the government operates everything; where Committee delegates organise everything; where the information is edited, cutting through the lines of least persistence and where equality of outcome ensures the finality of its long-term results. It's not that hard. We continue to organize it! What God can create – man can destroy!

We exist in an Age with more promises than perils, more opportunities than obstacles, with better health care, communication and affordability, yet they silently await the Mushroom clouds and for the smells of death to capture the planet like never before. They are as compliant as sheep to the slaughter. 'The Lord is my shepherd ...' Their fears keep them together, huddling and overwhelmed by our prospect of the inevitable!

Satanists believe that the fear inspired by the atomic bomb and other weapons yet to come will be so great that everyone will refrain from using them . . . (Material deleted) It will mean the division of the world among 2 or 3 vast superstates, unable to be overthrown by any internal rebellion.

Their structure will be hierarchic, with the Satanic caste at the top and outright slavery at the bottom, and the crushing out of liberty would exceed anything the world has yet seen. Within each state the necessary psychological atmosphere will be maintained by a complete severance from the outside world, and by a continuous phoney war against rival states. Civilizations of this type will remain stable for thousands of years. Have no fear!

Bibliography

Allen, D S and Delair, J B, *The Day The Earth Nearly Died* (Gateway Books, Bath, 1995)

Baigent, Michael, Leigh Richard, and Lincoln, Henry: *The Holy Blood and the Holy Grail* (Arrow Books; 2nd Revised edition, 1996)

Bamford, James: *Body of Secrets: How America's NSA & Britain's GCHQ Eavesdrop On The World* (Arrow Books Ltd; New edition, 2002)

Baron, S W: *A Social and Religious History of the Jews* (New York, 1957)

Bellamy, Dr Hans Schindler: *Moons, Myths and Man*. A reinterpretation (Faber & Faber, 1936, also 1949 revised)

Bellamy, Dr Hans Schindler: *The Great Idol of Tiahuanaco* (Faber & Faber, 1959, with Peter Allan)

Bentov, Itzhak: *Stalking the Wild Pendulum: On the Mechanics of Consciousness* (Inner Traditions Bear and Company; New edition, 1988)

Bigelsen, Harvey: *Holographic Blood* (HERF Publishing, 2007 – see also www.drbigelsen.com)

Bigelsen, Harvey: *Medical Conspiracy in America* (www.drbigelsen.com, 2009)

Booker, Christopher: *The Real Global Warming Disaster* (Continuum International Publishing Group, 2009)

Bronder, Dietrich: *Before Hitler Came* (Hans Pfeiffer, Hanover, 1964)

Brown, Dan: *The Da Vinci Code* (Corgi, 2004)

Brzezinski, Zbigniew: *The Grand Chessboard: American Primacy And It's Geostrategic Imperatives* (Basic Books, 1997)

Butler, Smedley: *War is a Racket: The Antiwar Classic by America's Most Decorated General* (Feral House; New edition, 2003, first published 1935)

Chomsky, Noam: *Necessary Illusions: Thought Control in Democratic Societies* (Pluto Press, 1989)

Childress, David Hatcher: *The Anti-Gravity Handbook* (Adventures Unlimited Press, 1993)

Cooper, Major Gordon (co-author): *We Seven* (Simon and Schuster, New York, 1962)

Cooper, William: *Behold a Pale Horse* (Windrush Publishing Services, 1995)

Cramer, Samuel Noah: *History Begins in Sumer: Twenty-seven 'Firsts' in Man's Recorded History* (Doubleday Anchor Books, 1959)

Cremo, Michael A, and Thompson, Richard L: *Forbidden Archaeology: The Hidden History of the Human Race* (Bhaktivedanta Book Trust; 2nd Revised edition, 1993)

Daschle, Tom (co-author): *Critical: What We Can Do About the Health-Care Crisis* (Thomas Dunne Books, 2008)

Deane, John Bathhurst: *Worship of the Serpent* (BiblioBazaar, 2009, first published 1933)

Engdahl, William F: *Seeds of Destruction: The Hidden Agenda of Genetic Manipulation* (Global Research, 2007)

Finkelstein, Norman: *The Holocaust Industry: Reflections on the Exploitation of Jewish Suffering* (Verso Books, 2003)

Frawley, David: *Gods, Sages, And Kings: Vedic Secrets Of Ancient Civilization* (Lotus Press, 2001)

Grof, Stanislav, *The Holotropic Mind: Three Levels of Human Consciousness and How They Shape Our Lives* (HarperSanFrancisco, 1993)

Grose, Peter: *Gentleman Spy: The Life of Allen Dulles* (Houghton Mifflin, 1994)

Gynn, Graham and Wright, Tony: *Left in the Dark* (Kaleidos Press; 2nd edition, 2008)

Hart, Alan: Zionism: *The Real Enemy of the Jews* (World Focus Publishing, 2007)

Halvorsen, Dr Richard: *The Truth About Vaccines: How We Are Used as Guinea Pigs Without Knowing It* (Gibson Square Books, 2009)

Hapsburg, Otto von: *The Social Order of Tomorrow* (O Wolff, 1958)

Huxley, Aldous: *Brave New World* (Vintage Classics, 2007, first published 1932)

Iserbyt, Charlotte: *The Deliberate Dumbing Down of America – a Chronological Paper Trail* (3d Research Co, 1999)

Kaku, Dr Michio: *Hyperspace: A Scientific Odyssey through Parallel Universes, Time Warps, and the Tenth Dimension* (Oxford Paperbacks; New edition, 1995)

Keel, John A: *Our Haunted Planet* (Galde Press Inc, 1999)

Knight, Christopher, and Butler, Alan: *Who Built The Moon?* (Watkins, 2007)

Koestler, Arthur: *The Thirteenth Tribe* (Random House, 1999)

Levant, Ezra: Shakedown: *How Our Government Is Undermining Democracy in the Name of Human Rights* (McClelland & Stewart, 2009)

Lindstrom, Martin: *Buyology: How Everything We Believe About Why We Buy is Wrong* (Random House Business Books, 2008)

Lipton, Bruce: *Biology of Belief: Unleashing the Power of Consciousness, Matter and Miracles* (Hay House, 2008)

Lockwood, Michael: *The Labyrinth of Time: Introducing the Universe* (Clarendon Press, 2007)

Mearsheimer, John J and Walt, Stephen M: *The Israel Lobby and U.S. Foreign Policy* (Farrar Straus Giroux, 2008)

Morton, Frederic: *The Rothschilds. A family portrait* (Secker & Warburg, 1962)

Mott, Michael: *Caverns, Cauldrons, and Concealed Creatures* (Hidden Mysteries, Texas, 2000)

Nagy, Dr Sandor: *The Forgotten Cradle of the Hungarian Culture* (Patria Publishing, Toronto, 1973)

Neil, William: *How We Were Made: A Book of Revelations Made* (Oracle Books, 2003)

Ouspensky, P D, Uspenskii, P D, Williamson, Marianne: *In Search of the Miraculous, The Definitive Exploration of G I Gurdjieff's Mystical Thought and Universal View* (Mariner Books; New edition, 2001)

Plaut, Gunther: *The Man Who Would Be Messiah* (Borgo Press, 1995)

Pike, Albert: *Morals and Dogma* (Morals and Dogma of the Ancient and Accepted Scottish Rite Freemasonry, Kessinger Publishing, 2002, first published 1871)

Rabin, Yitzhak: *The Rabin Memoirs* (Littlehampton Book Services, 1979)

Russell, Bertrand: *The Impact of Science on Society* (Ams Pr Inc, 1953)

Russell, Bertrand: *The Scientific Outlook* (George Allen & Unwin, 1931)

Roosevelt, Kermit: *Counter Coup: The Struggle for the Control of Iran* (Mcgraw-Hill, 1979)

Sabak, Pierre: *The Murder of Reality* (www.pierresabak.com, 2009)

Sachar, Howard: *A History of the Jews in America* (Vintage, 1993)

Sagan, Carl: *The Dragons of Eden: Speculations on the Evolution of Human Intelligence* (Ballantine Books Inc; Reprint edition, 1992)

Sand, Professor Shlomo: *The Invention of the Jewish People* (Verso, 2009)

Swerdlow, Stewart: *Blue Blood, True Blood* (Expansions Pub Co, 2002)

Solzhenitsyn, Aleksandr: *Gulag Archipelago, volume two* (Harper Perennial; Reissue edition, 2007)

Talbot, Michael: *The Holographic Universe* (HarperCollins Publishers Ltd; New Ed edition, 1996)

Tarpley, Webster Griffin: *Barack H Obama: The Unauthorized Biography* (Progressive Press, 2008)

Thaler, Richard H: Nudge: *Improving Decisions About Health, Wealth, and Happiness* (Penguin, 2009)

Thompson, Richard L: *Maya, The World as a Virtual-reality* (Govardhan Hill Publishing; illustrated edition, 2003)

Thompson, Thomas: *The Mythic Past: Biblical Archaeology and the Myth of Israel* (Basic Books, 2000)

Tracy, Professor Ann Blake: *Prozac: Panacea or Pandora* (Cassia Publications, 1994)

Walters, Guy: *Hunting Evil: The Nazi War Criminals Who Escaped and the Quest to Bring Them to Justice* (Broadway, 2010)

Wilson, Don: *Our Mysterious Spaceship Moon* (Dell, 1975)

Index

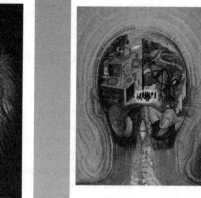

Other work by David Icke

The David Icke Guide to the Global Conspiracy (and how to end it)
A masterpiece of dot-connecting that is both extraordinary and unique. There is a 'wow', indeed many of them, on every page as Icke lifts the veil on the unseen world.

Infinite Love is the Only Truth, *Everything Else is Illusion*
Why the 'world' is a virtual-reality game that only exists because we believe it does. Icke explains how we 'live' in a 'holographic internet' in that our brains are connected to a central 'computer' that feeds us the same collective reality that we decode from waveforms and electrical signals into the holographic 3D 'world' that we all think we see.

Alice in Wonderland and the World Trade Center Disaster – Why the Official Story of 9/11 is a Monumental Lie
A shocking exposé of the Ministries of Mendacity that have told the world the Big Lie about what happened on September 11th, who did it, how and why. This 500 page book reveals the real agenda behind the 9/11 attacks and how they were orchestrated from within the borders of the United States and not from a cave in Afghanistan.

Tales from the Time Loop
In this 500-page, profusely-illustrated book, David Icke explores in detail the multi-levels of the global conspiracy. He exposes the five-sense level and demolishes the official story of the invasions of Iraq and Afghanistan; he explains the inter-dimensional manipulation; and he shows that what we think is the 'physical world' is all an illusion that only exists in our mind. Without this knowledge, the true nature of the conspiracy cannot be understood.

The Biggest Secret
An exposé of how the same interbreeding bloodlines have controlled the planet for thousands of years. It includes the horrific background to the British royal family, the murder of Princess Diana, and the true origins of major religions. A blockbuster.

Children of the Matrix
The companion book of The Biggest Secret that investigates the reptilian and other dimensional connections to the global conspiracy and reveals the world of illusion – the 'Matrix' – that holds the human race in daily slavery.

… And The Truth Shall Set You Free (21st century edition)
Icke exposes in more than 500 pages the interconnecting web that controls the world today. This book focuses on the last 200 years and particularly on what is happening around us today. Another highly acclaimed book, which has been constantly updated. A classic in its field.

I Am Me, I Am Free
Icke's book of solutions. With humour and powerful insight, he shines a light on the mental and emotional prisons we build for ourselves … prisons that disconnect us from our true and infinite potential to control our own destiny. A getaway car for the human psyche.

Earlier books by David Icke include The Robots' Rebellion (Gill & Macmillan), Truth Vibrations (Gill & Macmillan), Heal the World (Gill & Macmillan), Days of Decision (Jon Carpenter) and It Doesn't Have To Be Like This (Green Print). The last two books are out of print and no longer available.

Beyond the Cutting Edge – Exposing the Dreamworld We Believe to be Real
Since his extraordinary 'awakening' in 1990 and 1991, David Icke has been on a journey across the world, and within himself, to find the Big answers to the Big questions: Who are we? Where are we? What are we doing here? Who really controls this world and how and why? In this seven-hour presentation to 2,500 people at the Brixton Academy in London, David addresses all these questions and connects the dots between them to reveal a picture of life on earth that is truly beyond the cutting edge.

Freedom or Fascism: the time to choose – 3xDVD set
More than 2,000 people from all over Britain and across the world gather at London's famous Brixton Academy to witness an extraordinary event. David Icke weaves together more than 16 years of painstaking research and determined investigation into the Global Conspiracy and the extraordinary 'sting' being perpetrated on an amnesic human race. Icke is the Dot Connector and he uses hundreds of illustrations to reveal the hidden story behind apparently unconnected world events.

Revelations of a Mother Goddess – DVD
Arizona Wilder was mind-programmed from birth by Josef Mengele, the notorious, 'Angel of Death' in the Nazi concentration camps. In this interview with David Icke, she describes human sacrifice rituals at Glamis Castle and Balmoral in England, in which the Queen, the Queen Mother and other members of the Royal Family sacrificed children in Satanic ceremonies.

The Reptilian Agenda – DVD
In this memorable, almost six hours of interview, contained in parts one and two, Zulu shaman, Credo Mutwa, reveals his incredible wealth of knowledge about the black magicians of the Illuminati and how

they use their knowledge of the occult to control the world. Sit back and savour this wonderful man. You are in the presence of a genius and a giant.

Other books available

The Medical Mafia
The superb exposé of the medical system by Canadian doctor, Guylaine Lanctot, who also shows how and why 'alternative' methods are far more effective. Highly recommended.

What The Hell Am I Doing Here Anyway?
A second book by Guylaine Lanctot. We thirst for freedom, yet all the while we are imprisoned by conditioned beliefs.

Trance-Formation Of America
The staggering story of Cathy O'Brien, the mind-controlled slave of the US Government for some 25 years. Read this one sitting down. A stream of the world's most famous political names are revealed as they really are. Written by Cathy O'Brien and Mark Phillips.

Access Denied – For Reasons Of National Security
From the authors of *Trance-Formation of America*, this is the documented journey through CIA mind-control.

*All books, DVDs and videos are available from David Icke Books
(contact details on the back page)
or through the website:*
www.davidicke.com

Readings by post
with Carol Clarke

**To order David Icke's
books and DVDs, contact:**

David Icke Books Ltd
Suite 4
185a High Street
Ryde
Isle of Wight
PO33 2PN
England

Orders by telephone or fax:
+44 (0) 1983 566002

Orders by email:
info@davidickebooks.co.uk

Or order through the website:
www.davidickebooks.com

For other information visit:
www.davidicke.com